Webster's American English Dictionary

Expanded Edition

Created in Cooperation with the Editors of
MERRIAM-WEBSTER

FEDERAL
STREET
PRESS

A Division of Merriam-Webster, Incorporated
Springfield, Massachusetts

This edition published by Federal Street Press,
a division of Merriam-Webster, Incorporated
P.O. Box 281
Springfield, MA 01102

Federal Street Press books are available for bulk purchase for
sales promotion and premium use. For details write the manager of special sales, Federal Street Press, P.O. Box 281,
Springfield, MA 01102

ISBN-13 978-1-59695-154-9

Printed in the United States of America

3rd printing   Craftline, Ft. Wayne, IN   08/2015   Jouve

CONTENTS

PREFACE

This new edition contains new words and senses that have become established in the language since publication of the previous edition. It remains an extremely concise reference to those words that form the very core of the English vocabulary. It is intended to serve as a quick reference, especially for questions of spelling, pronunciation, and hyphenation of the most common words in everyday use.

Though small, this work shares many details of presentation with more comprehensive dictionaries. However, conciseness of presentation necessarily requires special treatment of entries, and this book has a number of special features uniquely its own. Users need to be familiar with the following major features of this dictionary.

Main entries follow one another in alphabetical order. Centered periods within the entries show points at which a hyphen may be put when the word is broken at the end of a line.

Homographs (words spelled the same but having different meanings) are run in to a single main entry when they are closely related. Second and succeeding homographs are represented by a swung dash: ～ Homographs of distinctly different origin (as **¹perch** and **²perch**) are given separate entries with preceding raised numerals.

Variant spellings that are quite common appear at the main entry following a comma (as **the·ater, the·atre**) and following other boldface entry words, such as inflected forms and run-on entries.

Inflected forms of nouns, verbs, adjectives, and adverbs are shown when they are irregular—as when requiring the dropping of a final *e* or changing a final *y* to *i* before the suffix: (as **prat·ed; prat·ing** at **prate**) or when the form of the base word itself changes: (as **swam...; swum** at **swim**)—or when there might be doubt about their spelling: (as *pl* **twos** at **two**). They are given either in full (as **worse...; worst** at **bad**) or cut back to a convenient point of division (as **-mat·ed; -mat·ing** at **es·ti·mate**). Common variants of inflected forms are shown even if they are regular (as **bused** *or* **bussed** at **bus**). When the inflected forms of a verb involve no irregularity except the doubling of a final consonant, the double consonant is shown instead of full or cut-back inflected forms (as *vb* **-gg-** at **hug**). A variant or inflected form whose alphabetical place is distant from the main entry is entered at its own place with a cross-reference in small capital letters to the main entry (as **laid** *past of* LAY).

Several other kinds of entries are also found in this dictionary. A **run-in entry** is a term related to a main entry that appears within a definition (as **cacao beans** at **ca·cao**). It is essentially defined in the context of the definition and is set off by parentheses. Derivative words, made up usually of the main entry and a common word element, such as a suffix, are shown as **undefined run-on entries** following all definitions of a main entry. These are set off by a dash (as — **man·u·al·ly** at **man·u·al** or — **hill·top** at **hill**). The meaning of an undefined run-on entry can be inferred from the meaning of the main entry where it appears and that of the added word element, shown elsewhere in the book. A **run-on phrase** is a group of two or more words having the main entry as a major element and having a special meaning of its own (as **knock out** at **knock** or **set forth** at **set**). Run-on phrases are always defined.

Lists of undefined words formed by the addition of a common English prefix to a word entered in the dictionary and having meanings that can be inferred from the meaning of the root word and that of the prefix will be found in a separate section at the bottom of the page at entries for the following prefixes: *anti-, bi-, co-, counter-, extra-, hyper-, in-, inter-, mini-, multi-, non-, over-, post-, pre-, re-, self-, sub-, super-, un-,* and *vice-.*

Pronunciation information is either given explicitly or implied for every entry in the dictionary. Pronunciation respellings are placed within reversed slanted lines (as \ˌjenəˈralətē\ at **ge·ner·al·i·ty**). Where the pronunciation is not indicated at a particular entry, or is indicated in a cutback form, the full pronunciation is to be inferred from an earlier indicated pronunciation. A full list of the pronunciation symbols used is shown on the page following this Preface.

The grammatical function of entry words is indicated by an italic **functional label** (as *vb, n,* or *prefix*).

A **hyphen** that is a fixed part of a hyphenated expression (such as *self-conscious*) is converted to a special "double hyphen" (⸗) when the compound expression appears in lightface type and when the fixed hyphen comes at the end of a line in this dictionary. This indicates to you that the hyphen is to be retained when the word is not at the end of a line. Fixed hyphens in boldface entry words are shown as short boldface dashes, which are a bit larger than ordinary hyphens. These short dashes or long hyphens in boldface words are retained at the end of a line in this dictionary.

Guide words are used at the top of pages to indicate the range of entries on those pages. In choosing guide words for a page, we select the alphabetically first and last spelled-out boldface words or phrases on that page. This means that any boldface entry— main entry, variant spelling, inflected form, run-in or run-on entry—can be used as a guide word. Please keep this in mind if the word used as a guide word does not happen to be the first or last main entry on the page. The guide words themselves are in alphabetical order throughout the book, so occasionally it has been necessary to modify this rule. When the alphabetically last entry on one page would come later than the alphabetically first entry on the following page, a different word is chosen as guide word. On pages that contain a substantial number of undefined words derived from a prefix entry, the undefined words are not considered when choosing guide words.

All **abbreviations** used in this book are listed, along with a number of other common abbreviations, in a special section immediately following the dictionary proper.

PRONUNCIATION SYMBOLS

ə   banana, collide, abut; raised \ᵊ\ in \ᵊl, ᵊn\ as in battle, cotton; in \lᵊ, mᵊ, rᵊ\ as in French table, prisme, titre

'ə, ˌə   humbug, abut

ər   operation, further

a   map, patch

ā   day, fate

ä   bother, cot, father

à   father as pronounced by those who do not rhyme it with *bother*

aů   now, out

b   baby, rib

ch   chin, catch

d   did, adder

e   set, red

ē   beat, nosebleed, easy

f   fifty, cuff

g   go, big

h   hat, ahead

hw   whale

i   tip, banish

ī   site, buy

j   job, edge

k   kin, cook

k̲   German ich, Buch

l   lily, cool

m   murmur, dim

n   nine, own; raised \ⁿ\ indicates that a preceding vowel or diphthong is pronounced through both nose and mouth, as in French *bon* \bōⁿ\

ŋ   sing, singer, finger, ink

ō   bone, hollow

ȯ   saw, cork

œ   French bœuf, German Hölle

œ̄   French feu, German Höhle

ȯi   toy, sawing

p   pepper, lip

r   rarity

s   source, less

sh   shy, mission

t   tie, attack

th   thin, ether

t̲h̲   then, either

ü   boot, few \'fyü\

ů   put, pure \'pyůr\

ᵫ   German füllen

ᵫ̄   French rue, German fühlen

v   vivid, give

w   we, away

y   yard, cue \'kyü\; raised \ʸ\ indicates that a preceding \l\, \n\, or \w\ is modified by the placing of the tongue tip against the lower front teeth, as in French *digne* \dēnʸ\

z   zone, raise

zh   vision, pleasure

\   slant line used in pairs to mark the beginning and end of a transcription

'   mark at the beginning of a syllable that has primary (strongest) stress: \'penmənˌship\

ˌ   mark at the beginning of a syllable that has secondary (next-strongest) stress: \'penmənˌship\

¹a \'ā\ *n*, *pl* **a's** *or* **as** \'āz\ : 1st letter of the alphabet

²a \ə, 'ā\ *indefinite article* : one or some — used to indicate an unspecified or unidentified individual

aard·vark \'ärd,värk\ *n* : ant-eating African mammal

aback \ə'bak\ *adv* : by surprise

aba·cus \'abəkəs\ *n*, *pl* **aba·ci** \'abə-,sī, -,kē\ *or* **aba·cus·es** : calculating instrument using rows of beads

abaft \ə'baft\ *adv* : toward or at the stern

ab·a·lo·ne \,abə'lōnē\ *n* : large edible shellfish

¹aban·don \ə'bandən\ *vb* : give up without intent to reclaim — **aban·don·ment** *n*

²abandon *n* : thorough yielding to impulses

aban·doned \ə'bandənd\ *adj* : morally unrestrained

abase \ə'bās\ *vb* **abased; abas·ing** : lower in dignity — **abase·ment** *n*

abash \ə'bash\ *vb* : embarrass — **abashment** *n*

abate \ə'bāt\ *vb* **abat·ed; abat·ing** : decrease or lessen

abate·ment \ə'bātmənt\ *n* : tax reduction

ab·at·toir \'abə,twär\ *n* : slaughterhouse

ab·bess \'abəs\ *n* : head of a convent

ab·bey \'abē\ *n*, *pl* **-beys** : monastery or convent

ab·bot \'abət\ *n* : head of a monastery

ab·bre·vi·ate \ə'brēvē,āt\ *vb* **-at·ed; -at·ing** : shorten — **ab·bre·vi·a·tion** \ə,brēvē'āshən\ *n*

ab·di·cate \'abdi,kāt\ *vb* **-cat·ed; -cat·ing** : renounce — **ab·di·ca·tion** \,abdi'kāshən\ *n*

ab·do·men \'abdəmən, ab'dōmən\ *n* **1** : body area between chest and pelvis **2** : hindmost part of an insect — **ab·dom·i·nal** \ab'dämən°l\ *adj* — **ab·dom·i·nal·ly** *adv*

ab·duct \ab'dəkt\ *vb* : kidnap — **ab-**

duc·tion \-'dəkshən\ *n* — **ab·duc·tor** \-'tər\ *n*

abed \ə'bed\ *adv or adj* : in bed

ab·er·ra·tion \,abə'rāshən\ *n* : deviation or distortion — **ab·er·rant** \a'berənt\ *adj*

abet \ə'bet\ *vb* **-tt-** : incite or encourage — **abet·tor, abet·ter** \-ər\ *n*

abey·ance \ə'bāəns\ *n* : state of inactivity

ab·hor \əb'hȯr, ab-\ *vb* **-rr-** : hate — **ab·hor·rence** \-əns\ *n* — **ab·hor·rent** \-ənt\ *adj*

abide \ə'bīd\ *vb* **abode** \-'bōd\ *or* **abid·ed; abid·ing 1** : endure **2** : remain, last, or reside

ab·ject \'ab,jekt, ab'-\ *adj* : low in spirit or hope — **ab·jec·tion** \ab-'jekshən\ *n* — **ab·ject·ly** *adv* — **ab·ject·ness** *n*

ab·jure \ab'jùr\ *vb* **1** : renounce **2** : abstain from — **ab·ju·ra·tion** \,abjə-'rāshən\ *n*

ablaze \ə'blāz\ *adj or adv* : on fire

able \'ābəl\ *adj* **abler** \-blər\; **ablest** \-bləst\ **1** : having sufficient power, skill, or resources **2** : skilled or efficient — **abil·i·ty** \ə'bilətē\ *n* — **ably** \'āblē\ *adv*

-able, -ible \əbəl\ *adj suffix* **1** : capable of, fit for, or worthy of **2** : tending, given, or liable to

ab·lu·tion \ə'blüshən, a'blü-\ *n* : washing of one's body

ab·ne·gate \'abni,gāt\ *vb* **-gat·ed; -gat·ing 1** : relinquish **2** : renounce — **ab·ne·ga·tion** \,abni'gāshən\ *n*

ab·nor·mal \ab'nȯrməl\ *adj* : deviating from the normal or average — **ab·nor·mal·i·ty** \,abnər'malətē, -nȯr-\ *n* — **ab·nor·mal·ly** *adv*

aboard \ə'bōrd\ *adv* : on, onto, or within a car, ship, or aircraft ~ *prep* : on or within

abode \ə'bōd\ *n* : residence

abol·ish \ə'bälish\ *vb* : do away with — **ab·o·li·tion** \,abə'lishən\ *n*

abom·i·na·ble \ə'bämənəbəl\ *adj* : thoroughly unpleasant or revolting

abom·i·nate \ə'bämə,nāt\ *vb* **-nat·ed; -nat·ing** : hate — **abom·i·na·tion** \ə,bämə'nāshən\ *n*

ab·orig·i·nal \,abə'rijənəl\ *adj* **1** : original **2** : primitive

ab·orig·i·ne \-'rijənē\ *n* : original inhabitant

abort \ə'bȯrt\ *vb* : terminate prematurely — **abor·tive** \-'bȯrtiv\ *adj*

abor·tion \ə'bȯrshən\ *n* : spontaneous or induced termination of pregnancy

abound \ə'baúnd\ *vb* : be plentiful

about \ə'baút\ *adv* : around ~ *prep* **1** : on every side of **2** : on the verge of **3** : having as a subject

above \ə'bəv\ *adv* : in or to a higher place ~ *prep* **1** : in or to a higher place than **2** : more than

above·board *adv or adj* : without deception

abrade \ə'brād\ *vb* **abrad·ed; abrad·ing** : wear away by rubbing — **abra·sion** \-'brāzhən\ *n*

abra·sive \ə'brāsiv\ *n* : substance for grinding, smoothing, or polishing ~ *adj* **1** : tending to abrade **2** : causing irritation — **abra·sive·ly** *adv* — **abra·sive·ness** *n*

abreast \ə'brest\ *adv or adj* **1** : side by side **2** : up to a standard or level

abridge \ə'brij\ *vb* **abridged; abridg·ing** : shorten or condense — **abridg·ment, abridge·ment** *n*

abroad \ə'brȯd\ *adv or adj* **1** : over a wide area **2** : outside one's country

ab·ro·gate \'abrəgāt\ *vb* **-gat·ed; -gat·ing** : annul or revoke — **ab·ro·ga·tion** \,abrə'gāshən\ *n*

abrupt \ə'brəpt\ *adj* **1** : sudden **2** : so quick as to seem rude — **abrupt·ly** *adv*

ab·scess \'ab,ses\ *n* : collection of pus surrounded by inflamed tissue — **ab·scessed** \-,sest\ *adj*

ab·scond \ab'skänd\ *vb* : run away and hide

ab·sent \'absənt\ *adj* : not present ~ **ab·sent** \ab'sent\ *vb* : keep oneself away — **ab·sence** \'absəns\ *n* — **absen·tee** \,absən'tē\ *n*

ab·sent·mind·ed \,absənt'mīndəd\ *adj* : unaware of one's surroundings or action — **ab·sent·mind·ed·ly** *adv* — **ab·sent·mind·ed·ness** *n*

ab·so·lute \'absə,lüt, ,absə'-\ *adj* **1**

: pure **2** : free from restriction **3** : definite — **ab·so·lute·ly** *adv*

ab·so·lu·tion \,absə'lüshən\ *n* : remission of sins

ab·solve \əb'zälv, -'sälv\ *vb* **-solved; -solv·ing** : set free of the consequences of guilt

ab·sorb \əb'sȯrb, -'zȯrb\ *vb* **1** : suck up or take in as a sponge does **2** : engage (one's attention) — **ab·sor·ben·cy** \-'sȯrbənsē, -'zȯr-\ *n* — **ab·sor·bent** \-bənt\ *adj or n* — **ab·sorb·ing** *adj*

ab·sorp·tion \əb'sȯrpshən, -'zȯrp-\ *n* : process of absorbing — **ab·sorp·tive** \-tiv\ *adj*

ab·stain \əb'stān\ *vb* : refrain from doing something — **ab·stain·er** *n* — **ab·sten·tion** \-'stenchən\ *n* — **ab·sti·nence** \'abstənəns\ *n*

ab·ste·mi·ous \ab'stēmēəs\ *adj* : sparing in use of food or drink — **ab·ste·mi·ous·ly** *adv* — **ab·ste·mi·ous·ness** *n*

ab·stract \ab'strakt, 'ab,-\ *adj* **1** : expressing a quality apart from an object **2** : not representing something specific ~ \'ab,-\ *n* : summary ~ \ab'-, 'ab,-\ *vb* **1** : remove or separate **2** : make an abstract of — **ab·stract·ly** *adv* — **ab·stract·ness** *n*

ab·strac·tion \ab'strakshən\ *n* **1** : act of abstracting **2** : abstract idea or work of art

ab·struse \əb'strüs, ab-\ *adj* : hard to understand — **ab·struse·ly** *adv* — **ab·struse·ness** *n*

ab·surd \əb'sərd, -'zərd\ *adj* : ridiculous or unreasonable — **ab·sur·di·ty** \-ətē\ *n* — **ab·surd·ly** *adv*

abun·dant \ə'bəndənt\ *adj* : more than enough — **abun·dance** \-dəns\ *n* — **abun·dant·ly** *adv*

abuse \ə'byüz\ *vb* **abused; abus·ing** **1** : misuse **2** : mistreat **3** : attack with words ~ \-'byüs\ *n* **1** : corrupt practice **2** : improper use **3** : mistreatment **4** : coarse and insulting speech — **abus·er** *n* — **abu·sive** \-'byüsiv\ *adj* — **abu·sive·ly** *adv* — **abu·sive·ness** *n*

abut \ə'bət\ *vb* **-tt-** : touch along a border — **abut·ter** *n*

abut·ment \ə'bətmənt\ *n* : part of a bridge that supports weight

abys·mal \ə'bizməl\ *adj* **1** : immeasurably deep **2** : wretched — **abys·mal·ly** *adv*

abyss \ə'bis\ *n* : immeasurably deep gulf

-ac \ˌak\ *n suffix* : one affected with

aca·cia \ə'kāshə\ *n* : leguminous tree or shrub

ac·a·dem·ic \ˌakə'demik\ *adj* 1 : relating to schools or colleges 2 : theoretical — **academic** *n* — **ac·a·dem·i·cal·ly** \-iklē\ *adv*

acad·e·my \ə'kadəmē\ *n, pl* **-mies** 1 : private high school 2 : society of scholars or artists

acan·thus \ə'kanthəs\ *n, pl* **acanthus** 1 : prickly Mediterranean herb 2 : ornament representing acanthus leaves

ac·cede \ak'sēd\ *vb* **-ced·ed; -ced·ing** 1 : become a party to an agreement 2 : express approval 3 : enter upon an office

ac·cel·er·ate \ik'selə,rāt, ak-\ *vb* **-at·ed; -at·ing** 1 : bring about earlier 2 : speed up — **ac·cel·er·a·tion** \-,selə'rāshən\ *n*

ac·cel·er·a·tor \ik'selə,rātər, ak-\ *n* : pedal for controlling the speed of a motor vehicle

ac·cent \'ak,sent\ *n* 1 : distinctive manner of pronunciation 2 : prominence given to one syllable of a word 3 : mark (as ´, `, ^) over a vowel in writing or printing to indicate pronunciation ~ \'akˌ-, ak'-\ *vb* : emphasize — **ac·cen·tu·al** \ak'senchəwəl\ *adj*

ac·cen·tu·ate \ak'senchə,wāt\ *vb* **-at·ed; -at·ing** : stress or show off by a contrast — **ac·cen·tu·a·tion** \-ˌsenchə'wāshən\ *n*

ac·cept \ik'sept, ak-\ *vb* 1 : receive willingly 2 : agree to — **ac·cept·abil·i·ty** \ikˌseptə'bilətē, ak-\ *n* — **ac·cept·able** \-'septəbəl\ *adj* — **ac·cep·tance** \-'septəns\ *n*

ac·cess \'ak,ses\ *n* : capability or way of approaching — **ac·ces·si·bil·i·ty** \ikˌsesə'bilətē, ak-\ *n* — **ac·ces·si·ble** \-'sesəbəl\ *adj*

ac·ces·sion \ik'seshən, ak-\ *n* 1 : something added 2 : act of taking office

ac·ces·so·ry \ik'sesərē, ak-\ *n, pl* **-ries** 1 : nonessential addition 2 : one guilty of aiding a criminal — **accessory** *adj*

ac·ci·dent \'aksədənt\ *n* 1 : event occurring by chance or unintentionally 2 : chance — **ac·ci·den·tal** \ˌaksə'dent°l\ *adj* — **ac·ci·den·tal·ly** *adv*

ac·claim \ə'klām\ *vb or n* : praise

ac·cla·ma·tion \ˌaklə'māshən\ *n* 1 : eager applause 2 : unanimous vote

ac·cli·mate \'aklə,māt, ə'klīmət\ *vb* **-mat·ed; -mat·ing** : acclimatize — **ac·cli·ma·tion** \ˌaklə'māshən, -ˌklī-\ *n*

ac·cli·ma·tize \ə'klīmə,tīz\ *vb* **-tized; -tiz·ing** : accustom to a new climate or situation — **ac·cli·ma·ti·za·tion** \-ˌklīmətə'zāshən\ *n*

ac·co·lade \'akə,lād\ *n* : expression of praise

ac·com·mo·date \ə'kämə,dāt\ *vb* **-dat·ed; -dat·ing** 1 : adapt 2 : provide with something needed 3 : hold without crowding

ac·com·mo·da·tion \ə,kämə'dāshən\ *n* 1 : quarters — usu. pl. 2 : act of accommodating

ac·com·pa·ny \ə'kəmpənē\ *vb* **-nied; -ny·ing** 1 : go or occur with 2 : play supporting music — **ac·com·pa·ni·ment** \-nəmənt\ *n* — **ac·com·pa·nist** \-nist\ *n*

ac·com·plice \ə'kämpləs, -'kəm-\ *n* : associate in crime

ac·com·plish \ə'kämplish, -'kəm-\ *vb* : do, fulfill, or bring about — **ac·com·plished** *adj* — **ac·com·plish·er** *n* — **ac·com·plish·ment** *n*

ac·cord \ə'kòrd\ *vb* 1 : grant 2 : agree ~ *n* 1 : agreement 2 : willingness to act — **ac·cor·dance** \-'kòrd°ns\ *n* — **ac·cor·dant** \-°nt\ *adj*

ac·cord·ing·ly \ə'kòrdiŋlē\ *adv* : consequently

according to *prep* 1 : in conformity with 2 : as stated by

ac·cor·di·on \ə'kòrdēən\ *n* : keyboard instrument with a bellows and reeds ~ *adj* : folding like an accordion bellows — **ac·cor·di·on·ist** \-nist\ *n*

ac·cost \ə'kòst\ *vb* : approach and speak to esp. aggressively

ac·count \ə'kaunt\ *n* 1 : statement of business transactions 2 : credit arrangement with a vendor 3 : report 4 : worth 5 : sum deposited in a bank ~ *vb* : give an explanation

ac·count·able \ə'kauntəbəl\ *adj* : responsible — **ac·count·abil·i·ty** \-ˌkauntə'bilətē\ *n*

ac·coun·tant \ə'kaunt°nt\ *n* : one skilled in accounting — **ac·coun·tan·cy** \-°nsē\ *n*

ac·count·ing \ə'kaúntiŋ\ n : financial record keeping

ac·cou·tre, ac·cou·ter \ə'kütər\ vb **-tred** or **-tered; -tring** or **-ter·ing** \-'kütəriŋ, -'kütriŋ\ : equip

ac·cou·tre·ment, ac·cou·ter·ment \ə'kütrəmənt, -'kütər-\ n **1** : accessory item — usu. pl. **2** : identifying characteristic

ac·cred·it \ə'kredət\ vb **1** : approve officially **2** : attribute — **ac·cred·i·ta·tion** \-ˌkredə'tāshən\ n

ac·crue \ə'krü\ vb **-crued; -cru·ing** : be added by periodic growth — **ac·cru·al** \-əl\ n

ac·cu·mu·late \ə'kyümyəˌlāt\ vb **-lat·ed; -lat·ing** : collect or pile up — **ac·cu·mu·la·tion** \-ˌkyümyə'lāshən\ n

ac·cu·rate \'akyərət\ adj : free from error — **ac·cu·ra·cy** \-rəsē\ n — **ac·cu·rate·ly** adv — **ac·cu·rate·ness** n

ac·cursed \ə'kərst, -'kərsəd\ **ac·curst** \ə'kərst\ adj **1** : being under a curse **2** : damnable

ac·cuse \ə'kyüz\ vb **-cused; -cus·ing** : charge with an offense — **ac·cu·sa·tion** \ˌakyə'zāshən\ n — **ac·cus·er** n

ac·cused \ə'kyüzd\ n, pl **-cused** : defendant in a criminal case

ac·cus·tom \ə'kəstəm\ vb : make familiar through use or experience

ace \'ās\ n : one that excels

acer·bic \ə'sərbik, a-\ adj : sour or biting in temper, mood, or tone

acet·amin·o·phen \əˌsētə'minəfən\ n : pain reliever

ac·e·tate \'asəˌtāt\ n : fabric or plastic derived from acetic acid

ace·tic acid \ə'sētik-\ n : acid found in vinegar

acet·y·lene \ə'setⁿlən, -ⁿlˌ ēn\ n : colorless gas used as a fuel in welding

ache \'āk\ vb **ached; ach·ing 1** : suffer a dull persistent pain **2** : yearn — **ache** n

achieve \ə'chēv\ vb **achieved; achiev·ing** : gain by work or effort — **achieve·ment** n — **achiev·er** n

ac·id \'asəd\ adj **1** : sour or biting to the taste **2** : sharp in manner **3** : of or relating to an acid ~ n : sour water-soluble chemical compound that reacts with a base to form a salt — **acid·ic** \ə'sidik\ adj — **acid·i·fy** \ə'sidəˌfī\ vb — **acid·i·ty** \-ətē\ n — **acid·ly** adv

ac·knowl·edge \ik'nälij, ak-\ vb

-edged; -edg·ing 1 : admit as true **2** : admit the authority of **3** : express thanks for — **ac·knowl·edg·ment** n

ac·me \'akmē\ n : highest point

ac·ne \'aknē\ n : skin disorder marked esp. by pimples

ac·o·lyte \'akəˌlīt\ n : assistant to a member of clergy in a religious service

acorn \'āˌkȯrn, -kərn\ n : nut of the oak

acous·tic \ə'küstik\ adj : relating to hearing or sound — **acous·ti·cal** \-stikəl\ adj — **acous·ti·cal·ly** \-klē\ adv

acous·tics \ə'küstiks\ n sing or pl **1** : science of sound **2** : qualities in a room that affect how sound is heard

ac·quaint \ə'kwānt\ vb **1** : inform **2** : make familiar

ac·quain·tance \ə'kwāntⁿns\ n **1** : personal knowledge **2** : person with whom one is acquainted — **ac·quain·tance·ship** n

ac·qui·esce \ˌakwē'es\ vb **-esced; -esc·ing** : consent or submit — **ac·qui·es·cence** \-'esⁿns\ n — **ac·qui·es·cent** \-ⁿnt\ adj — **ac·qui·es·cent·ly** adv

ac·quire \ə'kwīr\ vb **-quired; -quir·ing** : gain

ac·qui·si·tion \ˌakwə'zishən\ n : a gaining or something gained — **ac·qui·si·tive** \ə'kwizətiv\ adj

ac·quit \ə'kwit\ vb **-tt- 1** : pronounce not guilty **2** : conduct (oneself) usu. well — **ac·quit·tal** \-ⁿl\ n

acre \'ākər\ n **1** pl : lands **2** : 4840 square yards

acre·age \'ākərij\ n : area in acres

ac·rid \'akrəd\ adj : sharp and biting — **acrid·i·ty** \a'kridətē, ə-\ n — **ac·rid·ly** adv — **ac·rid·ness** n

ac·ri·mo·ny \'akrəˌmōnē\ n, pl **-nies** : harshness of language or feeling — **ac·ri·mo·ni·ous** \ˌakrə'mōnēəs\ adj — **ac·ri·mo·ni·ous·ly** adv

ac·ro·bat \'akrəˌbat\ n : performer of tumbling feats — **ac·ro·bat·ic** \ˌakrə'batik\ adj

across \ə'krȯs\ adv : to or on the opposite side ~ prep **1** : to or on the opposite side of **2** : on so as to cross

acryl·ic \ə'krilik\ n **1** : plastic used for molded parts or in paints **2** : synthetic textile fiber

act \'akt\ n **1** : thing done **2** : law **3** : main division of a play ~ vb **1**

: perform in a play **2** : conduct oneself **3** : operate **4** : produce an effect

ac•tion \'akshən\ *n* **1** : legal proceeding **2** : manner or method of performing **3** : activity **4** : thing done over a period of time or in stages **5** : combat **6** : events of a literary plot **7** : operating mechanism

ac•ti•vate \'aktə‚vāt\ *vb* **-vat•ed; -vat•ing** : make active or reactive — **ac•ti•va•tion** \‚aktə'vāshən\ *n*

ac•tive \'aktiv\ *adj* **1** : causing action or change **2** : lively, vigorous, or energetic **3** : erupting or likely to erupt **4** : now in operation — **active** *n* — **ac•tive•ly** *adv*

ac•tiv•i•ty \ak'tivətē\ *n, pl* **-ties** **1** : quality or state of being active **2** : what one is actively doing

ac•tor \'aktər\ *n* : one that acts

ac•tress \'aktrəs\ *n* : woman who acts in plays

ac•tu•al \'akchəwəl\ *adj* : really existing — **ac•tu•al•i•ty** \‚akchə'walətē\ *n* — **ac•tu•al•iza•tion** \‚akchəwələ-'zāshən\ *n* — **ac•tu•al•ize** \'akchəwə‚līz\ *vb* — **ac•tu•al•ly** *adv*

ac•tu•ary \'akchə‚werē\ *n, pl* **-ar•ies** : one who calculates insurance risks and premiums — **ac•tu•ar•i•al** \‚akchə'werēəl\ *adj*

ac•tu•ate \'akchə‚wāt\ *vb* **-at•ed; -at•ing** : put into action — **ac•tu•a•tor** \-‚wātər\ *n*

acu•men \ə'kyümən\ *n* : mental keenness

acu•punc•ture \'akyu‚pəŋkchər\ *n* : treatment by puncturing the body with needles — **acu•punc•tur•ist** \‚akyu'pəŋkchərist\ *n*

acute \ə'kyüt\ *adj* **acut•er; acut•est** **1** : sharp **2** : containing less than 90 degrees **3** : mentally alert **4** : severe — **acute•ly** *adv* — **acute•ness** *n*

ad \'ad\ *n* : advertisement

ad•age \'adij\ *n* : old familiar saying

ad•a•mant \'adəmənt, -‚mant\ *adj* : insistent — **ad•a•mant•ly** *adv*

adapt \ə'dapt\ *vb* : adjust to be suitable for a new use or condition — **adapt•abil•i•ty** \ə‚daptə'bilətē\ *n* — **adapt•able** *adj* — **ad•ap•ta•tion** \‚ad‚ap-'tāshən, -əp-\ *n* — **adap•ter** *n* — **adap•tive** \ə'daptiv\ *adj*

add \'ad\ *vb* **1** : join to something else so as to increase in amount **2** : say further **3** : find a sum — **ad•di•tion** \ə'dishən\ *n*

ad•der \'adər\ *n* **1** : poisonous European snake **2** : No. American snake

ad•dict \'adikt\ *n* : one who is psychologically or physiologically dependent (as on a drug) ~ \ə'dikt\ *vb* : cause to become an addict — **ad•dic•tion** \ə'dikshən\ *n* — **ad•dic•tive** \-'diktiv\ *adj*

ad•di•tion•al \ə'dishənəl\ *adj* : existing as a result of adding — **ad•di•tion•al•ly** *adv*

ad•di•tive \'adətiv\ *n* : substance added to another

ad•dle \'ad°l\ *vb* **-dled; -dling** : confuse

ad•dress \ə'dres\ *vb* **1** : direct one's remarks to **2** : mark an address on ~ \ə'dres, 'ad‚res\ *n* **1** : formal speech **2** : place where a person may be reached or mail may be delivered

ad•duce \ə'düs, -'dyüs\ *vb* **-duced; -duc•ing** : offer as proof

ad•e•noid \'ad‚nȯid, -°nȯid\ *n* : enlarged tissue near the opening of the nose into the throat — usu. pl. — **ade•noid, ad•e•noi•dal** \-əl\ *adj*

adept \ə'dept\ *adj* : highly skilled — **adept•ly** *adv* — **adept•ness** *n*

ad•e•quate \'adikwət\ *adj* : good or plentiful enough — **ad•e•qua•cy** \-kwəsē\ *n* — **ad•e•quate•ly** *adv*

ad•here \ad'hir, əd-\ *vb* **-hered; -her•ing** **1** : remain loyal **2** : stick fast — **ad•her•ence** \-'hirəns\ *n* — **ad•her•ent** \-ənt\ *adj or n*

ad•he•sion \ad'hēzhən, əd-\ *n* : act or state of adhering

ad•he•sive \-'hēsiv, -ziv\ *adj* : tending to adhere ~ *n* : adhesive substance

adieu \ə'dü, -dyü\ *n, pl* **adieus** *or* **adieux** \-'düz,-'dyüz\ : farewell

ad•ja•cent \ə'jās°nt\ *adj* : situated near or next

ad•jec•tive \'ajiktiv\ *n* : word that serves as a modifier of a noun — **ad•jec•ti•val** \‚ajik'tīvəl\ *adj* — **ad•jec•ti•val•ly** *adv*

ad•join \ə'jȯin\ *vb* : be next to

ad•journ \ə'jərn\ *vb* : end a meeting — **ad•journ•ment** *n*

ad•judge \ə'jəj\ *vb* **-judged; -judg•ing** **1** : think or pronounce to be **2** : award by judicial decision

ad•ju•di•cate \ə'jüdi‚kāt\ *vb* **-cat•ed; -cat•ing** : settle judicially — **ad•ju•di•ca•tion** \ə‚jüdi'kāshən\ *n*

ad•junct \'aj‚eŋkt\ *n* : something joined or added but not essential

ad·just \ə'jəst\ vb : fix, adapt, or set right — **ad·just·able** adj — **ad·just·er, ad·jus·tor** \ə'jəstər\ n — **ad·just·ment** \-mənt\ n

ad·ju·tant \'ajətənt\ n : aide esp. to a commanding officer

ad-lib \'ad'lib\ vb **-bb-** : speak without preparation — **ad–lib** n or adj

ad·min·is·ter \əd'minəstər\ vb **1** : manage **2** : give out esp. in doses — **ad·min·is·tra·ble** \-strəbəl\ adj

ad·min·is·tra·tion \əd,minə'strāshən, ad-\ n **1** : process of managing **2** : persons responsible for managing — **ad·min·is·tra·tive** \əd'minə,strātiv\ adj — **ad·min·is·tra·tive·ly** adv

ad·min·is·tra·tor \əd'minə,strātər\ n : one that manages

ad·mi·ra·ble \'admərəbəl\ adj : worthy of admiration — **ad·mi·ra·bly** \-blē\ adv

ad·mi·ral \'admərəl\ n : commissioned officer in the navy ranking next below a fleet admiral

ad·mire \əd'mīr\ vb **-mired; -mir·ing** : have high regard for — **ad·mi·ra·tion** \,admə'rāshən\ n — **ad·mir·er** n — **ad·mir·ing·ly** adv

ad·mis·si·ble \əd'misəbəl\ adj : that can be permitted — **ad·mis·si·bil·i·ty** \-,misə'bilətē\ n

ad·mis·sion \əd'mishən\ n **1** : act of admitting **2** : admittance or a fee paid for this **3** : acknowledgment of a fact

ad·mit \əd'mit\ vb **-tt- 1** : allow to enter **2** : permit **3** : recognize as genuine — **ad·mit·ted·ly** adv

ad·mit·tance \əd'mit³ns\ n : permission to enter

ad·mix·ture \ad'mikschər\ n **1** : thing added in mixing **2** : mixture

ad·mon·ish \ad'mänish\ vb : rebuke — **ad·mon·ish·ment** \-mənt\ n — **ad·mo·ni·tion** \,admə'nishən\ n — **ad·mon·i·to·ry** \ad'mänə,tōrē\ adj

ado \ə'dü\ n **1** : fuss **2** : trouble

ado·be \ə'dōbē\ n : sun-dried building brick

ad·o·les·cence \,ad³l'es³ns\ n : period of growth between childhood and maturity — **ad·o·les·cent** \-³nt\ adj or n

adopt \ə'däpt\ vb **1** : take (a child of other parents) as one's own child **2** : take up and practice as one's own — **adop·tion** \-'däpshən\ n

adore \ə'dōr\ vb **adored; ador·ing 1** : worship **2** : be extremely fond of —

ador·able adj — **ador·ably** adv — **ad·o·ra·tion** \,adə'rāshən\ n

adorn \ə'dórn\ vb : decorate with ornaments — **adorn·ment** n

adrift \ə'drift\ adv or adj **1** : afloat without motive power or moorings **2** : without guidance or purpose

adroit \ə'dróit\ adj : dexterous or shrewd — **adroit·ly** adv — **adroit·ness** n

adult \ə'dəlt, 'ad,əlt\ adj : fully developed and mature ~ n : grown-up person — **adult·hood** n

adul·ter·ate \ə'dəltə,rāt\ vb **-at·ed; -at·ing** : make impure by mixture — **adul·ter·a·tion** \-,dəltə'rāshən\ n

adul·tery \ə'dəltərē\ n, pl **-ter·ies** : sexual unfaithfulness of a married person — **adul·ter·er** \-tərər\ n — **adul·ter·ess** \-tərəs\ n — **adul·ter·ous** \-tərəs\ adj

ad·vance \əd'vans\ vb **-vanced; -vancing 1** : bring or move forward **2** : promote **3** : lend ~ n **1** : forward movement **2** : improvement **3** : offer ~ adj : being ahead of time — **ad·vance·ment** n

ad·van·tage \əd'vantij\ n **1** : superiority of position **2** : benefit or gain — **ad·van·ta·geous** \,ad,van'tājəs, -vən-\ adj — **ad·van·ta·geous·ly** adv

ad·vent \'ad,vent\ n **1** cap : period before Christmas **2** : a coming into being or use

ad·ven·ti·tious \,advən'tishəs\ adj : accidental — **ad·ven·ti·tious·ly** adv

ad·ven·ture \əd'venchər\ n **1** : risky undertaking **2** : exciting experience — **ad·ven·tur·er** \-chərər\ n — **ad·ven·ture·some** \-chərsəm\ adj — **ad·ven·tur·ous** \-chərəs\ adj

ad·verb \'ad,vərb\ n : word that modifies a verb, an adjective, or another adverb — **ad·ver·bi·al** \ad'vərbeəl\ adj — **ad·ver·bi·al·ly** adv

ad·ver·sary \'advər,serē\ n, pl **-sar·ies** : enemy or rival — **adversary** adj

ad·verse \ad'vərs, 'ad-,\ adj : opposing or unfavorable — **ad·verse·ly** adv

ad·ver·si·ty \ad'vərsətē\ n, pl **-ties** : hard times

ad·vert \ad'vərt\ vb : refer

ad·ver·tise \'advər,tīz\ vb **-tised; -tis·ing** : call public attention to — **ad·ver·tise·ment** \,advər'tīzmənt, əd-'vərtəzmənt\ n — **ad·ver·tis·er** n

ad·ver·tis·ing \'advər,tīziŋ\ n : business of preparing advertisements

ad·vice \əd'vīs\ *n* : recommendation with regard to a course of action

ad·vis·able \əd'vīzəbəl\ *adj* : wise or prudent — **ad·vis·abil·i·ty** \-ˌvīzə-'bilətē\ *n*

ad·vise \əd'vīz\ *vb* -vised; -vis·ing : give advice to — **ad·vis·er, ad·vis·or** \-'vīzər\ *n*

ad·vise·ment \əd'vīzmənt\ *n* : careful consideration

ad·vi·so·ry \əd'vīzərē\ *adj* : having power to advise

ad·vo·cate \'advəkət, -ˌkāt\ *n* : one who argues or pleads for a cause or proposal ～ \-ˌkāt\ *vb* -cat·ed; -cat·ing : recommend — **ad·vo·ca·cy** \-vəkəsē\ *n*

adze \'adz\ *n* : tool for shaping wood

ae·gis \'ējəs\ *n* : protection or sponsorship

ae·on \'ēən, 'ē,än\ *var of* EON

aer·ate \'ar,āt\ *vb* -at·ed; -at·ing : supply or impregnate with air — **aer·a·tion** \,ar'āshən\ *n* — **aer·a·tor** \'ar,ātər\ *n*

ae·ri·al \'arēəl\ *adj* : inhabiting, occurring in, or done in the air ～ *n* : antenna

ae·rie \'arē, 'irē\ *n* : eagle's nest

aer·o·bic \,ar'ōbik\ *adj* : using or needing oxygen

aer·o·bics \-biks\ *n sing or pl* : exercises that produce a marked increase in respiration and heart rate

aero·dy·nam·ics \,arōdī'namiks\ *n* : science of bodies in motion in a gas — **aero·dy·nam·ic** \-ik\ *adj* — **aero·dy·nam·i·cal·ly** \-iklē\ *adv*

aero·nau·tics \,arə'nòtiks\ *n* : science dealing with aircraft — **aero·nau·ti·cal** \-ikəl\ *adj*

aero·sol \'arə,säl, -,sòl\ *n* **1** : liquid or solid particles suspended in a gas **2** : substance sprayed as an aerosol

aero·space \'arō,spās\ *n* : earth's atmosphere and the space beyond — **aerospace** *adj*

aes·thet·ic \es'thetik\ *adj* : relating to beauty — **aes·thet·i·cal·ly** \-iklē\ *adv*

aes·thet·ics \-'thetiks\ *n* : branch of philosophy dealing with beauty

afar \ə'fär\ *adv* : from, at, or to a great distance — **afar** *n*

af·fa·ble \'afəbəl\ *adj* : easy to talk to — **af·fa·bil·i·ty** \,afə'bilətē\ *n* — **af·fa·bly** \'afəblē\ *adv*

af·fair \ə'far\ *n* : something that relates to or involves one

¹af·fect \ə'fekt, a-\ *vb* : assume for effect — **af·fec·ta·tion** \,af,ek'tā-shən\ *n*

²affect *vb* : produce an effect on

af·fect·ed \ə'fektəd, a-\ *adj* **1** : pretending to some trait **2** : artificially assumed to impress — **af·fect·ed·ly** *adv*

af·fect·ing \ə'fektiŋ, a-\ *adj* : arousing pity or sorrow — **af·fect·ing·ly** *adv*

af·fec·tion \ə'fekshən\ *n* : kind or loving feeling — **af·fec·tion·ate** \-shənət\ *adj* — **af·fec·tion·ate·ly** *adv*

af·fi·da·vit \,afə'dāvət\ *n* : sworn statement

af·fil·i·ate \ə'filē,āt\ *vb* -at·ed; -at·ing : become a member or branch — **af·fil·i·ate** \-ēət\ *n* — **af·fil·i·a·tion** \-ˌfilē'āshən\ *n*

af·fin·i·ty \ə'finətē\ *n, pl* -ties : close attraction or relationship

af·firm \ə'fərm\ *vb* : assert positively — **af·fir·ma·tion** \,afər'māshən\ *n*

af·fir·ma·tive \ə'fərmətiv\ *adj* : asserting the truth or existence of something ～ *n* : statement of affirmation or agreement

af·fix \ə'fiks\ *vb* : attach

af·flict \ə'flikt\ *vb* : cause pain and distress to — **af·flic·tion** \-'flikshən\ *n*

af·flu·ence \'af,lüəns; a'flü-, ə-\ *n* : wealth — **af·flu·ent** \-ənt\ *adj*

af·ford \ə'fòrd\ *vb* **1** : manage to bear the cost of **2** : provide

af·fray \ə'frā\ *n* : fight

af·front \ə'frənt\ *vb or n* : insult

af·ghan \'af,gan, -gən\ *n* : crocheted or knitted blanket

afire \ə'fīr\ *adj or adv* : being on fire

aflame \ə'flām\ *adj or adv* : flaming

afloat \ə'flōt\ *adj or adv* : floating

afoot \ə'füt\ *adv or adj* **1** : on foot **2** : in progress

afore·said \ə'fōr,sed\ *adj* : said or named before

afraid \ə'frād, *South also* ə'fred\ *adj* : filled with fear

afresh \ə'fresh\ *adv* : anew

aft \'aft\ *adv* : to or toward the stern or tail

af·ter \'aftər\ *adv* : at a later time ～ *prep* **1** : behind in place or time **2** : in pursuit of ～ *conj* : following the time when ～ *adj* **1** : later **2** : located toward the back

af·ter·life \\'aftər‚līf\ *n* : existence after death

af·ter·math \-‚math\ *n* : results

af·ter·noon \‚aftər'nün\ *n* : time between noon and evening

af·ter·thought *n* : later thought

af·ter·ward \'aftərwərd\, **af·ter·wards** \-wərdz\ *adv* : at a later time

again \ə'gen, -'gin\ *adv* **1** : once more **2** : on the other hand **3** : in addition

against \ə'genst\ *prep* **1** : directly opposite to **2** : in opposition to **3** : so as to touch or strike

agape \ə'gāp, -'gap\ *adj or adv* : having the mouth open in astonishment

ag·ate \'agət\ *n* : quartz with bands or masses of various colors

age \'āj\ *n* **1** : length of time of life or existence **2** : particular time in life (as majority or the latter part) **3** : quality of being old **4** : long time **5** : period in history ～ *vb* : become old or mature

-age \ij\ *n suffix* **1** : aggregate **2** : action or process **3** : result of **4** : rate of **5** : place of **6** : state or rank **7** : fee

aged *adj* **1** \'ājəd\ : old **2** \'ājd\ : allowed to mature

age·less \'ājləs\ *adj* : eternal

agen·cy \'ājənsē\ *n, pl* **-cies** **1** : one through which something is accomplished **2** : office or function of an agent **3** : government administrative division

agen·da \ə'jendə\ *n* : list of things to be done

agent \'ājənt\ *n* **1** : means **2** : person acting or doing business for another

ag·gran·dize \ə'gran‚dīz, 'agrən-\ *vb* **-dized; -diz·ing** : make great or greater — **ag·gran·dize·ment** \ə'grandəzmənt, -‚dīz-; ‚agrən'dīz-\ *n*

ag·gra·vate \'agrə‚vāt\ *vb* **-vat·ed; -vat·ing** **1** : make more severe **2** : irritate — **ag·gra·va·tion** \‚agrə-'vāshən\ *n*

ag·gre·gate \'agrigət\ *adj* : formed into a mass ～ \-‚gāt\ *vb* **-gat·ed; -gat·ing** : collect into a mass ～ \-gət\ *n* **1** : mass **2** : whole amount

ag·gres·sion \ə'greshən\ *n* **1** : unprovoked attack **2** : hostile behavior — **ag·gres·sor** \-'gresər\ *n*

ag·gres·sive \ə'gresiv\ *adj* **1** : easily provoked to fight **2** : hard working and enterprising — **ag·gres·sive·ly** *adv* — **ag·gres·sive·ness** *n*

ag·grieve \ə'grēv\ *vb* **-grieved; -griev-**

ing **1** : cause grief to **2** : inflict injury on

aghast \ə'gast\ *adj* : struck with amazement or horror

ag·ile \'ajəl\ *adj* : able to move quickly and easily — **agil·i·ty** \ə'jilətē\ *n*

ag·i·tate \'ajə‚tāt\ *vb* **-tat·ed; -tat·ing** **1** : shake or stir back and forth **2** : excite or trouble the mind of **3** : try to arouse public feeling — **ag·i·ta·tion** \‚ajə'tāshən\ *n* — **ag·i·ta·tor** \'ajə‚tātər\ *n*

ag·nos·tic \ag'nästik, əg-\ *n* : one who doubts the existence of God

ago \ə'gō\ *adj or adv* : earlier than the present

agog \ə'gäg\ *adj* : full of excitement

ag·o·nize \'agə‚nīz\ *vb* **-nized; -niz·ing** : suffer mental agony — **ag·o·niz·ing·ly** *adv*

ag·o·ny \'agənē\ *n, pl* **-nies** : extreme pain or mental distress

agrar·i·an \ə'grerēən\ *adj* : relating to land ownership or farming interests — **agrarian** *n* — **agrar·i·an·ism** *n*

agree \ə'grē\ *vb* **agreed; agree·ing** **1** : be of the same opinion **2** : express willingness **3** : get along together **4** : be similar **5** : be appropriate, suitable, or healthful

agree·able \-əbəl\ *adj* **1** : pleasing **2** : willing to give approval — **agree·able·ness** *n* — **agree·ably** *adv*

agree·ment \-mənt\ *n* **1** : harmony of opinion or purpose **2** : mutual understanding or arrangement

ag·ri·cul·ture \'agri‚kəlchər\ *n* : farming — **ag·ri·cul·tur·al** \‚agri'kəlchərəl\ *adj* — **ag·ri·cul·tur·ist** \-rist\, **ag·ri·cul·tur·al·ist** \-rəlist\ *n*

aground \ə'graünd\ *adv or adj* : on or onto the bottom or shore

ague \'āgyü\ *n* **1** : fever with recurrent chills and sweating **2** : malaria

ahead \ə'hed\ *adv or adj* **1** : in or toward the front **2** : into or for the future **3** : in a more advantageous position

ahead of *prep* **1** : in front or advance of **2** : in excess of

ahoy \ə'hói\ *interj* — used in hailing

aid \'ād\ *vb* : provide help or support ～ *n* : help

aide \'ād\ *n* : helper

AIDS \'ādz\ *n* : serious disease of the human immune system

ail \'āl\ *vb* **1** : trouble **2** : be ill

ai·le·ron \'ālə,rän\ *n* : movable part of an airplane wing

ail·ment \'ālmənt\ *n* : bodily disorder

aim \'ām\ *vb* **1** : point or direct (as a weapon) **2** : direct one's efforts ~ *n* **1** : an aiming or the direction of aiming **2** : object or purpose — **aim·less** *adj* — **aim·less·ly** *adv* — **aim·less·ness** *n*

air \'ar\ *n* **1** : mixture of gases surrounding the earth **2** : melody **3** : outward appearance **4** : artificial manner **5** : compressed air **6** : travel by or use of aircraft **7** : medium of transmission of radio waves ~ *vb* **1** : expose to the air **2** : broadcast — **air·borne** \-,bōrn\ *adj*

air–condition *vb* : equip with an apparatus (**air conditioner**) for filtering and cooling the air

air·craft *n, pl* **aircraft** : craft that flies

Aire·dale terrier \'ar,dāl-\ *n* : large terrier with a hard wiry coat

air·field *n* : airport or its landing field

air force *n* : military organization for conducting warfare by air

air·lift *n* : a transporting of esp. emergency supplies by aircraft — **airlift** *vb*

air·line *n* : air transportation system — **air·lin·er** *n*

air·mail *n* : system of transporting mail by airplane — **airmail** *vb*

air·man \-mən\ *n* **1** : aviator **2** : enlisted man in the air force in one of the 3 ranks below sergeant

airman basic *n* : enlisted man of the lowest rank in the air force

airman first class *n* : enlisted man in the air force ranking just below sergeant

air·plane *n* : fixed-wing aircraft heavier than air

air·port *n* : place for landing aircraft and usu. for receiving passengers

air·ship *n* : powered lighter-than-air aircraft

air·strip *n* : airfield runway

air·tight *adj* : tightly sealed to prevent flow of air

air·waves \'ar,wāvz\ *n pl* : medium of transmission of radio waves

airy \'arē\ *adj* **air·i·er; -est** **1** : delicate **2** : breezy

aisle \'īl\ *n* : passage between sections or rows

ajar \ə'jär\ *adj or adv* : partly open

akim·bo \ə'kimbō\ *adj or adv* : having the hand on the hip and the elbow turned outward

akin \ə'kin\ *adj* **1** : related by blood **2** : similar in kind

-al \əl\ *adj suffix* : of, relating to, or characterized by

al·a·bas·ter \'alə,bastər\ *n* : white or translucent mineral

alac·ri·ty \ə'lakrətē\ *n* : cheerful readiness

alarm \ə'lärm\ *n* **1** : warning signal or device **2** : fear at sudden danger ~ *vb* **1** : warn **2** : frighten

alas \ə'las\ *interj* — used to express unhappiness, pity, or concern

al·ba·tross \'albə,trós, -,träs\ *n, pl* **-tross** *or* **-tross·es** : large seabird

al·be·it \òl'bēət, al-\ *conj* : even though

al·bi·no \al'bīnō\ *n, pl* **-nos** : person or animal with abnormally white skin — **al·bi·nism** \'albə,nizəm\ *n*

al·bum \'albəm\ *n* **1** : book for displaying a collection (as of photographs) **2** : collection of recordings

al·bu·men \al'byümən\ *n* **1** : white of an egg **2** : albumin

al·bu·min \-mən\ *n* : protein found in blood, milk, egg white, and tissues

al·che·my \'alkəmē\ *n* : medieval chemistry — **al·che·mist** \'alkəmist\ *n*

al·co·hol \'alkə,hól\ *n* **1** : intoxicating agent in liquor **2** : liquor — **al·co·hol·ic** *adj*

al·co·hol·ic \,alkə'hólik, -'häl-\ *n* : person affected with alcoholism

al·co·hol·ism \'alkə,hól,izəm\ *n* : addiction to alcoholic beverages

al·cove \'al,kōv\ *n* : recess in a room or wall

al·der·man \'óldərmən\ *n* : city official

ale \'āl\ *n* : beerlike beverage — **ale·house** *n*

alert \ə'lərt\ *adj* **1** : watchful **2** : quick to perceive and act ~ *n* : alarm ~ *vb* : warn — **alert·ly** *adv* — **alert·ness** *n*

ale·wife *n* : fish of the herring family

al·fal·fa \al'falfə\ *n* : cloverlike forage plant

al·ga \'algə\ *n, pl* **-gae** \'al,jē\ : any of a group of lower plants that includes seaweed — **al·gal** \-gəl\ *adj*

al·ge·bra \'aljəbrə\ *n* : branch of mathematics — **al·ge·bra·ic** \,aljə'brāik\ *adj* — **al·ge·bra·i·cal·ly** \-'brāəklē\ *adv*

alias \'ālēəs, 'ālyəs\ *adv* : otherwise called ~ *n* : assumed name

al·i·bi \'alə,bī\ *n* **1** : defense of having been elsewhere when a crime was committed **2** : justification ~ *vb* **-bied; -bi·ing** : offer an excuse

alien \'ālēən, 'ālyən\ *adj* : foreign ~ *n* **1** : foreign-born resident **2** : extraterrestrial

alien·ate \'ālēə,nāt, 'ālyə-\ *vb* **-at·ed; -at·ing** : cause to be no longer friendly — **alien·ation** \,ālēə'nāshən, ,ālyə-\ *n*

alight \ə'līt\ *vb* : dismount

align \ə'līn\ *vb* : bring into line — **align·er** *n* — **align·ment** *n*

alike \ə'līk\ *adj* : identical or very similar ~ *adv* : equally

al·i·men·ta·ry \,alə'mentərē\ *adj* : relating to or functioning in nutrition

al·i·mo·ny \'alə,mōnē\ *n, pl* **-nies** : money paid to a separated or divorced spouse

alive \ə'līv\ *adj* **1** : having life **2** : lively or animated

al·ka·li \'alkə,lī\ *n, pl* **-lies** *or* **-lis** : strong chemical base — **al·ka·line** \-kələn, -,līn\ *adj* — **al·ka·lin·i·ty** \,alkə'linətē\ *n*

all \'ȯl\ *adj* **1** : the whole of **2** : greatest possible **3** : every one of ~ *adv* **1** : wholly **2** : so much **3** : for each side ~ *pron* **1** : whole number or amount **2** : everything or everyone

Al·lah \'älə, 'al-\ *n* : God of Islam

all–around *adj* : versatile

al·lay \ə'lā\ *vb* **1** : alleviate **2** : calm

al·lege \ə'lej\ *vb* **-leged; -leg·ing** : assert without proof — **al·le·ga·tion** \,ali'gāshən\ *n* — **al·leg·ed·ly** \ə'lejədlē\ *adv*

al·le·giance \ə'lējəns\ *n* : loyalty

al·le·go·ry \'alə,gōrē\ *n, pl* **-ries** : story in which figures and actions are symbols of general truths — **al·le·gor·i·cal** \,alə'gȯrikəl\ *adj*

al·le·lu·ia \,alə'lüyə\ *interj* : hallelujah

al·ler·gen \'alərjən\ *n* : something that causes allergy — **al·ler·gen·ic** \,alər'jenik\ *adj*

al·ler·gy \'alərjē\ *n, pl* **-gies** : abnormal reaction to a substance — **al·ler·gic** \ə'lərjik\ *adj* — **al·ler·gist** \'alərjist\ *n*

al·le·vi·ate \ə'lēvē,āt\ *vb* **-at·ed; -at·ing** : relieve or lessen — **al·le·vi·a·tion** \ə,lēvē'āshən\ *n*

al·ley \'alē\ *n, pl* **-leys** **1** : place for bowling **2** : narrow passage between buildings

al·li·ance \ə'līəns\ *n* : association

al·li·ga·tor \'alə,gātər\ *n* : large aquatic reptile related to the crocodiles

al·lit·er·a·tion \ə,litə'rāshən\ *n* : repetition of initial sounds of words — **al·lit·er·a·tive** \-'litə,rātiv\ *adj*

al·lo·cate \'alə,kāt\ *vb* **-cat·ed; -cat·ing** : assign — **al·lo·ca·tion** \,alə'kāshən\ *n*

al·lot \ə'lät\ *vb* **-tt-** : distribute as a share — **al·lot·ment** *n*

al·low \ə'laù\ *vb* **1** : admit or concede **2** : permit — **al·low·able** *adj*

al·low·ance \-əns\ *n* **1** : allotted share **2** : money given regularly for expenses

al·loy \'al,òi\ *n* : metals melted together — **al·loy** \ə'lòi\ *vb*

all right *adv or adj* **1** : satisfactorily **2** : yes **3** : certainly

all·spice \'ȯlspīs\ *n* : berry of a West Indian tree made into a spice

al·lude \ə'lüd\ *vb* **-lud·ed; -lud·ing** : refer indirectly — **al·lu·sion** \-'lüzhən\ *n* — **al·lu·sive** \-'lüsiv\ *adj*

al·lure \ə'lùr\ *vb* **-lured; -lur·ing** : entice ~ *n* : attractive power

al·ly \ə'lī, 'al,ī\ *vb* **-lied; -ly·ing** : enter into an alliance — **al·ly** \'al,ī, ə'lī\ *n*

-al·ly \əlē\ *adv suffix* : -ly

al·ma·nac \'ȯlmə,nak, 'al-\ *n* : annual information book

al·mighty \ȯl'mītē\ *adj* : having absolute power

al·mond \'ämənd, 'am-, 'alm-, 'älm-\ *n* : tree with nutlike fruit kernels

al·most \'ȯl,mōst, ȯl'-\ *adv* : very nearly

alms \'ämz, 'älmz, 'almz\ *n, pl* **alms** : charitable gift

aloft \ə'lȯft\ *adv* : high in the air

alo·ha \ä'lōhä\ *interj* — used to greet or bid farewell

alone \ə'lōn\ *adj* **1** : separated from others **2** : not including anyone or anything else — **alone** *adv*

along \ə'lȯŋ\ *prep* **1** : in line with the direction of **2** : at a point on or during ~ *adv* **1** : forward **2** : as a companion

along·side *adv or prep* : along or by the side

alongside of *prep* : alongside

aloof \ə'lüf\ *adj* : indifferent and reserved — **aloof·ness** *n*

aloud \ə'laùd\ *adv* : so as to be heard

al·paca \al'pakə\ *n* **1** : So. American mammal related to the llama **2** : alpaca wool or cloth made of this

al·pha·bet \'alfə,bet, -bət\ *n* : ordered set of letters of a language — **al·pha·bet·i·cal** \,alfə'betikəl\, **alpha·bet·ic** \-'betik\ *adj* — **al·pha·bet·i·cal·ly** \-klē\ *adv*

al·pha·bet·ize \'alfəbə,tīz\ *vb* **-ized; -iz·ing** : arrange in alphabetical order — **al·pha·bet·iz·er** *n*

al·ready \ol'redē\ *adv* : by a given time

al·so \'olsō\ *adv* : in addition

al·tar \'oltər\ *n* : structure for rituals

al·ter \'oltər\ *vb* : make different — **al·ter·a·tion** \,oltə'rāshən\ *n*

al·ter·ca·tion \,oltər'kāshən\ *n* : dispute

al·ter·nate \'oltərnət, 'al-\ *adj* **1** : arranged or succeeding by turns **2** : every other ~ \-,nāt\ *vb* **-nat·ed; -nat·ing** : occur or cause to occur by turns ~ \-nət\ *n* : substitute — **al·ter·nate·ly** *adv* — **al·ter·na·tion** \,oltər'nāshən, ,al-\ *n*

alternating current *n* : electric current that regularly reverses direction

al·ter·na·tive \ol'tərnətiv, al-\ *adj* : offering a choice — **alternative** *n*

al·ter·na·tor \'oltər,nātər, 'al-\ *n* : alternating-current generator

al·though \ol'thō\ *conj* : even though

al·tim·e·ter \al'timətər, 'altə,mētər\ *n* : instrument for measuring altitude

al·ti·tude \'altə,tüd, -,tyüd\ *n* **1** : distance up from the ground **2** : angular distance above the horizon

al·to \'altō\ *n, pl* **-tos** : lower female choral voice

al·to·geth·er \,oltə'gethər\ *adv* **1** : wholly **2** : on the whole

al·tru·ism \'altrú,izəm\ *n* : concern for others — **al·tru·ist** \-ist\ *n* — **al·tru·is·tic** \,altrú'istik\ *adj* — **al·tru·is·ti·cal·ly** \-tiklē\ *adv*

al·um \'aləm\ *n* : crystalline compound containing aluminum

alu·mi·num \ə'lümənəm\ *n* : silver-white malleable ductile light metallic element

alum·na \ə'ləmnə\ *n, pl* **-nae** \-,nē\ : woman graduate

alum·nus \ə'ləmnəs\ *n, pl* **-ni** \-,nī\ : graduate

al·ways \'olwēz, -wāz\ *adv* **1** : at all times **2** : forever

am *pres 1st sing of* BE

amal·gam \ə'malgəm\ *n* **1** : mercury alloy **2** : mixture

amal·gam·ate \ə'malgə,māt\ *vb* **-at·ed; -at·ing** : unite — **amal·ga·ma·tion** \-,malgə'māshən\ *n*

am·a·ryl·lis \,amə'riləs\ *n* : bulbous herb with clusters of large colored flowers like lilies

amass \ə'mas\ *vb* : gather

am·a·teur \'amə,tər, -,tùr, -,tyúr, -,chùr, -chər\ *n* **1** : person who does something for pleasure rather than for pay **2** : person who is not expert — **am·a·teur·ish** \,amə'tərish, -'tùr-, -'tyùr-\ *adj* — **ama·teur·ism** \'amə,tər,izəm, -,tùr-, -,tyùr-, -,chùr-, -chər-\ *n*

am·a·to·ry \'amə,tōrē\ *adj* : of or expressing sexual love

amaze \ə'māz\ *vb* **amazed; amaz·ing** : fill with wonder — **amaze·ment** *n* — **amaz·ing·ly** *adv*

am·a·zon \'amə,zän, -zən\ *n* : tall strong woman — **am·a·zo·ni·an** \,amə'zōnēən\ *adj*

am·bas·sa·dor \am'basədər\ *n* : representative esp. of a government — **am·bas·sa·do·ri·al** \-,basə'dō-rēəl\ *adj* — **am·bas·sa·dor·ship** *n*

am·ber \'ambər\ *n* : yellowish fossil resin or its color

am·ber·gris \'ambər,gris, -,grēs\ *n* : waxy substance from certain whales used in making perfumes

am·bi·dex·trous \,ambi'dekstrəs\ *adj* : equally skilled with both hands — **am·bi·dex·trous·ly** *adv*

am·bi·ence, am·bi·ance \'ambēəns, 'ämbē,äns\ *n* : pervading atmosphere

am·big·u·ous \am'bigyəwəs\ *adj* : having more than one interpretation — **am·bi·gu·i·ty** \,ambə'gyüətē\ *n*

am·bi·tion \am'bishən\ *n* : eager desire for success or power — **am·bi·tious** \shəs\ *adj* — **am·bi·tious·ly** *adv*

am·biv·a·lence \am'bivələns\ *n* : simultaneous attraction and repulsion — **am·biv·a·lent** \-lənt\ *adj*

am·ble \'ambəl\ *vb* **-bled; -bling** : go at a leisurely gait — **amble** *n*

am·bu·lance \'ambyələns\ *n* : vehicle for carrying injured or sick persons

am·bu·la·to·ry \'ambyələ,tōrē\ *adj* **1** : relating to or adapted to walking **2** : able to walk about

am·bush \'am,bùsh\ *n* : trap by which

a surprise attack is made from a place of hiding — **ambush** *vb*

ame·lio·rate \ə'mēlyə‚rāt\ *vb* **-rat·ed; -rat·ing** : make or grow better — **ame·lio·ra·tion** \-‚mēlyə'rāshən\ *n*

amen \'ā'men, 'ä-\ *interj* — used for affirmation esp. at the end of prayers

ame·na·ble \ə'mēnəbəl, -'men-\ *adj* : ready to yield or be influenced

amend \ə'mend\ *vb* **1** : improve **2** : alter in writing

amend·ment \-mənt\ *n* : change made in a formal document (as a law)

amends \ə'mendz\ *n sing or pl* : compensation for injury or loss

ame·ni·ty \ə'menətē, -'mē-\ *n, pl* **-ties 1** : agreeableness **2** *pl* : social conventions **3** : something serving to comfort or accommodate

am·e·thyst \'aməthəst\ *n* : purple gemstone

ami·a·ble \'āmēəbəl\ *adj* : easy to get along with — **ami·a·bil·i·ty** \‚āmēə'bilətē\ *n* — **ami·a·bly** \'āmēəblē\ *adv*

am·i·ca·ble \'amikəbəl\ *adj* : friendly — **am·i·ca·bly** \-blē\ *adv*

amid \ə'mid\, **amidst** \-'midst\ *prep* : in or into the middle of

amino acid \ə'mēnō-\ *n* : nitrogen-containing acid

amiss \ə'mis\ *adv* : in the wrong way ～ *adj* : wrong

am·me·ter \'am‚ētər\ *n* : instrument for measuring electric current

am·mo·nia \ə'mōnyə\ *n* **1** : colorless gaseous compound of nitrogen and hydrogen **2** : solution of ammonia in water

am·mu·ni·tion \‚amyə'nishən\ *n* **1** : projectiles fired from guns **2** : explosive items used in war

am·ne·sia \am'nēzhə\ *n* : sudden loss of memory — **am·ne·si·ac** \-zē‚ak, -zhē-\, **am·ne·sic** \-zik, -sik\ *adj or n*

am·nes·ty \'amnəstē\ *n, pl* **-ties** : a pardon for a group — **amnesty** *vb*

amoe·ba \ə'mēbə\ *n, pl* **-bas** *or* **-bae** \-‚bē\ : tiny one-celled animal that occurs esp. in water — **amoe·bic** \-bik\ *adj*

amok \ə'mək, -'mäk\ *adv* : in a violent or uncontrolled way

among \ə'məŋ\ *prep* **1** : in or through **2** : in the number or class of **3** : in shares to each of

am·o·rous \'amərəs\ *adj* **1** : inclined to love **2** : being in love **3** : indicative

of love — **am·o·rous·ly** *adv* — **am·o·rous·ness** *n*

amor·phous \ə'mórfəs\ *adj* : shapeless

am·or·tize \'amər‚tīz, ə'mór-\ *vb* **-tized; -tiz·ing** : get rid of (as a debt) gradually with periodic payments — **amor·ti·za·tion** \‚amərtə'zāshən, ə‚mórt-\ *n*

amount \ə'maúnt\ *vb* **1** : be equivalent **2** : reach a total ～ *n* : total number or quantity

amour \ə'múr, ä-, a-\ *n* **1** : love affair **2** : lover

am·pere \'am‚pir\ *n* : unit of electric current

am·per·sand \'ampər‚sand\ *n* : character & used for the word *and*

am·phib·i·ous \am'fibēəs\ *adj* **1** : able to live both on land and in water **2** : adapted for both land and water — **am·phib·i·an** \-ən\ *n*

am·phi·the·ater \'amfə‚thēətər\ *n* : oval or circular structure with rising tiers of seats around an arena

am·ple \'ampəl\ *adj* **-pler** \-plər\; **-plest** \-pləst\ **1** : large **2** : sufficient — **am·ply** \-plē\ *adv*

am·pli·fy \'amplə‚fī\ *vb* **-fied; -fy·ing** : make louder, stronger, or more thorough — **am·pli·fi·ca·tion** \‚ampləfə'kāshən\ *n* — **am·pli·fi·er** \'amplə‚fīər\ *n*

am·pli·tude \-‚tüd, -‚tyüd\ *n* **1** : fullness **2** : extent of a vibratory movement

am·pu·tate \'ampyə‚tāt\ *vb* **-tat·ed; -tat·ing** : cut off (a body part) — **am·pu·ta·tion** \‚ampyə'tāshən\ *n* — **am·pu·tee** \‚ampyə'tē\ *n*

amuck \ə'mək\ *var of* **AMOK**

am·u·let \'amyələt\ *n* : ornament worn as a charm against evil

amuse \ə'myüz\ *vb* **amused; amus·ing 1** : engage the attention of in an interesting and pleasant way **2** : make laugh — **amuse·ment** *n*

an \ən, 'an\ *indefinite article* : a — used before words beginning with a vowel sound

-an \ən\, **-ian** \ēən\, **-ean** \ēən\ *n suffix* **1** : one that belongs to **2** : one skilled in ～ *adj suffix* **1** : of or belonging to **2** : characteristic of or resembling

anach·ro·nism \ə'nakrə‚nizəm\ *n* : one that is chronologically out of place — **anach•ro•nis•tic** \ə͵nakrə-ˈnistik\ *adj*

an•a•con•da \͵anəˈkändə\ *n* : large So. American snake

ana•gram \ˈanə͵gram\ *n* : word or phrase made by transposing the letters of another word or phrase

anal \ˈānᵊl\ *adj* : relating to the anus

an•al•ge•sic \͵anᵊlˈjēzik, -sik\ *n* : pain reliever

anal•o•gy \əˈnaləjē\ *n, pl* **-gies** 1 : similarity between unlike things 2 : example of something similar — **an•a•log•i•cal** \͵anᵊlˈäjikəl\ *adj* — **an•a•log•i•cal•ly** \-iklē\ *adv* — **anal•o•gous** \əˈnaləgəs\ *adj*

anal•y•sis \əˈnaləsəs\ *n, pl* **-y•ses** \-͵sēz\ 1 : examination of a thing to determine its parts 2 : psychoanalysis — **an•a•lyst** \ˈanᵊlist\ *n* — **an•a•lyt•ic** \͵anᵊlˈitik\, **an•a•lyt•i•cal** \-ikəl\ *adj* — **an•a•lyt•i•cal•ly** \-iklē\ *adv*

an•a•lyze \ˈanᵊl͵īz\ *vb* **-lyzed; -lyz•ing** : make an analysis of

an•ar•chism \ˈanər͵kizəm, -͵när-\ *n* : theory that all government is undesirable — **an•ar•chist** \-kist\ *n or adj* — **an•ar•chis•tic** \͵anərˈkistik\ *adj*

an•ar•chy \ˈanərkē, -͵när-\ *n* : lack of government or order — **an•ar•chic** \aˈnärkik\ *adj* — **an•ar•chi•cal•ly** \-iklē\ *adv*

anath•e•ma \əˈnathəmə\ *n* 1 : solemn curse 2 : person or thing accursed or intensely disliked

anat•o•my \əˈnatəmē\ *n, pl* **-mies** : science dealing with the structure of organisms — **an•a•tom•ic** \͵anə-ˈtämik\, **an•a•tom•i•cal** \-ikəl\ *adj* — **an•a•tom•i•cal•ly** *adv* — **anat•o•mist** \əˈnatəmist\ *n*

-ance \əns\ *n suffix* 1 : action or process 2 : quality or state 3 : amount or degree

an•ces•tor \ˈan͵sestər\ *n* : one from whom an individual is descended

an•ces•tress \-trəs\ *n* : female ancestor

an•ces•try \-trē\ *n* 1 : line of descent 2 : ancestors — **an•ces•tral** \an-ˈsestrəl\ *adj*

an•chor \ˈaŋkər\ *n* 1 : heavy device that catches in the sea bottom to hold a ship in place 2 : anchorperson ∼ *vb* : hold or become held in place by or as if by an anchor — **an•chor•age** \-kərij\ *n*

an•chor•per•son \ˈaŋkər͵pərsən\ *n* : news broadcast coordinator

an•cho•vy \ˈan͵chōvē, anˈchō-\ *n, pl* **-vies** *or* **-vy** : small herringlike fish

an•cient \ˈānshənt\ *adj* 1 : having existed for many years 2 : belonging to times long past — **ancient** *n*

-ancy \ənsē\ *n suffix* : quality or state

and \ənd, ˈand\ *conj* — used to indicate connection or addition

and•iron \ˈan͵dīərn\ *n* : one of 2 metal supports for wood in a fireplace

an•drog•y•nous \anˈdräjənəs\ *adj* 1 : having characteristics of both male and female 2 : suitable for either sex

an•ec•dote \ˈanik͵dōt\ *n* : brief story — **an•ec•dot•al** \͵anikˈdōtᵊl\ *adj*

ane•mia \əˈnēmēə\ *n* : blood deficiency — **ane•mic** \əˈnēmik\ *adj*

anem•o•ne \əˈnemənē\ *n* : small herb with showy usu. white flowers

an•es•the•sia \͵anəsˈthēzhə\ *n* : loss of bodily sensation

an•es•thet•ic \͵anəsˈthetik\ *n* : agent that produces anesthesia — **anesthetic** *adj* — **anes•the•tist** \əˈnesthətist\ *n* — **anes•the•tize** \-thə-͵tīz\ *vb*

an•eu•rysm, an•eu•rism \ˈanyə-͵rizəm\ : blood-filled bulge of a blood vessel

anew \əˈnü, -ˈnyü\ *adv* : over again

an•gel \ˈānjəl\ *n* : spiritual being superior to humans — **an•gel•ic** \an-ˈjelik\, **an•gel•i•cal** \-ikəl\ *adj* — **angel•i•cal•ly** *adv*

an•ger \ˈaŋgər\ *n* : strong feeling of displeasure ∼ *vb* : make angry

an•gi•na \anˈjīnə\ *n* : painful disorder of heart muscles — **an•gi•nal** \anˈjīnᵊl\ *adj*

¹**an•gle** \ˈaŋgəl\ *n* 1 : figure formed by the meeting of 2 lines in a point 2 : sharp corner 3 : point of view ∼ *vb* **-gled; -gling** : turn or direct at an angle

²**angle** *vb* **an•gled; an•gling** : fish with a hook and line — **an•gler** \-glər\ *n* — **an•gle•worm** *n* — **an•gling** *n*

an•go•ra \aŋˈgōrə, an-\ *n* : yarn or cloth made from the hair of an Angora goat or rabbit

an•gry \ˈaŋgrē\ *adj* **-gri•er; -est** : feeling or showing anger — **an•gri•ly** \-grəlē\ *adv*

an•guish \ˈaŋgwish\ *n* : extreme pain or distress of mind — **an•guished** \-gwisht\ *adj*

an•gu•lar \'aŋgyələr\ *adj* **1** : having many or sharp angles **2** : thin and bony — **an•gu•lar•i•ty** \ˌaŋgyə'larətē\ *n*

an•i•mal \'anəməl\ *n* **1** : living being capable of feeling and voluntary motion **2** : lower animal as distinguished from humans

an•i•mate \'anəmət\ *adj* : having life ～ \-ˌmāt\ *vb* -mat•ed; -mat•ing **1** : give life or vigor to **2** : make appear to move — **an•i•mat•ed** *adj*

an•i•ma•tion \ˌanə'māshən\ *n* **1** : liveliness **2** : animated cartoon

an•i•ma•tron•ic \ˌanəmə'tränik\ : relating to an electrically animated mechanical figure

an•i•mos•i•ty \ˌanə'mäsətē\ *n, pl* **-ties** : resentment

an•i•mus \'anəməs\ *n* : deep-seated hostility

an•ise \'anəs\ *n* : herb related to the carrot with aromatic seeds (**ani•seed** \-ˌsēd\) used in flavoring

an•kle \'aŋkəl\ *n* : joint or region between the foot and the leg — **an•kle-bone** *n*

an•nals \'anᵊlz\ *n pl* : chronological record of history — **an•nal•ist** \-ᵊlist\ *n*

an•neal \ə'nēl\ *vb* **1** : make less brittle by heating and then cooling **2** : strengthen or toughen

an•nex \ə'neks, 'anˌeks\ *vb* : assume political control over (a territory) ～ \'anˌeks, -iks\ *n* : added building — **an•nex•a•tion** \ˌanˌek'sāshən\ *n*

an•ni•hi•late \ə'nīəˌlāt\ *vb* -lat•ed; -lat•ing : destroy — **an•ni•hi•la•tion** \-ˌnīə-'lāshən\ *n*

an•ni•ver•sa•ry \ˌanə'vərsərē\ *n, pl* **-ries** : annual return of the date of a notable event or its celebration

an•no•tate \'anəˌtāt\ *vb* -tat•ed; -tat•ing : furnish with notes — **an•no•ta•tion** \ˌanə'tāshən\ *n* — **an•no•ta•tor** \'anəˌtātər\ *n*

an•nounce \ə'naùns\ *vb* -nounced; -nounc•ing : make known publicly — **an•nounce•ment** *n* — **an•nounc•er** *n*

an•noy \ə'nói\ *vb* : disturb or irritate — **an•noy•ance** \-əns\ *n* — **an•noy•ing•ly** \-'nóiiŋlē\ *adv*

an•nu•al \'anyəwəl\ *adj* **1** : occurring once a year **2** : living only one year — **annual** *n* — **an•nu•al•ly** *adv*

an•nu•i•ty \ə'nüətē, -'nyü-\ *n, pl* **-ties**

: amount payable annually or the right to such a payment

an•nul \ə'nəl\ *vb* **-ll-** : make legally void — **an•nul•ment** *n*

an•ode \'anˌōd\ *n* **1** : positive electrode **2** : negative battery terminal — **an•od•ic** \a'nädik\ *adj*

anoint \ə'nóint\ *vb* : apply oil to as a rite — **anoint•ment** *n*

anom•a•ly \ə'näməlē\ *n, pl* **-lies** : something abnormal or unusual — **anom•a•lous** \ə'nämələs\ *adj*

anon•y•mous \ə'nänəməs\ *adj* : of unknown origin — **an•o•nym•i•ty** \ˌanə'nimətē\ *n* — **anon•y•mous•ly** *adv*

an•oth•er \ə'nəthər\ *adj* **1** : any or some other **2** : one more ～ *pron* **1** : one more **2** : one different

an•swer \'ansər\ *n* **1** : something spoken or written in reply to a question **2** : solution to a problem ～ *vb* **1** : reply to **2** : be responsible **3** : be adequate — **an•swer•er** *n*

an•swer•able \-rəbəl\ *adj* : responsible

ant \'ant\ *n* : small social insect — **ant-hill** *n*

-ant \ənt\ *n suffix* **1** : one that performs or causes an action **2** : thing that is acted upon ～ *adj suffix* **1** : performing an action or being in a condition **2** : causing an action or process

ant•ac•id \ant'asəd\ : agent that counteracts acidity

an•tag•o•nism \an'tagəˌnizəm\ *n* : active opposition or hostility — **an•tag•o•nist** \-ənist\ *n* — **an•tag•o•nis•tic** \-ˌtagə'nistik\ *adj*

an•tag•o•nize \an'tagəˌnīz\ *vb* -nized; -niz•ing : cause to be hostile

ant•arc•tic \ant'ärktik, -'ärtik\ *adj* : relating to the region near the south pole

antarctic circle *n* : circle parallel to the equator approximately 23°27' from the south pole

an•te•bel•lum \ˌanti'beləm\ *adj* : existing before the U.S. Civil War

an•te•ced•ent \ˌantə'sēdᵊnt\ *n* : one that comes before — **antecedent** *adj*

an•te•lope \'antᵊlˌōp\ *n, pl* **-lope** *or* **-lopes** : deerlike mammal related to the ox

an•ten•na \an'tenə\ *n, pl* **-nae** \-ˌnē\ *or* **-nas** **1** : one of the long slender paired sensory organs on the head of an arthropod **2** *pl* **-nas** : metallic device for sending or receiving radio waves

an·te·ri·or \an'tirēər\ *adj* : located before in place or time

an·them \'anthəm\ *n* : song or hymn of praise or gladness

an·ther \'anthər\ *n* : part of a seed plant that contains pollen

an·thol·o·gy \an'thäləjē\ *n, pl* **-gies** : literary collection

an·thra·cite \'anthrə,sīt\ *n* : hard coal

an·thro·poid \'anthrə,pȯid\ *n* : large ape — **anthropoid** *adj*

an·thro·pol·o·gy \,anthrə'päləjē\ *n* : science dealing with humans — **an·thro·po·log·i·cal** \-pə'läjikəl\ *adj* — **an·thro·pol·o·gist** \-'päləjist\ *n*

anti- \,antē, -,tī\ **ant-, anth-** *prefix* **1** : opposite in kind, position, or action **2** : opposing or hostile toward **3** : defending against **4** : curing or treating

an·ti·bi·ot·ic \,antēbī'ätik, -bē-\ *n* : substance that inhibits harmful microorganisms — **antibiotic** *adj*

an·ti·body \'anti,bädē\ *n* : bodily substance that counteracts the effects of a foreign substance or organism

an·tic \'antik\ *n* : playful act ~ *adj* : playful

an·tic·i·pate \an'tisə,pāt\ *vb* **-pat·ed; -pat·ing 1** : be prepared for **2** : look forward to — **an·tic·i·pa·tion** \-,tisə-'pāshən\ *n* — **an·tic·i·pa·to·ry** \-'tisəpə,tōrē\ *adj*

an·ti·cli·max \,antē'klī,maks\ *n* : something strikingly less important than what has preceded it — **an·ti·cli·mac·tic** \-klī'maktik\ *adj*

an·ti·dote \'anti,dōt\ *n* : remedy for poison

an·ti·freeze \'anti,frēz\ *n* : substance to prevent a liquid from freezing

an·ti·his·ta·mine \,anti'histə,mēn\ : drug for treating allergies and colds

an·ti·mo·ny \'antə,mōnē\ *n* : brittle white metallic chemical element

an·tip·a·thy \an'tipəthē\ *n, pl* **-thies** : strong dislike

---

List of self-explanatory words with the prefix *anti-*

antiabortion	anticigarette	antifatigue
antiacademic	anticlerical	antifemale
antiadministration	anticollision	antifeminine
antiaggression	anticolonial	antifeminism
antiaircraft	anticommunism	antifeminist
antialien	anticommunist	antifertility
antiapartheid	anticonservation	antiforeign
antiaristocratic	anticonservationist	antiforeigner
antiart	anticonsumer	antifraud
antiauthoritarian	anticonventional	antigambling
antiauthority	anticorrosion	antiglare
antibacterial	anticorrosive	antigovernment
antibias	anticorruption	antiguerrilla
antiblack	anticrime	antigun
antibourgeois	anticruelty	antihijack
antiboycott	anticult	antihomosexual
antibureaucratic	anticultural	antihuman
antiburglar	antidandruff	antihumanism
antiburglary	antidemocratic	antihumanistic
antibusiness	antidiscrimination	antihunting
anticancer	antidrug	anti–imperialism
anticapitalism	antidumping	anti–imperialist
anticapitalist	antiestablishment	anti–inflation
anti–Catholic	antievolution	anti–inflationary
anticensorship	antievolutionary	anti–institutional
anti–Christian	antifamily	anti–integration
anti–Christianity	antifascism	anti–intellectual
antichurch	antifascist	anti–intellectualism

an·ti·quar·i·an \ˌantə'kwerēən\ *adj*
: relating to antiquities or old books
— **antiquarian** *n*
an·ti·quary \'antəˌkwerē\ *n, pl* **-quar-
ies** : one who collects or studies
antiquities
an·ti·quat·ed \'antəˌkwātəd\ *adj* : out-
of-date
an·tique \an'tēk\ *adj* : very old or out-
of-date — **antique** *n*
an·tiq·ui·ty \an'tikwətē\ *n, pl* **-ties 1**
: ancient times **2** *pl* : relics of ancient
times
an·ti·sep·tic \ˌantə'septik\ *adj* : killing
or checking the growth of germs —
antiseptic *n* — **an·ti·sep·ti·cal·ly**
\-tiklē\ *adv*
an·tith·e·sis \an'tithəsəs\ *n, pl* **-e·ses**
\-ˌsēz\ : direct opposite
ant·ler \'antlər\ *n* : solid branched
horn of a deer — **ant·lered** \-lərd\ *adj*
ant·onym \'antəˌnim\ *n* : word of opposite meaning
anus \'ānəs\ *n* : the rear opening of the
alimentary canal

an·vil \'anvəl\ *n* : heavy iron block on
which metal is shaped
anx·i·ety \aŋ'zīətē\ *n, pl* **-eties** : uneasiness usu. over an expected misfortune
anx·ious \'aŋkshəs\ *adj* **1** : uneasy **2**
: earnestly wishing — **anx·ious·ly**
adv
any \'enē\ *adj* **1** : one chosen at random **2** : of whatever number or quantity ~ *pron* **1** : any one or ones **2**
: any amount ~ *adv* : to any extent or
degree
any·body \-bədē, -ˌbäd-\ *pron* : anyone
any·how \-ˌhau̇\ *adv* **1** : in any way **2**
: nevertheless
any·more \ˌenē'mōr\ *adv* : at the present time
any·one \-'enēˌwən\ *pron* : any person
any·place *adv* : anywhere
any·thing *pron* : any thing whatever
any·time *adv* : at any time whatever
any·way *adv* : anyhow

antijamming
anti–Jewish
antilabor
antiliberal
antiliberalism
antilitter
antilittering
antilynching
antimale
antimanagement
antimaterialism
antimaterialist
antimicrobial
antimilitarism
antimilitarist
antimilitary
antimiscegenation
antimonopolist
antimonopoly
antimosquito
antinoise
antiobesity
antiobscenity
antipapal
antipersonnel
antipolice
antipollution
antipornographic
antipornography
antipoverty

antiprofiteering
antiprogressive
antiprostitution
antirabies
antiracketeering
antiradical
antirape
antirealism
antirecession
antireform
antireligious
antirevolutionary
antiriot
antiromantic
antirust
antisegregation
antisex
antisexist
antisexual
antishoplifting
antislavery
antismoking
antismuggling
antismut
antispending
antistrike
antistudent
antisubmarine
antisubversion
antisubversive

antisuicide
antitank
antitax
antitechnological
antitechnology
antiterrorism
antiterrorist
antitheft
antitobacco
antitotalitarian
antitoxin
antitraditional
antitrust
antituberculosis
antitumor
antityphoid
antiulcer
antiunemployment
antiunion
antiuniversity
antiurban
antiviolence
antiviral
antivivisection
antiwar
anti–West
anti–Western
antiwhite
antiwoman

any•where *adv* : in or to any place

aor•ta \ā'ȯrtə\ *n, pl* **-tas** *or* **-tae** \-ē\ : main artery from the heart — **aor•tic** \ā'ȯrtik\ *adj*

apart \ə'pärt\ *adv* **1** : separately in place or time **2** : aside **3** : to pieces

apart•heid \ə'pär,tāt, -,tīt\ *n* : racial segregation

apart•ment \ə'pärtmənt\ *n* : set of usu. rented rooms

ap•a•thy \'apəthē\ *n* : lack of emotion or interest — **ap•a•thet•ic** \,apə-'thetik\ *adj* — **ap•a•thet•i•cal•ly** \-iklē\ *adv*

ape \'āp\ *n* : large tailless primate ~ *vb* **aped; ap•ing** : imitate

ap•er•ture \'apər,chu̇r, -chər\ *n* : opening

apex \'ā,peks\ *n, pl* **apex•es** *or* **api•ces** \'āpə,sēz, 'apə-\ : highest point

aphid \'āfid, 'a-\ *n* : small insect that sucks plant juices

aph•o•rism \'afə,rizəm\ *n* : short saying stating a general truth — **aph•oris•tic** \,afə'ristik\ *adj*

aph•ro•di•si•ac \,afrə'dēzē,ak, 'diz-\ *n* : substance that excites sexual desire

api•a•rist \'āpēərist\ *n* : beekeeper — **api•ary** \-pē,erē\ *n*

apiece \ə'pēs\ *adv* : for each one

aplen•ty \ə'plentē\ *adj* : plentiful or abundant

aplomb \ə'pläm, -'pləm\ *n* : complete calmness or self-assurance

apoc•a•lypse \ə'päkə,lips\ *n* : writing prophesying a cataclysm in which evil forces are destroyed — **apoc•a•lyp•tic** \-,päkə'liptik\ *adj*

apoc•ry•pha \ə'päkrəfə\ *n* : writings of dubious authenticity — **apoc•ry•phal** \-fəl\ *adj*

apol•o•get•ic \ə,pälə'jetik\ *adj* : expressing apology — **apol•o•get•i•cal•ly** \-iklē\ *adv*

apol•o•gize \ə'pälə,jīz\ *vb* **-gized; -giz•ing** : make an apology — **apol•o•gist** \-jist\ *n*

apol•o•gy \ə'päləjē\ *n, pl* **-gies 1** : formal justification **2** : expression of regret for a wrong

ap•o•plexy \'apə,pleksē\ *n* : sudden loss of consciousness caused by rupture or obstruction of an artery of the brain — **ap•o•plec•tic** \,apə'plektik\ *adj*

apos•ta•sy \ə'pästəsē\ *n, pl* **-sies** : abandonment of a former loyalty — **apos•tate** \ə'päs,tāt\ *adj or n*

apos•tle \ə'päsəl\ *n* : disciple or advocate — **apos•tle•ship** *n* — **ap•os•tolic** \,apə'stälik\ *adj*

apos•tro•phe \ə'pästrə,fē\ *n* : punctuation mark ' to indicate the possessive case or the omission of a letter or figure

apoth•e•cary \ə'päthə,kerē\ *n, pl* **-car•ies** : druggist

ap•pall \ə'pȯl\ *vb* : fill with horror or dismay

ap•pa•ra•tus \,apə'ratəs, -'rät-\ *n, pl* **-tus•es** *or* **-tus 1** : equipment **2** : complex machine or device

ap•par•el \ə'parəl\ *n* : clothing

ap•par•ent \ə'parənt\ *adj* **1** : visible **2** : obvious **3** : seeming — **ap•par•ent•ly** *adv*

ap•pa•ri•tion \,apə'rishən\ *n* : ghost

ap•peal \ə'pēl\ *vb* **1** : try to have a court case reheard **2** : ask earnestly **3** : have an attraction — **appeal** *n*

ap•pear \ə'pir\ *vb* **1** : become visible or evident **2** : come into the presence of someone **3** : seem

ap•pear•ance \ə'pirəns\ *n* **1** : act of appearing **2** : outward aspect

ap•pease \ə'pēz\ *vb* **-peased; -peas•ing** : pacify with concessions — **ap•pease•ment** *n*

ap•pel•late \ə'pelət\ *adj* : having power to review decisions

ap•pend \ə'pend\ *vb* : attach

ap•pend•age \ə'pendij\ *n* : something attached

ap•pen•dec•to•my \,apən'dektəmē\ *n, pl* **-mies** : surgical removal of the appendix

ap•pen•di•ci•tis \ə,pendə'sītəs\ *n* : inflammation of the appendix

ap•pen•dix \ə'pendiks\ *n, pl* **-dix•es** *or* **-di•ces** \-də,sēz\ **1** : supplementary matter **2** : narrow closed tube extending from lower right intestine

ap•pe•tite \'apə,tīt\ *n* **1** : natural desire esp. for food **2** : preference

ap•pe•tiz•er \-,tīzər\ *n* : food or drink to stimulate the appetite

ap•pe•tiz•ing \-ziŋ\ *adj* : tempting to the appetite — **ap•pe•tiz•ing•ly** *adv*

ap•plaud \ə'plȯd\ *vb* : show approval esp. by clapping

ap•plause \ə'plȯz\ *n* : a clapping in approval

ap•ple \\'apəl\ *n* : rounded fruit with firm white flesh

ap•ple•jack \-ˌjak\ *n* : brandy made from cider

ap•pli•ance \ə'plīəns\ *n* : household machine or device

ap•pli•ca•ble \'aplikəbəl, ə'plikə-\ *adj* : capable of being applied — **ap•pli•ca•bil•i•ty** \ˌaplikə'bilətē, əˌplikə-\ *n*

ap•pli•cant \'aplikənt\ *n* : one who applies

ap•pli•ca•tion \ˌaplə'kāshən\ *n* **1** : act of applying or thing applied **2** : constant attention **3** : request **4** : computer program that performs a major task

ap•pli•ca•tor \'apləˌkātər\ *n* : device for applying a substance

ap•pli•qué \ˌaplə'kā\ *n* : cut-out fabric decoration — **appliqué** *vb*

ap•ply \ə'plī\ *vb* **-plied; -ply•ing 1** : place in contact **2** : put to practical use **3** : devote (one's) attention or efforts to something **4** : submit a request **5** : have reference or a connection

ap•point \ə'póint\ *vb* **1** : set or assign officially **2** : equip or furnish — **ap•poin•tee** \əˌpóin'tē, ˌa-\ *n*

ap•point•ment \ə'póintmənt\ *n* **1** : act of appointing **2** : nonelective political job **3** : arrangement for a meeting

ap•por•tion \ə'pōrshən\ *vb* : distribute proportionately — **ap•por•tion•ment** *n*

ap•po•site \'apəzət\ *adj* : suitable — **ap•po•site•ly** *adv* — **ap•po•site•ness** *n*

ap•praise \ə'prāz\ *vb* **-praised; -prais•ing** : set value on — **ap•prais•al** \-'prāzəl\ *n* — **ap•prais•er** *n*

ap•pre•cia•ble \ə'prēshəbəl\ *adj* : considerable — **ap•pre•cia•bly** \-blē\ *adv*

ap•pre•ci•ate \ə'prēshēˌāt\ *vb* **-ated; -at•ing 1** : value justly **2** : be grateful for **3** : increase in value — **ap•pre•cia•tion** \-ˌprēshē'āshən\ *n*

ap•pre•cia•tive \ə'prēshətiv, -shēˌāt-\ *adj* : showing appreciation

ap•pre•hend \ˌapri'hend\ *vb* **1** : arrest **2** : look forward to in dread **3** : understand — **ap•pre•hen•sion** \-'henchən\ *n*

ap•pre•hen•sive \-'hensiv\ *adj* : fearful — **ap•pre•hen•sive•ly** *adv* — **ap•pre•hen•sive•ness** *n*

ap•pren•tice \ə'prentəs\ *n* : person learning a craft ~ *vb* **-ticed; -tic•ing** : employ or work as an apprentice — **ap•pren•tice•ship** *n*

ap•prise \ə'prīz\ *vb* **-prised; -pris•ing** : inform

ap•proach \ə'prōch\ *vb* **1** : move nearer or be close to **2** : make initial advances or efforts toward — **approach** *n* — **ap•proach•able** *adj*

ap•pro•ba•tion \ˌaprə'bāshən\ *n* : approval

ap•pro•pri•ate \ə'prōprēˌāt\ *vb* **-at•ed; -at•ing 1** : take possession of **2** : set apart for a particular use ~ \-prēət\ *adj* : suitable — **ap•pro•pri•ate•ly** *adv* — **ap•pro•pri•ate•ness** *n* — **ap•pro•pria•tion** \əˌprōprē-'āshən\ *n*

ap•prov•al \ə'prüvəl\ *n* : act of approving

ap•prove \ə'prüv\ *vb* **-proved; -proving** : accept as satisfactory

ap•prox•i•mate \ə'präksəmət\ *adj* : nearly correct or exact ~ \-ˌmāt\ *vb* **-mat•ed; -mat•ing** : come near — **ap•prox•i•mate•ly** *adv* — **ap•prox•i•ma•tion** \-ˌpräksə'māshən\ *n*

ap•pur•te•nance \ə'pərtnəns\ *n* : accessory — **ap•pur•te•nant** \-'pərtnənt\ *adj*

apri•cot \'aprəˌkät, 'ā-\ *n* : peachlike fruit

April \'āprəl\ *n* : 4th month of the year having 30 days

apron \'āprən\ *n* : protective garment

ap•ro•pos \ˌaprə'pō, 'aprəˌpō\ *adv* : suitably ~ *adj* : being to the point

apropos of *prep* : with regard to

apt \'apt\ *adj* **1** : suitable **2** : likely **3** : quick to learn — **apt•ly** *adv* — **apt•ness** *n*

ap•ti•tude \'aptəˌtüd, -ˌtyüd\ *n* **1** : capacity for learning **2** : natural ability

aqua \'akwə, 'äk-\ *n* : light greenish blue color

aquar•i•um \ə'kwarēəm\ *n, pl* **-iums** *or* **-ia** \-ēə\ : glass container for aquatic animals and plants

aquat•ic \ə'kwätik, -'kwat-\ *adj* : of or relating to water — **aquatic** *n*

aq•ue•duct \'akwəˌdəkt\ *n* : conduit for carrying running water

aq•ui•line \'akwəˌlīn, -lən\ *adj* : curved like an eagle's beak

-ar \ər\ *adj suffix* **1** : of, relating to, or being **2** : resembling

ar·a·besque \ˌarə'besk\ *n* : intricate design

ar·a·ble \'arəbəl\ *adj* : fit for crops

ar·bi·ter \'ärbətər\ *n* : final authority

ar·bi·trary \'ärbəˌtrerē\ *adj* **1** : selected at random **2** : autocratic — **ar·bi·trari·ly** \ˌärbə'trerəlē\ *adv* — **ar·bi·trari·ness** \'ärbəˌtrerēnəs\ *n*

ar·bi·trate \'ärbəˌtrāt\ *vb* **-trat·ed; -trat·ing** : settle a dispute as arbitrator — **ar·bi·tra·tion** \ˌärbə'trāshən\ *n*

ar·bi·tra·tor \'ärbəˌtrātər\ *n* : one chosen to settle a dispute

ar·bor \'ärbər\ *n* : shelter under branches or vines

ar·bo·re·al \är'bōrēəl\ *adj* : living in trees

arc \'ärk\ *n* **1** : part of a circle **2** : bright sustained electrical discharge ~ *vb* **arced** \'ärkt\; **arc·ing** \'ärkiŋ\ : form an arc

ar·cade \är'kād\ *n* : arched passageway between shops

ar·cane \är'kān\ *adj* : mysterious or secret

¹arch \'ärch\ *n* : curved structure spanning an opening ~ *vb* : cover with or form into an arch

²arch *adj* **1** : chief — usu. in combination **2** : mischievous — **arch·ly** *adv* — **arch·ness** *n*

ar·chae·ol·o·gy, ar·che·ol·o·gy \ˌärkē'äləjē\ *n* : study of past human life — **ar·chae·o·log·i·cal** \-kēə'läjikəl\ *adj* — **ar·chae·ol·o·gist** \-kē-'äləjist\ *n*

ar·cha·ic \är'kāik\ *adj* : belonging to an earlier time — **ar·cha·i·cal·ly** \-iklē\ *adv*

arch·an·gel \'ärkˌānjəl\ *n* : angel of high rank

arch·bish·op \ärch'bishəp\ *n* : chief bishop — **arch·bish·op·ric** \-əˌprik\ *n*

arch·di·o·cese \-'dīəsəs, -ˌsēz, -ˌsēs\ *n* : diocese of an archbishop

ar·chery \'ärchərē\ *n* : shooting with bow and arrows — **ar·cher** \-chər\ *n*

ar·che·type \'ärkiˌtīp\ *n* : original pattern or model

ar·chi·pel·a·go \ˌärkə'peləˌgō, ˌärchə-\ *n, pl* **-goes** *or* **-gos** : group of islands

ar·chi·tect \'ärkəˌtekt\ *n* : building designer

ar·chi·tec·ture \'ärkəˌtekchər\ *n* **1**

: building design **2** : style of building **3** : manner of organizing elements — **ar·chi·tec·tur·al** \ˌärkə'tekchərəl, -'tekshrəl\ *adj* — **ar·chi·tec·tur·al·ly** *adv*

ar·chives \'ärˌkīvz\ *n pl* : public records or their storage place — **archi·vist** \'ärkəvist, -ˌkī-\ *n*

arch·way *n* : passageway under an arch

arc·tic \'ärktik, 'ärt-\ *adj* **1** : relating to the region near the north pole **2** : frigid

arctic circle *n* : circle parallel to the equator approximately 23°27' from the north pole

-ard \ərd\ *n suffix* : one that is

ar·dent \'ärd⁰nt\ *adj* : characterized by warmth of feeling — **ar·dent·ly** *adv*

ar·dor \'ärdər\ *n* : warmth of feeling

ar·du·ous \'ärjəwəs\ *adj* : difficult — **ar·du·ous·ly** *adv* — **ar·du·ous·ness** *n*

are *pres 2d sing or pres pl of* BE

ar·ea \'arēə\ *n* **1** : space for something **2** : amount of surface included **3** : region **4** : range covered by a thing or concept

area code *n* : 3-digit area-identifying telephone number

are·na \ə'rēnə\ *n* **1** : enclosed exhibition area **2** : sphere of activity

ar·gon \'ärˌgän\ *n* : colorless odorless gaseous chemical element

ar·got \'ärgət, -ˌgō\ *n* : special language (as of the underworld)

argu·able \'ärgyəwəbəl\ *adj* : open to dispute

ar·gue \'ärgyü\ *vb* **-gued; -gu·ing** **1** : give reasons for or against something **2** : disagree in words

ar·gu·ment \'ärgyəmənt\ *n* **1** : reasons given to persuade **2** : dispute with words

ar·gu·men·ta·tive \ˌärgyə'mentətiv\ *adj* : inclined to argue

ar·gyle \'ärˌgīl\ *n* : colorful diamond pattern in knitting

aria \'ärēə\ *n* : opera solo

ar·id \'arəd\ *adj* : very dry — **arid·i·ty** \ə'ridətē\ *n*

arise \ə'rīz\ *vb* **arose** \-'rōz\; **aris·en** \-'riz⁰n\; **aris·ing** \-'rīziŋ\ **1** : get up **2** : originate

ar·is·toc·ra·cy \ˌarə'stäkrəsē\ *n, pl* **-cies** : upper class — **aris·to·crat** \ə'ristəˌkrat\ *n* — **aris·to·crat·ic** \əˌristə'kratik\ *adj*

arith·me·tic \ə'rithməˌtik\ *n* : mathematics that deals with numbers — **ar‑ith‑met‑ic** \ˌarith'metik\, **ar‑ith‑met‑i‑cal** \‑ikəl\ *adj*

ark \'ärk\ *n* : big boat

¹**arm** \'ärm\ *n* **1** : upper limb **2** : branch — **armed** \'ärmd\ *adj* — **arm‑less** *adj*

²**arm** *vb* : furnish with weapons ~ *n* **1** : weapon **2** : branch of the military forces **3** *pl* : family's heraldic designs

ar‑ma‑da \är'mädə, ‑'mäd‑\ *n* : naval fleet

ar‑ma‑dil‑lo \ˌärmə'dilō\ *n, pl* **‑los** : burrowing mammal covered with bony plates

ar‑ma‑ment \'ärməmənt\ *n* : military arms and equipment

ar‑ma‑ture \'ärmə‚chu̇r, ‑chər\ *n* : rotating part of an electric generator or motor

armed forces *n pl* : military

ar‑mi‑stice \'ärməstəs\ *n* : truce

ar‑mor \'ärmər\ *n* : protective covering — **ar‑mored** \‑mərd\ *adj*

ar‑mory \'ärmərē\ *n, pl* **‑mor‑ies** : factory or storehouse for arms

arm‑pit *n* : hollow under the junction of the arm and shoulder

ar‑my \'ärmē\ *n, pl* **‑mies 1** : body of men organized for war esp. on land **2** : great number

aro‑ma \ə'rōmə\ *n* : usu. pleasing odor — **ar‑o‑mat‑ic** \ˌarə'matik\ *adj*

around \ə'rau̇nd\ *adv* **1** : in or along a circuit **2** : on all sides **3** : near **4** : in an opposite direction ~ *prep* **1** : surrounding **2** : along the circuit of **3** : to or on the other side of **4** : near

arouse \ə'rau̇z\ *vb* **aroused; arous‑ing 1** : awaken from sleep **2** : stir up — **arous‑al** \‑'rau̇zəl\ *n*

ar‑raign \ə'rān\ *vb* **1** : call before a court to answer to an indictment **2** : accuse — **ar‑raign‑ment** *n*

ar‑range \ə'rānj\ *vb* **‑ranged; ‑rang‑ing 1** : put in order **2** : settle or agree on **3** : adapt (a musical composition) for voices or instruments — **ar‑range‑ment** *n* — **ar‑rang‑er** *n*

ar‑ray \ə'rā\ *vb* **1** : arrange in order **2** : dress esp. splendidly ~ *n* **1** : arrangement **2** : rich clothing **3** : imposing group

ar‑rears \ə'rirz\ *n pl* : state of being behind in paying debts

ar‑rest \ə'rest\ *vb* **1** : stop **2** : take into legal custody — **arrest** *n*

ar‑rive \ə'rīv\ *vb* **‑rived; ‑riv‑ing 1**

: reach a destination, point, or stage **2** : come near in time — **ar‑riv‑al** \‑əl\ *n*

ar‑ro‑gant \'arəgənt\ *adj* : showing an offensive sense of superiority — **ar‑ro‑gance** \‑gəns\ *n* — **ar‑ro‑gant‑ly** *adv*

ar‑ro‑gate \‑ˌgāt\ *vb* **‑gat‑ed; ‑gat‑ing** : to claim without justification

ar‑row \'arō\ *n* : slender missile shot from a bow — **ar‑row‑head** *n*

ar‑royo \ə'róiō, ‑ə\ *n, pl* **‑royos 1** : watercourse **2** : gully

ar‑se‑nal \'ärsᵊnəl\ *n* **1** : place where arms are made or stored **2** : store

ar‑se‑nic \'ärsᵊnik\ *n* : solid grayish poisonous chemical element

ar‑son \'ärsᵊn\ *n* : willful or malicious burning of property — **ar‑son‑ist** \‑ist\ *n*

art \'ärt\ *n* **1** : skill **2** : branch of learning **3** : creation of things of beauty or works so produced **4** : ingenuity

ar‑te‑rio‑scle‑ro‑sis \ärˌtirēōsklə‑'rōsəs\ *n* : hardening of the arteries — **ar‑te‑rio‑scle‑rot‑ic** \‑'rätik\ *adj or n*

ar‑tery \'ärtərē\ *n, pl* **‑ter‑ies 1** : tubular vessel carrying blood from the heart **2** : thoroughfare — **ar‑te‑ri‑al** \är'tirēəl\ *adj*

art‑ful \‑fəl\ *adj* **1** : ingenious **2** : crafty — **art‑ful‑ly** *adv* — **art‑ful‑ness** *n*

ar‑thri‑tis \är'thrītəs\ *n, pl* **‑ti‑des** \‑'thritə‚dēz\ : inflammation of the joints — **ar‑thrit‑ic** \‑'thritik\ *adj or n*

ar‑thro‑pod \'ärthrə‚päd\ *n* : invertebrate animal (as an insect or crab) with segmented body and jointed limbs — **arthropod** *adj*

ar‑ti‑choke \'ärtə‚chōk\ *n* : tall thistle‑like herb or its edible flower head

ar‑ti‑cle \'ärtikəl\ *n* **1** : distinct part of a written document **2** : nonfictional published piece of writing **3** : word (as *an, the*) used to limit a noun **4** : item or piece

ar‑tic‑u‑late \är'tikyələt\ *adj* : able to speak effectively ~ \‑ˌlāt\ *vb* **‑lated; ‑lat‑ing 1** : utter distinctly **2** : unite by joints — **ar‑tic‑u‑late‑ly** *adv* — **ar‑tic‑u‑late‑ness** *n* — **ar‑tic‑u‑la‑tion** \‑ˌtikyə'lāshən\ *n*

ar‑ti‑fact \'ärtə‚fakt\ *n* : object of esp. prehistoric human workmanship

ar·ti·fice \'ärtəfəs\ *n* **1** : trick or trick-ery **2** : ingenious device or ingenuity

ar·ti·fi·cial \‚ärtə'fishəl\ *adj* **1** : man-made **2** : not genuine — **ar·ti·fi·ci·al·i·ty** \-‚fishē'alətē\ *n* — **ar·ti·fi·cial·ly** *adv* — **ar·ti·fi·cial·ness** *n*

ar·til·lery \är'tilərē\ *n, pl* **-ler·ies** : large caliber firearms

ar·ti·san \'ärtəzən, -sən\ *n* : skilled craftsman

art·ist \'ärtist\ *n* : one who creates art — **ar·tis·tic** \är'tistik\ *adj* — **ar·tis·ti·cal·ly** \-iklē\ *adv* — **ar·tis·try** \'ärtəstrē\ *n*

art·less \'ärtləs\ *adj* : sincere or natural — **art·less·ly** *adv* — **art·less·ness** *n*

arty \'ärtē\ *adj* **art·i·er; -est** : preten-tiously artistic — **art·i·ly** \'ärt°lē\ *adv* — **art·i·ness** *n*

-ary \‚erē\ *adj suffix* : of, relating to, or connected with

as \əz, ‚az\ *adv* **1** : to the same degree **2** : for example ~ *conj* **1** : in the same way or degree as **2** : while **3** : because **4** : though ~ *pron* — used after *same* or *such* ~ *prep* : in the ca-pacity of

as·bes·tos \as'bestəs, az-\ *n* : fibrous incombustible mineral

as·cend \ə'send\ *vb* : move upward — **as·cen·sion** \-'senchən\ *n*

as·cen·dan·cy \ə'sendənsē\ *n* : domi-nation

as·cen·dant \ə'sendənt\ *n* : dominant position ~ *adj* **1** : moving upward **2** : dominant

as·cent \ə'sent\ *n* **1** : act of moving upward **2** : degree of upward slope

as·cer·tain \‚asər'tān\ *vb* : determine — **as·cer·tain·able** *adj*

as·cet·ic \ə'setik\ *adj* : self-denying — **ascetic** *n* — **as·cet·i·cism** \-'setə‚sizəm\ *n*

as·cribe \ə'skrīb\ *vb* **-cribed; -crib·ing** : attribute — **as·crib·able** *adj* — **as·crip·tion** \-'skripshən\ *n*

asep·tic \ā'septik\ *adj* : free of disease germs

¹ash \'ash\ *n* : tree related to the olives

²ash *n* : matter left when something is burned — **ash·tray** *n*

ashamed \ə'shāmd\ *adj* : feeling shame — **asham·ed·ly** \-'shā-mədlē\ *adv*

ash·en \'ashən\ *adj* : deadly pale

ashore \ə'shōr\ *adv* : on or to the shore

aside \ə'sīd\ *adv* **1** : toward the side **2** : out of the way

aside from *prep* **1** : besides **2** : except for

as·i·nine \'as°n‚īn\ *adj* : foolish — **as·i·nin·i·ty** \‚as°n'inətē\ *n*

ask \'ask\ *vb* **1** : call on for an answer or help **2** : utter (a question or re-quest) **3** : invite

askance \ə'skans\ *adv* **1** : with a side glance **2** : with mistrust

askew \ə'skyü\ *adv or adj* : out of line

asleep \ə'slēp\ *adv or adj* **1** : sleeping **2** : numbed **3** : inactive

as long as *conj* **1** : on condition that **2** : because

as of *prep* : from the time of

as·par·a·gus \ə'sparəgəs\ *n* : tall herb related to the lilies or its edible stalks

as·pect \'as‚pekt\ *n* **1** : way some-thing looks to the eye or mind **2** : phase

as·pen \'aspən\ *n* : poplar

as·per·i·ty \a'sperətē, ə-\ *n, pl* **-ties 1** : roughness **2** : harshness

as·per·sion \ə'spərzhən\ *n* : remark that hurts someone's reputation

as·phalt \'as‚fòlt\ *n* : dark tarlike sub-stance used in paving

as·phyx·ia \as'fiksēə\ *n* : lack of oxy-gen causing unconsciousness

as·phyx·i·ate \-sē‚āt\ *vb* **-at·ed; -at·ing** : suffocate — **as·phyx·i·a·tion** \-‚fiksē'āshən\ *n*

as·pi·ra·tion \‚aspə'rāshən\ *n* : strong desire to achieve a goal

as·pire \ə'spīr\ *vb* **-pired; -pir·ing** : have an ambition — **as·pir·ant** \'aspərənt, ə'spīrənt\ *n*

as·pi·rin \'asprən\ *n, pl* **aspirin** *or* **as·pirins** : pain reliever

ass \'as\ *n* **1** : long-eared animal re-lated to the horse **2** : stupid person

as·sail \ə'sāl\ *vb* : attack violently — **as·sail·able** *adj* — **as·sail·ant** *n*

as·sas·si·nate \ə'sas°n‚āt\ *vb* **-nat·ed; -nat·ing** : murder esp. for political reasons — **as·sas·sin** \-'sas°n\ *n* — **as·sas·si·na·tion** \-‚sas°n'āshən\ *n*

as·sault \ə'sòlt\ *n or vb* : attack

as·say \'as‚ā, a'sā\ *n* : analysis (as of an ore) to determine quality or prop-erties — **as·say** \a'sā, 'as‚ā\ *vb*

as·sem·ble \ə'sembəl\ *vb* **-bled; -bling 1** : collect into one place **2** : fit together the parts of

as·sem·bly \-blē\ *n, pl* **-blies 1** : meet-ing **2** *cap* : legislative body **3** : a fit-ting together of parts

as•sem•bly•man \-mən\ *n* : member of a legislative assembly

as•sem•bly•wom•an \-ˌwu̇-mən\ *n* : woman who is a member of a legislative assembly

as•sent \ə'sent\ *vb or n* : consent

as•sert \ə'sərt\ *vb* **1** : declare **2** : defend — **as•ser•tion** \-'sərshən\ *n* — **as•sert•ive** \-'sərtiv\ *adj* — **as•sert•ive•ness** *n*

as•sess \ə'ses\ *vb* **1** : impose (as a tax) **2** : evaluate for taxation — **as•sess•ment** *n* — **as•ses•sor** \-ər\ *n*

as•set \'asˌet\ *n* **1** *pl* : individually owned property **2** : advantage or resource

as•sid•u•ous \ə'sijəwəs\ *adj* : diligent — **as•si•du•i•ty** \ˌasə'düətē, -'dyü-\ *n* — **as•sid•u•ous•ly** *adv* — **as•sid•u•ous•ness** *n*

as•sign \ə'sīn\ *vb* **1** : transfer to another **2** : appoint to a duty **3** : designate as a task **4** : attribute — **as•sign•able** *adj* — **as•sign•ment** *n*

as•sim•i•late \ə'siməˌlāt\ *vb* **-lat•ed; -lat•ing** **1** : absorb as nourishment **2** : understand — **as•sim•i•la•tion** \-ˌsimə'lāshən\ *n*

as•sist \ə'sist\ *vb* : help — **assist** *n* — **assis•tance** \-'sistəns\ *n* — **as•sis•tant** \-tənt\ *n*

as•so•ci•ate \ə'sōshē,āt, -sē-\ *vb* **-at•ed; -at•ing** **1** : join in companionship or partnership **2** : connect in thought — **as•so•ci•ate** \-shēət, -sēət\ *n* — **as•so•ci•a•tion** \-ˌsō-shē'āshən, -sē-\ *n*

as soon as *conj* : when

as•sort•ed \ə'sórtəd\ *adj* : consisting of various kinds

as•sort•ment \-mənt\ *n* : assorted collection

as•suage \ə'swāj\ *vb* **-suaged; -suag•ing** : ease or satisfy

as•sume \ə'süm\ *vb* **-sumed; -sum•ing** **1** : take upon oneself **2** : pretend to have or be **3** : take as true

as•sump•tion \ə'səmpshən\ *n* : something assumed

as•sure \ə'shu̇r\ *vb* **-sured; -sur•ing** **1** : give confidence or conviction to **2** : guarantee — **as•sur•ance** \-əns\ *n*

as•ter \'astər\ *n* : herb with daisylike flowers

as•ter•isk \'astəˌrisk\ *n* : a character * used as a reference mark or as an indication of omission of words

astern \ə'stərn\ *adv or adj* **1** : behind **2** : at or toward the stern

as•ter•oid \'astəˌrȯid\ *n* : small planet between Mars and Jupiter

asth•ma \'azmə\ *n* : disorder marked by difficulty in breathing — **asth•mat•ic** \az'matik\ *adj or n*

astig•ma•tism \ə'stigməˌtizəm\ *n* : visual defect — **as•tig•mat•ic** \ˌastig-'matik\ *adj*

as to *prep* **1** : concerning **2** : according to

as•ton•ish \ə'stänish\ *vb* : amaze — **as•ton•ish•ing•ly** *adv* — **as•ton•ish•ment** *n*

as•tound \ə'stau̇nd\ *vb* : fill with confused wonder — **as•tound•ing•ly** *adv*

astrad•dle \ə'strad°l\ *adv or prep* : so as to straddle

as•tral \'astrəl\ *adj* : relating to or coming from the stars

astray \ə'strā\ *adv or adj* : off the right path

astride \ə'strīd\ *adv* : with legs apart or one on each side ∼ *prep* : with one leg on each side of

as•trin•gent \ə'strinjənt\ *adj* : causing shrinking or puckering of tissues — **as•trin•gen•cy** \-jənsē\ *n* — **as•trin•gent** *n*

as•trol•o•gy \ə'sträləjē\ *n* : prediction of events by the stars — **as•trol•o•ger** \-əjər\ *n* — **as•tro•log•i•cal** \ˌas-trə'läjikəl\ *adj*

as•tro•naut \'astrəˌnȯt\ *n* : space traveler

as•tro•nau•tics \ˌastrə'nȯtiks\ *n* : construction and operation of spacecraft — **as•tro•nau•tic** \-ik\, **as•tro•nau•ti•cal** \-ikəl\ *adj*

as•tro•nom•i•cal \ˌastrə'nämikəl\ *adj* **1** : relating to astronomy **2** : extremely large

as•tron•o•my \ə'stränəmē\ *n, pl* **-mies** : study of the celestial bodies — **as•tron•o•mer** \-əmər\ *n*

as•tute \ə'stüt, -'styüt\ *adj* : shrewd — **as•tute•ly** *adv* — **as•tute•ness** *n*

asun•der \ə'səndər\ *adv or adj* **1** : into separate pieces **2** : separated

asy•lum \ə'sīləm\ *n* **1** : refuge **2** : institution for care esp. of the insane

asym•met•ri•cal \ˌāsə'metrikəl\, **asym•met•ric** \-trik\ *adj* : not symmetrical — **asym•me•try** \ˌā'simə-trē\ *n*

at \ət, 'at\ *prep* **1** — used to indicate a point in time or space **2** — used to indicate a goal **3** — used to indicate condition, means, cause, or manner

at all *adv* : without restriction or under any circumstances

ate *past of* EAT

-ate \ət, ˌāt\ *n suffix* **1** : office or rank **2** : group of persons holding an office or rank ～ *adj suffix* **1** : brought into or being in a state **2** : marked by having

athe·ist \ˈāthēist\ *n* : one who denies the existence of God — **athe·ism** \-ˌizəm\ *n* — **athe·is·tic** \ˌāthēˈistik\ *adj*

ath·ero·scle·ro·sis \ˌathərōskləˈrōsəs\ *n* : arteriosclerosis with deposition of fatty substances in the arteries — **ath·ero·scle·rot·ic** \-ˈrätik\ *adj*

ath·lete \ˈathˌlēt\ *n* : one trained to compete in athletics

ath·let·ics \athˈletiks\ *n sing or pl* : exercises and games requiring physical skill — **ath·let·ic** \-ik\ *adj*

-a·tion \ˈāshən\ *n suffix* : action or process

-a·tive \ˌātiv, ətiv\ *adj suffix* **1** : of, relating to, or connected with **2** : tending to

atlas \ˈatləs\ *n* : book of maps

ATM \ˌāˌtēˈem\ *n* : computerized machine for performing basic bank functions

at·mo·sphere \ˈatməˌsfir\ *n* **1** : mass of air surrounding the earth **2** : surrounding influence — **at·mo·spher·ic** \ˌatməˈsfirik, -ˈsfer-\ *adj* — **at·mo·spher·i·cal·ly** \-iklē\ *adv*

atoll \ˈaˌtȯl, ˈā-, -ˌtäl\ *n* : ring-shaped coral island

at·om \ˈatəm\ *n* **1** : tiny bit **2** : smallest particle of a chemical element that can exist alone or in combination

atom·ic \əˈtämik\ *adj* **1** : relating to atoms **2** : nuclear

atomic bomb *n* : bomb utilizing the energy released by splitting the atom

at·om·iz·er \ˈatəˌmīzər\ *n* : device for dispersing a liquid as a very fine spray

atone \əˈtōn\ *vb* **atoned; aton·ing** : make amends — **atone·ment** *n*

atop \əˈtäp\ *prep* : on top of ～ *adv or adj* : on, to, or at the top

atri·um \ˈātrēəm\ *n, pl* **atria** \-trēə\ *or* **atriums 1** : open central room or court **2** : heart chamber that receives blood from the veins

atro·cious \əˈtrōshəs\ *adj* : appalling or abominable — **atro·cious·ly** *adv* — **atro·cious·ness** *n*

atroc·i·ty \əˈträsətē\ *n, pl* **-ties** : savage act

at·ro·phy \ˈatrəfē\ *n, pl* **-phies** : wasting away of a bodily part or tissue — **at·ro·phy** *vb*

at·ro·pine \ˈatrəˌpēn\ *n* : drug used esp. to relieve spasms

at·tach \əˈtach\ *vb* **1** : seize legally **2** : bind by personalities **3** : join — **at·tach·ment** *n*

at·ta·ché \ˌatəˈshā, ˌaˌta-, əˌta-\ *n* : technical expert on a diplomatic staff

at·tack \əˈtak\ *vb* **1** : try to hurt or destroy with violence or words **2** : set to work on ～ *n* **1** : act of attacking **2** : fit of sickness

at·tain \əˈtān\ *vb* **1** : achieve or accomplish **2** : reach — **at·tain·abil·i·ty** \əˌtānəˈbilətē\ *n* — **at·tain·able** *adj* — **at·tain·ment** *n*

at·tempt \əˈtempt\ *vb* : make an effort toward — **attempt** *n*

at·tend \əˈtend\ *vb* **1** : handle or provide for the care of something **2** : accompany **3** : be present at **4** : pay attention — **at·ten·dance** \-ˈtendəns\ *n* — **at·ten·dant** \-dənt\ *adj or n*

at·ten·tion \əˈtenchən\ *n* **1** : concentration of the mind on something **2** : notice or awareness — **at·ten·tive** \-ˈtentiv\ *adj* — **at·ten·tive·ly** *adv* — **at·ten·tive·ness** *n*

at·ten·u·ate \əˈtenyəˌwāt\ *vb* **-at·ed; -at·ing 1** : make or become thin **2** : weaken — **at·ten·u·a·tion** \-ˌtenyəˈwāshən\ *n*

at·test \əˈtest\ *vb* : certify or bear witness — **at·tes·ta·tion** \ˌaˌtesˈtāshən\ *n*

at·tic \ˈatik\ *n* : space just below the roof

at·tire \əˈtīr\ *vb* **-tired; -tir·ing** : dress — **attire** *n*

at·ti·tude \ˈatəˌtüd, -ˌtyüd\ *n* **1** : posture or relative position **2** : feeling, opinion, or mood

at·tor·ney \əˈtərnē\ *n, pl* **-neys** : legal agent

at·tract \əˈtrakt\ *vb* **1** : draw to oneself **2** : have emotional or aesthetic appeal for — **at·trac·tion** \-ˈtrakshən\ *n* — **at·trac·tive** \-ˈtraktiv\ *adj* — **at·trac·tive·ly** *adv* — **at·trac·tive·ness** *n* at•tri•bute \\'atrə,byüt\\ *n* : inherent characteristic ~ \\ə'tribyət\\ *vb* -trib•ut•ed; -trib•ut•ing **1** : regard as having a specific cause or origin **2** : regard as a characteristic — at•trib•ut•able *adj* — at•tri•bu•tion \\,atrə-'byüshən\\ *n*

at•tune \\ə'tün, -'tyün\\ *vb* : bring into harmony

au•burn \\'óbərn\\ *adj* : reddish brown

auc•tion \\'ókshən\\ *n* : public sale of property to the highest bidder — auc•tion *vb* — auc•tion•eer \\,ókshə'nir\\ *n*

au•dac•i•ty \\ó'dasətē\\ *n* : boldness or insolence — au•da•cious \\ó'dā-shəs\\ *adj*

au•di•ble \\'ódəbəl\\ *adj* : capable of being heard — au•di•bly \\-blē\\ *adv*

au•di•ence \\'ódēəns\\ *n* **1** : formal interview **2** : group of listeners or spectators

au•dio \\'ódē,ō\\ *adj* : relating to sound or its reproduction ~ *n* : television sound

au•dio•vi•su•al \\,ódēō'vizhəwəl\\ *adj* : relating to both hearing and sight

au•dit \\'ódət\\ *vb* : examine financial accounts — audit *n* — au•di•tor \\'ódətər\\ *n*

au•di•tion \\ó'dishən\\ *n* : tryout performance — audition *vb*

au•di•to•ri•um \\,ódə'tōrēəm\\ *n, pl* -ri•ums *or* -ria \\'-rēa\\ : room or building used for public performances

au•di•to•ry \\'ódə,tōrē\\ *adj* : relating to hearing

au•ger \\'ógər\\ *n* : tool for boring

aug•ment \\ og'ment\\ *vb* : enlarge or increase — aug•men•ta•tion \\,ógmən'tāshən\\ *n*

au•gur \\'ógər\\ *n* : prophet ~ *vb* : predict — au•gu•ry \\'ógyərē, -gər-\\ *n*

au•gust \\ó'gəst\\ *adj* : majestic

Au•gust \\'ógəst\\ *n* : 8th month of the year having 31 days

auk \\'ók\\ *n* : stocky diving seabird

aunt \\'ant, 'ȧnt\\ *n* **1** : sister of one's father or mother **2** : wife of one's uncle

au•ra \\'órə\\ *n* **1** : distinctive atmosphere **2** : luminous radiation

au•ral \\'órəl\\ *adj* : relating to the ear or to hearing

au•ri•cle \\'órikəl\\ *n* : atrium or ear-shaped pouch in the atrium of the heart

au•ro•ra bo•re•al•is \\ə'rōrə,bōrē'aləs\\ *n* : display of light in the night sky of northern latitudes

aus•pic•es \\'óspəsəz, -,sēz\\ *n pl* : patronage and protection

aus•pi•cious \\ó'spishəs\\ *adj* : favorable

aus•tere \\ó'stir\\ *adj* : severe — aus•tere•ly *adv* — aus•ter•i•ty \\ó'sterətē\\ *n*

au•then•tic \\ə'thentik, ó-\\ *adj* : genuine — au•then•ti•cal•ly \\-iklē\\ *adv* — au•then•tic•i•ty \\,ó,then'tisətē\\ *n*

au•then•ti•cate \\ə'thenti,kāt, ó-\\ *vb* -cat•ed; -cat•ing : prove genuine — au•then•ti•ca•tion \\-,thenti'kāshən\\ *n*

au•thor \\'óthər\\ *n* **1** : writer **2** : creator — au•thor•ship *n*

au•thor•i•tar•i•an \\ó,thärə'terēən, ə-, -,thór-\\ *adj* : marked by blind obedience to authority

au•thor•i•ta•tive \\ə'thärə,tātiv, ó-, -'thór-\\ *adj* : being an authority — au•thor•i•ta•tive•ly *adv* — au•thor•i•ta•tive•ness *n*

au•thor•i•ty \\ə'thärətē, ó-, -'thór-\\ *n, pl* -ties **1** : expert **2** : right, responsibility, or power to influence **3** *pl* : persons in official positions

au•tho•rize \\'óthə,rīz\\ *vb* -rized; -riz•ing : permit or give official approval for — au•tho•ri•za•tion \\,óthərə-'zāshən\\ *n*

au•tism \\'ó,tizəm\\ *n* : mental disorder marked by impaired ability to communicate and form social relationships and by repetitive behavior patterns

au•to \\'ótō\\ *n, pl* autos : automobile

au•to•bi•og•ra•phy \\,ótəbī'ägrəfē, -bē-\\ *n* : writer's own life story — au•to•bi•og•ra•pher \\-fər\\ *n* — au•to•bio•graph•i•cal \\-,bīə'grafikəl\\ *adj*

au•toc•ra•cy \\ó'täkrəsē\\ *n, pl* -cies : government by one person having unlimited power — au•to•crat \\'ótə-,krat\\ *n* — au•to•crat•ic \\,ótə-'kratik\\ *adj* — au•to•crat•i•cal•ly \\-iklē\\ *adv*

au•to•graph \\'ótə,graf\\ *n* : signature ~ *vb* : write one's name on

au•to•mate \\'ótə,māt\\ *vb* -mat•ed; -mat•ing : make automatic — au•to•ma•tion \\,ótə'māshən\\ *n*

au•to•mat•ic \\,ótə'matik\\ *adj* **1** : involuntary **2** : designed to function without human intervention ~ *n*

: automatic device (as a firearm) —
au•to•mat•i•cal•ly \-iklē\ adv
au•tom•a•ton \ò'tämətən, -ˌtän\ n, pl
-a•tons or -a•ta \-tə, -ˌtä\ : robot
au•to•mo•bile \ˌótəmō'bēl, -'mōˌbēl\
n : 4-wheeled passenger vehicle with
its own power source
au•to•mo•tive \ˌótə'mōtiv\ adj : relating to automobiles
au•ton•o•mous \ò'tänəməs\ adj : self-
governing — **au•ton•o•mous•ly** adv
— **au•ton•o•my** \-mē\ n
au•top•sy \'òˌtäpsē, 'òtəp-\ n, pl -sies
: medical examination of a corpse
au•tumn \'ótəm\ n : season between
summer and winter — **au•tum•nal**
\ò'təmnəl\ adj
aux•il•ia•ry \òg'zilyərē, -lərē\ adj 1
: being a supplement or reserve 2
: accompanying a main verb form to
express person, number, mood, or
tense — **auxiliary** n
avail \ə'vāl\ vb : be of use or make use
~ n : use
avail•able \ə'vāləbəl\ adj 1 : usable 2
: accessible — **avail•abil•i•ty** \-ˌvālə-
'bilətē\ n
av•a•lanche \'avəˌlanch\ n : mass of
sliding or falling snow or rock
av•a•rice \'avərəs\ n : greed — **av•a•ri•
cious** \ˌavə'rishəs\ adj
avenge \ə'venj\ vb **avenged; aveng•
ing** : take vengeance for — **aveng•er**
n
av•e•nue \'avəˌnü, -ˌnyü\ n 1 : way of
approach 2 : broad street
av•er•age \'avrij\ adj 1 : being about
midway between extremes 2 : ordinary ~ vb 1 : be usually 2 : find the
mean of ~ n : mean
averse \ə'vərs\ adj : feeling dislike
or reluctance — **aver•sion** \-'vər-
zhən\ n
avert \ə'vərt\ vb : turn away
avi•ary \'āvēˌerē\ n, pl -ar•ies : place
where birds are kept
avi•a•tion \ˌāvē'āshən, ˌav-\ n : operation or manufacture of airplanes —
avi•a•tor \'āvēˌātər, 'av-\ n
av•id \'avəd\ adj 1 : greedy 2 : enthusiastic — **avid•i•ty** \ə'vidətē, a-\ n
— **av•id•ly** adv
av•o•ca•do \ˌavə'kädō, ˌäv-\ n, pl
-dos : tropical fruit with green pulp
av•o•ca•tion \ˌavə'kāshən\ n : hobby
avoid \ə'vóid\ vb 1 : keep away from 2

: prevent the occurrence of 3 : refrain
from — **avoid•able** adj — **avoid•
ance** \-ᵊns\ n
av•oir•du•pois \ˌavərdə'póiz\ n : system of weight based on the pound of
16 ounces
avow \ə'vaù\ vb : declare openly —
avow•al \-'vaùəl\ n
await \ə'wāt\ vb : wait for
awake \ə'wāk\ vb **awoke** \-'wōk\;
awok•en \-'wōkən\ or **awaked;
awak•ing** : wake up — **awake** adj
awak•en \ə'wākən\ vb -**ened; -en•ing**
: wake up
award \ə'wórd\ vb : give (something
won or deserved) ~ n 1 : judgment
2 : prize
aware \ə'war\ adj : having realization
or consciousness — **aware•ness** n
awash \ə'wòsh, -'wäsh\ adv or adj
: flooded
away \ə'wā\ adv 1 : from this or that
place or time 2 : out of the way 3 : in
another direction 4 : from one's
possession ~ adj 1 : absent 2 : distant
awe \'ó\ n : respectful fear or wonder
~ vb **awed; aw•ing** : fill with awe —
awe•some \-səm\ adj — **awe•
struck** adj
aw•ful \'ófəl\ adj 1 : inspiring awe 2
: extremely disagreeable 3 : very
great — **aw•ful•ly** adv
awhile \ə'hwīl\ adv : for a while
awk•ward \'ókwərd\ adj 1 : clumsy 2
: embarrassing — **awk•ward•ly** adv
— **awk•ward•ness** n
awl \'ól\ n : hole-making tool
awn•ing \'ónin̄\ n : window cover
awry \ə'rī\ adv or adj : wrong
ax, axe \'aks\ n : chopping tool
ax•i•om \'aksēəm\ n : generally accepted truth — **ax•i•om•at•ic** \ˌak-
sēə'matik\ adj
ax•is \'aksəs\ n, pl **ax•es** \-ˌsēz\ : center of rotation — **ax•i•al** \-sēəl\ adj
— **ax•i•al•ly** adv
ax•le \'aksəl\ n : shaft on which a
wheel revolves
aye \'ī\ adv : yes ~ n : a vote of yes
aza•lea \ə'zālyə\ n : rhododendron
with funnel-shaped blossoms
az•i•muth \'azəməth\ n : horizontal direction expressed as an angle
azure \'azhər\ n : blue of the sky —
azure adj

B

b \'bē\ *n, pl* **b's** *or* **bs** \'bēz\ : 2d letter of the alphabet

bab•ble \'babəl\ *vb* **-bled; -bling** **1** : utter meaningless sounds **2** : talk foolishly or too much — **babble** *n* — **bab•bler** *n*

babe \'bāb\ *n* : baby

ba•bel \'bābəl, 'bab-\ *n* : noisy confusion

ba•boon \ba'bün\ *n* : large Asian or African ape with a doglike muzzle

ba•by \'bābē\ *n, pl* **-bies** : very young child ~ *vb* **-bied; -by•ing** : pamper — **baby** *adj* — **ba•by•hood** *n* — **ba•by•ish** *adj*

ba•by–sit *vb* **-sat; -sit•ting** : care for children while parents are away — **baby–sit•ter** *n*

bac•ca•lau•re•ate \,bakə'lorēət\ *n* : bachelor's degree

bac•cha•na•lia \,bakə'nālyə\ *n, pl* **-lia** : drunken orgy — **bac•cha•na•lian** \-yən\ *adj or n*

bach•e•lor \'bachələr\ *n* **1** : holder of lowest 4-year college degree **2** : unmarried man — **bach•e•lor•hood** *n*

ba•cil•lus \bə'siləs\ *n, pl* **-li** \-,lī\ : rod-shaped bacterium — **bac•il•lary** \'basə,lerē\ *adj*

back \'bak\ *n* **1** : part of a human or animal body nearest the spine **2** : part opposite the front **3** : player farthest from the opponent's goal ~ *adv* **1** : to or at the back **2** : ago **3** : to or in a former place or state **4** : in reply ~ *adj* **1** : located at the back **2** : not paid on time **3** : moving or working backward **4** : not current ~ *vb* **1** : support **2** : go or cause to go back **3** : form the back of — **back•ache** *n* — **back•er** *n* — **back•ing** *n* — **back•less** *adj* — **back•rest** *n*

back•bite *vb* **-bit; -bit•ten; -bit•ing** : say spiteful things about someone absent — **back•bit•er** *n*

back•bone *n* **1** : bony column in the back that encloses the spinal cord **2** : firm character

back•drop *n* : painted cloth hung across the rear of a stage

back•fire *n* : loud noise from the wrongly timed explosion of fuel in an engine ~ *vb* **1** : make or undergo a backfire **2** : have a result opposite of that intended

back•gam•mon \'bak,gamən\ *n* : board game

back•ground *n* **1** : scenery behind something **2** : sum of a person's experience or training

back•hand *n* : stroke (as in tennis) made with the back of the hand turned forward — **backhand** *adj or vb* — **back•hand•ed** *adj*

back•lash *n* : adverse reaction

back•log *n* : accumulation of things to be done — **backlog** *vb*

back•pack *n* : camping pack carried on the back ~ *vb* : hike with a backpack — **back•pack•er** *n*

back•slide *vb* **-slid; -slid** *or* **-slid•den** \-,slid³n\; **-slid•ing** : lapse in morals or religious practice — **back•slid•er** *n*

back•stage *adv or adj* : in or to an area behind a stage

back•up *n* : substitute

back•ward \'bakwərd\, **back•wards** *adv* **1** : toward the back **2** : with the back foremost **3** : in a reverse direction **4** : toward an earlier or worse state ~ *adj* **1** : directed, turned, or done backward **2** : retarded in development — **back•ward•ness** *n*

back•woods *n pl* : remote or isolated place

ba•con \'bākən\ *n* : salted and smoked meat from a pig

bac•te•ri•um \bak'tirēəm\ *n, pl* **-ria** \-ēə\ : microscopic plant — **bac•te•ri•al** \-ēəl\ *adj* — **bac•te•ri•o•log•ic** \-,tirēə'läjik\, **bac•te•ri•o•log•i•cal** \-əl\ *adj* — **bac•te•ri•ol•o•gist** \-ē-'äləjist\ *n* — **bac•te•ri•ol•o•gy** \-jē\ *n*

bad \'bad\ *adj* **worse** \'wərs\; **worst** \'wərst\ **1** : not good **2** : naughty **3** : faulty **4** : spoiled — **bad** *n or adv* — **bad•ly** *adv* — **bad•ness** *n*

bade *past of* BID

badge \ˈbaj\ *n* : symbol of status

bad•ger \ˈbajər\ *n* : burrowing mammal **~** *vb* : harass

bad•min•ton \ˈbadˌmintᵊn\ *n* : tennislike game played with a shuttlecock

bad–mouth \ˈbadˌmau̇th\ *vb* : criticize severely

baf•fle \ˈbafəl\ *vb* **-fled; -fling** : perplex **~** *n* : device to alter flow (as of liquid or sound) — **baf•fle•ment** *n*

bag \ˈbag\ *n* : flexible usu. closable container **~** *vb* **-gg-** **1** : bulge out **2** : put in a bag **3** : catch in hunting

bag•a•telle \ˌbagəˈtel\ *n* : trifle

ba•gel \ˈbāgəl\ *n* : hard doughnut-shaped roll

bag•gage \ˈbagij\ *n* : traveler's bags and belongings

bag•gy \ˈbagē\ *adj* **-gi•er; -est** : puffed out like a bag — **baggi•ness** *n*

bag•pipe *n* : musical instrument with a bag, a tube with valves, and sounding pipes — often pl.

[1]**bail** \ˈbāl\ *n* : container for scooping water out of a boat — **bail** *vb* — **bail•er** *n*

[2]**bail** *n* **1** : security given to guarantee a prisoner's appearance in court **2** : release secured by bail **~** *vb* : bring about the release of by giving bail

bai•liff \ˈbāləf\ *n* **1** : British sheriff's aide **2** : minor officer of a U.S. court

bai•li•wick \ˈbāliˌwik\ *n* : one's special field or domain

bail•out \ˈbāˌlau̇t\ *n* : rescue from financial distress

bait \ˈbāt\ *vb* **1** : harass with dogs usu. for sport **2** : furnish (a hook or trap) with bait **~** *n* : lure esp. for catching animals

bake \ˈbāk\ *vb* **baked; bak•ing** : cook in dry heat esp. in an oven **~** *n* : party featuring baked food — **bak•er** *n* — **bak•ery** \ˈbākərē\ *n* — **bake•shop** *n*

bal•ance \ˈbaləns\ *n* **1** : weighing device **2** : counteracting weight, force, or influence **3** : equilibrium **4** : that which remains **~** *vb* **-anced; -anc•ing** **1** : compute the balance **2** : equalize **3** : bring into harmony or proportion — **bal•anced** *adj*

bal•co•ny \ˈbalkənē\ *n, pl* **-nies** : platform projecting from a wall

bald \ˈbȯld\ *adj* **1** : lacking a natural or usual covering (as of hair) **2** : plain — **bald•ing** *adj* — **bald•ly** *adv* — **bald•ness** *n*

bal•der•dash \ˈbȯldərˌdash\ *n* : nonsense

bale \ˈbāl\ *n* : large bundle **~** *vb* **baled; bal•ing** : pack in a bale — **bal•er** *n*

bale•ful \ˈbālfəl\ *adj* **1** : deadly **2** : ominous

balk \ˈbȯk\ *n* : hindrance **~** *vb* **1** : thwart **2** : stop short and refuse to go on — **balky** *adj*

[1]**ball** \ˈbȯl\ *n* **1** : rounded mass **2** : game played with a ball **~** *vb* : form into a ball

[2]**ball** *n* : large formal dance — **ballroom** *n*

bal•lad \ˈbaləd\ *n* **1** : narrative poem **2** : slow romantic song — **bal•lad•eer** \ˌbaləˈdiər\ *n*

bal•last \ˈbaləst\ *n* : heavy material to steady a ship or balloon **~** *vb* : provide with ballast

bal•le•ri•na \ˌbaləˈrēnə\ *n* : female ballet dancer

bal•let \ˈbaˌlā, baˈlā\ *n* : theatrical dancing

bal•lis•tics \bəˈlistiks\ *n sing or pl* : science of projectile motion — **bal•listic** *adj*

bal•loon \bəˈlün\ *n* : inflated bag **~** *vb* **1** : travel in a balloon **2** : swell out — **bal•loon•ist** *n*

bal•lot \ˈbalət\ *n* **1** : paper used to cast a vote **2** : system of voting **~** *vb* : vote

bal•ly•hoo \ˈbalēˌhü\ *n* : publicity — **ballyhoo** *vb*

balm \ˈbäm, ˈbälm\ *n* **1** : fragrant healing or soothing preparation **2** : spicy fragrant herb

balmy \ˈbämē, ˈbälmē\ *adj* **balm•i•er; -est** : gently soothing — **balm•i•ness** *n*

ba•lo•ney \bəˈlōnē\ *n* : nonsense

bal•sa \ˈbȯlsə\ *n* : very light wood of a tropical tree

bal•sam \-səm\ *n* **1** : aromatic resinous plant substance **2** : balsam-yielding plant — **bal•sam•ic** \bȯlˈsamik\ *adj*

bal•us•ter \ˈbaləstər\ *n* : upright support for a rail

bal•us•trade \-ˌstrād\ *n* : row of balusters topped by a rail

bam•boo \bamˈbü\ *n* : tall tropical grass with strong hollow stems

bam•boo•zle \bamˈbüzəl\ *vb* **-zled; -zling** : deceive

ban \ˈban\ *vb* **-nn-** : prohibit **~** *n* : legal prohibition

ba·nal \bə'näl, -'nal; 'bān²l\ *adj* : ordinary and uninteresting — **ba·nal·ity** \bə'nalətē\ *n*

ba·nana \bə'nanə\ *n* : elongated fruit of a treelike tropical plant

¹band \'band\ *n* **1** : something that ties or binds **2** : strip or stripe different (as in color) from nearby matter **3** : range of radio wavelengths ~ *vb* **1** : enclose with a band **2** : unite for a common end — **band·ed** *adj* — **band·er** *n*

²band *n* **1** : group **2** : musicians playing together

ban·dage \'bandij\ *n* : material used esp. in dressing wounds ~ *vb* : dress or cover with a bandage

ban·dan·na, ban·dana \ban'danə\ *n* : large colored figured handkerchief

ban·dit \'bandət\ *n* : outlaw or robber — **ban·dit·ry** \-dətrē\ *n*

band·stand *n* : stage for band concerts

band·wag·on *n* : candidate, side, or movement gaining support

¹ban·dy \'bandē\ *vb* **-died; -dy·ing** : exchange in rapid succession

²bandy *adj* : curved outward

bane \'bān\ *n* **1** : poison **2** : cause of woe — **bane·ful** *adj*

¹bang \'baŋ\ *vb* : strike, thrust, or move usu. with a loud noise ~ *n* **1** : blow **2** : sudden loud noise ~ *adv* : directly

²bang *n* : fringe of short hair over the forehead — usu. pl. ~ *vb* : cut in bangs

ban·gle \'baŋgəl\ *n* : bracelet

ban·ish \'banish\ *vb* **1** : force by authority to leave a country **2** : expel — **ban·ish·ment** *n*

ban·is·ter \-əstər\ *n* **1** : baluster **:** handrail

ban·jo \'banˌjō\ *n, pl* **-jos** : stringed instrument with a drumlike body — **banjo·ist** *n*

¹bank \'baŋk\ *n* **1** : piled-up mass **2** : rising ground along a body of water **3** : sideways slope along a curve ~ *vb* **1** : form a bank **2** : cover (as a fire) to keep inactive **3** : incline (an airplane) laterally

²bank *n* : tier of objects

³bank *n* **1** : money institution **2** : reserve supply ~ *vb* : conduct business in a bank — **bank·book** *n* — **bank·er** *n* — **bank·ing** *n*

bank·rupt \'baŋˌkrəpt\ *n* : one required by law to forfeit assets to pay off debts ~ *adj* **1** : legally a bankrupt **2** : lacking something essential — **bankrupt** *vb* — **bank·rupt·cy** \-ˌkrəpsē\ *n*

ban·ner \'banər\ *n* : flag ~ *adj* : excellent

banns \'banz\ *n pl* : announcement in church of a proposed marriage

ban·quet \'baŋkwət\ *n* : ceremonial dinner — **banquet** *vb*

ban·shee \'banshē\ *n* : wailing female spirit that foretells death

ban·tam \'bantəm\ *n* : miniature domestic fowl

ban·ter \'bantər\ *n* : good-natured joking — **banter** *vb*

ban·yan \'banyən\ *n* : large tree that grows new trunks from the limbs

bap·tism \'bapˌtizəm\ *n* : Christian rite signifying spiritual cleansing — **bap·tis·mal** \bap'tizməl\ *adj*

bap·tize \bap'tīz, 'bapˌtīz\ *vb* **-tized; -tiz·ing** : administer baptism to

bar \'bär\ *n* **1** : long narrow object used esp. as a lever, fastening, or support **2** : barrier **3** : body of practicing lawyers **4** : wide stripe **5** : food counter **6** : place where liquor is served **7** : vertical line across the musical staff ~ *vb* **-rr- 1** : obstruct with a bar **2** : shut out **3** : prohibit ~ *prep* : excluding — **barred** *adj* — **bar·room** *n* — **bar·tend·er** *n*

barb \'bärb\ *n* : sharp projection pointing backward — **barbed** *adj*

bar·bar·ian \bär'barēən\ *adj* **1** : relating to people considered backward **2** : not refined — **barbarian** *n*

bar·bar·ic \-'barik\ *adj* : barbarian

bar·ba·rous \'bärbərəs\ *adj* **1** : lacking refinement **2** : mercilessly cruel — **bar·bar·ism** \-bəˌrizəm\ *n* — **bar·bar·i·ty** \bär'barətē\ *n* — **bar·ba·rous·ly** *adv*

bar·be·cue \'bärbiˌkyü\ *n* : gathering at which barbecued food is served ~ *vb* **-cued; -cu·ing** : cook over hot coals or on a spit often with a highly seasoned sauce

bar·ber \'bärbər\ *n* : one who cuts hair

bar·bi·tu·rate \bär'bichərət\ *n* : sedative or hypnotic drug

bard \'bärd\ *n* : poet

bare \'bar\ *adj* **bar·er; bar·est 1** : naked **2** : not concealed **3** : empty **4** : leaving nothing to spare **5** : plain ~ *vb* **bared; bar·ing** : make or lay bare — **bare·foot, bare·foot·ed** *adv or adj* — **bare–hand·ed** *adv or adj*

— bare•head•ed *adv or adj* — bare-ly *adv* — bare•ness *n*
bare•back, bare•backed *adv or adj* : without a saddle
bare•faced *adj* : open and esp. brazen
bar•gain \'bärgən\ *n* **1** : agreement **2** : something bought for less than its value ∼ *vb* **1** : negotiate **2** : barter
barge \'bärj\ *n* : broad flat-bottomed boat ∼ *vb* **barged; barg•ing** : move rudely or clumsily — **barge•man** *n*
bari•tone \'barə,tōn\ *n* : male voice between bass and tenor
bar•i•um \'bareəm\ *n* : silver-white metallic chemical element
¹**bark** \'bärk\ *vb* **1** : make the sound of a dog **2** : speak in a loud curt tone ∼ *n* : sound of a barking dog
²**bark** *n* : tough corky outer covering of a woody stem or root ∼ *vb* : remove bark or skin from
³**bark** *n* : sailing ship with a fore-and-aft rear sail
bark•er \'bärkər\ *n* : one who calls out to attract people to a show
bar•ley \'bärlē\ *n* : cereal grass or its seeds
barn \'bärn\ *n* : building for keeping hay or livestock — **barn•yard** *n*
bar•na•cle \'bärnikəl\ *n* : marine crustacean
barn•storm *vb* : tour through rural districts giving performances
ba•rom•e•ter \bə'rämətər\ *n* : instrument for measuring atmospheric pressure — **baro•met•ric** \,barə'metrik\ *adj*
bar•on \'barən\ *n* : British peer — **bar•on•age** \-ij\ *n* — **ba•ro•ni•al** \bə-'rōnēəl\ *adj* — **bar•ony** \'barənē\ *n*
bar•on•ess \-ənəs\ *n* **1** : baron's wife **2** : woman holding a baronial title
bar•on•et \-ənət\ *n* : man holding a rank between a baron and a knight — **bar•on•et•cy** \-sē\ *n*
ba•roque \bə'rōk, -'räk\ *adj* : elaborately ornamented
bar•racks \'barəks\ *n sing or pl* : soldiers' housing
bar•ra•cu•da \,barə'küdə\ *n, pl* **-da** *or* **-das** : large predatory sea fish
bar•rage \bə'räzh, -'räj\ *n* : heavy artillery fire
bar•rel \'barəl\ *n* **1** : closed cylindrical container **2** : amount held by a barrel **3** : cylindrical part ∼ *vb* **-reled** *or* **-relled; -rel•ing** *or* **-rel•ling 1** : pack in a barrel **2** : move at high speed

bar•ren \'barən\ *adj* **1** : unproductive of life **2** : uninteresting — **bar•ren•ness** *n*
bar•rette \bä'ret, bə-\ *n* : clasp for a woman's hair
bar•ri•cade \'barə,kād, ,barə'-\ *n* : barrier — **barricade** *vb*
bar•ri•er \'barēər\ *n* : something that separates or obstructs
bar•ring \'bärin\ *prep* : omitting
bar•ris•ter \'barəstər\ *n* : British trial lawyer
bar•row \'barō\ *n* : wheelbarrow
bar•ter \'bärtər\ *vb* : trade by exchange of goods — **barter** *n*
ba•salt \bə'sȯlt, 'bā,-\ *n* : dark fine-grained igneous rock — **ba•sal•tic** \bə'sȯltik\ *adj*
¹**base** \'bās\ *n, pl* **bas•es 1** : bottom **2** : fundamental part **3** : beginning point **4** : supply source of a force **5** : compound that reacts with an acid to form a salt ∼ *vb* **based; bas•ing** : establish — **base•less** *adj*
²**base** *adj* **bas•er; bas•est 1** : inferior **2** : contemptible — **base•ly** *adv* — **base•ness** *n*
base•ball *n* : game played with a bat and ball by 2 teams
base•ment \-mənt\ *n* : part of a building below ground level
bash \'bash\ *vb* : strike violently ∼ *n* : heavy blow
bash•ful \-fəl\ *adj* : self-conscious — **bash•ful•ness** *n*
ba•sic \'bāsik\ *adj* **1** : relating to or forming the base or essence **2** : relating to a chemical base — **ba•si•cally** *adv* — **ba•sic•i•ty** \bā'sisətē\ *n*
ba•sil \'bazəl, 'bās-, 'bāz-\ *n* : aromatic mint
ba•sil•i•ca \bə'silikə\ *n* : important church or cathedral
ba•sin \'bās³n\ *n* **1** : large bowl or pan **2** : region drained by a river
ba•sis \'bāsəs\ *n, pl* **ba•ses** \-,sēz\ **1** : something that supports **2** : fundamental principle
bask \'bask\ *vb* : enjoy pleasant warmth
bas•ket \'baskət\ *n* : woven container — **bas•ket•ful** *n*
bas•ket•ball *n* : game played with a ball on a court by 2 teams
bas–re•lief \,bäri'lēf\ *n* : flat sculpture with slightly raised design
¹**bass** \'bas\ *n, pl* **bass** *or* **bass•es** : spiny-finned sport and food fish

²bass \'bās\ *n* **1** : deep tone **2** : lowest choral voice

bas·set hound \'basət-\ *n* : short-legged dog with long ears

bas·si·net \ˌbasə'net\ *n* : baby's bed

bas·soon \bə'sün, ba-\ *n* : low-pitched wind instrument

bas·tard \'bastərd\ *n* **1** : illegitimate child **2** : offensive person ~ *adj* **1** : illegitimate **2** : inferior — **bastard·ize** *vb* — **bas·tardy** *n*

¹baste \'bāst\ *vb* **bast·ed; bast·ing** : sew temporarily with long stitches

²baste *vb* **bast·ed; bast·ing** : moisten at intervals while cooking

bas·tion \'baschən\ *n* : fortified position

¹bat \'bat\ *n* **1** : stick or club **2** : sharp blow ~ *vb* **-tt-** : hit with a bat

²bat *n* : small flying mammal

³bat *vb* **-tt-** : wink or blink

batch \'bach\ *n* : quantity used or produced at one time

bate \'bāt\ *vb* **bat·ed; bat·ing** : moderate or reduce

bath \'bath, 'bàth\ *n*, *pl* **baths** \'bathz, 'baths, 'bàthz, 'bàths\ **1** : a washing of the body **2** : water for washing the body **3** : liquid in which something is immersed **4** : bathroom **5** : large financial loss — **bath·tub** *n*

bathe \'bāth\ *vb* **bathed; bath·ing 1** : wash in liquid **2** : flow against so as to wet **3** : shine light over **4** : take a bath or a swim — **bath·er** *n*

bath·robe *n* : robe worn around the house

bath·room *n* : room with a bathtub or shower and usu. a sink and toilet

ba·tiste \bə'tēst\ *n* : fine sheer fabric

ba·ton \bə'tän\ *n* : musical conductor's stick

bat·tal·ion \bə'talyən\ *n* : military unit composed of a headquarters and two or more companies

bat·ten \'batⁿn\ *n* : strip of wood used to seal or reinforce ~ *vb* : furnish or fasten with battens

¹bat·ter \'batər\ *vb* : beat or damage with repeated blows

²batter *n* : mixture of flour and liquid

³batter *n* : player who bats

bat·tery \'batərē\ *n*, *pl* **-ter·ies 1** : illegal beating of a person **2** : group of artillery guns **3** : group of electric cells

bat·ting \'batiŋ\ *n* : layers of cotton or wool for stuffing

bat·tle \'batⁿl\ *n* : military fighting ~ *vb* **-tled; -tling** : engage in battle — **battle·field** *n*

bat·tle-ax *n* : long-handled ax formerly used as a weapon

bat·tle·ment \-mənt\ *n* : parapet on top of a wall

bat·tle·ship *n* : heavily armed warship

bat·ty \'batē\ *adj* **-ti·er; -est** : crazy

bau·ble \'bóbəl\ *n* : trinket

bawdy \'bódē\ *adj* **bawd·i·er; -est** : obscene or lewd — **bawd·i·ly** *adv* — **bawd·i·ness** *n*

bawl \'ból\ *vb* : cry loudly ~ *n* : long loud cry

¹bay \'bā\ *adj* : reddish brown ~ *n* : bay-colored animal

²bay *n* : European laurel

³bay *n* **1** : compartment **2** : area projecting out from a building and containing a window (**bay window**)

⁴bay *vb* : bark with deep long tones ~ *n* **1** : position of one unable to escape danger **2** : baying of dogs

⁵bay *n* : body of water smaller than a gulf and nearly surrounded by land

bay·ber·ry \-ˌberē\ *n* : shrub bearing small waxy berries

bay·o·net \'bāənət, ˌbāə'net\ *n* : dagger that fits on the end of a rifle ~ *vb* **-net·ed; -net·ing** : stab with a bayonet

bay·ou \'bīü, -ō\ *n* : creek flowing through marshy land

ba·zaar \bə'zär\ *n* **1** : market **2** : fair for charity

ba·zoo·ka \-'zükə\ *n* : weapon that shoots armor-piercing rockets

BB *n* : small shot pellet

be \'bē\ *vb* **was** \'wəz, 'wäz\, **were** \'wər\; **been** \'bin\; **be·ing** \'bēiŋ\; **am** \əm, 'am\, **is** \'iz, əz\, **are** \ər, 'är\ **1** : equal **2** : exist **3** : occupy a certain place **4** : occur ~ *verbal auxiliary* — used to show continuous action or to form the passive voice

beach \'bēch\ *n* : sandy shore of a sea, lake, or river ~ *vb* : drive ashore

beach·comb·er \-ˌkōmər\ *n* : one who searches the shore for useful objects

beach·head *n* : shore area held by an attacking force in an invasion

bea·con \'bēkən\ *n* : guiding or warning light or signal

bead \'bēd\ *n* : small round body esp. strung on a thread ~ *vb* : form into a bead — **bead·ing** *n* — **beady** *adj*

bea·gle \'bēgəl\ *n* : small short-legged hound

beak \'bēk\ *n* : bill of a bird — **beaked** *adj*

bea·ker \'bēkər\ *n* **1** : large drinking cup **2** : laboratory vessel

beam \'bēm\ *n* **1** : large long piece of timber or metal **2** : ray of light **3** : directed radio signals for the guidance of pilots ~ *vb* **1** : send out light **2** : smile **3** : aim a radio broadcast

bean \'bēn\ *n* : edible plant seed borne in pods

¹**bear** \'bar\ *n, pl* **bears 1** *or pl* **bear** : large heavy mammal with shaggy hair **2** : gruff or sullen person — **bear·ish** *adj*

²**bear** *vb* **bore** \'bōr\; **borne** \'bōrn\; **bear·ing 1** : carry **2** : give birth to or produce **3** : endure **4** : press **5** : go in an indicated direction — **bear·able** *adj* — **bear·er** *n*

beard \'bird\ *n* **1** : facial hair on a man **2** : tuft like a beard ~ *vb* : confront boldly — **beard·ed** *adj* — **beard·less** *adj*

bear·ing *n* **1** : way of carrying oneself **2** : supporting object or purpose **3** : significance **4** : machine part in which another part turns **5** : direction with respect esp. to compass points

beast \'bēst\ *n* **1** : animal **2** : brutal person — **beast·li·ness** *n* — **beast·ly** *adj*

beat \'bēt\ *vb* **beat; beat·en** \'bēt³n\ *or* **beat; beat·ing 1** : strike repeatedly **2** : defeat **3** : act or arrive before **4** : throb ~ *n* **1** : single stroke or pulsation **2** : rhythmic stress in poetry or music ~ *adj* : exhausted — **beat·er** *n*

be·atif·ic \ˌbēə'tifik\ *adj* : blissful

be·at·i·fy \bē'atəˌfī\ *vb* **-fied; -fy·ing** : make happy or blessed — **be·at·i·fi·ca·tion** \-ˌatəfə'kāshən\ *n*

be·at·i·tude \-'atəˌtüd, -ˌtyüd\ *n* : saying in the Sermon on the Mount (Matthew 5:3-12) beginning "Blessed are"

beau \'bō\ *n, pl* **beaux** \'bōz\ *or* **beaus** : suitor

beau·ty \'byütē\ *n, pl* **-ties** : qualities that please the senses or mind — **beau·te·ous** \-ēəs\ *adj* — **beau·te·ously** *adv* — **beau·ti·fi·ca·tion** \ˌbyütəfə'kāshən\ *n* — **beau·ti·fi·er** \'byütəˌfīər\ *n* — **beau·ti·ful** \-ifəl\

adj — **beau·ti·ful·ly** *adv* — **beau·ti·fy** \-əˌfī\ *vb*

bea·ver \'bēvər\ *n* : large fur-bearing rodent

be·cause \bi'kȯz, -'kəz\ *conj* : for the reason that

because of *prep* : by reason of

beck \'bek\ *n* : summons

beck·on \'bekən\ *vb* : summon esp. by a nod or gesture

be·come \bi'kəm\ *vb* **-came** \-'kām\; **-come; -com·ing 1** : come to be **2** : be suitable — **be·com·ing** *adj* — **be·com·ing·ly** *adv*

bed \'bed\ *n* **1** : piece of furniture to sleep on **2** : flat or level surface ~ *vb* **-dd-** : put or go to bed — **bed·spread** *n*

bed·bug *n* : wingless bloodsucking insect

bed·clothes *n pl* : bedding

bed·ding *n* **1** : sheets and blankets for a bed **2** : soft material (as hay) for an animal's bed

be·deck \bi'dek\ *vb* : adorn

be·dev·il \-'devəl\ *vb* : harass

bed·lam \'bedləm\ *n* : uproar and confusion

be·drag·gled \bi'dragəld\ *adj* : dirty and disordered

bed·rid·den \'bedˌrid³n\ *adj* : kept in bed by illness

bed·rock *n* : solid subsurface rock — **bedrock** *adj*

¹**bee** \'bē\ *n* : 4-winged honey-producing insect — **bee·hive** *n* — **bee·keep·er** *n* — **bees·wax** *n*

²**bee** *n* : neighborly work session

beech \'bēch\ *n, pl* **beech·es** *or* **beech** : tree with smooth gray bark and edible nuts (**beech·nuts**) — **beech·en** \-ən\ *adj*

beef \'bēf\ *n, pl* **beefs** \'bēfs\ *or* **beeves** \'bēvz\ : flesh of a steer, cow, or bull ~ *vb* : strengthen — used with *up* — **beef·steak** *n*

bee·line *n* : straight course

been *past part of* BE

beep \'bēp\ *n* : short usu. high-pitched warning sound — **beep** *vb* — **beep·er** *n*

beer \'bir\ *n* : alcoholic drink brewed from malt and hops — **beery** *adj*

beet \'bēt\ *n* : garden root vegetable

bee·tle \'bētəl\ *n* : 4-winged insect

be·fall \bi'fȯl\ *vb* **-fell; -fall·en** : happen to

be·fit \bi'fit\ *vb* : be suitable to

be·fore \bi'fōr\ adv **1** : in front **2** : earlier ~ prep **1** : in front of **2** : earlier than ~ conj : earlier than

be·fore·hand adv or adj : in advance

be·friend \bi'frend\ vb : act as friend to

be·fud·dle \-'fəd°l\ vb : confuse

beg \'beg\ vb **-gg-** : ask earnestly

be·get \bi'get\ vb **-got; -got·ten** or **-got; -get·ting** : become the father of

beg·gar \'begər\ n : one that begs ~ vb : make poor — **beg·gar·ly** adj — **beg·gary** n

be·gin \bi'gin\ vb **-gan** \-'gan\; **-gun** \-'gən\; **-gin·ning 1** : start **2** : come into being — **be·gin·ner** n

be·gone \bi'gȯn\ vb : go away

be·go·nia \-'gōnyə\ n : tropical herb with waxy flowers

be·grudge \-'grəj\ vb **1** : concede reluctantly **2** : look upon disapprovingly

be·guile \-'gīl\ vb **-guiled; -guil·ing 1** : deceive **2** : amuse

be·half \-'haf, -'häf\ n : benefit

be·have \-'hāv\ vb **-haved; -hav·ing** : act in a certain way

be·hav·ior \-'hāvyər\ n : way of behaving — **be·hav·ior·al** \-əl\ adj

be·head \-'hed\ vb : cut off the head of

be·hest \-'hest\ n : command

be·hind \bi'hīnd\ adv : at the back ~ prep **1** : in back of **2** : less than **3** : supporting

be·hold \-'hōld\ vb **-held; -hold·ing** : see — **be·hold·er** n

be·hold·en \-'hōldən\ adj : indebted

be·hoove \-'hüv\ vb **-hooved; -hooving** : be necessary for

beige \'bāzh\ n : yellowish brown — **beige** adj

be·ing \'bēiŋ\ n **1** : existence **2** : living thing

be·la·bor \bi'lābər\ vb : carry on to absurd lengths

be·lat·ed \-'lātəd\ adj : delayed

belch \'belch\ vb **1** : expel stomach gas orally **2** : emit forcefully — **belch** n

be·lea·guer \bi'lēgər\ vb **1** : besiege **2** : harass

bel·fry \'belfrē\ n, pl **-fries** : bell tower

be·lie \bi'lī\ vb **-lied; -ly·ing 1** : misrepresent **2** : prove false

be·lief \bə'lēf\ n **1** : trust **2** : something believed

be·lieve \-'lēv\ vb **-lieved; -liev·ing 1** : trust in **2** : accept as true **3** : hold as

an opinion — **be·liev·able** adj — **be·liev·ably** adv — **be·liev·er** n

be·lit·tle \bi'lit°l\ vb **-lit·tled; -lit·tling 1** : disparage **2** : make seem less

bell \'bel\ n : hollow metallic device that rings when struck ~ vb : provide with a bell

bel·la·don·na \,belə'dänə\ n : poisonous herb yielding a drug

belle \'bel\ n : beautiful woman

bel·li·cose \'beli,kōs\ adj : pugnacious — **bel·li·cos·i·ty** \,beli'käsətē\ n

bel·lig·er·ent \bə'lijərənt\ adj **1** : waging war **2** : truculent — **bel·lig·er·ence** \-rəns\ n — **bel·lig·er·en·cy** \-rənsē\ n — **belligerent** n

bel·low \'belō\ vb : make a loud deep roar or shout — **bellow** n

bel·lows \-ōz, -əz\ n sing or pl : device with sides that can be compressed to expel air

bell·weth·er \'bel'wethər, -,weth-\ n : leader

bel·ly \'belē\ n, pl **-lies** : abdomen ~ vb **-lied; -ly·ing** : bulge

be·long \bi'lȯŋ\ vb **1** : be suitable **2** : be owned **3** : be a part of

be·long·ings \-iŋz\ n pl : possessions

be·loved \bi'ləvəd, -'ləvd\ adj : dearly loved — **beloved** n

be·low \-'lō\ adv : in or to a lower place ~ prep : lower than

belt \'belt\ n **1** : strip (as of leather) worn about the waist **2** : endless band to impart motion **3** : distinct region ~ vb **1** : put a belt around **2** : thrash

be·moan \bi'mōn\ vb : lament

be·muse \-'myüz\ vb : confuse

bench \'bench\ n **1** : long seat **2** : judge's seat **3** : court

bend \'bend\ vb **bent** \'bent\; **bending 1** : curve or cause a change of shape in **2** : turn in a certain direction ~ n **1** : act of bending **2** : curve

be·neath \bi'nēth\ adv or prep : below

bene·dic·tion \,benə'dikshən\ n : closing blessing

bene·fac·tor \'benə,faktər\ n : one who gives esp. charitable aid

be·nef·i·cence \bə'nefəsəns\ n : quality of doing good — **be·nef·i·cent** \-sənt\ adj

ben·e·fi·cial \,benə'fishəl\ adj : being of benefit — **ben·e·fi·cial·ly** adv

ben·e·fi·cia·ry \-'fishē,erē, -'fishərē\ n, pl **-ries** : one who receives benefits

ben·e·fit \'benə,fit\ n **1** : something

that does good **2** : help **3** : fund=
raising event — **benefit** *vb*

be•nev•o•lence \bə'nevələns\ *n* **1**
: charitable nature **2** : act of kindness
— **be•nev•o•lent** \-lənt\ *adj* — **be-
nev•o•lent•ly** *adv*

be•night•ed \bi'nītəd\ *adj* : ignorant

be•nign \bi'nīn\ *adj* **1** : gentle or
kindly **2** : not malignant — **be•nig-
ni•ty** \-'nignətē\ *n*

be•nig•nant \-'nignənt\ *adj* : benign

bent \'bent\ *n* : aptitude or interest

be•numb \bi'nəm\ *vb* : make numb
esp. by cold

ben•zene \'ben,zēn\ *n* : colorless flammable liquid

be•queath \bi'kwēth, -'kwēth\ *vb* **1**
: give by will **2** : hand down

be•quest \bi'kwest\ *n* : something be-
queathed

be•rate \-'rāt\ *vb* : scold harshly

be•reaved \-'rēvd\ *adj* : suffering the
death of a loved one ~ *n, pl* **bereaved** : one who is bereaved — **be-
reave•ment** *n*

be•reft \-'reft\ *adj* : deprived of or
lacking something

be•ret \bə'rā\ *n* : round soft visorless
cap

beri•beri \,berē'berē\ *n* : thiamine=
deficiency disease

berm \'bərm\ *n* : bank of earth

ber•ry \'berē\ *n, pl* **-ries** : small pulpy
fruit

ber•serk \bər'sərk, -'zərk\ *adj* : crazed
— **berserk** *adv*

berth \'bərth\ *n* **1** : place where a ship
is anchored **2** : place to sit or sleep
esp. on a ship **3** : job ~ *vb* : to bring
or come into a berth

ber•yl \'berəl\ *n* : light-colored silicate
mineral

be•seech \bi'sēch\ *vb* **-sought** \-'sot\
or **-seeched; -seech•ing** : entreat

be•set \-'set\ *vb* **1** : harass **2** : hem in

be•side \-'sīd\ *prep* **1** : by the side of
2 : besides

be•sides \-'sīdz\ *adv* **1** : in addition **2**
: moreover ~ *prep* **1** : other than **2**
: in addition to

be•siege \-'sēj\ *vb* : lay siege to — **be-
sieg•er** *n*

be•smirch \-'smərch\ *vb* : soil

be•sot \-'sät\ *vb* **-tt-** : become drunk

be•speak \bi'spēk\ *vb* **-spoke; -spo-
ken; -speak•ing 1** : address **2** : indicate

best \'best\ *adj, superlative of* GOOD

1 : excelling all others **2** : most pro-
ductive **3** : largest ~ *adv superlative
of* WELL **1** : in the best way **2** : most
~ *n* : one that is best ~ *vb* : outdo

bes•tial \'beschəl, 'bēs-\ *adj* **1** : relating to beasts **2** : brutish — **bes•ti•al-
i•ty** \,beschē'alətē, ,bēs-\ *n*

be•stir \bi'stər\ *vb* : rouse to action

best man *n* : chief male attendant at a
wedding

be•stow \bi'stō\ *vb* : give — **be•stow-
al** \-əl\ *n*

bet \'bet\ *n* **1** : something risked or
pledged on the outcome of a contest
2 : the making of a bet ~ *vb* **bet;
bet•ting 1** : risk (as money) on an
outcome **2** : make a bet with

be•tide \bi'tīd\ *vb* : happen to

be•to•ken \bi'tōkən\ *vb* : give an indication of

be•tray \bi'trā\ *vb* **1** : seduce **2** : report or reveal to an enemy by treach-
ery **3** : abandon **4** : prove unfaithful
to **5** : reveal unintentionally — **be-
tray•al** *n* — **be•tray•er** *n*

be•troth \-'träth, -'trōth, -'trōth, *or
with* th\ *vb* : promise to marry — **be-
troth•al** *n* — **be•trothed** *n*

bet•ter \'betər\ *adj, comparative of*
GOOD **1** : more than half **2** : im-
proved in health **3** : of higher quality
~ *adv comparative of* WELL **1** : in a
superior manner **2** : more ~ *n* **1**
: one that is better **2** : advantage ~
vb **1** : improve **2** : surpass — **bet•ter-
ment** \-mənt\ *n*

bet•tor, bet•ter \'betər\ *n* : one who
bets

be•tween \bi'twēn\ *prep* **1** — used to
show two things considered together
2 : in the space separating **3** — used
to indicate a comparison or choice ~
adv : in an intervening space or interval

bev•el \'bevəl\ *n* : slant on an edge ~
vb **-eled** *or* **-elled; -el•ing** *or* **-el•ling
1** : cut or shape to a bevel **2** : incline

bev•er•age \'bevrij\ *n* : drink

bevy \'bevē\ *n, pl* **bev•ies** : large group

be•wail \bi'wāl\ *vb* : lament

be•ware \-'war\ *vb* : be cautious

be•wil•der \-'wildər\ *vb* : confuse —
be•wil•der•ment *n*

be•witch \-'wich\ *vb* **1** : affect by
witchcraft **2** : charm — **be•witch-
ment** *n*

be•yond \bē'yänd\ *adv* **1** : farther **2**
: besides ~ *prep* **1** : on or to the far-

ther side of **2** : out of the reach of **3** : besides

bi- \'bī, ˌbī\ *prefix* **1** : two **2** : coming or occurring every two **3** : twice, doubly, or on both sides

bi·an·nu·al \ˌbī'anyəwəl\ *adj* : occurring twice a year — **bi·an·nu·al·ly** *adv*

bi·as \'bīəs\ *n* **1** : line diagonal to the grain of a fabric **2** : prejudice ~ *vb* **-ased** *or* **-assed; -as·ing** *or* **-as·sing** : prejudice

bib \'bib\ *n* : shield tied under the chin to protect the clothes while eating

Bi·ble \'bībəl\ *n* **1** : sacred scriptures of Christians **2** : sacred scriptures of Judaism or of some other religion — **bib·li·cal** \'biblikəl\ *adj*

bib·li·og·ra·phy \ˌbiblē'ägrəfē\ *n, pl* **-phies** : list of writings on a subject or of an author — **bib·li·og·ra·pher** \-fər\ *n* — **bib·li·o·graph·ic** \-lēə-'grafik\ *adj*

bi·cam·er·al \'bī'kamərəl\ *adj* : having 2 legislative chambers

bi·car·bon·ate \-'kärbə،nāt, -nət\ *n* : acid carbonate

bi·cen·ten·ni·al \ˌbīsen'tenēəl\ *n* : 200th anniversary — **bicentennial** *adj*

bi·ceps \'bī،seps\ *n* : large muscle of the upper arm

bick·er \'bikər\ *vb or n* : squabble

bi·cus·pid \bī'kəspəd\ *n* : double= pointed tooth

bi·cy·cle \'bī،sikəl\ *n* : 2-wheeled vehicle moved by pedaling ~ *vb* **-cled; -cling** : ride a bicycle — **bi·cy·cler** \-klər\ *n* — **bi·cy·clist** \-list\ *n*

bid \'bid\ *vb* **bade** \'bad, 'bād\ *or* **bid; bid·den** \'bid°n\ *or* **bid; bid·ding 1** : order **2** : invite **3** : express **4** : make a bid ~ *n* **1** : act of bidding **2** : buyer's proposed price — **bid·da·ble** \-əbəl\ *adj* — **bid·der** *n*

bide \'bīd\ *vb* **bode** \'bōd\ *or* **bid·ed; bided; bid·ing 1** : wait **2** : dwell

bi·en·ni·al \bī'enēəl\ *adj* **1** : occurring once in 2 years **2** : lasting 2 years — **biennial** *n* — **bi·en·ni·al·ly** *adv*

bier \'bir\ *n* : stand for a coffin

bifocals \'bī،fōkəlz\ *n pl* : eyeglasses that correct for near and distant vision

big \'big\ *adj* **-gg-** : large in size, amount, or scope — **big·ness** *n*

big·a·my \'bigəmē\ *n* : marrying one person while still married to another — **big·a·mist** \-mist\ *n* — **big·a·mous** \-məs\ *adj*

big·horn *n, pl* **-horn** *or* **-horns** : wild mountain sheep

bight \'bīt\ *n* **1** : loop of a rope **2** : bay

big·ot \'bigət\ *n* : one who is intolerant of others — **big·ot·ed** \-ətəd\ *adj* — **big·ot·ry** \-ətrē\ *n*

big shot *n* : important person

big·wig *n* : big shot

bike \'bīk\ *n* : bicycle or motorcycle

bi·ki·ni \bə'kēnē\ *n* : woman's brief 2-piece bathing suit

bi·lat·er·al \'bī'latərəl\ *adj* : involving 2 sides — **bi·lat·er·al·ly** *adv*

bile \'bīl\ *n* **1** : greenish liver secretion that aids digestion **2** : bad temper

bi·lin·gual \bī'liŋgwəl\ *adj* : using 2 languages

bil·ious \'bilyəs\ *adj* : irritable — **bil·ious·ness** *n*

bilk \'bilk\ *vb* : cheat

¹bill \'bil\ *n* : jaws of a bird together with their horny covering ~ *vb* : caress fondly — **billed** *adj*

²bill *n* **1** : draft of a law **2** : list of things to be paid for **3** : printed advertisement **4** : piece of paper money ~ *vb* : submit a bill or account to

bill·board *n* : surface for displaying advertising bills

bil·let \'bilət\ *n* : soldiers' quarters ~ *vb* : lodge in a billet

bill·fold *n* : wallet

bil·liards \'bilyərdz\ *n* : game of driving balls into one another or into pockets on a table

bil·lion \'bilyən\ *n, pl* **billions** *or*

List of self-explanatory words with the prefix *bi-*

bicolored	bicultural	binational
biconcave	bidirectional	biparental
biconcavity	bifunctional	bipolar
biconvex	bimetal	biracial
biconvexity	bimetallic	

billion : 1000 millions — **billion** *adj* — **bil·lionth** \-yənth\ *adj or n*

bil·low \'bilō\ *n* **1** : great wave **2** : rolling mass ~ *vb* : swell out — **billowy** \'biləwē\ *adj*

billy goat *n* : male goat

bin \'bin\ *n* : storage box

bi·na·ry \'bīnərē\ *adj* : consisting of 2 things — **binary** *n*

bind \'bīnd\ *vb* **bound** \'baúnd\; **bind·ing** **1** : tie **2** : obligate **3** : unite into a mass **4** : bandage — **bind·er** *n* — **binding** *n*

binge \'binj\ *n* : spree

bin·go \'biŋgō\ *n, pl* **-gos** : game of covering numbers on a card

bin·oc·u·lar \bī'näkyələr, bə-\ *adj* : of or relating to both eyes ~ *n* : binocular optical instrument —usu. pl.

bio·chem·is·try \,bīō'keməstrē\ *n* : chemistry dealing with organisms — **bio·chemi·cal** *adj or n* — **biochem·ist** *n*

bio·de·grad·able \,bīōdi'grādəbəl\ *adj* : able to be reduced to harmless products by organisms — **bio·degrad·abil·i·ty** *n* — **bio·deg·ra·da·tion** *n* — **bio·de·grade** *vb*

bi·og·ra·phy \bī'ägrəfē, bē-\ *n, pl* **-phies** : written history of a person's life — **bi·og·ra·pher** \-fər\ *n* — **bi·o·graph·i·cal** \,bīə'grafikəl\ *adj*

bi·ol·o·gy \bī'äləjē\ *n* : science of living beings and life processes — **bi·o·log·ic** \,bīə'läjik\, **bi·o·log·i·cal** \-əl\ *adj* — **bi·ol·o·gist** \bī'äləjist\ *n*

bi·on·ic \bī'änik\ *adj* : having normal biological capabilities enhanced by electronic or mechanical devices

bio·phys·ics \,bīō'fiziks\ *n* : application of physics to biological problems — **bio·phys·i·cal** *adj* — **bio·phys·i·cist** *n*

bi·op·sy \'bī,äpsē\ *n, pl* **-sies** : removal of live bodily tissue for examination

bio·tech·nol·o·gy \,bīōtek'näləjē\ *n* : manufacture of products using techniques involving the manipulation of DNA

bi·par·ti·san \bī'pärtəzən, -sən\ *adj* : involving members of 2 parties

bi·ped \'bī,ped\ *n* : 2-footed animal

birch \'bərch\ *n* : deciduous tree with close-grained wood — **birch, birch·en** \-ən\ *adj*

bird \'bərd\ *n* : warm-blooded egg-laying vertebrate with wings and feathers — **bird·bath** *n* — **bird·house** *n* — **bird·seed** *n*

bird's—eye \'bərdz,ī\ *adj* **1** : seen from above **2** : cursory

birth \'bərth\ *n* **1** : act or fact of being born or of producing young **2** : origin — **birth·day** *n* — **birth·place** *n* — **birth·rate** *n*

birth·mark *n* : unusual blemish on the skin at birth

birth·right *n* : something one is entitled to by birth

bis·cuit \'biskət\ *n* : small bread made with leavening other than yeast

bi·sect \'bī,sekt\ *vb* : divide into 2 parts — **bi·sec·tion** \'bī,sekshən\ *n* — **bi·sec·tor** \-tər\ *n*

bish·op \'bishəp\ *n* : clergy member higher than a priest

bish·op·ric \-shə,prik\ *n* **1** : diocese **2** : office of bishop

bis·muth \'bizməth\ *n* : heavy brittle metallic chemical element

bi·son \'bīsⁿn, 'bīz-\ *n, pl* **-son** : large shaggy wild ox of central U.S.

bis·tro \'bēstrō, 'bis-\ *n, pl* **-tros** : small restaurant or bar

¹bit \'bit\ *n* **1** : part of a bridle that goes in a horse's mouth **2** : drilling tool

²bit *n* **1** : small piece or quantity **2** : small degree

bitch \'bich\ *n* : female dog ~ *vb* : complain

bite \'bīt\ *vb* **bit** \'bit\; **bit·ten** \'bitⁿn\; **bit·ing** \'bītiŋ\ **1** : to grip or cut with teeth or jaws **2** : dig in or grab and hold **3** : sting **4** : take bait ~ *n* **1** : act of biting **2** : bit of food **3** : wound made by biting — **bit·ing** *adj*

bit·ter \'bitər\ *adj* **1** : having an acrid lingering taste **2** : intense or severe **3** : extremely harsh or resentful — **bitter·ly** *adv* — **bit·ter·ness** *n*

bit·tern \'bitərn\ *n* : small heron

bi·tu·mi·nous coal \bə'tümənəs-, -'tyü-\ *n* : coal that yields volatile waste matter when heated

bi·valve \'bī,valv\ *n* : animal (as a clam) with a shell of 2 parts — **bi·valve** *adj*

biv·ouac \'bivə,wak\ *n* : temporary camp ~ *vb* **-ouacked; -ouack·ing** : camp

bi·zarre \bə'zär\ *adj* : very strange — **bi·zarre·ly** *adv*

blab \'blab\ *vb* **-bb-** : talk too much

black \'blak\ *adj* **1** : of the color black

2 : dark-skinned **3** : soiled **4** : lacking light **5** : wicked or evil **6** : gloomy ～ *n* **1** : black pigment or dye **2** : something black **3** : color of least lightness **4** : person of a dark-skinned race ～ *vb* : blacken — **black•ing** *n* — **black•ish** *adj* — **black•ly** *adv* — **black•ness** *n*

black–and–blue *adj* : darkly discolored from bruising

black•ball \'blak₁bȯl\ *vb* **1** : ostracize **2** : boycott — **blackball** *n*

black•ber•ry \'blak₁berē\ *n* : black or purple fruit of a bramble

black•bird *n* : bird of which the male is largely or wholly black

black•board *n* : dark surface for writing on with chalk

black•en \'blakən\ *vb* **1** : make or become black **2** : defame

black•guard \'blagərd, -₁ärd\ *n* : scoundrel

black•head *n* : small dark oily mass plugging the outlet of a skin gland

black hole *n* : invisible extremely massive celestial object

black•jack *n* **1** : flexible leather-covered club **2** : card game ～ *vb* : hit with a blackjack

black•list *n* : list of persons to be punished or boycotted — **blacklist** *vb*

black•mail *n* **1** : extortion by threat of exposure **2** : something extorted by blackmail — **blackmail** *vb* — **black•mail•er** *n*

black•out *n* **1** : darkness due to electrical failure **2** : brief fainting spell — **black out** *vb*

black•smith *n* : one who forges iron

black•top *n* : dark tarry material for surfacing roads — **blacktop** *vb*

blad•der \'bladər\ *n* : sac into which urine passes from the kidneys

blade \'blād\ *n* **1** : leaf esp. of grass **2** : something resembling the flat part of a leaf **3** : cutting part of an instrument or tool — **blad•ed** \'blādəd\ *adj*

blame \'blām\ *vb* **blamed; blam•ing 1** : find fault with **2** : hold responsible or responsible for — **blam•able** *adj* — **blame** *n* — **blame•less** *adj* — **blame•less•ly** *adv* — **blame•worthy** *adj*

blanch \'blanch\ *vb* : make or become white or pale

bland \'bland\ *adj* **1** : smooth in man-ner **2** : soothing **3** : tasteless — **bland•ly** *adv* — **bland•ness** *n*

blan•dish•ment \'blandishmənt\ *n* : flattering or coaxing speech or act

blank \'blaŋk\ *adj* **1** : showing or causing a dazed look **2** : lacking expression **3** : empty **4** : free from writing **5** : downright ～ *n* **1** : an empty space **2** : form with spaces to write in **3** : unfinished form (as of a key) **4** : cartridge with no bullet ～ *vb* : cover or close up — **blank•ly** *adv* — **blank•ness** *n*

blan•ket \'blaŋkət\ *n* **1** : heavy covering for a bed **2** : covering layer ～ *vb* : cover ～ *adj* : applying to a group

blare \'blar\ *vb* **blared; blar•ing** : make a loud harsh sound — **blare** *n*

blar•ney \'blärnē\ *n* : skillful flattery

bla•sé \blä'zā\ *adj* : indifferent to pleasure or excitement

blas•pheme \blas'fēm\ *vb* **-phemed; -phem•ing** : speak blasphemy — **blas•phem•er** *n*

blas•phe•my \'blasfəmē\ *n, pl* **-mies** : irreverence toward God or anything sacred — **blas•phe•mous** *adj*

blast \'blast\ *n* **1** : violent gust of wind **2** : explosion ～ *vb* : shatter by or as if by explosive — **blast off** *vb* : take off esp. in a rocket

bla•tant \'blāt²nt\ *adj* : offensively showy — **bla•tan•cy** \-ᵊnsē\ *n* — **bla•tant•ly** *adv*

¹**blaze** \'blāz\ *n* **1** : fire **2** : intense direct light **3** : strong display ～ *vb* **blazed; blaz•ing** : burn or shine brightly

²**blaze** *n* **1** : white stripe on an animal's face **2** : trail marker esp. on a tree ～ *vb* **blazed; blaz•ing** : mark with blazes

blaz•er \-ər\ *n* : sports jacket

bleach \'blēch\ *vb* : whiten — **bleach** *n*

bleach•ers \-ərz\ *n sing or pl* : uncovered stand for spectators

bleak \'blēk\ *adj* **1** : desolately barren **2** : lacking cheering qualities — **bleak•ish** *adj* — **bleak•ly** *adv* — **bleak•ness** *n*

bleary \'blirē\ *adj* : dull or dimmed esp. from fatigue

bleat \'blēt\ *n* : cry of a sheep or goat or a sound like it — **bleat** *vb*

bleed \'blēd\ *vb* **bled** \'bled\; **bleed•ing 1** : lose or shed blood **2** : feel distress **3** : flow from a wound **4**

: draw fluid from **5** : extort money from — **bleed•er** n

blem•ish \'blemish\ vb : spoil by a flaw ~ n : noticeable flaw

¹**blench** \'blench\ vb : flinch

²**blench** vb : grow or make pale

blend \'blend\ vb **1** : mix thoroughly **2** : combine into an integrated whole — **blend** n — **blend•er** n

bless \'bles\ vb **blessed** \'blest\; **bless•ing 1** : consecrate by religious rite **2** : invoke divine care for **3** : make happy — **bless•ed** \'blesəd\, **blest** \'blest\ adj — **bless•ed•ly** \'blesədlē\ adv — **bless•ed•ness** \'blesədnəs\ n — **bless•ing** n

blew past of BLOW

blight \'blīt\ n **1** : plant disorder marked by withering or an organism causing it **2** : harmful influence **3** : deteriorated condition ~ vb : affect with or suffer from blight

blimp \'blimp\ n : airship holding form by pressure of contained gas

blind \'blīnd\ adj **1** : lacking or quite deficient in ability to see **2** : not intelligently controlled **3** : having no way out ~ vb **1** : to make blind **2** : dazzle ~ n **1** : something to conceal or darken **2** : place of concealment — **blind•ly** adv — **blind•ness** n

blind•fold vb : cover the eyes of — **blindfold** n

blink \'bliŋk\ vb **1** : wink **2** : shine intermittently ~ n : wink

blink•er n : a blinking light

bliss \'blis\ n **1** : complete happiness **2** : heaven or paradise — **bliss•ful** adj — **bliss•ful•ly** adv

blis•ter \'blistər\ n **1** : raised area of skin containing watery fluid **2** : raised or swollen spot ~ vb : develop or cause blisters

blithe \'blīth, 'blīth\ adj **blith•er**; **blith•est** : cheerful — **blithe•ly** adv — **blithe•some** \-səm\ adj

blitz \'blits\ n **1** : series of air raids **2** : fast intensive campaign — **blitz** vb

bliz•zard \'blizərd\ n : severe snowstorm

bloat \'blōt\ vb : swell

blob \'bläb\ n : small lump or drop

bloc \'bläk\ n : group working together

block \'bläk\ n **1** : solid piece **2** : frame enclosing a pulley **3** : quantity considered together **4** : large building divided into separate units **5** : a city square or the distance along

one of its sides **6** : obstruction **7** : interruption of a bodily or mental function ~ vb : obstruct or hinder

block•ade \blä'kād\ n : isolation of a place usu. by troops or ships — **block-ade** vb — **block•ad•er** n

block•head n : stupid person

blond, blonde \'bländ\ adj **1** : fair in complexion **2** : of a light color — **blond, blonde** n

blood \'bləd\ n **1** : red liquid that circulates in the heart, arteries, and veins of animals **2** : lifeblood **3** : lineage — **blood•ed** adj — **blood•less** adj — **blood•stain** n — **blood-stained** adj — **blood•suck•er** n — **blood•suck•ing** n — **bloody** adj

blood•cur•dling adj : terrifying

blood•hound n : large hound with a keen sense of smell

blood•mo•bile \-mō₁bēl\ n : truck for collecting blood from donors

blood•shed n : slaughter

blood•shot adj : inflamed to redness

blood•stream n : blood in a circulatory system

blood•thirsty adj : eager to shed blood — **blood•thirst•i•ly** adv — **blood-thirst•i•ness** n

bloom \'blüm\ n **1** : flower **2** : period of flowering **3** : fresh or healthy look ~ vb **1** : yield flowers **2** : mature — **bloomy** adj

bloo•mers \'blümərz\ n pl : woman's underwear of short loose trousers

bloop•er \'blüpər\ n : public blunder

blos•som \'bläsəm\ n or vb : flower

blot \'blät\ n **1** : stain **2** : blemish ~ vb **-tt- 1** : spot **2** : dry with absorbent paper — **blot•ter** n

blotch \'bläch\ n : large spot — **blotch** vb — **blotchy** adj

blouse \'blaùs, 'blaùz\ n : loose garment reaching from the neck to the waist

¹**blow** \'blō\ vb **blew** \'blü\; **blown** \'blōn\; **blow•ing 1** : move forcibly **2** : send forth a current of air **3** : sound **4** : shape by blowing **5** : explode **6** : bungle ~ n **1** : gale **2** : act of blowing — **blow•er** n — **blowy** adj

²**blow** n **1** : forcible stroke **2** pl : fighting **3** : calamity

blow•out n : bursting of a tire

blow•torch n : small torch that uses a blast of air

¹**blub•ber** \'bləbər\ n : fat of whales

²**blubber** *vb* : cry noisily

blud•geon \'bləjən\ *n* : short club ∼ *vb* : hit with a bludgeon

blue \'blü\ *adj* **blu•er; blu•est 1** : of the color blue **2** : melancholy ∼ *n* : color of the clear sky — **blu•ish** \-ish\ *adj*

blue•bell *n* : plant with blue bell-shaped flowers

blue•ber•ry \-ˌberē\ *n* : edible blue or blackish berry

blue•bird *n* : small bluish songbird

blue•fish *n* : bluish marine food fish

blue jay *n* : American crested jay

blue•print *n* **1** : photographic print in white on blue of a mechanical drawing **2** : plan of action — **blueprint** *vb*

blues \'blüz\ *n pl* **1** : depression **2** : music in a melancholy style

¹**bluff** \'bləf \ *adj* **1** : rising steeply with a broad flat front **2** : frank ∼ *n* : cliff

²**bluff** *vb* : deceive by pretense ∼ *n* : act of bluffing — **bluff•er** \-ər\ *n*

blu•ing, blue•ing \'blüiŋ\ *n* : laundry preparation to keep fabrics white

blun•der \'bləndər\ *vb* **1** : move clumsily **2** : make a stupid mistake ∼ *n* : bad mistake

blun•der•buss \-ˌbəs\ *n* : obsolete short-barreled firearm

blunt \'blənt\ *adj* **1** : not sharp **2** : tactless ∼ *vb* : make dull — **blunt•ly** *adv* — **blunt•ness** *n*

blur \'blər\ *n* **1** : smear **2** : something perceived indistinctly ∼ *vb* **-rr-** : cloud or obscure — **blur•ry** \-ē\ *adj*

blurb \'blərb\ *n* : short publicity notice

blurt \'blərt\ *vb* : utter suddenly

blush \'bləsh\ *n* : reddening of the face — **blush** *vb* — **blush•ful** *adj*

blus•ter \'bləstər\ *vb* **1** : blow violently **2** : talk or act with boasts or threats — **blus•ter** *n* — **blus•tery** *adj*

boa \'bōə\ *n* **1** : a large snake (as the **boa con•stric•tor** \-kən'striktər\) that crushes its prey **2** : fluffy scarf

boar \'bōr\ *n* : male swine

board \'bōrd\ *n* **1** : long thin piece of sawed lumber **2** : flat thin sheet esp. for games **3** : daily meals furnished for pay **4** : official body ∼ *vb* **1** : go aboard **2** : cover with boards **3** : supply meals to — **board•er** *n*

board•walk *n* : wooden walk along a beach

boast \'bōst\ *vb* : praise oneself or one's possessions — **boast** *n* —

boast•er *n* — **boast•ful** *adj* — **boast•ful•ly** *adv*

boat \'bōt\ *n* : small vessel for traveling on water — **boat** *vb* — **boat•man** *n*

boat•swain \'bōsᵊn\ *n* : ship's officer in charge of the hull

¹**bob** \'bäb\ *vb* **-bb- 1** : move up and down **2** : appear suddenly

²**bob** *n* **1** : float **2** : woman's short haircut ∼ *vb* : cut hair in a bob

bob•bin \'bäbən\ *n* : spindle for holding thread

bob•ble \'bäbəl\ *vb* **-bled; -bling** : fumble — **bobble** *n*

bob•cat *n* : small American lynx

bob•o•link \'bäbəˌliŋk\ *n* : American songbird

bob•sled \'bäbˌsled\ *n* : racing sled — **bobsled** *vb*

bob•white \'bäb'hwīt\ *n* : quail

bock \'bäk\ *n* : dark beer

¹**bode** \'bōd\ *vb* **bod•ed; bod•ing** : indicate by signs

²**bode** *past of* BIDE

bod•ice \'bädəs\ *n* : close-fitting top of dress

bodi•ly \'bädᵊlē\ *adj* : relating to the body ∼ *adv* **1** : in the flesh **2** : as a whole

body \'bädē\ *n, pl* **bod•ies 1** : the physical whole of an organism **2** : human being **3** : main part **4** : mass of matter **5** : group — **bod•ied** *adj* — **bodi•less** \-iləs, -ᵊləs\ *adj* — **body•guard** *n*

bog \'bäg, 'bog\ *n* : swamp ∼ *vb* **-gg-** : sink in or as if in a bog — **bog•gy** *adj*

bo•gey \'bugē, 'bō-\ *n, pl* **-geys** : someone or something frightening

bog•gle \'bägəl\ *vb* **-gled; -gling** : overwhelm with amazement

bo•gus \'bōgəs\ *adj* : fake

bo•he•mi•an \bō'hēmēən\ *n* : one living unconventionally — **bohemian** *adj*

¹**boil** \'boil\ *n* : inflamed swelling

²**boil** *vb* **1** : heat to a temperature (**boiling point**) at which vapor forms **2** : cook in boiling liquid **3** : be agitated — **boil** *n*

boil•er \'boilər\ *n* : tank holding hot water or steam

bois•ter•ous \'boistərəs\ *adj* : noisily turbulent — **bois•ter•ous•ly** *adv*

bold \'bōld\ *adj* **1** : courageous **2** : in-

solent **3** : daring — **bold•ly** *adv* —
bold•ness *n*
bo•le•ro \bə'lerō\ *n, pl* **-ros 1** : Spanish dance **2** : short open jacket
boll \'bōl\ *n* : seed pod
boll weevil *n* : small grayish weevil that
infests the cotton plant
bo•lo•gna \bə'lōnē\ *n* : large smoked
sausage
bol•ster \'bōlstər\ *n* : long pillow ~
vb **-stered; -ster•ing** : support
bolt \'bōlt\ *n* **1** : flash of lightning **2**
: sliding bar used to fasten a door **3**
: roll of cloth **4** : threaded pin used
with a nut ~ *vb* **1** : move suddenly
2 : fasten with a bolt **3** : swallow
hastily
bomb \'bäm\ *n* : explosive device ~
vb : attack with bombs — **bomb-
proof** *adj*
bom•bard \bäm'bärd, bəm-\ *vb* : attack with or as if with artillery —
bom•bard•ment *n*
bom•bar•dier \ˌbämbə'dir\ *n* : one
who releases the bombs from a
bomber
bom•bast \'bäm₁bast\ *n* : pretentious
language — **bom•bas•tic** \bäm-
'bastik\ *adj*
bomb•er *n* **1** : one that bombs **2** : airplane for dropping bombs
bomb•shell *n* **1** : bomb **2** : great surprise
bona fide \'bōnə₁fīd, 'bän-; ˌbōnə-
'fīdē\ *adj* **1** : made in good faith **2**
: genuine
bo•nan•za \bə'nanzə\ *n* : something
yielding a rich return
bon•bon \'bän₁bän\ *n* : piece of candy
bond \'bänd\ *n* **1** *pl* : fetters **2** : uniting force **3** : obligation made binding
by money **4** : interest-bearing certificate ~ *vb* **1** : insure **2** : cause to adhere — **bond•hold•er** *n*
bond•age \'bändij\ *n* : slavery
¹**bonds•man** \'bändzmən\ *n* : slave
²**bondsman** *n* : surety
bone \'bōn\ *n* : skeletal material ~ *vb*
boned; bon•ing : to free from bones
— **bone•less** *adj* — **bony** \'bōnē\
adj
bon•er \'bōnər\ *n* : blunder
bon•fire \'bän₁fīr\ *n* : outdoor fire
bo•ni•to \bə'nētō\ *n, pl* **-tos** *or* **-to**
: medium-sized tuna
bon•net \'bänət\ *n* : hat for a woman or
infant
bo•nus \'bōnəs\ *n* : extra payment

boo \'bü\ *n, pl* **boos** : shout of disapproval — **boo** *vb*
boo•by \'bübē\ *n, pl* **-bies** : dunce
book \'bùk\ *n* **1** : paper sheets bound
into a volume **2** : long literary work
or a subdivision of one ~ *vb* : reserve — **book•case** *n* — **book•let**
\-lət\ *n* — **book•mark** *n* — **book-
sell•er** *n* — **book•shelf** *n*
book•end *n* : support to hold up a row
of books
book•ie \-ē\ *n* : bookmaker
book•ish \-ish\ *adj* : fond of books and
reading
book•keep•er *n* : one who keeps business accounts — **book•keep•ing** *n*
book•mak•er *n* : one who takes bets —
book•mak•ing *n*
book•worm *n* : one devoted to reading
¹**boom** \'büm\ *n* **1** : long spar to extend
the bottom of a sail **2** : beam projecting from the pole of a derrick
²**boom** *vb* **1** : make a deep hollow sound
2 : grow rapidly esp. in value ~ *n* **1**
: booming sound **2** : rapid growth
boo•mer•ang \'bümə₁raŋ\ *n* : angular
club that returns to the thrower
¹**boon** \'bün\ *n* : benefit
²**boon** *adj* : congenial
boon•docks \'bün₁däks\ *n pl* : rural
area
boor \'bùr\ *n* : rude person — **boor-
ish** *adj*
boost \'büst\ *vb* **1** : raise **2** : promote
— **boost** *n* — **boost•er** *n*
boot \'büt\ *n* **1** : covering for the foot
and leg **2** : kick ~ *vb* : kick
boo•tee, boo•tie \'bütē\ *n* : infant's
knitted sock
booth \'büth\ *n, pl* **booths** \'büthz,
'büths\ : small enclosed stall or seat-
ing area
boot•leg \'büt₁leg\ *vb* : make or sell
liquor illegally — **bootleg** *adj or n*
— **boot•leg•ger** *n*
boo•ty \'bütē\ *n, pl* **-ties** : plunder
booze \'büz\ *vb* **boozed; booz•ing**
: drink liquor to excess ~ *n* : liquor
— **booz•er** *n* — **boozy** *adj*
bo•rax \'bōr₁aks\ *n* : crystalline compound of boron
bor•der \'bòrdər\ *n* **1** : edge **2**
: boundary ~ *vb* **1** : put a border on
2 : be close
¹**bore** \'bōr\ *vb* **bored; bor•ing 1** : pierce
2 : make by piercing ~ *n* : cylindrical hole or its diameter — **bor•er** *n*
²**bore** *past of* BEAR

[3]**bore** *n* : one that is dull ~ *vb* **bored;
bor•ing** : tire with dullness — **boredom** \'bōrdəm\ *n*

born \'bȯrn\ *adj* **1** : brought into life **2**
: being such by birth

borne *past part of* BEAR

bo•ron \'bōr͵än\ *n* : dark-colored
chemical element

bor•ough \'bərō\ *n* : incorporated town
or village

bor•row \'bärō\ *vb* **1** : take as a loan **2**
: take into use

bo•som \'bu̇zəm, 'bu̇s-\ *n* : breast ~
adj : intimate — **bo•somed** *adj*

boss \'bȯs\ *n* : employer or supervisor
~ *vb* : supervise — **bossy** *adj*

bot•a•ny \'bät²nē\ *n* : plant biology —
bo•tan•i•cal \bə'tanikəl\ *adj* — **bot-
a•nist** \'bät²nist\ *n* — **bot•a•nize**
\-²n͵īz\ *vb*

botch \'bäch\ *vb* : do clumsily —
botch *n*

both \'bōth\ *adj or pron* : the one and
the other ~ *conj* — used to show
each of two is included

both•er \'bäthər\ *vb* **1** : annoy or
worry **2** : take the trouble — **bother**
n — **both•er•some** \-səm\ *adj*

bot•tle \'bät²l\ *n* : container with a narrow neck and no handles ~ *vb* **bot-
tled; bot•tling** : put into a bottle

bot•tle•neck *n* : place or cause of congestion

bot•tom \'bätəm\ *n* **1** : supporting surface **2** : lowest part or place — **bottom** *adj* — **bot•tom•less** *adj*

bot•u•lism \'bächə͵lizəm\ *n* : acute
food poisoning

bou•doir \'bü͵dwär, 'bu̇-, ͵bü'-,
͵bu̇'-\ *n* : woman's private room

bough \'bau̇\ *n* : large tree branch

bought *past of* BUY

bouil•lon \'bü͵yän; 'bu̇l͵yän, -yən\ *n*
: clear soup

boul•der \'bōldər\ *n* : large rounded
rock — **boul•dered** *adj*

bou•le•vard \'bu̇lə͵värd, 'bü-\ *n* : broad
thoroughfare

bounce \'bau̇ns\ *vb* **bounced; bouncing** **1** : spring back **2** : make bounce
— **bounce** *n* — **bouncy** \'bau̇nsē\
adj

[1]**bound** \'bau̇nd\ *adj* : intending to go

[2]**bound** *n* : limit or boundary ~ *vb* : be
a boundary of — **bound•less** *adj* —
bound•less•ness *n*

[3]**bound** *adj* **1** : obliged **2** : having a

binding **3** : determined **4** : incapable
of failing

[4]**bound** *n* : leap ~ *vb* : move by springing

bound•ary \'bau̇ndrē\ *n, pl* **-aries**
: line marking extent or separation

boun•ty \'bau̇ntē\ *n, pl* **-ties** **1** : generosity **2** : reward — **boun•te•ous**
\-ēəs\ *adj* — **boun•te•ous•ly** *adv* —
boun•ti•ful \-ifəl\ *adj* — **boun•ti•ful-
ly** *adv*

bou•quet \bō'kā, bü-\ *n* **1** : bunch of
flowers **2** : fragrance

bour•bon \'bərbən\ *n* : corn whiskey

bour•geoi•sie \͵bu̇rzh͵wä'zē\ *n* : middle class of society — **bour•geois**
\'bu̇rzh͵wä, bu̇rzh'wä\ *n or adj*

bout \'bau̇t\ *n* **1** : contest **2** : outbreak

bou•tique \bü'tēk\ *n* : specialty shop

bo•vine \'bō͵vīn, -͵vēn\ *adj* : relating
to cattle — **bovine** *n*

[1]**bow** \'bau̇\ *vb* **1** : submit **2** : bend the
head or body ~ *n* : act of bowing

[2]**bow** \'bō\ *n* **1** : bend or arch **2**
: weapon for shooting arrows **3** : knot
with loops **4** : rod with stretched
horsehairs for playing a stringed instrument ~ *vb* : curve or bend —
bow•man \-mən\ *n* — **bow•string** *n*

[3]**bow** \'bau̇\ *n* : forward part of a ship —
bow *adj*

bow•els \'bau̇əls\ *n pl* **1** : intestines **2**
: inmost parts

bow•er \'bau̇ər\ *n* : arbor

[1]**bowl** \'bōl\ *n* : concave vessel or part —
bowl•ful \-͵fu̇l\ *n*

[2]**bowl** *n* : round ball for bowling ~ *vb*
: roll a ball in bowling — **bowl•er** *n*

bowl•ing *n* : game in which balls are
rolled to knock down pins

[1]**box** \'bäks\ *n, pl* **box** *or* **box•es** : evergreen shrub — **box•wood** \-͵wu̇d\ *n*

[2]**box** *n* **1** : container usu. with 4 sides
and a cover **2** : small compartment
~ *vb* : put in a box

[3]**box** *n* : slap ~ *vb* **1** : slap **2** : fight with
the fists — **box•er** *n* — **box•ing** *n*

box•car *n* : roofed freight car

box office *n* : theater ticket office

boy \'bȯi\ *n* : male child — **boy•hood**
n — **boy•ish** *adj* — **boy•ish•ly** *adv*
— **boy•ish•ness** *n*

boy•cott \-͵kät\ *vb* : refrain from dealing with — **boycott** *n*

boy•friend \'bȯi͵frend\ *n* **1** : male
friend **2** : woman's regular male
companion

brace \'brās\ *n* **1** : crank for turning a

bit **2** : something that resists weight or supports **3** : punctuation mark { or } ∼ *vb* **braced; brac•ing 1** : make taut or steady **2** : invigorate **3** : strengthen

brace•let \'brāslət\ *n* : ornamental band for the wrist or arm

brack•et \'brakət\ *n* **1** : projecting support **2** : punctuation mark [or] **3** : class ∼ *vb* **1** : furnish or fasten with brackets **2** : place within brackets **3** : group

brack•ish \-ish\ *adj* : salty

brad \'brad\ *n* : nail with a small head

brag \'brag\ *vb* **-gg-** : boast — **brag** *n*

brag•gart \'bragərt\ *n* : boaster

braid \'brād\ *vb* : interweave ∼ *n* : something braided

braille \'brāl\ *n* : system of writing for the blind using raised dots

brain \'brān\ *n* **1** : organ of thought and nervous coordination enclosed in the skull **2** : intelligence ∼ *vb* : smash the skull of — **brained** *adj* — **brain•less** *adj* — **brainy** *adj*

braise \'brāz\ *vb* **braised; brais•ing** : cook (meat) slowly in a covered dish

brake \'brāk\ *n* : device for slowing or stopping ∼ *vb* **braked; brak•ing** : slow or stop by a brake

bram•ble \'brambəl\ *n* : prickly shrub

bran \'bran\ *n* : edible cracked grain husks

branch \'branch\ *n* **1** : division of a plant stem **2** : part ∼ *vb* **1** : develop branches **2** : diverge — **branched** *adj*

brand \'brand\ *n* **1** : identifying mark made by burning **2** : stigma **3** : distinctive kind (as of goods from one firm) ∼ *vb* : mark with a brand

bran•dish \'brandish\ *vb* : wave

brand–new *adj* : unused

bran•dy \'brandē\ *n, pl* **-dies** : liquor distilled from wine

brash \'brash\ *adj* **1** : impulsive **2** : aggressively self-assertive

brass \'bras\ *n* **1** : alloy of copper and zinc **2** : brazen self-assurance **3** : high-ranking military officers — **brassy** *adj*

bras•siere \brə'zir\ *n* : woman's undergarment to support the breasts

brat \'brat\ *n* : ill-behaved child — **brat•ti•ness** *n* — **brat•ty** *adj*

bra•va•do \brə'vädō\ *n, pl* **-does** *or* **-dos** : false bravery

¹brave \'brāv\ *adj* **brav•er; brav•est** : showing courage ∼ *vb* **braved; brav•ing** : face with courage — **brave•ly** *adv* — **brav•ery** \-ərē\ *n*

²brave *n* : American Indian warrior

bra•vo \'brävō\ *n, pl* **-vos** : shout of approval

brawl \'brȯl\ *n* : noisy quarrel or violent fight — **brawl** *vb* — **brawl•er** *n*

brawn \'brȯn\ *n* : muscular strength — **brawny** \-ē\ *adj* — **brawn•i•ness** *n*

bray \'brā\ *n* : harsh cry of a donkey — **bray** *vb*

bra•zen \'brāzᵊn\ *adj* **1** : made of brass **2** : bold — **bra•zen•ly** *adv* — **bra•zen•ness** *n*

bra•zier \'brāzhər\ *n* : charcoal grill

breach \'brēch\ *n* **1** : breaking of a law, obligation, or standard **2** : gap ∼ *vb* : make a breach in

bread \'bred\ *n* : baked food made of flour ∼ *vb* : cover with bread crumbs

breadth \'bredth\ *n* : width

bread•win•ner *n* : wage earner

break \'brāk\ *vb* **broke** \'brōk\; **broken** \'brōkən\; **break•ing 1** : knock into pieces **2** : transgress **3** : force a way into or out of **4** : exceed **5** : interrupt **6** : fail ∼ *n* **1** : act or result of breaking **2** : stroke of good luck — **break•able** *adj or n* — **break•age** \'brākij\ *n* — **break•er** *n* — **break in** *vb* **1** : enter by force **2** : interrupt **3** : train — **break out** *vb* **1** : erupt with force **2** : develop a rash

break•down *n* : physical or mental failure — **break down** *vb*

break•fast \'brekfəst\ *n* : first meal of the day — **breakfast** *vb*

breast \'brest\ *n* **1** : milk-producing gland esp. of a woman **2** : front part of the chest

breast•bone *n* : sternum

breath \'breth\ *n* **1** : slight breeze **2** : air breathed in or out — **breath•less** *adj* — **breath•less•ly** *adv* — **breath•less•ness** *n* — **breathy** \'brethē\ *adj*

breathe \'brēth\ *vb* **breathed; breathing 1** : draw air into the lungs and expel it **2** : live **3** : utter

breath•tak•ing *adj* : exciting

breech•es \'brichəz\ *n pl* : trousers ending near the knee

breed \'brēd\ *vb* **bred** \'bred\; **breeding 1** : give birth to **2** : propagate **3** : raise ∼ *n* **1** : kind of plant or animal usu. developed by humans **2** : class — **breed•er** *n*

breeze \'brēz\ *n* : light wind ~ *vb* **breezed; breez·ing** : move fast — **breezy** *adj*

breth·ren \'brethrən, -ərn\ *pl of* BROTHER

bre·via·ry \'brēvərē, 'bre-, -vyərē, -vē,erē\ *n, pl* -**ries** : prayer book used by Roman Catholic priests

brev·i·ty \'brevətē\ *n, pl* -**ties** : shortness or conciseness

brew \'brü\ *vb* : make by fermenting or steeping — **brew** *n* — **brew·er** *n* — **brew·ery** \'brüərē, 'brürē\ *n*

bri·ar *var of* BRIER

bribe \'brīb\ *vb* **bribed; brib·ing** : corrupt or influence by gifts ~ *n* : something offered or given in bribing — **brib·able** *adj* — **brib·ery** \-ərē\ *n*

bric–a–brac \'brikə,brak\ *n pl* : small ornamental articles

brick \'brik\ *n* : building block of baked clay — **brick** *vb* — **brick·lay·er** *n* — **brick·lay·ing** *n*

bride \'brīd\ *n* : woman just married or about to be married — **brid·al** \-ᵊl\ *adj*

bride·groom *n* : man just married or about to be married

brides·maid *n* : woman who attends a bride at her wedding

¹**bridge** \'brij\ *n* **1** : structure built for passage over a depression or obstacle **2** : upper part of the nose **3** : compartment from which a ship is navigated **4** : artificial replacement for missing teeth ~ *vb* : build a bridge over — **bridge·able** *adj*

²**bridge** *n* : card game for 4 players

bri·dle \'brīdᵊl\ *n* : headgear to control a horse ~ *vb* -**dled; -dling 1** : put a bridle on **2** : restrain **3** : show hostility or scorn

brief \'brēf\ *adj* : short or concise ~ *n* : concise summary (as of a legal case) ~ *vb* : give final instructions or essential information to — **brief·ly** *adv* — **brief·ness** *n*

brief·case *n* : case for papers

¹**bri·er** \'brīər\ *n* : thorny plant

²**brier** *n* : heath of southern Europe

¹**brig** \'brig\ *n* : 2-masted ship

²**brig** *n* : jail on a naval ship

bri·gade \brig'ād\ *n* **1** : large military unit **2** : group organized for a special activity

brig·a·dier general \,brigə'dir-\ *n* : officer ranking next below a major general

brig·and \'brigənd\ *n* : bandit — **brig·and·age** \-ij\ *n*

bright \'brīt\ *adj* **1** : radiating or reflecting light **2** : cheerful **3** : intelligent — **bright·en** \-ᵊn\ *vb* — **bright·en·er** \'brīt°nər\ *n* — **bright·ly** *adv* — **bright·ness** *n*

bril·liant \'brilyənt\ *adj* **1** : very bright **2** : splendid **3** : very intelligent — **bril·liance** \-yəns\ *n* — **bril·lian·cy** \-yənsē\ *n* — **bril·liant·ly** *adv*

brim \'brim\ *n* : edge or rim ~ *vb* : be or become full — **brim·less** *adj* — **brimmed** *adj*

brim·ful \-'fùl\ *adj* : full to the brim

brim·stone *n* : sulfur

brin·dled \'brind°ld\ *adj* : gray or tawny with dark streaks or flecks

brine \'brīn\ *n* **1** : salt water **2** : ocean — **brin·i·ness** *n* — **briny** *adj*

bring \'briŋ\ *vb* **brought** \'bròt\; **bring·ing 1** : cause to come with one **2** : persuade **3** : produce **4** : sell for — **bring·er** *n* — **bring about** *vb* : make happen — **bring up** *vb* **1** : care for and educate **2** : cause to be noticed

brink \'briŋk\ *n* : edge

bri·quette, bri·quet \bri'ket\ *n* : pressed mass (as of charcoal)

brisk \'brisk\ *adj* **1** : lively **2** : invigorating — **brisk·ly** *adv* — **brisk·ness** *n*

bris·ket \'briskət\ *n* : breast or lower chest of a quadruped

bris·tle \'brisəl\ *n* : short stiff hair ~ *vb* -**tled; -tling 1** : stand erect **2** : show angry defiance **3** : appear as if covered with bristles — **bris·tly** *adj*

brit·tle \'britᵊl\ *adj* -**tler; -tlest** : easily broken — **brit·tle·ness** *n*

broach \'brōch\ *n* : pointed tool (as for opening casks) ~ *vb* **1** : pierce (as a cask) to open **2** : introduce for discussion

broad \'bròd\ *adj* **1** : wide **2** : spacious **3** : clear or open **4** : obvious **5** : tolerant in outlook **6** : widely applicable **7** : dealing with essential points — **broad·en** \-ᵊn\ *vb* — **broad·ly** *adv* — **broad·ness** *n*

broad·cast *n* **1** : transmission by radio waves **2** : radio or television program ~ *vb* -**cast; -cast·ing 1** : scatter or sow in all directions **2** : make widely known **3** : send out on a broadcast — **broad·cast·er** *n*

broad·cloth *n* : fine cloth

broad•loom *adj* : woven on a wide loom esp. in solid color

broad–mind•ed *adj* : tolerant of varied opinions — **broad–mind•ed•ly** *adv* — **broad–mind•ed•ness** *n*

broad•side *n* **1** : simultaneous firing of all guns on one side of a ship **2** : verbal attack

bro•cade \brō′kād\ *n* : usu. silk fabric with a raised design

broc•co•li \′bräkəlē\ *n* : green vegetable akin to cauliflower

bro•chure \brō′shủr\ *n* : pamphlet

brogue \′brōg\ *n* : Irish accent

broil \′brȯil\ *vb* : cook by radiant heat — **broil** *n*

broil•er *n* **1** : utensil for broiling **2** : chicken fit for broiling

¹**broke** \′brōk\ *past of* BREAK

²**broke** *adj* : out of money

bro•ken \′brōkən\ *adj* : imperfectly spoken — **bro•ken•ly** *adv*

bro•ken•heart•ed \-′härtəd\ *adj* : overcome by grief or despair

bro•ker \′brōkər\ *n* : agent who buys and sells for a fee — **broker** *vb* — **bro•ker•age** \-kərij\ *n*

bro•mine \′brō₁mēn\ *n* : deep red liquid corrosive chemical element

bron•chi•tis \brän′kītəs, bräŋ-\ *n* : inflammation of the bronchi

bron•chus \′bräŋkəs\ *n, pl* **-chi** \-₁kī, -₁kē\ : division of the windpipe leading to a lung — **bron•chi•al** \-kēəl\ *adj*

bronze \′bränz\ *vb* **bronzed; bronz-ing** : make bronze in color ∼ *n* **1** : alloy of copper and tin **2** : yellowish brown \-ē\ *adj*

brooch \′brōch, ′brüch\ *n* : ornamental clasp or pin

brood \′brüd\ *n* : family of young ∼ *vb* **1** : sit on eggs to hatch them **2** : ponder ∼ *adj* : kept for breeding — **brood•er** *n* — **brood•ing•ly** *adv*

¹**brook** \′brủk\ *vb* : tolerate

²**brook** *n* : small stream

broom \′brüm, ′brủm\ *n* **1** : flowering shrub **2** : implement for sweeping — **broom•stick** *n*

broth \′brȯth\ *n, pl* **broths** \′brȯths, ′brȯthz\ : liquid in which meat has been cooked

broth•el \′bräthəl, ′brȯth-\ *n* : house of prostitutes

broth•er \′brəthər\ *n, pl* **brothers** *also* **breth•ren** \′brethrən, -ərn\ **1** : male sharing one or both parents

with another person **2** : kinsman — **broth•er•hood** *n* — **broth•er•li•ness** *n* — **broth•er•ly** *adj*

broth•er–in–law *n, pl* **brothers–in–law** : brother of one's spouse or husband of one's sister or of one's spouse's sister

brought *past of* BRING

brow \′braủ\ *n* **1** : eyebrow **2** : forehead **3** : edge of a steep place

brow•beat *vb* **-beat; -beat•en** *or* **-beat; -beat•ing** : intimidate

brown \′braủn\ *adj* **1** : of the color brown **2** : of dark or tanned complexion ∼ *n* : a color like that of coffee ∼ *vb* : make or become brown — **brown•ish** *adj*

browse \′braủz\ *vb* **browsed; brows-ing 1** : graze **2** : look over casually — **brows•er** *n*

brows•er \′braủzər\ *n* : computer program for accessing Web sites

bru•in \′brüən\ *n* : bear

bruise \′brüz\ *vb* **bruised; bruis•ing 1** : make a bruise on **2** : become bruised ∼ *n* : surface injury to flesh

brunch \′brənch\ *n* : late breakfast, early lunch, or combination of both

bru•net, bru•nette \brü′net\ *adj* : having dark hair and usu. dark skin — **bru•net, brunette** *n*

brunt \′brənt\ *n* : main impact

¹**brush** \′brəsh\ *n* **1** : small cut branches **2** : coarse shrubby vegetation

²**brush** *n* **1** : bristles set in a handle used esp. for cleaning or painting **2** : light touch ∼ *vb* **1** : apply a brush to **2** : remove with or as if with a brush **3** : dismiss in an offhand way **4** : touch lightly — **brush up** *vb* : renew one's skill

³**brush** *n* : skirmish

brush–off *n* : curt dismissal

brusque \′brəsk\ *adj* : curt or blunt in manner — **brusque•ly** *adv*

bru•tal \′brüt³l\ *adj* : like a brute and esp. cruel — **bru•tal•i•ty** \brü′talətē\ *n* — **bru•tal•ize** \′brüt³l₁īz\ *vb* — **bru•tal•ly** \-³lē\ *adv*

brute \′brüt\ *adj* **1** : relating to beasts **2** : unreasoning **3** : purely physical ∼ *n* **1** : beast **2** : brutal person — **brut•ish** \-ish\ *adj*

bub•ble \′bəbəl\ *vb* **-bled; -bling** : form, rise in, or give off bubbles ∼ *n* : globule of gas in or covered with a liquid — **bub•bly** \-əlē\ *adj*

bu·bo \'bübō, 'byü-\ n, pl **buboes** : inflammatory swelling of a lymph gland — **bu·bon·ic** \bü'bänik, 'byü-\ adj

buc·ca·neer \,bəkə'nir\ n : pirate

buck \'bək\ n, pl **buck** or **bucks** 1 : male animal (as a deer) 2 : dollar ~ vb 1 : jerk forward 2 : oppose

buck·et \'bəkət\ n : pail — **buck·et·ful** n

buck·le \'bəkəl\ n 1 : clasp (as on a belt) for two loose ends 2 : bend or fold ~ vb **-led; -ling** 1 : fasten with a buckle 2 : apply oneself 3 : bend or crumple

buck·ler \'bəklər\ n : shield

buck·shot n : coarse lead shot

buck·skin n : soft leather (as from the skin of a buck) — **buckskin** adj

buck·tooth n : large projecting front tooth — **buck–toothed** adj

buck·wheat n : herb whose seeds are used as a cereal grain or the seeds themselves

bu·col·ic \byü'kälik\ adj : pastoral

bud \'bəd\ n 1 : undeveloped plant shoot 2 : partly opened flower ~ vb **-dd-** 1 : form or put forth buds 2 : be or develop like a bud

Bud·dhism \'bü,dizəm, 'bù-\ n : religion of eastern and central Asia — **Bud·dhist** \'büdist, 'bùd-\ n or adj

bud·dy \'bədē\ n, pl **-dies** : friend

budge \'bəj\ vb **budged; budg·ing** : move from a place

bud·get \'bəjət\ n 1 : estimate of income and expenses 2 : plan for coordinating income and expenses 3 : money available for a particular use — **budget** vb or adj — **bud·get·ary** \-ə,terē\ adj

buff \'bəf\ n 1 : yellow to orange yellow color 2 : enthusiast ~ adj : of the color buff ~ vb : polish

buf·fa·lo \'bəfə,lō\ n, pl **-lo** or **-loes** : wild ox (as a bison)

¹**buff·er** \'bəfər\ n : shield or protector

²**buffer** n : one that buffs

¹**buf·fet** \'bəfət\ n : blow or slap ~ vb : hit esp. repeatedly

²**buf·fet** \,bə'fā, bü-\ n 1 : sideboard 2 : meal at which people serve themselves

buf·foon \,bə'fün\ n : clown — **buffoon·ery** \-ərē\ n

bug \'bəg\ n 1 : small usu. obnoxious crawling creature 2 : 4-winged sucking insect 3 : unexpected imperfec-

tion 4 : disease-producing germ 5 : hidden microphone ~ vb **-gg-** 1 : pester 2 : conceal a microphone in

bug·a·boo \'bəgə,bü\ n, pl **-boos** : bogey

bug·bear n : source of dread

bug·gy \'bəgē\ n, pl **-gies** : light carriage

bu·gle \'byügəl\ n : trumpetlike brass instrument — **bu·gler** \-glər\ n

build \'bild\ vb **built** \'bilt\; **build·ing** 1 : put together 2 : establish 3 : increase ~ n : physique — **build·er** n

build·ing \'bildiŋ\ n 1 : roofed and walled structure 2 : art or business of constructing buildings

bulb \'bəlb\ n 1 : large underground plant bud 2 : rounded or pear-shaped object — **bul·bous** \-əs\ adj

bulge \'bəlj\ n : swelling projecting part ~ vb **bulged; bulg·ing** : swell out

bulk \'bəlk\ n 1 : magnitude 2 : indigestible food material 3 : large mass 4 : major portion ~ vb : cause to swell or bulge — **bulky** \-ē\ adj

bulk·head n : ship's partition

¹**bull** \'bùl\ n : large adult male animal (as of cattle) ~ adj : male

²**bull** n 1 : papal letter 2 : decree

bull·dog n : compact short-haired dog

bull·doze \-,dōz\ vb 1 : move or level with a tractor (**bull·doz·er**) having a broad blade 2 : force

bul·let \'bùlət\ n : missile to be shot from a gun — **bul·let·proof** adj

bul·le·tin \'bùlətən\ n 1 : brief public report 2 : periodical

bull·fight n : sport of taunting and killing bulls — **bull·fight·er** n

bull·frog n : large deep-voiced frog

bull·head·ed adj : stupidly stubborn

bul·lion \'bùlyən\ n : gold or silver esp. in bars

bul·lock \'bùlək\ n 1 : young bull 2 : steer

bull's–eye n, pl **bull's–eyes** : center of a target

bul·ly \'bùlē\ n, pl **-lies** : one who hurts or intimidates others ~ vb **-lied; -ly·ing** : act like a bully toward

bul·rush \'bùl,rəsh\ n : tall coarse rush or sedge

bul·wark \'bùl,wərk, -,wórk; 'bəl-,wərk\ n 1 : wall-like defense 2 : strong support or protection

bum \'bəm\ vb **-mm-** 1 : wander as a

tramp **2** : get by begging ～ *n* : idle worthless person ～ *adj* : bad

bum·ble·bee \'bəmbəl,bē\ *n* : large hairy bee

bump \'bəmp\ *vb* : strike or knock forcibly ～ *n* **1** : sudden blow **2** : small bulge or swelling — **bumpy** *adj*

¹**bum·per** \'bəmpər\ *adj* : unusually large

²**bump·er** \'bəmpər\ *n* : shock-absorbing bar at either end of a car

bump·kin \'bəmpkən\ *n* : awkward country person

bun \'bən\ *n* : sweet biscuit or roll

bunch \'bənch\ *n* : group ～ *vb* : form into a group — **bunchy** *adj*

bun·dle \'bənd³l\ *n* **1** : several items bunched together **2** : something wrapped for carrying **3** : large amount ～ *vb* **-dled; -dling** : gather into a bundle

bun·ga·low \'bəngə,lō\ *n* : one-story house

bun·gle \'bəngəl\ *vb* **-gled; -gling** : do badly — **bungle** *n* — **bun·gler** *n*

bun·ion \'bənyən\ *n* : inflamed swelling of the first joint of the big toe

¹**bunk** \'bəŋk\ *n* : built-in bed that is often one of a tier ～ *vb* : sleep

²**bunk** *n* : nonsense

bun·ker \-ər\ *n* **1** : storage compartment **2** : protective embankment

bun·kum, bun·combe \'bəŋkəm\ *n* : nonsense

bun·ny \'bənē\ *n, pl* **-nies** : rabbit

¹**bun·ting** \'bəntiŋ\ *n* : small finch

²**bunting** *n* : flag material

buoy \'büē, 'bòi\ *n* : floating marker anchored in water ～ *vb* **1** : keep afloat **2** : raise the spirits of — **buoy·an·cy** \'bòiənsē, 'büyən-\ *n* — **buoy·ant** \-yənt\ *adj*

bur, burr \'bər\ *n* : rough or prickly covering of a fruit — **bur·ry** *adj*

bur·den \'bərd³n\ *n* **1** : something carried **2** : something oppressive **3** : cargo ～ *vb* : load or oppress — **bur·den·some** \-səm\ *adj*

bur·dock \'bər,däk\ *n* : tall coarse herb with prickly flower heads

bu·reau \'byürō\ *n* **1** : chest of drawers **2** : administrative unit **3** : business office

bu·reau·cra·cy \byü'räkrəsē\ *n, pl* **-cies 1** : body of government officials **2** : unwieldy administrative system — **bu·reau·crat** \'byürə,krat\ *n*

— **bu·reau·crat·ic** \,byürə'kratik\ *adj*

bur·geon \'bərjən\ *vb* : grow

bur·glary \'bərglərē\ *n, pl* **-glar·ies** : forcible entry into a building to steal — **bur·glar** \-glər\ *n* — **bur·glar·ize** \'bərglə,rīz\ *vb*

bur·gle \'bərgəl\ *vb* **-gled; -gling** : commit burglary on or in

Bur·gun·dy \'bərgəndē\ *n, pl* **-dies** : kind of table wine

buri·al \'berēəl\ *n* : act of burying

bur·lap \'bər,lap\ *n* : coarse fabric usu. of jute or hemp

bur·lesque \bər'lesk\ *n* **1** : witty or derisive imitation **2** : broadly humorous variety show ～ *vb* **-lesqued; -lesqu·ing** : mock

bur·ly \'bərlē\ *adj* **-li·er; -est** : strongly and heavily built

burn \'bərn\ *vb* **burned** \'bərnd, 'bərnt\ *or* **burnt** \'bərnt\; **burn·ing 1** : be on fire **2** : feel or look as if on fire **3** : alter or become altered by or as if by fire or heat **4** : cause or make by fire ～ *n* : injury or effect produced by burning — **burn·er** *n*

bur·nish \'bərnish\ *vb* : polish

burp \'bərp\ *n or vb* : belch

bur·ro \'bərō, 'bùr-\ *n, pl* **-os** : small donkey

bur·row \'bərō\ *n* : hole in the ground made by an animal ～ *vb* : make a burrow — **bur·row·er** *n*

bur·sar \'bərsər\ *n* : treasurer esp. of a college

bur·si·tis \bər'sītəs\ *n* : inflammation of a sac (**bur·sa** \'bərsə\) in a joint

burst \'bərst\ *vb* **burst** *or* **burst·ed; burst·ing 1** : fly apart or into pieces **2** : enter or emerge suddenly ～ *n* : sudden outbreak or effort

bury \'berē\ *vb* **bur·ied; bury·ing 1** : deposit in the earth **2** : hide

bus \'bəs\ *n, pl* **bus·es** *or* **bus·ses** : large motor-driven passenger vehicle ～ *vb* **bused** *or* **bussed; bus·ing** *or* **bus·sing** : travel or transport by bus

bus·boy *n* : waiter's helper

bush \'bùsh\ *n* **1** : shrub **2** : rough uncleared country **3** : a thick tuft or mat — **bushy** *adj*

bush·el \'bùshəl\ *n* : 4 pecks

bush·ing \'bùshiŋ\ *n* : metal lining used as a guide or bearing

busi·ness \'biznəs, -nəz\ *n* **1** : vocation **2** : commercial or industrial

enterprise **3** : personal concerns —
busi·ness·man \-ˌman\ *n* — **busi-ness·wom·an** \-ˌwùmən\ *n*

¹**bust** \'bəst\ *n* **1** : sculpture of the head and upper torso **2** : breasts of a woman

²**bust** *vb* **1** : burst or break **2** : tame ∼ *n* **1** : punch **2** : failure

¹**bus·tle** \'bəsəl\ *vb* **-tled; -tling** : move or work briskly ∼ *n* : energetic activity

²**bustle** *n* : pad or frame formerly worn under a woman's skirt

busy \'bizē\ *adj* **busi·er; -est 1** : engaged in action **2** : being in use **3** : full of activity ∼ *vb* **bus·ied; busy·ing** : make or keep busy — **busi·ly** *adv*

busy·body *n* : meddler

but \'bət\ *conj* **1** : if not for the fact **2** : that **3** : without the certainty that **4** : rather **5** : yet ∼ *prep* : other than

butch·er \'bùchər\ *n* **1** : one who slaughters animals or dresses their flesh **2** : brutal killer **3** : bungler — **butcher** *vb* — **butch·ery** \-ərē\ *n*

but·ler \'bətlər\ *n* : chief male household servant

¹**butt** \'bət\ *vb* : strike with a butt ∼ *n* : blow with the head or horns

²**butt** *n* **1** : target **2** : victim

³**butt** *vb* : join edge to edge

⁴**butt** *n* : large end or bottom

⁵**butt** *n* : large cask

butte \'byüt\ *n* : isolated steep hill

but·ter \'bətər\ *n* : solid edible fat churned from cream ∼ *vb* : spread with butter — **but·tery** *adj*

but·ter·cup *n* : yellow-flowered herb

but·ter·fat *n* : natural fat of milk and of butter

but·ter·fly *n* : insect with 4 broad wings

but·ter·milk *n* : liquid remaining after butter is churned

but·ter·nut *n* : edible nut of a tree related to the walnut or this tree

but·ter·scotch \-ˌskäch\ *n* : candy made from sugar, corn syrup, and water

but·tocks \'bətəks\ *n pl* : rear part of the hips

but·ton \'bətᵊn\ *n* **1** : small knob for fastening clothing **2** : buttonlike object ∼ *vb* : fasten with buttons

but·ton·hole *n* : hole or slit for a button ∼ *vb* : hold in talk

but·tress \'bətrəs\ *n* **1** : projecting structure to support a wall **2** : support — **buttress** *vb*

bux·om \'bəkəm\ *adj* : full-bosomed

buy \'bī\ *vb* **bought** \'bòt\; **buy·ing** : purchase ∼ *n* : bargain — **buy·er** *n*

buzz \'bəz\ *vb* : make a low humming sound ∼ *n* : act or sound of buzzing

buz·zard \'bəzərd\ *n* : large bird of prey

buzz·er *n* : signaling device that buzzes

buzz·word \'bəzˌwərd\ *n* : word or phrase in vogue

by \'bī\ *prep* **1** : near **2** : through **3** : beyond **4** : throughout **5** : no later than ∼ *adv* **1** : near **2** : farther

by·gone \'bīˌgòn\ *adj* : past — **by·gone** *n*

by·law, bye·law *n* : organization's rule

by·line *n* : writer's name on an article

by·pass *n* : alternate route ∼ *vb* : go around

by·prod·uct *n* : product in addition to the main product

by·stand·er *n* : spectator

by·way \'bīˌwā\ *n* : side road

by·word *n* : proverb

C

c \'sē\ *n, pl* **c's** *or* **cs** \'sēz\ : 3d letter of the alphabet

cab \'kab\ *n* **1** : light closed horse-drawn carriage **2** : taxicab **3** : compartment for a driver — **cab·bie, cab·by** *n* — **cab·stand** *n*

ca·bal \kə'bal\ *n* : group of conspirators

ca·bana \kə'banə, -nyə\ *n* : shelter at a beach or pool

cab·a·ret \ˌkabə'rā\ *n* : nightclub

cab·bage \'kabij\ *n* : vegetable with a dense head of leaves

cab·in \-ən\ *n* **1** : private room on a ship **2** : small house **3** : airplane compartment

cab·i·net \'kabnət\ *n* **1** : display case or cupboard **2** : advisory council of a head of state — **cab·i·net·mak·er** *n* — **cab·i·net·mak·ing** *n* — **cab·i·net·work** *n*

ca·ble \'kābəl\ *n* **1** : strong rope, wire, or chain **2** : cablegram **3** : bundle of electrical wires ~ *vb* **-bled; -bling** : send a cablegram to

ca·ble·gram \-ˌgram\ *n* : message sent by a submarine telegraph cable

ca·boose \kə'büs\ *n* : crew car on a train

ca·cao \kə'kaů, -'kāō\ *n, pl* **cacaos** : So. American tree whose seeds (**ca·cao beans**) yield cocoa and chocolate

cache \'kash\ *n* **1** : hiding place **2** : something hidden — **cache** *vb*

ca·chet \ka'shā\ *n* : prestige or a feature conferring this

cack·le \'kakəl\ *vb* **-led; -ling** : make a cry or laugh like the sound of a hen — **cackle** *n* — **cack·ler** *n*

ca·coph·o·ny \ka'käfənē\ *n, pl* **-nies** : harsh noise — **ca·coph·o·nous** \-nəs\ *adj*

cac·tus \'kaktəs\ *n, pl* **cac·ti** \-ˌtī\ *or* **-tus·es** : drought-resistant flowering plant with scales or prickles

cad \'kad\ *n* : ungentlemanly person — **cad·dish** \-ish\ *adj* — **cad·dish·ly** *adv*

ca·dav·er \kə'davər\ *n* : dead body — **ca·dav·er·ous** \-ərəs\ *adj*

cad·die, cad·dy \'kadē\ *n, pl* **-dies** : golfer's helper — **caddie, caddy** *vb*

cad·dy \'kadē\ *n, pl* **-dies** : small tea chest

ca·dence \'kādᵊns\ *n* : measure of a rhythmical flow — **ca·denced** \-ᵊnst\ *adj*

ca·det \kə'det\ *n* : student in a military academy

cadge \'kaj\ *vb* **cadged; cadg·ing** : beg — **cadg·er** *n*

cad·mi·um \'kadmēəm\ *n* : grayish metallic chemical element

cad·re \-rē\ *n* : nucleus of highly trained people

ca·fé \ka'fā, kə-\ *n* : restaurant

caf·e·te·ria \ˌkafə'tirēə\ *n* : self-service restaurant

caf·feine \ka'fēn, 'kaˌfēn\ *n* : stimulating alkaloid in coffee and tea

cage \'kāj\ *n* : box of wire or bars for confining an animal ~ *vb* **caged; cag·ing** : put or keep in a cage

ca·gey \-ē\ *adj* **-gi·er; -est** : shrewd — **ca·gi·ly** *adv* — **ca·gi·ness** *n*

cais·son \'kāˌsän, -sən\ *n* **1** : ammunition carriage **2** : watertight chamber for underwater construction

ca·jole \kə'jōl\ *vb* **-joled; -jol·ing** : persuade or coax — **ca·jol·ery** \-ərē\ *n*

cake \'kāk\ *n* **1** : food of baked or fried usu. sweet batter **2** : compacted mass ~ *vb* **caked; cak·ing** **1** : form into a cake **2** : encrust

cal·a·bash \'kaləˌbash\ *n* : gourd

cal·a·mine \'kaləˌmīn\ *n* : lotion of oxides of zinc and iron

ca·lam·i·ty \kə'lamətē\ *n, pl* **-ties** : disaster — **ca·lam·i·tous** \-ətəs\ *adj* — **ca·lam·i·tous·ly** *adv*

cal·ci·fy \'kalsəˌfī\ *vb* **-fied; -fy·ing** : harden — **cal·ci·fi·ca·tion** \ˌkalsəfə'kāshən\ *n*

cal·ci·um \'kalsēəm\ *n* : silver-white soft metallic chemical element

cal·cu·late \'kalkyəˌlāt\ *vb* **-lat·ed; -lat·ing** **1** : determine by mathematical processes **2** : judge — **cal·cu·la·ble** \-ləbəl\ *adj* — **cal·cu·la·tion** \ˌkalkyə'lāshən\ *n* — **cal·cu·la·tor** \'kalkyəˌlātər\ *n*

cal·cu·lat·ing *adj* : shrewd

cal·cu·lus \'kalkyələs\ *n, pl* **-li** \-ˌlī\ : higher mathematics dealing with rates of change

cal·dron *var of* **CAULDRON**

cal·en·dar \'kaləndər\ *n* : list of days, weeks, and months

¹calf \'kaf, 'käf\ *n, pl* **calves** \'kavz, 'kävz\ : young cow or related mammal — **calf·skin** *n*

²calf *n, pl* **calves** : back part of the leg below the knee

cal·i·ber, cal·i·bre \'kaləbər\ *n* **1** : diameter of a bullet or shell or of a gun bore **2** : degree of mental or moral excellence

cal·i·brate \'kaləˌbrāt\ *vb* **-brat·ed; -brat·ing** : adjust precisely — **cal·i·bra·tion** \ˌkalə'brāshən\ *n*

cal·i·co \'kaliˌkō\ *n, pl* **-coes** *or* **-cos** **1** : printed cotton fabric **2** : animal with fur having patches of different colors

cal·i·pers \'kaləpərz\ *n* : measuring instrument with two adjustable legs

ca·liph \'kāləf, 'kal-\ *n* : title of head of Islam — **ca·liph·ate** \-ˌāt, -ət\ *n*

cal·is·then·ics \ˌkaləs'theniks\ *n sing or pl* : stretching and jumping exercises — **cal·is·then·ic** *adj*

calk \'kók\ *var of* **CAULK**

call \'kól\ *vb* **1** : shout **2** : summon **3** : demand **4** : telephone **5** : make a visit **6** : name — **call** *n* — **call·er** *n*

— **call down** *vb* : reprimand — **call off** *vb* : cancel

call•ing *n* : vocation

cal•li•ope \kə'līə,pē, 'kalē,ōp\ *n* : musical instrument of steam whistles

cal•lous \'kaləs\ *adj* **1** : thickened and hardened **2** : unfeeling ~ *vb* : make callous — **cal•los•i•ty** \ka'läsətē\ *n* — **cal•lous•ly** *adv* — **cal•lous•ness** *n*

cal•low \'kalō\ *adj* : inexperienced or innocent — **cal•low•ness** *n*

cal•lus \'kaləs\ *n* : callous area on skin or bark ~ *vb* : form a callus

call–waiting *n* : telephone service by which during a call in progress an incoming call is signaled

calm \'käm, 'kälm\ *n* **1** : period or condition of peacefulness or stillness ~ *adj* : still or tranquil ~ *vb* : make calm — **calm•ly** *adv* — **calm•ness** *n*

ca•lor•ic \kə'lórik\ *adj* : relating to heat or calories

cal•o•rie \'kalərē\ *n* : unit for measuring heat and energy value of food

ca•lum•ni•ate \kə'ləmnē,āt\ *vb* **-ated; -at•ing** : slander — **ca•lum•ni•a•tion** \-,ləmnē'āshən\ *n*

cal•um•ny \'kaləmnē\ *n, pl* **-nies** : false and malicious charge — **ca•lum•ni•ous** \kə'ləmnēəs\ *adj*

calve \'kav, 'kàv\ *vb* **calved; calv•ing** : give birth to a calf

calves *pl of* CALF

ca•lyp•so \kə'lipsō\ *n, pl* **-sos** : West Indian style of music

ca•lyx \'kāliks, 'kal-\ *n, pl* **-lyx•es** *or* **-ly•ces** \-lə,sēz\ : sepals of a flower

cam \'kam\ *n* : machine part that slides or rotates irregularly to transmit linear motion

ca•ma•ra•de•rie \,käm'rädərē, ,kam-, -mə'-, -'rad-\ *n* : fellowship

cam•bric \'kāmbrik\ *n* : fine thin linen or cotton fabric

came *past of* COME

cam•el \'kaməl\ *n* : large hoofed mammal of desert areas

ca•mel•lia \kə'mēlyə\ *n* : shrub or tree grown for its showy roselike flowers or the flower itself

cam•eo \'kamē,ō\ *n, pl* **-eos** : gem carved in relief

cam•era \'kamrə\ *n* : box with a lens for taking pictures — **cam•era•man** \-,man, -mən\ *n*

cam•ou•flage \'kamə,fläzh, -,fläj\ *vb* : hide by disguising — **camouflage** *n*

camp \'kamp\ *n* **1** : place to stay temporarily esp. in a tent **2** : group living in a camp ~ *vb* : make or live in a camp — **camp•er** *n* — **camp•ground** *n* — **camp•site** *n*

cam•paign \kam'pān\ *n* : series of military operations or of activities meant to gain a result — **campaign** *vb*

cam•pa•ni•le \,kampə'nēlē, -'nēl\ *n, pl* **-ni•les** *or* **-ni•li** \-'nēlē\ : bell tower

cam•phor \'kamfər\ *n* : gummy volatile aromatic compound from an evergreen tree (**cam•phor tree**)

cam•pus \'kampəs\ *n* : grounds and buildings of a college or school

¹can \kən, 'kan\ *vb, past* **could** \kəd, 'kùd\; *pres sing & pl* **can** **1** : be able to **2** : be permitted to by conscience or feeling **3** : have permission or liberty to

²can \'kan\ *n* : metal container ~ *vb* **-nn-** : preserve by sealing in airtight cans or jars — **can•ner** *n* — **can•nery** \-ərē\ *n*

ca•nal \kə'nal\ *n* **1** : tubular passage in the body **2** : channel filled with water

can•a•pé \'kanəpē, -,pā\ *n* : appetizer

ca•nard \kə'närd\ *n* : false report

ca•nary \-'nerē\ *n, pl* **-nar•ies** : yellow or greenish finch often kept as a pet

can•cel \'kansəl\ *vb* **-celed** *or* **-celled; -cel•ing** *or* **-cel•ing 1** : cross out **2** : destroy, neutralize, or match the force or effect of — **cancel** *n* — **can•cel•la•tion** \,kansə'lāshən\ *n* — **can•cel•er, can•cel•ler** *n*

can•cer \'kansər\ *n* **1** : malignant tumor that tends to spread **2** : slowly destructive evil — **can•cer•ous** \-sərəs\ *adj* — **can•cer•ous•ly** *adv*

can•de•la•bra \,kandə'läbrə, -'lab-\ *n* : candelabrum

can•de•la•brum \-rəm\ *n, pl* **-bra** \-rə\ : ornamental branched candlestick

can•did \'kandəd\ *adj* **1** : frank **2** : unposed — **can•did•ly** *adv* — **can•did•ness** *n*

can•di•date \'kandə,dāt, -dət\ *n* : one who seeks an office or membership — **can•di•da•cy** \-dəsē\ *n*

can•dle \'kandᵊl\ *n* : tallow or wax molded around a wick and burned to give light — **can•dle•light** *n* — **can•dle•stick** *n*

can•dor \'kandər\ *n* : frankness

can•dy \-dē\ *n, pl* **-dies** : food made

from sugar ∼ vb **-died; -dy·ing** : encrust in sugar

cane \'kān\ n **1** : slender plant stem **2** : a tall woody grass or reed **3** : stick for walking or beating ∼ vb **caned; can·ing 1** : beat with a cane **2** : weave or make with cane — **can·er** n

ca·nine \'kā,nīn\ adj : relating to dogs ∼ n **1** : pointed tooth next to the incisors **2** : dog

can·is·ter \'kanəstər\ n : cylindrical container

can·ker \'kaŋkər\ n : mouth ulcer — **can·ker·ous** \-kərəs\ adj

can·na·bis \'kanəbəs\ n : preparation derived from hemp

can·ni·bal \'kanəbəl\ n : human or animal that eats its own kind — **can·ni·bal·ism** \-bə,lizəm\ n — **can·ni·bal·is·tic** \,kanəbə'listik\ adj

can·ni·bal·ize \'kanəbə,līz\ vb **-ized; -iz·ing 1** : take usable parts from **2** : practice cannibalism

can·non \'kanən\ n, pl **-nons** or **-non** : large heavy gun — **can·non·ball** n — **can·non·eer** \,kanə'nir\ n

can·non·ade \,kanə'nād\ n : heavy artillery fire ∼ vb **-ad·ed; -ad·ing** : bombard

can·not \'kan,ät; kə'nät\ : can not — **cannot but** : be bound to

can·ny \'kanē\ adj **-ni·er; -est** : shrewd — **can·ni·ly** adv — **can·ni·ness** n

ca·noe \kə'nü\ n : narrow sharp-ended boat propelled by paddles — **canoe** vb — **ca·noe·ist** n

¹can·on \'kanən\ n **1** : regulation governing a church **2** : authoritative list **3** : an accepted principle

²canon n : clergy member in a cathedral

ca·non·i·cal \kə'nänikəl\ adj **1** : relating to or conforming to a canon **2** : orthodox — **ca·non·i·cal·ly** adv

can·on·ize \'kanə,nīz\ vb **-ized** \-,nīzd\, **-iz·ing** : recognize as a saint — **can·on·iza·tion** \,kanənə-'zāshən\ n

can·o·py \'kanəpē\ n, pl **-pies** : overhanging cover — **canopy** vb

¹cant \'kant\ n **1** : slanting surface **2** : slant ∼ vb **1** : tip up **2** : lean to one side

²cant vb : talk hypocritically ∼ n **1** : jargon **2** : insincere talk

can't \'kant, 'kant\ : can not

can·ta·loupe \'kant³l,ōp\ n : muskmelon with orange flesh

can·tan·ker·ous \kan'taŋkərəs\ adj : hard to deal with — **can·tan·ker·ous·ly** adv — **can·tan·ker·ous·ness** n

can·ta·ta \kən'tätə\ n : choral work

can·teen \kan'tēn\ n **1** : place of recreation for service personnel **2** : water container

can·ter \'kantər\ n : slow gallop — **can·ter** vb

can·ti·cle \'kantikəl\ n : liturgical song

can·ti·le·ver \'kant³l,ēvər, -,ev-\ n : beam or structure supported only at one end

can·to \'kan,tō\ n, pl **-tos** : major division of a long poem

can·tor \'kantər\ n : synagogue official who sings liturgical music

can·vas \'kanvəs\ n **1** : strong cloth orig. used for making tents and sails **2** : set of sails **3** : oil painting

can·vass \-vəs\ vb : solicit votes, orders, or opinions from ∼ n : act of canvassing — **can·vass·er** n

can·yon \'kanyən\ n : deep valley with steep sides

cap \'kap\ n **1** : covering for the head **2** : top or cover like a cap **3** : upper limit ∼ vb **-pp- 1** : provide or protect with a cap **2** : climax — **cap·ful** \-,fùl\ n

ca·pa·ble \'kāpəbəl\ adj : able to do something — **ca·pa·bil·i·ty** \,kāpə-'bilətē\ n — **ca·pa·bly** \'kāpəblē\ adv

ca·pa·cious \kə'pāshəs\ adj : able to contain much

ca·pac·i·tance \kə'pasətəns\ n : ability to store electrical energy

ca·pac·i·tor \-sətər\ n : device for storing electrical energy

ca·pac·i·ty \-sətē\ n, pl **-ties 1** : ability to contain **2** : volume **3** : ability **4** : role or job ∼ adj : equaling maximum capacity

¹cape \'kāp\ n : point of land jutting out into water

²cape n : garment that drapes over the shoulders

¹ca·per \'kāpər\ n : flower bud of a shrub pickled for use as a relish

²caper vb : leap or prance about ∼ n **1** : frolicsome leap **2** : escapade

cap·il·lary \'kapə,lerē\ adj **1** : resembling a hair **2** : having a very small bore ∼ n, pl **-lar·ies** : tiny thin-walled blood vessel

¹**cap·i·tal** \'kapət³l\ adj **1** : punishable by death **2** : being in the series A, B, C rather than a, b, c **3** : relating to capital **4** : excellent ∼ n **1** : capital letter **2** : seat of government **3** : wealth **4** : total face value of a company's stock **5** : investors as a group

²**capital** n : top part of a column

cap·i·tal·ism \-ˌizəm\ n : economic system of private ownership of capital

cap·i·tal·ist \-ist\ n **1** : person with capital invested in business **2** : believer in capitalism ∼ adj **1** : owning capital **2** : practicing, advocating, or marked by capitalism — **cap·i·tal·is·tic** \ˌkapət³l'istik\ adj

cap·i·tal·ize \-ˌīz\ vb **-ized; -iz·ing** **1** : write or print with a capital letter **2** : use as capital **3** : supply capital for **4** : turn something to advantage — **cap·i·tal·iza·tion** \ˌkapət³lə'zāshən\ n

cap·i·tol \'kapət³l\ n : building in which a legislature sits

ca·pit·u·late \kə'pichəˌlāt\ vb **-lat·ed; -lat·ing** : surrender — **ca·pit·u·la·tion** \-ˌpichə'lāshən\ n

ca·pon \'kāˌpän, -pən\ n : castrated male chicken

ca·price \kə'prēs\ n : whim — **ca·pri·cious** \-'prishəs\ adj — **ca·pri·cious·ly** adv — **ca·pri·cious·ness** n

cap·size \'kapˌsīz, kap'sīz\ vb **-sized; -siz·ing** : overturn

cap·stan \'kapstən, -ˌstan\ n : upright winch

cap·sule \'kapsəl, -sül\ n **1** : enveloping cover (as for medicine) **2** : small pressurized compartment for astronauts ∼ adj : very brief or compact — **cap·su·lar** \-sələr\ adj — **cap·su·lat·ed** \-səˌlātəd\ adj

cap·tain \'kaptən\ n **1** : commander of a body of troops **2** : officer in charge of a ship **3** : commissioned officer in the navy ranking next below a rear admiral or a commodore **4** : commissioned officer (as in the army) ranking next below a major **5** : leader ∼ vb : be captain of — **cap·tain·cy** n

cap·tion \'kapshən\ n **1** : title **2** : explanation with an illustration — **caption** vb

cap·tious \'kapshəs\ adj : tending to find fault — **cap·tious·ly** adv

cap·ti·vate \'kaptəˌvāt\ vb **-vat·ed;** **-vat·ing** : attract and charm — **cap·ti·va·tion** \ˌkaptə'vāshən\ n — **cap·ti·va·tor** \'kaptəˌvātər\ n

cap·tive \-tiv\ adj **1** : made prisoner **2** : confined or under control — **captive** n — **cap·tiv·i·ty** \kap'tivətē\ n

cap·tor \'kaptər\ n : one that captures

cap·ture \-chər\ n : seizure by force or trickery ∼ vb **-tured; -tur·ing** : take captive

car \'kär\ n **1** : vehicle moved on wheels **2** : cage of an elevator

ca·rafe \kə'raf, -'räf\ n : decanter

car·a·mel \'karəməl, 'kärməl\ n **1** : burnt sugar used for flavoring and coloring **2** : firm chewy candy

¹**carat** var of KARAT

²**car·at** \'karət\ n : unit of weight for precious stones

car·a·van \'karəˌvan\ n : travelers journeying together (as in a line)

car·a·way \'karəˌwā\ n : aromatic herb with seeds used in seasoning

car·bine \'kärˌbēn, -ˌbīn\ n : short-barreled rifle

car·bo·hy·drate \ˌkärbō'hīˌdrāt, -drət\ n : compound of carbon, hydrogen, and oxygen

car·bon \'kärbən\ n **1** : chemical element occurring in nature esp. as diamond and graphite **2** : piece of carbon paper or a copy made with it

¹**car·bon·ate** \'kärbəˌnāt, -nət\ n : salt or ester of a carbon-containing acid

²**car·bon·ate** \-ˌnāt\ vb **-at·ed; -at·ing** : impregnate with carbon dioxide — **car·bon·ation** \ˌkärbə'nāshən\ n

carbon paper n : thin paper coated with a pigment for making copies

car·bun·cle \'kärˌbəŋkəl\ n : painful inflammation of the skin and underlying tissue

car·bu·re·tor \'kärbəˌrātər, -byə-\ n : device for mixing fuel and air

car·cass \'kärkəs\ n : dead body

car·cin·o·gen \kär'sinəjən\ n : agent causing cancer — **car·ci·no·gen·ic** \ˌkärsⁿō'jenik\ adj

car·ci·no·ma \ˌkärsⁿ'ōmə\ n, pl **-mas** or **-ma·ta** \-mətə\ : malignant tumor

¹**card** \'kärd\ vb : comb (fibers) before spinning ∼ n : device for carding fibers — **card·er** n

²**card** n **1** : playing card **2** pl : game played with playing cards **3** : small flat piece of paper

card·board n : stiff material like paper

car·di·ac \'kärdē͵ak\ *adj* : relating to the heart

car·di·gan \'kärdigən\ *n* : sweater with an opening in the front

¹**car·di·nal** \'kärd³nəl\ *n* **1** : official of the Roman Catholic Church **2** : bright red songbird

²**cardinal** *adj* : of basic importance

cardinal number *n* : number (as 1, 82, 357) used in counting

car·di·ol·o·gy \͵kärdē'äləjē\ *n* : study of the heart — **car·di·ol·o·gist** \-jist\ *n*

car·dio·vas·cu·lar \-ō'vaskyələr\ *adj* : relating to the heart and blood vessels

care \'ker\ *n* **1** : anxiety **2** : watchful attention **3** : supervision ~ *vb* **cared; car·ing 1** : feel anxiety or concern **2** : like **3** : provide care — **care·free** *adj* — **care·ful** \-fəl\ *adj* — **care·ful·ly** *adv* — **care·ful·ness** *n* — **care·giv·er** \-͵givər\ *n* — **care·less** *adj* — **care·less·ly** *adv* — **care·less·ness** *n*

ca·reen \kə'rēn\ *vb* **1** : sway from side to side **2** : career

ca·reer \kə'rir\ *n* : vocation ~ *vb* : go at top speed

ca·ress \kə'res\ *n* : tender touch ~ *vb* : touch lovingly or tenderly

car·et \'karət\ *n* : mark ∧ showing where something is to be inserted

care·tak·er *n* : one in charge for another or temporarily

car·go \'kärgō\ *n, pl* **-goes** *or* **-gos** : transported goods

car·i·bou \'karə͵bü\ *n, pl* **-bou** *or* **-bous** : large No. American deer

car·i·ca·ture \'karikə͵chůr\ *n* : distorted representation for humor or ridicule — **caricature** *vb* — **car·i·ca·tur·ist** \-ist\ *n*

car·ies \'karēz\ *n, pl* **caries** : tooth decay

car·il·lon \'karə͵län\ *n* : set of tuned bells

car·jack·ing \'kär͵jakiŋ\ *n* : theft of an automobile by force or intimidation — **car·jack·er** *n*

car·mine \'kärmən, -͵mīn\ *n* : vivid red

car·nage \'kärnij\ *n* : slaughter

car·nal \'kärn³l\ *adj* : sensual — **car·nal·i·ty** \kär'nalətē\ *n* — **car·nal·ly** *adv*

car·na·tion \kär'nāshən\ *n* : showy flower

car·ni·val \'kärnəvəl\ *n* **1** : festival **2** : traveling enterprise offering amusements

car·ni·vore \-͵vōr\ *n* : flesh-eating animal — **car·niv·o·rous** \kär'nivərəs\ *adj* — **car·niv·o·rous·ly** *adv* — **car·niv·o·rous·ness** *n*

car·ol \'karəl\ *n* : song of joy — **carol** *vb* — **car·ol·er, car·ol·ler** \-ələr\ *n*

car·om \-əm\ *n or vb* : rebound

ca·rouse \kə'rauz\ *vb* **-roused; -rousing** : drink and be boisterous — **carouse** *n* — **ca·rous·er** *n*

car·ou·sel, car·rou·sel \͵karə'sel, 'karə͵-\ *n* : merry-go-round

¹**carp** \'kärp\ *vb* : find fault

²**carp** *n, pl* **carp** *or* **carps** : freshwater fish

car·pel \'kärpəl\ *n* : modified leaf forming part of the ovary of a flower

car·pen·ter \'kärpəntər\ *n* : one who builds with wood — **carpenter** *vb* — **car·pen·try** \-trē\ *n*

car·pet \'kärpət\ *n* : fabric floor covering ~ *vb* : cover with a carpet — **car·pet·ing** \-iŋ\ *n*

car·port *n* : open-sided automobile shelter

car·riage \'karij\ *n* **1** : conveyance **2** : manner of holding oneself **3** : wheeled vehicle

car·ri·on \'karēən\ *n* : dead and decaying flesh

car·rot \'karət\ *n* : orange root vegetable

car·ry \'karē\ *vb* **-ried; -ry·ing 1** : move while supporting **2** : hold (oneself) in a specified way **3** : support **4** : keep in stock **5** : reach to a distance **6** : win — **car·ri·er** \-ēər\ *n* — **carry on** *vb* **1** : conduct **2** : behave excitedly — **carry out** *vb* : put into effect

cart \'kärt\ *n* : wheeled vehicle ~ *vb* : carry in a cart — **cart·age** \-ij\ *n* — **cart·er** *n*

car·tel \kär'tel\ *n* : business combination designed to limit competition

car·ti·lage \'kärt³lij\ *n* : elastic skeletal tissue — **car·ti·lag·i·nous** \͵kärt³l'ajənəs\ *adj*

car·tog·ra·phy \kär'tägrəfē\ *n* : making of maps — **car·tog·ra·pher** \-fər\ *n*

car·ton \'kärt³n\ *n* : cardboard box

car·toon \kär'tün\ *n* **1** : humorous drawing **2** : comic strip — **cartoon** *vb* — **car·toon·ist** *n*

car•tridge \'kärtrij\ *n* **1** : tube containing powder and a bullet or shot for a firearm **2** : container of material for insertion into an apparatus

carve \'kärv\ *vb* **carved; carv•ing 1** : cut with care **2** : cut into pieces or slices — **carv•er** *n*

cas•cade \kas'kād\ *n* : small steep waterfall ⁓ *vb* **-cad•ed; -cad•ing** : fall in a cascade

¹case \'kās\ *n* **1** : particular instance **2** : convincing argument **3** : inflectional form esp. of a noun or pronoun **4** : fact **5** : lawsuit **6** : instance of disease — **in case** : as a precaution — **in case of** : in the event of

²case *n* **1** : box **2** : outer covering ⁓ *vb* **cased; cas•ing 1** : enclose **2** : inspect

case•ment \-mənt\ *n* : window that opens like a door

cash \'kash\ *n* **1** : ready money **2** : money paid at the time of purchase ⁓ *vb* : give or get cash for

ca•shew \'kashü, kə'shü\ *n* : tropical American tree or its nut

¹ca•shier \ka'shir\ *vb* : dismiss in disgrace

²cash•ier *n* : person who receives and records payments

cash•mere \'kazh,mir, 'kash-\ *n* : fine goat's wool or a fabric of this

ca•si•no \kə'sēnō\ *n, pl* **-nos** : place for gambling

cask \'kask\ *n* : barrel-shaped container for liquids

cas•ket \'kaskət\ *n* : coffin

cas•se•role \'kasə,rōl\ *n* : baking dish or the food cooked in this

cas•sette \kə'set, ka-\ *n* : case containing magnetic tape

cas•sock \'kasək\ *n* : long clerical garment

cast \'kast\ *vb* **cast; cast•ing 1** : throw **2** : deposit (a ballot) **3** : assign parts in a play **4** : mold ⁓ *n* **1** : throw **2** : appearance **3** : rigid surgical dressing **4** : actors in a play

cas•ta•nets \,kastə'nets\ *n pl* : shells clicked together in the hand

cast•away \'kastə,wā\ *n* : survivor of a shipwreck — **castaway** *adj*

caste \'kast\ *n* : social class or rank

cast•er \'kastər\ *n* : small wheel on furniture

cas•ti•gate \'kastə,gāt\ *vb* **-gat•ed; -gat•ing** : chastise severely — **cas•ti-**

ga•tion \,kastə'gāshən\ *n* — **cas•ti-ga•tor** \'kastə,gātər\ *n*

cast iron *n* : hard brittle alloy of iron

cas•tle \'kasəl\ *n* : fortified building

cast–off *adj* : thrown away — **cast•off** *n*

cas•trate \'kas,trāt\ *vb* **-trat•ed; -trat•ing** : remove the testes of — **cas•tra•tion** \ka'strāshən\ *n*

ca•su•al \'kazhəwəl\ *adj* **1** : happening by chance **2** : showing little concern **3** : informal — **ca•su•al•ly** \-ē\ *adv* — **ca•su•al•ness** *n*

ca•su•al•ty \-tē\ *n, pl* **-ties 1** : serious or fatal accident **2** : one injured, lost, or destroyed

ca•su•ist•ry \'kazhəwəstrē\ *n, pl* **-ries** : rationalization — **ca•su•ist** \-wist\ *n*

cat \'kat\ *n* **1** : small domestic mammal **2** : related animal (as a lion) — **cat•like** *adj*

cat•a•clysm \'katə,klizəm\ *n* : violent change — **cat•a•clys•mal** \,katə-'klizməl\, **cat•a•clys•mic** \-'klizmik\ *adj*

cat•a•comb \'katə,kōm\ *n* : underground burial place

cat•a•log, cat•a•logue \'kat³l,ȯg\ *n* **1** : list **2** : book containing a description of items ⁓ *vb* **-loged** *or* **-logued; -log•ing** *or* **-logu•ing 1** : make a catalog of **2** : enter in a catalog — **cat•a•log•er, cat•a•logu•er** *n*

ca•tal•pa \kə'talpə\ *n* : tree with broad leaves and long pods

ca•tal•y•sis \kə'taləsəs\ *n, pl* **-y•ses** \-,sēz\ : increase in the rate of chemical reaction caused by a substance (**cat•a•lyst** \'kat³list\) that is itself unchanged — **cat•a•lyt•ic** \,kat³l-'itik\ *adj*

cat•a•ma•ran \,katəmə'ran\ *n* : boat with twin hulls

cat•a•mount \'katə,maunt\ *n* : cougar

cat•a•pult \'katə,pəlt, -,pult\ *n* : device for hurling or launching — **catapult** *vb*

cat•a•ract \'katə,rakt\ *n* **1** : large waterfall **2** : cloudiness of the lens of the eye

ca•tarrh \kə'tär\ *n* : inflammation of the nose and throat

ca•tas•tro•phe \kə'tastrə,fē\ *n* **1** : great disaster or misfortune **2** : utter failure — **cat•a•stroph•ic** \,katə-'sträfik\ *adj* — **cat•a•stroph•i•cal•ly** \-iklē\ *adv*

cat·bird *n* : American songbird

cat·call *n* : noise of disapproval

catch \'kach, 'kech\ *vb* **caught** \'kȯt\; **catch·ing** **1** : capture esp. after pursuit **2** : trap **3** : detect esp. by surprise **4** : grasp **5** : get entangled **6** : become affected with or by **7** : seize and hold firmly ∼ *n* **1** : act of catching **2** : something caught **3** : something that fastens **4** : hidden difficulty — **catch·er** *n*

catch·ing \-iŋ\ *adj* : infectious

catch·up \'kechəp, 'kach-; 'katsəp\ *var of* KETCHUP

catch·word *n* : slogan

catchy \-ē\ *adj* **catch·i·er; -est** : likely to catch interest

cat·e·chism \'katə,kizəm\ *n* : set of questions and answers esp. to teach religious doctrine

cat·e·gor·i·cal \,katə'gȯrikəl\ *adj* : absolute — **cat·e·gor·i·cal·ly** \-klē\ *adv*

cat·e·go·ry \'katə,gōrē\ *n, pl* **-ries** : group or class — **cat·e·go·ri·za·tion** \,katigərə'zāshən\ *n* — **cat·e·go·rize** \'katigə,rīz\ *vb*

ca·ter \'kātər\ *vb* **1** : provide food for **2** : supply what is wanted — **ca·ter·er** *n*

cat·er·cor·ner \,katē'kȯrnər, ,katə-, ,kitē-\, **cat·er·cor·nered** *adv or adj* : in a diagonal position

cat·er·pil·lar \'katər,pilər\ *n* : butterfly or moth larva

cat·er·waul \'katər,wȯl\ *vb* : make the harsh cry of a cat — **caterwaul** *n*

cat·fish *n* : big-headed fish with feelers about the mouth

cat·gut *n* : tough cord made usu. from sheep intestines

ca·thar·sis \kə'thärsəs\ *n, pl* **ca·thar·ses** \-,sēz\ : a purging — **ca·thar·tic** \kə'thärtik\ *adj or n*

ca·the·dral \-'thēdrəl\ *n* : principal church of a diocese

cath·e·ter \'kathətər\ *n* : tube for insertion into a body cavity

cath·ode \'kath,ōd\ *n* **1** : negative electrode **2** : positive battery terminal — **ca·thod·ic** \ka'thädik\ *adj*

cath·o·lic \'kathəlik\ *adj* **1** : universal **2** *cap* : relating to Roman Catholics

Cath·o·lic *n* : member of the Roman Catholic Church — **Ca·thol·i·cism** \kə'thälə,sizəm\ *n*

cat·kin \'katkən\ *n* : long dense flower cluster

cat·nap *n* : short light nap — **catnap** *vb*

cat·nip \-,nip\ *n* : aromatic mint relished by cats

cat's–paw *n, pl* **cat's–paws** : person used as if a tool

cat·sup \'kechəp, 'kach-; 'katsəp\ *var of* KETCHUP

cat·tail *n* : marsh herb with furry brown spikes

cat·tle \'katᵊl\ *n pl* : domestic bovines — **cat·tle·man** \-mən, -,man\ *n*

cat·ty \'katē\ *adj* **-ti·er; -est** : mean or spiteful — **cat·ti·ly** *adv* — **cat·ti·ness** *n*

cat·walk *n* : high narrow walk

Cau·ca·sian \kȯ'kāzhən\ *adj* : relating to the white race — **Caucasian** *n*

cau·cus \'kȯkəs\ *n* : political meeting — **caucus** *vb*

caught *past of* CATCH

cauldron \'kȯldrən\ *n* : large kettle

cau·li·flow·er \'kȯli,flaůər, 'käl-\ *n* : vegetable having a compact head of usu. white undeveloped flowers

caulk \'kȯk\ *vb* : make seams watertight — **caulk** *n* — **caulk·er** *n*

caus·al \'kȯzəl\ *adj* : relating to or being a cause — **cau·sal·i·ty** \kȯ'zalətē\ *n* — **caus·al·ly** \'kȯzəlē\ *adv*

cause \'kȯz\ *n* **1** : something that brings about a result **2** : reason **3** : lawsuit **4** : principle or movement to support ∼ *vb* **caused; caus·ing** : be the cause of — **cau·sa·tion** \kȯ'zāshən\ *n* — **caus·ative** \'kȯzətiv\ *adj* — **cause·less** *adj* — **caus·er** *n*

cause·way *n* : raised road esp. over water

caus·tic \'kȯstik\ *adj* **1** : corrosive **2** : sharp or biting — **caustic** *n*

cau·ter·ize \'kȯtə,rīz\ *vb* **-ized; -iz·ing** : burn to prevent infection or bleeding — **cau·ter·i·za·tion** \,kȯtərə'zāshən\ *n*

cau·tion \'kȯshən\ *n* **1** : warning **2** : care or prudence ∼ *vb* : warn — **cau·tion·ary** \-shə,nerē\ *adj*

cau·tious \'kȯshəs\ *adj* : taking caution — **cau·tious·ly** *adv* — **cau·tious·ness** *n*

cav·al·cade \,kavəl'kād, 'kavəl,-\ *n* **1** : procession on horseback **2** : series

cav·a·lier \,kavə'lir\ *n* : mounted soldier ∼ *adj* : disdainful or arrogant — **cav·a·lier·ly** *adv*

cav·al·ry \'kavəlrē\ *n, pl* **-ries** : troops on horseback or in vehicles — **cav·al·ry·man** \-mən, -,man\ *n*

cave \'kāv\ *n* : natural underground chamber — **cave in** *vb* : collapse

cav·ern \'kavərn\ *n* : large cave — **cav·ern·ous** *adj* — **cav·ern·ous·ly** *adv*

cav·i·ar, cav·i·are \'kavē,är, 'käv-\ *n* : salted fish roe

cav·il \'kavəl\ *vb* **-iled** *or* **-illed; -il·ing** *or* **-il·ling** : raise trivial objections — **cavil** *n* — **cav·il·er, cav·il·ler** *n*

cav·i·ty \'kavətē\ *n, pl* **-ties 1** : unfilled place within a mass **2** : decay in a tooth

ca·vort \kə'vȯrt\ *vb* : prance or caper

caw \'kȯ\ *vb* : utter the harsh call of the crow — **caw** *n*

cay·enne pepper \,kī'en-, ,kā-\ *n* : ground dried fruits of a hot pepper

CD \,sē'dē\ *n* : compact disc

cease \'sēs\ *vb* **ceased; ceas·ing** : stop

cease·less \-ləs\ *adj* : continuous

ce·dar \'sēdər\ *n* : cone-bearing tree with fragrant durable wood

cede \'sēd\ *vb* **ced·ed; ced·ing** : surrender — **ced·er** *n*

ceil·ing \'sēliŋ\ *n* **1** : overhead surface of a room **2** : upper limit

cel·e·brate \'selə,brāt\ *vb* **-brat·ed; -brat·ing 1** : perform with appropriate rites **2** : honor with ceremonies **3** : extol — **cel·e·brant** \-brənt\ *n* — **cel·e·bra·tion** \,selə'brāshən\ *n* — **cel·e·bra·tor** \'selə,brātər\ *n*

cel·e·brat·ed \-əd\ *adj* : renowned

ce·leb·ri·ty \sə'lebrətē\ *n, pl* **-ties 1** : renown **2** : well-known person

ce·ler·i·ty \sə'lerətē\ *n* : speed

cel·ery \'selərē\ *n, pl* **-er·ies** : herb grown for crisp edible stalks

ce·les·ta \sə'lestə\ **ce·leste** \sə'lest\ *n* : keyboard musical instrument

ce·les·tial \sə'leschəl\ *adj* **1** : relating to the sky **2** : heavenly

cel·i·ba·cy \'seləbəsē\ *n* **1** : state of being unmarried **2** : abstention from sexual intercourse — **cel·i·bate** \'seləbət\ *n or adj*

cell \'sel\ *n* **1** : small room **2** : tiny mass of protoplasm that forms the fundamental unit of living matter **3** : container holding an electrolyte for generating electricity — **celled** *adj*

cel·lar \'selər\ *n* : room or area below ground

cel·lo \'chelō\ *n, pl* **-los** : bass member of the violin family — **cel·list** \-ist\ *n*

cel·lo·phane \'selə,fān\ *n* : thin transparent cellulose wrapping

cell phone *n* : portable cordless telephone for use in a system of radio transmitters

cel·lu·lar \'selyələr\ *adj* : relating to or consisting of cells

cel·lu·lose \'selyə,lōs\ *n* : complex plant carbohydrate

Cel·sius \'selsēəs\ *adj* : relating to a thermometer scale on which the freezing point of water is 0° and the boiling point is 100°

ce·ment \si'ment\ *n* **1** : powdery mixture of clay and limestone that hardens when wetted **2** : binding agent ~ *vb* : unite or cover with cement

cem·e·tery \'semə,terē\ *n, pl* **-ter·ies** : burial ground

cen·ser \'sensər\ *n* : vessel for burning incense

cen·sor \'sensər\ *n* : one with power to suppress anything objectionable (as in printed matter) ~ *vb* : be a censor of — **cen·so·ri·al** \sen'sōrēəl\ *adj* — **cen·sor·ship** \-,ship\ *n*

cen·so·ri·ous \sen'sōrēəs\ *adj* : critical — **cen·so·ri·ous·ly** *adv* — **cen·so·ri·ous·ness** *n*

cen·sure \'senchər\ *n* : official reprimand ~ *vb* **-sured; -sur·ing** : find blameworthy — **cen·sur·able** *adj*

cen·sus \'sensəs\ *n* : periodic population count — **census** *vb*

cent \'sent\ *n* : monetary unit equal to ¹⁄₁₀₀ of a basic unit of value

cen·taur \'sen,tȯr\ *n* : mythological creature that is half man and half horse

cen·ten·ni·al \sen'tenēəl\ *n* : 100th anniversary — **centennial** *adj*

cen·ter \'sentər\ *n* **1** : middle point **2** : point of origin or greatest concentration **3** : region of concentrated population **4** : player near the middle of the team ~ *vb* **1** : place, fix, or concentrate at or around a center **2** : have a center — **cen·ter·piece** *n*

cen·ti·grade \'sentə,grād, 'sänt-\ *adj* : Celsius

cen·ti·me·ter \'sentə,mētər, 'sänt-\ *n* : ¹⁄₁₀₀ meter

cen·ti·pede \'sentə,pēd\ *n* : long flat many-legged arthropod

cen·tral \'sentrəl\ *adj* **1** : constituting or being near a center **2** : essential or principal — **cen·tral·ly** *adv*

cen·tral·ize \-trə,līz\ *vb* **-ized; -iz·ing**

: bring to a central point or under central control — **cen·tral·i·za·tion** \ˌsentrələˈzāshən\ n — **cen·tral·iz·er** n

cen·tre chiefly Brit var of **CENTER**

cen·trif·u·gal \senˈtrifyəgəl, -ˈtrifigəl\ adj : acting in a direction away from a center or axis

cen·tri·fuge \ˈsentrəˌfyüj\ n : machine that separates substances by spinning

cen·trip·e·tal \senˈtripətˀl\ adj : acting in a direction toward a center or axis

cen·tu·ri·on \senˈchùrēən, -ˈtùr-\ n : Roman military officer

cen·tu·ry \ˈsenchərē\ n, pl **-ries** : 100 years

ce·ram·ic \səˈramik\ n 1 pl : art or process of shaping and hardening articles from clay 2 : product of ceramics — **ceramic** adj

ce·re·al \ˈsirēəl\ adj : made of or relating to grain or to the plants that produce it ~ n 1 : grass yielding edible grain 2 : food prepared from a cereal grain

cer·e·bel·lum \ˌserəˈbeləm\ n, pl **-bellums** or **-bel·la** \-ˈbelə\ : part of the brain controlling muscular coordination — **cer·e·bel·lar** \-ər\ adj

ce·re·bral \səˈrēbrəl, ˈserə-\ adj 1 : relating to the brain, intellect, or cerebrum 2 : appealing to the intellect

cerebral palsy n : disorder caused by brain damage and marked esp. by defective muscle control

cer·e·brate \ˈserəˌbrāt\ vb **-brat·ed; -brat·ing** : think — **cer·e·bra·tion** \ˌserəˈbrāshən\ n

ce·re·brum \səˈrēbrəm, ˈserə-\ n, pl **-brums** or **-bra** \-brə\ : part of the brain that contains the higher nervous centers

cer·e·mo·ny \ˈserəˌmōnē\ n, pl **-nies** 1 : formal act prescribed by law, ritual, or convention 2 : prescribed procedures — **cer·e·mo·ni·al** \ˌserəˈmōnēəl\ adj or n — **cer·e·mo·ni·ous** \-nēəs\ adj

ce·rise \səˈrēs\ n : moderate red

cer·tain \ˈsərtˀn\ adj 1 : settled 2 : true 3 : specific but not named 4 : bound 5 : assured ~ pron : certain ones — **cer·tain·ly** adv — **cer·tain·ty** \-tē\ n

cer·tif·i·cate \sərˈtifikət\ n : document establishing truth or fulfillment

cer·ti·fy \ˈsərtəˌfī\ vb **-fied; -fy·ing** 1

: verify 2 : endorse — **cer·ti·fi·able** \-ˌfīəbəl\ adj — **cer·ti·fi·ably** \-blē\ adv — **cer·ti·fi·ca·tion** \ˌsərtəfəˈkāshən\ n — **cer·ti·fi·er** n

cer·ti·tude \ˈsərtəˌtüd, -ˌtyüd\ n : state of being certain

cer·vix \ˈsərviks\ n, pl **-vi·ces** \-vəˌsēz\ or **-vix·es** 1 : neck 2 : narrow end of the uterus — **cer·vi·cal** \-vikəl\ adj

ce·sar·e·an \siˈzarēən\ n : surgical operation to deliver a baby — **cesarean** adj

ce·si·um \ˈsēzēəm\ n : silver-white soft ductile chemical element

ces·sa·tion \seˈsāshən\ n : a halting

ces·sion \ˈseshən\ n : a yielding

cess·pool \ˈsesˌpül\ n : underground sewage pit

Cha·blis \ˈshabˌlē; shaˈblē\ n, pl **Chablis** \-ˌlēz, -ˈblēz\ : dry white wine

chafe \ˈchāf\ vb **chafed; chaf·ing** 1 : fret 2 : make sore by rubbing

chaff \ˈchaf\ n 1 : debris separated from grain 2 : something worthless

chaf·ing dish \ˈchāfiŋ-\ n : utensil for cooking at the table

cha·grin \shəˈgrin\ n : embarrassment or humiliation ~ vb : cause to feel chagrin

chain \ˈchān\ n 1 : flexible series of connected links 2 pl : fetters 3 : linked series ~ vb : bind or connect with a chain

chair \ˈcher\ n 1 : seat with a back 2 : position of authority or dignity 3 : chairman ~ vb : act as chairman of

chair·man \-mən\ n : presiding officer — **chair·man·ship** n

chair·wom·an \-ˌwùmən\ n : woman who is a presiding officer

chaise longue \ˈshāzˈlòŋ\ n, pl **chaise longues** \-ˈlòŋ, -ˈlòŋz\ : long chair for reclining

cha·let \shaˈlā\ n : Swiss mountain cottage with overhanging roof

chal·ice \ˈchaləs\ n : eucharistic cup

chalk \ˈchòk\ n 1 : soft limestone 2 : chalky material used as a crayon ~ vb : mark with chalk — **chalky** adj — **chalk up** vb 1 : credit 2 : achieve

chalk·board n : blackboard

chal·lenge \ˈchalənj\ vb **-lenged; -leng·ing** 1 : dispute 2 : invite or dare to act or compete — **challenge** n — **chal·leng·er** n

cham·ber \ˈchāmbər\ n 1 : room 2 : enclosed space 3 : legislative meet-

ing place or body **4** *pl* : judge's consultation room — **cham•bered** *adj*
cham•ber•maid *n* : bedroom maid
chamber music *n* : music by a small group for a small audience
cha•me•leon \kə'mēlyən\ *n* : small lizard whose skin changes color
cham•ois \'shamē\ *n, pl* **cham•ois** \-ē, -ēz\ **1** : goatlike antelope **2** : soft leather
¹champ \'champ, 'champ\ *vb* : chew noisily
²champ \'champ\ *n* : champion
cham•pagne \sham'pān\ *n* : sparkling white wine
cham•pi•on \'champēən\ *n* **1** : advocate or defender **2** : winning contestant ~ *vb* : protect or fight for
cham•pi•on•ship \-ˌship\ *n* **1** : title of a champion **2** : contest to pick a champion
chance \'chans\ *n* **1** : unpredictable element of existence **2** : opportunity **3** : probability **4** : risk **5** : raffle ticket ~ *vb* **chanced; chanc•ing 1** : happen **2** : encounter unexpectedly **3** : risk — **chance** *adj*
chan•cel \'chansəl\ *n* : part of a church around the altar
chan•cel•lery, chan•cel•lory \'chansələrē\ *n, pl* **-ler•ies** *or* **-lor•ies 1** : position of a chancellor **2** : chancellor's office
chan•cel•lor \-ələr\ *n* **1** : chief or high state official **2** : head of a university — **chan•cel•lor•ship** *n*
chan•cre \'shaŋkər\ *n* : skin ulcer esp. from syphilis
chancy \'chansē\ *adj* **chanc•i•er; -est** : risky
chan•de•lier \ˌshandə'lir\ *n* : hanging lighting fixture
chan•dler \'chandlər\ *n* : provisions dealer — **chan•dlery** *n*
change \'chānj\ *vb* **changed; changing 1** : make or become different **2** : exchange **3** : give or receive change for ~ *n* **1** : a changing **2** : excess from a payment **3** : money in smaller denominations **4** : coins — **change-able** *adj* — **change•less** *adj* — **chang•er** *n*
chan•nel \'chanªl\ *n* **1** : deeper part of a waterway **2** : means of passage or communication **3** : strait **4** : broadcast frequency ~ *vb* **-neled** *or* **-nelled; -nel•ing** *or* **-nel•ling** : make or direct through a channel

chant \'chant\ *vb* : sing or speak in one tone — **chant** *n* — **chant•er** *n*
chan•tey, chan•ty \'shantē, 'chant-\ *n, pl* **-teys** *or* **-ties** : sailors' work song
Cha•nu•kah \'känəkə, 'hän-\ *var of* HANUKKAH
cha•os \'kā,äs\ *n* : complete disorder — **cha•ot•ic** \kā'ätik\ *adj* — **cha•ot•i•cal•ly** \-iklē\ *adv*
¹chap \'chap\ *n* : fellow
²chap *vb* **-pp-** : dry and crack open usu. from wind and cold
cha•pel \'chapəl\ *n* : private or small place of worship
chap•er•on, chap•er•one \'shapəˌrōn\ : older person who accompanies young people at a social gathering ~ *vb* **-oned; -on•ing** : act as chaperon at or for — **chap•er•on•age** \-ij\ *n*
chap•lain \'chaplən\ *n* : clergy member in a military unit or a prison — **chap•lain•cy** \-sē\ *n*
chap•ter \'chaptər\ *n* **1** : main book division **2** : branch of a society
char \'chär\ *vb* **-rr- 1** : burn to charcoal **2** : scorch
char•ac•ter \'kariktər\ *n* **1** : letter or graphic mark **2** : trait or distinctive combination of traits **3** : peculiar person **4** : fictional person — **char•ac•ter•i•za•tion** \ˌkariktərə'zāshən\ *n* — **char•ac•ter•ize** \'kariktəˌrīz\ *vb*
char•ac•ter•is•tic \ˌkariktə'ristik\ *adj* : typical ~ *n* : distinguishing quality — **char•ac•ter•is•ti•cal•ly** \-tiklē\ *adv*
cha•rades \shə'rādz\ *n sing or pl* : pantomime guessing game
char•coal \'chärˌkōl\ *n* : porous carbon prepared by partial combustion
chard \'chärd\ *n* : leafy vegetable
charge \'chärj\ *vb* **charged; charging 1** : give an electric charge to **2** : impose a task or responsibility on **3** : command **4** : accuse **5** : rush forward in assault **6** : assume a debt for **7** : fix as a price ~ *n* **1** : excess or deficiency of electrons in a body **2** : tax **3** : responsibility **4** : accusation **5** : cost **6** : attack — **charge•able** *adj*
charg•er \-ər\ *n* : horse ridden in battle
char•i•ot \'charēət\ *n* : ancient 2-wheeled vehicle — **char•i•o•teer** \ˌcharēə'tir\ *n*
cha•ris•ma \kə'rizmə\ *n* : special abil-

ity to lead — **char·is·mat·ic** \ˌkarəz-ˈmatik\ *adj*

char·i·ty \ˈcharətē\ *n, pl* **-ties** 1 : love for mankind 2 : generosity or leniency 3 : alms 4 : institution for relief of the needy — **char·i·ta·ble** \-əbəl\ *adj* — **char·i·ta·ble·ness** *n* — **char·i·ta·bly** \-blē\ *adv*

char·la·tan \ˈshärlətən\ *n* : impostor

charm \ˈchärm\ *n* 1 : something with magic power 2 : appealing trait 3 : small ornament ~ *vb* : fascinate — **charm·er** *n* — **charm·ing** *adj* — **charm·ing·ly** *adv*

char·nel house \ˈchärnᵊl-\ *n* : place for dead bodies

chart \ˈchärt\ *n* 1 : map 2 : diagram ~ *vb* 1 : make a chart of 2 : plan

char·ter \-ər\ *n* 1 : document granting rights 2 : constitution ~ *vb* 1 : establish by charter 2 : rent — **char·ter·er** *n*

char·treuse \shärˈtrüz, -ˈtrüs\ *n* : brilliant yellow green

char·wom·an \ˈchärˌwumən\ *n* : cleaning woman

chary \ˈcharē\ *adj* **chari·er; -est** : cautious — **char·i·ly** \ˈcharəlē\ *adv*

¹**chase** \ˈchās\ *vb* **chased; chas·ing** 1 : follow trying to catch 2 : drive away — **chase** *n* — **chas·er** *n*

²**chase** *vb* **chased; chas·ing** : decorate (metal) by embossing or engraving

chasm \ˈkazəm\ *n* : gorge

chas·sis \ˈchasē, ˈshasē\ *n, pl* **chas·sis** \-ēz\ : supporting structural frame

chaste \ˈchāst\ *adj* **chast·er; chast·est** 1 : abstaining from all or unlawful sexual relations 2 : modest or decent 3 : severely simple — **chaste·ly** *adv* — **chaste·ness** *n* — **chas·ti·ty** \ˈchastətē\ *n*

chas·ten \ˈchāsᵊn\ *vb* : discipline

chas·tise \chasˈtīz\ *vb* **-tised; -tis·ing** 1 : punish 2 : censure — **chas·tise·ment** \-mənt, ˈchastəz-\ *n*

chat \ˈchat\ *n* : informal talk — **chat** *vb* — **chat·ty** \-ē\ *adj*

châ·teau \shaˈtō\ *n, pl* **-teaus** \-ˈtōz\ *or* **-teaux** \-ˈtō, -ˈtōz\ 1 : large country house 2 : French vineyard estate

chat·tel \ˈchatᵊl\ *n* : item of tangible property other than real estate

chat·ter \ˈchatər\ *vb* 1 : utter rapidly succeeding sounds 2 : talk fast or too much — **chatter** *n* — **chat·ter·er** *n*

chat·ter·box *n* : incessant talker

chauf·feur \ˈshōfər, shōˈfər\ *n* : hired car driver ~ *vb* : work as a chauffeur

chau·vin·ism \ˈshōvəˌnizəm\ *n* : excessive patriotism — **chau·vin·ist** \-vənist\ *n* — **chau·vin·is·tic** \ˌshōvəˈnistik\ *adj*

cheap \ˈchēp\ *adj* 1 : inexpensive 2 : shoddy — **cheap** *adv* — **cheap·en** \ˈchēpən\ *vb* — **cheap·ly** *adv* — **cheap·ness** *n*

cheap·skate *n* : stingy person

cheat \ˈchēt\ *n* 1 : act of deceiving 2 : one that cheats ~ *vb* 1 : deprive through fraud or deceit 2 : violate rules dishonestly — **cheat·er** *n*

check \ˈchek\ *n* 1 : sudden stoppage 2 : restraint 3 : test or standard for testing 4 : written order to a bank to pay money 5 : ticket showing ownership 6 : slip showing an amount due 7 : pattern in squares or fabric in such a pattern 8 : mark placed beside an item noted ~ *vb* 1 : slow down or stop 2 : restrain 3 : compare or correspond with a source or original 4 : inspect or test for condition 5 : mark with a check 6 : leave or accept for safekeeping or shipment 7 : checker — **check in** *vb* : report one's arrival — **check out** *vb* : settle one's account and leave

¹**check·er** \-ər\ *n* : piece in checkers ~ *vb* : mark with different colors or into squares

²**checker** *n* : one that checks

check·er·board \-ˌbōrd\ *n* : board of 64 squares of alternate colors

check·ers \ˈchekərz\ *n* : game for 2 played on a checkerboard

check·mate *vb* : thwart completely — **checkmate** *n*

check·point *n* : place where traffic is checked

check·up *n* : physical examination

ched·dar \ˈchedər\ *n* : hard smooth cheese

cheek \ˈchēk\ *n* 1 : fleshy side part of the face 2 : impudence — **cheeked** \ˈchēkt\ *adj* — **cheeky** *adj*

cheep \ˈchēp\ *vb* : utter faint shrill sounds — **cheep** *n*

cheer \ˈchir\ *n* 1 : good spirits 2 : food and drink for a feast 3 : shout of applause or encouragement ~ *vb* 1 : give hope or courage to 2 : make or become glad 3 : urge on or applaud with shouts — **cheer·er** *n* — **cheer·ful** \-fəl\ *adj* — **cheer·ful·ly**

adv — **cheer·ful·ness** *n* — **cheer-lead·er** *n* — **cheer·less** *adj* — **cheer·less·ly** *adv* — **cheer·less·ness** *n*

cheery \'chirē\ *adj* **cheer·i·er; -est** : cheerful — **cheer·i·ly** *adv* — **cheer·i·ness** *n*

cheese \'chēz\ *n* : curd of milk usu. pressed and cured — **cheesy** *adj*

cheese·cloth *n* : lightweight coarse cotton gauze

chee·tah \'chētə\ *n* : spotted swift= moving African cat

chef \'shef\ *n* : chief cook

chem·i·cal \'kemikəl\ *adj* **1** : relating to chemistry **2** : working or produced by chemicals ~ *n* : substance obtained by chemistry — **chem·i·cal·ly** \-klē\ *adv*

che·mise \shə'mēz\ *n* **1** : woman's one-piece undergarment **2** : loose dress

chem·ist \'kemist\ *n* **1** : one trained in chemistry **2** *Brit* : pharmacist

chem·is·try \-istrē\ *n, pl* **-tries** : science that deals with the composition and properties of substances

che·mo·ther·a·py \ˌkēmō'therəpē, ˌkemō-\ *n* : use of chemicals in the treatment of disease — **che·mo·ther·a·peu·tic** *adj*

che·nille \shə'nēl\ *n* : yarn with protruding pile or fabric of such yarn

cheque \'chek\ *chiefly Brit var of* CHECK 4

cher·ish \'cherish\ *vb* : hold dear

cher·ry \'cherē\ *n, pl* **-ries** : small fleshy fruit of a tree related to the roses or the tree or its wood

cher·ub \'cherəb\ *n* **1** *pl* **-u·bim** \-əˌbim, -yə-\ : angel **2** *pl* **-ubs** : chubby child — **che·ru·bic** \chə-'rübik\ *adj*

chess \'ches\ *n* : game for 2 played on a checkerboard — **chess·board** *n* — **chess·man** *n*

chest \'chest\ *n* **1** : boxlike container **2** : part of the body enclosed by the ribs and breastbone — **chest·ed** *adj*

chest·nut \'ches,nət\ *n* : nut of a tree related to the beech or the tree

chev·i·ot \'shevēət\ *n* **1** : heavy rough wool fabric **2** : soft-finished cotton fabric

chev·ron \'shevrən\ *n* : V-shaped insignia

chew \'chü\ *vb* : crush or grind with the teeth ~ *n* : something to chew —

chew·able *adj* — **chew·er** *n* — **chewy** *adj*

chic \'shēk\ *n* : smart elegance of dress or manner ~ *adj* **1** : stylish **2** : currently fashionable

chi·ca·nery \shik'ānərē\ *n, pl* **-ner·ies** : trickery

chick \'chik\ *n* : young chicken or bird

chick·a·dee \-əˌdē\ *n* : small grayish American bird

chick·en \'chikən\ *n* **1** : common domestic fowl or its flesh used as food **2** : coward

chicken pox *n* : acute contagious virus disease esp. of children

chi·cle \'chikəl\ *n* : gum from a tropical evergreen tree

chic·o·ry \'chikərē\ *n, pl* **-ries** : herb used in salad or its dried ground root used to adulterate coffee

chide \'chīd\ *vb* **chid** \'chid\ *or* **chid·ed** \'chīdəd\; **chid** *or* **chid·den** \'chidᵊn\ *or* **chided; chid·ing** \'chīdiŋ\ : scold

chief \'chēf\ *n* : leader ~ *adj* **1** : highest in rank **2** : most important — **chief·dom** *n* — **chief·ly** *adv*

chief·tain \'chēftən\ *n* : chief

chif·fon \shif'än, 'shif,-\ *n* : sheer fabric

chig·ger \'chigər\ *n* : bloodsucking mite

chi·gnon \'shēn,yän\ *n* : knot of hair

chil·blain \'chil,blān\ *n* : sore or inflamed swelling caused by cold

child \'chīld\ *n, pl* **chil·dren** \'chil-drən\ **1** : unborn or recently born person **2** : son or daughter — **child-bear·ing** *n or adj* — **child·birth** *n* — **child·hood** *n* — **child·ish** *adj* — **child·ish·ly** *adv* — **child·ish·ness** *n* — **child·less** *adj* — **child·less·ness** *n* — **child·like** *adj* — **child·proof** \-ˌprüf\ *adj*

chili, chile, chil·li \'chilē\ *n, pl* **chil·ies** *or* **chil·es** *or* **chil·lies** **1** : hot pepper **2** : spicy stew of ground beef, chilies, and beans

chill \'chil\ *vb* : make or become cold or chilly ~ *adj* : moderately cold ~ *n* **1** : feeling of coldness with shivering **2** : moderate coldness

chilly \-ē\ *adj* **chill·i·er; -est** : noticeably cold — **chill·i·ness** *n*

chime \'chīm\ *n* : set of tuned bells or their sound ~ *vb* : make bell-like sounds — **chime in** *vb* : break into or join in a conversation

chi•me•ra, chi•mae•ra \kī'mirə, kə-\ n 1 : imaginary monster 2 : illusion — chi•me•ri•cal \-'merikəl\ adj

chim•ney \'chimnē\ n, pl -neys 1 : passage for smoke 2 : glass tube around a lamp flame

chimp \'chimp, 'shimp\ n : chimpanzee

chim•pan•zee \ˌchimˌpan'zē, ˌshim-; chim'panzē, shim-\ n : small ape

chin \'chin\ n : part of the face below the mouth — chin•less adj

chi•na \'chīnə\ n 1 : porcelain ware 2 : domestic pottery

chin•chil•la \chin'chilə\ n : small So. American rodent with soft pearl-gray fur or this fur

chink \'chiŋk\ n : small crack ~ vb : fill chinks of

chintz \'chints\ n : printed cotton cloth

chip \'chip\ n 1 : small thin flat piece cut or broken off 2 : thin crisp morsel of food 3 : counter used in games 4 : flaw where a chip came off 5 : small slice of semiconductor containing electronic circuits ~ vb -pp- : cut or break chips from — chip in vb : contribute

chip•munk \-ˌməŋk\ n : small striped ground-dwelling rodent

chip•per \-ər\ adj : lively and cheerful

chi•rop•o•dy \kə'räpədē, shə-\ n : podiatry — chi•rop•o•dist \-ədist\ n

chi•ro•prac•tic \'kīrəˌpraktik\ n : system of healing based esp. on manipulation of body structures — chi•ro•prac•tor \-tər\ n

chirp \'chərp\ n : short sharp sound like that of a bird or cricket — chirp vb

chis•el \'chizəl\ n : sharp-edged metal tool ~ vb -eled or -elled; -el•ing or -el•ling 1 : work with a chisel 2 : cheat — chis•el•er \-ələr\ n

chit \'chit\ n : signed voucher for a small debt

chit•chat \-ˌchat\ n : casual conversation — chitchat vb

chiv•al•rous \'shivəlrəs\ adj 1 : relating to chivalry 2 : honest, courteous, or generous — chiv•al•rous•ly adv — chiv•al•rous•ness n

chiv•al•ry \-rē\ n, pl -ries 1 : system or practices of knighthood 2 : spirit or character of the ideal knight — chi•val•ric \shə'valrik\ adj

chive \'chīv\ n : herb related to the onion

chlo•ride \'klōrˌīd\ n : compound of chlorine

chlo•ri•nate \-əˌnāt\ vb -nat•ed; -nating : treat or combine with chlorine — chlo•ri•na•tion \ˌklōrə'nāshən\ n

chlo•rine \'klōrˌēn\ n : chemical element that is a heavy strong-smelling greenish yellow irritating gas

chlo•ro•form \'klōrəˌfórm\ n : etherlike colorless heavy fluid ~ vb : anesthetize or kill with chloroform

chlo•ro•phyll \'klōrəˌfil\ n : green coloring matter of plants

chock \'chäk\ n : wedge for blocking the movement of a wheel — chock vb

chock–full \'chək'fúl, 'chäk-\ adj : full to the limit

choc•o•late \'chäkələt, 'chók-\ n 1 : ground roasted cacao beans or a beverage made from them 2 : candy made of or with chocolate 3 : dark brown

choice \'chóis\ n 1 : act or power of choosing 2 : one selected 3 : variety offered for selection ~ adj choic•er; choic•est 1 : worthy of being chosen 2 : selected with care 3 : of high quality

choir \'kwīr\ n : group of singers esp. in church — choir•boy n — choir•mas•ter n

choke \'chōk\ vb choked; chok•ing 1 : hinder breathing 2 : clog or obstruct ~ n 1 : a choking or sound of choking 2 : valve for controlling air intake in a gasoline engine

chok•er \-ər\ n : tight necklace

chol•er \'kälər, 'kō-\ n : bad temper — chol•er•ic \'kälərik, kə'ler-\ adj

chol•era \'kälərə\ n : disease marked by severe vomiting and dysentery

cho•les•ter•ol \kə'lestəˌról, -ˌról\ n : waxy substance in animal tissues

choose \'chüz\ vb chose \'chōz\; cho•sen \'chōzᵊn\; choos•ing 1 : select after consideration 2 : decide 3 : prefer — choos•er n

choosy, choos•ey \'chüzē\ adj choos•i•er; -est : fussy in making choices

chop \'chäp\ vb -pp- 1 : cut by repeated blows 2 : cut into small pieces ~ n 1 : sharp downward blow 2 : small cut of meat often with part of a rib

chop•per \-ər\ *n* **1** : one that chops **2** : helicopter

chop•py \-ē\ *adj* **-pi•er; -est 1** : rough with small waves **2** : jerky or disconnected — **chop•pi•ly** *adv* — **chop•pi•ness** *n*

chops \'chäps\ *n pl* : fleshy covering of the jaws

chop•sticks *n pl* : pair of sticks used in eating in oriental countries

cho•ral \'kōrəl\ *adj* : relating to or sung by a choir or chorus or in chorus — **cho•ral•ly** *adv*

cho•rale \kə'ral, -'räl\ *n* **1** : hymn tune or harmonization of a traditional melody **2** : chorus or choir

¹**chord** \'kórd\ *n* : harmonious tones sounded together

²**chord** *n* **1** : cordlike anatomical structure **2** : straight line joining 2 points on a curve

chore \'chōr\ *n* **1** *pl* : daily household or farm work **2** : routine or disagreeable task

cho•re•og•ra•phy \,kōrē'ägrəfē\ *n, pl* **-phies** : art of composing and arranging dances — **cho•reo•graph** \'kōrēə,graf\ *vb* — **cho•re•og•ra•pher** \,kōrē'ägrəfər\ *n* — **cho•reo•graph•ic** \-ēə'grafik\ *adj*

cho•ris•ter \'kōrəstər\ *n* : choir singer

chor•tle \'chórtᵊl\ *vb* **-tled; -tling** : laugh or chuckle — **chortle** *n*

cho•rus \'kōrəs\ *n* **1** : group of singers or dancers **2** : part of a song repeated at intervals **3** : composition for a chorus ~ *vb* : sing or utter together

chose *past of* CHOOSE

cho•sen \'chōzᵊn\ *adj* : favored

¹**chow** \'chaú\ *n* : food

²**chow** *n* : thick-coated muscular dog

chow•der \'chaúdər\ *n* : thick soup usu. of seafood and milk

chow mein \'chaú'mān\ *n* : thick stew of shredded vegetables and meat

chris•ten \'krisᵊn\ *vb* **1** : baptize **2** : name — **chris•ten•ing** *n*

Chris•ten•dom \-dəm\ *n* : areas where Christianity prevails

Chris•tian \'krischən\ *n* : adherent of Christianity ~ *adj* : relating to or professing a belief in Christianity or Jesus Christ — **Chris•tian•ize** \'krischə,nīz\ *vb*

Chris•ti•an•i•ty \,krischē'anətē\ *n* : religion derived from the teachings of Jesus Christ

Christian name *n* : first name

Christ•mas \'krisməs\ *n* : December 25 celebrated as the birthday of Christ

chro•mat•ic \krō'matik\ *adj* **1** : relating to color **2** : proceeding by half steps of the musical scale

chrome \'krōm\ *n* : chromium or something plated with it

chro•mi•um \-ēəm\ *n* : a bluish white metallic element used esp. in alloys

chro•mo•some \'krōmə,sōm, -,zōm\ *n* : part of a cell nucleus that contains the genes — **chro•mo•som•al** \,krōmə'sōməl. -'zō-\ *adj*

chron•ic \'kränik\ *adj* : frequent or persistent — **chron•i•cal•ly** \-iklē\ *adv*

chron•i•cle \'känikəl\ *n* : history ~ *vb* **-cled; -cling** : record — **chron•i•cler** \-iklər\ *n*

chro•nol•o•gy \krə'näləjē\ *n, pl* **-gies** : list of events in order of their occurrence — **chron•o•log•i•cal** \,kränᵊl-'äjikəl\ *adj* — **chron•o•log•i•cal•ly** \-iklē\ *adv*

chro•nom•e•ter \krə'nämətər\ *n* : very accurate timepiece

chrys•a•lis \'krisələs\ *n, pl* **chry•sal•i•des** \kris'alə,dēz\ *or* **chrys•a•lis•es** : insect pupa enclosed in a shell

chry•san•the•mum \kris'anthəməm\ *n* : plant with showy flowers

chub•by \'chəbē\ *adj* **-bi•er; -est** : fat — **chub•bi•ness** *n*

¹**chuck** \'chək\ *vb* **1** : tap **2** : toss ~ *n* **1** : light pat under the chin **2** : toss

²**chuck** *n* **1** : cut of beef **2** : machine part that holds work or another part

chuck•le \'chəkəl\ *vb* **-led; -ling** : laugh quietly — **chuckle** *n*

chug \'chəg\ *n* : sound of a laboring engine ~ *vb* **-gg-** : work or move with chugs

chum \'chəm\ *n* : close friend ~ *vb* **-mm-** : be chums — **chum•my** \-ē\ *adj*

chump \'chəmp\ *n* : fool

chunk \'chəŋk\ *n* **1** : short thick piece **2** : sizable amount

chunky \-ē\ *adj* **chunk•i•er; -est 1** : stocky **2** : containing chunks

church \'chərch\ *n* **1** : building esp. for Christian public worship **2** : whole body of Christians **3** : denomination **4** : congregation — **church•go•er** *n* — **church•go•ing** *adj or n*

church•yard *n* : cemetery beside a church

churl \'chərl\ *n* : rude ill-bred person — **churl·ish** *adj*

churn \'chərn\ *n* : container in which butter is made ∼ *vb* **1** : agitate in a churn **2** : shake violently

chute \'shüt\ *n* : trough or passage

chut·ney \'chətnē\ *n, pl* **-neys** : sweet and sour relish

chutz·pah \'hutspə, 'kut-, -ˌspä\ *n* : nerve or insolence

ci·ca·da \sə'kādə\ *n* : stout-bodied insect with transparent wings

ci·der \'sīdər\ *n* : apple juice

ci·gar \sig'är\ *n* : roll of leaf tobacco for smoking

cig·a·rette \ˌsigə'ret, 'sigəˌret\ *n* : cut tobacco rolled in paper for smoking

cinch \'sinch\ *n* **1** : strap holding a saddle or pack in place **2** : sure thing — **cinch** *vb*

cin·cho·na \siŋ'kōnə\ *n* : So. American tree that yields quinine

cinc·ture \'siŋkchər\ *n* : belt or sash

cin·der \'sindər\ *n* **1** *pl* : ashes **2** : piece of partly burned wood or coal

cin·e·ma \'sinəmə\ *n* : movies or a movie theater — **cin·e·mat·ic** \ˌsinə-'matik\ *adj*

cin·na·mon \'sinəmən\ *n* : spice from an aromatic tree bark

ci·pher \'sīfər\ *n* **1** : zero **2** : code

cir·ca \'sərkə\ *prep* : about

cir·cle \'sərkəl\ *n* **1** : closed symmetrical curve **2** : cycle **3** : group with a common tie ∼ *vb* **-cled; -cling 1** : enclose in a circle **2** : move or revolve around

cir·cuit \'sərkət\ *n* **1** : boundary **2** : regular tour of a territory **3** : complete path of an electric current **4** : group of electronic components

cir·cu·itous \ˌsər'kyüətəs\ *adj* : circular or winding

cir·cuit·ry \'sərkətrē\ *n, pl* **-ries** : arrangement of an electric circuit

cir·cu·lar \'sərkyələr\ *adj* **1** : round **2** : moving in a circle ∼ *n* : advertising leaflet — **cir·cu·lar·i·ty** \ˌsərkyə-'larətē\ *n*

cir·cu·late \'sərkyəˌlāt\ *vb* **-lat·ed; -lat·ing** : move or cause to move in a circle or from place to place or person to person — **cir·cu·la·tion** \ˌsər-kyə'lāshən\ *n* — **cir·cu·la·to·ry** \'sərkyələˌtōrē\ *adj*

cir·cum·cise \'sərkəmˌsīz\ *vb* **-cised; -cis·ing** : cut off the foreskin of — **cir·cum·ci·sion** \ˌsərkəm'sizhən\ *n*

cir·cum·fer·ence \sər'kəmfrəns\ *n* : perimeter of a circle

cir·cum·flex \'sərkəmˌfleks\ *n* : phonetic mark (as ˆ)

cir·cum·lo·cu·tion \ˌsərkəmlō'kyü-shən\ *n* : excessive use of words

cir·cum·nav·i·gate \ˌsərkəm'navəˌgāt\ *vb* : sail completely around — **cir·cum·nav·i·ga·tion** *n*

cir·cum·scribe \'sərkəmˌskrīb\ *vb* **1** : draw a line around **2** : limit

cir·cum·spect \'sərkəmˌspekt\ *adj* : careful — **cir·cum·spec·tion** \ˌsər-kəm'spekshən\ *n*

cir·cum·stance \'sərkəmˌstans\ *n* **1** : fact or event **2** *pl* : surrounding conditions **3** *pl* : financial situation — **cir·cum·stan·tial** \ˌsərkəm'stan-chəl\ *adj*

cir·cum·vent \ˌsərkəm'vent\ *vb* : get around esp. by trickery — **cir·cum·ven·tion** \-'venchən\ *n*

cir·cus \'sərkəs\ *n* : show with feats of skill, animal acts, and clowns

cir·rho·sis \sə'rōsəs\ *n, pl* **-rho·ses** \-ˌsēz\ : fibrosis of the liver — **cir·rhot·ic** \-'rätik\ *adj or n*

cir·rus \'sirəs\ *n, pl* **-ri** \-ˌī\ : wispy white cloud

cis·tern \'sistərn\ *n* : underground water tank

cit·a·del \'sitəd'l, -əˌdel\ *n* : fortress

cite \'sīt\ *vb* **cit·ed; cit·ing 1** : summon before a court **2** : quote **3** : refer to esp. in commendation — **ci·ta·tion** \sī'tāshən\ *n*

cit·i·zen \'sitəzən\ *n* : member of a country — **cit·i·zen·ry** \-rē\ *n* — **cit·i·zen·ship** *n*

cit·ron \'sitrən\ *n* : lemonlike fruit

cit·rus \'sitrəs\ *n, pl* **-rus** *or* **-rus·es** : evergreen tree or shrub grown for its fruit (as the orange or lemon)

city \'sitē\ *n, pl* **cit·ies** : place larger or more important than a town

civ·ic \'sivik\ *adj* : relating to citizenship or civil affairs

civ·ics \-iks\ *n* : study of citizenship

civ·il \'sivəl\ *adj* **1** : relating to citizens **2** : polite **3** : relating to or being a lawsuit — **civ·il·ly** *adv*

ci·vil·ian \sə'vilyən\ *n* : person not in a military, police, or fire-fighting force

ci·vil·i·ty \sə'vilətē\ *n, pl* **-ties** : courtesy

civ·i·li·za·tion \ˌsivələ'zāshən\ *n* **1**

: high level of cultural development **2**
: culture of a time or place

civ•i•lize \\'sivə‚līz\\ *vb* **-lized; -liz•ing**
: raise from a primitive stage of cultural development — **civ•i•lized** *adj*

civil liberty *n* : freedom from arbitrary governmental interference — usu. pl.

civil rights *n pl* : nonpolitical rights of a citizen

civil service *n* : government service

civil war *n* : war among citizens of one country

clack \\'klak\\ *vb* : make or cause a clatter — **clack** *n*

clad \\'klad\\ *adj* : covered

claim \\'klām\\ *vb* **1** : demand or take as the rightful owner **2** : maintain ～ *n* **1** : demand of right or ownership **2** : declaration **3** : something claimed — **claim•ant** \\-ənt\\ *n*

clair•voy•ant \\klar'vȯiənt\\ *adj* : able to perceive things beyond the senses — **clair•voy•ance** \\-əns\\ *n* — **clairvoy•ant** *n*

clam \\'klam\\ *n* : bivalve mollusk

clam•ber \\'klambər\\ *vb* : climb awkwardly

clam•my \\'klamē\\ *adj* **-mi•er; -est** : being damp, soft, and usu. cool — **clammi•ness** *n*

clam•or \\-ər\\ *n* **1** : uproar **2** : protest — **clamor** *vb* — **clam•or•ous** *adj*

clamp \\'klamp\\ *n* : device for holding things together — **clamp** *vb*

clan \\'klan\\ *n* : group of related families — **clan•nish** *adj* — **clan•nish•ness** *n*

clan•des•tine \\klan'destən\\ *adj* : secret

clang \\'klaŋ\\ *n* : loud metallic ringing — **clang** *vb*

clan•gor \\-ər, -gər\\ *n* : jumble of clangs

clank \\'klaŋk\\ *n* : brief sound of struck metal — **clank** *vb*

clap \\'klap\\ *vb* **-pp- 1** : strike noisily **2** : applaud ～ *n* **1** : loud crash **2** : noise made by clapping the hands

clap•board \\'klabərd, 'klap-, -‚bȯrd\\ *n* : narrow tapered board used for siding

clap•per \\'klapər\\ *n* : tongue of a bell

claque \\'klak\\ *n* **1** : group hired to applaud at a performance **2** : group of sycophants

clar•et \\'klarət\\ *n* : dry red wine

clar•i•fy \\'klarə‚fī\\ *vb* **-fied; -fy•ing** : make or become clear — **clar•i•fi•ca•tion** \\‚klarəfə'kāshən\\ *n*

clar•i•net \\‚klarə'net\\ *n* : woodwind instrument shaped like a tube — **clar•i•net•ist, clar•i•net•tist** \\-ist\\ *n*

clar•i•on \\'klarēən\\ *adj* : loud and clear

clar•i•ty \\'klarətē\\ *n* : clearness

clash \\'klash\\ *vb* **1** : make or cause a clash **2** : be in opposition or disharmony ～ *n* **1** : crashing sound **2** : hostile encounter

clasp \\'klasp\\ *n* **1** : device for holding things together **2** : embrace or grasp ～ *vb* **1** : fasten **2** : embrace or grasp

class \\'klas\\ *n* **1** : group of the same status or nature **2** : social rank **3** : course of instruction **4** : group of students ～ *vb* : classify — **classless** *adj* — **class•mate** *n* — **classroom** *n*

clas•sic \\'klasik\\ *adj* **1** : serving as a standard of excellence **2** : classical ～ *n* : work of enduring excellence and esp. of ancient Greece or Rome — **clas•si•cal** \\-ikəl\\ *adj* — **clas•si•cal•ly** \\-klē\\ *adv* — **clas•si•cism** \\'klasə‚sizəm\\ *n* — **clas•si•cist** \\-sist\\ *n*

clas•si•fied \\'klasə‚fīd\\ *adj* : restricted for security reasons

clas•si•fy \\-‚fī\\ *vb* **-fied; -fy•ing** : arrange in or assign to classes — **clas•si•fi•ca•tion** \\‚klasəfə'kāshən\\ *n* — **clas•si•fi•er** \\'klasə‚fīər\\ *n*

clat•ter \\'klatər\\ *n* : rattling sound — **clatter** *vb*

clause \\'klȯz\\ *n* **1** : separate part of a document **2** : part of a sentence with a subject and predicate

claus•tro•pho•bia \\‚klȯstrə'fōbēə\\ *n* : fear of closed or narrow spaces — **claus•tro•pho•bic** \\-bik\\ *adj*

clav•i•chord \\'klavə‚kȯrd\\ *n* : early keyboard instrument

clav•i•cle \\'klavikəl\\ *n* : collarbone

claw \\'klȯ\\ *n* : sharp curved nail or process (as on the toe of an animal) ～ *vb* : scratch or dig — **clawed** *adj*

clay \\'klā\\ *n* : plastic earthy material — **clay•ey** \\-ē\\ *adj*

clean \\'klēn\\ *adj* **1** : free from dirt or disease **2** : pure or honorable **3** : thorough ～ *vb* : make or become clean — **clean** *adv* — **clean•er** *n* — **clean•ly** \\-lē\\ *adv* — **clean•ness** *n*

clean•ly \\'klenlē\\ *adj* **-li•er; -est** : clean — **clean•li•ness** *n*

cleanse \\'klenz\\ *vb* **cleansed; cleansing** : make clean — **cleans•er** *n*

clear \\'klir\\ *adj* **1** : bright **2** : free from

clouds **3** : transparent **4** : easily heard, seen or understood **5** : free from doubt **6** : free from restriction or obstruction ∼ *vb* **1** : make or become clear **2** : go away **3** : free from accusation or blame **4** : explain or settle **5** : net **6** : jump or pass without touching ∼ *n* : clear space or part — **clear** *adv* — **clear•ance** \'klirəns\ *n*

clear•ing \'klirin̄\ *n* : land cleared of wood

clear•ly *adv* **1** : in a clear manner **2** : it is obvious that

cleat \'klēt\ *n* : projection that strengthens or prevents slipping

cleav•age \'klēvij\ *n* **1** : a splitting apart **2** : depression between a woman's breasts

¹cleave \'klēv\ *vb* **cleaved** \'klēvd\ *or* **clove** \'klōv\; **cleav•ing** : adhere

²cleave *vb* **cleaved** \'klēvd\; **cleav•ing** : split apart

cleav•er \'klēvər\ *n* : heavy chopping knife

clef \'klef\ *n* : sign on the staff in music to show pitch

cleft \'kleft\ *n* : crack

clem•ent \'klemənt\ *adj* **1** : merciful **2** : temperate or mild — **clem•en•cy** \-ənsē\ *n*

clench \'klench\ *vb* **1** : hold fast **2** : close tightly

cler•gy \'klərjē\ *n* : body of religious officials — **cler•gy•man** \-jimən\ *n*

cler•ic \'klerik\ *n* : member of the clergy

cler•i•cal \-ikəl\ *adj* **1** : relating to the clergy **2** : relating to a clerk or office worker

clerk \'klərk, *Brit* 'klärk\ *n* **1** : official responsible for record-keeping **2** : person doing general office work **3** : salesperson in a store — **clerk** *vb* — **clerk•ship** *n*

clev•er \'klevər\ *adj* **1** : resourceful **2** : marked by wit or ingenuity — **clev•er•ly** *adv* — **clev•er•ness** *n*

clew *var of* CLUE

cli•ché \kli'shā\ *n* : trite phrase — **cli•chéd** \-'shād\ *adj*

click \'klik\ *n* : slight sharp noise ∼ *vb* : make or cause to make a click

cli•ent \'klīənt\ *n* **1** : person who engages professional services **2** : customer

cli•en•tele \,klīən'tel, ,klē-\ *n* : body of customers

cliff \'klif\ *n* : high steep face of rock

cli•mate \'klīmət\ *n* : average weather conditions over a period of years — **cli•mat•ic** \klī'matik\ *adj*

cli•max \'klī,maks\ *n* : the highest point ∼ *vb* : come to a climax — **cli•mac•tic** \klī'maktik\ *adj*

climb \'klīm\ *vb* **1** : go up or down by use of hands and feet **2** : rise ∼ *n* : a climbing — **climb•er** *n*

clinch \'klinch\ *vb* **1** : fasten securely **2** : settle **3** : hold fast or firmly — **clinch** *n* — **clinch•er** *n*

cling \'klin̄\ *vb* **clung** \'klən̄\; **cling•ing** **1** : adhere firmly **2** : hold on tightly

clin•ic \'klinik\ *n* : facility for diagnosis and treatment of outpatients — **clin•i•cal** \-əl\ *adj* — **clin•i•cal•ly** \-klē\ *adv*

clink \'klin̄k\ *vb* : make a slight metallic sound — **clink** *n*

clin•ker \'klin̄kər\ *n* : fused stony matter esp. in a furnace

¹clip \'klip\ *vb* **-pp-** : fasten with a clip ∼ *n* : device to hold things together

²clip *vb* **-pp-** **1** : cut or cut off **2** : hit ∼ *n* **1** : clippers **2** : sharp blow **3** : rapid pace

clip•per \'klipər\ *n* **1** *pl* : implement for clipping **2** : fast sailing ship

clique \'klēk, 'klik\ *n* : small exclusive group of people

cli•to•ris \'klitərəs, kli'tórəs\ *n*, *pl* **cli•to•ri•des** \-'tórə,dēz\ : small organ at the front of the vulva

cloak \'klōk\ *n* **1** : loose outer garment **2** : something that conceals ∼ *vb* : cover or hide with a cloak

clob•ber \'kläbər\ *vb* : hit hard

clock \'kläk\ *n* : timepiece not carried on the person ∼ *vb* : record the time of

clock•wise \-,wīz\ *adv or adj* : in the same direction as a clock's hands move

clod \'kläd\ *n* **1** : lump esp. of earth **2** : dull insensitive person

clog \'kläg\ *n* **1** : restraining weight **2** : thick-soled shoe ∼ *vb* **-gg-** **1** : impede with a clog **2** : obstruct passage through **3** : become plugged up

clois•ter \'klóistər\ *n* **1** : monastic establishment **2** : covered passage ∼ *vb* : shut away from the world

clone \'klōn\ *n* **1** : offspring produced from a single organism **2** : copy

¹close \'klōz\ *vb* **closed**; **clos•ing** **1**

: shut **2** : cease operation **3** : terminate **4** : bring or come together ~ *n*
: conclusion or end

²close \'klōs\ *adj* **clos•er; clos•est 1**
: confining **2** : secretive **3** : strict **4**
: stuffy **5** : having little space between items **6** : fitting tightly **7** : near
8 : intimate **9** : accurate **10** : nearly
even — **close** *adv* — **close•ly** *adv* —
close•ness *n*

clos•et \'kläzət, 'klòz-\ *n* : small compartment for household utensils or
clothing ~ *vb* : take into a private
room for a talk

clo•sure \'klōzhər\ *n* **1** : act of closing **2** : something that closes

clot \'klät\ *n* : dried mass of a liquid —
clot *vb*

cloth \'klòth\ *n, pl* **cloths** \'klòthz,
'klòths\ **1** : fabric **2** : tablecloth

clothe \'klōth\ *vb* **clothed** *or* **clad**
\'klad\; **cloth•ing** : dress

clothes \'klōthz, 'klōz\ *n pl* **1** : clothing **2** : bedclothes

cloth•ier \'klōthyər, -thēər\ *n* : maker
or seller of clothing

cloth•ing \'klōthiŋ\ *n* : covering for
the human body

cloud \'klaùd\ *n* **1** : visible mass of
particles in the air **2** : something that
darkens, hides, or threatens ~ *vb*
: darken or hide — **cloud•i•ness** *n* —
cloud•less *adj* — **cloudy** *adj*

cloud•burst *n* : sudden heavy rain

clout \'klaùt\ *n* **1** : blow **2** : influence
~ *vb* : hit forcefully

¹clove \'klōv\ *n* : section of a bulb

²clove *past of* CLEAVE

³clove *n* : dried flower bud of an East Indian tree used as a spice

clo•ver \'klōvər\ *n* : leguminous herb
with usu. 3-part leaves

clo•ver•leaf *n, pl* **-leafs** *or* **-leaves**
: highway interchange

clown \'klaùn\ *n* : funny costumed entertainer esp. in a circus ~ *vb* : act
like a clown — **clown•ish** *adj* —
clown•ish•ly *adv* — **clown•ish•ness**
n

cloy \'klòi\ *vb* : disgust with excess —
cloy•ing•ly \-iŋlē\ *adv*

club \'kləb\ *n* **1** : heavy wooden stick
2 : playing card of a suit marked
with a black figure like a clover leaf
3 : group associated for a common purpose ~ *vb* **-bb-** : hit with a
club

club•foot *n* : misshapen foot twisted out
of position from birth — **club•foot-
ed** \-,fútəd\ *adj*

cluck \'klək\ *n* : sound made by a hen
— **cluck** *vb*

clue \'klü\ *n* : piece of evidence that
helps solve a problem ~ *vb* **clued;
clue•ing** *or* **clu•ing** : provide with a
clue

clump \'kləmp\ *n* **1** : cluster **2** : heavy
tramping sound ~ *vb* : tread heavily

clum•sy \'kləmzē\ *adj* **-si•er; -est 1**
: lacking dexterity, nimbleness, or
grace **2** : tactless — **clum•si•ly** *adv*
— **clum•si•ness** *n*

clung *past of* CLING

clunk•er \'kləŋkər\ *n* : old automobile

clus•ter \'kləstər\ *n* : group ~ *vb*
: grow or gather in a cluster

clutch \'kləch\ *vb* : grasp ~ *n* **1**
: grasping hand or claws **2** : control
or power **3** : coupling for connecting
two working parts in machinery

clut•ter \'klətər\ *vb* : fill with things
that get in the way — **clutter** *n*

co- *prefix* : with, together, joint, or
jointly

List of self-explanatory words with the prefix *co-*

coact	codesign	coexist
coactor	codevelop	coexistence
coauthor	codeveloper	coexistent
coauthorship	codirect	cofeature
cocaptain	codirector	cofinance
cochairman	codiscoverer	cofound
cochampion	codrive	cofounder
cocomposer	codriver	coheir
coconspirator	coedit	coheiress
cocreator	coeditor	cohost
codefendant	coexecutor	cohostess

coach \'kōch\ *n* **1** : closed 2-door 4-wheeled carriage **2** : railroad passenger car **3** : bus **4** : 2d-class air travel **5** : one who instructs or trains performers ~ *vb* : instruct or direct as a coach

co·ag·u·late \kō'agyə‚lāt\ *vb* **-lat·ed; -lat·ing** : clot — **co·ag·u·lant** \-lənt\ *n* — **co·ag·u·la·tion** \-‚agyə'lāshən\ *n*

coal \'kōl\ *n* **1** : ember **2** : black solid mineral used as fuel — **coalfield** *n*

co·alesce \‚kōə'les\ *vb* **-alesced; -alesc·ing** : grow together — **co·ales·cence** \-'les°ns\ *n*

co·ali·tion \-'lishən\ *n* : temporary alliance

coarse \'kōrs\ *adj* **coars·er; coarsest** **1** : composed of large particles **2** : rough or crude — **coarse·ly** *adv* — **coars·en** \-°n\ *vb* — **coarseness** *n*

coast \'kōst\ *n* : seashore ~ *vb* : move without effort — **coast·al** \-°l\ *adj*

coast·er \-ər\ *n* **1** : one that coasts **2** : plate or mat to protect a surface

coast guard *n* : military force that guards or patrols a coast — **coast-guards·man** \'kōst‚gärdzmən\ *n*

coast·line *n* : shape of a coast

coat \'kōt\ *n* **1** : outer garment for the upper body **2** : external growth of fur or feathers **3** : covering layer ~ *vb* : cover with a coat — **coat·ed** *adj* — **coat·ing** *n*

coax \'kōks\ *vb* : move to action or achieve by gentle urging or flattery

cob \'käb\ *n* : corncob

co·balt \'kō‚bölt\ *n* : shiny silver-white magnetic metallic chemical element

cob·ble \'käbəl\ *vb* **cob·bled; cobbling** : make or put together hastily

cob·bler \'käblər\ *n* **1** : shoemaker **2** : deep-dish fruit pie

cob·ble·stone *n* : small round paving stone

co·bra \'kōbrə\ *n* : venomous snake

cob·web \'käb‚web\ *n* : network spun by a spider or a similar filament

co·caine \kō'kān, 'kō‚kān\ *n* : drug obtained from the leaves of a So. American shrub (**co·ca** \'kōkə\)

co·chlea \'kōklēə, 'käk-\ *n, pl* **-chleas** *or* **-chle·ae** \-lē‚ē, -‚ī\ : the usu. spiral part of the inner ear — **cochle·ar** \-lēər\ *adj*

cock \'käk\ *n* **1** : male fowl **2** : valve or faucet ~ *vb* **1** : draw back the hammer of a firearm **2** : tilt to one side — **cock·fight** *n*

cock·a·too \'käkə‚tü\ *n, pl* **-toos** : large Australian crested parrot

cock·eyed \'käk'īd\ *adj* **1** : tilted to one side **2** : slightly crazy

cock·le \'käkəl\ *n* : edible shellfish

cock·pit \'käk‚pit\ *n* : place for a pilot, driver, or helmsman

cock·roach *n* : nocturnal insect often infesting houses

cock·tail \'käk‚tāl\ *n* **1** : iced drink of liquor and flavorings **2** : appetizer

cocky \'käkē\ *adj* **cock·i·er; -est** : overconfident — **cock·i·ly** \-əlē\ *adv* — **cock·i·ness** *n*

co·coa \'kōkō\ *n* **1** : cacao **2** : powdered chocolate or a drink made from this

co·co·nut \'kōkə‚nət\ *n* : large nutlike fruit of a tropical palm (**coconut palm**)

co·coon \kə'kün\ *n* : case protecting an insect pupa

cod \'käd\ *n, pl* **cod** : food fish of the No. Atlantic

cod·dle \'käd°l\ *vb* **-dled; -dling** : pamper

---

coinvent	copartnership	copublisher
coinventor	copresident	corecipient
coinvestigator	coprincipal	coresident
coleader	coprisoner	cosignatory
comanagement	coproduce	cosigner
comanager	coproducer	cosponsor
co-organizer	coproduction	costar
co-own	copromoter	cowinner
co-owner	coproprietor	coworker
copartner	copublish	cowrite

code \'kōd\ *n* **1** : system of laws or rules **2** : system of signals

co·deine \'kō,dēn\ *n* : narcotic drug used in cough remedies

cod·ger \'käjər\ *n* : odd fellow

cod·i·cil \'kädəsəl, -,sil\ *n* : postscript to a will

cod·i·fy \'kädə,fī, 'kōd-\ *vb* **-fied; -fy·ing** : arrange systematically — **cod·i·fi·ca·tion** \,kädəfə'kāshən, ,kōd-\ *n*

co·ed \'kō,ed\ *n* : female student in a coeducational institution — **coed** *adj*

co·ed·u·ca·tion \,kō-\ *n* : education of the sexes together — **co·ed·u·ca·tion·al** *adj*

co·ef·fi·cient \,kōə'fishənt\ *n* **1** : number that is a multiplier of another **2** : number that serves as a measure of some property

co·erce \kō'ərs\ *vb* **-erced; -erc·ing** : force — **co·er·cion** \-'ərzhən, -shən\ *n* — **co·er·cive** \-'ərsiv\ *adj*

cof·fee \'kȯfē\ *n* : drink made from the roasted and ground seeds (**coffee beans**) of a tropical shrub — **cof·fee·house** *n* — **cof·fee·pot** *n*

cof·fer \'kȯfər\ *n* : box for valuables

cof·fin \-fən\ *n* : box for burial

cog \'käg\ *n* : tooth on the rim of a gear — **cogged** \'kägd\ *adj* — **cog·wheel** *n*

co·gent \'kōjənt\ *adj* : compelling or convincing — **co·gen·cy** \-jənsē\ *n*

cog·i·tate \'käjə,tāt\ *vb* **-tat·ed; -tat·ing** : think over — **cog·i·ta·tion** \,käjə'tāshən\ *n* — **cog·i·ta·tive** \'käjə,tātiv\ *adj*

co·gnac \'kōn,yak\ *n* : French brandy

cog·nate \'käg,nāt\ *adj* : related — **cog·nate** *n*

cog·ni·tion \käg'nishən\ *n* : act or process of knowing — **cog·ni·tive** \'kägnətiv\ *adj*

cog·ni·zance \'kägnəzəns\ *n* : notice or awareness — **cog·ni·zant** \'kägnəzənt\ *adj*

co·hab·it \kō'habət\ *vb* : live together as husband and wife — **co·hab·i·ta·tion** \-,habə'tāshən\ *n*

co·here \kō'hir\ *vb* **-hered; -her·ing** : stick together

co·her·ent \-'hirənt\ *adj* **1** : able to stick together **2** : logically consistent — **co·her·ence** \-əns\ *n* — **co·her·ent·ly** *adv*

co·he·sion \-'hēzhən\ *n* : a sticking together — **co·he·sive** \-siv\ *adj* —

co·he·sive·ly *adv* — **co·he·sive·ness** *n*

co·hort \'kō,hȯrt\ *n* **1** : group of soldiers **2** : companion

coif·fure \kwä'fyu̇r\ *n* : hair style

coil \'kȯil\ *vb* : wind in a spiral ~ *n* : series of loops (as of rope)

coin \'kȯin\ *n* : piece of metal used as money ~ *vb* **1** : make (a coin) by stamping **2** : create — **coin·age** \-ij\ *n* — **coin·er** *n*

co·in·cide \,kōən'sīd, 'kōən,sīd\ *vb* **-cid·ed; -cid·ing** **1** : be in the same place **2** : happen at the same time **3** : be alike — **co·in·ci·dence** \kō'insədəns\ *n* — **co·in·ci·dent** \-dənt\ *adj* — **co·in·ci·den·tal** \-,insə'dentʰl\ *adj*

co·itus \'kōətəs\ *n* : sexual intercourse — **co·ital** \-ətʰl\ *adj*

coke \'kōk\ *n* : fuel made by heating soft coal

co·la \'kōlə\ *n* : carbonated soft drink

col·an·der \'kələndər, 'käl-\ *n* : perforated utensil for draining food

cold \'kōld\ *adj* **1** : having a low or below normal temperature **2** : lacking warmth of feeling **3** : suffering from lack of warmth ~ *n* **1** : low temperature **2** : minor respiratory illness — **cold·ly** *adv* — **cold·ness** *n* — **in cold blood** : with premeditation

cold–blood·ed *adj* **1** : cruel or merciless **2** : having a body temperature that varies with the temperature of the environment

cole·slaw \'kōl,slȯ\ *n* : cabbage salad

col·ic \'kälik\ *n* : sharp abdominal pain — **col·icky** *adj*

col·i·se·um \,kälə'sēəm\ *n* : arena

col·lab·o·rate \kə'labə,rāt\ *vb* **-rat·ed; -rat·ing** **1** : work jointly with others **2** : help the enemy — **col·lab·o·ra·tion** \-,labə'rāshən\ *n* — **col·lab·o·ra·tor** \-'labə,rātər\ *n*

col·lapse \kə'laps\ *vb* **-lapsed; -laps·ing** **1** : fall in **2** : break down physically or mentally **3** : fold down ~ *n* : breakdown — **col·laps·ible** *adj*

col·lar \'kälər\ *n* : part of a garment around the neck ~ *vb* **1** : seize by the collar **2** : grab — **col·lar·less** *adj*

col·lar·bone *n* : bone joining the breastbone and the shoulder blade

col·lards \'kälərdz\ *n pl* : kale

col·late \kə'lāt; 'käl,āt, 'kōl-\ *vb* **-lat-**

ed; -lat•ing **1** : compare carefully **2** : assemble in order

col•lat•er•al \kə'latərəl\ adj **1** : secondary **2** : descended from the same ancestors but not in the same line **3** : similar ~ n : property used as security for a loan

col•league \'käl,ēg\ n : associate

col•lect \kə'lekt\ vb **1** : bring, come, or gather together **2** : receive payment of ~ adv or adj : to be paid for by the receiver — col•lect•ible, col•lect•able adj — col•lec•tion \-'lek-shən\ n — col•lec•tor \-'lektər\ n

col•lec•tive \-tiv\ adj : denoting or shared by a group ~ n : a cooperative unit — col•lec•tive•ly adv

col•lege \'kälij\ n : institution of higher learning granting a bachelor's degree — col•le•gian \kə'lējən\ n — col•le•giate \kə'lējət\ adj

col•lide \kə'līd\ vb -lid•ed; -lid•ing : strike together — col•li•sion \-'lizhən\ n

col•lie \'kälē\ n : large long-haired dog

col•loid \'käl,óid\ n : tiny particles in suspension in a fluid — col•loi•dal \kə'lóid°l\ adj

col•lo•qui•al \kə'lōkwēəl\ adj : used in informal conversation — col•lo•qui•al•ism \-ə,lizəm\ n

col•lu•sion \kə'lüzhən\ n : secret cooperation for deceit — col•lu•sive \-'lüsiv\ adj

co•logne \kə'lōn\ n : perfumed liquid

¹co•lon \'kōlən\ n, pl colons or co•la \-lə\ : lower part of the large intestine — co•lon•ic \kō'länik\ adj

²colon n, pl colons : punctuation mark : used esp. to direct attention to following matter

col•o•nel \'kərn°l\ n : commissioned officer (as in the army) ranking next below a brigadier general

col•o•nize \'kälə,nīz\ vb -nized; -nizing **1** : establish a colony in **2** : settle — col•o•ni•za•tion \,kälənə'zāshən\ n — col•o•niz•er n

col•on•nade \,kälə'nād\ n : row of supporting columns

col•o•ny \'kälənē\ n, pl -nies **1** : people who inhabit a new territory or the territory itself **2** : animals of one kind (as bees) living together — co•lo•nial \kə'lōnēəl\ adj or n — col•o•nist \'kälənist\ n

col•or \'kələr\ n **1** : quality of visible things distinct from shape that results

from light reflection **2** pl : flag **3** : liveliness ~ vb **1** : give color to **2** : blush — col•or•fast adj — col•or•ful adj — col•or•less adj

col•or–blind adj : unable to distinguish colors — color blindness n

col•ored \'kələrd\ adj **1** : having color **2** : of a race other than the white ~ n, pl colored or coloreds : colored person

co•los•sal \kə'läsəl\ adj : very large or great

co•los•sus \-səs\ n, pl -si \-'läs,ī\ : something of great size or scope

colt \'kōlt\ n : young male horse — colt•ish adj

col•umn \'käləm\ n **1** : vertical section of a printed page **2** : regular feature article (as in a newspaper) **3** : pillar **4** : row (as of soldiers) — co•lum•nar \kə'ləmnər\ adj — col•um•nist \'käləmnist\ n

co•ma \'kōmə\ n : deep prolonged unconsciousness — co•ma•tose \-,tōs, 'kämə-\ adj

comb \'kōm\ n **1** : toothed instrument for arranging the hair **2** : crest on a fowl's head — comb vb — combed \'kōmd\ adj

com•bat \kəm'bat, 'käm,bat\ vb -bat•ed or -bat•ted; -bat•ing or -batting : fight — com•bat \'käm,bat\ n — com•bat•ant \kəm'bat°nt\ n — com•bat•ive \kəm'bativ\ adj

com•bi•na•tion \,kämbə'nāshən\ n **1** : process or result of combining **2** : code for opening a lock

com•bine \kəm'bīn\ vb -bined; -bining : join together ~ \'käm,bīn\ n **1** : association for business or political advantage **2** : harvesting machine

com•bus•ti•ble \kəm'bəstəbəl\ adj : apt to catch fire — com•bus•ti•bil•i•ty \-,bəstə'bilətē\ n — combustible n

com•bus•tion \-'bəschən\ n : process of burning

come \'kəm\ vb came \'kām\; come; com•ing **1** : move toward or arrive at something **2** : reach a state **3** : originate or exist **4** : amount — come clean vb : confess — come into vb : acquire, achieve — come off vb : succeed — come to vb : regain consciousness — come to pass : happen — come to terms : reach an agreement

come•back *n* **1** : retort **2** : return to a former position — **come back** *vb*

co•me•di•an \kə'mēdēən\ *n* **1** : comic actor **2** : funny person **3** : entertainer specializing in comedy

co•me•di•enne \-ˌmēdē'en\ *n* : a woman who is a comedian

com•e•dy \'kämədē\ *n, pl* **-dies 1** : an amusing play **2** : humorous entertainment

come•ly \'kəmlē\ *adj* **-li•er; -est** : attractive — **come•li•ness** *n*

com•et \'kämət\ *n* : small bright celestial body having a tail

com•fort \'kəmfərt\ *n* **1** : consolation **2** : well-being or something that gives it ∼ *vb* **1** : give hope to **2** : console — **com•fort•able** \'kəmftəbəl, 'kəmfərt-\ *adj* — **com•fort•ably** \-blē\ *adv*

com•fort•er \'kəmfərtər\ *n* **1** : one that comforts **2** : quilt

com•ic \'kämik\ *adj* **1** : relating to comedy **2** : funny ∼ *n* **1** : comedian **2** : sequence of cartoons — **com•i•cal** *adj*

com•ing \'kəmiŋ\ *adj* : next

com•ma \'kämə\ *n* : punctuation mark , used esp. to separate sentence parts

com•mand \kə'mand\ *vb* **1** : order **2** : control ∼ *n* **1** : act of commanding **2** : an order given **3** : mastery **4** : troops under a commander — **com•man•dant** \'kämənˌdant, -ˌdänt\ *n*

com•man•deer \ˌkämən'dir\ *vb* : seize by force

com•mand•er \kə'mandər\ *n* **1** : officer commanding an army or subdivision of an army **2** : commissioned officer in the navy ranking next below a captain

com•mand•ment \-'mandmənt\ *n* : order

command sergeant major *n* : noncommissioned officer in the army ranking above a first sergeant

com•mem•o•rate \kə'meməˌrāt\ *vb* **-rat•ed; -rat•ing** : celebrate or honor — **com•mem•o•ra•tion** \-ˌmemə'rāshən\ *n* — **com•mem•o•ra•tive** \-'memrətiv, -'meməˌrāt-\ *adj*

com•mence \kə'mens\ *vb* **-menced; -menc•ing** : start

com•mence•ment \-mənt\ *n* **1** : beginning **2** : graduation ceremony

com•mend \kə'mend\ *vb* **1** : entrust **2** : recommend **3** : praise — **com-**

mend•able \-əbəl\ *adj* — **com•men•da•tion** \ˌkämən'dāshən, -ˌen-\ *n*

com•men•su•rate \kə'mensərət, -'mench-\ *adj* : equal in measure or extent

com•ment \'kämˌent\ *n* : statement of opinion or remark — **comment** *vb*

com•men•tary \-ənˌterē\ *n, pl* **-tar•ies** : series of comments

com•men•ta•tor \-ənˌtātər\ *n* : one who discusses news

com•merce \'kämərs\ *n* : business

com•mer•cial \kə'mərshəl\ *adj* : designed for profit or for mass appeal ∼ *n* : broadcast advertisement — **com•mer•cial•ize** \-ˌīz\ *vb* — **com•mer•cial•ly** \-ē\ *adv*

com•min•gle \kə'miŋgəl\ *vb* : mix

com•mis•er•ate \kə'mizəˌrāt\ *vb* **-at•ed; -at•ing** : sympathize — **com•mis•er•a•tion** \-ˌmizə'rāshən\ *n*

com•mis•sary \'käməˌserē\ *n, pl* **-sar•ies** : store esp. for military personnel

com•mis•sion \kə'mishən\ *n* **1** : order granting power or rank **2** : panel to judge, approve, or act **3** : the doing of an act **4** : agent's fee ∼ *vb* **1** : confer rank or authority to or for **2** : request something be done

com•mis•sion•er \-shənər\ *n* **1** : member of a commission **2** : head of a government department

com•mit \kə'mit\ *vb* **-tt- 1** : turn over to someone for safekeeping or confinement **2** : perform or do **3** : pledge — **com•mit•ment** *n*

com•mit•tee \kə'mitē\ *n* : panel that examines or acts on something

com•mo•di•ous \kə'mōdēəs\ *adj* : spacious

com•mod•i•ty \kə'mädətē\ *n, pl* **-ties** : article for sale

com•mo•dore \'käməˌdōr\ *n* **1** : former commissioned officer in the navy ranking next below a rear admiral **2** : officer commanding a group of merchant ships

com•mon \'kämən\ *adj* **1** : public **2** : shared by several **3** : widely known, found, or observed **4** : ordinary ∼ *n* : community land — **com•mon•ly** *adv* — **in common** : shared together

com•mon•place \'kämənˌplās\ *n* : cliché ∼ *adj* : ordinary

common sense *n* : good judgment

com•mon•weal \-ˌwēl\ *n* : general welfare

com•mon•wealth \-ˌwelth\ *n* : state

com•mo•tion \kə'mōshən\ *n* : disturbance

¹com•mune \kə'myün\ *vb* **-muned; -mun•ing** : communicate intimately

²com•mune \'käm‚yün; kə'myün\ *n* : community that shares all ownership and duties — **com•mu•nal** \-ᵊl\ *adj*

com•mu•ni•cate \kə'myünə‚kāt\ *vb* **-cat•ed; -cat•ing** 1 : make known 2 : transmit 3 : exchange information or opinions — **com•mu•ni•ca•ble** \-'myünikəbəl\ *adj* — **com•mu•ni•ca•tion** \-‚myünə'kāshən\ *n* — **com•mu•ni•ca•tive** \-'myüni‚kātiv, -kət-\ *adj*

Com•mu•nion \kə'myünyən\ *n* : Christian sacrament of partaking of bread and wine

com•mu•ni•qué \kə'myünə‚kā, -‚myünə'kā\ *n* : official bulletin

com•mu•nism \'kämyə‚nizəm\ *n* 1 : social organization in which goods are held in common 2 *cap* : political doctrine based on revolutionary Marxist socialism — **com•mu•nist** \-nist\ *n or adj, often cap* — **com•mu•nis•tic** \‚kämyə'nistik\ *adj, often cap*

com•mu•ni•ty \kə'myünətē\ *n, pl* **-ties** : body of people living in the same place under the same laws

com•mute \kə'myüt\ *vb* **-mut•ed; -mut•ing** 1 : reduce (a punishment) 2 : travel back and forth regularly ∼ *n* : trip made in commuting — **com•mu•ta•tion** \‚kämyə'tāshən\ *n* — **com•mut•er** *n*

¹com•pact \kəm'pakt, 'käm‚pakt\ *adj* 1 : hard 2 : small or brief ∼ *vb* : pack together ∼ \'käm‚pakt\ *n* 1 : cosmetics case 2 : small car — **com•pact•ly** *adv* — **com•pact•ness** *n*

²com•pact \'käm‚pakt\ *n* : agreement

compact disc *n* : plastic-coated disc with laser-readable recorded music

com•pan•ion \kəm'panyən\ *n* 1 : close friend 2 : one of a pair — **com•pan•ion•able** *adj* — **com•pan•ion•ship** *n*

com•pa•ny \'kəmpənē\ *n, pl* **-nies** 1 : business organization 2 : group of performers 3 : guests 4 : infantry unit

com•par•a•tive \kəm'parətiv\ *adj* 1 : relating to or being an adjective or adverb form that denotes increase 2 : relative — **comparative** *n* — **com•par•a•tive•ly** *adv*

com•pare \kəm'par\ *vb* **-pared; -par-** ing 1 : represent as similar 2 : check for likenesses or differences ∼ *n* : comparison — **com•pa•ra•ble** \'kämprəbəl\ *adj*

com•par•i•son \kəm'parəsən\ *n* 1 : act of comparing 2 : change in the form and meaning of an adjective or adverb to show different levels of quality, quantity, or relation

com•part•ment \kəm'pärtmənt\ *n* : section or room

com•pass \'kəmpəs, 'käm-\ *n* 1 : scope 2 : device for drawing circles 3 : device for determining direction

com•pas•sion \kəm'pashən\ *n* : pity — **com•pas•sion•ate** \-ənət\ *adj*

com•pat•i•ble \-'patəbəl\ *adj* : harmonious — **com•pat•i•bil•i•ty** \-‚patə'bilətē\ *n*

com•pa•tri•ot \kəm'pātrēət, -trē‚ät\ *n* : fellow countryman

com•pel \kəm'pel\ *vb* **-ll-** : cause through necessity

com•pen•di•ous \kam'pendēəs\ *adj* 1 : concise and comprehensive 2 : comprehensive

com•pen•di•um \-'pendēəm\ *n, pl* **-di•ums** *or* **-dia** \-dēə\ : summary

com•pen•sate \'kämpən‚sāt\ *vb* **-sat•ed; -sat•ing** 1 : offset or balance 2 : repay — **com•pen•sa•tion** \‚kämpən'sāshən\ *n* — **com•pen•sa•to•ry** \kəm'pensə‚tōrē\ *adj*

com•pete \kəm'pēt\ *vb* **-pet•ed; -pet-** ing : strive to win — **com•pe•ti•tion** \‚kämpə'tishən\ *n* — **com•pet•i•tive** \kəm'petətiv\ *adj* — **com•pet•i•tive•ness** *n* — **com•pet•i•tor** \kəm'petətər\ *n*

com•pe•tent \'kämpətənt\ *adj* : capable — **com•pe•tence** \-əns\ *n* — **com•pe•ten•cy** \-ənsē\ *n*

com•pile \kəm'pīl\ *vb* **-piled; -pil•ing** : collect or compose from several sources — **com•pi•la•tion** \‚kämpə'lāshən\ *n* — **com•pil•er** \kəm'pīlər\ *n*

com•pla•cen•cy \kəm'plāsᵊnsē\ *n* : self-satisfaction — **com•pla•cent** \-ᵊnt\ *adj*

com•plain \kəm'plān\ *vb* 1 : express grief, pain, or discontent 2 : make an accusation — **com•plain•ant** *n* — **com•plain•er** *n*

com•plaint \-'plānt\ *n* 1 : expression of grief or discontent 2 : ailment 3 : formal accusation

com•ple•ment \'kämpləmənt\ *n* 1

: something that completes **2** : full number or amount ~ \-ˌment\ *vb* : complete — **com·ple·men·ta·ry** \ˌkämpləˈmentərē\ *adj*

com·plete \kəmˈplēt\ *adj* **-plet·er; -est** **1** : having all parts **2** : finished **3** : total ~ *vb* **-plet·ed; -plet·ing** **1** : make whole **2** : finish — **com·plete·ly** *adv* — **com·plete·ness** *n* — **com·ple·tion** \-ˈplēshən\ *n*

com·plex \kämˈpleks, kəm-; ˈkämˌpleks\ *adj* **1** : having many parts **2** : intricate ~ \ˈkämˌpleks\ *n* : psychological problem — **com·plex·i·ty** \kəmˈpleksətē, käm-\ *n*

com·plex·ion \kəmˈplekshən\ *n* : hue or appearance of the skin esp. of the face — **com·plex·ioned** *adj*

com·pli·cate \ˈkämpləˌkāt\ *vb* **-cat·ed; -cat·ing** : make complex or hard to understand — **com·pli·cat·ed** \-əd\ *adj* — **com·pli·ca·tion** \ˌkämpləˈkāshən\ *n*

com·plic·i·ty \kəmˈplisətē\ *n, pl* **-ties** : participation in guilt

com·pli·ment \ˈkämpləmənt\ *n* **1** : flattering remark **2** *pl* : greeting ~ \-ˌment\ *vb* : pay a compliment to

com·pli·men·ta·ry \ˌkämpləˈmentərē\ *adj* **1** : praising **2** : free

com·ply \kəmˈplī\ *vb* **-plied; -ply·ing** : conform or yield — **com·pli·ance** \-əns\ *n* — **com·pli·ant** \-ənt\ *n*

com·po·nent \kəmˈpōnənt, ˈkämˌpō-\ *n* : part of something larger ~ *adj* : serving as a component

com·port \kəmˈpōrt\ *vb* **1** : agree **2** : behave — **com·port·ment** \-mənt\ *n*

com·pose \kəmˈpōz\ *vb* **-posed; -pos·ing** **1** : create (as by writing) or put together **2** : calm **3** : set type — **com·pos·er** *n* — **com·po·si·tion** \ˌkämpəˈzishən\ *n*

com·pos·ite \kämˈpäzət, kəm-\ *adj* : made up of diverse parts — **composite** *n*

com·post \ˈkämˌpōst\ *n* : decayed organic fertilizing material

com·po·sure \kəmˈpōzhər\ *n* : calmness

com·pote \ˈkämˌpōt\ *n* : fruits cooked in syrup

¹**com·pound** \ˈkämˌpau̇nd, kəmˈpau̇nd\ *vb* **1** : combine or add **2** : pay (interest) on principal and accrued interest ~ \ˈkämˌpau̇nd\ *adj* : made up of 2

or more parts ~ \ˈkämˌpau̇nd\ *n* : something that is compound

²**com·pound** \ˈkämˌpau̇nd\ *n* : enclosure

com·pre·hend \ˌkämpriˈhend\ *vb* **1** : understand **2** : include — **com·pre·hen·si·ble** \-ˈhensəbəl\ *adj* — **com·pre·hen·sion** \-ˈhenchən\ *n* — **com·pre·hen·sive** \-siv\ *adj*

com·press \kəmˈpres\ *vb* : squeeze together ~ \ˈkämˌpres\ *n* : pad for pressing on a wound — **com·pres·sion** \-ˈpreshən\ *n* — **com·pres·sor** \-ˈpresər\ *n*

compressed air *n* : air under pressure greater than that of the atmosphere

com·prise \kəmˈprīz\ *vb* **-prised; -pris·ing** **1** : contain or cover **2** : be made up of

com·pro·mise \ˈkämprəˌmīz\ *vb* **-mised; -mis·ing** : settle differences by mutual concessions — **compromise** *n*

comp·trol·ler \kənˈtrōlər, ˈkämpˌtrō-\ *n* : financial officer

com·pul·sion \kəmˈpəlshən\ *n* **1** : coercion **2** : irresistible impulse — **com·pul·sive** \-siv\ *adj* — **com·pul·so·ry** \-ˈpəlsərē\ *adj*

com·punc·tion \-ˈpəŋkshən\ *n* : remorse

com·pute \-ˈpyüt\ *vb* **-put·ed; -put·ing** : calculate — **com·pu·ta·tion** \ˌkämpyüˈtāshən\ *n*

com·put·er \kəmˈpyütər\ *n* : electronic data processing machine — **com·put·er·i·za·tion** \-ˌpyütərəˈzāshən\ *n* — **com·put·er·ize** \-ˈpyütəˌrīz\ *vb*

com·rade \ˈkämˌrad, -rəd\ *n* : companion — **com·rade·ship** *n*

¹**con** \ˈkän\ *adv* : against ~ *n* : opposing side or person

²**con** *vb* **-nn-** : swindle

con·cave \känˈkāv, ˈkänˌkāv\ *adj* : curved like the inside of a sphere — **con·cav·i·ty** \känˈkavətē\ *n*

con·ceal \kənˈsēl\ *vb* : hide — **con·ceal·ment** *n*

con·cede \-ˈsēd\ *vb* **-ced·ed; -ced·ing** : grant

con·ceit \-ˈsēt\ *n* : excessively high opinion of oneself — **con·ceit·ed** \-əd\ *adj*

con·ceive \-ˈsēv\ *vb* **-ceived; -ceiv·ing** **1** : become pregnant **2** : think of — **con·ceiv·able** \-ˈsēvəbəl\ *adj* — **con·ceiv·ably** \-blē\ *adv*

con·cen·trate \\'känsən‚trāt\\ *vb* **-trat-ed; -trat·ing 1** : gather together **2** : make stronger **3** : fix one's attention — **~** *n* : something concentrated — **con·cen·tra·tion** \\‚känsən'trāshən\\ *n*

con·cen·tric \\kən'sentrik\\ *adj* : having a common center

con·cept \\'kän‚sept\\ *n* : thought or idea

con·cep·tion \\kən'sepshən\\ *n* **1** : act of conceiving **2** : idea

con·cern \\kən'sərn\\ *vb* **1** : relate to **2** : involve **~** *n* **1** : affair **2** : worry **3** : business — **con·cerned** \\-'sərnd\\ *adj* — **con·cern·ing** \\-'sərniŋ\\ *prep*

con·cert \\'kän‚sərt\\ *n* **1** : agreement or joint action **2** : public performance of music — **con·cert·ed** \\kən-'sərtəd\\ *adj*

con·cer·ti·na \\‚känsər'tēnə\\ *n* : accordionlike instrument

con·cer·to \\kən'chertō\\ *n, pl* **-ti** \\-tē\\ *or* **-tos** : orchestral work with solo instruments

con·ces·sion \\-'seshən\\ *n* **1** : act of conceding **2** : something conceded **3** : right to do business on a property

conch \\'käŋk, 'känch\\ *n, pl* **conchs** \\'käŋks\\ *or* **conch·es** \\'känchəz\\ : large spiral-shelled marine mollusk

con·cil·ia·to·ry \\kən'silēə‚tōrē\\ *adj* : mollifying

con·cise \\kən'sīs\\ *adj* : said in few words — **con·cise·ly** *adv* — **con·cise·ness** *n* — **con·ci·sion** \\kən'sizhən\\ *n*

con·clave \\'kän‚klāv\\ *n* : private meeting

con·clude \\kən'klüd\\ *vb* **-clud·ed; -clud·ing 1** : end **2** : decide — **con·clu·sion** \\-'klüzhən\\ *n* — **con·clu·sive** \\-siv\\ *adj* — **con·clu·sive·ly** *adv*

con·coct \\kən'käkt, kän-\\ *vb* : prepare or devise — **con·coc·tion** \\-'käkshən\\ *n*

con·com·i·tant \\-'kämətənt\\ *adj* : accompanying — **concomitant** *n*

con·cord \\'kän‚kòrd, 'käŋ-\\ *n* : agreement

con·cor·dance \\kən'kòrd²ns\\ *n* **1** : agreement **2** : index of words — **con·cor·dant** \\-²nt\\ *adj*

con·course \\'kän‚kōrs\\ *n* : open space where crowds gather

con·crete \\kän'krēt, 'kän‚krēt\\ *adj* **1** : naming something real **2** : actual or

substantial **3** : made of concrete **~** \\'kän‚krēt, kän'krēt\\ *n* : hard building material made of cement, sand, gravel, and water

con·cre·tion \\kän'krēshən\\ *n* : hard mass

con·cu·bine \\'käŋkyù‚bīn\\ *n* : mistress

con·cur \\kən'kər\\ *vb* **-rr-** : agree — **con·cur·rence** \\-'kərəns\\ *n*

con·cur·rent \\-ənt\\ *adj* : happening at the same time

con·cus·sion \\kən'kəshən\\ *n* **1** : shock **2** : brain injury from a blow

con·demn \\-'dem\\ *vb* **1** : declare to be wrong, guilty, or unfit for use **2** : sentence — **con·dem·na·tion** \\‚kän‚dem'nāshən\\ *n*

con·dense \\kən'dens\\ *vb* **-densed; -dens·ing 1** : make or become more compact **2** : change from vapor to liquid — **con·den·sa·tion** \\‚kän‚den'sāshən, -dən-\\ *n* — **con·dens·er** *n*

con·de·scend \\‚kändi'send\\ *vb* **1** : lower oneself **2** : act haughtily — **con·de·scen·sion** \\-'senchən\\ *n*

con·di·ment \\'kändəmənt\\ *n* : pungent seasoning

con·di·tion \\kən'dishən\\ *n* **1** : necessary situation or stipulation **2** *pl* : state of affairs **3** : state of being **~** *vb* : put into proper condition — **con·di·tion·al** \\kən'dishənəl\\ *adj* — **con·di·tion·al·ly** \\-ē\\ *adv*

con·do·lence \\kən'dōləns\\ *n* : expression of sympathy — usu. pl.

con·do·min·i·um \\‚kändə'minēəm\\ *n, pl* **-ums** : individually owned apartment

con·done \\kən'dōn\\ *vb* **-doned; -don·ing** : overlook or forgive

con·dor \\'kändər, -‚dòr\\ *n* : large western American vulture

con·du·cive \\kən'düsiv, -'dyü-\\ *adj* : tending to help or promote

con·duct \\'kän‚dəkt\\ *n* **1** : management **2** : behavior **~** \\kən'dəkt\\ *vb* **1** : guide **2** : manage or direct **3** : be a channel for **4** : behave — **con·duc·tion** \\-'dəkshən\\ *n* — **con·duc·tive** \\-'dəktiv\\ *adj* — **con·duc·tiv·i·ty** \\‚kän‚dək'tivətē\\ *n* — **con·duc·tor** \\-'dəktər\\ *n*

con·duit \\'kän‚düət, -‚dyü-\\ *n* : channel (as for conveying fluid)

cone \\'kōn\\ *n* **1** : scaly fruit of pine

and related trees **2** : solid figure having a circular base and tapering sides

con·fec·tion \kən'fekshən\ *n* : sweet dish or candy — **con·fec·tion·er** \-shənər\ *n*

con·fed·er·a·cy \kən'fedərəsē\ *n*, *pl* **-cies 1** : league **2** *cap* : 11 southern states that seceded from the U.S. in 1860 and 1861

con·fed·er·ate \-rət\ *adj* **1** : united in a league **2** *cap* : relating to the Confederacy ⁓ *n* **1** : ally **2** *cap* : adherent of the Confederacy ⁓ \-'fedə,rāt\ *vb* **-at·ed; -at·ing** : unite — **con·fed·er·a·tion** \-,fedə'rāshən\ *n*

con·fer \kən'fər\ *vb* **-rr- 1** : give **2** : meet to exchange views — **con·fer·ee** \,känfə'rē\ *n* — **con·fer·ence** \'känfərəns\ *n*

con·fess \kən'fes\ *vb* **1** : acknowledge or disclose one's misdeed, fault, or sin **2** : declare faith in — **con·fes·sion** \-'feshən\ *n* — **con·fes·sion·al** \-'feshənəl\ *n or adj*

con·fes·sor \kən'fesər, 2 *also* ' kän-,fes-\ *n* **1** : one who confesses **2** : priest who hears confessions

con·fet·ti \kən'fetē\ *n* : bits of paper or ribbon thrown in celebration

con·fi·dant \'känfə,dant, -,dänt\ *n* : one to whom secrets are confided

con·fide \kən'fīd\ *vb* **-fid·ed; -fid·ing 1** : share private thoughts **2** : reveal in confidence

con·fi·dence \'känfədəns\ *n* **1** : trust **2** : self-assurance **3** : something confided — **con·fi·dent** \-dənt\ *adj* — **con·fi·den·tial** \,känfə'denchəl\ *adj* — **con·fi·den·tial·ly** \-ē\ *adv* — **con·fi·dent·ly** *adv*

con·fig·u·ra·tion \kən,figyə'rāshən\ *n* : arrangement

con·fine \kən'fīn\ *vb* **-fined; -fin·ing 1** : restrain or restrict to a limited area **2** : imprison — **con·fine·ment** *n* — **con·fin·er** *n*

confines \'kän,fīnz\ *n pl* : bounds

con·firm \kən'fərm\ *vb* **1** : ratify **2** : verify **3** : admit as a full member of a church or synagogue — **con·fir·ma·tion** \,känfər'māshən\ *n*

con·fis·cate \'känfə,skāt\ *vb* **-cat·ed; -cat·ing** : take by authority — **con·fis·ca·tion** \,känfə'skāshən\ *n* — **con·fis·ca·to·ry** \kən'fiskə,tōrē\ *adj*

con·fla·gra·tion \,känflə'grāshən\ *n* : great fire

con·flict \'kän,flikt\ *n* **1** : war **2** : clash of ideas ⁓ \kən'flikt\ *vb* : clash

con·form \kən'fórm\ *vb* **1** : make or be like **2** : obey — **con·for·mi·ty** \kən'fórmətē\ *n*

con·found \kən'faúnd, kän-\ *vb* : confuse

con·front \kən'frənt\ *vb* : oppose or face — **con·fron·ta·tion** \,känfrən-'tāshən\ *n*

con·fuse \kən'fyüz\ *vb* **-fused; -fus·ing 1** : make mentally uncertain **2** : jumble — **con·fu·sion** \-'fyüzhən\ *n*

con·fute \-'fyüt\ *vb* **-fut·ed; -fut·ing** : overwhelm by argument

con·geal \kən'jēl\ *vb* **1** : freeze **2** : become thick and solid

con·ge·nial \kən'jēnēəl\ *adj* : kindred or agreeable — **con·ge·ni·al·i·ty** *n*

con·gen·i·tal \kən'jenət³l\ *adj* : existing from birth

con·gest \kən'jest\ *vb* : overcrowd or overfill — **con·ges·tion** \-'jeschən\ *n* — **con·ges·tive** \-'jestiv\ *adj*

con·glom·er·ate \kən'glämərət\ *adj* : made up of diverse parts ⁓ \-ə,rāt\ *vb* **-at·ed; -at·ing** : form into a mass ⁓ \-ərət\ *n* : diversified corporation — **con·glom·er·a·tion** \-,glämə'rāshən\ *n*

con·grat·u·late \kən'grachə,lāt, -'graj-\ *vb* **-lat·ed; -lat·ing** : express pleasure to for good fortune — **con·grat·u·la·tion** \-,grachə'lāshən, -,graj-\ *n* — **con·grat·u·la·to·ry** \-'grachələ,tōrē, -'graj-\ *adj*

con·gre·gate \'käŋgri,gāt\ *vb* **-gat·ed; -gat·ing** : assemble

con·gre·ga·tion \,käŋgri'gāshən\ *n* **1** : assembly of people at worship **2** : religious group — **con·gre·ga·tion·al** \-shənəl\ *adj*

con·gress \'käŋgrəs\ *n* : assembly of delegates or of senators and representatives — **con·gres·sio·nal** \kən-'greshənəl, kän-\ *adj* — **con·gress·man** \'käŋgrəsmən\ *n* — **con·gress·wom·an** *n*

con·gru·ence \kən'grüəns, 'käŋgrəw-əns\ *n* : likeness — **con·gru·ent** \-ənt\ *adj*

con·gru·ity \kən'grüətē, kän-\ *n* : correspondence between things — **con·gru·ous** \'käŋgrəwəs\ *adj*

con·ic \'känik\ *adj* : relating to or like a cone — **con·i·cal** \-ikəl\ *adj*

co·ni·fer \\'känəfər, 'kōn-\\ *n* : cone-bearing tree — **co·nif·er·ous** \\kō-'nifərəs\\ *adj*

con·jec·ture \\kən'jekchər\\ *n or vb* : guess — **con·jec·tur·al** \\-əl\\ *adj*

con·join \\kən'join\\ *vb* : join together — **con·joint** \\-'joint\\ *adj*

con·ju·gal \\'känjigəl, kən'jü-\\ *adj* : relating to marriage

con·ju·gate \\'känjə,gāt\\ *vb* **-gat·ed; -gat·ing** : give the inflected forms of (a verb) — **con·ju·ga·tion** \\,känjə-'gāshən\\ *n*

con·junc·tion \\kən'jəŋkshən\\ *n* **1** : combination **2** : occurrence at the same time **3** : a word that joins other words together — **con·junc·tive** \\-tiv\\ *adj*

con·jure \\'känjər, 'kən-\\ *vb* **-jured; -jur·ing** **1** : summon by sorcery **2** : practice sleight of hand **3** : entreat — **con·jur·er, con·ju·ror** \\'känjərər, 'kən-\\ *n*

con·nect \\kə'nekt\\ *vb* : join or associate — **con·nect·able** *adj* — **con·nec·tion** \\-'nekshən\\ *n* — **con·nec·tive** \\-tiv\\ *n or adj* — **con·nec·tor** *n*

con·nive \\kə'nīv\\ *vb* **-nived; -niv·ing** **1** : pretend ignorance of wrongdoing **2** : cooperate secretly — **con·niv·ance** *n*

con·nois·seur \\,känə'sər, -'sur\\ *n* : expert judge esp. of art

con·note \\kə'nōt\\ *vb* **-not·ed; -not·ing** : suggest additional meaning — **con·no·ta·tion** \\,känə'tāshən\\ *n*

con·nu·bi·al \\kə'nübēəl, -'nyü-\\ *adj* : relating to marriage

con·quer \\'käŋkər\\ *vb* : defeat or overcome — **con·quer·or** \\-kərər\\ *n*

con·quest \\'kän,kwest, 'käŋ-\\ *n* **1** : act of conquering **2** : something conquered

con·science \\'känchəns\\ *n* : awareness of right and wrong

con·sci·en·tious \\,känchē'enchəs\\ *adj* : honest and hard-working — **con·sci·en·tious·ly** *adv*

con·scious \\'känchəs\\ *adj* **1** : aware **2** : mentally awake or alert **3** : intentional — **con·scious·ly** *adv* — **con·scious·ness** *n*

con·script \\kən'skript\\ *vb* : draft for military service — **con·script** \\'kän,skript\\ *n* — **con·scrip·tion** \\kən'skripshən\\ *n*

con·se·crate \\'känsə,krāt\\ *vb* **-crat·ed; -crat·ing** **1** : declare sacred **2**

: devote to a solemn purpose — **con·se·cra·tion** \\,känə'krāshən\\ *n*

con·sec·u·tive \\kən'sekyətiv\\ *adj* : following in order — **con·sec·u·tive·ly** *adv*

con·sen·sus \\-'sensəs\\ *n* **1** : agreement in opinion **2** : collective opinion

con·sent \\-'sent\\ *vb* : give permission or approval — **consent** *n*

con·se·quence \\'känsə,kwens\\ *n* **1** : result or effect **2** : importance — **con·se·quent** \\-kwənt, -,kwent\\ *adj* — **con·se·quent·ly** *adv*

con·se·quen·tial \\,känsə'kwenchəl\\ *adj* : important

con·ser·va·tion \\,känsər'vāshən\\ *n* : planned management of natural resources — **con·ser·va·tion·ist** \\-shən-ist\\ *n*

con·ser·va·tive \\kən'sərvətiv\\ *adj* **1** : disposed to maintain the status quo **2** : cautious — **con·ser·va·tism** \\-və,tizəm\\ *n* — **conservative** *n* — **con·ser·va·tive·ly** *adv*

con·ser·va·to·ry \\kən'sərvə,tōrē\\ *n, pl* **-ries** : school for art or music

con·serve \\-'sərv\\ *vb* **-served; -serv·ing** : keep from wasting ~ \\'kän-,sərv\\ *n* : candied fruit or fruit preserves

con·sid·er \\kən'sidər\\ *vb* **1** : think about **2** : give thoughtful attention to **3** : think that — **con·sid·er·ate** \\-'sidərət\\ *adj* — **con·sid·er·ation** \\-,sidə'rāshən\\ *n*

con·sid·er·able \\-'sidərəbəl\\ *adj* **1** : significant **2** : noticeably large — **con·sid·er·a·bly** \\-blē\\ *adv*

con·sid·er·ing *prep* : taking notice of

con·sign \\kən'sīn\\ *vb* **1** : transfer **2** : send to an agent for sale — **con·sign·ee** \\,känsə'nē, -,sī-; kən,sī-\\ *n* — **con·sign·ment** \\kən'sīnmənt\\ *n* — **con·sign·or** \\,känsə'nor, -,sī-; kən,sī-\\ *n*

con·sist \\kən'sist\\ *vb* **1** : be inherent — used with *in* **2** : be made up — used with *of*

con·sis·ten·cy \\-'sistənsē\\ *n, pl* **-cies** **1** : degree of thickness or firmness **2** : quality of being consistent

con·sis·tent \\-tənt\\ *adj* : being steady and regular — **con·sis·tent·ly** *adv*

¹con·sole \\kən'sōl\\ *vb* **-soled; -sol·ing** : soothe the grief of — **con·so·la·tion** \\,känsə'lāshən\\ *n*

²con·sole \\'kän,sōl\\ *n* : cabinet or part with controls

con·sol·i·date \kən'sälə,dāt\ *vb* **-dat·ed; -dat·ing** : unite or compact — **con·sol·i·da·tion** \-,sälə'dāshən\ *n*

con·som·mé \,känsə'mā\ *n* : clear soup

con·so·nance \'känsənəns\ *n* : agreement or harmony — **con·so·nant** \-nənt\ *adj* — **con·so·nant·ly** *adv*

con·so·nant \-nənt\ *n* **1** : speech sound marked by constriction or closure in the breath channel **2** : letter other than *a, e, i, o* and *u* — **con·so·nan·tal** \,känsə'nant°l\ *adj*

con·sort \'kän,sȯrt\ *n* : spouse ~ \kən'sȯrt\ *vb* : keep company

con·spic·u·ous \kən'spikyəwəs\ *adj* : very noticeable — **con·spic·u·ous·ly** *adv*

con·spire \kən'spīr\ *vb* **-spired; -spir·ing** : secretly plan an unlawful act — **con·spir·a·cy** \-'spirəsē\ *n* — **con·spir·a·tor** \-'spirətər\ *n* — **con·spir·a·to·ri·al** \-,spirə'tōrēəl\ *adj*

con·sta·ble \'känstəbəl, 'kən-\ *n* : police officer

con·stab·u·lary \kən'stabyə,lerē\ *n, pl* **-lar·ies** : police force

con·stant \'känstənt\ *adj* **1** : steadfast or faithful **2** : not varying **3** : continually recurring ~ *n* : something unchanging — **con·stan·cy** \-stənsē\ *n* — **con·stant·ly** *adv*

con·stel·la·tion \,känstə'lāshən\ *n* : group of stars

con·ster·na·tion \-stər'nāshən\ *n* : amazed dismay

con·sti·pa·tion \-stə'pāshən\ *n* : difficulty of defecation — **con·sti·pate** \'känstə,pāt\ *vb*

con·stit·u·ent \kən'stichəwənt\ *adj* **1** : component **2** : having power to elect ~ *n* **1** : component part **2** : one who may vote for a representative — **con·stit·u·en·cy** \-wənsē\ *n*

con·sti·tute \'känstə,tüt, -,tyüt\ *vb* **-tut·ed; -tut·ing** **1** : establish **2** : be all or a basic part of

con·sti·tu·tion \,känstə'tüshən, -'tyü-\ *n* **1** : physical composition or structure **2** : the basic law of an organized body or the document containing it — **con·sti·tu·tion·al** \-əl\ *adj* — **con·sti·tu·tion·al·i·ty** \-,tüshə'nalətē, -,tyü-\ *n*

con·strain \kən'strān\ *vb* **1** : compel **2** : confine **3** : restrain — **con·straint** \-'strānt\ *n*

con·strict \-'strikt\ *vb* : draw or squeeze together — **con·stric·tion** \-'strikshən\ *n* — **con·stric·tive** \-'striktiv\ *adj*

con·struct \kən'strəkt\ *vb* : build or make — **con·struc·tion** \-'strək-shən\ *n* — **con·struc·tive** \-tiv\ *adj*

con·strue \kən'strü\ *vb* **-strued; -stru·ing** : explain or interpret

con·sul \'känsəl\ *n* **1** : Roman magistrate **2** : government commercial official in a foreign country — **con·sul·ar** \-ələr\ *adj* — **con·sul·ate** \-lət\ *n*

con·sult \kən'səlt\ *vb* **1** : ask the advice or opinion of **2** : confer — **con·sul·tant** \-ənt\ *n* — **con·sul·ta·tion** \,känsəl'tāshən\ *n*

con·sume \kən'süm\ *vb* **-sumed; -sum·ing** : eat or use up — **con·sum·able** *adj* — **con·sum·er** *n*

con·sum·mate \kən'səmət\ *adj* : complete or perfect ~ \'känsə,māt\ *vb* **-mat·ed; -mat·ing** : make complete — **con·sum·ma·tion** \,känsə'mā-shən\ *n*

con·sump·tion \kən'səmpshən\ *n* **1** : act of consuming **2** : use of goods **3** : tuberculosis — **con·sump·tive** \-tiv\ *adj or n*

con·tact \'kän,takt\ *n* **1** : a touching **2** : association or relationship **3** : connection or communication ~ *vb* **1** : come or bring into contact **2** : communicate with

con·ta·gion \kən'tājən\ *n* **1** : spread of disease by contact **2** : disease spread by contact — **con·ta·gious** \-jəs\ *adj*

con·tain \-'tān\ *vb* **1** : enclose or include **2** : have or hold within **3** : restrain — **con·tain·er** *n* — **con·tain·ment** *n*

con·tam·i·nate \kən'tamə,nāt\ *vb* **-nat·ed; -nat·ing** : soil or infect by contact or association — **con·tam·i·na·tion** \-,tamə'nāshən\ *n*

con·tem·plate \'käntəm,plāt\ *vb* **-plat·ed; -plat·ing** : view or consider thoughtfully — **con·tem·pla·tion** \,käntəm'plāshən\ *n* — **con·tem·pla·tive** \kən'templətiv; 'käntəm,-plāt-\ *adj*

con·tem·po·ra·ne·ous \kən,tempə-'rānēəs\ *adj* : contemporary

con·tem·po·rary \-'tempə,rerē\ *adj* **1** : occurring or existing at the same time **2** : of the same age — **contem·porary** *n*

con·tempt \kən'tempt\ *n* **1** : feeling

of scorn **2** : state of being despised **3**
: disobedience to a court or legislature — **con·tempt·ible** \-ˈtempt-
əbəl\ adj

con·temp·tu·ous \-ˈtempchəwəs\ adj
: feeling or expressing contempt —
con·temp·tu·ous·ly adv

con·tend \-ˈtend\ vb **1** : strive against
rivals or difficulties **2** : argue **3**
: maintain or claim — **con·tend·er** n

¹**con·tent** \kən'tent\ adj : satisfied ~
vb : satisfy ~ n : ease of mind —
con·tent·ed adj — **con·tent·ed·ly**
adv — **con·tent·ed·ness** n — **con-
tent·ment** n

²**con·tent** \ˈkän,tent\ n **1** pl : something contained **2** pl : subject matter
(as of a book) **3** : essential meaning
4 : proportion contained

con·ten·tion \kən'tenchən\ n : state
of contending — **con·ten·tious**
\-chəs\ adj — **con·ten·tious·ly** adv

con·test \kən'test\ vb : dispute or
challenge ~ \ˈkän,test\ n **1** : struggle **2** : game — **con·test·able** \kən-
ˈtestəbəl\ adj — **con·tes·tant**
\-ˈtestənt\ n

con·text \ˈkän,tekst\ n : words surrounding a word or phrase

con·tig·u·ous \kən'tigyəwəs\ adj
: connected to or adjoining — **con·ti-
gu·i·ty** \,käntə'gyüətē\ n

con·ti·nence \ˈkäntᵊnəns\ n : self-
restraint — **con·ti·nent** \-nənt\ adj

con·ti·nent \ˈkäntᵊnənt\ n : great division of land on the globe — **con·ti-
nen·tal** \,käntᵊn'entᵊl\ adj

con·tin·gen·cy \kən'tinjənsē\ n, pl
-cies : possible event

con·tin·gent \-jənt\ adj : dependent on
something else ~ n : a quota from an
area or group

con·tin·u·al \kən'tinyəwəl\ adj **1**
: continuous **2** : steadily recurring —
con·tin·u·al·ly \-ē\ adv

con·tin·ue \kən'tinyü\ vb **-tin·ued;
-tin·u·ing 1** : remain in a place or
condition **2** : endure **3** : resume after
an intermission **4** : extend — **con-
tin·u·ance** \-yəwəns\ n — **con·tin-
u·ation** \-,tinyə'wāshən\ n

con·tin·u·ous \-'tinyəwəs\ adj : continuing without interruption — **con-
ti·nu·ity** \,käntᵊn'üətē, -'yü-\ n —
con·tin·u·ous·ly adv

con·tort \kən'tórt\ vb : twist out of
shape — **con·tor·tion** \-'tórshən\ n

con·tour \ˈkän,tůr\ n **1** : outline **2** pl
: shape

con·tra·band \ˈkäntrə,band\ n : illegal goods

con·tra·cep·tion \,käntrə'sepshən\ n
: prevention of conception — **con-
tra·cep·tive** \-'septiv\ adj or n

con·tract \ˈkän,trakt\ n : binding
agreement ~ \kən'trakt; 1 usu
ˈkän,trakt\ vb **1** : establish or undertake by contract **2** : become ill with
3 : make shorter — **con·trac·tion**
\kən'trakshən\ n — **con·trac·tor**
\ˈkän,traktər, kən'trak-\ n — **con-
trac·tu·al** \kən'trakchəwəl\ adj —
con·trac·tu·al·ly adv

con·tra·dict \,käntrə'dikt\ vb : state
the contrary of — **con·tra·dic·tion**
\-'dikshən\ n — **con·tra·dic·to·ry**
\-'diktərē\ adj

con·tral·to \kən'traltō\ n, pl -tos
: lowest female singing voice

con·trap·tion \kən'trapshən\ n : device or contrivance

con·trary \ˈkän,trerē; 4 often kən-
ˈtrerē\ adj **1** : opposite in character,
nature, or position **2** : mutually opposed **3** : unfavorable **4** : uncoopera-
tive or stubborn — **con·trari·ly**
\-,trerəlē, -'trer-\ adv — **con·trari-
wise** \-,wīz\ adv — **contrary** \ˈkän-
,trerē\ n

con·trast \ˈkän,trast\ n **1** : unlikeness
shown by comparing **2** : unlike color
or tone of adjacent parts ~ \kən-
ˈtrast\ vb **1** : show differences **2**
: compare so as to show differences

con·tra·vene \,käntrə'vēn\ vb **-vened;
-ven·ing** : go or act contrary to

con·trib·ute \kən'tribyət\ vb **-ut·ed;
-ut·ing** : give or help along with
others — **con·tri·bu·tion** \,käntrə-
ˈbyüshən\ n — **con·trib·u·tor** \kən-
ˈtribyətər\ n — **con·trib·u·to·ry**
\-yə,tōrē\ adj

con·trite \ˈkän,trīt, kən'trīt\ adj : re-
pentant — **con·tri·tion** \kən'tri-
shən\ n

con·trive \kən'trīv\ vb **-trived; -triv-
ing 1** : devise or make with ingenuity
2 : bring about — **con·triv·ance**
\-'trīvəns\ n — **con·triv·er** n

con·trol \-'trōl\ vb **-ll- 1** : exercise
power over **2** : dominate or rule ~ n
1 : power to direct or regulate **2**
: restraint **3** : regulating device —
con·trol·la·ble adj — **con·trol·ler**
\-'trōlər, 'kän,-\ n

con•tro•ver•sy \'käntrə‚vərsē\ *n, pl* **-sies** : clash of opposing views — **con•tro•ver•sial** \‚käntrə'vərshəl, -sēəl\ *adj*

con•tro•vert \'käntrə‚vərt, ‚käntrə'-\ *vb* : contradict — **con•tro•vert•ible** *adj*

con•tu•ma•cious \‚käntə'māshəs, -tyə-\ *adj* : rebellious

con•tu•me•ly \kən'tüməlē, 'käntü‚mēlē, -tyü-\ *n* : rudeness

con•tu•sion \kən'tüzhən, -tyü-\ *n* : bruise — **con•tuse** \-'tüz, -'tyüz\ *vb*

co•nun•drum \kə'nəndrəm\ *n* : riddle

con•va•lesce \‚känvə'les\ *vb* **-lesced; -lesc•ing** : gradually recover health — **con•va•les•cence** \-ᵊns\ *n* — **con•va•les•cent** \-ᵊnt\ *adj or n*

con•vec•tion \kən'vekshən\ *n* : circulation in fluids due to warmer portions rising and colder ones sinking — **con•vec•tion•al** \-'vekshənəl\ *adj* — **con•vec•tive** \-'vektiv\ *adj*

con•vene \kən'vēn\ *vb* **-vened; -ven•ing** : assemble or meet

con•ve•nience \-'vēnyəns\ *n* **1** : personal comfort or ease **2** : device that saves work

con•ve•nient \-nyənt\ *adj* **1** : suited to one's convenience **2** : near at hand — **con•ve•nient•ly** *adv*

con•vent \'känvənt, -‚vent\ *n* : community of nuns

con•ven•tion \kən'venchən\ *n* **1** : agreement esp. between nations **2** : large meeting **3** : body of delegates **4** : accepted usage or way of behaving — **con•ven•tion•al** \-'venchənəl\ *adj* — **con•ven•tion•al•ly** *adv*

con•verge \kən'vərj\ *vb* **-verged; -verg•ing** : approach a single point — **con•ver•gence** \-'vərjəns\ *n* — **con•ver•gent** \-jənt\ *adj*

con•ver•sant \-'vərsᵊnt\ *adj* : having knowledge and experience

con•ver•sa•tion \‚känvər'sāshən\ *n* : an informal talking together — **con•ver•sa•tion•al** \-shənəl\ *adj*

¹con•verse \kən'vərs\ *vb* **-versed; -vers•ing** : engage in conversation — **con•verse** \'kän‚vərs\ *n*

²con•verse \kən'vərs, 'kän‚vers\ *adj* : opposite — **con•verse** \'kän‚vərs\ *n* — **con•verse•ly** *adv*

con•ver•sion \kən'vərzhən\ *n* **1** : change **2** : adoption of religion

con•vert \kən'vərt\ *vb* **1** : turn from one belief or party to another **2** : change \~ \'kän‚vərt\ *n* : one who has undergone religious conversion — **con•vert•er, con•ver•tor** \kən-'vərtər\ *n* — **con•vert•ible** *adj*

con•vert•ible \kən'vərtəbəl\ *n* : automobile with a removable top

con•vex \kän'veks, 'kän‚-, kən'-\ *adj* : curved or rounded like the outside of a sphere — **con•vex•i•ty** \kən'veksətē, kän-\ *n*

con•vey \kən'vā\ *vb* **-veyed; -vey•ing** : transport or transmit — **con•vey•ance** \-'vāəns\ *n* — **con•vey•or** \-ər\ *n*

con•vict \kən'vikt\ *vb* : find guilty \~ \'kän‚vikt\ *n* : person in prison

con•vic•tion \kən'vikshən\ *n* **1** : act of convicting **2** : strong belief

con•vince \-'vins\ *vb* **-vinced; -vinc•ing** : cause to believe — **con•vinc•ing•ly** *adv*

con•viv•ial \-'vivyəl, -'vivēəl\ *adj* : cheerful or festive — **con•viv•i•al•i•ty** \-‚vivē'alətē\ *n*

con•voke \kən'vōk\ *vb* **-voked; -vok•ing** : call together to a meeting — **con•vo•ca•tion** \‚känvə'kāshən\ *n*

con•vo•lut•ed \'känvə‚lütəd\ *adj* **1** : intricately folded **2** : intricate

con•vo•lu•tion \‚känvə'lüshən\ *n* : convoluted structure

con•voy \'kän‚vȯi, kən'vȯi\ *vb* : accompany for protection \~ \'kän‚vȯi\ *n* : group of vehicles or ships moving together

con•vul•sion \kən'vəlshən\ *n* : violent involuntary muscle contraction — **con•vulse** \-'vəls\ *vb* — **con•vul•sive** \-'vəlsiv\ *adj*

coo \'kü\ *n* : sound of a pigeon — **coo** *vb*

cook \'kük\ *n* : one who prepares food \~ *vb* : prepare food — **cook•book** *n* — **cook•er** *n* — **cook•ery** \-ərē\ *n* — **cook•ware** *n*

cook•ie, cooky \'kükē\ *n, pl* **-ies** : small sweet flat cake

cool \'kül\ *adj* **1** : moderately cold **2** : not excited **3** : unfriendly \~ *vb* : make or become cool \~ *n* **1** : cool time or place **2** : composure — **cool•ant** \-ənt\ *n* — **cool•er** *n* — **cool•ly** *adv* — **cool•ness** *n*

coo•lie \'külē\ *n* : unskilled laborer in or from the Far East

coop \'küp, 'kùp\ *n* : enclosure usu.

for poultry ~ vb : confine in or as if in a coop

co·op \\'kō͜,äp\ n : cooperative

coo·per \\'küpər, 'kủp-\ n : barrel maker — **cooper** vb

co·op·er·ate \kō'äpə,rāt\ vb : act jointly — **co·op·er·a·tion** \-,äpə-'rāshən\ n

co·op·er·a·tive \kō'äpərətiv, -'äpə-,rāt-\ adj : willing to work with others ~ n : enterprise owned and run by those using its services

co–opt \kō'äpt\ vb 1 : elect as a colleague 2 : take over

co·or·di·nate \-'órd°nət\ adj : equal esp. in rank ~ n : any of a set of numbers used in specifying the location of a point on a surface or in space ~ \-°n,āt\ vb -nat·ed; -nat·ing 1 : make or become coordinate 2 : work or act together harmoniously — **co·or·di·nate·ly** adv — **co·or·di·na·tion** \-,órd°n'āshən\ n — **co·or·di·na·tor** \-°n,ātər\ n

coot \\'küt\ n 1 : dark-colored ducklike bird 2 : harmless simple person

cop \\'käp\ n : police officer

¹**cope** \\'kōp\ n : cloaklike ecclesiastical vestment

²**cope** vb **coped; cop·ing** : deal with difficulties

co·pi·lot \\'kō,pīlət\ n : assistant airplane pilot

cop·ing \\'kōpiŋ\ n : top layer of a wall

co·pi·ous \\'kōpēəs\ adj : very abundant — **co·pi·ous·ly** adv — **co·pi·ous·ness** n

cop·per \\'käpər\ n 1 : malleable reddish metallic chemical element 2 : penny — **cop·pery** adj

cop·per·head n : largely coppery brown venomous snake

co·pra \\'kōprə\ n : dried coconut meat

copse \\'käps\ n : thicket

cop·u·la \\'käpyələ\ n : verb linking subject and predicate — **cop·u·la·tive** \-,lātiv\ adj

cop·u·late \\'käpyə,lāt\ vb -lat·ed; -lat·ing : engage in sexual intercourse — **cop·u·la·tion** \,käpyə'lāshən\ n

copy \\'käpē\ n, pl **cop·ies** 1 : imitation or reproduction of an original 2 : writing to be set for printing ~ vb **cop·ied; copy·ing** 1 : make a copy of 2 : imitate — **copi·er** \-ər\ n — **copyist** n

copy·right n : sole right to a literary or artistic work ~ vb : get a copyright on

co·quette \kō'ket\ n : flirt

cor·al \\'kórəl\ n 1 : skeletal material of colonies of tiny sea polyps 2 : deep pink — **coral** adj

cord \\'kórd\ n 1 : usu. heavy string 2 : long slender anatomical structure 3 : measure of firewood equal to 128 cu. ft. 4 : small electrical cable ~ vb 1 : tie or furnish with a cord 2 : pile (wood) in cords

cor·dial \\'kórjəl\ adj : warmly welcoming ~ n : liqueur — **cor·di·al·i·ty** \,kórjē'alətē, kórd'yal-\ n — **cor·dial·ly** \\'kórjəlē\ adv

cor·don \\'kórd°n\ n : encircling line of troops or police — **cordon** vb

cor·do·van \\'kórdəvən\ n : soft fine-grained leather

cor·du·roy \\'kórdə,rói\ n 1 : heavy ribbed fabric 2 pl : trousers of corduroy

core \\'kōr\ n 1 : central part of some fruits 2 : inmost part ~ vb **cored; cor·ing** : take out the core of — **cor·er** n

cork \\'kórk\ n 1 : tough elastic bark of a European oak (**cork oak**) 2 : stopper of cork ~ vb : stop up with a cork — **corky** adj

cork·screw n : device for drawing corks from bottles

cor·mo·rant \\'kórmərənt, -,rant\ n : dark seabird

¹**corn** \\'kórn\ n : cereal grass or its seeds ~ vb : cure or preserve in brine — **corn·meal** n — **corn·stalk** n — **corn·starch** n

²**corn** n : local hardening and thickening of skin

corn·cob n : axis on which the kernels of Indian corn are arranged

cor·nea \\'kórnēə\ n : transparent part of the coat of the eyeball — **cor·ne·al** adj

cor·ner \\'kórnər\ n 1 : point or angle formed by the meeting of lines or sides 2 : place where two streets meet 3 : inescapable position 4 : control of the supply of something ~ vb 1 : drive into a corner 2 : get a corner on 3 : turn a corner

cor·ner·stone n 1 : stone at a corner of a wall 2 : something basic

cor·net \kór'net\ n : trumpetlike instrument

cor•nice \\'kórnəs\ *n* : horizontal wall projection

cor•nu•co•pia \\,kórnə'kōpēə, -nyə-\ *n* : goat's horn filled with fruits and grain emblematic of abundance

co•rol•la \kə'rälə\ *n* : petals of a flower

cor•ol•lary \\'kórə,lerē\ *n, pl* **-lar•ies 1** : logical deduction **2** : consequence or result

co•ro•na \kə'rōnə\ *n* : shining ring around the sun seen during eclipses

cor•o•nary \\'kórə,nerē\ *adj* : relating to the heart or its blood vessels ～ *n* **1** : thrombosis of an artery supplying the heart **2** : heart attack

cor•o•na•tion \\,kórə'nāshən\ *n* : crowning of a monarch

cor•o•ner \\'kórənər\ *n* : public official who investigates causes of suspicious deaths

¹cor•po•ral \\'kórpərəl\ *adj* : bodily

²corporal *n* : noncommissioned officer ranking next below a sergeant

cor•po•ra•tion \\,kórpə'rāshən\ *n* : legal creation with the rights and liabilities of a person — **cor•po•rate** \\'kórpərət\ *adj*

cor•po•re•al \kór'pōrēəl\ *adj* : physical or material — **cor•po•re•al•ly** *adv*

corps \\'kōr\ *n, pl* **corps** \\'kōrz\ **1** : subdivision of a military force **2** : working group

corpse \\'kórps\ *n* : dead body

cor•pu•lence \\'kórpyələns\ *n* : obesity — **cor•pu•lent** \-lənt\ *adj*

cor•pus \\'kórpəs\ *n, pl* **-po•ra** \-pərə\ **1** : corpse **2** : body of writings

cor•pus•cle \\'kór,pəsəl\ *n* : blood cell

cor•ral \kə'ral\ *n* : enclosure for animals — **corral** *vb*

cor•rect \kə'rekt\ *vb* **1** : make right **2** : chastise ～ *adj* **1** : true or factual **2** : conforming to a standard — **cor•rec•tion** \-'rekshən\ *n* — **cor•rec•tive** \-'rektiv\ *adj* — **cor•rect•ly** *adv* — **cor•rect•ness** *n*

cor•re•late \\'kórə,lāt\ *vb* **-lat•ed; -lat•ing** : show a connection between — **cor•re•late** \-lət, -,lāt\ *n* — **cor•re•la•tion** \\,kórə'lāshən\ *n*

cor•rel•a•tive \kə'relətiv\ *adj* : regularly used together — **correlative** *n*

cor•re•spond \\,kórə'spänd\ *vb* **1** : match **2** : communicate by letter — **cor•re•spon•dence** \-'spändəns\ *n* — **cor•re•spond•ing•ly** \-'spändiŋlē\ *adv*

cor•re•spon•dent \-'spändənt\ *n* **1** : person one writes to **2** : reporter

cor•ri•dor \\'kórədər, -,dór\ *n* : passageway connecting rooms

cor•rob•o•rate \kə'räbə,rāt\ *vb* **-rat•ed; -rat•ing** : support with evidence — **cor•rob•o•ra•tion** \-,räbə'rāshən\ *n*

cor•rode \kə'rōd\ *vb* **-rod•ed; -rod•ing** : wear away by chemical action — **cor•ro•sion** \-'rōzhən\ *n* — **cor•ro•sive** \-'rōsiv\ *adj or n*

cor•ru•gate \\'kórə,gāt\ *vb* **-gat•ed; -gat•ing** : form into ridges and grooves — **cor•ru•gat•ed** *adj* — **cor•ru•ga•tion** \\,kórə'gāshən\ *n*

cor•rupt \kə'rəpt\ *vb* **1** : change from good to bad **2** : bribe ～ *adj* : morally debased — **cor•rupt•ible** *adj* — **cor•rup•tion** \-'rəpshən\ *n*

cor•sage \kór'säzh, -'säj\ *n* : bouquet worn by a woman

cor•set \\'kórsət\ *n* : woman's stiffened undergarment

cor•tege \kór'tezh, 'kór,-\ *n* : funeral procession

cor•tex \\'kór,teks\ *n, pl* **-ti•ces** \\'kórtə-,sēz\ *or* **-tex•es** : outer or covering layer of an organism or part (as the brain) — **cor•ti•cal** \\'kórtikəl\ *adj*

cor•ti•sone \\'kórtə,sōn, -zōn\ *n* : adrenal hormone

cos•met•ic \käz'metik\ *n* : beautifying preparation ～ *adj* : relating to beautifying

cos•mic \\'käzmik\ *adj* **1** : relating to the universe **2** : vast or grand

cos•mo•naut \\'käzmə,nót\ *n* : Soviet or Russian astronaut

cos•mo•pol•i•tan \\,käzmə'pälət°n\ *adj* : belonging to all the world — **cosmopolitan** *n*

cos•mos \\'käzməs, -,mōs, -,mäs\ *n* : universe

Cos•sack \\'käs,ak, -ək\ *n* : Russian cavalryman

cost \\'kóst\ *n* **1** : amount paid for something **2** : loss or penalty ～ *vb* **cost; cost•ing 1** : require so much in payment **2** : cause to pay, suffer, or lose — **cost•li•ness** \-lēnəs\ *n* — **cost•ly** \-lē\ *adj*

cos•tume \\'käs,tüm, -,tyüm\ *n* : clothing

co•sy \\'kōzē\ *var of* COZY

cot \\'kät\ *n* : small bed

cote \\'kōt, 'kät\ *n* : small shed or coop

co•te•rie \\'kōtə,rē, ,kōtə'-\ *n* : exclusive group of persons

co‧til‧lion \kō'tilyən\ *n* : formal ball

cot‧tage \'kätij\ *n* : small house

cot‧ton \'kät°n\ *n* : soft fibrous plant substance or thread or cloth made of it — **cot‧ton‧seed** *n* — **cot‧tony** *adj*

cot‧ton‧mouth *n* : poisonous snake

couch \'kaúch\ *vb* **1** : lie or place on a couch **2** : phrase ∼ *n* : bed or sofa

couch potato *n* : one who spends a great deal of time watching television

cou‧gar \'kügər, -ˌgär\ *n* : large tawny wild American cat

cough \'kòf\ *vb* : force air from the lungs with short sharp noises — **cough** *n*

could \'kúd\ *past of* CAN

coun‧cil \'kaúnsəl\ *n* **1** : assembly or meeting **2** : body of lawmakers — **coun‧cil‧lor, coun‧cil‧or** \-sələr\ *n* — **coun‧cil‧man** \-mən\ *n* — **coun‧cil‧wom‧an** *n*

coun‧sel \'kaúnsəl\ *n* **1** : advice **2** : deliberation together **3** *pl* **-sel** : lawyer ∼ *vb* **-seled** *or* **-selled;** **-sel‧ing** *or* **-sel‧ling** **1** : advise **2** : consult together — **coun‧sel‧or, coun‧sel‧lor** \-sələr\ *n*

¹count \'kaúnt\ *vb* **1** : name or indicate one by one to find the total number **2** : recite numbers in order **3** : rely **4** : be of value or account ∼ *n* **1** : act of counting or the total obtained by counting **2** : charge in an indictment — **count‧able** *adj*

²count *n* : European nobleman

coun‧te‧nance \'kaúnt°nəns\ *n* : face or facial expression ∼ *vb* **-nanced; -nanc‧ing** : allow or encourage

¹count‧er \'kaúntər\ *n* **1** : piece for reckoning or games **2** : surface over which business is transacted

²count‧er *n* : one that counts

³coun‧ter *vb* : oppose ∼ *adv* : in an opposite direction ∼ *n* : offsetting force or move ∼ *adj* : contrary

counter- *prefix* **1** : contrary or opposite **2** : opposing **3** : retaliatory

coun‧ter‧act *vb* : lessen the force of — **coun‧ter‧ac‧tive** *adj*

coun‧ter‧bal‧ance *n* : balancing influence or weight ∼ *vb* : oppose or balance

coun‧ter‧clock‧wise *adv or adj* : opposite to the way a clock's hands move

coun‧ter‧feit \'kaúntərˌfit\ *vb* **1** : copy in order to deceive **2** : pretend ∼ *adj* : spurious ∼ *n* : fraudulent copy — **coun‧ter‧feit‧er** *n*

coun‧ter‧mand \-ˌmand\ *vb* : supersede with a contrary order

coun‧ter‧pane \-ˌpān\ *n* : bedspread

coun‧ter‧part *n* : one that is similar or corresponds

coun‧ter‧point *n* : music with interwoven melodies

coun‧ter‧sign *n* : secret signal ∼ *vb* : add a confirming signature to

count‧ess \'kaúntəs\ *n* : wife or widow of a count or an earl or a woman holding that rank in her own right

---

List of self-explanatory words with the prefix *counter-*

counteraccusation
counteraggression
counterargue
counterassault
counterattack
counterbid
counterblockade
counterblow
countercampaign
countercharge
counterclaim
countercomplaint
countercoup
countercriticism
counterdemand
counterdemonstration
counterdemonstrator
countereffort

counterevidence
counterguerrilla
counterinflationary
counterinfluence
countermeasure
countermove
countermovement
counteroffer
counterpetition
counterploy
counterpower
counterpressure
counterpropaganda
counterproposal
counterprotest
counterquestion
counterraid
counterrally

counterreform
counterresponse
counterretaliation
counterrevolution
counterrevolutionary
counterstrategy
counterstyle
countersue
countersuggestion
countersuit
countertendency
counterterror
counterterrorism
counterterrorist
counterthreat
counterthrust
countertrend

count·less \-ləs\ *adj* : too many to be numbered

coun·try \'kəntrē\ *n, pl* **-tries 1** : nation **2** : rural area ~ *adj* : rural — **coun·try·man** \-mən\ *n*

coun·try·side *n* : rural area or its people

coun·ty \'kaúntē\ *n, pl* **-ties** : local government division esp. of a state

coup \'kü\ *n, pl* **coups** \'küz\ **1** : brilliant sudden action or plan **2** : sudden overthrow of a government

coupe \'küp\ *n* : 2-door automobile with an enclosed body

cou·ple \'kəpəl\ *vb* **-pled; -pling** : link together ~ *n* **1** : pair **2** : two persons closely associated or married

cou·pling \'kəpliŋ\ *n* : connecting device

cou·pon \'kü,pän, 'kyü-\ *n* : certificate redeemable for goods or a cash discount

cour·age \'kərij\ *n* : ability to conquer fear or despair — **cou·ra·geous** \kə'rājəs\ *adj*

cou·ri·er \'kúrēər, 'kərē-\ *n* : messenger

course \'kōrs\ *n* **1** : progress **2** : ground over which something moves **3** : part of a meal served at one time **4** : method of procedure **5** : subject taught in a series of classes ~ *vb* **coursed; cours·ing 1** : hunt with dogs **2** : run speedily — **of course** : as might be expected

court \'kōrt\ *n* **1** : residence of a sovereign **2** : sovereign and his or her officials and advisers **3** : area enclosed by a building **4** : space marked for playing a game **5** : place where justice is administered ~ *vb* : woo — **court·house** *n* — **court·room** *n* — **court·ship** \-,ship\ *n*

cour·te·ous \'kərtēəs\ *adj* : showing politeness and respect for others — **cour·te·ous·ly** *adv*

cour·te·san \'kōrtəzən, 'kərt-\ *n* : prostitute

cour·te·sy \'kərtəsē\ *n, pl* -sies : courteous behavior

court·ier \'kōrtēər, 'kōrtyər\ *n* : person in attendance at a royal court

court·ly \'kōrtlē\ *adj* **-li·er; -est** : polite or elegant — **court·li·ness** *n*

court–mar·tial *n, pl* **courts–martial** : military trial court — **court–martial** *vb*

court·yard *n* : enclosure open to the sky that is attached to a house

cous·in \'kəz³n\ *n* : child of one's uncle or aunt

cove \'kōv\ *n* : sheltered inlet or bay

co·ven \'kəvən\ *n* : group of witches

cov·e·nant \'kəvənənt\ *n* : binding agreement — **cov·e·nant** \-nənt, -,nant\ *vb*

cov·er \'kəvər\ *vb* **1** : place something over or upon **2** : protect or hide **3** : include or deal with ~ *n* : something that covers — **cov·er·age** \-ərij\ *n*

cov·er·let \-lət\ *n* : bedspread

co·vert \'kō,vərt, 'kəvərt\ *adj* : secret ~ \'kəvərt, 'kō-\ *n* : thicket that shelters animals

cov·et \'kəvət\ *vb* : desire enviously — **cov·et·ous** *adj*

cov·ey \'kəvē\ *n, pl* **-eys 1** : bird with her young **2** : small flock (as of quail)

¹cow \'kaú\ *n* : large adult female animal (as of cattle) — **cow·hide** *n*

²cow *vb* : intimidate

cow·ard \'kaúərd\ *n* : one who lacks courage — **cow·ard·ice** \-əs\ *n* — **cow·ard·ly** *adv or adj*

cow·boy *n* : a mounted ranch hand who tends cattle

cow·er \'kaúər\ *vb* : shrink from fear or cold

cow·girl *n* : woman ranch hand who tends cattle

cowl \'kaúl\ *n* : monk's hood

cow·lick \'kaú,lik\ *n* : turned-up tuft of hair that resists control

cow·slip \-,slip\ *n* : yellow flower

cox·swain \'käkən, -,swān\ *n* : person who steers a boat

coy \'kói\ *adj* : shy or pretending shyness

coy·ote \'kī,ōt, kī'ōtē\ *n, pl* **coy·otes** *or* **coyote** : small No. American wolf

coz·en \'kəz³n\ *vb* : cheat

co·zy \'kōzē\ *adj* **-zi·er; -est** : snug

crab \'krab\ *n* : short broad shellfish with pincers

crab·by \'krabē\ *adj* **-bi·er; -est** : cross

¹crack \'krak\ *vb* **1** : break with a sharp sound **2** : fail in tone **3** : break without completely separating ~ *n* **1** : sudden sharp noise **2** : witty remark **3** : narrow break **4** : sharp blow **5** : try

²crack *adj* : extremely proficient

crack·down *n* : disciplinary action — **crack down** *vb*

crack·er \-ər\ *n* : thin crisp bakery product

crack·le \'krakəl\ *vb* -led; -ling 1 : make snapping noises 2 : develop fine cracks in a surface — **crackle** *n*

crack·pot \'krak,pät\ *n* : eccentric

crack–up *n* : crash

cra·dle \'krādʰl\ *n* : baby's bed ~ *vb* -dled; -dling 1 : place in a cradle 2 : hold securely

craft \'kraft\ *n* 1 : occupation requiring special skill 2 : craftiness 3 *pl usu* **craft** : structure designed to provide transportation 4 *pl usu* **craft** : small boat — **crafts·man** \'kraftsmən\ *n* — **crafts·man·ship** \-,ship\ *n*

crafty \'kraftē\ *adj* **craft·i·er; -est** : sly — **craft·i·ness** *n*

crag \'krag\ *n* : steep cliff — **crag·gy** \-ē\ *adj*

cram \'kram\ *vb* -mm- 1 : eat greedily 2 : pack in tight 3 : study intensely for a test

cramp \'kramp\ *n* 1 : sudden painful contraction of muscle 2 *pl* : sharp abdominal pains ~ *vb* 1 : affect with cramp 2 : restrain

cran·ber·ry \'kran,berē\ *n* : red acid berry of a trailing plant

crane \'krān\ *n* 1 : tall wading bird 2 : machine for lifting heavy objects ~ *vb* craned; cran·ing : stretch one's neck to see

cra·ni·um \'krānēəm\ *n, pl* -ni·ums *or* -nia \-nēə\ : skull — **cra·ni·al** \-əl\ *adj*

crank \'kraŋk\ *n* 1 : bent lever turned to operate a machine 2 : eccentric ~ *vb* : start or operate by turning a crank

cranky \'kraŋkē\ *adj* **crank·i·er; -est** : irritable

cran·ny \'kranē\ *n, pl* -nies : crevice

craps \'kraps\ *n* : dice game

crash \'krash\ *vb* 1 : break noisily 2 : fall and hit something with noise and damage ~ *n* 1 : loud sound 2 : action of crashing 3 : failure

crass \'kras\ *adj* : crude or unfeeling

crate \'krāt\ *n* : wooden shipping container — **crate** *vb*

cra·ter \'krātər\ *n* : volcanic depression

cra·vat \krə'vat\ *n* : necktie

crave \'krāv\ *vb* craved; crav·ing : long for — **crav·ing** *n*

cra·ven \'krāvən\ *adj* : cowardly — **cra·ven** *n*

craw·fish \'krȯ,fish\ *n* : crayfish

crawl \'krȯl\ *vb* 1 : move slowly (as by drawing the body along the ground) 2 : swarm with creeping things ~ *n* : very slow pace

cray·fish \'krā,fish\ *n* : lobsterlike freshwater crustacean

cray·on \'krā,än, -ən\ *n* : stick of chalk or wax used for drawing or coloring — **crayon** *vb*

craze \'krāz\ *vb* crazed; craz·ing : make or become insane ~ *n* : fad

cra·zy \'krāzē\ *adj* **cra·zi·er; -est** 1 : mentally disordered 2 : wildly impractical — **cra·zi·ly** *adv* — **cra·zi·ness** *n*

creak \'krēk\ *vb or n* : squeak — **creaky** *adj*

cream \'krēm\ *n* 1 : yellowish fat-rich part of milk 2 : thick smooth sauce, confection, or cosmetic 3 : choicest part ~ *vb* : beat into creamy consistency — **creamy** *adj*

cream·ery \-ərē\ *n, pl* -er·ies : place where butter and cheese are made

crease \'krēs\ *n* : line made by folding — **crease** *vb*

cre·ate \krē'āt\ *vb* -at·ed; -at·ing : bring into being — **cre·ation** \krē'āshən\ *n* — **cre·ative** \-'ātiv\ *adj* — **cre·ativ·i·ty** \,krēā'tivətē\ *n* — **cre·a·tor** \krē'ātər\ *n*

crea·ture \'krēchər\ *n* : lower animal or human being

cre·dence \'krēdʰns\ *n* : belief

cre·den·tials \kri'denchəlz\ *n pl* : evidence of qualifications or authority

cred·i·ble \'kredəbəl\ *adj* : believable — **cred·i·bil·i·ty** \,kredə'bilətē\ *n*

cred·it \'kredət\ *n* 1 : balance in a person's favor 2 : time given to pay for goods 3 : belief 4 : esteem 5 : source of honor ~ *vb* 1 : believe 2 : give credit to

cred·it·able \-əbəl\ *adj* : worthy of esteem or praise — **cred·it·ably** \-əblē\ *adv*

cred·i·tor \-ər\ *n* : person to whom money is owed

cred·u·lous \'krejələs\ *adj* : easily convinced — **cre·du·li·ty** \kri'dülətē, -'dyü-\ *n*

creed \'krēd\ *n* : statement of essential beliefs

creek \'krēk, 'krik\ *n* : small stream

creel \'krēl\ *n* : basket for carrying fish

creep \'krēp\ *vb* crept \'krept\; creep·ing 1 : crawl 2 : grow over

a surface like ivy — **creep** *n* —
creep•er *n*
cre•mate \'krē,māt\ *vb* **-mat•ed;**
-mat•ing : burn up (a corpse) — **cre-
ma•tion** \kri'māshən\ *n* — **cre•ma-
to•ry** \'krēmə,tōrē, 'krem-\ *n*
cre•o•sote \'krēə,sōt\ *n* : oily wood
preservative
crepe, crêpe \'krāp\ *n* : light crinkled
fabric
cre•scen•do \krə'shendō\ *adv or adj*
: growing louder — **crescendo** *n*
cres•cent \'kres°nt\ *n* : shape of the
moon between new moon and first
quarter
crest \'krest\ *n* **1** : tuft on a bird's head
2 : top of a hill or wave **3** : part of a
coat of arms ~ *vb* : rise to a crest —
crest•ed \-təd\ *adj*
crest•fall•en *adj* : sad
cre•tin \'krēt°n\ *n* : stupid person
cre•vasse \kri'vas\ *n* : deep fissure esp.
in a glacier
crev•ice \'krevəs\ *n* : narrow fissure
crew \'krü\ *n* : body of workers (as on
a ship) — **crew•man** \-mən\ *n*
crib \'krib\ *n* **1** : manger **2** : grain
storage bin **3** : baby's bed ~ *vb* **-bb-**
: put in a crib
crib•bage \'kribij\ *n* : card game
scored by moving pegs on a board
(**cribbage board**)
crick \'krik\ *n* : muscle spasm
¹crick•et \'krikət\ *n* : insect noted for
the chirping of the male
²cricket *n* : bat and ball game played on a
field with wickets
cri•er \'krīər\ *n* : one who calls out an-
nouncements
crime \'krīm\ *n* : serious violation of
law
crim•i•nal \'krimən°l\ *adj* : relating to
or being a crime or its punishment ~
n : one who commits a crime
crimp \'krimp\ *vb* : cause to become
crinkled, wavy, or bent — **crimp** *n*
crim•son \'krimzən\ *n* : deep red —
crimson *adj*
cringe \'krinj\ *vb* **cringed; cring•ing**
: shrink in fear
crin•kle \'krinkəl\ *vb* **-kled; -kling**
: wrinkle — **crinkle** *n* — **crin•kly**
\-klē\ *adj*
crin•o•line \'krin°lən\ *n* **1** : stiff cloth
2 : full stiff skirt or petticoat
crip•ple \'kripəl\ *n* : disabled person
~ *vb* **-pled; -pling** : disable

cri•sis \'krīsəs\ *n, pl* **cri•ses** \-,sēz\
: decisive or critical moment
crisp \'krisp\ *adj* **1** : easily crumbled
2 : firm and fresh **3** : lively **4** : invigorating — **crisp** *vb* — **crisp•ly** *adv*
— **crisp•ness** *n* — **crispy** *adj*
criss•cross \'kris,krós\ *n* : pattern of
crossed lines ~ *vb* : mark with or follow a crisscross
cri•te•ri•on \krī'tirēən\ *n, pl* **-ria** \-ēə\
: standard
crit•ic \'kritik\ *n* : judge of literary or
artistic works
crit•i•cal \-ikəl\ *adj* **1** : inclined to criticize **2** : being a crisis **3** : relating to
criticism or critics — **crit•i•cal•ly**
\-iklē\ *adv*
crit•i•cize \'kritə,sīz\ *vb* **-cized; -ciz-**
ing 1 : judge as a critic **2** : find fault
— **crit•i•cism** \-ə,sizəm\ *n*
cri•tique \krə'tēk\ *n* : critical estimate
croak \'krōk\ *n* : hoarse harsh cry (as
of a frog) — **croak** *vb*
cro•chet \krō'shā\ *n* : needlework
done with a hooked needle — **cro-
chet** *vb*
crock \'kräk\ *n* : thick earthenware pot
or jar — **crock•ery** \-ərē\ *n*
croc•o•dile \'kräkə,dīl\ *n* : large reptile of tropical waters
cro•cus \'krōkəs\ *n, pl* **-cus•es** : herb
with spring flowers
crone \'krōn\ *n* : ugly old woman
cro•ny \'krōnē\ *n, pl* **-nies** : chum
crook \'krúk\ *n* **1** : bent or curved tool
or part **2** : thief ~ *vb* : curve sharply
crook•ed \'krúkəd\ *adj* **1** : bent **2**
: dishonest — **crook•ed•ness** *n*
croon \'krün\ *vb* : sing softly —
croon•er *n*
crop \'kräp\ *n* **1** : pouch in the throat
of a bird or insect **2** : short riding
whip **3** : something that can be har-
vested ~ *vb* **-pp- 1** : trim **2** : appear
unexpectedly — used with *up*
cro•quet \krō'kā\ *n* : lawn game of
driving balls through wickets
cro•quette \-'ket\ *n* : mass of minced
food deep-fried
cro•sier \'krōzhər\ *n* : bishop's staff
cross \'krós\ *n* **1** : figure or structure
consisting of an upright and a cross
piece **2** : interbreeding of unlike
strains ~ *vb* **1** : intersect **2** : cancel
3 : go or extend across **4** : interbreed
~ *adj* **1** : going across **2** : contrary
3 : marked by bad temper — **crossing** *n* — **cross•ly** *adv*

cross•bow \-,bō\ *n* : short bow mounted on a rifle stock

cross•breed *vb* **-bred; -breed•ing** : hybridize

cross–ex•am•ine *vb* : question about earlier testimony — **cross–ex•am•i•na•tion** *n*

cross–eyed *adj* : having the eye turned toward the nose

cross–re•fer *vb* : refer to another place (as in a book) — **cross–ref•er•ence** *n*

cross•roads *n* : place where 2 roads cross

cross section *n* : representative portion

cross•walk *n* : path for pedestrians crossing a street

cross•ways *adv* : crosswise

cross–wise \-,wīz\ *adv* : so as to cross something — **crosswise** *adj*

crotch \'krăch\ *n* : angle formed by the parting of 2 legs or branches

crotch•ety \'krăchətē\ *adj* : cranky, ill= natured

crouch \'kraùch\ *vb* : stoop over — **crouch** *n*

croup \'krüp\ *n* : laryngitis of infants

crou•ton \'krü,tän\ *n* : bit of toast

¹crow \'krō\ *n* : large glossy black bird

²crow *vb* **1** : make the loud sound of the cock **2** : gloat ~ *n* : cry of the cock

crow•bar *n* : metal bar used as a pry or lever

crowd \'kraùd\ *vb* : collect or cram together ~ *n* : large number of people

crown \'kraùn\ *n* **1** : wreath of honor or victory **2** : royal headdress **3** : top or highest part ~ *vb* **1** : place a crown on **2** : honor — **crowned** \'kraùnd\ *adj*

cru•cial \'krüshəl\ *adj* : vitally important

cru•ci•ble \'krüsəbəl\ *n* : heat-resisting container

cru•ci•fix \'krüsə,fiks\ *n* : representation of Christ on the cross

cru•ci•fix•ion \,krüsə'fikshən\ *n* : act of crucifying

cru•ci•fy \'krüsə,fī\ *vb* **-fied; -fy•ing 1** : put to death on a cross **2** : persecute

crude \'krüd\ *adj* **crud•er; -est 1** : not refined **2** : lacking grace or elegance ~ *n* : unrefined petroleum — **crude•ly** *adv* — **cru•di•ty** \-ətē\ *n*

cru•el \'krüəl\ *adj* **-el•er** *or* **-el•ler; -el•est** *or* **-el•lest** : causing suffering to others — **cru•el•ly** \-ē\ *adv* — **cru•el•ty** \tē\ *n*

cru•et \'krüət\ *n* : bottle for salad dressings

cruise \'krüz\ *vb* **cruised; cruis•ing 1** : sail to several ports **2** : travel at the most efficient speed — **cruise** *n*

cruis•er \'krüzər\ *n* **1** : warship **2** : police car

crumb \'krəm\ *n* : small fragment

crum•ble \'krəmbəl\ *vb* **-bled; -bling** : break into small pieces — **crum•bly** \-blē\ *adj*

crum•ple \'krəmpəl\ *vb* **-pled; -pling 1** : crush together **2** : collapse

crunch \'krənch\ *vb* : chew or press with a crushing noise ~ *n* : crunching sound — **crunchy** *adj*

cru•sade \krü'sād\ *n* **1** *cap* : medieval Christian expedition to the Holy Land **2** : reform movement — **crusade** *vb* — **cru•sad•er** *n*

crush \'krəsh\ *vb* **1** : squeeze out of shape **2** : grind or pound to bits **3** : suppress ~ *n* **1** : severe crowding **2** : infatuation

crust \'krəst\ *n* **1** : hard outer part of bread or a pie **2** : hard surface layer — **crust•al** *adj* — **crusty** *adj*

crus•ta•cean \,krəs'tāshən\ *n* : aquatic arthropod having a firm shell

crutch \'krəch\ *n* : support for use by the disabled in walking

crux \'krəks, 'krüks\ *n, pl* **crux•es 1** : hard problem **2** : crucial point

cry \'krī\ *vb* **cried; cry•ing 1** : call out **2** : weep ~ *n, pl* **cries 1** : shout **2** : fit of weeping **3** : characteristic sound of an animal

crypt \'kript\ *n* : underground chamber

cryp•tic \'kriptik\ *adj* : enigmatic

cryp•tog•ra•phy \krip'tägrəfē\ *n* : coding and decoding of messages — **cryp•tog•ra•pher** \-fər\ *n*

crys•tal \'krist³l\ *n* **1** : transparent quartz **2** : something (as glass) like crystal **3** : body formed by solidification that has a regular repeating atomic arrangement — **crys•tal•line** \-tələn\ *adj*

crys•tal•ize \-tə,līz\ *vb* **-lized; -liz•ing** : form crystals or a definite shape — **crys•tal•li•za•tion** \,kristələ'zāshən\ *n*

cub \'kəb\ *n* : young animal

cub•by•hole \'kəbē,hōl\ *n* : small confined space

cube \'kyüb\ *n* **1** : solid having 6 equal square sides **2** : product obtained by taking a number 3 times as a factor

~ *vb* **cubed; cub·ing 1** : raise to the 3d power **2** : form into a cube **3** : cut into cubes — **cu·bic** \'kyübik\ *adj*

cu·bi·cle \-bikəl\ *n* : small room

cu·bit \'kyübət\ *n* : ancient unit of length equal to about 18 inches

cuck·old \'kəkəld, 'kùk-\ *n* : man whose wife is unfaithful — **cuckold** *vb*

cuck·oo \'kükü, 'kùk-\ *n, pl* **-oos** : brown European bird **~** *adj* : silly

cu·cum·ber \'kyü,kəmbər\ *n* : fleshy fruit related to the gourds

cud \'kəd\ *n* : food chewed again by ruminating animals

cud·dle \'kədᵊl\ *vb* **-dled; -dling** : lie close

cud·gel \'kəjəl\ *n or vb* : club

¹cue \'kyü\ *n* : signal — **cue** *vb*

²cue *n* : stick used in pool

¹cuff \'kəf\ *n* **1** : part of a sleeve encircling the wrist **2** : folded trouser hem

²cuff *vb or n* : slap

cui·sine \kwi'zēn\ *n* : manner of cooking

cu·li·nary \'kələ,nerē, 'kyülə-\ *adj* : of or relating to cookery

cull \'kəl\ *vb* : select

cul·mi·nate \'kəlmə,nāt\ *vb* **-nat·ed; -nat·ing** : rise to the highest point — **cul·mi·na·tion** \,kəlmə'nāshən\ *n*

cul·pa·ble \'kəlpəbəl\ *adj* : deserving blame

cul·prit \'kəlprət\ *n* : guilty person

cult \'kəlt\ *n* **1** : religious system **2** : faddish devotion — **cult·ist** *n*

cul·ti·vate \'kəltə,vāt\ *vb* **-vat·ed; -vat·ing 1** : prepare for crops **2** : foster the growth of **3** : refine — **cul·ti·va·tion** \,kəltə'vāshən\ *n*

cul·ture \'kəlchər\ *n* **1** : cultivation **2** : refinement of intellectual and artistic taste **3** : particular form or stage of civilization — **cul·tur·al** \'kəlchərəl\ *adj* — **cul·tured** \'kəlchərd\ *adj*

cul·vert \'kəlvərt\ *n* : drain crossing under a road or railroad

cum·ber·some \'kəmbərsəm\ *adj* : awkward to handle due to bulk

cu·mu·la·tive \'kyümyələtiv, -,lāt-\ *adj* : increasing by additions

cu·mu·lus \'kyümyələs\ *n, pl* **-li** \-,lī, -,lē\ : massive rounded cloud

cun·ning \'kəniŋ\ *adj* **1** : crafty **2** : clever **3** : appealing **~** *n* **1** : skill **2** : craftiness

cup \'kəp\ *n* **1** : small drinking vessel **2** : contents of a cup **3** : a half pint **~** *vb* **-pp-** : shape like a cup — **cup·ful** *n*

cup·board \'kəbərd\ *n* : small storage closet

cup·cake *n* : small cake

cu·pid·i·ty \kyù'pidətē\ *n, pl* **-ties** : excessive desire for money

cu·po·la \'kyüpələ, -,lō\ *n* : small rooftop structure

cur \'kər\ *n* : mongrel dog

cu·rate \'kyùrət\ *n* : member of the clergy — **cu·ra·cy** \-əsē\ *n*

cu·ra·tor \kyù'rātər\ *n* : one in charge of a museum or zoo

curb \'kərb\ *n* **1** : restraint **2** : raised edging along a street **~** *vb* : hold back

curd \'kərd\ *n* : coagulated milk

cur·dle \'kərdᵊl\ *vb* **-dled; -dling 1** : form curds **2** : sour

cure \'kyùr\ *n* **1** : recovery from disease **2** : remedy **~** *vb* **cured; cur·ing 1** : restore to health **2** : process for storage or use — **cur·able** *adj*

cur·few \'kər,fyü\ *n* : requirement to be off the streets at a set hour

cu·rio \'kyürē,ō\ *n, pl* **-ri·os** : rare or unusual article

cu·ri·ous \'kyürēəs\ *adj* **1** : eager to learn **2** : strange — **cu·ri·os·i·ty** \,kyürē'äsətē\ *n* — **cu·ri·ous·ness** *n*

curl \'kərl\ *vb* **1** : form into ringlets **2** : curve **~** *n* **1** : ringlet of hair **2** : something with a spiral form — **curl·er** *n* — **curly** *adj*

cur·lew \'kərlü, -,lyü\ *n, pl* **-lews** *or* **-lew** : long-legged brownish bird

curli·cue \'kərli,kyü\ *n* : fanciful curve

cur·rant \'kərənt\ *n* **1** : small seedless raisin **2** : berry of a shrub

cur·ren·cy \'kərənsē\ *n, pl* **-cies 1** : general use or acceptance **2** : money

cur·rent \'kərənt\ *adj* : occurring in or belonging to the present **~** *n* **1** : swiftest part of a stream **2** : flow of electricity

cur·ric·u·lum \kə'rikyələm\ *n, pl* **-la** \-lə\ : course of study

¹cur·ry \'kərē\ *vb* **-ried; -ry·ing** : brush (a horse) with a wire brush (**cur·ry·comb** \-,kōm\) — **curry fa·vor** : seek favor by flattery

²curry *n, pl* **-ries** : blend of pungent spices or a food seasoned with this

curse \\'kərs\ *n* **1** : a calling down of evil or harm upon one **2** : affliction ~ *vb* **cursed; curs•ing 1** : call down injury upon **2** : swear at **3** : afflict

cur•sor \\'kərsər\ *n* : indicator on a computer screen

cur•so•ry \\'kərsərē\ *adj* : hastily done

curt \\'kərt\ *adj* : rudely abrupt — **curt•ly** *adv* — **curt•ness** *n*

cur•tail \kər'tāl\ *vb* : shorten — **curtail•ment** *n*

cur•tain \\'kərtᵊn\ *n* : hanging screen that can be drawn back or raised — **curtain** *vb*

curt•sy, curt•sey \\'kərtsē\ *n, pl* **-sies** *or* **-seys** : courteous bow made by bending the knees — **curtsy, curtsey** *vb*

cur•va•ture \\'kərvə,chủr\ *n* : amount or state of curving

curve \\'kərv\ *vb* **curved; curv•ing** : bend from a straight line or course ~ *n* **1** : a bending without angles **2** : something curved

cush•ion \\'kủshən\ *n* **1** : soft pillow **2** : something that eases or protects ~ *vb* **1** : provide with a cushion **2** : soften the force of

cusp \\'kəsp\ *n* : pointed end

cus•pid \\'kəspəd\ *n* : a canine tooth

cus•pi•dor \\'kəspə,dȯr\ *n* : spittoon

cus•tard \\'kəstərd\ *n* : sweetened cooked mixture of milk and eggs

cus•to•dy \\'kəstədē\ *n, pl* **-dies** : immediate care or charge — **cus•to•di•al** \,kəs'tōdēəl\ *adj* — **cus•to•di•an** \-dēən\ *n*

cus•tom \\'kəstəm\ *n* **1** : habitual course of action **2** *pl* : import taxes ~ *adj* : made to personal order — **cus•tom•ar•i•ly** \,kəstə'merəlē\ *adv* — **cus•tom•ary** \\'kəstə,merē\ *adj* — **custom–built** *adj* — **cus•tom–made** *adj*

cus•tom•er \\'kəstəmər\ *n* : buyer

cut \\'kət\ *vb* **cut; cut•ting 1** : penetrate or divide with a sharp edge **2** : experience the growth of (a tooth) through the gum **3** : shorten **4** : remove by severing **5** : intersect ~ *n* **1** : something separated by cutting **2** : reduction — **cut in** *vb* : thrust oneself between others

cu•ta•ne•ous \kyủ'tānēəs\ *adj* : relating to the skin

cute \\'kyủt\ *adj* **cut•er; -est** : pretty

cu•ti•cle \\'kyủtikəl\ *n* : outer layer (as of skin)

cut•lass \\'kətləs\ *n* : short heavy curved sword

cut•lery \-lərē\ *n* : cutting utensils

cut•let \-lət\ *n* : slice of meat

cut•ter \\'kətər\ *n* **1** : tool or machine for cutting **2** : small armed motorboat **3** : light sleigh

cut•throat *n* : murderer ~ *adj* : ruthless

-cy \sē\ *n suffix* **1** : action or practice **2** : rank or office **3** : body **4** : state or quality

cy•a•nide \\'sīə,nīd, -nəd\ *n* : poisonous chemical salt

cy•ber- *comb form* : computer : computer network

cy•ber•space \\'sībər,spās\ *n* : online world of the Internet

cy•cle \\'sīkəl, 4 also 'sikəl\ *n* **1** : period of time for a series of repeated events **2** : recurring round of events **3** : long period of time **4** : bicycle or motorcycle ~ *vb* **-cled; -cling** : ride a cycle — **cy•clic** \\'sīklik, 'sik-\, **cy•cli•cal** \-əl\ *adj* — **cy•clist** \\'sīklist, 'sik-\ *n*

cy•clone \\'sī,klōn\ *n* : tornado — **cy•clon•ic** \sī'klänik\ *adj*

cy•clo•pe•dia, cy•clo•pae•dia \,sīklə'pēdēə\ *n* : encyclopedia

cyl•in•der \\'siləndər\ *n* **1** : long round body or figure **2** : rotating chamber in a revolver **3** : piston chamber in an engine — **cy•lin•dri•cal** \sə'lindrikəl\ *adj*

cym•bal \\'simbəl\ *n* : one of 2 concave brass plates clashed together

cyn•ic \\'sinik\ *n* : one who attributes all actions to selfish motives — **cyn•i•cal** \-ikəl\ *adj* — **cyn•i•cism** \-ə,sizəm\ *n*

cy•no•sure \\'sīnə,shủur, 'sin-\ *n* : center of attraction

cy•press \\'sīprəs\ *n* : evergreen tree related to the pines

cyst \\'sist\ *n* : abnormal bodily sac — **cys•tic** \\'sistik\ *adj*

czar \\'zär\ *n* : ruler of Russia until 1917 — **czar•ist** *n or adj*

D

d \'dē\ *n, pl* **d's** *or* **ds** \'dēz\ : 4th letter of the alphabet

¹dab \'dab\ *n* : gentle touch or stroke ∼ *vb* **-bb-** : touch or apply lightly

²dab *n* : small amount

dab•ble \'dabəl\ *vb* **-bled; -bling 1** : splash **2** : work without serious effort — **dab•bler** \-blər\ *n*

dachs•hund \'däks,hunt\ *n* : small dog with a long body and short legs

dad \'dad\ *n* : father

dad•dy \'dadē\ *n, pl* **-dies** : father

daf•fo•dil \'dafə,dil\ *n* : narcissus with trumpetlike flowers

daft \'daft\ *adj* : foolish — **daft•ness** *n*

dag•ger \'dagər\ *n* : knife for stabbing

dahl•ia \'dalyə, 'däl-\ *n* : tuberous herb with showy flowers

dai•ly \'dālē\ *adj* **1** : occurring, done, or used every day or every weekday **2** : computed in terms of one day ∼ *n, pl* **-lies** : daily newspaper — **daily** *adv*

dain•ty \'dāntē\ *n, pl* **-ties** : something delicious ∼ *adj* **-ti•er; -est** : delicately pretty — **dain•ti•ly** *adv* — **dain•ti•ness** *n*

dairy \'darē\ *n, pl* **-ies** : farm that produces or company that processes milk — **dairy•maid** *n* — **dairy•man** \-mən, -,man\ *n*

da•is \'dāəs\ *n* : raised platform (as for a speaker)

dai•sy \'dāzē\ *n, pl* **-sies** : tall leafy-stemmed plant bearing showy flowers

dale \'dāl\ *n* : valley

dal•ly \'dalē\ *vb* **-lied; -ly•ing 1** : flirt **2** : dawdle — **dal•li•ance** \-əns\ *n*

dal•ma•tian \dal'māshən\ *n* : large dog having a spotted white coat

¹dam \'dam\ *n* : female parent of a domestic animal

²dam *n* : barrier to hold back water — **dam** *vb*

dam•age \'damij\ *n* **1** : loss or harm due to injury **2** *pl* : compensation for loss or injury ∼ *vb* **-aged; -ag•ing** : do damage to

dam•ask \'daməsk\ *n* : firm lustrous figured fabric

dame \'dām\ *n* : woman of rank or authority

damn \'dam\ *vb* **1** : condemn to hell **2** : curse — **dam•na•ble** \-nəbəl\ *adj* — **dam•na•tion** \dam'nāshən\ *n* — **damned** *adj*

damp \'damp\ *n* : moisture ∼ *vb* **1** : reduce the draft in **2** : restrain **3** : moisten ∼ *adj* : moist — **damp•ness** *n*

damp•en \'dampən\ *vb* **1** : diminish in activity or vigor **2** : make or become damp

damp•er \'dampər\ *n* : movable plate to regulate a flue draft

dam•sel \'damzəl\ *n* : young woman

dance \'dans\ *vb* **danced; danc•ing** : move rhythmically to music ∼ *n* : act of dancing or a gathering for dancing — **danc•er** *n*

dan•de•li•on \'dand³l,īən\ *n* : common yellow-flowered herb

dan•der \'dandər\ *n* : temper

dan•druff \'dandrəf\ *n* : whitish thin dry scales of skin on the scalp

dan•dy \'dandē\ *n, pl* **-dies 1** : man too concerned with clothes **2** : something excellent ∼ *adj* **-di•er; -est** : very good

dan•ger \'dānjər\ *n* **1** : exposure to injury or evil **2** : something that may cause injury — **dan•ger•ous** \'dānjərəs\ *adj*

dan•gle \'daŋgəl\ *vb* **-gled; -gling 1** : hang and swing freely **2** : be left without support or connection **3** : allow or cause to hang **4** : offer as an inducement

dank \'daŋk\ *adj* : unpleasantly damp

dap•per \'dapər\ *adj* : neat and stylishly dressed

dap•ple \'dapəl\ *vb* **-pled; -pling** : mark with colored spots

dare \'dar\ *vb* **dared; dar•ing 1** : have sufficient courage **2** : urge or provoke to contend — **dare** *n* — **dar•ing** \'dariŋ\ *n or adj*

dare•dev•il *n* : recklessly bold person

dark \'därk\ *adj* **1** : having little or no light **2** : not light in color **3** : gloomy

~ *n* : absence of light — **dark•en** \-ən\ *vb* — **dark•ly** *adv* — **dark-ness** *n*

dar•ling \'därliŋ\ *n* **1** : beloved **2** : favorite **~** *adj* **1** : dearly loved **2** : very pleasing

darn \'därn\ *vb* : mend with interlacing stitches — **darn•er** *n*

dart \'därt\ *n* **1** : small pointed missile **2** *pl* : game of throwing darts at a target **3** : tapering fold in a garment **4** : quick movement **~** *vb* : move suddenly or rapidly

dash \'dash\ *vb* **1** : smash **2** : knock or hurl violently **3** : ruin **4** : perform or finish hastily **5** : move quickly **~** *n* **1** : sudden burst, splash, or stroke **2** : punctuation mark — **3** : tiny amount **4** : showiness or liveliness **5** : sudden rush **6** : short race **7** : dashboard

dash•board *n* : instrument panel

dash•ing \'dashiŋ\ *adj* : dapper and charming

das•tard \'dastərd\ *n* : one who sneakingly commits malicious acts

das•tard•ly \-lē\ *adj* : base or malicious

da•ta \'dātə, 'dat-, 'dät-\ *n sing or pl* : factual information

da•ta•base \-,bās\ *n* : data organized for computer search

¹date \'dāt\ *n* : edible fruit of a palm

²date *n* **1** : day, month, or year when something is done or made **2** : historical time period **3** : social engagement or the person one goes out with **~** *vb* **dat•ed; dat•ing 1** : determine or record the date of **2** : have a date with **3** : originate — **to date** : up to now

dat•ed \-əd\ *adj* : old-fashioned

da•tum \'dātəm, 'dat-, 'dät-\ *n, pl* **-ta** \-ə\ *or* **-tums** : piece of data

daub \'dob\ *vb* : smear **~** *n* : something daubed on — **daub•er** *n*

daugh•ter \'dotər\ *n* : human female offspring

daugh•ter–in–law *n, pl* **daughters–in–law** : wife of one's son

daunt \'dont\ *vb* : lessen the courage of

daunt•less \-ləs\ *adj* : fearless

dav•en•port \'davən,port\ *n* : sofa

daw•dle \'dod°l\ *vb* **-dled; -dling 1** : waste time **2** : loiter

dawn \'don\ *vb* **1** : grow light as the sun rises **2** : begin to appear, develop, or be understood **~** *n* : first appearance (as of daylight)

day \'dā\ *n* **1** : period of light between one night and the next **2** : 24 hours **3** : specified date **4** : particular time or age **5** : period of work for a day — **day•light** *n* — **day•time** *n*

day•break *n* : dawn

day•dream *n* : fantasy of wish fulfillment — **daydream** *vb*

daylight saving time *n* : time one hour ahead of standard time

daze \'dāz\ *vb* **dazed; daz•ing 1** : stun by a blow **2** : dazzle — **daze** *n*

daz•zle \'dazəl\ *vb* **-zled; -zling 1** : overpower with light **2** : impress greatly — **dazzle** *n*

DDT \,dē,dē'tē\ *n* : long-lasting insecticide

dea•con \'dēkən\ *n* : subordinate church officer

dea•con•ess \'dēkənəs\ *n* : woman who assists in church ministry

dead \'ded\ *adj* **1** : lifeless **2** : unresponsive or inactive **3** : exhausted **4** : obsolete **5** : precise **~** *n, pl* **dead 1** : one that is dead — usu. with *the* **2** : most lifeless time **~** *adv* **1** : completely **2** : directly — **dead•en** \'ded°n\ *vb*

dead•beat *n* : one who will not pay debts

dead end *n* : end of a street with no exit — **dead–end** *adj*

dead heat *n* : tie in a contest

dead•line *n* : time by which something must be finished

dead•lock *n* : struggle that neither side can win — **deadlock** *vb*

dead•ly \'dedlē\ *adj* **-li•er; -est 1** : capable of causing death **2** : very accurate **3** : fatal to spiritual progress **4** : suggestive of death **5** : very great **~** *adv* : extremely — **dead•li•ness** *n*

dead•pan *adj* : expressionless — **deadpan** *n or vb or adv*

dead•wood *n* : something useless

deaf \'def\ *adj* : unable or unwilling to hear — **deaf•en** \-ən\ *vb* — **deaf-ness** *n*

deaf–mute *n* : deaf person unable to speak

deal \'dēl\ *n* **1** : indefinite quantity **2** : distribution of playing cards **3** : negotiation or agreement **4** : treatment received **5** : bargain **~** *vb* **dealt** \'delt\; **deal•ing** \'dēliŋ\ **1** : distribute playing cards **2** : be concerned with **3** : administer or deliver **4** : take action **5** : sell **6** : reach a state of acceptance — **deal•er** *n* — **deal•ing** *n*

dean \'dēn\ *n* **1** : head of a group of clergy members **2** : university or school administrator **3** : senior member

dear \'dir\ *adj* **1** : highly valued or loved **2** : expensive ~ *n* : loved one — **dear•ly** *adv* — **dear•ness** *n*

dearth \'dərth\ *n* : scarcity

death \'deth\ *n* **1** : end of life **2** : cause of loss of life **3** : state of being dead **4** : destruction or extinction — **death•less** *adj* — **death•ly** *adj or adv*

de•ba•cle \di'bäkəl, -'bakəl\ *n* : disaster or fiasco

de•bar \di'bär\ *vb* : bar from something

de•bark \-'bärk\ *vb* : disembark — **de•bar•ka•tion** \,dē,bär'kāshən\ *n*

de•base \di'bās\ *vb* : disparage — **de•base•ment** *n*

de•bate \-'bāt\ *vb* **-bat•ed; -bat•ing** : discuss a question by argument — **de•bat•able** *adj* — **debate** *n* — **de•bat•er** *n*

de•bauch \-'bóch\ *vb* : seduce or corrupt — **de•bauch•ery** \-ərē\ *n*

de•bil•i•tate \-'bilə,tāt\ *vb* **-tat•ed; -tat•ing** : make ill or weak

de•bil•i•ty \-'bilətē\ *n, pl* **-ties** : physical weakness

deb•it \'debət\ *n* : account entry of a payment or debt ~ *vb* : record as a debit

deb•o•nair \,debə'nar\ *adj* : suave

de•bris \də'brē, dā-; 'dā,brē\ *n, pl* **-bris** \-'brēz, -,brēz\ : remains of something destroyed

debt \'det\ *n* **1** : sin **2** : something owed **3** : state of owing — **debt•or** \-ər\ *n*

de•bunk \dē'bəŋk\ *vb* : expose as false

de•but \'dā,byü, dā'byü\ *n* **1** : first public appearance **2** : formal entrance into society — **debut** *vb* — **deb•u•tante** \'debyü,tänt\ *n*

de•cade \'dek,ād, -əd; de'kād\ *n* : 10 years

dec•a•dence \'dekədəns, di'kād°ns\ *n* : deterioration — **dec•a•dent** \-ənt, -°nt\ *adj or n*

de•cal \'dē,kal, di'kal, 'dekəl\ *n* : picture or design for transfer from prepared paper

de•camp \di'kamp\ *vb* : depart suddenly

de•cant \di'kant\ *vb* : pour gently

de•cant•er \-ər\ *n* : ornamental bottle

de•cap•i•tate \di'kapə,tāt\ *vb* **-tat•ed; -tat•ing** : behead — **de•cap•i•ta•tion** \-,kapə'tāshən\ *n*

de•cay \di'kā\ *vb* **1** : decline in condition **2** : decompose — **decay** *n*

de•cease \-'sēs\ *n* : death — **decease** *vb*

de•ceit \-'sēt\ *n* **1** : deception **2** : dishonesty — **de•ceit•ful** \-fəl\ *adj* — **de•ceit•ful•ly** *adv* — **de•ceit•ful•ness** *n*

de•ceive \-'sēv\ *vb* **-ceived; -ceiv•ing** : trick or mislead — **de•ceiv•er** *n*

de•cel•er•ate \dē'selə,rāt\ *vb* **-at•ed; -at•ing** : slow down

De•cem•ber \di'sembər\ *n* : 12th month of the year having 31 days

de•cent \'dēs°nt\ *adj* **1** : good, right, or just **2** : clothed **3** : not obscene **4** : fairly good — **de•cen•cy** \-°nsē\ *n* — **de•cent•ly** *adv*

de•cep•tion \di'sepshən\ *n* **1** : act or fact of deceiving **2** : fraud — **de•cep•tive** \-'septiv\ *adj* — **de•cep•tive•ly** *adv* — **de•cep•tive•ness** *n*

de•cide \di'sīd\ *vb* **-cid•ed; -cid•ing 1** : make a choice or judgment **2** : bring to a conclusion **3** : cause to decide

de•cid•ed *adj* **1** : unquestionable **2** : resolute — **de•cid•ed•ly** *adv*

de•cid•u•ous \di'sijəwəs\ *adj* : having leaves that fall annually

dec•i•mal \'desəməl\ *n* : fraction in which the denominator is a power of 10 expressed by a point (**decimal point**) placed at the left of the numerator — **decimal** *adj*

de•ci•pher \di'sīfər\ *vb* : make out the meaning of — **de•ci•pher•able** *adj*

de•ci•sion \-'sizhən\ *n* **1** : act or result of deciding **2** : determination

de•ci•sive \-'sīsiv\ *adj* **1** : having the power to decide **2** : conclusive **3** : showing determination — **de•ci•sive•ly** *adv* — **de•ci•sive•ness** *n*

deck \'dek\ *n* **1** : floor of a ship **2** : pack of playing cards ~ *vb* **1** : array or dress up **2** : knock down

de•claim \di'klām\ *vb* : speak loudly or impressively — **dec•la•ma•tion** \,deklə'māshən\ *n*

de•clare \di'klar\ *vb* **-clared; -clar•ing 1** : make known formally **2** : state emphatically — **dec•la•ra•tion** \,deklə'rāshən\ *n* — **de•clar•a•tive** \di'klarətiv\ *adj* — **de•clar•a•to•ry** \di'klarə,tōrē\ *adj* — **de•clar•er** *n*

de·clen·sion \di'klenchən\ *n* : inflectional forms of a noun, pronoun, or adjective

de·cline \di'klīn\ *vb* **-clined; -clin·ing** **1** : turn or slope downward **2** : wane **3** : refuse to accept **4** : inflect ~ *n* **1** : gradual wasting away **2** : change to a lower state or level **3** : a descending slope — **dec·li·na·tion** \,dek-lə'nāshən\ *n*

de·code \dē'kōd\ *vb* : decipher (a coded message) — **de·cod·er** *n*

de·com·mis·sion \,dēkə'mishən\ *vb* : remove from service

de·com·pose \,dēkəm'pōz\ *vb* **1** : separate into parts **2** : decay — **de·com·po·si·tion** \dē,kämpə'zishən\ *n*

de·con·ges·tant \,dēkən'jestənt\ *n* : agent that relieves congestion

de·cor, dé·cor \dā'kòr, 'dā,kòr\ *n* : room design or decoration

dec·o·rate \'dekə,rāt\ *vb* **-rat·ed; -rat·ing** **1** : add something attractive to **2** : honor with a medal — **dec·o·ra·tion** \,dekə'rāshən\ *n* — **dec·o·ra·tive** \'dekərətiv\ *adj* — **dec·o·ra·tor** \'dekə,rātər\ *n*

de·co·rum \di'kōrəm\ *n* : proper behavior — **dec·o·rous** \'dekərəs, di-'kōrəs\ *adj*

de·coy \'dē,kòi, di'-\ *n* : something that tempts or draws attention from another ~ *vb* : tempt

de·crease \di'krēs\ *vb* **-creased; -creas·ing** : grow or cause to grow less — **decrease** \'dē,krēs\ *n*

de·cree \di'krē\ *n* : official order — **de·cree** *vb*

de·crep·it \di'krepət\ *adj* : impaired by age

de·cre·scen·do \,dākrə'shendō\ *adv or adj* : with a decrease in volume

de·cry \di'krī\ *vb* : express strong disapproval of

ded·i·cate \'dedi,kāt\ *vb* **-cat·ed; -cat·ing** **1** : set apart for a purpose (as honor or worship) **2** : address to someone as a compliment — **ded·i·ca·tion** \,dedi'kāshən\ *n* — **ded·i·ca·to·ry** \'dedikə,tōrē\ *adj*

de·duce \di'düs, -'dyüs\ *vb* **-duced; -duc·ing** : derive by reasoning — **de·duc·ible** *adj*

de·duct \-'dəkt\ *vb* : subtract — **de·duct·ible** *adj*

de·duc·tion \-'dəkshən\ *n* **1** : subtrac-

tion **2** : reasoned conclusion — **de·duc·tive** \-'dəktiv\ *adj*

deed \'dēd\ *n* **1** : exploit **2** : document showing ownership ~ *vb* : convey by deed

deem \'dēm\ *vb* : think

deep \'dēp\ *adj* **1** : extending far or a specified distance down, back, within, or outward **2** : occupied **3** : dark and rich in color **4** : low in tone ~ *adv* **1** : deeply **2** : far along in time ~ *n* : deep place — **deep·en** \'dēpən\ *vb* — **deep·ly** *adv*

deep–seat·ed \-'sētəd\ *adj* : firmly established

deer \'dir\ *n, pl* **deer** : ruminant mammal with antlers in the male — **deer·skin** *n*

de·face \di'fās\ *vb* : mar the surface of — **de·face·ment** *n* — **de·fac·er** *n*

de·fame \di'fām\ *vb* **-famed; -fam·ing** : injure the reputation of — **def·a·ma·tion** \,defə'māshən\ *n* — **de·fam·a·to·ry** \di'famə,tōrē\ *adj*

de·fault \di'fòlt\ *n* : failure in a duty — **default** *vb* — **de·fault·er** *n*

de·feat \di'fēt\ *vb* **1** : frustrate **2** : win victory over ~ *n* : loss of a battle or contest

def·e·cate \'defi,kāt\ *vb* **-cat·ed; -cat·ing** : discharge feces from the bowels — **def·e·ca·tion** \,defi'kāshən\ *n*

de·fect \'dē,fekt, di'fekt\ *n* : imperfection ~ \di'-\ *vb* : desert — **de·fec·tion** \-'fekshən\ *n* — **de·fec·tor** \-'fektər\ *n*

de·fec·tive \di'fektiv\ *adj* : faulty or deficient — **defective** *n*

de·fend \-'fend\ *vb* **1** : protect from danger or harm **2** : take the side of — **de·fend·er** *n*

de·fen·dant \-'fendənt\ *n* : person charged or sued in a court

de·fense \-'fens\ *n* **1** : act of defending **2** : something that defends **3** : party, group, or team that opposes another — **de·fense·less** *adj* — **de·fen·si·ble** *adj* — **de·fen·sive** *adj or n*

¹**de·fer** \di'fər\ *vb* **-rr-** : postpone — **de·fer·ment** \di'fərmənt\ *n* — **de·fer·ra·ble** \-əbəl\ *adj*

²**defer** *vb* **-rr-** : yield to the opinion or wishes of another — **def·er·ence** \'defrəns\ *n* — **def·er·en·tial** \,defə'renchəl\ *adj*

de·fi·ance \di'fiəns\ *n* : disposition to resist — **de·fi·ant** \-ənt\ *adj*

de·fi·cient \di'fishənt\ *adj* **1** : lacking

something necessary 2 : not up to standard — **de·fi·cien·cy** \-'fishən-sē\ *n*

def·i·cit \'defəsət\ *n* : shortage esp. in money

de·file \di'fīl\ *vb* **-filed; -fil·ing 1** : make filthy or corrupt **2** : profane or dishonor — **de·file·ment** *n*

de·fine \di'fīn\ *vb* **-fined; -fin·ing 1** : fix or mark the limits of **2** : clarify in outline **3** : set forth the meaning of — **de·fin·able** *adj* — **de·fin·ably** *adv* — **de·fin·er** *n* — **def·i·ni·tion** \,defə'nishən\ *n*

def·i·nite \'defənət\ *adj* **1** : having distinct limits **2** : clear in meaning, intent, or identity **3** : typically designating an identified or immediately identifiable person or thing — **def·i·nite·ly** *adv*

de·fin·i·tive \di'finətiv\ *adj* **1** : conclusive **2** : authoritative

de·flate \di'flāt\ *vb* **-flat·ed; -flat·ing 1** : release air or gas from **2** : reduce — **de·fla·tion** \-'flāshən\ *n*

de·flect \-'flekt\ *vb* : turn aside — **de·flec·tion** \-'flekshən\ *n*

de·fog \-'fóg, -'fäg\ *vb* : remove condensed moisture from — **de·fog·ger** *n*

de·fo·li·ate \dē'fōlē,āt\ *vb* **-at·ed; -at·ing** : deprive of leaves esp. prematurely — **de·fo·li·ant** \-lēənt\ *n* — **de·fo·li·a·tion** \-,fōlē'āshən\ *n*

de·form \di'fórm\ *vb* **1** : distort **2** : disfigure — **de·for·ma·tion** \,dē-,fór'māshən, ,defər-\ *n* — **de·for·mi·ty** \di'fórmətē\ *n*

de·fraud \di'fród\ *vb* : cheat

de·fray \-'frā\ *vb* : pay

de·frost \-'fróst\ *vb* **1** : thaw out **2** : free from ice — **de·frost·er** *n*

deft \'deft\ *adj* : quick and skillful — **deft·ly** *adv* — **deft·ness** *n*

de·funct \di'fəŋkt\ *adj* : dead

de·fy \-'fī\ *vb* **-fied; -fy·ing 1** : challenge **2** : boldly refuse to obey

de·gen·er·ate \di'jenərət\ *adj* : degraded or corrupt ~ *n* : degenerate person ~ \-ə,rāt\ *vb* : become degenerate — **de·gen·er·a·cy** \-ərəsē\ *n* — **de·gen·er·a·tion** \-,jenə'rā-shən\ *n* — **de·gen·er·a·tive** \-'jenə-,rātiv\ *adj*

de·grade \di'grād\ *vb* **1** : reduce from a higher to a lower rank or degree **2** : debase **3** : decompose — **de·grad-**

able \-əbəl\ *adj* — **deg·ra·da·tion** \,degrə'dāshən\ *n*

de·gree \di'grē\ *n* **1** : step in a series **2** : extent, intensity, or scope **3** : title given to a college graduate **4** : a 360th part of the circumference of a circle **5** : unit for measuring temperature

de·hy·drate \dē'hī,drāt\ *vb* **1** : remove water from **2** : lose liquid — **de·hy·dra·tion** \,dēhī'drāshən\ *n*

de·i·fy \'dēə,fī, 'dā-\ *vb* **-fied; -fy·ing** : make a god of — **de·i·fi·ca·tion** \,dēəfə'kāshən, ,dā-\ *n*

deign \'dān\ *vb* : condescend

de·i·ty \'dēətē, 'dā-\ *n, pl* **-ties 1** *cap* : God **2** : a god or goddess

de·ject·ed \di'jektəd\ *adj* : sad — **de·jec·tion** \-shən\ *n*

de·lay \di'lā\ *n* : a putting off of something ~ *vb* **1** : postpone **2** : stop or hinder for a time

de·lec·ta·ble \di'lektəbəl\ *adj* : delicious

del·e·gate \'deligət, -,gāt\ *n* : representative ~ \-,gāt\ *vb* **-gat·ed; -gat·ing 1** : entrust to another **2** : appoint as one's delegate — **del·e·ga·tion** \,deli'gāshən\ *n*

de·lete \di'lēt\ *vb* **-let·ed; -let·ing** : eliminate something written — **de·le·tion** \-'lēshən\ *n*

del·e·te·ri·ous \,delə'tirēəs\ *adj* : harmful

de·lib·er·ate \di'libərət\ *adj* **1** : determined after careful thought **2** : intentional **3** : not hurried ~ \-ə,rāt\ *vb* **-at·ed; -at·ing** : consider carefully — **de·lib·er·ate·ly** *adv* — **de·lib·er·ate·ness** *n* — **de·lib·er·a·tion** \-,libə'rāshən\ *n* — **de·lib·er·a·tive** \-'libə,rātiv, -rət-\ *adj*

del·i·ca·cy \'delikəsē\ *n, pl* **-cies 1** : something special and pleasing to eat **2** : fineness **3** : frailty

del·i·cate \'delikət\ *adj* **1** : subtly pleasing to the senses **2** : dainty and charming **3** : sensitive or fragile **4** : requiring fine skill or tact — **del·i·cate·ly** *adv*

del·i·ca·tes·sen \,delikə'tesᵊn\ *n* : store that sells ready-to-eat food

de·li·cious \di'lishəs\ *adj* : very pleasing esp. in taste or aroma — **de·li·cious·ly** *adv* — **de·li·cious·ness** *n*

de·light \di'līt\ *n* **1** : great pleasure **2** : source of great pleasure ~ *vb* **1** : take great pleasure **2** : satisfy

greatly — **de·light·ful** \-fəl\ *adj* —
de·light·ful·ly *adv*
de·lin·eate \di'linē͜āt\ *vb* -eat·ed;
-eat·ing : sketch or portray — **de·lin·ea·tion** \-͜linē'āshən\ *n*
de·lin·quent \-'liŋkwənt\ *n* : delin-
quent person ∼ *adj* 1 : violating
duty or law 2 : overdue in payment
— **de·lin·quen·cy** \-kwənsē\ *n*
de·lir·i·um \di'lirēəm\ *n* : mental disturbance — **de·lir·i·ous** \-ēəs\ *adj*
de·liv·er \di'livər\ *vb* 1 : set free 2
: hand over 3 : assist in birth 4 : say
or speak 5 : send to an intended destination — **de·liv·er·ance** \-ərəns\ *n*
— **de·liv·er·er** *n* — **de·liv·ery** \-ərē\
n
dell \'del\ *n* : small secluded valley
del·ta \'deltə\ *n* : triangle of land at the
mouth of a river
de·lude \di'lüd\ *vb* -lud·ed; -lud·ing
: mislead or deceive
del·uge \'delyüj\ *n* 1 : flood 2
: drenching rain ∼ *vb* -uged; -ug-
ing 1 : flood 2 : overwhelm
de·lu·sion \di'lüzhən\ *n* : false belief
de·luxe \di'lúks, -'ləks, -'lüks\ *adj*
: very luxurious or elegant
delve \'delv\ *vb* delved; delv·ing 1
: dig 2 : seek information in records
dem·a·gogue, dem·a·gog \'demə͜gäg\
n : politician who appeals to emotion
and prejudice — **dem·a·gogu·ery**
\-͜gägərē\ *n* — **dem·a·gogy** \-͜gägē,
-͜gäjē\ *n*
de·mand \di'mand\ *n* 1 : act of demanding 2 : something claimed as
due 3 : ability and desire to buy 4
: urgent need ∼ *vb* 1 : ask for with
authority 2 : require
de·mar·cate \di'mär͜kāt, 'dē͜mär-\
vb -cat·ed; -cat·ing : ma͜k the limits
of — **de·mar·ca·tion** \͜dē͜mär'kā-
shən\ *n*
de·mean \di'mēn\ *vb* : degrade
de·mean·or \-'mēnər\ *n* : behavior
de·ment·ed \-'mentəd\ *adj* : crazy
de·mer·it \-'merət\ *n* : mark given an
offender
demi·god \'demi͜gäd\ *n* : mythological being less powerful than a god
de·mise \di'mīz\ *n* 1 : death 2 : loss
of status
demi·tasse \'demi͜tas\ *n* : small cup
of coffee
de·mo·bi·lize \di'mōbə͜līz, dē-\ *vb*
: disband from military service — **de-**

mo·bi·li·za·tion \-͜mōbələ'zāshən\
n
de·moc·ra·cy \di'mäkrəsē\ *n, pl* **-cies**
1 : government in which the supreme
power is held by the people 2 : political unit with democratic government
dem·o·crat \'demə͜krat\ *n* : adherent
of democracy
dem·o·crat·ic \͜demə'kratik\ *adj* : relating to or favoring democracy —
dem·o·crat·i·cal·ly \-tiklē\ *adv* —
de·moc·ra·tize \di'mäkrə͜tīz\ *vb*
de·mol·ish \di'mälish\ *vb* 1 : tear
down or smash 2 : put an end to —
de·mo·li·tion \͜demə'lishən, ͜dē-\ *n*
de·mon \'dēmən\ *n* : evil spirit — **de-
mon·ic** \di'mänik\ *adj*
dem·on·strate \'demən͜strāt\ *vb*
-strat·ed; -strat·ing : show clearly
or publicly 2 : prove 3 : explain —
de·mon·stra·ble \di'mänstrəbəl\
adj — **de·mon·stra·bly** \-blē\ *adv*
— **dem·on·stra·tion** \͜demən'strā-
shən\ *n* — **de·mon·stra·tive** \di-
'mänstrətiv\ *adj or n* — **dem·on-
stra·tor** \'demən͜strātər\ *n*
de·mor·al·ize \di'mórə͜līz\ *vb* : destroy the enthusiasm of
de·mote \di'mōt\ *vb* -mot·ed; -mot-
ing : reduce to a lower rank — **de-
mo·tion** \-'mōshən\ *n*
de·mur \di'mər\ *vb* -rr- : object — **de-
mur** *n*
de·mure \di'myúr\ *adj* : modest — **de-
mure·ly** *adv*
den \'den\ *n* 1 : animal's shelter 2
: hiding place 3 : cozy private little
room
de·na·ture \dē'nāchər\ *vb* -tured;
-tur·ing : make (alcohol) unfit for
drinking
de·ni·al \di'nīəl\ *n* : rejection of a request or of the validity of a statement
den·i·grate \'deni͜grāt\ *vb* -grat·ed;
-grat·ing : speak ill of
den·im \'denəm\ *n* 1 : durable twilled
cotton fabric 2 *pl* : pants of denim
den·i·zen \'denəzən\ *n* : inhabitant
de·nom·i·na·tion \di͜nämə'nāshən\ *n*
1 : religious body 2 : value or size
in a series — **de·nom·i·na·tion·al**
\-shənəl\ *adj*
de·nom·i·na·tor \-'nämə͜nātər\ *n*
: part of a fraction below the line
de·note \di'nōt\ *vb* 1 : mark out
plainly 2 : mean — **de·no·ta·tion**
\͜dēnō'tāshən\ *n* — **de·no·ta·tive**
\'dēnō͜tātiv, di'nōtətiv\ *adj*

de•noue•ment \ˌdāˌnü'mäⁿ\ *n* : final outcome (as of a drama)

de•nounce \di'naůns\ *vb* **-nounced; -nounc•ing** **1** : pronounce blameworthy or evil **2** : inform against

dense \'dens\ *adj* **dens•er; -est** **1** : thick, compact, or crowded **2** : stupid — **dense•ly** *adv* — **dense•ness** *n* — **den•si•ty** \'densətē\ *n*

dent \'dent\ *n* : small depression — **dent** *vb*

den•tal \'dent°l\ *adj* : relating to teeth or dentistry

den•ti•frice \'dentəfrəs\ *n* : preparation for cleaning teeth

den•tin \'dent°n\, **den•tine** \'den,tēn, ˌden'-\ *n* : bonelike component of teeth

den•tist \'dentist\ *n* : one who cares for and replaces teeth — **den•tist•ry** *n*

den•ture \'denchər\ *n* : artificial teeth

de•nude \di'nüd, -'nyüd\ *vb* **-nud•ed; -nud•ing** : strip of covering

de•nun•ci•a•tion \diˌnənsē'āshən\ *n* : act of denouncing

de•ny \-'nī\ *vb* **-nied; -ny•ing** **1** : declare untrue **2** : disavow **3** : refuse to grant

de•odor•ant \dē'ōdərənt\ *n* : preparation to prevent unpleasant odors — **de•odor•ize** \-ˌrīz\ *vb*

de•part \di'pärt\ *vb* **1** : go away or away from **2** : die — **de•par•ture** \-'pärchər\ *n*

de•part•ment \di'pärtmənt\ *n* **1** : area of responsibility or interest **2** : functional division — **de•part•men•tal** \diˌpärt'ment°l, ˌdē-\ *adj*

de•pend \di'pend\ *vb* **1** : rely for support **2** : be determined by or based on something else — **de•pend•abil•i•ty** \-ˌpendə'bilətē\ *n* — **de•pend•able** *adj* — **de•pen•dence** \di'pendəns\ *n* — **de•pen•den•cy** \-dənsē\ *n* — **de•pen•dent** \-ənt\ *adj or n*

de•pict \di'pikt\ *vb* : show by or as if by a picture — **de•pic•tion** \-'pikshən\ *n*

de•plete \di'plēt\ *vb* **-plet•ed; -plet•ing** : use up resources of — **de•ple•tion** \-'plēshən\ *n*

de•plore \-'plōr\ *vb* **-plored; -plor•ing** : regret strongly — **de•plor•able** \-əbəl\ *adj*

de•ploy \-'ploi\ *vb* : spread out for battle — **de•ploy•ment** \-mənt\ *n*

de•port \di'pōrt\ *vb* **1** : behave **2** : send out of the country — **de•por-**

ta•tion \ˌdēˌpōr'tāshən\ *n* — **de•port•ment** \di'pōrtmənt\ *n*

de•pose \-'pōz\ *vb* **-posed; -pos•ing** **1** : remove (a ruler) from office **2** : testify — **de•po•si•tion** \ˌdepə'zishən, ˌdē-\ *n*

de•pos•it \di'päzət\ *vb* **-it•ed; -it•ing** : place esp. for safekeeping ∼ *n* **1** : state of being deposited **2** : something deposited **3** : act of depositing **4** : natural accumulation — **de•pos•i•tor** \-'päzətər\ *n*

de•pos•i•to•ry \di'päzəˌtōrē\ *n, pl* **-ries** : place for deposit

de•pot *1 usu* 'depō, *2 usu* 'dēp-\ *n* **1** : place for storage **2** : bus or railroad station

de•prave \di'prāv\ *vb* **-praved; -prav•ing** : corrupt morally — **de•praved** *adj* — **de•prav•i•ty** \-'pravətē\ *n*

dep•re•cate \'depriˌkāt\ *vb* **-cat•ed; -cat•ing** **1** : express disapproval of **2** : belittle — **dep•re•ca•tion** \ˌdepri'kāshən\ *n* — **dep•re•ca•tory** \'deprikəˌtōrē\ *adj*

de•pre•ci•ate \di'prēshēˌāt\ *vb* **-at•ed; -at•ing** **1** : lessen in value **2** : belittle — **de•pre•ci•a•tion** \-ˌprēshē'āshən\ *n*

dep•re•da•tion \ˌdeprə'dāshən\ *n* : a laying waste or plundering — **dep•re•date** \'deprəˌdāt\ *vb*

de•press \di'pres\ *vb* **1** : press down **2** : lessen the activity or force of **3** : discourage **4** : decrease the market value of — **de•pres•sant** \-°nt\ *n or adj* — **de•pressed** *adj* — **de•pres•sive** \-iv\ *adj or n* — **de•pres•sor** \-ər\ *n*

de•pres•sion \di'preshən\ *n* **1** : act of depressing or state of being depressed **2** : depressed place **3** : period of low economic activity

de•prive \-'prīv\ *vb* **-prived; -priv•ing** : take or keep something away from — **de•pri•va•tion** \ˌdeprə'vāshən\ *n*

depth \'depth\ *n, pl* **depths** **1** : something that is deep **2** : distance down from a surface **3** : distance from front to back **4** : quality of being deep

dep•u•ta•tion \ˌdepyə'tāshən\ *n* : delegation

dep•u•ty \'depyətē\ *n, pl* **-ties** : person appointed to act for another — **dep•u•tize** \-yəˌtīz\ *vb*

de•rail \di'rāl\ *vb* : leave the rails — **de•rail•ment** *n*

de•range \-'rānj\ *vb* **-ranged; -rang-**

ing 1 : disarrange or upset **2** : make insane — **de·range·ment** n

der·by \'dərbē, *Brit* 'där-\ n, pl **-bies 1** : horse race **2** : stiff felt hat with dome-shaped crown

de·reg·u·late \dē'regyù,lāt\ vb : remove restrictions on — **de·reg·u·la·tion** \-,regyù'lāshən\ n

der·e·lict \'derə,likt\ adj **1** : abandoned **2** : negligent ~ n **1** : something abandoned **2** : bum — **der·e·lic·tion** \,derə'likshən\ n

de·ride \di'rīd\ vb **-rid·ed; -rid·ing** : make fun of — **de·ri·sion** \-'rizhən\ n — **de·ri·sive** \-'rīsiv\ adj — **de·ri·sive·ly** adv — **de·ri·sive·ness** n

de·rive \di'rīv\ vb **-rived; -riv·ing 1** : obtain from a source or parent **2** : come from a certain source **3** : infer or deduce — **der·i·va·tion** \,derə-'vāshən\ n — **de·riv·a·tive** \di'rivə-tiv\ adj or n

der·ma·tol·o·gy \,dərmə'täləjē\ n : study of the skin and its disorders — **der·ma·tol·o·gist** \-jist\ n

de·ro·ga·tive \di'rägətiv\ adj : derogatory

de·rog·a·to·ry \di'rägə,tōrē\ adj : intended to lower the reputation

der·rick \'derik\ n **1** : hoisting apparatus **2** : framework over an oil well

de·scend \di'send\ vb **1** : move or climb down **2** : derive **3** : extend downward **4** : appear suddenly (as in an attack) — **de·scen·dant, de·scen·dent** \-ənt\ adj or n — **de·scent** \di'sent\ n

de·scribe \-'skrīb\ vb **-scribed; -scrib·ing** : represent in words — **de·scrib·able** adj — **de·scrip·tion** \-'skripshən\ n — **de·scrip·tive** \-'skriptiv\ adj

de·scry \di'skrī\ vb **-scried; -scry·ing** : catch sight of

des·e·crate \'desi,krāt\ vb **-crat·ed; -crat·ing** : treat (something sacred) with disrespect — **des·e·cra·tion** \,desi'krāshən\ n

de·seg·re·gate \dē'segrə,gāt\ vb : eliminate esp. racial segregation in — **de·seg·re·ga·tion** n

¹**des·ert** \'dezərt\ n : dry barren region — **desert** adj

²**de·sert** \di'zərt\ n : what one deserves

³**de·sert** \di'zərt\ vb : abandon — **de·sert·er** n — **de·ser·tion** \-'zərshən\ n

de·serve \-'zərv\ vb **-served; -serv·ing** : be worthy of

des·ic·cate \'desi,kāt\ vb **-cat·ed; -cat·ing** : dehydrate — **des·ic·ca·tion** \,desi'kāshən\ n

de·sign \di'zīn\ vb **1** : create and work out the details of **2** : make a pattern or sketch of ~ n **1** : mental project or plan **2** : purpose **3** : preliminary sketch **4** : underlying arrangement of elements **5** : decorative pattern — **de·sign·er** n

des·ig·nate \'dezig,nāt\ vb **-nat·ed; -nat·ing 1** : indicate, specify, or name **2** : appoint — **des·ig·na·tion** \,dezig'nāshən\ n

de·sire \di'zīr\ vb **-sired; -sir·ing 1** : feel desire for **2** : request ~ n **1** : strong conscious impulse to have, be, or do something **2** : something desired — **de·sir·abil·i·ty** \-,zīrə-'bilətē\ n — **de·sir·able** \-'zīrəbəl\ adj — **de·sir·able·ness** n — **de·sir·ous** \-'zīrəs\ adj

de·sist \di'zist, -'sist\ vb : stop

desk \'desk\ n : table esp. for writing and reading

des·o·late \'desələt, 'dez-\ adj **1** : lifeless **2** : disconsolate ~ \-,lāt\ vb **-lat·ed; -lat·ing** : lay waste — **des·o·la·tion** \,desə'lāshən, ,dez-\ n

de·spair \di'spar\ vb : lose all hope ~ n : loss of hope

des·per·a·do \,despə'rädō, -'rād-\ n, pl **-does** or **-dos** : desperate criminal

des·per·ate \'despərət\ adj **1** : hopeless **2** : rash **3** : extremely intense — **des·per·ate·ly** adv — **des·per·a·tion** \,despə'rāshən\ n

de·spi·ca·ble \di'spikəbel, 'despik-\ adj : deserving scorn

de·spise \di'spīz\ vb **-spised; -spis·ing** : feel contempt for

de·spite \-'spīt\ prep : in spite of

de·spoil \-'spȯil\ vb : strip of possessions or value

de·spon·den·cy \-'spändənsē\ n : dejection — **de·spon·dent** \-dənt\ adj

des·pot \'despət, -,pät\ n : tyrant — **des·pot·ic** \des'pätik\ adj — **des·po·tism** \'despə,tizəm\ n

des·sert \di'zərt\ n : sweet food, fruit, or cheese ending a meal

des·ti·na·tion \,destə'nāshən\ n : place where something or someone is going

des·tine \'destən\ *vb* **-tined; -tin·ing**
1 : designate, assign, or determine in
advance **2** : direct

des·ti·ny \'destənē\ *n, pl* **-nies** : that
which is to happen in the future

des·ti·tute \'destə‚tüt, -‚tyüt\ *adj* **1**
: lacking something **2** : very poor
— **des·ti·tu·tion** \‚destə'tüshən,
-'tyü-\ *n*

de·stroy \di'strói\ *vb* : kill or put an
end to

de·stroy·er \-'stróiər\ *n* **1** : one that
destroys **2** : small speedy warship

de·struc·tion \-'strəkshən\ *n* **1** : action of destroying **2** : ruin — **de-**
struc·ti·bil·i·ty \-‚strəktə'bilətē\ *n*
— **de·struc·ti·ble** \-'strəktəbəl\ *adj*
— **de·struc·tive** \-'strəktiv\ *adj*

des·ul·to·ry \'desəl‚tōrē\ *adj* : aimless

de·tach \di'tach\ *vb* : separate

de·tached \-'tacht\ *adj* **1** : separate **2**
: aloof or impartial

de·tach·ment \-'tachmənt\ *n* **1** : separation **2** : troops or ships on special
service **3** : aloofness **4** : impartiality

de·tail \di'tāl, 'dē‚tāl\ *n* : small item or
part ~ *vb* : give details of

de·tain \di'tān\ *vb* **1** : hold in custody
2 : delay

de·tect \di'tekt\ *vb* : discover — **de-**
tect·able *adj* — **de·tec·tion** \-'tek-
shən\ *n* — **de·tec·tor** \-tər\ *n*

de·tec·tive \-'tektiv\ *n* : one who investigates crime

dé·tente \dā'tänt\ *n* : relaxation of ten-
sions between nations

de·ten·tion \di'tenchən\ *n* : confinement

de·ter \-'tər\ *vb* **-rr-** : discourage or prevent — **de·ter·rence** \-əns\ *n* — **de-**
ter·rent \-ənt\ *adj or n*

de·ter·gent \di'tərjənt\ *n* : cleansing
agent

de·te·ri·o·rate \-'tirēə‚rāt\ *vb* **-rat·ed;**
-rat·ing : make or become worse —
de·te·ri·o·ra·tion \-‚tirēə'rāshən\ *n*

de·ter·mi·na·tion \di‚tərmə'nāshən\
n **1** : act of deciding or fixing **2**
: firm purpose

de·ter·mine \-'tərmən\ *vb* **-mined;**
-min·ing 1 : decide on, establish, or
settle **2** : find out **3** : bring about as a
result

de·test \-'test\ *vb* : hate — **de·test-**
able *adj* — **de·tes·ta·tion** \‚dē‚tes-
'tāshən\ *n*

det·o·nate \'detən‚āt\ *vb* **-nat·ed;**
-nat·ing : explode — **det·o·na·tion**
\‚detən'āshən\ *n* — **det·o·na·tor**
\'detən‚ātər\ *n*

de·tour \'dē‚túr\ *n* : temporary indirect
route — **detour** *vb*

de·tract \di'trakt\ *vb* : take away —
de·trac·tion \-'trakshən\ *n* — **de-**
trac·tor \-'traktər\ *n*

det·ri·ment \'detrəmənt\ *n* : damage
— **det·ri·men·tal** \‚detrə'mentᵊl\
adj — **det·ri·men·tal·ly** *adv*

deuce \'düs, 'dyüs\ *n* **1** : 2 in cards or
dice **2** : tie in tennis **3** : devil — used
as an oath

deut·sche mark \'dóichə-\ *n* : monetary unit of Germany

de·val·ue \dē'val‚yü\ *vb* : reduce the
value of — **de·val·u·a·tion** *n*

dev·as·tate \'devə‚stāt\ *vb* **-tat·ed;**
-tat·ing : ruin — **dev·as·ta·tion**
\‚devə'stāshən\ *n*

de·vel·op \di'veləp\ *vb* **1** : grow, increase, or evolve gradually **2** : cause
to grow, increase, or reach full potential — **de·vel·op·er** *n* — **de·vel-**
op·ment *n* — **de·vel·op·men·tal**
\-‚veləp'mentᵊl\ *adj*

de·vi·ate \'dēvē‚āt\ *vb* **-at·ed; -at·ing**
: change esp. from a course or stan-
dard — **de·vi·ant** \-vēənt\ *adj or n*
— **de·vi·ate** \-vēət, -vē‚āt\ *n* — **de-**
vi·a·tion \‚dēvē'āshən\ *n*

de·vice \di'vīs\ *n* **1** : specialized piece
of equipment or tool **2** : design

dev·il \'devəl\ *n* **1** : personified
supreme spirit of evil **2** : demon **3**
: wicked person ~ *vb* **-iled** *or* **-illed;**
-il·ing *or* **-il·ling 1** : season highly **2**
: pester — **dev·il·ish** \'devəlish\ *adj*
— **dev·il·ry** \'devəlrē\, **dev·il·try**
\-trē\ *n*

de·vi·ous \'dēvēəs\ *adj* : tricky

de·vise \di'vīz\ *vb* **-vised; -vis·ing 1**
: invent **2** : plot **3** : give by will

de·void \-'vóid\ *adj* : entirely lacking

de·vote \di'vōt\ *vb* **-vot·ed; -vot·ing**
: set apart for a special purpose

de·vot·ed *adj* : faithful

dev·o·tee \‚devə'tē, -'tā\ *n* : ardent follower

de·vo·tion \di'vōshən\ *n* **1** : prayer —
usu. pl. **2** : loyalty and dedication —
de·vo·tion·al \-shənəl\ *adj*

de·vour \di'vaùər\ *vb* : consume rav-
enously — **de·vour·er** *n*

de·vout \-'vaùt\ *adj* **1** : devoted to religion **2** : serious — **de·vout·ly** *adv*
— **de·vout·ness** *n*

dew \'dü, 'dyü\ *n* : moisture condensed at night — **dew·drop** *n* — **dewy** *adj*

dex·ter·ous \'dekstrəs\ *adj* : skillful with the hands — **dex·ter·i·ty** \dek-'sterətē\ *n* — **dex·ter·ous·ly** *adv*

dex·trose \'dek,strōs\ *n* : plant or blood sugar

di·a·be·tes \,dīə'bētēz, -'bētəs\ *n* : disorder in which the body has too little insulin and too much sugar — **di·a·bet·ic** \-'betik\ *adj or n*

di·a·bol·ic \,dīə'bälik\, **di·a·bol·i·cal** \-ikəl\ *adj* : fiendish

di·a·crit·ic \-'kritik\ *n* : mark accompanying a letter and indicating a specific sound value — **di·a·crit·i·cal** \-'kritikəl\ *adj*

di·a·dem \'dīə,dem\ *n* : crown

di·ag·no·sis \,dīig'nōsəs, -əg-\ *n, pl* **-no·ses** \-,sēz\ : identifying of a disease from its symptoms — **di·ag·nose** \'dīig,nōs, -əg-\ *vb* — **di·ag·nos·tic** \,dīig'nästik, -əg-\ *adj*

di·ag·o·nal \dī'agənəl\ *adj* : extending from one corner to the opposite corner ~ *n* : diagonal line, direction, or arrangement — **di·ag·o·nal·ly** *adv*

di·a·gram \'dīə,gram\ *n* : explanatory drawing or plan ~ *vb* **-gramed** *or* **-grammed; -gram·ing** *or* **-gram·ming** : represent by a diagram — **di·a·gram·mat·ic** \,dīəgrə'matik\ *adj*

di·al \'dīəl\ *n* **1** : face of a clock, meter, or gauge **2** : control knob or wheel ~ *vb* **-aled** *or* **-alled; -al·ing** *or* **-al·ling** : turn a dial to call, operate, or select

di·a·lect \'dīə,lekt\ *n* : variety of language confined to a region or group

di·a·logue \-,lóg\ *n* : conversation

di·am·e·ter \dī'amətər\ *n* **1** : straight line through the center of a circle **2** : thickness

di·a·met·ric \,dīə'metrik\ **di·a·met·ri·cal** \-trikəl\ *adj* : completely opposite — **di·a·met·ri·cal·ly** \-iklē\ *adv*

di·a·mond \'dīmənd, 'dīə-\ *n* **1** : hard brilliant mineral that consists of crystalline carbon **2** : flat figure having 4 equal sides, 2 acute angles, and 2 obtuse angles **3** : playing card of a suit marked with a red diamond **4** : baseball field

di·a·per \'dīpər\ *n* : baby's garment for receiving bodily wastes ~ *vb* : put a diaper on

di·a·phragm \'dīə,fram\ *n* **1** : sheet of muscle between the chest and abdominal cavity **2** : contraceptive device

di·ar·rhea \,dīə'rēə\ *n* : abnormally watery discharge from bowels

di·a·ry \'dīərē\ *n, pl* **-ries** : daily record of personal experiences — **di·a·rist** \'dīərist\ *n*

di·a·tribe \'dīə,trīb\ *n* : biting or abusive denunciation

dice \'dīs\ *n, pl* **dice** : die or a game played with dice ~ *vb* **diced; dic·ing** : cut into small cubes

dick·er \'dikər\ *vb* : bargain

dic·tate \'dik,tāt\ *vb* **-tat·ed; -tat·ing** **1** : speak for a person or a machine to record **2** : command ~ *n* : order — **dic·ta·tion** \dik'tāshən\ *n*

dic·ta·tor \'dik,tātər\ *n* : person ruling absolutely and often brutally — **dic·ta·to·ri·al** \,diktətōrēəl\ *adj* — **dic·ta·tor·ship** \dik'tātər,ship, 'dik,-\ *n*

dic·tion \'dikshən\ *n* **1** : choice of the best word **2** : precise pronunciation

dic·tio·nary \-shə,nerē\ *n, pl* **-nar·ies** : reference book of words with information about their meanings

dic·tum \'diktəm\ *n, pl* **-ta** \-tə\ : authoritative or formal statement

did *past of* DO

di·dac·tic \dī'daktik\ *adj* : intended to teach a moral lesson

¹die \'dī\ *vb* **died; dy·ing** \'dīiŋ\ **1** : stop living **2** : pass out of existence **3** : stop or subside **4** : long

²die \'dī\ *n* **1** *pl* **dice** \'dīs\ : small marked cube used in gambling **2** *pl* **dies** \'dīz\ : form for stamping or cutting

die·sel \'dēzəl, -səl\ *n* : engine in which high compression causes ignition of the fuel

di·et \'dīət\ *n* : food and drink regularly consumed (as by a person) ~ *vb* : eat less or according to certain rules — **di·etary** \'dīə,terē\ *adj or n* — **di·et·er** *n*

di·etet·ics \,dīə'tetiks\ *n sing or pl* : science of nutrition — **di·etet·ic** *adj* — **di·eti·tian, di·eti·cian** \-'tishən\ *n*

dif·fer \'difər\ *vb* **1** : be unlike **2** : vary **3** : disagree — **dif·fer·ence** \'difrəns\ *n*

dif·fer·ent \-rənt\ *adj* : not the same — **dif·fer·ent·ly** *adv*

dif·fer·en·ti·ate \,difə'renchē,āt\ *vb* **-at·ed; -at·ing** **1** : make or become different **2** : attain a specialized adult form during development **3** : distinguish — **dif•fer•en•ti•a•tion** \-ˌren-chēˈāshən\ *n*

dif•fi•cult \ˈdifikəlt\ *adj* : hard to do, understand, or deal with

dif•fi•cul•ty \-kəltē\ *n, pl* **-ties 1** : difficult nature **2** : great effort **3** : something hard to do, understand, or deal with

dif•fi•dent \ˈdifədənt\ *adj* : reserved — **dif•fi•dence** \-əns\ *n*

dif•fuse \difˈyüs\ *adj* **1** : wordy **2** : not concentrated ~ \-ˈyüz\ *vb* **-fused; -fus•ing** : pour out or spread widely — **dif•fu•sion** \-ˈyüzhən\ *n*

dig \ˈdig\ *vb* **dug** \ˈdəg\; **dig•ging 1** : turn up soil **2** : hollow out or form by removing earth **3** : uncover by turning up earth ~ *n* **1** : thrust **2** : cutting remark — **dig in** *vb* **1** : establish a defensive position **2** : begin working or eating — **dig up** *vb* : discover

¹di•gest \ˈdīˌjest\ *n* : body of information in shortened form

²di•gest \dīˈjest, də-\ *vb* **1** : think over **2** : convert (food) into a form that can be absorbed **3** : summarize — **di•gest•ible** *adj* — **di•ges•tion** \-ˈjeschən\ *n* — **di•ges•tive** \-ˈjestiv\ *adj*

dig•it \ˈdijət\ *n* **1** : any of the figures 1 to 9 inclusive and usu. the symbol 0 **2** : finger or toe

dig•i•tal \-ᵊl\ *adj* : providing information in numerical digits — **dig•i•tal•ly** *adv*

digital camera *n* : camera that records images as digital data instead of on film

dig•ni•fy \ˈdignəˌfī\ *vb* **-fied; -fy•ing** : give dignity or attention to

dig•ni•tary \-ˌterē\ *n, pl* **-taries** : person of high position

dig•ni•ty \ˈdignətē\ *n, pl* **-ties 1** : quality or state of being worthy or honored **2** : formal reserve (as of manner)

di•gress \dīˈgres, də-\ *vb* : wander from the main subject — **di•gres•sion** \-ˈgreshən\ *n*

dike \ˈdīk\ *n* : earth bank or dam

di•lap•i•dat•ed \dəˈlapəˌdātəd\ *adj* : fallen into partial ruin — **di•lap•i•da•tion** \-ˌlapəˈdāshən\ *n*

di•late \dīˈlāt, ˈdīˌlāt\ *vb* **-lat•ed; -lat•ing** : swell or expand — **dil•a•ta•tion** \ˌdiləˈtāshən\ *n* — **di•la•tion** \dīˈlāshən\ *n*

dil•a•to•ry \ˈdiləˌtōrē\ *adj* **1** : delaying **2** : tardy or slow

di•lem•ma \dəˈlemə\ *n* **1** : undesirable choice **2** : predicament

dil•et•tante \ˈdiləˌtänt, -ˌtant; ˌdiləˈtänt, -ˈtant\ *n, pl* **-tantes** *or* **-tan•ti** \-ˈtäntē, -ˈtantē\ : one who dabbles in a field of interest

dil•i•gent \ˈdiləjənt\ *adj* : attentive and busy — **dil•i•gence** \-jəns\ *n* — **dil•i•gent•ly** *adv*

dill \ˈdil\ *n* : herb with aromatic leaves and seeds

dil•ly•dal•ly \ˈdilēˌdalē\ *vb* : waste time by delay

di•lute \dīˈlüt, də-\ *vb* **-lut•ed; -lut•ing** : lessen the consistency or strength of by mixing with something else ~ *adj* : weak — **di•lu•tion** \-ˈlüshən\ *n*

dim \ˈdim\ *adj* **-mm- 1** : not bright or distinct **2** : having no luster **3** : not seeing or understanding clearly — **dim** *vb* — **dim•ly** *adv* — **dim•mer** *n* — **dim•ness** *n*

dime \ˈdīm\ *n* : U.S. coin worth $\frac{1}{10}$ dollar

di•men•sion \dəˈmenchən, dī-\ *n* **1** : measurement of extension (as in length, height, or breadth) **2** : extent — **di•men•sion•al** \-ˈmenchənəl\ *adj*

di•min•ish \dəˈminish\ *vb* **1** : make less or cause to appear less **2** : dwindle

di•min•u•tive \dəˈminyətiv\ *adj* : extremely small

dim•ple \ˈdimpəl\ *n* : small depression esp. in the cheek or chin

din \ˈdin\ *n* : loud noise

dine \ˈdīn\ *vb* **dined; din•ing** : eat dinner

din•er \ˈdīnər\ *n* **1** : person eating dinner **2** : railroad dining car or restaurant resembling one

din•ghy \ˈdiŋē, -gē, -kē\ *n, pl* **-ghies** : small boat

din•gy \ˈdinjē\ *adj* **-gi•er; -est 1** : dirty **2** : shabby — **din•gi•ness** *n*

din•ner \ˈdinər\ *n* : main daily meal

di•no•saur \ˈdīnəˌsȯr\ *n* : extinct often huge reptile

dint \ˈdint\ *n* : force — in the phrase *by dint of*

di•o•cese \ˈdīəsəs, -ˌsēz, -ˌsēs\ *n, pl* **-ces•es** \-səz, ˈdīəˌsēz\ : territorial jurisdiction of a bishop — **di•oc•e•san** \dī'äsəsən, ͵dīə'sēzⁿn\ *adj or n*

dip \'dip\ *vb* **-pp-** **1** : plunge into a liquid **2** : take out with a ladle **3** : lower and quickly raise again **4** : sink or slope downward suddenly ∼ *n* **1** : plunge into water for sport **2** : sudden downward movement or incline — **dip•per** *n*

diph•the•ria \dif'thirēə\ *n* : acute contagious disease

diph•thong \'dif͵thȯŋ\ *n* : two vowel sounds joined to form one speech sound (as *ou* in *out*)

di•plo•ma \də'plōmə\ *n, pl* **-mas** : record of graduation from a school

di•plo•ma•cy \-məsē\ *n* **1** : business of conducting negotiations between nations **2** : tact — **dip•lo•mat** \'diplə͵mat\ *n* — **dip•lo•mat•ic** \͵diplə'matik\ *adj*

dire \'dīr\ *adj* **dir•er; -est** **1** : very horrible **2** : extreme

di•rect \də'rekt, dī-\ *vb* **1** : address **2** : cause to move or to follow a certain course **3** : show (someone) the way **4** : regulate the activities or course of **5** : request with authority ∼ *adj* **1** : leading to or coming from a point without deviation or interruption **2** : frank — **direct** *adv* — **di•rect•ly** *adv* — **di•rect•ness** *n* — **di•rec•tor** \-tər\ *n*

direct current *n* : electric current flowing in one direction only

di•rec•tion \də'rekshən, dī-\ *n* **1** : supervision **2** : order **3** : course along which something moves — **di•rec•tion•al** \-shənəl\ *adj*

di•rec•tive \-tiv\ *n* : order

di•rec•to•ry \-tərē\ *n, pl* **-ries** : alphabetical list of names and addresses

dirge \'dərj\ *n* : funeral hymn

di•ri•gi•ble \'dirəjəbəl, də'rijə-\ *n* : airship

dirt \'dərt\ *n* **1** : mud, dust, or grime that makes something unclean **2** : soil

dirty \-ē\ *adj* **dirt•i•er; -est** **1** : not clean **2** : unfair **3** : indecent ∼ *vb* **dirt•ied; dirty•ing** : make or become dirty — **dirt•i•ness** *n*

dis•able \dis'ābəl\ *vb* **-abled; -abling** : make unable to function — **dis•abil•i•ty** \͵disə'bilətē\ *n*

dis•abuse \͵disə'byüz\ *vb* : free from error or misconception

dis•ad•van•tage \͵disəd'vantij\ *n* : something that hinders success — **dis•ad•van•ta•geous** *adj*

dis•af•fect \͵disə'fekt\ *vb* : cause discontent in — **dis•af•fec•tion** *n*

dis•agree \͵disə'grē\ *vb* **1** : fail to agree **2** : differ in opinion — **dis•agree•ment** *n*

dis•agree•able \-əbəl\ *adj* : unpleasant

dis•al•low \͵disə'laů\ *vb* : refuse to admit or recognize

dis•ap•pear \͵disə'pir\ *vb* **1** : pass out of sight **2** : cease to be — **dis•ap•pear•ance** *n*

dis•ap•point \͵disə'pȯint\ *vb* : fail to fulfill the expectation or hope of — **dis•ap•point•ment** *n*

dis•ap•prove \-ə'prüv\ *vb* **1** : condemn or reject **2** : feel or express dislike or rejection — **dis•ap•prov•al** *n* — **dis•ap•prov•ing•ly** *adv*

dis•arm \dis'ärm\ *vb* **1** : take weapons from **2** : reduce armed forces **3** : make harmless or friendly — **dis•ar•ma•ment** \-'ärməmənt\ *n*

dis•ar•range \͵disə'rānj\ *vb* : throw into disorder — **dis•ar•range•ment** *n*

dis•ar•ray \͵disə'rā\ *n* : disorder

dis•as•ter \diz'astər, dis-\ *n* : sudden great misfortune — **di•sas•trous** \-'astrəs\ *adj*

dis•avow \͵disə'vaů\ *vb* : deny responsibility for — **dis•avow•al** \-'vaůəl\ *n*

dis•band \dis'band\ *vb* : break up the organization of

dis•bar \dis'bär\ *vb* : expel from the legal profession — **dis•bar•ment** *n*

dis•be•lieve \͵disbi'lēv\ *vb* : hold not worthy of belief — **dis•be•lief** *n*

dis•burse \dis'bərs\ *vb* **-bursed; -burs•ing** : pay out — **dis•burse•ment** *n*

disc *var of* DISK

dis•card \dis'kärd, 'dis͵kärd\ *vb* : get rid of as unwanted — **dis•card** \'dis͵kärd\ *n*

dis•cern \dis'ərn, diz-\ *vb* : discover with the eyes or the mind — **dis•cern•ible** *adj* — **dis•cern•ment** *n*

dis•charge \dis'chärj, 'dis͵chärj\ *vb* **1** : unload **2** : shoot **3** : set free **4** : dismiss from service **5** : let go or let off **6** : give forth fluid ∼ \'dis͵-, dis'-\ *n* **1** : act of discharging **2** : a flowing out (as of blood) **3** : dismissal

dis•ci•ple \di'sīpəl\ *n* : one who helps spread another's teachings

dis·ci·pli·nar·i·an \ˌdisəplə'nerēən\ n : one who enforces order

dis·ci·pline \'disəplən\ n 1 : field of study 2 : training that corrects, molds, or perfects 3 : punishment 4 : control gained by obedience or training ~ vb **-plined; -plin·ing** 1 : punish 2 : train in self-control — **dis·ci·plin·ary** \'disəplə,nerē\ adj

dis·claim \dis'klām\ vb : disavow

dis·close \-'klōz\ vb : reveal — **dis·clo·sure** \-'klōzhər\ n

dis·col·or \dis'kələr\ vb : change the color of esp. for the worse — **dis·col·or·ation** \dis,kələ'rāshən\ n

dis·com·fit \dis'kəmfət\ vb : upset — **dis·com·fi·ture** \dis'kəmfə,chúr\ n

dis·com·fort \dis'kəmfərt\ n : uneasiness

dis·con·cert \ˌdiskən'sərt\ vb : upset

dis·con·nect \ˌdiskə'nekt\ vb : undo the connection of

dis·con·so·late \dis'känsələt\ adj : hopelessly sad

dis·con·tent \ˌdiskən'tent\ n : uneasiness of mind — **dis·con·tent·ed** adj

dis·con·tin·ue \diskən'tinyü\ vb : end — **dis·con·tin·u·ance** n — **dis·con·ti·nu·i·ty** \dis,käntə'nüətē, -'nyü-\ n — **dis·con·tin·u·ous** \ˌdiskən-'tinyəwəs\ adj

dis·cord \'dis,kórd\ n : lack of harmony — **dis·cor·dant** \dis'kórd°nt\ adj — **dis·cor·dant·ly** adv

dis·count \'dis,kaùnt\ n : reduction from a regular price ~ \'dis,-, dis'-\ vb 1 : reduce the amount of 2 : disregard — **discount** adj — **dis·count·er** n

dis·cour·age \dis'kərij\ vb **-aged; -ag·ing** 1 : deprive of courage, confidence, or enthusiasm 2 : dissuade — **dis·cour·age·ment** n

dis·course \'dis,kōrs\ n 1 : conversation 2 : formal treatment of a subject ~ \dis'-\ vb **-coursed; -cours·ing** : talk at length

dis·cour·te·ous \dis'kərtēəs\ adj : lacking courtesy — **dis·cour·te·ous·ly** adv — **dis·cour·te·sy** n

dis·cov·er \dis'kəvər\ vb 1 : make known 2 : obtain the first sight or knowledge of 3 : find out — **dis·cov·er·er** n — **dis·cov·ery** \-ərē\ n

dis·cred·it \dis'kredət\ vb 1 : disbelieve 2 : destroy confidence in ~ n 1 : loss of reputation 2 : disbelief — **dis·cred·it·able** adj

dis·creet \dis'krēt\ adj : capable of keeping a secret — **dis·creet·ly** adv

dis·crep·an·cy \dis'krepənsē\ n, pl **-cies** : difference or disagreement

dis·crete \dis'krēt, 'dis,-\ adj : individually distinct

dis·cre·tion \dis'kreshən\ n 1 : discreet quality 2 : power of decision or choice — **dis·cre·tion·ary** adj

dis·crim·i·nate \dis'krimə,nāt\ vb **-na·ted; -nat·ing** 1 : distinguish 2 : show favor or disfavor unjustly — **dis·crim·i·na·tion** \-,krimə'nāshən\ n — **dis·crim·i·na·to·ry** \-'krimənə-,tōrē\ adj

dis·cur·sive \dis'kərsiv\ adj : passing from one topic to another — **dis·cur·sive·ly** adv — **dis·cur·sive·ness** n

dis·cus \'diskəs\ n, pl **-cus·es** : disk hurled for distance in a contest

dis·cuss \dis'kəs\ vb : talk about or present — **dis·cus·sion** \-'kəshən\ n

dis·dain \dis'dān\ n : feeling of contempt ~ vb : look upon or reject with disdain — **dis·dain·ful** \-fəl\ adj — **dis·dain·ful·ly** adv

dis·ease \di'zēz\ n : condition of a body that impairs its functioning — **dis·eased** \-'zēzd\ adj

dis·em·bark \ˌdisəm'bärk\ vb : get off a ship — **dis·em·bar·ka·tion** \dis-,em,bär'kāshən\ n

dis·em·bod·ied \ˌdisəm'bädēd\ adj : having no substance or reality

dis·en·chant \ˌdisən'chant\ vb : to free from illusion — **dis·en·chant·ment** n

dis·en·chant·ed \-'chantəd\ adj : disappointed

dis·en·gage \-°n'gāj\ vb : release — **dis·en·gage·ment** n

dis·en·tan·gle \-°n'taŋgəl\ vb : free from entanglement

dis·fa·vor \dis'fāvər\ n : disapproval

dis·fig·ure \dis'figyər\ vb : spoil the appearance of — **dis·fig·ure·ment** n

dis·fran·chise \dis'fran,chīz\ vb : deprive of the right to vote — **dis·fran·chise·ment** n

dis·gorge \dis'górj\ vb : spew forth

dis·grace \dis'grās\ vb : bring disgrace to ~ n 1 : shame 2 : cause of shame — **dis·grace·ful** \-fəl\ adj — **dis·grace·ful·ly** adv

dis·grun·tle \dis'grənt°l\ vb **-tled; -tling** : put in bad humor

dis·guise \dis'gīz\ vb **-guised; -guis-**

ing : hide the true identity or nature of ~ *n* : something that conceals

dis·gust \dis'gəst\ *n* : strong aversion ~ *vb* : provoke disgust in — **dis·gust·ed·ly** *adv* — **dis·gust·ing·ly** *adv*

dish \'dish\ *n* **1** : vessel for serving food or the food it holds **2** : food prepared in a particular way ~ *vb* : put in a dish — **dish·cloth** *n* — **dish·rag** *n* — **dish·wash·er** *n* — **dish·wa·ter** *n*

dis·har·mo·ny \dis'härmənē\ *n* : lack of harmony — **dis·har·mo·ni·ous** \ˌdishär'mōnēəs\ *adj*

dis·heart·en \dis'härtᵊn\ *vb* : discourage

di·shev·el \di'shevəl\ *vb* -eled *or* -elled; -el·ing *or* -el·ling : throw into disorder — **di·shev·eled, di·shev·elled** *adj*

dis·hon·est \dis'änəst\ *adj* : not honest — **dis·hon·est·ly** *adv* — **dis·hon·es·ty** *n*

dis·hon·or \dis'änər\ *n or vb* : disgrace — **dis·hon·or·able** *adj* — **dis·hon·or·ably** *adv*

dis·il·lu·sion \ˌdisə'lüzhən\ *vb* : to free from illusion — **dis·il·lu·sion·ment** *n*

dis·in·cli·na·tion \disˌinklə'nāshən\ *n* : slight aversion — **dis·in·cline** \ˌdisᵊn'klīn\ *vb*

dis·in·fect \ˌdisᵊn'fekt\ *vb* : destroy disease germs in or on — **dis·in·fec·tant** \-'fektənt\ *adj or n* — **dis·in·fec·tion** \-'fekshən\ *n*

dis·in·gen·u·ous \ˌdisᵊn'jenyəwəs\ *adj* : lacking in candor

dis·in·her·it \-ᵊn'herət\ *vb* : prevent from inheriting property

dis·in·te·grate \dis'intəˌgrāt\ *vb* : break into parts or small bits — **dis·in·te·gra·tion** \disˌintə'grāshən\ *n*

dis·in·ter·est·ed \dis'intərəstəd, -ˌres-\ *adj* **1** : not interested **2** : not prejudiced — **dis·in·ter·est·ed·ness** *n*

dis·joint·ed \dis'jóintəd\ *adj* **1** : separated at the joint **2** : incoherent

disk \'disk\ *n* : something round and flat

dis·like \dis'līk\ *vb* : regard with dislike ~ *n* : feeling that something is unpleasant and to be avoided

dis·lo·cate \'dislōˌkāt, dis'-\ *vb* : move out of the usual or proper place — **dis·lo·ca·tion** \ˌdislō'kāshən\ *n*

dis·lodge \dis'läj\ *vb* : force out of a place

dis·loy·al \dis'lóiəl\ *adj* : not loyal — **dis·loy·al·ty** *n*

dis·mal \'dizməl\ *adj* : showing or causing gloom — **dis·mal·ly** *adv*

dis·man·tle \dis'mantᵊl\ *vb* -tled; -tling : take apart

dis·may \dis'mā\ *vb* -mayed; -may·ing : discourage — **dismay** *n*

dis·mem·ber \dis'membər\ *vb* : cut into pieces — **dis·mem·ber·ment** *n*

dis·miss \dis'mis\ *vb* **1** : send away **2** : remove from service **3** : put aside or out of mind — **dis·miss·al** *n*

dis·mount \dis'maúnt\ *vb* **1** : get down from something **2** : take apart

dis·obey \ˌdisə'bā\ *vb* : refuse to obey — **dis·obe·di·ence** \-'bēdēəns\ *n* — **dis·obe·di·ent** \-ənt\ *adj*

dis·or·der \dis'órdər\ *n* **1** : lack of order **2** : breach of public order **3** : abnormal state of body or mind — **disorder** *vb* — **dis·or·der·li·ness** *n* — **dis·or·der·ly** *adj*

dis·or·ga·nize \dis'órgəˌnīz\ *vb* : throw into disorder — **dis·or·ga·ni·za·tion** *n*

dis·own \dis'ōn\ *vb* : repudiate

dis·par·age \-'parij\ *vb* -aged; -ag·ing : say bad things about — **dis·par·age·ment** *n*

dis·pa·rate \dis'parət, 'dispərət\ *adj* : different in quality or character — **dis·par·i·ty** \dis'parətē\ *n*

dis·pas·sion·ate \dis'pashənət\ *adj* : not influenced by strong feeling — **dis·pas·sion·ate·ly** *adv*

dis·patch \dis'pach\ *vb* **1** : send **2** : attend to rapidly **3** : kill **4** : defeat ~ *n* **1** : message **2** : news item from a correspondent **3** : promptness and efficiency — **dis·patch·er** *n*

dis·pel \dis'pel\ *vb* -ll- : clear away

dis·pen·sa·ry \-'pensərē\ *n, pl* -ries : place where medical or dental aid is provided

dis·pen·sa·tion \ˌdispən'sāshən\ *n* **1** : system of principles or rules **2** : exemption from a rule **3** : act of dispensing

dis·pense \dis'pens\ *vb* -pensed; -pens·ing **1** : portion out **2** : make up and give out (remedies) — **dis·pens·er** *n* — **dispense with** : do without

dis·perse \-'pərs\ *vb* -persed; -pers-

ing : scatter — **dis•per•sal** \-'pərsəl\
n — **dis•per•sion** \-'perzhən\ *n*

dis•place \-'plās\ *vb* **1** : expel or force
to flee from home or native land **2**
: take the place of — **dis•place•ment**
\-mənt\ *n*

dis•play \-'plā\ *vb* : present to view —
display *n*

dis•please \-'plēz\ *vb* : arouse the dislike of — **dis•plea•sure** \-'plezhər\
n

dis•port \dis'pōrt\ *vb* **1** : amuse **2**
: frolic

dis•pose \dis'pōz\ *vb* **-posed; -pos-**
ing **1** : give a tendency to **2** : settle
— **dis•pos•able** \-'pōzəbəl\ *adj* —
dis•pos•al \-'pōzəl\ *n* — **dis•pos•er**
n — **dispose of** **1** : determine
the fate, condition, or use of **2** : get
rid of

dis•po•si•tion \,dispə'zishən\ *n* **1** : act
or power of disposing of **2** : arrangement **3** : natural attitude

dis•pos•sess \,dispə'zes\ *vb* : deprive
of possession or occupancy — **dis-**
pos•ses•sion \-'zeshən\ *n*

dis•pro•por•tion \,disprə'pōrshən\ *n*
: lack of proportion — **dis•pro•por-**
tion•ate \-shənət\ *adj*

dis•prove \dis'prüv\ *vb* : prove false

dis•pute \dis'pyüt\ *vb* **-put•ed; -put-**
ing **1** : argue **2** : deny the truth or
rightness of **3** : struggle against or
over ~ *n* : debate or quarrel — **dis-**
put•able \-əbəl, 'dispyət-\ *adj* —
dis•pu•ta•tion \,dispyə'tāshən\ *n*

dis•qual•i•fy \dis'kwälə,fī\ *vb* : make
ineligible — **dis•qual•i•fi•ca•tion** *n*

dis•qui•et \dis'kwīət\ *vb* : make uneasy or restless ~ *n* : anxiety

dis•re•gard \,disri'gärd\ *vb* : pay no attention to ~ *n* : neglect

dis•re•pair \,disri'par\ *n* : need of repair

dis•rep•u•ta•ble \dis'repyətəbəl\ *adj*
: having a bad reputation

dis•re•pute \,disri'pyüt\ *n* : low regard

dis•re•spect \,disri'spekt\ *n* : lack of
respect — **dis•re•spect•ful** *adj*

dis•robe \dis'rōb\ *vb* : undress

dis•rupt \dis'rəpt\ *vb* : throw into disorder — **dis•rup•tion** \-'rəpshən\ *n*
— **dis•rup•tive** \-'rəptiv\ *adj*

dis•sat•is•fac•tion \dis,satəs'fakshən\
n : lack of satisfaction

dis•sat•is•fy \dis'satəs,fī\ *vb* : fail to
satisfy

dis•sect \di'sekt\ *vb* : cut into parts

esp. to examine — **dis•sec•tion**
\-'sekshən\ *n*

dis•sem•ble \di'sembəl\ *vb* **-bled;**
-bling : disguise feelings or intention
— **dis•sem•bler** *n*

dis•sem•i•nate \di'semə,nāt\ *vb* **-nat-**
ed; -nat•ing : spread around — **dis-**
sem•i•na•tion \-,semə'nāshən\ *n*

dis•sen•sion \di'senchən\ *n* : discord

dis•sent \di'sent\ *vb* : object or disagree ~ *n* : difference of opinion —
dis•sent•er *n*

dis•ser•ta•tion \,disər'tāshən\ *n* : long
written study of a subject

dis•ser•vice \dis'sərvəs\ *n* : injury

dis•si•dent \'disədənt\ *n* : one who
differs openly with an establishment
— **dis•si•dence** \-əns\ *n* — **dissi-**
dent *adj*

dis•sim•i•lar \di'simələr\ *adj* : different — **dis•sim•i•lar•i•ty** \di,simə-
'larətē\ *n*

dis•si•pate \'disə,pāt\ *vb* **-pat•ed;**
-pat•ing **1** : break up and drive off **2**
: squander — **dis•si•pa•tion** \,dis-
ə'pāshən\ *n*

dis•so•ci•ate \dis'ōsē,āt, -shē-\ *vb*
-at•ed; -at•ing : separate from association — **dis•so•ci•a•tion** \dis,ōsē-
'āshən, -shē-\ *n*

dis•so•lute \'disə,lüt\ *adj* : loose in
morals or conduct

dis•so•lu•tion \,disə'lüshən\ *n* : act or
process of dissolving

dis•solve \di'zälv\ *vb* **1** : break up or
bring to an end **2** : pass or cause to
pass into solution

dis•so•nance \'disənəns\ *n* : discord
— **dis•so•nant** \-nənt\ *adj*

dis•suade \di'swād\ *vb* **-suad•ed;**
-suad•ing : persuade not to do something — **dis•sua•sion** \-'swāzhən\ *n*

dis•tance \'distəns\ *n* **1** : measure of
separation in space or time **2** : reserve

dis•tant \-tənt\ *adj* **1** : separate in
space **2** : remote in time, space, or relationship **3** : reserved — **dis•tant•ly**
adv

dis•taste \dis'tāst\ *n* : dislike — **dis-**
taste•ful *adj*

dis•tem•per \dis'tempər\ *n* : serious
virus disease of dogs

dis•tend \dis'tend\ *vb* : swell out —
dis•ten•sion, dis•ten•tion \-'ten-
chən\ *n*

dis•till \di'stil\ *vb* : obtain by distillation — **dis•til•late** \'distə,lāt, -lət\ *n*

— **dis·till·er** *n* — **dis·till·ery** \di-'stilərē\ *n*

dis·til·la·tion \,distə'lāshən\ *n* : purification of liquid by evaporating then condensing

dis·tinct \dis'tiŋkt\ *adj* 1 : distinguishable from others 2 : readily discerned — **dis·tinc·tive** \-tiv\ *adj* — **dis·tinc·tive·ly** *adv* — **dis·tinc·tive·ness** *n* — **dis·tinct·ly** *adv* — **dis·tinct·ness** *n*

dis·tinc·tion \-'tiŋkshən\ *n* 1 : act of distinguishing 2 : difference 3 : special recognition

dis·tin·guish \-'tiŋgwish\ *vb* 1 : perceive as different 2 : set apart 3 : discern 4 : make outstanding — **dis·tin·guish·able** *adj* — **dis·tin·guished** \-gwisht\ *adj*

dis·tort \dis'tȯrt\ *vb* : twist out of shape, condition, or true meaning — **dis·tor·tion** \-'tȯrshən\ *n*

dis·tract \di'strakt\ *vb* : divert the mind or attention of — **dis·trac·tion** \-'strakshən\ *n*

dis·traught \dis'trȯt\ *adj* : agitated with mental conflict

dis·tress \-'tres\ *n* 1 : suffering 2 : misfortune 3 : state of danger or great need ~ *vb* : subject to strain or distress — **dis·tress·ful** *adj*

dis·trib·ute \-'tribyət\ *vb* -ut·ed; -ut·ing 1 : divide among many 2 : spread or hand out — **dis·tri·bu·tion** \,distrə'byüshən\ *n* — **dis·trib·u·tive** \dis'tribyətiv\ *adj* — **dis·trib·u·tor** \-ər\ *n*

dis·trict \'dis,trikt\ *n* : territorial division

dis·trust \dis'trəst\ *vb or n* : mistrust — **dis·trust·ful** \-fəl\ *adj*

dis·turb \dis'tərb\ *vb* 1 : interfere with 2 : destroy the peace, composure, or order of — **dis·tur·bance** \-'tərbəns\ *n* — **dis·turb·er** *n*

dis·use \dis'yüs\ *n* : lack of use

ditch \'dich\ *n* : trench ~ *vb* 1 : dig a ditch in 2 : get rid of

dith·er \'dithər\ *n* : highly nervous or excited state

dit·to \'ditō\ *n, pl* -tos : more of the same

dit·ty \'ditē\ *n, pl* -ties : short simple song

di·uret·ic \,dīyù'retik\ *adj* : tending to increase urine flow — **diuretic** *n*

di·ur·nal \dī'ərn³l\ *adj* 1 : daily 2 : of or occurring in the daytime

di·van \'dī,van, di'-\ *n* : couch

dive \'dīv\ *vb* **dived** \'dīvd\ *or* **dove** \'dōv\; **dived; div·ing** 1 : plunge into water headfirst 2 : submerge 3 : descend quickly ~ *n* 1 : act of diving 2 : sharp decline — **div·er** *n*

di·verge \də'vərj, dī-\ *vb* -verged; -verg·ing 1 : move in different directions 2 : differ — **di·ver·gence** \-'vərjəns\ *n* — **di·ver·gent** \-jənt\ *adj*

di·vers \'dīvərz\ *adj* : various

di·verse \dī'vərs, də-, 'dī,vərs\ *adj* : involving different forms — **di·ver·si·fi·ca·tion** \də,vərsəfə'kāshən, dī-\ *n* — **di·ver·si·fy** \-'vərsə,fī\ *vb* — **di·ver·si·ty** \-sətē\ *n*

di·vert \də'vərt, dī-\ *vb* 1 : turn from a course or purpose 2 : distract 3 : amuse — **di·ver·sion** \-'vərzhən\ *n*

di·vest \dī'vest, də-\ *vb* : strip of clothing, possessions, or rights

di·vide \də'vīd\ *vb* -vid·ed; -vid·ing 1 : separate 2 : distribute 3 : share 4 : subject to mathematical division ~ *n* : watershed — **di·vid·er** *n*

div·i·dend \'divə,dend\ *n* 1 : individual share 2 : bonus 3 : number to be divided

div·i·na·tion \,divə'nāshən\ *n* : practice of trying to foretell future events

di·vine \də'vīn\ *adj* -vin·er; -est 1 : relating to or being God or a god 2 : supremely good ~ *n* : clergy member ~ *vb* -vined; -vin·ing 1 : infer 2 : prophesy — **di·vine·ly** *adv* — **di·vin·er** *n* — **di·vin·i·ty** \də'vinətē\ *n*

di·vis·i·ble \-'vizəbəl\ *adj* : capable of being divided — **di·vis·i·bil·i·ty** \-,vizə'bilətē\ *n*

di·vi·sion \-'vizhən\ *n* 1 : distribution 2 : part of a whole 3 : disagreement 4 : process of finding out how many times one number is contained in another

di·vi·sive \də'vīsiv, -'vi-, -ziv\ *adj* : creating dissension

di·vi·sor \-'vīzər\ *n* : number by which a dividend is divided

di·vorce \də'vōrs\ *n* : legal breaking up of a marriage — **divorce** *vb*

di·vor·cée \-,vōr'sā, -'sē\ *n* : divorced woman

di·vulge \də'vəlj, dī-\ *vb* -vulged; -vulg·ing : reveal

diz·zy \'dizē\ *adj* -zi·er; -est 1 : having a sensation of whirling 2 : causing or caused by giddiness — **diz•zi•ly** *adv* — **diz•zi•ness** *n*

DNA \ˌdēˌen'ā\ *n* : compound in cell nuclei that is the basis of heredity

do \'dü\ *vb* **did** \'did\; **done** \'dən\; **do•ing** \'düiŋ\; **does** \'dəz\ **1** : work to accomplish (an action or task) **2** : behave **3** : prepare or fix up **4** : fare **5** : finish **6** : serve the needs or purpose of **7** — used as an auxiliary verb — **do•er** \'düər\ *n* — **do away with 1** : get rid of **2** : destroy — **do by** : deal with — **do in** *vb* **1** : ruin **2** : kill

doc•ile \'däsəl\ *adj* : easily managed — **do•cil•i•ty** \dä'silətē\ *n*

¹**dock** \'däk\ *vb* **1** : shorten **2** : reduce

²**dock** *n* **1** : berth between 2 piers to receive ships **2** : loading wharf or platform ∼ *vb* : bring or come into dock — **dock•work•er** *n*

³**dock** *n* : place in a court for a prisoner

dock•et \'däkət\ *n* **1** : record of the proceedings in a legal action **2** : list of legal causes to be tried — **docket** *vb*

doc•tor \'däktər\ *n* **1** : person holding one of the highest academic degrees **2** : one (as a surgeon) skilled in healing arts ∼ *vb* **1** : give medical treatment to **2** : repair or alter — **doc•tor•al** \-tərəl\ *adj*

doc•trine \'däktrən\ *n* : something taught — **doc•tri•nal** \-trən³l\ *adj*

doc•u•ment \'däkyəmənt\ *n* : paper that furnishes information or legal proof — **doc•u•ment** \-ˌment\ *vb* — **doc•u•men•ta•tion** \ˌdäkyəmən-'tāshən\ *n* — **doc•u•ment•er** *n*

doc•u•men•ta•ry \ˌdäkyə'mentərē\ *adj* **1** : of or relating to documents **2** : giving a factual presentation — **documentary** *n*

dod•der \'dädər\ *vb* : become feeble usu. from age

dodge \'däj\ *vb* **dodged; dodg•ing 1** : move quickly aside or out of the way of **2** : evade — **dodge** *n*

do•do \'dōdō\ *n, pl* **-does** *or* **-dos 1** : heavy flightless extinct bird **2** : stupid person

doe \'dō\ *n, pl* **does** *or* **doe** : adult female deer — **doe•skin** \-ˌskin\ *n*

does *pres 3d sing of* DO

doff \'däf\ *vb* : remove

dog \'dȯg\ *n* : flesh-eating domestic mammal ∼ *vb* **1** : hunt down or track like a hound **2** : harass — **dog-**

catch•er *n* — **dog•gy** \-ē\ *n or adj* — **dog•house** *n*

dog–ear \'dȯgˌir\ *n* : turned-down corner of a page — **dog–ear** *vb* — **dog–eared** \-ˌird\ *adj*

dog•ged \'dȯgəd\ *adj* : stubbornly determined

dog•ma \'dȯgmə\ *n* : tenet or code of tenets

dog•ma•tism \-ˌtizəm\ *n* : unwarranted stubbornness of opinion — **dog•ma•tic** \dȯg'matik\ *adj*

dog•wood *n* : flowering tree

doi•ly \'dȯilē\ *n, pl* **-lies** : small decorative mat

do•ings \'düiŋz\ *n pl* : events

dol•drums \'dōldrəmz,'däl-\ *n pl* : spell of listlessness, despondency, or stagnation

dole \'dōl\ *n* : distribution esp. of money to the needy or unemployed — **dole out** *vb* : give out esp. in small portions

dole•ful \'dōlfəl\ *adj* : sad — **dole•ful•ly** *adv*

doll \'däll, 'dȯl\ *n* : small figure of a person used esp. as a child's toy

dol•lar \'dälər\ *n* : any of various basic monetary units (as in the U.S. and Canada)

dol•ly \'dälē\ *n, pl* **-lies** : small cart or wheeled platform

dol•phin \'dälfən\ *n* **1** : sea mammal related to the whales **2** : saltwater food fish

dolt \'dōlt\ *n* : stupid person — **dolt•ish** *adj*

-dom \dəm\ *n suffix* **1** : office or realm **2** : state or fact of being **3** : those belonging to a group

do•main \dō'mān, də-\ *n* **1** : territory over which someone reigns **2** : sphere of activity or knowledge

dome \'dōm\ *n* **1** : large hemispherical roof **2** : roofed stadium

do•mes•tic \də'mestik\ *adj* **1** : relating to the household or family **2** : relating and limited to one's own country **3** : tame ∼ *n* : household servant — **do•mes•ti•cal•ly** \-tiklē\ *adv*

do•mes•ti•cate \-ti,kāt\ *vb* **-cat•ed; -cat•ing** : tame — **do•mes•ti•ca•tion** \-ˌmesti'kāshən\ *n*

do•mi•cile \'dämə,sīl, 'dō-; 'däməsəl\ *n* : home — **domicile** *vb*

dom•i•nance \'dämənəns\ *n* : control — **dom•i•nant** \-nənt\ *adj*

dom•i•nate \-₁nāt\ *vb* **-nat•ed; -nat•ing**
1 : have control over **2** : rise high
above — **dom•i•na•tion** \₁dämə'nā-
shən\ *n*

dom•i•neer \₁dämə'nir\ *vb* : exercise
arbitrary control

do•min•ion \də'minyən\ *n* **1**
: supreme authority **2** : governed territory

dom•i•no \'dämə₁nō\ *n, pl* **-noes** *or*
-nos : flat rectangular block used as a
piece in a game (**dominoes**)

don \'dän\ *vb* **-nn-** : put on (clothes)

do•nate \'dō₁nāt\ *vb* **-nat•ed; -nat•ing**
: make a gift of — **do•na•tion**
\dō'nāshən\ *n*

¹done \'dən\ *past part of* DO

²done *adj* **1** : finished or ended **2**
: cooked sufficiently

don•key \'däŋkē, 'dəŋ-\ *n, pl* **-keys**
: sturdy domestic ass

do•nor \'dōnər\ *n* : one that gives

doo•dle \'düdᵊl\ *vb* **-dled; -dling**
: draw or scribble aimlessly — **doo-
dle** *n*

doom \'düm\ *n* **1** : judgment **2** : fate
3 : ruin — **doom** *vb*

door \'dōr\ *n* : passage for entrance or
a movable barrier that can open or
close such a passage — **door•jamb** *n*
— **door•knob** *n* — **door•mat** *n* —
door•step *n* — **door•way** *n*

dope \'dōp\ **1** : narcotic preparation **2**
: stupid person **3** : information ~ *vb*
doped; dop•ing : drug

dor•mant \'dórmənt\ *adj* : not actively
growing or functioning — **dor-
man•cy** \-mənsē\ *n*

dor•mer \'dórmər\ *n* : window built
upright in a sloping roof

dor•mi•to•ry \'dórmə₁tōrē\ *n, pl* **-ries**
: residence hall (as at a college)

dor•mouse \'dór₁maùs\ *n* : squirrel-
like rodent

dor•sal \'dórsəl\ *adj* : relating to or on
the back — **dor•sal•ly** *adv*

do•ry \'dōrē\ *n, pl* **-ries** : flat-bottomed
boat

dose \'dōs\ *n* : quantity (as of medicine) taken at one time ~ *vb* **dosed;
dos•ing** : give medicine to — **dos-
age** \'dōsij\ *n*

dot \'dät\ *n* **1** : small spot **2** : small
round mark made with or as if with a
pen ~ *vb* **-tt-** : mark with dots

dot•age \'dōtij\ *n* : senility

dote \'dōt\ *vb* **dot•ed; dot•ing 1** : act
feebleminded **2** : be foolishly fond

dou•ble \'dəbəl\ *adj* **1** : consisting of
2 members or parts **2** : being twice as
great or as many **3** : folded in two ~
n **1** : something twice another **2**
: one that resembles another ~ *adv*
: doubly ~ *vb* **-bled; -bling 1** : make
or become twice as great **2** : fold or
bend **3** : clench

dou•ble–cross *vb* : deceive by trickery
— **dou•ble–cross•er** *n*

dou•bly \'dəblē\ *adv* : to twice the degree

doubt \'daùt\ *vb* **1** : be uncertain about
2 : mistrust **3** : consider unlikely ~
n **1** : uncertainty **2** : mistrust **3** : inclination not to believe — **doubt•ful**
\-fəl\ *adj* — **doubt•ful•ly** *adv* —
doubt•less \-ləs\ *adv*

douche \'düsh\ *n* : jet of fluid for
cleaning a body part

dough \'dō\ *n* : stiff mixture of flour
and liquid — **doughy** \'dōē\ *adj*

dough•nut \-₁nət\ *n* : small fried ring=
shaped cake

dough•ty \'daùtē\ *adj* **-ti•er; -est**
: able, strong, or valiant

dour \'daùər, 'dùr\ *adj* **1** : severe **2**
: gloomy or sullen — **dour•ly** *adv*

douse \'daùs, 'daùz\ *vb* **doused;
dous•ing 1** : plunge into or drench
with water **2** : extinguish

¹dove \'dəv\ *n* : small wild pigeon

²dove \'dōv\ *past of* DIVE

dove•tail \'dəv₁tāl\ *vb* : fit together
neatly

dow•a•ger \'daùijər\ *n* **1** : widow with
wealth or a title **2** : dignified elderly
woman

dowdy \'daùdē\ *adj* **dowd•i•er; -est**
: lacking neatness and charm

dow•el \'daùəl\ *n* **1** : peg used for fastening two pieces **2** : wooden rod

dow•er \'daùər\ *n* : property given a
widow for life ~ *vb* : supply with a
dower

¹down \'daùn\ *adv* **1** : toward or in a
lower position or state **2** : to a lying
or sitting position **3** : as a cash deposit **4** : on paper ~ *adj* **1** : lying on
the ground **2** : directed or going
downward **3** : being at a low level ~
prep : toward the bottom of ~ *vb* **1**
: cause to go down **2** : defeat

²down *n* : fluffy feathers

down•cast *adj* **1** : sad **2** : directed
down

down•fall *n* : ruin or cause of ruin

down•grade n : downward slope ~ vb : lower in grade or position

down•heart•ed adj : sad

down•pour n : heavy rain

down•right adv : thoroughly ~ adj : absolute or thorough

downs \'daůnz\ n pl : rolling treeless uplands

down•size \'daůn‚sīz\ vb : reduce in size

down•stairs adv : on or to a lower floor and esp. the main floor — **down•stairs** adj or n

down–to–earth adj : practical

down•town adv : to, toward, or in the business center of a town — **down•town** n or adj

down•trod•den \'daůn‚träd°n\ adj : suffering oppression

down•ward \'daůnwərd\, **down•wards** \-wərdz\ adv : to a lower place or condition — **downward** adj

down•wind adv or adj : in the direction the wind is blowing

downy \'daůnē\ adj **-i•er; -est** : resembling or covered with down

dow•ry \'daůrē\ n, pl **-ries** : property a woman gives her husband in marriage

dox•ol•o•gy \däk'sälɔjē\ n, pl **-gies** : hymn of praise to God

doze \'dōz\ vb **dozed; doz•ing** : sleep lightly — **doze** n

doz•en \'dəz°n\ n, pl **-ens** or **-en** : group of 12 — **doz•enth** \-°nth\ adj

drab \'drab\ adj **-bb-** : dull — **drab•ly** adv — **drab•ness** n

dra•co•ni•an \drā'kōnēən, dra-\ adj, often cap : harsh, cruel

draft \'draft, 'dráft\ n **1** : act of drawing or hauling **2** : act of drinking **3** : amount drunk at once **4** : preliminary outline or rough sketch **5** : selection from a pool or the selection process **6** : order for the payment of money **7** : air current ~ vb **1** : select usu. on a compulsory basis **2** : make a preliminary sketch, version, or plan of ~ adj : drawn from a container — **draft•ee** \draf'tē, dráf-\ n — **drafty** \'draftē\ adj

drafts•man \'draftsmən, 'dráft-\ n : person who draws plans

drag \'drag\ n **1** : something dragged over a surface or through water **2** : something that hinders progress or is boring **3** : act or an instance of dragging ~ vb **-gg- 1** : haul **2** : move or work with difficulty **3** : pass slowly **4** : search or fish with a drag — **drag•ger** n

drag•net \-‚net\ n **1** : trawl **2** : planned actions for finding a criminal

dra•gon \'dragən\ n : fabled winged serpent

drag•on•fly n : large 4-winged insect

drain \'drān\ vb **1** : draw off or flow off gradually or completely **2** : exhaust ~ n : means or act of draining — **drain•age** \-ij\ n — **drain•er** n — **drain•pipe** n

drake \'drāk\ n : male duck

dra•ma \'drämə, 'dram-\ n **1** : composition for theatrical presentation esp. on a serious subject **2** : series of events involving conflicting forces — **dra•mat•ic** \drə'matik\ adj — **dra•mat•i•cal•ly** \-iklē\ adv — **dram•a•tist** \'dramətist, 'dräm-\ n — **dram•a•ti•za•tion** \‚dramətə'zāshən, ‚dräm-\ n — **dra•ma•tize** \'dramə‚tīz, 'dräm-\ vb

drank past of **DRINK**

drape \'drāp\ vb **draped; drap•ing 1** : cover or adorn with folds of cloth **2** : cause to hang in flowing lines or folds ~ n : curtain

drap•ery \'drāpərē\ n, pl **-er•ies** : decorative fabric hung esp. as a heavy curtain

dras•tic \'drastik\ adj : extreme or harsh — **dras•ti•cal•ly** \-tiklē\ adj

draught \'dráft\, **draughty** \'dráftē\ chiefly Brit var of **DRAFT, DRAFTY**

draw \'drȯ\ vb **drew** \'drü\; **drawn** \'drȯn\; **draw•ing 1** : move or cause to move (as by pulling) **2** : attract or provoke **3** : extract **4** : take or receive (as money) **5** : bend a bow in preparation for shooting **6** : leave a contest undecided **7** : sketch **8** : write out **9** : deduce ~ n **1** : act, process, or result of drawing **2** : tie — **draw out** : cause to speak candidly — **draw up 1** : write out **2** : pull oneself erect **3** : bring or come to a stop

draw•back n : disadvantage

draw•bridge n : bridge that can be raised

draw•er \'drȯr, 'drȯər\ n **1** : one that draws **2** : sliding boxlike compartment **3** pl : underpants

draw•ing \'drȯiŋ\ n **1** : occasion of choosing by lot **2** : act or art of making a figure, plan, or sketch with lines **3** : something drawn

drawl \'drȯl\ *vb* : speak slowly — **drawl** *n*

dread \'dred\ *vb* : feel extreme fear or reluctance ~ *n* : great fear ~ *adj* : causing dread — **dread•ful** \-fəl\ *adj* — **dread•ful•ly** *adv*

dream \'drēm\ *n* **1** : series of thoughts or visions during sleep **2** : dreamlike vision **3** : something notable **4** : ideal ~ *vb* **dreamed** \'dremt, 'drēmd\ *or* **dreamt** \'dremt\; **dream•ing 1** : have a dream **2** : imagine — **dream•er** *n* — **dream•like** *adj* — **dreamy** *adj*

drea•ry \'drirē\ *adj* **-ri•er; -est** : dismal — **drea•ri•ly** \'drirəlē\ *adv*

¹dredge \'drej\ *n* : machine for removing earth esp. from under water ~ *vb* **dredged; dredg•ing** : dig up or search with a dredge — **dredg•er** *n*

²dredge *vb* **dredged; dredg•ing** : coat (food) with flour

dregs \'dregz\ *n pl* **1** : sediment **2** : most worthless part

drench \'drench\ *vb* : wet thoroughly

dress \'dres\ *vb* **1** : put clothes on **2** : decorate **3** : prepare (as a carcass) for use **4** : apply dressings, remedies, or fertilizer to ~ *n* **1** : apparel **2** : single garment of bodice and skirt ~ *adj* : suitable for a formal event — **dress•mak•er** *n* — **dress•mak•ing** *n*

dress•er \'dresər\ *n* : bureau with a mirror

dress•ing *n* **1** : act or process of dressing **2** : sauce or a seasoned mixture **3** : material to cover an injury

dressy \'dresē\ *adj* **dress•i•er; -est 1** : showy in dress **2** : stylish

drew *past of* DRAW

drib•ble \'dribəl\ *vb* **-bled; -bling 1** : fall or flow in drops **2** : drool — **dribble** *n*

drier *comparative of* DRY

driest *superlative of* DRY

drift \'drift\ *n* **1** : motion or course of something drifting **2** : mass piled up by wind **3** : general intention or meaning ~ *vb* **1** : float or be driven along (as by a current) **2** : wander without purpose **3** : pile up under force — **drift•er** *n* — **drift•wood** *n*

¹drill \'dril\ *vb* **1** : bore with a drill **2** : instruct by repetition ~ *n* **1** : tool for boring holes **2** : regularly practiced exercise — **drill•er** *n*

²drill *n* : seed-planting implement

³drill *n* : twill-weave cotton fabric

drily *var of* DRYLY

drink \'driŋk\ *vb* **drank** \'draŋk\; **drunk** \'drəŋk\ *or* **drank; drink•ing 1** : swallow liquid **2** : absorb **3** : drink alcoholic beverages esp. to excess ~ *n* **1** : beverage **2** : alcoholic liquor — **drink•able** *adj* — **drink•er** *n*

drip \'drip\ *vb* **-pp-** : fall or let fall in drops ~ *n* **1** : a dripping **2** : sound of falling drops

drive \'drīv\ *vb* **drove** \'drōv\; **driv•en** \'drivən\; **driv•ing 1** : urge or force onward **2** : direct the movement or course of **3** : compel **4** : cause to become **5** : propel forcefully ~ *n* **1** : trip in a vehicle **2** : intensive campaign **3** : aggressive or dynamic quality **4** : basic need — **driv•er** *n*

drive–in *adj* : accommodating patrons in cars — **drive–in** *n*

driv•el \'drivəl\ *vb* **-eled** *or* **-elled; -el•ing** *or* **-el•ling 1** : drool **2** : talk stupidly ~ *n* : nonsense

drive•way *n* : usu. short private road from the street to a house

driz•zle \'drizəl\ *n* : fine misty rain — **drizzle** *vb*

droll \'drōl\ *adj* : humorous or whimsical — **droll•ery** *n* — **drol•ly** *adv*

drom•e•dary \'drämə,derē\ *n, pl* **-dar•ies** : speedy one-humped camel

drone \'drōn\ *n* **1** : male honeybee **2** : deep hum or buzz ~ *vb* **droned; dron•ing** : make a dull monotonous sound

drool \'drül\ *vb* : let liquid run from the mouth

droop \'drüp\ *vb* **1** : hang or incline downward **2** : lose strength or spirit — **droop** *n* — **droopy** \-ē\ *adj*

drop \'dräp\ *n* **1** : quantity of fluid in one spherical mass **2** *pl* : medicine used by drops **3** : decline or fall **4** : distance something drops ~ *vb* **-pp- 1** : fall in drops **2** : let fall **3** : convey **4** : go lower or become less strong or less active — **drop•let** \-lət\ *n* — **drop back** *vb* : move toward the rear — **drop behind** : fail to keep up — **drop in** *vb* : pay an unexpected visit

drop•per *n* : device that dispenses liquid by drops

drop•sy \'dräpsē\ *n* : edema

dross \'dräs\ *n* : waste matter

drought \'draut\ *n* : long dry spell

¹drove \'drōv\ *n* : crowd of moving people or animals

²drove *past of* DRIVE

drown \'draun\ *vb* **1** : suffocate in water **2** : overpower or become overpowered

drowse \'drauz\ *vb* **drowsed; drowsing** : doze — **drowse** *n*

drowsy \'drauzē\ *adj* **drows•i•er; -est** : sleepy — **drows•i•ly** *adv* — **drows•i•ness** *n*

drub \'drəb\ *vb* **-bb-** : beat severely

drudge \'drəj\ *vb* **drudged; drudg•ing** : do hard or boring work — **drudge** *n* — **drudg•ery** \-ərē\ *n*

drug \'drəg\ *n* **1** : substance used as or in medicine **2** : narcotic ~ *vb* **-gg-** : affect with drugs — **drug•gist** \-ist\ *n* — **drug•store** *n*

dru•id \'drüəd\ *n* : ancient Celtic priest

drum \'drəm\ *n* **1** : musical instrument that is a skin-covered cylinder beaten usu. with sticks **2** : drum-shaped object (as a container) ~ *vb* **-mm-** **1** : beat a drum **2** : drive, force, or bring about by steady effort — **drum•beat** *n* — **drum•mer** *n*

drum•stick *n* **1** : stick for beating a drum **2** : lower part of a fowl's leg

drunk \'drəŋk\ *adj* : having the faculties impaired by alcohol ~ *n* : one who is drunk — **drunk•ard** \'drəŋkərd\ *n* — **drunk•en** \-kən\ *adj* — **drunk•en•ly** *adv* — **drunk•en•ness** *n*

dry \'drī\ *adj* **dri•er** \'drīər\; **dri•est** \'drīəst\ **1** : lacking water or moisture **2** : thirsty **3** : marked by the absence of alcoholic beverages **4** : uninteresting **5** : not sweet ~ *vb* **dried; dry•ing** : make or become dry — **dry•ly** *adv* — **dry•ness** *n*

dry–clean *vb* : clean (fabrics) chiefly with solvents other than water — **dry cleaning** *n*

dry•er \'drīər\ *n* : device for drying

dry goods *n pl* : textiles, clothing, and notions

dry ice *n* : solid carbon dioxide

du•al \'düəl, 'dyü-\ *adj* : twofold — **du•al•ism** \-ə,lizəm\ *n* — **du•al•i•ty** \dü'alətē, dyü-\ *n*

dub \'dəb\ *vb* **-bb-** : name

du•bi•ous \'dübēəs, 'dyü-\ *adj* **1** : uncertain **2** : questionable — **du•bi•ous•ly** *adv* — **du•bi•ous•ness** *n*

du•cal \'dükəl, 'dyü-\ *adj* : relating to a duke or dukedom

duch•ess \'dəchəs\ *n* **1** : wife of a duke **2** : woman holding a ducal title

duchy \-ē\ *n, pl* **-ies** : territory of a duke or duchess

¹**duck** \'dək\ *n* : swimming bird related to the goose and swan ~ *vb* **1** : thrust or plunge under water **2** : lower the head or body suddenly **3** : evade — **duck•ling** \-liŋ\ *n*

²**duck** *n* : cotton fabric

duct \'dəkt\ *n* : canal for conveying a fluid — **duct•less** \-ləs\ *adj*

duc•tile \'dəkt°l\ *adj* : able to be drawn out or shaped — **duc•til•i•ty** \,dək-'tilətē\ *n*

dude \'düd, 'dyüd\ *n* **1** : dandy **2** : guy

dud•geon \'dəjən\ *n* : ill humor

due \'dü, 'dyü\ *adj* **1** : owed **2** : appropriate **3** : attributable **4** : scheduled ~ *n* **1** : something due **2** *pl* : fee ~ *adv* : directly

du•el \'düəl, 'dyü-\ *n* : combat between 2 persons — **duel** *vb* — **du•el•ist** *n*

du•et \dü'et, dyü-\ *n* : musical composition for 2 performers

due to *prep* : because of

dug *past of* DIG

dug•out \'dəg,aut\ *n* **1** : boat made by hollowing out a log **2** : shelter made by digging

duke \'dük, 'dyük\ *n* : nobleman of the highest rank — **duke•dom** *n*

dull \'dəl\ *adj* **1** : mentally slow **2** : blunt **3** : not brilliant or interesting — **dull** *vb* — **dul•lard** \'dələrd\ *n* — **dull•ness** *n* — **dul•ly** *adv*

du•ly \'dülē, 'dyü-\ *adv* : in a due manner or time

dumb \'dəm\ *adj* **1** : mute **2** : stupid — **dumb•ly** *adv*

dumb•bell \'dəm,bel\ *n* **1** : short bar with weights on the ends used for exercise **2** : stupid person

dumb•found, dum•found \,dəm-'faund\ *vb* : amaze

dum•my \'dəmē\ *n, pl* **-mies 1** : stupid person **2** : imitative substitute

dump \'dəmp\ *vb* : let fall in a pile ~ *n* : place for dumping something (as refuse) — **in the dumps** : sad

dump•ling \'dəmpliŋ\ *n* : small mass of boiled or steamed dough

dumpy \'dəmpē\ *adj* **dump•i•er; -est** : short and thick in build

¹**dun** \'dən\ *adj* : brownish gray

²**dun** *vb* **-nn-** : hound for payment of a debt

dunce \'dəns\ *n* : stupid person

dune \'dün, 'dyün\ *n* : hill of sand

dung \'dəŋ\ *n* : manure

dun·ga·ree \,dəŋgə'rē\ *n* **1** : blue denim **2** *pl* : work clothes made of dungaree

dun·geon \'dənjən\ *n* : underground prison

dunk \'dəŋk\ *vb* : dip or submerge temporarily in liquid

duo \'düō, 'dyüō\ *n, pl* **du·os** : pair

du·o·de·num \,düə'dēnəm, ,dyü-; dü-'äd²nəm, dyü-\ *n, pl* **-na** \-'dēnə, -²nə\ *or* **-nums** : part of the small intestine nearest the stomach — **du·o·de·nal** \-'dēn²l, -²nəl\ *adj*

dupe \'düp, dyüp\ *n* : one easily deceived or cheated — **dupe** *vb*

du·plex \'dü,pleks, 'dyü-\ *adj* : double ~ *n* : 2-family house

du·pli·cate \'düplikət, 'dyü-\ *adj* **1** : consisting of 2 identical items **2** : being just like another ~ *n* : exact copy ~ \-,kāt\ *vb* **-cat·ed; -cat·ing** **1** : make an exact copy of **2** : repeat or equal — **du·pli·ca·tion** \,düpli-'kāshən, ,dyü-\ *n* — **du·pli·ca·tor** \'düpli,kātər, dyü-\ *n*

du·plic·i·ty \dü'plisətē, ,dyü-\ *n, pl* **-ties** : deception

du·ra·ble \'dürəbəl, 'dyür-\ *adj* : lasting a long time — **du·ra·bil·i·ty** \,dürə'bilətē, ,dyür-\ *n*

du·ra·tion \du'rāshən, dyu-\ *n* : length of time something lasts

du·ress \du'res, dyu-\ *n* : coercion

dur·ing \'dürin, 'dyür-\ *prep* **1** : throughout **2** : at some point in

dusk \'dəsk\ *n* : twilight — **dusky** *adj*

dust \'dəst\ *n* : powdered matter ~ *vb* **1** : remove dust from **2** : sprinkle with fine particles — **dust·er** *n* — **dust·pan** *n* — **dusty** *adj*

du·ty \'dütē, 'dyü-\ *n, pl* **-ties** **1** : action required by one's occupation or position **2** : moral or legal obligation **3** : tax — **du·te·ous** \-əs\ *adj* — **du·ti·able** \-əbəl\ *adj* — **du·ti·ful** \'dütifəl, 'dyü-\ *adj*

DVD \,dē,vē'dē\ *n* : digital video disk

dwarf \'dwȯrf\ *n, pl* **dwarfs** \'dwȯrfs\ *or* **dwarves** \'dwȯrvz\ : one that is much below normal size ~ *vb* **1** : stunt **2** : cause to seem smaller — **dwarf·ish** *adj*

dwell \'dwel\ *vb* **dwelt** \'dwelt\ *or* **dwelled** \'dweld, 'dwelt\; **dwell·ing** **1** : reside **2** : keep the attention directed — **dwell·er** *n* — **dwell·ing** *n*

dwin·dle \'dwind²l\ *vb* **-dled; -dling** : become steadily less

dye \'dī\ *n* : coloring material ~ *vb* **dyed; dye·ing** : give a new color to

dying *pres part of* DIE

dyke *var of* DIKE

dy·nam·ic \dī'namik\ *adj* **1** : relating to physical force producing motion **2** : energetic or forceful

dy·na·mite \'dīnə,mīt\ *n* : explosive made of nitroglycerin — **dynamite** *vb*

dy·na·mo \-,mō\ *n, pl* **-mos** : electrical generator

dy·nas·ty \'dīnəstē, -,nas-\ *n, pl* **-ties** : succession of rulers of the same family — **dy·nas·tic** \dī'nastik\ *adj*

dys·en·tery \'dis²n,terē\ *n, pl* **-ter·ies** : disease marked by diarrhea

dys·lex·ia \dis'leksēə\ *n* : disturbance of the ability to read — **dys·lex·ic** \-sik\ *adj*

dys·pep·sia \-'pepshə, -sēə\ *n* : indigestion — **dys·pep·tic** \-'peptik\ *adj or n*

dys·tro·phy \'distrəfē\ *n, pl* **-phies** : disorder involving nervous and muscular tissue

E

e \'ē\ *n, pl* **e's** *or* **es** \'ēz\ : 5th letter of the alphabet

e- *comb form* : electronic

each \'ēch\ *adj* : being one of the class named ~ *pron* : every individual one ~ *adv* : apiece

ea·ger \'ēgər\ *adj* : enthusiastic or anxious — **ea·ger·ly** *adv* — **ea·ger·ness** *n*

ea·gle \'ēgəl\ *n* : large bird of prey

-ean — see -AN

¹ear \'ir\ *n* : organ of hearing or the outer part of this — **ear·ache** *n* — **eared** *adj* — **ear·lobe** \-,lōb\ *n*

²**ear** *n* : fruiting head of a cereal

ear•drum *n* : thin membrane that receives and transmits sound waves in the ear

earl \'ərl\ *n* : British nobleman — **earl-dom** \-dəm\ *n*

ear•ly \'ərlē\ *adj* **-li•er; -est 1** : relating to or occurring near the beginning or before the usual time **2** : ancient — **early** *adv*

ear•mark *vb* : designate for a specific purpose

earn \'ərn\ *vb* **1** : receive as a return for service **2** : deserve

ear•nest \'ərnəst\ *n* : serious state of mind — **earnest** *adj* — **ear•nest•ly** *adv* — **ear•nest•ness** *n*

earn•ings \'ərniŋz\ *n pl* : something earned

ear•phone *n* : device that reproduces sound and is worn over or in the ear

ear•ring *n* : earlobe ornament

ear•shot *n* : range of hearing

earth \'ərth\ *n* **1** : soil or land **2** : planet inhabited by man — **earth•li-ness** *n* — **earth•ly** *adj* — **earth•ward** \-wərd\ *adv*

earth•en \'ərthən\ *adj* : made of earth or baked clay — **earth•en•ware** \-ˌwar\ *n*

earth•quake *n* : shaking or trembling of the earth

earth•worm *n* : long segmented worm

earthy \'ərthē\ *adj* **earth•i•er; -est 1** : relating to or consisting of earth **2** : practical **3** : coarse — **earth•i•ness** *n*

ease \'ēz\ *n* **1** : comfort **2** : naturalness of manner **3** : freedom from difficulty ~ *vb* **eased; eas•ing 1** : relieve from distress **2** : lessen the tension of **3** : make easier

ea•sel \'ēzəl\ *n* : frame to hold a painter's canvas

east \'ēst\ *adv* : to or toward the east ~ *adj* : situated toward or at or coming from the east ~ *n* **1** : direction of sunrise **2** *cap* : regions to the east — **east•er•ly** \'ēstərlē\ *adv or adj* — **east•ward** *adv or adj* — **east•wards** *adv*

Eas•ter \'ēstər\ *n* : church feast celebrating Christ's resurrection

east•ern \'ēstərn\ *adj* **1** *cap* : relating to a region designated East **2** : lying toward or coming from the east — **East•ern•er** *n*

easy \'ēzē\ *adj* **eas•i•er; -est 1**

: marked by ease **2** : lenient — **eas-i•ly** \'ēzəlē\ *adv* — **eas•i•ness** \-ēnəs\ *n*

easy•go•ing *adj* : relaxed and casual

eat \'ēt\ *vb* **ate** \'āt\; **eat•en** \'ēt°n\; **eat•ing 1** : take in as food **2** : use up or corrode — **eat•able** *adj or n* — **eat•er** *n*

eaves \'ēvz\ *n pl* : overhanging edge of a roof

eaves•drop *vb* : listen secretly — **eaves•drop•per** *n*

ebb \'eb\ *n* **1** : outward flow of the tide **2** : decline ~ *vb* **1** : recede from the flood state **2** : wane

eb•o•ny \'ebənē\ *n, pl* **-nies** : hard heavy wood of tropical trees ~ *adj* **1** : made of ebony **2** : black

ebul•lient \i'bulyənt, -'bəl-\ *adj* : exuberant — **ebul•lience** \-yəns\ *n*

ec•cen•tric \ik'sentrik\ *adj* **1** : odd in behavior **2** : being off center — **eccentric** *n* — **ec•cen•tri•cal•ly** \-triklē\ *adv* — **ec•cen•tric•i•ty** \ˌek,sen'trisətē\ *n*

ec•cle•si•as•tic \ik,lēzē'astik\ *n* : clergyman

ec•cle•si•as•ti•cal \-tikəl\, **ecclesias-tic** *adj* : relating to a church — **ec•cle-si•as•ti•cal•ly** \-tiklē\ *adv*

ech•e•lon \'eshəˌlän\ *n* **1** : steplike arrangement **2** : level of authority

echo \'ekō\ *n, pl* **ech•oes** : repetition of a sound caused by a reflection of the sound waves — **echo** *vb*

èclair \ā'klar\ *n* : custard-filled pastry

eclec•tic \e'klektik, i-\ *adj* : drawing or drawn from varied sources

eclipse \i'klips\ *n* : total or partial obscuring of one celestial body by another — **eclipse** *vb*

ecol•o•gy \i'käləjē, e-\ *n, pl* **-gies** : science concerned with the interaction of organisms and their environment — **eco•log•i•cal** \ˌēkə'läjikəl, ˌek-\ *adj* — **eco•log•i•cal•ly** *adv* — **ecol•o-gist** \i'käləjist, e-\ *n*

eco•nom•ic \ˌekə'nämik, ˌēkə-\ *adj* : relating to the producing and the buying and selling of goods and services

eco•nom•ics \-'nämiks\ *n* : branch of knowledge dealing with goods and services — **econ•o•mist** \i'känəmist\ *n*

econ•o•mize \i'känəˌmīz\ *vb* **-mized; -miz•ing** : be thrifty — **econ•o-miz•er** *n*

econ•o•my \-əmē\ *n, pl* **-mies 1** : thrifty use of resources **2** : economic system — **eco•nom•i•cal** \ˌekə'nämikəl, ˌēkə-\ *adj* — **ec•o•nom•i•cal•ly** *adv* — **economy** *adj*

ecru \'ekrü, 'ākrü\ *n* : beige

ec•sta•sy \'ekstəsē\ *n, pl* **-sies** : extreme emotional excitement — **ec•stat•ic** \ek'statik, ik-\ *adj* — **ec•stat•i•cal•ly** \-iklē\ *adv*

ec•u•men•i•cal \ˌekyə'menikəl\ *adj* : promoting worldwide Christian unity

ec•ze•ma \ig'zēmə, 'egzəmə, 'eksə-\ *n* : itching skin inflammation

¹-ed \d *after a vowel or* b, g, j, l, m, n, ŋ, r, th, v, z, zh; əd, id *after* d, t; t *after other sounds*\ *vb suffix or adj suffix* **1** — used to form the past participle of regular verbs **2** : having or having the characteristics of

²-ed *vb suffix* — used to form the past tense of regular verbs

ed•dy \'edē\ *n, pl* **-dies** : whirlpool — **eddy** *vb*

ede•ma \i'dēmə\ *n* : abnormal accumulation of fluid in the body tissues — **edem•a•tous** \-'demətəs\ *adj*

Eden \'ēd³n\ *n* : paradise

edge \'ej\ *n* **1** : cutting side of a blade **2** : line where something begins or ends ~ *vb* **edged; edg•ing 1** : give or form an edge **2** : move gradually **3** : narrowly defeat — **edg•er** *n*

edge•wise \-ˌwīz\ *adv* : sideways

edgy \'ejē\ *adj* **edg•i•er; -est** : nervous — **edg•i•ness** *n*

ed•i•ble \'edəbəl\ *adj* : fit or safe to be eaten — **ed•i•bil•i•ty** \ˌedə'bilətē\ *n* — **edible** *n*

edict \'ē,dikt\ *n* : order or decree

ed•i•fi•ca•tion \ˌedəfə'kāshən\ *n* : instruction or information — **ed•i•fy** \'edə,fī\ *vb*

ed•i•fice \'edəfəs\ *n* : large building

ed•it \'edət\ *vb* **1** : revise and prepare for publication **2** : delete — **ed•i•tor** \-ər\ *n* — **ed•i•tor•ship** *n*

edi•tion \i'dishən\ *n* **1** : form in which a text is published **2** : total number published at one time

ed•i•to•ri•al \ˌedə'tōrēəl\ *adj* **1** : relating to an editor or editing **2** : expressing opinion ~ *n* : article (as in a newspaper) expressing the views of an editor — **ed•i•to•ri•al•ize** \-ēə,līz\ *vb* — **ed•i•to•ri•al•ly** *adv*

ed•u•cate \'ejə,kāt\ *vb* **-cat•ed; -cat-**

ing 1 : give instruction to **2** : develop mentally and morally **3** : provide with information — **ed•u•ca•ble** \'ejəkəbəl\ *adj* — **ed•u•ca•tion** \ˌejə'kāshən\ *n* — **ed•u•ca•tion•al** \-shənəl\ *adj* — **ed•u•ca•tor** \-ər\ *n*

eel \'ēl\ *n* : snakelike fish

ee•rie \'irē\ *adj* **-ri•er; -est** : weird — **ee•ri•ly** \'irəlē\ *adv*

ef•face \i'fās, e-\ *vb* **-faced; -fac•ing** : obliterate by rubbing out — **ef•face•ment** *n*

ef•fect \i'fekt\ *n* **1** : result **2** : meaning **3** : influence **4** *pl* : goods or possessions ~ *vb* : cause to happen — **in effect** : in substance

ef•fec•tive \i'fektiv\ *adj* **1** : producing a strong or desired effect **2** : being in operation — **ef•fec•tive•ly** *adv* — **ef•fec•tive•ness** *n*

ef•fec•tu•al \i'fekchəwəl\ *adj* : producing an intended effect — **ef•fec•tu•al•ly** *adv* — **ef•fec•tu•al•ness** *n*

ef•fem•i•nate \ə'femənət\ *adj* : having qualities more typical of women than men — **ef•fem•i•na•cy** \-nəsē\ *n*

ef•fer•vesce \ˌefər'ves\ *vb* **-vesced; -vesc•ing 1** : bubble and hiss as gas escapes **2** : show exhilaration — **ef•fer•ves•cence** \-'ves³ns\ *n* — **ef•fer•ves•cent** \-³nt\ *adj* — **ef•fer•ves•cent•ly** *adv*

ef•fete \e'fēt\ *adj* **1** : worn out **2** : weak or decadent **3** : effeminate

ef•fi•ca•cious \ˌefə'kāshəs\ *adj* : effective — **ef•fi•ca•cy** \'efikəsē\ *n*

ef•fi•cient \i'fishənt\ *adj* : working well with little waste — **ef•fi•cien•cy** \-ənsē\ *n* — **ef•fi•cient•ly** *adv*

ef•fi•gy \'efəjē\ *n, pl* **-gies** : usu. crude image of a person

ef•flu•ent \'e,flüənt, e'flü-\ *n* : something that flows out — **effluent** *adj*

ef•fort \'efərt\ *n* **1** : a putting forth of strength **2** : use of resources toward a goal **3** : product of effort — **ef•fort•less** *adj* — **ef•fort•less•ly** *adv*

ef•fron•tery \i'frəntərē\ *n, pl* **-ter•ies** : insolence

ef•fu•sion \i'fyüzhən, e-\ *n* : a gushing forth — **ef•fu•sive** \-'fyüsiv\ *adj* — **ef•fu•sive•ly** *adv*

¹egg \'eg, 'āg\ *vb* : urge to action

²egg *n* **1** : rounded usu. hard-shelled reproductive body esp. of birds and reptiles from which the young hatches **2** : ovum — **egg•shell** *n*

egg•nog \-₁näg\ *n* : rich drink of eggs and cream

egg•plant *n* : edible purplish fruit of a plant related to the potato

ego \'ēgō\ *n, pl* **egos** : self-esteem

ego•cen•tric \₁ēgō'sentrik\ *adj* : self-centered

ego•tism \'ēgə₁tizəm\ *n* : exaggerated sense of self-importance — **ego•tist** \-tist\ *n* — **ego•tis•tic** \₁ēgə'tistik\, **ego•tis•ti•cal** \-tikəl\ *adj* — **ego•tis•ti•cal•ly** *adv*

egre•gious \i'grējəs\ *adj* : notably bad — **egre•gious•ly** *adv*

egress \'ē₁gres\ *n* : a way out

egret \'ēgrət, i'gret, 'egrət\ *n* : long-plumed heron

ei•der•down \'īdər₁daün\ *n* : soft down obtained from a northern sea duck (**eider**)

eight \'āt\ *n* **1** : one more than 7 **2** : 8th in a set or series **3** : something having 8 units — **eight** *adj or pron* — **eighth** \'ātth\ *adj or adv or n*

eigh•teen \āt'tēn\ *n* : one more than 17 — **eigh•teen** *adj or pron* — **eigh•teenth** \-'tēnth\ *adj or n*

eighty \'ātē\ *n, pl* **eight•ies** : 8 times 10 — **eight•i•eth** \'ātēəth\ *adj or n* — **eighty** *adj or pron*

ei•ther \'ēthər, 'ī-\ *adj* **1** : both **2** : being the one or the other of two ~ *pron* : one of two or more ~ *conj* : one or the other

ejac•u•late \i'jakyə₁lāt\ *vb* **-lat•ed; -lat•ing 1** : say suddenly **2** : eject a fluid (as semen) — **ejac•u•la•tion** \-₁jakyə'lāshən\ *n*

eject \i'jekt\ *vb* : drive or throw out — **ejec•tion** \-'jekshən\ *n*

eke \'ēk\ *vb* **eked; ek•ing** : barely gain with effort — usu. with *out*

elab•o•rate \i'labərət\ *adj* **1** : planned in detail **2** : complex and ornate ~ \-ə₁rāt\ *vb* **-rat•ed; -rat•ing** : work out in detail — **elab•o•rate•ly** *adv* — **elab•o•rate•ness** *n* — **elab•o•ra•tion** \-₁labə'rāshən\ *n*

elapse \i'laps\ *vb* **elapsed; elaps•ing** : slip by

elas•tic \i'lastik\ *adj* **1** : springy **2** : flexible ~ *n* **1** : elastic material **2** : rubber band — **elas•tic•i•ty** \-₁las-'tisətē, ₁ē₁las-\ *n*

elate \i'lāt\ *vb* **elat•ed; elat•ing** : fill with joy — **ela•tion** \-'lāshən\ *n*

el•bow \'el₁bō\ *n* **1** : joint of the arm **2** : elbow-shaped bend or joint ~ *vb* : push aside with the elbow

el•der \'eldər\ *adj* : older ~ *n* **1** : one who is older **2** : church officer

el•der•ber•ry \'eldər₁berē\ *n* : edible black or red fruit or a tree or shrub bearing these

el•der•ly \'eldərlē\ *adj* : past middle age

el•dest \'eldəst\ *adj* : oldest

elect \i'lekt\ *adj* : elected but not yet in office ~ *n* **elect** *pl* : exclusive group ~ *vb* : choose esp. by vote — **elec•tion** \i'lekshən\ *n* — **elec•tive** \i'lektiv\ *n or adj* — **elec•tor** \i'lektər\ *n* — **elec•tor•al** \-tərəl\ *adj*

elec•tor•ate \i'lektərət\ *n* : body of persons entitled to vote

elec•tric \i'lektrik\ *adj* **1** *or* **elec•tri•cal** \-trikəl\ : relating to or run by electricity **2** : thrilling — **elec•tri•cal•ly** *adv*

elec•tri•cian \i₁lek'trishən\ *n* : person who installs or repairs electrical equipment

elec•tric•i•ty \-'trisətē\ *n, pl* **-ties 1** : fundamental form of energy occurring naturally (as in lightning) or produced artificially **2** : electric current

elec•tri•fy \i'lektrə₁fī\ *vb* **-fied; -fy•ing 1** : charge with electricity **2** : equip for use of electric power **3** : thrill — **elec•tri•fi•ca•tion** \-₁lektrəfə'kāshən\ *n*

elec•tro•car•dio•gram \i₁lektrō-'kärdēə₁gram\ *n* : tracing made by an electrocardiograph

elec•tro•car•dio•graph \-₁graf\ *n* : instrument for monitoring heart function

elec•tro•cute \i'lektrə₁kyüt\ *vb* **-cut•ed; -cut•ing** : kill by an electric shock — **elec•tro•cu•tion** \-₁lektrə'kyü-shən\ *n*

elec•trode \i'lek₁trōd\ *n* : conductor at a nonmetallic part of a circuit

elec•trol•y•sis \i₁lek'träləsəs\ *n* **1** : production of chemical changes by passage of an electric current through a substance **2** : destruction of hair roots with an electric current — **elec•tro•lyt•ic** \-trə'litik\ *adj*

elec•tro•lyte \i'lektrə₁līt\ *n* : nonmetallic electric conductor

elec•tro•mag•net \i₁lektrō'magnət\ *n* : magnet made using electric current

elec•tro•mag•ne•tism \-nə₁tizəm\ *n* : natural force responsible for interac-

tions between charged particles —
elec·tro·mag·net·ic \-mag'netik\
adj — **elec·tro·mag·net·i·cal·ly**
\-iklē\ *adv*
elec·tron \i'lek,trän\ *n* : negatively
charged particle within the atom
elec·tron·ic \i,lek'tränik\ *adj* : relating to electrons or electronics —
elec·tron·i·cal·ly \-iklē\ *adv*
elec·tron·ics \-iks\ *n* : physics of electrons and their use esp. in devices
elec·tro·plate \i'lektrə,plāt\ *vb* : coat
(as with metal) by electrolysis
el·e·gance \'eligəns\ *n* : refined grace-
fulness — **el·e·gant** \-gənt\ *adj* —
el·e·gant·ly *adv*
el·e·gy \'eləjē\ *n, pl* **-gies** : poem expressing grief for one who is dead —
ele·gi·ac \,elə'jīək, -,ak\ *adj*
el·e·ment \'eləmənt\ *n* **1** *pl* : weather
conditions **2** : natural environment **3**
: constituent part **4** *pl* : simplest principles **5** : substance that has atoms of
only one kind — **el·e·men·tal** \,elə'-
ment°l\ *adj*
el·e·men·ta·ry \,elə'mentrē\ *adj* **1**
: simple **2** : relating to the basic subjects of education
el·e·phant \'eləfənt\ *n* : huge mammal
with a trunk and 2 ivory tusks
el·e·vate \'elə,vāt\ *vb* **-vat·ed; -vat·ing**
1 : lift up **2** : exalt
el·e·va·tion \,elə'vāshən\ *n* : height or
a high place
el·e·va·tor \'elə,vātər\ *n* **1** : cage or
platform for raising or lowering
something **2** : grain storehouse
elev·en \i'levən\ *n* **1** : one more than
10 **2** : 11th in a set or series **3**
: something having 11 units —
eleven *adj or pron* — **elev·enth**
\-ənth\ *adj or n*
elf \'elf\ *n, pl* **elves** \'elvz\ : mischievous fairy — **elf·in** \'elfən\ *adj* —
elf·ish \'elfish\ *adj*
elic·it \i'lisət\ *vb* : draw forth
el·i·gi·ble \'eləjəbəl\ *adj* : qualified to
participate or to be chosen — **el·i·gi·**
bil·i·ty \,eləjə'bilətē\ *n*
elim·i·nate \i'limə,nāt\ *vb* **-nat·ed;**
-nat·ing : get rid of — **elim·i·na·tion**
\i,limə'nāshən\ *n*
elite \ā'lēt\ *n* : choice or select group
elix·ir \i'liksər\ *n* : medicinal solution
elk \'elk\ *n* : large deer
el·lipse \i'lips, e-\ *n* : oval
el·lip·sis \-'lipsəs\ *n, pl* **-lip·ses**

\-,sēz\ **1** : omission of a word **2**
: marks (as . . .) to show omission
el·lip·ti·cal \-'tikəl\, **el·lip·tic** \-'tik\
adj **1** : relating to or shaped like an
ellipse **2** : relating to or marked by
ellipsis
elm \'elm\ *n* : tall shade tree
el·o·cu·tion \,elə'kyüshən\ *n* : art of
public speaking
elon·gate \i'lón,gāt\ *vb* **-gat·ed; -gat·**
ing : make or grow longer — **elon·**
ga·tion \,ē,lón'gāshən\ *n*
elope \i'lōp\ *vb* **eloped; elop·ing** : run
away esp. to be married — **elope·**
ment *n* — **elop·er** *n*
el·o·quent \'eləkwənt\ *adj* : forceful
and persuasive in speech — **el·o·**
quence \-kwəns\ *n* — **el·o·quent·ly**
adv
else \'els\ *adv* **1** : in a different way,
time, or place **2** : otherwise ~ *adj* **1**
: other **2** : more
else·where *adv* : in or to another place
elu·ci·date \i'lüsə,dāt\ *vb* **-dat·ed;**
-dat·ing : explain — **elu·ci·da·tion**
\i,lüsə'dāshən\ *n*
elude \ē'lüd\ *vb* **elud·ed; elud·ing**
: evade — **elu·sive** \ē'lüsiv\ *adj* —
elu·sive·ly *adv* — **elu·sive·ness** *n*
elves *pl of* ELF
ema·ci·ate \i'māshē,āt\ *vb* **-at·ed; -at·**
ing : become or make very thin —
ema·ci·a·tion \i,māsē'āshən, -shē-\ *n*
e–mail \'ē,māl\ *n* : message sent or received via computers
em·a·nate \'emə,nāt\ *vb* **-nat·ed;**
-nat·ing : come forth — **em·a·na·**
tion \,emə'nāshən\ *n*
eman·ci·pate \i'mansə,pāt\ *vb* **-pat·ed;**
-pat·ing : set free — **eman·ci·pa·**
tion \i,mansə'pāshən\ *n* — **eman·**
ci·pa·tor \i'mansə,pātər\ *n*
emas·cu·late \i'maskyə,lāt\ *vb* **-lat·ed;**
-lat·ing **1** : castrate **2** : weaken —
emas·cu·la·tion \i,maskyə'lāshən\
n
em·balm \im'bäm, -'bälm\ *vb* : preserve (a corpse) — **em·balm·er** *n*
em·bank·ment \im'baŋkmənt\ *n*
: protective barrier of earth
em·bar·go \im'bärgō\ *n, pl* **-goes**
: ban on trade — **embargo** *vb*
em·bark \-'bärk\ *vb* **1** : go on board a
ship or airplane **2** : make a start —
em·bar·ka·tion \,em,bär'kāshən\ *n*
em·bar·rass \im'barəs\ *vb* : cause dis-

tress and self-consciousness — **em·bar·rass·ment** *n*

em·bas·sy \'embəsē\ *n, pl* **-sies** : residence and offices of an ambassador

em·bed \im'bed\ *vb* **-dd-** : fix firmly

em·bel·lish \-'belish\ *vb* : decorate — **em·bel·lish·ment** *n*

em·ber \'embər\ *n* : smoldering fragment from a fire

em·bez·zle \im'bezəl\ *vb* **-zled; -zling** : steal (money) by falsifying records — **em·bez·zle·ment** *n* — **em·bez·zler** \-ələr\ *n*

em·bit·ter \im'bitər\ *vb* : make bitter

em·bla·zon \-'blāz°n\ *vb* : display conspicuously

em·blem \'embləm\ *n* : symbol — **em·blem·at·ic** \,emblə'matik\ *adj*

em·body \im'bädē\ *vb* **-bod·ied; -body·ing** : give definite form or expression to — **em·bodi·ment** \-'bädimənt\ *n*

em·boss \-'bäs, -'bòs\ *vb* : ornament with raised work

em·brace \-'brās\ *vb* **-braced; -bracing** 1 : clasp in the arms 2 : welcome 3 : include — **embrace** *n*

em·broi·der \-'bròidər\ *vb* : ornament with or do needlework — **em·broi·dery** \-ərē\ *n*

em·broil \im'bròil\ *vb* : involve in conflict or difficulties

em·bryo \'embrē,ō\ *n* : living being in its earliest stages of development — **em·bry·on·ic** \,embrē'änik\ *adj*

emend \ē'mend\ *vb* : correct — **emen·da·tion** \,ē,men'dāshən\ *n*

em·er·ald \'emrəld, 'emə-\ *n* : green gem ~ *adj* : bright green

emerge \i'mərj\ *vb* **emerged; emerging** : rise, come forth, or appear — **emer·gence** \-'mərjəns\ *n* — **emer·gent** \-jənt\ *adj*

emer·gen·cy \i'mərjənsē\ *n, pl* **-cies** : condition requiring prompt action

em·ery \'emərē\ *n, pl* **-er·ies** : dark granular mineral used for grinding

emet·ic \i'metik\ *n* : agent that induces vomiting — **emetic** *adj*

em·i·grate \'emə,grāt\ *vb* **-grat·ed; -grat·ing** : leave a country to settle elsewhere — **em·i·grant** \-igrənt\ *n* — **em·i·gra·tion** \,emə'grāshən\ *n*

em·i·nence \'emənəns\ *n* 1 : prominence or superiority 2 : person of high rank

em·i·nent \-nənt\ *adj* : prominent — **em·i·nent·ly** *adv*

em·is·sary \'emə,serē\ *n, pl* **-sar·ies** : agent

emis·sion \ē'mishən\ *n* : substance discharged into the air

emit \ē'mit\ *vb* **-tt-** : give off or out

emol·u·ment \i'mälyəmənt\ *n* : salary or fee

emote \i'mōt\ *vb* **emot·ed; emot·ing** : express emotion

emo·tion \i'mōshən\ *n* : intense feeling — **emo·tion·al** \-shənəl\ *adj* — **emo·tion·al·ly** *adv*

em·per·or \'empərər\ *n* : ruler of an empire

em·pha·sis \'emfəsəs\ *n, pl* **-pha·ses** \-,sēz\ : stress

em·pha·size \-,sīz\ *vb* **-sized; -siz·ing** : stress

em·phat·ic \im'fatik, em-\ *adj* : uttered with emphasis — **em·phat·i·cal·ly** \-iklē\ *adv*

em·pire \'em,pīr\ *n* : large state or a group of states

em·pir·i·cal \im'pirikəl\ *adj* : based on observation — **em·pir·i·cal·ly** \-iklē\ *adv*

em·ploy \im'plòi\ *vb* 1 : use 2 : occupy ~ *n* : paid occupation — **em·ploy·ee, em·ploye** \im,plòi'ē, -'plòi,ē\ *n* — **em·ploy·er** *n* — **em·ploy·ment** \-mənt\ *n*

em·pow·er \im'pauər\ *vb* : give power to — **em·pow·er·ment** *n*

em·press \'emprəs\ *n* 1 : wife of an emperor 2 : woman emperor

emp·ty \'emptē\ *adj* 1 : containing nothing 2 : not occupied 3 : lacking value, sense, or purpose ~ *vb* **-tied; -ty·ing** : make or become empty — **emp·ti·ness** \-tēnəs\ *n*

emu \'ēmyü\ *n* : Australian bird related to the ostrich

em·u·late \'emyə,lāt\ *vb* **-lat·ed; -lat·ing** : try to equal or excel — **em·u·la·tion** \,emyə'lāshən\ *n*

emul·si·fy \i'məlsə,fī\ *vb* **-fied; -fy·ing** : convert into an emulsion — **emul·si·fi·ca·tion** \i,məlsəfə'kāshən\ *n* — **emul·si·fi·er** \-'məlsə,fīər\ *n*

emul·sion \i'məlshən\ *n* 1 : mixture of mutually insoluble liquids 2 : light-sensitive coating on photographic film

-en \ən,°n\ *vb suffix* 1 : become or cause to be 2 : cause or come to have

en·able \in'ābəl\ *vb* **-abled; -abling** : give power, capacity, or ability to

en•act \in'akt\ *vb* **1** : make into law **2** : act out — **en•act•ment** *n*

enam•el \in'aməl\ *n* **1** : glasslike substance used to coat metal or pottery **2** : hard outer layer of a tooth **3** : glossy paint — **enamel** *vb*

en•am•or \in'amər\ *vb* : excite with love

en•camp \in'kamp\ *vb* : make camp — **en•camp•ment** *n*

en•case \in'kās\ *vb* : enclose in or as if in a case

-ence \əns,³ns\ *n suffix* **1** : action or process **2** : quality or state

en•ceph•a•li•tis \in,sefə'lītəs\ *n, pl* -**lit•i•des** \-'litə,dēz\ : inflammation of the brain

en•chant \in'chant\ *vb* **1** : bewitch **2** : fascinate — **en•chant•er** *n* — **en•chant•ment** *n* — **en•chant•ress** \-'chantrəs\ *n*

en•cir•cle \in'sərkəl\ *vb* : surround

en•close \in'klōz\ *vb* **1** : shut up or surround **2** : include — **en•clo•sure** \in'klōzhər\ *n*

en•co•mi•um \en'kōmēəm\ *n, pl* -**mi•ums** *or* -**mia** \-mēə\ : high praise

en•com•pass \in'kəmpəs, -'käm-\ *vb* : surround or include

en•core \'än,kōr\ *n* : further performance

en•coun•ter \in'kauntər\ *vb* **1** : fight **2** : meet unexpectedly — **encounter** *n*

en•cour•age \in'kərij\ *vb* -**aged; -ag•ing 1** : inspire with courage and hope **2** : foster — **en•cour•age•ment** *n*

en•croach \in'krōch\ *vb* : enter upon another's property or rights — **en•croach•ment** *n*

en•crust \in'krəst\ *vb* : form a crust on

en•cum•ber \in'kəmbər\ *vb* : burden — **en•cum•brance** \-brəns\ *n*

-en•cy \ənsē,³n-\ *n suffix* : -ence

en•cyc•li•cal \in'siklikəl, en-\ *n* : papal letter to bishops

en•cy•clo•pe•dia \in,sīklə'pēdēə\ *n* : reference work on many subjects — **en•cy•clo•pe•dic** \-'pēdik\ *adj*

end \'end\ *n* **1** : point at which something stops or no longer exists **2** : cessation **3** : purpose ∼ *vb* **1** : stop or finish **2** : be at the end of — **end•less** *adj* — **end•less•ly** *adv*

en•dan•ger \in'dānjər\ *vb* : bring into danger

en•dear \in'dir\ *vb* : make dear — **en•dear•ment** \-mənt\ *n*

en•deav•or \in'devər\ *vb or n* : attempt

end•ing \'endiŋ\ *n* : end

en•dive \'en,dīv\ *n* : salad plant

en•do•crine \'endəkrən, -,krīn, -,krēn\ *adj* : producing secretions distributed by the bloodstream

en•dorse \in'dòrs\ *vb* -**dorsed; -dors•ing 1** : sign one's name to **2** : approve — **en•dorse•ment** *n*

en•dow \in'daú\ *vb* **1** : furnish with funds **2** : furnish naturally — **en•dow•ment** *n*

en•dure \in'dúr, -'dyúr\ *vb* -**dured; -dur•ing 1** : last **2** : suffer patiently **3** : tolerate — **en•dur•able** *adj* — **en•dur•ance** \-əns\ *n*

en•e•ma \'enəmə\ *n* : injection of liquid into the rectum

en•e•my \-mē\ *n, pl* -**mies** : one that attacks or tries to harm another

en•er•get•ic \,enər'jetik\ *adj* : full of energy or activity — **en•er•get•i•cal•ly** \-iklē\ *adv*

en•er•gize \'enər,jīz\ *vb* -**gized; -giz•ing** : give energy to

en•er•gy \'enərjē\ *n, pl* -**gies 1** : capacity for action **2** : vigorous action **3** : capacity for doing work

en•er•vate \'enər,vāt\ *vb* -**vat•ed; -vat•ing** : make weak or listless — **en•er•va•tion** \,enər'vāshən\ *n*

en•fold \in'fōld\ *vb* : surround or embrace

en•force \-'fōrs\ *vb* **1** : compel **2** : carry out — **en•force•able** \-əbəl\ *adj* — **en•force•ment** *n*

en•fran•chise \-'fran,chīz\ *vb* -**chised; -chis•ing** : grant voting rights to — **en•fran•chise•ment** \-,chīzmənt, -chəz-\ *n*

en•gage \in'gāj\ *vb* -**gaged; -gag•ing 1** : participate or cause to participate **2** : bring or come into working contact **3** : bind by a pledge to marry **4** : hire **5** : bring or enter into conflict — **en•gage•ment** \-mənt\ *n*

en•gag•ing *adj* : attractive

en•gen•der \in'jendər\ *vb* -**dered; -der•ing** : create

en•gine \'enjən\ *n* **1** : machine that converts energy into mechanical motion **2** : locomotive

en•gi•neer \,enjə'nir\ *n* **1** : one trained in engineering **2** : engine operator ∼ *vb* : lay out or manage as an engineer

en•gi•neer•ing \-iŋ\ *n* : practical application of science and mathematics

en•grave \in'grāv\ vb -graved; -graving : cut into a surface — en•grav•er n — en•grav•ing n

en•gross \-'grōs\ vb : occupy fully

en•gulf \-'gəlf\ vb : swallow up

en•hance \-'hans\ vb -hanced; -hancing : improve in value — en•hancement n

enig•ma \i'nigmə\ n : puzzle or mystery — enig•mat•ic \,enig'matik, ,ē-\ adj — enig•mat•i•cal•ly adv

en•join \in'jóin\ vb 1 : command 2 : forbid

en•joy \-'jói\ vb : take pleasure in — en•joy•able adj — en•joy•ment n

en•large \-'lärj\ vb -larged; -larging : make or grow larger — en•largement n — en•larg•er n

en•light•en \-'līt³n\ vb : give knowledge or spiritual insight to — en•light•en•ment n

en•list \-'list\ vb 1 : join the armed forces 2 : get the aid of — en•list•ee \-,lis'tē\ n — en•list•ment \-'listmənt\ n

en•liv•en \in'līvən\ vb : give life or spirit to

en•mi•ty \'enmətē\ n, pl -ties : mutual hatred

en•no•ble \in'ōbəl\ vb -bled; -bling : make noble

en•nui \,än'wē\ n : boredom

enor•mi•ty \i'nòrmətē\ n, pl -ties 1 : great wickedness 2 : huge size

enor•mous \i'nòrməs\ adj : great in size, number, or degree — enor•mous•ly adv — enor•mous•ness n

enough \i'nəf\ adj : adequate ～ adv 1 : in an adequate manner 2 : in a tolerable degree ～ pron : adequate number, quantity, or amount

en•quire \in'kwīr\, en•qui•ry \'in-,kwīrē, in'-; 'inkwərē, 'iŋ-\ var of INQUIRE, INQUIRY

en•rage \in'rāj\ vb : fill with rage

en•rich \-'rich\ vb : make rich — en•rich•ment n

en•roll, en•rol \-'rōl\ vb -rolled; -rolling 1 : enter on a list 2 : become enrolled — en•roll•ment n

en route \än'rüt, en-, in-\ adv or adj : on or along the way

en•sconce \in'skäns\ vb -sconced; -sconc•ing : settle snugly

en•sem•ble \än'sämbəl\ n 1 : small group 2 : complete costume

en•shrine \in'shrīn\ vb 1 : put in a shrine 2 : cherish

en•sign \'ensən, 1 also 'en,sīn\ n 1 : flag 2 : lowest ranking commissioned officer in the navy

en•slave \in'slāv\ vb : make a slave of — en•slave•ment n

en•snare \-'snar\ vb : trap

en•sue \-'sü\ vb -sued; -su•ing : follow as a consequence

en•sure \-'shùr\ vb -sured; -sur•ing : guarantee

en•tail \-'tāl\ vb : involve as a necessary result

en•tan•gle \-'taŋgəl\ vb : tangle — en•tan•gle•ment n

en•ter \'entər\ vb 1 : go or come in or into 2 : start 3 : set down (as in a list)

en•ter•prise \'entər,prīz\ n 1 : an undertaking 2 : business organization 3 : initiative

en•ter•pris•ing \-,prīziŋ\ adj : showing initiative

en•ter•tain \,entər'tān\ vb 1 : treat or receive as a guest 2 : hold in mind 3 : amuse — en•ter•tain•er n — en•ter•tain•ment n

en•thrall, en•thral \in'thròl\ vb -thralled; -thrall•ing : hold spellbound

en•thu•si•asm \-'thüzē,azəm, -'thyü-\ n : strong excitement of feeling or its cause — en•thu•si•ast \-,ast, -əst\ n — en•thu•si•as•tic \-,thüzē'astik, -,thyü-\ adj — en•thu•si•as•ti•cal•ly \-tiklē\ adv

en•tice \-'tīs\ vb -ticed; -tic•ing : tempt — en•tice•ment n

en•tire \in'tīr\ adj : complete or whole — en•tire•ly adv — en•tire•ty \-'tīrətē, -'tīrtē\ n

en•ti•tle \-'tīt³l\ vb -tled; -tling 1 : name 2 : give a right to

en•ti•ty \'entətē\ n, pl -ties : something with separate existence

en•to•mol•o•gy \,entə'mäləjē\ n : study of insects — en•to•mo•log•i•cal \-mə'läjikəl\ adj — en•to•mol•o•gist \-'mäləjist\ n

en•tou•rage \,äntù'räzh\ n : retinue

en•trails \'entrəlz, -,trālz\ n pl : intestines

¹**en•trance** \'entrəns\ n 1 : act of entering 2 : means or place of entering — en•trant \'entrənt\ n

²**en•trance** \in'trans\ vb -tranced; -tranc•ing : fascinate or delight

en•trap \in'trap\ vb : trap — en•trap•ment n

en·treat \-'trēt\ vb : ask urgently —
en·treaty \-'trētē\ n
en·trée, en·tree \'än₁trā\ n : principal
dish of the meal
en·trench \in'trench\ vb : establish in
a strong position — en·trench·ment
n
en·tre·pre·neur \₁äntrəprə'nər\ n : organizer or promoter of an enterprise
en·trust \in'trəst\ vb : commit to another with confidence
en·try \'entrē\ n, pl -tries 1 : entrance
2 : an entering in a record or an item
so entered
en·twine \in'twīn\ vb : twine together
or around
enu·mer·ate \i'nümə₁rāt, -'nyü-\ vb
-at·ed; -at·ing 1 : count 2 : list —
enu·mer·a·tion \i₁nümə'rāshən,
-₁nyü-\ n
enun·ci·ate \ē'nənsē₁āt\ vb -at·ed;
-at·ing 1 : announce 2 : pronounce
— enun·ci·a·tion \-₁nənsē'āshən\ n
en·vel·op \in'veləp\ vb : surround —
en·vel·op·ment n
en·ve·lope \'envə₁lōp, 'än-\ n : paper
container for a letter
en·vi·ron·ment \in'vīrənmənt\ n
: surroundings — en·vi·ron·men·tal
\-₁vīrən'mentᵊl\ adj
en·vi·ron·men·tal·ist \-ᵊlist\ n : person
concerned about the environment
en·vi·rons \in'vīrənz\ n pl : vicinity
en·vis·age \in'vizij\ vb -aged; -ag·ing
: have a mental picture of
en·vi·sion \-'vizhən\ vb : picture to
oneself
en·voy \'en₁vói, 'än-\ n : diplomat
en·vy \'envē\ n 1 : resentful awareness
of another's advantage 2 : object of
envy ~ vb -vied; -vy·ing : feel envy
toward or on account of — en·vi·
able \-vēəbəl\ adj — en·vi·ous
\-vēəs\ adj — en·vi·ous·ly adv
en·zyme \'en₁zīm\ n : biological catalyst
eon \'ēon, ē₁än\ n : indefinitely long
time
ep·au·let \₁epə'let\ n : shoulder ornament on a uniform
ephem·er·al \i'femərəl\ adj : short-
lived
ep·ic \'epik\ n : long poem about a hero
— epic adj
ep·i·cure \'epi₁kyúr\ n : person with
fastidious taste esp. in food and wine
— ep·i·cu·re·an \₁epikyù'rēən,
-'kyúrē-\ n or adj

ep·i·dem·ic \₁epə'demik\ adj : affecting many persons at one time — epi-
demic n
epi·der·mis \₁epə'dərməs\ n : outer
layer of skin
ep·i·gram \'epə₁gram\ n : short witty
poem or saying
ep·i·lep·sy \'epə₁lepsē\ n, pl -sies
: nervous disorder marked by convulsive attacks — ep·i·lep·tic \₁epə'lep-
tik\ adj or n
epis·co·pal \i'piskəpəl\ adj : governed
by bishops
ep·i·sode \'epə₁sōd, -₁zōd\ n : occurrence — ep·i·sod·ic \₁epə'sädik,
-'zäd-\ adj
epis·tle \i'pisəl\ n : letter
ep·i·taph \'epə₁taf \ n : inscription in
memory of a dead person
ep·i·thet \'epə₁thet, -thət\ n : charac-
terizing often abusive word or phrase
epit·o·me \i'pitəmē\ n 1 : summary 2
: ideal example — epit·o·mize
\-₁mīz\ vb
ep·och \'epək, 'ep₁äk\ n : extended
period — ep·och·al \'epəkəl, 'ep-
₁äkəl\ adj
ep·oxy \'ep₁äksē, ep'äksē\ n : synthetic resin used esp. in adhesives ~
vb -ox·ied or -oxyed; -oxy·ing : glue
with epoxy
equa·ble \'ekwəbəl, 'ekwə-\ adj : free
from unpleasant extremes — eq·ua-
bil·i·ty \₁ekwə'bilətē, ₁ē-\ n — eq·
ua·bly \-blē\ adv
equal \'ēkwəl\ adj : of the same quantity, value, quality, number, or status
as another ~ n : one that is equal ~
vb equaled or equalled; equal·ing
or equal·ling : be or become equal to
— equal·i·ty \i'kwälətē\ n —
equal·ize \'ēkwə₁līz\ vb — equal·ly
\'ēkwəlē\ adv
equa·nim·i·ty \₁ēkwə'nimətē, ek-\ n,
pl -ties : calmness
equate \i'kwāt\ vb equat·ed; equat-
ing : treat or regard as equal
equa·tion \i'kwāzhən, -shən\ n
: mathematical statement that two
things are equal
equa·tor \i'kwātər\ n : imaginary circle that separates the northern and
southern hemispheres — equa·to-
ri·al \₁ēkwə'tōrēəl, ₁ek-\ adj
eques·tri·an \i'kwestrēən\ adj : relating to horseback riding ~ n : horseback rider

equi·lat·er·al \ˌēkwə'latərəl\ *adj* : having equal sides

equi·lib·ri·um \-'librēəm\ *n, pl* **-ri·ums** *or* **-ria** \-reə\ : state of balance

equine \'ē,kwīn, 'ek,wīn\ *adj* : relating to the horse — **equine** *n*

equi·nox \'ēkwə,näks, 'ek-\ *n* : time when day and night are everywhere of equal length

equip \i'kwip\ *vb* **-pp-** : furnish with needed resources — **equip·ment** \-mənt\ *n*

eq·ui·ta·ble \'ekwətəbəl\ *adj* : fair

eq·ui·ty \'ekwətē\ *n, pl* **-ties** **1** : justice **2** : value of a property less debt

equiv·a·lent \i'kwivələnt\ *adj* : equal — **equiv·a·lence** \-ləns\ *n* — **equivalent** *n*

equiv·o·cal \i'kwivəkəl\ *adj* : ambiguous or uncertain

equiv·o·cate \i'kwivə,kāt\ *vb* **-cat·ed; -cat·ing** **1** : use misleading language **2** : avoid answering definitely — **equiv·o·ca·tion** \-ˌkwivə'kāshən\ *n*

¹**-er** \ər\ *adj suffix or adv suffix* — used to form the comparative degree of adjectives and adverbs and esp. those of one or two syllables

²**-er** \ər\, **-ier** \ēər, yər\, **-yer** \yər\ *n suffix* **1** : one that is associated with **2** : one that performs or is the object of an action **3** : one that is

era \'irə, 'erə, 'ērə\ *n* : period of time associated with something

erad·i·cate \i'radə,kāt\ *vb* **-cat·ed; -cat·ing** : do away with

erase \i'rās\ *vb* **erased; eras·ing** : rub or scratch out — **eras·er** *n* — **era·sure** \i'rāshər\ *n*

ere \'er\ *prep or conj* : before

erect \i'rekt\ *adj* : not leaning or lying down ~ *vb* **1** : build **2** : bring to an upright position — **erec·tion** \i'rekshən\ *n*

er·mine \'ərmən\ *n* : weasel with white winter fur or its fur

erode \i'rōd\ *vb* **erod·ed; erod·ing** : wear away gradually

ero·sion \i'rōzhən\ *n* : process of eroding

erot·ic \i'rätik\ *adj* : sexually arousing — **erot·i·cal·ly** \-iklē\ *adv* — **erot·i·cism** \i'rätə,sizəm\ *n*

err \'er, 'ər\ *vb* : be or do wrong

er·rand \'erənd\ *n* : short trip taken to do something often for another

er·rant \-ənt\ *adj* **1** : traveling about **2** : going astray

er·rat·ic \ir'atik\ *adj* **1** : eccentric **2** : inconsistent — **er·rat·i·cal·ly** \-iklē\ *adv*

er·ro·ne·ous \ir'ōnēəs, e'rō-\ *adj* : wrong — **er·ro·ne·ous·ly** *adv*

er·ror \'erər\ *n* **1** : something that is not accurate **2** : state of being wrong

er·satz \'er,säts\ *adj* : phony

erst·while \'ərst,hwīl\ *adv* : in the past ~ *adj* : former

er·u·di·tion \ˌerə'dishən, ˌeryə-\ *n* : great learning — **er·u·dite** \'erə,dīt, 'eryə-\ *adj*

erupt \i'rəpt\ *vb* : burst forth esp. suddenly and violently — **erup·tion** \i'rəpshən\ *n* — **erup·tive** \-tiv\ *adj*

-ery \ərē\ *n suffix* **1** : character or condition **2** : practice **3** : place of doing

¹**-es** \əz, iz *after* s, z, sh, ch; z *after* v *or a vowel*\ *n pl suffix* — used to form the plural of some nouns

²**-es** *vb suffix* — used to form the 3d person singular present of some verbs

es·ca·late \'eskə,lāt\ *vb* **-lat·ed; -lat·ing** : become quickly larger or greater — **es·ca·la·tion** \ˌeskə'lāshən\ *n*

es·ca·la·tor \'eskə,lātər\ *n* : moving stairs

es·ca·pade \'eskə,pād\ *n* : mischievous adventure

es·cape \is'kāp\ *vb* **-caped; -cap·ing** : get away or get away from ~ *n* **1** : flight from or avoidance of something unpleasant **2** : leakage **3** : means of escape ~ *adj* : providing means of escape — **es·cap·ee** \is,kā'pē, ,es-\ *n*

es·ca·role \'eskə,rōl\ *n* : salad green

es·carp·ment \is'kärpmənt\ *n* : cliff

es·chew \is'chü\ *vb* : shun

es·cort \'es,kòrt\ *n* : one accompanying another — **es·cort** \is'kòrt, es-\ *vb*

es·crow \'es,krō\ *n* : deposit to be delivered upon fulfillment of a condition

esoph·a·gus \i'säfəgəs\ *n, pl* **-gi** \-,gī, -,jī\ : muscular tube connecting the mouth and stomach

es·o·ter·ic \ˌesə'terik\ *adj* : mysterious or secret

es·pe·cial·ly \is'peshəlē\ *adv* : particularly or notably

es·pi·o·nage \'espēə,näzh, -nij\ *n* : practice of spying

es·pous·al \is'pauzəl\ *n* **1** : betrothal **2** : wedding **3** : a taking up as a supporter — **es·pouse** \-'pauz\ *vb*

espres·so \e'spresō\ *n, pl* **-sos** : strong steam-brewed coffee

es·py \is'pī\ *vb* **-pied; -py·ing** : catch sight of

es·quire \'es,kwīr\ *n* — used as a title of courtesy

-ess \əs, ,es\ *n suffix* : female

es·say \'es,ā\ *n* : literary composition ~ *vb* \e'sā, 'es,ā\ : attempt — **es·say·ist** \'es,āist\ *n*

es·sence \'es°ns\ *n* **1** : fundamental nature or quality **2** : extract **3** : perfume

es·sen·tial \i'senchəl\ *adj* : basic or necessary — **essential** *n* — **es·sen·tial·ly** *adv*

-est \əst, ist\ *adj suffix or adv suffix* — used to form the superlative degree of adjectives and adverbs and esp. those of 1 or 2 syllables

es·tab·lish \is'tablish\ *vb* **1** : bring into existence **2** : put on a firm basis **3** : cause to be recognized

es·tab·lish·ment \-mənt\ *n* **1** : business or a place of business **2** : an establishing or being established **3** : controlling group

es·tate \is'tāt\ *n* **1** : one's possessions **2** : large piece of land with a house

es·teem \is'tēm\ *n or vb* : regard

es·ter \'estər\ *n* : organic chemical compound

esthetic *var of* AESTHETIC

es·ti·ma·ble \'estəməbəl\ *adj* : worthy of esteem

es·ti·mate \'estə,māt\ *vb* **-mat·ed; -mat·ing** : judge the approximate value, size, or cost ~ \-mət\ *n* **1** : rough or approximate calculation **2** : statement of the cost of a job — **es·ti·ma·tion** \,estə'māshən\ *n* — **es·ti·ma·tor** \'estə,mātər\ *n*

es·trange \is'trānj\ *vb* **-tranged; -trang·ing** : make hostile — **es·trange·ment** *n*

es·tro·gen \'estrəjən\ *n* : hormone that produces female characteristics

es·tu·ary \'eschə,werē\ *n, pl* **-ar·ies** : arm of the sea at a river's mouth

et cet·era \et'setərə, -'setrə\ : and others esp. of the same kind

etch \'ech\ *vb* : produce by corroding parts of a surface with acid — **etch·er** *n* — **etch·ing** *n*

eter·nal \i'tərn°l\ *adj* : lasting forever — **eter·nal·ly** *adv*

eter·ni·ty \-nətē\ *n, pl* **-ties** : infinite duration

eth·ane \'eth,ān\ *n* : gaseous hydrocarbon

eth·a·nol \'ethə,nól, -,nōl\ *n* : alcohol

ether \'ēthər\ *n* : light flammable liquid used as an anesthetic

ethe·re·al \i'thirēəl\ *adj* **1** : celestial **2** : exceptionally delicate

eth·i·cal \'ethikəl\ *adj* **1** : relating to ethics **2** : honorable — **eth·i·cal·ly** *adv*

eth·ics \-iks\ *n sing or pl* **1** : study of good and evil and moral duty **2** : moral principles or practice

eth·nic \'ethnik\ *adj* : relating to races or groups of people with common customs ~ *n* : member of a minority ethnic group

eth·nol·o·gy \eth'näləjē\ *n* : study of the races of human beings — **eth·no·log·i·cal** \,ethnə'läjikəl\ *adj* — **eth·nol·o·gist** \eth'näləjist\ *n*

et·i·quette \'etikət, -,ket\ *n* : good manners

et·y·mol·o·gy \,etə'mäləjē\ *n, pl* **-gies** **1** : history of a word **2** : study of etymologies — **et·y·mo·log·i·cal** \-mə-'läjikəl\ *adj* — **et·y·mol·o·gist** \-'mäləjist\ *n*

eu·ca·lyp·tus \,yükə'liptəs\ *n, pl* **-ti** \-,tī\ *or* **-tus·es** : Australian evergreen tree

Eu·cha·rist \'yükərəst\ *n* : Communion — **eu·cha·ris·tic** \,yükə'ristik\ *adj*

eu·lo·gy \'yüləjē\ *n, pl* **-gies** : speech in praise — **eu·lo·gis·tic** \,yülə'jistik\ *adj* — **eu·lo·gize** \'yülə,jīz\ *vb*

eu·nuch \'yünək\ *n* : castrated man

eu·phe·mism \'yüfə,mizəm\ *n* : substitution of a pleasant expression for an unpleasant or offensive one — **eu·phe·mis·tic** \,yüfə'mistik\ *adj*

eu·pho·ni·ous \yù'fōnēəs\ *adj* : pleasing to the ear — **eu·pho·ny** \'yüfənē\ *n*

eu·pho·ria \yù'fōrēə\ *n* : elation — **eu·phor·ic** \-'fórik\ *adj*

eu·ro \'yùrō\ *n, pl* **euros** : commmon monetary unit of most of the European Union

eu·tha·na·sia \,yüthə'nāzhə, -zhēə\ *n* : mercy killing

evac·u·ate \i'vakyə,wāt\ *vb* **-at·ed; -at·ing** **1** : discharge wastes from the body **2** : remove or withdraw from — **evac·u·a·tion** \i,vakyə'wāshən\ *n*

evade \i'vād\ *vb* **evad·ed; evad·ing** : manage to avoid eval·u·ate \i'valyə‚wāt\ vb -at·ed; -at·ing : appraise — eval·u·a·tion \i‚valyə'wāshən\ n

evan·gel·i·cal \‚ē‚van'jelikəl, ‚evən-\ adj : relating to the Christian gospel

evan·ge·lism \i'vanjə‚lizəm\ n : the winning or revival of personal commitments to Christ — evan·ge·list \i'vanjəlist\ n — evan·ge·lis·tic \i‚vanjə'listik\ adj

evap·o·rate \i'vapə‚rāt\ vb -rat·ed; -rat·ing 1 : pass off in or convert into vapor 2 : disappear quickly — evap·o·ra·tion \i‚vapə'rāshən\ n — evap-ora·tor \i'vapə‚rātər\ n

eva·sion \i'vāzhən\ n : act or instance of evading — eva·sive \i'vāsiv\ adj — eva·sive·ness n

eve \'ēv\ n : evening

even \'ēvən\ adj 1 : smooth 2 : equal or fair 3 : fully revenged 4 : divisible by 2 ~ adv 1 : already 2 — used for emphasis ~ vb : make or become even — even·ly adv — even·ness n

eve·ning \'ēvniŋ\ n : early part of the night

event \i'vent\ n 1 : occurrence 2 : noteworthy happening 3 : eventuality — event·ful adj

even·tu·al \i'venchəwəl\ adj : later — even·tu·al·ly adv

even·tu·al·i·ty \i‚venchə'walətē\ n, pl -ties : possible occurrence or outcome

ev·er \'evər\ adv 1 : always 2 : at any time 3 : in any case

ev·er·green adj : having foliage that remains green — evergreen n

ev·er·last·ing \‚evər'lastiŋ\ adj : lasting forever

ev·ery \'evrē\ adj 1 : being each one of a group 2 : all possible

ev·ery·body \'evri‚bädē, -bəd-\ pron : every person

ev·ery·day adj : ordinary

ev·ery·one \-‚wən\ pron : every person

ev·ery·thing pron : all that exists

ev·ery·where adv : in every place or part

evict \i'vikt\ vb : force (a person) to move from a property — evic·tion \i'vikshən\ n

ev·i·dence \'evədəns\ n 1 : outward sign 2 : proof or testimony

ev·i·dent \-ənt\ adj : clear or obvious — ev·i·dent·ly \-ədəntlē, -ə‚dent-\ adv

evil \'ēvəl\ adj evil·er or evil·ier; evil-

est or evil·lest : wicked ~ n 1 : sin 2 : source of sorrow or distress — evil·do·er \‚ēvəl'düər\ n — evil·ly adv

evince \i'vins\ vb evinced; evinc·ing : show

evis·cer·ate \i'visə‚rāt\ vb -at·ed; -at·ing : remove the viscera of — evis·cer·a·tion \i‚visə'rāshən\ n

evoke \i'vōk\ vb evoked; evok·ing : call forth or up — evo·ca·tion \‚ēvō'kāshən, ‚evə-\ n — evoc·a·tive \i'väkətiv\ adj

evo·lu·tion \‚evə'lüshən\ n : process of change by degrees — evo·lu·tion·ary \-shə‚nerē\ adj

evolve \i'välv\ vb evolved; evolv·ing : develop or change by degrees

ewe \'yü\ n : female sheep

ew·er \'yüər\ n : water pitcher

ex·act \ig'zakt\ vb : compel to furnish ~ adj : precisely correct — ex·act·ing adj — ex·ac·tion \-'zakshən\ n — ex·ac·ti·tude \-'zaktə‚tüd, -‚tyüd\ n — ex·act·ly adv — ex·act·ness n

ex·ag·ger·ate \ig'zajə‚rāt\ vb -at·ed; -at·ing : say more than is true — ex·ag·ger·at·ed·ly adv — ex·ag·ger·a·tion \-‚zajə'rāshən\ n — ex·ag·ger·a·tor \-'zajərātər\ n

ex·alt \ig'zòlt\ vb : glorify — ex·al·ta·tion \‚eg‚zòl'tāshən, ‚ek‚sòl-\ n

ex·am \ig'zam\ n : examination

ex·am·ine \-ən\ vb -ined; -in·ing 1 : inspect closely 2 : test by questioning — ex·am·i·na·tion \-‚zamə'nāshən\ n

ex·am·ple \ig'zampəl\ n 1 : representative sample 2 : model 3 : problem to be solved for teaching purposes

ex·as·per·ate \ig'zaspə‚rāt\ vb -at·ed; -at·ing : thoroughly annoy — ex·as·per·a·tion \-‚zaspə'rāshən\ n

ex·ca·vate \'ekskə‚vāt\ vb -vat·ed; -vat·ing : dig or hollow out — ex·ca·va·tion \‚ekskə'vāshən\ n — ex·ca·va·tor \'ekskə‚vātər\ n

ex·ceed \ik'sēd\ vb 1 : go or be beyond the limit of 2 : do better than

ex·ceed·ing·ly adv : extremely

ex·cel \ik'sel\ vb -ll- : do extremely well or far better than

ex·cel·lence \'eksələns\ n : quality of being excellent

ex·cel·len·cy \-lənsē\ n, pl -cies — used as a title of honor

ex·cel·lent \'eksələnt\ *adj* : very good — **ex·cel·lent·ly** *adv*

ex·cept \ik'sept\ *vb* : omit ~ *prep* : excluding ~ *conj* : but — **ex·cep·tion** \-'sepshən\ *n*

ex·cep·tion·al \-'sepshənəl\ *adj* : superior — **ex·cep·tion·al·ly** *adv*

ex·cerpt \'ek,sərpt, 'eg,zərpt\ *n* : brief passage ~ \ek'-, eg'-, 'ek,-, 'eg,-\ *vb* : select an excerpt

ex·cess \ik'ses, 'ek,ses\ *n* : amount left over — **excess** *adj* — **ex·ces·sive** \ik'sesiv\ *adj* — **ex·ces·sive·ly** *adv*

ex·change \iks'chānj, 'eks,chānj\ *n* **1** : the giving or taking of one thing in return for another **2** : marketplace esp. for securities ~ *vb* **-changed; -chang·ing** : transfer in return for some equivalent — **ex·change·able** \iks'chānjəbəl\ *adj*

¹**ex·cise** \'ek,sīz, -,sīs\ *n* : tax

²**ex·cise** \ik'sīz\ *vb* **-cised; -cis·ing** : cut out — **ex·ci·sion** \-'sizhən\ *n*

ex·cite \ik'sīt\ *vb* **-cit·ed; -cit·ing** **1** : stir up **2** : kindle the emotions of — **ex·cit·abil·i·ty** \-,sītə'bilətē\ *n* — **ex·cit·able** \-'sītəbəl\ *adj* — **ex·ci·ta·tion** \,ek,sī'tāshən, -ə-\ *n* — **ex·cit·ed·ly** *adv* — **ex·cite·ment** \ik'sītmənt\ *n*

ex·claim \iks'klām\ *vb* : cry out esp. in delight — **ex·cla·ma·tion** \,ek-sklə'māshən\ *n* — **ex·clam·a·to·ry** \iks'klamə,tōrē\ *adj*

exclamation point *n* : punctuation mark ! used esp. after an interjection or exclamation

ex·clude \iks'klüd\ *vb* **-clud·ed; -clud·ing** : leave out — **ex·clu·sion** \-'klüzhən\ *n*

ex·clu·sive \-'klüsiv\ *adj* **1** : reserved for particular persons **2** : stylish **3** : sole — **exclusive** *n* — **ex·clu·sive·ly** *adv* — **ex·clu·sive·ness** *n*

ex·com·mu·ni·cate \,ekskə'myünə,kāt\ *vb* : expel from a church — **ex·com·mu·ni·ca·tion** \-,myünə'kā-shən\ *n*

ex·cre·ment \'ekskrəmənt\ *n* : bodily waste

ex·crete \ik'skrēt\ *vb* **-cret·ed; -cret·ing** : eliminate wastes from the body — **ex·cre·tion** \-'skrēshən\ *n* — **ex·cre·to·ry** \'ekskrə,tōrē\ *adj*

ex·cru·ci·at·ing \ik'skrüshē,ātiŋ\ *adj* : intensely painful — **ex·cru·ci·at·ing·ly** *adv*

ex·cul·pate \'ekskəl,pāt\ *vb* **-pat·ed; -pat·ing** : clear from alleged fault

ex·cur·sion \ik'skərzhən\ *n* : pleasure trip

ex·cuse \ik'skyüz\ *vb* **-cused; -cus·ing** **1** : pardon **2** : release from an obligation **3** : justify ~ \-'skyüs\ *n* **1** : justification **2** : apology

ex·e·cute \'eksi,kyüt\ *vb* **-cut·ed; -cut·ing** **1** : carry out fully **2** : enforce **3** : put to death — **ex·e·cu·tion** \,eksi'kyüshən\ *n* — **ex·e·cu·tion·er** \-shənər\ *n*

ex·ec·u·tive \ig'zekyətiv\ *adj* : relating to the carrying out of decisions, plans, or laws ~ *n* **1** : branch of government with executive duties **2** : administrator

ex·ec·u·tor \-yətər\ *n* : person named in a will to execute it

ex·ec·u·trix \ig'zekyə,triks\ *n, pl* **ex·ec·u·tri·ces** \-,zekyə'trī,sēz\ *or* **ex·ec·u·trix·es** : woman executor

ex·em·pla·ry \ig'zemplərē\ *adj* : so commendable as to serve as a model

ex·em·pli·fy \-plə,fī\ *vb* **-fied; -fy·ing** : serve as an example of — **ex·em·pli·fi·ca·tion** \-,zempləfə'kāshən\ *n*

ex·empt \ig'zempt\ *adj* : being free from some liability ~ *vb* : make exempt — **ex·emp·tion** \-'zempshən\ *n*

ex·er·cise \'eksər,sīz\ *n* **1** : a putting into action **2** : exertion to develop endurance or a skill **3** *pl* : public ceremony ~ *vb* **-cised; -cis·ing** **1** : exert **2** : engage in exercise — **ex·er·cis·er** *n*

ex·ert \ig'zərt\ *vb* : put into action — **ex·er·tion** \-'zərshən\ *n*

ex·hale \eks'hāl\ *vb* **-haled; -hal·ing** : breathe out — **ex·ha·la·tion** \ek-shə'lāshən\ *n*

ex·haust \ig'zóst\ *vb* **1** : draw out or develop completely **2** : use up **3** : tire or wear out ~ *n* : waste steam or gas from an engine or a system for removing it — **ex·haus·tion** \-'zó-schən\ *n* — **ex·haus·tive** \-'zóstiv\ *adj*

ex·hib·it \ig'zibət\ *vb* : display esp. publicly ~ *n* **1** : act of exhibiting **2** : something exhibited — **ex·hi·bi·tion** \,eksə'bishən\ *n* — **ex·hib·i·tor** \ig'zibətər\ *n*

ex·hil·a·rate \ig'zilə,rāt\ *vb* **-rat·ed; -rat·ing** : thrill — **ex·hil·a·ra·tion** \-,zilə'rāshən\ *n*

ex·hort \-'zȯrt\ vb : urge earnestly — **ex·hor·ta·tion** \ˌeks·ȯr'tāshən, ˌegz-, -ər-\ n

ex·hume \igz'üm, -'yüm; iks'yüm, -'hyüm\ vb -**humed; -hum·ing** : dig up (a buried corpse) — **ex·hu·ma·tion** \ˌeksyü'māshən, -hyü-; ˌegzü-, -zyü-\ n

ex·i·gen·cies \'eksəjənsēz, ig'zijən-\ n pl : requirements (as of a situation)

ex·ile \'eg,zīl, 'ek,sīl\ n 1 : banishment 2 : person banished from his or her country — **exile** vb

ex·ist \ig'zist\ vb 1 : have real or actual being 2 : live — **ex·is·tence** \-əns\ n — **ex·is·tent** \-ənt\ adj

ex·it \'egzət, 'eksət\ n 1 : departure 2 : way out of an enclosed space 3 : way off an expressway — **exit** vb

ex·o·dus \'eksədəs\ n : mass departure

ex·on·er·ate \ig'zänə,rāt\ vb -**at·ed; -at·ing** : free from blame — **ex·on·er·a·tion** \-,zänə'rāshən\ n

ex·or·bi·tant \ig'zȯrbətənt\ adj : exceeding what is usual or proper

ex·or·cise \'ek,sȯr,sīz, -sər-\ vb -**cised; -cis·ing** : drive out (as an evil spirit) — **ex·or·cism** \-,sizəm\ n — **ex·or·cist** \-,sist\ n

ex·ot·ic \ig'zätik\ adj : foreign or strange — **exotic** n — **ex·ot·i·cal·ly** \-iklē\ adv

ex·pand \ik'spand\ vb : enlarge

ex·panse \-'spans\ n : very large area

ex·pan·sion \-'spanchən\ n 1 : act or process of expanding 2 : expanded part

ex·pan·sive \-'spansiv\ adj 1 : tending to expand 2 : warmly benevolent 3 : of large extent — **ex·pan·sive·ly** adv — **ex·pan·sive·ness** n

ex·pa·tri·ate \ek'spātrē,āt, -ət\ n : exile — **expatriate** \-,āt\ adj or vb

ex·pect \ik'spekt\ vb 1 : look forward to 2 : consider probable or one's due — **ex·pec·tan·cy** \-ənsē\ n — **ex·pec·tant** \-ənt\ adj — **ex·pec·tant·ly** adv — **ex·pec·ta·tion** \ˌek,spek-'tāshən\ n

ex·pe·di·ent \ik'spēdēənt\ adj : convenient or advantageous rather than right or just ~ n : convenient often makeshift means to an end

ex·pe·dite \'ekspə,dīt\ vb -**dit·ed; -dit·ing** : carry out or handle promptly — **ex·pe·dit·er** n

ex·pe·di·tion \ˌekspə'dishən\ n : long journey for work or research or the people making this

ex·pe·di·tious \-əs\ adj : prompt and efficient

ex·pel \ik'spel\ vb -**ll-** : force out

ex·pend \-'spend\ vb 1 : pay out 2 : use up — **ex·pend·able** adj

ex·pen·di·ture \-'spendichər, -də,chùr\ n : act of using or spending

ex·pense \ik'spens\ n : cost — **ex·pen·sive** \-'spensiv\ adj — **ex·pen·sive·ly** adv

ex·pe·ri·ence \ik'spirēəns\ n 1 : a participating in or living through an event 2 : an event that affects one 3 : knowledge from doing ~ vb -**enced; -enc·ing** : undergo

ex·per·i·ment \ik'sperəmənt\ n : test to discover something ~ vb : make experiments — **ex·per·i·men·tal** \-,sperə'ment°l\ adj — **ex·per·i·men·ta·tion** \-mən'tāshən\ n — **ex·per·i·men·ter** \-'sperə,mentər\ n

ex·pert \'ek,spərt\ adj : thoroughly skilled ~ n : person with special skill — **ex·pert·ly** adv — **ex·pert·ness** n

ex·per·tise \ˌekspər'tēz\ n : skill

ex·pi·ate \'ekspē,āt\ vb : make amends for — **ex·pi·a·tion** \ˌekspē'āshən\ n

ex·pire \ik'spīr, ek-\ vb -**pired; -pir·ing** 1 : breathe out 2 : die 3 : end — **ex·pi·ra·tion** \ˌekspə'rāshən\ n

ex·plain \ik'splān\ vb 1 : make clear 2 : give the reason for — **ex·plain·able** \-əbəl\ adj — **ex·pla·na·tion** \ˌeksplə'nāshən\ n — **ex·plan·a·to·ry** \ik'splanə,tōrē\ adj

ex·ple·tive \'eksplətiv\ n : usu. profane exclamation

ex·pli·ca·ble \ek'splikəbəl, 'eksplik-\ adj : capable of being explained

ex·plic·it \ik'splisət\ adj : absolutely clear or precise — **ex·plic·it·ly** adv — **ex·plic·it·ness** n

ex·plode \ik'splōd\ vb -**plod·ed; -plod·ing** 1 : discredit 2 : burst or cause to burst violently 3 : increase rapidly

ex·ploit \'ek,splȯit\ n : heroic act ~ \ik'splȯit\ vb 1 : utilize 2 : use unfairly — **ex·ploi·ta·tion** \ˌek,splȯi-'tāshən\ n

ex·plore \ik'splōr\ vb -**plored; -plor·ing** : examine or range over thoroughly — **ex·plo·ra·tion** \ˌeksplə-

'rāshən\ *n* — **ex•plor•ato•ry** \ik-
'splōrə,tōrē\ *adj* — **ex•plor•er** *n*
ex•plo•sion \ik'splōzhən\ *n* : process
or instance of exploding
ex•plo•sive \-siv\ *adj* **1** : able to cause
explosion **2** : likely to explode — **ex-**
plosive *n* — **ex•plo•sive•ly** *adv*
ex•po•nent \ik'spōnənt, 'ek,spō-\ *n*
1 : mathematical symbol showing
how many times a number is to be repeated as a factor **2** : advocate — **ex-**
po•nen•tial \,ekspə'nenchəl\ *adj* —
ex•po•nen•tial•ly *adv*
ex•port \ek'spōrt, 'ek,spōrt\ *vb* : send
to foreign countries — **export** \'ek,-\
n — **ex•por•ta•tion** \,ek,spōr'tā-
shən\ *n* — **ex•port•er** \ek'spōrtər,
'ek,spōrt-\ *n*
ex•pose \ik'spōz\ *vb* **-posed; -pos-**
ing **1** : deprive of shelter or protection **2** : subject (film) to light **3**
: make known — **ex•po•sure**
\-'spōzhər\ *n*
ex•po•sé, ex•po•se \,ekspō'zā\ *n* : exposure of something discreditable
ex•po•si•tion \,ekspə'zishən\ *n* : public exhibition
ex•pound \ik'spaủnd\ *vb* : set forth or
explain in detail
¹**ex•press** \-'spres\ *adj* **1** : clear **2**
: specific **3** : traveling at high speed
with few stops — **express** *adv or n*
— **ex•press•ly** *adv*
²**express** *vb* **1** : make known in words or
appearance **2** : press out (as juice)
ex•pres•sion \-'spreshən\ *n* **1** : utterance **2** : mathematical symbol **3**
: significant word or phrase **4** : look
on one's face — **ex•pres•sive**
\-'spresiv\ *adj* — **ex•pres•sive-**
ness *n*
ex•press•way \ik'spres,wā\ *n* : high=
speed divided highway with limited
access
ex•pul•sion \ik'spəlshən\ *n* : an ex-
pelling or being expelled
ex•pur•gate \'ekspər,gāt\ *vb* **-gat•ed;**
-gat•ing : censor — **ex•pur•ga•tion**
\,ekspər'gāshən\ *n*
ex•qui•site \ek'skwizət, 'ekskwiz-\
adj **1** : flawlessly beautiful and delicate **2** : keenly discriminating
ex•tant \'ekstənt, ek'stant\ *adj* : existing
ex•tem•po•ra•ne•ous \ek,stempə-
'rānēəs\ *adj* : impromptu — **ex•tem-**
po•ra•ne•ous•ly *adv*
ex•tend \ik'stend\ *vb* **1** : stretch forth

or out **2** : prolong **3** : enlarge — **ex-**
tend•able \-'stendəbəl\ *adj*
ex•ten•sion \-'stenchən\ *n* **1** : an extending or being extended **2** : additional part **3** : extra telephone connection
ex•ten•sive \-'stensiv\ *adj* : of considerable extent — **ex•ten•sive•ly** *adv*
ex•tent \-'stent\ *n* : range, space, or degree to which something extends
ex•ten•u•ate \ik'stenyə,wāt\ *vb* **-at-**
ed; -at•ing : lessen the seriousness of
— **ex•ten•u•a•tion** \-,stenyə'wā-
shən\ *n*
ex•te•ri•or \ek'stirēər\ *adj* : external
~ *n* : external part or surface
ex•ter•mi•nate \ik'stərmə,nāt\ *vb*
-nat•ed; -nat•ing : destroy utterly —
ex•ter•mi•na•tion \-,stərmə'nā-
shən\ *n* — **ex•ter•mi•na•tor** \-'stərmə,nātər\ *n*
ex•ter•nal \ek'stərn°l\ *adj* : relating to
or on the outside — **ex•ter•nal•ly** *adv*
ex•tinct \ik'stiŋkt\ *adj* : no longer existing — **ex•tinc•tion** \-'stiŋkshən\
n
ex•tin•guish \-'stiŋgwish\ *vb* : cause to
stop burning — **ex•tin•guish•able**
adj — **ex•tin•guish•er** *n*
ex•tir•pate \'ekstər,pāt\ *vb* **-pat•ed;**
-pat•ing : destroy
ex•tol \ik'stōl\ *vb* **-ll-** : praise highly
ex•tort \-'stȯrt\ *vb* : obtain by force or
improper pressure — **ex•tor•tion**
\-'stȯrshən\ *n* — **ex•tor•tion•er** *n* —
ex•tor•tion•ist *n*
ex•tra \'ekstrə\ *adj* **1** : additional **2**
: superior — **extra** *n or adv*
extra- *prefix* : outside or beyond
ex•tract \ik'strakt\ *vb* **1** : pull out
forcibly **2** : withdraw (as a juice) ~
\'ek,-\ *n* **1** : excerpt **2** : product (as a
juice) obtained by extracting — **ex-**
tract•able *adj* — **ex•trac•tion** \ik's-
trakshən\ *n* — **ex•trac•tor** \-tər\ *n*
ex•tra•cur•ric•u•lar \,ekstrəkə'rik-
yələr\ *adj* : lying outside the regular
curriculum
ex•tra•dite \'ekstrə,dīt\ *vb* **-dit•ed;**
-dit•ing : bring or deliver a suspect to
a different jurisdiction for trial — **ex-**
tra•di•tion \,ekstrə'dishən\ *n*
ex•tra•mar•i•tal \,ekstrə'marət°l\ *adj*
: relating to sexual relations of a married person outside of the marriage
ex•tra•ne•ous \ek'strānēəs\ *adj* : not
essential or relevant — **ex•tra•ne-**
ous•ly *adv*
ex•traor•di•nary \ik'strȯrd°n,erē, ,ek-

strə'ȯrd-\ *adj* : notably unusual or exceptional — **ex·traor·di·nari·ly** \ik͵strȯrd°n'erəlē, ͵ekstrə͵ȯrd-\ *adv*

ex·tra·sen·so·ry \͵ekstrə'sensərē\ *adj* : outside the ordinary senses

ex·tra·ter·res·tri·al \͵ekstrətə'restrēəl\ *n* : one existing or coming from outside the earth ~ *adj* : relating to an extraterrestrial

ex·trav·a·gant \ik'stravigənt\ *adj* : wildly excessive, lavish, or costly — **ex·trav·a·gance** \-gəns\ *n* — **ex·trav·a·gant·ly** *adv*

ex·trav·a·gan·za \-͵stravə'ganzə\ *n* : spectacular event

ex·tra·ve·hic·u·lar \͵ekstrəvē'hikyələr\ *adj* : occurring outside a spacecraft

ex·treme \ik'strēm\ *adj* **1** : very great or intense **2** : very severe **3** : not moderate **4** : most remote ~ *n* **1** : extreme state **2** : something located at one end or the other of a range — **ex·treme·ly** *adv*

ex·trem·i·ty \-'stremətē\ *n, pl* **-ties 1** : most remote part **2** : human hand or foot **3** : extreme degree or state (as of need)

ex·tri·cate \'ekstrə͵kāt\ *vb* **-cat·ed; -cat·ing** : set or get free from an entanglement or difficulty — **ex·tri·ca·ble** \ik'strikəbəl, ek-; 'ekstrik-\ *adj* — **ex·tri·ca·tion** \͵ekstrə'kāshən\ *n*

ex·tro·vert \'ekstrə͵vərt\ *n* : gregarious person — **ex·tro·ver·sion** \͵ekstrə'vərzhən\ *n* — **ex·tro·vert·ed** \'ekstrə͵vərtəd\ *adj*

ex·trude \ik'strüd\ *vb* **-trud·ed; -trud·ing** : to force or push out

ex·u·ber·ant \ig'zübərənt\ *adj* : joyously unrestrained — **ex·u·ber·ance** \-rəns\ *n* — **ex·u·ber·ant·ly** *adv*

ex·ude \ig'züd\ *vb* **-ud·ed; -ud·ing 1** : discharge slowly through pores **2** : display conspicuously

ex·ult \ig'zəlt\ *vb* : rejoice — **ex·ul·tant** \-'zəlt°nt\ *adj* — **ex·ul·tant·ly** *adv* — **ex·ul·ta·tion** \͵eksəl'tāshən, ͵egzəl-\ *n*

-ey — see **-Y**

eye \'ī\ *n* **1** : organ of sight consisting of a globular structure (**eye·ball**) in a socket of the skull with thin movable covers (**eye·lids**) bordered with hairs (**eye·lash·es**) **2** : vision **3** : judgment **4** : something suggesting an eye ~ *vb* **eyed; eye·ing** *or* **ey·ing** : look at — **eye·brow** \-͵braū\ *n* — **eyed** \'īd\ *adj* — **eye·strain** *n*

eye·drop·per *n* : dropper

eye·glass·es *n pl* : glasses

eye·let \'īlət\ *n* : hole (as in cloth) for a lacing or rope

eye·open·er *n* : something startling — **eye·open·ing** *adj*

eye·piece *n* : lens at the eye end of an optical instrument

eye·sight *n* : sight

eye·sore *n* : unpleasant sight

eye·tooth *n* : upper canine tooth

eye·wit·ness *n* : person who actually sees something happen

ey·rie \'īrē, *or like* AERIE\ *var of* AERIE

F

f \'ef\ *n, pl* **f's** *or* **fs** \'efs\ : 6th letter of the alphabet

fa·ble \'fābəl\ *n* **1** : legendary story **2** : story that teaches a lesson — **fa·bled** \-bəld\ *adj*

fab·ric \'fabrik\ *n* **1** : structure **2** : material made usu. by weaving or knitting fibers

fab·ri·cate \'fabri͵kāt\ *vb* **-cat·ed; -cat·ing 1** : construct **2** : invent — **fab·ri·ca·tion** \͵fabri'kāshən\ *n*

fab·u·lous \'fabyələs\ *adj* **1** : like, told in, or based on fable **2** : incredible or marvelous — **fab·u·lous·ly** *adv*

fa·cade \fə'säd\ *n* **1** : principal face of a building **2** : false or superficial appearance

face \'fās\ *n* **1** : front or principal surface (as of the head) **2** : presence **3** : facial expression **4** : grimace **5** : outward appearance ~ *vb* **faced; fac·ing 1** : challenge or resist firmly or brazenly **2** : cover with different material **3** : sit or stand with the face toward **4** : have the front oriented toward — **faced** \'fāst\ adj — **face•less** adj — **fa•cial** \'fāshəl\ adj or n

face•down adv : with the face downward

face–lift \'fās,lift\ n **1** : cosmetic surgery on the face **2** : modernization

fac•et \'fasət\ n **1** : surface of a cut gem **2** : phase — **fac•et•ed** adj

fa•ce•tious \fə'sēshəs\ adj : jocular — **fa•ce•tious•ly** adv — **fa•ce•tious•ness** n

fac•ile \'fasəl\ adj **1** : easy **2** : fluent

fa•cil•i•tate \fə'silə,tāt\ vb -tat•ed; -tat•ing : make easier

fa•cil•i•ty \fə'silətē\ n, pl -ties **1** : ease in doing or using **2** : something built or installed to serve a purpose or facilitate an activity

fac•ing \'fāsiŋ\ n : lining or covering or material for this

fac•sim•i•le \fak'siməlē\ n : exact copy

fact \'fakt\ n **1** : act or action **2** : something that exists or is real **3** : piece of information — **fac•tu•al** \'fakchəwəl\ adj — **fac•tu•al•ly** adv

fac•tion \'fakshən\ n : part of a larger group — **fac•tion•al•ism** \-shənə,l izəm\ n

fac•tious \'fakshəs\ adj : causing discord

fac•ti•tious \fak'tishəs\ adj : artificial

fac•tor \'faktər\ n **1** : something that has an effect **2** : gene **3** : number used in multiplying

fac•to•ry \'faktərē\ n, pl -ries : place for manufacturing

fac•to•tum \fak'tōtəm\ n : person (as a servant) with varied duties

fac•ul•ty \'fakəltē\ n, pl -ties **1** : ability to act **2** : power of the mind or body **3** : body of teachers or department of instruction

fad \'fad\ n : briefly popular practice or interest — **fad•dish** adj — **fad•dist** n

fade \'fād\ vb fad•ed; fad•ing **1** : wither **2** : lose or cause to lose freshness or brilliance **3** : grow dim **4** : vanish

fag \'fag\ vb -gg- **1** : drudge **2** : tire or exhaust

fag•ot, fag•got \'fagət\ n : bundle of twigs

Fahr•en•heit \'farən,hīt\ adj : relating to a thermometer scale with the boiling point at 212 degrees and the freezing point at 32 degrees

fail \'fāl\ vb **1** : decline in health **2** : die away **3** : stop functioning **4** : be unsuccessful **5** : become bankrupt **6** : disappoint **7** : neglect ~ n : act of failing

fail•ing n : slight defect in character or conduct ~ prep : in the absence or lack of

faille \'fīl\ n : closely woven ribbed fabric

fail•ure \'fālyər\ n **1** : absence of expected action or performance **2** : bankruptcy **3** : deficiency **4** : one that has failed

faint \'fānt\ adj **1** : cowardly or spiritless **2** : weak and dizzy **3** : lacking vigor **4** : indistinct ~ vb : lose consciousness ~ n : act or condition of fainting — **faint•heart•ed** adj — **faint•ly** adv — **faint•ness** n

¹**fair** \'far\ adj **1** : pleasing in appearance **2** : not stormy or cloudy **3** : just or honest **4** : conforming with the rules **5** : open to legitimate pursuit or attack **6** : light in color **7** : adequate — **fair•ness** n

²**fair** adv chiefly Brit : FAIRLY

³**fair** n : exhibition for judging or selling — **fair•ground** n

fair•ly \'farlē\ adv **1** : in a manner of speaking **2** : without bias **3** : somewhat

fairy \'farē\ n, pl fair•ies : usu. small imaginary being — **fairy tale** n

fairy•land \-,land\ n **1** : land of fairies **2** : beautiful or charming place

faith \'fāth\ n, pl faiths \'fāths, 'fāthz\ **1** : allegiance **2** : belief and trust in God **3** : confidence **4** : system of religious beliefs — **faith•ful** \-fəl\ adj — **faith•ful•ly** adv — **faith•ful•ness** n — **faith•less** adj — **faith•less•ly** adv — **faith•less•ness** n

fake \'fāk\ vb faked; fak•ing **1** : falsify **2** : counterfeit ~ n : copy, fraud, or impostor ~ adj : not genuine — **fak•er** n

fa•kir \fə'kir\ n : wandering beggar of India

fal•con \'falkən, 'fȯl-\ n : small long-winged hawk used esp. for hunting — **fal•con•ry** \-rē\ n

fall \'fȯl\ vb fell \'fel\; fall•en \'fȯlən\; fall•ing **1** : go down by gravity **2** : hang freely **3** : go lower **4** : be defeated or ruined **5** : commit a sin **6** : happen at a certain time **7** : become gradually ~ n **1** : act of falling **2**

: autumn **3** : downfall **4** *pl* : waterfall **5** : distance something falls

fal•la•cy \'faləsē\ *n, pl* **-cies 1** : false idea **2** : false reasoning — **fal•la•cious** \fə'lāshəs\ *adj*

fal•li•ble \'faləbəl\ *adj* : capable of making a mistake — **fal•li•bly** \-blē\ *adv*

fall•out *n* **1** : radioactive particles from a nuclear explosion **2** : secondary effects

fal•low \'falō\ *adj* **1** : plowed but not planted **2** : dormant — **fallow** *n or vb*

false \'fóls\ *adj* **fals•er; fals•est 1** : not genuine, true, faithful, or permanent **2** : misleading — **false•ly** *adv* — **false•ness** *n* — **fal•si•fi•ca•tion** \ˌfólsəfə'kāshən\ *n* — **fal•si•fy** \'fólsəˌfī\ *vb* — **fal•si•ty** \'fólsətē\ *n*

false•hood \'fóls ˌhùd\ *n* : lie

fal•set•to \fól'setō\ *n, pl* **-tos** : artificially high singing voice

fal•ter \'fóltər\ *vb* **-tered; -ter•ing 1** : move unsteadily **2** : hesitate — **fal•ter•ing•ly** *adv*

fame \'fām\ *n* : public reputation — **famed** \'fāmd\ *adj*

fa•mil•ial \fə'milyəl\ *adj* : relating to a family

¹fa•mil•iar \fə'milyər\ *n* **1** : companion **2** : guardian spirit

²familiar *adj* **1** : closely acquainted **2** : forward **3** : frequently seen or experienced — **fa•mil•iar•i•ty** \fəˌmil'yarətē, -ˌmilē'yar-\ *n* — **fa•mil•iar•ize** \fə'milyəˌrīz\ *vb* — **fa•mil•iar•ly** *adv*

fam•i•ly \'famlē\ *n, pl* **-lies 1** : persons of common ancestry **2** : group living together **3** : parents and children **4** : group of related individuals

fam•ine \'famən\ *n* : extreme scarcity of food

fam•ish \'famish\ *vb* : starve

fa•mous \'fāməs\ *adj* : widely known or celebrated

fa•mous•ly *adv* : very well

¹fan \'fan\ *n* : device for producing a current of air ∼ *vb* **-nn- 1** : move air with a fan **2** : direct a current of air upon **3** : stir to activity

²fan *n* : enthusiastic follower or admirer

fa•nat•ic \fə'natik\, **fa•nat•i•cal** \-ikəl\ *adj* : excessively enthusiastic or devoted — **fanatic** *n* — **fa•nat•i•cism** \-'natəˌsizəm\ *n*

fan•ci•er \'fansēər\ *n* : one devoted to raising a particular plant or animal

fan•cy \'fansē\ *n, pl* **-cies 1** : liking **2** : whim **3** : imagination ∼ *vb* **-cied; -cy•ing 1** : like **2** : imagine ∼ *adj* **-cier; -est 1** : not plain **2** : of superior quality — **fan•ci•ful** \-sifəl\ *adj* — **fan•ci•ful•ly** \-fəlē\ *adv* — **fan•ci•ly** *adv*

fan•dan•go \fan'daŋgō\ *n, pl* **-gos** : lively Spanish dance

fan•fare \'fanˌfar\ *n* **1** : a sounding of trumpets **2** : showy display

fang \'faŋ\ *n* : long sharp tooth

fan•light *n* : semicircular window

fan•ta•sia \fan'tāzhə, -zēə; ˌfantə'zēə\ *n* : music written to fancy rather than to form

fan•tas•tic \fan'tastik\ *adj* **1** : imaginary or unrealistic **2** : exceedingly or unbelievably great — **fan•tas•ti•cal•ly** \-tiklē\ *adv*

fan•ta•sy \'fantəsē\ *n* **1** : imagination **2** : product (as a daydream) of the imagination **3** : fantasia — **fan•ta•size** \'fantəˌsīz\ *vb*

FAQ *abbr* frequently asked questions

far \'fär\ *adv* **far•ther** \-thər\ *or* **fur•ther** \'fər-\; **far•thest** *or* **fur•thest** \-thəst\ **1** : at or to a distance **2** : much **3** : to a degree **4** : to an advanced point or extent ∼ *adj* **farther** *or* **further; far•thest** *or* **furthest 1** : remote **2** : long **3** : being more distant

far•away *adj* : distant

farce \'färs\ *n* **1** : satirical comedy with an improbable plot **2** : ridiculous display — **far•ci•cal** \-sikəl\ *adj*

¹fare \'far\ *vb* **fared; far•ing** : get along

²fare *n* **1** : price of transportation **2** : range of food

fare•well \far'wel\ *n* **1** : wish of welfare at parting **2** : departure — **farewell** *adj*

far–fetched \'fär'fecht\ *adj* : improbable

fa•ri•na \fə'rēnə\ *n* : fine meal made from cereal grains

farm \'färm\ *n* : place where something is raised for food ∼ *vb* **1** : use (land) as a farm **2** : raise plants or animals for food — **farm•er** *n* — **farm•hand** \-ˌhand\ *n* — **farm•house** *n* — **farm•ing** *n* — **farm•land** \-ˌland\ *n* — **farm•yard** *n*

far–off *adj* : remote in time or space

far•ri•er \'färēər\ *n* : blacksmith who shoes horses

far·row \'farō\ *vb* : give birth to a litter of pigs — **farrow** *n*

far·sight·ed *adj* **1** : better able to see distant things than near **2** : judicious or shrewd — **far·sight·ed·ness** *n*

far·ther \'färthər\ *adv* **1** : at or to a greater distance or more advanced point **2** : to a greater degree or extent ~ *adj* : more distant

far·ther·most *adj* : most distant

far·thest \'färthəst\ *adj* : most distant ~ *adv* **1** : to or at the greatest distance **2** : to the most advanced point **3** : by the greatest extent

fas·ci·cle \'fasikəl\ *n* **1** : small bundle **2** : division of a book published in parts — **fas·ci·cled** \-kəld\ *adj*

fas·ci·nate \'fas°n,āt\ *vb* -nat·ed; -nat·ing : transfix and hold spellbound — **fas·ci·na·tion** \,fas°n-'āshən\ *n*

fas·cism \'fash,izəm\ *n* : dictatorship that exalts nation and race — **fas·cist** \-ist\ *n or adj* — **fas·cis·tic** \fa'shistik\ *adj*

fash·ion \'fashən\ *n* **1** : manner **2** : prevailing custom or style ~ *vb* : form or construct — **fash·ion·able** \-ənəbəl\ *adj* — **fash·ion·ably** \-blē\ *adv*

¹**fast** \'fast\ *adj* **1** : firmly fixed, bound, or shut **2** : faithful **3** : moving or acting quickly **4** : indicating ahead of the correct time **5** : deep and undisturbed **6** : permanently dyed **7** : wild or promiscuous ~ *adv* **1** : so as to be secure or bound **2** : soundly or deeply **3** : swiftly

²**fast** *vb* : abstain from food or eat sparingly ~ *n* : act or time of fasting

fas·ten \'fas°n\ *vb* : attach esp. by pinning or tying — **fas·ten·er** *n* — **fas·ten·ing** *n*

fas·tid·i·ous \fas'tidēəs\ *adj* : hard to please — **fas·tid·i·ous·ly** *adv* — **fas·tid·i·ous·ness** *n*

fat \'fat\ *adj* -tt- **1** : having much fat **2** : thick ~ *n* : animal tissue rich in greasy or oily matter — **fat·ness** *n* — **fat·ten** \'fat°n\ *vb* — **fat·ty** *adj or n*

fa·tal \'fāt°l\ *adj* : causing death or ruin — **fa·tal·i·ty** \fā'talətē, fə-\ *n* — **fa·tal·ly** *adv*

fa·tal·ism \'fāt°l,izəm\ *n* : belief that fate determines events — **fa·tal·ist** \-ist\ *n* — **fa·tal·is·tic** \,fāt°l'istik\ *adj* — **fa·tal·is·ti·cal·ly** \-tiklē\ *adv*

fate \'fāt\ *n* **1** : principle, cause, or will held to determine events **2** : end or outcome — **fat·ed** *adj* — **fate·ful** \-fəl\ *adj* — **fate·ful·ly** *adv*

fa·ther \'fäthər, 'fath-\ *n* **1** : male parent **2** *cap* : God **3** : originator — **father** *vb* — **fa·ther·hood** \-,hůd\ *n* — **fa·ther·land** \-,land\ *n* — **fa·ther·less** *adj* — **fa·ther·ly** *adj*

father–in–law *n, pl* **fathers–in–law** : father of one's spouse

fath·om \'fathəm\ *n* : nautical unit of length equal to 6 feet ~ *vb* : understand — **fath·om·able** *adj* — **fath·om·less** *adj*

fa·tigue \fə'tēg\ *n* **1** : weariness from labor or use **2** : tendency to break under repeated stress ~ *vb* -tigued; -tigu·ing : tire out

fat·u·ous \'fachəwəs\ *adj* : foolish or stupid — **fat·u·ous·ly** *adv* — **fat·u·ous·ness** *n*

fau·cet \'fósət, 'fäs-\ *n* : fixture for drawing off a liquid

fault \'fólt\ *n* **1** : weakness in character **2** : something wrong or imperfect **3** : responsibility for something wrong **4** : fracture in the earth's crust ~ *vb* : find fault in or with — **fault·find·er** *n* — **fault·find·ing** *n* — **fault·i·ly** \'fóltəlē\ *adv* — **fault·less** *adj* — **fault·less·ly** *adv* — **faulty** *adj*

fau·na \'fónə\ *n* : animals or animal life esp. of a region — **fau·nal** \-°l\ *adj*

faux pas \'fō'pä\ *n, pl* **faux pas** *same or* -'päz\ : social blunder

fa·vor \'fāvər\ *n* **1** : approval **2** : partiality **3** : act of kindness ~ *vb* : regard or treat with favor — **fa·vor·able** \'fāvərəbəl\ *adj* — **fa·vor·ably** \-blē\ *adv*

fa·vor·ite \'fāvərət\ *n* : one favored — **favorite** *adj* — **fa·vor·it·ism** \-,izəm\ *n*

¹**fawn** \'fón\ *vb* : seek favor by groveling

²**fawn** *n* : young deer

faze \'fāz\ *vb* **fazed; faz·ing** : disturb the composure of

fear \'fir\ *n* : unpleasant emotion caused by expectation or awareness of danger ~ *vb* : be afraid of — **fear·ful** \-fəl\ *adj* — **fear·ful·ly** *adv* — **fear·less** *adj* — **fear·less·ly** *adv* — **fear·less·ness** *n* — **fear·some** \-səm\ *adj*

fea·si·ble \'fēzəbəl\ *adj* : capable of being done — **fea·si·bil·i·ty** \,fēzə'bilətē\ *n* — **fea·si·bly** \'fēzəblē\ *adv*

feast \'fēst\ *n* **1** : large or fancy meal **2**

: religious festival ～ *vb* : eat plentifully

feat \'fēt\ *n* : notable deed

feath•er \'fethər\ *n* : one of the light horny outgrowths that form the external covering of a bird's body — **feather** *vb* — **feath•ered** \-ərd\ *adj* — **feath•er•less** *adj* — **feath•ery** *adj*

fea•ture \'fēchər\ *n* **1** : shape or appearance of the face **2** : part of the face **3** : prominent characteristic **4** : special attraction ～ *vb* : give prominence to — **fea•ture•less** *adj*

Feb•ru•ary \'febyə,werē, 'febə-, 'febrə-\ *n* : 2d month of the year having 28 and in leap years 29 days

fe•ces \'fē,sēz\ *n pl* : intestinal body waste — **fe•cal** \-kəl\ *adj*

feck•less \'fekləs\ *adj* : irresponsible

fe•cund \'fekənd, 'fē-\ *adj* : prolific — **fe•cun•di•ty** \fi'kəndətē, fe-\ *n*

fed•er•al \'fedrəl, -dərəl\ *adj* : of or constituting a government with power distributed between a central authority and constituent units — **fed•er•al•ism** \-rə,lizəm\ *n* — **fed•er•al•ist** \-list\ *n or adj* — **fed•er•al•ly** *adv*

fed•er•ate \'fedə,rāt\ *vb* **-at•ed; -at•ing** : join in a federation

fed•er•a•tion \,fedə'rāshən\ *n* : union of organizations

fe•do•ra \fi'dōrə\ *n* : soft felt hat

fed up *adj* : out of patience

fee \'fē\ *n* : fixed charge

fee•ble \'fēbəl\ *adj* **-bler; -blest** : weak or ineffective — **fee•ble•mind•ed** \,fēbəl'mīndəd\ *adj* — **fee•ble•mind•ed•ness** *n* — **fee•ble•ness** *n* — **fee•bly** \-blē\ *adv*

feed \'fēd\ *vb* **fed** \'fed\; **feed•ing 1** : give food to **2** : eat **3** : furnish ～ *n* : food for livestock — **feed•er** *n*

feel \'fēl\ *vb* **felt** \'felt\; **feel•ing 1** : perceive or examine through physical contact **2** : think or believe **3** : be conscious of **4** : seem **5** : have sympathy ～ *n* **1** : sense of touch **2** : quality of a thing imparted through touch — **feel•er** *n*

feel•ing \'fēliŋ\ *n* **1** : sense of touch **2** : state of mind **3** *pl* : sensibilities **4** : opinion

feet *pl of* FOOT

feign \'fān\ *vb* : pretend

feint \'fānt\ *n* : mock attack intended to distract attention — **feint** *vb*

fe•lic•i•tate \fi'lisə,tāt\ *vb* **-tat•ed; -tat-**

ing : congratulate — **fe•lic•i•ta•tion** \-,lisə'tāshən\ *n*

fe•lic•i•tous \fi'lisətəs\ *adj* : aptly expressed — **fe•lic•i•tous•ly** *adv*

fe•lic•i•ty \-'lisətē\ *n, pl* **-ties 1** : great happiness **2** : pleasing faculty esp. in art or language

fe•line \'fē,līn\ *adj* : relating to cats — **feline** *n*

¹fell \'fel\ *vb* : cut or knock down

²fell *past of* FALL

fel•low \'felō\ *n* **1** : companion or associate **2** : man or boy — **fel•low•ship** \-,ship\ *n*

fel•low•man \,felō'man\ *n* : kindred human being

fel•on \'felən\ *n* : one who has committed a felony

fel•o•ny \'felənē\ *n, pl* **-nies** : serious crime — **fe•lo•ni•ous** \fə'lōnēəs\ *adj*

¹felt \'felt\ *n* : cloth made of pressed wool and fur

²felt *past of* FEEL

fe•male \'fē,māl\ *adj* : relating to or being the sex that bears young — **female** *n*

fem•i•nine \'femənən\ *adj* : relating to the female sex — **fem•i•nin•i•ty** \,femə'ninətē\ *n*

fem•i•nism \'femə,nizəm\ *n* : organized activity on behalf of women's rights — **fem•i•nist** \-nist\ *n or adj*

fe•mur \'fēmər\ *n, pl* **fe•murs** *or* **fem•o•ra** \'femərə\ : long bone of the thigh — **fem•o•ral** \'femərəl\ *adj*

fence \'fens\ *n* : enclosing barrier esp. of wood or wire ～ *vb* **fenced; fenc•ing 1** : enclose with a fence **2** : practice fencing — **fenc•er** *n*

fenc•ing \'fensiŋ\ *n* **1** : combat with swords for sport **2** : material for building fences

fend \'fend\ *vb* : ward off

fend•er \'fendər\ *n* : guard over an automobile wheel

fen•nel \'fen³l\ *n* : herb related to the carrot

fer•ment \fər'ment\ *vb* : cause or undergo fermentation ～ \'fər,ment\ *n* : agitation

fer•men•ta•tion \,fərmən'tāshən, -,men-\ *n* : chemical decomposition of an organic substance in the absence of oxygen

fern \'fərn\ *n* : flowerless seedless green plant

fe•ro•cious \fə'rōshəs\ *adj* : fierce or savage — **fe•ro•cious•ly** *adv* — **fe•ro-**

cious•ness *n* — fe•roc•i•ty \-'räs-ətē\ *n*

fer•ret \'ferət\ *n* : white European pole-cat ~ *vb* : find out by searching

fer•ric \'ferik\, fer•rous \'ferəs\ *adj* : relating to or containing iron

fer•rule \'ferəl\ *n* : metal band or ring

fer•ry \'ferē\ *vb* -ried; -ry•ing : carry by boat over water ~ *n, pl* -ries : boat used in ferrying — fer•ry•boat *n*

fer•tile \'fərt°l\ *adj* 1 : producing plentifully 2 : capable of developing or reproducing — fer•til•i•ty \fər'tilətē\ *n*

fer•til•ize \'fərt°l,īz\ *vb* -ized; -iz•ing : make fertile — fer•til•iza•tion \,fərt°lə'zāshən\ *n* — fer•til•iz•er *n*

fer•vid \'fərvəd\ *adj* : ardent or zealous — fer•vid•ly *adv*

fer•vor \'fərvər\ *n* : passion — fer•ven•cy \-vənsē\ *n* — fer•vent \-vənt\ *adj* — fer•vent•ly *adv*

fes•ter \'festər\ *vb* 1 : form pus 2 : become more bitter or malignant

fes•ti•val \'festəvəl\ *n* : time of celebration

fes•tive \-tiv\ *adj* : joyous or happy — fes•tive•ly *adv* — fes•tiv•i•ty \fes-'tivətē\ *n*

fes•toon \fes'tün\ *n* : decorative chain or strip hanging in a curve — festoon *vb*

fe•tal \'fēt°l\ *adj* : of, relating to, or being a fetus

fetch \'fech\ *vb* 1 : go or come after and bring or take back 2 : sell for

fetch•ing \'fechiŋ\ *adj* : attractive — fetch•ing•ly *adv*

fête \'fāt, 'fet\ *n* : lavish party ~ *vb* fêt•ed; fêt•ing : honor or commemorate with a fête

fet•id \'fetəd\ *adj* : having an offensive smell

fe•tish \'fetish\ *n* 1 : object believed to have magical powers 2 : object of unreasoning devotion or concern

fet•lock \'fet,läk\ *n* : projection on the back of a horse's leg above the hoof

fet•ter \'fetər\ *n* : chain or shackle for the feet — fetter *vb*

fet•tle \'fet°l\ *n* : state of fitness

fe•tus \'fētəs\ *n* : vertebrate not yet born or hatched

feud \'fyüd\ *n* : prolonged quarrel — feud *vb*

feu•dal \'fyüd°l\ *adj* : of or relating to feudalism

feu•dal•ism \-,izəm\ *n* : medieval political order in which land is granted in return for service — feu•dal•is•tic \,fyüd°l'istik\ *adj*

fe•ver \'fēvər\ *n* 1 : abnormal rise in body temperature 2 : state of heightened emotion — fe•ver•ish *adj* — fe•ver•ish•ly *adv*

few \'fyü\ *pron* : not many ~ *adj* : some but not many — often with *a* ~ *n* : small number — often with *a*

few•er \-ər\ *pron* : smaller number of things

fez \'fez\ *n, pl* fez•zes : round flat-crowned hat

fi•an•cé \,fē,än'sā\ *n* : man one is engaged to

fi•an•cée \,fē,än'sā\ *n* : woman one is engaged to

fi•as•co \fē'askō\ *n, pl* -coes : ridiculous failure

fi•at \'fēat, -,at, -,ät; 'fīat, -,at\ *n* : decree

fib \'fib\ *n* : trivial lie — fib *vb* — fib•ber *n*

fi•ber, fi•bre \'fībər\ *n* 1 : threadlike substance or structure (as a muscle cell or fine root) 2 : indigestible material in food 3 : element that gives texture or substance — fi•brous \-brəs\ *adj*

fi•ber•board *n* : construction material made of compressed fibers

fi•ber•glass *n* : glass in fibrous form in various products (as insulation)

fi•bril•la•tion \,fibrə'lāshən, ,fīb-\ *n* : rapid irregular contractions of heart muscle — fib•ril•late \'fibrə,lāt, 'fīb-\ *vb*

fib•u•la \'fibyələ\ *n, pl* -lae \-lē, -lī\ *or* -las : outer of the two leg bones below the knee — fib•u•lar \-lər\ *adj*

fick•le \'fikəl\ *adj* : unpredictably changeable — fick•le•ness *n*

fic•tion \'fikshən\ *n* : a made-up story or literature consisting of these — fic•tion•al \-shənəl\ *adj*

fic•ti•tious \fik'tishəs\ *adj* : made up or pretended

fid•dle \'fid°l\ *n* : violin ~ *vb* -dled; -dling 1 : play on the fiddle 2 : move the hands restlessly — fid•dler \'fidlər, -°lər\ *n*

fid•dle•sticks *n* : nonsense — used as an interjection

fi•del•i•ty \fə'delətē, fī-\ *n, pl* -ties 1 : quality or state of being faithful 2 : quality of reproduction

fid•get \'fijət\ *n* **1** *pl* : restlessness **2** : one that fidgets ~ *vb* : move restlessly — **fid•gety** *adj*

fi•du•ci•a•ry \fə'düshē͵erē, -'dyü-, -shərē\ *adj* : held or holding in trust — **fiduciary** *n*

field \'fēld\ *n* **1** : open country **2** : cleared land **3** : land yielding some special product **4** : sphere of activity **5** : area for sports **6** : region or space in which a given effect (as magnetism) exists ~ *vb* : put into the field — **field** *adj* — **field•er** *n*

fiend \'fēnd\ *n* **1** : devil **2** : extremely wicked person — **fiend•ish** *adj* — **fiend•ish•ly** *adv*

fierce \'firs\ *adj* **fierc•er; -est 1** : violently hostile or aggressive **2** : intense **3** : menacing looking — **fierce•ly** *adv* — **fierce•ness** *n*

fi•ery \'fīərē\ *adj* **fi•er•i•er; -est 1** : burning **2** : hot or passionate — **fi•eri•ness** \'fīərēnəs\ *n*

fi•es•ta \fē'estə\ *n* : festival

fife \'fīf\ *n* : small flute

fif•teen \fif'tēn\ *n* : one more than 14 — **fifteen** *adj or pron* — **fif•teenth** \-'tēnth\ *adj or n*

fifth \'fifth\ *n* **1** : one that is number 5 in a countable series **2** : one of 5 equal parts of something — **fifth** *adj or adv*

fif•ty \'fiftē\ *n, pl* **-ties** : 5 times 10 — **fif•ti•eth** \-tēəth\ *adj or n* — **fifty** *adj or pron*

fif•ty-fif•ty *adv or adj* : shared equally

fig \'fig\ *n* : pear-shaped edible fruit

fight \'fīt\ *vb* **fought** \'fȯt\; **fight•ing 1** : contend against another in battle **2** : box ~ *n* **1** : hostile encounter **2** : boxing match **3** : verbal disagreement — **fight•er** *n*

fig•ment \'figmənt\ *n* : something imagined or made up

fig•u•ra•tive \'figyərətiv, -gə-\ *adj* : metaphorical — **fig•u•ra•tive•ly** *adv*

fig•ure \'figyər, -gər\ *n* **1** : symbol representing a number **2** *pl* : arithmetical calculations **3** : price **4** : shape or outline **5** : illustration **6** : pattern or design **7** : prominent person ~ *vb* **-ured; -ur•ing 1** : be important **2** : calculate — **fig•ured** *adj*

fig•u•rine \͵figyə'rēn\ *n* : small statue

fil•a•ment \'filəmənt\ *n* : fine thread or threadlike part — **fil•a•men•tous** \͵filə'mentəs\ *adj*

fil•bert \'filbərt\ *n* : edible nut of a European hazel

filch \'filch\ *vb* : steal furtively

¹file \'fīl\ *n* : tool for smoothing or sharpening ~ *vb* **filed; fil•ing** : rub or smooth with a file

²file *vb* **filed; fil•ing 1** : arrange in order **2** : enter or record officially ~ *n* : device for keeping papers in order

³file *n* : row of persons or things one behind the other ~ *vb* **filed; fil•ing** : march in file

fil•ial \'filēəl, 'filyəl\ *adj* : relating to a son or daughter

fil•i•bus•ter \'filə͵bəstər\ *n* : long speeches to delay a legislative vote — **filibuster** *vb* — **fil•i•bus•ter•er** *n*

fil•i•gree \'filə͵grē\ *n* : ornamental designs of fine wire — **fil•i•greed** \͵grēd\ *adj*

fill \'fil\ *vb* **1** : make or become full **2** : stop up **3** : feed **4** : satisfy **5** : occupy fully **6** : spread through ~ *n* **1** : full supply **2** : material for filling — **fill•er** *n* — **fill in** *vb* **1** : provide information to or for **2** : substitute

fil•let \'filət, fi'lā, 'fil͵ā\ *n* : piece of boneless meat or fish ~ *vb* : cut into fillets

fill•ing *n* : material used to fill something

fil•ly \'filē\ *n, pl* **-lies** : young female horse

film \'film\ *n* **1** : thin skin or membrane **2** : thin coating or layer **3** : strip of material used in taking pictures **4** : movie ~ *vb* : make a movie of — **filmy** *adj*

film•strip *n* : strip of film with photographs for still projection

fil•ter \'filtər\ *n* **1** : device for separating matter from a fluid **2** : device (as on a camera lens) that absorbs light ~ *vb* **1** : pass through a filter **2** : remove by means of a filter — **fil•ter•able** *adj* — **fil•tra•tion** \fil'trāshən\ *n*

filth \'filth\ *n* : repulsive dirt or refuse — **filth•i•ness** *n* — **filthy** \'filthē\ *adj*

fin \'fin\ *n* **1** : thin external process controlling movement in an aquatic animal **2** : fin-shaped part (as on an airplane) **3** : flipper — **finned** \'find\ *adj*

fi•na•gle \fə'nāgəl\ *vb* **-gled; -gling** : get by clever or tricky means — **fi•na•gler** *n*

fi•nal \'fīnᵊl\ *adj* **1** : not to be changed

2 : ultimate **3** : coming at the end —
final n — **fi·nal·ist** \'fīn°list\ n — **fi·nal·i·ty** \fī'nalətē, fə-\ n — **fi·nal·ize** \-ˌīz\ vb — **fi·nal·ly** adv
fi·na·le \fə'nalē, fi'näl-\ n : last or climactic part
fi·nance \fə'nans, 'fī,nans\ n **1** pl : money resources **2** : management of money affairs ~ vb **-nanc·ing 1** : raise funds for **2** : give necessary funds to **3** : sell on credit
fi·nan·cial \fə'nanchəl, fī-\ adj : relating to finance — **fi·nan·cial·ly** adv
fi·nan·cier \ˌfinən'sir, ˌfī,nan-\ n : person who invests large sums of money
finch \'finch\ n : songbird (as a sparrow or linnet) with a strong bill
find \'fīnd\ vb **found** \'faůnd\; **find·ing 1** : discover or encounter **2** : obtain by effort **3** : experience or feel **4** : gain or regain the use of **5** : decide on (a verdict) ~ n **1** : act or instance of finding **2** : something found — **find·er** n — **find·ing** n — **find out** vb : learn, discover, or verify something
fine \'fīn\ n : money paid as a penalty ~ vb **fined; fin·ing** : impose a fine on ~ adj **fin·er; -est 1** : free from impurity **2** : small or thin **3** : not coarse **4** : superior in quality or appearance ~ adv : finely — **fine·ly** adv — **fine·ness** n
fin·ery \'fīnərē\ n, pl **-er·ies** : showy clothing and jewels
fi·nesse \fə'nes\ n **1** : delicate skill **2** : craftiness — **finesse** vb
fin·ger \'fiŋgər\ n **1** : one of the 5 divisions at the end of the hand and esp. one other than the thumb **2** : something like a finger **3** : part of a glove for a finger ~ vb **1** : touch with the fingers **2** : identify as if by pointing — **fin·gered** adj — **fin·ger·nail** n — **fin·ger·tip** n
fin·ger·ling \-gərliŋ\ n : small fish
fin·ger·print n : impression of the pattern of marks on the tip of a finger — **fingerprint** vb
fin·icky \'finikē\ adj : excessively particular in taste or standards
fin·ish \'finish\ vb **1** : come or bring to an end **2** : use or dispose of entirely **3** : put a final coat or surface on ~ n **1** : end **2** : final treatment given a surface — **fin·ish·er** n
fi·nite \'fī,nīt\ adj : having definite limits

fink \'fiŋk\ n : contemptible person
fiord var of FJORD
fir \'fər\ n : evergreen tree or its wood
fire \'fīr\ n **1** : light or heat and esp. the flame of something burning **2** : destructive burning (as of a house) **3** : enthusiasm **4** : the shooting of weapons ~ vb **fired; fir·ing 1** : kindle **2** : stir up or enliven **3** : dismiss from employment **4** : shoot **5** : bake — **fire·bomb** n or vb — **fire·fight·er** n — **fire·less** adj — **fire·proof** adj or vb — **fire·wood** n
fire·arm n : weapon (as a rifle) that works by an explosion of gunpowder
fire·ball n **1** : ball of fire **2** : brilliant meteor
fire·boat n : boat equipped for fighting fire
fire·box n **1** : chamber (as of a furnace) that contains a fire **2** : fire-alarm box
fire·break n : cleared land for checking a forest fire
fire·bug n : person who deliberately sets destructive fires
fire·crack·er n : small firework that makes noise
fire·fight·er \'fīr,fītər\ n : a person who fights fires
fire·fly n : night-flying beetle that produces a soft light
fire·place n : opening made in a chimney to hold an open fire
fire·plug n : hydrant
fire·side n **1** : place near the fire or hearth **2** : home ~ adj : having an informal quality
fire·trap n : place apt to catch on fire
fire·work n : device that explodes to produce noise or a display of light
¹firm \'fərm\ adj **1** : securely fixed in place **2** : strong or vigorous **3** : not subject to change **4** : resolute ~ vb : make or become firm — **firm·ly** adv — **firm·ness** n
²firm n : business enterprise
fir·ma·ment \'fərməmənt\ n : sky
first \'fərst\ adj **1** : being number one **2** : foremost ~ adv **1** : before any other **2** : for the first time ~ n **1** : number one **2** : one that is first — **first class** n — **first–class** adj or adv — **first·ly** adv — **first–rate** adj or adv
first aid n : emergency care
first lieutenant n : commissioned officer ranking next below a captain
first sergeant n **1** : noncommissioned

officer serving as the chief assistant to the commander of a military unit **2** : rank in the army below a sergeant major and in the marine corps below a master gunnery sergeant

firth \'fərth\ *n* : estuary

fis·cal \'fiskəl\ *adj* : relating to money — **fis·cal·ly** *adv*

fish \'fish\ *n, pl* **fish** *or* **fish·es** : water animal with fins, gills, and usu. scales ~ *vb* **1** : try to catch fish **2** : grope — **fish·er** *n* — **fish·hook** *n* — **fish·ing** *n*

fish·er·man \-mən\ *n* : one who fishes

fish·ery \'fishərē\ *n, pl* **-er·ies** : fishing business or a place for this

fishy \'fishē\ *adj* **fish·i·er; -est 1** : relating to or like fish **2** : questionable

fis·sion \'fishən, 'fizh-\ *n* : splitting of an atomic nucleus — **fis·sion·able** \-ənəbəl\ *adj*

fis·sure \'fishər\ *n* : crack

fist \'fist\ *n* : hand doubled up — **fist·ed** \'fistəd\ *adj* — **fist·ful** \-ˌfūl\ *n*

fist·i·cuffs \'fistiˌkəfs\ *n pl* : fist fight

¹fit \'fit\ *n* : sudden attack of illness or emotion

²fit *adj* **-tt- 1** : suitable **2** : qualified **3** : sound in body ~ *vb* **-tt- 1** : be suitable to **2** : insert or adjust correctly **3** : make room for **4** : supply or equip **5** : belong ~ *n* : state of fitting or being fitted — **fit·ly** *adv* — **fit·ness** *n* — **fit·ter** *n*

fit·ful \'fitfəl\ *adj* : restless — **fit·ful·ly** *adv*

fit·ting *adj* : suitable ~ *n* : a small part

five \'fīv\ *n* **1** : one more than 4 **2** : 5th in a set or series **3** : something having 5 units — **five** *adj or pron*

fix \'fiks\ *vb* **1** : attach **2** : establish **3** : make right **4** : prepare **5** : improperly influence ~ *n* **1** : predicament **2** : determination of location — **fix·er** *n*

fix·a·tion \fik'sāshən\ *n* : obsessive attachment — **fix·ate** \'fikˌsāt\ *vb*

fixed \'fikst\ *adj* **1** : stationary **2** : settled — **fixed·ly** \'fikədlē\ *adv* — **fixed·ness** \-nəs\ *n*

fix·ture \'fikschər\ *n* : permanent part of something

fizz \'fiz\ *vb* : make a hissing sound ~ *n* : effervescence

fiz·zle \'fizəl\ *vb* **-zled; -zling 1** : fizz **2** : fail ~ *n* : failure

fjord \fē'òrd\ *n* : inlet of the sea between cliffs

flab \'flab\ *n* : flabby flesh

flab·ber·gast \'flabərˌgast\ *vb* : astound

flab·by \'flabē\ *adj* **-bi·er; -est** : not firm — **flab·bi·ness** *n*

flac·cid \'flaksəd, 'flasəd\ *adj* : not firm

¹flag \'flag\ *n* : flat stone

²flag *n* **1** : fabric that is a symbol (as of a country) **2** : something used to signal ~ *vb* **-gg-** : signal with a flag — **flag·pole** *n* — **flag·staff** *n*

³flag *vb* **-gg-** : lose strength or spirit

flag·el·late \'flajəˌlāt\ *vb* **-lat·ed; -lat·ing** : whip — **flag·el·la·tion** \ˌflajə'lāshən\ *n*

flag·on \'flagən\ *n* : container for liquids

fla·grant \'flāgrənt\ *adj* : conspicuously bad — **fla·grant·ly** *adv*

flag·ship *n* : ship carrying a commander

flag·stone *n* : flag

flail \'flāl\ *n* : tool for threshing grain ~ *vb* : beat with or as if with a flail

flair \'flar\ *n* : natural aptitude

flak \'flak\ *n, pl* **flak 1** : antiaircraft fire **2** : criticism

flake \'flāk\ *n* : small flat piece ~ *vb* **flaked; flak·ing** : separate or form into flakes

flam·boy·ant \flam'bòiənt\ *adj* : showy — **flam·boy·ance** \-əns\ *n* — **flam·boy·ant·ly** *adv*

flame \'flām\ *n* **1** : glowing part of a fire **2** : state of combustion **3** : burning passion — **flame** *vb* — **flam·ing** *adj*

fla·min·go \flə'miŋgō\ *n, pl* **-gos** : long-legged long-necked tropical water bird

flam·ma·ble \'flaməbəl\ *adj* : easily ignited

flange \'flanj\ *n* : rim

flank \'flaŋk\ *n* : side of something ~ *vb* **1** : attack or go around the side of **2** : be at the side of

flan·nel \'flanᵊl\ *n* : soft napped fabric

flap \'flap\ *n* **1** : slap **2** : something flat that hangs loose ~ *vb* **-pp- 1** : move (wings) up and down **2** : swing back and forth noisily

flap·jack \-ˌjak\ *n* : pancake

flare \'flar\ *vb* **flared; flar·ing** : become suddenly bright or excited ~ *n* : blaze of light

flash \'flash\ *vb* **1** : give off a sudden flame or burst of light **2** : appear or pass suddenly ~ *n* **1** : sudden burst of light or inspiration **2** : instant ~ *adj* : coming suddenly

flash•light *n* : small battery-operated light

flashy \'flashē\ *adj* **flash•i•er; -est** : showy — **flash•i•ly** *adv* — **flash•i•ness** *n*

flask \'flask\ *n* : flattened bottle

flat \'flat\ *adj* **-tt- 1** : smooth **2** : broad and thin **3** : definite **4** : uninteresting **5** : deflated **6** : below the true pitch ~ *n* **1** : level surface of land **2** : flat note in music **3** : apartment **4** : deflated tire ~ *adv* **-tt- 1** : exactly **2** : below the true pitch ~ *vb* **-tt-** : make flat — **flat•ly** *adv* — **flat•ness** *n* — **flat•ten** \-ᵊn\ *vb*

flat•car *n* : railroad car without sides

flat•fish *n* : flattened fish with both eyes on the upper side

flat•foot *n, pl* **flat•feet** : foot condition in which the arch is flattened — **flat–foot•ed** *adj*

flat–out *adj* **1** : being maximum effort or speed **2** : downright

flat•ter \'flatər\ *vb* **1** : praise insincerely **2** : judge or represent too favorably — **flat•ter•er** *n* — **flat•tery** \'flatərē\ *n*

flat•u•lent \'flachələnt\ *adj* : full of gas — **flat•u•lence** \-ləns\ *n*

flat•ware *n* : eating utensils

flaunt \'flȯnt\ *vb* : display ostentatiously — **flaunt** *n*

fla•vor \'flāvər\ *n* **1** : quality that affects the sense of taste **2** : something that adds flavor ~ *vb* : give flavor to — **fla•vor•ful** *adj* — **fla•vor•ing** *n* — **fla•vor•less** *adj*

flaw \'flȯ\ *n* : fault — **flaw•less** *adj* — **flaw•less•ly** *adv* — **flaw•less•ness** *n*

flax \'flaks\ *n* : plant from which linen is made

flax•en \'flaksən\ *adj* : made of or like flax

flay \'flā\ *vb* **1** : strip off the skin of **2** : criticize harshly

flea \'flē\ *n* : leaping bloodsucking insect

fleck \'flek\ *vb or n* : streak or spot

fledg•ling \'flejliŋ\ *n* : young bird

flee \'flē\ *vb* **fled** \'fled\; **flee•ing** : run away

fleece \'flēs\ *n* : sheep's wool ~ *vb* **fleeced; fleec•ing 1** : shear **2** : get money from dishonestly — **fleecy** *adj*

¹**fleet** \'flēt\ *vb* : pass rapidly ~ *adj*

: swift — **fleet•ing** *adj* — **fleet•ness** *n*

²**fleet** *n* : group of ships

fleet admiral *n* : commissioned officer of the highest rank in the navy

flesh \'flesh\ *n* **1** : soft parts of an animal's body **2** : soft plant tissue (as fruit pulp) — **fleshed** \'flesht\ *adj* — **fleshy** *adj* — **flesh out** *vb* : make fuller

flesh•ly \'fleshlē\ *adj* : sensual

flew *past of* FLY

flex \'fleks\ *vb* : bend

flex•i•ble \'fleksəbəl\ *adj* **1** : capable of being flexed **2** : adaptable — **flex•i•bil•i•ty** \,fleksə'bilətē\ *n* — **flex•i•bly** \-səblē\ *adv*

flick \'flik\ *n* : light jerky stroke ~ *vb* **1** : strike lightly **2** : flutter

flick•er \'flikər\ *vb* **1** : waver **2** : burn unsteadily ~ *n* **1** : sudden movement **2** : wavering light

fli•er \'flīər\ *n* **1** : aviator **2** : advertising circular

¹**flight** \'flīt\ *n* **1** : act or instance of flying **2** : ability to fly **3** : a passing through air or space **4** : series of stairs — **flight•less** *adj*

²**flight** *n* : act or instance of running away

flighty \-ē\ *adj* **flight•i•er; -est** : capricious or silly — **flight•i•ness** *n*

flim•flam \'flim,flam\ *n* : trickery

flim•sy \-zē\ *adj* **-si•er; -est 1** : not strong or well made **2** : not believable — **flim•si•ly** *adv* — **flim•si•ness** *n*

flinch \'flinch\ *vb* : shrink from pain

fling \'fliŋ\ *vb* **flung** \'fləŋ\; **fling•ing 1** : move brusquely **2** : throw ~ *n* **1** : act or instance of flinging **2** : attempt **3** : period of self-indulgence

flint \'flint\ *n* : hard quartz that gives off sparks when struck with steel — **flinty** *adj*

flip \'flip\ *vb* **-pp- 1** : cause to turn over quickly or many times **2** : move with a quick push ~ *adj* : insolent — **flip** *n*

flip•pant \'flipənt\ *adj* : not serious enough — **flip•pan•cy** \-ənsē\ *n*

flip•per \'flipər\ *n* : paddlelike limb (as of a seal) for swimming

flirt \'flərt\ *vb* **1** : be playfully romantic **2** : show casual interest ~ *n* : one who flirts — **flir•ta•tion** \,flər'tāshən\ *n* — **flir•ta•tious** \-shəs\ *adj*

flit \'flit\ *vb* **-tt-** : dart

float \'flōt\ *n* **1** : something that floats **2** : vehicle carrying an exhibit ~ *vb*

1 : rest on or in a fluid without sinking **2** : wander **3** : finance by issuing stock or bonds — **float•er** n

flock \'fläk\ n : group of animals (as birds) or people ～ vb : gather or move as a group

floe \'flō\ n : mass of floating ice

flog \'fläg\ vb **-gg-** : beat with a rod or whip — **flog•ger** n

flood \'fləd\ n **1** : great flow of water over the land **2** : overwhelming volume ～ vb : cover or fill esp. with water — **flood•wa•ter** n

floor \'flōr\ n **1** : bottom of a room on which one stands **2** : story of a building **3** : lower limit ～ vb **1** : furnish with a floor **2** : knock down **3** : amaze — **floor•board** n — **floor•ing** \-iŋ\ n

floo•zy, floo•zie \'flüzē\ n, pl **-zies** : promiscuous young woman

flop \'fläp\ vb **-pp- 1** : flap **2** : slump heavily **3** : fail — **flop** n

flop•py \'fläpē\ adj **-pi•er; -est** : soft and flexible

flo•ra \'flōrə\ n : plants or plant life of a region

flo•ral \'flōrəl\ adj : relating to flowers

flor•id \'flórəd\ adj **1** : very flowery in style **2** : reddish

flo•rist \'flórist\ n : flower dealer

floss \'fläs\ n **1** : soft thread for embroidery **2** : thread used to clean between teeth — **floss** vb

flo•ta•tion \flō'tāshən\ n : process or instance of floating

flo•til•la \flō'tilə\ n : small fleet

flot•sam \'flätsəm\ n : floating wreckage

¹**flounce** \'flaůns\ vb **flounced; flouncing** : move with exaggerated jerky motions — **flounce** n

²**flounce** n : fabric border or wide ruffle

¹**floun•der** \'flaůndər\ n, pl **flounder** or **flounders** : flatfish

²**flounder** vb **1** : struggle for footing **2** : proceed clumsily

flour \'flaůr\ n : finely ground meal ～ vb : coat with flour — **floury** adj

flour•ish \'flərish\ vb **1** : thrive **2** : wave threateningly ～ n **1** : embellishment **2** : fanfare **3** : wave **4** : showiness of action

flout \'flaůt\ vb : treat with disdain

flow \'flō\ vb **1** : move in a stream **2** : proceed smoothly and readily ～ n : uninterrupted stream

flow•er \'flaůər\ n **1** : showy plant

shoot that bears seeds **2** : state of flourishing ～ vb **1** : produce flowers **2** : flourish — **flow•ered** adj — **flow•er•less** adj — **flow•er•pot** n — **flow•ery** \-ē\ adj

flown past part of FLY

flu \'flü\ n **1** : influenza **2** : minor virus ailment

flub \'fləb\ vb **-bb-** : bungle — **flub** n

fluc•tu•ate \'fləkchə,wāt\ vb **-at•ed; -at•ing** : change rapidly esp. up and down — **fluc•tu•a•tion** \,fləkchə-'wāshən\ n

flue \'flü\ n : smoke duct

flu•ent \'flüənt\ adj : speaking with ease — **flu•en•cy** \-ənsē\ n — **flu•ent•ly** adv

fluff \'fləf\ n **1** : something soft and light **2** : blunder ～ vb **1** : make fluffy **2** : make a mistake — **fluffy** \-ē\ adj

flu•id \'flüəd\ adj : flowing ～ n : substance that can flow — **flu•id•i•ty** \flü'idətē\ n — **flu•id•ly** adv

fluid ounce n : unit of liquid measure equal to ¹⁄₁₆ pint

fluke \'flük\ n : stroke of luck

flume \'flüm\ n : channel for water

flung past of FLING

flunk \'fləŋk\ vb : fail in school work

flun•ky, flun•key \'fləŋkē\ n, pl **-kies** or **-keys** : lackey

flu•o•res•cence \,flůr'es°ns, ,flór-\ n : emission of light after initial absorption — **flu•o•resce** \-'es\ vb — **flu•o•res•cent** \-'es°nt\ adj

flu•o•ri•date \'flórə,dāt, 'flůr-\ vb **-dat•ed; -dat•ing** : add fluoride to — **flu•o•ri•da•tion** \,flórə'dāshən, ,flůr-\ n

flu•o•ride \'flór,īd, 'flůr-\ n : compound of fluorine

flu•o•rine \'flůr,ēn, -ən\ n : toxic gaseous chemical element

flu•o•ro•car•bon \,flórō'kärbən, ,flůr-\ n : compound containing fluorine and carbon

flu•o•ro•scope \'flůrə,skōp\ n : instrument for internal examination — **flu•o•ro•scop•ic** \,flůrə'skäpik\ adj — **flu•o•ros•co•py** \,flůr'äskəpē\ n

flur•ry \'flərē\ n, pl **-ries 1** : light snowfall **2** : bustle **3** : brief burst of activity — **flurry** vb

¹**flush** \'fləsh\ vb : cause (a bird) to fly from cover

²**flush** n **1** : sudden flow (as of water) **2** : surge of emotion **3** : blush ～ vb **1**

: blush **2** : wash out with a rush of liquid ⁓ *adj* **1** : filled to overflowing **2** : of a reddish healthy color **3** : smooth or level **4** : abutting — **flush** *adv*

³**flush** *n* : cards of the same suit

flus·ter \ˈfləstər\ *vb* : upset — **fluster** *n*

flute \ˈflüt\ *n* **1** : pipelike musical instrument **2** : groove — **flut·ed** *adj* — **flut·ing** *n* — **flut·ist** \-ist\ *n*

flut·ter \ˈflətər\ *vb* **1** : flap the wings rapidly **2** : move with quick wavering or flapping motions **3** : behave in an agitated manner ⁓ *n* **1** : a fluttering **2** : state of confusion — **flut·tery** \-ərē\ *adj*

flux \ˈfləks\ *n* : state of continuous change

¹**fly** \ˈflī\ *vb* **flew** \ˈflü\; **flown** \ˈflōn\; **fly·ing 1** : move through the air with wings **2** : float or soar **3** : flee **4** : move or pass swiftly **5** : operate an airplane

²**fly** *n, pl* **flies** : garment closure

³**fly** *n, pl* **flies** : winged insect

fly·er *var of* FLIER

fly·pa·per *n* : sticky paper for catching flies

fly·speck *n* **1** : speck of fly dung **2** : something tiny

fly·wheel *n* : rotating wheel that regulates the speed of machinery

foal \ˈfōl\ *n* : young horse — **foal** *vb*

foam \ˈfōm\ *n* **1** : mass of bubbles on top of a liquid **2** : material of cellular form ⁓ *vb* : form foam — **foamy** *adj*

fob \ˈfäb\ *n* : short chain for a pocket watch

fo'c's'le *var of* FORECASTLE

fo·cus \ˈfōkəs\ *n, pl* **-ci** \-ˌsī\ **1** : point at which reflected or refracted rays meet **2** : adjustment (as of eyeglasses) for clear vision **3** : central point ⁓ *vb* : bring to a focus — **fo·cal** \-kəl\ *adj* — **fo·cal·ly** *adv*

fod·der \ˈfädər\ *n* : food for livestock

foe \ˈfō\ *n* : enemy

fog \ˈfòg, ˈfäg\ *n* **1** : fine particles of water suspended near the ground **2** : mental confusion ⁓ *vb* **-gg-** : obscure or be obscured with fog — **fog·gy** *adj*

fog·horn *n* : warning horn sounded in a fog

fo·gy \ˈfōgē\ *n, pl* **-gies** : person with old-fashioned ideas

foi·ble \ˈfòibəl\ *n* : minor character fault

¹**foil** \ˈfòil\ *vb* : defeat ⁓ *n* : light fencing sword

²**foil** *n* **1** : thin sheet of metal **2** : one that sets off another by contrast

foist \ˈfòist\ *vb* : force another to accept

¹**fold** \ˈfōld\ *n* **1** : enclosure for sheep **2** : group with a common interest

²**fold** *vb* **1** : lay one part over another **2** : embrace ⁓ *n* : part folded

fold·er \ˈfōldər\ *n* **1** : one that folds **2** : circular **3** : folded cover or envelope for papers

fol·de·rol \ˈfäldəˌräl\ *n* : nonsense

fo·liage \ˈfōlēij, -lij\ *n* : plant leaves

fo·lio \ˈfōlēˌō\ *n, pl* **-li·os** : sheet of paper folded once

folk \ˈfōk\ *n, pl* **folk** *or* **folks 1** : people in general **2** *folks pl* : one's family ⁓ *adj* : relating to the common people

folk·lore *n* : customs and traditions of a people — **folk·lor·ist** *n*

folksy \ˈfōksē\ *adj* **folks·i·er; -est** : friendly and informal

fol·li·cle \ˈfälikəl\ *n* : small anatomical cavity or gland

fol·low \ˈfälō\ *vb* **1** : go or come after **2** : pursue **3** : obey **4** : proceed along **5** : keep one's attention fixed on **6** : result from — **fol·low·er** *n*

fol·low·ing \ˈfäləwiŋ\ *adj* : next ⁓ *n* : group of followers ⁓ *prep* : after

fol·ly \ˈfälē\ *n, pl* **-lies** : foolishness

fo·ment \fōˈment\ *vb* : incite

fond \ˈfänd\ *adj* **1** : strongly attracted **2** : affectionate **3** : dear — **fond·ly** *adv* — **fond·ness** *n*

fon·dle \ˈfändᵊl\ *vb* **-dled; -dling** : touch lovingly

fon·due \fänˈdü, -ˈdyü\ *n* : preparation of melted cheese

font \ˈfänt\ *n* **1** : baptismal basin **2** : fountain

food \ˈfüd\ *n* : material eaten to sustain life

fool \ˈfül\ *n* **1** : stupid person **2** : jester ⁓ *vb* **1** : waste time **2** : meddle **3** : deceive — **fool·ery** \ˈfülərē\ *n* — **fool·ish** \ˈfülish\ *adj* — **fool·ish·ly** *adv* — **fool·ish·ness** *n* — **fool·proof** *adj*

fool·har·dy \ˈfülˌhärdē\ *adj* : rash — **fool·har·di·ness** *n*

foot \ˈfut\ *n, pl* **feet** \ˈfēt\ **1** : end part of a leg **2** : unit of length equal to ⅓ yard **3** : unit of verse meter **4** : bottom — **foot·age** \-ij\ *n* — **foot·ed** *adj* — **foot·path** *n* — **foot·print** *n* —

foot•race *n* — **foot•rest** *n* — **foot-wear** *n*

foot•ball *n* : ball game played by 2 teams on a rectangular field

foot•bridge *n* : bridge for pedestrians

foot•hill *n* : hill at the foot of higher hills

foot•hold *n* : support for the feet

foot•ing *n* **1** : foothold **2** : basis

foot•lights *n pl* : stage lights along the floor

foot•lock•er *n* : small trunk

foot•loose *adj* : having no ties

foot•man \'fütmən\ *n* : male servant

foot•note *n* : note at the bottom of a page

foot•step *n* **1** : step **2** : distance covered by a step **3** : footprint

foot•stool *n* : stool to support the feet

foot•work *n* : skillful movement of the feet (as in boxing)

fop \'fäp\ *n* : dandy — **fop•pery** \-ərē\ *n* — **fop•pish** *adj*

for \'for\ *prep* **1** — used to show preparation or purpose **2** : because of **3** — used to show a recipient **4** : in support of **5** : so as to support or help cure **6** : so as to be equal to **7** : concerning **8** : through the period of ~ *conj* : because

for•age \'forij\ *n* : food for animals ~ *vb* **-aged; -ag•ing 1** : hunt food **2** : search for provisions

for•ay \'for,ā\ *n or vb* : raid

¹**for•bear** \for'bar\ *vb* **-bore** \-'bor\; **-borne** \-'born\; **-bear•ing 1** : refrain from **2** : be patient — **for•bear•ance** \-'barəns\ *n*

²**forbear** *var of* FOREBEAR

for•bid \fər'bid\ *vb* **-bade** \-'bad, -'bād\ *or* **-bad** \-'bad\; **-bid•den** \-'bid°n\; **-bid•ding 1** : prohibit **2** : order not to do something

for•bid•ding *adj* : tending to discourage

force \'fors\ *n* **1** : exceptional strength or energy **2** : military strength **3** : body (as of persons) available for a purpose **4** : violence **5** : influence (as a push or pull) that causes motion ~ *vb* **forced; forc•ing 1** : compel **2** : gain against resistance **3** : break open — **force•ful** \-fəl\ *adj* — **force•ful•ly** *adv* — **in force 1** : in great numbers **2** : valid

for•ceps \'forsəps\ *n, pl* **forceps** : surgical instrument for grasping objects

forc•ible \'forsəbəl\ *adj* **1** : done by force **2** : showing force — **forc•i•bly** \-blē\ *adv*

ford \'ford\ *n* : place to wade across a stream ~ *vb* : wade across

fore \'for\ *adv* : in or toward the front ~ *adj* : being or coming before in time, place, or order ~ *n* : front

fore–and–aft *adj* : lengthwise

fore•arm \'for,ärm\ *n* : part of the arm between the elbow and the wrist

fore•bear \'for,bar\ *n* : ancestor

fore•bod•ing \for'bōdiŋ\ *n* : premonition of disaster — **fore•bod•ing** *adj*

fore•cast \'for,kast\ *vb* **-cast; -cast•ing** : predict — **forecast** *n* — **fore•cast•er** *n*

fore•cas•tle \'fōksəl\ *n* : forward part of a ship

fore•close \for'klōz\ *vb* : take legal measures to terminate a mortgage — **fore•clo•sure** \-'klōzhər\ *n*

fore•fa•ther \'for,fäthər\ *n* : ancestor

fore•fin•ger \'for,fiŋgər\ *n* : finger next to the thumb

fore•foot \'for,füt\ *n* : front foot of a quadruped

fore•front \'for,frənt\ *n* : foremost position or place

¹**fore•go** \for'gō\ *vb* **-went; -gone; -go•ing** : precede

²**forego** *var of* FORGO

fore•go•ing *adj* : preceding

fore•gone *adj* : determined in advance

fore•ground \'for,graùnd\ *n* : part of a scene nearest the viewer

fore•hand \'for,hand\ *n* : stroke (as in tennis) made with the palm of the hand turned forward — **forehand** *adj*

fore•head \'forəd, 'for,hed\ *n* : part of the face above the eyes

for•eign \'forən\ *adj* **1** : situated outside a place or country and esp. one's own country **2** : belonging to a different place or country **3** : not pertinent **4** : related to or dealing with other nations — **for•eign•er** \-ər\ *n*

fore•know \for'nō\ *vb* **-knew; -known; -know•ing** : know beforehand — **fore•knowl•edge** *n*

fore•leg \'for,leg\ *n* : front leg

fore•lock \'for,läk\ *n* : front lock of hair

fore•man \'formən\ *n* **1** : spokesman of a jury **2** : workman in charge

fore•most \'for,mōst\ *adj* : first in time, place, or order — **foremost** *adv*

fore•noon \'for,nün\ *n* : morning

fo•ren•sic \fə'rensik\ *adj* : relating to courts or public speaking or debate

fo·ren·sics \-siks\ *n pl* : art or study of speaking or debating

fore·or·dain \ˌfōrȯr'dān\ *vb* : decree beforehand

fore·quar·ter \'fōrˌkwȯrtər\ *n* : front half on one side of the body of a quadruped

fore·run·ner \'fōrˌrənər\ *n* : one that goes before

fore·see \fōr'sē\ *vb* **-saw; -seen; -see·ing** : see or realize beforehand — **fore·see·able** *adj*

fore·shad·ow \fōr'shadō\ *vb* : hint or suggest beforehand

fore·sight \'fōrˌsīt\ *n* : care or provision for the future — **fore·sight·ed** *adj* — **fore·sight·ed·ness** *n*

for·est \'fȯrəst\ *n* : large thick growth of trees and underbrush — **for·est·ed** \'fȯrəstəd\ *adj* — **for·est·er** \-əstər\ *n* — **for·est·land** \-ˌland\ *n* — **for·est·ry** \-əstrē\ *n*

fore·stall \fōr'stȯl, fȯr-\ *vb* : prevent by acting in advance

foreswear *var of* FORSWEAR

fore·taste \'fōrˌtāst\ *n* : advance indication or notion ~ *vb* : anticipate

fore·tell \fōr'tel\ *vb* **-told; -tell·ing** : predict

fore·thought \'fōrˌthȯt\ *n* : foresight

for·ev·er \fȯr'evər\ *adv* **1** : for a limitless time **2** : always

for·ev·er·more \-ˌevər'mōr\ *adv* : forever

fore·warn \fōr'wȯrn\ *vb* : warn beforehand

fore·word \'fōrwərd\ *n* : preface

for·feit \'fȯrfət\ *n* : something forfeited ~ *vb* : lose or lose the right to by an error or crime — **for·fei·ture** \-fəˌchūr\ *n*

¹forge \'fōrj\ *n* : smithy ~ *vb* **forged; forg·ing 1** : form (metal) by heating and hammering **2** : imitate falsely esp. to defraud — **forg·er** *n* — **forg·ery** \-ərē\ *n*

²forge *vb* **forged; forg·ing** : move ahead steadily

for·get \fər'get\ *vb* **-got** \-'gät\; **-got·ten** \-'gät³n\ *or* **-got; -get·ting 1** : be unable to think of or recall **2** : fail to think of at the proper time — **for·get·ta·ble** *adj* — **for·get·ful** \-fəl\ *adj* — **for·get·ful·ly** *adv*

forget–me–not *n* : small herb with blue or white flowers

for·give \fər'giv\ *vb* **-gave** \-'gāv\; **-giv·en** \-'givən\; **-giv·ing** : pardon — **for·giv·able** *adj* — **for·give·ness** *n*

for·giv·ing *adj* **1** : able to forgive **2** : allowing room for error or weakness

for·go, fore·go \fȯr'gō\ *vb* **-went; -gone; -go·ing** : do without

fork \'fȯrk\ *n* **1** : implement with prongs for lifting, holding, or digging **2** : forked part **3** : a dividing into branches or a place where something branches ~ *vb* **1** : divide into branches **2** : move with a fork — **forked** \'fȯrkt, 'fȯrkəd\ *adj*

fork·lift *n* : machine for lifting with steel fingers

for·lorn \fər'lȯrn\ *adj* **1** : deserted **2** : wretched — **for·lorn·ly** *adv*

form \'fȯrm\ *n* **1** : shape **2** : set way of doing or saying something **3** : document with blanks to be filled in **4** : manner of performing with respect to what is expected **5** : mold **6** : kind or variety **7** : one of the ways in which a word is changed to show difference in use ~ *vb* **1** : give form or shape to **2** : train **3** : develop **4** : constitute — **for·ma·tive** \-tiv\ *adj* — **form·less** \-ləs\ *adj*

for·mal \'fȯrməl\ *adj* : following established custom ~ *n* : formal social event — **for·mal·i·ty** \fȯr'malətē\ *n* — **for·mal·ize** \'fȯrməˌlīz\ *vb* — **for·mal·ly** *adv*

form·al·de·hyde \fȯr'maldəˌhīd\ *n* : colorless pungent gas used as a preservative and disinfectant

for·mat \'fȯrˌmat\ *n* : general style or arrangement of something — **format** *vb*

for·ma·tion \fȯr'māshən\ *n* **1** : a giving form to something **2** : something formed **3** : arrangement

for·mer \'fȯrmər\ *adj* : coming before in time — **for·mer·ly** *adv*

for·mi·da·ble \'fȯrmədəbəl, fȯr'mid-\ *adj* **1** : causing fear or dread **2** : very difficult — **for·mi·da·bly** \-blē\ *adv*

for·mu·la \'fȯrmyələ\ *n, pl* **-las** *or* **-lae** \-ˌlē, -ˌlī\ **1** : set form of words for ceremonial use **2** : recipe **3** : milk mixture for a baby **4** : group of symbols or figures briefly expressing information **5** : set form or method

for·mu·late \-ˌlāt\ *vb* **-lat·ed; -lat·ing** : design, devise — **for·mu·la·tion** \ˌfȯrmyə'lāshən\ *n*

for·ni·ca·tion \ˌfȯrnə'kāshən\ *n* : illicit sexual intercourse — **for•ni•cate** \'fòrnə‚kāt\ *vb* — **for•ni•ca•tor** \-‚kātər\ *n*

for•sake \fər'sāk\ *vb* **-sook** \-'sùk\; **-sak•en** \-'sākən\; **-sak•ing** : renounce completely

for•swear \fòr'swar\ *vb* **-swore; -sworn; -swear•ing 1** : renounce under oath **2** : perjure

for•syth•ia \fər'sithēə\ *n* : shrub grown for its yellow flowers

fort \'fòrt\ *n* **1** : fortified place **2** : permanent army post

forte \'fòrt, 'fòr‚tā\ *n* : something at which a person excels

forth \'fòrth\ *adv* : forward

forth•com•ing *adj* **1** : coming or available soon **2** : open and direct

forth•right *adj* : direct — **forth•right•ly** *adv* — **forth•right•ness** *n*

forth•with *adv* : immediately

for•ti•fy \'fòrtə‚fī\ *vb* **-fied; -fy•ing** : make strong — **for•ti•fi•ca•tion** \‚fòrtəfə'kāshən\ *n*

for•ti•tude \'fòrtə‚tüd, -‚tyüd\ *n* : ability to endure

fort•night \'fòrt‚nīt\ *n* : 2 weeks — **fort•night•ly** *adj or adv*

for•tress \'fòrtrəs\ *n* : strong fort

for•tu•itous \fòr'tüətəs, -'tyü-\ *adj* : accidental

for•tu•nate \'fòrchənət\ *adj* **1** : coming by good luck **2** : lucky — **for•tu•nate•ly** *adv*

for•tune \'fòrchən\ *n* **1** : prosperity attained partly through luck **2** : good or bad luck **3** : destiny **4** : wealth

for•tune–tell•er \-‚telər\ *n* : one who foretells a person's future — **for•tune–tell•ing** \-iŋ\ *n or adj*

for•ty \'fòrtē\ *n, pl* **forties** : 4 times 10 — **for•ti•eth** \-ēəth\ *adj or n* — **forty** *adj or pron*

fo•rum \'fōrəm\ *n, pl* **-rums 1** : Roman marketplace **2** : medium for open discussion

for•ward \'fòrwərd\ *adj* **1** : being near or at or belonging to the front **2** : brash ~ *adv* : toward what is in front ~ *n* : player near the front of his team ~ *vb* **1** : help onward **2** : send on — **for•ward•er** \-wərdər\ *n* — **for•ward•ness** *n*

for•wards \'fòrwərdz\ *adv* : forward

fos•sil \'fäsəl\ *n* : preserved trace of an ancient plant or animal ~ *adj* : being or originating from a fossil — **fos•sil•ize** *vb*

fos•ter \'fòstər\ *adj* : being, having, or relating to substitute parents ~ *vb* : help to grow or develop

fought *past of* FIGHT

foul \'faùl\ *adj* **1** : offensive **2** : clogged with dirt **3** : abusive **4** : wet and stormy **5** : unfair ~ *n* : a breaking of the rules in a game ~ *adv* : foully ~ *vb* **1** : make or become foul or filthy **2** : tangle — **foul•ly** *adv* — **foul•mouthed** \-'maùthd, -'maùtht\ *adj* — **foul•ness** *n*

fou•lard \fù'lärd\ *n* : lightweight silk

foul–up *n* : error or state of confusion — **foul up** *vb* : bungle

[1]**found** \'faùnd\ *past of* FIND

[2]**found** *vb* : establish — **found•er** *n*

foun•da•tion \faùn'dāshən\ *n* **1** : act of founding **2** : basis for something **3** : endowed institution **4** : supporting structure — **foun•da•tion•al** \-shənəl\ *adj*

foun•der \'faùndər\ *vb* : sink

found•ling \'faùndliŋ\ *n* : abandoned infant that is found

found•ry \'faùndrē\ *n, pl* **-dries** : place where metal is cast

fount \'faùnt\ *n* : fountain

foun•tain \'faùntⁿn\ *n* **1** : spring of water **2** : source **3** : artificial jet of water

four \'fōr\ *n* **1** : one more than 3 **2** : 4th in a set or series **3** : something having 4 units — **four** *adj or pron*

four•fold *adj* : quadruple — **four•fold** *adv*

four•score *adj* : 80

four•some \'fōrsəm\ *n* : group of 4

four•teen \fōr'tēn\ *n* : one more than 13 — **fourteen** *adj or pron* — **four•teenth** \-'tēnth\ *adj or n*

fourth \'fōrth\ *n* **1** : one that is 4th **2** : one of 4 equal parts of something — **fourth** *adj or adv*

fowl \'faùl\ *n, pl* **fowl** *or* **fowls 1** : bird **2** : chicken

fox \'fäks\ *n, pl* **fox•es 1** : small mammal related to wolves **2** : clever person ~ *vb* : trick — **foxy** \'fäksē\ *adj*

fox•glove *n* : flowering plant that provides digitalis

fox•hole \'fäks‚hōl\ *n* : pit for protection against enemy fire

foy•er \'fòiər, 'fòi‚yä\ *n* : entrance hallway

fra•cas \'frākəs, 'frak-\ *n, pl* **-cas•es** \-əsəz\ : brawl

frac•tion \'frakshən\ *n* **1** : number indicating one or more equal parts of a whole **2** : portion — **frac·tion·al** \-shənəl\ *adj* — **frac·tion·al·ly** *adv*

frac·tious \'frakshəs\ *adj* : hard to control

frac·ture \'frakchər\ *n* : a breaking of something — **fracture** *vb*

frag·ile \'frajəl, -ˌīl\ *adj* : easily broken — **fra·gil·i·ty** \frə'jilətē\ *n*

frag·ment \'fragmənt\ *n* : part broken off ~ \-ˌment\ *vb* : break into parts — **frag·men·tary** \'fragmənˌterē\ *adj* — **frag·men·ta·tion** \ˌfragmən'tāshən, -ˌmen-\ *n*

fra·grant \'frāgrənt\ *adj* : sweet-smelling — **fra·grance** \-grəns\ *n* — **fra·grant·ly** *adv*

frail \'frāl\ *adj* : weak or delicate — **frail·ty** \-tē\ *n*

frame \'frām\ *vb* **framed; fram·ing 1** : plan **2** : formulate **3** : construct or arrange **4** : enclose in a frame **5** : make appear guilty ~ *n* **1** : makeup of the body **2** : supporting or enclosing structure **3** : state or disposition (as of mind) — **frame·work** *n*

franc \'frank\ *n* : monetary unit (as of France)

fran·chise \'franˌchīz\ *n* **1** : special privilege **2** : the right to vote — **fran·chi·see** \ˌfranˌchī'zē, -chə-\ *n*

fran·gi·ble \'franjəbəl\ *adj* : breakable — **fran·gi·bil·i·ty** \ˌfranjə'bilətē\ *n*

¹**frank** \'frank\ *adj* : direct and sincere — **frank·ly** *adv* — **frank·ness** *n*

²**frank** *vb* : mark (mail) with a sign showing it can be mailed free ~ *n* : sign on franked mail

frank·furt·er \'frankfərtər, -ˌfərt-\, **frank·furt** \-fərt\ *n* : cooked sausage

frank·in·cense \'frankənˌsens\ *n* : incense resin

fran·tic \'frantik\ *adj* : wildly excited — **fran·ti·cal·ly** \-iklē\ *adv*

fra·ter·nal \frə'tərn°l\ *adj* **1** : brotherly **2** : of a fraternity — **fra·ter·nal·ly** *adv*

fra·ter·ni·ty \frə'tərnətē\ *n, pl* **-ties** : men's student social group

frat·er·nize \'fratərˌnīz\ *vb* **-nized; -niz·ing 1** : mingle as friends **2** : associate with members of a hostile group — **frat·er·ni·za·tion** \ˌfratərnə'zāshən\ *n*

frat·ri·cide \'fratrəˌsīd\ *n* : killing of a sibling — **frat·ri·cid·al** \ˌfratrə-'sīd°l\ *adj*

fraud \'frȯd\ *n* : trickery — **fraud·u-**

lent \'frȯjələnt\ *adj* — **fraud·u·lent·ly** *adv*

fraught \'frȯt\ *adj* : full of or accompanied by something specified

¹**fray** \'frā\ *n* : fight

²**fray** *vb* **1** : wear by rubbing **2** : separate the threads of **3** : irritate

fraz·zle \'frazəl\ *vb* **-zled; -zling** : wear out ~ *n* : exhaustion

freak \'frēk\ *n* **1** : something abnormal or unusual **2** : enthusiast — **freak·ish** *adj* — **freak out** *vb* **1** : experience nightmarish hallucinations from drugs **2** : distress or become distressed

freck·le \'frekəl\ *n* : brown spot on the skin — **freckle** *vb*

free \'frē\ *adj* **fre·er; fre·est 1** : having liberty or independence **2** : not taxed **3** : given without charge **4** : voluntary **5** : not in use **6** : not fastened ~ *adv* : without charge ~ *vb* **freed; free·ing** : set free — **free** *adv* — **free·born** *adj* — **free·dom** \'frēdəm\ *n* — **free·ly** *adv*

free·boo·ter \-ˌbütər\ *n* : pirate

free–for–all *n* : fight with no rules

free·load *vb* : live off another's generosity — **free·load·er** *n*

free·stand·ing *adj* : standing without support

free·way \'frēˌwā\ *n* : expressway

free will *n* : independent power to choose — **free·will** *adj*

freeze \'frēz\ *vb* **froze** \'frōz\; **fro·zen** \'frōz°n\; **freez·ing 1** : harden into ice **2** : become chilled **3** : damage by frost **4** : stick fast **5** : become motionless **6** : fix at one stage or level ~ *n* **1** : very cold weather **2** : state of being frozen — **freez·er** *n*

freeze–dry *vb* : preserve by freezing then drying — **freeze–dried** *adj*

freight \'frāt\ *n* **1** : carrying of goods or payment for this **2** : shipped goods ~ *vb* : load or ship goods — **freight·er** *n*

french fry *vb* : fry in deep fat — **french fry** *n*

fre·net·ic \fri'netik\ *adj* : frantic — **fre·net·i·cal·ly** \-iklē\ *adv*

fren·zy \'frenzē\ *n, pl* **-zies** : violent agitation — **fren·zied** \-zēd\ *adj*

fre·quen·cy \'frēkwənsē\ *n, pl* **-cies 1** : frequent or regular occurrence **2** : number of cycles or sound waves per second

fre·quent \'frēkwənt\ *adj* : happening

often ~ \frē'kwent, 'frēkwənt\ *vb*
: go to habitually — **fre·quent·er** *n*
— **fre·quent·ly** *adv*
fres·co \'freskō\ *n, pl* **-coes** : painting
on fresh plaster
fresh \'fresh\ *adj* **1** : not salt **2** : pure
3 : not preserved **4** : not stale **5** : like
new **6** : insolent — **fres·hen** \-ən\
vb — **fresh·ly** *adv* — **fresh·ness** *n*
fresh·et \-ət\ *n* : overflowing stream
fresh·man \-mən\ *n* : first-year student
fresh·wa·ter \-'wȯ-\ *n* : water that is not salty
fret \'fret\ *vb* **-tt-** **1** : worry or become
irritated **2** : fray **3** : agitate ~ *n* **1**
: worn spot **2** : irritation — **fret·ful**
\-fəl\ *adj* — **fret·ful·ly** *adv*
fri·a·ble \'frīəbəl\ *adj* : easily pulverized
fri·ar \'frīər\ *n* : member of a religious
order
fri·ary \-ē\ *n, pl* **-ar·ies** : monastery of
friars
fric·as·see \'frikə‚sē, ‚frikə'-\ *n*
: meat stewed in a gravy ~ *vb* **-seed;**
-see·ing : stew in gravy
fric·tion \'frikshən\ *n* **1** : a rubbing
between 2 surfaces **2** : clash of opinions — **fric·tion·al** *adj*
Fri·day \'frīdā\ *n* : 6th day of the week
friend \'frend\ *n* : person one likes —
friend·less \-ləs\ *adj* — **friend·li-**
ness \-lēnəs\ *n* — **friend·ly** *adj* —
friend·ship \-‚ship\ *n*
frieze \'frēz\ *n* : ornamental band
around a room
frig·ate \'frigət\ *n* : warship smaller
than a destroyer
fright \'frīt\ *n* : sudden fear — **frigh·ten**
\-ᵊn\ *vb* — **fright·ful** \-fəl\ *adj* —
fright·ful·ly *adv* — **fright·ful·ness** *n*
frig·id \'frijəd\ *adj* : intensely cold —
fri·gid·i·ty \frij'idətē\ *n*
frill \'fril\ *n* **1** : ruffle **2** : pleasing but
nonessential addition — **frilly** *adj*
fringe \'frinj\ *n* **1** : ornamental border
of short hanging threads or strips **2**
: edge — **fringe** *vb*
frisk \'frisk\ *vb* **1** : leap about **2**
: search (a person) esp. for weapons
frisky \'friskē\ *adj* **frisk·i·er; -est**
: playful — **frisk·i·ly** *adv* — **frisk·i-**
ness *n*
¹**frit·ter** \'fritər\ *n* : fried batter containing fruit or meat
²**fritter** *vb* : waste little by little
friv·o·lous \'frivələs\ *adj* : not important or serious — **fri·vol·i·ty** \friv-
'älətē\ *n* — **friv·o·lous·ly** *adv*

frizz \'friz\ *vb* : curl tightly — **frizz** *n* —
frizzy *adj*
fro \'frō\ *adv* : away
frock \'fräk\ *n* **1** : loose outer garment
2 : dress
frog \'frȯg, 'fräg\ *n* **1** : leaping amphibian **2** : hoarseness **3** : ornamental braid fastener **4** : small holder for
flowers
frog·man \-‚man, -mən\ *n* : underwater swimmer
frol·ic \'frälik\ *vb* **-icked; -ick·ing**
: romp ~ *n* : fun — **frol·ic·some**
\-səm\ *adj*
from \'frəm, 'främ\ *prep* — used to
show a starting point
frond \'fränd\ *n* : fern or palm leaf
front \'frənt\ *n* **1** : face **2** : behavior **3**
: main side of a building **4** : forward
part **5** : boundary between air masses
~ *vb* **1** : have the main side adjacent
to something **2** : serve as a front —
fron·tal \-ᵊl\ *adj*
front·age \'frəntij\ *n* : length of
boundary line on a street
fron·tier \‚frən'tir\ *n* : outer edge of
settled territory — **fron·tiers·man**
\-'tirzmən\ *n*
fron·tis·piece \'frəntə‚spēs\ *n* : illustration facing a title page
frost \'frȯst\ *n* **1** : freezing temperature
2 : ice crystals on a surface ~ *vb* **1**
: cover with frost **2** : put icing on (a
cake) — **frosty** *adj*
frost·bite \-‚bīt\ *n* : partial freezing of
part of the body — **frost·bit·ten**
\-‚bitᵊn\ *adj*
frost·ing *n* : icing
froth \'frȯth\ *n, pl* **froths** \'frȯths,
'frȯthz\ : bubbles on a liquid —
frothy *adj*
fro·ward \'frōwərd\ *adj* : willful
frown \'fraun\ *vb or n* : scowl
frow·sy, frow·zy \'frauzē\ *adj* **-si·er** *or*
-zi·er; -est : untidy
froze *past of* FREEZE
frozen *past part of* FREEZE
fru·gal \'frügəl\ *adj* : thrifty — **fru·gal-**
i·ty \frü'galətē\ *n* — **fru·gal·ly** *adv*
fruit \'früt\ *n* **1** : usu. edible and sweet
part of a seed plant **2** : result ~ *vb*
: bear fruit — **fruit·cake** *n* — **fruit·ed**
\-əd\ *adj* — **fruit·ful** *adj* — **fruit·ful-**
ness *n* — **fruit·less** *adj* — **fruit-**
less·ly *adv* — **fruity** *adj*
fru·ition \frü'ishən\ *n* : completion
frumpy \'frəmpē\ *adj* **frump·i·er; -est**
: dowdy

frus•trate \'frəs,trāt\ *vb* **-trat•ed; -trat-ing 1** : block **2** : cause to fail — **frus•trat•ing•ly** *adv* — **frus•tra•tion** \,frəs'trāshən\ *n*

¹**fry** \'frī\ *vb* **fried; fry•ing 1** : cook esp. with fat or oil **2** : be cooked by frying ~ *n, pl* **fries 1** : something fried **2** : social gathering with fried food

²**fry** *n, pl* **fry** : recently hatched fish

fud•dle \'fəd°l\ *vb* **-dled; -dling** : muddle

fud•dy–dud•dy \'fədē,dədē\ *n, pl* **-dies** : one who is old-fashioned or unimaginative

fudge \'fəj\ *vb* **fudged; fudg•ing** : cheat or exaggerate ~ *n* : creamy candy

fu•el \'fyüəl\ *n* : material burned to produce heat or power ~ *vb* **-eled** *or* **-elled; -el•ing** *or* **-el•ling** : provide with or take in fuel

fu•gi•tive \'fyüjətiv\ *adj* **1** : running away or trying to escape **2** : not lasting — **fugitive** *n*

-ful \'fəl\ *adj suffix* **1** : full of **2** : having the qualities of **3** : -able ~ *n suffix* : quantity that fills

ful•crum \'fulkrəm, 'fəl-\ *n, pl* **-crums** *or* **-cra** \-krə\ : support on which a lever turns

ful•fill, ful•fil \ful'fil\ *vb* **-filled; -fill•ing 1** : perform **2** : satisfy — **ful•fill•ment** *n*

¹**full** \'ful\ *adj* **1** : filled **2** : complete **3** : rounded **4** : having an abundance of something ~ *adv* : entirely ~ *n* : utmost degree — **full•ness** *n* — **ful•ly** *adv*

²**full** *vb* : shrink and thicken woolen cloth — **full•er** *n*

full–fledged \'ful'flejd\ *adj* : fully developed

ful•some \'fulsəm\ *adj* : copious verging on excessive

fum•ble \'fəmbəl\ *vb* **-bled; -bling** : fail to hold something properly — **fumble** *n*

fume \'fyüm\ *n* : irritating gas ~ *vb* **fumed; fum•ing 1** : give off fumes **2** : show annoyance

fu•mi•gate \'fyümə,gāt\ *vb* **-gat•ed; -gat•ing** : treat with pest-killing fumes — **fu•mi•gant** \'fyümigənt\ *n* — **fu•mi•ga•tion** \,fyümə'gāshən\ *n*

fun \'fən\ *n* **1** : something providing amusement or enjoyment **2** : enjoyment ~ *adj* : full of fun

func•tion \'fəŋkshən\ *n* **1** : special

purpose **2** : formal ceremony or social affair ~ *vb* : have or carry on a function — **func•tion•al** \-shənəl\ *adj* — **func•tion•al•ly** *adv*

func•tion•ary \-shə,nerē\ *n, pl* **-ar•ies** : official

fund \'fənd\ *n* **1** : store **2** : sum of money intended for a special purpose **3** *pl* : available money ~ *vb* : provide funds for

fun•da•men•tal \,fəndə'ment°l\ *adj* **1** : basic **2** : of central importance or necessity — **fundamental** *n* — **fun•da•men•tal•ly** *adv*

fu•ner•al \'fyünərəl\ *n* : ceremony for a dead person — **funeral** *adj* — **fu•ne•re•al** \fyü'nirēəl\ *adj*

fun•gi•cide \'fənjə,sīd, 'fəŋgə-\ *n* : agent that kills fungi — **fun•gi•cid•al** \,fənjə'sīd°l, ,fəŋgə-\ *adj*

fun•gus \'fəŋgəs\ *n, pl* **fun•gi** \'fən,jī, 'fəŋ,gī\ : lower plant that lacks chlorophyll — **fun•gal** \'fəŋgəl\ *adj* — **fun•gous** \-gəs\ *adj*

funk \'fəŋk\ *n* : state of depression

funky \'fəŋkē\ *adj* **funk•i•er; -est** : unconventional and unsophisticated

fun•nel \'fən°l\ *n* **1** : cone-shaped utensil with a tube for directing the flow of a liquid **2** : ship's smokestack ~ *vb* **-neled; -nel•ing** : move to a central point or into a central channel

fun•nies \'fənēz\ *n pl* : section of comic strips

fun•ny \'fənē\ *adj* **-ni•er; -est 1** : amusing **2** : strange

fur \'fər\ *n* **1** : hairy coat of a mammal **2** : article of clothing made with fur — **fur** *adj* — **furred** \'fərd\ *adj* — **fur•ry** \-ē\ *adj*

fur•bish \'fərbish\ *vb* : make lustrous or new looking

fu•ri•ous \'fyürēəs\ *adj* : fierce or angry — **fu•ri•ous•ly** *adv*

fur•long \'fər,lόŋ\ *n* : a unit of distance equal to 220 yards

fur•lough \'fərlō\ *n* : authorized absence from duty — **furlough** *vb*

fur•nace \'fərnəs\ *n* : enclosed structure in which heat is produced

fur•nish \'fərnish\ *vb* **1** : provide with what is needed **2** : make available for use

fur•nish•ings \-iŋs\ *n pl* **1** : articles or accessories of dress **2** : furniture

fur•ni•ture \'fərnichər\ *n* : movable articles for a room

fu•ror \'fyur̩ȯr\ *n* **1** : anger **2** : sensational craze

fur•ri•er \'fərēər\ *n* : dealer in furs

fur•row \'fərō\ *n* **1** : trench made by a plow **2** : wrinkle or groove — **furrow** *vb*

fur•ther \'fərthər\ *adv* **1** : at or to a more advanced point **2** : more ~ *adj* : additional ~ *vb* : promote — **further•ance** \-ərəns\ *n*

fur•ther•more \'fərthər̩mȯr\ *adv* : in addition

fur•ther•most \-̩mōst\ *adj* : most distant

fur•thest \'fərthəst\ *adv or adj* : farthest

fur•tive \'fərtiv\ *adj* : slyly or secretly done — **fur•tive•ly** *adv* — **fur•tive•ness** *n*

fu•ry \'fyurē\ *n, pl* **-ries 1** : intense rage **2** : violence

¹**fuse** \'fyüz\ *n* **1** : cord lighted to transmit fire to an explosive **2** *usu* **fuze** : device for exploding a charge ~ *or* **fuze** *vb* **fused** *or* **fuzed; fus•ing** *or* **fuz•ing** : equip with a fuse

²**fuse** *vb* **fused; fus•ing 1** : melt and run together **2** : unite ~ *n* : electrical safety device — **fus•ible** *adj*

fu•se•lage \'fyüsə̩läzh, -zə-\ *n* : main body of an aircraft

fu•sil•lade \'fyüsə̩läd, -̩läd, ̩fyüsə'-, -zə-\ *n* : volley of fire

fu•sion \'fyüzhən\ *n* **1** : process of merging by melting **2** : union of atomic nuclei

fuss \'fəs\ *n* **1** : needless bustle or excitement **2** : show of attention **3** : objection or protest ~ *vb* : make a fuss

fuss•bud•get \-̩bəjət\ *n* : one who fusses or is fussy about trifles

fussy \'fəsē\ *adj* **fuss•i•er; -est 1** : irritable **2** : paying very close attention to details — **fuss•i•ly** *adv* — **fuss•i•ness** *n*

fu•tile \'fyüt³l, 'fyü̩tīl\ *adj* : useless or vain — **fu•til•i•ty** \fyü'tilətē\ *n*

fu•ton \'fü̩tän\ *n* : a cotton-filled mattress

fu•ture \'fyüchər\ *adj* : coming after the present ~ *n* **1** : time yet to come **2** : what will happen — **fu•tur•is•tic** \̩fyüchə'ristik\ *adj*

fuze *var of* FUSE

fuzz \'fəz\ *n* : fine particles or fluff

fuzzy \-ē\ *adj* **fuzz•i•er; -est 1** : covered with or like fuzz **2** : indistinct — **fuzz•i•ness** *n*

-fy \̩fī\ *vb suffix* : make — **-fi•er** \̩fīər\ *n suffix*

G

g \'jē\ *n, pl* **g's** *or* **gs** \'jēz\ **1** : 7th letter of the alphabet **2** : unit of gravitational force

gab \'gab\ *vb* **-bb-** : chatter — **gab** *n* — **gab•by** \'gabē\ *adj*

gab•ar•dine \'gabər̩dēn\ *n* : durable twilled fabric

ga•ble \'gābəl\ *n* : triangular part of the end of a building — **ga•bled** \-bəld\ *adj*

gad \'gad\ *vb* **-dd-** : roam about

gad•fly *n* : persistently critical person

gad•get \'gajət\ *n* : device — **gad•get•ry** \'gajətrē\ *n*

gaff \'gaf\ *n* : metal hook for lifting fish — **gaff** *vb*

gaffe \'gaf\ *n* : social blunder

gag \'gag\ *vb* **-gg- 1** : prevent from speaking or crying out by stopping up the mouth **2** : retch or cause to retch

~ *n* **1** : something that stops up the mouth **2** : laugh-provoking remark or act

gage *var of* GAUGE

gag•gle \'gagəl\ *n* : flock of geese

gai•ety \'gāətē\ *n, pl* **-eties** : high spirits

gai•ly \'gālē\ *adv* : in a gay manner

gain \'gān\ *n* **1** : profit **2** : obtaining of profit or possessions **3** : increase ~ *vb* **1** : get possession of **2** : win **3** : arrive at **4** : increase or increase in **5** : profit — **gain•er** *n* — **gain•ful** *adj* — **gain•ful•ly** *adv*

gain•say \gān'sā\ *vb* **-said** \-'sād, -'sed\; **-say•ing; -says** \-'sāz, -'sez\ : deny or dispute — **gain•say•er** *n*

gait \'gāt\ *n* : manner of walking or running — **gait•ed** *adj*

gal \'gal\ *n* : girl

ga·la \\'gālə, 'galə, 'gälə\\ *n* : festive celebration — **gala** *adj*

gal·axy \\'galəksē\\ *n, pl* **-ax·ies** : very large group of stars — **ga·lac·tic** \gə'laktik\ *adj*

gale \\'gāl\\ *n* **1** : strong wind **2** : outburst

¹**gall** \\'gól\\ *n* **1** : bile **2** : insolence

²**gall** *n* **1** : skin sore caused by chafing **2** : swelling of plant tissue caused by parasites ⁓ *vb* **1** : chafe **2** : irritate or vex

gal·lant \gə'lant, -'länt; 'galənt\ *n* : man very attentive to women ⁓ \\'galənt; gə'lant, -'länt\ *adj* **1** : splendid **2** : brave **3** : polite and attentive to women — **gal·lant·ly** *adv* — **gal·lant·ry** \\'galəntrē\ *n*

gall·blad·der *n* : pouch attached to the liver in which bile is stored

gal·le·on \\'galyən\\ *n* : large sailing ship formerly used esp. by the Spanish

gal·lery \\'galərē\\ *n, pl* **-ler·ies** **1** : outdoor balcony **2** : long narrow passage or hall **3** : room or building for exhibiting art **4** : spectators — **gal·ler·ied** \-rēd\ *adj*

gal·ley \\'galē\\ *n, pl* **-leys** **1** : old ship propelled esp. by oars **2** : kitchen of a ship or airplane

gal·li·um \\'galēəm\\ *n* : bluish white metallic chemical element

gal·li·vant \\'galə,vant\\ *vb* : travel or roam about for pleasure

gal·lon \\'galən\\ *n* : unit of liquid measure equal to 4 quarts

gal·lop \\'galəp\\ *n* : fast 3-beat gait of a horse — **gallop** *vb* — **gal·lop·er** *n*

gal·lows \\'galōz\\ *n, pl* **-lows** *or* **-lows·es** : upright frame for hanging criminals

gall·stone *n* : abnormal concretion in the gallbladder or bile passages

ga·lore \gə'lōr\\ *adj* : in abundance

ga·losh \gə'läsh\\ *n* : overshoe — usu. pl.

gal·va·nize \\'galvə,nīz\\ *vb* **-nized; -niz·ing** **1** : shock into action **2** : coat (iron or steel) with zinc — **gal·va·ni·za·tion** \,galvənə'zāshən\ *n* — **gal·va·niz·er** *n*

gam·bit \\'gambit\\ *n* **1** : opening tactic in chess **2** : stratagem

gam·ble \\'gambəl\\ *vb* **-bled; -bling** **1** : play a game for stakes **2** : bet **3** : take a chance ⁓ *n* : risky undertaking — **gam·bler** \-blər\ *n*

gam·bol \\'gambəl\\ *vb* **-boled** *or* **-bolled; -bol·ing** *or* **-bol·ling** : skip about in play — **gambol** *n*

game \\'gām\\ *n* **1** : playing activity **2** : competition according to rules **3** : animals hunted for sport or food ⁓ *vb* **gamed; gam·ing** : gamble ⁓ *adj* **1** : plucky **2** : lame — **game·ly** *adv* — **game·ness** *n*

game·cock *n* : fighting cock

game·keep·er *n* : person in charge of game animals or birds

gam·ete \gə'mēt, 'gam,ēt\ *n* : mature germ cell — **ga·met·ic** \gə'metik\ *adj*

ga·mine \ga'mēn\\ *n* : charming tomboy

gam·ut \\'gamət\\ *n* : entire range or series

gamy *or* **gam·ey** \\'gāmē\\ *adj* **gam·i·er; -est** : having the flavor of game esp. when slightly tainted — **gam·i·ness** *n*

¹**gan·der** \\'gandər\\ *n* : male goose

²**gander** *n* : glance

gang \\'gaŋ\\ *n* **1** : group of persons working together **2** : group of criminals ⁓ *vb* : attack in a gang — **with up**

gan·gling \\'gaŋgliŋ\\ *adj* : lanky

gan·gli·on \\'gaŋglēən\\ *n, pl* **-glia** \-glēə\ : mass of nerve cells

gang·plank *n* : platform used in boarding or leaving a ship

gan·grene \\'gaŋ,grēn, gaŋ'-, 'gan-, gan-\ *n* : local death of body tissue — **gangrene** *vb* — **gan·gre·nous** \\'gaŋgrənəs\ *adj*

gang·ster \\'gaŋstər\\ *n* : member of criminal gang

gang·way \-,wā\\ *n* : passage in or out

gan·net \\'ganət\\ *n* : large fish-eating marine bird

gan·try \\'gantrē\\ *n, pl* **-tries** : frame structure supported over or around something

gap \\'gap\\ *n* **1** : break in a barrier **2** : mountain pass **3** : empty space

gape \\'gāp\\ *vb* **gaped; gap·ing** **1** : open widely **2** : stare with mouth open — **gape** *n*

ga·rage \gə'räzh, -'räj\\ *n* : shelter or repair shop for automobiles ⁓ *vb* **-raged; -rag·ing** : put or keep in a garage

garb \\'gärb\\ *n* : clothing ⁓ *vb* : dress

gar·bage \\'gärbij\\ *n* **1** : food waste **2** : trash — **gar·bage·man** *n*

gar•ble \'gärbəl\ *vb* **-bled; -bling** : distort the meaning of

gar•den \'gärd⁰n\ *n* **1** : plot for growing fruits, flowers, or vegetables **2** : public recreation area ⁓ *vb* : work in a garden — **gar•den•er** \'gärd⁰nər\ *n*

gar•de•nia \gär'dēnyə\ *n* : tree or shrub with fragrant white or yellow flowers or the flower

gar•gan•tuan \gär'ganchəwən\ *adj* : having tremendous size or volume

gar•gle \'gärgəl\ *vb* **-gled; -gling** : rinse the throat with liquid — **gargle** *n*

gar•goyle \'gär₁gȯil\ *n* : waterspout in the form of a grotesque human or animal

gar•ish \'garish\ *adj* : offensively bright or gaudy

gar•land \'gärlənd\ *n* : wreath ⁓ *vb* : form into or deck with a garland

gar•lic \'gärlik\ *n* : herb with pungent bulbs used in cooking — **gar•licky** \-likē\ *adj*

gar•ment \'gärmənt\ *n* : article of clothing

gar•ner \'gärnər\ *vb* : acquire by effort

gar•net \'gärnət\ *n* : deep red mineral

gar•nish \'gärnish\ *vb* : add decoration to (as food) — **garnish** *n*

gar•nish•ee \₁gärnə'shē\ *vb* **-eed; -ee•ing** : take (as a debtor's wages) by legal authority

gar•nish•ment \'gärnishmənt\ *n* : attachment of property to satisfy a creditor

gar•ret \'garət\ *n* : attic

gar•ri•son \'garəsən\ *n* : military post or the troops stationed there — **garrison** *vb*

gar•ru•lous \'garələs\ *adj* : talkative — **gar•ru•li•ty** \gə'rülətē\ *n* — **gar•ru•lous•ly** *adv* — **gar•ru•lous•ness** *n*

gar•ter \'gärtər\ *n* : band to hold up a stocking or sock

gas \'gas\ *n, pl* **gas•es 1** : fluid (as hydrogen or air) that tends to expand indefinitely **2** : gasoline ⁓ *vb* **gassed; gas•sing** : treat with gas **2** : fill with gasoline — **gas•eous** \'gasēəs, 'gashəs\ *adj*

gash \'gash\ *n* : deep long cut — **gash** *vb*

gas•ket \'gaskət\ *n* : material or a part used to seal a joint

gas•light *n* : light of burning illuminating gas

gas•o•line \'gasə₁lēn, ₁gasə'-\ *n* : flammable liquid from petroleum

gasp \'gasp\ *vb* **1** : catch the breath audibly **2** : breathe laboriously — **gasp** *n*

gas•tric \'gastrik\ *adj* : relating to or located near the stomach

gas•tron•o•my \gas'tränəmē\ *n* : art of good eating — **gas•tro•nom•ic** \₁gastrə'nämik\ *adj*

gate \'gāt\ *n* : an opening for passage in a wall or fence — **gate•keep•er** *n* — **gate•post** *n*

gate•way *n* : way in or out

gath•er \'gathər\ *vb* **1** : bring or come together **2** : harvest **3** : pick up little by little **4** : deduce — **gath•er•er** *n* — **gath•er•ing** *n*

gauche \'gōsh\ *adj* : crude or tactless

gaudy \'gȯdē\ *adj* **gaud•i•er; -est** : tastelessly showy — **gaud•i•ly** \'gȯd⁰lē\ *adv* — **gaud•i•ness** *n*

gauge \'gāj\ *n* : instrument for measuring ⁓ *vb* **gauged; gaug•ing** : measure

gaunt \'gȯnt\ *adj* : thin or emaciated — **gaunt•ness** *n*

¹gaunt•let \-lət\ *n* **1** : protective glove **2** : challenge to combat

²gauntlet *n* : ordeal

gauze \'gȯz\ *n* : thin often transparent fabric — **gauzy** *adj*

gave *past of* GIVE

gav•el \'gavəl\ *n* : mallet of a presiding officer, auctioneer, or judge

gawk \'gȯk\ *vb* : stare stupidly

gawky \-ē\ *adj* **gawk•i•er; -est** : clumsy

gay \'gā\ *adj* **1** : merry **2** : bright and lively **3** : homosexual — **gay** *n*

gaze \'gāz\ *vb* **gazed; gaz•ing** : fix the eyes in a steady intent look — **gaze** *n* — **gaz•er** *n*

ga•zelle \gə'zel\ *n* : small swift antelope

ga•zette \-'zet\ *n* : newspaper

gaz•et•teer \₁gazə'tir\ *n* : geographical dictionary

gear \'gir\ *n* **1** : clothing **2** : equipment **3** : toothed wheel — **gear** *vb*

gear•shift *n* : mechanism by which automobile gears are shifted

geek \'gēk\ *n* : socially inept person

geese *pl of* GOOSE

gei•sha \'gāshə, 'gē-\ *n, pl* **-sha** *or* **-shas** : Japanese girl or woman trained to entertain men

gel•a•tin \'jelət⁰n\ *n* : sticky substance

obtained from animal tissues by boiling — **ge·lat·i·nous** \jə'latᵊnəs\ *adj*

geld \'geld\ *vb* : castrate

geld·ing \-iŋ\ *n* : castrated horse

gem \'jem\ *n* : cut and polished valuable stone — **gem·stone** *n*

gen·der \'jendər\ *n* **1** : sex **2** : division of a class of words (as nouns) that determines agreement of other words

gene \'jēn\ *n* : segment of DNA that controls inheritance of a trait

ge·ne·al·o·gy \,jēnē'äləjē, ,jen-, -'al-\ *n, pl* **-gies** : study of family pedigrees — **ge·ne·a·log·i·cal** \-ēə'läjikəl\ *adj* — **ge·ne·a·log·i·cal·ly** *adv* — **ge·ne·al·o·gist** \-ē'äləjist, -'al-\ *n*

genera *pl of* GENUS

gen·er·al \'jenrəl, 'jenə-\ *adj* **1** : relating to the whole **2** : applicable to all of a group **3** : common or widespread ~ *n* **1** : something that involves or is applicable to the whole **2** : commissioned officer in the army, air force, or marine corps ranking above a lieutenant general — **gen·er·al·ly** *adv* — **in general** : for the most part

gen·er·al·i·ty \,jenə'ralətē\ *n, pl* **-ties** : general statement

gen·er·al·ize \'jenrə,līz, 'jenə-\ *vb* **-ized; -iz·ing** : reach a general conclusion esp. on the basis of particular instances — **gen·er·al·iza·tion** \,jenrələ'zāshən, ,jenə-\ *n*

general of the air force : commissioned officer of the highest rank in the air force

general of the army : commissioned officer of the highest rank in the army

gen·er·ate \'jenə,rāt\ *vb* **-at·ed; -at·ing** : create or produce

gen·er·a·tion \,jenə'rāshən\ *n* **1** : living beings constituting a single step in a line of descent **2** : production — **gen·er·a·tive** \'jenə,rātiv, -rət-\ *adj*

gen·er·a·tor \'jenə,rātər\ *n* **1** : one that generates **2** : machine that turns mechanical into electrical energy

ge·ner·ic \jə'nerik\ *adj* **1** : general **2** : not protected by a trademark **3** : relating to a genus — **generic** *n*

gen·er·ous \'jenərəs\ *adj* : freely giving or sharing — **gen·er·os·i·ty** \,jenə'räsətē\ *n* — **gen·er·ous·ly** *adv* — **gen·er·ous·ness** *n*

ge·net·ics \jə'netiks\ *n* : biology dealing with heredity and variation — **ge-**

net·ic \-ik\ *adj* — **ge·net·i·cal·ly** *adv* — **ge·net·i·cist** \-'netəsist\ *n*

ge·nial \'jēnēəl\ *adj* : cheerful — **ge·nial·i·ty** \,jēnē'alətē\ *n* — **ge·nial·ly** *adv*

ge·nie \'jēnē\ *n* : supernatural spirit that often takes human form

gen·i·tal \'jenətᵊl\ *adj* : concerned with reproduction — **gen·i·tal·ly** \-təlē\ *adv*

gen·i·ta·lia \,jenə'tālyə\ *n pl* : external genital organs

gen·i·tals \'jenətᵊlz\ *n pl* : genitalia

ge·nius \'jēnyəs\ *n* **1** : single strongly marked capacity **2** : extraordinary intellectual power or a person having such power

geno·cide \'jenə,sīd\ *n* : systematic destruction of a racial or cultural group

genre \'zhänrə, 'zhäⁿrə\ *n* : category esp. of literary composition

gen·teel \jen'tēl\ *adj* : polite or refined

gen·tile \'jen,tīl\ *n* : person who is not Jewish — **gentile** *adj*

gen·til·i·ty \jen'tilətē\ *n, pl* **-ties 1** : good birth and family **2** : good manners

gen·tle \'jentᵊl\ *adj* **-tler; -tlest 1** : of a family of high social station **2** : not harsh, stern, or violent **3** : soft or delicate ~ *vb* **-tled; -tling** : make gentle — **gen·tle·ness** *n* — **gen·tly** *adv*

gen·tle·man \-mən\ *n* : man of good family or manners — **gen·tle·man·ly** *adv*

gen·tle·wom·an \-,wùmən\ *n* : woman of good family or breeding

gen·try \'jentrē\ *n, pl* **-tries** : people of good birth or breeding

gen·u·flect \'jenyə,flekt\ *vb* : bend the knee in worship — **gen·u·flec·tion** \,jenyə'flekshən\ *n*

gen·u·ine \'jenyəwən\ *adj* : being the same in fact as in appearance — **gen·u·ine·ly** *adv* — **gen·u·ine·ness** *n*

ge·nus \'jēnəs\ *n, pl* **gen·era** \'jenərə\ : category of biological classification

ge·ode \'jē,ōd\ *n* : stone having a mineral-lined cavity

geo·de·sic \,jēə'desik, -'dēs-\ *adj* : made of a framework of linked polygons

ge·og·ra·phy \jē'ägrəfē\ *n* **1** : study of the earth and its climate, products, and inhabitants **2** : natural features of a region — **ge·og·ra·pher** \-fər\ *n* — **geo·graph·ic** \,jēə-**

'grafik\, **geo•graph•i•cal** \-ikəl\ *adj*
— **geo•graph•i•cal•ly** *adv*
ge•ol•o•gy \jē'äləjē\ *n* : study of the
history of the earth and its life esp. as
recorded in rocks — **geo•log•ic**
\ˌjēə'läjik\, **geo•log•i•cal** \-ikəl\ *adj*
— **geo•log•i•cal•ly** *adv* — **ge•ol•o•
gist** \jē'äləjist\ *n*
ge•om•e•try \jē'ämətrē\ *n, pl* **-tries**
: mathematics of the relations, prop-
erties, and measurements of solids,
surfaces, lines, and angles — **geo•
met•ric** \ˌjēə'metrik\, **geo•met•ri•
cal** \-rikəl\ *adj*
geo•ther•mal \ˌjēo'thərməl\ *adj* : relating to or derived from the heat of
the earth's interior
ge•ra•ni•um \jə'rānēəm\ *n* : garden
plant with clusters of white, pink, or
scarlet flowers
ger•bil \'jərbəl\ *n* : burrowing desert
rodent
ge•ri•at•ric \ˌjerē'atrik\ *adj* **1** : relating to aging or the aged **2** : old
ge•ri•at•rics \-triks\ *n* : medicine dealing with the aged and aging
germ \'jərm\ *n* **1** : microorganism **2**
: source or rudiment
ger•mane \jər'mān\ *adj* : relevant
ger•ma•ni•um \-'mānēəm\ *n* : grayish
white hard chemical element
ger•mi•cide \'jərmə,sīd\ *n* : agent that
destroys germs — **ger•mi•cid•al**
\ˌjərmə'sīdᵊl\ *adj*
ger•mi•nate \'jərmə,nāt\ *vb* **-nat•ed;
-nat•ing** : begin to develop — **ger•mi•
na•tion** \ˌjərmə'nāshən\ *n*
ger•ry•man•der \'ˌjerē'mandər, 'je-
rēˌ-, ˌgerē'-, 'gerēˌ-\ *vb* : divide into
election districts so as to give one political party an advantage — **gerry•
mander** *n*
ger•und \'jerənd\ *n* : word having the
characteristics of both verb and noun
ge•sta•po \gə'stäpō\ *n, pl* **-pos** : secret
police
ges•ta•tion \je'stāshən\ *n* : pregnancy
or incubation — **ges•tate** \'jes,tāt\ *vb*
ges•ture \'jeschər\ *n* **1** : movement of
the body or limbs that expresses
something **2** : something said or
done for its effect on the attitudes of
others — **ges•tur•al** \-chərəl\ *adj* —
gesture *vb*
ge•sund•heit \gə'zunt,hīt\ *interj* —
used to wish good health to one who
has just sneezed
get \'get\ *vb* **got** \'gät\; **got** *or* **got•ten**

\'gätᵊn\; **get•ting 1** : gain or be in
possession of **2** : succeed in coming
or going **3** : cause to come or go or to
be in a certain condition or position **4**
: become **5** : be subjected to **6** : understand **7** : be obliged — **get along**
vb **1** : get by **2** : be on friendly terms
— **get by** *vb* : meet one's needs
get•away \'getəˌwā\ *n* **1** : escape **2** : a
starting or getting under way
gey•ser \'gīzər\ *n* : spring that intermittently shoots up hot water and
steam
ghast•ly \'gastlē\ *adj* **-li•er; -est** : horrible or shocking
gher•kin \'gərkən\ *n* : small pickle
ghet•to \'getō\ *n, pl* **-tos** *or* **-toes** : part
of a city in which members of a mi-
nority group live
ghost \'gōst\ *n* : disembodied soul —
ghost•ly *adv*
ghost•write *vb* **-wrote; -writ•ten** : write
for and in the name of another —
ghost•writ•er *n*
ghoul \'gül\ *n* : legendary evil being
that feeds on corpses — **ghoul•ish**
adj
GI \ˌjē'ī\ *n, pl* **GI's** *or* **GIs** : member of
the U.S. armed forces
gi•ant \'jīənt\ *n* **1** : huge legendary being **2** : something very large or very
powerful — **giant** *adj*
gib•ber \'jibər\ *vb* **-bered; -ber•ing**
: speak rapidly and foolishly
gib•ber•ish \'jibərish\ *n* : unintelligi-
ble speech or language
gib•bon \'gibən\ *n* : manlike ape
gibe \'jīb\ *vb* **gibed; gib•ing** : jeer at —
gibe *n*
gib•lets \'jibləts\ *n pl* : edible fowl viscera
gid•dy \'gidē\ *adj* **-di•er; -est 1** : silly
2 : dizzy — **gid•di•ness** *n*
gift \'gift\ *n* **1** : something given **2**
: talent — **gift•ed** *adj*
gi•gan•tic \jī'gantik\ *adj* : very big
gig•gle \'gigəl\ *vb* **-gled; -gling** : laugh
in a silly manner — **giggle** *n* — **gig•
gly** \-əlē\ *adj*
gig•o•lo \'jigəˌlō\ *n, pl* **-los** : man living
on the earnings of a woman
Gi•la monster \'hēlə-\ *n* : large venomous lizard
gild \'gild\ *vb* **gild•ed** \'gildəd\ *or* **gilt**
\'gilt\; **gild•ing** : cover with or as if
with gold
gill \'gil\ *n* : organ of a fish for obtaining oxygen from water

gilt \'gilt\ *adj* : gold-colored ~ *n* : gold or goldlike substance on the surface of an object

gim·bal \'gimbəl, 'jim-\ *n* : device that allows something to incline freely

gim·let \'gimlət\ *n* : small tool for boring holes

gim·mick \'gimik\ *n* : new and ingenious scheme, feature, or device — **gim·mick·ry** *n* — **gim·micky** \-ikē\ *adj*

gimpy \'gimpē\ *adj* : lame

¹gin \'jin\ *n* : machine to separate seeds from cotton — **gin** *vb*

²gin *n* : clear liquor flavored with juniper berries

gin·ger \'jinjər\ *n* : pungent aromatic spice from a tropical plant — **gin·ger·bread** *n*

gin·ger·ly *adv* : very cautiously

ging·ham \'giŋəm\ *n* : cotton clothing fabric

gin·gi·vi·tis \,jinjə'vītəs\ *n* : inflammation of the gums

gink·go \'giŋkō\ *n, pl* **-goes** *or* **-gos** : tree of eastern China

gin·seng \'jin,siŋ, -,seŋ, -saŋ\ *n* : aromatic root of a Chinese herb

gi·raffe \jə'raf\ *n* : African mammal with a very long neck

gird \'gərd\ *vb* **gird·ed** \'gərdəd\ *or* **girt** \'gərt\; **gird·ing** **1** : encircle or fasten with or as if with a belt **2** : prepare

gird·er \'gərdər\ *n* : horizontal supporting beam

gir·dle \'gərd³l\ *n* : woman's supporting undergarment ~ *vb* : surround

girl \'gərl\ *n* **1** : female child **2** : young woman **3** : sweetheart — **girl·hood** \-,hud\ *n* — **girl·ish** *adj*

girl·friend *n* : frequent or regular female companion of a boy or man

girth \'gərth\ *n* : measure around something

gist \'jist\ *n* : main point or part

give \'giv\ *vb* **gave** \'gāv\; **giv·en** \'givən\; **giv·ing** **1** : put into the possession or keeping of another **2** : pay **3** : perform **4** : contribute or donate **5** : produce **6** : utter **7** : yield to force, strain, or pressure ~ *n* : capacity or tendency to yield to force or strain — **give in** *vb* : surrender — **give out** *vb* : become used up or exhausted — **give up** *vb* **1** : let out of one's control **2** : cease from trying, doing, or hoping

give·away *n* **1** : unintentional betrayal **2** : something given free

giv·en \'givən\ *adj* **1** : prone or disposed **2** : having been specified

giz·zard \'gizərd\ *n* : muscular usu. horny-lined enlargement following the crop of a bird

gla·cial \'glāshəl\ *adj* **1** : relating to glaciers **2** : very slow — **gla·cial·ly** *adv*

gla·cier \'glāshər\ *n* : large body of ice moving slowly

glad \'glad\ *adj* **-dd-** **1** : experiencing or causing pleasure, joy, or delight **2** : very willing — **glad·den** \-³n\ *vb* — **glad·ly** *adv* — **glad·ness** *n*

glade \'glād\ *n* : grassy open space in a forest

glad·i·a·tor \'glādē,ātər\ *n* : one who fought to the death for the entertainment of ancient Romans — **glad·i·a·to·ri·al** \,gladēə'tōrēəl\ *adj*

glad·i·o·lus \,gladē'ōləs\ *n, pl* **-li** \-lē, -,lī\ : plant related to the irises

glam·our, glam·or \'glamər\ *n* : romantic or exciting attractiveness — **glam·or·ize** \-ə,rīz\ *vb* — **glam·or·ous** \-ərəs\ *adj*

glance \'glans\ *vb* **glanced; glanc·ing** **1** : strike and fly off to one side **2** : give a quick look ~ *n* : quick look

gland \'gland\ *n* : group of cells that secretes a substance — **glan·du·lar** \'glanjələr\ *adj*

glans \'glanz\ *n, pl* **glan·des** \'glan-,dēz\ : conical vascular body forming the end of the penis or clitoris

glare \'glar\ *vb* **glared; glar·ing** **1** : shine with a harsh dazzling light **2** : stare angrily ~ *n* **1** : harsh dazzling light **2** : angry stare

glar·ing \'glariŋ\ *adj* : painfully obvious — **glar·ing·ly** *adv*

glass \'glas\ *n* **1** : hard usu. transparent material made by melting sand and other materials **2** : something made of glass **3** *pl* : lenses used to correct defects of vision — **glass** *adj* — **glass·ful** \-,fül\ *n* — **glass·ware** \-,war\ *n* — **glassy** *adj*

glass·blow·ing *n* : art of shaping a mass of molten glass by blowing air into it — **glass·blow·er** *n*

glau·co·ma \glau'kōmə, glò-\ *n* : state of increased pressure within the eyeball

glaze \'glāz\ *vb* **glazed; glaz·ing** **1**

: furnish with glass **2** : apply glaze to ~ *n* : glassy surface or coating

gla·zier \'glāzhər\ *n* : one who sets glass in window frames

gleam \'glēm\ *n* **1** : transient or partly obscured light **2** : faint trace ~ *vb* : send out gleams

glean \'glēn\ *vb* : collect little by little — **glean·able** *adj* — **glean·er** *n*

glee \'glē\ *n* : joy — **glee·ful** *adj*

glen \'glen\ *n* : narrow hidden valley

glib \'glib\ *adj* **-bb-** : speaking or spoken with ease — **glib·ly** *adv*

glide \'glīd\ *vb* **glid·ed; glid·ing** : move or descend smoothly and effortlessly — **glide** *n*

glid·er \'glīdər\ *n* **1** : winged aircraft having no engine **2** : swinging porch seat

glim·mer \'glimər\ *vb* : shine faintly or unsteadily ~ *n* **1** : faint light **2** : small amount

glimpse \'glimps\ *vb* **glimpsed; glimps·ing** : take a brief look at — **glimpse** *n*

glint \'glint\ *vb* : gleam or sparkle — **glint** *n*

glis·ten \'glis°n\ *vb* : shine or sparkle by reflection — **glisten** *n*

glit·ter \'glitər\ *vb* : shine with brilliant or metallic luster ~ *n* : small glittering ornaments — **glit·tery** *adj*

glitz \'glits\ *n* : extravagant showiness — **glitzy** \'glitsē\ *adj*

gloat \'glōt\ *vb* : think of something with triumphant delight

glob \'gläb\ *n* : large rounded lump

glob·al \'glōbəl\ *adj* : worldwide — **glob·al·ly** *adv*

globe \'glōb\ *n* **1** : sphere **2** : the earth or a model of it

glob·u·lar \'gläbyələr\ *adj* **1** : round **2** : made up of globules

glob·ule \'gläbyül\ *n* : tiny ball

glock·en·spiel \'gläkən‚shpēl\ *n* : portable musical instrument consisting of tuned metal bars

gloom \'glüm\ *n* **1** : darkness **2** : sadness — **gloom·i·ly** *adv* — **gloom·i·ness** *n* — **gloomy** *adj*

glop \'gläp\ *n* : messy mass or mixture

glo·ri·fy \'glōrə‚fī\ *vb* **-fied; -fy·ing 1** : make to seem glorious **2** : worship — **glo·ri·fi·ca·tion** \‚glōrəfə-'kāshən\ *n*

glo·ry \'glōrē\ *n, pl* **-ries 1** : praise or honor offered in worship **2** : cause for praise or renown **3** : magnificence

4 : heavenly bliss ~ *vb* **-ried; -ry·ing** : rejoice proudly — **glo·ri·ous** \'glōrēəs\ *adj* — **glo·ri·ous·ly** *adv*

¹**gloss** \'gläs, 'glòs\ *n* : luster — **gloss·i·ly** \-əlē\ *adv* — **gloss·i·ness** \-ēnəs\ *n* — **glossy** \-ē\ *adj* — **gloss over** *vb* **1** : mask the true nature of **2** : deal with only superficially

²**gloss** *n* : brief explanation or translation ~ *vb* : translate or explain

glos·sa·ry \'gläsərē, 'glòs-\ *n, pl* **-ries** : dictionary — **glos·sar·i·al** \glä-'sarēəl, glò-\ *adj*

glove \'gləv\ *n* : hand covering with sections for each finger

glow \'glō\ *vb* **1** : shine with or as if with intense heat **2** : show exuberance ~ *n* : brightness or warmth of color or feeling

glow·er \'glaùər\ *vb* : stare angrily — **glower** *n*

glow·worm *n* : insect or insect larva that emits light

glu·cose \'glü‚kōs\ *n* : sugar found esp. in blood, plant sap, and fruits

glue \'glü\ *n* : substance used for sticking things together — **glue** *vb* — **glu·ey** \'glüē\ *adj*

glum \'gləm\ *adj* **-mm- 1** : sullen **2** : dismal

glut \'glət\ *vb* **-tt-** : fill to excess — **glut** *n*

glu·ten \'glüt°n\ *n* : gluey protein substance in flour

glu·ti·nous \'glüt°nəs\ *adj* : sticky

glut·ton \'glət°n\ *n* : one who eats to excess — **glut·ton·ous** \'glət°nəs\ *adj* — **glut·tony** \'glət°nē\ *n*

gnarled \'närld\ *adj* **1** : knotty **2** : gloomy or sullen

gnash \'nash\ *vb* : grind (as teeth) together

gnat \'nat\ *n* : small biting fly

gnaw \'nò\ *vb* : bite or chew on

gnome \'nōm\ *n* : dwarf of folklore — **gnom·ish** *adj*

gnu \'nü, 'nyü\ *n, pl* **gnu** *or* **gnus** : large African antelope

go \'gō\ *vb* **went** \'went\; **gone** \'gòn, 'gän\; **go·ing** \'goiŋ\; **goes** \'gōz\ **1** : move, proceed, run, or pass **2** : leave **3** : extend or lead **4** : sell or amount — **with** *for* **5** : happen **6** — used in present participle to show intent or imminent action **7** : become **8** : fit or harmonize **9** : belong ~ *n, pl* **goes 1** : act or manner of going **2** : vigor **3** : attempt — **go back on** : betray — **go by the board** : be discarded — **go for** : favor — **go off** : explode — **go one better** : outdo — **go over 1** : examine **2** : study — **go to town** : be very successful — **on the go** : constantly active

goad \'gōd\ *n* : something that urges — **goad** *vb*

goal \'gōl\ *n* **1** : mark to reach in a race **2** : purpose **3** : object in a game through which a ball is propelled

goal•ie \'gōlē\ *n* : player who defends the goal

goal•keep•er *n* : goalie

goat \'gōt\ *n* : horned ruminant mammal related to the sheep — **goat•skin** *n*

goa•tee \gō'tē\ *n* : small pointed beard

gob \'gäb\ *n* : lump

¹**gob•ble** \'gäbəl\ *vb* **-bled; -bling** : eat greedily

²**gobble** *vb* **-bled; -bling** : make the noise of a turkey (**gobbler**)

gob•ble•dy•gook \'gäbəldē,gúk, -'gük\ *n* : nonsense

gob•let \'gäblət\ *n* : large stemmed drinking glass

gob•lin \'gäblən\ *n* : ugly mischievous sprite

god \'gäd, 'gòd\ *n* **1** *cap* : supreme being **2** : being with supernatural powers — **god•like** *adj* — **god•ly** *adj*

god•child *n* : person one sponsors at baptism — **god•daugh•ter** *n* — **god•son** *n*

god•dess \'gädəs, 'gòd-\ *n* : female god

god•less \-ləs\ *adj* : not believing in God — **god•less•ness** *n*

god•par•ent *n* : sponsor at baptism — **god•fa•ther** *n* — **god•moth•er** *n*

god•send \-,send\ *n* : something needed that comes unexpectedly

goes *pres 3d sing of* GO

go•get•ter \'gō,getər\ *n* : enterprising person — **go•get•ting** \-iŋ\ *adj or n*

gog•gle \'gägəl\ *vb* **-gled; -gling** : stare wide-eyed

gog•gles \-əlz\ *n pl* : protective glasses

go•ings–on \,gōiŋz'òn, -'än\ *n pl* : events

goi•ter \'gòitər\ *n* : abnormally enlarged thyroid gland

gold \'gōld\ *n* : malleable yellow metallic chemical element — **gold•smith** \-,smith\ *n*

gold•brick \-,brik\ *n* : person who shirks duty — **goldbrick** *vb*

gold•en \'gōldən\ *adj* **1** : made of, containing, or relating to gold **2** : having the color of gold **3** : precious or favorable

gold•en•rod \'gōldən,räd\ *n* : herb having tall stalks with tiny yellow flowers

gold•finch \'gōld,finch\ *n* : yellow American finch

gold•fish \-,fish\ *n* : small usu. orange or golden carp

golf \'gälf, 'gòlf\ *n* : game played by hitting a small ball (**golf ball**) with clubs (**golf clubs**) into holes placed in a field (**golf course**) — **golf** *vb* — **golf•er** *n*

go•nad \'gō,nad\ *n* : sex gland

gon•do•la \'gändələ (*usual for 1*), gän'dō-\ *n* **1** : long narrow boat used on the canals of Venice **2** : car suspended from a cable

gon•do•lier \,gändə'lir\ *n* : person who propels a gondola

gone \'gòn\ *adj* **1** : past **2** : involved

gon•er \'gònər\ *n* : hopeless case

gong \'gäŋ, 'gòŋ\ *n* : metallic disk that makes a deep sound when struck

gon•or•rhea \,gänə'rēə\ *n* : bacterial inflammatory venereal disease of the genital tract

goo \'gü\ *n* : thick or sticky substance — **goo•ey** \-ē\ *adj*

good \'gúd\ *adj* bet•ter \'betər\; best \'best\ **1** : satisfactory **2** : salutary **3** : considerable **4** : desirable **5** : well-behaved, kind, or virtuous ∼ *n* **1** : something good **2** : benefit **3** *pl* : personal property **4** *pl* : wares ∼ *adv* : well — **good–heart•ed** \-'härtəd\ *adj* — **good–look•ing** *adj* — **good-na•tured** *adj* — **good•ness** *n* — **for good** : forever

good–bye, good–by \gúd'bī\ *n* : parting remark

good–for–noth•ing *n* : idle worthless person

Good Friday *n* : Friday before Easter observed as the anniversary of the crucifixion of Christ

good•ly *adj* **-li•er; -est** : considerable

good•will *n* **1** : good intention **2** : kindly feeling

goody \'gúdē\ *n, pl* **good•ies** : something that is good esp. to eat

goody–goody *adj* : affectedly or annoyingly sweet or self-righteous — **goody–goody** *n*

goof \'güf\ *vb* **1** : blunder **2** : waste time — usu. with *off* or *around* — **goof** *n* — **goof–off** *n*

goofy \'güfē\ adj **goof•i•er; -est** : crazy — **goof•i•ness** n

goose \'güs\ n, pl **geese** \'gēs\ : large bird with webbed feet

goose•ber•ry \'güs,berē, 'güz-\ n : berry of a shrub related to the currant

goose bumps n pl : roughening of the skin caused by fear, excitement, or cold

goose•flesh n : goose bumps

goose pimples n pl : goose bumps

go•pher \'gōfər\ n : burrowing rodent

¹**gore** \'gōr\ n : blood

²**gore** vb **gored; gor•ing** : pierce or wound with a horn or tusk

¹**gorge** \'gȯrj\ n : narrow ravine

²**gorge** vb **gorged; gorg•ing** : eat greedily

gor•geous \'gȯrjəs\ adj : supremely beautiful

go•ril•la \gə'rilə\ n : African manlike ape

gory \'gōrē\ adj **gor•i•er; -est** : bloody

gos•hawk \'gäs,hȯk\ n : long-tailed hawk with short rounded wings

gos•ling \'gäzliŋ, 'gȯz-\ n : young goose

gos•pel \'gäspəl\ n 1 : teachings of Christ and the apostles 2 : something accepted as infallible truth — **gospel** adj

gos•sa•mer \'gäsəmər, gäz-\ n 1 : film of cobweb 2 : light filmy substance

gos•sip \'gäsəp\ n 1 : person who reveals personal information 2 : rumor or report of an intimate nature ∼ vb : spread gossip — **gos•sipy** \-ē\ adj

got past of GET

Goth•ic \'gäthik\ adj : relating to a medieval style of architecture

gotten past part of GET

gouge \'gaúj\ n 1 : rounded chisel 2 : cavity or groove scooped out ∼ vb **gouged; goug•ing** 1 : cut or scratch a groove in 2 : overcharge

gou•lash \'gü,läsh, -,lash\ n : beef stew with vegetables and paprika

gourd \'gōrd, 'gúrd\ n 1 : any of a group of vines including the cucumber, squash, and melon 2 : inedible hard-shelled fruit of a gourd

gour•mand \'gúr,mänd\ n : person who loves good food and drink

gour•met \'gúr,mā, gúr'mā\ n : connoisseur of food and drink

gout \'gaút\ n : disease marked by painful inflammation and swelling of the joints — **gouty** adj

gov•ern \'gəvərn\ vb 1 : control and direct policy in 2 : guide or influence strongly 3 : restrain — **gov•ern•ment** \-ərmənt\ n — **gov•ern•men•tal** \,gəvər'ment³l\ adj

gov•ern•ess \'gəvərnəs\ n : female teacher in a private home

gov•er•nor \'gəvənər, 'gəvər-\ n 1 : head of a political unit 2 : automatic speed-control device — **gov•er•nor•ship** n

gown \'gaún\ n 1 : loose flowing outer garment 2 : woman's formal evening dress — **gown** vb

grab \'grab\ vb **-bb-** : take by sudden grasp — **grab** n

grace \'grās\ n 1 : unmerited divine assistance 2 : short prayer before or after a meal 3 : respite 4 : ease of movement or bearing ∼ vb **graced; grac•ing** 1 : honor 2 : adorn — **graceful** \-fəl\ adj — **grace•ful•ly** adv — **grace•ful•ness** n — **grace•less** adj

gra•cious \'grāshəs\ adj : marked by kindness and courtesy or charm and taste — **gra•cious•ly** adv — **gra•cious•ness** n

grack•le \'grakəl\ n : American blackbird

gra•da•tion \grā'dāshən, grə-\ n : step, degree, or stage in a series

grade \'grād\ n 1 : stage in a series, order, or ranking 2 : division of school representing one year's work 3 : mark of accomplishment in school 4 : degree of slope ∼ vb **grad•ed; grad•ing** 1 : arrange in grades 2 : make level or evenly sloping 3 : give a grade to — **grad•er** n

grade school n : school including the first 4 or 8 grades

gra•di•ent \'grādēənt\ n : slope

grad•u•al \'grajəwəl\ adj : going by steps or degrees — **grad•u•al•ly** adv

grad•u•ate \'grajəwət\ n : holder of a diploma ∼ adj : of or relating to studies beyond the bachelor's degree ∼ \-ə,wāt\ vb **-at•ed; -at•ing** 1 : grant or receive a diploma 2 : mark with degrees of measurement — **grad•u•a•tion** \,grajə'wāshən\ n

graf•fi•to \grə'fētō, grə-\ n, pl **-ti** \-ē\ : inscription on a wall

graft \'graft\ vb : join one thing to another so that they grow together ∼ n

1 : grafted plant **2** : the getting of money dishonestly or the money so gained — **graft•er** n

grain \'grān\ n **1** : seeds or fruits of cereal grasses **2** : small hard particle **3** : arrangement of fibers in wood — **grained** \'grānd\ adj — **grainy** adj

gram \'gram\ n : metric unit of weight equal to 1/1000 kilogram

gram•mar \'gramər\ n : study of words and their functions and relations in the sentence — **gram•mar•i•an** \grə-'mareēən\ n — **gram•mat•i•cal** \-'matikəl\ adj — **gram•mat•i•cal•ly** adv

grammar school n : grade school

gra•na•ry \'grānərē, 'gran-\ n, pl -ries : storehouse for grain

grand \'grand\ adj **1** : large or striking in size or scope **2** : fine and imposing **3** : very good — **grand•ly** adv — **grand•ness** n

grand•child \-,chīld\ n : child of one's son or daughter — **grand•daugh•ter** n — **grand•son** n

gran•deur \'granjər\ n : quality or state of being grand

gran•dil•o•quence \gran'diləkwəns\ n : pompous speaking — **gran•dil•o•quent** \-kwənt\ adj

gran•di•ose \'grandē,ōs, ,grandē-\ adj **1** : impressive **2** : affectedly splendid — **gran•di•ose•ly** adv

grand•par•ent \'grand,parənt\ n : parent of one's father or mother — **grand•fa•ther** \-,fäthər, -,fäth-\ n — **grand•moth•er** \-,məthər\ n

grand•stand \-,stand\ n : usu. roofed stand for spectators

grange \'grānj\ n : farmers association

gran•ite \'granət\ n : hard igneous rock

grant \'grant\ vb **1** : consent to **2** : give **3** : admit as true ~ n **1** : act of granting **2** : something granted — **grant•ee** \grant'ē\ n — **grant•er** \'grantər\ n — **grant•or** \-ər, -,ȯr\ n

gran•u•late \'granyə,lāt\ vb -lat•ed; -lat•ing : form into grains or crystals — **gran•u•la•tion** \,granyə'lāshən\ n

gran•ule \'granyül\ n : small particle — **gran•u•lar** \-yələr\ adj — **gran•u•lar•i•ty** \,granyə'larətē\ n

grape \'grāp\ n : smooth juicy edible berry of a woody vine (**grape•vine**)

grape•fruit n : large edible yellow-skinned citrus fruit

graph \'graf\ n : diagram that shows relationships between things — **graph** vb

graph•ic \'grafik\ adj **1** : vividly described **2** : relating to the arts (**graphic arts**) of representation and printing on flat surfaces ~ n **1** : picture used for illustration **2** pl : computer screen display — **graph•i•cal•ly** \-iklē\ adv

graph•ite \'graf,īt\ n : soft carbon used for lead pencils and lubricants

grap•nel \'grapnəl\ n : small anchor with several claws

grap•ple \'grapəl\ vb -pled; -pling **1** : seize or hold with or as if with a hooked implement **2** : wrestle

grasp \'grasp\ vb **1** : take or seize firmly **2** : understand ~ n **1** : one's hold or control **2** : one's reach **3** : comprehension

grass \'gras\ n : plant with jointed stem and narrow leaves — **grassy** adj

grass•hop•per \-,häpər\ n : leaping plant-eating insect

grass•land n : land covered with grasses

¹grate \'grāt\ n **1** : grating **2** : frame of iron bars to hold burning fuel

²grate vb grat•ed; -ing **1** : pulverize by rubbing against something rough **2** : irritate — **grat•er** n — **grat•ing•ly** adv

grate•ful \'grātfəl\ adj : thankful or appreciative — **grate•ful•ly** adv — **grate•ful•ness** n

grat•i•fy \'gratə,fī\ vb -fied; -fy•ing : give pleasure to — **grat•i•fi•ca•tion** \,gratəfə'kāshən\ n

grat•ing \'grātiŋ\ n : framework with bars across it

gra•tis \'gratəs, 'grāt-\ adv or adj : free

grat•i•tude \'gratə,tüd, -,tyüd\ n : state of being grateful

gra•tu•itous \grə'tüətəs, -'tyü-\ adj **1** : free **2** : uncalled-for

gra•tu•ity \-ətē\ n, pl -ities : tip

¹grave \'grāv\ n : place of burial — **grave•stone** n — **grave•yard** n

²grave adj grav•er; grav•est **1** : threatening great harm or danger **2** : solemn — **grave•ly** adv — **grave•ness** n

grav•el \'gravəl\ n : loose rounded fragments of rock — **grav•el•ly** adj

grav•i•tate \'gravə,tāt\ vb -tat•ed; -tat•ing : move toward something

grav•i•ta•tion \,gravə'tāshən\ n : natural force of attraction that tends to draw bodies together — **grav•i•ta•tion•al** \-shənəl\ adj

grav•i•ty \'gravətē\ *n, pl* **-ties** **1** : serious importance **2** : gravitation

gra•vy \'grāvē\ *n, pl* **-vies** : sauce made from thickened juices of cooked meat

gray \'grā\ *adj* **1** : of the color gray **2** : having gray hair ∼ *n* : neutral color between black and white ∼ *vb* : make or become gray — **gray•ish** \-ish\ *adj* — **gray•ness** *n*

¹**graze** \'grāz\ *vb* **grazed; graz•ing** : feed on herbage or pasture — **graz•er** *n*

²**graze** *vb* **grazed; graz•ing** : touch lightly in passing

grease \'grēs\ *n* : thick oily material or fat ∼ \'grēs, 'grēz\ *vb* **greased; greas•ing** : smear or lubricate with grease — **greasy** \'grēsē, -zē\ *adj*

great \'grāt\ *adj* **1** : large in size or number **2** : larger than usual — **great•ly** *adv* — **great•ness** *n*

grebe \'grēb\ *n* : diving bird related to the loon

greed \'grēd\ *n* : selfish desire beyond reason — **greed•i•ly** \-ᵊlē\ *adv* — **greed•i•ness** \-ēnəs\ *n* — **greedy** \'grēdē\ *adj*

green \'grēn\ *adj* **1** : of the color green **2** : unripe **3** : inexperienced ∼ *vb* : become green ∼ *n* **1** : color between blue and yellow **2** *pl* : leafy parts of plants — **green•ish** *adj* — **green•ness** *n*

green•ery \'grēnərē\ *n, pl* **-er•ies** : green foliage or plants

green•horn *n* : inexperienced person

green•house *n* : glass structure for the growing of plants

greet \'grēt\ *vb* **1** : address with expressions of kind wishes **2** : react to — **greet•er** *n*

greet•ing *n* **1** : friendly address on meeting **2** *pl* : best wishes

gre•gar•i•ous \gri'garēəs\ *adj* : social or companionable — **gre•gar•i•ous•ly** *adv* — **gre•gar•i•ous•ness** *n*

grem•lin \'gremlən\ *n* : small mischievous gnome

gre•nade \grə'nād\ *n* : small missile filled with explosive or chemicals

grew *past of* GROW

grey *var of* GRAY

grey•hound \'grā,haund\ *n* : tall slender dog noted for speed

grid \'grid\ *n* **1** : grating **2** : evenly spaced horizontal and vertical lines (as on a map)

grid•dle \'gridᵊl\ *n* : flat metal surface for cooking

grid•iron \'grid,īərn\ *n* **1** : grate for broiling **2** : football field

grief \'grēf\ *n* **1** : emotional suffering caused by or as if by bereavement **2** : disaster

griev•ance \'grēvəns\ *n* : complaint

grieve \'grēv\ *vb* **grieved; griev•ing** : feel or cause to feel grief or sorrow

griev•ous \'grēvəs\ *adj* **1** : oppressive **2** : causing grief or sorrow — **griev•ous•ly** *adv*

grill \'gril\ *vb* **1** : cook on a grill **2** : question intensely ∼ *n* **1** : griddle **2** : informal restaurant

grille, grill \'gril\ *n* : grating forming a barrier or screen — **grill•work** *n*

grim \'grim\ *adj* **-mm-** **1** : harsh and forbidding in appearance **2** : relentless — **grim•ly** *adv* — **grim•ness** *n*

gri•mace \'grimas, grim'ās\ *n* : facial expression of disgust — **grimace** *vb*

grime \'grīm\ *n* : embedded or accumulated dirt — **grimy** *adj*

grin \'grin\ *vb* **-nn-** : smile so as to show the teeth — **grin** *n*

grind \'grīnd\ *vb* **ground** \'graund\; **grind•ing** **1** : reduce to powder **2** : wear down or sharpen by friction **3** : operate or produce by turning a crank ∼ *n* : monotonous labor or routine — **grind•er** *n* — **grind•stone** \'grīn,stōn\ *n*

grip \'grip\ *vb* **-pp-** : seize or hold firmly ∼ *n* **1** : grasp **2** : control **3** : device for holding

gripe \'grīp\ *vb* **griped; grip•ing** **1** : cause pains in the bowels **2** : complain — **gripe** *n*

grippe \'grip\ *n* : influenza

gris•ly \'grizlē\ *adj* **-li•er; -est** : horrible or gruesome

grist \'grist\ *n* : grain to be ground or already ground — **grist•mill** *n*

gris•tle \'grisəl\ *n* : cartilage — **gris•tly** \-lē\ *adj*

grit \'grit\ *n* **1** : hard sharp granule **2** : material composed of granules **3** : unyielding courage ∼ *vb* **-tt-** : press with a grating noise — **grit•ty** *adj*

grits \'grits\ *n pl* : coarsely ground hulled grain

griz•zled \'grizəld\ *adj* : streaked with gray

groan \'grōn\ *vb* **1** : moan **2** : creak under a strain — **groan** *n*

gro•cer \'grōsər\ *n* : food dealer — **gro•cery** \'grōsrē, 'grōsh-, -ərē\ *n*

grog \'gräg\ *n* : rum diluted with water

grog•gy \-ē\ *adj* **-gi•er; -est** : dazed and unsteady on the feet — **grog•gi•ly** *adv* — **grog•gi•ness** *n*

groin \'groin\ *n* : juncture of the lower abdomen and inner thigh

grom•met \'grämət, 'gröm-\ *n* : eyelet

groom \'grüm, 'grům\ *n* **1** : one who cares for horses **2** : bridegroom ~ *vb* **1** : clean and care for (as a horse) **2** : make neat or attractive **3** : prepare

groove \'grüv\ *n* **1** : long narrow channel **2** : fixed routine — **groove** *vb*

grope \'grōp\ *vb* **groped; grop•ing** : search for by feeling

gros•beak \'grōs₁bēk\ *n* : finch with large conical bill

¹**gross** \'grōs\ *adj* **1** : glaringly noticeable **2** : bulky **3** : consisting of an overall total exclusive of deductions **4** : vulgar ~ *n* : the whole before any deductions ~ *vb* : earn as a total — **gross•ly** *adv* — **gross•ness** *n*

²**gross** *n, pl* **gross** : 12 dozen

gro•tesque \grō'tesk\ *adj* **1** : absurdly distorted or repulsive **2** : ridiculous — **gro•tesque•ly** *adv*

grot•to \'grätō\ *n, pl* **-toes** : cave

grouch \'graůch\ *n* : complaining person — **grouch** *vb* — **grouchy** *adj*

¹**ground** \'graůnd\ *n* **1** : bottom of a body of water **2** *pl* : sediment **3** : basis for something **4** : surface of the earth **5** : conductor that makes electrical connection with the earth or a framework ~ *vb* **1** : force or bring down to the ground **2** : give basic knowledge to **3** : connect with an electrical ground — **ground•less** *adj*

²**ground** *past of* GRIND

ground•hog *n* : woodchuck

ground•wa•ter *n* : underground water

ground•work *n* : foundation

group \'grüp\ *n* : number of associated individuals ~ *vb* : gather or collect into groups

grou•per \'grüpər\ *n* : large fish of warm seas

grouse \'graůs\ *n, pl* **grouse** *or* **grouses** : ground-dwelling game bird

grout \'graůt\ *n* : mortar for filling cracks — **grout** *vb*

grove \'grōv\ *n* : small group of trees

grov•el \'grävəl, 'grəv-\ *vb* **-eled** *or* **-elled; -el•ing** *or* **-el•ling** : abase oneself

grow \'grō\ *vb* **grew** \'grü\; **grown** \'grōn\; **grow•ing** **1** : come into existence and develop to maturity **2** : be able to grow **3** : advance or increase **4** : become **5** : cultivate — **grow•er** *n*

growl \'graůl\ *vb* : utter a deep threatening sound — **growl** *n*

grown–up \'grōn₁əp\ *n* : adult — **grown–up** *adj*

growth \'grōth\ *n* **1** : stage in growing **2** : process of growing **3** : result of something growing

grub \'grəb\ *vb* **-bb-** **1** : root out by digging **2** : search about ~ *n* **1** : thick wormlike larva **2** : food

grub•by \'grəbē\ *adj* **-bi•er; -est** : dirty — **grub•bi•ness** *n*

grub•stake *n* : supplies for a prospector

grudge \'grəj\ *vb* **grudged; grudg•ing** : be reluctant to give ~ *n* : feeling of ill will

gru•el \'grüəl\ *n* : thin porridge

gru•el•ing, gru•el•ling \-əliŋ\ *adj* : requiring extreme effort

grue•some \'grüsəm\ *adj* : horribly repulsive

gruff \'grəf\ *adj* : rough in speech or manner — **gruff•ly** *adv*

grum•ble \'grəmbəl\ *vb* **-bled; -bling** : mutter in discontent — **grum•bler** \-blər\ *n*

grumpy \-pē\ *adj* **grump•i•er; -est** : cross — **grump•i•ly** *adv* — **grump•i•ness** *n*

grunge \'grənj\ *n* **1** : something shabby, tattered, or dirty **2** : rock music expressing alienation and discontent — **grun•gy** \'grənjē\ *adj*

grun•ion \'grənyən\ *n* : fish of the California coast

grunt \'grənt\ *n* : deep guttural sound — **grunt** *vb*

gua•no \'gwänō\ *n* : excrement of seabirds used as fertilizer

guar•an•tee \₁garən'tē\ *n* **1** : assurance of the fulfillment of a condition **2** : something given or held as a security ~ *vb* **-teed; -tee•ing** **1** : promise to be responsible for **2** : state with certainty — **guar•an•tor** \₁garən'tór\ *n*

guar•an•ty \'garəntē\ *n, pl* **-ties** **1** : promise to answer for another's failure to pay a debt **2** : guarantee **3** : pledge ~ *vb* **-tied; -ty•ing** : guarantee

guard \'gärd\ *n* **1** : defensive position **2** : act of protecting **3** : an individual or group that guards against danger **4** : protective or safety device ~ *vb* **1** : protect or watch over **2** : take precautions — **guard·house** *n* — **guard-room** *n*

guard·ian \\'gärdēən\ *n* : one who has responsibility for the care of the person or property of another — **guardian·ship** *n*

gua·va \\'gwävə\ *n* : shrubby tropical tree or its mildly acid fruit

gu·ber·na·to·ri·al \ˌgübənə'tōrēəl, ˌgyü-\ *adj* : relating to a governor

guer·ril·la, gue·ril·la \gə'rilə\ *n* : soldier engaged in small-scale harassing tactics

guess \\'ges\ *vb* **1** : form an opinion from little evidence **2** : state correctly solely by chance **3** : think or believe — **guess** *n*

guest \\'gest\ *n* **1** : person to whom hospitality (as of a house) is extended **2** : patron of a commercial establishment (as a hotel) **3** : person not a regular cast member who appears on a program

guf·faw \gə'fȯ, 'gəfˌȯ\ *n* : loud burst of laughter — **guf·faw** \gə'fȯ\ *vb*

guide \\'gīd\ *n* **1** : one that leads or gives direction to another **2** : device on a machine to direct motion ~ *vb* **guid·ed; guid·ing 1** : show the way to **2** : direct — **guid·able** *adj* — **guid·ance** \\'gīdᵊns\ *n* — **guide·book** *n*

guide·line \-ˌlīn\ *n* : summary of procedures regarding policy or conduct

guild \\'gild\ *n* : association

guile \\'gīl\ *n* : craftiness — **guile·ful** *adj* — **guile·less** *adj* — **guile·less·ness** *n*

guil·lo·tine \\'gilə,tēn, ˌgēyə'tēn, 'gēyəˌ-\ *n* : machine for beheading persons — **guillotine** *vb*

guilt \\'gilt\ *n* **1** : fact of having committed an offense **2** : feeling of responsibility for offenses — **guilt·i·ly** *adv* — **guilt·i·ness** *n* — **guilty** \\'giltē\ *adj*

guin·ea \\'ginē\ *n* **1** : old gold coin of United Kingdom **2** : 21 shillings

guinea pig *n* : small So. American rodent

guise \\'gīz\ *n* : external appearance

gui·tar \gə'tär, gi-\ *n* : 6-stringed musical instrument played by plucking

gulch \\'gəlch\ *n* : ravine

gulf \\'gəlf\ *n* **1** : extension of an ocean or a sea into the land **2** : wide gap

¹gull \\'gəl\ *n* : seabird with webbed feet

²gull *vb* : make a dupe of ~ *n* : dupe — **gull·ible** *adj*

gul·let \\'gələt\ *n* : throat

gul·ly \\'gəlē\ *n, pl* **-lies** : trench worn by running water

gulp \\'gəlp\ *vb* : swallow hurriedly or greedily — **gulp** *n*

¹gum \\'gəm\ *n* : tissue along the jaw at the base of the teeth

²gum *n* **1** : sticky plant substance **2** : gum usu. of sweetened chicle prepared for chewing — **gum·my** *adj*

gum·bo \\'gəmbō\ *n* : thick soup

gum·drop *n* : gumlike candy

gump·tion \\'gəmpshən\ *n* : initiative

gun \\'gən\ *n* **1** : cannon **2** : portable firearm **3** : discharge of a gun **4** : something like a gun ~ *vb* **-nn-** : hunt with a gun — **gun·fight** *n* — **gun·fight·er** *n* — **gun·fire** *n* — **gun·man** \-mən\ *n* — **gun·pow·der** *n* — **gun·shot** *n* — **gun·smith** *n*

gun·boat *n* : small armed ship

gun·ner \\'gənər\ *n* : person who uses a gun

gun·nery sergeant \\'gənərē-\ *n* : noncommissioned officer in the marine corps ranking next below a master sergeant

gun·ny·sack \\'gənēˌsak\ *n* : burlap sack

gun·sling·er \\'gənˌsliŋər\ *n* : skilled gunman in the old West

gun·wale \\'gən²l\ *n* : upper edge of a boat's side

gup·py \\'gəpē\ *n, pl* **-pies** : tiny tropical fish

gur·gle \\'gərgəl\ *vb* **-gled; -gling** : make a sound like that of a flowing and gently splashing liquid — **gurgle** *n*

gu·ru \\'gü,rü\ *n, pl* **-rus 1** : personal religious teacher in Hinduism **2** : expert

gush \\'gəsh\ *vb* : pour forth violently or enthusiastically — **gush·er** \\'gəshər\ *n*

gushy \-ē\ *adj* **gush·i·er; -est** : effusively sentimental

gust \\'gəst\ *n* **1** : sudden brief rush of wind **2** : sudden outburst — **gust** *vb* — **gusty** *adj*

gus·ta·to·ry \\'gəstəˌtōrē\ *adj* : relating to the sense of taste

gus·to \\'gəstō\ *n* : zest

gut \\'gət\ *n* **1** *pl* : intestines **2** : digestive canal **3** *pl* : courage ~ *vb* **-tt-** : eviscerate

gut·ter \\'gətər\ *n* : channel for carrying off rainwater

gut·tur·al \\'gətərəl\ *adj* : sounded in the throat — **guttural** *n*

¹guy \'gī\ *n* : rope, chain, or rod attached to something to steady it — **guy** *vb*

²guy *n* : person

guz•zle \'gəzəl\ *vb* **-zled; -zling** : drink greedily

gym \'jim\ *n* : gymnasium

gym•na•si•um \jim'nāzēəm, -zhəm\ *n, pl* **-si•ums** *or* **-sia** \-zēə, -zhə\ : place for indoor sports

gym•nas•tics \jim'nastiks\ *n* : physical exercises performed in a gymnasium — **gym•nast** \'jim₁nast\ *n* — **gym•nas•tic** *adj*

gy•ne•col•o•gy \₁gīnə'käləjē, ₁jin-\ *n* : branch of medicine dealing with the diseases of women — **gy•ne•co•log•ic** \-ikə'läjik\, **gy•ne•co•log•i•cal** \-ikəl\ *adj* — **gy•ne•col•o•gist** \-ə'käləjist\ *n*

gyp \'jip\ *n* **1** : cheat **2** : trickery — **gyp** *vb*

gyp•sum \'jipsəm\ *n* : calcium-containing mineral

gy•rate \'jī₁rāt\ *vb* **-rat•ed; -rat•ing** : revolve around a center — **gy•ra•tion** \jī'rāshən\ *n*

gy•ro•scope \'jīrō₁skōp\ *n* : wheel mounted to spin rapidly about an axis that is free to turn in various directions

H

h \'āch\ *n, pl* **h's** *or* **hs** \'āchəz\ : 8th letter of the alphabet

hab•er•dash•er \'habər₁dashər\ *n* : men's clothier — **hab•er•dash•ery** \-ərē\ *n*

hab•it \'habət\ *n* **1** : monk's or nun's clothing **2** : usual behavior **3** : addiction — **hab•it–form•ing** *adj*

hab•it•able \-əbəl\ *adj* : capable of being lived in

hab•i•tat \'habə₁tat\ *n* : place where a plant or animal naturally occurs

hab•i•ta•tion \₁habə'tāshən\ *n* **1** : occupancy **2** : dwelling place

ha•bit•u•al \hə'bichəwəl\ *adj* **1** : commonly practiced or observed **2** : doing, practicing, or acting by habit — **ha•bit•u•al•ly** *adv*

ha•bit•u•ate \hə'bichə₁wāt\ *vb* **-at•ed; -at•ing** : accustom

ha•ci•en•da \₁häsē'endə\ *n* : ranch house

¹hack \'hak\ *vb* **1** : cut with repeated irregular blows **2** : cough in a short dry manner **3** : manage successfully — **hack** *n* — **hack•er** *n*

²hack *n* **1** : horse or vehicle for hire **2** : saddle horse **3** : writer for hire — **hack** *adj* — **hack•man** \-mən\ *n*

hack•le \'hakəl\ *n* **1** : long feather on the neck or back of a bird **2** *pl* : hairs that can be erected **3** *pl* : temper

hack•ney \-nē\ *n, pl* **-neys 1** : horse for riding or driving **2** : carriage for hire

hack•neyed \-nēd\ *adj* : trite

hack•saw *n* : saw for metal

had *past of* **HAVE**

had•dock \'hadək\ *n, pl* **haddock** : Atlantic food fish

Ha•des \'hādēz\ *n* **1** : mythological abode of the dead **2** *often not cap* : hell

haft \'haft\ *n* : handle of a weapon or tool

hag \'hag\ *n* **1** : witch **2** : ugly old woman

hag•gard \'hagərd\ *adj* : worn or emaciated — **hag•gard•ly** *adv*

hag•gle \'hagəl\ *vb* **-gled; -gling** : argue in bargaining — **hag•gler** *n*

¹hail \'hāl\ *n* **1** : precipitation in small lumps of ice **2** : something like a rain of hail ∼ *vb* : rain hail — **hail•stone** *n* — **hail•storm** *n*

²hail *vb* **1** : greet or salute **2** : summon ∼ *n* : expression of greeting or praise — often used as an interjection

hair \'har\ *n* : threadlike growth from the skin — **hair•brush** *n* — **hair•cut** *n* — **hair•dress•er** *n* — **haired** *adj* — **hair•i•ness** *n* — **hair•less** *adj* — **hair•pin** *n* — **hair•style** *n* — **hair•styl•ing** *n* — **hair•styl•ist** *n* — **hairy** *adj*

hair•breadth \-₁bredth\, **hairs•breadth** \'harz-\ *n* : tiny distance or margin

hair•do \-₁dü\ *n, pl* **-dos** : style of wearing hair

hair•line *n* **1** : thin line **2** : outline of the hair on the head

hair•piece *n* : toupee

hair–rais•ing *adj* : causing terror or astonishment

hake \'hāk\ *n* : marine food fish

hal•cy•on \'halsēən\ *adj* : prosperous or most pleasant

¹**hale** \'hāl\ *adj* : healthy or robust

²**hale** *vb* **haled; hal•ing** 1 : haul 2 : compel to go

half \'haf, 'håf\ *n, pl* **halves** \'havz, 'håvz\ : either of 2 equal parts ～ *adj* 1 : being a half or nearly a half 2 : partial — **half** *adv*

half brother *n* : brother related through one parent only

half•heart•ed \-'härtəd\ *adj* : without enthusiasm — **half•heart•ed•ly** *adv*

half–life *n* : time for half of something to undergo a process

half sister *n* : sister related through one parent only

half•way *adj* : midway between 2 points — **half•way** *adv*

half–wit \-ˌwit\ *n* : foolish person — **half–wit•ted** \-ˌwitəd\ *adj*

hal•i•but \'haləbət\ *n, pl* **halibut** : large edible marine flatfish

hal•i•to•sis \ˌhalə'tōsəs\ *n* : bad breath

hall \'hòl\ *n* 1 : large public or college or university building 2 : lobby 3 : auditorium

hal•le•lu•jah \ˌhalə'lüyə\ *interj* — used to express praise, joy, or thanks

hall•mark \'hòlˌmärk\ *n* : distinguishing characteristic

hal•low \'halō\ *vb* : consecrate — **hallowed** \-ōd, -əwəd\ *adj*

Hal•low•een \ˌhalə'wēn, ˌhäl-\ *n* : evening of October 31 observed esp. by children in merrymaking and masquerading

hal•lu•ci•na•tion \həˌlüs°n'āshən\ *n* : perception of objects that are not real — **hal•lu•ci•nate** \ha'lus°nˌāt\ *vb* — **hal•lu•ci•na•to•ry** \-'lüs°nəˌtōrē\ *adj*

hal•lu•ci•no•gen \hə'lüs°nəjən\ *n* : substance that induces hallucinations — **hal•lu•ci•no•gen•ic** \-ˌlüs°nə'jenik\ *adj*

hall•way *n* : entrance hall

ha•lo \'hālō\ *n, pl* **-los** or **-loes** : circle of light appearing to surround a shining body

¹**halt** \'hòlt\ *adj* : lame

²**halt** *vb* : stop or cause to stop — **halt** *n*

hal•ter \'hòltər\ *n* 1 : rope or strap for leading or tying an animal 2 : brief

blouse held up by straps ～ *vb* : catch (an animal) with a halter

halt•ing \'hòltiŋ\ *adj* : uncertain — **halt•ing•ly** *adv*

halve \'hav, 'håv\ *vb* **halved; halv•ing** 1 : divide into halves 2 : reduce to half

halves *pl of* HALF

ham \'ham\ *n* 1 : thigh — usu. pl. 2 : cut esp. of pork from the thigh 3 : showy actor 4 : amateur radio operator ～ *vb* **-mm-** : overplay a part — **ham** *adj*

ham•burg•er \'hamˌbərgər\, **ham•burg** \-ˌbərg\ *n* : ground beef or a sandwich made with this

ham•let \'hamlət\ *n* : small village

ham•mer \'hamər\ *n* 1 : hand tool for pounding 2 : gun part whose striking explodes the charge ～ *vb* : beat, drive, or shape with a hammer — **hammer out** *vb* : produce with effort

ham•mer•head *n* 1 : striking part of a hammer 2 : shark with a hammerlike head

ham•mock \'hamək\ *n* : swinging bed hung by cords at each end

¹**ham•per** \'hampər\ *vb* : impede

²**hamper** *n* : large covered basket

ham•ster \'hamstər\ *n* : stocky short-tailed rodent

ham•string \'hamˌstriŋ\ *vb* **-strung** \-ˌstrəŋ\: **-string•ing** \-ˌstriŋiŋ\ 1 : cripple by cutting the leg tendons 2 : make ineffective or powerless

hand \'hand\ *n* 1 : end of a front limb adapted for grasping 2 : side 3 : promise of marriage 4 : handwriting 5 : assistance or participation 6 : applause 7 : cards held by a player 8 : worker ～ *vb* : lead, assist, give, or pass with the hand — **hand•clasp** *n* — **hand•craft** *vb* — **hand•ful** *n* — **hand•gun** *n* — **hand•less** *adj* — **hand•made** *adj* — **hand•rail** *n* — **hand•saw** *n* — **hand•wo•ven** *adj* — **hand•writ•ing** *n* — **hand•writ•ten** *adj*

hand•bag *n* : woman's purse

hand•ball *n* : game played by striking a ball with the hand

hand•bill *n* : printed advertisement or notice distributed by hand

hand•book *n* : concise reference book

hand•cuffs *n pl* : locking bracelets that bind the wrists together — **handcuff** *vb*

hand•i•cap \'handēˌkap\ *n* 1 : advantage given or disadvantage imposed to equalize a competition **2** : disadvantage — **handicap** *vb* — **hand·i·capped** *adj* — **hand·i·cap·per** *n*

hand·i·craft \'handē‚kraft\ *n* **1** : manual skill **2** : article made by hand — **hand·i·craft·er** *n*

hand·i·work \-‚wərk\ *n* : work done personally or by the hands

hand·ker·chief \'haŋkərchəf, -‚chēf\ *n, pl* **-chiefs** \-chəfs, -‚chēfs\ : small piece of cloth carried for personal use

han·dle \'hand°l\ *n* : part to be grasped ∼ *vb* **-dled; -dling 1** : touch, hold, or manage with the hands **2** : deal with **3** : deal or trade in — **han·dle·bar** *n* — **han·dled** \-d°ld\ *adj* — **han·dler** \'handlər\ *n*

hand·maid·en *n* : female attendant

hand·out *n* : something given out

hand·pick *vb* : select personally

hand·shake *n* : clasping of hands (as in greeting)

hand·some \'hansəm\ *adj* **-som·er; -est 1** : sizable **2** : generous **3** : nice-looking — **hand·some·ly** *adv* — **hand·some·ness** *n*

hand·spring *n* : somersault on the hands

hand·stand *n* : a balancing upside down on the hands

handy \'handē\ *adj* **hand·i·er; -est 1** : conveniently near **2** : easily used **3** : dexterous — **hand·i·ly** *adv* — **handi·ness** *n*

handy·man \-‚man\ *n* : one who does odd jobs

hang \'haŋ\ *vb* **hung** \'həŋ\; **hang·ing 1** : fasten or remain fastened to an elevated point without support from below **2** : suspend by the neck until dead — past tense often *hanged* **3** : droop ∼ *n* **1** : way a thing hangs **2** : an understanding of something — **hang·er** *n* — **hang·ing** *n*

han·gar \'haŋər\ *n* : airplane shelter

hang·dog \'haŋ‚dȯg\ *adj* : ashamed or guilty

hang·man \-mən\ *n* : public executioner

hang·nail *n* : loose skin near a fingernail

hang·out *n* : place where one likes to spend time

hang·over *n* : sick feeling following heavy drinking

hank \'haŋk\ *n* : coil or loop

han·ker \'haŋkər\ *vb* : desire strongly — **han·ker·ing** *n*

han·ky–pan·ky \‚haŋkē'paŋkē\ *n* : questionable or underhanded activity

han·som \'hansəm\ *n* : 2-wheeled covered carriage

Ha·nuk·kah \'k̲änəkə, 'hän-\ *n* : 8-day Jewish holiday commemorating the rededication of the Temple of Jerusalem after its defilement by Antiochus of Syria

hap·haz·ard \hap'hazərd\ *adj* : having no plan or order — **hap·haz·ard·ly** *adv*

hap·less \'hapləs\ *adj* : unfortunate — **hap·less·ly** *adv* — **hap·less·ness** *n*

hap·pen \'hapən\ *vb* **1** : take place **2** : be fortunate to encounter something unexpectedly — often used with infinitive

hap·pen·ing \-əniŋ\ *n* : occurrence

hap·py \'hapē\ *adj* **-pi·er; -est 1** : fortunate **2** : content, pleased, or joyous — **hap·pi·ly** \'hapəlē\ *adv* — **hap·pi·ness** *n*

ha·rangue \hə'raŋ\ *n* : ranting or scolding speech — **harangue** *vb* — **ha·rangu·er** \-'raŋər\ *n*

ha·rass \hə'ras, 'harəs\ *vb* **1** : disturb and impede by repeated raids **2** : annoy continually — **ha·rass·ment** *n*

har·bin·ger \'härbənjər\ *n* : one that announces or foreshadows what is coming

har·bor \-bər\ *n* : protected body of water suitable for anchorage ∼ *vb* **1** : give refuge to **2** : hold as a thought or feeling

hard \'härd\ *adj* **1** : not easily penetrated **2** : firm or definite **3** : close or searching **4** : severe or unfeeling **5** : strenuous or difficult **6** : physically strong or intense — **hard** *adv* — **hard·ness** *n*

hard·en \'härd°n\ *vb* : make or become hard or harder — **hard·en·er** *n*

hard·head·ed \‚härd'hedəd\ *adj* **1** : stubborn **2** : realistic — **hard·head·ed·ly** *adv* — **hard·head·ed·ness** *n*

hard–heart·ed \-'härtəd\ *adj* : lacking sympathy — **hard–heart·ed·ly** *adv* — **hard–heart·ed·ness** *n*

hard·ly \'härdlē\ *adv* **1** : only just **2** : certainly not

hard–nosed \-‚nōzd\ *adj* : tough or uncompromising

hard·ship \-‚ship\ *n* : suffering or privation

hard·tack \-‚tak\ *n* : hard biscuit

hard·ware *n* **1** : cutlery or tools made

of metal **2** : physical components of a vehicle or apparatus

hard·wood *n* : wood of a broad-leaved usu. deciduous tree — **hardwood** *adj*

har·dy \'härdē\ *adj* **-di·er; -est** : able to withstand adverse conditions — **har·di·ly** *adv* — **har·di·ness** *n*

hare \'har\ *n, pl* **hare** *or* **hares** : long-eared mammal related to the rabbit

hare·brained \-,brānd\ *adj* : foolish

hare·lip *n* : deformity in which the upper lip is vertically split — **hare·lipped** \-,lipt\ *adj*

ha·rem \'harəm\ *n* : house or part of a house allotted to women in a Muslim household or the women and servants occupying it

hark \'härk\ *vb* : listen

har·le·quin \'härlikən, -kwən\ *n* : clown

har·lot \'härlət\ *n* : prostitute

harm \'härm\ *n* **1** : physical or mental damage **2** : mischief ~ *vb* : cause harm — **harm·ful** \-fəl\ *adj* — **harm·ful·ly** *adv* — **harm·ful·ness** *n* — **harm·less** *adj* — **harm·less·ly** *adv* — **harm·less·ness** *n*

har·mon·ic \här'mänik\ *adj* **1** : of or relating to musical harmony **2** : pleasing to hear — **har·mon·i·cal·ly** \-iklē\ *adv*

har·mon·i·ca \här'mänikə\ *n* : small wind instrument with metallic reeds

har·mo·ny \'härmənē\ *n, pl* **-nies** **1** : musical combination of sounds **2** : pleasing arrangement of parts **3** : lack of conflict **4** : internal calm — **har·mo·ni·ous** \här'mōnēəs\ *adj* — **har·mo·ni·ous·ly** *adv* — **har·mo·ni·ous·ness** *n* — **har·mo·ni·za·tion** \,härmənə'zāshən\ *n* — **har·mo·nize** \'härmə,nīz\ *vb*

har·ness \'härnəs\ *n* : gear of a draft animal ~ *vb* **1** : put a harness on **2** : put to use

harp \'härp\ *n* : musical instrument with many strings plucked by the fingers ~ *vb* **1** : play on a harp **2** : dwell on a subject tiresomely — **harp·er** *n* — **harp·ist** *n*

har·poon \här'pün\ *n* : barbed spear used in hunting whales — **harpoon** *vb* — **har·poon·er** *n*

harp·si·chord \'härpsi,kord\ *n* : keyboard instrument with strings that are plucked

har·py \'härpē\ *n, pl* **-pies** : shrewish woman

har·row \'harō\ *n* : implement used to break up soil ~ *vb* **1** : cultivate with a harrow **2** : distress

har·ry \'harē\ *vb* **-ried; -ry·ing** : torment by or as if by constant attack

harsh \'härsh\ *adj* **1** : disagreeably rough **2** : severe — **harsh·ly** *adv* — **harsh·ness** *n*

har·um–scar·um \,harəm'skarəm\ *adv* : recklessly

har·vest \'härvəst\ *n* **1** : act or time of gathering in a crop **2** : mature crop — **harvest** *vb* — **har·vest·er** *n*

has *pres 3d sing of* HAVE

hash \'hash\ *vb* : chop into small pieces ~ *n* : chopped meat mixed with potatoes and browned

hasp \'hasp\ *n* : hinged strap fastener esp. for a door

has·sle \'hasəl\ *n* **1** : quarrel **2** : struggle **3** : cause of annoyance — **hassle** *vb*

has·sock \'hasək\ *n* : cushion used as a seat or leg rest

haste \'hāst\ *n* **1** : rapidity of motion **2** : rash action **3** : excessive eagerness — **hast·i·ly** \'hāstəlē\ *adv* — **hast·i·ness** \-stēnəs\ *n* — **hasty** \-stē\ *adj*

has·ten \'hāsᵊn\ *vb* : hurry

hat \'hat\ *n* : covering for the head

¹hatch \'hach\ *n* : small door or opening — **hatch·way** *n*

²hatch *vb* : emerge from an egg — **hatch·ery** \-ərē\ *n*

hatch·et \'hachət\ *n* : short-handled ax

hate \'hāt\ *n* : intense hostility and aversion ~ *vb* **hat·ed; hat·ing** **1** : express or feel hate **2** : dislike — **hate·ful** \-fəl\ *adj* — **hate·ful·ly** *adv* — **hate·ful·ness** *n* — **hat·er** *n*

ha·tred \'hātrəd\ *n* : hate

hat·ter \'hatər\ *n* : one that makes or sells hats

haugh·ty \'hotē\ *adj* **-ti·er; -est** : disdainfully proud — **haugh·ti·ly** *adv* — **haugh·ti·ness** *n*

haul \'hol\ *vb* **1** : draw or pull **2** : transport or carry ~ *n* **1** : amount collected **2** : load or the distance it is transported — **haul·er** *n*

haunch \'honch\ *n* : hip or hindquarter — usu. pl.

haunt \'hont\ *vb* **1** : visit often **2** : visit or inhabit as a ghost ~ *n* : place frequented — **haunt·er** *n* — **haunt·ing·ly** *adv*

have \'hav, *in sense 2 before* "to" *usu*

¹haf** *vb* **had \'had\; hav•ing \'havin\; has \'haz, *in sense 2 before "to" usu* **'has\ 1 :** hold in possession, service, or affection **2 :** be compelled or forced to **3** — used as an auxiliary with the past participle to form the present perfect, past perfect, or future perfect **4 :** obtain or receive **5 :** undergo **6 :** cause to **7 :** bear — **have to do with :** have in the way of connection or relation with or effect on

ha•ven \'hāvən** *n* **: place of safety

hav•oc \'havək** *n* **1 : wide destruction **2 :** great confusion

¹hawk \'hȯk** *n* **: bird of prey with a strong hooked bill and sharp talons

²hawk *vb* **:** offer for sale by calling out in the street — **hawk•er** *n*

haw•ser \'hȯzər** *n* **: large rope

haw•thorn \'hȯ,thȯrn** *n* **: spiny shrub or tree with pink or white fragrant flowers

hay \'hā** *n* **: herbs (as grass) cut and dried for use as fodder — **hay** *vb* — **hay•loft** *n* — **hay•mow \-,mau** *n* — **hay•stack** *n*

hay•cock \'hā,käk** *n* **: small pile of hay

hay•rick \-,rik** *n* **: large outdoor stack of hay

hay•seed \'hā,sēd** *n* **: bumpkin

hay•wire *adj* **:** being out of order

haz•ard \'hazərd** *n* **1 : source of danger **2 :** chance **~** *vb* **:** venture or risk — **haz•ard•ous** *adj*

¹haze \'hāz** *n* **: fine dust, smoke, or light vapor in the air that reduces visibility

²haze *vb* **hazed; haz•ing :** harass by abusive and humiliating tricks

ha•zel \'hāzəl** *n* **1 : shrub or small tree bearing edible nuts (**ha•zel•nuts**) **2** **:** light brown color

hazy \'hāzē** *adj* **haz•i•er; -est 1 : obscured by haze **2 :** vague or indefinite — **haz•i•ly** *adv* — **haz•i•ness** *n*

he \'hē** *pron* **1 : that male one **2 :** a or the person

head \'hed** *n* **1 : front or upper part of the body **2 :** mind **3 :** upper or higher end **4 :** director or leader **5 :** place of leadership or honor **~** *adj* **:** principal or chief **~** *vb* **1 :** provide with or form a head **2 :** put, stand, or be at the head **3 :** point or proceed in a certain direction — **head•ache** *n* — **head•band** *n* — **head•dress** *n* — **head•ed** *adj* — **head•first** *adv or adj* — **head•gear** *n* — **head•less** *adj* — **head•rest** *n* — **head•ship** *n* — **head•wait•er** *n*

head•ing \-in** *n* **1 : direction in which a plane or ship heads **2 :** something (as a title) standing at the top or beginning

head•land \'hedlənd, -,land** *n* **: promontory

head•light *n* **:** light on the front of a vehicle

head•line *n* **:** introductory line of a newspaper story printed in large type

head•long \-'lȯn** *adv* **1 : head foremost **2 :** in a rash or reckless manner — **head•long \-,lȯn** *adj*

head•mas•ter *n* **:** man who is head of a private school

head•mis•tress *n* **:** woman who is head of a private school

head–on *adj* **:** having the front facing in the direction of initial contact — **head–on** *adv*

head•phone *n* **:** an earphone held on by a band over the head — usu. pl.

head•quar•ters *n sing or pl* **:** command or administrative center

head•stone *n* **:** stone at the head of a grave

head•strong *adj* **:** stubborn or willful

head•wa•ters *n pl* **:** source of a stream

head•way *n* **:** forward motion

heady \'hedē** *adj* **head•i•er; -est 1 **:** intoxicating **2 :** shrewd

heal \'hēl** *vb* **: make or become sound or whole — **heal•er** *n*

health \'helth** *n* **: sound physical or mental condition

health•ful \-fəl** *adj* **: beneficial to health — **health•ful•ly** *adv* — **health•ful•ness** *n*

healthy \'helthē** *adj* **health•i•er; -est **:** enjoying or typical of good health — **health•i•ly** *adv* — **health•i•ness** *n*

heap \'hēp** *n* **: pile **~** *vb* **:** throw or lay in a heap

hear \'hir** *vb* **heard \'hərd\; hear•ing \'hirin\ 1 : perceive by the ear **2** **:** heed **3 :** learn

hear•ing *n* **1 :** process or power of perceiving sound **2 :** earshot **3 :** session in which witnesses are heard

hear•ken \'härkən** *vb* **: give attention

hear•say *n* **:** rumor

hearse \'hərs** *n* **: vehicle for carrying the dead to the grave

heart \'härt** *n* **1 : hollow muscular organ that keeps up the circulation of the blood **2** : playing card of a suit marked with a red heart **3** : whole personality or the emotional or moral part of it **4** : courage **5** : essential part — **heart•beat** n — **heart•ed** adj

heart•ache n : anguish of mind

heart•break n : crushing grief — **heart•break•er** n — **heart•break•ing** adj — **heart•bro•ken** adj

heart•burn n : burning distress in the heart area after eating

heart•en \'härt°n\ vb : encourage

hearth \'härth\ n **1** : area in front of a fireplace **2** : home — **hearth•stone** n

heart•less \'härtləs\ adj : cruel

heart•rend•ing \-ˌrendiŋ\ adj : causing intense grief or anguish

heart•sick adj : very despondent

heart•strings n pl : deepest emotions

heart•throb n : sweetheart

heart•warm•ing adj : inspiring sympathetic feeling

heart•wood n : central portion of wood

hearty \'härtē\ adj **heart•i•er; -est 1** : vigorously healthy **2** : nourishing — **heart•i•ly** adv — **heart•i•ness** n

heat \'hēt\ vb : make or become warm or hot ~ n **1** : condition of being hot **2** : form of energy that causes a body to rise in temperature **3** : intensity of feeling — **heat•ed•ly** adv — **heat•er** n

heath \'hēth\ n **1** : often evergreen shrubby plant of wet acid soils **2** : tract of wasteland — **heathy** adj

hea•then \'hēthən\ n, pl **-thens** or **-then** : uncivilized or godless person — **heathen** adj

heath•er \'hethər\ n : evergreen heath with lavender flowers — **heath•ery** adj

heat•stroke n : disorder that follows prolonged exposure to excessive heat

heave \'hēv\ vb **heaved** or **hove** \'hōv\; **heav•ing 1** : rise or lift upward **2** : throw **3** : rise and fall ~ n **1** : an effort to lift or raise **2** : throw

heav•en \'hevən\ n **1** pl : sky **2** : abode of the Deity and of the blessed dead **3** : place of supreme happiness — **heav•en•ly** adj — **heav•en•ward** adv or adj

heavy \'hevē\ adj **heavi•er; -est 1** : having great weight **2** : hard to bear **3** : greater than the average — **heav•i•ly** adv — **heavi•ness** n — **heavy-weight** n

heavy–du•ty adj : able to withstand unusual strain

heavy•set adj : stocky and compact in build

heck•le \'hekəl\ vb **-led; -ling** : harass with gibes — **heck•ler** \'heklər\ n

hec•tic \'hektik\ adj : filled with excitement, activity, or confusion — **hec•ti•cal•ly** \-tiklē\ adv

hedge \'hej\ n **1** : fence or boundary of shrubs or small trees **2** : means of protection ~ vb **hedged; hedg•ing 1** : protect oneself against loss **2** : evade the risk of commitment — **hedg•er** n

hedge•hog n : spiny mammal (as a porcupine)

he•do•nism \'hēd°nˌizəm\ n : way of life devoted to pleasure — **he•do•nist** \-°nist\ n — **he•do•nis•tic** \ˌhēd°n-'istik\ adj

heed \'hēd\ vb : pay attention ~ n : attention — **heed•ful** \-fəl\ adj — **heed•ful•ly** adv — **heed•ful•ness** n — **heed•less** adj — **heed•less•ly** adv — **heed•less•ness** n

¹**heel** \'hēl\ n **1** : back of the foot **2** : crusty end of a loaf of bread **3** : solid piece forming the back of the sole of a shoe — **heel•less** \'hēlləs\ adj

²**heel** vb : tilt to one side

heft \'heft\ n : weight ~ vb : judge the weight of by lifting

hefty \'heftē\ adj **heft•i•er; -est** : big and bulky

he•ge•mo•ny \hi'jemənē\ n : preponderant influence over others

heif•er \'hefər\ n : young cow

height \'hīt, 'hītth\ n **1** : highest part or point **2** : distance from bottom to top **3** : altitude

height•en \'hīt°n\ vb : increase in amount or degree

hei•nous \'hānəs\ adj : shockingly evil — **hei•nous•ly** adv — **hei•nous•ness** n

heir \'ar\ n : one who inherits or is entitled to inherit property

heir•ess \'arəs\ n : female heir esp. to great wealth

heir•loom \'arˌlüm\ n : something handed on from one generation to another

held past of **HOLD**

he•li•cal \'helikəl, 'hē-\ adj : spiral

he•li•cop•ter \'heləˌkäptər, 'hē-\ n : aircraft supported in the air by rotors

he•lio•trope \'hēlyəˌtrōp\ n : garden

herb with small fragrant white or purple flowers

he·li·um \'hēlēəm\ *n* : very light nonflammable gaseous chemical element

he·lix \'hēliks\ *n, pl* **-li·ces** \'helə,sēz, 'hē-\ : something spiral

hell \'hel\ *n* 1 : nether world in which the dead continue to exist 2 : realm of the devil 3 : place or state of torment or destruction — **hell·ish** *adj*

hell·gram·mite \'helgrə,mīt\ *n* : aquatic insect larva

hel·lion \'helyən\ *n* : troublesome person

hel·lo \hə'lō, he-\ *n, pl* **-los** : expression of greeting

helm \'helm\ *n* : lever or wheel for steering a ship — **helms·man** \'helmzmən\ *n*

hel·met \'helmət\ *n* : protective covering for the head

help \'help\ *vb* 1 : supply what is needed 2 : be of use 3 : refrain from or prevent ∼ *n* 1 : something that helps or a source of help 2 : one who helps another — **help·er** *n* — **help·ful** \-fəl\ *adj* — **help·ful·ly** *adv* — **help·ful·ness** *n* — **help·less** *adj* — **help·less·ly** *adv* — **help·less·ness** *n*

help·ing \'helpiŋ\ *n* : portion of food

help·mate *n* 1 : helper 2 : wife

help·meet \-,mēt\ *n* : helpmate

hel·ter–skel·ter \,heltər'skeltər\ *adv* : in total disorder

hem \'hem\ *n* : border of an article of cloth doubled back and stitched down ∼ *vb* **-mm-** 1 : sew a hem 2 : surround restrictively — **hem·line** *n*

he·ma·tol·o·gy \,hēmə'täləjē\ *n* : study of the blood and blood-forming organs — **hema·to·log·ic** \-mət²l-'äjik\ *adj* — **he·ma·tol·o·gist** \-'täləjist\ *n*

hemi·sphere \'hemə,sfir\ *n* : one of the halves of the earth divided by the equator into northern and southern parts (**northern hemisphere, southern hemisphere**) or by a meridian into eastern and western parts (**eastern hemisphere, western hemisphere**) — **hemi·spher·ic** \,hemə'sfirik, -'sfer-\, **hemi·spher·i·cal** \-'sfirikəl, -'sfer-\ *adj*

hem·lock \'hem,läk\ *n* 1 : poisonous herb related to the carrot 2 : evergreen tree related to the pines

he·mo·glo·bin \'hēmə,glōbən\ *n* : iron-containing compound found in red blood cells

he·mo·phil·ia \,hēmə'filēə\ *n* : hereditary tendency to severe prolonged bleeding — **he·mo·phil·i·ac** \-ē,ak\ *adj or n*

hem·or·rhage \'hemərij\ *n* : large discharge of blood — **hemorrhage** *vb* — **hem·or·rhag·ic** \,hemə'rajik\ *adj*

hem·or·rhoids \'hemə,róidz\ *n pl* : swollen mass of dilated veins at or just within the anus

hemp \'hemp\ *n* : tall Asian herb grown for its tough fiber

hen \'hen\ *n* : female domestic fowl

hence \'hens\ *adv* 1 : away 2 : therefore 3 : from this source or origin

hence·forth *adv* : from this point on

hence·for·ward *adv* : henceforth

hench·man \'henchmən\ *n* : trusted follower

hen·na \'henə\ *n* : reddish brown dye from a tropical shrub used esp. on hair

hen·peck \'hen,pek\ *vb* : subject (one's husband) to persistent nagging

he·pat·ic \hi'patik\ *adj* : relating to or resembling the liver

hep·a·ti·tis \,hepə'tītəs\ *n, pl* **-tit·i·des** \-'titə,dēz\ : disease in which the liver becomes inflamed

her \'hər\ *adj* : of or relating to her or herself ∼ \ər, (')hər\ *pron objective case of* SHE

her·ald \'herəld\ *n* 1 : official crier or messenger 2 : harbinger ∼ *vb* : give notice

her·ald·ry \'herəldrē\ *n, pl* **-ries** : practice of devising and granting stylized emblems (as for a family) — **he·ral·dic** \he'raldik, hə-\ *adj*

herb \'ərb, 'hərb\ *n* 1 : seed plant that lacks woody tissue 2 : plant or plant part valued for medicinal or savory qualities — **her·ba·ceous** \,ər'bāshəs, ,hər-\ *adj* — **herb·age** \'ərbij, 'hər-\ *n or adj* — **herb·al** \-bəl\ *n or adj* — **herb·al·ist** \-bəlist\ *n*

her·bi·cide \'ərbə,sīd, 'hər-\ *n* : agent that destroys plants — **her·bi·cid·al** \,ərbə'sīd²l, ,hər-\ *adj*

her·biv·o·rous \,ər'bivərəs, ,hər-\ *adj* : feeding on plants — **her·bi·vore** \'ərbə,vōr, 'hər-\ *n*

her·cu·le·an \,hərkyə'lēən, ,hər'kyü-lēən\ *adj* : of extraordinary power, size, or difficulty

herd \'hərd\ *n* : group of animals of

one kind ⁓ *vb* : assemble or move in a herd — **herd•er** *n* — **herds•man** \'hərdzmən\ *n*

here \'hir\ *adv* **1** : in, at, or to this place **2** : now **3** : at or in this point or particular **4** : in the present life or state ⁓ *n* : this place — **here•abouts** \'hirə,bauts\, **here•about** \-,baut\ *adv*

here•af•ter *adv* : in some future time or state ⁓ *n* : existence beyond earthly life

here•by *adv* : by means of this

he•red•i•tary \hə'redə,terē\ *adj* **1** : genetically passed or passable from parent to offspring **2** : passing by inheritance

he•red•i•ty \-ətē\ *n* : the passing of characteristics from parent to offspring

here•in *adv* : in this

here•of *adv* : of this

here•on *adv* : on this

her•e•sy \'herəsē\ *n, pl* **-sies** : opinion or doctrine contrary to church dogma — **her•e•tic** \-,tik\ *n* — **he•re•ti•cal** \hə'retikəl\ *adj*

here•to *adv* : to this document

here•to•fore \'hirtü,fōr\ *adv* : up to this time

here•un•der *adv* : under this

here•un•to *adv* : to this

here•upon *adv* : on this

here•with *adv* **1** : with this **2** : hereby

her•i•tage \'herətij\ *n* **1** : inheritance **2** : birthright

her•maph•ro•dite \hər'mafrə,dīt\ *n* : animal or plant having both male and female reproductive organs — **hermaphrodite** *adj* — **her•maph•ro•dit•ic** \-,mafrə'ditik\ *adj*

her•met•ic \hər'metik\ *adj* : sealed airtight — **her•met•i•cal•ly** \-iklē\ *adv*

her•mit \'hərmət\ *n* : one who lives in solitude

her•nia \'hərnēə\ *n, pl* **-ni•as** *or* **-ni•ae** \-nē,ē, -nē,ī\ : protrusion of a bodily part through the weakened wall of its enclosure — **her•ni•ate** \-nē,āt\ *vb*

he•ro \'hērō, 'hirō\ *n, pl* **-roes** : one that is much admired or shows great courage — **he•ro•ic** \hi'rōik\ *adj* — **he•ro•i•cal•ly** \-iklē\ *adv* — **he•ro•ics** \-iks\ *n pl* — **her•o•ism** \'herə,wizəm\ *n*

her•o•in \'herəwən\ *n* : strongly addictive narcotic

her•o•ine \'herəwən\ *n* : woman of heroic achievements or qualities

her•on \'herən\ *n* : long-legged long-billed wading bird

her•pes \'hərpēz\ *n* : virus disease characterized by the formation of blisters

her•pe•tol•o•gy \,hərpə'täləjē\ *n* : study of reptiles and amphibians — **her•pe•tol•o•gist** \-pə'täləjist\ *n*

her•ring \'heriŋ\ *n, pl* **-ring** *or* **-rings** : narrow-bodied Atlantic food fish

hers \'hərz\ *pron* : one or the ones belonging to her

her•self \hər'self\ *pron* : she, her — used reflexively or for emphasis

hertz \'herts, 'hərts\ *n, pl* **hertz** : unit of frequency equal to one cycle per second

hes•i•tant \'hezətənt\ *adj* : tending to hesitate — **hes•i•tance** \-tens\ *n* — **hes•i•tan•cy** \-tənsē\ *n* — **hes•i•tant•ly** *adv*

hes•i•tate \'hezə,tāt\ *vb* **-tat•ed; -tat•ing** **1** : hold back esp. in doubt **2** : pause — **hes•i•ta•tion** \,hezə'tāshən\ *n*

het•er•o•ge•neous \,hetərə'jēnēəs, -nyəs\ *adj* : consisting of dissimilar ingredients or constituents — **het•er•o•ge•ne•ity** \-jə'nēətē\ *n* — **het•ero•ge•neous•ly** *adv*

het•ero•sex•u•al \,hetərō'sekshəwəl\ *adj* : oriented toward the opposite sex — **heterosexual** *n* — **het•ero•sex•u•al•i•ty** \-,sekshə'walətē\ *n*

hew \'hyü\ *vb* **hewed** *or* **hewn** \'hyün\; **hew•ing** **1** : cut or shape with or as if with an ax **2** : conform strictly — **hew•er** *n*

hex \'heks\ *vb* : put an evil spell on — **hex** *n*

hexa•gon \'heksə,gän\ *n* : 6-sided polygon — **hex•ag•o•nal** \hek'sagən°l\ *adj*

hey•day \'hā,dā\ *n* : time of flourishing

hi•a•tus \hī'ātəs\ *n* : lapse in continuity

hi•ba•chi \hi'bächē\ *n* : brazier

hi•ber•nate \'hībər,nāt\ *vb* **-nat•ed; -nat•ing** : pass the winter in a torpid or resting state — **hi•ber•na•tion** \,hībər'nāshən\ *n* — **hi•ber•na•tor** \'hībər,nātər\ *n*

hic•cup \'hikəp\ *vb* **-cuped; -cup•ing** : to inhale spasmodically and make a peculiar sound ⁓ *n pl* : attack of hiccuping

hick \'hik\ *n* : awkward provincial person — **hick** *adj*

hick•o•ry \'hikərē\ *n, pl* **-ries** : No.

American hardwood tree — **hickory** *adj*

¹hide \'hīd\ *vb* **hid** \'hid\; **hid·den** \'hid³n\ *or* **hid; hid·ing** : put or remain out of sight — **hid·er** *n*

²hide *n* : animal skin

hide·bound \'hīd₁baund\ *adj* : inflexible or conservative

hid·eous \'hidēəs\ *adj* : very ugly — **hid·eous·ly** *adv* — **hid·eous·ness** *n*

hie \'hī\ *vb* **hied; hy·ing** *or* **hie·ing** : hurry

hi·er·ar·chy \'hīə₁rärkē\ *n, pl* **-chies** : persons or things arranged in a graded series — **hi·er·ar·chi·cal** \₁hīə'rärkikəl\ *adj*

hi·er·o·glyph·ic \₁hīərə'glifik\ *n* : character in the picture writing of the ancient Egyptians

high \'hī\ *adj* **1** : having large extension upward **2** : elevated in pitch **3** : exalted in character **4** : of greater degree or amount than average **5** : expensive **6** : excited or stupefied by alcohol or a drug ~ *adv* : at or to a high place or degree ~ *n* **1** : elevated point or level **2** : automobile gear giving the highest speed — **high·ly** *adv*

high·boy *n* : high chest of drawers on legs

high·brow \-₁brau\ *n* : person of superior learning or culture — **highbrow** *adj*

high–definition *adj* : being or relating to a television system with twice as many scan lines per frame as a conventional system

high–flown *adj* : pretentious

high–hand·ed *adj* : willful and arrogant — **high–hand·ed·ly** *adv* — **high–hand·ed·ness** *n*

high·land \'hīlənd\ *n* : hilly country — **high·land·er** \-ləndər\ *n*

high·light *n* : event or detail of major importance ~ *vb* **1** : emphasize **2** : be a highlight of

high·ness \-nəs\ *n* **1** : quality or degree of being high **2** — used as a title (as for kings)

high–rise *adj* : having several stories

high school *n* : school usu. including grades 9 to 12 or 10 to 12

high–spir·it·ed *adj* : lively

high·way *n* : public road

high·way·man \-mən\ *n* : one who robs travelers on a road

hi·jack \'hī₁jak\ *vb* : steal esp. by commandeering a vehicle — **hijack** *n* — **hi·jack·er** *n*

hike \'hīk\ *vb* **hiked; hik·ing** **1** : raise quickly **2** : take a long walk ~ *n* **1** : long walk **2** : increase — **hik·er** *n*

hi·lar·i·ous \hi'larēəs, hī-\ *adj* : extremely funny — **hi·lar·i·ous·ly** *adv* — **hi·lar·i·ty** \-ətē\ *n*

hill \'hil\ *n* : place where the land rises — **hill·side** *n* — **hill·top** *n* — **hilly** *adj*

hill·bil·ly \'hil₁bilē\ *n, pl* **-lies** : person from a backwoods area

hill·ock \'hilək\ *n* : small hill

hilt \'hilt\ *n* : handle of a sword

him \'him\ *pron, objective case of* HE

him·self \him'self\ *pron* : he, him — used reflexively or for emphasis

¹hind \'hīnd\ *n* : female deer

²hind *adj* : back

hin·der \'hindər\ *vb* : obstruct or hold back

hind·most *adj* : farthest to the rear

hind·quar·ter *n* : back half of a complete side of a carcass

hin·drance \'hindrəns\ *n* : something that hinders

hind·sight *n* : understanding of an event after it has happened

Hin·du·ism \'hindü₁izəm\ *n* : body of religious beliefs and practices native to India — **Hin·du** *n or adj*

hinge \'hinj\ *n* : jointed piece on which a swinging part (as a door) turns ~ *vb* **hinged; hing·ing** **1** : attach by or furnish with hinges **2** : depend

hint \'hint\ *n* **1** : indirect suggestion **2** : clue **3** : very small amount — **hint** *vb*

hin·ter·land \'hintər₁land\ *n* : remote region

hip \'hip\ *n* : part of the body on either side just below the waist — **hip·bone** *n*

hip·po·pot·a·mus \₁hipə'pätəməs\ *n, pl* **-mus·es** *or* **-mi** \-₁mī\ : large thick-skinned African river animal

hire \'hīr\ *n* **1** : payment for labor **2** : employment **3** : one who is hired ~ *vb* **hired; hir·ing** : employ for pay

hire·ling \-liŋ\ *n* : one who serves another only for gain

hir·sute \'hər₁süt, 'hir-\ *adj* : hairy

his \'hiz\ *adj* : of or belonging to him ~ *pron* : ones belonging to him

hiss \'his\ *vb* **1** : make a sibilant sound **2** : show dislike by hissing — **hiss** *n*

his·to·ri·an \his'tōrēən\ *n* : writer of history

his·to·ry \'histərē\ *n, pl* **-ries** **1** : chronological record of significant events **2** : study of past events **3** : an established record — **his·tor·ic** \his-'tȯrik\, **his·tor·i·cal** \-ikəl\ *adj* — **his·tor·i·cal·ly** \-klē\ *adv*

his·tri·on·ics \ˌhistrē'äniks\ *n pl* : exaggerated display of emotion

hit \'hit\ *vb* **hit; hit·ting 1** : reach with a blow **2** : come or cause to come in contact **3** : affect detrimentally ~ *n* **1** : blow **2** : great success — **hit·ter** *n*

hitch \'hich\ *vb* **1** : move by jerks **2** : catch by a hook **3** : hitchhike ~ *n* **1** : jerk **2** : sudden halt

hitch·hike \'hich,hīk\ *vb* : travel by securing free rides from passing vehicles — **hitch·hik·er** *n*

hith·er \'hithər\ *adv* : to this place

hith·er·to \-,tü\ *adv* : up to this time

hive \'hīv\ *n* **1** : container housing honeybees **2** : colony of bees — **hive** *vb*

hives \'hīvz\ *n sing or pl* : allergic disorder with itchy skin patches

HMO \ˌāch,em,'ō\ *n* : comprehensive health-care organization financed by clients

hoard \'hōrd\ *n* : hidden accumulation — **hoard** *vb* — **hoard·er** *n*

hoar·frost \'hōr,frȯst\ *n* : frost

hoarse \'hōrs\ *adj* **hoars·er; -est 1** : harsh in sound **2** : speaking in a harsh strained voice — **hoarse·ly** *adv* — **hoarse·ness** *n*

hoary \'hōrē\ *adj* **hoar·i·er; -est** : gray or white with age — **hoar·i·ness** *n*

hoax \'hōks\ *n* : act intended to trick or dupe — **hoax** *vb* — **hoax·er** *n*

hob·ble \'häbəl\ *vb* **-bled; -bling** : limp along ~ *n* : hobbling movement

hob·by \'häbē\ *n, pl* **-bies** : interest engaged in for relaxation — **hob·by·ist** \-ēist\ *n*

hob·gob·lin \'häb,gäblən\ *n* **1** : mischievous goblin **2** : bogey

hob·nail \-,nāl\ *n* : short nail for studding shoe soles — **hob·nailed** \-,nāld\ *adj*

hob·nob \-,näb\ *vb* **-bb-** : associate socially

ho·bo \'hōbō\ *n, pl* **-boes** : tramp

¹hock \'häk\ *n* : joint or region in the hind limb of a quadruped corresponding to the human ankle

²hock *n or vb* : pawn

hock·ey \'häkē\ *n* : game played on ice or a field by 2 teams

hod \'häd\ *n* : carrier for bricks or mortar

hodge·podge \'häj,päj\ *n* : heterogeneous mixture

hoe \'hō\ *n* : long-handled tool for cultivating or weeding — **hoe** *vb*

hog \'hȯg, 'häg\ *n* **1** : domestic adult swine **2** : glutton ~ *vb* : take selfishly — **hog·gish** *adj*

hogs·head \'hȯgz,hed, 'hägz-\ *n* : large cask or barrel

hog·wash *n* : nonsense

hoist \'hȯist\ *vb* : lift ~ *n* **1** : lift **2** : apparatus for hoisting

hok·ey \'hōkē\ *adj* **hok·i·er; -est 1** : tiresomely simple or sentimental **2** : phony

¹hold \'hōld\ *vb* **held** \'held\; **hold·ing 1** : possess **2** : restrain **3** : have a grasp on **4** : remain or keep in a particular situation or position **5** : contain **6** : regard **7** : cause to occur **8** : occupy esp. by appointment or election ~ *n* **1** : act or manner of holding **2** : restraining or controlling influence — **hold·er** *n* — **hold forth** : speak at length — **hold to** : adhere to — **hold with** : agree with

²hold *n* : cargo area of a ship

hold·ing \'hōldiŋ\ *n* : property owned — usu. pl.

hold·up *n* **1** : robbery at the point of a gun **2** : delay

hole \'hōl\ *n* **1** : opening into or through something **2** : hollow place (as a pit) **3** : den — **hole** *vb*

hol·i·day \'hälə,dā\ *n* **1** : day of freedom from work **2** : vacation — **holi·day** *vb*

ho·li·ness \'hōlēnəs\ *n* : quality or state of being holy — used as a title for a high religious official

ho·lis·tic \hō'listik\ *adj* : relating to a whole (as the body)

hol·ler \'hälər\ *vb* : cry out — **holler** *n*

hol·low \'hälō\ *adj* **-low·er** \-əwər\; **-est 1** : sunken **2** : having a cavity within **3** : sounding like a noise made in an empty place **4** : empty of value or meaning ~ *vb* : make or become hollow ~ *n* **1** : surface depression **2** : cavity — **hol·low·ness** *n*

hol·ly \'hälē\ *n, pl* **-lies** : evergreen tree or shrub with glossy leaves

hol·ly·hock \-,häk, -,hȯk\ *n* : tall perennial herb with showy flowers

ho·lo·caust \'hälə,kȯst, 'hō-, 'hȯ-\ *n* : thorough destruction esp. by fire

hol·stein \'hōl͵stēn, -͵stīn\ *n* : large black-and-white dairy cow

hol·ster \'hōlstər\ *n* : case for a pistol

ho·ly \'hōlē\ *adj* **-li·er; -est 1** : sacred **2** : spiritually pure

hom·age \'ämij, 'hä-\ *n* : reverent regard

home \'hōm\ **1** : residence **2** : congenial environment **3** : place of origin or refuge ~ *vb* **homed; hom·ing** : go or return home — **home·bred** *adj* — **home·com·ing** *n* — **home-grown** *adj* — **home·land** \-͵land\ — **home·less** *adj* — **home·made** \-'mād\ *adj*

home·ly \-lē\ *adj* **-li·er; -est** : plain or unattractive — **home·li·ness** *n*

home·mak·er *n* : one who manages a household — **home·mak·ing** *n*

home·sick *adj* : longing for home — **home·sick·ness** *n*

home·spun \-͵spən\ *adj* : simple

home·stead \-͵sted\ *n* : home and land occupied and worked by a family — **home·stead·er** \-ər\ *n*

home·stretch *n* **1** : last part of a racetrack **2** : final stage

home·ward \-wərd\, **home·wards** \-wərdz\ *adv* : toward home — **homeward** *adj*

home·work *n* : school lessons to be done outside the classroom

hom·ey \'hōmē\ *adj* **hom·i·er; -est** : characteristic of home

ho·mi·cide \'hämə͵sīd, 'hō-\ *n* : the killing of one human being by another — **hom·i·cid·al** \͵hämə'sīdəl, ͵hō-\ *adj*

hom·i·ly \'häməlē\ *n, pl* **-lies** : sermon

hom·i·ny \'hämənē\ *n* : type of processed hulled corn

ho·mo·ge·neous \͵hōmə'jēnēəs, -nyəs\ *adj* : of the same or a similar kind — **ho·mo·ge·ne·i·ty** \-jə'nēətē\ *n* — **ho·mo·ge·neous·ly** *adv*

ho·mog·e·nize \hō'mäjə͵nīz, hə-\ *vb* **-nized; -niz·ing** : make the particles in (as milk) of uniform size and even distribution — **ho·mog·e·ni·za·tion** \-͵mäjənə'zāshən\ *n* — **ho·mog·e·niz·er** *n*

ho·mo·graph \'hämə͵graf, 'hō-\ *n* : one of 2 or more words (as the noun *conduct* and the verb *conduct*) spelled alike but different in origin or meaning or pronunciation

hom·onym \'hämə͵nim, 'hō-\ *n* **1** : homophone **2** : homograph **3** : one of 2 or more words (as *pool* of water and *pool* the game) spelled and pronounced alike but different in meaning

ho·mo·phone \'hämə͵fōn, 'hō-\ *n* : one of 2 or more words (as *to, too,* and *two*) pronounced alike but different in origin or meaning or spelling

Ho·mo sa·pi·ens \͵hōmō'sapēənz, -'sä-\ *n* : humankind

ho·mo·sex·u·al \͵hōmə'sekshəwəl\ *adj* : oriented toward one's own sex — **homosexual** *n* — **ho·mo·sex·u·al·i·ty** \-͵sekshə'walətē\ *n*

hone \'hōn\ *vb* : sharpen with or as if with an abrasive stone

hon·est \'änəst\ *adj* **1** : free from deception **2** : trustworthy **3** : frank — **hon·est·ly** *adv* — **hon·esty** \-əstē\ *n*

hon·ey \'hənē\ *n, pl* **-eys** : sweet sticky substance made by bees (**hon·ey·bees**) from the nectar of flowers

hon·ey·comb *n* : mass of 6-sided wax cells built by honeybees or something like it ~ *vb* : make or become full of holes like a honeycomb

hon·ey·moon *n* : holiday taken by a newly married couple — **honey·moon** *vb*

hon·ey·suck·le \-͵səkəl\ *n* : shrub or vine with flowers rich in nectar

honk \'häŋk, 'hȯŋk\ *n* : cry of a goose or a similar sound — **honk** *vb* — **honk·er** *n*

hon·or \'änər\ *n* **1** : good name **2** : outward respect or symbol of this **3** : privilege **4** : person of superior rank or position — used esp. as a title **5** : something or someone worthy of respect **6** : integrity ~ *vb* **1** : regard with honor **2** : confer honor on **3** : fulfill the terms of — **hon·or·able** \'änərəbəl\ *adj* — **hon·or·ably** \-blē\ *adv* — **hon·or·ari·ly** \͵änə'rerəlē\ *adv* — **hon·or·ary** \'änə͵rerē\ *adj* — **hon·or·ee** \͵änə'rē\ *n*

hood \'hu̇d\ *n* **1** : part of a garment that covers the head **2** : covering over an automobile engine compartment — **hood·ed** *adj*

-hood \͵hu̇d\ *n suffix* **1** : state, condition, or quality **2** : individuals sharing a state or character

hood·lum \'hu̇dləm, 'hüd-\ *n* : thug

hood·wink \'hu̇d͵wiŋk\ *vb* : deceive

hoof \'hu̇f, 'hüf\ *n, pl* **hooves** \'hu̇vz, 'hüvz\ *or* **hoofs** : horny covering of the toes of some mammals (as horses or cattle) — **hoofed** \'hůft, 'hüft\ *adj*

hook \'hůk\ *n* : curved or bent device for catching, holding, or pulling ～ *vb* : seize or make fast with a hook — **hook•er** *n*

hook•worm *n* : parasitic intestinal worm

hoo•li•gan \'hüligən\ *n* : thug

hoop \'hüp\ *n* : circular strip, figure, or object

hoot \'hüt\ *vb* **1** : shout in contempt **2** : make the cry of an owl — **hoot** *n* — **hoot•er** *n*

¹**hop** \'häp\ *vb* **-pp-** : move by quick springy leaps — **hop** *n*

²**hop** *n* : vine whose ripe dried flowers are used to flavor malt liquors

hope \'hōp\ *vb* **hoped; hop•ing** : desire with expectation of fulfillment ～ *n* **1** : act of hoping **2** : something hoped for — **hope•ful** \-fəl\ *adj* — **hope•ful•ly** *adv* — **hope•ful•ness** *n* — **hope•less** *adj* — **hope•less•ly** *adv* — **hope•less•ness** *n*

hop•per \'häpər\ *n* : container that releases its contents through the bottom

horde \'hōrd\ *n* : throng or swarm

ho•ri•zon \hə'rīz³n\ *n* : apparent junction of earth and sky

hor•i•zon•tal \ˌhōrə'zänt³l\ *adj* : parallel to the horizon — **hor•i•zon•tal•ly** *adv*

hor•mone \'hȯrˌmōn\ *n* : cell product in body fluids that has a specific effect on other cells — **hor•mon•al** \hȯr'mōn³l\ *adj*

horn \'hȯrn\ *n* **1** : hard bony projection on the head of a hoofed animal **2** : brass wind instrument — **horned** *adj* — **horn•less** *adj*

hor•net \'hȯrnət\ *n* : large social wasp

horny \'hȯrnē\ *adj* **horn•i•er; -est 1** : made of horn **2** : hard or callous **3** : sexually aroused

horo•scope \'hȯrəˌskōp\ *n* : astrological forecast

hor•ren•dous \hȯ'rendəs\ *adj* : horrible

hor•ri•ble \'hȯrəbəl\ *adj* **1** : having or causing horror **2** : highly disagreeable — **hor•ri•ble•ness** *n* — **hor•ri•bly** \-blē\ *adv*

hor•rid \'hȯrəd\ *adj* : horrible — **hor•rid•ly** *adv*

hor•ri•fy \'hȯrəˌfī\ *vb* **-fied; -fy•ing** : cause to feel horror

hor•ror \'hȯrər\ *n* **1** : intense fear,

dread, or dismay **2** : intense repugnance **3** : something horrible

hors d'oeuvre \ȯr'dərv\ *n, pl* **hors d'oeuvres** \-'dərvz\ : appetizer

horse \'hȯrs\ *n* : large solid-hoofed domesticated mammal — **horse•back** *n or adv* — **horse•hair** *n* — **horse•hide** *n* — **horse•less** *adj* — **horse•man** \-mən\ *n* — **horse•man•ship** *n* — **horse•wom•an** *n* — **hors•ey, horsy** *adj*

horse•fly *n* : large fly with bloodsucking female

horse•play *n* : rough boisterous play

horse•pow•er *n* : unit of mechanical power

horse•rad•ish *n* : herb with a pungent root used as a condiment

horse•shoe *n* : U-shaped protective metal plate fitted to the rim of a horse's hoof

hor•ti•cul•ture \'hȯrtəˌkəlchər\ *n* : science of growing fruits, vegetables, and flowers — **hor•ti•cul•tur•al** \ˌhȯrtə'kəlchərəl\ *adj* — **hor•ti•cul•tur•ist** \-rist\ *n*

ho•san•na \hō'zanə, -'zän-\ *interj* — used as a cry of acclamation and adoration — **hosanna** *n*

hose \'hōz\ *n* **1** *pl* **hose** : stocking or sock **2** *pl* **hos•es** : flexible tube for conveying fluids ～ *vb* **hosed; hos•ing** : spray, water, or wash with a hose

ho•siery \'hōzhərē, 'hōzə-\ *n* : stockings or socks

hos•pice \'häspəs\ *n* **1** : lodging (as for travelers) maintained by a religious order **2** : facility or program for caring for dying persons

hos•pi•ta•ble \hä'spitəbəl, 'häsˌpit-\ *adj* : given to generous and cordial reception of guests — **hos•pi•ta•bly** \-blē\ *adv*

hos•pi•tal \'häsˌpit³l\ *n* : institution where the sick or injured receive medical care — **hos•pi•tal•i•za•tion** \ˌhäsˌpit³lə'zāshən\ *n* — **hos•pi•tal•ize** \'häsˌpit³lˌīz\ *vb*

hos•pi•tal•i•ty \ˌhäspə'talətē\ *n, pl* **-ties** : hospitable treatment, reception, or disposition

¹**host** \'hōst\ *n* **1** : army **2** : multitude

²**host** *n* : one who receives or entertains guests — **host** *vb*

³**host** *n* : eucharistic bread

hos•tage \'hästij\ *n* : person held to guarantee that promises be kept or demands met

hos•tel \'häst°l\ *n* : lodging for youth — **hos•tel•er** *n*

hos•tel•ry \-rē\ *n, pl* **-ries** : hotel

host•ess \'hōstəs\ *n* : woman who is host

hos•tile \'häst°l, -ˌtīl\ *adj* : openly or actively unfriendly or opposed to someone or something — **hostile** *n* — **hos•tile•ly** *adv* — **hos•til•i•ty** \häs'tilətē\ *n*

hot \'hät\ *adj* **-tt-** **1** : having a high temperature **2** : giving a sensation of heat or burning **3** : ardent **4** : pungent — **hot** *adv* — **hot•ly** *adv* — **hot•ness** *n*

hot•bed *n* : environment that favors rapid growth

hot dog *n* : frankfurter

ho•tel \hō'tel\ *n* : building where lodging and personal services are provided

hot•head•ed *adj* : impetuous — **hot•head** *n* — **hot•head•ed•ly** *adv* — **hot•head•ed•ness** *n*

hot•house *n* : greenhouse

hound \'haund\ *n* : long-eared hunting dog ~ *vb* : pursue relentlessly

hour \'aùər\ *n* **1** : 24th part of a day **2** : time of day — **hour•ly** *adv or adj*

hour•glass *n* : glass vessel for measuring time

house \'haùs\ *n, pl* **hous•es** \'haùzəz\ **1** : building to live in **2** : household **3** : legislative body **4** : business firm ~ \'haùz\ *vb* **housed; hous•ing** : provide with or take shelter — **house•boat** \'haùsˌbōt\ *n* — **house•clean** \'haùsˌklēn\ *vb* — **house•clean•ing** *n* — **house•ful** \-ˌfùl\ *n* — **house•maid** *n* — **house•wares** *n pl* — **house•work** *n*

house•bro•ken \-ˌbrōkən\ *adj* : trained in excretory habits acceptable in indoor living

house•fly *n* : two-winged fly common about human habitations

house•hold \-ˌhōld\ *n* : those who dwell as a family under the same roof ~ *adj* **1** : domestic **2** : common or familiar — **house•hold•er** *n*

house•keep•ing \-ˌkēpiŋ\ *n* : care and management of a house or institution — **house•keep•er** *n*

house•warm•ing *n* : party to celebrate moving into a house

house•wife \'haùsˌwīf\ *n* : married woman in charge of a household —

house•wife•ly *adj* — **house•wif•ery** \-ˌwīfərē\

hous•ing \'haùziŋ\ *n* **1** : dwellings for people **2** : protective covering

hove *past of* HEAVE

hov•el \'həvəl, 'häv-\ *n* : small wretched house

hov•er \'həvər, 'häv-\ *vb* **1** : remain suspended in the air **2** : move about in the vicinity

how \'haù\ *adv* **1** : in what way or condition **2** : for what reason **3** : to what extent ~ *conj* : the way or manner in which

how•ev•er \haù'evər\ *conj* : in whatever manner ~ *adv* **1** : to whatever degree or in whatever manner **2** : in spite of that

how•it•zer \'haùətsər\ *n* : short cannon

howl \'haùl\ *vb* : emit a loud long doleful sound like a dog — **howl** *n* — **howl•er** *n*

hoy•den \'hòid°n\ *n* : girl or woman of saucy or carefree behavior

hub \'həb\ *n* : central part of a circular object (as of a wheel) — **hub•cap** *n*

hub•bub \'həbˌəb\ *n* : uproar

hu•bris \'hyübrəs\ *n* : excessive pride

huck•le•ber•ry \'həkəlˌberē\ *n* **1** : shrub related to the blueberry or its berry **2** : blueberry

huck•ster \'həkstər\ *n* : peddler

hud•dle \'həd°l\ *vb* **-dled; -dling** **1** : crowd together **2** : confer — **hud•dle** *n*

hue \'hyü\ *n* : color or gradation of color — **hued** \'hyüd\ *adj*

huff \'həf\ *n* : fit of pique — **huffy** *adj*

hug \'həg\ *vb* **-gg-** **1** : press tightly in the arms **2** : stay close to — **hug** *n*

huge \'hyüj\ *adj* **hug•er; hug•est** : very large or extensive — **huge•ly** *adv* — **huge•ness** *n*

hu•la \'hülə\ *n* : Polynesian dance

hulk \'həlk\ *n* **1** : bulky or unwieldy person or thing **2** : old ship unfit for service — **hulk•ing** *adj*

hull \'həl\ *n* **1** : outer covering of a fruit or seed **2** : frame or body of a ship or boat ~ *vb* : remove the hulls of — **hull•er** *n*

hul•la•ba•loo \'hələbəˌlü\ *n, pl* **-loos** : uproar

hum \'həm\ *vb* **-mm-** **1** : make a prolonged sound like that of the speech sound \m\ **2** : be busily active **3** : run smoothly **4** : sing with closed lips — **hum** *n* — **hum•mer** *n*

hu•man \\'hyümən, 'yü-\ *adj* **1** : of or relating to the species people belong to **2** : by, for, or like people — **human** *n* — **hu•man•kind** *n* — **hu•man•ly** *adv* — **hu•man•ness** *n*

hu•mane \hyü'mān, ˌyü-\ *adj* : showing compassion or consideration for others — **hu•mane•ly** *adv* — **hu•mane•ness** *n*

hu•man•ism \\'hyümə.nizəm, 'yü-\ *n* : doctrine or way of life centered on human interests or values — **hu•man•ist** \-nist\ *n or adj* — **hu•man•is•tic** \ˌhyümə'nistik, ˌyü-\ *adj*

hu•man•i•tar•i•an \hyüˌmanə'terēən, yü-\ *n* : person promoting human welfare — **humanitarian** *adj* — **hu•man•i•tari•an•ism** *n*

hu•man•i•ty \hyü'manətē, yü-\ *n, pl* **-ties 1** : human or humane quality or state **2** : the human race

hu•man•ize \\'hyümə.nīz, 'yü-\ *vb* **-ized; -iz•ing** : make human or humane — **hu•man•iza•tion** \ˌhyümənə'zāshən, ˌyü-\ *n* — **hu•man•iz•er** *n*

hu•man•oid \\'hyümə.nȯid, 'yü-\ *adj* : having human form — **humanoid** *n*

hum•ble \\'həmbəl\ *adj* **-bler; -blest 1** : not proud or haughty **2** : not pretentious ~ *vb* **-bled; -bling** : make humble — **hum•ble•ness** *n* — **humbler** *n* — **hum•bly** \-blē\ *adv*

hum•bug \\'həm.bəg\ *n* : nonsense

hum•drum \-.drəm\ *adj* : monotonous

hu•mid \\'hyüməd, 'yü-\ *adj* : containing or characterized by moisture — **hu•mid•i•fi•ca•tion** \hyüˌmidəfə'kāshən\ *n* — **hu•mid•i•fi•er** \-'midə.fīər\ *n* — **hu•mid•i•fy** \-.fī\ *vb* — **hu•mid•ly** *adv*

hu•mid•i•ty \hyü'midətē, yü-\ *n, pl* **-ties** : atmospheric moisture

hu•mi•dor \\'hyümə.dȯr, 'yü-\ *n* : humidified storage case (as for cigars)

hu•mil•i•ate \hyü'milē.āt, yü-\ *vb* **-at•ed; -at•ing** : injure the self-respect of — **hu•mil•i•at•ing•ly** *adv* — **hu•mil•i•ation** \-.milē'āshən\ *n*

hu•mil•i•ty \hyü'milətē, yü-\ *n* : humble quality or state

hum•ming•bird \\'həmiŋ.bərd\ *n* : tiny American bird that can hover

hum•mock \\'həmək\ *n* : mound or knoll — **hum•mocky** \-məkē\ *adj*

hu•mor \\'hyümər, 'yü-\ *n* **1** : mood **2** : quality of being laughably ludicrous or incongruous **3** : appreciation of what is ludicrous or incongruous **4**

: something intended to be funny ~ *vb* : comply with the wishes or mood of — **hu•mor•ist** \-ərist\ *n* — **hu•mor•less** *adj* — **hu•mor•less•ly** *adv* — **hu•mor•less•ness** *n* — **hu•mor•ous** \\'hyümərəs, 'yü-\ *adj* — **hu•mor•ous•ly** *adv* — **hu•mor•ous•ness** *n*

hump \\'həmp\ *n* : rounded protuberance — **humped** *adj*

hump•back *n* : hunchback — **hump•backed** *adj*

hu•mus \\'hyüməs, 'yü-\ *n* : dark organic part of soil

hunch \\'hənch\ *vb* : assume or cause to assume a bent or crooked posture ~ *n* : strong intuitive feeling

hunch•back *n* **1** : back with a hump **2** : person with a crooked back — **hunch•backed** *adj*

hun•dred \\'həndrəd\ *n, pl* **-dreds** *or* **-dred** : 10 times 10 — **hundred** *adj* — **hun•dredth** \-drədth\ *adj or n*

¹**hung** *past of* HANG

²**hung** *adj* : unable to reach a verdict

hun•ger \\'həŋgər\ *n* **1** : craving or urgent need for food **2** : strong desire — **hunger** *vb* — **hun•gri•ly** \-grəlē\ *adv* — **hun•gry** *adj*

hunk \\'həŋk\ *n* : large piece

hun•ker \\'həŋkər\ *vb* : settle in for a sustained period — used with *down*

hunt \\'hənt\ *vb* **1** : pursue for food or sport **2** : try to find ~ *n* : act or instance of hunting — **hunt•er** *n*

hur•dle \\'hərd³l\ *n* **1** : barrier to leap over in a race **2** : obstacle — **hurdle** *vb* — **hur•dler** *n*

hurl \\'hərl\ *vb* : throw with violence — **hurl** *n* — **hurl•er** *n*

hur•rah \hu̇'rä, -'rȯ\ *interj* — used to express joy or approval

hur•ri•cane \\'hərə.kān\ *n* : tropical storm with winds of 74 miles per hour or greater

hur•ry \\'hərē\ *vb* **-ried; -ry•ing** : go or cause to go with haste ~ *n* : extreme haste — **hur•ried•ly** *adv* — **hur•ried•ness** *n*

hurt \\'hərt\ *vb* **hurt; hurt•ing 1** : feel or cause pain **2** : do harm to ~ *n* **1** : bodily injury **2** : harm — **hurt•ful** \-fəl\ *adj* — **hurt•ful•ness** *n*

hur•tle \\'hərt³l\ *vb* **-tled; -tling** : move rapidly or forcefully

hus•band \\'həzbənd\ *n* : married man ~ *vb* : manage prudently

hus•band•ry \-bəndrē\ *n* **1** : careful use **2** : agriculture

hush \'həsh\ *vb* : make or become quiet ~ *n* : silence

husk \'həsk\ *n* : outer covering of a seed or fruit ~ *vb* : strip the husk from — **husk•er** *n*

¹**hus•ky** \'həskē\ *adj* **-ki•er; -est** : hoarse — **hus•ki•ly** *adv* — **hus•ki•ness** *n*

²**husky** *adj* **-ki•er; -est** : burly — **husk•i•ness** *n*

³**husky** *n, pl* **-kies** : working dog of the arctic

hus•sy \'həsē, -zē\ *n, pl* **-sies 1** : brazen woman **2** : mischievous girl

hus•tle \'həsəl\ *vb* **-tled; -tling 1** : hurry **2** : work energetically — **hustle** *n* — **hus•tler** \'həslər\ *n*

hut \'hət\ *n* : small often temporary dwelling

hutch \'həch\ *n* **1** : cupboard with open shelves **2** : pen for an animal

hy•a•cinth \'hīə,sinth\ *n* : bulbous herb grown for bell-shaped flowers

hy•brid \'hībrəd\ *n* : offspring of genetically differing parents — **hybrid** *adj* — **hy•brid•iza•tion** \,hībrədə'zā-shən\ *n* — **hy•brid•ize** \'hībrəd,īz\ *vb* — **hy•brid•iz•er** *n*

hy•drant \'hīdrənt\ *n* : pipe from which water may be drawn to fight fires

hy•drau•lic \hī'dròlik\ *adj* : operated by liquid forced through a small hole — **hy•drau•lics** \-liks\ *n*

hy•dro•car•bon \,hīdrə'kärbən\ *n* : organic compound of carbon and hydrogen

hy•dro•elec•tric \,hīdrōi'lektrik\ *adj* : producing electricity by waterpower — **hy•dro•elec•tric•i•ty** \-,lek'trisətē\ *n*

hy•dro•gen \'hīdrəjən\ *n* : very light gaseous colorless odorless flammable chemical element

hydrogen bomb *n* : powerful bomb that derives its energy from the union of atomic nuclei

hy•dro•pho•bia \,hīdrə'fōbēə\ *n* : rabies

hy•dro•plane \'hīdrə,plān\ *n* : speedboat that skims the water

hy•drous \'hīdrəs\ *adj* : containing water

hy•e•na \hī'ēnə\ *n* : nocturnal carnivorous mammal of Asia and Africa

hy•giene \'hī,jēn\ *n* : conditions or practices conducive to health — **hy•gien•ic** \hī'jenik, -'jēn-; ,hījē'enik\ *adj* — **hy•gien•i•cal•ly** \-iklē\ *adv* — **hy•gien•ist** \hī'jēnist, -'jen-; 'hī-,jēn-\ *n*

hy•grom•e•ter \hī'grämətər\ *n* : instrument for measuring atmospheric humidity

hying *pres part of* HIE

hymn \'him\ *n* : song of praise esp. to God — **hymn** *vb*

hym•nal \'himnəl\ *n* : book of hymns

hype \'hīp\ *vb* **hyped; hyp•ing** : publicize extravagantly — **hype** *n*

hyper- *prefix* **1** : above or beyond **2** : excessively or excessive

hy•per•bo•le \hī'pərbəlē\ *n* : extravagant exaggeration

hy•per•ten•sion \'hīpər,tenchən\ *n* : high blood pressure — **hy•per•ten•sive** \,hīpər'tensiv\ *adj or n*

hy•phen \'hīfən\ *n* : punctuation mark - used to divide or compound words — **hyphen** *vb*

hy•phen•ate \'hīfə,nāt\ *vb* **-at•ed; -at•ing** : connect or divide with a hyphen — **hy•phen•ation** \,hīfə'nāshən\ *n*

hyp•no•sis \hip'nōsəs\ *n, pl* **-no•ses** \-,sēz\ : induced state like sleep in which the subject is responsive to suggestions of the inducer (**hyp•no•tist** \'hipnətist\) — **hyp•no•tism** \'hipnə,tizəm\ *n* — **hyp•no•tiz•able** \,hipnə'tīzəbəl\ *adj* — **hyp•no•tize** \'hipnə,tīz\ *vb*

List of self-explanatory words with the prefix *hyper-*

hyperacid	hyperenergetic	hypersensitive
hyperacidity	hyperexcitable	hypersensitiveness
hyperactive	hyperfastidious	hypersensitivity
hyperacute	hyperintense	hypersexual
hyperaggressive	hypermasculine	hypersusceptible
hypercautious	hypernationalistic	hypertense
hypercorrect	hyperreactive	hypervigilant
hypercritical	hyperrealistic	
hyperemotional	hyperromantic	

hyp•not•ic \hip'nätik\ adj : relating to hypnosis — **hypnotic** n — **hyp•not•i•cal•ly** \-iklē\ adv

hy•po•chon•dria \,hīpə'kändrēə\ n : morbid concern for one's health — **hy•po•chon•dri•ac** \-drē,ak\ adj or n

hy•poc•ri•sy \hip'äkrəsē\ n, pl **-sies** : a feigning to be what one is not — **hyp•o•crite** \'hipə,krit\ n — **hyp•o•crit•i•cal** \,hipə'kritikəl\ adj — **hyp•o•crit•i•cal•ly** adv

hy•po•der•mic \,hīpə'dərmik\ adj : administered or used in making an injection beneath the skin ～ n : hypodermic syringe

hy•pot•e•nuse \hī'pätə,nüs, -,nüz, -,nyüs, -,nyüz\ n : side of a right-angled triangle opposite the right angle

hy•poth•e•sis \hī'päthəsəs\ n, pl **-e•ses** \-,sēz\ : assumption made in order to test its consequences — **hy•poth•e•size** \-,sīz\ vb — **hy•po•thet•i•cal** \,hīpə'thetikəl\ adj — **hy•po•thet•i•cal•ly** adv

hys•ter•ec•to•my \,histə'rektəmē\ n, pl **-mies** : surgical removal of the uterus

hys•te•ria \his'terēə, -tir-\ n : uncontrollable fear or outburst of emotion — **hys•ter•i•cal** \-'terikəl\ adj — **hys•ter•i•cal•ly** adv

hys•ter•ics \-'teriks\ n pl : uncontrollable laughter or crying

---

I

i \'ī\ n, pl **i's** or **is** \'īz\ : 9th letter of the alphabet

I \'ī\ pron : the speaker

-ial adj suffix : of, relating to, or characterized by

-ian — see -AN

ibis \'ībəs\ n, pl **ibis** or **ibis•es** : wading bird with a down-curved bill

-ible — see -ABLE

ibu•pro•fen \,ībyü'prōfən\ n : drug used to relieve inflammation, pain, and fever

-ic \ik\ adj suffix 1 : of, relating to, or being 2 : containing 3 : characteristic of 4 : marked by 5 : caused by

-i•cal \ikəl\ adj suffix : -ic — **-i•cal•ly** \iklē, -kəlē\ adv suffix

ice \'īs\ n 1 : frozen water 2 : flavored frozen dessert ～ vb **iced; ic•ing** 1 : freeze 2 : chill 3 : cover with icing

ice•berg \'īs,bərg\ n : large floating mass of ice

ice•box n : refrigerator

ice•break•er n : ship equipped to cut through ice

ice cream n : sweet frozen food

ice–skate vb : skate on ice — **ice skater** n

ich•thy•ol•o•gy \,ikthē'äləjē\ n : study of fishes — **ich•thy•ol•o•gist** \-jist\ n

ici•cle \'ī,sikəl\ n : hanging mass of ice

ic•ing \'īsiŋ\ n : sweet usu. creamy coating for baked goods

icon \'ī,kän\ n 1 : religious image 2 : small picture on a computer screen identified with an available function

icon•o•clast \ī'känə,klast\ n : attacker of cherished beliefs or institutions — **icon•o•clasm** \-,klazəm\ n

icy \'īsē\ adj **ic•i•er; -est** 1 : covered with or consisting of ice 2 : very cold — **ic•i•ly** adv — **ic•i•ness** n

id \'id\ n : unconscious instinctual part of the mind

idea \ī'dēə\ n 1 : something imagined in the mind 2 : purpose or plan

ide•al \ī'dēəl\ adj 1 : imaginary 2 : perfect ～ n 1 : standard of excellence 2 : model 3 : aim — **ide•al•ly** adv

ide•al•ism \ī'dēə,lizəm\ n : adherence to ideals — **ide•al•ist** \-list\ n — **ide•al•is•tic** \ī,dēə'listik\ adj — **ide•al•is•ti•cal•ly** \-tiklē\ adv

ide•al•ize \ī'dēə,līz\ vb **-ized; -iz•ing** : think of or represent as ideal — **ide•al•i•za•tion** \-,dēələ'zāshən\ n

iden•ti•cal \ī'dentikəl\ adj 1 : being the same 2 : exactly or essentially alike

iden•ti•fi•ca•tion \ī,dentəfə'kāshən\ n 1 : act of identifying 2 : evidence of identity

iden•ti•fy \ī'dentə,fī\ vb **-fied; -fy•ing** 1 : associate 2 : establish the identity of — **iden•ti•fi•able** \ī,dentə'fīəbəl\ adj — **iden•ti•fi•er** \ī'dentə,fīər\ n

iden•ti•ty \ī'dentətē\ n, pl **-ties** 1 : sameness of essential character 2

: individuality **3** : fact of being what is supposed

ide·ol·o·gy \ˌīdē'äləjē, ˌid-\ *n, pl* **-gies** : body of beliefs — **ide·o·log·i·cal** \ˌīdēə'läjikəl, ˌid-\ *adj*

id·i·om \'idēəm\ *n* **1** : language peculiar to a person or group **2** : expression with a special meaning — **id·i·om·at·ic** \ˌidēə'matik\ *adj* — **id·i·om·at·i·cal·ly** \-iklē\ *adv*

id·io·syn·cra·sy \ˌidēō'siŋkrəsē\ *n, pl* **-sies** : personal peculiarity — **id·io·syn·crat·ic** \-sin'kratik\ *adj* — **id·io·syn·crat·i·cal·ly** \-'kratiklē\ *adv*

id·i·ot \'idēət\ *n* : mentally retarded or foolish person — **id·i·o·cy** \-əsē\ *n* — **id·i·ot·ic** \ˌidē'ätik\ *adj* — **id·i·ot·i·cal·ly** \-iklē\ *adv*

idle \'īd°l\ *adj* **idler; idlest 1** : worthless **2** : inactive **3** : lazy ~ *vb* **idled; idling** : spend time doing nothing — **idle·ness** *n* — **idler** *n* — **idly** \'īdlē\ *adv*

idol \'īd°l\ *n* **1** : image of a god **2** : object of devotion — **idol·iza·tion** \ˌīd°lə'zāshən\ *n* — **idol·ize** \'īd°līz\ *vb*

idol·a·ter, idol·a·tor \ī'dälətər\ *n* : worshiper of idols — **idol·a·trous** \-trəs\ *adj* — **idol·a·try** \-trē\ *n*

idyll \'īd°l\ *n* : period of peace and contentment — **idyl·lic** \ī'dilik\ *adj*

-ier — see **-ER**

if \'if\ *conj* **1** : in the event that **2** : whether **3** : even though

-i·fy \ˌə'ˌfī\ *vb suffix* : -fy

ig·loo \'iglü\ *n, pl* **-loos** : hut made of snow blocks

ig·nite \ig'nīt\ *vb* **-nit·ed; -nit·ing** : set afire or catch fire — **ig·nit·able** \-'nītəbəl\ *adj*

ig·ni·tion \ig'nishən\ *n* **1** : a setting on fire **2** : process or means of igniting fuel

ig·no·ble \ig'nōbəl\ *adj* : not honorable — **ig·no·bly** \-blē\ *adv*

ig·no·min·i·ous \ˌignə'minēəs\ *adj* **1** : dishonorable **2** : humiliating — **ig·no·min·i·ous·ly** *adv* — **ig·no·mi·ny** \'ignəˌminē, ig'nämənē\ *n*

ig·no·ra·mus \ˌignə'rāməs\ *n* : ignorant person

ig·no·rant \'ignərənt\ *adj* **1** : lacking knowledge **2** : showing a lack of knowledge or intelligence **3** : unaware — **ig·no·rance** \-rəns\ *n* — **ig·no·rant·ly** *adv*

ig·nore \ig'nōr\ *vb* **-nored; -nor·ing** : refuse to notice

igua·na \i'gwänə\ *n* : large tropical American lizard

ilk \'ilk\ *n* : kind

ill \'il\ *adj* **worse** \'wərs\; **worst** \'wərst\ **1** : sick **2** : bad **3** : rude or unacceptable **4** : hostile ~ *adv* **worse; worst 1** : with displeasure **2** : harshly **3** : scarcely **4** : badly ~ *n* **1** : evil **2** : misfortune **3** : sickness

il·le·gal \il'lēgəl\ *adj* : not lawful — **il·le·gal·i·ty** \ili'galətē\ *n* — **il·le·gal·ly** \il'lēgəlē\ *adv*

il·leg·i·ble \il'lejəbəl\ *adj* : not legible — **il·leg·i·bil·i·ty** \ilˌlejə'bilətē\ *n* — **il·leg·i·bly** \il'lejəblē\ *adv*

il·le·git·i·mate \ˌili'jitəmət\ *adj* **1** : born of unmarried parents **2** : illegal — **il·le·git·i·ma·cy** \-əməsē\ *n* — **il·le·git·i·mate·ly** *adv*

il·lic·it \il'lisət\ *adj* : not lawful — **il·lic·it·ly** *adv*

il·lim·it·able \il'limətəbəl\ *adj* : boundless — **il·lim·it·ably** \-blē\ *adv*

il·lit·er·ate \il'litərət\ *adj* : unable to read or write — **il·lit·er·a·cy** \-ərəsē\ *n* — **illiterate** *n*

ill–na·tured \-'nāchərd\ *adj* : cross — **ill–na·tured·ly** *adv*

ill·ness \'ilnəs\ *n* : sickness

il·log·i·cal \il'läjikəl\ *adj* : contrary to sound reasoning — **il·log·i·cal·ly** *adv*

ill–starred \'il'stärd\ *adj* : unlucky

il·lu·mi·nate \il'üməˌnāt\ *vb* **-nat·ed; -nat·ing 1** : light up **2** : make clear — **il·lu·mi·nat·ing·ly** \-ˌnātiŋlē\ *adv* — **il·lu·mi·na·tion** \-ˌümə'nāshən\ *n*

ill–use \-'yüz\ *vb* : abuse — **ill–use** \-'yüs\ *n*

il·lu·sion \il'üzhən\ *n* **1** : mistaken idea **2** : misleading visual image

il·lu·so·ry \il'üsərē, -'üz-\ *adj* : based on or producing illusion

il·lus·trate \'iləsˌtrāt\ *vb* **-trat·ed; -trat·ing 1** : explain by example **2** : provide with pictures or figures — **il·lus·tra·tor** \-ər\ *n*

il·lus·tra·tion \ˌiləs'trāshən\ *n* **1** : example that explains **2** : pictorial explanation

il·lus·tra·tive \il'əstrətiv\ *adj* : designed to illustrate — **il·lus·tra·tive·ly** *adv*

il·lus·tri·ous \-trēəs\ *adj* : notably or

brilliantly outstanding — **il•lus•tri-ous•ness** *n*

ill will *n* : unfriendly feeling

im•age \'imij\ *n* **1** : likeness **2** : visual counterpart of an object formed by a lens or mirror **3** : mental picture ~ *vb* **-aged; -ag•ing** : create a representation of

im•ag•ery \'imijrē\ *n* **1** : images **2** : figurative language

imag•i•nary \im'ajə,nerē\ *adj* : existing only in the imagination

imag•i•na•tion \im,ajə'nāshən\ *n* **1** : act or power of forming a mental image **2** : creative ability — **imag•i-na•tive** \im'ajənətiv, -ə,nātiv\ *adj* — **imag•i•na•tive•ly** *adv*

imag•ine \im'ajən\ *vb* **-ined; -in•ing** : form a mental picture of something not present — **imag•in•able** \-'ajənəbəl\ *adj* — **imag•in•ably** \-blē\ *adv*

im•bal•ance \im'baləns\ *n* : lack of balance

im•be•cile \'imbəsəl, -,sil\ *n* : idiot — **imbecile, im•be•cil•ic** \,imbə'silik\ *adj* — **im•be•cil•i•ty** \-'silətē\ *n*

im•bibe \im'bīb\ *vb* **-bibed; -bib•ing** : drink — **im•bib•er** *n*

im•bro•glio \im'brōlyō\ *n, pl* **-glios** : complicated situation

im•bue \-'byü\ *vb* **-bued; -bu•ing** : fill (as with color or a feeling)

im•i•tate \'imə,tāt\ *vb* **-tat•ed; -tat•ing** **1** : follow as a model **2** : mimic — **im•i•ta•tive** \-,tātiv\ *adj* — **im•i•ta-tor** \-ər\ *n*

im•i•ta•tion \,imə'tāshən\ *n* **1** : act of imitating **2** : copy — **imitation** *adj*

im•mac•u•late \im'akyələt\ *adj* : without stain or blemish — **im•mac•u-late•ly** *adv*

im•ma•te•ri•al \,imə'tirēəl\ *adj* **1** : spiritual **2** : not relevant — **im•ma-te•ri•al•i•ty** \-,tirē'alətē\ *n*

im•ma•ture \,imə'tür, -'tyùr\ *adj* : not yet mature — **im•ma•tu•ri•ty** \-ətē\ *n*

im•mea•sur•able \im'ezhərəbəl\ *adj* : indefinitely extensive — **im•mea-sur•ably** \-blē\ *adv*

im•me•di•a•cy \im'ēdēəsē\ *n, pl* **-cies** : quality or state of being urgent

im•me•di•ate \-ēət\ *adj* **1** : direct **2** : being next in line **3** : made or done at once **4** : not distant — **im•me•di-ate•ly** *adv*

im•me•mo•ri•al \,imə'mōrēəl\ *adj* : old beyond memory

im•mense \im'ens\ *adj* : vast — **im-mense•ly** *adv* — **im•men•si•ty** \-'ensətē\ *n*

im•merse \im'ərs\ *vb* **-mersed; -mers-ing** **1** : plunge or dip esp. into liquid **2** : engross — **im•mer•sion** \-'ərzhən\ *n*

im•mi•grant \'imigrənt\ *n* : one that immigrates

im•mi•grate \'imə,grāt\ *vb* **-grat•ed; -grat•ing** : come into a place and take up residence — **im•mi•gra•tion** \,imə'grāshən\ *n*

im•mi•nent \'imənənt\ *adj* : ready to take place — **im•mi•nence** \-nəns\ *n* — **im•mi•nent•ly** *adv*

im•mo•bile \im'ōbəl\ *adj* : incapable of being moved — **im•mo•bil•i•ty** \,imō'bilətē\ *n* — **im•mo•bi•lize** \im'ōbəlīz\ *vb*

im•mod•er•ate \im'ädərət\ *adj* : not moderate — **im•mod•er•a•cy** \-ərəsē\ *n* — **im•mod•er•ate•ly** *adv*

im•mod•est \im'ädəst\ *adj* : not modest — **im•mod•est•ly** *adv* — **im-mod•es•ty** \-əstē\ *n*

im•mo•late \'imə,lāt\ *vb* **-lat•ed; -lat-ing** : offer in sacrifice — **im•mo•la-tion** \,imə'lāshən\ *n*

im•mor•al \im'órəl\ *adj* : not moral — **im•mo•ral•i•ty** \,imó'ralətē, ,imə-\ *n* — **im•mor•al•ly** *adv*

im•mor•tal \im'órt³l\ *adj* **1** : not mortal **2** : having lasting fame ~ *n* : one exempt from death or oblivion — **im•mor•tal•i•ty** \,im,ór-'talətē\ *n* — **im•mor•tal•ize** \im'órt³l,īz\ *vb*

im•mov•able \im'üvəbəl\ *adj* **1** : stationary **2** : unyielding — **im•mov-abil•i•ty** \,im,üvə'bilətē\ *n* — **im-mov•ably** *adv*

im•mune \im'yün\ *adj* : not liable esp. to disease — **im•mu•ni•ty** \im-'yünətē\ *n* — **im•mu•ni•za•tion** \,imyənə'zāshən\ *n* — **im•mu•nize** \'imyə,nīz\ *vb*

im•mu•nol•o•gy \,imyə'näləjē\ *n* : science of immunity to disease — **im•mu•no•log•ic** \-yən³l'äjik\, **im-mu•no•log•i•cal** \-ikəl\ *adj* — **im-mu•no•nol•o•gist** \,imyə'näləjist\ *n*

im•mu•ta•ble \im'yütəbəl\ *adj* : unchangeable — **im•mu•ta•bil•i•ty** \im-,yütə'bilətē\ *n* — **im•mu•ta•bly** *adv*

imp \'imp\ *n* **1** : demon **2** : mischievous child

im·pact \im'pakt\ *vb* **1** : press close **2** : have an effect on ~ \'im,pakt\ *n* **1** : forceful contact **2** : influence

im·pact·ed \im'paktəd\ *adj* : wedged between the jawbone and another tooth

im·pair \im'par\ *vb* : diminish in quantity, value, or ability — **im·pair·ment** *n*

im·pa·la \im'palə\ *n, pl* **impalas** *or* **impala** : large African antelope

im·pale \im'pāl\ *vb* **-paled; -pal·ing** : pierce with something pointed

im·pal·pa·ble \im'palpəbəl\ *adj* : incapable of being felt — **im·pal·pa·bly** *adv*

im·pan·el \im'panⁿl\ *vb* : enter in or on a panel

im·part \-'pärt\ *vb* : give from or as if from a store

im·par·tial \im'pärshəl\ *adj* : not partial — **im·par·tial·i·ty** \im,pärshē-'alətē\ *n* — **im·par·tial·ly** *adv*

im·pass·able \im'pasəbəl\ *adj* : not passable — **im·pass·ably** \-'pasəblē\ *adv*

im·passe \'im,pas\ *n* : inescapable predicament

im·pas·sioned \im'pashənd\ *adj* : filled with passion

im·pas·sive \im'pasiv\ *adj* : showing no feeling or interest — **im·pas·sive·ly** *adv* — **im·pas·siv·i·ty** \,im,pas-'ivətē\ *n*

im·pa·tiens \im'pāshənz, -shəns\ *n* : annual herb with showy flowers

im·pa·tient \im'pāshənt\ *adj* : not patient — **im·pa·tience** \-shəns\ *n* — **im·pa·tient·ly** *adv*

im·peach \im'pēch\ *vb* **1** : charge (an official) with misconduct **2** : cast doubt on **3** : remove from office for misconduct — **im·peach·ment** *n*

im·pec·ca·ble \im'pekəbəl\ *adj* : faultless — **im·pec·ca·bly** *adv*

im·pe·cu·nious \,impi'kyünēəs\ *adj* : broke — **im·pe·cu·nious·ness** *n*

im·pede \im'pēd\ *vb* **-ped·ed; -ped·ing** : interfere with

im·ped·i·ment \-'pedəmənt\ *n* **1** : hindrance **2** : speech defect

im·pel \-'pel\ *vb* **-pelled; -pel·ling** : urge forward

im·pend \-'pend\ *vb* : be about to occur

im·pen·e·tra·ble \im'penətrəbəl\ *adj* : incapable of being penetrated or understood — **im·pen·e·tra·bil·i·ty** \im,penətrə'bilətē\ *n* — **im·pen·e·tra·bly** *adv*

im·pen·i·tent \im'penətənt\ *adj* : not penitent — **im·pen·i·tence** \-təns\ *n*

im·per·a·tive \im'perətiv\ *adj* **1** : expressing a command **2** : urgent ~ *n* **1** : imperative mood or verb form **2** : unavoidable fact, need, or obligation — **im·per·a·tive·ly** *adv*

im·per·cep·ti·ble \,impər'septəbəl\ *adj* : not perceptible — **im·per·cep·ti·bly** *adv*

im·per·fect \im'pərfikt\ *adj* : not perfect — **im·per·fec·tion** *n* — **im·per·fect·ly** *adv*

im·pe·ri·al \im'pirēəl\ *adj* **1** : relating to an empire or an emperor **2** : royal

im·pe·ri·al·ism \im'pirēə,lizəm\ *n* : policy of controlling other nations — **im·pe·ri·al·ist** \-list\ *n or adj* — **im·pe·ri·al·is·tic** \-,pirēə'listik\ *adj* — **im·pe·ri·al·is·ti·cal·ly** \-tiklē\ *adv*

im·per·il \im'perəl\ *vb* **-iled** *or* **-illed; -il·ing** *or* **-il·ling** : endanger

im·pe·ri·ous \im'pirēəs\ *adj* : arrogant or domineering — **im·pe·ri·ous·ly** *adv*

im·per·ish·able \im'perishəbəl\ *adj* : not perishable

im·per·ma·nent \-'pərmənənt\ *adj* : not permanent — **im·per·ma·nent·ly** *adv*

im·per·me·able \-'pərmēəbəl\ *adj* : not permeable

im·per·mis·si·ble \,impər'misəbəl\ *adj* : not permissible

im·per·son·al \im'pərsⁿnəl\ *adj* : not involving human personality or emotion — **im·per·son·al·i·ty** \im,pərsⁿn-'alətē\ *n* — **im·per·son·al·ly** *adv*

im·per·son·ate \im'pərsⁿn,āt\ *vb* **-at·ed; -at·ing** : assume the character of — **im·per·son·a·tion** \-,pərsⁿn-'āshən\ *n* — **im·per·son·a·tor** \-'pərsⁿn,ātər\ *n*

im·per·ti·nent \im'pərtⁿnənt\ *adj* **1** : irrelevant **2** : insolent — **im·per·ti·nence** \-ⁿnəns\ *n* — **im·per·ti·nent·ly** *adv*

im·per·turb·able \,impər'tərbəbəl\ *adj* : calm and steady

im·per·vi·ous \im'pərvēəs\ *adj* : incapable of being penetrated or affected

im·pet·u·ous \im'pechəwəs\ *adj* : impulsive — **im·pet·u·os·i·ty** \im-,pechə'wäsətē\ *n* — **im·pet·u·ous·ly** *adv*

im·pe·tus \'impətəs\ *n* : driving force

im·pi·ety \im'pīətē\ *n* : quality or state of being impious

im·pinge \im'pinj\ *vb* **-pinged; -ping·ing** : encroach — **im·pinge·ment** \-mənt\ *n* im•pi•ous \'impēəs, im'pī-\ *adj* : not pious

imp•ish \'impish\ *adj* : mischievous — imp•ish•ly *adv* — imp•ish•ness *n*

im•pla•ca•ble \im'plakəbəl, -'plā-\ *adj* : not capable of being appeased or changed — im•pla•ca•bil•i•ty \im-ˌplakə'bilətē, -ˌplā-\ *n* — im•pla•ca•bly \im'plakəblē\ *adv*

im•plant \im'plant\ *vb* 1 : set firmly or deeply 2 : fix in the mind or spirit ~ \'im,plant\ *n* : something implanted in tissue — im•plan•ta•tion \ˌim-ˌplan'tāshən\ *n*

im•plau•si•ble \im'plózəbəl\ *adj* : not plausible — im•plau•si•bil•i•ty \im-ˌplózə'bilətē\ *n*

im•ple•ment \'impləmənt\ *n* : tool, utensil ~ \-ˌment\ *vb* : put into practice — im•ple•men•ta•tion \ˌimplə-mən'tāshən\ *n*

im•pli•cate \'implə,kāt\ *vb* -cat•ed; -cat•ing : involve

im•pli•ca•tion \ˌimplə'kāshən\ *n* 1 : an implying 2 : something implied

im•plic•it \im'plisət\ *adj* 1 : understood though only implied 2 : complete and unquestioning — im•plic•it•ly *adv*

im•plode \im'plōd\ *vb* -plod•ed; -plod•ing : burst inward — im•plo•sion \-'plōzhən\ *n* — im•plo•sive \-'plōsiv\ *adj*

im•plore \im'plōr\ *vb* -plored; -plor•ing : entreat

im•ply \-'plī\ *vb* -plied; -ply•ing : express indirectly

im•po•lite \ˌimpə'līt\ *adj* : not polite

im•pol•i•tic \im'pälə,tik\ *adj* : not politic

im•pon•der•a•ble \im'pändərəbəl\ *adj* : incapable of being precisely evaluated — imponderable *n*

im•port \im'pōrt\ *vb* 1 : mean 2 : bring in from an external source ~ \'im,pōrt\ *n* 1 : meaning 2 : importance 3 : something imported — im•por•ta•tion \ˌim,pōr'tāshən\ *n* — im•port•er *n*

im•por•tant \im'pōrtənt\ *adj* : having great worth, significance, or influence — im•por•tance \-ᵊns\ *n* — im•por•tant•ly *adv*

im•por•tu•nate \im'pōrchənət\ *adj* : troublesomely persistent or urgent

im•por•tune \im,pər'tün, -'tyün; im-'pōrchən\ *vb* -tuned; -tun•ing : urge or beg persistently — im•por•tu•ni•ty \ˌimpər'tünətē, -'tyü-\ *n*

im•pose \im'pōz\ *vb* -posed; -pos-

ing 1 : establish as compulsory 2 : take unwarranted advantage of — im•po•si•tion \ˌimpə'zishən\ *n*

im•pos•ing \im'pōziŋ\ *adj* : impressive — im•pos•ing•ly *adv*

im•pos•si•ble \im'päsəbəl\ *adj* 1 : incapable of occurring 2 : enormously difficult — im•pos•si•bil•i•ty \im-ˌpäsə'bilətē\ *n* — im•pos•si•bly \im-'päsəblē\ *adv*

im•post \'im,pōst\ *n* : tax

im•pos•tor, im•pos•ter \im'pästər\ *n* : one who assumes an identity or title to deceive — im•pos•ture \-'päschər\ *n*

im•po•tent \'impətənt\ *adj* 1 : lacking power 2 : sterile — im•po•tence \-pətəns\ *n* — im•po•ten•cy \-ənsē\ *n* — im•po•tent•ly *adv*

im•pound \im'paund\ *vb* : seize and hold in legal custody — im•pound•ment *n*

im•pov•er•ish \im'pävərish\ *vb* : make poor — im•pov•er•ish•ment *n*

im•prac•ti•ca•ble \im'praktikəbəl\ *adj* : not practicable

im•prac•ti•cal \-'praktikəl\ *adj* : not practical

im•pre•cise \ˌimpri'sīs\ *adj* : not precise — im•pre•cise•ly *adv* — im•pre•cise•ness *n* — im•pre•ci•sion \-'sizhən\ *n*

im•preg•na•ble \im'pregnəbəl\ *adj* : able to resist attack — im•preg•na•bil•i•ty \im,pregnə'bilətē\ *n*

im•preg•nate \im'preg,nāt\ *vb* -nat•ed; -nat•ing 1 : make pregnant 2 : cause to be filled, permeated, or saturated — im•preg•na•tion \ˌim-ˌpreg'nāshən\ *n*

im•pre•sa•rio \ˌimprə'särē,ō\ *n, pl* -ri•os : one who sponsors an entertainment

¹im•press \im'pres\ *vb* 1 : apply with or produce by pressure 2 : press, stamp, or print in or upon 3 : produce a vivid impression of 4 : affect (as the mind) forcibly

²im•press \im'pres\ *vb* : force into naval service — im•press•ment *n*

im•pres•sion \im'preshən\ *n* 1 : mark made by impressing 2 : marked influence or effect 3 : printed copy 4 : vague notion or recollection — im•pres•sion•able \-'preshənəbəl\ *adj*

im•pres•sive \im'presiv\ *adj* : making a marked impression — im•pres•sive•ly *adv* — im•pres•sive•ness *n*

im•pri•ma•tur \ˌimprə'mä,tùr\ *n* : official approval (as of a publication by a censor)

im·print \im'print, 'im‚-\ *vb* : stamp or mark by or as if by pressure ~ \'im‚-\ *n* : something imprinted or printed

im·pris·on \im'priz²n\ *vb* : put in prison — **im·pris·on·ment** \-mənt\ *n*

im·prob·a·ble \im'präbəbəl\ *adj* : unlikely to be true or to occur — **im·prob·a·bil·i·ty** \im‚präbə'bilətē\ *n* — **im·prob·a·bly** *adv*

im·promp·tu \im'prämptü, -tyü\ *adj* : not planned beforehand — **impromptu** *adv or n*

im·prop·er \im'präpər\ *adj* : not proper — **im·prop·er·ly** *adv*

im·pro·pri·ety \‚imprə'prīətē\ *n, pl* **-eties** : state or instance of being improper

im·prove \im'prüv\ *vb* **-proved; -proving** : grow or make better — **im·prov·able** \-'prüvəbəl\ *adj* — **im·prove·ment** *n*

im·prov·i·dent \im'prävədənt\ *adj* : not providing for the future — **im·prov·i·dence** \-əns\ *n*

im·pro·vise \'imprə‚vīz\ *vb* **-vised; -vis·ing** : make, invent, or arrange offhand — **im·pro·vi·sa·tion** \im‚prävə-'zāshən, ‚imprəvə-\ *n* — **im·pro·vis·er, im·pro·vi·sor** \'imprə‚vīzər\ *n*

im·pru·dent \im'prüd²nt\ *adj* : not prudent — **im·pru·dence** \-²ns\ *n*

im·pu·dent \'impyədənt\ *adj* : insolent — **im·pu·dence** \-əns\ *n* — **im·pu·dent·ly** *adv*

im·pugn \im'pyün\ *vb* : attack as false

im·pulse \'im‚pəls\ *n* **1** : moving force **2** : sudden inclination

im·pul·sive \im'pəlsiv\ *adj* : acting on impulse — **im·pul·sive·ly** *adv* — **im·pul·sive·ness** *n*

im·pu·ni·ty \im'pyünətē\ *n* : exemption from punishment or harm

im·pure \im'pyür\ *adj* : not pure — **im·pu·ri·ty** \-'pyürətē\ *n*

im·pute \im'pyüt\ *vb* **-put·ed; -put·ing** : credit to or blame on a person or cause — **im·pu·ta·tion** \‚impyə-'tāshən\ *n*

in \'in\ *prep* **1** — used to indicate location, inclusion, situation, or manner **2** : into **3** : during ~ *adv* : to or toward the inside ~ *adj* : located inside

in- \in\ *prefix* **1** : not **2** : lack of

in·ad·ver·tent \‚inəd'vərt²nt\ *adj* : unintentional — **in·ad·ver·tence** \-²ns\ *n* — **in·ad·ver·ten·cy** \-²nsē\ *n* — **in·ad·ver·tent·ly** *adv*

in·alien·able \in'ālyənəbəl, -'ālēənə-\ *adj* : incapable of being transferred or given up — **in·alien·abil·i·ty** \in‚ālyənə'bilətē, -'ālēənə-\ *n* — **in·alien·ably** *adv*

inane \in'ān\ *adj* **inan·er; -est** : silly or stupid — **inan·i·ty** \in'anətē\ *n*

in·an·i·mate \in'anəmət\ *adj* : not animate or animated — **in·an·i·mate·ly** *adv* — **in·an·i·mate·ness** *n*

in·ap·pre·cia·ble \‚inə'prēshəbəl\ *adj* : too small to be perceived — **in·ap·pre·cia·bly** *adv*

in·ar·tic·u·late \‚inär'tikyələt\ *adj* : without the power of speech or effective expression — **in·ar·tic·u·late·ly** *adv*

in·as·much as \‚inaz'məchaz\ *conj* : because

in·at·ten·tion \‚inə'tenchən\ *n* : failure to pay attention

in·au·gu·ral \in'ȯgyərəl, -gərəl\ *adj* : relating to an inauguration ~ *n* **1** : inaugural speech **2** : inauguration

in·au·gu·rate \in'ȯgyə‚rāt, -gə-\ *vb* **-rat·ed; -rat·ing** **1** : install in office **2** : start — **in·au·gu·ra·tion** \-‚ȯgyə-'rāshən, -gə-\ *n*

in·board \‚in‚bȯrd\ *adv* : inside a vehicle or craft — **inboard** *adj*

in·born \'in‚bȯrn\ *adj* : present from birth

in·bred \'in‚bred\ *adj* : deeply ingrained in one's nature

in·breed·ing \'in‚brēdiŋ\ *n* : interbreeding of closely related individuals — **in·breed** \-‚brēd\ *vb*

in·cal·cu·la·ble \in'kalkyələbəl\ *adj*

List of self-explanatory words with the prefix _in-_

inability	**inactivity**	**inadvisable**
inaccessibility	**inadequacy**	**inapparent**
inaccessible	**inadequate**	**inapplicable**
inaccuracy	**inadequately**	**inapposite**
inaccurate	**inadmissibility**	**inappositely**
inaction	**inadmissible**	**inappositeness**
inactive	**inadvisability**	**inappreciative**

: too large to be calculated — **in•cal•cu•la•bly** *adv*

in•can•des•cent \ˌinkən'des⁼nt\ *adj* **1** : glowing with heat **2** : brilliant — **in•can•des•cence** \-⁼ns\ *n*

in•can•ta•tion \ˌinˌkan'tāshən\ *n* : use of spoken or sung charms or spells as a magic ritual

in•ca•pac•i•tate \ˌinkə'pasəˌtāt\ *vb* -tat•ed; -tat•ing : disable

in•ca•pac•i•ty \ˌinkə'pasətē\ *n, pl* -ties : quality or state of being incapable

in•car•cer•ate \in'kärsəˌrāt\ *vb* -at•ed; -at•ing : imprison — **in•car•cer•a•tion** \inˌkärsə'rāshən\ *n*

in•car•nate \in'kärnət, -ˌnāt\ *adj* : having bodily form and substance — **in•car•nate** \-ˌnāt\ *vb* — **in•car•na•tion** \-ˌkär'nāshən\ *n*

in•cen•di•ary \in'sendēˌerē\ *adj* **1** : pertaining to or used to ignite fire **2** : tending to excite — **incendiary** *n*

in•cense \'inˌsens\ *n* : material burned to produce a fragrant odor or its smoke ∼ \in'sens\ *vb* -censed; -cens•ing : make very angry

in•cen•tive \in'sentive\ *n* : inducement to do something

in•cep•tion \in'sepshən\ *n* : beginning

in•ces•sant \in'ses⁼nt\ *adj* : continuing without interruption — **in•ces•sant•ly** *adv*

in•cest \'inˌsest\ *n* : sexual intercourse between close relatives — **in•ces•tu•ous** \in'seschəwəs\ *adj*

inch \'inch\ *n* : unit of length equal to ¹⁄₁₂ foot ∼ *vb* : move by small degrees

in•cho•ate \in'kōət, 'inkəˌwāt\ *adj* : new and not fully formed or ordered

in•ci•dent \'insədənt\ *n* : occurrence — **in•ci•dence** \-əns\ *n* — **incident** *adj*

in•ci•den•tal \ˌinsə'dent⁼l\ *adj* **1** : subordinate, nonessential, or attendant **2** : met by chance ∼ *n* **1** : something incidental **2** *pl* : minor expenses that are not itemized — **in•ci•den•tal•ly** *adv*

in•cin•er•ate \in'sinəˌrāt\ *vb* -at•ed;

-at•ing : burn to ashes — **in•cin•er•a•tor** \-ˌrātər\ *n*

in•cip•i•ent \in'sipēənt\ *adj* : beginning to be or appear

in•cise \in'sīz\ *vb* -cised; -cis•ing : carve into

in•ci•sion \in'sizhən\ *n* : surgical cut

in•ci•sive \in'sīsiv\ *adj* : keen and discerning — **in•ci•sive•ly** *adv*

in•ci•sor \in'sīzər\ *n* : tooth for cutting

in•cite \in'sīt\ *vb* -cit•ed; -cit•ing : arouse to action — **in•cite•ment** *n*

in•ci•vil•i•ty \ˌinsə'vilətē\ *n* : rudeness

in•clem•ent \in'klemənt\ *adj* : stormy — **in•clem•en•cy** \-ənsē\ *n*

in•cline \in'klīn\ *vb* -clined; -clin•ing **1** : bow **2** : tend toward an opinion **3** : slope ∼ *n* : slope — **in•cli•na•tion** \ˌinklə'nāshən\ *n* — **in•clin•er** *n*

inclose, inclosure *var of* ENCLOSE, ENCLOSURE

in•clude \in'klüd\ *vb* -clud•ed; -clud•ing : take in or comprise — **in•clu•sion** \in'klüzhən\ *n* — **in•clu•sive** \-'klüsiv\ *adj*

in•cog•ni•to \ˌinˌkäg'nētō, in'kägnəˌtō\ *adv or adj* : with one's identity concealed

in•come \'inˌkəm\ *n* : money gained (as from work or investment)

in•com•ing \'inˌkəmiŋ\ *adj* : coming in

in•com•mu•ni•ca•do \ˌinkəˌmyünə'kädō\ *adv or adj* : without means of communication

in•com•pa•ra•ble \in'kämpərəbəl\ *adj* : eminent beyond comparison

in•com•pe•tent \in'kämpətənt\ *adj* : lacking sufficient knowledge or skill — **in•com•pe•tence** \-pətəns\ *n* — **in•com•pe•ten•cy** \-ənsē\ *n* — **incompetent** *n*

in•con•ceiv•able \ˌinkən'sēvəbəl\ *adj* **1** : impossible to comprehend **2** : unbelievable — **in•con•ceiv•ably** \-blē\ *adv*

in•con•gru•ous \in'käŋgrəwəs\ *adj* : inappropriate or out of place — **in•con•gru•i•ty** \ˌinkən'grüətē, -ˌkän-\ *n* — **in•con•gru•ous•ly** *adv*

in•con•se•quen•tial \ˌinˌkänsə'kwen-

---

inapproachable	inartistically	inauthentic
inappropriate	inattentive	incapability
inappropriately	inattentively	incapable
inappropriateness	inattentiveness	incautious
inapt	inaudible	incoherence
inarguable	inaudibly	incoherent
inartistic	inauspicious	incoherently

chəl\ *adj* : unimportant — **in·con·se·quence** \in'känsə,kwens\ *n* — **in·con·se·quen·tial·ly** *adv*

in·con·sid·er·able \,inkən'sidərəbəl\ *adj* : trivial

in·con·sol·able \,inkən'sōləbəl\ *adj* : incapable of being consoled — **in·con·sol·ably** *adv*

in·con·ve·nience \,inkən'vēnyəns\ *n* 1 : discomfort 2 : something that causes trouble or annoyance ～ *vb* : cause inconvenience to — **in·con·ve·nient** \,inkən'vēnyənt\ *adj* — **in·con·ve·nient·ly** *adv*

in·cor·po·rate \in'kórpə,rāt\ *vb* -rat·ed; -rat·ing 1 : blend 2 : form into a legal body — **in·cor·po·rat·ed** *adj* — **in·cor·po·ra·tion** \-,kórpə'rāshən\ *n*

in·cor·ri·gi·ble \in'kórəjəbəl\ *adj* : incapable of being corrected or reformed — **in·cor·ri·gi·bil·i·ty** \in,kórəjə'bilətē\ *n*

in·crease \in'krēs, 'in,krēs\ *vb* -creased; -creas·ing : make or become greater ～ \'in,-, in'-\ *n* 1 : enlargement in size 2 : something added — **in·creas·ing·ly** \-'krēsiŋlē\ *adv*

in·cred·i·ble \in'kredəbəl\ *adj* : too extraordinary to be believed — **in·cred·ibil·i·ty** \in,kredə'bilətē\ *n* — **in·cred·i·bly** \in'kredəblē\ *adv*

in·cred·u·lous \in'krejələs\ *adj* : skeptical — **in·cre·du·li·ty** \,inkri'dül·ətē, -'dyü-\ *n* — **in·cred·u·lous·ly** *adv*

in·cre·ment \'iŋkrəmənt, 'in-\ *n* : increase or amount of increase — **in·cre·men·tal** \,iŋkrə'ment'l, ,in-\ *adj*

in·crim·i·nate \in'krimə,nāt\ *vb* -nat·ed; -nat·ing : show to be guilty of a crime — **in·crim·i·na·tion** \-,krimə'nāshən\ *n* — **in·crim·i·na·to·ry** \-'krimənə,tōrē\ *adj*

in·cu·bate \'iŋkyə,bāt, 'in-\ *vb* -bat·ed; -bat·ing : keep (as eggs) under conditions favorable for development — **in·cu·ba·tion** \,iŋkyə'bāshən,

,in-\ *n* — **in·cu·ba·tor** \'iŋkyə,bātər, 'in-\ *n*

in·cul·cate \in'kəl,kāt, 'in,kəl-\ *vb* -cat·ed; -cat·ing : instill by repeated teaching — **in·cul·ca·tion** \,in,kəl-'kāshən\ *n*

in·cum·bent \in'kəmbənt\ *n* : holder of an office ～ *adj* : obligatory — **in·cum·ben·cy** \-bənsē\ *n*

in·cur \in'kər\ *vb* -rr- : become liable or subject to

in·cur·sion \in'kərzhən\ *n* : invasion

in·debt·ed \in'detəd\ *adj* : owing something — **in·debt·ed·ness** *n*

in·de·ci·sion \,indi'sizhən\ *n* : inability to decide

in·deed \in'dēd\ *adv* : without question

in·de·fat·i·ga·ble \indi'fatigəbəl\ *adj* : not tiring — **in·de·fat·i·ga·bly** \-blē\ *adv*

in·def·i·nite \in'defənət\ *adj* 1 : not defining or identifying 2 : not precise 3 : having no fixed limit — **in·def·i·nite·ly** *adv*

in·del·i·ble \in'deləbəl\ *adj* : not capable of being removed or erased — **in·del·i·bly** *adv*

in·del·i·cate \in'delikət\ *adj* : improper — **in·del·i·ca·cy** \in'deləkəsē\ *n*

in·dem·ni·fy \in'demnə,fī\ *vb* -fied; -fy·ing : repay for a loss — **in·dem·ni·fi·ca·tion** \-,demnəfə'kāshən\ *n*

in·dem·ni·ty \in'demnətē\ *n, pl* -ties : security against loss or damage

¹**in·dent** \in'dent\ *vb* : leave a space at the beginning of a paragraph

²**indent** *vb* : force inward so as to form a depression or dent

in·den·ta·tion \,in,den'tashən\ *n* 1 : notch, recess, or dent 2 : action of indenting 3 : space at the beginning of a paragraph

in·den·ture \in'denchər\ *n* : contract binding one person to work for another for a given period — usu. in pl. ～ *vb* -tured; -tur·ing : bind by indentures

Independence Day *n* : July 4 observed as a legal holiday in commemoration of the adoption of the Declaration of Independence in 1776

in·de·pen·dent \ˌində'pendənt\ *adj* **1** : not governed by another **2** : not requiring or relying on something or somebody else **3** : not easily influenced — **in·de·pen·dence** \-dəns\ *n* — **independent** *n* — **in·de·pen·dent·ly** *adv*

in·de·ter·mi·nate \ˌindi'tərmənət\ *adj* : not definitely determined — **in·de·ter·mi·na·cy** \-nəsē\ *n* — **in·de·ter·mi·nate·ly** *adv*

in·dex \'inˌdeks\ *n, pl* **-dex·es** *or* **-di·ces** \-dəˌsēz\ **1** : alphabetical list of items (as topics in a book) **2** : a number that serves as a measure or indicator of something ~ *vb* **1** : provide with an index **2** : serve as an index of

index finger *n* : forefinger

in·di·cate \'indəˌkāt\ *vb* **-cat·ed; -cat·ing** **1** : point out or to **2** : show indirectly **3** : state briefly — **in·di·ca·tion** \ˌində'kāshən\ *n* — **in·di·ca·tor** \'indəˌkātər\ *n*

in·dic·a·tive \in'dikətiv\ *adj* : serving to indicate

in·dict \in'dīt\ *vb* : charge with a crime — **in·dict·able** *adj* — **in·dict·ment** *n*

in·dif·fer·ent \in'difrənt\ *adj* **1** : having no preference **2** : showing neither interest nor dislike **3** : mediocre — **in·dif·fer·ence** \-'difrəns\ *n* — **in·dif·fer·ent·ly** *adv*

in·dig·e·nous \in'dijənəs\ *adj* : native to a particular region

in·di·gent \'indijənt\ *adj* : needy — **in·di·gence** \-jəns\ *n*

in·di·ges·tion \ˌindī'jeschən, -də-\ *n* : discomfort from inability to digest food

in·dig·na·tion \ˌindig'nāshən\ *n* : anger aroused by something unjust or unworthy — **in·dig·nant** \in'dignənt\ *adj* — **in·dig·nant·ly** *adv*

in·dig·ni·ty \in'dignətē\ *n, pl* **-ties** **1** : offense against self-respect **2** : humiliating treatment

in·di·go \'indiˌgō\ *n, pl* **-gos** *or* **-goes**

1 : blue dye **2** : deep reddish blue color

in·di·rect \ˌində'rekt, -dī-\ *adj* : not straight or straightforward — **in·di·rec·tion** \-'rekshən\ *n* — **in·di·rect·ly** *adv* — **in·di·rect·ness** *n*

in·dis·crim·i·nate \ˌindis'krimənət\ *adj* **1** : not careful or discriminating **2** : haphazard — **in·dis·crim·i·nate·ly** *adv*

in·dis·pens·able \ˌindis'pensəbəl\ *adj* : absolutely essential — **in·dis·pens·abil·i·ty** \-ˌpensə'bilətē\ *n* — **indispensable** *n* — **in·dis·pens·ably** \-'pensəblē\ *adv*

in·dis·posed \-'pōzd\ *adj* : slightly ill — **in·dis·po·si·tion** \inˌdispə'zishən\ *n*

in·dis·sol·u·ble \ˌindis'älyəbəl\ *adj* : not capable of being dissolved or broken

in·di·vid·u·al \ˌində'vijəwəl\ *n* **1** : single member of a category **2** : person — **individual** *adj* — **in·di·vid·u·al·ly** *adv*

in·di·vid·u·al·ist \-əwəlist\ *n* : person who is markedly independent in thought or action

in·di·vid·u·al·i·ty \-ˌvijə'walətē\ *n* : special quality that distinguishes an individual

in·di·vid·u·al·ize \-'vijəwəˌlīz\ *vb* **-ized; -iz·ing** **1** : make individual **2** : treat individually

in·doc·tri·nate \in'däktrəˌnāt\ *vb* **-nat·ed; -nat·ing** : instruct in fundamentals (as of a doctrine) — **in·doc·tri·na·tion** \inˌdäktrə'nāshən\ *n*

in·do·lent \'indələnt\ *adj* : lazy — **in·do·lence** \-ləns\ *n*

in·dom·i·ta·ble \in'dämətəbəl\ *adj* : invincible — **in·dom·i·ta·bly** \-blē\ *adv*

in·door \'in'dōr\ *adj* : relating to the inside of a building

in·doors \in'dōrz\ *adv* : in or into a building

in·du·bi·ta·ble \in'dübətəbəl, -'dyü-\ *adj* : being beyond question — **in·du·bi·ta·bly** \-blē\ *adv*

---

inconstancy	incorporeally	incurious
inconstant	incorrect	indecency
inconstantly	incorrectly	indecent
inconsumable	incorrectness	indecently
incontestable	incorruptible	indecipherable
incontestably	inculpable	indecisive
incorporeal	incurable	indecisively

in•duce \in'düs, -'dyüs\ *vb* **-duced;**
-duc•ing 1 : persuade **2** : bring
about — **in•duce•ment** *n* — **in•duc•**
er *n*

in•duct \in'dəkt\ *vb* **1** : put in office **2**
: admit as a member **3** : enroll (as for
military service) — **in•duct•ee** \in-
,dək'tē\ *n*

in•duc•tion \in'dəkshən\ *n* **1** : act or
instance of inducting **2** : reasoning
from particular instances to a general
conclusion

in•duc•tive \in'dəktiv\ *adj* : reasoning
by induction

in•dulge \in'dəlj\ *vb* **-dulged; -dulg•ing**
: yield to the desire of or for — **in-**
dul•gence \-'dəljəns\ *n* — **in•dul•**
gent \-jənt\ *adj* — **in•dul•gent•ly**
adv

in•dus•tri•al \in'dəstrēəl\ *adj* **1** : relating to industry **2** : heavy-duty — **in-**
dus•tri•al•ist \-əlist\ *n* — **in•dus•tri•**
al•iza•tion \-,dəstrēələ'zāshən\ *n*
— **in•dus•tri•al•ize** \-'dəstrēə,līz\
vb — **in•dus•tri•al•ly** *adv*

in•dus•tri•ous \in'dəstrēəs\ *adj* : diligent or busy — **in•dus•tri•ous•ly** *adv*
— **in•dus•tri•ous•ness** *n*

in•dus•try \'indəstrē\ *n, pl* **-tries 1**
: diligence **2** : manufacturing enter-
prises or activity

in•ebri•at•ed \i'nēbrē,ātəd\ *adj* : drunk
— **in•ebri•a•tion** \-,ēbrē'āshən\ *n*

in•ef•fa•ble \in'efəbəl\ *adj* : incapable
of being expressed in words — **in•ef-**
fa•bly \-blē\ *adv*

in•ept \in'ept\ *adj* **1** : inappropriate or
foolish **2** : generally incompetent —
in•ep•ti•tude \in'eptə,tüd, -,tyüd\ *n*
— **in•ept•ly** *adv* — **in•ept•ness** *n*

in•equal•i•ty \,ini'kwälətē\ *n* : quality
of being unequal or uneven

in•ert \in'ərt\ *adj* **1** : powerless to
move or act **2** : sluggish — **in•ert•ly**
adv — **in•ert•ness** *n*

in•er•tia \in'ərshə\ *n* : tendency of
matter to remain at rest or in motion
— **in•er•tial** \-shəl\ *adj*

in•es•cap•able \,inə'skāpəbəl\ *adj*

: inevitable — **in•es•cap•ably** \-blē\
adv

in•es•ti•ma•ble \in'estəməbəl\ *adj*
: incapable of being estimated — **in-**
es•ti•ma•bly \-blē\ *adv*

in•ev•i•ta•ble \in'evətəbəl\ *adj* : incapable of being avoided or escaped —
in•ev•i•ta•bil•i•ty \in,evətə'bilətē\ *n*
— **in•ev•i•ta•bly** \in'evətəblē\ *adv*

in•ex•cus•able \,inik'skyüzəbəl\ *adj*
: being without excuse or justification
— **in•ex•cus•ably** \-blē\ *adv*

in•ex•haust•ible \,inig'zόstəbəl\ *adj*
: incapable of being used up or tired
out — **in•ex•haust•ibly** \-blē\ *adv*

in•ex•o•ra•ble \in'eksərəbəl\ *adj* : unyielding or relentless — **in•ex•o•ra•**
bly *adv*

in•fal•li•ble \in'faləbəl\ *adj* : incapable
of error — **in•fal•li•bil•i•ty** \in,falə-
'bilətē\ *n* — **in•fal•li•bly** *adv*

in•fa•mous \'infəməs\ *adj* : having the
worst kind of reputation — **in•fa•**
mous•ly *adv*

in•fa•my \-mē\ *n, pl* **-mies** : evil reputation

in•fan•cy \'infənsē\ *n, pl* **-cies 1**
: early childhood **2** : early period of
existence

in•fant \'infənt\ *n* : baby

in•fan•tile \'infən,tīl, -t°l, -,tēl\ *adj* **1**
: relating to infants **2** : childish

in•fan•try \'infəntrē\ *n, pl* **-tries** : soldiers that fight on foot

in•fat•u•ate \in'fachə,wāt\ *vb* **-at•ed;**
-at•ing : inspire with foolish love or
admiration — **in•fat•u•a•tion** \-,fachə-
'wāshən\ *n*

in•fect \in'fekt\ *vb* : contaminate with
disease-producing matter — **in•fec-**
tion \-'fekshən\ *n* — **in•fec•tious**
\-shəs\ *adj* — **in•fec•tive** \-'fektiv\
adj

in•fer \in'fər\ *vb* **-rr-** : deduce — **in•fer-**
ence \'infərəns\ *n* — **in•fer•en•tial**
\,infə'renchəl\ *adj*

in•fe•ri•or \in'firēər\ *adj* **1** : being
lower in position, degree, rank, or

merit **2** : of lesser quality — **inferior**
n — **in•fe•ri•or•i•ty** \inˌfirē'ȯrətē\ *n*
in•fer•nal \in'fərn°l\ *adj* : of or like
hell — often used as a general expression of disapproval — **in•fer•nal•ly**
adv
in•fer•no \in'fərnō\ *n, pl* **-nos** : place
or condition suggesting hell
in•fest \in'fest\ *vb* : swarm or grow
in or over — **in•fes•ta•tion** \ˌinˌfes-
'tāshən\ *n*
in•fi•del \'infəd°l, -fəˌdel\ *n* : one who
does not believe in a particular religion
in•fi•del•i•ty \ˌinfə'delətē, -fī-\ *n, pl*
-ties : lack of faithfulness
in•field \'inˌfēld\ *n* : baseball field inside the base lines — **in•field•er** *n*
in•fil•trate \in'filˌtrāt, 'infil-\ *vb* **-trat-
ed; -trat•ing** : enter or become established in without being noticed —
in•fil•tra•tion \ˌinfil'trāshən\ *n*
in•fi•nite \'infənət\ *adj* **1** : having no
limit or extending indefinitely **2** : vast
— **infinite** *n* — **in•fi•nite•ly** *adv* —
in•fin•i•tude \in'finəˌtüd, -tyüd\ *n*
in•fin•i•tes•i•mal \ˌinˌfinə'tesəməl\ *adj*
: immeasurably small — **in•fin•i•tes-
i•mal•ly** *adv*
in•fin•i•tive \in'finətiv\ *n* : verb form in
English usu. used with *to*
in•fin•i•ty \in'finətē\ *n, pl* **-ties 1**
: quality or state of being infinite **2**
: indefinitely great number or amount
in•firm \in'fərm\ *adj* : feeble from age
— **in•fir•mi•ty** \-'fərmətē\ *n*
in•fir•ma•ry \in'fərmərē\ *n, pl* **-ries**
: place for the care of the sick
in•flame \in'flām\ *vb* **-flamed; -flam-
ing 1** : excite to intense action or
feeling **2** : affect or become affected
with inflammation — **in•flam•ma•to-
ry** \-'flaməˌtōrē\ *adj*
in•flam•ma•ble \in'flaməbəl\ *adj*
: flammable
in•flam•ma•tion \ˌinflə'māshən\ *n*
: response to injury in which an affected area becomes red and painful
and congested with blood

in•flate \in'flāt\ *vb* **-flat•ed; -flat•ing 1**
: swell or puff up (as with gas) **2** : expand or increase abnormally — **in-
flat•able** *adj*
in•fla•tion \in'flāshən\ *n* **1** : act of in-
flating **2** : continual rise in prices —
in•fla•tion•ary \-shəˌnerē\ *adj*
in•flec•tion \in'flekshən\ *n* **1** : change
in pitch or loudness of the voice **2**
: change in form of a word — **in•flect**
\-'flekt\ *vb* — **in•flec•tion•al** \-'flek-
shənəl\ *adj*
in•flict \in'flikt\ *vb* : give by or as if by
hitting — **in•flic•tion** \-'flikshən\ *n*
in•flu•ence \'inˌflüəns\ *n* **1** : power or
capacity of causing an effect in indirect or intangible ways **2** : one that
exerts influence ⁓ *vb* **-enced; -enc-
ing** : affect or alter by influence — **in-
flu•en•tial** \ˌinflü'enchəl\ *adj*
in•flu•en•za \ˌinflü'enzə\ *n* : acute
very contagious virus disease
in•flux \'inˌfləks\ *n* : a flowing in
in•form \in'fȯrm\ *vb* : give information
or knowledge to — **in•for•mant** \-ənt\
n — **in•form•er** *n*
in•for•mal \in'fȯrməl\ *adj* **1** : without
formality or ceremony **2** : for ordinary or familiar use — **in•for•mal•i•ty**
\ˌinfȯr'malətē, -fər-\ *n* — **in•for•mal-
ly** *adv*
in•for•ma•tion \ˌinfər'māshən\ *n*
: knowledge obtained from investigation, study, or instruction — **in•for-
ma•tion•al** \-shənəl\ *adj*
in•for•ma•tive \in'fȯrmətiv\ *adj* : giving knowledge
in•frac•tion \in'frakshən\ *n* : violation
in•fra•red \ˌinfrə'red\ *adj* : being, relating to, or using radiation of wavelengths longer than those of red light
— **infrared** *n*
in•fra•struc•ture \'infrəˌstrəkchər\ *n*
: foundation of a system or organization
in•fringe \in'frinj\ *vb* **-fringed; -fring-
ing** : violate another's right or privilege — **in•fringe•ment** *n*
in•fu•ri•ate \in'fyurēˌāt\ *vb* **-at•ed; -at-**

indivisibility	ineffectually	inelegance
indivisible	ineffectualness	inelegant
ineducable	inefficiency	ineligibility
ineffective	inefficient	ineligible
ineffectively	inefficiently	ineradicable
ineffectiveness	inelastic	inessential
ineffectual	inelasticity	inexact

ing : make furious — **in•fu•ri•at•ing•ly** \-ˌātiŋlē\ adv

in•fuse \in'fyüz\ vb -fused; -fus•ing 1 : instill a principle or quality in 2 : steep in liquid without boiling — **in•fu•sion** \-'fyüzhən\ n

¹**-ing** \iŋ\ vb suffix or adj suffix — used to form the present participle and sometimes an adjective resembling a present participle

²**-ing** n suffix 1 : action or process 2 : something connected with or resulting from an action or process

in•ge•nious \in'jēnyəs\ adj : very clever — **in•ge•nious•ly** adv — **in•ge•nious•ness** n

in•ge•nue, in•gé•nue \'anjə,nü, 'än-; 'aⁿzhə-, 'äⁿ-\ n : naive young woman

in•ge•nu•ity \ˌinjə'nüətē, -'nyü-\ n, pl -ities : skill or cleverness in planning or inventing

in•gen•u•ous \in'jenyəwəs\ adj : innocent and candid — **in•gen•u•ous•ly** adv — **in•gen•u•ous•ness** n

in•gest \in'jest\ vb : eat — **in•ges•tion** \-'jeschən\ n

in•gle•nook \'iŋgəl,nùk\ n : corner by the fireplace

in•got \'iŋgət\ n : block of metal

in•grained \in'grānd\ adj : deep-seated

in•grate \'in,grāt\ n : ungrateful person

in•gra•ti•ate \in'grāshē,āt\ vb -at•ed; -at•ing : gain favor for (oneself) — **in•gra•ti•at•ing** adj

in•gre•di•ent \in'grēdēənt\ n : one of the substances that make up a mixture

in•grown \'in,grōn\ adj : grown in and esp. into the flesh

in•hab•it \in'habət\ vb : live or dwell in — **in•hab•it•able** adj — **in•hab•it•ant** \-ətənt\ n

in•hale \in'hāl\ vb -haled; -hal•ing : breathe in — **in•hal•ant** \-ənt\ n — **in•ha•la•tion** \ˌinhə'lāshən, ˌinə-\ n — **in•hal•er** n

in•here \in'hir\ vb -hered; -her•ing : be inherent

in•her•ent \in'hirənt, -'her-\ adj : being an essential part of something —

in•her•ent•ly adv

in•her•it \in'herət\ vb : receive from one's ancestors — **in•her•it•able** \-'əbəl\ adj — **in•her•i•tance** \-ətəns\ n — **in•her•i•tor** \-ətər\ n

in•hib•it \in'hibət\ vb : hold in check — **in•hi•bi•tion** \ˌinhə'bishən, ˌinə-\ n

in•hu•man \in'hyümən, -'yü-\ adj : cruel or impersonal — **in•hu•man•i•ty** \-hyü'manətē, -yü-\ n — **in•hu•man•ly** adv — **in•hu•man•ness** n

in•im•i•cal \in'imikəl\ adj : hostile or harmful — **in•im•i•cal•ly** adv

in•im•i•ta•ble \in'imətəbəl\ adj : not capable of being imitated

in•iq•ui•ty \in'ikwətē\ n, pl -ties : wickedness — **in•iq•ui•tous** \-wətəs\ adj

ini•tial \in'ishəl\ adj 1 : of or relating to the beginning 2 : first ∼ n : 1st letter of a word or name ∼ vb -tialed or -tialled; -tial•ing or -tial•ling : put initials on — **ini•tial•ly** adv

ini•ti•ate \in'ishē,āt\ vb -at•ed; -at•ing 1 : start 2 : induct into membership 3 : instruct in the rudiments of something — **initiate** \-'ishēət\ n — **ini•ti•a•tion** \-ˌishē'āshən\ n — **ini•tia•to•ry** \-'ishēə,tōrē\ adj

ini•tia•tive \in'ishətiv\ n 1 : first step 2 : readiness to undertake something on one's own

in•ject \in'jekt\ vb : force or introduce into something — **in•jec•tion** \-'jekshən\ n

in•junc•tion \in'jəŋkshən\ n : court writ requiring one to do or to refrain from doing a specified act

in•jure \'injər\ vb -jured; -jur•ing : do damage, hurt, or a wrong to

in•ju•ry \'injərē\ n, pl -ries 1 : act that injures 2 : hurt, damage, or loss sustained — **in•ju•ri•ous** \in'jùrēəs\ adj

in•jus•tice \in'jəstəs\ n : unjust act

ink \'iŋk\ n : usu. liquid and colored material for writing and printing ∼ vb : put ink on — **ink•well** \-ˌwel\ n — **inky** adj

in•kling \'iŋkliŋ\ n : hint or idea

in·land \'in,land, -lənd\ *n* : interior of a country — **inland** *adj or adv*

in–law \'in,lȯ\ *n* : relative by marriage

in·lay \in'lā, 'in,lā\ *vb* **-laid** \-'lād\; **-lay·ing** : set into a surface for decoration ~ \'in,lā\ *n* **1** : inlaid work **2** : shaped filling cemented into a tooth

in·let \'in,let, -lət\ *n* : small bay

in·mate \'in,māt\ *n* : person confined to an asylum or prison

in me·mo·ri·am \,inmə'mōrēəm\ *prep* : in memory of

in·most \'in,mōst\ *adj* : deepest within

inn \'in\ *n* : hotel

in·nards \'inərdz\ *n pl* : internal parts

in·nate \in'āt\ *adj* **1** : inborn **2** : inherent — **in·nate·ly** *adv*

in·ner \'inər\ *adj* : being on the inside

in·ner·most \'inər,mōst\ *adj* : farthest inward

in·ner·sole \,inər'sōl\ *n* : insole

in·ning \'iniŋ\ *n* : baseball team's turn at bat

inn·keep·er \'in,kēpər\ *n* : owner of an inn

in·no·cent \'inəsənt\ *adj* **1** : free from guilt **2** : harmless **3** : not sophisticated — **in·no·cence** \-səns\ *n* — **innocent** *n* — **in·no·cent·ly** *adv*

in·noc·u·ous \in'äkyəwəs\ *adj* **1** : harmless **2** : inoffensive

in·no·va·tion \,inə'vāshən\ *n* : new idea or method — **in·no·vate** \'inə,vāt\ *vb* — **in·no·va·tive** \'inə,vātiv\ *adj* — **in·no·va·tor** \-,vātər\ *n*

in·nu·en·do \,inyə'wendō\ *n, pl* **-dos** *or* **-does** : insinuation

in·nu·mer·a·ble \in'ümərəbəl, -'yüm-\ *adj* : countless

in·oc·u·late \in'äkyə,lāt\ *vb* **-lat·ed**; **-lat·ing** : treat with something esp. to establish immunity — **in·oc·u·la·tion** \-,äkyə'lāshən\ *n*

in·op·por·tune \in,äpər'tün, -'tyün\ *adj* : inconvenient — **in·op·por·tune·ly** *adv*

in·or·di·nate \in'ȯrdᵊnət\ *adj* : unusual or excessive — **in·or·di·nate·ly** *adv*

in·or·gan·ic \,in,ȯr'ganik\ *adj* : made of mineral matter

in·pa·tient \'in,pāshənt\ *n* : patient who stays in a hospital

in·put \'in,pu̇t\ *n* : something put in — **input** *vb*

in·quest \'in,kwest\ *n* : inquiry esp. before a jury

in·quire \in'kwīr\ *vb* **-quired**; **-quir·ing** **1** : ask **2** : investigate — **in·quir·er** *n* — **in·quir·ing·ly** *adv* — **in·qui·ry** \'in,kwīrē, in'kwīrē; 'inkwərē, 'iŋ-\ *n*

in·qui·si·tion \,inkwə'zishən, ,iŋ-\ *n* **1** : official inquiry **2** : severe questioning — **in·quis·i·tor** \in'kwizətər\ *n* — **in·quis·i·to·ri·al** \-,kwizə-'tōrēəl\ *adj*

in·quis·i·tive \in'kwizətiv\ *adj* : curious — **in·quis·i·tive·ly** *adv* — **in·quis·i·tive·ness** *n*

in·road \'in,rōd\ *n* : encroachment

in·rush \'in,rəsh\ *n* : influx

in·sane \in'sān\ *adj* **1** : not sane **2** : absurd — **in·sane·ly** *adv* — **in·san·i·ty** \in'sanətē\ *n*

in·sa·tia·ble \in'sāshəbəl\ *adj* : incapable of being satisfied — **in·sa·tia·bil·i·ty** \in,sāshə'bilətē\ *n* — **in·sa·tia·bly** *adv*

in·scribe \in'skrīb\ *vb* **1** : write **2** : engrave **3** : dedicate (a book) to someone — **in·scrip·tion** \-'skripshən\ *n*

in·scru·ta·ble \in'skrütəbəl\ *adj* : mysterious — **in·scru·ta·bly** *adv*

in·seam \'in,sēm\ *n* : inner seam (of a garment)

in·sect \'in,sekt\ *n* : small usu. winged animal with 6 legs

in·sec·ti·cide \in'sektə,sīd\ *n* : insect poison — **in·sec·ti·cid·al** \in,sektə-'sīdᵊl\ *adj*

in·se·cure \,insi'kyu̇r\ *adj* **1** : uncertain **2** : unsafe **3** : fearful — **in·se·cure·ly** *adv* — **in·se·cu·ri·ty** \-'kyu̇rətē\ *n*

in·sem·i·nate \in'semə,nāt\ *vb* **-nat·ed**; **-nat·ing** : introduce semen into

---

— in·sem·i·na·tion \-ˌsemə'nāshən\ n

in·sen·si·ble \in'sensəbəl\ adj 1 : unconscious 2 : unable to feel 3 : unaware — in·sen·si·bil·i·ty \inˌsensə-'bilətē\ n — in·sen·si·bly adv

in·sen·tient \in'senchənt\ adj : lacking feeling — in·sen·tience \-chəns\ n

in·sert \in'sərt\ vb : put in — insert \'inˌsərt\ n — in·ser·tion \in-'sərshən\ n

in·set \'inˌset\ vb inset or in·set·ted; in·set·ting : set in — inset n

in·shore \'in'shōr\ adj 1 : situated near shore 2 : moving toward shore ~ adv : toward shore

in·side \in'sīd, 'inˌsīd\ n 1 : inner side 2 pl : innards ~ prep 1 : in or into the inside of 2 : within ~ adv 1 : on the inner side 2 : into the interior — inside adj — in·sid·er \in'sīdər\ n

inside of prep : inside

in·sid·i·ous \in'sidēəs\ adj 1 : treacherous 2 : seductive — in·sid·i·ous·ly adv — in·sid·i·ous·ness n

in·sight \'inˌsīt\ n : understanding — in·sight·ful \in'sītfəl-\ adj

in·sig·nia \in'signēə\, in·sig·ne \-ˌnē\ n, pl -nia or -ni·as : badge of authority or office

in·sin·u·ate \in'sinyəˌwāt\ vb -at·ed; -at·ing 1 : imply 2 : bring in artfully — in·sin·u·a·tion \inˌsinyə'wāshən\ n

in·sip·id \in'sipəd\ adj 1 : tasteless 2 : not stimulating — in·si·pid·i·ty \ˌinsə'pidətē\ n

in·sist \in'sist\ vb : be firmly demanding — in·sis·tence \in'sistəns\ n — in·sis·tent \-tənt\ adj — in·sis·tent·ly adv

insofar as \ˌinsō'färaz\ conj : to the extent that

in·sole \'inˌsōl\ n : inside sole of a shoe

in·so·lent \'insələnt\ adj : contemptuously rude — in·so·lence \-ləns\ n

in·sol·vent \in'sälvənt\ adj : unable or insufficient to pay debts — in·sol·ven·cy \-vənsē\ n

in·som·nia \in'sämnēə\ n : inability to sleep — in·som·ni·ac \-nē-ˌak\ n

in·so·much as \ˌinsō'məchaz\ conj : inasmuch as

insomuch that conj : to such a degree that

in·sou·ci·ance \in'süsēəns, aⁿsü'syäⁿs\ n : lighthearted indifference — in·sou·ci·ant \in'süsēənt, aⁿsü'syäⁿ\ adj

in·spect \in'spekt\ vb : view closely and critically — in·spec·tion \-'spekshən\ n — in·spec·tor \-tər\ n

in·spire \in'spīr\ vb -spired; -spir·ing 1 : inhale 2 : influence by example 3 : bring about 4 : stir to action — in·spi·ra·tion \ˌinspə'rāshən\ n — in·spi·ra·tion·al \-'rāshənəl\ adj — in·spir·er n

in·stall, in·stal \in'stòl\ vb -stalled; -stall·ing 1 : induct into office 2 : set up for use — in·stal·la·tion \ˌinstə-'lāshən\ n

in·stall·ment \in'stòlmənt\ n : partial payment

in·stance \'instəns\ n 1 : request or instigation 2 : example

in·stant \'instənt\ n : moment ~ adj 1 : immediate 2 : ready to mix — in·stan·ta·neous \ˌinstən'tānēəs\ adj — in·stan·ta·neous·ly adv — in·stant·ly adv

in·stead \in'sted\ adv : as a substitute or alternative

instead of prep : as a substitute for or alternative to

in·step \'inˌstep\ n : part of the foot in front of the ankle

in·sti·gate \'instəˌgāt\ vb -gat·ed; -gat·ing : incite — in·sti·ga·tion \ˌinstə'gāshən\ n — in·sti·ga·tor \'instəˌgātər\ n

in·still \in'stil\ vb -stilled; -still·ing : impart gradually

in·stinct \'inˌstiŋkt\ n 1 : natural talent 2 : natural inherited or subconsciously motivated behavior — in·stinc·tive \in'stiŋktiv\ adj — in·stinc·tive·ly adv — in·stinc·tu·al \in'stiŋkchəwəl\ adj

in·sti·tute \'instəˌtüt, -ˌtyüt\ vb -tuted; -tut·ing : establish, start, or organize ~ n 1 : organization promoting a cause 2 : school

in·sti·tu·tion \ˌinstə'tüshən, -'tyü-\ n 1 : act of instituting 2 : custom 3 : corporation or society of a public character — in·sti·tu·tion·al \-shənəl\ adj — in·sti·tu·tion·al·ize \-ˌīz\ vb — in·sti·tu·tion·al·ly adv

in·struct \in'strəkt\ vb 1 : teach 2 : give an order to — in·struc·tion \in'strəkshən\ n — in·struc·tion·al \-shənəl\ adj — in·struc·tive \in-'strəktiv\ adj — in·struc·tor \in-'strəktər\ n — in·struc·tor·ship \-ˌship\ n

in·stru·ment \'instrəmənt\ n 1 : something that produces music 2 : means 3 : device for doing work and esp. precision work 4 : legal document — in·stru·men·tal \ˌinstrə-'mentºl\ adj — in·stru·men·tal·ist \-ist\ n — in·stru·men·tal·i·ty \ˌinstrəmən'talətē, -ˌmen-\ n — in·stru·men·ta·tion \ˌinstrəmən'tā-shən, -ˌmen-\ n

in·sub·or·di·nate \ˌinsə'bord°nət\ adj : not obeying — in·sub·or·di·na·tion \-ˌbord°n'āshən\ n

in·suf·fer·able \in'səfərəbəl\ adj : unbearable — in·suf·fer·ably \-blē\ adv

in·su·lar \'insülər, -syü-\ adj 1 : relating to or residing on an island 2 : narrow-minded — in·su·lar·i·ty \ˌinsü'larətē, -syü-\ n

in·su·late \'insəˌlāt\ vb -lat·ed; -lat·ing : protect from heat loss or electricity — in·su·la·tion \ˌinsə'lāshən\ n — in·su·la·tor \'insəˌlātər\ n

in·su·lin \'insələn\ n : hormone used by diabetics

in·sult \in'səlt\ vb : treat with contempt ~ \'inˌsəlt\ n : insulting act or remark — in·sult·ing·ly \-iŋlē\ adv

in·su·per·a·ble \in'süpərəbəl\ adj : too difficult — in·su·per·a·bly \-blē\ adv

in·sure \in'shùr\ vb -sured; -sur·ing 1 : guarantee against loss 2 : make certain — in·sur·able \-əbəl\ adj — in·sur·ance \-əns\ n — in·sured \in'shùrd\ n — in·sur·er n

in·sur·gent \in'sərjənt\ n : rebel — in·sur·gence \-jəns\ n — in·sur·gen·cy \-jənsē\ n — in·sur·gent adj

in·sur·mount·able \ˌinsər'maùntəbəl\ adj : too great to be overcome — in·sur·mount·ably \-blē\ adv

in·sur·rec·tion \ˌinsə'rekshən\ n : revolution — in·sur·rec·tion·ist n

in·tact \in'takt\ adj : undamaged

in·take \'inˌtāk\ n 1 : opening through which something enters 2 : act of taking in 3 : amount taken in

in·te·ger \'intijər\ n : number that is not a fraction and does not include a fraction

in·te·gral \'intigrəl\ adj : essential

in·te·grate \'intəˌgrāt\ vb -grat·ed; -grat·ing 1 : unite 2 : end segregation of or at — in·te·gra·tion \ˌintə-'grāshən\ n

in·teg·ri·ty \in'tegrətē\ n 1 : soundness 2 : adherence to a code of values 3 : completeness

in·tel·lect \'intºlˌekt\ n : power of knowing or thinking — in·tel·lec·tu·al \ˌintºl'ekchəwəl\ adj or n — in·tel·lec·tu·al·ism \-chəwəˌlizəm\ n — in·tel·lec·tu·al·ly adv

in·tel·li·gence \in'teləjəns\ n 1 : ability to learn and understand 2 : mental acuteness 3 : information

in·tel·li·gent \in'teləjənt\ adj : having or showing intelligence — in·tel·li·gent·ly adv

in·tel·li·gi·ble \in'teləjəbəl\ adj : understandable — in·tel·li·gi·bil·i·ty \-ˌtel-əjə'bilətē\ n — in·tel·li·gi·bly adv

in·tem·per·ance \in'tempərəns\ n : lack of moderation — in·tem·per·ate \-pərət\ adj — in·tem·per·ate·ness n

in·tend \in'tend\ vb : have as a purpose

in·tend·ed \-'tendəd\ n : engaged person — intended adj

in·tense \in'tens\ adj 1 : extreme 2 : deeply felt — in·tense·ly adv — in·ten·si·fi·ca·tion \-ˌtensəfə'kāshən\ n — in·ten·si·fy \-'tensəˌfī\ vb — in·ten·si·ty \in'tensətē\ n — in·ten·sive \in'tensiv\ adj — in·ten·sive·ly adv

¹in·tent \in'tent\ n : purpose — in·ten·tion \-'tenchən\ n — in·ten·tion·al \-'tenchənəl\ adj — in·ten·tion·al·ly adv

²intent adj : concentrated — in·tent·ly adv — in·tent·ness n

in·ter \in'tər\ vb -rr- : bury

inviable
invisibility
invisible

invisibly
involuntarily
involuntary

invulnerability
invulnerable
invulnerably

inter- *prefix* : between or among

in·ter·ac·tion \ˌintər'akshən\ *n* : mutual influence — **in·ter·act** \-'akt\ *vb* — **in·ter·ac·tive** *adj*

in·ter·breed \ˌintər'brēd\ *vb* -bred \-'bred\; -breed·ing : breed together

in·ter·ca·late \in'tərkə,lāt\ *vb* -lat·ed; -lat·ing : insert — **in·ter·ca·la·tion** \-ˌtərkə'lāshən\ *n*

in·ter·cede \ˌintər'sēd\ *vb* -ced·ed; -ced·ing : act to reconcile — **in·ter·ces·sion** \-'seshən\ *n* — **in·ter·ces·sor** \-'sesər\ *n*

in·ter·cept \ˌintər'sept\ *vb* : interrupt the progress of — **intercept** \'intərˌsept\ *n* — **in·ter·cep·tion** \ˌintər'sepshən\ *n* — **in·ter·cep·tor** \-'septər\ *n*

in·ter·change \ˌintər'chānj\ *vb* 1 : exchange 2 : change places ~ \'intərˌchānj\ *n* 1 : exchange 2 : junction of highways — **in·ter·change·able** \ˌintər'chānjəbəl\ *adj*

in·ter·course \'intərˌkōrs\ *n* 1 : relations between persons or nations 2 : copulation

in·ter·de·pen·dent \ˌintərdi'pendənt\ *adj* : mutually dependent — **in·ter·de·pen·dence** \-dəns\ *n*

in·ter·dict \ˌintər'dikt\ *vb* 1 : prohibit 2 : destroy or cut (an enemy supply line) — **in·ter·dic·tion** \-'dikshən\ *n*

in·ter·est \'intrəst, -təˌrest\ *n* 1 : right 2 : benefit 3 : charge for borrowed money 4 : readiness to pay special attention 5 : quality that causes interest ~ *vb* 1 : concern 2 : get the attention of — **in·ter·est·ing** *adj* — **in·ter·est·ing·ly** *adv*

in·ter·face \'intərˌfās\ *n* : common boundary — **in·ter·fa·cial** \ˌintər'fāshəl\ *adj*

in·ter·fere \ˌintər'fir\ *vb* -fered; -fer·ing 1 : collide or be in opposition 2

: try to run the affairs of others — **in·ter·fer·ence** \-'firəns\ *n*

in·ter·im \'intərəm\ *n* : time between — **interim** *adj*

in·te·ri·or \in'tirēər\ *adj* : being on the inside ~ *n* 1 : inside 2 : inland area

in·ter·ject \ˌintər'jekt\ *vb* : stick in between

in·ter·jec·tion \-'jekshən\ *n* : an exclamatory word — **in·ter·jec·tion·al·ly** \-shənəlē\ *adv*

in·ter·lace \ˌintər'lās\ *vb* : cross or cause to cross one over another

in·ter·lin·ear \ˌintər'linēər\ *adj* : between written or printed lines

in·ter·lock \ˌintər'läk\ *vb* 1 : interlace 2 : connect for mutual effect — **inter·lock** \'intərˌläk\ *n*

in·ter·lop·er \ˌintər'lōpər\ *n* : intruder or meddler

in·ter·lude \'intərˌlüd\ *n* : intervening period

in·ter·mar·ry \ˌintər'marē\ *vb* 1 : marry each other 2 : marry within a group — **in·ter·mar·riage** \-'marij\ *n*

in·ter·me·di·ary \ˌintər'mēdē,erē\ *n*, *pl* -ar·ies : agent between individuals or groups — **intermediary** *adj*

in·ter·me·di·ate \ˌintər'mēdēət\ *adj* : between extremes — **intermediate** *n*

in·ter·ment \in'tərmənt\ *n* : burial

in·ter·mi·na·ble \in'tərmənəbəl\ *adj* : endless — **in·ter·mi·na·bly** *adv*

in·ter·min·gle \ˌintər'miŋgəl\ *vb* : mingle

in·ter·mis·sion \ˌintər'mishən\ *n* : break in a performance

in·ter·mit·tent \-'mit³nt\ *adj* : coming at intervals — **in·ter·mit·tent·ly** *adv*

in·ter·mix \ˌintər'miks\ *vb* : mix together — **in·ter·mix·ture** \-'mikschər\ *n*

¹in·tern \'in,tərn, in'tərn\ *vb* : confine esp. during a war — **in·tern·ee** \ˌin,tər'nē\ *n* — **in·tern·ment** *n*

List of self-explanatory words with the prefix *inter-*

interagency	intercommunal	interfaculty
interatomic	intercommunity	interfamily
interbank	intercompany	interfiber
interborough	intercontinental	interfraternity
intercampus	intercounty	intergalactic
interchurch	intercultural	intergang
intercity	interdenominational	intergovernmental
interclass	interdepartmental	intergroup
intercoastal	interdivisional	interhemispheric
intercollegiate	interelectronic	interindustry
intercolonial	interethnic	interinstitutional

²**in•tern** \'in₁tərn\ *n* : advanced student (as in medicine) gaining supervised experience ～ *vb* : act as an intern — **in•tern•ship** *n*

in•ter•nal \in'tərn°l\ *adj* **1** : inward **2** : inside of the body **3** : relating to or existing in the mind — **in•ter•nal•ly** *adv*

in•ter•na•tion•al \₁intər'nashənəl\ *adj* : affecting 2 or more nations ～ *n* : something having international scope — **in•ter•na•tion•al•ism** \-₁izəm\ *n* — **in•ter•na•tion•al•ize** \-₁iz\ *vb* — **in•ter•na•tion•al•ly** *adv*

In•ter•net \'intər₁net\ *n* : network that connects computer networks worldwide

in•ter•nist \'in₁tərnist\ *n* : specialist in nonsurgical medicine

in•ter•play \'intər₁plā\ *n* : interaction

in•ter•po•late \in'tərpə₁lāt\ *vb* **-lat•ed**; **-lat•ing** : insert — **in•ter•po•la•tion** \-₁tərpə'lāshən\ *n*

in•ter•pose \₁intər'pōz\ *vb* **-posed**; **-pos•ing** **1** : place between **2** : intrude — **in•ter•po•si•tion** \-pə'zishən\ *n*

in•ter•pret \in'tərprət\ *vb* : explain the meaning of — **in•ter•pre•ta•tion** \in₁tərprə'tāshən\ *n* — **in•ter•pre•ta•tive** \-'tərprə₁tātiv\ *adj* — **in•ter•pret•er** *n* — **in•ter•pre•tive** \-'tərprətiv\ *adj*

in•ter•re•late \₁intəri'lāt\ *vb* : have a mutual relationship — **in•ter•re•lat•ed•ness** \-'lātədnəs\ *n* — **in•ter•re•la•tion** \-'lāshən\ *n* — **in•ter•re•la•tion•ship** *n*

in•ter•ro•gate \in'terə₁gāt\ *vb* **-gat•ed**; **-gat•ing** : question — **in•ter•ro•ga•tion** \-₁terə'gāshən\ *n* — **in•ter•rog•a•tive** \₁intə'rägətiv\ *adj or n* — **in•ter•ro•ga•tor** \-'terə₁gātər\ *n* — **in•ter•rog•a•to•ry** \₁intə'rägə₁tōrē\ *adj*

in•ter•rupt \₁intə'rəpt\ *vb* : intrude so as to hinder or end continuity — **in•ter-**

rupt•er *n* — **in•ter•rup•tion** \-'rəpshən\ *n* — **in•ter•rup•tive** \-'rəptiv\ *adv*

in•ter•sect \₁intər'sekt\ *vb* **1** : cut across or divide **2** : cross — **in•ter•sec•tion** \-'sekshən\ *n*

in•ter•sperse \₁intər'spərs\ *vb* **-spersed**; **-spers•ing** : insert at intervals — **in•ter•per•sion** \-'spərzhən\ *n*

in•ter•stice \in'tərstəs\ *n, pl* **-stic•es** \-stə₁sēz, -stəsəz\ : space between — **in•ter•sti•tial** \₁intər'stishəl\ *adj*

in•ter•twine \₁intər'twīn\ *vb* : twist together — **in•ter•twine•ment** *n*

in•ter•val \'intərvəl\ *n* **1** : time between **2** : space between

in•ter•vene \₁intər'vēn\ *vb* **-vened**; **-ven•ing** **1** : happen between events **2** : intercede — **in•ter•ven•tion** \-'venchən\ *n*

in•ter•view \'intər₁vyü\ *n* : a meeting to get information — **interview** *vb* — **in•ter•view•er** *n*

in•ter•weave \₁intər'wēv\ *vb* **-wove** \-'wōv\; **-wo•ven** \-'wōvən\; **-weav•ing** : weave together — **in•ter•wo•ven** \-'wōvən\ *adj*

in•tes•tate \in'tes₁tāt, -tət\ *adj* : not leaving a will

in•tes•tine \in'testən\ *n* : tubular part of the digestive system after the stomach including a long narrow upper part (**small intestine**) followed by a broader shorter lower part (**large intestine**) — **in•tes•ti•nal** \-tən°l\ *adj*

in•ti•mate \'intə₁māt\ *vb* **-mat•ed**; **-mat•ing** : hint ～ \'intəmət\ *adj* **1** : very friendly **2** : suggesting privacy **3** : very personal ～ *n* : close friend — **in•ti•ma•cy** \'intəməsē\ *n* — **in•ti•mate•ly** *adv* — **in•ti•ma•tion** \₁intə-'māshən\ *n*

in•tim•i•date \in'timə₁dāt\ *vb* **-dat•ed**;

---

interisland	interprovincial	intertribal
interlibrary	interracial	intertroop
intermolecular	interregional	intertropical
intermountain	interreligious	interuniversity
interoceanic	interscholastic	interurban
interoffice	intersectional	intervalley
interparticle	interstate	intervillage
interparty	interstellar	interwar
interpersonal	intersystem	interzonal
interplanetary	interterm	interzone
interpopulation	interterminal	

-dat•ing : make fearful — **in•tim•i•da•tion** \-ˌtiməˈdāshən\ n

in•to \ˈintü\ prep 1 : to the inside of 2 : to the condition of 3 : against

in•to•na•tion \ˌintōˈnāshən\ n : way of singing or speaking

in•tone \inˈtōn\ vb -toned; -ton•ing : chant

in•tox•i•cate \inˈtäkəˌkāt\ vb -cat•ed; -cat•ing : make drunk — **in•tox•i•cant** \-sikənt\ n or adj — **in•tox•i•ca•tion** \-ˌtäkəˈkāshən\ n

in•tra•mu•ral \ˌintrəˈmyürəl\ adj : within a school

in•tran•si•gent \inˈtransəjənt\ adj : uncompromising — **in•tran•si•gence** \-jəns\ n — **intransigent** n

in•tra•ve•nous \ˌintrəˈvēnəs\ adj : by way of the veins — **in•tra•ve•nous•ly** adv

in•trep•id \inˈtrepəd\ adj : fearless — **in•tre•pid•i•ty** \ˌintrəˈpidətē\ n

in•tri•cate \ˈintrikət\ adj : very complex and delicate — **in•tri•ca•cy** \-trikəsē\ n — **in•tri•cate•ly** adv

in•trigue \inˈtrēg\ vb -trigued; -trigu•ing 1 : scheme 2 : arouse curiosity of ~ n : secret scheme — **in•trigu•ing•ly** \-iŋlē\ adv

in•trin•sic \inˈtrinzik, -sik\ adj : essential — **in•trin•si•cal•ly** \-ziklē, -si-\ adv

in•tro•duce \ˌintrəˈdüs, -ˈdyüs\ vb -duced; -duc•ing 1 : bring in esp. for the 1st time 2 : cause to be acquainted 3 : bring to notice 4 : put in — **in•tro•duc•tion** \ˈdəkshən\ n — **in•tro•duc•to•ry** \-ˈdəktərē\ adj

in•tro•spec•tion \ˌintrəˈspekshən\ n : examination of one's own thoughts or feelings — **in•tro•spec•tive** \-ˈspektiv\ adj — **in•tro•spec•tive•ly** adv

in•tro•vert \ˈintrəˌvərt\ n : shy or reserved person — **in•tro•ver•sion** \ˌintrəˈvərzhən\ n — **introvert** adj — **in•tro•vert•ed** \ˈintrəˌvərtəd\ adj

in•trude \inˈtrüd\ vb -trud•ed; -trud•ing 1 : thrust in 2 : encroach — **in•trud•er** n — **in•tru•sion** \-ˈtrüzhən\ n — **in•tru•sive** \-ˈtrüsiv\ adj — **in•tru•sive•ness** n

in•tu•i•tion \ˌintüˈishən, -tyü-\ n : quick and ready insight — **in•tu•it** \inˈtüət, -ˈtyü-\ vb — **in•tu•i•tive** \-ətiv\ adj — **in•tu•i•tive•ly** adv

in•un•date \ˈinənˌdāt\ vb -dat•ed; -dat-ing : flood — **in•un•da•tion** \ˌinənˈdāshən\ n

in•ure \inˈür, -ˈyür\ vb -ured; -ur•ing : accustom to accept something undesirable

in•vade \inˈvād\ vb -vad•ed; -vad•ing : enter for conquest — **in•vad•er** n — **in•va•sion** \-ˈvāzhən\ n

[1]**in•val•id** \inˈvaləd\ adj : not true or legal — **in•va•lid•i•ty** \ˌinvəˈlidətē\ n — **in•val•id•ly** adv

[2]**in•va•lid** \ˈinvaləd\ adj : sickly ~ n : one chronically ill

in•val•i•date \inˈvaləˌdāt\ vb : make invalid — **in•val•i•da•tion** \inˌvalə-ˈdāshən\ n

in•valu•able \inˈvalyəwəbəl\ adj : extremely valuable

in•va•sive \inˈvāsiv\ adj : involving entry into the body

in•vec•tive \inˈvektiv\ n : abusive language — **invective** adj

in•veigh \inˈvā\ vb : protest or complain forcefully

in•vei•gle \inˈvāgəl, -ˈvē-\ vb -gled; -gling : win over or get by flattery

in•vent \inˈvent\ vb 1 : think up 2 : create for the 1st time — **in•ven•tion** \-ˈvenchən\ n — **in•ven•tive** \-ˈventiv\ adj — **in•ven•tive•ness** n — **in•ven•tor** \-ˈventər\ n

in•ven•to•ry \ˈinvənˌtōrē\ n, pl -ries 1 : list of goods 2 : stock — **inventory** vb

in•verse \inˈvərs, ˈinˌvərs\ adj or n : opposite — **in•verse•ly** adv

in•vert \inˈvərt\ vb 1 : turn upside down or inside out 2 : reverse — **in•ver•sion** \-ˈvərzhən\ n

in•ver•te•brate \inˈvərtəbrət, -ˌbrāt\ adj : lacking a backbone ~ n : invertebrate animal

in•vest \inˈvest\ vb 1 : give power or authority to 2 : endow with a quality 3 : commit money to someone else's use in hope of profit — **in•vest•ment** \-mənt\ n — **in•ves•tor** \-ˈvestər\ n

in•ves•ti•gate \inˈvestəˌgāt\ vb -gat•ed; -gat•ing : study closely and systematically — **in•ves•ti•ga•tion** \-ˌvestə-ˈgāshən\ n — **in•ves•ti•ga•tive** \-ˈvestəˌgātiv\ adj — **in•ves•ti•ga•tor** \-ˈvestəˌgātər\ n

in•ves•ti•ture \inˈvestəˌchùr, -chər\ n : act of establishing in office

in•vet•er•ate \inˈvetərət\ adj : acting out of habit

in·vid·i·ous \in'vidēəs\ *adj* : harmful or obnoxious — **in·vid·i·ous·ly** *adv*

in·vig·o·rate \in'vigə‚rāt\ *vb* **-rat·ed; -rat·ing** : give life and energy to — **in·vig·o·ra·tion** \-‚vigə'rāshən\ *n*

in·vin·ci·ble \in'vinsəbəl\ *adj* : incapable of being conquered — **in·vin·ci·bil·i·ty** \in‚vinsə'bilətē\ *n* — **in·vin·ci·bly** \in'vinsəblē\ *adv*

in·vi·o·la·ble \in'vīələbəl\ *adj* : safe from violation or desecration — **in·vi·o·la·bil·i·ty** \in‚vīələ'bilətē\ *n*

in·vi·o·late \in'vīələt\ *adj* : not violated or profaned

in·vite \in'vīt\ *vb* **-vit·ed; -vit·ing** **1** : entice **2** : increase the likelihood of **3** : request the presence or participation of **4** : encourage — **in·vi·ta·tion** \‚invə'tāshən\ *n* — **in·vit·ing** \in'vītiŋ\ *adj*

in·vo·ca·tion \‚invə'kāshən\ *n* **1** : prayer **2** : incantation

in·voice \'in‚vois\ *n* : itemized bill for goods shipped ~ *vb* **-voiced; -voic·ing** : bill

in·voke \in'vōk\ *vb* **-voked; -vok·ing** **1** : call on for help **2** : cite as authority **3** : conjure **4** : carry out

in·volve \in'välv\ *vb* **-volved; -volv·ing** **1** : draw in as a participant **2** : relate closely **3** : require as a necessary part **4** : occupy fully — **in·volve·ment** *n*

in·volved \-'välvd\ *adj* : intricate

¹in·ward \'inwərd\ *adj* : inside

²inward, in·wards \-wərdz\ *adv* : toward the inside, center, or inner being

in·ward·ly *adv* **1** : mentally or spiritually **2** : internally **3** : to oneself

io·dide \'īə‚dīd\ *n* : compound of iodine

io·dine \'īə‚dīn, -əd°n\ *n* **1** : nonmetallic chemical element **2** : solution of iodine used as an antiseptic

io·dize \'īə‚dīz\ *vb* **-dized; -diz·ing** : treat with iodine or an iodide

ion \īən, 'ī‚än\ *n* : electrically charged particle — **ion·ic** \īänik\ *adj* — **ion·iz·able** \'īə‚nīzəbəl\ *adj* — **ion·iza·tion** \‚īənə'zāshən\ *n* — **ion·ize** \'īə‚nīz\ *vb* — **ion·iz·er** \'īə‚nīzər\ *n*

-ion *n suffix* **1** : act or process **2** : state or condition

ion·o·sphere \ī'änə‚sfir\ *n* : layer of the upper atmosphere containing ionized gases — **ion·o·spher·ic** \ī‚änə-'sfirik, -'sfer-\ *adj*

io·ta \ī'ōtə\ *n* : small quantity

IOU \‚ī‚ō'yü\ *n* : acknowledgment of a debt

IRA \‚ī‚är'ā\ *n* : individual retirement savings account

iras·ci·ble \ir'asəbəl, ī'ras-\ *adj* : marked by hot temper — **iras·ci·bil·i·ty** \-‚asə'bilətē, -‚ras-\ *n*

irate \ī'rāt\ *adj* : roused to intense anger — **irate·ly** *adv*

ire \'īr\ *n* : anger

ir·i·des·cence \‚irə'des°ns\ *n* : rainbowlike play of colors — **ir·i·des·cent** \-°nt\ *adj*

iris \'īrəs\ *n, pl* **iris·es** *or* **iri·des** \'īrə‚dēz, 'ir-\ **1** : colored part around the pupil of the eye **2** : plant with long leaves and large showy flowers

irk \'ərk\ *vb* : annoy — **irk·some** \-əm\ *adj* — **irk·some·ly** *adv*

iron \'īərn\ *n* **1** : heavy metallic chemical element **2** : something made of iron **3** : heated device for pressing clothes **4** : hardness, determination ~ *vb* : press or smooth out with an iron — **iron·ware** *n* — **iron·work** *n* — **iron·work·er** *n* — **iron·works** *n pl*

iron·clad \-'klad\ *adj* **1** : sheathed in iron armor **2** : strict or exacting

iron·ing \'īərniŋ\ *n* : clothes to be ironed

iron·wood \-‚wùd\ *n* : tree or shrub with very hard wood or this wood

iro·ny \'īrənē\ *n, pl* **-nies** **1** : use of words to express the opposite of the literal meaning **2** : incongruity between the actual and expected result of events — **iron·ic** \ī'ränik\, **iron·i·cal** \-ikəl\ *adj* — **iron·i·cal·ly** \-iklē\ *adv*

ir·ra·di·ate \ir'ādē‚āt\ *vb* **-at·ed; -at·ing** : treat with radiation — **ir·ra·di·a·tion** \-‚ādē'āshən\ *n*

ir·ra·tio·nal \ir'ashənəl\ *adj* **1** : incapable of reasoning **2** : not based on reason — **ir·ra·tio·nal·i·ty** \ir‚ashə-'nalətē\ *n* — **ir·ra·tio·nal·ly** *adv*

ir·rec·on·cil·able \ir‚ekən'sīləbəl\ *adj* : impossible to reconcile — **ir·rec·on·cil·abil·i·ty** \-‚sīlə'bilətē\ *n*

ir·re·cov·er·able \‚iri'kəvərəbəl\ *adj* : not capable of being recovered — **ir·re·cov·er·ably** \-blē\ *adv*

ir·re·deem·able \‚iri'dēməbəl\ *adj* : not redeemable

ir·re·duc·ible \‚iri'düsəbəl, -'dyü-\ *adj* : not reducible — **ir·re·duc·ibly** \-blē\ *adv* ir·re·fut·able \,iri'fyütəbəl, ir'refyət-\ adj : impossible to refute

ir·reg·u·lar \ir'egyələr\ adj : not regular or normal — **irregular** n — **ir·reg·u·lar·i·ty** \ir,egyə'larətē\ n — **ir·reg·u·lar·ly** adv

ir·rel·e·vant \ir'eləvənt\ adj : not relevant — **ir·rel·e·vance** \-vəns\ n

ir·re·li·gious \,iri'lijəs\ adj : not following religious practices

ir·rep·a·ra·ble \ir'epərəbəl\ adj : impossible to make good, undo, or remedy

ir·re·place·able \,iri'plāsəbəl\ adj : not replaceable

ir·re·press·ible \-'presəbəl\ adj : impossible to repress or control

ir·re·proach·able \-'prōchəbəl\ adj : blameless

ir·re·sist·ible \-'zistəbəl\ adj : impossible to successfully resist — **ir·re·sist·ibly** \-blē\ adv

ir·res·o·lute \ir'ezəlüt\ adj : uncertain — **ir·res·o·lute·ly** adv — **ir·res·o·lu·tion** \-,ezə'lüshən\ n

ir·re·spec·tive of \,iri'spektiv-\ prep : without regard to

ir·re·spon·si·ble \,iri'spänsəbəl\ adj : not responsible — **ir·re·spon·si·bil·i·ty** \-,spänsə'bilətē\ n — **ir·re·spon·si·bly** adv

ir·re·triev·able \,iri'trēvəbəl\ adj : not retrievable

ir·rev·er·ence \ir'evərəns\ n 1 : lack of reverence 2 : irreverent act or utterance — **ir·rev·er·ent** \-rənt\ adj

ir·re·vers·ible \,iri'vsərəbəl\ adj : incapable of being reversed

ir·rev·o·ca·ble \ir'evəkəbəl\ adj : incapable of being revoked — **ir·rev·o·ca·bly** \-blē\ adv

ir·ri·gate \'irə,gāt\ vb -gat·ed; -gat·ing : supply with water by artificial means — **ir·ri·ga·tion** \,irə'gāshən\ n

ir·ri·tate \'irə,tāt\ vb -tat·ed; -tat·ing 1 : excite to anger 2 : make sore or inflamed — **ir·ri·ta·bil·i·ty** \,irətə-'bilətē\ n — **ir·ri·ta·ble** \'irətəbəl\ adj — **ir·ri·ta·bly** \'irətəblē\ adv — **ir·ri·tant** \'irətənt\ adj or n — **ir·ri·tat·ing·ly** adv — **ir·ri·ta·tion** \,irə'tā·shən\ n

is pres 3d sing of BE

-ish \ish\ adj suffix 1 : characteristic of 2 : somewhat

Is·lam \is'läm, iz-, -'läm\ n : religious faith of Muslims — **Is·lam·ic** \-ik\ adj

is·land \'īlənd\ n : body of land surrounded by water — **is·land·er** \'īləndər\ n

isle \'īl\ n : small island

is·let \'īlət\ n : small island

-ism \,izəm\ n suffix 1 : act or practice 2 : characteristic manner 3 : condition 4 : doctrine

iso·late \'īsə,lāt\ vb -lat·ed; -lat·ing : place or keep by itself — **iso·la·tion** \,īsə'lāshən\ n

iso·met·rics \,īsə'metriks\ n sing or pl : exercise against unmoving resistance — **isometric** adj

isos·ce·les \ī'säsə,lēz\ adj : having 2 equal sides

iso·tope \'īsə,tōp\ n : species of atom of a chemical element — **iso·to·pic** \,īsə'täpik, -'tō-\ adj

is·sue \'ishü\ vb -sued; -su·ing 1 : go, come, or flow out 2 : descend from a specified ancestor 3 : emanate or result 4 : put forth or distribute officially ~ n 1 : action of issuing 2 : offspring 3 : result 4 : point of controversy 5 : act of giving out or printing 6 : quantity given out or printed — **is·su·ance** \'ishəwəns\ n — **is·su·er** n

-ist \ist\ n suffix 1 : one that does 2 : one that plays 3 : one that specializes in 4 : follower of a doctrine

isth·mus \'isməs\ n : narrow strip of land connecting 2 larger portions

it \'it\ pron 1 : that one — used of a lifeless thing or an abstract entity 2 — used as an anticipatory subject or object ~ n : player who tries to catch others (as in a game of tag)

ital·ic \ə'talik, i-, ī-\ n : style of type with slanting letters — **italic** adj — **ital·i·ci·za·tion** \ə,taləsə'zāshən, i-, ī-\ n — **ital·i·cize** \ə'talə,sīz, i-, ī-\ vb

itch \'ich\ n 1 : uneasy irritating skin sensation 2 : skin disorder 3 : persistent desire — **itch** vb — **itchy** adj

item \'ītəm\ n 1 : particular in a list, account, or series 2 : piece of news — **item·iza·tion** \,ītəmə'zāshən\ n — **item·ize** \'ītə,mīz\ vb

itin·er·ant \ī'tinərənt, ə-\ adj : traveling from place to place

itin·er·ary \ī'tinə,rerē, ə-\ n, pl -ar·ies : route or outline of a journey

its \'its\ adj : relating to it

it·self \it'self\ pron : it — used reflexively or for emphasis

-ity \ətē\ *n suffix* : quality, state, or degree

-ive \iv\ *adj suffix* : that performs or tends toward an action

ivo•ry \'īvərē\ *n, pl* **-ries** **1** : hard creamy-white material of elephants' tusks **2** : pale yellow color

ivy \'īvē\ *n, pl* **ivies** : trailing woody vine with evergreen leaves

-ize \ˌīz\ *vb suffix* **1** : cause to be, become, or resemble **2** : subject to an action **3** : treat or combine with **4** : engage in an activity

J

j \'jā\ *n, pl* **j's** *or* **js** \'jāz\ : 10th letter of the alphabet

jab \'jab\ *vb* **-bb-** : thrust quickly or abruptly ⁓ *n* : short straight punch

jab•ber \'jabər\ *vb* : talk rapidly or unintelligibly — **jabber** *n*

jack \'jak\ *n* **1** : mechanical device to raise a heavy body **2** : small flag **3** : small 6-pointed metal object used in a game (**jacks**) **4** : electrical socket ⁓ *vb* **1** : raise with a jack **2** : increase

jack•al \'jakəl, -ˌȯl\ *n* : wild dog

jack•ass *n* **1** : male ass **2** : stupid person

jack•et \'jakət\ *n* : garment for the upper body

jack•ham•mer \'jakˌhamər\ *n* : pneumatic tool for drilling

jack•knife \'jakˌnīf\ *n* : pocketknife ⁓ *vb* : fold like a jackknife

jack-o'-lan•tern \'jakəˌlantərn\ *n* : lantern made of a carved pumpkin

jack•pot \'jakˌpät\ *n* : sum of money won

jack•rab•bit \-ˌrabət\ *n* : large hare of western No. America

jade \'jād\ *n* : usu. green gemstone

jad•ed \'jādəd\ *adj* : dulled or bored by having too much

jag•ged \'jagəd\ *adj* : sharply notched

jag•uar \'jagˌwär, 'jagyə-\ *n* : black-spotted tropical American cat

jai alai \'hīˌlī\ *n* : game with a ball propelled by a basket on the hand

jail \'jāl\ *n* : prison — **jail** *vb* — **jailbreak** *n* — **jail•er, jail•or** *n*

ja•la•pe•ño \ˌhäləˈpänˌyō, -ˌpēnō\ *n* : Mexican hot pepper

ja•lopy \jəˈläpē\ *n, pl* **-lopies** : dilapidated vehicle

jal•ou•sie \'jaləsē\ *n* : door or window with louvers

jam \'jam\ *vb* **-mm-** **1** : press into a tight position **2** : cause to become wedged and unworkable ⁓ *n* **1** : crowded mass that blocks or impedes **2** : difficult situation **3** : thick sweet food made of cooked fruit

jamb \'jam\ *n* : upright framing piece of a door

jam•bo•ree \ˌjambəˈrē\ *n* : large festive gathering

jan•gle \'jaŋgəl\ *vb* **-gled; -gling** : make a harsh ringing sound — **jangle** *n*

jan•i•tor \'janətər\ *n* : person who has the care of a building — **jan•i•to•ri•al** \ˌjanəˈtōrēəl\ *adj*

Jan•u•ary \'janyəˌwerē\ *n* : 1st month of the year having 31 days

¹jar \'jär\ *vb* **-rr-** **1** : have a harsh or disagreeable effect **2** : vibrate or shake ⁓ *n* **1** : jolt **2** : painful effect

²jar *n* : wide-mouthed container

jar•gon \'järgən, -ˌgän\ *n* : special vocabulary of a group

jas•mine \'jazmən\ *n* : climbing shrub with fragrant flowers

jas•per \'jaspər\ *n* : red, yellow, or brown opaque quartz

jaun•dice \'jȯndəs\ *n* : yellowish discoloration of skin, tissues, and body fluids

jaun•diced \-dəst\ *adj* : exhibiting envy or hostility

jaunt \'jȯnt\ *n* : short pleasure trip

jaun•ty \'jȯntē\ *adj* **-ti•er; -est** : lively in manner or appearance — **jaun•ti•ly** \'jȯntʰlē\ *adv* — **jaun•ti•ness** *n*

jav•e•lin \'javələn\ *n* : light spear

jaw \'jȯ\ *n* **1** : either of the bony or cartilaginous structures that support the mouth **2** : one of 2 movable parts for holding or crushing ⁓ *vb* : talk indignantly or at length — **jaw•bone** \-ˌbōn\ *n* — **jawed** \'jȯd\ *adj*

jay \'jā\ *n* : noisy brightly colored bird

jay•bird *n* : jay

jay•walk vb : cross a street carelessly — **jay•walk•er** n

jazz \'jaz\ vb : enliven ~ n **1** : kind of American music involving improvisation **2** : empty talk — **jazzy** adj

jeal•ous \'jeləs\ adj : suspicious of a rival or of one believed to enjoy an advantage — **jeal•ous•ly** adv — **jeal•ou•sy** \-əsē\ n

jeans \'jēnz\ n pl : pants made of durable twilled cotton cloth

jeep \'jēp\ n : 4-wheel army vehicle

jeer \'jir\ vb **1** : speak or cry out in derision **2** : ridicule ~ n : taunt

Je•ho•vah \ji'hōvə\ n : God

je•june \ji'jün\ adj : dull or childish

jell \'jel\ vb **1** : come to the consistency of jelly **2** : take shape

jel•ly \'jelē\ n, pl **-lies** : a substance (as food) with a soft somewhat elastic consistency — **jelly** vb

jel•ly•fish n : sea animal with a saucer-shaped jellylike body

jen•ny \'jenē\ n, pl **-nies** : female bird or donkey

jeop•ar•dy \'jepərdē\ n : exposure to death, loss, or injury — **jeop•ar•dize** \-ər͵dīz\ vb

jerk \'jərk\ vb **1** : give a sharp quick push, pull, or twist **2** : move in short abrupt motions ~ n **1** : short quick pull or twist **2** : stupid or foolish person — **jerk•i•ly** adv — **jerky** adj

jer•kin \'jərkən\ n : close-fitting sleeveless jacket

jer•ry–built \'jerē͵bilt\ adj : built cheaply and flimsily

jer•sey \'jərzē\ n, pl **-seys 1** : plain knit fabric **2** : knitted shirt

jest \'jest\ n : witty remark — **jest** vb

jest•er \'jestər\ n : one employed to entertain a court

¹jet \'jet\ n : velvet-black coal used for jewelry

²jet vb **-tt- 1** : spout or emit in a stream **2** : travel by jet ~ n **1** : forceful rush of fluid through a narrow opening **2** : jet-propelled airplane

jet–propelled adj : driven by an engine (**jet engine**) that produces propulsion (**jet propulsion**) by the rearward discharge of a jet of fluid

jet•sam \'jetsəm\ n : jettisoned goods

jet•ti•son \'jetəsən\ vb **1** : throw (goods) overboard **2** : discard — **jettison** n

jet•ty \'jetē\ n, pl **-ties** : pier or wharf

Jew \'jü\ n : one whose religion is Judaism — **Jew•ish** adj

jew•el \'jüəl\ n **1** : ornament of precious metal **2** : gem ~ vb **-eled** or **-elled; -el•ing** or **-el•ling** : adorn with jewels — **jew•el•er, jew•el•ler** \-ər\ n — **jew•el•ry** \-rē\ n

jib \'jib\ n : triangular sail

jibe \'jīb\ vb **jibed; jib•ing** : be in agreement

jif•fy \'jifē\ n, pl **-fies** : short time

jig \'jig\ n : lively dance ~ vb **-gg-** : dance a jig

jig•ger \'jigər\ n : measure used in mixing drinks

jig•gle \'jigəl\ vb **-gled; -gling** : move with quick little jerks — **jiggle** n

jig•saw n : machine saw with a narrow blade that moves up and down

jilt \'jilt\ vb : drop (a lover) unfeelingly

jim•my \'jimē\ n, pl **-mies** : small crowbar ~ vb **-mied; -my•ing** : pry open

jim•son•weed \'jimsən͵wēd\ n : coarse poisonous weed

jin•gle \'jiŋgəl\ vb **-gled; -gling** : make a light tinkling sound ~ n **1** : light tinkling sound **2** : short verse or song

jin•go•ism \'jiŋgō͵izəm\ n : extreme chauvinism or nationalism — **jin•go•ist** \-ist\ n — **jin•go•is•tic** \͵jiŋgō-'istik\ adj

jinx \'jiŋks\ n : one that brings bad luck — **jinx** vb

jit•ney \'jitnē\ n, pl **-neys** : small bus

jit•ters \'jitərz\ n pl : extreme nervousness — **jit•tery** \-ərē\ adj

job \'jäb\ n **1** : something that has to be done **2** : regular employment — **job•hold•er** n — **job•less** adj

job•ber \'jäbər\ n : middleman

jock•ey \'jäkē\ n, pl **-eys** : one who rides a horse in a race ~ vb **-eyed; -ey•ing** : manipulate or maneuver adroitly

jo•cose \jō'kōs\ adj : jocular

joc•u•lar \'jäkyələr\ adj : marked by jesting — **joc•u•lar•i•ty** \͵jäkyə-'larətē\ n — **joc•u•lar•ly** adv

jo•cund \'jäkənd\ adj : full of mirth or gaiety

jodh•purs \'jädpərz\ n pl : riding breeches

¹jog \'jäg\ vb **-gg- 1** : give a slight shake or push to **2** : run or ride at a slow pace ~ n **1** : slight shake **2** : slow pace — **jog•ger** n

²jog n : brief abrupt change in direction or line

join \'jȯin\ vb **1** : come or bring to-

gether **2** : become a member of —
join·er *n*

joint \'joint\ *n* **1** : point of contact between bones **2** : place where 2 parts
connect **3** : often disreputable place
~ *adj* : common to 2 or more —
joint·ed *adj* — **joint·ly** *adv*

joist \'joist\ *n* : beam supporting a floor
or ceiling

joke \'jōk\ *n* : something said or done
to provoke laughter ~ *vb* **joked; joking** : make jokes — **jok·er** *n* — **jok-
ing·ly** \'jōkiŋlē\ *adv*

jol·li·ty \'jälətē\ *n, pl* **-ties** : gaiety or
merriment

jol·ly \'jälē\ *adj* **-li·er; -est** : full of high
spirits

jolt \'jōlt\ *vb* **1** : move with a sudden
jerky motion **2** : give a jolt to ~ *n* **1**
: abrupt jerky blow or movement **2**
: sudden shock — **jolt·er** *n*

jon·quil \'jänkwəl\ *n* : narcissus with
white or yellow flowers

josh \'jäsh\ *vb* : tease or joke

jos·tle \'jäsəl\ *vb* **-tled; -tling** : push or
shove

jot \'jät\ *n* : least bit ~ *vb* **-tt-** : write
briefly and hurriedly

jounce \'jauns\ *vb* **jounced; jounc-
ing** : jolt — **jounce** *n*

jour·nal \'jərnᵊl\ *n* **1** : brief account of
daily events **2** : periodical (as a
newspaper)

jour·nal·ism \'jərnᵊl,izəm\ *n* : business of reporting or printing news —
jour·nal·ist \-ist\ *n* — **jour·nal·is·tic**
\,jərnᵊl'istik\ *adj*

jour·ney \'jərnē\ *n, pl* **-neys** : a going
from one place to another ~ *vb*
-neyed; -ney·ing : make a journey

jour·ney·man \-mən\ *n* : worker who
has learned a trade and works for another person

joust \'jaust\ *n* : combat on horseback
between 2 knights with lances —
joust *vb*

jo·vial \'jōvēəl\ *adj* : marked by good
humor — **jo·vi·al·i·ty** \,jōvē'alətē\ *n*
— **jo·vi·al·ly** \'jōvēəlē\ *adv*

¹jowl \'jaul\ *n* : loose flesh about the
lower jaw or throat

²jowl *n* **1** : lower jaw **2** : cheek

joy \'joi\ *n* **1** : feeling of happiness **2**
: source of happiness — **joy** *vb* — **joy-
ful** *adj* — **joy·ful·ly** *adv* — **joy·less**
adj — **joy·ous** \'joiəs\ *adj* — **joy-
ous·ly** *adv* — **joy·ous·ness** *n*

joy·ride *n* : reckless ride for pleasure —
joy·rid·er *n* — **joy·rid·ing** *n*

ju·bi·lant \'jübələnt\ *adj* : expressing
great joy — **ju·bi·lant·ly** *adv* — **ju·bi-
la·tion** \,jübə'lāshən\ *n*

ju·bi·lee \'jübə,lē\ *n* **1** : 50th anniversary **2** : season or occasion of celebration

Ju·da·ism \'jüdə,izəm\ *n* : religion developed among the ancient Hebrews
— **Ju·da·ic** \jü'dāik\ *adj*

judge \'jəj\ *vb* **judged; judg·ing** **1**
: form an opinion **2** : decide as a
judge ~ *n* **1** : public official authorized to decide questions brought before a court **2** : one who gives an
authoritative opinion — **judge·ship** *n*

judg·ment, judge·ment \'jəjmənt\ *n*
1 : decision or opinion given after
judging **2** : capacity for judging —
judg·men·tal \,jəj'mentəl\ *adj* —
judg·men·tal·ly *adv*

ju·di·ca·ture \'jüdikə,chur\ *n* : administration of justice

ju·di·cial \jü'dishəl\ *adj* : relating to
judicature or the judiciary — **ju·di-
cial·ly** *adv*

ju·di·cia·ry \jü'dishē,erē, -'dishərē\ *n*
: system of courts of law or the
judges of them — **judiciary** *adj*

ju·di·cious \jü'dishəs\ *adj* : having or
characterized by sound judgment —
ju·di·cious·ly *adv*

ju·do \'jüdō\ *n* : form of wrestling —
judo·ist *n*

jug \'jəg\ *n* : large deep container with a
narrow mouth and a handle

jug·ger·naut \'jəgər,not\ *n* : massive
inexorable force or object

jug·gle \'jəgəl\ *vb* **-gled; -gling** **1**
: keep several objects in motion in the
air at the same time **2** : manipulate
for an often tricky purpose — **jug-
gler** \'jəglər\ *n*

jug·u·lar \'jəgyələr\ *adj* : in or on the
throat or neck

juice \'jüs\ *n* **1** : extractable fluid contents of cells or tissues **2** : electricity
— **juic·er** *n* — **juic·i·ly** \'jüsəlē\ *adv*
— **juic·i·ness** \-sēnəs\ *n* — **juicy**
\'jüsē\ *adj*

ju·jube \'jü,jüb, 'jüjü,bē\ *n* : gummy
candy

juke·box \'jük,bäks\ *n* : coin-operated
machine for playing music recordings

ju·lep \'jüləp\ *n* : mint-flavored bour-
bon drink

Ju·ly \ju̇'lī\ *n* : 7th month of the year having 31 days

jum·ble \'jəmbəl\ *vb* **-bled; -bling** : mix in a confused mass — **jumble** *n*

jum·bo \'jəmbō\ *n, pl* **-bos** : very large version — **jumbo** *adj*

jump \'jəmp\ *vb* **1** : rise into or through the air esp. by muscular effort **2** : pass over **3** : give a start **4** : rise or increase sharply ~ *n* **1** : a jumping **2** : sharp sudden increase **3** : initial advantage

¹jump·er \'jəmpər\ *n* : one that jumps

²jumper *n* : sleeveless one-piece dress

jumpy \'jəmpē\ *adj* **jump·i·er; -est** : nervous or jittery

junc·tion \'jəŋkshən\ *n* **1** : a joining **2** : place or point of meeting

junc·ture \'jəŋkchər\ *n* **1** : joint or connection **2** : critical time or state of affairs

June \'jün\ *n* : 6th month of the year having 30 days

jun·gle \'jəŋgəl\ *n* : thick tangled mass of tropical vegetation

ju·nior \'jünyər\ *n* **1** : person who is younger or of lower rank than another **2** : student in the next-to-last year ~ *adj* : younger or lower in rank

ju·ni·per \'jünəpər\ *n* : evergreen shrub or tree

¹junk \'jəŋk\ *n* **1** : discarded articles **2** : shoddy product ~ *vb* : discard or scrap — **junky** *adj*

²junk *n* : flat-bottomed ship of Chinese waters

jun·ket \'jəŋkət\ *n* : trip made by an official at public expense

jun·ta \'hu̇ntə, 'jəntə, 'həntə\ *n* : group of persons controlling a government

ju·ris·dic·tion \ju̇rəs'dikshən\ *n* **1** : right or authority to interpret and apply the law **2** : limits within which authority may be exercised — **ju·ris·dic·tion·al** \-shənəl\ *adj*

ju·ris·pru·dence \-'prüdᵊns\ *n* **1** : system of laws **2** : science or philosophy of law

ju·rist \'ju̇rist\ *n* : judge

ju·ror \'ju̇rər\ *n* : member of a jury

ju·ry \'ju̇rē\ *n, pl* **-ries** : body of persons sworn to give a verdict on a matter

just \'jəst\ *adj* **1** : reasonable **2** : correct or proper **3** : morally or legally right **4** : deserved ~ *adv* **1** : exactly **2** : very recently **3** : barely **4** : only **5** : quite **6** : possibly — **just·ly** *adv* — **just·ness** *n*

jus·tice \'jəstəs\ *n* **1** : administration of what is just **2** : judge **3** : administration of law **4** : fairness

jus·ti·fy \'jəstə,fī\ *vb* **-fied; -fy·ing** : prove to be just, right, or reasonable — **jus·ti·fi·able** *adj* — **jus·ti·fi·ca·tion** \,jəstəfə'kāshən\ *n*

jut \'jət\ *vb* **-tt-** : stick out

jute \'jüt\ *n* : strong glossy fiber from a tropical plant

ju·ve·nile \'jüvə,nīl, -vənᵊl\ *adj* : relating to children or young people ~ *n* : young person

jux·ta·pose \'jəkstə,pōz\ *vb* **-posed; -pos·ing** : place side by side — **jux·ta·po·si·tion** \,jəkstəpə'zishən\ *n*

K

k \'kā\ *n, pl* **k's** *or* **ks** \'kāz\ : 11th letter of the alphabet

kai·ser \'kīzər\ *n* : German ruler

kale \'kāl\ *n* : curly cabbage

ka·lei·do·scope \kə'līdə,skōp\ *n* : device containing loose bits of colored material reflecting in many patterns — **ka·lei·do·scop·ic** \-,līdə'skäpik\ *adj* — **ka·lei·do·scop·i·cal·ly** \-iklē\ *adv*

kan·ga·roo \,kaŋgə'rü\ *n, pl* **-roos** : large leaping Australian mammal

ka·o·lin \'kāələn\ *n* : fine white clay

kar·a·o·ke \,karē'ōkē\ *n* : device that plays accompaniments for singers

kar·at \'karət\ *n* : unit of gold content

ka·ra·te \kə'rätē\ *n* : art of self-defense by crippling kicks and punches

ka·ty·did \'kātē,did\ *n* : large American grasshopper

kay·ak \'kī,ak\ *n* : Eskimo canoe

ka·zoo \kə'zü\ *n, pl* **-zoos** : toy musical instrument

keel \'kēl\ *n* : central lengthwise strip

on the bottom of a ship — **keeled** \'kēld\ *adj*

keen \'kēn\ *adj* **1** : sharp **2** : severe **3** : enthusiastic **4** : mentally alert — **keen•ly** *adv* — **keen•ness** *n*

keep \'kēp\ *vb* kept \'kept\; **keep•ing 1** : perform **2** : guard **3** : maintain **4** : retain in one's possession **5** : detain **6** : continue in good condition **7** : refrain ~ *n* **1** : fortress **2** : means by which one is kept — **keep•er** *n*

keep•ing \'kēpiŋ\ *n* : conformity

keep•sake \'kēp,sāk\ *n* : souvenir

keg \'keg\ *n* : small cask or barrel

kelp \'kelp\ *n* : coarse brown seaweed

ken \'ken\ *n* : range of sight or understanding

ken•nel \'ken³l\ *n* : dog shelter — **kennel** *vb*

ker•chief \'kərchəf, -,chēf\ *n* : square of cloth worn as a head covering

ker•nel \'kərn³l\ *n* **1** : inner softer part of a seed or nut **2** : whole seed of a cereal **3** : central part

ker•o•sene, ker•o•sine \'kerə,sēn, ,kerə'-\ *n* : thin flammable oil from petroleum

ketch•up \'kechəp, 'ka-\ *n* : spicy tomato sauce

ket•tle \'ket³l\ *n* : vessel for boiling liquids

ket•tle•drum \-,drum\ *n* : brass or copper kettle-shaped drum

¹**key** \'kē\ *n* **1** : usu. metal piece to open a lock **2** : explanation **3** : lever pressed by a finger in playing an instrument or operating a machine **4** : leading individual or principle **5** : system of musical tones or pitch ~ *vb* : attune ~ *adj* : basic — **key•hole** *n* — **key up** *vb* : make nervous

²**key** *n* : low island or reef

key•board *n* : arrangement of keys

key•note \-,nōt\ *n* **1** : 1st note of a scale **2** : central fact, idea, or mood ~ *vb* **1** : set the keynote of **2** : deliver the major speech

key•stone *n* : wedge-shaped piece at the crown of an arch

kha•ki \'kakē, 'käk-\ *n* : light yellowish brown color

khan \'kän, 'kan\ *n* : Mongol leader

kib•butz \kib'üts, -'üts\ *n, pl* -**but•zim** \-,üt'sēm, -,üt-\ : Israeli communal farm or settlement

ki•bitz•er \'kibətsər, kə'bit-\ *n* : one who offers unwanted advice — **kib•itz** \'kibəts\ *vb*

kick \'kik\ *vb* **1** : strike out or hit with the foot **2** : object strongly **3** : recoil ~ *n* **1** : thrust with the foot **2** : recoil of a gun **3** : stimulating effect — **kick•er** *n*

kid \'kid\ *n* **1** : young goat **2** : child ~ *vb* -**dd**- **1** : deceive as a joke **2** : tease — **kid•der** *n* — **kid•ding•ly** *adv*

kid•nap \'kid,nap\ *vb* -**napped** *or* -**naped** \-,napt\; -**nap•ping** *or* -**nap•ing** : carry a person away by illegal force — **kid•nap•per, kid•nap•er** *n*

kid•ney \'kidnē\ *n, pl* -**neys** : either of a pair of organs that excrete urine

kill \'kil\ *vb* **1** : deprive of life **2** : finish **3** : use up (time) ~ *n* : act of killing — **kill•er** *n*

kiln \'kil, 'kiln\ *n* : heated enclosure for burning, firing, or drying — **kiln** *vb*

ki•lo \'kēlō\ *n, pl* -**los** : kilogram

kilo•cy•cle \'kilə,sīkəl\ *n* : kilohertz

ki•lo•gram \'kēlə,gram, 'kilə-\ *n* : metric unit of weight equal to 2.2 pounds

ki•lo•hertz \'kilə,hərts, 'kēlə-, -,herts\ *n* : 1000 hertz

ki•lo•me•ter \kil'ämətər, 'kilə,mēt-\ *n* : 1000 meters

ki•lo•volt \'kilə,vōlt\ *n* : 1000 volts

kilo•watt \'kilə,wät\ *n* : 1000 watts

kilt \'kilt\ *n* : knee-length pleated skirt

kil•ter \'kiltər\ *n* : proper condition

ki•mo•no \kə'mōnō\ *n, pl* -**nos** : loose robe

kin \'kin\ *n* **1** : one's relatives **2** : kinsman

kind \'kīnd\ *n* **1** : essential quality **2** : group with common traits **3** : variety ~ *adj* **1** : of a sympathetic nature **2** : arising from sympathy — **kind•heart•ed** *adj* — **kind•ness** *n*

kin•der•gar•ten \'kindər,gärt³n\ *n* : class for young children — **kin•der•gart•ner** \-,gärtnər\ *n*

kin•dle \'kind³l\ *vb* -**dled**; -**dling 1** : set on fire or start burning **2** : stir up

kin•dling \'kindliŋ, 'kinlən\ *n* : material for starting a fire

kind•ly \'kīndlē\ *adj* -**li•er**; -**est** : of a sympathetic nature ~ *adv* **1** : sympathetically **2** : courteously — **kind•li•ness** *n*

kin•dred \'kindrəd\ *n* **1** : related individuals **2** : kin ~ *adj* : of a like nature

kin•folk \'kin,fōk\, **kinfolks** *n pl* : kin

king \'kiŋ\ *n* : male sovereign — **king-**

dom \-dəm\ n — **king·less** adj — **king·ly** adj — **king·ship** n

king·fish·er \-,fishər\ n : bright-colored crested bird

kink \'kiŋk\ n **1** : short tight twist or curl **2** : cramp — **kinky** adj

kin·ship n : relationship

kins·man \'kinzmən\ n : male relative

kins·wom·an \-,wùmən\ n : female relative

kip·per \'kipər\ n : dried or smoked fish — **kipper** vb

kiss \'kis\ vb : touch with the lips as a mark of affection — **kiss** n

kit \'kit\ n : set of articles (as tools or parts)

kitch·en \'kichən\ n : room with cooking facilities

kite \'kīt\ n **1** : small hawk **2** : covered framework flown at the end of a string

kith \'kith\ n : familiar friends

kit·ten \'kit³n\ n : young cat — **kit·ten·ish** adj

¹kit·ty \'kitē\ n, pl **-ties** : kitten

²kitty n, pl **-ties** : fund or pool (as in a card game)

kit·ty–cor·ner, kit·ty–cor·nered var of CATERCORNER

ki·wi \'kē,wē\ n **1** : small flightless New Zealand bird **2** : brownish egg-shaped subtropical fruit

klep·to·ma·nia \,kleptə'mānēə\ n : neurotic impulse to steal — **klep·to·ma·ni·ac** \-nē,ak\ n

knack \'nak\ n **1** : clever way of doing something **2** : natural aptitude

knap·sack \'nap,sak\ n : bag for carrying supplies on one's back

knave \'nāv\ n : rogue — **knav·ery** \'nāvərē\ n — **knav·ish** \'nāvish\ adj

knead \'nēd\ vb **1** : work and press with the hands **2** : massage — **knead·er** n

knee \'nē\ n : joint in the middle part of the leg — **kneed** \'nēd\ adj

knee·cap \'nē,kap\ n : bone forming the front of the knee

kneel \'nēl\ vb **knelt** \'nelt\ or **kneeled; kneel·ing** : rest on one's knees

knell \'nel\ n : stroke of a bell

knew past of KNOW

knick·ers \'nikərz\ n pl : pants gathered at the knee

knick·knack \'nik,nak\ n : small decorative object

knife \'nīf\ n, pl **knives** \'nīvz\ : sharp blade with a handle ~ vb **knifed; knif·ing** : stab or cut with a knife

knight \'nīt\ n **1** : mounted warrior of feudal times **2** : man honored by a sovereign ~ vb : make a knight of — **knight·hood** n — **knight·ly** adv

knit \'nit\ vb **knit** or **knit·ted; knit·ting 1** : link firmly or closely **2** : form a fabric by interlacing yarn or thread ~ n : knitted garment — **knit·ter** n

knob \'näb\ n : rounded protuberance or handle — **knobbed** \'näbd\ adj — **knob·by** \'näbē\ adj

knock \'näk\ vb **1** : strike with a sharp blow **2** : collide **3** : find fault with ~ n : sharp blow — **knock out** vb : make unconscious

knock·er n : device hinged to a door to knock with

knoll \'nōl\ n : small round hill

knot \'nät\ n **1** : interlacing (as of string) that forms a lump **2** : base of a woody branch in the stem **3** : group **4** : one nautical mile per hour ~ vb **-tt-** : tie in or with a knot — **knot·ty** adj

know \'nō\ vb **knew** \'nü, 'nyü\; **known** \'nōn\; **know·ing 1** : perceive directly or understand **2** : be familiar with — **know·able** adj — **know·er** n

know·ing \'nōiŋ\ adj : shrewdly and keenly alert — **know·ing·ly** adv

knowl·edge \'nälij\ n **1** : understanding gained by experience **2** : range of information — **knowl·edge·able** adj

knuck·le \'nəkəl\ n : rounded knob at a finger joint

ko·ala \kō'älə\ n : gray furry Australian animal

kohl·ra·bi \kōl'rabē, -'räb-\ n, pl **-bies** : cabbage that forms no head

Ko·ran \kə'ran, -'rän\ n : book of Islam containing revelations made to Muhammad by Allah

ko·sher \'kōshər\ adj : ritually fit for use according to Jewish law

kow·tow \kaù'taù, 'kaù,taù\ vb : show excessive deference

kryp·ton \'krip,tän\ n : gaseous chemical element used in lamps

ku·dos \'kyü,däs, 'kü-, -,dōz\ n : fame and renown

kum·quat \'kəm,kwät\ n : small citrus fruit

Kwan·zaa, Kwan·za \'kwänzə\ n : African-American festival held from December 26 to January 1 ~

L

l \'el\ *n, pl* **l's** *or* **ls** \'elz\ : 12th letter of the alphabet

lab \'lab\ *n* : laboratory

la·bel \'lābəl\ *n* **1** : identification slip **2** : identifying word or phrase ～ *vb* **-beled** *or* **-belled;** — **bel·ing** *or* — **bel·ling** : put a label on

la·bi·al \'lābēəl\ *adj* : of or relating to the lips

la·bor \'lābər\ *n* **1** : physical or mental effort **2** : physical efforts of childbirth **3** : task **4** : people who work manually ～ *vb* : work esp. with great effort — **la·bor·er** *n*

lab·o·ra·to·ry \'labrə,tōrē\ *n, pl* **-ries** : place for experimental testing

Labor Day *n* : 1st Monday in September observed as a legal holiday in recognition of working people

la·bo·ri·ous \lə'bōrēəs\ *adj* : requiring great effort — **la·bo·ri·ous·ly** *adv*

lab·y·rinth \'labə,rinth\ *n* : maze — **lab·y·rin·thine** \,labə'rinthən\ *adj*

lace \'lās\ *n* **1** : cord or string for tying **2** : fine net usu. figured fabric ～ *vb* **laced; lac·ing 1** : tie **2** : adorn with lace — **lacy** \'lāsē\ *adj*

lac·er·ate \'lasə,rāt\ *vb* **-at·ed; -at·ing** : tear roughly — **lac·er·a·tion** \,lasə'rāshən\ *n*

lach·ry·mose \'lakrə,mōs\ *adj* : tearful

lack \'lak\ *vb* : be missing or deficient in ～ *n* : deficiency

lack·a·dai·si·cal \,lakə'dāzikəl\ *adj* : lacking spirit — **lack·a·dai·si·cal·ly** \-klē\ *adv*

lack·ey \'lakē\ *n, pl* **-eys 1** : footman or servant **2** : toady

lack·lus·ter \'lak,ləstər\ *adj* : dull

la·con·ic \lə'känik\ *adj* : sparing of words — **la·con·i·cal·ly** \-iklē\ *adv*

lac·quer \'lakər\ *n* : glossy surface coating — **lacquer** *vb*

la·crosse \lə'krós\ *n* : ball game played with long-handled rackets

lac·tate \'lak,tāt\ *vb* **-tat·ed; -tat·ing** : secrete milk — **lac·ta·tion** \lak'tāshən\ *n*

lac·tic \'laktik\ *adj* : relating to milk

la·cu·na \lə'künə, -'kyü-\ *n, pl* **-nae** \-,nē\ *or* **-nas** : blank space or missing part

lad \'lad\ *n* : boy

lad·der \'ladər\ *n* : device with steps or rungs for climbing

lad·en \'lād°n\ *adj* : loaded

la·dle \'lād°l\ *n* : spoon with a deep bowl **-ladle** *vb*

la·dy \'lādē\ *n, pl* **-dies 1** : woman of rank or authority **2** : woman

la·dy·bird \'lādē,bərd\ *n* : ladybug

la·dy·bug \-,bəg\ *n* : brightly colored beetle

lag \'lag\ *vb* **-gg-** : fail to keep up ～ *n* **1** : a falling behind **2** : interval

la·ger \'lägər\ *n* : beer

lag·gard \'lagərd\ *adj* : slow ～ *n* : one that lags — **lag·gard·ly** *adv*

la·gniappe \'lan,yap\ *n* : bonus

la·goon \lə'gün\ *n* : shallow sound, channel, or pond near or connecting with a larger body of water

laid *past of* LAY

lain *past part of* LIE

lair \'lar\ *n* : den

lais·sez–faire \,les,ā'far\ *n* : doctrine opposing government interference in business

la·ity \'lāətē\ *n* : people of a religious faith who are not clergy members

lake \'lāk\ *n* : inland body of water

la·ma \'lämə\ *n* : Buddhist monk

lamb \'lam\ *n* : young sheep or its flesh used as food

lam·baste, lam·bast \lam'bāst, -'bast\ *vb* **1** : beat **2** : censure

lam·bent \'lambənt\ *adj* : light or bright — **lam·bent·ly** *adv*

lame \'lām\ *adj* **lam·er; lam·est 1** : having a limb disabled **2** : weak ～ *vb* **lamed; lam·ing** : make lame — **lame·ly** *adv* **-lame·ness** *n*

la·mé \lä'mā, la-\ *n* : cloth with tinsel threads

lame·brain \'lām,brān\ *n* : fool

la·ment \lə'ment\ *vb* **1** : mourn **2** : express sorrow for ～ *n* **1** : mourning **2** : complaint — **lam·en·ta·ble** \'laməntəbəl, lə'mentə-\ *adj* — **lam·en·ta·bly** \-blē\ *adv* — **lam·en·ta·tion** \,lamən'tāshən\ *n*

lam·i·nat·ed \'lamə͵nātəd\ *adj* : made of thin layers of material — **lam·i·nate** \-͵nāt\ *vb* — **lam·i·nate** \-nət\ *n or adj* — **lam·i·na·tion** \͵lamə'nāshən\ *n*

lamp \'lamp\ *n* : device for producing light or heat

lam·poon \lam'pün\ *n* : satire — **lampoon** *vb*

lam·prey \'lamprē\ *n, pl* **-preys** : sucking eellike fish

lance \'lans\ *n* : spear ~ *vb* **lanced; lanc·ing** : pierce or open with a lancet

lance corporal *n* : enlisted man in the marine corps ranking above a private first class and below a corporal

lan·cet \'lansət\ *n* : pointed surgical instrument

land \'land\ *n* **1** : solid part of the surface of the earth **2** : country ~ *vb* **1** : go ashore **2** : catch or gain **3** : touch the ground or a surface — **land·less** *adj* — **land·own·er** *n*

land·fill *n* : dump

land·ing \'landiŋ\ *n* **1** : action of one that lands **2** : place for loading passengers and cargo **3** : level part of a staircase

land·la·dy \'land͵lādē\ *n* : woman landlord

land·locked *adj* : enclosed by land

land·lord *n* : owner of property

land·lub·ber \-͵ləbər\ *n* : one with little sea experience

land·mark \-͵märk\ *n* **1** : object that marks a boundary or serves as a guide **2** : event that marks a turning point

land·scape \-͵skāp\ *n* : view of natural scenery ~ *vb* **-scaped; -scap·ing** : beautify a piece of land (as by decorative planting)

land·slide *n* **1** : slipping down of a mass of earth **2** : overwhelming victory

land·ward \'landwərd\ *adj* : toward the land — **landward** *adv*

lane \'lān\ *n* : narrow way

lan·guage \'laŋgwij\ *n* : words and the methods of combining them for communication

lan·guid \'laŋgwəd\ *adj* **1** : weak **2** : sluggish — **lan·guid·ly** *adv* — **languid·ness** *n*

lan·guish \'laŋgwish\ *vb* : become languid or discouraged

lan·guor \'laŋgər\ *n* : listless indolence — **lan·guor·ous** *adj* — **lan·guorous·ly** *adv*

lank \'laŋk\ *adj* **1** : thin **2** : limp

lanky *adj* **lank·i·er; -est** : tall and thin

lan·o·lin \'lan°lən\ *n* : fatty wax from sheep's wool used in ointments

lan·tern \'lantərn\ *n* : enclosed portable light

¹lap \'lap\ *n* **1** : front part of the lower trunk and thighs of a seated person **2** : overlapping part **3** : one complete circuit completing a course (as around a track or pool) ~ *vb* **-pp-** : fold over

²lap *vb* **-pp- 1** : scoop up with the tongue **2** : splash gently

lap·dog *n* : small dog

la·pel \lə'pel\ *n* : fold of the front of a coat

lap·i·dary \'lapə͵derē\ *n* : one who cuts and polishes gems ~ *adj* : relating to gems

lapse \'laps\ *n* **1** : slight error **2** : termination of a right or privilege **3** : interval ~ *vb* **lapsed; laps·ing 1** : slip **2** : subside **3** : cease

lap·top \'lap͵täp\ *adj* : of a size that may be used on one's lap

lar·board \'lärbərd\ *n* : port side

lar·ce·ny \'lärs°nē\ *n, pl* **-nies** : theft — **lar·ce·nous** \'lärs°nəs\ *adj*

larch \'lärch\ *n* : tree like a pine that loses its needles

lard \'lärd\ *n* : pork fat

lar·der \'lärdər\ *n* : pantry

large \'lärj\ *adj* **larg·er; larg·est** : greater than average — **large·ly** *adv* — **large·ness** *n*

lar·gesse, lar·gess \lär'zhes, -'jes; 'lär͵-\ *n* : liberal giving

lar·i·at \'larēət\ *n* : lasso

¹lark \'lärk\ *n* : small songbird

²lark *vb or n* : romp

lar·va \'lärvə\ *n, pl* **-vae** \-͵vē\ : wormlike form of an insect — **lar·val** \-vəl\ *adj*

lar·yn·gi·tis \͵larən'jītəs\ *n* : inflammation of the larynx

lar·ynx \'lariŋks\ *n, pl* **-ryn·ges** \lə'rin͵jēz\ *or* **-ynx·es** : upper part of the trachea — **la·ryn·ge·al** \͵larən'jēəl, lə'rinjēəl\ *adj*

la·sa·gna \lə'zäny°\ *n* : flat noodles baked usu. with tomato sauce, meat, and cheese

las·civ·i·ous \lə'sivēəs\ *adj* : lewd — **las·civ·i·ous·ness** *n*

la·ser \'lāzər\ *n* : device that produces an intense light beam

¹lash \'lash\ *vb* : whip ~ *n* **1** : stroke esp. of a whip **2** : eyelash

²lash *vb* : bind with a rope or cord

lass \'las\ *n* : girl

lass•ie \'lasē\ *n* : girl

las•si•tude \'lasə̱tüd, -ˌtyüd\ *n* 1 : fatigue 2 : listlessness

las•so \'lasō, la'sü\ *n, pl* -sos *or* -soes : rope with a noose for catching livestock — lasso *vb*

¹last \'last\ *vb* : continue in existence or operation

²last *adj* 1 : final 2 : previous 3 : least likely ∼ *adv* 1 : at the end 2 : most recently 3 : in conclusion ∼ *n* : something that is last — last•ly *adv* — at last : finally

³last *n* : form on which a shoe is shaped

latch \'lach\ *vb* : catch or get hold ∼ *n* : catch that holds a door closed

late \'lāt\ *adj* lat•er; lat•est 1 : coming or staying after the proper time 2 : advanced toward the end 3 : recently deceased 4 : recent — late *adv* — late•com•er \-ˌkəmər\ *n* — late•ly *adv* — late•ness *n*

la•tent \'lāt°nt\ *adj* : present but not visible or expressed — la•ten•cy \-°nsē\ *n*

lat•er•al \'latərəl\ *adj* : on or toward the side — lat•er•al•ly *adv*

la•tex \'lāˌteks\ *n, pl* -ti•ces \'lātəˌsēz, 'lat-\ *or* -tex•es : emulsion of synthetic rubber or plastic

lath \'lath, 'lath\ *n, pl* laths *or* lath : building material (as a thin strip of wood) used as a base for plaster — lath *vb* — lath•ing \-iŋ\ *n*

lathe \'lāth\ *n* : machine that rotates material for shaping

lath•er \'lathər\ *n* : foam ∼ *vb* : form or spread lather

lat•i•tude \'latəˌtüd, -ˌtyüd\ *n* 1 : distance north or south from the earth's equator 2 : freedom of action

la•trine \lə'trēn\ *n* : toilet

lat•ter \'latər\ *adj* 1 : more recent 2 : being the second of 2 — lat•ter•ly *adv*

lat•tice \'latəs\ *n* : framework of crossed strips

laud *vb or n* : praise — laud•able *adj* — laud•ably *adv*

laugh \'laf, 'làf\ *vb* : show mirth, joy, or scorn with a smile and explosive sound — laugh *n* — laugh•able *adj* — laugh•ing•ly \-iŋlē\ *adv*

laugh•ing•stock \'lafiŋˌstäk, 'làf-\ *n* : object of ridicule

laugh•ter \'laftər, 'làf-\ *n* : action or sound of laughing

¹launch \'lónch\ *vb* 1 : hurl or send off 2 : set afloat 3 : start — launch *n* — launch•er *n*

²launch *n* : small open boat

laun•der \'lóndər\ *vb* : wash or iron fabrics — laun•der•er *n* — laun•dress \-drəs\ *n* — laun•dry \-drē\ *n*

lau•re•ate \'lórēət\ *n* : recipient of honors — laureate *adj*

lau•rel \'lórəl\ *n* 1 : small evergreen tree 2 : honor

la•va \'lävə, 'lav-\ *n* : volcanic molten rock

lav•a•to•ry \'lavəˌtōrē\ *n, pl* -ries : bathroom

lav•en•der \'lavəndər\ *n* 1 : aromatic plant used for perfume 2 : pale purple color

lav•ish \'lavish\ *adj* : expended profusely ∼ *vb* : expend or give freely — lav•ish•ly *adv* — lav•ish•ness *n*

law \'ló\ *n* 1 : established rule of conduct 2 : body of such rules 3 : principle of construction or procedure 4 : rule stating uniform behavior under uniform conditions 5 : lawyer's profession — law•break•er *n* — law•giv•er *n* — law•less *adj* — law•less•ly *adv* — law•less•ness *n* — law•mak•er *n* — law•man \-mən\ *n* — law•suit *n*

law•ful \'lófəl\ *adj* : permitted by law — law•ful•ly *adv*

lawn \'lón\ *n* : grass-covered yard

law•yer \'lóyər\ *n* : legal practitioner

lax \'laks\ *adj* : not strict or tense — lax•i•ty \'laksətē\ *n* — lax•ly *adv*

lax•a•tive \'lakətiv\ *n* : drug relieving constipation

¹lay \'lā\ *vb* laid \'lād\; lay•ing 1 : put or set down 2 : produce eggs 3 : bet 4 : impose as a duty or burden 5 : put forward ∼ *n* : way something lies or is laid

²lay *past of* LIE

³lay *n* : song

⁴lay *adj* : of the laity — lay•man \-mən\ *n* — lay•wom•an \-ˌwumən\ *n*

lay•er \'lāər\ *n* 1 : one that lays 2 : one thickness over or under another

lay•off \'lāˌóf\ *n* : temporary dismissal of a worker

lay•out \'lāˌaùt\ *n* : arrangement

la•zy \'lāzē\ *adj* -zi•er; -est : disliking activity or exertion — la•zi•ly \'lāzəlē\ *adv* -la•zi•ness *n*

lea \'lē, 'lā\ *n* : meadow

leach \'lēch\ *vb* : remove (a soluble part) with a solvent

¹lead \'lēd\ *vb* led \'led\; lead•ing 1 : guide on a way 2 : direct the activity

of **3** : go at the head of **4** : tend to a definite result ∼ *n* : position in front — **lead•er** *n* — **lead•er•less** *adj* — **lead•er•ship** *n*

²**lead** \'led\ *n* **1** : heavy bluish white chemical element **2** : marking substance in a pencil — **lead•en** \'led°n\ *adj*

leaf \'lēf\ *n, pl* **leaves** \'lēvz\ **1** : green outgrowth of a plant stem **2** : leaflike thing ∼ *vb* **1** : produce leaves **2** : turn book pages — **leaf•age** \'lēfij\ *n* — **leafed** \'lēft\ *adj* — **leaf•less** *adj* — **leafy** *adj* — **leaved** \'lēfd\ *adj*

leaf•let \'lēflət\ *n* : pamphlet

¹**league** \'lēg\ *n* : unit of distance equal to about 3 miles

²**league** *n* : association for a common purpose — **league** *vb* — **leagu•er** *n*

leak \'lēk\ *vb* **1** : enter or escape through a leak **2** : become or make known ∼ *n* : opening that accidentally admits or lets out a substance — **leak•age** \'lēkij\ *n* — **leaky** *adj*

¹**lean** \'lēn\ *vb* **1** : bend from a vertical position **2** : rely on for support **3** : incline in opinion — **lean** *n*

²**lean** *adj* **1** : lacking in flesh **2** : lacking richness — **lean•ness** \'lēnnəs\ *n*

leap \'lēp\ *vb* **leapt** *or* **leaped** \'lēpt, 'lept\; **leap•ing** : jump — **leap** *n*

leap year *n* : 366-day year

learn \'lərn\ *vb* **1** : gain understanding or skill by study or experience **2** : memorize **3** : find out — **learn•er** *n*

learn•ed \-əd\ *adj* : having great learning — **learn•ed•ness** *n*

learn•ing \-iŋ\ *n* : knowledge

lease \'lēs\ *n* : contract transferring real estate for a term and usu. for rent ∼ *vb* **leased; leas•ing** : grant by or hold under a lease

leash \'lēsh\ *n* : line to hold an animal — **leash** *vb*

least \'lēst\ *adj* **1** : lowest in importance or position **2** : smallest **3** : scantiest ∼ *n* : one that is least ∼ *adv* : in the smallest or lowest degree

leath•er \'lethər\ *n* : dressed animal skin — **leath•ern** \-ərn\ *adj* — **leath•ery** *adj*

¹**leave** \'lēv\ *vb* **left** \'left\; **leav•ing** **1** : bequeath **2** : allow or cause to remain **3** : have as a remainder **4** : go away ∼ *n* **1** : permission **2** : authorized absence **3** : departure

²**leave** *vb* **leaved; leav•ing** : leaf

leav•en \'levən\ *n* : substance for producing fermentation ∼ *vb* : raise dough with a leaven

leaves *pl of* LEAF

lech•ery \'lechərē\ *n* : inordinate indulgence in sex — **lech•er** \'lechər\ *n* — **lech•er•ous** \-chərəs\ *adj* — **lech•er•ous•ly** *adv* — **lech•er•ous•ness** *n*

lec•ture \'lekchər\ *n* **1** : instructive talk **2** : reprimand — **lecture** *vb* — **lec•tur•er** *n* — **lec•ture•ship** *n*

led *past of* LEAD

ledge \'lej\ *n* : shelflike projection

led•ger \'lejər\ *n* : account book

lee \'lē\ *n* : side sheltered from the wind — **lee** *adj*

leech \'lēch\ *n* : segmented freshwater worm that feeds on blood

leek \'lēk\ *n* : onionlike herb

leer \'lir\ *n* : suggestive or malicious look — **leer** *vb*

leery \'lirē\ *adj* : suspicious or wary

lees \'lēz\ *n pl* : dregs

lee•ward \'lēwərd, 'lüərd\ *adj* : situated away from the wind ∼ *n* : the lee side

lee•way \'lē₁wā\ *n* : allowable margin

¹**left** \'left\ *adj* : on the same side of the body as the heart ∼ *n* : left hand — **left** *adv*

²**left** *past of* LEAVE

leg \'leg\ *n* **1** : limb of an animal that supports the body **2** : something like a leg **3** : clothing to cover the leg ∼ *vb* **-gg-** : walk or run — **leg•ged** \'legəd\ *adj* — **leg•less** *adj*

leg•a•cy \'legəsē\ *n, pl* **-cies** : inheritance

le•gal \'lēgəl\ *adj* **1** : relating to law or lawyers **2** : lawful — **le•gal•is•tic** \₁lēgə'listik\ *adj* — **le•gal•i•ty** \li'galətē\ *n* — **le•gal•ize** \'lēgə₁līz\ *vb* — **le•gal•ly** \-gəlē\ *adv*

leg•ate \'legət\ *n* : official representative

le•ga•tion \li'gāshən\ *n* **1** : diplomatic mission **2** : official residence and office of a diplomat

leg•end \'lejənd\ *n* **1** : story handed down from the past **2** : inscription **3** : explanation of map symbols — **leg•end•ary** \-ən₁derē\ *adj*

leg•er•de•main \₁lejərdə'mān\ *n* : sleight of hand

leg•ging, leg•gin \'legən, -iŋ\ *n* : leg covering

leg•i•ble \'lejəbəl\ *adj* : capable of being read — **leg·i·bil·i·ty** \ˌlejə-ˈbilətē\ *n* — **leg·i·bly** \ˈlejəblē\ *adv*

le·gion \ˈlējən\ *n* **1** : large army unit **2** : multitude **3** : association of former servicemen — **le·gion·ary** \-ˌerē\ *n* — **le·gion·naire** \ˌlējən'ar\ *n*

leg·is·late \ˈlejəˌslāt\ *vb* **-lat·ed; -lat·ing** : enact or bring about with laws — **leg·is·la·tion** \ˌlejə'slāshən\ *n* — **leg·is·la·tive** \ˈlejəˌslātiv\ *adj* — **leg·is·la·tor** \-ər\ *n*

leg·is·la·ture \ˈlejəˌslāchər\ *n* : organization with authority to make laws

le·git·i·mate \li'jitəmət\ *adj* **1** : lawfully begotten **2** : genuine **3** : conforming with law or accepted standards — **le·git·i·ma·cy** \-məsē\ *n* — **le·git·i·mate·ly** *adv* — **le·git·i·mize** \-mīz\ *vb*

le·gume \ˈlegˌyüm, li'gyüm\ *n* : plant bearing pods — **le·gu·mi·nous** \li'gyümənəs\ *adj*

lei \ˈlā\ *n* : necklace of flowers

lei·sure \ˈlēzhər, 'lezh-, 'lāzh-\ *n* **1** : free time **2** : ease **3** : convenience — **lei·sure·ly** *adj or adv*

lem·ming \ˈlemiŋ\ *n* : short-tailed rodent

lem·on \ˈlemən\ *n* : yellow citrus fruit — **lem·ony** *adj*

lem·on·ade \ˌlemə'nād\ *n* : sweetened lemon beverage

lend \ˈlend\ *vb* **lent** \ˈlent\; **lend·ing** **1** : give for temporary use **2** : furnish — **lend·er** *n*

length \ˈleŋth\ *n* **1** : longest dimension **2** : duration in time **3** : piece to be joined to others — **length·en** \ˈleŋthən\ *vb* — **length·wise** *adv or adj* — **lengthy** *adj*

le·nient \ˈlēnēənt, -nyənt\ *adj* : of mild and tolerant disposition or effect — **le·ni·en·cy** \ˈlēnēənsē -nyənsē\ *n* — **le·ni·ent·ly** *adv*

len·i·ty \ˈlenətē\ *n* : leniency

lens \ˈlenz\ *n* **1** : curved piece for forming an image in an optical instrument **2** : transparent body in the eye that focuses light rays

Lent \ˈlent\ *n* : 40-day period of penitence and fasting from Ash Wednesday to Easter — **Lent·en** \-ˀn\ *adj*

len·til \ˈlentˀl\ *n* : legume with flat edible seeds

le·o·nine \ˈlēəˌnīn\ *adj* : like a lion

leop·ard \ˈlepərd\ *n* : large tawny black-spotted cat

le·o·tard \ˈlēəˌtärd\ *n* : close-fitting garment

lep·er \ˈlepər\ *n* : person with leprosy

lep·re·chaun \ˈleprəˌkän\ *n* : mischievous Irish elf

lep·ro·sy \ˈleprəsē\ *n* : chronic bacterial disease — **lep·rous** \-rəs\ *adj*

les·bi·an \ˈlezbēən\ *n* : female homosexual — **lesbian** *adj* — **les·bi·an·ism** \-ˌizəm\ *n*

le·sion \ˈlēzhən\ *n* : abnormal area in the body due to injury or disease

less \ˈles\ *adj* **1** : fewer **2** : of lower rank, degree, or importance **3** : smaller ~ *adv* : to a lesser degree ~ *n, pl* **less** : smaller portion ~ *prep* : minus — **less·en** \-ˀn\ *vb*

-less \ləs\ *adj suffix* **1** : not having **2** : unable to act or be acted on

les·see \le'sē\ *n* : tenant under a lease

less·er \ˈlesər\ *adj* : of less size, quality, or significance

les·son \ˈlesˀn\ *n* **1** : reading or exercise to be studied by a pupil **2** : something learned

les·sor \ˈlesˌȯr, le'sȯr\ *n* : one who transfers property by a lease

lest \ˌlest\ *conj* : for fear that

¹let \ˈlet\ *n* : hindrance or obstacle

²let *vb* **let; let·ting** **1** : cause to **2** : rent **3** : permit

-let \lət\ *n suffix* : small one

le·thal \ˈlēthəl\ *adj* : deadly — **le·thal·ly** *adv*

leth·ar·gy \ˈlethərjē\ *n* **1** : drowsiness **2** : state of being lazy or indifferent — **le·thar·gic** \li'thärjik\ *adj*

let·ter \ˈletər\ *n* **1** : unit of an alphabet **2** : written or printed communication **3** *pl* : literature or learning **4** : literal meaning ~ *vb* : mark with letters — **let·ter·er** *n*

let·tuce \ˈletəs\ *n* : garden plant with crisp leaves

leu·ke·mia \lü'kēmēə\ *n* : cancerous blood disease — **leu·ke·mic** \-mik\ *adj or n*

lev·ee \ˈlevē\ *n* : embankment to prevent flooding

lev·el \ˈlevəl\ *n* **1** : device for establishing a flat surface **2** : horizontal surface **3** : position in a scale ~ *vb* **-eled** *or* **-elled; -el·ing** *or* **-el·ling** **1** : make flat or level **2** : aim **3** : raze ~ *adj* **1** : having an even surface **2** : of the same height or rank — **lev·el·er** *n* — **lev·el·ly** *adv* — **lev·el·ness** *n*

le·ver \ˈlevər, 'lē-\ *n* : bar for prying or

dislodging something — **le·ver·age** \'levərij, 'lēv-\ n

le·vi·a·than \li'vīəthən\ n 1 : large sea animal 2 : enormous thing

lev·i·ty \'levətē\ n : unseemly frivolity

levy \'levē\ n, pl **lev·ies** : imposition or collection of a tax ~ vb **lev·ied; levy·ing** 1 : impose or collect legally 2 : enlist for military service 3 : wage

lewd \'lüd\ adj 1 : sexually unchaste 2 : vulgar — **lewd·ly** adv — **lewd·ness** n

lex·i·cog·ra·phy \ˌleksə'kägrəfē\ n : dictionary making — **lex·i·cog·ra·pher** \-fər\ n — **lex·i·co·graph·i·cal** \-kō'grafikəl\, **lex·i·co·graph·ic** \-ik\ adj

lex·i·con \'leksəˌkän\ n, pl **-i·ca** \-sikə\ or **-icons** : dictionary

li·a·ble \'līəbəl\ adj 1 : legally obligated 2 : probable 3 : susceptible — **li·a·bil·i·ty** \ˌlīə'bilətē\ n

li·ai·son \'lēəˌzän, lē'ā-\ n 1 : close bond 2 : communication between groups

li·ar \'līər\ n : one who lies

li·bel \'lībəl\ n : action, crime, or an instance of injuring a person's reputation esp. by something written ~ vb **-beled** or **-belled; -bel·ing** or **-bel·ling** : make or publish a libel — **li·bel·er** n — **li·bel·ist** n — **li·bel·ous, li·bel·lous** \-bələs\ adj

lib·er·al \'librəl, 'libə-\ adj : not stingy, narrow, or conservative — **liberal** n — **lib·er·al·ism** \-ˌizəm\ n — **lib·er·al·i·ty** \ˌlibə'ralətē\ n — **lib·er·al·ize** \'librə-ˌlīz, 'libə-\ vb — **lib·er·al·ly** \-rəlē\ adv

lib·er·ate \'libəˌrāt\ vb **-at·ed; -at·ing** : set free — **lib·er·a·tion** \ˌlibə'rā-shən\ n — **lib·er·a·tor** \'libəˌrātər\ n

lib·er·tine \'libərˌtēn\ n : one who leads a dissolute life

lib·er·ty \'libərtē\ n, pl **-ties** 1 : quality or state of being free 2 : action going beyond normal limits

li·bi·do \lə'bēdō, -'bīd-\ n, pl **-dos** : sexual drive — **li·bid·i·nal** \lə-'bid°nəl\ adj — **li·bid·i·nous** \-əs\ adj

li·brary \'līˌbrerē\ n, pl **-brar·ies** 1 : place where books are kept for use 2 : collection of books — **li·brar·i·an** \lī'brerēən\ n

li·bret·to \lə'bretō\ n, pl **-tos** or **-ti** \-ē\ : text of an opera — **li·bret·tist** \-ist\ n

lice pl of LOUSE

li·cense, li·cence \'līs°ns\ n 1 : legal permission to engage in some activity 2 : document or tag providing proof of a license 3 : irresponsible use

of freedom — **license** vb — **li·cens·ee** \ˌlīs°n'sē\ n

li·cen·tious \lī'senchəs\ adj : disregarding sexual restraints — **li·cen·tious·ly** adv — **li·cen·tious·ness** n

li·chen \'līkən\ n : complex lower plant made up of an alga and a fungus

lic·it \'lisət\ adj : lawful

lick \'lik\ vb 1 : draw the tongue over 2 : beat ~ n 1 : stroke of the tongue 2 : small amount

lic·o·rice \'likərish, -rəs\ n : dried root of a European legume or candy flavored by it

lid \'lid\ n 1 : movable cover 2 : eyelid

¹lie \'lī\ vb lay \'lā\; lain \'lān\; ly·ing \'līiŋ\ 1 : be in, rest in, or assume a horizontal position 2 : occupy a certain relative position ~ n : position in which something lies

²lie vb lied; ly·ing \'līiŋ\ : tell a lie ~ n : untrue statement

liege \'lēj\ n : feudal superior or vassal

lien \'lēn, 'lēən\ n : legal claim on the property of another

lieu·ten·ant \lü'tenənt\ n 1 : representative 2 : first lieutenant or second lieutenant 3 : commissioned officer in the navy ranking next below a lieutenant commander — **lieu·ten·an·cy** \-ənsē\ n

lieutenant colonel n : commissioned officer (as in the army) ranking next below a colonel

lieutenant commander n : commissioned officer in the navy ranking next below a commander

lieutenant general n : commissioned officer (as in the army) ranking next below a general

lieutenant junior grade n, pl **lieutenants junior grade** : commissioned officer in the navy ranking next below a lieutenant

life \'līf\ n, pl **lives** \'līvz\ 1 : quality that distinguishes a vital and functional being from a dead body or inanimate matter 2 : physical and mental experiences of an individual 3 : biography 4 : period of existence 5 : way of living 6 : liveliness — **life·less** adj — **life·like** adj

life·blood n : basic source of strength and vitality

life·boat n : boat for saving lives at sea

life·guard n : one employed to safeguard bathers

life·long adj : continuing through life

life·sav·ing *n* : art or practice of saving lives — **life·sav·er** \-ˌsāvər\ *n*

life·style \'līf,stīl\ *n* : a way of life

life·time *n* : duration of an individual's existence

lift \'lift\ *vb* **1** : move upward or cause to move upward **2** : put an end to — **lift** *n* — **lift·er** *n*

lift·off \'lift,óf\ *n* : vertical takeoff by a rocket

lig·a·ment \'ligəmənt\ *n* : band of tough tissue that holds bones together

lig·a·ture \'ligə,chúr, -chər\ *n* : something that binds or ties

¹**light** \'līt\ *n* **1** : radiation that makes vision possible **2** : daylight **3** : source of light **4** : public knowledge **5** : aspect **6** : celebrity **7** : flame for lighting ~ *adj* **1** : bright **2** : weak in color ~ *vb* lit \'lit\ *or* **light·ed**; **light·ing 1** : make or become light **2** : cause to burn — **light·er** *n* — **light·ness** *n* — **light·proof** *adj*

²**light** *adj* : not heavy, serious, or abundant — **light** *adv* — **light·ly** *adv* — **light·ness** *n* — **light·weight** *adj*

³**light** *vb* **light·ed** *or* **lit** \'lit\; **light·ing** : settle or dismount

¹**light·en** \'līt°n\ *vb* **1** : make light or bright **2** : give out flashes of lightning

²**lighten** *vb* **1** : relieve of a burden **2** : become lighter

light·heart·ed \-'härtəd\ *adj* : free from worry — **light·heart·ed·ly** *adv* — **light·heart·ed·ness** *n*

light·house *n* : structure with a powerful light for guiding sailors

light·ning \'lītniŋ\ *n* : flashing discharge of atmospheric electricity

light–year \'līt,yir\ *n* : distance traveled by light in one year equal to about 5.88 trillion miles

lig·nite \'lig,nīt\ *n* : brownish black soft coal

¹**like** \'līk\ *vb* **liked**; **lik·ing 1** : enjoy **2** : desire ~ *n* : preference — **lik·able**, **like·able** \'līkəbəl\ *adj*

²**like** *adj* : similar ~ *prep* **1** : similar or similarly to **2** : typical of **3** : such as ~ *n* : counterpart ~ *conj* : as or as if — **like·ness** *n* — **like·wise** *adv*

-like \ˌlīk\ *adj comb form* : resembling or characteristic of

like·li·hood \'līklē,húd\ *n* : probability

like·ly \'līklē\ *adj* **-li·er; -est 1** : probable **2** : believable ~ *adv* : in all probability

lik·en \'līkən\ *vb* : compare

lik·ing \'līkiŋ\ *n* : favorable regard

li·lac \'līlək, -ˌlak, -ˌläk\ *n* : shrub with clusters of fragrant pink, purple, or white flowers

lilt \'lilt\ *n* : rhythmical swing or flow

lily \'lilē\ *n, pl* **lil·ies** : tall bulbous herb with funnel-shaped flowers

lima bean \'līmə-\ *n* : flat edible seed of a plant or the plant itself

limb \'lim\ *n* **1** : projecting appendage used in moving or grasping **2** : tree branch — **limb·less** *adj*

lim·ber \'limbər\ *adj* : supple or agile ~ *vb* : make or become limber

lim·bo \'limbō\ *n, pl* **-bos** : place or state of confinement or oblivion

¹**lime** \'līm\ *n* : caustic white oxide of calcium

²**lime** *n* : small green lemonlike citrus fruit — **lime·ade** \-ˌād\ *n*

lime·light *n* : center of public attention

lim·er·ick \'limərik\ *n* : light poem of 5 lines

lime·stone *n* : rock that yields lime when burned

lim·it \'limət\ *n* **1** : boundary **2** : something that restrains or confines ~ *vb* : set limits on — **lim·i·ta·tion** \ˌlimə'tāshən\ *n* — **lim·it·less** *adj*

lim·ou·sine \'limə,zēn, ˌlimə'-\ *n* : large luxurious sedan

limp \'limp\ *vb* : walk lamely ~ *n* : limping movement or gait ~ *adj* : lacking firmness and body — **limp·ly** *adv* — **limp·ness** *n*

lim·pid \'limpəd\ *adj* : clear or transparent

lin·den \'lindən\ *n* : tree with large heart-shaped leaves

¹**line** \'līn\ *vb* **lined**; **lin·ing** : cover the inner surface of — **lin·ing** *n*

²**line** *n* **1** : cord, rope, or wire **2** : row or something like a row **3** : note **4** : course of action or thought **5** : state of agreement **6** : occupation **7** : limit **8** : transportation system **9** : long narrow mark ~ *vb* **lined**; **lin·ing 1** : mark with a line **2** : place in a line **3** : form a line

lin·e·age \'linēij\ *n* : descent from a common ancestor

lin·e·al \'linēəl\ *adj* **1** : linear **2** : in a direct line of ancestry

lin·ea·ments \'linēəmənts\ *n pl* : features or contours esp. of a face

lin·e·ar \'linēər\ *adj* **1** : straight **2** : long and narrow

lin·en \'linən\ *n* **1** : cloth or thread made of flax **2** : household articles made of linen cloth

lin·er \'līnər\ *n* **1** : one that lines **2** : ship or airplane belonging to a line

line·up \'līn,əp\ *n* **1** : line of persons for inspection or identification **2** : list of players in a game

-ling \liŋ\ *n suffix* **1** : one linked with **2** : young, small, or minor one

lin·ger \'liŋgər\ *vb* : be slow to leave or act — **lin·ger·er** *n*

lin·ge·rie \,länjə'rā, ,lanzhə-, -'rē\ *n* : women's underwear

lin·go \'liŋgō\ *n, pl* **-goes** : usu. strange language

lin·guist \'liŋgwist\ *n* **1** : person skilled in speech or languages **2** : student of language — **lin·guis·tic** \liŋ-'gwistik\ *adj* — **lin·guis·tics** *n pl*

lin·i·ment \'linəmənt\ *n* : liquid medication rubbed on the skin

link \'liŋk\ *n* **1** : connecting structure (as a ring of a chain) **2** : bond — **link** *vb* — **link·age** \-ij\ *n* — **link·er** *n*

li·no·leum \lə'nōlēəm\ *n* : floor covering with hard surface

lin·seed \'lin,sēd\ *n* : seeds of flax yielding an oil (**linseed oil**)

lint \'lint\ *n* : fine fluff or loose short fibers from fabric

lin·tel \'lintᵊl\ *n* : horizontal piece over a door or window

li·on \'līən\ *n* : large cat of Africa and Asia — **li·on·ess** \'līənəs\ *n*

li·on·ize \'līə,nīz\ *vb* **-ized; -iz·ing** : treat as very important — **li·on·iza·tion** \,līənə'zāshən\ *n*

lip \'lip\ *n* **1** : either of the 2 fleshy folds surrounding the mouth **2** : edge of something hollow — **lipped** \'lipt\ *adj* — **lip·read·ing** *n*

li·po·suc·tion \'lipə,səkshən, 'lī-\ *n* : surgical removal of fat deposits (as from the thighs)

lip·stick \'lip,stik\ *n* : stick of cosmetic to color lips

liq·ue·fy \'likwə,fī\ *vb* **-fied; -fy·ing** : make or become liquid — **liq·ue·fi·er** \'likwə,fīər\ *n*

li·queur \li'kər\ *n* : sweet or aromatic alcoholic liquor

liq·uid \'likwəd\ *adj* **1** : flowing freely like water **2** : neither solid nor gaseous **3** : of or convertible to cash — **liquid** *n* — **li·quid·i·ty** \lik'widətē\ *n*

liq·ui·date \'likwə,dāt\ *vb* **-dat·ed;** **-dat·ing 1** : pay off **2** : dispose of — **liq·ui·da·tion** \,likwə'dāshən\ *n*

li·quor \'likər\ *n* : liquid substance and esp. a distilled alcoholic beverage

lisp \'lisp\ *vb* : pronounce *s* and *z* imperfectly — **lisp** *n*

lis·some \'lisəm\ *adj* : supple or agile

¹list \'list\ *n* **1** : series of names or items ~ *vb* **1** : make a list of **2** : put on a list

²list *vb* : tilt or lean over ~ *n* : slant

lis·ten \'lisᵊn\ *vb* **1** : pay attention in order to hear **2** : heed — **lis·ten·er** \'lisᵊnər\ *n*

list·less \'listləs\ *adj* : having no desire to act — **list·less·ly** *adv* — **list·less·ness** *n*

lit \'lit\ *past of* LIGHT

lit·a·ny \'litᵊnē\ *n, pl* **-nies 1** : prayer said as a series of responses to a leader **2** : long recitation

li·ter \'lētər\ *n* : unit of liquid measure equal to about 1.06 quarts

lit·er·al \'litərəl\ *adj* : being exactly as stated — **lit·er·al·ly** *adv*

lit·er·ary \'litə,rerē\ *adj* : relating to literature

lit·er·ate \'litərət\ *adj* : able to read and write — **lit·er·a·cy** \'litərəsē\ *n*

lit·er·a·ture \'litərə,chùr, -chər\ *n* : writings of enduring interest

lithe \'līth, 'līth\ *adj* **1** : supple **2** : graceful — **lithe·some** \-səm\ *adj*

lith·o·graph \'lithə,graf\ *n* : print from a drawing on metal or stone — **li·thog·ra·pher** \lith'ägrəfər, 'lithə,grafər\ *n* — **lith·o·graph·ic** \,lithə'grafik\ *adj* — **li·thog·ra·phy** \lə'thägrəfē\ *n*

lit·i·gate \'litə,gāt\ *vb* **-gat·ed; -gat·ing** : carry on a lawsuit — **lit·i·gant** \'litigənt\ *n* — **lit·i·ga·tion** \,litə'gā-shən\ *n* — **li·ti·gious** \lə'tijəs, li-\ *adj* — **li·ti·gious·ness** *n*

lit·mus \'litməs\ *n* : coloring matter that turns red in acid solutions and blue in alkaline

lit·ter \'litər\ *n* **1** : animal offspring of one birth **2** : stretcher **3** : rubbish **4** : material to absorb animal waste ~ *vb* **1** : give birth to young **2** : strew with litter

lit·tle \'litᵊl\ *adj* **lit·tler** *or* **less** \'les\ *or* **less·er** \'lesər\; **lit·tlest** *or* **least** \'lēst\ **1** : not big **2** : not much **3** : not important ~ *adv* **less** \'les\; **least** \'lēst\ **1** : slightly **2** : not often ~ *n* : small amount — **lit·tle·ness** *n*

lit·ur·gy \'litərjē\ *n, pl* **-gies** : rite of

worship — **li•tur•gi•cal** \lə'tərjikəl\ *adj* — **li•tur•gi•cal•ly** \-klē\ *adv* — **lit•ur•gist** \'litərjist\ *n*

liv•able \'livəbəl\ *adj* : suitable for living in or with — **liv•a•bil•i•ty** \ˌlivə-'bilətē\ *n*

¹**live** \'liv\ *vb* **lived; liv•ing 1** : be alive **2** : conduct one's life **3** : subsist **4** : reside

²**live** \'līv\ *adj* **1** : having life **2** : burning **3** : connected to electric power **4** : not exploded **5** : of continuing interest **6** : involving the actual presence of real people

live•li•hood \'līvlēˌhud\ *n* : means of subsistence

live•long \'liv'lȯŋ\ *adj* : whole

live•ly \'līvlē\ *adj* **-li•er; -est** : full of life and vigor — **live•li•ness** *n*

liv•en \'līvən\ *vb* : enliven

liv•er \'livər\ *n* : organ that secretes bile

liv•ery \'livərē\ *n, pl* **-er•ies 1** : servant's uniform **2** : care of horses for pay — **liv•er•ied** \-rēd\ *adj* — **liv•ery•man** \-mən\ *n*

lives *pl of* LIFE

live•stock \'livˌstäk\ *n* : farm animals

liv•id \'livəd\ *adj* **1** : discolored by bruising **2** : pale **3** : enraged

liv•ing \'liviŋ\ *adj* : having life ⁓ *n* : livelihood

liz•ard \'lizərd\ *n* : reptile with 4 legs and a long tapering tail

lla•ma \'lämə\ *n* : So. American mammal related to the camel

load \'lōd\ *n* **1** : cargo **2** : supported weight **3** : burden **4** : a large quantity — usu. pl. ⁓ *vb* **1** : put a load on **2** : burden **3** : put ammunition in

¹**loaf** \'lōf\ *n, pl* **loaves** \'lōvz\ : mass of bread

²**loaf** *vb* : waste time — **loaf•er** *n*

loam \'lōm, 'lüm\ *n* : soil — **loamy** *adj*

loan \'lōn\ *n* **1** : money borrowed at interest **2** : something lent temporarily **3** : grant of use ⁓ *vb* : lend

loath \'lōth, 'lōth\ *adj* : very reluctant

loathe \'lōth\ *vb* **loathed; loath•ing** : hate

loath•ing \'lōthiŋ\ *n* : extreme disgust

loath•some \'lōthsəm, 'lōth-\ *adj* : repulsive

lob \'läb\ *vb* **-bb-** : throw or hit in a high arc **-lob** *n*

lob•by \'läbē\ *n, pl* **-bies 1** : public waiting room at the entrance of a building **2** : persons lobbying ⁓ *vb*

-bied; -by•ing : try to influence legislators — **lob•by•ist** *n*

lobe \'lōb\ *n* : rounded part — **lo•bar** \'lōbər\ *adj* — **lobed** \'lōbd\ *adj*

lo•bot•o•my \lō'bätəmē\ *n, pl* **-mies** : surgical severance of nerve fibers in the brain

lob•ster \'läbstər\ *n* : marine crustacean with 2 large pincerlike claws

lo•cal \'lōkəl\ *adj* : confined to or serving a limited area — **local** *n* — **lo•cal•ly** *adv*

lo•cale \lō'kal\ *n* : setting for an event

lo•cal•i•ty \lō'kalətē\ *n, pl* **-ties** : particular place

lo•cal•ize \'lōkəˌlīz\ *vb* **-ized; -iz•ing** : confine to a definite place — **lo•cal•i•za•tion** \ˌlōkələ'zāshən\ *n*

lo•cate \'lōˌkāt, lō'kāt\ *vb* **-cat•ed; -cat•ing 1** : settle **2** : find a site for **3** : discover the place of — **lo•ca•tion** \lō'kāshən\ *n*

¹**lock** \'läk\ *n* : tuft or strand of hair

²**lock** *n* **1** : fastener using a bolt **2** : enclosure in a canal to raise or lower boats ⁓ *vb* **1** : make fast with a lock **2** : confine **3** : interlock

lock•er \'läkər\ *n* : storage compartment

lock•et \'läkət\ *n* : small case worn on a necklace

lock•jaw *n* : tetanus

lock•out *n* : closing of a plant by an employer during a labor dispute

lock•smith \-ˌsmith\ *n* : one who makes or repairs locks

lo•co•mo•tion \ˌlōkə'mōshən\ *n* : power of moving — **lo•co•mo•tive** \-'mōtiv\ *adj*

lo•co•mo•tive \-'mōtiv\ *n* : vehicle that moves railroad cars

lo•co•weed \'lōkōˌwēd\ *n* : western plant poisonous to livestock

lo•cust \'lōkəst\ *n* **1** : migratory grasshopper **2** : cicada **3** : tree with hard wood or this wood

lo•cu•tion \lō'kyüshən\ *n* : way of saying something

lode \'lōd\ *n* : ore deposit

lode•stone *n* : magnetic rock

lodge \'läj\ *vb* **lodged; lodg•ing 1** : provide quarters for **2** : come to rest **3** : file ⁓ *n* **1** : special house (as for hunters) **2** : animal's den **3** : branch of a fraternal organization — **lodg•er** \'läjər\ *n* — **lodg•ing** *n* — **lodg•ment, lodge•ment** \-mənt\ *n*

loft \'lóft\ *n* **1** : attic **2** : upper floor (as of a warehouse)

lofty \'lóftē\ *adj* **loft•i•er; -est 1** : noble **2** : proud **3** : tall or high — **loft•i•ly** *adv* — **loft•i•ness** *n*

log \'lóg, 'läg\ *n* **1** : unshaped timber **2** : daily record of a ship's or plane's progress ~ *vb* **-gg- 1** : cut (trees) for lumber **2** : enter in a log — **log•ger** \-ər\ *n*

log•a•rithm \'lógə,rithəm, 'läg-\ *n* : exponent to which a base number is raised to produce a given number

loge \'lōzh\ *n* : box in a theater

log•ger•head \'lógər,hed, 'läg-\ *n* : large Atlantic sea turtle — **at log•gerheads** : in disagreement

log•ic \'läjik\ *n* **1** : science of reasoning **2** : sound reasoning — **log•i•cal** \-ikəl\ *adj* — **log•i•cal•ly** *adv* — **lo•gi•cian** \lō'jishən\ *n*

lo•gis•tics \lō'jistiks\ *n sing or pl* : procurement and movement of people and supplies — **lo•gis•tic** *adj*

logo \'lōgō, 'lóg-, 'läg-\ *n, pl* **log•os** \-ōz\ : advertising symbol

loin \'lóin\ *n* **1** : part of the body on each side of the spine between the hip and lower ribs **2** *pl* : pubic regions

loi•ter \'lóitər\ *vb* : remain around a place idly — **loi•ter•er** *n*

loll \'läl\ *vb* : lounge

lol•li•pop, lol•ly•pop \'läli,päp\ *n* : hard candy on a stick

lone \'lōn\ *adj* **1** : alone or isolated **2** : only — **lone•li•ness** *n* — **lone•ly** *adj* — **lon•er** \'lōnər\ *n*

lone•some \-səm\ *adj* : sad from lack of company — **lone•some•ly** *adv* — **lone•some•ness** *n*

long \'lóŋ\ *adj* **lon•ger** \'lóŋgər\; **long•est** \'lóŋgəst\ **1** : extending far or for a considerable time **2** : having a specified length **3** : tedious **4** : well supplied — used with *on* ~ *adv* : for a long time ~ *n* : long period ~ *vb* : feel a strong desire — **long•ing** \'lóŋiŋ\ *n* — **long•ing•ly** *adv*

lon•gev•i•ty \län'jevətē\ *n* : long life

long•hand *n* : handwriting

long•horn *n* : cattle with long horns

lon•gi•tude \'länjə,tüd, -,tyüd\ *n* : angular distance east or west from a meridian

lon•gi•tu•di•nal \,länjə'tüd³nəl, -'tyüd-\ *adj* : lengthwise — **lon•gi•tu•di•nal•ly** *adv*

long•shore•man \'lóŋ'shōrmən\ *n* : one who loads and unloads ships

look \'lúk\ *vb* **1** : see **2** : seem **3** : direct one's attention **4** : face ~ *n* **1** : action of looking **2** : appearance of the face **3** : aspect — **look after** : take care of — **look for 1** : expect **2** : search for

look•out *n* **1** : one who watches **2** : careful watch

¹loom \'lüm\ *n* : frame or machine for weaving

²loom *vb* : appear large and indistinct or impressive

loon \'lün\ *n* : black-and-white diving bird

loo•ny, loo•ney \'lünē\ *adj* **-ni•er; -est** : crazy

loop \'lüp\ *n* **1** : doubling of a line that leaves an opening **2** : something like a loop **-loop** *vb*

loop•hole \'lüp,hōl\ *n* : means of evading

loose \'lüs\ *adj* **loos•er; -est 1** : not fixed tight **2** : not restrained **3** : not dense **4** : slack **5** : not exact ~ *vb* **loosed; loos•ing 1** : release **2** : untie or relax — **loose** *adv* — **loose•ly** *adv* — **loos•en** \'lüs³n\ *vb* — **loose•ness** *n*

loot \'lüt\ *n or vb* : plunder — **loot•er** *n*

lop \'läp\ *vb* **-pp-** : cut off

lope \'lōp\ *n* : bounding gait — **lope** *vb*

lop•sid•ed \'läp'sīdəd\ *adj* **1** : leaning to one side **2** : not symmetrical — **lop•sid•ed•ly** *adv* — **lop•sid•ed•ness** *n*

lo•qua•cious \lō'kwāshəs\ *adj* : very talkative — **lo•quac•i•ty** \-'kwasətē\ *n*

lord \'lórd\ *n* **1** : one with authority over others **2** : British nobleman

lord•ly \-lē\ *adj* **-li•er; -est** : haughty

lord•ship \-,ship\ *n* : rank of a lord

Lord's Supper *n* : Communion

lore \'lōr\ *n* : traditional knowledge

lose \'lüz\ *vb* **lost** \'lóst\; **los•ing** \'lüziŋ\ **1** : have pass from one's possession **2** : be deprived of **3** : waste **4** : be defeated in **5** : fail to keep to or hold **6** : get rid of — **los•er** *n*

loss \'lós\ *n* **1** : something lost **2** *pl* : killed, wounded, or captured soldiers **3** : failure to win

lost \'lóst\ *adj* **1** : not used, won, or claimed **2** : unable to find the way

lot \'lät\ *n* **1** : object used in deciding something by chance **2** : share **3** : fate **4** : plot of land **5** : much

loth \'lōth, 'lōt͟h\ *var of* LOATH

lo•tion \'lōshən\ *n* : liquid to rub on the skin

lot•tery \'lätərē\ *n, pl* **-ter•ies** : drawing of lots with prizes going to winners

lo•tus \'lōtəs\ *n* **1** : legendary fruit that causes forgetfulness **2** : water lily

loud \'laud\ *adj* **1** : high in volume of sound **2** : noisy **3** : obtrusive in color or pattern — **loud** *adv* — **loud•ly** *adv* — **loud•ness** *n*

loud•speak•er *n* : device that amplifies sound

lounge \'launj\ *vb* **lounged; loung•ing** : act or move lazily ~ *n* : room with comfortable furniture

lour \'lauər\ *var of* LOWER

louse \'laus\ *n, pl* **lice** \'līs\ : parasitic wingless usu. flat insect

lousy \'lauzē\ *adj* **lous•i•er; -est** **1** : infested with lice **2** : not good — **lous•i•ly** *adv* — **lous•i•ness** *n*

lout \'laut\ *n* : stupid awkward person — **lout•ish** *adj* — **lout•ish•ly** *adv*

lou•ver, lou•vre \'lüvər\ *n* : opening having parallel slanted slats for ventilation or such a slat

love \'ləv\ *n* **1** : strong affection **2** : warm attachment **3** : beloved person ~ *vb* **loved; lov•ing** **1** : feel affection for **2** : enjoy greatly — **lov•able** \-əbəl\ *adj* — **love•less** *adj* — **lov•er** *n* — **lov•ing•ly** *adv*

love•lorn \-,lorn\ *adj* : deprived of love or of a lover

love•ly \'ləvlē\ *adj* **-li•er; -est** : beautiful — **love•li•ness** *n* — **lovely** *adv*

¹**low** \'lō\ *vb or n* : moo

²**low** *adj* **low•er; low•est** **1** : not high or tall **2** : below normal level **3** : not loud **4** : humble **5** : sad **6** : less than usual **7** : falling short of a standard **8** : unfavorable ~ *n* **1** : something low **2** : automobile gear giving the slowest speed — **low** *adv* — **low•ness** *n*

low•brow \'lō,brau\ *n* : person with little taste or intellectual interest

¹**low•er** \'lauər\ *vb* **1** : scowl **2** : become dark and threatening

²**low•er** \'lōər\ *adj* : relatively low (as in rank)

³**low•er** \'lōər\ *vb* **1** : drop **2** : let descend **3** : reduce in amount

low•land \'lōlənd, -,land\ *n* : low flat country

low•ly \'lōlē\ *adj* — **li•er; -est** **1** : humble **2** : low in rank — **low•li•ness** *n*

loy•al \'loiəl\ *adj* : faithful to a country, cause, or friend — **loy•al•ist** *n* — **loy•al•ly** *adv* — **loy•al•ty** \'loiəltē\ *n*

loz•enge \'läz°nj\ *n* : small medicated candy

lu•bri•cant \'lübrikənt\ *n* : material (as grease) to reduce friction

lu•bri•cate \-,kāt\ *vb* **-cat•ed; -cat•ing** : apply a lubricant to — **lu•bri•ca•tion** \,lübrə'kāshən\ *n* — **lu•bri•ca•tor** \'lübrə,kātər\ *n*

lu•cid \'lüsəd\ *adj* **1** : mentally sound **2** : easily understood — **lu•cid•i•ty** \lü'sidətē\ *n* — **lu•cid•ly** *adv* — **lu•cid•ness** *n*

luck \'lək\ *n* **1** : chance **2** : good fortune — **luck•i•ly** *adv* — **luck•i•ness** *n* — **luck•less** *adj* — **lucky** *adj*

lu•cra•tive \'lükrətiv\ *adj* : profitable — **lu•cra•tive•ly** *adv* — **lu•cra•tive•ness** *n*

Lud•dite \'lə,dīt\ *n* : one who opposes technological change

lu•di•crous \'lüdəkrəs\ *adj* : comically ridiculous — **lu•di•crous•ly** *adv* — **lu•di•crous•ness** *n*

lug \'ləg\ *vb* **-gg-** : drag or carry laboriously

lug•gage \'ləgij\ *n* : baggage

lu•gu•bri•ous \lu'gübrēəs\ *adj* : mournful often to an exaggerated degree — **lu•gu•bri•ous•ly** *adv* — **lu•gu•bri•ous•ness** *n*

luke•warm \'lük'worm\ *adj* **1** : moderately warm **2** : not enthusiastic

lull \'ləl\ *vb* : make or become quiet or relaxed ~ *n* : temporary calm

lul•la•by \'lələ,bī\ *n, pl* **-bies** : song to lull children to sleep

lum•ba•go \,ləm'bāgō\ *n* : rheumatic back pain

lum•ber \'ləmbər\ *n* : timber dressed for use ~ *vb* : cut logs — **lum•ber•man** *n* — **lum•ber•yard** *n*

lum•ber•jack \-,jak\ *n* : logger

lu•mi•nary \'lümə,nerē\ *n, pl* **-nar•ies** : very famous person

lu•mi•nes•cence \,lümə'nes°ns\ *n* : low-temperature emission of light — **lu•mi•nes•cent** \-°nt\ *adj*

lu•mi•nous \'lümənəs\ *adj* : emitting light — **lu•mi•nance** \-nəns\ *n* — **lu•mi•nos•i•ty** \,lümə'näsətē\ *n* — **lu•mi•nous•ly** *adv*

lump \'ləmp\ *n* **1** : mass of irregular shape **2** : abnormal swelling ~ *vb* : heap together — **lump•ish** *adj* — **lumpy** *adj*

lu·na·cy \'lünəsē\ *n, pl* **-cies** : state of insanity

lu·nar \'lünər\ *adj* : of the moon

lu·na·tic \'lünə,tik\ *adj* : insane — **lunatic** *n*

lunch \'lənch\ *n* : noon meal ⁓ *vb* : eat lunch

lun·cheon \'lənchən\ *n* : usu. formal lunch

lung \'ləŋ\ *n* : breathing organ in the chest — **lunged** \'ləŋd\ *adj*

lunge \'lənj\ *n* **1** : sudden thrust **2** : sudden move forward — **lunge** *vb*

lurch \'lərch\ *n* : sudden swaying — **lurch** *vb*

lure \'lùr\ *n* **1** : something that attracts **2** : artificial fish bait ⁓ *vb* **lured; luring** : attract

lu·rid \'lùrəd\ *adj* **1** : gruesome **2** : sensational — **lu·rid·ly** *adv*

lurk \'lərk\ *vb* : lie in wait

lus·cious \'ləshəs\ *adj* **1** : pleasingly sweet in taste or smell **2** : sensually appealing — **lus·cious·ly** *adv* — **lus·cious·ness** *n*

lush \'ləsh\ *adj* : covered with abundant growth

lust \'ləst\ *n* **1** : intense sexual desire **2** : intense longing — **lust** *vb* — **lust·ful** *adj*

lus·ter, lus·tre \'ləstər\ *n* **1** : brightness from reflected light **2** : magnificence — **lus·ter·less** *adj* — **lus·trous** \-trəs\ *adj*

lusty \'ləstē\ *adj* **lust·i·er; -est** : full of vitality — **lust·i·ly** *adv* — **lust·i·ness** *n*

lute \'lüt\ *n* : pear-shaped stringed instrument — **lute·nist, lu·ta·nist** \'lüt°nist\ *n*

lux·u·ri·ant \,ləg'zhùrēənt, ,lək-'shùr-\ *adj* **1** : growing plentifully **2** : rich and varied — **lux·u·ri·ance** \-ēəns\ *n* — **lux·u·ri·ant·ly** *adv*

lux·u·ri·ate \-ē,āt\ *vb* **-at·ed; -at·ing** : revel

lux·u·ry \'ləkshərē, 'ləgzh-\ *n, pl* **-ries 1** : great comfort **2** : something adding to pleasure or comfort — **lux·u·ri·ous** \,ləg'zhùrēəs, ,lək'shùr-\ *adj* — **lux·u·ri·ous·ly** *adv*

-ly \lē\ *adv suffix* **1** : in a specified way **2** : from a specified point of view

ly·ce·um \lī'sēəm, 'līsē-\ *n* : hall for public lectures

lye \'lī\ *n* : caustic alkaline substance

lying *pres part of* LIE

lymph \'limf\ *n* : bodily liquid consisting chiefly of blood plasma and white blood cells — **lym·phat·ic** \lim'fatik\ *adj*

lynch \'linch\ *vb* : put to death by mob action — **lynch·er** *n*

lynx \'liŋks\ *n, pl* **lynx** *or* **lynx·es** : wildcat

lyre \'līr\ *n* : ancient Greek stringed instrument

lyr·ic \'lirik\ *adj* **1** : suitable for singing **2** : expressing direct personal emotion ⁓ *n* **1** : lyric poem **2** *pl* : words of a song — **lyr·i·cal** \-ikəl\ *adj*

M

m \'em\ *n, pl* **m's** *or* **ms** \'emz\ : 13th letter of the alphabet

ma'am \'mam\ *n* : madam

ma·ca·bre \mə'käb, -'käbər, -'käbrə\ *adj* : gruesome

mac·ad·am \mə'kadəm\ *n* : pavement of cemented broken stone — **mac·ad·am·ize** \-,īz\ *vb*

mac·a·ro·ni \,makə'rōnē\ *n* : tube-shaped pasta

mac·a·roon \,makə'rün\ *n* : cookie of ground almonds or coconut

ma·caw \mə'kò\ *n* : large long-tailed parrot

¹mace \'mās\ *n* **1** : heavy spiked club **2** : ornamental staff as a symbol of authority

²mace *n* : spice from the fibrous coating of the nutmeg

ma·chete \mə'shetē\ *n* : large heavy knife

mach·i·na·tion \,makə'nāshən, ,mashə-\ *n* : plot or scheme — **mach·i·nate** \'makə,nāt, 'mash-\ *vb*

ma·chine \mə'shēn\ *n* : combination of mechanical or electrical parts ⁓ *vb* **-chined; -chin·ing** : modify by machine-operated tools — **ma·chin·able** *adj* — **ma·chin·ery** \-ərē\ *n* — **ma·chin·ist** *n*

mack•er•el \'makərəl\ *n, pl* **-el** *or* **-els** : No. Atlantic food fish

mack•i•naw \'makə,nó\ *n* : short heavy plaid coat

mac•ra•mé \,makrə'mā\ *n* : coarse lace or fringe made by knotting

mac•ro \'makrō\ *adj* : very large

mac•ro•cosm \'makrə,käzəm\ *n* : universe

mad \'mad\ *adj* **-dd-** **1** : insane or rabid **2** : rash and foolish **3** : angry **4** : carried away by enthusiasm — **mad•den** \'mad°n\ *vb* — **mad•den•ing•ly** \'mad°niṇlē\ *adv* — **mad•ly** *adv* — **mad•ness** *n*

mad•am \'madəm\ *n, pl* **mes•dames** \mā'däm\ — used in polite address to a woman

ma•dame \mə'dam, *before a surname* also 'madəm\ *n, pl* **mes•dames** \mā'däm\ — used as a title for a woman not of English-speaking nationality

mad•cap \'mad,kap\ *adj* : wild or zany — **madcap** *n*

made *past of* MAKE

Ma•dei•ra \mə'dirə\ *n* : amber-colored dessert wine

ma•de•moi•selle \,madmwə'zel, -mə-'zel\ *n, pl* **ma•de•moi•selles** \-'zelz\ *or* **mes•de•moi•selles** \,mādmwə-'zel\ : an unmarried girl or woman — used as a title for a woman esp. of French nationality

mad•house *n* **1** : insane asylum **2** : place of great uproar or confusion

mad•man \-,man, -mən\ *n* : lunatic

mad•ri•gal \'madrigəl\ *n* : elaborate song for several voice parts

mad•wom•an \'mad,wumən\ *n* : woman who is insane

mael•strom \'mālstrəm\ *n* **1** : whirlpool **2** : tumult

mae•stro \'mīstrō\ *n, pl* **-stros** *or* **-stri** \-,strē\ : eminent composer or conductor

Ma•fia \'mäfēə\ *n* : secret criminal organization

ma•fi•o•so \,mäfē'ōsō\ *n, pl* **-si** \-sē\ : member of the Mafia

mag•a•zine \'magə,zēn\ *n* **1** : storehouse **2** : publication issued at regular intervals **3** : cartridge container in a gun

ma•gen•ta \mə'jentə\ *n* : deep purplish red color

mag•got \'magət\ *n* : wormlike fly larva — **mag•goty** *adj*

mag•ic \'majik\ *n* **1** : art of using supernatural powers **2** : extraordinary power or influence **3** : sleight of hand — **magic, mag•i•cal** \-ikəl\ *adj* — **mag•i•cal•ly** *adv* — **ma•gi•cian** \mə'jishən\ *n*

mag•is•te•ri•al \,majə'stirēəl\ *adj* **1** : authoritative **2** : relating to a magistrate

mag•is•trate \'majə,strāt\ *n* : judge — **mag•is•tra•cy** \-strəsē\ *n*

mag•ma \'magmə\ *n* : molten rock

mag•nan•i•mous \mag'nanəməs\ *adj* : noble or generous — **mag•na•nim•i•ty** \,magnə'nimətē\ *n* — **mag•nan•i•mous•ly** *adv*

mag•ne•sia \mag'nēzhə, -shə\ *n* : oxide of magnesium used as a laxative

mag•ne•sium \mag'nēzēəm, -zhəm\ *n* : silver-white metallic chemical element

mag•net \'magnət\ *n* **1** : body that attracts iron **2** : something that attracts — **mag•net•ic** \mag'netik\ *adj* — **mag•net•i•cal•ly** \-iklē\ *adv* — **mag•ne•tism** \'magnə,tizəm\ *n*

mag•ne•tite \'magnə,tīt\ *n* : black iron ore

mag•ne•tize \'magnə,tīz\ *vb* **-tized;** **-tiz•ing** **1** : attract like a magnet **2** : give magnetic properties to — **mag•ne•tiz•able** *adj* — **mag•ne•ti•za•tion** \,magnətə'zāshən\ *n* — **mag•ne•tiz•er** *n*

mag•nif•i•cent \mag'nifəsənt\ *adj* : splendid — **mag•nif•i•cence** \-səns\ *n* — **mag•nif•i•cent•ly** *adv*

mag•ni•fy \'magnə,fī\ *vb* **-fied; -fy•ing** **1** : intensify **2** : enlarge — **mag•ni•fi•ca•tion** \,magnəfə'kāshən\ *n* — **mag•ni•fi•er** \'magnə,fīər\ *n*

mag•ni•tude \'magnə,tüd, -,tyüd\ *n* **1** : greatness of size or extent **2** : quantity

mag•no•lia \mag'nōlyə\ *n* : shrub with large fragrant flowers

mag•pie \'mag,pī\ *n* : long-tailed black-and-white bird

ma•hog•a•ny \mə'hägənē\ *n, pl* **-nies** : tropical evergreen tree or its reddish brown wood

maid \'mād\ *n* **1** : unmarried young woman **2** : female servant

maid•en \'mād°n\ *n* : unmarried young woman ~ *adj* **1** : unmarried **2** : first — **maid•en•hood** \-,hud\ *n* — **maid•en•ly** *adj*

maid·en·hair \-ˌhar\ *n* : fern with delicate feathery fronds

¹mail \'māl\ *n* **1** : something sent or carried in the postal system **2** : postal system ~ *vb* : send by mail — **mail·box** *n* — **mail·man** \-ˌman, -mən\ *n*

²mail *n* : armor of metal links or plates

maim \'mām\ *vb* : seriously wound or disfigure

main \'mān\ *n* **1** : force **2** : ocean **3** : principal pipe, duct, or circuit of a utility system ~ *adj* : chief — **main·ly** *adv*

main·frame \'mānˌfrām\ *n* : large fast computer

main·land \'mānˌland, -lənd\ *n* : part of a country on a continent

main·stay *n* : chief support

main·stream *n* : prevailing current or direction of activity or influence — **mainstream** *adj*

main·tain \mān'tān\ *vb* **1** : keep in an existing state (as of repair) **2** : sustain **3** : declare — **main·tain·abil·i·ty** \-ˌtānə'bilətē\ *n* — **main·tain·able** \-'tānəbəl\ *adj* — **main·te·nance** \'māntᵊnəns\ *n*

mai·tre d'hô·tel \ˌmātrədō'tel, ˌme-\ *n* : head of a dining room staff

maize \'māz\ *n* : corn

maj·es·ty \'majəstē\ *n, pl* **-ties 1** : sovereign power or dignity — used as a title **2** : grandeur or splendor — **ma·jes·tic** \mə'jestik\ *adj* — **ma·jes·ti·cal·ly** \-tiklē\ *adv*

ma·jor \'mājər\ *adj* **1** : larger or greater **2** : noteworthy or conspicuous ~ *n* **1** : commissioned officer (as in the army) ranking next below a lieutenant colonel **2** : main field of study ~ *vb* **-jored; -jor·ing** : pursue an academic major

ma·jor·do·mo \ˌmājər'dōmō\ *n, pl* **-mos** : head steward

major general *n* : commissioned officer (as in the army) ranking next below a lieutenant general

ma·jor·i·ty \mə'jórətē\ *n, pl* **-ties 1** : age of full civil rights **2** : quantity more than half

make \'māk\ *vb* **made** \'mād\; **making 1** : cause to exist, occur, or appear **2** : fashion or manufacture **3** : formulate in the mind **4** : constitute **5** : prepare **6** : cause to be or become **7** : carry out or perform **8** : compel **9** : gain **10** : have an effect — used with *for* ~ *n* : brand — **mak·er** *n* —

make do *vb* : get along with what is available — **make good** *vb* **1** : repay **2** : succeed — **make out** *vb* **1** : draw up or write **2** : discern or understand **3** : fare — **make up** *vb* **1** : invent **2** : become reconciled **3** : compensate for

make–be·lieve *n* : a pretending to believe ~ *adj* : imagined or pretended

make·shift *n* : temporary substitute — **makeshift** *adj*

make–up \-ˌəp\ *n* **1** : way in which something is constituted **2** : cosmetics

mal·ad·just·ed \ˌmalə'jəstəd\ *adj* : poorly adjusted (as to one's environment) — **mal·ad·just·ment** \-'jəstmənt\ *n*

mal·adroit \ˌmalə'dróit\ *adj* : clumsy or inept

mal·a·dy \'malədē\ *n, pl* **-dies** : disease or disorder

mal·aise \mə'lāz, ma-\ *n* : sense of being unwell

mal·a·mute \'maləˌmyüt\ *n* : powerful heavy-coated dog

mal·a·prop·ism \'maləˌpräpˌizəm\ *n* : humorous misuse of a word

ma·lar·ia \mə'lerēə\ *n* : disease transmitted by a mosquito — **ma·lar·i·al** \-əl\ *adj*

ma·lar·key \mə'lärkē\ *n* : foolishness

mal·con·tent \ˌmalkən'tent\ *n* : discontented person — **malcontent** *adj*

male \'māl\ *adj* **1** : relating to the sex that performs a fertilizing function **2** : masculine ~ *n* : male individual — **male·ness** *n*

mal·e·dic·tion \ˌmalə'dikshən\ *n* : curse

mal·e·fac·tor \'maləˌfaktər\ *n* : one who commits an offense esp. against the law

ma·lef·i·cent \mə'lefəsənt\ *adj* : harmful

ma·lev·o·lent \mə'levələnt\ *adj* : malicious or spiteful — **ma·lev·o·lence** \-ləns\ *n*

mal·fea·sance \mal'fēzᵊns\ *n* : misconduct by a public official

mal·for·ma·tion \ˌmalfór'māshən\ *n* : distortion or faulty formation — **mal·formed** \mal'fórmd\ *adj*

mal·func·tion \mal'fəŋkshən\ *vb* : fail to operate properly — **malfunction** *n*

mal·ice \'maləs\ *n* : desire to cause pain or injury to another — **ma·li-**

cious \mə'lishəs\ *adj* — **ma·li-cious·ly** *adv*

ma·lign \mə'līn\ *adj* 1 : wicked 2 : malignant ∼ *vb* : speak evil of

ma·lig·nant \mə'lignənt\ *adj* 1 : harmful 2 : likely to cause death — **ma·lig·nan·cy** \-nənsē\ *n* — **ma·lig·nant·ly** *adv* — **ma·lig·ni·ty** \-nətē\ *n*

ma·lin·ger \mə'liŋgər\ *vb* : pretend illness to avoid duty — **ma·lin·ger·er** *n*

mall \'mȯl\ *n* 1 : shaded promenade 2 : concourse providing access to rows of shops

mal·lard \'malərd\ *n, pl* **-lard** *or* **-lards** : common wild duck

mal·lea·ble \'malēəbəl\ *adj* 1 : easily shaped 2 : adaptable — **mal·le·a·bil·i·ty** \ˌmalēə'bilətē\ *n*

mal·let \'malət\ *n* : hammerlike tool

mal·nour·ished \mal'nərisht\ *adj* : poorly nourished

mal·nu·tri·tion \ˌmalnu'trishən, -nyu-\ *n* : inadequate nutrition

mal·odor·ous \mal'ōdərəs\ *adj* : foul-smelling — **mal·odor·ous·ly** *adv* — **mal·odor·ous·ness** *n*

mal·prac·tice \-'praktəs\ *n* : failure of professional duty

malt \'mȯlt\ *n* : sprouted grain used in brewing

mal·treat \mal'trēt\ *vb* : treat badly — **mal·treat·ment** *n*

ma·ma, mam·ma \'mämə\ *n* : mother

mam·mal \'maməl\ *n* : warm-blooded vertebrate animal that nourishes its young with milk — **mam·ma·li·an** \mə'mālēən, ma-\ *adj or n*

mam·ma·ry \'mamərē\ *adj* : relating to the milk-secreting glands (**mammary glands**) of mammals

mam·mo·gram \'maməˌgram\ *n* : X-ray photograph of the breasts

mam·moth \'maməth\ *n* : large hairy extinct elephant ∼ *adj* : enormous

man \'man\ *n, pl* **men** \'men\ 1 : human being 2 : adult male 3 : mankind ∼ *vb* **-nn-** : supply with people for working — **man·hood** *n* — **man·hunt** *n* — **man·like** *adj* — **man·li·ness** *n* — **man·ly** *adj or adv* — **man–made** *adj* — **man·nish** *adj* — **man·nish·ly** *adv* — **man·nish·ness** *n* — **man–size, man–sized** *adj*

man·a·cle \'manikəl\ *n* : shackle for the hands or wrists — **manacle** *vb*

man·age \'manij\ *vb* **-aged; -ag·ing** 1 : control 2 : direct or carry on business or affairs 3 : cope — **man·age·abil-**

i·ty \ˌmanijə'bilətē\ *n* — **man·age·able** \'manijəbəl\ *adj* — **man·age·able·ness** *n* — **man·age·ably** \-blē\ *adv* — **man·age·ment** \'manijmənt\ *n* — **man·ag·er** \'manijər\ *n* — **man·a·ge·ri·al** \ˌmanə'jirēəl\ *adj*

man·da·rin \'mandərən\ *n* : Chinese imperial official

man·date \'manˌdāt\ *n* : authoritative command

man·da·to·ry \'mandəˌtōrē\ *adj* : obligatory

man·di·ble \'mandəbəl\ *n* : lower jaw — **man·dib·u·lar** \man'dibyələr\ *adj*

man·do·lin \ˌmandə'lin, 'mandᵊlən\ *n* : stringed musical instrument

man·drake \'manˌdrāk\ *n* : herb with a large forked root

mane \'mān\ *n* : animal's neck hair — **maned** \'mānd\ *adj*

ma·neu·ver \mə'nüvər, -'nyü-\ *n* 1 : planned movement of troops or ships 2 : military training exercise 3 : clever or skillful move or action — **maneuver** *vb* — **ma·neu·ver·abil·i·ty** \-ˌnüvərə'bilətē, -ˌnyü-\ *n*

man·ful \'manfəl\ *adj* : courageous — **man·ful·ly** *adv*

man·ga·nese \'maŋgəˌnēz, -ˌnēs\ *n* : gray metallic chemical element

mange \'mānj\ *n* : skin disease of domestic animals — **mangy** \'mānjē\ *adj*

man·ger \'mānjər\ *n* : feeding trough for livestock

man·gle \'maŋgəl\ *vb* **-gled; -gling** 1 : mutilate 2 : bungle — **man·gler** *n*

man·go \'maŋgō\ *n, pl* **-goes** : juicy yellowish red tropical fruit

man·grove \'manˌgrōv, 'maŋ-\ *n* : tropical tree growing in salt water

man·han·dle *vb* : handle roughly

man·hole *n* : entry to a sewer

ma·nia \'mānēə, -nyə\ *n* 1 : insanity marked by uncontrollable emotion or excitement 2 : excessive enthusiasm — **ma·ni·ac** \-nēˌak\ *n* — **ma·ni·a·cal** \mə'nīəkəl\ *adj* — **man·ic** \'manik\ *adj or n*

man·i·cure \'manəˌkyur\ *n* : treatment for the fingernails ∼ *vb* **-cured; -cur·ing** 1 : do manicure work on 2 : trim precisely — **man·i·cur·ist** \-ˌkyurist\ *n*

¹man·i·fest \'manəˌfest\ *adj* : clear to the senses or to the mind ∼ *vb* : make evident — **man·i·fes·ta·tion**

\,manəfə'stāshən\ *n* — **man·i·fest·ly** *adv*

²**manifest** *n* : invoice of cargo or list of passengers

man·i·fes·to \,manə'festō\ *n, pl* **-tos** *or* **-toes** : public declaration of policy or views

man·i·fold \'manə,fōld\ *adj* : marked by diversity or variety ∼ *n* : pipe fitting with several outlets for connections

ma·nila paper \mə'nilə-\ *n* : durable brownish paper

ma·nip·u·late \mə'nipyə,lāt\ *vb* **-lat·ed; -lat·ing** **1** : treat or operate manually or mechanically **2** : influence esp. by cunning — **ma·nip·u·la·tion** \mə,nipyə'lāshən\ *n* — **ma·nip·u·la·tive** \-'nipyə,lātiv, -lətiv\ *adj* — **ma·nip·u·la·tor** \-,lātər\ *n*

man·kind \'man'kīnd\ *n* : human race

man·na \'manə\ *n* : something valuable that comes unexpectedly

manned \'mand\ *adj* : carrying or performed by a man

man·ne·quin \'manikən\ *n* : dummy used to display clothes

man·ner \'manər\ *n* **1** : kind **2** : usual way of acting **3** : artistic method **4** *pl* : social conduct

man·nered \-ərd\ *adj* **1** : having manners of a specified kind **2** : artificial

man·ner·ism \'manə,rizəm\ *n* : individual peculiarity of action

man·ner·ly \-lē\ *adj* : polite — **man·ner·li·ness** *n* — **mannerly** *adv*

man-of-war \,manə'wȯr, -əv'wȯr\ *n, pl* **men-of-war** \,men-\ : warship

man·or \'manər\ *n* : country estate — **ma·no·ri·al** \mə'nȯrēəl\ *adj*

man·pow·er *n* : supply of people available for service

man·sard \'man,särd\ *n* : roof with two slopes on all sides and the lower slope the steeper

manse \'mans\ *n* : parsonage

man·ser·vant *n, pl* **men·ser·vants** : a male servant

man·sion \'manchən\ *n* : very big house

man·slaugh·ter *n* : unintentional killing of a person

man·tel \'mant³l\ *n* : shelf above a fireplace

man·tis \'mantəs\ *n, pl* **-tis·es** *or* **-tes** \'man,tēz\ : large green insect-eating insect with stout forelegs

man·tle \'mant³l\ *n* **1** : sleeveless cloak **2** : something that covers, enfolds, or envelops — **mantle** *vb*

man·tra \'mantrə\ *n* : mystical chant

man·u·al \'manyəwəl\ *adj* : involving the hands or physical force ∼ *n* : handbook — **man·u·al·ly** *adv*

man·u·fac·ture \,manyə'fakchər, ,manə-\ *n* : process of making wares by hand or by machinery ∼ *vb* **-tured; -tur·ing** : make from raw materials — **man·u·fac·tur·er** *n*

ma·nure \mə'nůr, -'nyůr\ *n* : animal excrement used as fertilizer

manu·script \'manyə,skript\ *n* **1** : something written or typed **2** : document submitted for publication

many \'menē\ *adj* **more** \'mȯr\; **most** \'mōst\ : consisting of a large number — **many** *n or pron*

map \'map\ *n* : representation of a geographical area ∼ *vb* **-pp-** **1** : make a map of **2** : plan in detail — **map·pa·ble** \-əbəl\ *adj* — **map·per** *n*

ma·ple \'māpəl\ *n* : tree with hard light-colored wood

mar \'mär\ *vb* **-rr-** : damage

mar·a·schi·no \,marə'skēnō, -'shē-\ *n, pl* **-nos** : preserved cherry

mar·a·thon \'marə,thän\ *n* **1** : long-distance race **2** : test of endurance — **mar·a·thon·er** \-,thänər\ *n*

ma·raud \mə'rȯd\ *vb* : roam about in search of plunder — **ma·raud·er** *n*

mar·ble \'märbəl\ *n* **1** : crystallized limestone **2** : small glass ball used in a children's game (**marbles**)

mar·bling \-bəliŋ\ *n* : intermixture of fat and lean in meat

march \'märch\ *vb* : move with regular steps or in a purposeful manner ∼ *n* **1** : distance covered in a march **2** : measured stride **3** : forward movement **4** : music for marching — **march·er** *n*

March *n* : 3d month of the year having 31 days

mar·chio·ness \'märshənəs\ *n* : woman holding the rank of a marquess

Mar·di Gras \'märdē,grä\ *n* : Tuesday before the beginning of Lent often observed with parades and merry-making

mare \'mar\ *n* : female horse

mar·ga·rine \'märjərən\ *n* : butter substitute made usu. from vegetable oils

mar·gin \'märjən\ *n* **1** : edge **2** : spare amount, measure, or degree

mar·gin·al \-jənəl\ *adj* **1** : relating to

or situated at a border or margin **2** : close to the lower limit of acceptability — **mar·gin·al·ly** *adv*

mari·gold \'marə₁gōld\ *n* : garden plant with showy flower heads

mar·i·jua·na \₁marə'wänə, -'hwä-\ *n* : intoxicating drug obtained from the hemp plant

ma·ri·na \mə'rēnə\ *n* : place for mooring pleasure boats

mar·i·nate \'marə₁nāt\ *vb* **-nat·ed; -nat·ing** : soak in a savory sauce

ma·rine \mə'rēn\ *adj* **1** : relating to the sea **2** : relating to marines ∼ *n* : infantry soldier associated with a navy

mar·i·ner \'marənər\ *n* : sailor

mar·i·o·nette \₁marēə'net\ *n* : puppet

mar·i·tal \'marət⁰l\ *adj* : relating to marriage

mar·i·time \'marə₁tīm\ *adj* : relating to the sea or commerce on the sea

mar·jo·ram \'märjərəm\ *n* : aromatic mint used as a seasoning

mark \'märk\ *n* **1** : something aimed at **2** : something (as a line) designed to record position **3** : visible sign **4** : written symbol **5** : grade **6** : lasting impression **7** : blemish ∼ *vb* **1** : designate or set apart by a mark or make a mark on **2** : characterize **3** : remark — **mark·er** *n*

marked \'märkt\ *adj* : noticeable — **mark·ed·ly** \'märkədlē\ *adv*

mar·ket \'märkət\ *n* **1** : buying and selling of goods or the place this happens **2** : demand for commodities **3** : store ∼ *vb* : sell — **mar·ket·able** *adj*

mar·ket·place *n* **1** : market **2** : world of trade or economic activity

marks·man \'märksmən\ *n* : good shooter — **marks·man·ship** *n*

mar·lin \'märlən\ *n* : large oceanic fish

mar·ma·lade \'märmə₁lād\ *n* : jam with pieces of fruit and rind

mar·mo·set \'märmə₁set\ *n* : small bushy-tailed monkey

mar·mot \'märmət\ *n* : burrowing rodent

¹**ma·roon** \mə'rün\ *vb* : isolate without hope of escape

²**maroon** *n* : dark red color

mar·quee \mär'kē\ *n* : canopy over an entrance

mar·quess \'märkwəs\, **mar·quis** \'märkwəs, mär'kē\ *n, pl* **-quess·es**

or **-quis·es** or **-quis** : British noble ranking next below a duke

mar·quise \mär'kēz\ *n, pl* **mar·quises** \-'kēz, -'kēzəz\ : marchioness

mar·riage \'marij\ *n* **1** : state of being married **2** : wedding ceremony — **mar·riage·able** *adj*

mar·row \'marō\ *n* : soft tissue in the cavity of bone

mar·ry \'marē\ *vb* **-ried; -ry·ing 1** : join as husband and wife **2** : take or give in marriage — **mar·ried** *adj or n*

marsh \'märsh\ *n* : soft wet land — **marshy** *adj*

mar·shal \'märshəl\ *n* **1** : leader of ceremony **2** : usu. high military or administrative officer ∼ *vb* **-shaled** or **-shalled; -shal·ing** or **-shal·ling 1** : arrange in order, rank, or position **2** : lead with ceremony

marsh·mal·low \'märsh₁melō, -₁malō\ *n* : spongy candy

mar·su·pi·al \mär'süpēəl\ *n* : mammal that nourishes young in an abdominal pouch — **marsupial** *adj*

mart \'märt\ *n* : market

mar·ten \'märt⁰n\ *n, pl* **-ten** or **-tens** : weasellike mammal with soft fur

mar·tial \'märshəl\ *adj* **1** : relating to war or an army **2** : warlike

mar·tin \'märt⁰n\ *n* : small swallow

mar·ti·net \₁märt⁰n'et\ *n* : strict disciplinarian

mar·tyr \'märtər\ *n* : one who dies or makes a great sacrifice for a cause ∼ *vb* : make a martyr of — **mar·tyr·dom** \-dəm\ *n*

mar·vel \'märvəl\ *vb* **-veled** or **-velled; -vel·ing** or **-vel·ling** : feel surprise or wonder ∼ *n* : something amazing — **mar·vel·ous, mar·vel·lous** \'märvələs\ *adj* — **mar·vel·ous·ly** *adv* — **mar·vel·ous·ness** *n*

Marx·ism \'märk₁sizəm\ *n* : political and social principles of Karl Marx — **Marx·ist** \-sist\ *n or adj*

mas·cara \mas'karə\ *n* : eye cosmetic

mas·cot \'mas₁kät, -kət\ *n* : one believed to bring good luck

mas·cu·line \'maskyələn\ *adj* : relating to the male sex — **mas·cu·lin·i·ty** \₁maskyə'linətē\ *n*

mash \'mash\ *n* **1** : crushed steeped grain for fermenting **2** : soft pulpy mass ∼ *vb* **1** : reduce to a pulpy mass **2** : smash — **mash·er** *n*

mask \'mask\ *n* : disguise for the face

~ *vb* **1** : disguise **2** : cover to protect — **mask•er** *n*

mas•och•ism \'masə‚kizəm, 'maz-\ *n* : pleasure in being abused — **mas•och•ist** \-kist\ *n* — **mas•och•is•tic** \‚masə'kistik, ‚maz-\ *adj*

ma•son \'mās°n\ *n* : workman who builds with stone or brick — **ma•son•ry** \-rē\ *n*

mas•quer•ade \‚maskə'rād\ *n* **1** : costume party **2** : disguise ~ *vb* -**ad•ed**; -**ad•ing 1** : disguise oneself **2** : take part in a costume party — **mas•quer•ad•er** *n*

mass \'mas\ *n* **1** : large amount of matter or number of things **2** : expanse or magnitude **3** : great body of people — usu. pl. ~ *vb* : form into a mass — **mass•less** \-ləs\ *adj* — **massy** *adj*

Mass *n* : worship service of the Roman Catholic Church

mas•sa•cre \'masikər\ *n* : wholesale slaughter — **massacre** *vb*

mas•sage \mə'säzh, -'säj\ *n* : a rubbing of the body — **massage** *vb*

mas•seur \ma'sər\ *n* : man who massages

mas•seuse \-'sœz, -'süz\ *n* : woman who massages

mas•sive \'masiv\ *adj* **1** : being a large mass **2** : large in scope — **mas•sive•ly** *adv* — **mas•sive•ness** *n*

mast \'mast\ *n* : tall pole esp. for supporting sails — **mast•ed** *adj*

mas•ter \'mastər\ *n* **1** : male teacher **2** : holder of an academic degree between a bachelor's and a doctor's **3** : one highly skilled **4** : one in authority ~ *vb* **1** : subdue **2** : become proficient in — **mas•ter•ful** \-fəl\ *adj* — **mas•ter•ful•ly** *adv* — **mas•ter•ly** *adj* — **mas•tery** \'mastərē\ *n*

master chief petty officer *n* : petty officer of the highest rank in the navy

master gunnery sergeant *n* : noncommissioned officer in the marine corps ranking above a master sergeant

mas•ter•piece \'mastər‚pēs\ *n* : great piece of work

master sergeant *n* **1** : noncommissioned officer in the army ranking next below a sergeant major **2** : noncommissioned officer in the air force ranking next below a senior master sergeant **3** : noncommissioned officer in the marine corps ranking next below a master gunnery sergeant

mas•ter•work *n* : masterpiece

mas•tic \'mastik\ *n* : pasty glue

mas•ti•cate \'mastə‚kāt\ *vb* -**cat•ed**; -**cat•ing** : chew — **mas•ti•ca•tion** \‚mastə'kāshən\ *n*

mas•tiff \'mastəf\ *n* : large dog

mas•to•don \'mastə‚dän\ *n* : extinct elephantlike animal

mas•toid \'mas‚tòid\ *n* : bone behind the ear — **mastoid** *adj*

mas•tur•ba•tion \‚mastər'bāshən\ *n* : stimulation of sex organs by hand — **mas•tur•bate** \'mastər‚bāt\ *vb*

¹**mat** \'mat\ *n* **1** : coarse woven or plaited fabric **2** : mass of tangled strands **3** : thick pad ~ *vb* -**tt**- : form into a mat

²**mat** *vb* -**tt**- **1** : make matte **2** : provide (a picture) with a mat ~ *or* **matt** *or* **matte** *n* : border around a picture

³**mat** *var of* MATTE

mat•a•dor \'matə‚dòr\ *n* : bullfighter

¹**match** \'mach\ *n* **1** : one equal to another **2** : one able to cope with another **3** : suitable pairing **4** : game **5** : marriage ~ *vb* **1** : set in competition **2** : marry **3** : be or provide the equal of **4** : fit or go together — **match•less** *adj* — **match•mak•er** *n*

²**match** *n* : piece of wood or paper material with a combustible tip

mate \'māt\ *n* **1** : companion **2** : subordinate officer on a ship **3** : one of a pair ~ *vb* **mat•ed**; **mat•ing 1** : fit together **2** : come together as a pair **3** : copulate

ma•te•ri•al \mə'tirēəl\ *adj* **1** : natural **2** : relating to matter **3** : important **4** : of a physical or worldly nature ~ *n* : stuff something is made of — **ma•te•ri•al•ly** *adv*

ma•te•ri•al•ism \mə'tirēə‚lizəm\ *n* **1** : theory that matter is the only reality **2** : preoccupation with material and not spiritual things — **ma•te•ri•al•ist** \-list\ *n or adj* — **ma•te•ri•al•is•tic** \-‚tirēə'listik\ *adj*

ma•te•ri•al•ize \mə'tirēə‚līz\ *vb* -**ized**; -**iz•ing** : take or cause to take bodily form — **ma•te•ri•al•i•za•tion** \mə-‚tirēələ'zāshən\ *n*

ma•té•ri•el, ma•te•ri•el \mə‚tirē'el\ *n* : military supplies

ma•ter•nal \mə'tərn°l\ *adj* : motherly — **ma•ter•nal•ly** *adv*

ma•ter•ni•ty \mə'tərnətē\ *n, pl* -**ties 1** : state of being a mother **2** : hospital's childbirth facility ~ *adj* **1**

: worn during pregnancy **2** : relating to the period close to childbirth

math \'math\ *n* : mathematics

math•e•mat•ics \ˌmathə'matiks\ *n pl* : science of numbers and of shapes in space — **math•e•mat•i•cal** \-ikəl\ *adj* — **math•e•mat•i•cal•ly** *adv* — **mathe•ma•ti•cian** \ˌmathəmə'tishən\ *n*

mat•i•nee, mat•i•née \ˌmat'n'ā\ *n* : afternoon performance

mat•ins \'mat'nz\ *n* : morning prayers

ma•tri•arch \'mātrē,ärk\ *n* : woman who rules a family — **ma•tri•ar•chal** \ˌmātrē'ärkəl\ *adj* — **ma•tri•ar•chy** \'mātrē,ärkē\ *n*

ma•tri•cide \'matrə,sīd, 'mā-\ *n* : murder of one's mother — **ma•tri•cid•al** \ˌmatrə'sīd'l, ˌmā-\ *adj*

ma•tric•u•late \mə'trikyə,lāt\ *vb* **-lated; -lat•ing** : enroll in school — **ma•tric•u•la•tion** \-ˌtrikyə'lāshən\ *n*

mat•ri•mo•ny \'matrə,mōnē\ *n* : marriage — **mat•ri•mo•ni•al** \ˌmatrə'mōnēəl\ *adj* — **mat•ri•mo•ni•al•ly** *adv*

ma•trix \'mātriks\ *n, pl* **-tri•ces** \'mātrə,sēz, 'ma-\ *or* **-trix•es** \'mātriksəz\ : something (as a mold) that gives form, foundation, or origin to something else enclosed in it

ma•tron \'mātrən\ *n* **1** : dignified mature woman **2** : woman supervisor — **ma•tron•ly** *adj*

matte \'mat\ *adj* : not shiny

mat•ter \'matər\ *n* **1** : subject of interest **2** *pl* : circumstances **3** : trouble **4** : physical substance ∼ *vb* : be important

mat•tock \'matək\ *n* : a digging tool

mat•tress \'matrəs\ *n* : pad to sleep on

ma•ture \mə'túr, -'tyúr, -'chùr\ *adj* **-tur•er; -est 1** : carefully considered **2** : fully grown or developed **3** : due for payment ∼ *vb* **-tured; -tur•ing** : become mature — **mat•u•ra•tion** \ˌmachə'rāshən\ *n* — **ma•ture•ly** *adv* — **ma•tu•ri•ty** \-ətē\ *n*

maud•lin \'mòdlən\ *adj* : excessively sentimental

maul \'mòl\ *n* : heavy hammer ∼ *vb* **1** : beat **2** : handle roughly

mau•so•le•um \ˌmòsə'lēəm, ˌmòzə-\ *n, pl* **-leums** *or* **-lea** \-'lēə\ : large above-ground tomb

mauve \'mōv, 'mòv\ *n* : lilac color

ma•ven, ma•vin \'māvən\ *n* : expert

mav•er•ick \'mavrik\ *n* **1** : unbranded range animal **2** : nonconformist

maw \'mò\ *n* **1** : stomach **2** : throat, esophagus, or jaws

mawk•ish \'mòkish\ *adj* : sickly sentimental — **mawk•ish•ly** *adv* — **mawk•ish•ness** *n*

max•im \'maksəm\ *n* : proverb

max•i•mum \'maksəməm\ *n, pl* **-ma** \-səmə\ *or* **-mums 1** : greatest quantity **2** : upper limit **3** : largest number — **maximum** *adj* — **max•i•mize** \-sə,mīz\ *vb*

may \'mā\ *verbal auxiliary, past* **might** \'mīt\; *pres sing & pl* **may 1** : have permission **2** : be likely to **3** — used to express desire, purpose, or contingency

May \'mā\ *n* : 5th month of the year having 31 days

may•ap•ple *n* : woodland herb having edible fruit

may•be \'mābē\ *adv* : perhaps

may•flow•er *n* : spring-blooming herb

may•fly *n* : fly with an aquatic larva

may•hem \'mā,hem, 'māəm\ *n* **1** : crippling or mutilation of a person **2** : needless damage

may•on•naise \'māə,nāz\ *n* : creamy white sandwich spread

may•or \'māər, 'mer\ *n* : chief city official — **may•or•al** \-əl\ *adj* — **may•or•al•ty** \-əltē\ *n*

maze \'māz\ *n* : confusing network of passages — **mazy** *adj*

ma•zur•ka \mə'zərkə\ *n* : Polish dance

me \'mē\ *pron, objective case of* I

mead \'mēd\ *n* : alcoholic beverage brewed from honey

mead•ow \'medō\ *n* : low-lying usu. level grassland — **mead•ow•land** \-ˌland\ *n*

mead•ow•lark *n* : songbird with a yellow breast

mea•ger, mea•gre \'mēgər\ *adj* **1** : thin **2** : lacking richness or strength — **mea•ger•ly** *adv* — **mea•ger•ness** *n*

¹meal \'mēl\ *n* **1** : food to be eaten at one time **2** : act of eating — **mealtime** *n*

²meal *n* : ground grain — **mealy** *adj*

¹mean \'mēn\ *adj* **1** : humble **2** : worthy of or showing little regard **3** : stingy **4** : malicious — **mean•ly** *adv* — **mean•ness** *n*

²mean \'mēn\ *vb* **meant** \'ment\; **mean•ing** \'mēnin\ **1** : intend **2** : serve to convey, show, or indicate **3** : be important

³mean *n* **1** : middle point **2** *pl* : something that helps gain an end **3** *pl* : material resources **4** : sum of several quantities divided by the number of quantities ~ *adj* : being a mean

me·an·der \mē'andər\ *vb* **-dered; -der·ing 1** : follow a winding course **2** : wander aimlessly — **meander** *n*

mean·ing \'mēniŋ\ *n* **1** : idea conveyed or intended to be conveyed **2** : aim — **mean·ing·ful** \-fəl\ *adj* — **mean·ing·ful·ly** *adv* — **mean·ing·less** *adj*

mean·time \'mēn,tīm\ *n* : intervening time — **meantime** *adv*

mean·while \-,hwīl\ *n* : meantime ~ *adv* **1** : meantime **2** : at the same time

mea·sles \'mēzəlz\ *n pl* : disease that is marked by red spots on the skin

mea·sly \'mēzlē\ *adj* **-sli·er; -est** : contemptibly small in amount

mea·sure \'mezhər, 'māzh-\ *n* **1** : moderate amount **2** : dimensions or amount **3** : something to show amount **4** : unit or system of measurement **5** : act of measuring **6** : means to an end ~ *vb* **-sured; -sur·ing 1** : find out or mark off size or amount of **2** : have a specified measurement — **mea·sur·able** \'mezhərəbəl, 'māzh-\ *adj* — **mea·sur·ably** \-blē\ *adv* — **mea·sure·less** *adj* — **mea·sure·ment** *n* — **mea·sur·er** *n*

meat \'mēt\ *n* **1** : food **2** : animal flesh used as food — **meat·ball** *n* — **meaty** *adj*

me·chan·ic \mi'kanik\ *n* : worker who repairs cars

me·chan·i·cal \mi'kanikəl\ *adj* **1** : relating to machines or mechanics **2** : involuntary — **me·chan·i·cal·ly** *adv*

me·chan·ics \-iks\ *n sing or pl* **1** : branch of physics dealing with energy and forces in relation to bodies **2** : mechanical details

mech·a·nism \'mekə,nizəm\ *n* **1** : piece of machinery **2** : technique for gaining a result **3** : basic processes producing a phenomenon — **mech·a·nis·tic** \,mekə'nistik\ *adj* — **mech·a·ni·za·tion** \,mekənə'zāshən\ *n* — **mech·a·nize** \'mekə,nīz\ *vb* — **mech·a·niz·er** *n*

med·al \'med°l\ *n* **1** : religious pin or pendant **2** : coinlike commemorative metal piece

med·al·ist, med·al·list \'med°list\ *n* : person awarded a medal

me·dal·lion \mə'dalyən\ *n* : large medal

med·dle \'med°l\ *vb* **-dled; -dling** : interfere — **med·dler** \'med°lər\ *n* — **med·dle·some** \'med°lsəm\ *adj*

me·dia \'mēdēə\ *n pl* : communications organizations

me·di·an \'mēdēən\ *n* : middle value in a range — **median** *adj*

me·di·ate \'mēdē,āt\ *vb* **-at·ed; -at·ing** : help settle a dispute — **me·di·a·tion** \,mēdē'āshən\ *n* — **me·di·a·tor** \'mēdē,ātər\ *n*

med·ic \'medik\ *n* : medical worker esp. in the military

med·i·ca·ble \'medikəbəl\ *adj* : curable

med·ic·aid \'medi,kād\ *n* : government program of medical aid for the poor

med·i·cal \'medikəl\ *adj* : relating to medicine — **med·i·cal·ly** \-klē\ *adv*

medi·care \'medi,ker\ *n* : government program of medical care for the aged

med·i·cate \'medə,kāt\ *vb* **-cat·ed; -cat·ing** : treat with medicine

med·i·ca·tion \,medə'kāshən\ *n* **1** : act of medicating **2** : medicine

med·i·cine \'medəsən\ *n* **1** : preparation used to treat disease **2** : science dealing with the cure of disease — **me·dic·i·nal** \mə'dis°nəl\ *adj* — **me·dic·i·nal·ly** *adv*

me·di·e·val, me·di·ae·val \,mēdē'ēval, ,med-, ,mid-; ,mē'dē-, ,me-, ,mi-\ *adj* : of or relating to the Middle Ages — **me·di·eval·ist** \-ist\ *n*

me·di·o·cre \,mēdē'ōkər\ *adj* : not very good — **me·di·oc·ri·ty** \-'äkrətē\ *n*

med·i·tate \'medə,tāt\ *vb* **-tat·ed; -tat·ing** : contemplate — **med·i·ta·tion** \,medə'tāshən\ *n* — **med·i·ta·tive** \'medə,tātiv\ *adj* — **med·i·ta·tive·ly** *adv*

me·di·um \'mēdēəm\ *n, pl* **-diums** *or* **-dia** \-ēə\ **1** : middle position or degree **2** : means of effecting or conveying something **3** : surrounding substance **4** : means of communication **5** : mode of artistic expression — **medium** *adj*

med·ley \'medlē\ *n, pl* **-leys** : series of songs performed as one

meek \'mēk\ *adj* **1** : mild-mannered **2** : lacking spirit — **meek·ly** *adv* — **meek·ness** *n*

meer·schaum \'mirshəm, -,shȯm\ *n* : claylike tobacco pipe

¹meet \'mēt\ *vb* **met** \'met\; **meet·ing**

1 : run into **2** : join **3** : oppose **4** : assemble **5** : satisfy **6** : be introduced to ~ *n* : sports team competition

²**meet** *adj* : proper

meet·ing \'mētiŋ\ *n* : a getting together — **meet·ing·house** *n*

mega·byte \'megəbīt\ *n* : unit of computer storage capacity

mega·hertz \-,hərts, -,herts\ *n* : one million hertz

mega·phone \'megə,fōn\ *n* : cone-shaped device to intensify or direct the voice

mel·an·choly \'melən,kälē\ *n* : depression — **mel·an·chol·ic** \,melən-'kälik\ *adj* — **melancholy** *adj*

mel·a·no·ma \,melə'nōmə\ *n, pl* -mas : usu. malignant skin tumor

me·lee \'mā,lā, mā'lā\ *n* : brawl

me·lio·rate \'mēlyə,rāt, 'mēlēə-\ *vb* -rat·ed; -rat·ing : improve — **me·lio·ra·tion** \,mēlyə'rāshən, ,mēlēə-\ *n* — **me·lio·ra·tive** \'mēlyə,rātiv, 'mēlēə-\ *adj*

mel·lif·lu·ous \me'lifləwəs, mə-\ *adj* : sweetly flowing — **mel·lif·lu·ous·ly** *adv* — **mel·lif·lu·ous·ness** *n*

mel·low \'melō\ *adj* **1** : grown gentle or mild **2** : rich and full — **mellow** *vb* — **mel·low·ness** *n*

melo·dra·ma \'melə,drämə, -,dram-\ *n* : overly theatrical play — **melo·dra·mat·ic** \,melədrə'matik\ *adj* — **melo·dra·mat·i·cal·ly** \-tiklē\ *adv*

mel·o·dy \'melədē\ *n, pl* -dies **1** : agreeable sound **2** : succession of musical notes — **me·lod·ic** \mə-'lädik\ *adj* — **me·lod·i·cal·ly** \-iklē\ *adv* — **me·lo·di·ous** \mə'lōdēəs\ *adj* — **me·lo·di·ous·ly** *adv* — **me·lo·di·ous·ness** *n*

mel·on \'melən\ *n* : gourdlike fruit

melt \'melt\ *vb* **1** : change from solid to liquid usu. by heat **2** : dissolve or disappear gradually **3** : move or be moved emotionally

mem·ber \'membər\ *n* **1** : part of a person, animal, or plant **2** : one of a group **3** : part of a whole — **member·ship** \-,ship\ *n*

mem·brane \'mem,brān\ *n* : thin layer esp. in an organism — **mem·bra·nous** \-brənəs\ *adj*

me·men·to \mi'mentō\ *n, pl* -tos or -toes : souvenir

memo \'memō\ *n, pl* **mem·os** : memorandum

mem·oirs \'mem,wärz\ *n pl* : autobiography

mem·o·ra·bil·ia \,memərə'bilēə, -'bilyə\ *n pl* **1** : memorable things **2** : mementos

mem·o·ra·ble \'memərəbəl\ *adj* : worth remembering — **mem·o·ra·bil·i·ty** \,memərə'bilətē\ *n* — **mem·o·ra·ble·ness** *n* — **mem·o·ra·bly** \-blē\ *adv*

mem·o·ran·dum \,memə'randəm\ *n, pl* -dums *or* -da \-də\ : informal note

me·mo·ri·al \mə'mōrēəl\ *n* : something (as a monument) meant to keep remembrance alive — **memorial** *adj* — **me·mo·ri·al·ize** *vb*

Memorial Day *n* : last Monday in May or formerly May 30 observed as a legal holiday in commemoration of dead servicemen

mem·o·ry \'memrē, 'memə-\ *n, pl* -ries **1** : power of remembering **2** : something remembered **3** : commemoration **4** : time within which past events are remembered — **mem·o·ri·za·tion** \,memərə'zāshən\ *n* — **mem·o·rize** \'memə,rīz\ *vb* — **mem·o·riz·er** *n*

men *pl of* MAN

men·ace \'menəs\ *n* : threat of danger ~ *vb* -aced; -ac·ing **1** : threaten **2** : endanger — **men·ac·ing·ly** *adv*

me·nag·er·ie \mə'najərē\ *n* : collection of wild animals

mend \'mend\ *vb* **1** : improve **2** : repair **3** : heal — **mend** *n* — **mend·er** *n*

men·da·cious \men'dāshəs\ *adj* : dishonest — **men·da·cious·ly** *adv* — **men·dac·i·ty** \-'dasətē\ *n*

men·di·cant \'mendikənt\ *n* : beggar — **men·di·can·cy** \-kənsē\ *n* — **mendicant** *adj*

men·ha·den \men'hād°n, mən-\ *n, pl* -den : fish related to the herring

me·nial \'mēnēəl, -nyəl\ *adj* **1** : relating to servants **2** : humble ~ *n* : domestic servant — **me·ni·al·ly** *adv*

men·in·gi·tis \,menən'jītəs\ *n, pl* -git·i·des \-'jitə,dēz\ : disease of the brain and spinal cord

meno·pause \'menə,póz\ *n* : time when menstruation ends — **meno·paus·al** \,menə'pózəl\ *adj*

me·no·rah \mə'nōrə\ *n* : candelabrum used in Jewish worship

men·stru·a·tion \,menstrə'wāshən, men'strā-\ *n* : monthly discharge of blood from the uterus — **men·stru·al**

\\'menstrəwəl\\ *adj* — **men•stru•ate**
\\'menstrə,wāt, -,strāt\\ *vb*
-ment \\mənt\\ *n suffix* **1** : result or means
of an action **2** : action or process **3**
: place of an action **4** : state or condition
men•tal \\'mentʲl\\ *adj* : relating to the
mind or its disorders — **men•tal•i•ty**
\\men'talətē\\ *n* — **men•tal•ly** *adv*
men•thol \\'men,thòl, -,thōl\\ *n* : soothing substance from oil of peppermint
— **men•tho•lat•ed** \\-thə,lātəd\\ *adj*
men•tion \\'menchən\\ *vb* : refer to —
mention *n*
men•tor \\'men,tòr, 'mentər\\ *n* : instructor
menu \\'menyü\\ *n* **1** : restaurant's list
of food **2** : list of offerings
me•ow \\mē'aù\\ *n* : characteristic cry of
a cat — **meow** *vb*
mer•can•tile \\'mərkən,tēl, -,tīl\\ *adj*
: relating to merchants or trade
mer•ce•nary \\'mərsʲn,erē\\ *n, pl* **-naries** : hired soldier ∼ *adj* : serving only
for money
mer•chan•dise \\'mərchən,dīz, -,dīs\\
n : goods bought and sold ∼ *vb*
-dised; -dis•ing : buy and sell —
mer•chan•dis•er *n*
mer•chant \\'mərchənt\\ *n* : one who
buys and sells
merchant marine *n* : commercial ships
mer•cu•ri•al \\,mər'kyùrēəl\\ *adj* : unpredictable — **mer•cu•ri•al•ly** *adv* —
mer•cu•ri•al•ness *n*
mer•cu•ry \\'mərkyərē\\ *n* : heavy liquid metallic chemical element
mer•cy \\'mərsē\\ *n, pl* **-cies** **1** : show of
pity or leniency **2** : divine blessing —
mer•ci•ful \\-sifəl\\ *adj* — **mer•ci•fully** *adv* — **mer•ci•less** \\-siləs\\ *adj* —
mer•ci•less•ly *adv* — **mercy** *adj*
mere \\'mir\\ *adj, superlative* **mer•est**
: nothing more than — **mere•ly** *adv*
merge \\'mərj\\ *vb* **merged; merg•ing**
1 : unite **2** : blend — **merg•er**
\\'mərjər\\ *n*
me•rid•i•an \\mə'ridēən\\ *n* : imaginary
circle on the earth's surface passing
through the poles — **meridian** *adj*
me•ringue \\mə'raŋ\\ *n* : baked dessert
topping of beaten egg whites
me•ri•no \\mə'rēnō\\ *n, pl* **-nos** **1** : kind
of sheep **2** : fine soft woolen yarn
mer•it \\'merət\\ *n* **1** : praiseworthy
quality **2** *pl* : rights and wrongs of a
legal case ∼ *vb* : deserve — **mer•ito•ri•ous** \\,merə'tōrēəs\\ *adj* —

mer•i•to•ri•ous•ly *adv* — **mer•i•to•rious•ness** *n*
mer•lot \\mer'lō\\ *n* : dry red wine
mer•maid \\'mər,mād\\ *n* : legendary
female sea creature
mer•ry \\'merē\\ *adj* **-ri•er; -est** : full of
high spirits — **mer•ri•ly** *adv* — **merri•ment** \\'merimənt\\ *n* — **mer•rymak•er** \\'merē,mākər\\ *n* — **mer•rymak•ing** \\'merē,mākiŋ\\ *n*
merry–go–round *n* : revolving amusement ride
me•sa \\'māsə\\ *n* : steep flat-topped hill
mesdames *pl of* MADAM *or of*
MADAME *or of* MRS.
mesdemoiselles *pl of* MADEMOI
SELLE
mesh \\'mesh\\ *n* **1** : one of the openings in a net **2** : net fabric **3** : working contact ∼ *vb* : fit together
properly — **meshed** \\'mesht\\ *adj*
mes•mer•ize \\'mezmə,rīz\\ *vb* **-ized;
-iz•ing** : hypnotize
mess \\'mes\\ *n* **1** : meal eaten by a
group **2** : confused, dirty, or offensive state ∼ *vb* **1** : make dirty or untidy **2** : putter **3** : interfere — **messy**
adj
mes•sage \\'mesij\\ *n* : news, information, or a command sent by one person to another
mes•sen•ger \\'mesʲnjər\\ *n* : one who
carries a message or does an errand
Mes•si•ah \\mə'sīə\\ *n* **1** : expected deliverer of the Jews **2** : Jesus Christ **3**
not cap : great leader
messieurs *pl of* MONSIEUR
Messrs. *pl of* MR.
mes•ti•zo \\me'stēzō\\ *n, pl* **-zos** : person of mixed blood
met *past of* MEET
me•tab•o•lism \\mə'tabə,lizəm\\ *n* : biochemical processes necessary to life
— **met•a•bol•ic** \\,metə'bälik\\ *adj* —
me•tab•o•lize \\mə'tabə,līz\\ *vb*
met•al \\'metʲl\\ *n* : shiny substance that
can be melted and shaped and conducts heat and electricity — **me•tallic** \\mə'talik\\ *adj* — **met•al•ware**
— **met•al•work** *n* — **met•al•work•er**
n — **met•al•work•ing** *n*
met•al•lur•gy \\'metʲl,ərjē\\ *n* : science
of metals — **met•al•lur•gi•cal** \\,metʲl
'ərjikəl\\ *adj* — **met•al•lur•gist**
\\'metʲl,ərjist\\ *n*
meta•mor•pho•sis \\,metə'mòrfəsəs\\
n, pl **-pho•ses** \\-,sēz\\ : sudden and

drastic change (as of form) — **meta-mor·phose** \-ˌfōz, -ˌfōs\ *vb*

met·a·phor \'metə,fȯr, -fər\ *n* : use of a word denoting one kind of object or idea in place of another to suggest a likeness between them — **met·a-phor·i·cal** \ˌmetə'fȯrikəl\ *adj*

meta·phys·ics \ˌmetə'fiziks\ *n* : study of the causes and nature of things — **meta·phys·i·cal** \-'fizəkəl\ *adj*

mete \'mēt\ *vb* **met·ed; met·ing** : allot

me·te·or \'mētēər, -ē,ȯr\ *n* : small body that produces a streak of light as it burns up in the atmosphere

me·te·or·ic \ˌmētē'ȯrik\ *adj* **1** : relating to a meteor **2** : sudden and spectacular — **me·te·or·i·cal·ly** \-iklē\ *adv*

me·te·or·ite \'mētēə,rīt\ *n* : meteor that reaches the earth

me·te·o·rol·o·gy \ˌmētēə'rälejē\ *n* : science of weather — **me·te·o·ro-log·ic** \ˌmētē,ȯrə'läjik\, **me·te·o·ro-log·i·cal** \-'läjikəl\ *adj* — **me·te·o-rol·o·gist** \-ē·ə'rälejist\ *n*

¹**me·ter** \'mētər\ *n* : rhythm in verse or music

²**meter** *n* : unit of length equal to 39.37 inches

³**meter** *n* : measuring instrument

meth·a·done \'methə,dōn\ *n* : synthetic addictive narcotic

meth·ane \'meth,ān\ *n* : colorless odorless flammable gas

meth·a·nol \'methə,nȯl, -,nōl\ *n* : volatile flammable poisonous liquid

meth·od \'methəd\ *n* **1** : procedure for achieving an end **2** : orderly arrangement or plan — **me·thod·i·cal** \mə-'thädikəl\ *adj* — **me·thod·i·cal·ly** \-klē\ *adv* — **me·thod·i·cal·ness** *n*

me·tic·u·lous \mə'tikyələs\ *adj* : extremely careful in attending to details — **me·tic·u·lous·ly** *adv* — **me·tic·u-lous·ness** *n*

met·ric \'metrik\, **met·ri·cal** \-trikəl\ *adj* : relating to meter or the metric system — **met·ri·cal·ly** *adv*

metric system *n* : system of weights and measures using the meter and kilogram

met·ro·nome \'metrə,nōm\ *n* : instrument that ticks regularly to mark a beat in music

me·trop·o·lis \mə'träpələs\ *n* : major city — **met·ro·pol·i·tan** \ˌmetrə-'pälət°n\ *adj*

met·tle \'met°l\ *n* : spirit or courage — **met·tle·some** \-səm\ *adj*

mez·za·nine \'mez°n,ēn, ˌmez°n'ēn\ *n* **1** : intermediate level between 2 main floors **2** : lowest balcony

mez·zo-so·pra·no \ˌmetsōsə'pranō, ˌmedz-\ *n* : voice between soprano and contralto

mi·as·ma \mī'azmə\ *n* **1** : noxious vapor **2** : harmful influence — **mi·as-mic** \-mik\ *adj*

mi·ca \'mīkə\ *n* : mineral separable into thin transparent sheets

mice *pl of* MOUSE

mi·cro \'mīkrō\ *adj* : very small

mi·crobe \'mī,krōb\ *n* : disease-causing microorganism — **mi·cro·bi·al** \mī-'krōbēəl\ *adj*

mi·cro·bi·ol·o·gy \ˌmīkrōbī'äləjē\ *n* : biology dealing with microscopic life — **mi·cro·bi·o·log·i·cal** \'mīkrō-,bīə'läjikəl\ *adj* — **mi·cro·bi·ol·o-gist** \ˌmīkrōbī'äləjist\ *n*

mi·cro·com·put·er \'mīkrōkəm-,pyütər\ *n* : small computer that uses a microprocessor

mi·cro·cosm \'mīkrə,käzəm\ *n* : one thought of as a miniature universe

mi·cro·film \-,film\ *n* : small film recording printed matter — **micro-film** *vb*

mi·crom·e·ter \mī'krämətər\ *n* : instrument for measuring minute distances

mi·cro·min·i·a·tur·ized \ˌmīkrō-'minēəchə,rīzd, -'minichə-\ *adj* : reduced to a very small size — **mi-cro·min·i·a·tur·iza·tion** \-,minēə-,chùrə'zāshən, -,mini,chùr-, -chər-\ *n*

mi·cron \'mī,krän\ *n* : one millionth of a meter

mi·cro·or·gan·ism \ˌmīkrō'ȯrgə-,nizəm\ *n* : very tiny living thing

mi·cro·phone \'mīkrə,fōn\ *n* : instrument for changing sound waves into variations of an electric current

mi·cro·pro·ces·sor \'mīkrō,präse-sər\ *n* : miniaturized computer processing unit on a single chip

mi·cro·scope \-,skōp\ *n* : optical device for magnifying tiny objects — **mi·cro·scop·ic** \ˌmīkrə'skäpik\ *adj* — **mi·cro·scop·i·cal·ly** *adv* — **mi-cros·copy** \mī'kräskəpē\ *n*

mi·cro·wave \'mīkrə,wāv\ *n* **1** : short radio wave **2** : oven that cooks food using microwaves ~ *vb* : heat or cook in a microwave oven — **mi•cro•wav•able, mi•cro•wave•able** \ˌmīkrə-'wāvəbəl\ *adj*

mid \'mid\ *adj* : middle — **mid•point** *n* — **mid•stream** *n* — **mid•sum•mer** *n* — **mid•town** *n or adj* — **mid•week** *n* — **mid•win•ter** *n* — **mid•year** *n*

mid•air *n* : a point in the air well above the ground

mid•day *n* : noon

mid•dle \'midᵊl\ *adj* 1 : equally distant from the extremes 2 : being at neither extreme ~ *n* : middle part or point

Middle Ages *n pl* : period from about A.D. 500 to about 1500

mid•dle•man \-ˌman\ *n* : dealer or agent between the producer and consumer

mid•dling \'midliŋ, -lən\ *adj* 1 : of middle or medium size, degree, or quality 2 : mediocre

midge \'mij\ *n* : very tiny fly

midg•et \'mijət\ *n* : very small person or thing

mid•land \'midlənd, -ˌland\ *n* : interior of a country

mid•most *adj* : being nearest the middle — **midmost** *adv*

mid•night *n* : 12 o'clock at night

mid•riff \'midˌrif\ *n* : mid-region of the torso

mid•ship•man \'midˌshipmən, ˌmid-'ship-\ *n* : student naval officer

midst \'midst\ *n* : position close to or surrounded by others — **midst** *prep*

mid•way \'midˌwā\ *n* : concessions and amusements at a carnival ~ *adv* : in the middle

mid•wife \'midˌwīf\ *n* : person who aids at childbirth — **mid•wife•ry** \midˈwifərē, -ˈwīf-\ *n*

mien \'mēn\ *n* : appearance

miff \'mif\ *vb* : upset or peeve

¹**might** \'mīt\ *past of* MAY — used to express permission or possibility or as a polite alternative to *may*

²**might** *n* : power or resources

mighty \'mītē\ *adj* **might•i•er; -est** 1 : very strong 2 : great — **might•i•ly** *adv* — **might•i•ness** *n* — **mighty** *adv*

mi•graine \'mīˌgrān\ *n* : severe headache often with nausea

mi•grant \'mīgrənt\ *n* : one who moves frequently to find work

mi•grate \'mīˌgrāt\ *vb* **-grat•ed; -grat•ing** 1 : move from one place to another 2 : pass periodically from one region or climate to another — **mi-**

gra•tion \mī'grāshən\ *n* — **mi•gra•to•ry** \'mīgrəˌtōrē\ *adj*

mild \'mīld\ *adj* 1 : gentle in nature or behavior 2 : moderate in action or effect — **mild•ly** *adv* — **mild•ness** *n*

mil•dew \'milˌdü, -ˌdyü\ *n* : whitish fungal growth — **mildew** *vb*

mile \'mīl\ *n* : unit of length equal to 5280 feet

mile•age \'mīlij\ *n* 1 : allowance per mile for traveling expenses 2 : amount or rate of use expressed in miles

mile•stone *n* : significant point in development

mi•lieu \mēl'yü, -'yœ̄\ *n, pl* **-lieus** *or* **-lieux** \-'yüz, -'yœ̄\ : surroundings or setting

mil•i•tant \'milətənt\ *adj* : aggressively active or hostile — **mil•i•tan•cy** \-tənsē\ *n* — **militant** *n* — **mil•i•tant•ly** *adv*

mil•i•tar•ism \'milətəˌrizəm\ *n* : dominance of military ideals or of a policy of aggressive readiness for war — **mil•i•ta•rist** \-rist\ *n* — **mil•i•tar•is•tic** \ˌmilətə'ristik\ *adj*

mil•i•tary \'miləˌterē\ *adj* 1 : relating to soldiers, arms, or war 2 : relating to or performed by armed forces ~ *n* : armed forces or the people in them — **mil•i•tar•i•ly** \ˌmilə'terəlē\ *adv*

mil•i•tate \-ˌtāt\ *vb* **-tat•ed; -tat•ing** : have an effect

mi•li•tia \mə'lishə\ *n* : civilian soldiers — **mi•li•tia•man** \-mən\ *n*

milk \'milk\ *n* : white nutritive fluid secreted by female mammals for feeding their young ~ *vb* 1 : draw off the milk of 2 : draw something from as if by milking — **milk•er** *n* — **milk•i•ness** \-ēnəs\ *n* — **milky** *adj*

milk•man \-ˌman, -mən\ *n* : man who sells or delivers milk

milk•weed *n* : herb with milky juice

¹**mill** \'mil\ *n* 1 : building in which grain is ground into flour 2 : manufacturing plant 3 : machine used esp. for forming or processing ~ *vb* 1 : subject to a process in a mill 2 : move in a circle — **mill•er** *n*

²**mill** *n* : ¹⁄₁₀ cent

mil•len•ni•um \mə'lenēəm\ *n, pl* **-nia** \-ēə\ *or* **-niums** : a period of 1000 years

mil•let \'milət\ *n* : cereal and forage grass with small seeds

mil•li•gram \'miləˌgram\ *n* : ¹⁄₁₀₀₀ gram

mil·li·li·ter \-ˌlētər\ *n* : ¹⁄₁₀₀₀ liter

mil·li·me·ter \-ˌmētər\ : ¹⁄₁₀₀₀ meter

mil·li·ner \'milənər\ *n* : person who makes or sells women's hats — **mil·li·nery** \'milə,nerē\ *n*

mil·lion \'milyən\ *n, pl* **millions** *or* **million** : 1000 thousands — **million** *adj* — **mil·lionth** \-yənth\ *adj or n*

mil·lion·aire \ˌmilyə'nar, 'milyə,nar\ *n* : person worth a million or more (as of dollars)

mil·li·pede \'milə,pēd\ *n* : longbodied arthropod with 2 pairs of legs on most segments

mill·stone *n* : either of 2 round flat stones used for grinding grain

mime \'mīm\ *n* **1** : mimic **2** : pantomime — **mime** *vb*

mim·eo·graph \'mimēə,graf\ *n* : machine for making many stencil copies — **mimeograph** *vb*

mim·ic \'mimik\ *n* : one that mimics ~ *vb* **-icked; -ick·ing 1** : imitate closely **2** : ridicule by imitation — **mim·ic·ry** \'mimikrē\ *n*

min·a·ret \ˌminə'ret\ *n* : tower attached to a mosque

mince \'mins\ *vb* **minced; minc·ing 1** : cut into small pieces **2** : choose (one's words) carefully **3** : walk in a prim affected manner

mind \'mīnd\ *n* **1** : memory **2** : the part of an individual that feels, perceives, and esp. reasons **3** : intention **4** : normal mental condition **5** : opinion **6** : intellectual ability ~ *vb* **1** : attend to **2** : obey **3** : be concerned about **4** : be careful — **mind·ed** *adj* — **mind·less** \'mīndləs\ *adj* — **mind·less·ly** *adv* — **mind·less·ness** *n*

mind·ful \-fəl\ *adj* : aware or attentive — **mind·ful·ly** *adv* — **mind·ful·ness** *n*

¹mine \'mīn\ *pron* : that which belongs to me

²mine \'mīn\ *n* **1** : excavation from which minerals are taken **2** : explosive device placed in the ground or water for destroying enemy vehicles or vessels that later pass ~ *vb* **mined; min·ing 1** : get ore from **2** : place military mines in — **mine·field** *n* — **min·er** *n*

min·er·al \'minərəl\ *n* **1** : crystalline substance not of organic origin **2** : useful natural substance (as coal) obtained from the ground — **mineral** *adj*

min·er·al·o·gy \ˌminə'räləjē, -'ral-\ *n* : science dealing with minerals — **min·er·al·og·i·cal** \ˌminərə'läjikəl\ *adj* — **min·er·al·o·gist** \ˌminə-'räləjist, -'ral-\ *n*

min·gle \'miŋgəl\ *vb* **-gled; -gling** : bring together or mix

mini- *comb form* : miniature or of small dimensions

min·ia·ture \'minēə,chur, 'mini,chur, -chər\ *n* : tiny copy or very small version — **miniature** *adj* — **min·ia·tur·ist** \-,chùrist, -chər-\ *n* — **min·ia·tur·ize** \-ēəchə,rīz, -ichə-\ *vb*

mini·bike \'minē,bīk\ *n* : small motorcycle

mini·bus \-,bəs\ *n* : small bus

mini·com·put·er \-kəm,pyütər\ *n* : computer intermediate between a mainframe and a microcomputer in size and speed

mini·course \-,kōrs\ *n* : short course of study

min·i·mal \'minəməl\ *adj* : relating to or being a minimum — **min·i·mal·ly** *adv*

min·i·mize \'minə,mīz\ *vb* **-mized; -miz·ing 1** : reduce to a minimum **2** : underestimate intentionally

min·i·mum \'minəməm\ *n, pl* **-ma** \-mə\ *or* **-mums** : lowest quantity or amount — **minimum** *adj*

min·ion \'minyən\ *n* **1** : servile dependent **2** : subordinate official

mini·se·ries \'minē,sirēz\ *n* : television story in several parts

mini·skirt \-,skərt\ *n* : very short skirt

min·is·ter \'minəstər\ *n* **1** : Protestant member of the clergy **2** : high officer of state **3** : diplomatic representative ~ *vb* : give aid or service — **min·is·te·ri·al** \ˌminə'stirēəl\ *adj* — **min·is·tra·tion** *n*

min·is·try \'minəstrē\ *n, pl* **-tries 1** : office or duties of a minister **2** : body of ministers **3** : government department headed by a minister

mini·van \'minē,van\ *n* : small van

mink \'miŋk\ *n, pl* **mink** *or* **minks** : weasellike mammal or its soft brown fur

min·now \'minō\ *n, pl* **-nows** : small freshwater fish

mi·nor \'mīnər\ *adj* **1** : less in size, importance, or value **2** : not serious ~ *n* **1** : person not yet of legal age **2** : secondary field of academic specialization

mi·nor·i·ty \mə'nórətē, mī-\ *n, pl*

-ties 1 : time or state of being a minor **2** : smaller number (as of votes) **3** : part of a population differing from others (as in race or religion)

min•strel \'minstrəl\ *n* **1** : medieval singer of verses **2** : performer in a program usu. of black American songs and jokes — **min•strel•sy** \-sē\ *n*

¹mint \'mint\ *n* **1** : fragrant herb that yields a flavoring oil **2** : mint-flavored piece of candy — **minty** *adj*

²mint *n* **1** : place where coins are made **2** : vast sum ~ *adj* : unused — **mint** *vb* — **mint•er** *n*

min•u•et \ˌminyə'wet\ *n* : slow graceful dance

mi•nus \'mīnəs\ *prep* **1** : diminished by **2** : lacking ~ *n* : negative quantity or quality

mi•nus•cule \'minəsˌkyül, min'əs-\, **min•is•cule** \'minəs-\ *adj* : very small

¹min•ute \'minət\ *n* **1** : 60th part of an hour or of a degree **2** : short time **3** *pl* : official record of a meeting

²mi•nute \mī'nüt, mə-, -'nyüt\ *adj* **-nut•er; -est 1** : very small **2** : marked by close attention to details — **mi•nute•ly** *adv* — **mi•nute•ness** *n*

mir•a•cle \'mirikəl\ *n* **1** : extraordinary event taken as a sign of divine intervention in human affairs **2** : marvel — **mi•rac•u•lous** \mə'rakyələs\ *adj* — **mi•rac•u•lous•ly** *adv*

mi•rage \mə'räzh\ *n* : distant illusion caused by atmospheric conditions (as in the desert)

mire \'mīr\ *n* : heavy deep mud ~ *vb* **mired; mir•ing** : stick or sink in mire — **miry** *adj*

mir•ror \'mirər\ *n* : smooth surface (as of glass) that reflects images ~ *vb* : reflect in or as if in a mirror

mirth \'mərth\ *n* : gladness and laughter — **mirth•ful** \-fəl\ *adj* — **mirth•ful•ly** *adv* — **mirth•ful•ness** *n* — **mirth•less** *adj*

mis•an•thrope \'misⁿnˌthrōp\ *n* : one who hates mankind — **mis•an•throp•ic** \ˌmisⁿn'thräpik\ *adj* — **mis•an•thro•py** \mis'anthrəpē\ *n*

mis•ap•pre•hend \ˌmisˌaprə'hend\ *vb* : misunderstand — **mis•ap•pre•hen•sion** *n*

mis•ap•pro•pri•ate \ˌmisə'prōprē ˌāt\ *vb* : take dishonestly for one's own use — **mis•ap•pro•pri•a•tion** *n*

mis•be•got•ten \-bi'gätⁿn\ *adj* **1** : illegitimate **2** : ill-conceived

mis•be•have \ˌmisbi'hāv\ *vb* : behave improperly — **mis•be•hav•er** *n* — **mis•be•hav•ior** *n*

mis•cal•cu•late \mis'kalkyəˌlāt\ *vb* : calculate wrongly — **mis•cal•cu•la•tion** *n*

mis•car•ry \ˌmis'karē, 'misˌkarē\ *vb* **1** : give birth prematurely before the fetus can survive **2** : go wrong or be unsuccessful — **mis•car•riage** \-rij\ *n*

mis•ce•ge•na•tion \misˌejə'nāshən, ˌmisijə'nā-\ *n* : marriage between persons of different races

mis•cel•la•neous \ˌmisə'lānēəs\ *adj* : consisting of many things of different kinds — **mis•cel•la•neous•ly** *adv* — **mis•cel•la•neous•ness** *n*

mis•cel•la•ny \'misəˌlānē\ *n, pl* **-nies** : collection of various things

mis•chance \mis'chans\ *n* : bad luck

mis•chief \'mischəf\ *n* : conduct esp. of a child that annoys or causes minor damage

mis•chie•vous \'mischəvəs\ *adj* **1** : causing annoyance or minor injury **2** : irresponsibly playful — **mis•chie•vous•ly** *adv* — **mis•chie•vous•ness** *n*

mis•con•ceive \ˌmiskən'sēv\ *vb* : interpret incorrectly — **mis•con•cep•tion** *n*

mis•con•duct \mis'kändəkt\ *n* **1** : mismanagement **2** : bad behavior

mis•con•strue \ˌmiskən'strü\ *vb* : misinterpret — **mis•con•struc•tion** *n*

mis•cre•ant \'miskrēənt\ *n* : one who behaves criminally or viciously — **miscreant** *adj*

mis•deed \mis'dēd\ *n* : wrong deed

mis•de•mean•or \ˌmisdi'mēnər\ *n* : crime less serious than a felony

mi•ser \'mīzər\ *n* : person who hoards and is stingy with money — **mi•ser•li•ness** \-lēnəs\ *n* — **mi•ser•ly** *adj*

mis•er•a•ble \'mizərəbəl\ *adj* **1** : wretchedly deficient **2** : causing extreme discomfort **3** : shameful — **mis•er•a•ble•ness** *n* — **mis•er•a•bly** \-blē\ *adv*

mis•ery \'mizərē\ *n, pl* **-er•ies** : suffering and want caused by distress or poverty

mis•fire \mis'fīr\ *vb* **1** : fail to fire **2** : miss an intended effect — **mis•fire** \'misˌfīr\ *n*

mis•fit \'misˌfit, mis'fit\ *n* : person poorly adjusted to his environment

mis·for·tune \mis'fòrchən\ *n* **1** : bad luck **2** : unfortunate condition or event

mis·giv·ing \mis'givin\ *n* : doubt or concern

mis·guid·ed \mis'gīdəd\ *adj* : mistaken, uninformed, or deceived

mis·hap \'mis‚hap\ *n* : accident

mis·in·form \‚mis²n'fòrm\ *vb* : give wrong information to — **mis·in·for·ma·tion** \‚mis‚infər'māshən\ *n*

mis·in·ter·pret \‚mis²n'tərprət\ *vb* : understand or explain wrongly — **mis·in·ter·pre·ta·tion** \-‚tərprə'tāshən\ *n*

mis·judge \mis'jəj\ *vb* : judge incorrectly or unjustly — **mis·judg·ment** *n*

mis·lay \mis'lā\ *vb* **-laid; -lay·ing** : misplace

mis·lead \mis'lēd\ *vb* **-led; -lead·ing** : lead in a wrong direction or into error — **mis·lead·ing·ly** *adv*

mis·man·age \mis'manij\ *vb* : manage badly — **mis·man·age·ment** *n*

mis·no·mer \mis'nōmər\ *n* : wrong name

mi·sog·y·nist \mə'säjənist\ *n* : one who hates or distrusts women — **mi·sog·y·nis·tic** \mə‚säjə'nistik\ *adj* — **mi·sog·y·ny** \-nē\ *n*

mis·place \mis'plās\ *vb* : put in a wrong or unremembered place

mis·print \'mis‚print, mis'-\ *n* : error in printed matter

mis·pro·nounce \‚misprə'naúns\ *vb* : pronounce incorrectly — **mis·pro·nun·ci·a·tion** *n*

mis·quote \mis'kwōt\ *vb* : quote incorrectly — **mis·quo·ta·tion** \‚miskwō'tāshən\ *n*

mis·read \mis'rēd\ *vb* **-read; -read·ing** : read or interpret incorrectly

mis·rep·re·sent \‚mis‚repri'zent\ *vb* : represent falsely or unfairly — **mis·rep·re·sen·ta·tion** *n*

mis·rule \mis'rül\ *vb* : govern badly ~ *n* **1** : bad or corrupt government **2** : disorder

¹miss \'mis\ *vb* **1** : fail to hit, reach, or contact **2** : notice the absence of **3** : fail to obtain **4** : avoid **5** : omit — **miss** *n*

²miss *n* : young unmarried woman or girl — often used as a title

mis·sal \'misəl\ *n* : book containing what is said at mass during the year

mis·shap·en \mis'shāpən\ *adj* : distorted

mis·sile \'misəl\ *n* : object (as a stone or rocket) thrown or shot

miss·ing \'misiŋ\ *adj* : absent or lost

mis·sion \'mishən\ *n* **1** : ministry sent by a church to spread its teaching **2** : group of diplomats sent to a foreign country **3** : task

mis·sion·ary \'mishə‚nerē\ *adj* : relating to religious missions ~ *n, pl* **-ar·ies** : person sent to spread religious faith

mis·sive \'misiv\ *n* : letter

mis·spell \mis'spel\ *vb* : spell incorrectly — **mis·spell·ing** *n*

mis·state \mis'stāt\ *vb* : state incorrectly — **mis·state·ment** *n*

mis·step \'mis‚step\ *n* **1** : wrong step **2** : mistake

mist \'mist\ *n* : particles of water falling as fine rain

mis·take \mə'stāk\ *n* **1** : misunderstanding or wrong belief **2** : wrong action or statement — **mistake** *vb*

mis·tak·en \-'stākən\ *adj* : having a wrong opinion or incorrect information — **mis·tak·en·ly** *adv*

mis·ter \'mistər\ *n* : sir — used without a name in addressing a man

mis·tle·toe \'misəl‚tō\ *n* : parasitic green shrub with waxy white berries

mis·treat \mis'trēt\ *vb* : treat badly — **mis·treat·ment** *n*

mis·tress \'mistrəs\ *n* **1** : woman in control **2** : a woman not his wife with whom a married man has recurrent sexual relations

mis·tri·al \mis'trīəl\ *n* : trial that has no legal effect

mis·trust \-'trəst\ *n* : lack of confidence ~ *vb* : have no confidence in — **mis·trust·ful** \-fəl\ *adj* — **mis·trust·ful·ly** *adv* — **mis·trust·ful·ness** *n*

misty \'mistē\ *adj* **mist·i·er; -est** **1** : obscured by mist **2** : tearful — **mist·i·ly** *adv* — **mist·i·ness** *n*

mis·un·der·stand \‚mis‚əndər'stand\ *vb* **1** : fail to understand **2** : interpret incorrectly

mis·un·der·stand·ing \-'standiŋ\ *n* **1** : wrong interpretation **2** : disagreement

mis·use \mis'yüz\ *vb* **1** : use incorrectly **2** : mistreat — **misuse** \-'yüs\ *n*

mite \'mīt\ *n* **1** : tiny spiderlike animal **2** : small amount

mi·ter, mi·tre \'mītər\ *n* **1** : bishop's headdress **2** : angular joint in wood

~ *vb* **-tered** *or* **-tred; -ter•ing** *or* **-tring** \'mītəriŋ\ : bevel the ends of for a miter joint

mit•i•gate \'mitə͵gāt\ *vb* **-gat•ed; -gat•ing** : make less severe — **mit•i•ga•tion** \͵mitə'gāshən\ *n* — **mit•i•ga•tive** \'mitə͵gātiv\ *adj*

mi•to•sis \mī'tōsəs\ *n, pl* **-to•ses** \-͵sēz\ : process of forming 2 cell nuclei from one — **mi•tot•ic** \-'tätik\ *adj*

mitt \'mit\ *n* : mittenlike baseball glove

mit•ten \'mit⁰n\ *n* : hand covering without finger sections

mix \'miks\ *vb* : combine or join into one mass or group ~ *n* : commercially prepared food mixture — **mix•able** *adj* — **mix•er** *n* — **mix up** *vb* : confuse

mix•ture \'mikschər\ *n* : act or product of mixing

mix–up *n* : instance of confusion

mne•mon•ic \ni'mänik\ *adj* : relating to or assisting memory

moan \'mōn\ *n* : low prolonged sound of pain or grief — **moan** *vb*

moat \'mōt\ *n* : deep wide trench around a castle

mob \'mäb\ *n* **1** : large disorderly crowd **2** : criminal gang ~ *vb* **-bb-** : crowd around and attack or annoy

mo•bile \'mōbəl, -͵bēl, -͵bīl\ *adj* : capable of moving or being moved ~ \'mō͵bēl\ *n* : suspended art construction with freely moving parts — **mo•bil•i•ty** \mō'bilətē\ *n*

mo•bi•lize \'mōbə͵līz\ *vb* **-lized; -liz•ing** : assemble and make ready for war duty — **mo•bi•li•za•tion** \͵mōbələ'zāshən\ *n*

moc•ca•sin \'mäkəsən\ *n* **1** : heelless shoe **2** : venomous U.S. snake

mo•cha \'mōkə\ *n* **1** : mixture of coffee and chocolate **2** : dark brown color

mock \'mäk, 'mòk\ *vb* **1** : ridicule **2** : mimic in derision ~ *adj* **1** : simulated **2** : phony — **mock•er** *n* — **mock•ery** \-ərē\ *n* — **mock•ing•ly** *adv*

mock•ing•bird \'mäkiŋ͵bərd, 'mòk-\ *n* : songbird that mimics other birds

mode \'mōd\ *n* **1** : particular form or variety **2** : style — **mod•al** \-⁰l\ *adj* — **mod•ish** \'mōdish\ *adj*

mod•el \'mäd⁰l\ *n* **1** : structural design **2** : miniature representation **3** : something worthy of copying **4** : one who poses for an artist or displays clothes **5** : type or design ~ *vb* **-eled** *or* **-elled; -el•ing** *or* **-el•ling 1** : shape **2** : work as a model ~ *adj* **1** : serving as a pattern **2** : being a miniature representation of

mo•dem \'mōdəm, -͵dem\ *n* : device by which a computer communicates with another computer over telephone lines

mod•er•ate \'mädərət\ *adj* : avoiding extremes ~ \'mädə͵rāt\ *vb* **-at•ed; -at•ing 1** : lessen the intensity of **2** : act as a moderator — **moderate** *n* — **mod•er•ate•ly** *adv* — **mod•er•ate•ness** *n* — **mod•er•a•tion** \͵mädə'rāshən\ *n*

mod•er•a•tor \'mädə͵rātər\ *n* : one who presides

mod•ern \'mädərn\ *adj* : relating to or characteristic of the present — **modern** *n* — **mo•der•ni•ty** \mə'dərnətē\ *n* — **mod•ern•i•za•tion** \͵mädərnə'zāshən\ *n* — **mod•ern•ize** \'mädər͵nīz\ *vb* — **mod•ern•iz•er** \'mädər-͵nīzər\ *n* — **mod•ern•ly** *adv* — **mod•ern•ness** *n*

mod•est \'mädəst\ *adj* **1** : having a moderate estimate of oneself **2** : reserved or decent in thoughts or actions **3** : limited in size, amount, or aim — **mod•est•ly** *adv* — **mod•es•ty** \-əstē\ *n*

mod•i•cum \'mädikəm\ *n* : small amount

mod•i•fy \'mädə͵fī\ *vb* **-fied; -fy•ing 1** : limit the meaning of **2** : change — **mod•i•fi•ca•tion** \͵mädəfə'kāshən\ *n* — **mod•i•fi•er** \'mädə͵fīər\ *n*

mod•u•lar \'mäjələr\ *adj* : built with standardized units — **mod•u•lar•ized** \-lə͵rīzd\ *adj*

mod•u•late \'mäjə͵lāt\ *vb* **-lat•ed; -lat•ing 1** : keep in proper measure or proportion **2** : vary a radio wave — **mod•u•la•tion** \͵mäjə'lāshən\ *n* — **mod•u•la•tor** \'mäjə͵lātər\ *n* — **mod•u•la•to•ry** \-lə͵tōrē\ *adj*

mod•ule \'mäjül\ *n* : standardized unit

mo•gul \'mōgəl\ *n* : important person

mo•hair \'mō͵har\ *n* : fabric made from the hair of the Angora goat

moist \'mòist\ *adj* : slightly or moderately wet — **moist•en** \'mòis⁰n\ *vb* — **moist•en•er** \'mòis⁰nər\ *n* — **moist•ly** *adv* — **moist•ness** *n*

mois•ture \'mòischər\ *n* : small amount of liquid that causes damp-

ness — **mois•tur•ize** \-chə₁rīz\ *vb*
— **mois•tur•iz•er** *n*
mo•lar \'mōlər\ *n* : grinding tooth —
molar *adj*
mo•las•ses \mə'lasəz\ *n* : thick brown
syrup from raw sugar
¹**mold** \'mōld\ *n* : crumbly organic soil
²**mold** *n* : frame or cavity for forming ∼
vb : shape in or as if in a mold —
mold•er *n*
³**mold** *n* : surface growth of fungus ∼ *vb*
: become moldy — **mold•i•ness**
\'mōldēnəs\ *n* — **moldy** *adj*
mold•er \'mōldər\ *vb* : crumble
mold•ing \'mōldiŋ\ *n* : decorative surface, plane, or strip
¹**mole** \'mōl\ *n* : spot on the skin
²**mole** *n* : small burrowing mammal —
mole•hill *n*
mol•e•cule \'mäli₁kyül\ *n* : small particle of matter — **mo•lec•u•lar**
\mə'lekyələr\ *adj*
mole•skin \-₁skin\ *n* : heavy cotton
fabric
mo•lest \mə'lest\ *vb* **1** : annoy or disturb **2** : force physical and usu. sexual contact on — **mo•les•ta•tion**
\₁mōl₁es'tāshən, ₁mäl-\ *n* — **mo•**
lest•er *n*
mol•li•fy \'mälə₁fī\ *vb* **-fied; -fy•ing**
: soothe in temper — **mol•li•fi•ca•**
tion \₁mäləfə'kāshən\ *n*
mol•lusk, mol•lusc \'mäləsk\ *n* : shelled
aquatic invertebrate — **mol•lus•can**
\mə'ləskən\ *adj*
mol•ly•cod•dle \'mälē₁käd³l\ *vb* **-dled;**
-dling : pamper
molt \'mōlt\ *vb* : shed hair, feathers,
outer skin, or horns periodically —
molt *n* — **molt•er** *n*
mol•ten \'mōlt³n\ *adj* : fused or lique-
fied by heat
mom \'mäm, 'məm\ *n* : mother
mo•ment \'mōmənt\ *n* **1** : tiny portion
of time **2** : time of excellence **3** : importance
mo•men•tar•i•ly \₁mōmən'terəlē\ *adv*
1 : for a moment **2** : at any moment
mo•men•tary \'mōmən₁terē\ *adj*
: continuing only a moment — **mo•**
men•tar•i•ness *n*
mo•men•tous \mō'mentəs\ *adj* : very
important — **mo•men•tous•ly** *adv* —
mo•men•tous•ness *n*
mo•men•tum \-əm\ *n, pl* **-ta** \-ə\ *or*
-tums : force of a moving body
mon•arch \'mänərk, -₁ärk\ *n* : ruler of

a kingdom or empire — **mo•nar•chi•**
cal \mə'närkikəl\ *adj*
mon•ar•chist \'mänərkist\ *n* : believer
in monarchical government — **mon•**
ar•chism \-₁kizəm\ *n*
mon•ar•chy \'mänərkē\ *n, pl* **-chies**
: realm of a monarch
mon•as•tery \'mänə₁sterē\ *n, pl* **-ter•**
ies : house for monks
mo•nas•tic \mə'nastik\ *adj* : relating
to monasteries, monks, or nuns — **mo•**
nastic *n* — **mo•nas•ti•cal•ly** \-tiklē\
adv — **mo•nas•ti•cism** \-tə₁sizəm\ *n*
Mon•day \'məndā, -dē\ *n* : 2d day of
the week
mon•e•tary \'mänə₁terē, 'mən-\ *adj*
: relating to money
mon•ey \'mənē\ *n, pl* **-eys** *or* **-ies**
\'mənēz\ **1** : something (as coins or
paper currency) used in buying **2**
: wealth — **mon•eyed** \-ēd\ *adj* —
mon•ey•lend•er *n*
mon•ger \'məŋgər, 'mäŋ-\ *n* : dealer
mon•gol•ism \'mäŋgə₁lizəm\ *n* : con-
genital mental retardation — **Mon•**
gol•oid \-gə₁lȯid\ *adj or n*
mon•goose \'män₁güs, 'mäŋ-\ *n, pl*
-goos•es : small agile mammal esp.
of India
mon•grel \'mäŋgrəl, 'məŋ-\ *n* : offspring of mixed breed
mon•i•tor \'mänətər\ *n* **1** : student assistant **2** : television screen ∼ *vb*
: watch or observe esp. for quality
monk \'məŋk\ *n* : member of a religious order living in a monastery —
monk•ish *adj*
mon•key \'məŋkē\ *n, pl* **-keys** : small
long-tailed arboreal primate ∼ *vb* **1**
: fool **2** : tamper
mon•key•shines \-₁shīnz\ *n pl* : pranks
monks•hood \'məŋks₁hùd\ *n* : poisonous herb with showy flowers
mon•o•cle \'mänikəl\ *n* : eyeglass for
one eye
mo•nog•a•my \mə'nägəmē\ *n* **1**
: marriage with one person at a time
2 : practice of having a single mate
for a period of time — **mo•nog•a•**
mist \mə'nägəmist\ *n* — **mo•nog•**
a•mous \-məs\ *adj*
mono•gram \'mänə₁gram\ *n* : sign of
identity made of initials — **mono•**
gram *vb*
mono•graph \-₁graf\ *n* : learned trea-
tise
mono•lin•gual \₁mänə'liŋgwəl\ *adj*
: using only one language

mono·lith \'män^əlˌ ith\ *n* **1** : single great stone **2** : single uniform massive whole — **mono·lith·ic** \ˌmän^əl-'ithik\ *adj*

mono·logue \'män^əlˌ òg\ *n* : long speech — **mono·logu·ist** \-ˌògist\, **mo·no·lo·gist** \mə'näləjist, 'män^əl-ˌògist\ *n*

mono·nu·cle·o·sis \ˌmänōˌnüklē'ōsəs, -ˌnyü-\ *n* : acute infectious disease

mo·nop·o·ly \mə'näpəlē\ *n, pl* **-lies 1** : exclusive ownership or control of a commodity **2** : one controlling a monopoly — **mo·nop·o·list** \-list\ *n* — **mo·nop·o·lis·tic** \məˌnäpə'listik\ *adj* — **mo·nop·o·li·za·tion** \-lə-'zāshən\ *n* — **mo·nop·o·lize** \mə-'näpəˌlīz\ *vb*

mono·rail \'mänəˌrāl\ *n* : single rail for a vehicle or a vehicle or system using it

mono·syl·lab·ic \ˌmänəsə'labik\ *adj* : consisting of or using words of only one syllable — **mono·syl·la·ble** \'mänəˌsiləbəl\ *n*

mono·the·ism \'mänōthēˌizəm\ *n* : doctrine or belief that there is only one deity — **mono·the·ist** \-ˌthēist\ *n* — **mono·the·is·tic** \ˌmänōthē-'istik\ *adj*

mono·tone \'mänəˌtōn\ *n* : succession of words in one unvarying tone

mo·not·o·nous \mə'nät^ənəs\ *adj* **1** : sounded in one unvarying tone **2** : tediously uniform — **mo·not·o·nous·ly** *adv* — **mo·not·o·nous·ness** *n* — **mo·not·o·ny** \-^ənē\ *n*

mon·ox·ide \mə'näkˌsīd\ *n* : oxide containing one atom of oxygen in a molecule

mon·sieur \məs'yər, məsh-\ *n, pl* **mes·sieurs** \-yərz, mā'syərz\ : man of high rank or station — used as a title for a man esp. of French nationality

mon·si·gnor \män'sēnyər\ *n, pl* **mon·si·gnors** *or* **mon·si·gno·ri** \ˌmän-ˌsēn'yōrē\ : Roman Catholic prelate — used as a title

mon·soon \män'sün\ *n* : periodic rainy season

mon·ster \'mänstər\ *n* **1** : abnormal or terrifying animal **2** : ugly, wicked, or cruel person — **mon·stros·i·ty** \män'sträsətē\ *n* — **mon·strous** \'mänstrəs\ *adj* — **mon·strous·ly** *adv*

mon·tage \män'täzh\ *n* : artistic composition of several different elements

month \'mənth\ *n* : 12th part of a year — **month·ly** *adv or adj or n*

mon·u·ment \'mänyəmənt\ *n* : structure erected in remembrance

mon·u·men·tal \ˌmänyə'ment^əl\ *adj* **1** : serving as a monument **2** : outstanding **3** : very great — **mon·u·men·tal·ly** *adv*

moo \'mü\ *vb* : make the noise of a cow — **moo** *n*

mood \'müd\ *n* : state of mind or emotion

moody \'müdē\ *adj* **mood·i·er; -est 1** : sad **2** : subject to changing moods and esp. to bad moods — **mood·i·ly** \'müd^əlē\ *adv* — **mood·i·ness** \-ēnəs\ *n*

moon \'mün\ *n* : natural satellite (as of earth) — **moon·beam** *n* — **moon·light** *n* — **moon·lit** *adj*

moon·light \-ˌlīt\ *vb* **-ed; -ing** : hold a 2d job — **moon·light·er** *n*

moon·shine *n* **1** : moonlight **2** : meaningless talk **3** : illegally distilled liquor

¹**moor** \'mùr\ *n* : open usu. swampy wasteland — **moor·land** \-lənd, -ˌland\ *n*

²**moor** *vb* : fasten with line or anchor

moor·ing \-iŋ\ *n* : place where boat can be moored

moose \'müs\ *n, pl* **moose** : large heavy-antlered deer

moot \'müt\ *adj* : open to question

mop \'mäp\ *n* : floor-cleaning implement ∼ *vb* **-pp-** : use a mop on

mope \'mōp\ *vb* **moped; mop·ing** : be sad or listless

mo·ped \'mōˌped\ *n* : low-powered motorbike

mo·raine \mə'rān\ *n* : glacial deposit of earth and stones

mor·al \'mórəl\ *adj* **1** : relating to principles of right and wrong **2** : conforming to a standard of right behavior **3** : relating to or acting on the mind, character, or will ∼ *n* **1** : point of a story **2** *pl* : moral practices or teachings — **mor·al·ist** \'mórəlist\ *n* — **mor·al·is·tic** \ˌmórə'listik\ *adj* — **mor·al·i·ty** \mə'ralətē\ *n* — **mor·al·ize** \'mórəˌlīz\ *vb* — **mor·al·ly** *adv*

mo·rale \mə'ral\ *n* : emotional attitude

mo·rass \mə'ras\ *n* : swamp

mor·a·to·ri·um \ˌmórə'tōrēəm\ *n, pl* **-ri·ums** *or* **-ria** \-ēə\ : suspension of activity

mo·ray \'mòrˌā, mə'rā\ *n* : savage eel

mor·bid \\'mórbəd\\ *adj* **1** : relating to disease **2** : gruesome — **mor·bid·i·ty** \\mór'bidətē\\ *n* — **mor·bid·ly** *adv* — **mor·bid·ness** *n*

mor·dant \\'mórd°nt\\ *adj* : sarcastic — **mor·dant·ly** *adv*

more \\'mōr\\ *adj* **1** : greater **2** : additional ~ *adv* **1** : in addition **2** : to a greater degree ~ *n* **1** : greater quantity **2** : additional amount ~ *pron* : additional ones

mo·rel \\mə'rel\\ *n* : pitted edible mushroom

more·over \\mōr'ōvər\\ *adv* : in addition

mo·res \\'mór͵āz, -ēz\\ *n pl* : customs

morgue \\'mórg\\ *n* : temporary holding place for dead bodies

mor·i·bund \\'mórə͵bənd\\ *adj* : dying

morn \\'mórn\\ *n* : morning

morn·ing \\'mórniŋ\\ *n* : time from sunrise to noon

mo·ron \\'mōr͵än\\ *n* **1** : mentally retarded person **2** : very stupid person — **mo·ron·ic** \\mə'ränik\\ *adj* — **mo·ron·i·cal·ly** *adv*

mo·rose \\mə'rōs\\ *adj* : sullen — **mo·rose·ly** *adv* — **mo·rose·ness** *n*

mor·phine \\'mór͵fēn\\ *n* : addictive painkilling drug

mor·row \\'märō\\ *n* : next day

Morse code \\'mórs-\\ *n* : code of dots and dashes or long and short sounds used for transmitting messages

mor·sel \\'mórsəl\\ *n* : small piece or quantity

mor·tal \\'mórt°l\\ *adj* **1** : causing or subject to death **2** : extreme — **mortal** *n* — **mor·tal·i·ty** \\mór'talətē\\ *n* — **mor·tal·ly** \\'mórt°lē\\ *adv*

mor·tar \\'mórtər\\ *n* **1** : strong bowl **2** : short-barreled cannon **3** : masonry material used to cement bricks or stones in place — **mortar** *vb*

mort·gage \\'mórgij\\ *n* : transfer of property rights as security for a loan — **mortgage** *vb* — **mort·gag·ee** \\͵mórgi'jē\\ *n* — **mort·ga·gor** \\͵mórgi'jór\\ *n*

mor·ti·fy \\'mórtə͵fī\\ *vb* **-fied; -fy·ing** **1** : subdue by abstinence or self-inflicted pain **2** : humiliate — **mor·ti·fi·ca·tion** \\͵mórtəfə'kāshən\\ *n*

mor·tu·ary \\'mórchə͵werē\\ *n, pl* **-aries** : place where dead bodies are kept until burial

mo·sa·ic \\mō'zāik\\ *n* : inlaid stone decoration — **mosaic** *adj*

Mos·lem \\'mäzləm\\ *var of* MUSLIM

mosque \\'mäsk\\ *n* : building where Muslims worship

mos·qui·to \\mə'skētō\\ *n, pl* **-toes** : biting bloodsucking insect

moss \\'mós\\ *n* : green seedless plant — **mossy** *adj*

most \\'mōst\\ *adj* **1** : majority of **2** : greatest ~ *adv* : to the greatest or a very great degree ~ *n* : greatest amount ~ *pron* : greatest number or part

-most \\͵mōst\\ *adj suffix* : most : most toward

most·ly \\'mōstlē\\ *adv* : mainly

mote \\'mōt\\ *n* : small particle

mo·tel \\mō'tel\\ *n* : hotel with rooms accessible from the parking lot

moth \\'móth\\ *n* : small pale insect related to the butterflies

moth·er \\'məthər\\ *n* **1** : female parent **2** : source ~ *vb* **1** : give birth to **2** : cherish or protect — **moth·er·hood** \\-͵hùd\\ *n* — **moth·er·land** \\-͵land\\ *n* — **moth·er·less** *adj* — **moth·er·ly** *adj*

moth·er–in–law *n, pl* **mothers–in–law** : spouse's mother

mo·tif \\mō'tēf\\ *n* : dominant theme

mo·tion \\'mōshən\\ *n* **1** : act or instance of moving **2** : proposal for action ~ *vb* : direct by a movement — **mo·tion·less** *adj* — **mo·tion·less·ly** *adv* — **mo·tion·less·ness** *n*

motion picture *n* : movie

mo·ti·vate \\'mōtə͵vāt\\ *vb* **-vat·ed; -vat·ing** : provide with a motive — **mo·ti·va·tion** \\͵mōtə'vāshən\\ *n* — **mo·ti·va·tor** \\'mōtə͵vātər\\ *n*

mo·tive \\'mōtiv\\ *n* : cause of a person's action ~ *adj* **1** : moving to action **2** : relating to motion — **mo·tive·less** *adj*

mot·ley \\'mätlē\\ *adj* : of diverse colors or elements

mo·tor \\'mōtər\\ *n* : unit that supplies power or motion ~ *vb* : travel by automobile — **mo·tor·ist** \\-ist\\ *n* — **mo·tor·ize** \\'mōtə͵rīz\\ *vb*

mo·tor·bike *n* : lightweight motorcycle

mo·tor·boat *n* : engine-driven boat

mo·tor·car *n* : automobile

mo·tor·cy·cle *n* : 2-wheeled automotive vehicle — **mo·tor·cy·clist** *n*

mo·tor·truck *n* : automotive truck

mot·tle \\'mät°l\\ *vb* **-tled; -tling** : mark with spots of different color

mot·to \\'mätō\\ *n, pl* **-toes** : brief guiding rule

mould \\'mōld\\ *var of* MOLD

mound \\'maund\\ *n* : pile (as of earth)

¹mount \\'maunt\\ *n* : mountain

²mount *vb* **1** : increase in amount **2** : get up on **3** : put in position ~ *n* **1** : frame or support **2** : horse to ride — **mount•able** *adj* — **mount•er** *n*

moun•tain \\'maunt°n\\ *n* : elevated land higher than a hill — **moun•tain•ous** \\'maunt°nəs\\ *adj* — **moun•tain•top** *n*

moun•tain•eer \\,maunt°n'ir\\ *n* : mountain resident or climber

moun•te•bank \\'maunti,baŋk\\ *n* : impostor

mourn \\'mōrn\\ *vb* : feel or express grief — **mourn•er** *n* — **mourn•ful** \\-fəl\\ *adj* — **mourn•ful•ly** *adv* — **mourn•ful•ness** *n* — **mourn•ing** *n*

mouse \\'maus\\ *n, pl* **mice** \\'mīs\\ **1** : small rodent **2** : device for controlling cursor movement on a computer display — **mouse•trap** *n or vb* — **mousy, mous•ey** \\'mausē, -zē\\ *adj*

mousse \\'müs\\ *n* **1** : light chilled dessert **2** : foamy hair-styling preparation

mous•tache \\'məs,tash, məs'tash\\ *var of* MUSTACHE

mouth \\'mauth\\ *n* : opening through which an animal takes in food ~ \\'mauth\\ *vb* **1** : speak **2** : repeat without comprehension or sincerity **3** : form soundlessly with the lips — **mouthed** \\'mauthd, 'mautht\\ *adj* — **mouth•ful** \\-,fül\\ *n*

mouth•piece *n* **1** : part (as of a musical instrument) held in or to the mouth **2** : spokesman

mou•ton \\'mü,tän\\ *n* : processed sheepskin

move \\'müv\\ *vb* **moved; mov•ing 1** : go or cause to go to another point **2** : change residence **3** : change or cause to change position **4** : take or cause to take action **5** : make a formal request **6** : stir the emotions ~ *n* **1** : act or instance of moving **2** : step taken to achieve a goal — **mov•able, move•able** \\-əbəl\\ *adj* — **move•ment** *n* — **mov•er** *n*

mov•ie \\'müvē\\ *n* : projected picture in which persons and objects seem to move

¹mow \\'mau\\ *n* : part of a barn where hay or straw is stored

²mow \\'mō\\ *vb* **mowed; mowed** *or* **mown** \\'mōn\\; **mow•ing** : cut with a machine — **mow•er** *n*

Mr. \\'mistər\\ *n, pl* **Messrs.** \\'mesərz\\ — conventional title for a man

Mrs. \\'misəz, -səs, *esp South* 'mizəz, -əs\\ *n, pl* **Mes•dames** \\mā'däm, -'dam\\ — conventional title for a married woman

Ms. \\'miz\\ *n* — conventional title for a woman

much \\'məch\\ *adj* **more** \\'mōr\\; **most** \\'mōst\\ : great in quantity, extent, or degree ~ *adv* **more; most** : to a great degree or extent ~ *n* : great quantity, extent, or degree

mu•ci•lage \\'myüsəlij\\ *n* : weak glue

muck \\'mək\\ *n* : manure, dirt, or mud — **mucky** *adj*

mu•cus \\'myükəs\\ *n* : slippery protective secretion of membranes (**mucous membranes**) lining body cavities — **mu•cous** \\-kəs\\ *adj*

mud \\'məd\\ *n* : soft wet earth — **mud•di•ly** \\'məd°lē\\ *adv* — **mud•di•ness** \\-ēnəs\\ *n* — **mud•dy** *adj or vb*

mud•dle \\'məd°l\\ *vb* **-dled; -dling 1** : make, be, or act confused **2** : make a mess of — **muddle** *n* — **mud•dle•head•ed** \\,məd°l'hedəd\\ *adj*

mu•ez•zin \\mü'ez°n, myü-\\ *n* : Muslim who calls the hour of daily prayer

¹muff \\'məf\\ *n* : tubular hand covering

²muff *vb* : bungle — **muff** *n*

muf•fin \\'məfən\\ *n* : soft cake baked in a cup-shaped container

muf•fle \\'məfəl\\ *vb* **-fled; -fling 1** : wrap up **2** : dull the sound of — **muf•fler** \\'məflər\\ *n*

muf•ti \\'məftē\\ *n* : civilian clothes

¹mug \\'məg\\ *n* : drinking cup ~ *vb* **-gg-** : make faces

²mug *vb* **-gg-** : assault with intent to rob — **mug•ger** *n*

mug•gy \\'məgē\\ *adj* **-gi•er; -est** : hot and humid — **mug•gi•ness** *n*

Mu•ham•mad•an \\mō'hamədən, -'häm-; mü-\\ *n* : Muslim — **Mu•ham•mad•an•ism** \\-,izəm\\ *n*

mu•lat•to \\mü'lätō, -'lat-\\ *n, pl* **-toes** *or* **-tos** : person of mixed black and white ancestry

mul•ber•ry \\'məl,berē\\ *n* : tree with small edible fruit

mulch \\'məlch\\ *n* : protective ground covering — **mulch** *vb*

mulct \\'məlkt\\ *n or vb* : fine

¹mule \\'myül\\ *n* **1** : offspring of a male ass and a female horse **2** : stubborn person — **mul•ish** \\'myülish\\ *adj* — **mul•ish•ly** *adv* — **mu•lish•ness** *n*

²**mule** *n* : backless shoe

mull \'məl\ *vb* : ponder

mul•let \'mələt\ *n, pl* **-let** *or* **-lets** : marine food fish

multi- *comb form* **1** : many or multiple **2** : many times over

mul•ti•far•i•ous \,məltə'farēəs\ *adj* : diverse

mul•ti•lat•er•al \,məlti'latərəl, -,tī-\ *adj* : having many sides or participants

mul•ti•lin•gual \-'liŋgwəl\ *adj* : knowing or using several languages — **mul•ti•lin•gual•ism** \-gwə,lizəm\ *n*

mul•ti•na•tion•al \-'nashənəl\ *adj* **1** : relating to several nations or nationalities **2** : having divisions in several countries — **multinational** *n*

mul•ti•ple \'məltəpəl\ *adj* **1** : several or many **2** : various ∼ *n* : product of one number by another

multiple sclerosis \-sklə'rōsəs\ *n* : brain or spinal disease affecting muscle control

mul•ti•pli•ca•tion \,məltəplə'kāshən\ *n* **1** : increase **2** : short method of repeated addition

mul•ti•plic•i•ty \,məltə'plisətē\ *n, pl* **-ties** : great number or variety

mul•ti•ply \'məltə,plī\ *vb* **-plied; -plying** **1** : increase in number **2** : perform multiplication — **mul•ti•pli•er** \-,plīər\ *n*

mul•ti•tude \'məltə,tüd, -,tyüd\ *n*

: great number — **mul•ti•tu•di•nous** \,məltə'tüd°nəs, -'tyü-\ *adj*

¹**mum** \'məm\ *adj* : silent

²**mum** *n* : chrysanthemum

mum•ble \'məmbəl\ *vb* **-bled; -bling** : speak indistinctly — **mumble** *n* — **mum•bler** *n*

mum•mer \'məmər\ *n* **1** : actor esp. in a pantomime **2** : disguised merrymaker — **mum•mery** *n*

mum•my \'məmē\ *n, pl* **-mies** : embalmed body — **mum•mi•fi•ca•tion** \,məmifə'kāshən\ *n* — **mum•mi•fy** \'məmi,fī\ *vb*

mumps \'məmps\ *n sing or pl* : virus disease with swelling esp. of the salivary glands

munch \'mənch\ *vb* : chew

mun•dane \,mən'dān, 'mən,-\ *adj* **1** : relating to the world **2** : lacking concern for the ideal or spiritual — **mun•dane•ly** *adv*

mu•nic•i•pal \myù'nisəpəl\ *adj* : of or relating to a town or city — **mu•nic•i•pal•i•ty** \myù,nisə'palətē\ *n*

mu•nif•i•cent \myù'nifəsənt\ *adj* : generous — **mu•nif•i•cence** \-səns\ *n*

mu•ni•tion \myù'nishən\ *n* : armaments

mu•ral \'myùrəl\ *adj* : relating to a wall ∼ *n* : wall painting — **mu•ra•list** *n*

mur•der \'mərdər\ *n* : unlawful killing of a person ∼ *vb* : commit a murder — **mur•der•er** *n* — **mur•der•ess**

List of self-explanatory words with the prefix *multi-*

multiarmed	multifunction	multipurpose
multibarreled	multifunctional	multiracial
multibillion	multigrade	multiroom
multibranched	multiheaded	multisense
multibuilding	multihospital	multiservice
multicenter	multihued	multisided
multichambered	multilane	multispeed
multichannel	multilevel	multistage
multicolored	multimedia	multistep
multicounty	multimember	multistory
multicultural	multimillion	multisyllabic
multidimensional	multimillionaire	multitalented
multidirectional	multipart	multitrack
multidisciplinary	multipartite	multiunion
multidiscipline	multiparty	multiunit
multidivisional	multiplant	multiuse
multifaceted	multipolar	multivitamin
multifamily	multiproblem	multiwarhead
multifilament	multiproduct	multiyear

\-əs\ *n* — **mur•der•ous** \-əs\ *adj* — **mur•der•ous•ly** *adv*

murk \'mərk\ *n* : darkness — **murk•i•ly** \'mərkəlē\ *adv* — **murk•i•ness** \-kēnəs\ *n* — **murky** *adj*

mur•mur \'mərmər\ *n* **1** : muttered complaint **2** : low indistinct sound — **murmur** *vb* — **mur•mur•er** *n* — **mur•mur•ous** *adj*

mus•ca•tel \ˌməskə'tel\ *n* : sweet wine

mus•cle \'məsəl\ *n* **1** : body tissue capable of contracting to produce motion **2** : strength ～ *vb* **-cled; -cling** : force one's way — **mus•cled** *adj* — **mus•cu•lar** \'məskyələr\ *adj* — **mus•cu•lar•i•ty** \ˌməskyə'larətē\ *n*

muscular dystrophy *n* : disease marked by progressive wasting of muscles

mus•cu•la•ture \'məskyələˌchùr\ *n* : bodily muscles

¹**muse** \'myüz\ *vb* **mused; mus•ing** : ponder — **mus•ing•ly** *adv*

²**muse** *n* : source of inspiration

mu•se•um \myù'zēəm\ *n* : institution displaying objects of interest

mush \'məsh\ *n* **1** : corn meal boiled in water or something of similar consistency **2** : sentimental nonsense — **mushy** *adj*

mush•room \'məshˌrüm, -ˌrùm\ *n* : caplike organ of a fungus ～ *vb* : grow rapidly

mu•sic \'myüzik\ *n* : vocal or instrumental sounds — **mu•si•cal** \-zikəl\ *adj or n* — **mu•si•cal•ly** *adv*

mu•si•cian \myù'zishən\ *n* : composer or performer of music — **mu•si•cian•ly** *adj* — **mu•si•cian•ship** *n*

musk \'məsk\ *n* : strong-smelling substance from an Asiatic deer used in perfume — **musk•i•ness** \'məskēnəs\ *n* — **musky** *adj*

mus•kel•lunge \'məskəˌlənj\ *n, pl* **-lunge** : large No. American pike

mus•ket \'məskət\ *n* : former shoulder firearm — **mus•ke•teer** \ˌməskə'tir\ *n*

musk•mel•on \'məskˌmelən\ *n* : small edible melon

musk–ox \'məskˌäks\ *n* : shaggy-coated wild ox of the arctic

musk•rat \-ˌrat\ *n, pl* **-rat** *or* **-rats** : No. American aquatic rodent

Mus•lim \'məzləm, 'mùs-, 'mùz-\ *n* : adherent of Islam — **Muslim** *adj*

mus•lin \'məzlən\ *n* : cotton fabric

muss \'məs\ *n* : untidy state ～ *vb* : disarrange — **muss•i•ly** \'məsəlē\

adv — **muss•i•ness** \-ēnəs\ *n* — **mussy** *adj*

mus•sel \'məsəl\ *n* : edible mollusk

must \'məst\ *vb* — used as an auxiliary esp. to express a command, obligation, or necessity ～ \'məst\ *n* : something necessary

mus•tache \'məsˌtash, məs'-\ *n* : hair of the human upper lip

mus•tang \'məsˌtaŋ\ *n* : wild horse of Western America

mus•tard \'məstərd\ *n* : pungent yellow seasoning

mus•ter \'məstər\ *vb* **1** : assemble **2** : rouse ～ *n* : assembled group

musty \'məstē\ *adj* **mus•ti•er; -est** : stale — **must•i•ly** *adv* — **must•i•ness** *n*

mu•ta•ble \'myütəbəl\ *adj* : changeable — **mu•ta•bil•i•ty** \ˌmyütə'bilətē\ *n*

mu•tant \'myüt°nt\ *adj* : relating to or produced by mutation — **mutant** *n*

mu•tate \'myüˌtāt\ *vb* **-tat•ed; -tat•ing** : undergo mutation — **mu•ta•tive** \'myüˌtātiv, 'myütət-\ *adj*

mu•ta•tion \myü'tāshən\ *n* : change in a hereditary character — **mu•ta•tion•al** *adj*

mute \'myüt\ *adj* **mut•er; mut•est 1** : unable to speak **2** : silent ～ *n* **1** : one who is mute **2** : muffling device ～ *vb* **mut•ed; mut•ing** : muffle — **mute•ly** *adv* — **mute•ness** *n*

mu•ti•late \'myüt°lˌāt\ *vb* **-lat•ed; -lat•ing** : damage seriously (as by cutting off or altering an essential part) — **mu•ti•la•tion** \ˌmyüt°l'āshən\ *n* — **mu•ti•la•tor** \'myüt°lˌātər\ *n*

mu•ti•ny \'myütənē\ *n, pl* **-nies** : rebellion — **mu•ti•neer** \ˌmyüt°n'ir\ *n* — **mu•ti•nous** \'myüt°nəs\ *adj* — **mu•ti•nous•ly** *adv* — **mutiny** *vb*

mutt \'mət\ *n* : mongrel

mut•ter \'mətər\ *vb* **1** : speak indistinctly or softly **2** : grumble — **mut•ter** *n*

mut•ton \'mət°n\ *n* : flesh of a mature sheep — **mut•tony** *adj*

mu•tu•al \'myüchəwəl\ *adj* **1** : given or felt by one another in equal amount **2** : common — **mu•tu•al•ly** *adv*

muz•zle \'məzəl\ *n* **1** : nose and jaws of an animal **2** : muzzle covering to immobilize an animal's jaws **3** : discharge end of a gun ～ *vb* **-zled; -zling** : restrain with or as if with a muzzle

my \'mī\ *adj* **1** : relating to me or my-self **2** — used interjectionally esp. to express surprise

my·nah, my·na \'mīnə\ *n* : dark crested Asian bird

my·o·pia \mī'ōpēə\ *n* : nearsightedness — **my·o·pic** \-'ōpik, -'äpik\ *adj* — **my·o·pi·cal·ly** *adv*

myr·i·ad \'mirēəd\ *n* : indefinitely large number — **myriad** *adj*

myrrh \'mər\ *n* : aromatic plant gum

myr·tle \'mərt°l\ *n* : shiny evergreen

my·self \mī'self\ *pron* : I, me — used reflexively or for emphasis

mys·tery \'mistərē\ *n, pl* **-ter·ies 1** : religious truth **2** : something not understood **3** : puzzling or secret quality or state — **mys·te·ri·ous** \mis-'tirēəs\ *adj* — **mys·te·ri·ous·ly** *adv* — **mys·te·ri·ous·ness** *n*

mys·tic \'mistik\ *adj* : mystical or mys-terious ~ *n* : one who has mys-tical experiences — **mys·ti·cism** \-tə,sizəm\ *n*

mys·ti·cal \'mistikəl\ *adj* **1** : spiritual **2** : relating to direct communion with God — **mys·ti·cal·ly** *adj*

mys·ti·fy \'mistə,fī\ *vb* **-fied; -fy·ing** : perplex — **mys·ti·fi·ca·tion** \,mistəfə'kāshən\ *n*

mys·tique \mis'tēk\ *n* : aura of mys-tery surrounding something

myth \'mith\ *n* **1** : legendary narrative explaining a belief or phenomenon **2** : imaginary person or thing — **myth·i·cal** \-ikəl\ *adj*

my·thol·o·gy \mith'äləjē\ *n, pl* **-gies** : body of myths — **myth·o·log·i·cal** \,mithə'läjikəl\ *adj* — **my·thol·o·gist** \mith'äləjist\ *n*

N

n \'en\ *n, pl* **n's** *or* **ns** \'enz\ : 14th let-ter of the alphabet

nab \'nab\ *vb* **-bb-** : seize or arrest

na·cho \'nächō\ *n* : tortilla chip topped with a savory mixture and cheese and broiled

na·dir \'nā,dir, 'nādər\ *n* : lowest point

¹nag \'nag\ *n* : old or decrepit horse

²nag *vb* **-gg- 1** : complain **2** : scold or urge continually **3** : be persistently an-noying ~ *n* : one who nags habitually

na·iad \'nāəd, 'nī-, -,ad\ *n, pl* **-iads** *or* **-ia·des** \-ə,dēz\ : mythological water nymph

nail \'nāl\ *n* **1** : horny sheath at the end of each finger and toe **2** : pointed metal fastener ~ *vb* : fasten with a nail — **nail·er** *n*

na·ive, na·ïve \nä'ēv\ *adj* **-iv·er; -est 1** : innocent and unsophisticated **2** : easily deceived — **na·ive·ly** *adv* — **na·ive·ness** *n*

na·ive·té \,nä,ēvə'tā, nä'ēvə,-\ *n* : quality or state of being naive

na·ked \'nākəd, 'nekəd\ *adj* **1** : hav-ing no clothes on **2** : uncovered **3** : plain or obvious **4** : unaided — **na·ked·ly** *adv* — **na·ked·ness** *n*

nam·by–pam·by \,nambē'pambē\ *adj* : weak or indecisive

name \'nām\ *n* **1** : word by which a person or thing is known **2** : dis-paraging word for someone **3** : dis-tinguished reputation ~ *vb* **named; nam·ing 1** : give a name to **2** : men-tion or identify by name **3** : nominate or appoint ~ *adj* **1** : relating to a name **2** : prominent — **name·able** *adj* — **name·less** *adj* — **name·less-ly** *adv*

name·ly \'nāmlē\ *adv* : that is to say

name·sake \-,sāk\ *n* : one named after another

nano·tech·nol·o·gy \,nanōtek'näləjē\ *n* : manipulation of materials on an atomic or molecular scale

¹nap \'nap\ *vb* **-pp- 1** : sleep briefly **2** : be off guard ~ *n* : short sleep

²nap *n* : soft downy surface — **nap·less** *adj* — **napped** \'napt\ *adj*

na·palm \'nā,pälm, -,päm\ *n* : gaso-line in the form of a jelly

nape \'nāp, 'nap\ *n* : back of the neck

naph·tha \'nafthə\ *n* : flammable sol-vent

nap·kin \'napkən\ *n* : small cloth for use at the table

nar·cis·sism \'närsə,sizəm\ *n* : self=love — **nar·cis·sist** \-sist\ *n or adj* — **nar·cis·sis·tic** \,närsə'sistik\ *adj*

nar•cis•sus \när'sisəs\ *n, pl* **-cis•sus** *or* **-cis•sus•es** *or* **-cis•si** \-'sis,ī, -,ē\ : plant with flowers usu. borne separately

nar•cot•ic \när'kätik\ *n* : painkilling addictive drug — **narcotic** *adj*

nar•rate \'nar,āt\ *vb* **nar•rat•ed; nar•rat•ing** : tell (a story) — **nar•ra•tion** \na-'rāshən\ *n* — **nar•ra•tive** \'narətiv\ *n or adj* — **nar•ra•tor** \'nar,ātər\ *n*

nar•row \'narō\ *adj* **1** : of less than standard width **2** : limited **3** : not liberal **4** : barely successful ~ *vb* : make narrow — **nar•row•ly** *adv* — **nar•row•ness** *n*

nar•row–mind•ed \,narō'mīndəd\ *adj* : shallow, provincial, or bigoted

nar•rows \'narōz\ *n pl* : narrow passage

nar•whal \'när,hwäl, 'närwəl\ *n* : sea mammal with a tusk

nasal \'nāzəl\ *adj* : relating to or uttered through the nose — **na•sal•ly** *adv*

nas•tur•tium \nə'stərshəm, na-\ *n* : herb with showy flowers

nas•ty \'nastē\ *adj* **nas•ti•er; -est** **1** : filthy **2** : indecent **3** : malicious or spiteful **4** : difficult or disagreeable **5** : unfair — **nas•ti•ly** \'nastəlē\ *adv* — **nas•ti•ness** \-tēnəs\ *n*

na•tal \'nāt°l\ *adj* : relating to birth

na•tion \'nāshən\ *n* **1** : people of similar characteristics **2** : community with its own territory and government — **na•tion•al** \'nashənəl\ *adj or n* — **na•tion•al•ly** *adv* — **na•tion•hood** *n* — **na•tion•wide** *adj*

na•tion•al•ism \'nashənəl,izəm\ *n* : devotion to national interests, unity, and independence — **na•tion•al•ist** \-ist\ *n or adj* — **na•tion•al•is•tic** \,nashənəl'istik\ *adj*

na•tion•al•i•ty \,nashə'nalətē\ *n, pl* **-ties 1** : national character **2** : membership in a nation **3** : political independence **4** : ethnic group

na•tion•al•ize \'nashənəl,īz\ *vb* **-ized; -iz•ing 1** : make national **2** : place under government control — **na•tion•al•i•za•tion** \,nashənələ'zāshən\ *n*

na•tive \'nātiv\ *adj* **1** : belonging to a person at or by way of birth **2** : born or produced in a particular place ~ *n* : one who belongs to a country by birth

Na•tiv•i•ty \nə'tivətē, nā-\ *n, pl* **-ties 1** : birth of Christ **2** *not cap* : birth

nat•ty \'natē\ *adj* **-ti•er; -est** : smartly dressed — **nat•ti•ly** \'nat°lē\ *adv*

nat•u•ral \'nachərəl\ *adj* **1** : relating to or determined by nature **2** : not artificial **3** : simple and sincere **4** : lifelike ~ *n* : one having an innate talent — **nat•u•ral•ness** *n*

nat•u•ral•ism \'nachərə,lizəm\ *n* : realism in art and literature — **nat•u•ral•is•tic** \,nachərə'listik\ *adj*

nat•u•ral•ist \-list\ *n* **1** : one who practices naturalism **2** : student of animals or plants

nat•u•ral•ize \-,līz\ *vb* **-ized; -iz•ing 1** : become or cause to become established **2** : confer citizenship on — **nat•u•ral•i•za•tion** \,nachərələ'zāshən\ *n*

nat•u•ral•ly \'nachərəlē\ *adv* **1** : in a natural way **2** : as might be expected

na•ture \'nāchər\ *n* **1** : basic quality of something **2** : kind **3** : disposition **4** : physical universe **5** : natural environment

naught \'nȯt, 'nät\ *n* **1** : nothing **2** : zero

naugh•ty \'nȯtē, 'nät-\ *adj* **-ti•er; -est** **1** : disobedient or misbehaving **2** : improper — **naught•i•ly** \'nȯt°lē, 'nät-\ *adv* — **naught•i•ness** \-ēnəs\ *n*

nau•sea \'nȯzēə, -shə\ *n* **1** : sickness of the stomach with a desire to vomit **2** : extreme disgust — **nau•seous** \-shəs, -zēəs\ *adj*

nau•se•ate \'nȯzē,āt, -zhē-, -sē-, -shē-\ *vb* **-ated; -at•ing** : affect or become affected with nausea — **nau•se•at•ing•ly** \-,ātiŋlē\ *adv*

nau•ti•cal \'nȯtikəl\ *adj* : relating to ships and sailing — **nau•ti•cal•ly** *adv*

nau•ti•lus \'nȯt°ləs\ *n, pl* **-lus•es** *or* **-li** \-°l,ī, -,ē\ : sea mollusk with a spiral shell

na•val \'nāvəl\ *adj* : relating to a navy

nave \'nāv\ *n* : central part of a church

na•vel \'nāvəl\ *n* : depression in the abdomen

nav•i•ga•ble \'navigəbəl\ *adj* : capable of being navigated — **nav•i•ga•bil•i•ty** \,navigə'bilətē\ *n*

nav•i•gate \'navə,gāt\ *vb* **-gat•ed; -gat•ing 1** : sail on or through **2** : direct the course of — **nav•i•ga•tion** \,navə'gāshən\ *n* — **nav•i•ga•tor** \'navə,gātər\ *n*

na•vy \'nāvē\ *n, pl* **-vies 1** : fleet **2** : nation's organization for sea warfare

nay \'nā\ *adv* : no — used in oral voting ~ *n* : negative vote

Na•zi \'nätsē, 'nat-\ *n* : member of a German fascist party from 1933 to 1945 — **Nazi** *adj* — **Na•zism** \'nät,sizəm, 'nat-\, **Na•zi•ism** \-sē,izəm\ *n*

near \'nir\ *adv* : at or close to ～ *prep* : close to ～ *adj* **1** : not far away **2** : very much like ～ *vb* : approach — **near•ly** *adv* — **near•ness** *n*

near•by \nir'bī, 'nirˌbī\ *adv or adj* : near

near•sight•ed \'nir'sītəd\ *adj* : seeing well at short distances only — **near-sight•ed•ly** *adv* — **near•sight•ed-ness** *n*

neat \'nēt\ *adj* **1** : not diluted **2** : tastefully simple **3** : orderly and clean — **neat** *adv* — **neat•ly** *adv* — **neat-ness** *n*

neb•u•la \'nebyələ\ *n, pl* **-lae** \-ˌlē, -ˌlī\ : large cloud of interstellar gas — **neb•u•lar** \-lər\ *adj*

neb•u•lous \-ləs\ *adj* : indistinct

nec•es•sary \'nesəˌserē\ *n, pl* **-saries** : indispensable item ～ *adj* **1** : inevitable **2** : compulsory **3** : positively needed — **nec•es•sar•i•ly** \ˌnesə-'serəlē\ *adv*

ne•ces•si•tate \ni'sesəˌtāt\ *vb* **-tat•ed; -tat•ing** : make necessary

ne•ces•si•ty \ni'sesətē\ *n, pl* **-ties 1** : very great need **2** : something that is necessary **3** : poverty **4** : circumstances that cannot be changed

neck \'nek\ *n* **1** : body part connecting the head and trunk **2** : part of a garment at the neck **3** : narrow part ～ *vb* : kiss and caress — **necked** \'nekt\ *adj*

neck•er•chief \'nekərchəf, -ˌchēf\ *n, pl* **-chiefs** \-chəfs, -ˌchēfs\ : cloth worn tied around the neck

neck•lace \'nekləs\ *n* : ornament worn around the neck

neck•tie *n* : ornamental cloth tied under a collar

nec•ro•man•cy \'nekrəˌmansē\ *n* : art of conjuring up the spirits of the dead — **nec•ro•man•cer** \-sər\ *n*

ne•cro•sis \nə'krōsəs, ne-\ *n, pl* **-cro-ses** \-ˌsēz\ : death of body tissue

nec•tar \'nektər\ *n* : sweet plant secretion

nec•tar•ine \ˌnektə'rēn\ *n* : smooth-skinned peach

née, nee \'nā\ *adj* — used to identify a married woman by maiden name

need \'nēd\ *n* **1** : obligation **2** : lack of something or what is lacking **3** : poverty ～ *vb* **1** : be in want **2** : have cause for **3** : be under obligation — **need•ful** \-fəl\ *adj* — **need-less** *adj* — **need•less•ly** *adv* — **needy** *adj*

nee•dle \'nēd²l\ *n* **1** : pointed sewing implement or something like it **2** : movable bar in a compass **3** : hollow instrument for injecting or withdrawing material ～ *vb* **-dled; -dling** : incite to action by repeated gibes — **nee•dle•work** \-ˌwərk\ *n*

nee•dle•point \'nēd²lˌpȯint\ *n* **1** : lace fabric **2** : embroidery on canvas — **needlepoint** *adj*

ne•far•i•ous \ni'farēəs\ *adj* : very wicked — **ne•far•i•ous•ly** *adv*

ne•gate \ni'gāt\ *vb* **-gat•ed; -gat•ing 1** : deny **2** : nullify — **ne•ga•tion** \-'gāshən\ *n*

neg•a•tive \'negətiv\ *adj* **1** : marked by denial or refusal **2** : showing a lack of something suspected or desirable **3** : less than zero **4** : having more electrons than protons **5** : having light and shadow images reversed ～ *n* **1** : negative word or vote **2** : a negative number **3** : negative photographic image — **neg•a•tive•ly** *adv* — **neg•a•tive•ness** *n* — **neg•a•tiv•i-ty** \ˌnegə'tivətē\ *n*

ne•glect \ni'glekt\ *vb* **1** : disregard **2** : leave unattended to ～ *n* **1** : act of neglecting **2** : condition of being neglected — **ne•glect•ful** *adj*

neg•li•gee \ˌneglə'zhā\ *n* : woman's loose robe

neg•li•gent \'neglijənt\ *adj* : marked by neglect — **neg•li•gence** \-jəns\ *n* — **neg•li•gent•ly** *adv*

neg•li•gi•ble \'neglijəbəl\ *adj* : insignificant

ne•go•ti•ate \ni'gōshēˌāt\ *vb* **-at•ed; -at•ing 1** : confer with another to settle a matter **2** : obtain cash for **3** : get through successfully — **ne•go•tia•ble** \-shəbəl, -shēə-\ *adj* — **ne•go•ti•a-tion** \-ˌgōshē'āshən, -shē'ā-\ *n* — **ne•go•ti•a•tor** \-'gōshēˌātər\ *n*

Ne•gro \'nēgrō\ *n, pl* **-groes** *sometimes offensive* : member of the dark-skinned race native to Africa — **Ne-gro** *adj* — **Ne•groid** \'nēˌgrȯid\ *n or adj, often not cap*

neigh \'nā\ *n* : cry of a horse — **neigh** *vb*

neigh•bor \'nābər\ *n* **1** : one living nearby **2** : fellowman ～ *vb* : be near or next to — **neigh•bor•hood** \-ˌhud\ *n* — **neigh•bor•li•ness** *n* — **neigh-bor•ly** *adv*

nei•ther \'nēthər, 'nī-\ *pron or adj* : not the one or the other ～ *conj* **1** : not either **2** : nor

nem•e•sis \'neməsəs\ *n, pl* **-e•ses** \-ə‚sēz\ **1** : old and usu. frustrating rival **2** : retaliation

ne•ol•o•gism \nē'älə‚jizəm\ *n* : new word

ne•on \'nē‚än\ *n* : gaseous colorless chemical element that emits a reddish glow in electric lamps — **neon** *adj*

neo•phyte \'nēə‚fīt\ *n* : beginner

neph•ew \'nefyü, *chiefly Brit* 'nev-\ *n* : a son of one's brother, sister, brother-in-law, or sister-in-law

nep•o•tism \'nepə‚tizəm\ *n* : favoritism shown in hiring a relative

nerd \'nərd\ *n* : one who is not stylish or socially at ease — **nerdy** *adj*

nerve \'nərv\ *n* **1** : strand of body tissue that connects the brain with other parts of the body **2** : self-control **3** : daring **4** *pl* : nervousness — **nerved** \'nərvd\ *adj* — **nerve•less** *adj*

ner•vous \'nərvəs\ *adj* **1** : relating to or made up of nerves **2** : easily excited **3** : timid or fearful — **ner•vous•ly** *adv* — **ner•vous•ness** *n*

nervy \'nərvē\ *adj* **nerv•i•er; -est** : insolent or presumptuous

-ness \nəs\ *n suffix* : condition or quality

nest \'nest\ *n* **1** : shelter prepared by a bird for its eggs **2** : place where eggs (as of insects or fish) are laid and hatched **3** : snug retreat **4** : set of objects fitting one inside or under another ~ *vb* : build or occupy a nest

nes•tle \'nesəl\ *vb* **-tled; -tling** : settle snugly (as in a nest)

¹net \'net\ *n* : fabric with spaces between strands or something made of this ~ *vb* **-tt-** : cover with or catch in a net

²net *adj* : remaining after deductions ~ *vb* **-tt-** : have as profit

neth•er \'nethər\ *adj* : situated below

net•tle \'netᵊl\ *n* : coarse herb with stinging hairs ~ *vb* **-tled; -tling** : provoke or vex — **net•tle•some** *adj*

net•work *n* : system of crossing or connected elements

neu•ral \'nurəl, 'nyur-\ *adj* : relating to a nerve

neu•ral•gia \nu'raljə, nyu-\ *n* : pain along a nerve — **neu•ral•gic** \-jik\ *adj*

neu•ri•tis \nu'rītəs, nyu-\ *n, pl* **-rit•i•des** \-'ritə‚dēz\ *or* **-ri•tis•es** : inflammation of a nerve

neu•rol•o•gy \nu'räləjē, nyu-\ *n* : study of the nervous system — **neu•ro•log•i•cal** \‚nurə'läjikəl, ‚nyur-\, **neu•ro•log•ic** \-ik\ *adj* — **neu•rol•o•gist** \nu'räləjist, nyu-\ *n*

neu•ro•sis \nu'rōsəs, nyu-\ *n, pl* **-ro•ses** \-‚sēz\ : nervous disorder

neu•rot•ic \nu'rätik, nyu-\ *adj* : relating to neurosis ~ *n* : unstable person — **neu•rot•i•cal•ly** *adv*

neu•ter \'nütər, 'nyü-\ *adj* : neither masculine nor feminine ~ *vb* : castrate or spay

neu•tral \-trəl\ *adj* **1** : not favoring either side **2** : being neither one thing nor the other **3** : not decided in color **4** : not electrically charged ~ *n* **1** : one that is neutral **2** : position of gears that are not engaged — **neu•tral•i•za•tion** \‚nütrələ'zāshən, ‚nyü-\ *n* — **neu•tral•ize** \'nütrə‚līz, 'nyü-\ *vb*

neu•tral•i•ty \nü'tralətē, nyü-\ *n* : state of being neutral

neu•tron \'nü‚trän, 'nyü-\ *n* : uncharged atomic particle

nev•er \'nevər\ *adv* **1** : not ever **2** : not in any degree, way, or condition

nev•er•more *adv* : never again

nev•er•the•less *adv* : in spite of that

new \'nü, 'nyü\ *adj* **1** : not old or familiar **2** : different from the former **3** : recently discovered or learned **4** : not accustomed **5** : refreshed or regenerated **6** : being such for the first time ~ *adv* : newly — **new•ish** *adj* — **new•ness** *n*

new•born *adj* **1** : recently born **2** : born anew ~ *n, pl* **-born** *or* **-borns** : newborn individual

new•ly \-lē\ *adv* : recently

news \'nüz, 'nyüz\ *n* : report of recent events — **news•let•ter** *n* — **news•mag•a•zine** *n* — **news•man** \-mən, -‚man\ *n* — **news•pa•per** *n* — **news•pa•per•man** \-‚man\ *n* — **news•stand** *n* — **news•wom•an** \-‚wumən\ *n* — **news•wor•thy** *adj*

news•cast \-‚kast\ *n* : broadcast of news — **news•cast•er** \-‚kastər\ *n*

news•print *n* : paper made from wood pulp

newsy \'nüzē, 'nyü-\ *adj* **news•i•er; -est** : filled with news

newt \'nüt, 'nyüt\ *n* : small salamander

New Year *n* : New Year's Day

New Year's Day *n* : January 1 observed as a legal holiday

next \'nekst\ *adj* : immediately preceding or following ~ *adv* **1** : in the time or place nearest **2** : at the first time yet to come ~ *prep* : nearest to

nex•us \'neksəs\ *n, pl* **-us•es** \-səsəz\ *or* **-us** \-səs, -‚süs\ : connection

nib \'nib\ *n* : pen point

nib·ble \'nibəl\ *vb* -**bled; -bling** : bite gently or bit by bit — *n* : small bite

nice \'nīs\ *adj* **nic·er; nic·est** 1 : fastidious 2 : very precise or delicate 3 : pleasing 4 : respectable — **nice·ly** *adv* — **nice·ness** *n*

nice·ty \'nīsətē\ *n, pl* -**ties** 1 : dainty or elegant thing 2 : fine detail 3 : exactness

niche \'nich\ *n* 1 : recess in a wall 2 : fitting place, work, or use

nick \'nik\ *n* 1 : small broken area or chip 2 : critical moment — *vb* : make a nick in

nick·el \'nikəl\ *n* 1 : hard silver-white metallic chemical element used in alloys 2 : U.S. 5-cent piece

nick·name \'nik,nām\ *n* : informal substitute name — **nickname** *vb*

nic·o·tine \'nikə,tēn\ *n* : poisonous and addictive substance in tobacco

niece \'nēs\ *n* : a daughter of one's brother, sister, brother-in-law, or sister-in-law

nig·gard·ly \'nigərdlē\ *adj* : stingy — **nig·gard** *n* — **nig·gard·li·ness** *n*

nig·gling \'nigəliŋ\ *adj* : petty and annoying

nigh \'nī\ *adv or adj or prep* : near

night \'nīt\ *n* 1 : period between dusk and dawn 2 : the coming of night — **night** *adj* — **night·ly** *adj or adv* — **night·time** *n*

night·clothes *n pl* : garments worn in bed

night·club \-,kləb\ *n* : place for drinking and entertainment open at night

night crawler *n* : earthworm

night·fall *n* : the coming of night

night·gown *n* : gown worn for sleeping

night·in·gale \'nīt³n,gāl, -iŋ-\ *n* : Old World thrush that sings at night

night·mare \'nīt,mar\ *n* : frightening dream — **nightmare** *adj* — **night·mar·ish** \-,marish\ *adj*

night·shade \'nīt,shād\ *n* : group of plants that include poisonous forms and food plants (as the potato and eggplant)

nil \'nil\ *n* : nothing

nim·ble \'nimbəl\ *adj* -**bler; -blest** 1 : agile 2 : clever — **nim·ble·ness** *n* — **nim·bly** \-blē\ *adv*

nine \'nīn\ *n* 1 : one more than 8 2 : 9th in a set or series — **nine** *adj or pron* — **ninth** \'nīnth\ *adj or adv or n*

nine·pins *n* : bowling game using 9 pins

nine·teen \nīn'tēn\ *n* : one more than

18 — **nineteen** *adj or pron* — **nine·teenth** \-'tēnth\ *adj or n*

nine·ty \'nīntē\ *n, pl* -**ties** : 9 times 10 — **nine·ti·eth** \-ēəth\ *adj or n* — **ninety** *adj or pron*

nin·ny \'ninē\ *n, pl* **nin·nies** : fool

¹nip \'nip\ *vb* -**pp**- 1 : catch hold of and squeeze tightly 2 : pinch or bite off 3 : destroy the growth or fulfillment of — *n* 1 : biting cold 2 : tang 3 : pinch or bite

²nip *n* : small quantity of liquor — *vb* -**pp**- : take liquor in nips

nip·per \'nipər\ *n* 1 : one that nips 2 *pl* : pincers 3 : small boy

nip·ple \'nipəl\ *n* : tip of the breast or something resembling it

nip·py \'nipē\ *adj* -**pi·er; -est** 1 : pungent 2 : chilly

nir·va·na \nir'vänə\ *n* : state of blissful oblivion

nit \'nit\ *n* : egg of a parasitic insect

ni·ter \'nītər\ *n* : potassium nitrate used in gunpowder or fertilizer or in curing meat

ni·trate \'nī,trāt, -trət\ *n* : chemical salt used esp. in curing meat

ni·tric acid \'nītrik-\ *n* : liquid acid used in making dyes, explosives, and fertilizers

ni·trite \-,trīt\ *n* : chemical salt used in curing meat

ni·tro·gen \'nītrəjən\ *n* : tasteless odorless gaseous chemical element

ni·tro·glyc·er·in, **ni·tro·glyc·er·ine** \,nītrō'glisərən\ *n* : heavy oily liquid used as an explosive and as a blood-vessel relaxer

nit·wit \'nit,wit\ *n* : stupid person

no \'nō\ *adv* 1 — used to express the negative 2 : in no respect or degree 3 : not so 4 — used as an interjection of surprise or doubt — *adj* 1 : not any 2 : not a — *n, pl* **noes** *or* **nos** \'nōz\ 1 : refusal 2 : negative vote

no·bil·i·ty \nō'bilətē\ *n* 1 : quality or state of being noble 2 : class of people of noble rank

no·ble \'nōbəl\ *adj* -**bler; -blest** 1 : illustrious 2 : aristocratic 3 : stately 4 : of outstanding character — *n* : nobleman — **no·ble·ness** *n* — **no·bly** *adv*

no·ble·man \-mən\ *n* : member of the nobility

no·ble·wom·an \-,wùmən\ *n* : a woman of noble rank

no·body \'nōbədē, -,bädē\ *pron* : no person — *n, pl* -**bod·ies** : person of no influence or importance

no–brain•er \'nō'brānər\ : something that requires a minimum of thought

noc•tur•nal \näk'tərn³l\ adj : relating to, occurring at, or active at night

noc•turne \'näk,tərn\ n : dreamy musical composition

nod \'näd\ vb **-dd- 1** : bend the head downward or forward (as in bowing or going to sleep or as a sign of assent) **2** : move up and down **3** : show by a nod of the head — **nod** n

node \'nōd\ n : stem part from which a leaf arises — **nod•al** \-³l\ adj

nod•ule \'näjül\ n : small lump or swelling — **nod•u•lar** \'näjələr\ adj

no•el \nō³el\ n **1** : Christmas carol **2** cap : Christmas season

noes pl of NO

nog•gin \'nägən\ n **1** : small mug **2** : person's head

no•how \'nō,haú\ adv : in no manner

noise \'nóiz\ n : loud or unpleasant sound ~ vb **noised; nois•ing** : spread by rumor — **noise•less** adj

— **noise•less•ly** adv — **noise•mak•er** n — **nois•i•ly** \'nóizəlē\ adv — **nois•i•ness** \-zēnəs\ n — **noisy** \'nóizē\ adj

noi•some \'nóisəm\ adj : harmful or offensive

no•mad \'nō,mad\ n : one who has no permanent home — **nomad** adj — **no•mad•ic** \nō'madik\ adj

no•men•cla•ture \'nōmən,klāchər\ n : system of names

nom•i•nal \'nämən³l\ adj **1** : being something in name only **2** : small or negligible — **nom•i•nal•ly** adv

nom•i•nate \'nämə,nāt\ vb **-nat•ed; -nat•ing** : propose or choose as a candidate — **nom•i•na•tion** \,nämə'nāshən\ n

nom•i•na•tive \'nämənətiv\ adj : relating to or being a grammatical case marking typically the subject of a verb — **nominative** n

nom•i•nee \,nämə'nē\ n : person nominated

non- \'nän, ,nän\ prefix **1** : not, reverse of, or absence of **2** : not important

---

List of self-explanatory words with the prefix _non-_

nonabrasive
nonabsorbent
nonacademic
nonaccredited
nonacid
nonaddictive
nonadhesive
nonadjacent
nonadjustable
nonaffiliated
nonaggression
nonalcoholic
nonaligned
nonappearance
nonautomatic
nonbeliever
nonbinding
nonbreakable
noncancerous
noncandidate
non-Catholic
non-Christian
nonchurchgoer
noncitizen
nonclassical
nonclassified
noncombat
noncombatant

noncombustible
noncommercial
noncommunist
noncompliance
nonconflicting
nonconforming
nonconsecutive
nonconstructive
noncontagious
noncontrollable
noncontroversial
noncorrosive
noncriminal
noncritical
noncumulative
noncurrent
nondeductible
nondeferrable
nondegradable
nondelivery
nondemocratic
nondenominational
nondestructive
nondiscrimination
nondiscriminatory
noneducational
nonelastic
nonelected

nonelective
nonelectric
nonelectronic
nonemotional
nonenforcement
nonessential
nonexclusive
nonexistence
nonexistent
nonexplosive
nonfat
nonfatal
nonfattening
nonfictional
nonflammable
nonflowering
nonfunctional
nongovernmental
nongraded
nonhazardous
nonhereditary
nonindustrial
nonindustrialized
noninfectious
noninflationary
nonintegrated
nonintellectual
noninterference

non•age \\'nänij, 'nōnij\\ *n* : period of youth and esp. legal minority

nonce \\'näns\\ *n* : present occasion ~ *adj* : occurring, used, or made only once

non•cha•lant \\,nänshə'länt\\ *adj* : showing indifference — **non•cha•lance** \\-'läns\\ *n* — **non•cha•lant•ly** *adv*

non•com•mis•sioned officer \\,nänkə-'mishənd-\\ *n* : subordinate officer in the armed forces appointed from enlisted personnel

non•com•mit•tal \\,nänkə'mit°l\\ *adj* : indicating neither consent nor dissent

non•con•duc•tor *n* : substance that is a very poor conductor

non•con•form•ist *n* : one who does not conform to an established belief or mode of behavior — **non•con•for•mi•ty** *n*

non•de•script \\,nändi'skript\\ *adj* : lacking distinctive qualities

none \\'nən\\ *pron* : not any ~ *adv* : not at all

non•en•ti•ty *n* : one of no consequence

none•the•less \\,nənthə'les\\ *adv* : nevertheless

non•pa•reil \\,nänpə'rel\\ *adj* : having no equal ~ *n* **1** : one who has no equal **2** : chocolate candy disk

non•par•ti•san *adj* : not influenced by political party bias

non•per•son *n* : person without social or legal status

non•plus \\,nän'pləs\\ *vb* **-ss-** : perplex

non•pre•scrip•tion *adj* : available without a doctor's prescription

non•pro•lif•er•a•tion *adj* : aimed at ending increased use of nuclear arms

non•sched•uled *adj* : licensed to carry by air without a regular schedule

non•sense \\'nän,sens, -səns\\ *n* : foolish or meaningless words or actions — **non•sen•si•cal** \\nän'sensikəl\\ *adj* — **non•sen•si•cal•ly** *adv*

non•sup•port *n* : failure in a legal obligation to provide for someone's needs

non•vi•o•lence *n* : avoidance of violence esp. in political demonstrations — **non•vi•o•lent** *adj*

nonintoxicating	nonpolitical	nonskier
noninvasive	nonpolluting	nonsmoker
non-Jewish	nonporous	nonsmoking
nonlegal	nonpregnant	nonspeaking
nonlethal	nonproductive	nonspecialist
nonliterary	nonprofessional	nonspecific
nonliving	nonprofit	nonstandard
nonmagnetic	nonracial	nonstick
nonmalignant	nonradioactive	nonstop
nonmedical	nonrated	nonstrategic
nonmember	nonrealistic	nonstudent
nonmetal	nonrecurring	nonsugar
nonmetallic	nonrefillable	nonsurgical
nonmilitary	nonrefundable	nonswimmer
nonmusical	nonreligious	nontaxable
nonnative	nonrenewable	nonteaching
nonnegotiable	nonrepresentative	nontechnical
nonobjective	nonresident	nontoxic
nonobservance	nonresponsive	nontraditional
nonorthodox	nonrestricted	nontransferable
nonparallel	nonreversible	nontropical
nonparticipant	nonsalable	nontypical
nonparticipating	nonscientific	nonunion
nonpaying	nonscientist	nonuser
nonpayment	nonsegregated	nonvenomous
nonperformance	non–self–governing	nonverbal
nonperishable	nonsexist	nonvoter
nonphysical	nonsexual	nonwhite
nonpoisonous	nonsignificant	nonworker

noo•dle \'nüd³l\ *n* : ribbon-shaped food paste

nook \'nuk\ *n* **1** : inside corner **2** : private place

noon \'nün\ *n* : middle of the day — **noon** *adj*

noon•day \-ˌdā\ *n* : noon

no one *pron* : no person

noon•time *n* : noon

noose \'nüs\ *n* : rope loop that slips down tight

nor \nór\ *conj* : and not — used esp. after *neither* to introduce and negate the 2d member of a series

norm \'nórm\ *n* **1** : standard usu. derived from an average **2** : typical widespread practice or custom

nor•mal \'nórmǝl\ *adj* : average, regular, or standard — **nor•mal•cy** \-sē\ *n* — **nor•mal•i•ty** \nór'malǝtē\ *n* — **nor•mal•i•za•tion** \ˌnórmǝlǝ'zāshǝn\ *n* — **nor•mal•ize** \'nórmǝˌlīz\ *vb* — **nor•mal•ly** *adv*

north \'nórth\ *adv* : to or toward the north ∼ *adj* : situated toward, at, or coming from the north ∼ *n* **1** : direction to the left of one facing east **2** *cap* : regions to the north — **north•er•ly** \'nórthǝrlē\ *adv or adj* — **north•ern** \-ǝrn\ *adj* — **North•ern•er** *n* — **north•ern•most** \-ˌmōst\ *adj* — **north•ward** \-wǝrd\ *adv or adj* — **north•wards** \-wǝrdz\ *adv*

north•east \nórth'ēst\ *n* **1** : direction between north and east **2** *cap* : regions to the northeast — **northeast** *adj or adv* — **north•east•er•ly** \-ǝrlē\ *adv or adj* — **north•east•ern** \-ǝrn\ *adj*

northern lights *n pl* : aurora borealis

north pole *n* : northernmost point of the earth

north•west \-'west\ *n* **1** : direction between north and west **2** *cap* : regions to the northwest — **northwest** *adj or adv* — **north•west•er•ly** \-ǝrlē\ *adv or adj* — **north•west•ern** \-ǝrn\ *adj*

nose \'nōz\ *n* **1** : part of the face containing the nostrils **2** : sense of smell **3** : front part ∼ *vb* **nosed; nos•ing 1** : detect by smell **2** : push aside with the nose **3** : pry **4** : inch ahead — **nose•bleed** *n* — **nosed** \'nōzd\ *adj* — **nose out** *vb* : narrowly defeat

nose•gay \-ˌgā\ *n* : small bunch of flowers

nos•tal•gia \nä'staljǝ, nǝ-\ *n* : wistful yearning for something past — **nos•tal•gic** \-jik\ *adj*

nos•tril \'nästrǝl\ *n* : opening of the nose

nos•trum \-trǝm\ *n* : questionable remedy

nosy, nos•ey \'nōzē\ *adj* **nos•i•er; -est** : tending to pry

not \'nät\ *adv* — used to make a statement negative

no•ta•ble \'nōtǝbǝl\ *adj* **1** : noteworthy **2** : distinguished ∼ *n* : notable person — **no•ta•bil•i•ty** \nōtǝ'bilǝtē\ *n* — **no•ta•bly** \'nōtǝblē\ *adv*

no•ta•rize \'nōtǝˌrīz\ *vb* **-rized; -riz•ing** : attest as a notary public

no•ta•ry public \'nōtǝrē-\ *n, pl* **-ries public** *or* **-ry publics** : public official who attests writings to make them legally authentic

no•ta•tion \nō'tāshǝn\ *n* **1** : note **2** : act, process, or method of marking things down

notch \'näch\ *n* : V-shaped hollow — **notch** *vb*

note \'nōt\ *vb* **not•ed; not•ing 1** : notice **2** : write down ∼ *n* **1** : musical tone **2** : written comment or record **3** : short informal letter **4** : notice or heed — **note•book** *n*

not•ed \'nōtǝd\ *adj* : famous

note•wor•thy \-ˌwǝrthē\ *adj* : worthy of special mention

noth•ing \'nǝthiŋ\ *pron* **1** : no thing **2** : no part **3** : one of no value or importance ∼ *adv* : not at all ∼ *n* **1** : something that does not exist **2** : zero **3** : one of little or no importance — **noth•ing•ness** *n*

no•tice \'nōtǝs\ *n* **1** : warning or announcement **2** : attention ∼ *vb* **-ticed; -tic•ing** : take notice of — **no•tice•able** *adj* — **no•tice•ably** *adv*

no•ti•fy \'nōtǝˌfī\ *vb* **-fied; -fy•ing** : give notice of or to — **no•ti•fi•ca•tion** \ˌnōtǝfǝ'kāshǝn\ *n*

no•tion \'nōshǝn\ *n* **1** : idea or opinion **2** : whim

no•to•ri•ous \nō'tōrēǝs\ *adj* : widely and unfavorably known — **no•to•ri•e•ty** \ˌnōtǝ'rīǝtē\ *n* — **no•to•ri•ous•ly** *adv*

not•with•stand•ing \ˌnätwith'standiŋ, -with-\ *prep* : in spite of ∼ *adv* : nevertheless ∼ *conj* : although

nou•gat \'nügǝt\ *n* : nuts or fruit pieces in a sugar paste

nought \'nót, 'nät\ *var of* NAUGHT

noun \'naun\ *n* : word that is the name of a person, place, or thing

nour•ish \'nǝrish\ *vb* : promote the

growth of — **nour•ish•ing** *adj* — **nour•ish•ment** *n*

no•va \'nōvə\ *n, pl* **-vas** *or* **-vae** \-ˌvē, -ˌvī\ : star that suddenly brightens and then fades gradually

nov•el \'nävəl\ *adj* : new or strange ∼ *n* : long invented prose story — **nov•el•ist** \-əlist\ *n*

nov•el•ty \'nävəltē\ *n, pl* **-ties** 1 : something new or unusual 2 : newness 3 : small manufactured article — usu. pl.

No•vem•ber \nō'vembər\ *n* : 11th month of the year having 30 days

nov•ice \'nävəs\ *n* 1 : one preparing to take vows in a religious order 2 : one who is inexperienced or untrained

no•vi•tiate \nō'vishət, nə-\ *n* : period or state of being a novice

now \'naů\ *adv* 1 : at the present time or moment 2 : forthwith 3 : under these circumstances ∼ *conj* : in view of the fact ∼ *n* : present time

now•a•days \'naůəˌdāz\ *adv* : now

no•where \-ˌhwer\ *adv* : not anywhere — **no•where** *n*

nox•ious \'näkshəs\ *adj* : harmful

noz•zle \'näzəl\ *n* : device to direct or control a flow of fluid

nu•ance \'nü,äns, 'nyü-\ *n* : subtle distinction or variation

nub \'nəb\ *n* 1 : knob or lump 2 : gist

nu•bile \'nü,bīl, 'nyü-, -bəl\ *adj* 1 : of marriageable condition or age 2 : sexually attractive

nu•cle•ar \'nüklēər, 'nyü-\ *adj* 1 : relating to the atomic nucleus or atomic energy 2 : relating to a weapon whose power is from a nuclear reaction

nu•cle•us \'nüklēəs, 'nyü-\ *n, pl* **-clei** \-klē,ī\ : central mass or part (as of a cell or an atom)

nude \'nüd, 'nyüd\ *adj* **nud•er; nud•est** : naked ∼ *n* : nude human figure — **nu•di•ty** \'nüdətē, 'nyü-\ *n*

nudge \'nəj\ *vb* **nudged; nudg•ing** : touch or push gently — **nudge** *n*

nud•ism \'nüd,izəm, 'nyü-\ *n* : practice of going nude — **nud•ist** \'nüdist, 'nyü-\ *n*

nug•get \'nəgət\ *n* : lump of gold

nui•sance \'nüs°ns, 'nyü-\ *n* : something annoying

null \'nəl\ *adj* : having no legal or binding force — **nul•li•ty** \'nələtē\ *n*

nul•li•fy \'nələ,fī\ *vb* **-fied; -fy•ing** : make null or valueless — **nul•li•fi•ca•tion** \ˌnələfə'kāshən\ *n*

numb \'nəm\ *adj* : lacking feeling — **numb** *vb* — **numb•ly** *adv* — **numb•ness** *n*

num•ber \'nəmbər\ *n* 1 : total of individuals taken together 2 : indefinite total 3 : unit of a mathematical system 4 : numeral 5 : one in a sequence ∼ *vb* 1 : count 2 : assign a number to 3 : comprise in number — **num•ber•less** *adj*

nu•mer•al \'nümərəl, 'nyü-\ *n* : conventional symbol representing a number

nu•mer•a•tor \'nümə,rātər, 'nyü-\ *n* : part of a fraction above the line

nu•mer•i•cal \nů'merikəl, nyü-\, **nu•mer•ic** \-'merik\ *adj* 1 : relating to numbers 2 : expressed in or involving numbers — **nu•mer•i•cal•ly** *adv*

nu•mer•ol•o•gy \ˌnümə'räləjē, ˌnyü-\ *n* : occult study of numbers — **nu•mer•ol•o•gist** \-jist\ *n*

nu•mer•ous \'nümərəs, 'nyü-\ *adj* : consisting of a great number

nu•mis•mat•ics \ˌnüməz'matiks, ˌnyü-\ *n* : study or collection of monetary objects — **nu•mis•mat•ic** \-ik\ *adj* — **nu•mis•ma•tist** \nü'mizmətist, nyü-\ *n*

num•skull \'nəm,skəl\ *n* : stupid person

nun \'nən\ *n* : woman belonging to a religious order — **nun•nery** \-ərē\ *n*

nup•tial \'nəpshəl\ *adj* : relating to marriage or a wedding ∼ *n* : marriage or wedding — usu. pl.

nurse \'nərs\ *n* 1 : one hired to care for children 2 : person trained to care for sick people ∼ *vb* **nursed; nurs•ing** 1 : suckle 2 : care for

nurs•ery \'nərsərē\ *n, pl* **-er•ies** 1 : place where children are cared for 2 : place where young plants are grown

nursing home *n* : private establishment providing care for persons who are unable to care for themselves

nur•ture \'nərchər\ *n* 1 : training or upbringing 2 : food or nourishment ∼ *vb* **-tured; -tur•ing** 1 : care for or feed 2 : educate

nut \'nət\ *n* 1 : dry hard-shelled fruit or seed with a firm inner kernel 2 : metal block with a screw hole through it 3 : foolish, eccentric, or crazy person 4 : enthusiast — **nut•crack•er** *n* — **nut•shell** *n* — **nut•ty** *adj*

nut•hatch \'nət,hach\ *n* : small bird

nut·meg \\'nət,meg, -,māg\ *n* : nutlike aromatic seed of a tropical tree

nu·tri·ent \\'nütrēənt, 'nyü-\ *n* : something giving nourishment — **nutrient** *adj*

nu·tri·ment \-trəmənt\ *n* : nutrient

nu·tri·tion \nú'trishən, nyü-\ *n* : act or process of nourishing esp. with food — **nu·tri·tion·al** \-'trishənəl\ *adj* — **nu·tri·tious** \-'trishəs\ *adj* — **nu·tri·tive** \\'nütrətiv, 'nyü-\ *adj*

nuts \\'nəts\ *adj* **1** : enthusiastic **2** : crazy

nuz·zle \\'nəzəl\ *vb* **-zled; -zling 1** : touch with or as if with the nose **2** : snuggle

ny·lon \\'nī,län\ *n* **1** : tough synthetic material used esp. in textiles **2** *pl* : stockings made of nylon

nymph \\'nimf\ *n* **1** : lesser goddess in ancient mythology **2** : girl **3** : immature insect

O

o \\'ō\ *n, pl* **o's** *or* **os** \\'ōz\ **1** : 15th letter of the alphabet **2** : zero

O *var of* OH

oaf \\'ōf\ *n* : stupid or awkward person — **oaf·ish** \\'ōfish\ *adj*

oak \\'ōk\ *n, pl* **oaks** *or* **oak** : tree bearing a thin-shelled nut or its wood — **oak·en** \\'ōkən\ *adj*

oar \\'ōr\ *n* : pole with a blade at the end used to propel a boat

oar·lock \-,läk\ *n* : u-shaped device for holding an oar

oa·sis \ō'āsəs\ *n, pl* **oa·ses** \-,sēz\ : fertile area in a desert

oat \\'ōt\ *n* : cereal grass or its edible seed — **oat·cake** *n* — **oat·en** \-°n\ *adj* — **oat·meal** *n*

oath \\'ōth\ *n, pl* **oaths** \\'ōthz, 'ōths\ **1** : solemn appeal to God as a pledge of sincerity **2** : profane utterance

ob·du·rate \\'äbdúret, -dyü-\ *adj* : stubbornly resistant — **ob·du·ra·cy** \-rəsē\ *n*

obe·di·ent \ō'bēdēənt\ *adj* : willing to obey — **obe·di·ence** \-əns\ *n* — **obe·di·ent·ly** *adv*

obei·sance \ō'bēsəns, -'bās-\ *n* : bow of respect or submission

obe·lisk \\'äbə,lisk\ *n* : 4-sided tapering pillar

obese \ō'bēs\ *adj* : extremely fat — **obe·si·ty** \-'bēsətē\ *n*

obey \ō'bā\ *vb* **obeyed; obey·ing 1** : follow the commands or guidance of **2** : behave in accordance with

ob·fus·cate \\'äbfə,skāt\ *vb* **-cat·ed; -cat·ing** : confuse — **ob·fus·ca·tion** \,äbfəs'kāshən\ *n*

obit·u·ary \ə'bichə,werē\ *n, pl* **-ar·ies** : death notice

¹ob·ject \\'äbjikt\ *n* **1** : something that

may be seen or felt **2** : purpose **3** : noun or equivalent toward which the action of a verb is directed or which follows a preposition

²object \əb'jekt\ *vb* : offer opposition or disapproval — **ob·jec·tion** \-'jekshən\ *n* — **ob·jec·tion·able** \-shənəbəl\ *adj* — **ob·jec·tion·ably** \-blē\ *adv* — **ob·jec·tor** \-'jektər\ *n*

ob·jec·tive \əb'jektiv\ *adj* **1** : relating to an object or end **2** : existing outside an individual's thoughts or feelings **3** : treating facts without distortion **4** : relating to or being a grammatical case marking objects ~ *n* : aim or end of action — **ob·jec·tive·ly** *adv* — **ob·jec·tive·ness** *n* — **ob·jec·tiv·i·ty** \,äb,jek'tivətē\ *n*

ob·li·gate \\'äblə,gāt\ *vb* **-gat·ed; -gat·ing** : bind legally or morally — **ob·li·ga·tion** \,äblə'gāshən\ *n* — **oblig·a·to·ry** \ə'bligə,tōrē, 'äbligə-\ *adj*

oblige \ə'blīj\ *vb* **obliged; oblig·ing 1** : compel **2** : do a favor for — **oblig·ing** *adj* — **oblig·ing·ly** *adv*

oblique \ō'blēk, -'blīk\ *adj* **1** : lying at a slanting angle **2** : indirect — **oblique·ly** *adv* — **oblique·ness** *n* — **obliq·ui·ty** \-'blikwətē\ *n*

oblit·er·ate \ə'blitə,rāt\ *vb* **-at·ed; -at·ing** : completely remove or destroy — **oblit·er·a·tion** \-,blitə'rāshən\ *n*

obliv·i·on \ə'blivēən\ *n* **1** : state of having lost conscious awareness **2** : state of being forgotten

obliv·i·ous \-ēəs\ *adj* : not aware or mindful — with *to* or *of* — **obliv·i·ous·ly** *adv* — **obliv·i·ous·ness** *n*

ob·long \\'äb,lȯŋ\ *adj* : longer in one direction than in the other with opposite sides parallel — **oblong** *n*

ob·lo·quy \\'äbləkwē\ *n, pl* **-quies 1**
: strongly condemning utterance **2**
: bad repute

ob·nox·ious \äb'näkshəs, əb-\ *adj*
: repugnant — **ob·nox·ious·ly** *adv* —
ob·nox·ious·ness *n*

oboe \'ōbō\ *n* : slender woodwind instrument with a reed mouthpiece —
obo·ist \'o͏̣bōist\ *n*

ob·scene \äb'sēn, əb-\ *adj* : repug-
nantly indecent — **ob·scene·ly** *adv*
— **ob·scen·i·ty** \-'senətē\ *n*

ob·scure \äb'skyur, əb-\ *adj* **1** : dim
or hazy **2** : not well known **3** : vague
~ *vb* : make indistinct or unclear —
ob·scure·ly *adv* — **ob·scu·ri·ty**
\-'skyurətē\ *n*

ob·se·quies \'äbsəkwēz\ *n pl* : funeral
or burial rites

ob·se·qui·ous \əb'sēkwēəs\ *adj* : excessively attentive or flattering —
ob·se·qui·ous·ly *adv* — **ob·se·qui·
ous·ness** *n*

ob·ser·va·to·ry \əb'zərvə͏̣tōrē\ *n, pl*
-ries : place for observing astronomi-
cal phenomena

ob·serve \əb'zərv\ *vb* **-served; -serv-
ing 1** : conform to **2** : celebrate **3**
: see, watch, or notice **4** : remark —
ob·serv·able *adj* — **ob·ser·vance**
\-'zərvəns\ *n* — **ob·ser·vant** \-vənt\
adj — **ob·ser·va·tion** \͏̣äbsər'vā-
shən, -zər-\ *n*

ob·sess \əb'ses\ *vb* : preoccupy intensely or abnormally — **ob·ses·
sion** \äb'seshən, əb-\ *n* — **ob·ses·
sive** \-'sesiv\ *adj* — **ob·ses·sive·ly**
adv

ob·so·les·cent \͏̣äbsə'les°nt\ *adj* : going out of use — **ob·so·les·cence**
\-°ns\ *n*

ob·so·lete \͏̣äbsə'lēt, 'äbsə͏̣-\ *adj* : no
longer in use

ob·sta·cle \'äbstikəl\ *n* : something
that stands in the way or opposes

ob·stet·rics \əb'stetriks\ *n sing or pl*
: branch of medicine that deals with
childbirth — **ob·stet·ric** \-rik\, **ob-
stet·ri·cal** \-rikəl\ *adj* — **ob·ste·tri·
cian** \͏̣äbstə'trishən\ *n*

ob·sti·nate \'äbstənət\ *adj* : stubborn
— **ob·sti·na·cy** \-nəsē\ *n* — **ob·sti·
nate·ly** *adv*

ob·strep·er·ous \əb'strepərəs\ *adj*
: uncontrollably noisy or defiant —
ob·strep·er·ous·ness *n*

ob·struct \əb'strəkt\ *vb* : block or impede — **ob·struc·tion** \-'strəkshən\

n — **ob·struc·tive** \-'strəktiv\ *adj*
— **ob·struc·tor** \-tər\ *n*

ob·tain \əb'tān\ *vb* **1** : gain by effort **2**
: be generally recognized — **ob·tain·
able** *adj*

ob·trude \əb'trüd\ *vb* **-trud·ed; -trud-
ing 1** : thrust out **2** : intrude — **ob-
tru·sion** \-'trüzhən\ *n* — **ob·tru·
sive** \-'trüsiv\ *adj* — **ob·tru·sive·ly**
adv — **ob·tru·sive·ness** *n*

ob·tuse \äb'tüs, əb-, -'tyüs\ *adj* **1**
: slow-witted **2** : exceeding 90 but
less than 180 degrees — **ob·tuse·ly**
adv — **ob·tuse·ness** *n*

ob·verse \'äb͏̣vərs, äb'-\ *n* : principal
side (as of a coin)

ob·vi·ate \'äbvē͏̣āt\ *vb* **-at·ed; -at·ing**
: make unnecessary

ob·vi·ous \'äbvēəs\ *adj* : plain or un-
mistakable — **ob·vi·ous·ly** *adv* —
ob·vi·ous·ness *n*

oc·ca·sion \ə'kāzhən\ *n* **1** : favorable
opportunity **2** : cause **3** : time of an
event **4** : special event ~ *vb* : cause
— **oc·ca·sion·al** \-'kāzhənəl\ *adj*
— **oc·ca·sion·al·ly** *adv*

oc·ci·den·tal \͏̣äksə'dent°l\ *adj* : western — **Occidental** *n*

oc·cult \ə'kəlt, 'äk͏̣əlt\ *adj* **1** : secret
or mysterious **2** : relating to supernatural agencies — **oc·cult·ism** \-'kəl-
͏̣tizəm\ *n* — **oc·cult·ist** \-tist\ *n*

oc·cu·pan·cy \'äkyəpənsē\ *n, pl* **-cies**
: an occupying

oc·cu·pant \-pənt\ *n* : one who occupies

oc·cu·pa·tion \͏̣äkyə'pāshən\ *n* **1**
: vocation **2** : action or state of occupying — **oc·cu·pa·tion·al** \-shənəl\
adj — **oc·cu·pa·tion·al·ly** *adv*

oc·cu·py \'äkyə͏̣pī\ *vb* **-pied; -py·ing
1** : engage the attention of **2** : fill up
3 : take or hold possession of **4** : reside in — **oc·cu·pi·er** \-͏̣pīər\ *n*

oc·cur \ə'kər\ *vb* **-rr- 1** : be found or met
with **2** : take place **3** : come to mind

oc·cur·rence \ə'kərəns\ *n* : something
that takes place

ocean \'ōshən\ *n* **1** : whole body of
salt water **2** : very large body of water — **ocean·front** *n* — **ocean·go·
ing** *adj* — **oce·an·ic** \͏̣ōshē'anik\
adj

ocean·og·ra·phy \͏̣ōshə'nägrəfē\ *n*
: science dealing with the ocean —
ocean·og·ra·pher \-fər\ *n* —
ocean·o·graph·ic \-nə'grafik\ *adj*

oce·lot \'äsə͏̣lät, 'ōsə-\ *n* : medium·
sized American wildcat

ocher, ochre \'ōkər\ *n* : red or yellow pigment

o'·clock \ə'kläk\ *adv* : according to the clock

oc·ta·gon \'äktə‚gän\ *n* : 8-sided polygon — **oc·tag·o·nal** \äk'tagən°l\ *adj*

oc·tave \'äktiv\ *n* : musical interval of 8 steps or the notes within this interval

Oc·to·ber \äk'tōbər\ *n* : 10th month of the year having 31 days

oc·to·pus \'äktəpəs\ *n, pl* **-pus·es** *or* **-pi** \-‚pī\ : sea mollusk with 8 arms

oc·u·lar \'äkyələr\ *adj* : relating to the eye

oc·u·list \'äkyəlist\ *n* **1** : ophthalmologist **2** : optometrist

odd \'äd\ *adj* **1** : being only one of a pair or set **2** : not divisible by two without a remainder **3** : additional to what is usual or to the number mentioned **4** : queer — **odd·ly** *adv* — **odd·ness** *n*

odd·i·ty \'ädətē\ *n, pl* **-ties** : something odd

odds \'ädz\ *n pl* **1** : difference by which one thing is favored **2** : disagreement **3** : ratio between winnings and the amount of the bet

ode \'ōd\ *n* : solemn lyric poem

odi·ous \'ōdēəs\ *adj* : hated — **odi·ous·ly** *adv* — **odi·ous·ness** *n*

odi·um \'ōdēəm\ *n* **1** : merited loathing **2** : disgrace

odor \'ōdər\ *n* : quality that affects the sense of smell — **odor·less** *adj* — **odor·ous** *adj*

od·ys·sey \'ädəsē\ *n, pl* **-seys** : long wandering

o'er \'ōr\ *adv or prep* : OVER

of \'əv, 'äv\ *prep* **1** : from **2** : distinguished by **3** : because of **4** : made or written by **5** : made with, being, or containing **6** : belonging to or connected with **7** : about **8** : that is **9** : concerning **10** : before

off \'òf\ *adv* **1** : from a place **2** : unattached or removed **3** : to a state of being no longer in use **4** : away from work **5** : at a distance in time or space ~ *prep* **1** : away from **2** : at the expense of **3** : not engaged in or abstaining from **4** : below the usual level of ~ *adj* **1** : not operating, up to standard, or correct **2** : remote **3** : provided for

of·fal \'òfəl\ *n* **1** : waste **2** : viscera and trimmings of a butchered animal

of·fend \ə'fend\ *vb* **1** : sin or act in vi-

olation **2** : hurt, annoy, or insult — **of·fend·er** *n*

of·fense, of·fence \ə'fens, 'äf‚ens\ *n* : attack, misdeed, or insult

of·fen·sive \ə'fensiv, 'äf‚en-\ *adj* : causing offense ~ *n* : attack — **of·fen·sive·ly** *adv* — **of·fen·sive·ness** *n*

of·fer \'òfər\ *vb* **1** : present for acceptance **2** : propose **3** : put up (an effort) ~ *n* **1** : proposal **2** : bid — **of·fer·ing** *n*

of·fer·to·ry \'òfər‚tōrē\ *n, pl* **-ries** : presentation of offerings or its musical accompaniment

off·hand *adv or adj* : without previous thought or preparation

of·fice \'òfəs\ *n* **1** : position of authority (as in government) **2** : rite **3** : place where a business is transacted — **of·fice·hold·er** *n*

of·fi·cer \'òfəsər\ *n* **1** : one charged with law enforcement **2** : one who holds an office of trust or authority **3** : one who holds a commission in the armed forces

of·fi·cial \ə'fishəl\ *n* : one in office ~ *adj* : authorized or authoritative — **of·fi·cial·dom** \-dəm\ *n* — **of·fi·cial·ly** *adv*

of·fi·ci·ant \ə'fishēənt\ *n* : clergy member who officiates at a religious rite

of·fi·ci·ate \ə'fishē‚āt\ *vb* **-at·ed; -at·ing** : perform a ceremony or function

of·fi·cious \ə'fishəs\ *adj* : volunteering one's services unnecessarily — **of·fi·cious·ly** *adv* — **of·fi·cious·ness** *n*

off·ing \'òfiŋ\ *n* : future

off·set \'òf‚set\ *vb* **-set; -set·ting** : provide an opposite or equaling effect to

off·shoot \'òf‚shüt\ *n* : outgrowth

off·shore *adv* : at a distance from the shore ~ *adj* : moving away from or situated off the shore

off·spring \'òf‚spriŋ\ *n, pl* **offspring** : one coming into being through animal or plant reproduction

of·ten \'òfən, 'òft-\ *adv* : many times — **of·ten·times, oft·times** *adv*

ogle \'ōgəl\ *vb* **ogled; ogling** : stare at lustily — **ogle** *n* — **ogler** \-ələr\ *n*

ogre \'ōgər\ *n* **1** : monster **2** : dreaded person

oh \'ō\ *interj* **1** — used to express an emotion **2** — used in direct address

ohm \'ōm\ *n* : unit of electrical resistance — **ohm·me·ter** \'ōm‚mētər\ *n*

oil \'òil\ *n* **1** : greasy liquid substance

2 : petroleum ~ *vb* : put oil in or on — **oil•er** *n* — **oil•i•ness** \'óilēnəs\ *n* — **oily** \'óilē\ *adj*

oil•cloth *n* : cloth treated with oil or paint and used for coverings

oil•skin *n* : oiled waterproof cloth

oink \'óiŋk\ *n* : natural noise of a hog — **oink** *vb*

oint•ment \'óintmənt\ *n* : oily medicinal preparation

OK *or* **okay** \ō'kā\ *adv or adj* : all right ~ *vb* **OK'd** *or* **okayed; OK'•ing** *or* **okay•ing** : approve ~ *n* : approval

okra \'ōkrə, *South also* -krē\ *n* : leafy vegetable with edible green pods

old \'ōld\ *adj* **1** : of long standing **2** : of a specified age **3** : relating to a past era **4** : having existed a long time — **old•ish** \'ōldish\ *adj*

old•en \'ōldən\ *adj* : of or relating to a bygone era

old–fash•ioned \-'fashənd\ *adj* **1** : out-of-date **2** : conservative

old maid *n* : spinster

old–tim•er \ōld'tīmər\ *n* **1** : veteran **2** : one who is old

ole•an•der \'ōlē,andər\ *n* : poisonous evergreen shrub

oleo•mar•ga•rine \,ōlēō'märjərən\ *n* : margarine

ol•fac•to•ry \äl'faktərē, ōl-\ *adj* : relating to the sense of smell

oli•gar•chy \'älə,gärkē, 'ōlə-\ *n, pl* **-chies 1** : government by a few people **2** : those holding power in an oligarchy — **oli•garch** \-,gärk\ *n* — **oli•gar•chic** \,älə'gärkik, ,ōlə-\, **oli•gar•chi•cal** \-kikəl\ *adj*

ol•ive \'äliv, -əv\ *n* **1** : evergreen tree bearing small edible fruit or the fruit **2** : dull yellowish green color

om•buds•man \'äm,búdzmən, äm-'búdz-\ *n, pl* **-men** \-mən\ : complaint investigator

om•e•let, om•e•lette \'ämələt\ *n* : beaten eggs lightly fried and folded

omen \'ōmən\ *n* : sign or warning of the future

om•i•nous \'ämənəs\ *adj* : presaging evil — **om•i•nous•ly** *adv* — **om•i•nous•ness** *n*

omit \ō'mit\ *vb* **-tt- 1** : leave out **2** : fail to perform — **omis•si•ble** \ō-'misəbəl\ *adj* — **omis•sion** \-'mishən\ *n*

om•nip•o•tent \äm'nipətənt\ *adj* : almighty — **om•nip•o•tence** \-əns\ *n* — **om•nip•o•tent•ly** *adv*

om•ni•pres•ent \,ämni'prez°nt\ *adj* : ever-present — **om•ni•pres•ence** \-°ns\ *n*

om•ni•scient \äm'nishənt\ *adj* : all-knowing — **om•ni•science** \-əns\ *n* — **om•ni•scient•ly** *adv*

om•niv•o•rous \äm'nivərəs\ *adj* **1** : eating both meat and vegetables **2** : avid — **om•niv•o•rous•ly** *adv*

on \'ón, 'än\ *prep* **1** : in or to a position over and in contact with **2** : at or to **3** : about **4** : from **5** : with regard to **6** : in a state or process **7** : during the time of ~ *adv* **1** : in or into contact with **2** : forward **3** : into operation

once \'wəns\ *adv* **1** : one time only **2** : at any one time **3** : formerly ~ *n* : one time ~ *conj* : as soon as ~ *adj* : former — **at once 1** : simultaneously **2** : immediately

once–over *n* : swift examination

on•com•ing *adj* : approaching

one \'wən\ *adj* **1** : being a single thing **2** : being one in particular **3** : being the same in kind ~ *pron* **1** : certain indefinitely indicated person or thing **2** : a person in general ~ *n* **1** : 1st in a series **2** : single person or thing — **one•ness** *n*

oner•ous \'änərəs, 'ōnə-\ *adj* : imposing a burden

one•self \,wən'self\ *pron* : one's own self — usu. used reflexively or for emphasis

one–sid•ed \-'sīdəd\ *adj* **1** : occurring on one side only **2** : partial

one–time *adj* : former

one–way *adj* : made or for use in only one direction

on•go•ing *adj* : continuing

on•ion \'ənyən\ *n* : plant grown for its pungent edible bulb or this bulb

on•ly \'ōnlē\ *adj* : alone in its class ~ *adv* **1** : merely or exactly **2** : solely **3** : at the very least **4** : as a result ~ *conj* : but

on•set *n* : start

on•shore *adj* **1** : moving toward shore **2** : lying on or near the shore — **on•shore** *adv*

on•slaught \'än,slót, 'ón-\ *n* : attack

on•to \'óntü, 'än-\ *prep* : to a position or point on

onus \'ōnəs\ *n* : burden (as of obligation or blame)

on•ward \'ónwərd, 'än-\ *adv or adj* : forward

on•yx \'äniks\ *n* : quartz used as a gem

ooze \'üz\ *n* : soft mud ~ *vb* **oozed;**
ooz•ing : flow or leak out slowly —
oozy \'üzē\ *adj*
opac•i•ty \ō'pasətē\ *n* : quality or state
of being opaque or an opaque spot
opal \'ōpəl\ *n* : gem with delicate colors
opaque \ō'pāk\ *adj* **1** : blocking light
2 : not easily understood **3** : dull-
witted — **opaque•ly** *adv*
open \'ōpən\ *adj* **1** : not shut or shut
up **2** : not secret or hidden **3** : frank
or generous **4** : extended **5** : free
from controls **6** : not decided ~ *vb*
1 : make or become open **2** : make or
become functional **3** : start ~ *n*
: outdoors — **open•er** \-ər\ *n* —
open•ly *adv* — **open•ness** *n*
open•hand•ed \-'handəd\ *adj* : generous — **open•hand•ed•ly** *adv*
open•ing \'ōpəniŋ\ *n* **1** : act or instance of making open **2** : something
that is open **3** : opportunity
op•era \'äpərə, 'äprə\ *n* : drama set to
music — **op•er•at•ic** \,äpə'ratik\ *adj*
op•er•a•ble \'äpərəbəl\ *adj* **1** : usable
or in working condition **2** : suitable
for surgical treatment
op•er•ate \'äpə,rāt\ *vb* **-at•ed; -at•ing**
1 : perform work **2** : perform an
operation **3** : manage — **op•er•a•tor**
\-,rātər\ *n*
op•er•a•tion \,äpə'rāshən\ *n* **1** : act or
process of operating **2** : surgical work
on a living body **3** : military action or
mission — **op•er•a•tion•al** \-shənəl\
adj
op•er•a•tive \'äpərətiv, -,rāt-\ *adj*
: working or having an effect
op•er•et•ta \,äpə'retə\ *n* : light opera
oph•thal•mol•o•gy \,äf,thal'mäləjē\ *n*
: branch of medicine dealing with the
eye — **oph•thal•mol•o•gist** \-jist\ *n*
opi•ate \'ōpēət, -pē,āt\ *n* : preparation
or derivative of opium
opine \ō'pīn\ *vb* **opined; opin•ing**
: express an opinion
opin•ion \ə'pinyən\ *n* **1** : belief **2**
: judgment **3** : formal statement by an
expert
opin•ion•at•ed \-yə,nātəd\ *adj* : stubborn in one's opinions
opi•um \'ōpēəm\ *n* : addictive narcotic
drug that is the dried juice of a poppy
opos•sum \ə'päsəm\ *n* : common tree-
dwelling nocturnal mammal
op•po•nent \ə'pōnənt\ *n* : one that opposes
op•por•tune \,äpər'tün, -'tyün\ *adj*

: suitable or timely — **op•por•tune•ly**
adv
op•por•tun•ism \-'tü,nizəm, -'tyü-\ *n*
: a taking advantage of opportunities
— **op•por•tun•ist** \-nist\ *n* — **op-
por•tu•nis•tic** \-tü'nistik, -tyü-\ *adj*
op•por•tu•ni•ty \-'tünətē, -'tyü-\ *n, pl*
-ties : favorable time
op•pose \ə'pōz\ *vb* **-posed; -pos•ing**
1 : place opposite or against something **2** : resist — **op•po•si•tion**
\,äpə'zishən\ *n*
op•po•site \'äpəzət\ *n* : one that is opposed ~ *adj* **1** : set facing something that is at the other side or end **2**
: opposed or contrary ~ *adv* : on opposite sides ~ *prep* : across from —
op•po•site•ly *adv*
op•press \ə'pres\ *vb* **1** : persecute
2 : weigh down — **op•pres•sion**
\ə'preshən\ *n* — **op•pres•sive**
\-'presiv\ *adj* — **op•pres•sive•ly**
adv — **op•pres•sor** \-'presər\ *n*
op•pro•bri•ous \ə'prōbrēəs\ *adj* : expressing or deserving opprobrium
— **op•pro•bri•ous•ly** *adv*
op•pro•bri•um \-brēəm\ *n* **1** : something that brings disgrace **2** : infamy
opt \'äpt\ *vb* : choose
op•tic \'äptik\ *adj* : relating to vision or
the eye
op•ti•cal \'äptikəl\ *adj* : relating to op-
tics, vision, or the eye
op•ti•cian \äp'tishən\ *n* : maker of or
dealer in eyeglasses
op•tics \'äptiks\ *n pl* : science of light
and vision
op•ti•mal \'äptəməl\ *adj* : most favorable — **op•ti•mal•ly** *adv*
op•ti•mism \'äptə,mizəm\ *n* : tendency to hope for the best — **op•ti-
mist** \-mist\ *n* — **op•ti•mis•tic**
\,äptə'mistik\ *adj* — **op•ti•mis•ti-
cal•ly** *adv*
op•ti•mum \'äptəməm\ *n, pl* **-ma**
\-mə\ : amount or degree of something most favorable to an end — **op-
timum** *adj*
op•tion \'äpshən\ *n* **1** : ability to choose
2 : right to buy or sell a stock **3** : alternative — **op•tion•al** \-shənəl\ *adj*
op•tom•e•try \äp'tämətrē\ *n* : profession of examining the eyes — **op-
tom•e•trist** \-trist\ *n*
op•u•lent \'äpyələnt\ *adj* : lavish —
op•u•lence \-ləns\ *n* — **op•u•lent•ly**
adv

opus \'ōpəs\ *n, pl* **opera** \'ōpərə, 'äpə-\ : work esp. of music

or \'ȯr\ *conj* — used to indicate an alternative

-or \ər\ *n suffix* : one that performs an action

or•a•cle \'ȯrəkəl\ *n* **1** : one held to give divinely inspired answers or revelations **2** : wise person or an utterance of such a person — **orac•u•lar** \ȯ'rakyələr\ *adj*

oral \'ȯrəl\ *adj* **1** : spoken **2** : relating to the mouth — **oral•ly** *adv*

or•ange \'ȯrinj\ *n* **1** : reddish yellow citrus fruit **2** : color between red and yellow — **or•ange•ade** \ȯrinj'ād\ *n*

orang•u•tan \ə'raŋə̩taŋ, -̩tan\ *n* : large reddish brown ape

ora•tion \ə'rāshən\ *n* : elaborate formal speech

or•a•tor \'ȯrətər\ *n* : one noted as a public speaker

or•a•to•rio \ȯrə'tōrē̩ō\ *n, pl* **-ri•os** : major choral work

or•a•to•ry \'ȯrə̩tōrē\ *n* : art of public speaking — **or•a•tor•i•cal** \ȯrə-'tȯrikəl\ *adj*

orb \'ȯrb\ *n* : spherical body

or•bit \'ȯrbət\ *n* : path made by one body revolving around another ~ *vb* : revolve around — **or•bit•al** \-ᵊl\ *adj* — **or•bit•er** *n*

or•chard \'ȯrchərd\ *n* : place where fruit or nut trees are grown — **or•chard•ist** \-ist\ *n*

or•ches•tra \'ȯrkəstrə\ *n* **1** : group of musicians **2** : front seats of a theater's main floor — **or•ches•tral** \ȯr-'kestrəl\ *adj* — **or•ches•tral•ly** *adv*

or•ches•trate \'ȯrkə̩strāt\ *vb* **-trated; -trat•ing 1** : compose or arrange for an orchestra **2** : arrange or combine for best effect — **or•ches•tra•tion** \ȯrkə'strāshən\ *n*

or•chid \'ȯrkəd\ *n* : plant with showy 3-petal flowers or its flower

or•dain \ȯr'dān\ *vb* **1** : admit to the clergy **2** : decree

or•deal \ȯr'dēl, 'ȯr̩dēl\ *n* : severely trying experience

or•der \'ȯrdər\ *n* **1** : rank, class, or special group **2** : arrangement **3** : rule of law **4** : authoritative regulation or instruction **5** : working condition **6** : special request for a purchase or what is purchased ~ *vb* **1** : arrange **2** : give an order to **3** : place an order for

or•der•ly \-lē\ *adj* **1** : being in order or

tidy **2** : well behaved ~ *n, pl* **-lies 1** : officer's attendant **2** : hospital attendant — **or•der•li•ness** *n*

or•di•nal \'ȯrdᵊnəl\ *n* : number indicating order in a series

or•di•nance \-ᵊnəns\ *n* : municipal law

or•di•nary \'ȯrdᵊn̩erē\ *adj* : of common occurrence, quality, or ability — **or•di•nar•i•ly** \ȯrdᵊn'erəlē\ *adv*

or•di•na•tion \ȯrdᵊn'āshən\ *n* : act of ordaining

ord•nance \'ȯrdnəns\ *n* : military supplies

ore \'ȯr\ *n* : mineral containing a valuable constituent

oreg•a•no \ə'regə̩nō\ *n* : mint used as a seasoning and source of oil

or•gan \'ȯrgən\ *n* **1** : air-powered or electronic keyboard instrument **2** : animal or plant structure with special function **3** : periodical

or•gan•ic \ȯr'ganik\ *adj* **1** : relating to a bodily organ **2** : relating to living things **3** : relating to or containing carbon or its compounds **4** : relating to foods produced without the use of laboratory-made products — **or•gan•i•cal•ly** *adv*

or•gan•ism \'ȯrgə̩nizəm\ *n* : a living thing

or•gan•ist \'ȯrgənist\ *n* : organ player

or•ga•nize \'ȯrgə̩nīz\ *vb* **-nized; -niz•ing** : form parts into a functioning whole — **or•ga•ni•za•tion** \ȯrgənə-'zāshən\ *n* — **or•ga•ni•za•tion•al** \-shənəl\ *adj* — **or•ga•niz•er** *n*

or•gasm \'ȯr̩gazəm\ *n* : climax of sexual excitement — **or•gas•mic** \ȯr'gazmik\ *adj*

or•gy \'ȯrjē\ *n, pl* **-gies** : unrestrained indulgence (as in sexual activity)

ori•ent \'ōrē̩ent\ *vb* **1** : set in a definite position **2** : acquaint with a situation — **ori•en•ta•tion** \ōrēən'tāshən\ *n*

ori•en•tal \ōrē'entᵊl\ *adj* : Eastern — **Oriental** *n*

or•i•fice \'ȯrəfəs\ *n* : opening

or•i•gin \'ȯrəjən\ *n* **1** : ancestry **2** : rise, beginning, or derivation from a source — **orig•i•nate** \ə'rijə̩nāt\ *vb* — **orig•i•na•tor** \-ər\ *n*

orig•i•nal \ə'rijənəl\ *n* : something from which a copy is made ~ *adj* **1** : first **2** : not copied from something else **3** : inventive — **orig•i•nal•i•ty** *n* — **orig•i•nal•ly** *adv*

ori•ole \'ōrē̩ōl, -ēəl\ *n* : American songbird

or•na•ment \'ȯrnəmənt\ *n* : something

that adorns ~ *vb* : provide with ornament — **or•na•men•tal** \,órnə'-ment³l\ *adj* — **or•na•men•ta•tion** \-mən'tāshən\ *n*

or•nate \ór'nāt\ *adj* : elaborately decorated — **or•nate•ly** *adv* — **or•nate•ness** *n*

or•nery \'órnərē, 'än-\ *adj* : irritable

or•ni•thol•o•gy \,órnə'thäləjē\ *n, pl* -**gies** : study of birds — **or•ni•tho•log•i•cal** \-thə'läjikəl\ *adj* — **or•ni•thol•o•gist** \-'thäləjist\ *n*

or•phan \'órfən\ *n* : child whose parents are dead — **orphan** *vb* — **or•phan•age** \-ənij\ *n*

or•tho•don•tics \,órthə'däntiks\ *n* : dentistry dealing with straightening teeth — **or•tho•don•tist** \-'däntist\ *n*

or•tho•dox \'órthə,däks\ *adj* 1 : conforming to established doctrine 2 *cap* : of or relating to a Christian church originating in the Eastern Roman Empire — **or•tho•doxy** \-,däksē\ *n*

or•thog•ra•phy \ór'thägrəfē\ *n* : spelling — **or•tho•graph•ic** \,órthə'grafik\ *adj*

or•tho•pe•dics \,órthə'pēdiks\ *n sing or pl* : correction or prevention of skeletal deformities — **or•tho•pe•dic** \-ik\ *adj* — **or•tho•pe•dist** \-'pē-dist\ *n*

-**o•ry** \,órē, ,órē, ərē\ *adj suffix* 1 : of, relating to, or characterized by 2 : serving for, producing, or maintaining

os•cil•late \'äsə,lāt\ *vb* -**lat•ed; -lat•ing** : swing back and forth — **os•cil•la•tion** \,äsə'lāshən\ *n*

os•mo•sis \äz'mōsəs, äs-\ *n* : diffusion esp. of water through a membrane — **os•mot•ic** \-'mätik\ *adj*

os•prey \'äsprē, -,prā\ *n, pl* -**preys** : large fish-eating hawk

os•si•fy \'äsə,fī\ *vb* -**fied; -fy•ing** : make or become hardened or set in one's ways

os•ten•si•ble \ä'stensəbəl\ *adj* : seeming — **os•ten•si•bly** \-blē\ *adv*

os•ten•ta•tion \,ästən'tāshən\ *n* : pretentious display — **os•ten•ta•tious** \-shəs\ *adj* — **os•ten•ta•tious•ly** *adv*

os•te•op•a•thy \,ästē'äpəthē\ *n* : system of healing that emphasizes manipulation (as of joints) — **os•te•o•path** \'ästēə,path\ *n* — **os•te•o•path•ic** \,ästēə'pathik\ *adj*

os•te•o•po•ro•sis \,ästēōpə'rōsəs\ *n, pl* -**ro•ses** \-,sēz\ : condition characterized by fragile and porous bones

os•tra•cize \'ästrə,sīz\ *vb* -**cized; -ciz-**

ing : exclude by common consent — **os•tra•cism** \-,sizəm\ *n*

os•trich \'ästrich, 'ós-\ *n* : very large flightless bird

oth•er \'əthər\ *adj* 1 : being the one left 2 : alternate 3 : additional ~ *pron* 1 : remaining one 2 : different one

oth•er•wise *adv* 1 : in a different way 2 : in different circumstances 3 : in other respects — **otherwise** *adj*

ot•ter \'ätər\ *n* : fish-eating mammal with webbed feet

ot•to•man \'ätəmən\ *n* : upholstered footstool

ought \'ót\ *verbal auxiliary* — used to express obligation, advisability, or expectation

ounce \'aúns\ *n* 1 : unit of weight equal to about 28.3 grams 2 : unit of capacity equal to about 29.6 milliliters

our \'är, 'aúr\ *adj* : of or relating to us

ours \'aúrz, 'ärz\ *pron* : that which belongs to us

our•selves \är'selvz, aúr-\ *pron* : we, us — used reflexively or for emphasis

-**ous** \əs\ *adj suffix* : having or having the qualities of

oust \'aúst\ *vb* : expel or eject

oust•er \'aústər\ *n* : expulsion

out \'aút\ *adv* 1 : away from the inside or center 2 : beyond control 3 : to extinction, exhaustion, or completion 4 : in or into the open ~ *vb* : become known ~ *adj* 1 : situated outside 2 : absent ~ *prep* 1 : out through 2 : outward on or along — **out•bound** *adj* — **out•build•ing** *n*

out•age \'aútij\ *n* : period of no electricity

out•board \'aút,bórd\ *adv* : outside a boat or ship — **outboard** *adj*

out•break \'aút,brāk\ *n* : sudden occurrence

out•burst \-,bərst\ *n* : violent expression of feeling

out•cast \-,kast\ *n* : person cast out by society

out•come \-,kəm\ *n* : result

out•crop \'aút,kräp\ *n* : part of a rock stratum that appears above the ground — **outcrop** *vb*

out•cry \-,krī\ *n* : loud cry

out•dat•ed \aút'dātəd\ *adj* : out-of-date

out•dis•tance *vb* : go far ahead of

out•do \aút'dü\ *vb* -**did** \-'did\; -**done** \-'dən\; -**do•ing** \-'düiŋ\; -**does** \-'dəz\ : do better than

out·doors \aut'dōrz\ *adv* : in or into the open air ~ *n* : open air — **out·door** *adj*

out·er \'autər\ *adj* **1** : external **2** : farther out — **out·er·most** *adj*

out·field \'aut,fēld\ *n* : baseball field beyond the infield — **out·field·er** \-,fēldər\ *n*

out·fit \'aut,fit\ *n* **1** : equipment for a special purpose **2** : group ~ *vb* **-tt-** : equip — **out·fit·ter** *n*

out·go \'aut,gō\ *n, pl* **outgoes** : expenditure

out·go·ing \'aut,gōiŋ\ *adj* **1** : retiring from a position **2** : friendly

out·grow \aut'grō\ *vb* **-grew** \-'grü\; **-grown** \-'grōn\; **-grow·ing** **1** : grow faster than **2** : grow too large for

out·growth \'aut,grōth\ *n* **1** : product of growing out **2** : consequence

out·ing \'autiŋ\ *n* : excursion

out·land·ish \aut'landish\ *adj* : very strange — **out·land·ish·ly** *adv*

outlast *vb* : last longer than

out·law \'aut,lȯ\ *n* : lawless person ~ *vb* : make illegal

out·lay \'aut,lā\ *n* : expenditure

out·let \'aut,let, -lət\ *n* **1** : exit **2** : means of release **3** : market for goods **4** : electrical device that gives access to wiring

out·line \'aut,līn\ *n* **1** : line marking the outer limits **2** : summary ~ *vb* **1** : draw the outline of **2** : indicate the chief parts of

out·live \aut'liv\ *vb* : live longer than

out·look \'aut,lùk\ *n* **1** : viewpoint **2** : prospect for the future

out·ly·ing \'aut,līiŋ\ *adj* : far from a central point

out·ma·neu·ver \,autmə'nüvər, -'nyü,-\ *vb* : defeat by more skillful maneuvering

out·mod·ed \aut'mōdəd\ *adj* : out-of-date

out·num·ber \-'nəmbər\ *vb* : exceed in number

out of *prep* **1** : out from within **2** : beyond the limits of **3** : among **4** — used to indicate absence or loss **5** : because of **6** : from or with

out–of–date *adj* : no longer in fashion or in use

out·pa·tient *n* : person treated at a hospital who does not stay overnight

out·post *n* : remote military post

out·put *n* : amount produced ~ *vb* **-put·ted** *or* **-put; -put·ting** : produce

out·rage \'aut,rāj\ *n* **1** : violent or shameful act **2** : injury or insult **3** : extreme anger ~ *vb* **-raged; -rag·ing** **1** : subject to violent injury **2** : make very angry

out·ra·geous \aut'rājəs\ *adj* : extremely offensive or shameful — **out·ra·geous·ly** *adv* — **out·ra·geous·ness** *n*

out·right *adv* **1** : completely **2** : instantly ~ *adj* **1** : complete **2** : given without reservation

out·set *n* : beginning

out·side \aut'sīd, 'aut,-\ *n* **1** : place beyond a boundary **2** : exterior **3** : utmost limit ~ *adj* **1** : outer **2** : coming from without **3** : remote ~ *adv* : on or to the outside ~ *prep* **1** : on or to the outside of **2** : beyond the limits of

outside of *prep* **1** : outside **2** : besides

out·sid·er \-'sīdər\ *n* : one who does not belong to a group

out·skirts *n pl* : outlying parts (as of a city)

out·smart \aut'smärt\ *vb* : outwit

out·source \'aut,sȯrs\ *vb* **-sourced; -sourc·ing** : obtain from an outside supplier

out·spo·ken *adj* : direct and open in speech — **out·spo·ken·ness** *n*

out·stand·ing *adj* **1** : unpaid **2** : very good — **out·stand·ing·ly** *adv*

out·strip \aut'strip\ *vb* **1** : go faster than **2** : surpass

¹out·ward \'autwərd\ *adj* **1** : being toward the outside **2** : showing outwardly

²outward, out·wards \-wərdz\ *adv* : toward the outside — **out·ward·ly** *adv*

out·wit \aut'wit\ *vb* : get the better of by superior cleverness

ova *pl of* **OVUM**

oval \'ōvəl\ *adj* : egg-shaped — **oval** *n*

ova·ry \'ōvərē\ *n, pl* **-ries** **1** : egg-producing organ **2** : seed-producing part of a flower — **ovar·i·an** \ō'-varēən\ *adj*

ova·tion \ō'vāshən\ *n* : enthusiastic applause

ov·en \'əvən\ *n* : chamber (as in a stove) for baking

over \'ōvər\ *adv* **1** : across **2** : upside down **3** : in excess or addition **4** : above **5** : at an end **6** : again ~ *prep* **1** : above in position or authority **2** : more than **3** : along, through, or across **4** : because of ~ *adj* **1** : upper **2** : remaining **3** : ended

over- *prefix* **1** : so as to exceed or surpass **2** : excessive or excessively

¹**over•age** \ˌōvərˈāj\ *adj* : too old

²**overage** \ˈōvərij\ *n* : surplus

over•all \ˌōvərˈȯl\ *adj* : including everything

over•alls \ˈōvərˌȯlz\ *n pl* : pants with an extra piece covering the chest

over•awe *vb* : subdue by awe

over•bear•ing \-ˈbariŋ\ *adj* : arrogant

over•blown \-ˈblōn\ *adj* : pretentious

over•board *adv* : over the side into the water

over•cast *adj* : clouded over ⁓ *n* : cloud covering

over•coat *n* : outer coat

over•come *vb* -came \-ˈkām\; -come; -com•ing **1** : defeat **2** : make helpless or exhausted

over•do *vb* -did; -done; -do•ing; -does : do too much

over•draft *n* : overdrawn sum

over•draw *vb* -drew; -drawn; -draw•ing : write checks for more than one's bank balance

over•flow \ˌōvərˈflō\ *vb* **1** : flood **2** : flow over — **overflow** \ˈōvərˌflō\ *n*

over•grow *vb* -grew; -grown; -grow•ing : grow over

over•hand *adj* : made with the hand brought down from above — **overhand** *adv* — **over•hand•ed** \-ˌhandəd\ *adv or adj*

over•hang *vb* -hung; -hang•ing : jut out over ⁓ *n* : something that overhangs

over•haul *vb* **1** : repair **2** : overtake

over•head \ˌōvərˈhed\ *adv* : aloft ⁓ \ˈōvərˌ-\ *adj* : situated above ⁓ \ˈōvərˌ-\ *n* : general business expenses

over•hear *vb* -heard; -hear•ing : hear without the speaker's knowledge

over•joyed *adj* : filled with joy

over•kill \ˈōvərˌkil\ *n* : large excess

over•land \-ˌland, -lənd\ *adv or adj* : by, on, or across land

over•lap *vb* : lap over — **overlap** \ˈōvərˌlap\ *n*

over•lay \ˌōvərˈlā\ *vb* -laid; -lay•ing : lay over or across — **over•lay** \ˈōvərˌlā\ *n*

over•look \ˌōvərˈlu̇k\ *vb* **1** : look down on **2** : fail to see **3** : ignore **4**

List of self-explanatory words with the prefix *over-*

overabundance
overabundant
overachiever
overactive
overaggressive
overambitious
overanalyze
overanxiety
overanxious
overarousal
overassertive
overbake
overbid
overbill
overbold
overborrow
overbright
overbroad
overbuild
overburden
overbusy
overbuy
overcapacity
overcapitalize
overcareful
overcautious
overcharge
overcivilized
overclean

overcommit
overcompensate
overcomplicate
overconcern
overconfidence
overconfident
overconscientious
overconsume
overconsumption
overcontrol
overcook
overcorrect
overcritical
overcrowd
overdecorate
overdependence
overdependent
overdevelop
overdose
overdramatic
overdramatize
overdress
overdrink
overdue
overeager
overeat
overeducated
overelaborate
overemotional

overemphasis
overemphasize
overenergetic
overenthusiastic
overestimate
overexaggerate
overexaggeration
overexcite
overexcited
overexercise
overexert
overexertion
overexpand
overexpansion
overexplain
overexploit
overexpose
overextend
overextension
overexuberant
overfamiliar
overfatigued
overfeed
overfertilize
overfill
overfond
overgeneralization
overgeneralize
overgenerous

: pardon **5** : supervise ~ \\'ōvər,-\\ *n*
: observation point

over•ly \\'ōvərlē\\ *adv* : excessively

over•night *adv* **1** : through the night **2** : suddenly — **overnight** *adj*

over•pass *n* : bridge over a road

over•pow•er *vb* : conquer

over•reach \\,ōvər'rēch\\ *vb* : try or seek too much

over•ride *vb* **-rode; -rid•den; -rid•ing** : neutralize action of

over•rule *vb* : rule against or set aside

over•run *vb* **-ran; -run•ning 1** : swarm or flow over **2** : go beyond ~ *n* : an exceeding of estimated costs

over•seas *adv or adj* : beyond or across the sea

over•see \\,ōvər'sē\\ *vb* **-saw; -seen; -seeing** : supervise — **over•seer** \\'ōvər,siər\\ *n*

over•shad•ow *vb* : exceed in importance

over•shoe *n* : protective outer shoe

over•shoot *vb* **-shot; -shoot•ing** : shoot or pass beyond

over•sight *n* : inadvertent omission or error

over•sleep *vb* **-slept; -sleep•ing** : sleep longer than intended

over•spread *vb* **-spread; -spread•ing** : spread over or above

over•state *vb* : exaggerate — **over•state•ment** *n*

over•stay *vb* : stay too long

over•step *vb* : exceed

overt \\ō'vərt, 'ō,vərt\\ *adj* : not secret — **overt•ly** *adv*

over•take *vb* **-took; -tak•en; -tak•ing** : catch up with

over•throw \\,ōvər'thrō\\ *vb* **-threw; -thrown; -throw•ing 1** : upset **2** : defeat — **over•throw** \\'ōvər,-\\ *n*

over•time *n* : extra working time — **overtime** *adv*

over•tone *n* **1** : higher tone in a complex musical tone **2** : suggestion

over•ture \\'ōvər,chùr, -chər\\ *n* **1** : opening offer **2** : musical introduction

over•turn *vb* **1** : turn over **2** : nullify

over•view *n* : brief survey

over•ween•ing \\,ōvər'wēniŋ\\ *adj* **1** : arrogant **2** : excessive

over•whelm \\,ōvər'hwelm\\ *vb* : overcome completely — **over•whelming•ly** \\-'hwelmiŋlē\\ *adv*

over•wrought \\,ōvər'ròt\\ *adj* : extremely excited

---

overglamorize	overparticular	overserious
overgraze	overpay	oversexed
overharvest	overpayment	oversimple
overhasty	overplay	oversimplify
overheat	overpopulated	oversolicitous
overidealize	overpraise	overspecialize
overimaginative	overprescribe	overspend
overimpress	overpressure	overstaff
overindebtedness	overprice	overstimulation
overindulge	overprivileged	overstock
overindulgence	overproduce	overstrain
overindulgent	overproduction	overstress
overinflate	overpromise	overstretch
overinsistent	overprotect	oversubtle
overintense	overprotective	oversupply
overintensity	overqualified	oversuspicious
overinvestment	overrate	oversweeten
overladen	overreact	overtax
overlarge	overreaction	overtighten
overlend	overrefined	overtip
overload	overregulate	overtired
overlong	overregulation	overtrain
overloud	overreliance	overtreat
overmedicate	overrepresented	overuse
overmodest	overrespond	overutilize
overmuch	overripe	overvalue
overobvious	oversaturate	overweight
overoptimistic	oversell	overwork
overorganize	oversensitive	overzealous

ovoid \'ō̩vȯid\, **ovoi·dal** \ō'vȯid°l\ *adj* : egg-shaped

ovu·late \'ävyə̩lāt, 'ōv-\ *vb* **-lat·ed; -lat·ing** : produce eggs from an ovary — **ovu·la·tion** \̩ävyə'lāshən, ̩ōv-\ *n*

ovum \'ōvəm\ *n, pl* **ova** \-və\ : female germ cell

owe \'ō\ *vb* **owed; ow·ing 1** : have an obligation to pay **2** : be indebted to or for

owing to *prep* : because of

owl \'au̇l\ *n* : nocturnal bird of prey — **owl·ish** *adj* — **owl·ish·ly** *adv*

own \'ōn\ *adj* : belonging to oneself ~ *vb* **1** : have as property **2** : acknowl-edge ~ *pron* : one or ones belonging to oneself — **own·er** *n* — **own·er·ship** *n*

ox \'äks\ *n, pl* **ox·en** \'äksən\ : bovine mammal and esp. a castrated bull

ox·ide \'äk̩sīd\ *n* : compound of oxygen

ox·i·dize \'äksə̩dīz\ *vb* **-dized; -diz·ing** : combine with oxygen — **ox·i·da·tion** \̩äksə'dāshən\ *n* — **ox·i·diz·er** *n*

ox·y·gen \'äksijən\ *n* : gaseous chemi-cal element essential for life

oys·ter \'ȯistər\ *n* : bivalve mollusk — **oys·ter·ing** \-riŋ\ *n*

ozone \'ō̩zōn\ *n* : very reactive bluish form of oxygen

P

p \'pē\ *n, pl* **p's** *or* **ps** \'pēz\ : 16th let-ter of the alphabet

pace \'pās\ *n* **1** : walking step **2** : rate of progress ~ *vb* **paced; pac·ing 1** : go at a pace **2** : cover with slow steps **3** : set the pace of

pace·mak·er *n* : electrical device to regulate heartbeat

pachy·derm \'paki̩dərm\ *n* : elephant

pa·cif·ic \pə'sifik\ *adj* : calm or peace-ful

pac·i·fism \'pasə̩fizəm\ *n* : opposition to war or violence — **pac·i·fist** \-fist\ *n or adj* — **pac·i·fis·tic** \̩pasə'fistik\ *adj*

pac·i·fy \'pasə̩fī\ *vb* **-fied; -fy·ing** : make calm — **pac·i·fi·ca·tion** \̩pasəfə'kāshən\ *n* — **pac·i·fi·er** \'pasə̩fīər\ *n*

pack \'pak\ *n* **1** : compact bundle **2** : group of animals ~ *vb* **1** : put into a container **2** : fill tightly or com-pletely **3** : send without ceremony — **pack·er** *n*

pack·age \'pakij\ *n* : items bundled to-gether ~ *vb* **-aged; -ag·ing** : enclose in a package

pack·et \'pakət\ *n* : small package

pact \'pakt\ *n* : agreement

pad \'pad\ *n* **1** : cushioning part or thing **2** : floating leaf of a water plant **3** : tablet of paper ~ *vb* **-dd- 1** : fur-nish with a pad **2** : expand with need-less matter — **pad·ding** *n*

pad·dle \'pad°l\ *n* : implement with a flat blade ~ *vb* **-dled; -dling** : move, beat, or stir with a paddle

pad·dock \'padək\ *n* : enclosed area for racehorses

pad·dy \'padē\ *n, pl* **-dies** : wet land where rice is grown

pad·lock *n* : lock with a U-shaped catch — **padlock** *vb*

pae·an \'pēən\ *n* : song of praise

pa·gan \'pāgən\ *n or adj* : heathen — **pa·gan·ism** \-̩izəm\ *n*

¹page \'pāj\ *n* : messenger ~ *vb* **paged; pag·ing** : summon by re-peated calls — **pag·er** *n*

²page *n* **1** : single leaf (as of a book) or one side of the leaf **2** : informa-tion at a single World Wide Web ad-dress

pag·eant \'pajənt\ *n* : elaborate spec-tacle or procession — **pag·eant·ry** \-əntrē\ *n*

pa·go·da \pə'gōdə\ *n* : tower with roofs curving upward

paid *past of* PAY

pail \'pāl\ *n* : cylindrical container with a handle — **pail·ful** \-̩fu̇l\ *n*

pain \'pān\ *n* **1** : punishment or penalty **2** : suffering of body or mind **3** *pl* : great care ~ *vb* : cause or ex-perience pain — **pain·ful** \-fəl\ *adj* — **pain·ful·ly** *adv* — **pain·kill·er** *n* — **pain·kill·ing** *adj* — **pain·less** *adj* — **pain·less·ly** *adv*

pains·tak·ing \'pān͵stākiŋ\ *adj* : taking pains — **painstaking** *n* — **pains-tak·ing·ly** *adv*

paint \'pānt\ *vb* **1** : apply color or paint to **2** : portray esp. in color ⁓ *n* : mixture of pigment and liquid — **paint·brush** *n* — **paint·er** *n* — **paint·ing** *n*

pair \'par\ *n* : a set of two ⁓ *vb* : put or go together as a pair

pa·ja·mas \pə'jäməz, -'jam-\ *n pl* : loose suit for sleeping

pal \'pal\ *n* : close friend

pal·ace \'paləs\ *n* **1** : residence of a chief of state **2** : mansion — **pa·la·tial** \pə'lāshəl\ *adj*

pal·at·able \'palətəbəl\ *adj* : agreeable to the taste

pal·ate \'palət\ *n* **1** : roof of the mouth **2** : taste — **pal·a·tal** \-ət°l\ *adj*

pa·la·ver \pə'lavər, -'läv-\ *n* : talk — **palaver** *vb*

¹pale \'pāl\ *adj* **pal·er; pal·est 1** : lacking in color or brightness **2** : light in color or shade ⁓ *vb* **paled; pal·ing** : make or become pale — **pale·ness** *n*

²pale *n* **1** : fence stake **2** : enclosed place

pa·le·on·tol·o·gy \͵pālē͵än'täləjē\ *n* : branch of biology dealing with ancient forms of life known from fossils — **pa·le·on·tol·o·gist** \-͵än'täləjist, -ən-\ *n*

pal·ette \'palət\ *n* : board on which paints are laid and mixed

pal·i·sade \͵palə'sād\ *n* **1** : high fence **2** : line of cliffs

¹pall \'pól\ *n* **1** : cloth draped over a coffin **2** : something that produces gloom

²pall *vb* : lose in interest or attraction

pall·bear·er *n* : one who attends the coffin at a funeral

¹pal·let \'palət\ *n* : makeshift bed

²pallet *n* : portable storage platform

pal·li·ate \'palē͵āt\ *vb* **-at·ed; -at·ing 1** : ease without curing **2** : cover or conceal by excusing — **pal·li·a·tion** \͵palē'āshən\ *n* — **pal·li·a·tive** \'palē-͵ātiv\ *adj or n*

pal·lid \'paləd\ *adj* : pale

pal·lor \'palər\ *n* : paleness

¹palm \'päm, 'pälm\ *n* **1** : tall tropical tree crowned with large leaves **2** : symbol of victory

²palm *n* : underside of the hand ⁓ *vb* **1**

: conceal in the hand **2** : impose by fraud

palm·ist·ry \'päməstrē, 'pälmə-\ *n* : reading a person's character or future in his palms — **palm·ist** \'pämist, 'pälm-\ *n*

palmy \'pämē, 'pälmē\ *adj* **palm·i·er; -est** : flourishing

pal·o·mi·no \͵palə'mēnō\ *n, pl* **-nos** : light-colored horse

pal·pa·ble \'palpəbəl\ *adj* **1** : capable of being touched **2** : obvious — **pal·pa·bly** \-blē\ *adv*

pal·pi·tate \'palpə͵tāt\ *vb* **-tat·ed; -tat·ing** : beat rapidly — **pal·pi·ta·tion** \͵palpə'tāshən\ *n*

pal·sy \'pólzē\ *n, pl* **-sies 1** : paralysis **2** : condition marked by tremor — **pal·sied** \-zēd\ *adj*

pal·try \'póltrē\ *adj* **-tri·er; -est** : trivial

pam·per \'pampər\ *vb* : spoil or indulge

pam·phlet \'pamflət\ *n* : unbound publication — **pam·phle·teer** \͵pamflə-'tir\ *n*

pan \'pan\ *n* : broad, shallow, and open container ⁓ *vb* **1** : wash gravel in a pan to search for gold **2** : criticize severely

pan·a·cea \͵panə'sēə\ *n* : remedy for all ills or difficulties

pan·cake *n* : fried flat cake

pan·cre·as \'paŋkrēəs, 'pan-\ *n* : gland that produces insulin — **pan·cre·at·ic** \͵paŋkrē'atik, ͵pan-\ *adj*

pan·da \'pandə\ *n* : black-and-white bearlike animal

pan·de·mo·ni·um \͵pandə'mōnēəm\ *n* : wild uproar

pan·der \'pandər\ *n* **1** : pimp **2** : one who caters to others' desires or weaknesses ⁓ *vb* : act as a pander

pane \'pān\ *n* : sheet of glass

pan·e·gy·ric \͵panə'jirik\ *n* : eulogistic oration — **pan·e·gyr·ist** \-'jirist\ *n*

pan·el \'pan°l\ *n* **1** : list of persons (as jurors) **2** : discussion group **3** : flat piece of construction material **4** : board with instruments or controls ⁓ *vb* **-eled** *or* **-elled; -el·ing** *or* **-el·ling** : decorate with panels — **pan·el·ing** *n* — **pan·el·ist** \-ist\ *n*

pang \'paŋ\ *n* : sudden sharp pain

pan·han·dle \'pan͵hand°l\ *vb* **-dled; -dling** : ask for money on the street — **pan·han·dler** \-ər\ *n*

pan·ic \'panik\ *n* : sudden overpowering fright ~ *vb* **-icked; -ick·ing** : affect or be affected with panic — **pan·icky** \-ikē\ *adj*

pan·o·ply \'panəplē\ *n, pl* **-plies 1** : full suit of armor **2** : impressive array

pan·o·ra·ma \,panə'ramə, -'räm-\ *n* : view in every direction — **pan·o·ram·ic** \-'ramik\ *adj*

pan·sy \'panzē\ *n, pl* **-sies** : low= growing garden herb with showy flowers

pant \'pant\ *vb* **1** : breathe with great effort **2** : yearn ~ *n* : panting sound

pan·ta·loons \,pant⁰l'ünz\ *n pl* : pants

pan·the·on \'panthē,än, -ən\ *n* **1** : the gods of a people **2** : group of famous people

pan·ther \'panthər\ *n* : large wild cat

pant·ies \'pantēz\ *n pl* : woman's or child's short underpants

pan·to·mime \'pantə,mīm\ *n* **1** : play without words **2** : expression by bodily or facial movements ~ *vb* : represent by pantomime

pan·try \'pantrē\ *n, pl* **-tries** : storage room for food and dishes

pants \'pants\ *n pl* **1** : 2-legged outer garment **2** : panties

pap \'pap\ *n* : soft food

pa·pa·cy \'pāpəsē\ *n, pl* **-cies 1** : office of pope **2** : reign of a pope

pa·pal \'pāpəl\ *adj* : relating to the pope

pa·pa·ya \pə'pīə\ *n* : tropical tree with large yellow edible fruit

pa·per \'pāpər\ *n* **1** : pliable substance used to write or print on, to wrap things in, or to cover walls **2** : printed or written document **3** : newspaper — **paper** *adj or vb* — **pa·per·hang·er** *n* — **pa·per·weight** *n* — **pa·pery** \'pāpərē\ *adj*

pa·per·board *n* : cardboard

pa·pier–mâ·ché \,pāpərmə'shā, ,pap-,yämə-, -ma-\ *n* : molding material of waste paper

pa·poose \pa'püs, pə-\ *n* : young child of American Indian parents

pa·pri·ka \pə'prēkə, pa-\ *n* : mild red spice from sweet peppers

pa·py·rus \pə'pīrəs\ *n, pl* **-rus·es** *or* **-ri** \-,rē, -,rī\ **1** : tall grasslike plant **2** : paper from papyrus

par \'pär\ *n* **1** : stated value **2** : common level **3** : accepted standard or normal condition — **par** *adj*

par·a·ble \'parəbəl\ *n* : simple story illustrating a moral truth

para·chute \'parə,shüt\ *n* : large umbrella-shaped device for making a descent through air — **parachute** *vb* — **para·chut·ist** \-,shütist\ *n*

pa·rade \pə'rād\ *n* **1** : pompous display **2** : ceremonial formation and march ~ *vb* **-rad·ed; -rad·ing 1** : march in a parade **2** : show off

par·a·digm \'parə,dīm, -,dim\ *n* : model

par·a·dise \'parə,dīs, -,dīz\ *n* : place of bliss

par·a·dox \'parə,däks\ *n* : statement that seems contrary to common sense yet is perhaps true — **par·a·dox·i·cal** \,parə'däksikəl\ *adj* — **par·a·dox·i·cal·ly** *adv*

par·af·fin \'parəfən\ *n* : white waxy substance used esp. for making candles and sealing foods

par·a·gon \'parə,gän, -gən\ *n* : model of perfection

para·graph \'parə,graf\ *n* : unified division of a piece of writing ~ *vb* : divide into paragraphs

par·a·keet \'parə,kēt\ *n* : small slender parrot

par·al·lel \'parə,lel\ *adj* **1** : lying or moving in the same direction but always the same distance apart **2** : similar ~ *n* **1** : parallel line, curve, or surface **2** : line of latitude **3** : similarity ~ *vb* **1** : compare **2** : correspond to — **par·al·lel·ism** \-,izəm\ *n*

par·al·lel·o·gram \,parə'lelə,gram\ *n* : 4-sided polygon with opposite sides equal and parallel

pa·ral·y·sis \pə'raləsəs\ *n, pl* **-y·ses** \-,sēz\ : loss of function and esp. of voluntary motion — **par·a·lyt·ic** \,parə'litik\ *adj or n*

par·a·lyze \'parə,līz\ *vb* **-lyzed; -lyz·ing** : affect with paralysis — **par·a·lyz·ing·ly** *adv*

para·med·ic \,parə'medik\ *n* : person trained to provide initial emergency medical treatment

pa·ram·e·ter \pə'ramətər\ *n* : characteristic element — **para·met·ric** \,parə'metrik\ *adj*

par·a·mount \'parə,maùnt\ *adj* : superior to all others

par·amour \'parə,mùr\ *n* : illicit lover

para·noia \,parə'nòiə\ *n* : mental disorder marked by irrational suspicion — **para•noid** \'parə͵nȯid\ *adj or n*

par•a•pet \'parəpət, -͵pet\ *n* : protecting rampart in a fort

par•a•pher•na•lia \͵parəfə'nālyə, -fər-\ *n sing or pl* : equipment

para•phrase \'parə͵frāz\ *n* : restatement of a text giving the meaning in different words — **paraphrase** *vb*

para•ple•gia \͵parə'plējə, -jēə\ *n* : paralysis of the lower trunk and legs — **para•ple•gic** \-jik\ *adj or n*

par•a•site \'parə͵sīt\ *n* : organism living on another — **par•a•sit•ic** \͵parə-'sitik\ *adj* — **par•a•sit•ism** \'parəse-͵tizəm, -͵sīt͵iz-\ *n*

para•sol \'parə͵sȯl\ *n* : umbrella used to keep off the sun

para•troops \-͵trüps\ *n pl* : troops trained to parachute from an airplane — **para•troop•er** \-͵trüpər\ *n*

par•boil \'pär͵bȯil\ *vb* : boil briefly

par•cel \'pärsəl\ *n* **1** : lot **2** : package ~ *vb* **-celed** *or* **-celled; -cel•ing** *or* **-cel•ling** : divide into portions

parch \'pärch\ *vb* : toast or shrivel with dry heat

parch•ment \'pärchmənt\ *n* : animal skin prepared to write on

par•don \'pärdᵊn\ *n* : excusing of an offense ~ *vb* : free from penalty — **par•don•able** \'pärdᵊnəbəl\ *adj* — **par•don•er** \-ᵊnər\ *n*

pare \'par\ *vb* **pared; par•ing 1** : trim off an outside part **2** : reduce as if by paring — **par•er** *n*

par•e•gor•ic \͵parə'gȯrik\ *n* : tincture of opium and camphor

par•ent \'parənt\ *n* : one that begets or brings up offspring — **par•ent•age** \-ij\ *n* — **pa•ren•tal** \pə'rentᵊl\ *adj* — **par•ent•hood** *n*

pa•ren•the•sis \pə'renthəsəs\ *n, pl* **-the•ses** \-͵sēz\ **1** : word or phrase inserted in a passage **2** : one of a pair of punctuation marks ( ) — **par•en•thet•ic** \͵parən'thetik\, **par•en•thet•i•cal** \-ikəl\ *adj* — **par•en•thet•i•cal•ly** *adv*

par•fait \pär'fā\ *n* : layered cold dessert

pa•ri•ah \pə'rīə\ *n* : outcast

par•ish \'parish\ *n* : local church community

pa•rish•io•ner \pə'rishənər\ *n* : member of a parish

par•i•ty \'parətē\ *n, pl* **-ties** : equality

park \'pärk\ *n* : land set aside for recre-

ation or for its beauty ~ *vb* : leave a vehicle standing

par•ka \'pärkə\ *n* : usu. hooded heavy jacket

park•way \'pärk͵wā\ *n* : broad landscaped thoroughfare

par•lance \'pärləns\ *n* : manner of speaking

par•lay \'pär͵lā\ *n* : the risking of a stake plus its winnings — **parlay** *vb*

par•ley \'pärlē\ *n, pl* **-leys** : conference about a dispute — **parley** *vb*

par•lia•ment \'pärləmənt\ *n* : legislative assembly — **par•lia•men•tar•i•an** *n* — **par•lia•men•ta•ry** \͵pärlə-'mentərē\ *adj*

par•lor \'pärlər\ *n* **1** : reception room **2** : place of business

pa•ro•chi•al \pə'rōkēəl\ *adj* **1** : relating to a church parish **2** : provincial — **pa•ro•chi•al•ism** \-ə͵lizəm\ *n*

par•o•dy \'parədē\ *n, pl* **-dies** : humorous or satirical imitation — **parody** *vb*

pa•role \pə'rōl\ *n* : conditional release of a prisoner — **parole** *vb* — **pa•rol•ee** \-͵rō'lē, -'rō͵lē\ *n*

par•ox•ysm \'parək͵sizəm, pə'räk-\ *n* : convulsion

par•quet \'pär͵kā, pär'kā\ *n* : flooring of patterned wood inlay

par•ra•keet *var of* PARAKEET

par•rot \'parət\ *n* : bright-colored tropical bird

par•ry \'parē\ *vb* **-ried; -ry•ing 1** : ward off a blow **2** : evade adroitly — **parry** *n*

parse \'pärs\ *vb* **parsed; pars•ing** : analyze grammatically

par•si•mo•ny \'pärsə͵mōnē\ *n* : extreme frugality — **par•si•mo•ni•ous** \͵pärsə'mōnēəs\ *adj* — **par•si•mo•ni•ous•ly** *adv*

pars•ley \'pärslē\ *n* : garden plant used as a seasoning or garnish

pars•nip \'pärsnəp\ *n* : carrotlike vegetable with a white edible root

par•son \'pärsᵊn\ *n* : minister

par•son•age \'pärsᵊnij\ *n* : parson's house

part \'pärt\ *n* **1** : one of the units into which a larger whole is divided **2** : function or role ~ *vb* **1** : take leave **2** : separate **3** : go away **4** : give up

par•take \pär'tāk, pər-\ *vb* **-took; -tak•en; -tak•ing** : have or take a share — **par•tak•er** *n*

par·tial \'pärshəl\ *adj* **1** : favoring one over another **2** : affecting a part only — **par·tial·i·ty** \ˌpärshē'alətē\ *n* — **par·tial·ly** \'pärshəlē\ *adv*

par·tic·i·pate \pər'tisəˌpāt, pär-\ *vb* **-pat·ed; -pat·ing** : take part in something — **par·tic·i·pant** \-pənt\ *adj or n* — **par·tic·i·pa·tion** \-ˌtisə'pāshən\ *n* — **par·tic·i·pa·to·ry** \-'tisəpəˌtōrē\ *adj*

par·ti·ci·ple \'pärtəˌsipəl\ *n* : verb form with functions of both verb and adjective — **par·ti·cip·i·al** \ˌpärtə'sipēəl\ *adj*

par·ti·cle \'pärtikəl\ *n* : small bit

par·tic·u·lar \pär'tikyələr\ *adj* **1** : relating to a specific person or thing **2** : individual **3** : hard to please ~ *n* : detail — **par·tic·u·lar·ly** *adv*

par·ti·san \'pärtəzen, -sən\ *n* **1** : adherent **2** : guerrilla — **partisan** *adj* — **par·ti·san·ship** *n*

par·tite \'pärˌtīt\ *adj* : divided into parts

par·ti·tion \pər'tishən, pär-\ *n* **1** : distribution **2** : something that divides — **partition** *vb*

part·ly \'pärtlē\ *adv* : in some degree

part·ner \'pärtnər\ *n* **1** : associate **2** : companion **3** : business associate — **part·ner·ship** *n*

part of speech : class of words distinguished esp. according to function

par·tridge \'pärtrij\ *n, pl* **-tridge** *or* **-tridg·es** : stout-bodied game bird

par·ty \'pärtē\ *n, pl* **-ties** **1** : political organization **2** : participant **3** : company of persons esp. with a purpose **4** : social gathering

par·ve·nu \'pärvəˌnü, -ˌnyü\ *n* : social upstart

pass \'pas\ *vb* **1** : move past, over, or through **2** : go away or die **3** : allow to elapse **4** : go unchallenged **5** : transfer or undergo transfer **6** : render a judgment **7** : occur **8** : enact **9** : undergo testing successfully **10** : be regarded **11** : decline ~ *n* **1** : low place in a mountain range **2** : act of passing **3** : accomplishment **4** : permission to leave, enter, or move about — **pass·able** *adj* — **pass·ably** *adv* — **pass·er** *n* — **pass·er·by** *n*

pas·sage \'pasij\ *n* **1** : process of passing **2** : means of passing **3** : voyage **4** : right to pass **5** : literary selection — **pas·sage·way** *n*

pass·book *n* : bankbook

pas·sé \pa'sā\ *adj* : out-of-date

pas·sen·ger \'pas⁰njər\ *n* : traveler in a conveyance

pass·ing \'pasiŋ\ *n* : death

pas·sion \'pashən\ *n* **1** : strong feeling esp. of anger, love, or desire **2** : object of affection or enthusiasm — **pas·sion·ate** \'pashənət\ *adj* — **pas·sion·ate·ly** *adv* — **pas·sion·less** *adj*

pas·sive \'pasiv\ *adj* **1** : not active but acted upon **2** : submissive — **passive** *n* — **pas·sive·ly** *adv* — **pas·siv·i·ty** \pa'sivətē\ *n*

Pass·over \'pasˌōvər\ *n* : Jewish holiday celebrated in March or April in commemoration of the Hebrews' liberation from slavery in Egypt

pass·port \'pasˌpōrt\ *n* : government document needed for travel abroad

pass·word *n* **1** : word or phrase spoken to pass a guard **2** : sequence of characters needed to get into a computer system

past \'past\ *adj* **1** : ago **2** : just gone by **3** : having existed before the present **4** : expressing past time ~ *prep or adv* : beyond ~ *n* **1** : time gone by **2** : verb tense expressing time gone by **3** : past life

pas·ta \'pästə\ *n* : fresh or dried shaped dough

paste \'pāst\ *n* **1** : smooth ground food **2** : moist adhesive ~ *vb* **past·ed; past·ing** : attach with paste — **pasty** *adj*

paste·board *n* : cardboard

pas·tel \pas'tel\ *n* : light color — **pastel** *adj*

pas·teur·ize \'paschəˌrīz, 'pastə-\ *vb* **-ized; -iz·ing** : heat (as milk) so as to kill germs — **pas·teur·i·za·tion** \ˌpaschərə'zāshən, ˌpastə-\ *n*

pas·time \'pasˌtīm\ *n* : amusement

pas·tor \'pastər\ *n* : priest or minister serving a church or parish — **pas·tor·ate** \-tərət\ *n*

pas·to·ral \'pastərəl\ *adj* **1** : relating to rural life **2** : of or relating to spiritual guidance or a pastor ~ *n* : literary work dealing with rural life

pas·try \'pāstrē\ *n, pl* **-ries** : sweet baked goods

pas·ture \'paschər\ *n* : land used for grazing ~ *vb* **-tured; -tur·ing** : graze

pat \'pat\ *n* **1** : light tap **2** : small mass

~ *vb* **-tt-** : tap gently ~ *adj or adv* **1** : apt or glib **2** : unyielding

patch \'pach\ *n* **1** : piece used for mending **2** : small area distinct from surrounding area ~ *vb* **1** : mend with a patch **2** : make of fragments **3** : repair hastily — **patchy** \-ē\ *adj*

patch•work *n* : something made of pieces of different materials, shapes, or colors

pate \'pāt\ *n* : crown of the head

pa•tel•la \pə'telə\ *n, pl* **-lae** \-'tel͵ē, -͵ī\ *or* **-las** : kneecap

pa•tent *adj* **1** \'pat°nt, 'pāt-\ : obvious **2** \'pat-\ : protected by a patent ~ \'pat-\ *n* : document conferring or securing a right ~ \'pat-\ *vb* : secure by patent — **pat•ent•ly** *adv*

pa•ter•nal \pə'tərn°l\ *adj* **1** : fatherly **2** : related through or inherited from a father — **pa•ter•nal•ly** *adv*

pa•ter•ni•ty \pə'tərnətē\ *n* : fatherhood

path \'path, 'páth\ *n* **1** : trodden way **2** : route or course — **path•find•er** *n* — **path•way** *n* — **path•less** *adj*

pa•thet•ic \pə'thetik\ *adj* : pitiful — **pa•thet•i•cal•ly** *adv*

pa•thol•o•gy \pə'thäləjē\ *n, pl* **-gies 1** : study of disease **2** : physical abnormality — **path•o•log•i•cal** \͵pathə-'läjikəl\ *adj* — **pa•thol•o•gist** \pə-'thäləjist\ *n*

pa•thos \'pā͵thäs\ *n* : element evoking pity

pa•tience \'pāshəns\ *n* : habit or fact of being patient

pa•tient \'pāshənt\ *adj* : bearing pain or trials without complaint ~ *n* : one under medical care — **pa•tient•ly** *adv*

pa•ti•na \pə'tēnə, 'patənə\ *n, pl* **-nas** \-nəz\ *or* **-nae** \-͵nē, -͵nī\ : green film formed on copper and bronze

pa•tio \'patē͵ō, 'pät-\ *n, pl* **-ti•os 1** : courtyard **2** : paved recreation area near a house

pa•tri•arch \'pātrē͵ärk\ *n* **1** : man revered as father or founder **2** : venerable old man — **pa•tri•ar•chal** \͵pātrē'ärkəl\ *adj* — **pa•tri•ar•chy** \-͵ärkē\ *n*

pa•tri•cian \pə'trishən\ *n* : person of high birth — **patrician** *adj*

pat•ri•mo•ny \'patrə͵mōnē\ *n* : something inherited — **pat•ri•mo•ni•al** \͵patrə'mōnēəl\ *adj*

pa•tri•ot \'pātrēət, -͵ät\ *n* : one who loves his or her country — **pa•tri•ot-**

ic \͵pātrē'ätik\ *adj* — **pa•tri•ot•i•cal•ly** *adv* — **pa•tri•o•tism** \'pātrēə-͵tizəm\ *n*

pa•trol \pə'trōl\ *n* **1** : a going around for observation or security **2** : group on patrol ~ *vb* **-ll-** : carry out a patrol

pa•trol•man \-mən\ *n* : police officer

pa•tron \'pātrən\ *n* **1** : special protector **2** : wealthy supporter **3** : customer

pa•tron•age \'patrənij, 'pā-\ *n* **1** : support or influence of a patron **2** : trade of customers **3** : control of government appointments

pa•tron•ess \'pātrənəs\ *n* : woman who is a patron

pa•tron•ize \'pātrə͵nīz, 'pa-\ *vb* **-ized; -iz•ing 1** : be a customer of **2** : treat with condescension

¹**pat•ter** \'patər\ *vb* : talk glibly or mechanically ~ *n* : rapid talk

²**patter** *vb* : pat or tap rapidly ~ *n* : quick succession of pats or taps

pat•tern \'patərn\ *n* **1** : model for imitation or for making things **2** : artistic design **3** : noticeable formation or set of characteristics ~ *vb* : form according to a pattern

pat•ty \'patē\ *n, pl* **-ties** : small flat cake

pau•ci•ty \'pósətē\ *n* : shortage

paunch \'pónch\ *n* : large belly — **paunchy** *adj*

pau•per \'pópər\ *n* : poor person — **pau•per•ism** \-pə͵rizəm\ *n* — **pau•per•ize** \-pə͵rīz\ *vb*

pause \'póz\ *n* : temporary stop ~ *vb* **paused; paus•ing** : stop briefly

pave \'pāv\ *vb* **paved; pav•ing** : cover to smooth or firm the surface — **pave•ment** \-mənt\ *n* — **pav•ing** *n*

pa•vil•ion \pə'vilyən\ *n* **1** : large tent **2** : light structure used for entertainment or shelter

paw \'pó\ *n* : foot of a 4-legged clawed animal ~ *vb* **1** : handle clumsily or rudely **2** : touch or strike with a paw

pawn \'pón\ *n* **1** : goods deposited as security for a loan **2** : state of being pledged ~ *vb* : deposit as a pledge — **pawn•bro•ker** *n* — **pawn•shop** *n*

pay \'pā\ *vb* **paid** \'pād\; **pay•ing 1** : make due return for goods or services **2** : discharge indebtedness for **3** : requite **4** : give freely or as fitting **5** : be profitable ~ *n* **1** : status of being paid **2** : something paid — **pay-**

able *adj* — **pay•check** *n* — **pay•ee** \pā'ē\ *n* — **pay•er** *n* — **pay•ment** *n*

PC \ˌpē'sē\ *n, pl* **PCs** *or* **PC's** : microcomputer

pea \'pē\ *n* : round edible seed of a leguminous vine

peace \'pēs\ *n* **1** : state of calm and quiet **2** : absence of war or strife — **peace•able** \-əbəl\ *adj* — **peace•ably** \-blē\ *adv* — **peace•ful** \-fəl\ *adj* — **peace•ful•ly** *adv* — **peace•keep•er** *n* — **peace•keep•ing** *n* — **peace•mak•er** *n* — **peace•time** *n*

peach \'pēch\ *n* : sweet juicy fruit of a flowering tree or this tree

pea•cock \'pē,käk\ *n* : brilliantly colored male pheasant

peak \'pēk\ *n* **1** : pointed or projecting part **2** : top of a hill **3** : highest level — *vb* : reach a maximum — **peak** *adj*

peak•ed \'pēkəd\ *adj* : sickly

peal \'pēl\ *n* : loud sound (as of ringing bells) — *vb* : give out peals

pea•nut \'pē,nət\ *n* : annual herb that bears underground pods or the pod or the edible seed inside

pear \'par\ *n* : fleshy fruit of a tree related to the apple

pearl \'pərl\ *n* : gem formed within an oyster — **pearly** \'pərlē\ *adj*

peas•ant \'pez°nt\ *n* : tiller of the soil — **peas•ant•ry** \-°ntrē\ *n*

peat \'pēt\ *n* : decayed organic deposit often dried for fuel — **peaty** *adj*

peb•ble \'pebəl\ *n* : small stone — **peb•bly** *adj*

pe•can \pi'kän, -'kan\ *n* : hickory tree bearing a smooth-shelled nut or the nut

pec•ca•dil•lo \ˌpekə'dilō\ *n, pl* **-loes** *or* **-los** : slight offense

¹peck \'pek\ *n* : unit of dry measure equal to 8 quarts

²peck *vb* : strike or pick up with the bill — *n* : quick sharp stroke

pec•tin \'pektən\ *n* : water-soluble plant substance that causes fruit jellies to set — **pec•tic** \-tik\ *adj*

pec•to•ral \'pektərəl\ *adj* : relating to the breast or chest

pe•cu•liar \pi'kyülyər\ *adj* **1** : characteristic of only one **2** : strange — **pe•cu•liar•i•ty** \-ˌkyül'yarətē, -ē'ar-\ *n* — **pe•cu•liar•ly** *adv*

pe•cu•ni•ary \pi'kyünē,erē\ *adj* : relating to money

ped•a•go•gy \'pedə,gōjē, -,gäj-\ *n* : art or profession of teaching — **ped•a•gog•ic** \ˌpedə'gäjik, -'gōj-\, **ped•a-**

gog•i•cal \-ikəl\ *adj* — **ped•a•gogue** \'pedə,gäg\ *n*

ped•al \'ped°l\ *n* : lever worked by the foot — *adj* : relating to the foot — *vb* : use a pedal

ped•ant \'ped°nt\ *n* : learned bore — **pe•dan•tic** \pi'dantik\ *adj* — **ped•ant•ry** \'ped°ntrē\ *n*

ped•dle \'ped°l\ *vb* **-dled; -dling** : offer for sale — **ped•dler** \'pedlər\ *n*

ped•es•tal \'pedəst°l\ *n* : support or foot of something upright

pe•des•tri•an \pə'destrēən\ *adj* **1** : ordinary **2** : walking — *n* : person who walks

pe•di•at•rics \ˌpēdē'atriks\ *n* : branch of medicine dealing with children — **pe•di•at•ric** \-trik\ *adj* — **pe•di•a•tri•cian** \ˌpēdēə'trishən\ *n*

ped•i•gree \'pedə,grē\ *n* : line of ancestors or a record of it

ped•i•ment \'pedəmənt\ *n* : triangular gablelike decoration on a building

peek \'pēk\ *vb* **1** : look furtively **2** : glance — **peek** *n*

peel \'pēl\ *vb* **1** : strip the skin or rind from **2** : lose the outer layer — *n* : skin or rind — **peel•ing** *n*

¹peep \'pēp\ *vb or n* : cheep

²peep *vb* **1** : look slyly **2** : begin to emerge — *n* : brief look — **peep•er** *n* — **peep•hole** *n*

¹peer \'pir\ *n* **1** : one's equal **2** : nobleman — **peer•age** \-ij\ *n*

²peer *vb* : look intently or curiously

peer•less \-ləs\ *adj* : having no equal

peeve \'pēv\ *vb* **peeved; peev•ing** : make resentful — *n* : complaint — **peev•ish** \-ish\ *adj* — **peev•ish•ly** *adv* — **peev•ish•ness** *n*

peg \'peg\ *n* : small pinlike piece — *vb* **-gg- 1** : put a peg into **2** : fix or mark with or as if with pegs

pei•gnoir \pān'wär, pen-\ *n* : negligee

pe•jo•ra•tive \pi'jórətiv\ *adj* : having a negative or degrading effect — *n* : a degrading word or phrase — **pe•jo•ra•tive•ly** *adv*

pel•i•can \'pelikən\ *n* : large-billed seabird

pel•la•gra \pə'lagrə, -'lāg-\ *n* : protein=deficiency disease

pel•let \'pelət\ *n* : little ball — **pel•let•al** \-°l\ *adj* — **pel•let•ize** \-,īz\ *vb*

pell—mell \'pel'mel\ *adv* : in confusion or haste

pel·lu·cid \pə'lüsəd\ *adj* : very clear

¹pelt \'pelt\ *n* : skin of a fur-bearing animal

²pelt *vb* : strike with blows or missiles

pel·vis \'pelvəs\ *n, pl* **-vis·es** \-vəsəz\ *or* **-ves** \-,vēz\ : cavity formed by the hip bones — **pel·vic** \-vik\ *adj*

¹pen \'pen\ *n* : enclosure for animals ∼ *vb* **-nn-** : shut in a pen

²pen *n* : tool for writing with ink ∼ *vb* **-nn-** : write

pe·nal \'pēnᵊl\ *adj* : relating to punishment

pe·nal·ize \'pēnᵊl,īz, 'pen-\ *vb* **-ized; -iz·ing** : put a penalty on

pen·al·ty \'penᵊltē\ *n, pl* **-ties 1** : punishment for crime **2** : disadvantage, loss, or hardship due to an action

pen·ance \'penəns\ *n* : act performed to show repentance

pence \'pens\ *pl of* PENNY

pen·chant \'penchənt\ *n* : strong inclination

pen·cil \'pensəl\ *n* : writing or drawing tool with a solid marking substance (as graphite) as its core ∼ *vb* **-ciled** *or* **-cilled; -cil·ing** *or* **-cil·ling** : draw or write with a pencil

pen·dant \'pendənt\ *n* : hanging ornament

pen·dent, pen·dant \'pendənt\ *adj* : hanging

pend·ing \'pendiŋ\ *prep* : while awaiting ∼ *adj* : not yet decided

pen·du·lous \'penjələs, -dyùləs\ *adj* : hanging loosely

pen·du·lum \-ləm\ *n* : a hanging weight that is free to swing

pen·e·trate \'penə,trāt\ *vb* **-trat·ed; -trat·ing 1** : enter into **2** : permeate **3** : see into — **pen·e·tra·ble** \-trəbəl\ *adj* — **pen·e·tra·tion** \,penə'trāshən\ *n* — **pen·e·tra·tive** \'penə,trātiv\ *adj*

pen·guin \'pengwən, 'peŋ-\ *n* : short-legged flightless seabird

pen·i·cil·lin \,penə'silən\ *n* : antibiotic usu. produced by a mold

pen·in·su·la \pə'ninsələ, -'ninchə-\ *n* : land extending out into the water — **pen·in·su·lar** \-lər\ *adj*

pe·nis \'pēnəs\ *n, pl* **-nes** \-,nēz\ *or* **-nis·es** : male organ of copulation

pen·i·tent \'penətənt\ *adj* : feeling sorrow for sins or offenses ∼ *n* : penitent person — **pen·i·tence** \-təns\ *n* — **pen·i·ten·tial** \,penə'tenchəl\ *adj*

pen·i·ten·tia·ry \,penə'tenchərē\ *n, pl* **-ries** : state or federal prison

pen·man·ship \'penmən,ship\ *n* : art or practice of writing

pen·nant \'penənt\ *n* : nautical or championship flag

pen·ny \'penē\ *n, pl* **-nies** \-ēz\ *or* **pence** \'pens\ **1** : monetary unit equal to 1/100 pound **2** *pl* **-nies** : cent — **pen·ni·less** \'peniləs\ *adj*

pen·sion \'penchən\ *n* : retirement income ∼ *vb* : pay a pension to — **pen·sion·er** *n*

pen·sive \'pensiv\ *adj* : thoughtful — **pen·sive·ly** *adv*

pent \'pent\ *adj* : confined

pent·a·gon \'pentə,gän\ *n* : 5-sided polygon — **pen·tag·o·nal** \pen-'tagənᵊl\ *adj*

pen·tam·e·ter \pen'tamətər\ *n* : line of verse containing 5 metrical feet

pent·house \'pent,haùs\ *n* : rooftop apartment

pen·u·ry \'penyərē\ *n* **1** : poverty **2** : thrifty or stingy manner — **pe·nu·ri·ous** \pə'nùreəs, -'nyùr-\ *adj*

pe·on \'pē,än, -ən\ *n, pl* **-ons** *or* **-o·nes** \pā'ōnēz\ : landless laborer in Spanish America — **pe·on·age** \-ənij\ *n*

pe·o·ny \'pēənē\ *n, pl* **-nies** : garden plant having large flowers

peo·ple \'pēpəl\ *n, pl* **people 1** *pl* : human beings in general **2** *pl* : human beings in a certain group (as a family) or community **3** *pl* **peoples** : tribe, nation, or race ∼ *vb* **-pled; -pling** : constitute the population of

pep \'pep\ *n* : brisk energy ∼ *vb* **pepped; pep·ping** : put pep into — **pep·py** *adj*

pep·per \'pepər\ *n* **1** : pungent seasoning from the berry (**peppercorn**) of a shrub **2** : vegetable grown for its hot or sweet fruit ∼ *vb* : season with pepper — **pep·pery** \-ərē\ *adj*

pep·per·mint \-,mint, -mənt\ *n* : pungent aromatic mint

pep·per·o·ni \,pepə'rōnē\ *n* : spicy beef and pork sausage

pep·tic \'peptik\ *adj* : relating to digestion or the effect of digestive juices

per \'pər\ *prep* **1** : by means of **2** : for each **3** : according to

per·am·bu·late \pə'rambyə,lāt\ *vb* **-lat·ed; -lat·ing** : walk — **per·am·bu·la·tion** \-,rambyə'lāshən\ *n*

per•cale \ˌpər'kāl, 'pər-ˌ; ˌpər'kal\ *n* : fine woven cotton cloth

per•ceive \pər'sēv\ *vb* **-ceived; -ceiving** **1** : realize **2** : become aware of through the senses — **per•ceiv•able** *adj*

per•cent \pər'sent\ *adv* : in each hundred ~ *n, pl* **-cent** *or* **-cents** **1** : one part in a hundred **2** : percentage

per•cent•age \pər'sentij\ *n* : part expressed in hundredths

per•cen•tile \pər'sen,tīl\ *n* : a standing on a scale of 0–100

per•cep•ti•ble \pər'septəbəl\ *adj* : capable of being perceived — **per•cep•ti•bly** \-blē\ *adv*

per•cep•tion \pər'sepshən\ *n* **1** : act or result of perceiving **2** : ability to understand

per•cep•tive \pər'septiv\ *adj* : showing keen perception — **per•cep•tive•ly** *adv*

¹**perch** \'pərch\ *n* : roost for birds ~ *vb* : roost

²**perch** *n, pl* **perch** *or* **perch•es** : freshwater spiny-finned food fish

per•co•late \'pərkə,lāt\ *vb* **-lat•ed; -lat•ing** : trickle or filter down through a substance — **per•co•la•tor** \-ˌlātər\ *n*

per•cus•sion \pər'kəshən\ *n* **1** : sharp blow **2** : musical instrument sounded by striking

pe•remp•to•ry \pə'remptərē\ *adj* **1** : imperative **2** : domineering — **pe•remp•to•ri•ly** \-tərəlē\ *adv*

pe•ren•ni•al \pə'renēəl\ *adj* **1** : present at all seasons **2** : continuing from year to year **3** : recurring regularly ~ *n* : perennial plant — **pe•ren•ni•al•ly** *adv*

per•fect \'pərfikt\ *adj* **1** : being without fault or defect **2** : exact **3** : complete ~ \pər'fekt\ *vb* : make perfect — **per•fect•ibil•i•ty** \pərˌfektə'bilətē\ *n* — **per•fect•ible** \pər'fektəbəl\ *adj* — **per•fect•ly** *adv* — **per•fect•ness** *n*

per•fec•tion \pər'fekshən\ *n* **1** : quality or state of being perfect **2** : highest degree of excellence — **per•fec•tion•ist** \-shənist\ *n*

per•fid•i•ous \pər'fidēəs\ *adj* : treacherous — **per•fid•i•ous•ly** *adv*

per•fo•rate \'pərfə,rāt\ *vb* **-rat•ed; -rat•ing** : make a hole in — **per•fo•ra•tion** \ˌpərfə'rāshən\ *n*

per•force \pər'fōrs\ *adv* : of necessity

per•form \pər'fȯrm\ *vb* **1** : carry out **2** : do in a set manner **3** : give a performance — **per•form•er** *n*

per•for•mance \pər'fȯrˌməns\ *n* **1** : act or process of performing **2** : public presentation

per•fume \'pərˌfyüm, pər'-\ *n* **1** : pleasant odor **2** : something that gives a scent ~ \pər'-, 'pərˌ-\ *vb* **-fumed; -fum•ing** : add scent to

per•func•to•ry \pər'fəŋktərē\ *adj* : done merely as a duty — **per•func•to•ri•ly** \-tərəlē\ *adv*

per•haps \pər'haps\ *adv* : possibly but not certainly

per•il \'perəl\ *n* : danger — **per•il•ous** *adj* — **per•il•ous•ly** *adv*

pe•rim•e•ter \pə'rimətər\ *n* : outer boundary of a body or figure

pe•ri•od \'pirēəd\ *n* **1** : punctuation mark . used esp. to mark the end of a declarative sentence or an abbreviation **2** : division of time **3** : stage in a process or development

pe•ri•od•ic \ˌpirē'ädik\ *adj* : occurring at regular intervals — **pe•ri•od•i•cal•ly** *adv*

pe•ri•od•i•cal \ˌpirē'ädikəl\ *n* : newspaper or magazine

pe•riph•ery \pə'rifərē\ *n, pl* **-er•ies** : outer boundary — **pe•riph•er•al** \-ərəl\ *adj*

peri•scope \'perə,skōp\ *n* : optical instrument for viewing from a submarine

per•ish \'perish\ *vb* : die or spoil — **per•ish•able** \-əbəl\ *adj or n*

per•ju•ry \'pərjərē\ *n* : lying under oath — **per•jure** \'pərjər\ *vb* — **per•jur•er** *n*

¹**perk** \'pərk\ *vb* **1** : thrust (as the head) up jauntily **2** : freshen **3** : gain vigor or spirit — **perky** *adj*

²**perk** *vb* : percolate

³**perk** *n* : privilege or benefit in addition to regular pay

per•ma•nent \'pərmənənt\ *adj* : lasting ~ *n* : hair wave — **per•ma•nence** \-nəns\ *n* — **per•ma•nent•ly** *adv*

per•me•able \'pərmēəbəl\ *adj* : permitting fluids to seep through — **per•me•a•bil•i•ty** \ˌpərmēə'bilətē\ *n*

per•me•ate \'pərmē,āt\ *vb* **-at•ed; -at•ing** **1** : seep through **2** : pervade — **per•me•ation** \ˌpərmē'āshən\ *n*

per•mis•si•ble \pər'misəbəl\ *adj* : that may be permitted

per·mis·sion \pər'mishən\ *n* : formal consent

per·mis·sive \pər'misiv\ *adj* : granting freedom esp. to excess — **per·miss·ive·ly** *adv* — **per·mis·sive·ness** *n*

per·mit \pər'mit\ *vb* **-tt-** 1 : approve 2 : make possible ~ \'pər₁-, pər'-\ *n* : license

per·ni·cious \pər'nishəs\ *adj* : very harmful — **per·ni·cious·ly** *adv*

per·ox·ide \pə'räk₁sīd\ *n* : compound (as hydrogen peroxide) in which oxygen is joined to oxygen

per·pen·dic·u·lar \₁pərpən'dikyələr\ *adj* 1 : vertical 2 : meeting at a right angle — **perpendicular** *n* — **per·pen·dic·u·lar·i·ty** \-₁dikyə'larətē\ *n* — **per·pen·dic·u·lar·ly** *adv*

per·pe·trate \'pərpə₁trāt\ *vb* **-trat·ed; -trat·ing** : be guilty of doing — **per·pe·tra·tion** \₁pərpə'trāshən\ *n* — **per·pe·tra·tor** \'pərpə₁trātər\ *n*

per·pet·u·al \pər'pechəwəl\ *adj* 1 : continuing forever 2 : occurring continually — **per·pet·u·al·ly** *adv* — **per·pe·tu·ity** \₁pərpə'tüətē, -'tyü-\ *n*

per·pet·u·ate \pər'pechə₁wāt\ *vb* **-at·ed; -at·ing** : make perpetual — **per·pet·u·a·tion** \-₁pechə'wāshən\ *n*

per·plex \pər'pleks\ *vb* : confuse — **per·plex·i·ty** \-ətē\ *n*

per·se·cute \'pərsi₁kyüt\ *vb* **-cut·ed; -cut·ing** : harass, afflict — **per·se·cu·tion** \₁pərsi'kyüshən\ *n* — **per·se·cu·tor** \'pərsi₁kyütər\ *n*

per·se·vere \₁pərsə'vir\ *vb* **-vered; -ver·ing** : persist — **per·se·ver·ance** \-'virəns\ *n*

per·sist \pər'sist, -'zist\ *vb* 1 : go on resolutely in spite of difficulties 2 : continue to exist — **per·sis·tence** \-'sistəns, -'zis-\ *n* — **per·sis·ten·cy** \-tənsē\ *n* — **per·sis·tent** \-tənt\ *adj* — **per·sis·tent·ly** *adv*

per·son \'pərsᵊn\ *n* 1 : human being 2 : human being's body or individuality 3 : reference to the speaker, one spoken to, or one spoken of

per·son·able \'pərsᵊnəbəl\ *adj* : having a pleasing personality

per·son·age \'pərsᵊnij₁\ *n* : person of rank or distinction

per·son·al \'pərsᵊnəl\ *adj* 1 : relating to a particular person 2 : done in person 3 : affecting one's body 4 : offensive to a certain individual — **per·son·al·ly** *adv*

per·son·al·i·ty \₁pərsᵊn'alətē\ *n, pl* **-ties** 1 : manner and disposition of an individual 2 : distinctive or well-known person

per·son·al·ize \'pərsᵊnə₁līz\ *vb* **-ized; -iz·ing** : mark as belonging to a particular person

per·son·i·fy \pər'sänə₁fī\ *vb* **-fied; -fy·ing** 1 : represent as a human being 2 : be the embodiment of — **per·son·i·fi·ca·tion** \-₁sänəfə'kāshən\ *n*

per·son·nel \₁pərsᵊn'el\ *n* : body of persons employed

per·spec·tive \pər'spektiv\ *n* 1 : apparent depth and distance in painting 2 : view of things in their true relationship or importance

per·spi·ca·cious \₁pərspə'kāshəs\ *adj* : showing keen understanding or discernment — **per·spi·cac·i·ty** \-'kasətē\ *n*

per·spire \pər'spīr\ *vb* **-spired; -spir·ing** : sweat — **per·spi·ra·tion** \₁pərspə'rāshən\ *n*

per·suade \pər'swād\ *vb* **-suad·ed; -suad·ing** : win over to a belief or course of action by argument or entreaty — **per·sua·sion** \pər'swāzhən\ *n* — **per·sua·sive** \-'swāsiv, -ziv\ *adj* — **per·sua·sive·ly** *adv* — **per·sua·sive·ness** *n*

pert \'pərt\ *adj* : flippant or irreverent

per·tain \pər'tān\ *vb* 1 : belong 2 : relate

per·ti·nent \'pərtᵊnənt\ *adj* : relevant — **per·ti·nence** \-əns\ *n*

per·turb \pər'tərb\ *vb* : make uneasy — **per·tur·ba·tion** \₁pərtər'bāshən\ *n*

pe·ruse \pə'rüz\ *vb* **-rused; -rus·ing** : read attentively — **pe·rus·al** \-'rüzəl\ *n*

per·vade \pər'vād\ *vb* **-vad·ed; -vad·ing** : spread through every part of — **per·va·sive** \-'vāsiv, -ziv\ *adj*

per·verse \pər'vərs\ *adj* 1 : corrupt 2 : unreasonably contrary — **per·verse·ly** *adv* — **per·verse·ness** *n* — **per·ver·sion** \pər'vərzhən\ *n* — **per·ver·si·ty** \-'vərsətē\ *n*

per·vert \pər'vərt\ *vb* : corrupt or distort ~ \'pər₁-\ *n* : one that is perverted

pe·so \'pāsō\ *n, pl* **-sos** : monetary unit (as of Mexico)

pes·si·mism \'pesə₁mizəm\ *n* : inclination to expect the worst — **pes·si·mist** \-mist\ *n* — **pes·si·mis·tic** \₁pesə'mistik\ *adj*

pest \'pest\ *n* **1** : nuisance **2** : plant or animal detrimental to humans or their crops — **pes·ti·cide** \'pestə‚sīd\ *n*

pes·ter \'pestər\ *vb* **-tered; -ter·ing** : harass with petty matters

pes·ti·lence \'pestələns\ *n* : plague — **pes·ti·lent** \-lənt\ *adj*

pes·tle \'pesəl, 'pest'l\ *n* : implement for grinding substances in a mortar

pet \'pet\ *n* **1** : domesticated animal kept for pleasure **2** : favorite ~ *vb* **-tt-** : stroke gently or lovingly

pet·al \'pet'l\ *n* : modified leaf of a flower head

pe·tite \pə'tēt\ *adj* : having a small trim figure

pe·ti·tion \pə'tishən\ *n* : formal written request ~ *vb* : make a request — **pe·ti·tion·er** *n*

pet·ri·fy \'petrə‚fī\ *vb* **-fied; -fy·ing 1** : change into stony material **2** : make rigid or inactive (as from fear) — **pet·ri·fac·tion** \‚petrə'fakshən\ *n*

pe·tro·leum \pə'trōlēəm\ *n* : raw oil obtained from the ground

pet·ti·coat \'petē‚kōt\ *n* : skirt worn under a dress

pet·ty \'petē\ *adj* **-ti·er; -est 1** : minor **2** : of no importance **3** : narrow-minded or mean — **pet·ti·ly** \'pet'lē\ *adv* — **pet·ti·ness** *n*

petty officer *n* : subordinate officer in the navy or coast guard

pet·u·lant \'pechələnt\ *adj* : irritable — **pet·u·lance** \-ləns\ *n* — **pet·u·lant·ly** *adv*

pe·tu·nia \pi'tünyə, -'tyü-\ *n* : tropical herb with bright flowers

pew \'pyü\ *n* : bench with a back used in a church

pew·ter \'pyütər\ *n* : alloy of tin used for household utensils

pH \‚pē'āch\ *n* : number expressing relative acidity and alkalinity

pha·lanx \'fā‚laŋks\ *n, pl* **-lanx·es** *or* **-lan·ges** \fə'lan‚jēz\ **1** : body (as of troops) in compact formation **2** *pl* **phalanges** : digital bone of the hand or foot

phal·lus \'faləs\ *n, pl* **-li** \'fal‚ī\ *or* **-lus·es** : penis — **phal·lic** *adj*

phantasy *var of* FANTASY

phan·tom \'fantəm\ *n* : something that only appears to be real — **phantom** *adj*

pha·raoh \'ferō, 'fārō\ *n* : ruler of ancient Egypt

phar·ma·ceu·ti·cal \‚färmə'sütikəl\ *adj* : relating to pharmacy or the making and selling of medicinal drugs — **pharmaceutical** *n*

phar·ma·col·o·gy \‚färmə'käləjē\ *n* : science of drugs esp. as related to medicinal uses — **phar·ma·co·log·i·cal** \-ikəl\ *adj* — **phar·ma·col·o·gist** \-'käləjist\ *n*

phar·ma·cy \'färməsē\ *n, pl* **-cies 1** : art or practice of preparing and dispensing medical drugs **2** : drugstore — **phar·ma·cist** \-sist\ *n*

phar·ynx \'fariŋks\ *n, pl* **pha·ryn·ges** \fə'rin‚jēz\ : space behind the mouth into which the nostrils, esophagus, and windpipe open — **pha·ryn·ge·al** \fə'rinjəl, ‚farən'jēəl\ *adj*

phase \'fāz\ *n* **1** : particular appearance or stage in a recurring series of changes **2** : stage in a process — **phase in** *vb* : introduce in stages — **phase out** *vb* : discontinue gradually

pheas·ant \'fez'nt\ *n, pl* **-ant** *or* **-ants** : long-tailed brilliantly colored game bird

phe·nom·e·non \fi'nämə‚nän, -nən\ *n, pl* **-na** \-nə\ *or* **-nons 1** : observable fact or event **2** *pl* **-nons** : prodigy — **phe·nom·e·nal** \-'nämən'l\ *adj*

phi·lan·der·er \fə'landərər\ *n* : one who makes love without serious intent

phi·lan·thro·py \fə'lanthrəpē\ *n, pl* **-pies** : charitable act or gift or an organization that distributes such gifts — **phil·an·throp·ic** \‚filən'thräpik\ *adj* — **phi·lan·thro·pist** \fə'lanthrəpist\ *n*

phi·lat·e·ly \fə'lat'lē\ *n* : collection and study of postage stamps — **phi·lat·e·list** \-'list\ *n*

phi·lis·tine \'filə‚stēn, fə'listən\ *n* : one who is smugly indifferent to intellectual or artistic values — **philistine** *adj*

philo·den·dron \‚filə'dendrən\ *n, pl* **-drons** *or* **-dra** \-drə\ : plant grown for its showy leaves

phi·los·o·pher \fə'läsəfər\ *n* **1** : reflective thinker **2** : student of philosophy

phi·los·o·phy \fə'läsəfē\ *n, pl* **-phies 1** : critical study of fundamental beliefs **2** : sciences and liberal arts exclusive of medicine, law, and theology **3** : system of ideas **4** : sum of personal convictions — **phil·o·soph·ic** \‚filə'säfik\, **phil·o·soph·i-**

cal \-ikəl\ *adj* — **phil•o•soph•i•cal•ly** \-klē\ *adv* — **phi•los•o•phize** \fə'läsə,fīz\ *vb*

phle•bi•tis \fli'bītəs\ *n* : inflammation of a vein

phlegm \'flem\ *n* : thick mucus in the nose and throat

phlox \'fläks\ *n, pl* **phlox** *or* **phlox•es** : herb grown for its flower clusters

pho•bia \'fōbēə\ *n* : irrational persistent fear

phoe•nix \'fēniks\ *n* : legendary bird held to burn itself to death and rise fresh and young from its ashes

phone \'fōn\ *n* : telephone ∼ *vb* **phoned; phon•ing** : call on a telephone

pho•neme \'fō,nēm\ *n* : basic distinguishable unit of speech — **pho•ne•mic** \fō'nēmik\ *adj*

pho•net•ics \fə'netiks\ *n* : study of speech sounds — **pho•net•ic** \-ik\ *adj* — **pho•ne•ti•cian** \,fōnə'tishən\ *n*

pho•nics \'fäniks\ *n* : method of teaching reading by stressing sound values of syllables and words

pho•no•graph \'fōnə,graf\ *n* : instrument that reproduces sounds from a grooved disc

pho•ny, pho•ney \'fōnē\ *adj* **-ni•er; -est** : not sincere or genuine — **phony** *n*

phos•phate \'fäs,fāt\ *n* : chemical salt used in fertilizers — **phos•phat•ic** \fäs'fatik\ *adj*

phos•phor \'fäsfər\ *n* : phosphorescent substance

phos•pho•res•cence \,fäsfə'res⁰ns\ *n* : luminescence from absorbed radiation — **phos•pho•res•cent** \-⁰nt\ *adj*

phos•pho•rus \'fäsfərəs\ *n* : poisonous waxy chemical element — **phos•phor•ic** \fäs'fórik, -'fär-\ *adj* — **phos•pho•rous** \'fäsfərəs, fäs-'fōrəs\ *adj*

pho•to \'fōtō\ *n, pl* **-tos** : photograph — **photo** *vb or adj*

pho•to•copy \'fōtə,käpē\ *n* : photographic copy (as of a printed page) — **photocopy** *vb*

pho•to•elec•tric \,fōtōi'lektrik\ *adj* : relating to an electrical effect due to the interaction of light with matter

pho•to•ge•nic \,fōtə'jenik\ *adj* : suitable for being photographed

pho•to•graph \'fōtə,graf\ *n* : picture taken by photography — **photograph** *vb* — **pho•tog•ra•pher** \fə'tägrəfər\ *n*

pho•tog•ra•phy \fə'tägrəfē\ *n* : process of using light to produce images on a sensitized surface — **pho•to•graph•ic** \,fōtə'grafik\ *adj* — **pho•to•graph•i•cal•ly** *adv*

pho•to•syn•the•sis \,fōtō'sinthəsəs\ *n* : formation of carbohydrates by chlorophyll-containing plants exposed to sunlight — **pho•to•syn•the•size** \-,sīz\ *vb* — **pho•to•syn•thet•ic** \-sin'thetik\ *adj*

phrase \'frāz\ *n* **1** : brief expression **2** : group of related words that express a thought ∼ *vb* **phrased; phras•ing** : express in a particular manner

phrase•ol•o•gy \,frāzē'äləjē\ *n, pl* **-gies** : manner of phrasing

phy•lum \'fīləm\ *n, pl* **-la** \-lə\ : major division of the plant or animal kingdom

phys•i•cal \'fizikəl\ *adj* **1** : relating to nature **2** : material as opposed to mental or spiritual **3** : relating to the body ∼ *n* : medical examination — **phys•i•cal•ly** \-klē\ *adv*

phy•si•cian \fə'zishən\ *n* : doctor of medicine

physician's assistant *n* : person certified to provide basic medical care under a physician's supervision

phys•i•cist \'fizəsist\ *n* : specialist in physics

phys•ics \'fiziks\ *n* : science that deals with matter and motion

phys•i•og•no•my \,fizē'ägnəmē\ *n, pl* **-mies** : facial appearance esp. as a reflection of inner character

phys•i•ol•o•gy \,fizē'äləjē\ *n* : functional processes in an organism — **phys•i•o•log•i•cal** \-ē⁰'läjikəl\, **phys•i•o•log•ic** \-ik\ *adj* — **phys•i•ol•o•gist** \-ē'äləjist\ *n*

phy•sique \fə'zēk\ *n* : build of a person's body

pi \'pī\ *n, pl* **pis** \'pīz\ : symbol π denoting the ratio of the circumference of a circle to its diameter or the ratio itself

pi•a•nist \pē'anist, 'pēənist\ *n* : one who plays the piano

pi•ano \pē'anō\ *n, pl* **-anos** : musical instrument with strings sounded by hammers operated from a keyboard

pi•az•za \pē'azə, -'äz-, -tsə\ *n, pl* **-zas** *or* **-ze** \-tsä\ : public square in a town

pic•a•yune \,pikē'yün\ *adj* : trivial or petty

pic·co·lo \'pikə,lō\ *n, pl* **-los** : small shrill flute

¹**pick** \'pik\ *vb* **1** : break up with a pointed instrument **2** : remove bit by bit **3** : gather by plucking **4** : select **5** : rob **6** : provoke **7** : unlock with a wire **8** : eat sparingly ～ *n* **1** : act of choosing **2** : choicest one — **pick·er** *n* — **pick up** *vb* **1** : improve **2** : put in order

²**pick** *n* : pointed digging tool

pick·ax *n* : pick

pick·er·el \'pikərəl\ *n, pl* **-el** *or* **-els** : small pike

pick·et \'pikət\ *n* **1** : pointed stake (as for a fence) **2** : worker demonstrating on strike ～ *vb* : demonstrate as a picket

pick·le \'pikəl\ *n* **1** : brine or vinegar solution for preserving foods or a food preserved in a pickle **2** : bad state — **pickle** *vb*

pick·pock·et *n* : one who steals from pockets

pick·up \'pik,əp\ *n* **1** : revival or acceleration **2** : light truck with an open body

pic·nic \'pik,nik\ *n* : outing with food usu. eaten in the open ～ *vb* **-nicked; -nick·ing** : go on a picnic

pic·to·ri·al \pik'tōrēəl\ *adj* : relating to pictures

pic·ture \'pikchər\ *n* **1** : representation by painting, drawing, or photography **2** : vivid description **3** : copy **4** : movie ～ *vb* **-tured; -tur·ing** : form a mental image of

pic·tur·esque \,pikchə'resk\ *adj* : attractive enough for a picture

pie \'pī\ *n* : pastry crust and a filling

pie·bald \'pī,bȯld\ *adj* : blotched with white and black

piece \'pēs\ *n* **1** : part of a whole **2** : one of a group or set **3** : single item **4** : product of creative work ～ *vb* **pieced; piec·ing** : join into a whole

piece·meal \'pēs,mēl\ *adv or adj* : gradually

pied \'pīd\ *adj* : colored in blotches

pier \'pir\ *n* **1** : support for a bridge span **2** : deck or wharf built out over water **3** : pillar

pierce \'pirs\ *vb* **pierced; pierc·ing** **1** : enter or thrust into or through **2** : penetrate **3** : see through

pi·ety \'pīətē\ *n, pl* **-eties** : devotion to religion

pig \'pig\ *n* **1** : young swine **2** : dirty or greedy individual **3** : iron casting — **pig·gish** \-ish\ *adj* — **pig·let** \-lət\ *n* — **pig·pen** *n* — **pig·sty** *n*

pi·geon \'pijən\ *n* : stout-bodied short= legged bird

pi·geon·hole *n* : small open compartment for letters or documents ～ *vb* **1** : place in a pigeonhole **2** : classify

pig·gy·back \'pigē,bak\ *adv or adj* : up on the back and shoulders

pig·head·ed \-'hedəd\ *adj* : stubborn

pig·ment \'pigmənt\ *n* : coloring matter — **pig·men·ta·tion** *n*

pigmy *var of* **PYGMY**

pig·tail *n* : tight braid of hair

¹**pike** \'pīk\ *n, pl* **pike** *or* **pikes** : large freshwater fish

²**pike** *n* : former weapon consisting of a long wooden staff with a steel point

³**pike** *n* : turnpike

pi·laf, pi·laff \pi'läf, 'pē,läf\, **pi·lau** \pi'lȯ, -'lȯ; 'pēlȯ, -lȯ\ *n* : dish of seasoned rice

¹**pile** \'pīl\ *n* : supporting pillar driven into the ground

²**pile** *n* : quantity of things thrown on one another ～ *vb* **piled; pil·ing** : heap up, accumulate

³**pile** *n* : surface of fine hairs or threads — **piled** *adj*

piles \'pīls\ *n pl* : hemorrhoids

pil·fer \'pilfər\ *vb* : steal in small quantities

pil·grim \'pilgrəm\ *n* **1** : one who travels to a shrine or holy place in devotion **2** *cap* : one of the English settlers in America in 1620

pil·grim·age \-grəmij\ *n* : pilgrim's journey

pill \'pil\ *n* : small rounded mass of medicine — **pill·box** *n*

pil·lage \'pilij\ *vb* **-laged; -lag·ing** : loot and plunder — **pillage** *n*

pil·lar \'pilər\ *n* : upright usu. supporting column — **pil·lared** *adj*

pil·lo·ry \'pilərē\ *n, pl* **-ries** : wooden frame for public punishment with holes for the head and hands ～ *vb* **-ried; -ry·ing** **1** : set in a pillory **2** : expose to public scorn

pil·low \'pilō\ *n* : soft cushion for the head — **pil·low·case** *n*

pi·lot \'pīlət\ *n* **1** : helmsman **2** : person licensed to take ships into and out of a port **3** : guide **4** : one that flies an aircraft or spacecraft ∼ *vb* : act as pilot of — **pi•lot•less** *adj*

pi•men•to \pə'mentō\ *n*, *pl* **-tos** *or* **-to** **1** : allspice **2** : pimiento

pi•mien•to \pə'mentō, -'myen-\ *n*, *pl* **-tos** : mild red sweet pepper

pimp \'pimp\ *n* : man who solicits clients for a prostitute — **pimp** *vb*

pim•ple \'pimpəl\ *n* : small inflamed swelling on the skin — **pim•ply** \-pəlē\ *adj*

pin \'pin\ *n* **1** : fastener made of a small pointed piece of wire **2** : ornament or emblem fastened to clothing with a pin **3** : wooden object used as a target in bowling ∼ *vb* **-nn-** **1** : fasten with a pin **2** : hold fast or immobile — **pin•hole** *n*

pin•a•fore \'pinə,fōr\ *n* : sleeveless dress or apron fastened at the back

pin•cer \'pinsər\ *n* **1** *pl* : gripping tool with 2 jaws **2** : pincerlike claw

pinch \'pinch\ *vb* **1** : squeeze between the finger and thumb or between the jaws of a tool **2** : compress painfully **3** : restrict **4** : steal ∼ *n* **1** : emergency **2** : painful effect **3** : act of pinching **4** : very small quantity

pin•cush•ion *n* : cushion for storing pins

¹pine \'pīn\ *n* : evergreen cone-bearing tree or its wood

²pine *vb* **pined; pin•ing** **1** : lose health through distress **2** : yearn for intensely

pine•ap•ple *n* : tropical plant bearing an edible juicy fruit

pin•feath•er *n* : new feather just coming through the skin

¹pin•ion \'pinyən\ *vb* : restrain by binding the arms

²pinion *n* : small gear

¹pink \'piŋk\ *n* **1** : plant with narrow leaves and showy flowers **2** : highest degree

²pink *n* : light red color — **pink** *adj* — **pink•ish** *adj*

pink•eye *n* : contagious eye inflammation

pin•na•cle \'pinikəl\ *n* : highest point

pi•noch•le \'pē,nəkəl\ *n* : card game played with a 48-card deck

pin•point *vb* : locate, hit, or aim with great precision

pint \'pīnt\ *n* : 1/2 quart

pin•to \'pin,tō\ *n*, *pl* **pintos** : spotted horse or pony

pin•worm *n* : small parasitic intestinal worm

pi•o•neer \,pīə'nir\ *n* **1** : one that originates or helps open up a new line of thought or activity **2** : early settler ∼ *vb* : act as a pioneer

pi•ous \'pīəs\ *adj* **1** : conscientious in religious practices **2** : affectedly religious — **pi•ous•ly** *adv*

pipe \'pīp\ *n* **1** : tube that produces music when air is forced through **2** : bagpipe **3** : long tube for conducting a fluid **4** : smoking tool ∼ *vb* **piped;** **pip•ing** **1** : play on a pipe **2** : speak in a high voice **3** : convey by pipes — **pip•er** *n*

pipe•line *n* **1** : line of pipe **2** : channel for information

pip•ing \'pīpiŋ\ *n* **1** : music of pipes **2** : narrow fold of material used to decorate edges or seams

pi•quant \'pēkənt\ *adj* **1** : tangy **2** : provocative or charming — **pi•quan•cy** \-kənsē\ *n*

pique \'pēk\ *n* : resentment ∼ *vb* **piqued; piqu•ing** **1** : offend **2** : arouse by provocation

pi•qué, pi•que \pi'kā\ *n* : durable ribbed clothing fabric

pi•ra•cy \'pīrəsē\ *n*, *pl* **-cies** **1** : robbery on the seas **2** : unauthorized use of another's production or invention

pi•ra•nha \pə'ranyə, -'ränə\ *n* : small So. American fish with sharp teeth

pi•rate \'pīrət\ *n* : one who commits piracy — **pirate** *vb* — **pi•rat•i•cal** \pə-'ratikəl, pī-\ *adj*

pir•ou•ette \,pirə'wet\ *n* : ballet turn on the toe or ball of one foot — **pirouette** *vb*

pis *pl of* PI

pis•ta•chio \pə'stashē,ō, -'stäsh-\ *n*, *pl* **-chios** : small tree bearing a greenish edible seed or its seed

pis•til \'pist°l\ *n* : female reproductive organ in a flower — **pis•til•late** \'pistə,lāt\ *adj*

pis•tol \'pist°l\ *n* : firearm held with one hand

pis•ton \'pistən\ *n* : sliding piece that receives and transmits motion usu. inside a cylinder

¹pit \'pit\ *n* **1** : hole or shaft in the ground **2** : sunken or enclosed place for a special purpose **3** : hell **4** : hollow or indentation ∼ *vb* **-tt-** **1** : form pits in **2** : become marred with pits

²**pit** *n* : stony seed of some fruits ~ *vb* -**tt**- : remove the pit from

pit bull *n* : powerful compact dog bred for fighting

¹**pitch** \'pich\ *n* : resin from conifers — **pitchy** *adj*

²**pitch** *vb* **1** : erect and fix firmly in place **2** : throw **3** : set at a particular tone level **4** : fall headlong ~ *n* **1** : action or manner of pitching **2** : degree of slope **3** : relative highness of a tone **4** : sales talk — **pitched** *adj*

¹**pitch•er** \'pichər\ *n* : container for liquids

²**pitcher** *n* : one that pitches (as in baseball)

pitch•fork *n* : long-handled fork for pitching hay

pit•e•ous \'pitēəs\ *adj* : arousing pity — **pit•e•ous•ly** *adv*

pit•fall \'pit,fȯl\ *n* : hidden danger

pith \'pith\ *n* **1** : spongy plant tissue **2** : essential or meaningful part — **pithy** *adj*

piti•able \'pitēəbəl\ *adj* : pitiful

piti•ful \'pitifəl\ *adj* **1** : arousing or deserving pity **2** : contemptible — **piti•ful•ly** *adv*

pit•tance \'pit°ns\ *n* : small portion or amount

pi•tu•i•tary \pə'tüə,terē, -'tyü-\ *adj* : relating to or being a small gland attached to the brain

pity \'pitē\ *n, pl* **pi•ties** **1** : sympathetic sorrow **2** : something to be regretted ~ *vb* **pit•ied; pity•ing** : feel pity for — **piti•less** *adj* — **piti•less•ly** *adv*

piv•ot \'pivət\ *n* : fixed pin on which something turns ~ *vb* : turn on or as if on a pivot — **piv•ot•al** *adj*

pix•ie, pixy \'piksē\ *n, pl* **pix•ies** : mischievous sprite

piz•za \'pētsə\ *n* : thin pie of bread dough spread with a spiced mixture (as of tomatoes, cheese, and meat)

piz•zazz, pi•zazz \pə'zaz\ *n* : glamour

piz•ze•ria \,pētsə'rēə\ *n* : pizza restaurant

plac•ard \'plakərd, -,ärd\ *n* : poster ~ *vb* : display placards in or on

pla•cate \'plā,kāt, 'plak,āt\ *vb* -**cat•ed; -cat•ing** : appease — **pla•ca•ble** \'plakəbəl, 'plākə-\ *adj*

place \'plās\ *n* **1** : space or room **2** : indefinite area **3** : a particular building, locality, area, or part **4** : relative position in a scale or sequence **5** : seat **6** : job ~ *vb* **placed; plac•ing** **1** : put in a place **2** : identify — **place•ment** *n*

pla•ce•bo \plə'sēbō\ *n, pl* -**bos** : something inactive prescribed as a remedy for its psychological effect

pla•cen•ta \plə'sentə\ *n, pl* -**tas** *or* -**tae** \-,ē\ : structure in a uterus by which a fetus is nourished — **pla•cen•tal** \-'sent°l\ *adj*

plac•id \'plasəd\ *adj* : undisturbed or peaceful — **pla•cid•i•ty** \pla'sidətē\ *n* — **plac•id•ly** *adv*

pla•gia•rize \'plājə,rīz\ *vb* -**rized; -riz•ing** : use (words or ideas) of another as if your own — **pla•gia•rism** \-,rizəm\ *n* — **pla•gia•rist** \-rist\ *n*

plague \'plāg\ *n* **1** : disastrous evil **2** : destructive contagious bacterial disease ~ *vb* **plagued; plagu•ing** **1** : afflict with disease or disaster **2** : harass

plaid \'plad\ *n* : woolen fabric with a pattern of crossing stripes or the pattern itself — **plaid** *adj*

plain \'plān\ *n* : expanse of relatively level treeless country ~ *adj* **1** : lacking ornament **2** : not concealed or disguised **3** : easily understood **4** : frank **5** : not fancy or pretty — **plain•ly** *adv* — **plain•ness** \'plānnəs\ *n*

plain•tiff \'plāntəf\ *n* : complaining party in a lawsuit

plain•tive \'plāntiv\ *adj* : expressive of suffering or woe — **plain•tive•ly** *adv*

plait \'plāt, 'plat\ *n* **1** : pleat **2** : braid of hair or straw — **plait** *vb*

plan \'plan\ *n* **1** : drawing or diagram **2** : method for accomplishing something ~ *vb* -**nn**- **1** : form a plan of **2** : intend — **plan•less** *adj* — **plan•ner** *n*

¹**plane** \'plān\ *vb* **planed; plan•ing** : smooth or level off with a plane ~ *n* : smoothing or shaping tool — **plan•er** *n*

²**plane** *n* **1** : level surface **2** : level of existence, consciousness, or development **3** : airplane ~ *adj* **1** : flat **2** : dealing with flat surfaces or figures

plan•et \'planət\ *n* : celestial body that revolves around the sun — **plan•e•tary** \-ə,terē\ *adj*

plan•e•tar•i•um \,planə'terēəm\ *n, pl* -**iums** *or* -**ia** \-ēə\ : building or room housing a device to project images of celestial bodies

plank \'plaŋk\ *n* **1** : heavy thick board

2 : article in the platform of a political party — **plank•ing** n

plank•ton \'plaŋktən\ n : tiny aquatic animal and plant life — **plank•ton•ic** \plaŋk'tänik\ adj

plant \'plant\ vb **1** : set in the ground to grow **2** : place firmly or forcibly ~ n **1** : living thing without sense organs that cannot move about **2** : land, buildings, and machinery used esp. in manufacture

¹**plan•tain** \'plant°n\ n : short-stemmed herb with tiny greenish flowers

²**plantain** n : banana plant with starchy greenish fruit

plan•ta•tion \plan'tāshən\ n : agricultural estate usu. worked by resident laborers

plant•er \'plantər\ n **1** : plantation owner **2** : plant container

plaque \'plak\ n **1** : commemorative tablet **2** : film layer on a tooth

plas•ma \'plazmə\ n **1** : watery part of blood **2** : highly ionized gas — **plas•mat•ic** \plaz'matik\ adj

plasma TV n : television screen in which cells of plasma emit light upon receiving an electric current

plas•ter \'plastər\ n **1** : medicated dressing **2** : hardening paste for coating walls and ceilings ~ vb : cover with plaster — **plas•ter•er** n

plas•tic \'plastik\ adj : capable of being molded ~ n : material that can be formed into rigid objects, films, or filaments — **plas•tic•i•ty** \plas'tisətē\ n

plate \'plāt\ n **1** : flat thin piece **2** : plated metalware **3** : shallow usu. circular dish **4** : denture or the part of it that fits to the mouth **5** : something printed from an engraving ~ vb **plat•ed; plat•ing** : overlay with metal — **plat•ing** n

pla•teau \pla'tō\ n, pl **-teaus** or **-teaux** \-'tōz\ : large level area of high land

plat•form \'plat‚förm\ n **1** : raised flooring or stage **2** : declaration of principles for a political party

plat•i•num \'plat°nəm\ n : heavy grayish-white metallic chemical element

plat•i•tude \'platə‚tüd, -‚tyüd\ n : trite remark — **plat•i•tu•di•nous** \‚platə-'tüd°nəs, -'tyüd-\ adj

pla•toon \plə'tün\ n : small military unit

platoon sergeant n : noncommissioned officer in the army ranking below a first sergeant

plat•ter \'platər\ n : large serving plate

platy•pus \'platipəs\ n : small aquatic egg-laying mammal

plau•dit \'plódət\ n : act of applause

plau•si•ble \'plózəbəl\ adj : reasonable or believeable — **plau•si•bil•i•ty** \‚plózə'bilətē\ n — **plau•si•bly** \-blē\ adv

play \'plā\ n **1** : action in a game **2** : recreational activity **3** : light or fitful movement **4** : free movement **5** : stage representation of a drama ~ vb **1** : engage in recreation **2** : move or toy with aimlessly **3** : perform music **4** : act in a drama — **play•act•ing** n — **play•er** n — **play•ful** \-fəl\ adj — **play•ful•ly** adv — **play•ful•ness** n — **play•pen** n — **play•suit** n — **play•thing** n

play•ground n : place for children to play

play•house n **1** : theater **2** : small house for children to play in

playing card n : one of a set of 24 to 78 cards marked to show its rank and suit and used to play a game of cards

play•mate n : companion in play

play•off n : contest or series of contests to determine a champion

play•wright \-‚rīt\ n : writer of plays

pla•za \'plazə, 'pläz-\ n **1** : public square **2** : shopping mall

plea \'plē\ n **1** : defendant's answer to charges **2** : urgent request

plead \'plēd\ vb **plead•ed** \'plēdəd\ or **pled** \'pled\; **plead•ing 1** : argue for or against in court **2** : answer to a charge or indictment **3** : appeal earnestly — **plead•er** n

pleas•ant \'plez°nt\ adj **1** : giving pleasure **2** : marked by pleasing behavior or appearance — **pleas•ant•ly** adv — **pleas•ant•ness** n

pleas•ant•ries \-°ntrēz\ n pl : pleasant and casual conversation

please \'plēz\ vb **pleased; pleas•ing 1** : give pleasure or satisfaction to **2** : desire or intend

pleas•ing \'plēzin\ adj : giving pleasure — **pleas•ing•ly** adv

plea•sur•able \'plezhərəbəl\ adj : pleasant — **plea•sur•ably** \-blē\ adv

plea•sure \'plezhər\ n **1** : desire or inclination **2** : enjoyment **3** : source of delight

pleat \'plēt\ *vb* : arrange in pleats ~ *n* : fold in cloth

ple·be·ian \pli'bēən\ *n* : one of the common people ~ *adj* : ordinary

pledge \'plej\ *n* **1** : something given as security **2** : promise or vow ~ *vb* **pledged; pledg·ing 1** : offer as or bind by a pledge **2** : promise

ple·na·ry \'plēnərē, 'plen-\ *adj* : full

pleni·po·ten·tia·ry \,plenəpə'tenchərē, -'tenchē,erē\ *n* : diplomatic agent having full authority — **plenipoten·tiary** *adj*

plen·i·tude \'plenə,tüd, -,tyüd\ *n* **1** : completeness **2** : abundance

plen·te·ous \'plentēəs\ *adj* : existing in plenty

plen·ty \'plentē\ *n* : more than adequate number or amount — **plen·ti·ful** \'plentifəl\ *adj* — **plen·ti·ful·ly** *adv*

pleth·o·ra \'plethərə\ *n* : excess

pleu·ri·sy \'plùrəsē\ *n* : inflammation of the chest membrane

pli·able \'plīəbəl\ *adj* : flexible

pli·ant \'plīənt\ *adj* : flexible — **pli·an·cy** \-ənsē\ *n*

pli·ers \'plīərz\ *n pl* : pinching or gripping tool

¹**plight** \'plīt\ *vb* : pledge

²**plight** *n* : bad state

plod \'pläd\ *vb* **-dd- 1** : walk heavily or slowly **2** : work laboriously and monotonously — **plod·der** *n* — **plod·ding·ly** \-iŋlē\ *adv*

plot \'plät\ *n* **1** : small area of ground **2** : ground plan **3** : main story development (as of a book or movie) **4** : secret plan for doing something ~ *vb* **-tt- 1** : make a plot or plan of **2** : plan or contrive — **plot·ter** *n*

plo·ver \'pləvər, 'plōvər\ *n, pl* **-ver** or **-vers** : shorebird related to the sandpiper

plow, plough \'plaù\ *n* **1** : tool used to turn soil **2** : device for pushing material aside ~ *vb* **1** : break up with a plow **2** : cleave or move through like a plow — **plow·man** \-mən, -,man\ *n*

plow·share \-,sher\ *n* : plow part that cuts the earth

ploy \'plòi\ *n* : clever maneuver

pluck \'plək\ *vb* **1** : pull off or out **2** : tug or twitch ~ *n* **1** : act or instance of plucking **2** : spirit or courage

plucky \'pləkē\ *adj* **pluck·i·er; -est** : courageous or spirited

plug \'pləg\ *n* **1** : something for seal-ing an opening **2** : electrical connector at the end of a cord **3** : piece of favorable publicity ~ *vb* **-gg- 1** : stop or make tight or secure by inserting a plug **2** : publicize

plum \'pləm\ *n* **1** : smooth-skinned juicy fruit **2** : fine reward

plum·age \'plümij\ *n* : feathers of a bird — **plum·aged** \-mijd\ *adj*

plumb \'pləm\ *n* : weight on the end of a line (**plumb line**) to show vertical direction ~ *adv* **1** : vertically **2** : completely ~ *vb* : sound or test with a plumb ~ *adj* : vertical

plumb·er \'pləmər\ *n* : one who repairs usu. water pipes and fixtures

plumb·ing \'pləmiŋ\ *n* : system of water pipes in a building

plume \'plüm\ *n* : large, conspicuous, or showy feather ~ *vb* **plumed; plum·ing 1** : provide or deck with feathers **2** : indulge in pride — **plumed** \'plümd\ *adj*

plum·met \'pləmət\ *vb* : drop straight down

¹**plump** \'pləmp\ *vb* : drop suddenly or heavily ~ *adv* **1** : straight down **2** : in a direct manner

²**plump** *adj* : having a full rounded form — **plump·ness** *n*

plun·der \'pləndər\ *vb* : rob or take goods by force (as in war) ~ *n* : something taken in plundering — **plun·der·er** *n*

plunge \'plənj\ *vb* **plunged; plung·ing 1** : thrust or drive with force **2** : leap or dive into water **3** : begin an action suddenly **4** : dip or move suddenly forward or down ~ *n* : act or instance of plunging — **plung·er** *n*

plu·ral \'plùrəl\ *adj* : relating to a word form denoting more than one — **plural** *n*

plu·ral·i·ty \plù'ralətē\ *n, pl* **-ties** : greatest number of votes cast when not a majority

plu·ral·ize \'plùrə,līz\ *vb* **-ized; -iz·ing** : make plural — **plu·ral·i·za·tion** \,plùrələ'zāshən\ *n*

plus \'pləs\ *prep* : with the addition of ~ *n* **1** : sign + (**plus sign**) in mathematics to indicate addition **2** : added or positive quantity **3** : advantage ~ *adj* : being more or in addition ~ *conj* : and

plush \'pləsh\ *n* : fabric with a long pile ~ *adj* : luxurious — **plush·ly** *adv* — **plushy** *adj* — **plush·ness** *n*

plu·toc·ra·cy \plü'täkrəsē\ *n, pl* **-cies**
1 : government by the wealthy **2** : a controlling class of the wealthy — **plu·to·crat** \'plütə,krat\ *n* — **plu·to·crat·ic** \,plütə'kratik\ *adj*

plu·to·ni·um \plü'tōnēəm\ *n* : radioactive chemical element

¹ply \'plī\ *n, pl* **plies** : fold, thickness, or strand of which something is made

²ply *vb* **plied; ply·ing 1** : use or work at **2** : keep supplying something to **3** : travel regularly usu. by sea

ply·wood *n* : sheets of wood glued and pressed together

pneu·mat·ic \nu'matik, nyu-\ *adj* **1** : moved by air pressure **2** : filled with compressed air — **pneu·mat·i·cal·ly** *adv*

pneu·mo·nia \nu'mōnyə, nyu-\ *n* : inflammatory lung disease

¹poach \'pōch\ *vb* : cook in simmering liquid

²poach *vb* : hunt or fish illegally — **poach·er** *n*

pock \'päk\ *n* : small swelling on the skin or its scar — **pock·mark** *n* — **pock·marked** *adj*

pock·et \'päkət\ *n* **1** : small open bag sewn into a garment **2** : container or receptacle **3** : isolated area or group ∼ *vb* : put in a pocket — **pock·et·ful** \-,ful\ *n*

pock·et·book *n* **1** : purse **2** : financial resources

pock·et·knife *n* : knife with a folding blade carried in the pocket

pod \'päd\ *n* **1** : dry fruit that splits open when ripe **2** : compartment on a ship or craft

po·di·a·try \pə'dīətrē, pō-\ *n* : branch of medicine dealing with the foot — **po·di·a·trist** \pə'dīətrist, pō-\ *n*

po·di·um \'pōdēəm\ *n, pl* **-di·ums** *or* **-dia** \-ēə\ : dais

po·em \'pōəm\ *n* : composition in verse

po·et \'pōət\ *n* : writer of poetry

po·et·ry \'pōətrē\ *n* **1** : metrical writing **2** : poems — **po·et·ic** \pō'etik\, **po·et·i·cal** \-ikəl\ *adj*

po·grom \'pōgrəm, pə'gräm, 'pägrəm\ *n* : organized massacre

poi·gnant \'póinyənt\ *adj* **1** : emotionally painful **2** : deeply moving — **poi·gnan·cy** \-nyənsē\ *n*

poin·set·tia \póin'setēə, -'setə\ *n* : showy tropical American plant

point \'póint\ *n* **1** : individual often es-

sential detail **2** : purpose **3** : particular place, time, or stage **4** : sharp end **5** : projecting piece of land **6** : dot or period **7** : division of the compass **8** : unit of counting ∼ *vb* **1** : sharpen **2** : indicate direction by extending a finger **3** : direct attention to **4** : aim — **point·ed·ly** \-ədlē\ *adv* — **point·less** *adj*

point-blank *adj* **1** : so close to a target that a missile fired goes straight to it **2** : direct — **point-blank** *adv*

point·er \'póintər\ *n* **1** : one that points out **2** : large short-haired hunting dog **3** : hint or tip

poise \'póiz\ *vb* **poised; pois·ing** : balance ∼ *n* : self-possessed calmness

poi·son \'póiz²n\ *n* : chemical that can injure or kill ∼ *vb* **1** : injure or kill with poison **2** : apply poison to **3** : affect destructively — **poi·son·er** *n* — **poi·son·ous** \'póiz²nəs\ *adj*

poke \'pōk\ *vb* **poked; pok·ing 1** : prod **2** : dawdle ∼ *n* : quick thrust

¹pok·er \'pōkər\ *n* : rod for stirring a fire

²poker *n* : card game for gambling

po·lar \'pōlər\ *adj* : relating to a geographical or magnetic pole

po·lar·ize \'pōlə,rīz\ *vb* **-ized; -iz·ing 1** : cause to have magnetic poles **2** : break up into opposing groups — **po·lar·i·za·tion** \,pōlərə'zāshən\ *n*

¹pole \'pōl\ *n* : long slender piece of wood or metal

²pole *n* **1** : either end of the earth's axis **2** : battery terminal **3** : either end of a magnet

pole·cat \'pōl,kat\ *n, pl* **polecats** *or* **polecat 1** : European carnivorous mammal **2** : skunk

po·lem·ics \pə'lemiks\ *n sing or pl* : practice of disputation — **po·lem·i·cal** \-ikəl\ *adj* — **po·lem·i·cist** \-əsist\ *n*

po·lice \pə'lēs\ *n, pl* **police 1** : department of government that keeps public order and enforces the laws **2** : members of the police ∼ *vb* **-liced; -lic·ing** : regulate and keep in order — **po·lice·man** \-mən\ *n* — **po·lice·wom·an** *n*

police officer *n* : member of the police

¹pol·i·cy \'päləsē\ *n, pl* **-cies** : course of action selected to guide decisions

²policy *n, pl* **-cies** : insurance contract — **pol·i·cy·hold·er** *n*

po•lio \'pōlē,ō\ *n* : poliomyelitis — **po-lio** *adj*

po•lio•my•eli•tis \-,mīə'lītəs\ *n* : acute virus disease of the spinal cord

pol•ish \'pälish\ *vb* **1** : make smooth and glossy **2** : develop or refine ~ *n* **1** : shiny surface **2** : refinement

po•lite \pə'līt\ *adj* **-lit•er; -est** : marked by courteous social conduct — **po-lite•ly** *adv* — **po•lite•ness** *n*

pol•i•tic \'pälə,tik\ *adj* : shrewdly tact-ful

politically correct *adj* : seeking to avoid offending members of a differ-ent group

pol•i•tics \'pälə,tiks\ *n sing or pl* : practice of government and manag-ing of public affairs — **po•lit•i•cal** \pə'litikəl\ *adj* — **po•lit•i•cal•ly** *adv* — **pol•i•ti•cian** \,pälə'tishən\ *n*

pol•ka \'pōlkə\ *n* : lively couple dance — **polka** *vb*

pol•ka dot \'pōkə,dät\ *n* : one of a se-ries of regular dots in a pattern

poll \'pōl\ *n* **1** : head **2** : place where votes are cast — usu. pl. **3** : a sam-pling of opinion ~ *vb* **1** : cut off **2** : receive or record votes **3** : question in a poll — **poll•ster** \-stər\ *n*

pol•len \'pälən\ *n* : spores of a seed plant

pol•li•na•tion \,pälə'nāshən\ *n* : the carrying of pollen to fertilize the seed — **pol•li•nate** \'pälə,nāt\ *vb* — **pol-li•na•tor** \-ər\ *n*

pol•lute \pə'lüt\ *vb* **-lut•ed; -lut•ing** : contaminating with waste products — **pol•lut•ant** \-'lüt°nt\ *n* — **pol•lut-er** *n* — **pol•lu•tion** \-'lüshən\ *n*

pol•ly•wog, pol•li•wog \'pälē,wäg\ *n* : tadpole

po•lo \'pōlō\ *n* : game played by 2 teams on horseback using long-handled mallets to drive a wooden ball

pol•ter•geist \'pōltər,gīst\ *n* : mischie-vous ghost

pol•troon \päl'trün\ *n* : coward

poly•es•ter \'pälē,estər\ *n* : synthetic fiber

po•lyg•a•my \pə'ligəmē\ *n* : marriage to several spouses at the same time — **po•lyg•a•mist** \-mist\ *n* — **po•lyg•a-mous** \-məs\ *adj*

poly•gon \'päli,gän\ *n* : closed plane figure with straight sides

poly•mer \'päləmər\ *n* : chemical com-pound of molecules joined in long strings — **po•lym•er•i•za•tion** \pə-,limərə'zāshən\ *n* — **po•lym•er•ize** \pə'limə,rīz\ *vb*

poly•tech•nic \,päli'teknik\ *adj* : re-lating to many technical arts or ap-plied sciences

poly•the•ism \'pälithē,izəm\ *n* : wor-ship of many gods — **poly•the•ist** \-,thēist\ *adj or n*

poly•un•sat•u•rat•ed \,päle,ən'sachə-,rātəd\ *adj* : having many double or triple bonds in a molecule

pome•gran•ate \'päm,granət, 'pämə-\ *n* : tropical reddish fruit with many seeds

pom•mel \'pəməl, 'päm-\ *n* **1** : knob on the hilt of a sword **2** : knob at the front of a saddle ~ \'pəməl\ *vb* **-meled** *or* **-melled; -mel•ing** *or* **-mel-ling** : pummel

pomp \'pämp\ *n* **1** : brilliant display **2** : ostentation

pomp•ous \'pämpəs\ *adj* : pretentiously dignified — **pom•pos•i•ty** \päm-'päsətē\ *n* — **pomp•ous•ly** *adv*

pon•cho \'pänchō\ *n, pl* **-chos** : blan-ketlike cloak

pond \'pänd\ *n* : small body of water

pon•der \'pändər\ *vb* : consider

pon•der•ous \'pändərəs\ *adj* **1** : very heavy **2** : clumsy **3** : oppressively dull

pon•tiff \'päntəf\ *n* : pope — **pon•tif•i-cal** \pän'tifikəl\ *adj*

pon•tif•i•cate \pän'tifə,kāt\ *vb* **-cat-ed; -cat•ing** : talk pompously

pon•toon \pän'tün\ *n* : flat-bottomed boat or float

po•ny \'pōnē\ *n, pl* **-nies** : small horse

po•ny•tail \-,tāl\ *n* : hair arrangement like the tail of a pony

poo•dle \'püd°l\ *n* : dog with a curly coat

¹**pool** \'pül\ *n* **1** : small body of water **2** : puddle

²**pool** *n* **1** : amount contributed by par-ticipants in a joint venture **2** : game of pocket billiards ~ *vb* : combine in a common fund

poor \'pur, 'pōr\ *adj* **1** : lacking mate-rial possessions **2** : less than adequate **3** : arousing pity **4** : unfavorable — **poor•ly** *adv*

¹**pop** \'päp\ *vb* **-pp-** **1** : move suddenly **2** : burst with or make a sharp sound **3** : protrude ~ *n* **1** : sharp explosive sound **2** : flavored soft drink

²**pop** *adj* : popular

pop•corn \'päp,kórn\ *n* : corn whose

kernels burst open into a light mass when heated

pope \\'pōp\ *n, often cap* : head of the Roman Catholic Church

pop·lar \\'päplər\ *n* : slender quick=growing tree

pop·lin \\'päplən\ *n* : strong plain=woven fabric with crosswise ribs

pop·over \\'päp,ōvər\ *n* : hollow muffin made from egg-rich batter

pop·py \\'päpē\ *n, pl* **-pies** : herb with showy flowers

pop·u·lace \\'päpyələs\ *n* **1** : common people **2** : population

pop·u·lar \\'päpyələr\ *adj* **1** : relating to the general public **2** : widely accepted **3** : commonly liked — **pop·u·lar·i·ty** \,päpyə'larətē\ *n* — **pop·u·lar·ize** \\'päpyələ,rīz\ *vb* — **pop·u·lar·ly** \-lərlē\ *adv*

pop·u·late \\'päpyə,lāt\ *vb* **-lat·ed; -lat·ing** : inhabit or occupy

pop·u·la·tion \,päpyə'lāshən\ *n* : people or number of people in an area

pop·u·list \\'päpyəlist\ *n* : advocate of the rights of the common people — **pop·u·lism** \-,lizəm\ *n*

pop·u·lous \\'päpyələs\ *adj* : densely populated — **pop·u·lous·ness** *n*

por·ce·lain \\'pōrsələn\ *n* : fine-grained ceramic ware

porch \\'pōrch\ *n* : covered entrance

por·cu·pine \\'pórkyə,pīn\ *n* : mammal with sharp quills

¹**pore** \\'pōr\ *vb* **pored; por·ing** : read attentively

²**pore** *n* : tiny hole (as in the skin) — **pored** *adj*

pork \\'pōrk\ *n* : pig meat

pork barrel *n* : government projects benefiting political patrons

por·nog·ra·phy \pór'nägrəfē\ *n* : depiction of erotic behavior intended to cause sexual excitement — **por·no·graph·ic** \,pórnə'grafik\ *adj*

po·rous \\'pōrəs\ *adj* : permeable to fluids — **po·ros·i·ty** \pə'räsətē\ *n*

por·poise \\'pórpəs\ *n* **1** : small whale with a blunt snout **2** : dolphin

por·ridge \\'pórij\ *n* : soft boiled cereal

por·rin·ger \\'pórənjər\ *n* : low one=handled metal bowl or cup

¹**port** \\'pōrt\ *n* **1** : harbor **2** : city with a harbor

²**port** *n* **1** : inlet or outlet (as in an engine) for a fluid **2** : porthole

³**port** *n* : left side of a ship or airplane looking forward — **port** *adj*

⁴**port** *n* : sweet wine

por·ta·ble \\'pōrtəbəl\ *adj* : capable of being carried — **portable** *n*

por·tage \\'pōrtij, pór'täzh\ *n* : carrying of boats overland between navigable bodies of water or the route where this is done — **portage** *vb*

por·tal \\'pōrt²l\ *n* : entrance

por·tend \pór'tend\ *vb* : give a warning of beforehand

por·tent \\'pór,tent\ *n* : something that foreshadows a coming event — **por·ten·tous** \pór'tentəs\ *adj*

por·ter \\'pōrtər\ *n* : baggage carrier

por·ter·house \-,haùs\ *n* : choice cut of steak

port·fo·lio \pōrt'fōlē,ō\ *n, pl* **-lios 1** : portable case for papers **2** : office or function of a diplomat **3** : investor's securities

port·hole \\'pōrt,hōl\ *n* : window in the side of a ship or aircraft

por·ti·co \\'pōrti,kō\ *n, pl* **-coes** or **-cos** : colonnade forming a porch

por·tion \\'pōrshən\ *n* : part or share of a whole ∼ *vb* : divide into or allot portions

port·ly \\'pōrtlē\ *adj* **-li·er; -est** : somewhat stout

por·trait \\'pōrtrət, -,trāt\ *n* : picture of a person — **por·trait·ist** \-ist\ *n* — **por·trai·ture** \\'pōrtrə,chùr\ *n*

por·tray \pór'trā\ *vb* **1** : make a picture of **2** : describe in words **3** : play the role of — **por·tray·al** *n*

por·tu·la·ca \,pōrchə'lakə\ *n* : tropical herb with showy flowers

pose \\'pōz\ *vb* **posed; pos·ing 1** : assume a posture or attitude **2** : propose **3** : pretend to be what one is not ∼ *n* **1** : sustained posture **2** : pretense — **pos·er** *n*

posh \\'päsh\ *adj* : elegant

po·si·tion \pə'zishən\ *n* **1** : stand taken on a question **2** : place or location **3** : status **4** : job — **position** *vb*

pos·i·tive \\'päzətiv\ *adj* **1** : definite **2** : confident **3** : relating to or being an adjective or adverb form that denotes no increase **4** : greater than zero **5** : having a deficiency of electrons **6** : affirmative — **pos·i·tive·ly** *adv* — **pos·i·tive·ness** *n*

pos·se \\'päsē\ *n* : emergency assistants of a sheriff

pos•sess \pə'zes\ *vb* **1** : have as property or as a quality **2** : control — **pos•ses•sion** \-'zeshən\ *n* — **pos•ses•sor** \-'zesər\ *n*

pos•ses•sive \pə'zesiv\ *adj* **1** : relating to a grammatical case denoting ownership **2** : jealous — **possessive** *n* — **pos•ses•sive•ness** *n*

pos•si•ble \'päsəbəl\ *adj* **1** : that can be done **2** : potential — **pos•si•bil•i•ty** \ˌpäsə'bilətē\ *n* — **pos•si•bly** *adv*

pos•sum \'päsəm\ *n* : opossum

¹post \'pōst\ *n* : upright stake serving to support or mark ~ *vb* : put up or announce by a notice

²post *vb* **1** : mail **2** : inform

³post *n* **1** : sentry's station **2** : assigned task **3** : army camp ~ *vb* : station

post- *prefix* : after or subsequent to

post•age \'pōstij\ *n* : fee for mail

post•al \'pōst°l\ *adj* : relating to the mail

post•card *n* : card for mailing a message

post•date \ˌpōst'dāt\ *vb* : assign a date to that is later than the actual date of execution

post•er \'pōstər\ *n* : large usu. printed notice

pos•te•ri•or \pō'stirēər, pä-\ *adj* **1** : later **2** : situated behind ~ *n* : buttocks

pos•ter•i•ty \pä'sterətē\ *n* : all future generations

post•haste \'pōst'hāst\ *adv* : speedily

post•hu•mous \'päschəməs\ *adj* : occurring after one's death — **post•hu•mous•ly** *adv*

post•man \'pōstmən, -ˌman\ *n* : mail carrier

post•mark *n* : official mark on mail — **postmark** *vb*

post•mas•ter *n* : chief of a post office

post me•ri•di•em \'pōstmə'ridēəm, -ēˌem\ *adj* : being after noon

post•mor•tem \ˌpōst'mȯrtəm\ *adj* : occurring or done after death ~ *n* **1** : medical examination of a corpse **2** : analysis after an event

post office *n* : agency or building for mail service

post•op•er•a•tive \ˌpōst'äpərətiv, -'äpəˌrāt-\ *adj* : following surgery

post•paid *adv* : with postage paid by the sender

post•par•tum \-'pärtəm\ *adj* : following childbirth — **postpartum** *adv*

post•pone \-'pōn\ *vb* **-poned; -pon•ing** : put off to a later time — **post•pone•ment** *n*

post•script \'pōstˌskript\ *n* : added note

pos•tu•lant \'päschələnt\ *n* : candidate for a religious order

pos•tu•late \'päschəˌlāt\ *vb* **-lat•ed; -lat•ing** : assume as true ~ *n* : assumption

pos•ture \'päschər\ *n* : bearing of the body ~ *vb* **-tured; -tur•ing** : strike a pose

po•sy \'pōzē\ *n, pl* **-sies** : flower or bunch of flowers

pot \'pät\ *n* : rounded container ~ *vb* **-tt-** : place in a pot — **pot•ful** *n*

po•ta•ble \'pōtəbəl\ *adj* : drinkable

pot•ash \'pätˌash\ *n* : white chemical salt of potassium used esp. in agriculture

po•tas•si•um \pə'tasēəm\ *n* : silver-white metallic chemical element

po•ta•to \pə'tātō\ *n, pl* **-toes** : edible plant tuber

List of self-explanatory words with the prefix *post-*

postadolescent	postgraduation	postpuberty
postattack	postharvest	postrecession
postbaccalaureate	posthospital	postretirement
postbiblical	postimperial	postrevolutionary
postcollege	postinaugural	postseason
postcolonial	postindustrial	postsecondary
postelection	postinoculation	postsurgical
postexercise	postmarital	posttreatment
postflight	postmenopausal	posttrial
postgame	postnatal	postvaccination
postgraduate	postnuptial	postwar
	postproduction	

pot•bel•ly n : paunch — **pot•bel•lied** adj

po•tent \'pōt°nt\ adj : powerful or effective — **po•ten•cy** \-°nsē\ n

po•ten•tate \'pōt°n₁tāt\ n : powerful ruler

po•ten•tial \pə'tenchəl\ adj : capable of becoming actual ∼ n 1 : something that can become actual 2 : degree of electrification with reference to a standard — **po•ten•ti•al•i•ty** \pə₁tenchē'alətē\ n — **po•ten•tial•ly** adv

poth•er \'päthər\ n : fuss

pot•hole \'pät₁hōl\ n : large hole in a road surface

po•tion \'pōshən\ n : liquid medicine or poison

pot•luck n : whatever food is available

pot•pour•ri \₁pōpú'rē\ n 1 : mix of flowers, herbs, and spices used for scent 2 : miscellaneous collection

pot•shot n 1 : casual or easy shot 2 : random critical remark

pot•ter \'pätər\ n : pottery maker

pot•tery \'pätərē\ n, pl -ter•ies : objects (as dishes) made from clay

pouch \'paúch\ n 1 : small bag 2 : bodily sac

poul•tice \'pōltəs\ n : warm medicated dressing — **poultice** vb

poul•try \'pōltrē\ n : domesticated fowl

pounce \'paúns\ vb **pounced; pouncing** : spring or swoop upon and seize

¹**pound** \'paúnd\ n 1 : unit of weight equal to 16 ounces 2 : monetary unit (as of the United Kingdom) — **poundage** \-ij\ n

²**pound** n : shelter for stray animals

³**pound** vb 1 : crush by beating 2 : strike heavily 3 : drill 4 : move along heavily

pour \'pōr\ vb 1 : flow or supply esp. copiously 2 : rain hard

pout \'paút\ vb : look sullen — **pout** n

pov•er•ty \'pävərtē\ n 1 : lack of money or possessions 2 : poor quality

pow•der \'paúdər\ n : dry material of fine particles ∼ vb : sprinkle or cover with powder — **pow•dery** adj

pow•er \'paúər\ n 1 : position of authority 2 : ability to act 3 : one that has power 4 : physical might 5 : force or energy used to do work ∼

vb : supply with power — **pow•er•ful** \-fəl\ adj — **pow•er•ful•ly** adv — **pow•er•less** adj

pow•er•house n : dynamic or energetic person

pow•wow \'paú₁waú\ n : conference

pox \'päks\ n, pl **pox** or **pox•es** : disease marked by skin rash

prac•ti•ca•ble \'praktikəbəl\ adj : feasible — **prac•ti•ca•bil•i•ty** \₁praktikə'bilətē\ n

prac•ti•cal \'praktikəl\ adj 1 : relating to practice 2 : virtual 3 : capable of being put to use 4 : inclined to action as opposed to speculation — **prac•ti•cal•i•ty** \₁prakti'kalətē\ n — **prac•ti•cal•ly** \'praktiklē\ adv

prac•tice, prac•tise \'praktəs\ vb **-ticed** or **-tised; -tic•ing** or **-tis•ing** 1 : perform repeatedly to become proficient 2 : do or perform customarily 3 : be professionally engaged in ∼ n 1 : actual performance 2 : habit 3 : exercise for proficiency 4 : exercise of a profession

prac•ti•tio•ner \prak'tishənər\ n : one who practices a profession

prag•ma•tism \'pragmə₁tizəm\ n : practical approach to problems — **prag•mat•ic** \prag'matik\ adj — **prag•mat•i•cal•ly** adv

prai•rie \'prerē\ n : broad grassy rolling tract of land

praise \'prāz\ vb **praised; prais•ing** 1 : express approval of 2 : glorify — **praise** n — **praise•wor•thy** adj

prance \'prans\ vb **pranced; prancing** 1 : spring from the hind legs 2 : swagger — **prance** n — **prancer** n

prank \'praŋk\ n : playful or mischievous act — **prank•ster** \-stər\ n

prate \'prāt\ vb **prat•ed; prat•ing** : talk long and foolishly

prat•fall \'prat₁fól\ n : fall on the buttocks

prat•tle \'prat°l\ vb **-tled; -tling** : babble — **prattle** n

prawn \'prón\ n : shrimplike crustacean

pray \'prā\ vb 1 : entreat 2 : ask earnestly for something 3 : address God or a god

prayer \'prer\ n 1 : earnest request 2 : an addressing of God or a god 3 : words used in praying — **prayer•ful** adj — **prayer•ful•ly** adv

praying mantis n : mantis

pre- *prefix* : before, prior to, or in advance

preach \'prēch\ *vb* **1** : deliver a sermon **2** : advocate earnestly — **preach•er** *n* — **preach•ment** *n*

pre•am•ble \'prē,ambəl\ *n* : introduction

pre•can•cer•ous \,prē'kansərəs\ *adj* : likely to become cancerous

pre•car•i•ous \pri'karēəs\ *adj* : dangerously insecure — **pre•car•i•ous•ly** *adv* — **pre•car•i•ous•ness** *n*

pre•cau•tion \pri'kôshən\ *n* : care taken beforehand — **pre•cau•tion•ary** \-shə,nerē\ *adj*

pre•cede \pri'sēd\ *vb* **-ced•ed; -ced•ing** : be, go, or come ahead of — **pre•ce•dence** \'presədəns, pri'sēd°ns\ *n*

prec•e•dent \'presədənt\ *n* : something said or done earlier that serves as an example

pre•cept \'prē,sept\ *n* : rule of action or conduct

pre•cinct \'prē,siŋkt\ *n* **1** : district of a city **2** *pl* : vicinity

pre•cious \'preshəs\ *adj* **1** : of great value **2** : greatly cherished **3** : affected

prec•i•pice \'presəpəs\ *n* : steep cliff

pre•cip•i•tate \pri'sipə,tāt\ *vb* **-tat•ed; -tat•ing** **1** : cause to happen quickly or abruptly **2** : cause to separate out of a liquid **3** : fall as rain, snow, or hail ~ *n* : solid matter precipitated from a liquid ~ \-'sipətət, -ə,tāt\ *adj* : unduly hasty — **pre•cip•i•tate•ly** *adv* — **pre•cip•i•tate•ness** *n* — **pre•cip•i•tous** \pri'sipətəs\ *adj* — **pre•cip•i•tous•ly** *adv*

pre•cip•i•ta•tion \pri,sipə'tāshən\ *n* **1** : rash haste **2** : rain, snow, or hail

pré•cis \prā'sē\ *n, pl* **pré•cis** \-'sēz\ : concise summary of essentials

pre•cise \pri'sīs\ *adj* **1** : definite **2** : highly accurate — **pre•cise•ly** *adv* — **pre•cise•ness** *n*

pre•ci•sion \pri'sizhən\ *n* : quality or state of being precise

pre•clude \pri'klüd\ *vb* **-clud•ed; -clud•ing** : make impossible

pre•co•cious \pri'kōshəs\ *adj* : exceptionally advanced — **pre•co•cious•ly** *adv* — **pre•coc•i•ty** \pri'käsətē\ *n*

pre•cur•sor \pri'kərsər\ *n* : harbinger

pred•a•to•ry \'predə,tōrē\ *adj* : preying upon others — **pred•a•tor** \'predətər\ *n*

pre•de•ces•sor \'predə,sesər, 'prēd-\ *n* : a previous holder of a position

pre•des•tine \prē'destən\ *vb* : settle beforehand — **pre•des•ti•na•tion** \-,destə'nāshən\ *n*

pre•dic•a•ment \pri'dikəmənt\ *n* : difficult situation

pred•i•cate \'predikət\ *n* : part of a sentence that states something about the subject ~ \'predə,kāt\ *vb* **-cat•ed; -cat•ing** **1** : affirm **2** : establish — **pred•i•ca•tion** \,predə'kāshən\ *n*

pre•dict \pri'dikt\ *vb* : declare in advance — **pre•dict•abil•i•ty** \-,dikte'bilətē\ *n* — **pre•dict•able** \-'diktəbəl\ *adj* — **pre•dict•ably** \-blē\ *adv* — **pre•dic•tion** \-'dikshən\ *n*

pre•di•lec•tion \,predəl'ekshən, ,prēd-\ *n* : established preference

pre•dis•pose \,prēdis'pōz\ *vb* : cause to be favorable or susceptible to something beforehand — **pre•dis•po•si•tion** \,prē,dispə'zishən\ *n*

pre•dom•i•nate \pri'dämə,nāt\ *vb* : be

List of self-explanatory words with the prefix *pre-*

preadmission	prebreakfast	preconception
preadolescence	precalculus	preconcert
preadolescent	precancel	precondition
preadult	precancellation	preconstructed
preanesthetic	preclear	preconvention
prearrange	preclearance	precook
prearrangement	precollege	precool
preassembled	precolonial	precut
preassign	precombustion	predawn
prebattle	precompute	predefine
prebiblical	preconceive	predeparture

superior — **pre·dom·i·nance** \-nəns\ n — **pre·dom·i·nant** \-nənt\ adj — **pre·dom·i·nant·ly** adv

pre·em·i·nent \prē'emənənt\ adj : having highest rank — **pre·em·i·nence** \-nəns\ n — **pre·em·i·nent·ly** adv

pre·empt \prē'empt\ vb 1 : seize for oneself 2 : take the place of — **pre·emp·tion** \-'empshən\ n — **pre·emp·tive** \-'emptiv\ adj

preen \'prēn\ vb : dress or smooth up (as feathers)

pre·fab·ri·cat·ed \'prē'fabrə₁kātəd\ adj : manufactured for rapid assembly elsewhere — **pre·fab·ri·ca·tion** \₁prē-₁fabri'kāshən\ n

pref·ace \'prefəs\ n : introductory comments ~ vb -aced; -ac·ing : introduce with a preface — **pref·a·to·ry** \'prefe₁tōrē\ adj

pre·fect \'prē₁fekt\ n : chief officer or judge — **pre·fec·ture** \-₁fekchər\ n

pre·fer \pri'fər\ vb -rr- 1 : like better 2 : bring (as a charge) against a person — **pref·er·a·ble** \'prefərəbəl\ adj — **pref·er·a·bly** adv — **pref·er·ence** \-ərəns\ n — **pref·er·en·tial** \₁prefə-'renchəl\ adj

pre·fer·ment \pri'fərmənt\ n : promotion

pre·fig·ure \prē'figyər\ vb : foreshadow

¹**pre·fix** \'prē₁fiks, prē'fiks\ vb : place before

²**pre·fix** \'prē₁fiks\ n : affix at the beginning of a word

preg·nant \'pregnənt\ adj 1 : containing unborn young 2 : meaningful — **preg·nan·cy** \-nənsē\ n

pre·hen·sile \prē'hensəl, -₁sīl\ adj : adapted for grasping

pre·his·tor·ic \₁prēhis'tórik\, **pre·his·tor·i·cal** \-ikəl\ adj : relating to the period before written history

prej·u·dice \'prejədəs\ n 1 : damage esp. to one's rights 2 : unreasonable attitude for or against something ~ vb -diced; -dic·ing 1 : damage 2 : cause to have prejudice — **prej·u·di·cial** \₁prejə'dishəl\ adj

prel·ate \'prelət\ n : clergy member of high rank — **prel·a·cy** \-əsē\ n

pre·lim·i·nary \pri'limə₁nerē\ n, pl -nar·ies : something that precedes or introduces — **preliminary** adj

pre·lude \'prel₁üd, -₁yüd; 'prā₁lüd\ n : introductory performance, event, or musical piece

pre·ma·ture \₁prēmə'túər, -'tyúr, -'chúr\ adj : coming before the usual or proper time — **pre·ma·ture·ly** adv

pre·med·i·tate \pri'medə₁tāt\ vb : plan beforehand — **pre·med·i·ta·tion** \-₁medə'tāshən\ n

pre·mier \pri'mir, -'myir; 'prēmēər\ adj : first in rank or importance ~ n : prime minister — **pre·mier·ship** n

pre·miere \pri'myer, -'mir\ n : 1st performance ~ vb -miered; -mier·ing : give a 1st performance of

prem·ise \'preməs\ n 1 : statement made or implied as a basis of argument 2 pl : piece of land with the structures on it

pre·mi·um \'prēmēəm\ n 1 : bonus 2 : sum over the stated value 3 : sum paid for insurance 4 : high value

pre·mo·ni·tion \₁prēmə'nishən, ₁premə-\ n : feeling that something is about to happen — **pre·mon·i·to·ry** \pri'mänə₁tōrē\ adj

pre·oc·cu·pied \prē'äkyə₁pīd\ adj : lost in thought

pre·oc·cu·py \-₁pī\ vb : occupy the attention of — **pre·oc·cu·pa·tion** \prē-₁äkyə'pāshən\ n

---

predesignate	prefight	premarital
predetermine	preform	premenopausal
predischarge	pregame	premenstrual
predrill	preheat	premix
preelection	preinaugural	premodern
preelectric	preindustrial	premodify
preemployment	preinterview	premoisten
preestablish	prejudge	premold
preexist	prekindergarten	prenatal
preexistence	prelaunch	prenotification
preexistent	prelife	prenotify

pre·pare \pri'par\ *vb* **-pared; -par·ing** **1** : make or get ready often beforehand **2** : put together or compound — **prep·a·ra·tion** \ˌprepə'rāshən\ *n* — **pre·pa·ra·to·ry** \pri'parəˌtōrē\ *adj* — **pre·pared·ness** \-'parədnəs\ *n*

pre·pon·der·ant \pri'pändərənt\ *adj* : having great weight, power, importance, or numbers — **pre·pon·der·ance** \-rəns\ *n* — **pre·pon·der·ant·ly** *adv*

prep·o·si·tion \ˌprepə'zishən\ *n* : word that combines with a noun or pronoun to form a phrase — **prep·o·si·tion·al** \-'zishənəl\ *adj*

pre·pos·sess·ing \ˌprēpə'zesiŋ\ *adj* : tending to create a favorable impression

pre·pos·ter·ous \pri'pästərəs\ *adj* : absurd

pre·req·ui·site \prē'rekwəzət\ *n* : something required beforehand — **prerequisite** *adj*

pre·rog·a·tive \pri'rägətiv\ *n* : special right or power

pre·sage \'presij, pri'sāj\ *vb* **-saged; -sag·ing 1** : give a warning of **2** : predict — **pres·age** \'presij\ *n*

pres·by·ter \'prezbətər\ *n* : priest or minister

pre·science \'prēshəns, 'presh-\ *n* : foreknowledge of events — **pre·scient** \-ənt\ *adj*

pre·scribe \pri'skrīb\ *vb* **-scribed; -scrib·ing 1** : lay down as a guide **2** : direct the use of as a remedy

pre·scrip·tion \pri'skripshən\ *n* : written direction for the preparation and use of a medicine or the medicine prescribed

pres·ence \'prez³ns\ *n* **1** : fact or condition of being present **2** : appearance or bearing

¹pres·ent \'prez³nt\ *n* : gift

²pre·sent \pri'zent\ *vb* **1** : introduce **2** : bring before the public **3** : make a gift to or of **4** : bring before a court for inquiry — **pre·sent·able** *adj* — **pre·sen·ta·tion** \ˌprē ˌzen'tāshən, ˌprez³n-\ *n* — **pre·sent·ment** \pri'zentmənt\ *n*

³pres·ent \'prez³nt\ *adj* : now existing, in progress, or attending ~ *n* : present time

pre·sen·ti·ment \pri'zentəmənt\ *n* : premonition

pres·ent·ly \'prez³ntlē\ *adv* **1** : soon **2** : now

present participle *n* : participle that typically expresses present action

pre·serve \pri'zərv\ *vb* **-served; -serv·ing 1** : keep safe from danger or spoilage **2** : maintain ~ *n* **1** : preserved fruit — often in pl. **2** : area for protection of natural resources — **pres·er·va·tion** \ˌprezər'vāshən\ *n* — **pre·ser·va·tive** \pri'zərvətiv\ *adj or n* — **pre·serv·er** \-'zərvər\ *n*

pre·side \pri'zīd\ *vb* **-sid·ed; -sid·ing 1** : act as chairman **2** : exercise control

pres·i·dent \'prezədənt\ *n* **1** : one chosen to preside **2** : chief official (as of a company or nation) — **pres·i·den·cy** \-ənsē\ *n* — **pres·i·den·tial** \ˌprezə'denchəl\ *adj*

press \'pres\ *n* **1** : crowded condition **2** : machine or device for exerting pressure and esp. for printing **3** : pressure **4** : printing or publishing establishment **5** : news media and esp. newspapers ~ *vb* **1** : lie against and exert pressure on **2** : smooth with an iron or squeeze with something heavy **3** : urge **4** : crowd **5** : force one's way — **press·er** *n*

press·ing *adj* : urgent

pres·sure \'preshər\ *n* **1** : burden of distress or urgent business **2** : direct

---

prenuptial	prepubertal	presale
preopening	prepublication	preschool
preoperational	prepunch	preseason
preoperative	prepurchase	preselect
preordain	prerecorded	preset
prepackage	preregister	preshrink
prepay	preregistration	preshrunk
preplan	prerehearsal	presoak
preprocess	prerelease	presort
preproduction	preretirement	prestamp
preprofessional	prerevolutionary	presterilize
preprogram	prerinse	prestrike

application of force — **pressure** *vb* — **pres•sur•i•za•tion** \,preshərə-'zāshən\ *n* — **pres•sur•ize** \-,īz\ *vb*
pres•ti•dig•i•ta•tion \,prestə,dijə'-tāshən\ *n* : sleight of hand
pres•tige \pres'tēzh, -'tēj\ *n* : estimation in the eyes of people — **pres•ti•gious** \-'tijəs\ *adj*
pres•to \'prestō\ *adv or adj* : quickly
pre•sume \pri'züm\ *vb* **-sumed; -sum•ing** **1** : assume authority without right to do so **2** : take for granted — **pre•sum•able** \-'züməbəl\ *adj* — **pre•sum•ably** \-blē\ *adv*
pre•sump•tion \pri'zəmpshən\ *n* **1** : presumptuous attitude or conduct **2** : belief supported by probability — **pre•sump•tive** \-tiv\ *adj*
pre•sump•tu•ous \pri'zəmpchəwəs\ *adj* : too bold or forward — **pre•sump•tu•ous•ly** *adv*
pre•sup•pose \,prēsə'pōz\ *vb* : take for granted — **pre•sup•po•si•tion** \,prē,səpə'zishən\ *n*
pre•tend \pri'tend\ *vb* **1** : act as if something is real or true when it is not **2** : act in a way that is false **3** : lay claim — **pre•tend•er** *n*
pre•tense, pre•tence \'prē,tens, pri'tens\ *n* **1** : insincere effort **2** : deception — **pre•ten•sion** \pri-'tenchən\ *n*
pre•ten•tious \pri'tenchəs\ *adj* : overly showy or self-important — **pre•ten•tious•ly** *adv* — **pre•ten•tious•ness** *n*
pre•ter•nat•u•ral \,prētər'nachərəl\ *adj* **1** : exceeding what is natural **2** : inexplicable by ordinary means — **pre•ter•nat•u•ral•ly** *adv*
pre•text \'prē,tekst\ *n* : falsely stated purpose
pret•ty \'pritē, 'pùrt-\ *adj* **-ti•er; -est** : pleasing by delicacy or attractiveness ~ *adv* : in some degree ~ *vb* **-tied; -ty•ing** : make pretty — **pret•ti•ly** \'prit³lē\ *adv* — **pret•ti•ness** *n*
pret•zel \'pretsəl\ *n* : twisted thin bread that is glazed and salted
pre•vail \pri'vāl\ *vb* **1** : triumph **2** : urge successfully **3** : be frequent, widespread, or dominant

prev•a•lent \'prevələnt\ *adj* : widespread — **prev•a•lence** \-ləns\ *n*
pre•var•i•cate \pri'varə,kāt\ *vb* **-cat•ed; -cat•ing** : deviate from the truth — **pre•var•i•ca•tion** \-,varə-'kāshən\ *n* — **pre•var•i•ca•tor** \-'varə,kātər\ *n*
pre•vent \pri'vent\ *vb* : keep from happening or acting — **pre•vent•able** *adj* — **pre•ven•tion** \-'venchən\ *n* — **pre•ven•tive** \-'ventiv\ *adj or n* — **pre•ven•ta•tive** \-'ventətiv\ *adj or n*
pre•view \'prē,vyü\ *vb* : view or show beforehand — **preview** *n*
pre•vi•ous \'prēvēəs\ *adj* : having gone, happened, or existed before — **pre•vi•ous•ly** *adv*
prey \'prā\ *n, pl* **preys** **1** : animal taken for food by another **2** : victim ~ *vb* **1** : seize and devour animals as prey **2** : have a harmful effect on
price \'prīs\ *n* : cost ~ *vb* **priced; pric•ing** : set a price on
price•less \-ləs\ *adj* : too precious to have a price
pric•ey \'prīsē\ *adj* **pric•i•er; -est** : expensive
prick \'prik\ *n* **1** : tear or small wound made by a point **2** : something sharp or pointed ~ *vb* : pierce slightly with a sharp point — **prick•er** *n*
prick•le \'prikəl\ *n* **1** : small sharp spine or thorn **2** : slight stinging pain ~ *vb* **-led; -ling** : tingle — **prick•ly** \'priklē\ *adj*
pride \'prīd\ *n* : quality or state of being proud ~ *vb* **prid•ed; prid•ing** : indulge in pride — **pride•ful** *adj*
priest \'prēst\ *n* : person having authority to perform the sacred rites of a religion — **priest•hood** *n* — **priest•li•ness** \-lēnəs\ *n* — **priest•ly** *adj*
priest•ess \'prēstəs\ *n* : woman who is a priest
prig \'prig\ *n* : one who irritates by rigid or pointed observance of proprieties — **prig•gish** \-ish\ *adj* — **prig•gish•ly** *adv*
prim \'prim\ *adj* **-mm-** : stiffly formal and proper — **prim•ly** *adv* — **prim•ness** *n*

pri·mal \'prīməl\ *adj* **1** : original or primitive **2** : most important

pri·ma·ry \'prī,merē, 'prīmərē\ *adj* : first in order of time, rank, or importance ~ *n, pl* **-ries** : preliminary election — **pri·mar·i·ly** \prī'merəlē\ *adv*

primary school *n* : elementary school

pri·mate *n* **1** \'prī,māt, -mət\ : highest-ranking bishop **2** \-,māt\ : mammal of the group that includes humans and monkeys

prime \'prīm\ *n* : earliest or best part or period ~ *adj* : standing first (as in significance or quality) ~ *vb* **primed; prim·ing 1** : fill or load **2** : lay a preparatory coating on

prime minister *n* : chief executive of a parliamentary government

¹prim·er \'primər\ *n* : small introductory book

²prim·er \'primər\ *n* **1** : device for igniting an explosive **2** : material for priming a surface

pri·me·val \prī'mēvəl\ *adj* : relating to the earliest ages

prim·i·tive \'primətiv\ *adj* **1** : relating to or characteristic of an early stage of development **2** : of or relating to a tribal people or culture ~ *n* : one that is primitive — **prim·i·tive·ly** *adv* — **prim·i·tive·ness** *n*

pri·mor·di·al \prī'mórdēəl\ *adj* : primeval

primp \'primp\ *vb* : dress or groom in a finicky manner

prim·rose \'prim,rōz\ *n* : low herb with clusters of showy flowers

prince \'prins\ *n* **1** : ruler **2** : son of a king or queen — **prince·ly** *adj*

prin·cess \'prinsəs, -,ses\ *n* **1** : daughter of a king or queen **2** : wife of a prince

prin·ci·pal \'prinsəpəl\ *adj* : most important ~ *n* **1** : leading person **2** : head of a school **3** : sum lent at interest — **prin·ci·pal·ly** *adv*

prin·ci·pal·i·ty \,prinsə'palətē\ *n, pl* **-ties** : territory of a prince

prin·ci·ple \'prinsəpəl\ *n* **1** : general or fundamental law **2** : rule or code of conduct or devotion to such a code

print \'print\ *n* **1** : mark or impression made by pressure **2** : printed state or form **3** : printed matter **4** : copy made by printing **5** : cloth with a figure stamped on it ~ *vb* **1** : produce impressions of (as from type)

2 : write in letters like those of printer's type — **print·able** *adj* — **print·er** *n*

print·ing \'printiŋ\ *n* : art or business of a printer

print·out \'print,aút\ *n* : printed output produced by a computer — **print out** *vb*

¹pri·or \'prīər\ *n* : head of a religious house — **pri·o·ry** \'prīərē\ *n*

²prior *adj* : coming before in time, order, or importance — **pri·or·i·ty** \prī'órətē\ *n*

pri·or·ess \'prīərəs\ *n* : nun who is head of a religious house

prism \'prizəm\ *n* : transparent 3-sided object that separates light into colors — **pris·mat·ic** \priz'matik\ *adj*

pris·on \'priz°n\ *n* : place where criminals are confined

pris·on·er \'priz°nər\ *n* : person on trial or in prison

pris·sy \'prisē\ *adj* **-si·er; -est** : overly prim — **pris·si·ness** *n*

pris·tine \'pris,tēn, pris'-\ *adj* : pure

pri·va·cy \'prīvəsē\ *n, pl* **-cies** : quality or state of being apart from others

pri·vate \'prīvət\ *adj* **1** : belonging to a particular individual or group **2** : carried on independently **3** : withdrawn from company or observation ~ *n* : enlisted person of the lowest rank in the marine corps or of one of the two lowest ranks in the army — **pri·vate·ly** *adv*

pri·va·teer \,prīvə'tir\ *n* : private ship armed to attack enemy ships and commerce

private first class *n* : enlisted person ranking next below a corporal in the army and next below a lance corporal in the marine corps

pri·va·tion \prī'vāshən\ *n* : lack of what is needed for existence

priv·i·lege \'privəlij\ *n* : right granted as an advantage or favor — **priv·i·leged** *adj*

privy \'privē\ *adj* **1** : private or secret **2** : having access to private or secret information ~ *n, pl* **priv·ies** : outdoor toilet — **priv·i·ly** \'privəlē\ *adv*

¹prize \'prīz\ *n* **1** : something offered or striven for in competition or in contests of chance **2** : something very desirable — **prize** *adj* — **prize·win·ner** *n* — **prize·win·ning** *adj*

²prize *vb* **prized; priz·ing** : value highly

³prize *vb* **prized; priz·ing** : pry

prize•fight *n* : professional boxing match — **prize•fight•er** *n* — **prize•fight•ing** *n*

¹**pro** \'prō\ *n* : favorable argument or person ~ *adv* : in favor

²**pro** *n or adj* : professional

prob•a•ble \'präbəbəl\ *adj* : seeming true or real or to have a good chance of happening — **prob•a•bil•i•ty** \,präbə'bilətē\ *n* — **prob•a•bly** \'präbəblē\ *adv*

pro•bate \'prō,bāt\ *n* : judicial determination of the validity of a will ~ *vb* -**bat•ed**; -**bat•ing** : establish by probate

pro•ba•tion \prō'bāshən\ *n* **1** : period of testing and trial **2** : freedom for a convict during good behavior under supervision — **pro•ba•tion•ary** \-shə,nerē\ *adj* — **pro•ba•tion•er** *n*

probe \'prōb\ *n* **1** : slender instrument for examining a cavity **2** : investigation ~ *vb* **probed; prob•ing 1** : examine with a probe **2** : investigate

pro•bi•ty \'prōbətē\ *n* : honest behavior

prob•lem \'präbləm\ *n* **1** : question to be solved **2** : source of perplexity or vexation — **problem** *adj* — **prob•lem•at•ic** \,präblə'matik\ *adj* — **prob•lem•at•i•cal** \-ikəl\ *adj*

pro•bos•cis \prə'bäsəs\ *n, pl* -**cis•es** *also* -**ci•des** \-ə,dēz\ : long flexible snout

pro•ce•dure \prə'sējər\ *n* **1** : way of doing something **2** : series of steps in regular order — **pro•ce•dur•al** \-'sējərəl\ *adj*

pro•ceed \prō'sēd\ *vb* **1** : come forth **2** : go on in an orderly way **3** : begin and carry on an action **4** : advance

pro•ceed•ing *n* **1** : procedure **2** *pl* : something said or done or its official record

pro•ceeds \'prō,sēdz\ *n pl* : total money taken in

pro•cess \'präs,es, 'prōs-\ *n, pl* -**cess•es** \-,esəz, -əsəz, -ə,sēz\ **1** : something going on **2** : natural phenomenon marked by gradual changes **3** : series of actions or operations directed toward a result **4** : summons **5** : projecting part ~ *vb* : subject to a process — **pro•ces•sor** \-ər\ *n*

pro•ces•sion \prə'seshən\ *n* : group moving along in an orderly way

pro•ces•sion•al \-'seshənəl\ *n* : music for a procession

pro•claim \prō'klām\ *vb* : announce publicly or with conviction — **proc•la•ma•tion** \,präklə'māshən\ *n*

pro•cliv•i•ty \prō'klivətē\ *n, pl* -**ties** : inclination

pro•cras•ti•nate \prə'krastə,nāt\ *vb* -**nat•ed**; -**nat•ing** : put something off until later — **pro•cras•ti•na•tion** \-,krastə'nāshən\ *n* — **pro•cras•ti•na•tor** \-'krastə,nātər\ *n*

pro•cre•ate \'prōkrē,āt\ *vb* -**at•ed**; -**at•ing** : produce offspring — **pro•cre•ation** \,prōkrē'āshən\ *n* — **pro•cre•ative** \'prōkrē,ātiv\ *adj* — **pro•cre•ator** \-,ātər\ *n*

proc•tor \'präktər\ *n* : supervisor of students (as at an examination) — **proctor** *vb*

pro•cure \prə'kyúr\ *vb* -**cured**; -**cur•ing** : get possession of — **pro•cur•able** \-'kyúrəbəl\ *adj* — **pro•cure•ment** *n* — **pro•cur•er** *n*

prod \'präd\ *vb* -**dd-** : push with or as if with a pointed instrument — **prod** *n*

prod•i•gal \'prädigəl\ *adj* : recklessly extravagant or wasteful — **prodigal** *n* — **prod•i•gal•i•ty** \,prädə'galətē\ *n*

pro•di•gious \prə'dijəs\ *adj* : extraordinary in size or degree — **pro•di•gious•ly** *adv*

prod•i•gy \'prädəjē\ *n, pl* -**gies** : extraordinary person or thing

pro•duce \prə'düs, -'dyüs\ *vb* -**duced**; -**duc•ing 1** : present to view **2** : give birth to **3** : bring into existence ~ \'präd,üs, 'prōd-, -,yüs\ *n* **1** : product **2** : agricultural products — **pro•duc•er** \prə'düsər, -'dyü-\ *n*

prod•uct \'präd,əkt\ *n* **1** : number resulting from multiplication **2** : something produced

pro•duc•tion \prə'dəkshən\ *n* : act, process, or result of producing — **pro•duc•tive** \-'dəktiv\ *adj* — **pro•duc•tive•ness** *n* — **pro•duc•tiv•i•ty** \,prō,dək'tivətē, ,prä-\ *n*

prof \'präf\ *n* : professor

pro•fane \prō'fān\ *vb* -**faned**; -**fan•ing** : treat with irreverence ~ *adj* **1** : not concerned with religion **2** : serving to debase what is holy — **pro•fane•ly** *adv* — **pro•fane•ness** *n* — **pro•fan•i•ty** \prō'fanətē\ *n*

pro•fess \prə'fes\ *vb* **1** : declare openly **2** : confess one's faith in — **pro•fessed•ly** \-ədlē\ *adv*

pro•fes•sion \prə'feshən\ *n* **1** : open

declaration of belief **2** : occupation requiring specialized knowledge and academic training

pro•fes•sion•al \prə'feshənəl\ *adj* **1** : of, relating to, or engaged in a profession **2** : playing sport for pay — **professional** *n* — **pro•fes•sion•al•ism** *n* — **pro•fes•sion•al•ize** *vb* — **pro•fes•sion•al•ly** *adv*

pro•fes•sor \prə'fesər\ *n* : university or college teacher — **pro•fes•so•ri•al** \‚prōfə'sōrēəl, ‚präfə-\ *adj* — **pro•fes•sor•ship** *n*

prof•fer \'präfər\ *vb* **-fered; -fer•ing** : offer — **proffer** *n*

pro•fi•cient \prə'fishənt\ *adj* : very good at something — **pro•fi•cien•cy** \-ənsē\ *n* — **proficient** *n* — **pro•fi•cient•ly** *adv*

pro•file \'prō‚fīl\ *n* : picture in outline — **profile** *vb*

prof•it \'präfət\ *n* **1** : valuable return **2** : excess of the selling price of goods over cost ~ *vb* : gain a profit — **prof•it•able** \'präfətəbəl\ *adj* — **prof•it•ably** *adv* — **prof•it•less** *adj*

prof•i•teer \‚präfə'tir\ *n* : one who makes an unreasonable profit — **prof•iteer** *vb*

prof•li•gate \'präfligət, -lə‚gāt\ *adj* **1** : shamelessly immoral **2** : wildly extravagant — **prof•li•ga•cy** \-gəsē\ *n* — **profligate** *n* — **prof•li•gate•ly** *adv*

pro•found \prə'faúnd\ *adj* **1** : marked by intellectual depth or insight **2** : deeply felt — **pro•found•ly** *adv* — **pro•fun•di•ty** \-'fəndətē\ *n*

pro•fuse \prə'fyüs\ *adj* : pouring forth liberally — **pro•fuse•ly** *adv* — **pro•fu•sion** \-'fyüzhən\ *n*

pro•gen•i•tor \prō'jenətər\ *n* : direct ancestor

prog•e•ny \'präjənē\ *n, pl* **-nies** : offspring

pro•ges•ter•one \prō'jestə‚rōn\ *n* : female hormone

prog•no•sis \präg'nōsəs\ *n, pl* **-no•ses** \-‚sēz\ : prospect of recovery from disease

prog•nos•ti•cate \präg'nästə‚kāt\ *vb* **-cat•ed; -cat•ing** : predict from signs or symptoms — **prog•nos•ti•ca•tion** \-‚nästə'kāshən\ *n* — **prog•nos•ti•ca•tor** \-'nästə‚kātər\ *n*

pro•gram \'prō‚gram, -grəm\ *n* **1** : outline of the order to be pursued or the subjects included (as in a performance) **2** : plan of procedure **3** : coded instructions for a computer ~ *vb* **-grammed** *or* **-gramed; -gram•ming** *or* **-gram•ing** **1** : enter in a program **2** : provide a computer with a program — **pro•gram•ma•bil•i•ty** \‚prō‚gramə'bilətē\ *n* — **pro•gram•ma•ble** \'prō‚graməbəl\ *adj* — **pro•gram•mer** \'prō‚gramər\ *n*

prog•ress \'prägrəs, -‚res\ *n* : movement forward or to a better condition ~ \prə'gres\ *vb* **1** : move forward **2** : improve — **pro•gres•sive** \-'gresiv\ *adj* — **pro•gres•sive•ly** *adv*

pro•gres•sion \prə'greshən\ *n* **1** : act of progressing **2** : continuous connected series

pro•hib•it \prō'hibət\ *vb* : prevent by authority

pro•hi•bi•tion \‚prōə'bishən\ *n* **1** : act of prohibiting **2** : legal restriction on sale or manufacture of alcoholic beverages — **pro•hi•bi•tion•ist** \-'bishənist\ *n* — **pro•hib•i•tive** \prō'hibətiv\ *adj* — **pro•hib•i•tive•ly** *adv* — **pro•hib•i•to•ry** \-'hibə‚tōrē\ *adj*

proj•ect \'präj‚ekt, -ikt\ *n* : planned undertaking ~ \prə'jekt\ *vb* **1** : design or plan **2** : protrude **3** : throw forward — **pro•jec•tion** \-'jekshən\ *n*

pro•jec•tile \prə'jekt³l\ *n* : missile hurled by external force

pro•jec•tor \-'jektər\ *n* : device for projecting pictures on a screen

pro•le•tar•i•an \‚prōlə'terēən\ *n* : member of the proletariat — **proletarian** *adj*

pro•le•tar•i•at \-ēət\ *n* : laboring class

pro•lif•er•ate \prə'lifə‚rāt\ *vb* **-at•ed; -at•ing** : grow or increase in number rapidly — **pro•lif•er•a•tion** \-‚lifə'rāshən\ *n*

pro•lif•ic \prə'lifik\ *adj* : producing abundantly — **pro•lif•i•cal•ly** *adv*

pro•logue \'prō‚lóg, -‚läg\ *n* : preface

pro•long \prə'lóŋ\ *vb* : lengthen in time or extent — **pro•lon•ga•tion** \‚prō‚lóŋ'gāshən\ *n*

prom \'präm\ *n* : formal school dance

prom•e•nade \‚prämə'nād, -'näd\ *n* **1** : leisurely walk **2** : place for strolling — **promenade** *vb*

prom•i•nence \'prämənəns\ *n* **1** : quality, state, or fact of being readily noticeable or distinguished **2** : something that stands out — **prom•i-**

nent \-nənt\ adj — **prom•i•nent•ly** adv

pro•mis•cu•ous \prə'miskyəwəs\ adj : having a number of sexual partners — **prom•is•cu•ity** \ˌprämis'kyüətē, ˌprō,mis-\ n — **pro•mis•cu•ous•ly** adv — **pro•mis•cu•ous•ness** n

prom•ise \'präməs\ n 1 : statement that one will do or not do something 2 : basis for expectation — **promise** vb — **prom•is•so•ry** \-ə,sōrē\ adj

prom•is•ing \'präməsiŋ\ adj : likely to succeed — **prom•is•ing•ly** adv

prom•on•to•ry \'prämən,tōrē\ n, pl -ries : point of land jutting into the sea

pro•mote \prə'mōt\ vb -mot•ed; -mot•ing 1 : advance in rank 2 : contribute to the growth, development, or prosperity of — **pro•mot•er** n — **pro•mo•tion** \-'mōshən\ n — **pro•mo•tion•al** \-'mōshənəl\ adj

[1]**prompt** \'prämpt\ vb 1 : incite 2 : give a cue to (an actor or singer) — **prompt•er** n

[2]**prompt** adj : ready and quick — **prompt•ly** adv — **prompt•ness** n

prone \'prōn\ adj 1 : having a tendency 2 : lying face downward — **prone•ness** \'prōnnəs\ n

prong \'prȯŋ\ n : sharp point of a fork — **pronged** \'prȯŋd\ adj

pro•noun \'prō,naun\ n : word used as a substitute for a noun

pro•nounce \prə'nauns\ vb -nounced; -nounc•ing 1 : utter officially or as an opinion 2 : say or speak esp. correctly — **pro•nounce•able** adj — **pro•nounce•ment** n — **pro•nun•ci•a•tion** \-,nənsē'āshən\ n

pro•nounced \-'naunst\ adj : decided

[1]**proof** \'prüf\ n 1 : evidence of a truth or fact 2 : trial impression or print

[2]**proof** adj : designed for or successful in resisting or repelling

proof•read vb : read and mark corrections in — **proof•read•er** n

prop \'präp\ vb -pp- 1 : support 2 : sustain — **prop** n

pro•pa•gan•da \ˌpräpə'gandə, ˌprōpə-\ n : the spreading of ideas or information to further or damage a cause — **pro•pa•gan•dist** \-dist\ n — **pro•pa•gan•dize** \-,dīz\ vb

prop•a•gate \'präpə,gāt\ vb -gat•ed; -gat•ing 1 : reproduce biologically 2 : cause to spread — **prop•a•ga•tion** \ˌpräpə'gāshən\ n

pro•pane \'prō,pān\ n : heavy flammable gaseous fuel

pro•pel \prə'pel\ vb -ll- : drive forward — **pro•pel•lant, pro•pel•lent** n or adj

pro•pel•ler \prə'pelər\ n : hub with revolving blades that propels a craft

pro•pen•si•ty \prə'pensətē\ n, pl -ties : particular interest or inclination

prop•er \'präpər\ adj 1 : suitable or right 2 : limited to a specified thing 3 : correct 4 : strictly adhering to standards of social manners, dignity, or good taste — **prop•er•ly** adv

prop•er•ty \'präpərtē\ n, pl -ties 1 : quality peculiar to an individual 2 : something owned 3 : piece of real estate 4 : ownership

proph•e•cy \'präfəsē\ n, pl -cies : prediction

proph•e•sy \-,sī\ vb -sied; -sy•ing : predict — **proph•e•si•er** \-,sīər\ n

proph•et \'präfət\ n : one who utters revelations or predicts events — **proph•et•ess** \-əs\ n — **pro•phet•ic** \prə'fetik\ adj — **pro•phet•i•cal•ly** adv

pro•pin•qui•ty \prə'piŋkwətē\ n : nearness

pro•pi•ti•ate \prō'pishē,āt\ vb -at•ed; -at•ing : gain or regain the favor of — **pro•pi•ti•a•tion** \-,pishē'āshən\ n — **pro•pi•tia•to•ry** \-'pishēə,tōrē\ adj

pro•pi•tious \prə'pishəs\ adj : favorable

pro•po•nent \prə'pōnənt\ n : one who argues in favor of something

pro•por•tion \prə'pōrshən\ n 1 : relation of one part to another or to the whole with respect to magnitude, quantity, or degree 2 : symmetry 3 : share ~ vb : adjust in size in relation to others — **pro•por•tion•al** \-shənəl\ adj — **pro•por•tion•al•ly** adv — **pro•por•tion•ate** \-shənət\ adj — **pro•por•tion•ate•ly** adv

pro•pose \prə'pōz\ vb -posed; -pos•ing 1 : plan or intend 2 : make an offer of marriage 3 : present for consideration — **pro•pos•al** \-'pōzəl\ n

prop•o•si•tion \ˌpräpə'zishən\ n : something proposed ~ vb : suggest sexual intercourse to

pro•pound \prə'paund\ vb : set forth for consideration

pro•pri•etor \prə'prīətər\ n : owner — **pro•pri•etary** \prə'prīə,terē\ adj —

pro•pri•etor•ship *n* — **pro•pri•etress** \-'prīətrəs\ *n*

pro•pri•ety \prə'prīətē\ *n, pl* **-eties** : standard of acceptability in social conduct

pro•pul•sion \prə'pəlshən\ *n* **1** : action of propelling **2** : driving power — **pro•pul•sive** \-siv\ *adj*

pro•sa•ic \prō'zāik\ *adj* : dull

pro•scribe \prō'skrīb\ *vb* **-scribed; -scrib•ing** : prohibit — **pro•scrip•tion** \-'skripshən\ *n*

prose \'prōz\ *n* : ordinary language

pros•e•cute \'präsi,kyüt\ *vb* **-cut•ed; -cut•ing** **1** : follow to the end **2** : seek legal punishment of — **pros•e•cu•tion** \,präsi'kyüshən\ *n* — **pros•e•cu•tor** \'präsi,kyütər\ *n*

pros•e•lyte \'präsə,līt\ *n* : new convert — **pros•e•ly•tize** \'präsələ,tīz\ *vb*

pros•pect \'präs,pekt\ *n* **1** : extensive view **2** : something awaited **3** : potential buyer ~ *vb* : look for mineral deposits — **pro•spec•tive** \prə'spektiv, 'präs,pek-\ *adj* — **pro•spec•tive•ly** *adv* — **pros•pec•tor** \-,pektər, -'pek-\ *n*

pro•spec•tus \prə'spektəs\ *n* : introductory description of an enterprise

pros•per \'präspər\ *vb* : thrive or succeed — **pros•per•ous** \-pərəs\ *adj*

pros•per•i•ty \präs'perətē\ *n* : economic well-being

pros•tate \'präs,tāt\ *n* : glandular body about the base of the male urethra — **prostate** *adj*

pros•the•sis \präs'thēsəs, 'prästhə-\ *n, pl* **-the•ses** \-,sēz\ : artificial replacement for a body part — **pros•thet•ic** \präs'thetik\ *adj*

pros•ti•tute \'prästə,tüt, -,tyüt\ *vb* **-tut•ed; -tut•ing** **1** : offer sexual activity for money **2** : put to corrupt or unworthy purposes ~ *n* : one who engages in sexual activities for money — **pros•ti•tu•tion** \,prästə'tüshən, -'tyü-\ *n*

pros•trate \'präs,trāt\ *adj* : stretched out with face on the ground ~ *vb* **-trat•ed; -trat•ing** **1** : fall or throw (oneself) into a prostrate position **2** : reduce to helplessness — **pros•tra•tion** \präs'trāshən\ *n*

pro•tag•o•nist \prō'tagənist\ *n* : main character in a drama or story

pro•tect \prə'tekt\ *vb* : shield from injury — **pro•tec•tor** \-tər\ *n*

pro•tec•tion \prə'tekshən\ *n* **1** : act of protecting **2** : one that protects — **pro•tec•tive** \-'tektiv\ *adj*

pro•tec•tor•ate \-tərət\ *n* : state dependent upon the authority of another state

pro•té•gé \'prōtə,zhā\ *n* : one under the care and protection of an influential person

pro•tein \'prō,tēn\ *n* : complex combination of amino acids present in living matter

pro•test \'prō,test\ *n* **1** : organized public demonstration of disapproval **2** : strong objection ~ \prə'test\ *vb* **1** : assert positively **2** : object strongly — **pro•tes•ta•tion** \,prätəs'tāshən\ *n* — **pro•test•er, pro•tes•tor** \'prō-,testər\ *n*

Prot•es•tant \'prätəstənt\ *n* : Christian not of a Catholic or Orthodox church — **Prot•es•tant•ism** \'prätəstənt-,izəm\ *n*

pro•to•col \'prōtə,kȯl\ *n* : diplomatic etiquette

pro•ton \'prō,tän\ *n* : positively charged atomic particle

pro•to•plasm \'prōtə,plazəm\ *n* : complex colloidal living substance of plant and animal cells — **pro•to•plas•mic** \,prōtə'plazmik\ *adj*

pro•to•type \'prōtə,tīp\ *n* : original model

pro•to•zo•an \,prōtə'zōən\ *n* : single-celled lower invertebrate animal

pro•tract \prō'trakt\ *vb* : prolong

pro•trac•tor \-'traktər\ *n* : instrument for drawing and measuring angles

pro•trude \prō'trüd\ *vb* **-trud•ed; -trud•ing** : stick out or cause to stick out — **pro•tru•sion** \-'trüzhən\ *n*

pro•tu•ber•ance \prō'tübərəns, -'tyü-\ *n* : something that protrudes — **pro•tu•ber•ant** *adj*

proud \'praud\ *adj* **1** : having or showing excessive self-esteem **2** : highly pleased **3** : having proper self-respect **4** : glorious — **proud•ly** *adv*

prove \'prüv\ *vb* **proved; proved** *or* **prov•en** \'prüvən\; **prov•ing** **1** : test by experiment or by a standard **2** : establish the truth of by argument or evidence **3** : turn out esp. after trial or test — **prov•able** \'prüvəbəl\ *adj*

prov•en•der \'prävəndər\ *n* : dry food for domestic animals

prov•erb \'präv,ərb\ *n* : short meaningful popular saying — **pro•ver•bi•al** \prə'vərbēəl\ *adj*

pro•vide \prə'vīd\ *vb* **-vid•ed; -vid•ing** **1** : take measures beforehand **2** : make a stipulation **3** : supply what is needed — **pro•vid•er** *n*

pro•vid•ed *conj* : if

prov•i•dence \'prävədəns\ *n* **1** *often cap* : divine guidance **2** *cap* : God **3** : quality of being provident

prov•i•dent \-ədənt\ *adj* **1** : making provision for the future **2** : thrifty — **prov•i•dent•ly** *adv*

prov•i•den•tial \ˌprävə'denchəl\ *adj* **1** : relating to Providence **2** : opportune

pro•vid•ing *conj* : provided

prov•ince \'prävəns\ *n* **1** : administrative district **2** *pl* : all of a country outside the metropolis **3** : sphere

pro•vin•cial \prə'vinchəl\ *adj* **1** : relating to a province **2** : limited in outlook — **pro•vin•cial•ism** \-ˌizəm\ *n*

pro•vi•sion \prə'vizhən\ *n* **1** : act of providing **2** : stock of food — usu. in pl. **3** : stipulation ~ *vb* : supply with provisions

pro•vi•sion•al \-'vizhənəl\ *adj* : provided for a temporary need — **pro•vi•sion•al•ly** *adv*

pro•vi•so \prə'vīzō\ *n, pl* **-sos** or **-soes** : stipulation

pro•voke \prə'vōk\ *vb* **-voked; -vok•ing** **1** : incite to anger **2** : stir up on purpose — **prov•o•ca•tion** \ˌprävə'kāshən\ *n* — **pro•voc•a•tive** \prə'väkətiv\ *adj*

prow \'prau̇\ *n* : bow of a ship

prow•ess \'prau̇əs\ *n* **1** : valor **2** : extraordinary ability

prowl \'prau̇l\ *vb* : roam about stealthily — **prowl** *n* — **prowl•er** *n*

prox•i•mate \'präksəmət\ *adj* : very near

prox•im•i•ty \präk'simətē\ *n* : nearness

proxy \'präksē\ *n, pl* **prox•ies** : authority to act for another — **proxy** *adj*

prude \'prüd\ *n* : one who shows extreme modesty — **prud•ery** \'prüdərē\ *n* — **prud•ish** \'prüdish\ *adj*

pru•dent \'prüdᵊnt\ *adj* **1** : shrewd **2** : cautious **3** : thrifty — **pru•dence** \-ᵊns\ *n* — **pru•den•tial** \prü-'denchəl\ *adj* — **pru•dent•ly** *adv*

¹prune \'prün\ *n* : dried plum

²prune *vb* **pruned; prun•ing** : cut off unwanted parts

pru•ri•ent \'pru̇rēənt\ *adj* : lewd — **pru•ri•ence** \-ēəns\ *n*

¹pry \'prī\ *vb* **pried; pry•ing** : look closely or inquisitively

²pry *vb* **pried; pry•ing** : raise, move, or pull apart with a lever

psalm \'säm, 'sälm\ *n* : sacred song or poem — **psalm•ist** *n*

pseu•do•nym \'südᵊnˌim\ *n* : fictitious name — **pseu•don•y•mous** \sü'dänəməs\ *adj*

pso•ri•a•sis \sə'rīəsəs\ *n* : chronic skin disease

psy•che \'sīkē\ *n* : soul or mind

psy•chi•a•try \sə'kīətrē, sī-\ *n* : branch of medicine dealing with mental, emotional, and behavioral disorders — **psy•chi•at•ric** \ˌsīkē'atrik\ *adj* — **psy•chi•a•trist** \sə'kīətrist, sī-\ *n*

psy•chic \'sīkik\ *adj* **1** : relating to the psyche **2** : sensitive to supernatural forces ~ *n* : person sensitive to supernatural forces — **psy•chi•cal•ly** *adv*

psy•cho•anal•y•sis \ˌsīkōə'naləsəs\ *n* : study of the normally hidden content of the mind esp. to resolve conflicts — **psy•cho•an•a•lyst** \-'anᵊlist\ *n* — **psy•cho•an•al•yt•ic** \-ˌanᵊl'itik\ *adj* — **psy•cho•an•a•lyze** \-'anᵊlˌīz\ *vb*

psy•chol•o•gy \sī'käləjē\ *n, pl* **-gies 1** : science of mind and behavior **2** : mental and behavioral aspect (as of an individual) — **psy•cho•log•i•cal** \ˌsīkə'läjikəl\ *adj* — **psy•cho•log•i•cal•ly** *adv* — **psy•chol•o•gist** \sī-'käləjist\ *n*

psy•cho•path \'sīkəˌpath\ *n* : mentally ill or unstable person — **psy•cho•path•ic** \ˌsīkə'pathik\ *adj*

psy•cho•sis \sī'kōsəs\ *n, pl* **-cho•ses** \-ˌsēz\ : mental derangement (as paranoia) — **psy•chot•ic** \-'kätik\ *adj or n*

psy•cho•so•mat•ic \ˌsīkəsə'matik\ *adj* : relating to bodily symptoms caused by mental or emotional disturbance

psy•cho•ther•a•py \ˌsīkō'therəpē\ *n* : treatment of mental disorder by psychological means — **psy•cho•ther•a•pist** \-pist\ *n*

pto•maine \'tōˌmān\ *n* : bacterial decay product

pu•ber•ty \'pyübərtē\ *n* : time of sexual maturity

pu•bic \'pyübik\ *adj* : relating to the lower abdominal region

pub•lic \'pəblik\ *adj* **1** : relating to the

people as a whole **2** : civic **3** : not private **4** : open to all **5** : well-known **~** *n* : people as a whole — **pub·lic·ly** *adv*

pub·li·ca·tion \ˌpəblə'kāshən\ *n* **1** : process of publishing **2** : published work

pub·lic·i·ty \pə'blisətē\ *n* **1** : news information given out to gain public attention **2** : public attention

pub·li·cize \'pəblə,sīz\ *vb* **-cized; -ciz·ing** : bring to public attention — **pub·li·cist** \-sist\ *n*

pub·lish \'pəblish\ *vb* **1** : announce publicly **2** : reproduce for sale esp. by printing — **pub·lish·er** *n*

puck·er \'pəkər\ *vb* : pull together into folds or wrinkles **~** *n* : wrinkle

pud·ding \'pùdiŋ\ *n* : creamy dessert

pud·dle \'pəd³l\ *n* : very small pool of water

pudgy \'pəjē\ *adj* **pudg·i·er; -est** : short and plump

pu·er·ile \'pyùrəl\ *adj* : childish

puff \'pəf\ *vb* **1** : blow in short gusts **2** : pant **3** : enlarge **~** *n* **1** : short discharge (as of air) **2** : slight swelling **3** : something light and fluffy — **puffy** *adj*

pug \'pəg\ *n* : small stocky dog

pu·gi·lism \'pyüjə,lizəm\ *n* : boxing — **pu·gi·list** \-list\ *n* — **pu·gi·lis·tic** \ˌpyüjə'listik\ *adj*

pug·na·cious \ˌpəg'nāshəs\ *adj* : prone to fighting — **pug·nac·i·ty** \-'nasətē\ *n*

puke \'pyük\ *vb* **puked; puk·ing** : vomit — **puke** *n*

pul·chri·tude \'pəlkrə,tüd, -,tyüd\ *n* : beauty — **pul·chri·tu·di·nous** \ˌpəlkrə'tüd³nəs, -'tyüd-\ *adj*

pull \'pùl\ *vb* **1** : exert force so as to draw (something) toward or out **2** : move **3** : stretch or tear **~** *n* **1** : act of pulling **2** : influence **3** : device for pulling something — **pull·er** *n*

pul·let \'pùlət\ *n* : young hen

pul·ley \'pùlē\ *n, pl* **-leys** : wheel with a grooved rim

Pull·man \'pùlmən\ *n* : railroad car with berths

pull·over \'pùl,ōvər\ *adj* : put on by being pulled over the head — **pullover** *n*

pul·mo·nary \'pùlmə,nerē, 'pəl-\ *adj* : relating to the lungs

pulp \'pəlp\ *n* **1** : soft part of a fruit or

vegetable **2** : soft moist mass (as of mashed wood) — **pulpy** *adj*

pul·pit \'pùl,pit\ *n* : raised desk used in preaching

pul·sate \'pəl,sāt\ *vb* **-sat·ed; -sat·ing** : expand and contract rhythmically — **pul·sa·tion** \ˌpəl'sāshən\ *n*

pulse \'pəls\ *n* : arterial throbbing caused by heart contractions — **pulse** *vb*

pul·ver·ize \'pəlvə,rīz\ *vb* **-ized; -iz·ing** : beat or grind into a powder

pu·ma \'pümə, 'pyü-\ *n* : cougar

pum·ice \'pəməs\ *n* : light porous volcanic glass used in polishing

pum·mel \'pəməl\ *vb* **-meled; -mel·ing** : beat

¹**pump** \'pəmp\ *n* : device for moving or compressing fluids **~** *vb* **1** : raise (as water) with a pump **2** : fill by means of a pump — with *up* **3** : move like a pump — **pump·er** *n*

²**pump** *n* : woman's low shoe

pum·per·nick·el \'pəmpər,nikəl\ *n* : dark rye bread

pump·kin \'pəŋkən, 'pəmpkən\ *n* : large usu. orange fruit of a vine related to the gourd

pun \'pən\ *n* : humorous use of a word in a way that suggests two or more interpretations — **pun** *vb*

¹**punch** \'pənch\ *vb* **1** : strike with the fist **2** : perforate with a punch **~** *n* : quick blow with the fist — **punch·er** *n*

²**punch** *n* : tool for piercing or stamping

³**punch** *n* : mixed beverage often including fruit juice

punc·til·i·ous \pəŋk'tilēəs\ *adj* : marked by precise accordance with conventions

punc·tu·al \'pəŋkchəwəl\ *adj* : prompt — **punc·tu·al·i·ty** \ˌpəŋkchə'walətē\ *n* — **punc·tu·al·ly** *adv*

punc·tu·ate \'pəŋkchə,wāt\ *vb* **-at·ed; -at·ing** : mark with punctuation

punc·tu·a·tion \ˌpəŋkchə'wāshən\ *n* : standardized marks in written matter to clarify the meaning and separate parts

punc·ture \'pəŋkchər\ *n* : act or result of puncturing **~** *vb* **-tured; -tur·ing** : make a hole in

pun·dit \'pəndət\ *n* **1** : learned person **2** : expert or critic

pun·gent \'pənjənt\ *adj* : having a sharp or stinging odor or taste — **pun·gen·cy** \-jənsē\ *n* — **pun·gent·ly** *adv*

pun·ish \'pənish\ *vb* : impose a penalty

on or for — **pun•ish•able** *adj* —
pun•ish•ment *n*
pu•ni•tive \'pyünətiv\ *adj* : inflicting
punishment
pun•kin *var of* PUMPKIN
¹**punt** \'pənt\ *n* : long narrow flat=
bottomed boat ~ *vb* : propel (a boat)
by pushing with a pole
²**punt** *vb* : kick a ball dropped from the
hands ~ *n* : act of punting a ball
pu•ny \'pyünē\ *adj* **-ni•er; -est** : slight
in power or size
pup \'pəp\ *n* : young dog
pu•pa \'pyüpə\ *n, pl* **-pae** \-ıpē, -ıpī\
or **-pas** : insect (as a moth) when it is
in a cocoon — **pu•pal** \-pəl\ *adj*
¹**pu•pil** \'pyüpəl\ *n* : young person in
school
²**pupil** *n* : dark central opening of the iris
of the eye
pup•pet \'pəpət\ *n* : small doll moved
by hand or by strings — **pup•pe•teer**
\ıpəpə'tir\ *n*
pup•py \'pəpē\ *n, pl* **-pies** : young dog
pur•chase \'pərchəs\ *vb* **-chased;
-chas•ing** : obtain in exchange for
money ~ *n* **1** : act of purchasing **2**
: something purchased **3** : secure
grasp — **pur•chas•er** *n*
pure \'pyùr\ *adj* **pur•er; pur•est** : free
of foreign matter, contamination, or
corruption — **pure•ly** *adv*
pu•ree \pyù'rā, -'rē\ *n* : thick liquid
mass of food — **puree** *vb*
pur•ga•to•ry \'pərgəıtōrē\ *n, pl* **-ries**
: intermediate state after death for
purification by expiating sins — **pur•
ga•tor•i•al** \ıpərgə'tōrēəl\ *adj*
purge \'pərj\ *vb* **purged; purg•ing 1**
: purify esp. from sin **2** : have or
cause emptying of the bowels **3**
: get rid of ~ *n* **1** : act or result of
purging **2** : something that purges —
pur•ga•tive \'pərgətiv\ *adj or n*
pu•ri•fy \'pyùrəıfī\ *vb* **-fied; -fy•ing**
: make or become pure — **pu•ri•fi•ca•
tion** \ıpyùrəfə'kāshən\ *n* — **pu•ri•
fi•er** \-ıfīər\ *n*
Pu•rim \'pùrim\ *n* : Jewish holiday celebrated in February or March in commemoration of the deliverance of the
Jews from the massacre plotted by
Haman
pu•ri•tan \'pyùrət°n\ *n* : one who practices or preaches a very strict moral
code — **pu•ri•tan•i•cal** \ıpyürə-
'tanikəl\ *adj* — **pu•ri•tan•i•cal•ly** *adv*

pu•ri•ty \'pyùrətē\ *n* : quality or state
of being pure
purl \'pərl\ *n* : stitch in knitting ~ *vb*
: knit in purl stitch
pur•loin \pər'lòin, 'pərılòin\ *vb* : steal
pur•ple \'pərpəl\ *n* : bluish red color —
pur•plish \'pərpəlish\ *adj*
pur•port \pər'pōrt\ *vb* : convey outwardly as the meaning ~ \'pərıpōrt\
n : meaning — **pur•port•ed•ly** \-ədlē\
adv
pur•pose \'pərpəs\ *n* **1** : something
(as a result) aimed at **2** : resolution
~ *vb* **-posed; -pos•ing** : intend —
pur•pose•ful \-fəl\ *adj* — **pur•pose•
ful•ly** *adv* — **pur•pose•less** *adj* —
pur•pose•ly *adv*
purr \'pər\ *n* : low murmur typical of a
contented cat — **purr** *vb*
¹**purse** \'pərs\ *n* **1** : bag or pouch for
money and small objects **2** : financial
resource **3** : prize money
²**purse** *vb* **pursed; purs•ing** : pucker
pur•su•ance \pər'süəns\ *n* : act of carrying out or into effect
pur•su•ant to \-'süənt-\ *prep* : according to
pur•sue \pər'sü\ *vb* **-sued; -su•ing 1**
: follow in order to overtake **2** : seek
to accomplish **3** : proceed along **4**
: engage in — **pur•su•er** *n*
pur•suit \pər'süt\ *n* **1** : act of pursuing
2 : occupation
pur•vey \pər'vā\ *vb* **-veyed; -vey•ing**
: supply (as provisions) usu. as a business — **pur•vey•or** \-ər\ *n*
pus \'pəs\ *n* : thick yellowish fluid (as
in a boil)
push \'pùsh\ *vb* **1** : press against to
move forward **2** : urge on or provoke
~ *n* **1** : vigorous effort **2** : act of
pushing — **push•cart** *n* — **push•er**
\'pùshər\ *n*
pushy \'pùshē\ *adj* **push•i•er; -est**
: objectionably aggressive
pu•sil•lan•i•mous \ıpyüsə'lanəməs\
adj : cowardly
pussy \'pùsē\ *n, pl* **puss•ies** : cat
pus•tule \'pəschül\ *n* : pus-filled pim-
ple
put \'pùt\ *vb* **put; put•ting 1** : bring to
a specified position or condition **2**
: subject to pain, suffering, or death **3**
: impose or cause to exist **4** : express
5 : cause to be used or employed —
put off *vb* : postpone or delay — **put
out** *vb* : bother or inconvenience —

put up *vb* **1** : prepare for storage **2** : lodge **3** : contribute or pay — **put up with** : endure

pu•tre•fy \'pyütrə͵fī\ *vb* **-fied; -fy•ing** : make or become putrid — **pu•tre•fac•tion** \͵pyütrə'fakshən\ *n*

pu•trid \'pyütrəd\ *adj* : rotten — **pu•trid•i•ty** \pyü'tridətē\ *n*

put•ty \'pətē\ *n, pl* **-ties** : doughlike cement — **putty** *vb*

puz•zle \'pəzəl\ *vb* **-zled; -zling 1** : confuse **2** : attempt to solve — with *out* or *over* ∼ *n* : something that confuses or tests ingenuity — **puz•zle•ment** *n* — **puz•zler** \-ələr\ *n*

pyg•my \'pigmē\ *n, pl* **-mies** : dwarf — **pygmy** *adj*

py•lon \'pī͵län, -lən\ *n* : tower or tall post

pyr•a•mid \'pirə͵mid\ *n* : structure with a square base and 4 triangular sides meeting at a point

pyre \'pīr\ *n* : material heaped for a funeral fire

py•ro•ma•nia \͵pīrō'mānēə\ *n* : irresistible impulse to start fires — **py•ro•ma•ni•ac** \-nē͵ak\ *n*

py•ro•tech•nics \͵pīrə'tekniks\ *n pl* : spectacular display (as of fireworks) — **py•ro•tech•nic** \-nik\ *adj*

Pyr•rhic \'pirik\ *adj* : achieved at excessive cost

py•thon \'pī͵thän, -thən\ *n* : very large constricting snake

Q

q \'kyü\ *n, pl* **q's** *or* **qs** \'kyüz\ : 17th letter of the alphabet

¹**quack** \'kwak\ *vb* : make a cry like that of a duck — **quack** *n*

²**quack** *n* : one who pretends to have medical or healing skill — **quack** *adj* — **quack•ery** \-ərē\ *n*

quad•ran•gle \'kwäd͵raŋgəl\ *n* : rectangular courtyard

quad•rant \'kwädrənt\ *n* : 1/4 of a circle

quad•ri•lat•er•al \͵kwädrə'latərəl\ *n* : 4-sided polygon

qua•drille \kwä'dril, kə-\ *n* : square dance for 4 couples

quad•ru•ped \'kwädrə͵ped\ *n* : animal having 4 feet

qua•dru•ple \kwä'drüpəl, -'drəp-; 'kwädrəp-\ *vb* **-pled; -pling** \-pliŋ\ : multiply by 4 ∼ *adj* : being 4 times as great or as many

qua•dru•plet \kwä'drəplət, -'drüp-; 'kwädrəp-\ *n* : one of 4 offspring born at one birth

quaff \'kwäf, 'kwaf\ *vb* : drink deeply or repeatedly — **quaff** *n*

quag•mire \'kwag͵mīr, 'kwäg-\ *n* : soft land or bog

qua•hog \'kō͵hȯg, 'kwȯ-, 'kwō-, -͵häg\ *n* : thick-shelled clam

¹**quail** \'kwāl\ *n, pl* **quail** *or* **quails** : short-winged plump game bird

²**quail** *vb* : cower in fear

quaint \'kwānt\ *adj* : pleasingly old= fashioned or odd — **quaint•ly** *adv* — **quaint•ness** *n*

quake \'kwāk\ *vb* **quaked; quak•ing** : shake or tremble ∼ *n* : earthquake

qual•i•fi•ca•tion \͵kwäləfə'kāshən\ *n* **1** : limitation or stipulation **2** : special skill or experience for a job

qual•i•fy \'kwälə͵fī\ *vb* **-fied; -fy•ing 1** : modify or limit **2** : fit by skill or training for some purpose **3** : become eligible — **qual•i•fied** *adj* — **qual•i•fi•er** \-͵fīər\ *n*

qual•i•ty \'kwälətē\ *n, pl* **-ties 1** : peculiar and essential character, nature, or feature **2** : excellence or distinction

qualm \'kwäm, 'kwälm, 'kwȯm\ *n* : sudden feeling of doubt or uneasiness

quan•da•ry \'kwändrē\ *n, pl* **-ries** : state of perplexity or doubt

quan•ti•ty \'kwäntətē\ *n, pl* **-ties 1** : something that can be measured or numbered **2** : considerable amount

quan•tum theory \'kwäntəm-\ *n* : theory in physics that radiant energy (as light) is composed of separate packets of energy

quar•an•tine \'kwȯrən͵tēn\ *n* **1** : restraint on the movements of persons or goods to prevent the spread of pests or disease **2** : place or period of quarantine — **quarantine** *vb*

quar•rel \'kwórəl\ *n* : basis of conflict — **quarrel** *vb* — **quar•rel•some** \-səm\ *adj*

¹**quar•ry** \'kwórē\ *n, pl* **-ries** : prey

²**quarry** *n, pl* **-ries** : excavation for obtaining stone — **quarry** *vb*

quart \'kwórt\ *n* : unit of liquid measure equal to .95 liter or of dry measure equal to 1.10 liters

quar•ter \'kwórtər\ *n* **1** : 1/4 part **2** : 1/4 of a dollar **3** : city district **4** *pl* : place to live esp. for a time **5** : mercy ～ *vb* : divide into 4 equal parts

quar•ter•ly \'kwórtərlē\ *adv or adj* : at 3-month intervals ～ *n, pl* **-lies** : periodical published 4 times a year

quar•ter•mas•ter *n* **1** : ship's helmsman **2** : army supply officer

quar•tet \kwór'tet\ *n* **1** : music for 4 performers **2** : group of 4

quar•to \'kwórtō\ *n, pl* **-tos** : book printed on pages cut 4 from a sheet

quartz \'kwórts\ *n* : transparent crystalline mineral

quash \'kwäsh, 'kwósh\ *vb* **1** : set aside by judicial action **2** : suppress summarily and completely

qua•si \'kwā,zī, -sī; 'kwäzē, 'kwäs-; 'kwäzē\ *adj* : similar or nearly identical

qua•train \'kwä,trān\ *n* : unit of 4 lines of verse

qua•ver \'kwāvər\ *vb* : tremble or trill — **quaver** *n*

quay \'kē, 'kā, 'kwā\ *n* : wharf

quea•sy \'kwēzē\ *adj* **-si•er; -est** : nauseated — **quea•si•ly** \-zəlē\ *adv* — **quea•si•ness** \-zēnəs\ *n*

queen \'kwēn\ *n* **1** : wife or widow of a king **2** : female monarch **3** : woman of rank, power, or attractiveness **4** : fertile female of a social insect — **queen•ly** *adj*

queer \'kwir\ *adj* : differing from the usual or normal — **queer•ly** *adv* — **queer•ness** *n*

quell \'kwel\ *vb* : put down by force

quench \'kwench\ *vb* **1** : put out **2** : satisfy (a thirst) — **quench•able** *adj* — **quench•er** *n*

quer•u•lous \'kwerələs, -yələs\ *adj* : fretful or whining — **quer•u•lous•ly** *adv* — **quer•u•lous•ness** *n*

que•ry \'kwirē, 'kwer-\ *n, pl* **-ries** : question — **query** *vb*

quest \'kwest\ *n or vb* : search

ques•tion \'kweschən\ *n* **1** : something asked **2** : subject for debate **3** : dispute ～ *vb* **1** : ask questions **2** : doubt or dispute **3** : subject to analysis — **ques•tion•er** *n*

ques•tion•able \'kweschənəbəl\ *adj* **1** : not certain **2** : of doubtful truth or morality — **ques•tion•ably** \-blē\ *adv*

question mark *n* : a punctuation mark ? used esp. at the end of a sentence to indicate a direct question

ques•tion•naire \,kweschə'nar\ *n* : set of questions

queue \'kyü\ *n* **1** : braid of hair **2** : a waiting line ～ *vb* **queued; queuing** *or* **queue•ing** : line up

quib•ble \'kwibəl\ *n* : minor objection — **quibble** *vb* — **quib•bler** *n*

quick \'kwik\ *adj* **1** : rapid **2** : alert or perceptive ～ *n* : sensitive area of living flesh — **quick** *adv* — **quick•ly** *adv* — **quick•ness** *n*

quick•en \'kwikən\ *vb* **1** : come to life **2** : increase in speed

quick•sand *n* : deep mass of sand and water

quick•sil•ver *n* : mercury

qui•es•cent \kwī'es³nt\ *adj* : being at rest — **qui•es•cence** \-əns\ *n*

qui•et \'kwīət\ *adj* **1** : marked by little motion or activity **2** : gentle **3** : free from noise **4** : not showy **5** : secluded ～ *vb* : pacify — **quiet** *adv or n* — **qui•et•ly** *adv* — **qui•et•ness** *n*

qui•etude \'kwīə,tüd, -,tyüd\ *n* : quietness or repose

quill \'kwil\ *n* **1** : a large stiff feather **2** : porcupine's spine

quilt \'kwilt\ *n* : padded bedspread ～ *vb* : stitch or sew in layers with padding in between

quince \'kwins\ *n* : hard yellow applelike fruit

qui•nine \'kwī,nīn\ *n* : bitter drug used against malaria

quin•tes•sence \kwin'tes³ns\ *n* **1** : purest essence of something **2** : most typical example — **quin•tes•sen•tial** \,kwintə'senchəl\ *adj* — **quin•tes•sen•tial•ly** *adv*

quin•tet \kwin'tet\ *n* **1** : music for 5 performers **2** : group of 5

quin•tu•ple \kwin'tüpəl, -'tyüp-, -'təp-; 'kwintəp-\ *adj* **1** : having 5 units or members **2** : being 5 times as great or as many — **quintuple** *n or vb*

quin•tu•plet \-plət\ *n* : one of 5 offspring at one birth

quip \'kwip\ *vb* **-pp-** : make a clever remark — **quip** *n*

quire \'kwīr\ *n* : 24 or 25 sheets of paper of the same size and quality

quirk \'kwərk\ *n* : peculiarity of action or behavior — **quirky** *adj*

quit \'kwit\ *vb* **quit; quit•ting 1** : stop **2** : leave — **quit•ter** *n*

quite \'kwīt\ *adv* **1** : completely **2** : to a considerable extent

quits \'kwits\ *adj* : even or equal with another (as by repaying a debt)

¹**quiv•er** \'kwivər\ *n* : case for arrows

²**quiver** *vb* : shake or tremble — **quiver** *n*

quix•ot•ic \kwik'sätik\ *adj* : idealistic to an impractical degree — **quix•ot•i•cal•ly** \-tiklē\ *adv*

quiz \'kwiz\ *n, pl* **quiz•zes** : short test ~ *vb* **-zz-** : question closely

quiz•zi•cal \'kwizikəl\ *adj* **1** : teasing **2** : curious

quoit \'kȯit, 'kwȯit, 'kwät\ *n* : ring thrown at a peg in a game (**quoits**)

quon•dam \'kwändəm, -ˌdam\ *adj* : former

quo•rum \'kwȯrəm\ *n* : required number of members present

quo•ta \'kwōtə\ *n* : proportional part or share

quotation mark *n* : one of a pair of punctuation marks " " or ' ' used esp. to indicate the beginning and the end of a quotation

quote \'kwōt\ *vb* **quot•ed; quot•ing 1** : repeat (another's words) exactly **2** : state (a price) — **quot•able** *adj* — **quo•ta•tion** \kwō'tāshən\ *n* — **quote** *n*

quo•tient \'kwōshənt\ *n* : number obtained from division

R

r \'är\ *n, pl* **r's** *or* **rs** \'ärz\ : 18th letter of the alphabet

rab•bet \'rabət\ *n* : groove in a board

rab•bi \'rabˌī\ *n* : Jewish religious leader — **rab•bin•ic** \rə'binik\, **rab•bin•i•cal** \-ikəl\ *adj*

rab•bin•ate \'rabənət, -ˌnāt\ *n* : office of a rabbi

rab•bit \'rabət\ *n, pl* **-bit** *or* **-bits** : long-eared burrowing mammal

rab•ble \'rabəl\ *n* : mob

ra•bid \'rabəd\ *adj* **1** : violent **2** : fanatical **3** : affected with rabies — **ra•bid•ly** *adv*

ra•bies \'rābēz\ *n, pl* **rabies** : acute deadly virus disease

rac•coon \ra'kün\ *n, pl* **-coon** *or* **-coons** : tree-dwelling mammal with a black mask and a bushy ringed tail

¹**race** \'rās\ *n* **1** : strong current of water **2** : contest of speed **3** : election campaign ~ *vb* **raced; rac•ing 1** : run in a race **2** : rush — **race•course** *n* — **rac•er** *n* — **race•track** *n*

²**race** *n* **1** : family, tribe, people, or nation of the same stock **2** : division of mankind based on hereditary traits — **ra•cial** \'rāshəl\ *adj* — **ra•cial•ly** *adv*

race•horse *n* : horse used for racing

rac•ism \'rāsˌizəm\ *n* : discrimination based on the belief that some races are by nature superior — **rac•ist** \-ist\ *n*

rack \'rak\ *n* **1** : framework for display or storage **2** : instrument that stretches the body for torture ~ *vb* : torture with or as if with a rack

¹**rack•et** \'rakət\ *n* : bat with a tight netting across an open frame

²**racket** *n* **1** : confused noise **2** : fraudulent scheme — **rack•e•teer** \ˌrakə'tir\ *n* — **rack•e•teer•ing** *n*

ra•con•teur \ˌrakˌän'tər\ *n* : storyteller

racy \'rāsē\ *adj* **rac•i•er; -est** : risqué — **rac•i•ly** *adv* — **rac•i•ness** *n*

ra•dar \'rāˌdär\ *n* : radio device for determining distance and direction of distant objects

ra•di•al \'rādēəl\ *adj* : having parts arranged like rays coming from a common center — **ra•di•al•ly** *adv*

ra•di•ant \'rādēənt\ *adj* **1** : glowing **2** : beaming with happiness **3** : transmitted by radiation — **ra•di•ance** \-əns\ *n* — **ra•di•ant•ly** *adv*

ra•di•ate \'rādēˌāt\ *vb* **-at•ed; -at•ing 1** : issue rays or in rays **2** : spread from a center — **ra•di•a•tion** \ˌrādē'āshən\ *n*

ra·di·a·tor \'rādē₁ātər\ *n* : cooling or heating device

rad·i·cal \'radikəl\ *adj* **1** : fundamental **2** : extreme ∼ *n* : person favoring extreme changes — **rad·i·cal·ism** \-₁izəm\ *n* — **rad·i·cal·ly** *adv*

radii *pl of* RADIUS

ra·dio \'rādē₁ō\ *n, pl* **-di·os 1** : wireless transmission or reception of sound by means of electric waves **2** : radio receiving set ∼ *vb* : send a message to by radio — **radio** *adj*

ra·dio·ac·tiv·i·ty \₁rādēō₁ak'tivətē\ *n* : property of an element that emits energy through nuclear disintegration — **ra·dio·ac·tive** \-'aktiv\ *adj*

ra·di·ol·o·gy \₁rādē'äləjē\ *n* : medical use of radiation — **ra·di·ol·o·gist** \-jist\ *n*

rad·ish \'radish\ *n* : pungent fleshy root usu. eaten raw

ra·di·um \'rādēəm\ *n* : metallic radioactive chemical element

ra·di·us \'rādēəs\ *n, pl* **-dii** \-ē₁ī\ **1** : line from the center of a circle or sphere to the circumference or surface **2** : area defined by a radius

ra·don \'rā₁dän\ *n* : gaseous radioactive chemical element

raff·ish \'rafish\ *adj* : flashily vulgar — **raff·ish·ly** *adv* — **raff·ish·ness** *n*

raf·fle \'rafəl\ *n* : lottery among people who have bought tickets ∼ *vb* **-fled; -fling** : offer in a raffle

¹raft \'raft\ *n* : flat floating platform ∼ *vb* : travel or transport by raft

²raft *n* : large amount or number

raf·ter \'raftər\ *n* : beam supporting a roof

¹rag \'rag\ *n* : waste piece of cloth

²rag *n* : composition in ragtime

rag·a·muf·fin \'ragə₁məfən\ *n* : ragged dirty person

rage \'rāj\ *n* **1** : violent anger **2** : vogue ∼ *vb* **raged; rag·ing 1** : be extremely angry or violent **2** : be out of control

rag·ged \'ragəd\ *adj* : torn — **rag·ged·ly** *adv* — **rag·ged·ness** *n*

ra·gout \ra'gü\ *n* : meat stew

rag·time *n* : syncopated music

rag·weed *n* : coarse weedy herb with allergenic pollen

raid \'rād\ *n* : sudden usu. surprise attack — **raid** *vb* — **raid·er** *n*

¹rail \'rāl\ *n* **1** : bar serving as a guard or barrier **2** : bar forming a track for wheeled vehicles **3** : railroad

²rail *vb* : scold someone vehemently — **rail·er** *n*

rail·ing \'rāliŋ\ *n* : rail or a barrier of rails

rail·lery \'rālərē\ *n, pl* **-ler·ies** : good-natured ridicule

rail·road \'rāl₁rōd\ *n* : road for a train laid with iron rails and wooden ties ∼ *vb* : force something hastily — **rail·road·er** *n* — **rail·road·ing** *n*

rail·way \-₁wā\ *n* : railroad

rai·ment \'rāmənt\ *n* : clothing

rain \'rān\ *n* **1** : water falling in drops from the clouds **2** : shower of objects ∼ *vb* : fall as or like rain — **rain·coat** *n* — **rain·drop** *n* — **rain·fall** *n* — **rain·mak·er** *n* — **rain·mak·ing** *n* — **rain·storm** *n* — **rain·water** *n* — **rainy** *adj*

rain·bow \-₁bō\ *n* : arc of colors formed by the sun shining through moisture

raise \'rāz\ *vb* **raised; rais·ing 1** : lift **2** : arouse **3** : erect **4** : collect **5** : breed, grow, or bring up **6** : increase **7** : make light ∼ *n* : increase esp. in pay — **rais·er** *n*

rai·sin \'rāzᵊn\ *n* : dried grape

ra·ja, ra·jah \'räjə\ *n* : Indian prince

¹rake \'rāk\ *n* : garden tool for smoothing or sweeping ∼ *vb* **raked; rak·ing 1** : gather, loosen, or smooth with or as if with a rake **2** : sweep with gunfire

²rake *n* : dissolute man

rak·ish \'rākish\ *adj* : smart or jaunty — **rak·ish·ly** *adv* — **rak·ish·ness** *n*

ral·ly \'ralē\ *vb* **-lied; -ly·ing 1** : bring or come together **2** : revive or recover **3** : make a comeback ∼ *n, pl* **-lies 1** : act of rallying **2** : mass meeting

ram \'ram\ *n* **1** : male sheep **2** : beam used in battering down walls or doors ∼ *vb* **-mm- 1** : force or drive in or through **2** : strike against violently

RAM \'ram\ *n* : main internal storage area in a computer

ram·ble \'rambəl\ *vb* **-bled; -bling** : wander — **ramble** *n* — **ram·bler** \-blər\ *n*

ram·bunc·tious \ram'bəŋkshəs\ *adj* : unruly

ram·i·fi·ca·tion \₁raməfə'kāshən\ *n* : consequence

ram·i·fy \'ramə₁fī\ *vb* **-fied; -fy·ing** : branch out

ramp \'ramp\ *n* : sloping passage or connecting roadway

ram·page \'ram₁pāj, ram'pāj\ *vb* **-paged; -pag·ing** : rush about wildly ∼ \'ram₁-\ *n* : violent or riotous action or behavior

ram·pant \'rampənt\ *adj* : widespread — **ram·pant·ly** *adv*

ram·part \'ram₁pärt\ *n* : embankment of a fortification

ram·rod *n* : rod used to load or clean a gun ∼ *adj* : strict or inflexible

ram·shack·le \'ram₁shakəl\ *adj* : shaky

ran *past of* RUN

ranch \'ranch\ *n* **1** : establishment for the raising of cattle, sheep, or horses **2** : specialized farm ∼ *vb* : operate a ranch — **ranch·er** *n*

ran·cid \'ransəd\ *adj* : smelling or tasting as if spoiled — **ran·cid·i·ty** \ran-'sidətē\ *n*

ran·cor \'raŋkər\ *n* : bitter deep-seated ill will — **ran·cor·ous** *adj*

ran·dom \'randəm\ *adj* : occurring by chance — **ran·dom·ly** *adv* — **ran·dom·ness** *n* — **at random** : without definite aim or method

ran·dom·ize \'randə₁mīz\ *vb* **-ized; -izing** : select, assign, or arrange in a random way

rang *past of* RING

range \'rānj\ *n* **1** : series of things in a row **2** : open land for grazing **3** : cooking stove **4** : variation within limits **5** : place for target practice **6** : extent ∼ *vb* **ranged; rang·ing** **1** : arrange **2** : roam at large, freely, or over **3** : vary within limits

rang·er \'rānjər\ *n* : officer who manages and protects public lands

rangy \'rānjē\ *adj* **rang·i·er; -est** : being slender with long limbs — **rang·i·ness** *n*

¹rank \'raŋk\ *adj* **1** : vigorous in growth **2** : unpleasantly strong-smelling — **rank·ly** *adv* — **rank·ness** *n*

²rank *n* **1** : line of soldiers **2** : orderly arrangement **3** : grade of official standing **4** : position within a group ∼ *vb* **1** : arrange in formation or according to class **2** : take or have a relative position

rank and file *n* : general membership

ran·kle \'raŋkəl\ *vb* **-kled; -kling** : cause anger, irritation, or bitterness

ran·sack \'ran₁sak\ *vb* : search through and rob

ran·som \'ransəm\ *n* : something demanded for the freedom of a captive ∼ *vb* : gain the freedom of by paying a price — **ran·som·er** *n*

rant \'rant\ *vb* : talk or scold violently — **rant·er** *n* — **rant·ing·ly** *adv*

¹rap \'rap\ *n* : sharp blow or rebuke ∼ *vb* **-pp-** : strike or criticize sharply

²rap *vb* **-pp-** : talk freely

ra·pa·cious \rə'pāshəs\ *adj* **1** : excessively greedy **2** : ravenous — **ra·pa·cious·ly** *adv* — **ra·pa·cious·ness** *n* — **ra·pac·i·ty** \-'pasətē\ *n*

¹rape \'rāp\ *n* : herb grown as a forage crop and for its seeds (**rape·seed**)

²rape *vb* **raped; rap·ing** : force to have sexual intercourse — **rape** *n* — **rap·er** *n* — **rap·ist** \'rāpist\ *n*

rap·id \'rapəd\ *adj* : very fast — **ra·pid·i·ty** \rə'pidətē\ *n* — **rap·id·ly** *adv*

rap·ids \-ədz\ *n pl* : place in a stream where the current is swift

ra·pi·er \'rāpēər\ *n* : narrow 2-edged sword

rap·ine \'rapən, -₁īn\ *n* : plunder

rap·port \ra'pōr\ *n* : harmonious relationship

rapt \'rapt\ *adj* : engrossed — **rapt·ly** *adv* — **rapt·ness** *n*

rap·ture \'rapchər\ *n* : spiritual or emotional ecstasy — **rap·tur·ous** \-chərəs\ *adj* — **rap·tur·ous·ly** *adv*

¹rare \'rar\ *adj* **rar·er; rar·est** : having a portion relatively uncooked

²rare *adj* **rar·er; rar·est** **1** : not dense **2** : unusually fine **3** : seldom met with — **rare·ly** *adv* — **rare·ness** *n* — **rar·i·ty** \'rarətē\ *n*

rar·e·fy \'rarə₁fī\ *vb* **-fied; -fy·ing** : make or become rare, thin, or less dense — **rar·e·fac·tion** \₁rarə'fakshən\ *n*

rar·ing \'rarən, -iŋ\ *adj* : full of enthusiasm

ras·cal \'raskəl\ *n* : mean, dishonest, or mischievous person — **ras·cal·i·ty** \ras'kalətē\ *n* — **ras·cal·ly** \'raskəlē\ *adj*

¹rash \'rash\ *adj* : too hasty in decision or action — **rash·ly** *adv* — **rash·ness** *n*

²rash *n* : a breaking out of the skin with red spots

rasp \'rasp\ *vb* **1** : rub with or as if with a rough file **2** : speak in a grating tone ∼ *n* : coarse file

rasp·ber·ry \'raz₁berē\ *n* : edible red or black berry

rat \'rat\ *n* : destructive rodent larger than the mouse ∼ *vb* : betray or inform on

ratch·et \'rachət\ *n* : notched device for allowing motion in one direction

rate \'rāt\ *n* **1** : quantity, amount, or degree measured in relation to some other quantity **2** : rank ∼ *vb* **rat·ed; rat·ing 1** : estimate or determine the rank or quality of **2** : deserve

rath·er \'rathər, 'rəth-, 'räth-\ *adv* **1** : preferably **2** : on the other hand **3** : more properly **4** : somewhat

rat·i·fy \'ratə,fī\ *vb* **-fied; -fy·ing** : approve and accept formally — **rat·i·fi·ca·tion** \,ratəfə'kāshən\ *n*

rat·ing \'rātiŋ\ *n* : classification according to grade

ra·tio \'rāshēō\ *n, pl* **-tios** : relation in number, quantity, or degree between things

ra·tion \'rashən, 'rāshən\ *n* : share or allotment (as of food) ∼ *vb* : use or allot sparingly

ra·tio·nal \'rashənəl\ *adj* **1** : having reason or sanity **2** : relating to reason — **ra·tio·nal·ly** *adv*

ra·tio·nale \,rashə'nal\ *n* **1** : explanation of principles of belief or practice **2** : underlying reason

ra·tio·nal·ize \'rashənə,līz\ *vb* **-ized; -iz·ing** : justify (as one's behavior or weaknesses) esp. to oneself — **ra·tio·nal·i·za·tion** \,rashənələ'zāshən\ *n*

rat·tan \ra'tan, rə-\ *n* : palm with long stems used esp. for canes and wickerwork

rat·tle \'ratᵊl\ *vb* **-tled; -tling 1** : make a series of clattering sounds **2** : say briskly **3** : confuse or upset ∼ *n* **1** : series of clattering sounds **2** : something (as a toy) that rattles

rat·tler \'ratlər\ *n* : rattlesnake

rat·tle·snake *n* : American venomous snake with a rattle at the end of the tail

rat·ty \'ratē\ *adj* **rat·ti·er; -est** : shabby

rau·cous \'rȯkəs\ *adj* : harsh or boisterous — **rau·cous·ly** *adv* — **rau·cous·ness** *n*

rav·age \'ravij\ *n* : destructive effect ∼ *vb* **-aged; -ag·ing** : lay waste — **rav·ag·er** *n*

rave \'rāv\ *vb* **raved; rav·ing 1** : talk wildly in or as if in delirium **2** : talk with extreme enthusiasm ∼ *n* **1** : act of raving **2** : enthusiastic praise

rav·el \'ravəl\ *vb* **-eled** *or* **-elled; -el·ing** *or* **-el·ling 1** : unravel **2** : tangle ∼ *n* **1** : something tangled **2** : loose thread

ra·ven \'rāvən\ *n* : large black bird ∼ *adj* : black and shiny

rav·en·ous \'ravənəs\ *adj* : very hungry — **rav·en·ous·ly** *adv* — **rav·en·ous·ness** *n*

ra·vine \rə'vēn\ *n* : narrow steep-sided valley

rav·ish \'ravish\ *vb* **1** : seize and take away by violence **2** : overcome with joy or delight **3** : rape — **rav·ish·er** *n* — **rav·ish·ment** *n*

raw \'rȯ\ *adj* **raw·er** \'rȯər\; **raw·est** \'rȯəst\ **1** : not cooked **2** : not processed **3** : not trained **4** : having the surface rubbed off **5** : cold and damp **6** : vulgar — **raw·ness** *n*

raw·hide \'rȯ,hīd\ *n* : untanned skin of cattle

ray \'rā\ *n* **1** : thin beam of radiant energy (as light) **2** : tiny bit

ray·on \'rā,än\ *n* : fabric made from cellulose fiber

raze \'rāz\ *vb* **razed; raz·ing** : destroy or tear down

ra·zor \'rāzər\ *n* : sharp cutting instrument used to shave off hair

re- \rē, ͵rē, 'rē\ *prefix* **1** : again or anew **2** : back or backward

reach \'rēch\ *vb* **1** : stretch out **2** : touch or try to touch or grasp **3** : extend to or arrive at **4** : communicate with ∼ *n* **1** : act of reaching **2** : distance one can reach **3** : ability to reach — **reach·able** *adj* — **reach·er** *n*

re·act \rē'akt\ *vb* **1** : act in response to some influence or stimulus **2** : undergo chemical change — **re·ac·tive** \-'aktiv\ *adj*

re·ac·tion \rē'akshən\ *n* **1** : action or emotion caused by and directly related to or counter to another action **2** : chemical change

re·ac·tion·ary \-shə,nerē\ *adj* : relat-

List of self-explanatory words with the prefix *re-*

reaccelerate	reacquire	readjustment
reaccept	reactivate	readmit
reacclimatize	reactivation	readopt
reaccredit	readdress	reaffirm
reacquaint	readjust	realign

ing to or favoring return to an earlier political order or policy — **reac-tionary** n

re·ac·tor \rē'aktər\ n 1 : one that reacts 2 : device for the controlled release of nuclear energy

read \'rēd\ vb **read** \'red\; **read·ing** \'rēdiŋ\ 1 : understand written language 2 : utter aloud printed words 3 : interpret 4 : study 5 : indicate ~ \'red\ adj : informed by reading — **read·a·bil·i·ty** \ˌrēdə'bilətē\ n — **read·able** adj — **read·ably** adv — **read·er** n — **read·er·ship** n

read·ing \'rēdiŋ\ n 1 : something read or for reading 2 : particular version, interpretation, or performance 3 : data indicated by an instrument

ready \'redē\ adj **read·i·er; -est** 1 : prepared or available for use or action 2 : willing to do something ~ vb **read·ied; ready·ing** : make ready ~ n : state of being ready — **read·i·ly** adv — **read·i·ness** n

re·al \'rēl\ adj 1 : relating to fixed or immovable things (as land) 2 : genuine 3 : not imaginary ~ adv : very — **re·al·ness** n — **for real** 1 : in earnest 2 : genuine

real estate n : property in houses and land

re·al·ism \'rēəˌlizəm\ n 1 : disposition to deal with facts practically 2 : faithful portrayal of reality — **re·al·ist** \-list\ adj or n — **re·al·is·tic** \ˌrēə'listik\ adj — **re·al·is·ti·cal·ly** \-tiklē\ adv

re·al·i·ty \rē'alətē\ n, pl **-ties** 1 : quality or state of being real 2 : something real

re·al·ize \'rēəˌlīz\ vb **-ized; -iz·ing** 1 : make actual 2 : obtain 3 : be aware of — **re·al·iz·able** adj — **re·al·i·za·tion** \ˌrēələ'zāshən\ n

re·al·ly \'rēlē, 'ril-\ adv : in truth

realm \'relm\ n 1 : kingdom 2 : sphere

¹ream \'rēm\ n : quantity of paper that is 480, 500, or 516 sheets

²ream vb : enlarge, shape, or clean with a specially shaped tool (**reamer**)

reap \'rēp\ vb : cut or clear (as a crop) with a scythe or machine — **reap·er** n

¹rear \'rir\ vb 1 : raise upright 2 : breed or bring up 3 : rise on the hind legs

²rear n 1 : back 2 : position at the back of something ~ adj : being at the back — **rear·ward** \-wərd\ adj or adv

rear admiral n : commissioned officer in the navy or coast guard ranking next below a vice admiral

rea·son \'rēzᵊn\ n 1 : explanation or justification 2 : motive for action or belief 3 : power or process of thinking ~ vb 1 : use the faculty of reason 2 : try to persuade another — **rea·son·er** n — **rea·son·ing** \'rēzᵊniŋ\ n

rea·son·able \'rēzᵊnəbəl\ adj 1 : being within the bounds of reason 2 : inexpensive — **rea·son·able·ness** n — **rea·son·ably** \-blē\ adv

re·as·sure \ˌrēə'shůr\ vb : restore one's confidence — **re·as·sur·ance** \-'shůrəns\ n — **re·as·sur·ing·ly** adv

re·bate \'rēˌbāt\ n : return of part of a payment — **rebate** vb

reb·el \'rebəl\ n : one that resists authority ~ \ri'bel\ vb **-belled; -bel·ling** 1 : resist authority 2 : feel or exhibit anger — **rebel** \'rebəl\ adj

re·bel·lion \ri'belyən\ n : resistance to authority and esp. to one's government

re·bel·lious \-yəs\ adj 1 : engaged in rebellion 2 : inclined to resist authority — **re·bel·lious·ly** adv — **re·bel·lious·ness** n

re·birth \'rē'bərth\ n 1 : new or second birth 2 : revival

re·bound \'rē'baůnd, ri-\ vb 1 : spring back on striking something 2 : recover from a reverse ~ \'rēˌ-\ n 1 : action of rebounding 2 : reaction to a reverse

re·buff \ri'bəf\ vb : refuse or repulse rudely — **rebuff** n

re·buke \-'byük\ vb **-buked; -buk·ing** : reprimand sharply — **rebuke** n

re·bus \'rēbəs\ n : riddle representing syllables or words with pictures

re·but \ri'bət\ vb **-but·ted; -but·ting** : refute — **re·but·ter** n

re·but·tal \-ᵊl\ n : opposing argument

re·cal·ci·trant \ri'kalsətrənt\ adj 1 : stubbornly resisting authority 2 : re-

sistant to handling or treatment — **re-cal-ci-trance** \-trəns\ n
re-call \ri'kȯl\ vb 1 : call back 2 : remember 3 : revoke ~ \ri'-, 'rē,-\ n 1 : a summons to return 2 : remembrance 3 : act of revoking
re-cant \ri'kant\ vb : take back (something said) publicly
re-ca-pit-u-late \,rēkə'pichə,lāt\ vb : summarize — **re-ca-pit-u-la-tion** \-,pichə'lāshən\ n
re-cede \ri'sēd\ vb -ced-ed; -ced-ing 1 : move back or away 2 : slant backward
re-ceipt \-'sēt\ n 1 : act of receiving 2 : something (as payment) received — usu. in pl. 3 : writing acknowledging something received
re-ceive \ri'sēv\ vb -ceived; -ceiv-ing 1 : take in or accept 2 : greet or entertain (visitors) 3 : pick up radio waves and convert into sounds or pictures — **re-ceiv-able** adj
re-ceiv-er \ri'sēvər\ n 1 : one that receives 2 : one having charge of property or money involved in a lawsuit 3 : apparatus for receiving radio waves — **re-ceiv-er-ship** n
re-cent \'rēs³nt\ adj 1 : having lately come into existence 2 : of the present time or time just past — **re-cent-ly** adv — **re-cent-ness** n
re-cep-ta-cle \ri'septikəl\ n : container
re-cep-tion \ri'sepshən\ n 1 : act of receiving 2 : social gathering at which guests are formally welcomed
re-cep-tion-ist \-shənist\ n : person employed to greet callers
re-cep-tive \ri'septiv\ adj : open and responsive to ideas, impressions, or suggestions — **re-cep-tive-ly** adv — **re-cep-tive-ness** n — **re-cep-tiv-i-ty** \,rē,sep'tivətē\ n
re-cess \'rē,ses, ri'ses\ n 1 : indentation in a line or surface 2 : suspension of a session for rest ~ vb 1 : make a recess in or put into a recess 2 : interrupt a session for a recess
re-ces-sion \ri'seshən\ n 1 : departing procession 2 : period of reduced economic activity

rec-i-pe \'resə,pē\ n : instructions for making something
re-cip-i-ent \ri'sipēənt\ n : one that receives
re-cip-ro-cal \ri'siprəkəl\ adj 1 : affecting each in the same way 2 : so related that one is equivalent to the other — **re-cip-ro-cal-ly** adv — **re-ci-proc-i-ty** \,resə'präsətē\ n
re-cip-ro-cate \-,kāt\ vb : make a return for something done or given — **re-cip-ro-ca-tion** \-,siprə'kāshən\ n
re-cit-al \ri'sīt³l\ n 1 : public reading or recitation 2 : music or dance concert or exhibition by pupils — **re-cit-al-ist** \-³list\ n
rec-i-ta-tion \,resə'tāshən\ n : a reciting or recital
re-cite \ri'sīt\ vb -cit-ed; -cit-ing 1 : repeat verbatim 2 : recount — **re-cit-er** n
reck-less \'rekləs\ adj : lacking caution — **reck-less-ly** adv — **reck-less-ness** n
reck-on \'rekən\ vb 1 : count or calculate 2 : consider
reck-on-ing n 1 : act or instance of reckoning 2 : settling of accounts
re-claim \ri'klām\ vb 1 : change to a desirable condition 2 : obtain from a waste product or by-product 3 : demand or obtain the return of — **re-claim-able** adj — **rec-la-ma-tion** \,reklə'māshən\ n
re-cline \ri'klīn\ vb -clined; -clin-ing : lean backward or lie down
rec-luse \'rek,lüs, ri'klüs\ n : one who leads a secluded or solitary life
rec-og-ni-tion \,rekig'nishən\ n : act of recognizing or state of being recognized
re-cog-ni-zance \ri'känəzəns, -'käg-\ n : promise recorded before a court
rec-og-nize \'rekig,nīz\ vb 1 : identify as previously known 2 : take notice of 3 : acknowledge esp. with appreciation — **rec-og-niz-able** \'rekəg,nīzəbəl\ adj — **rec-og-niz-ably** \-blē\ adv
re-coil \ri'kȯil\ vb : draw or spring back ~ \'rē,-, ri'-\ n : action of recoiling
rec-ol-lect \,rekə'lekt\ vb : remember

---

reassemble
reassert
reassess
reassessment
reassign

reassignment
reattach
reattain
reawaken
rebalance

rebaptize
rebid
rebind
reborn
rebroadcast

rec·ol·lec·tion \ˌrekəˈlekshən\ *n* **1** : act or power of recollecting **2** : something recollected

rec·om·mend \ˌrekəˈmend\ *vb* **1** : present as deserving of acceptance or trial **2** : advise — **rec·om·mend·able** \-ˈmendəbəl\ *adj*

rec·om·men·da·tion \ˌrekəmənˈdāshən\ *n* **1** : act of recommending **2** : something recommended or that recommends

rec·om·pense \ˈrekəmˌpens\ *n* : compensation — **recompense** *vb*

rec·on·cile \ˈrekənˌsīl\ *vb* **-ciled; -cil·ing** **1** : cause to be friendly again **2** : adjust or settle **3** : bring to acceptance — **rec·on·cil·able** *adj* — **rec·on·cile·ment** *n* — **rec·on·cil·er** *n* — **rec·on·cil·i·a·tion** \ˌrekənˌsilēˈāshən\ *n*

re·con·dite \ˈrekənˌdīt, riˈkän-\ *adj* **1** : hard to understand **2** : little known

re·con·di·tion \ˌrēkənˈdishən\ *vb* : restore to good condition

re·con·nais·sance \riˈkänəzəns, -səns\ *n* : exploratory survey of enemy territory

re·con·noi·ter, re·con·noi·tre \ˌrēkəˈnóitər, ˌrekə-\ *vb* **-tered** *or* **-tred; -ter·ing** *or* **-tring** : make a reconnaissance of

re·cord \riˈkórd\ *vb* **1** : set down in writing **2** : register permanently **3** : indicate **4** : preserve (as sound or images) for later reproduction ~ \ˈrekərd\ *n* **1** : something recorded **2** : best performance

re·cord·er \riˈkórdər\ *n* **1** : person or device that records **2** : wind instrument with finger holes

¹**re·count** \riˈkaúnt\ *vb* : relate in detail

²**re·count** \ˈrē-\ *vb* : count again — **re·count** \ˈrēˌ-, ˌrē-\ *n*

re·coup \riˈküp\ *vb* : make up for (an expense or loss)

re·course \ˈrēˌkórs, riˈ-\ *n* : source of aid or a turning to such a source

re·cov·er \riˈkəvər\ *vb* **1** : regain position, poise, or health **2** : recoup — **re·cov·er·able** *adj* — **re·cov·ery** \-ˈkəvərē\ *n*

rec·re·a·tion \ˌrekrēˈāshən\ *n* : a refreshing of strength or spirits as a change from work or study — **rec·re·a·tion·al** \-shənəl\ *adj*

re·crim·i·na·tion \riˌkriməˈnāshən\ *n* : retaliatory accusation — **re·crim·i·nate** *vb*

re·cruit \riˈkrüt\ *n* : newly enlisted member ~ *vb* : enlist the membership or services of — **re·cruit·er** *n* — **re·cruit·ment** *n*

rect·an·gle \ˈrekˌtaŋgəl\ *n* : 4-sided figure with 4 right angles — **rect·an·gu·lar** \rekˈtaŋgyələr\ *adj*

rec·ti·fy \ˈrektəˌfī\ *vb* **-fied; -fy·ing** : make or set right — **rec·ti·fi·ca·tion** \ˌrektəfəˈkāshən\ *n*

rec·ti·tude \ˈrektəˌtüd, -ˌtyüd\ *n* : moral integrity

rec·tor \ˈrektər\ *n* : pastor

rec·to·ry \ˈrektərē\ *n, pl* **-ries** : rector's residence

rec·tum \ˈrektəm\ *n, pl* **-tums** *or* **-ta** \-tə\ : last part of the intestine joining the colon and anus — **rec·tal** \-t°l\ *adj*

re·cum·bent \riˈkəmbənt\ *adj* : lying down

re·cu·per·ate \riˈküpəˌrāt, -ˈkyü-\ *vb* **-at·ed; -at·ing** : recover (as from illness) — **re·cu·per·a·tion** \-ˌküpəˈrāshən, -ˌkyü-\ *n* — **re·cu·per·a·tive** \-ˈküpərātiv, -ˈkyü-\ *adj*

re·cur \riˈkər\ *vb* **-rr- 1** : return in thought or talk **2** : occur again — **re·cur·rence** \-ˈkərəns\ *n* — **re·cur·rent** \-ənt\ *adj*

re·cy·cle \rēˈsīkəl\ *vb* : process (as glass or cans) in order to regain a material for human use — **re·cy·cla·ble** \-kələbəl\ *adj*

red \ˈred\ *n* **1** : color of blood or of the ruby **2** *cap* : communist — **red** *adj* — **red·dish** *adj* — **red·ness** *n*

red·den \ˈred°n\ *vb* : make or become red or reddish

re·deem \riˈdēm\ *vb* **1** : regain, free, or rescue by paying a price **2** : atone for **3** : free from sin **4** : convert into something of value — **re·deem·able** *adj* — **re·deem·er** *n*

re·demp·tion \-ˈdempshən\ *n* : act of

rebuild	recertification	recheck
rebury	recertify	rechristen
recalculate	rechannel	recirculate
recapture	recharge	recirculation
recast	rechargeable	reclassification

redeeming — **re•demp•tive** \-tiv\ *adj*
— **re•demp•to•ry** \-‘tərē\ *adj*
red•head \-ˌhed\ *n* : one having red hair — **red•head•ed** \-‘hedəd\ *adj*
re•o•lent \‘red°lənt\ *adj* **1** : having a fragrance **2** : suggestive — **red•o•lence** \-əns\ *n* — **red•o•lent•ly** *adv*
re•dou•ble \rē‘dəbəl\ *vb* **1** : make twice as great in size or amount **2** : intensify
re•doubt \ri‘daut\ *n* : small fortification
re•doubt•able \-əbəl\ *adj* : arousing dread
re•dound \ri‘daund\ *vb* : have an effect
re•dress \ri‘dres\ *vb* : set right ∼ *n* **1** : relief or remedy **2** : compensation
red tape *n* : complex obstructive official routine
re•duce \ri‘düs, -‘dyüs\ *vb* **1** : lessen **2** : put in a lower rank **3** : lose weight — **re•duc•er** *n* — **re•duc•ible** \-‘düsəbəl, -‘dyü-\ *adj*
re•duc•tion \ri‘dəkshən\ *n* **1** : act of reducing **2** : amount lost in reducing **3** : something made by reducing
re•dun•dant \ri‘dəndənt\ *adj* : using more words than necessary — **re•dun•dan•cy** \-dənsē\ *n* — **re•dun•dant•ly** *adv*
red•wood *n* : tall coniferous timber tree
reed \‘rēd\ *n* **1** : tall slender grass of wet areas **2** : elastic strip that vibrates to produce tones in certain wind instruments — **reedy** *adj*
reef \‘rēf\ *n* : ridge of rocks or sand at or near the surface of the water
reek \‘rēk\ *n* : strong or disagreeable fume or odor ∼ *vb* : give off a reek
¹reel \‘rēl\ *n* : revolvable device on which something flexible is wound or a quantity of something wound on it ∼ *vb* **1** : wind on a reel **2** : pull in by reeling — **reel•able** *adj* — **reel•er** *n*
²reel *vb* **1** : whirl or waver as from a blow **2** : walk or move unsteadily ∼ *n* : reeling motion
³reel *n* : lively dance
re•fer \ri‘fər\ *vb* **-rr- 1** : direct or send to some person or place **2** : submit for consideration or action **3** : have connection **4** : mention or allude to

something — **re•fer•able** \‘refərəbəl, ri‘fərə-\ *adj* — **re•fer•ral** \ri‘fərəl\ *n*
ref•er•ee \ˌrefə‘rē\ *n* **1** : one to whom an issue is referred for settlement **2** : sports official ∼ *vb* **-eed; -ee•ing** : act as referee
ref•er•ence \‘refərəns\ *n* **1** : act of referring **2** : a bearing on a matter **3** : consultation for information **4** : person who can speak for one's character or ability or a recommendation given by such a person
ref•er•en•dum \ˌrefə‘rendəm\ *n, pl* **-da** \-də\ *or* **-dums** : a submitting of legislative measures for voters' approval or rejection
re•fill \ˌrē‘fil\ *vb* : fill again — **re•fill** \‘rēˌ-\ *n* — **re•fill•able** *adj*
re•fine \ri‘fīn\ *vb* **-fined; -fin•ing 1** : free from impurities or waste matter **2** : improve or perfect **3** : free or become free of what is coarse or uncouth — **re•fine•ment** \-mənt\ *n* — **re•fin•er** *n*
re•fin•ery \ri‘fīnərē\ *n, pl* **-er•ies** : place for refining (as oil or sugar)
re•flect \ri‘flekt\ *vb* **1** : bend or cast back (as light or heat) **2** : bring as a result **3** : cast reproach or blame **4** : ponder — **re•flec•tion** \-‘flekshən\ *n* — **re•flec•tive** \-tiv\ *adj* — **re•flec•tor** \ri‘flektər\ *n*
re•flex \‘rēˌfleks\ *n* : automatic response to a stimulus ∼ *adj* **1** : bent back **2** : relating to a reflex — **re•flex•ly** *adv*
re•flex•ive \ri‘fleksiv\ *adj* : of or relating to an action directed back upon the doer or the grammatical subject — **reflexive** *n* — **re•flex•ive•ly** *adv* — **re•flex•ive•ness** *n*
re•form \ri‘fórm\ *vb* : make or become better esp. by correcting bad habits — **reform** *n* — **re•form•able** *adj* — **re•for•ma•tive** \-‘fórmətiv\ *adj* — **re•form•er** *n*
re•for•ma•to•ry \ri‘fórməˌtōrē\ *n, pl* **-ries** : penal institution for reforming young offenders
re•fract \ri‘frakt\ *vb* : subject to refraction

reclassify	**reconnect**	**reconsolidate**
recolonize	**reconquer**	**reconstruct**
recombine	**reconquest**	**recontaminate**
recompute	**reconsider**	**reconvene**
reconceive	**reconsideration**	**reconvict**

re•frac•tion \-'frakshən\ *n* : the bending of a ray (as of light) when it passes from one medium into another — **re•frac•tive** \-tiv\ *adj*

re•frac•to•ry \ri'fraktərē\ *adj* : obstinate or unmanageable

re•frain \ri'frān\ *vb* : hold oneself back ⁓ *n* : verse recurring regularly in a song — **re•frain•ment** *n*

re•fresh \ri'fresh\ *vb* **1** : make or become fresh or fresher **2** : supply or take refreshment — **re•fresh•er** *n* — **re•fresh•ing•ly** *adv*

re•fresh•ment \-mənt\ *n* **1** : act of refreshing **2** *pl* : light meal

re•frig•er•ate \ri'frijə,rāt\ *vb* -at•ed; -at•ing : chill or freeze (food) for preservation — **re•frig•er•ant** \-ərənt\ *adj or n* — **re•frig•er•a•tion** \-,frijə-'rāshən\ *n* — **re•frig•er•a•tor** \-'frijə-,rātər\ *n*

ref•uge \'ref,yüj\ *n* **1** : protection from danger **2** : place that provides protection

ref•u•gee \,refyu'jē\ *n* : person who flees for safety

re•fund \ri'fənd, 'rē,fənd\ *vb* : give or put back (money) ⁓ \'rē,-\ *n* **1** : act of refunding **2** : sum refunded — **re•fund•able** *adj*

re•fur•bish \ri'fərbish\ *vb* : renovate

¹**re•fuse** \ri'fyüz\ *vb* -fused; -fus•ing : decline to accept, do, or give — **re•fus•al** \-'fyüzəl\ *n*

²**ref•use** \'ref,yüs, -,yüz\ *n* : worthless matter

re•fute \ri'fyüt\ *vb* -fut•ed; -fut•ing : prove to be false — **ref•u•ta•tion** \,refyu'tāshən\ *n* — **re•fut•er** \ri-'fyütər\ *n*

re•gal \'rēgəl\ *adj* **1** : befitting a king **2** : stately — **re•gal•ly** *adv*

re•gale \ri'gāl\ *vb* -galed; -gal•ing **1** : entertain richly or agreeably **2** : delight

re•ga•lia \ri'gālyə\ *n pl* **1** : symbols of royalty **2** : insignia of an office or order **3** : finery

re•gard \ri'gärd\ *n* **1** : consideration **2** : feeling of approval and liking **3** *pl* : friendly greetings **4** : relation ⁓ *vb*

1 : pay attention to **2** : show respect for **3** : have an opinion of **4** : look at **5** : relate to — **re•gard•ful** *adj* — **re•gard•less** *adj*

re•gard•ing *prep* : concerning

regardless of \ri'gärdləs-\ *prep* : in spite of

re•gen•er•ate \ri'jenərət\ *adj* **1** : formed or created again **2** : spiritually reborn ⁓ \-'jenə,rāt\ *vb* **1** : reform completely **2** : replace (a lost body part) by new tissue growth **3** : give new life to — **re•gen•er•a•tion** \-,jenə'rāshən\ *n* — **re•gen•er•a•tive** \-'jenə,rātiv\ *adj* — **re•gen•er•a•tor** \-,rātər\ *n*

re•gent \'rējənt\ *n* **1** : person who rules during the childhood, absence, or incapacity of the sovereign **2** : member of a governing board — **re•gen•cy** \-jənsē\ *n*

re•gime \rā'zhēm, ri-\ *n* : government in power

reg•i•men \'rejəmən\ *n* : systematic course of treatment or training

reg•i•ment \'rejəmənt\ *n* : military unit ⁓ \-,ment\ *vb* **1** : organize rigidly for control **2** : make orderly — **reg•i•men•tal** \,rejə'mentəl\ *adj* — **reg•i•men•ta•tion** \-mən'tāshən\ *n*

re•gion \'rējən\ *n* : indefinitely defined area — **re•gion•al** \'rējənəl\ *adj* — **re•gion•al•ly** *adv*

reg•is•ter \'rejəstər\ *n* **1** : record of items or details or a book for keeping such a record **2** : device to regulate ventilation **3** : counting or recording device **4** : range of a voice or instrument ⁓ *vb* **1** : enter in a register **2** : record automatically **3** : get special care for mail by paying more postage

reg•is•trar \-,strär\ *n* : official keeper of records

reg•is•tra•tion \,rejə'strāshən\ *n* **1** : act of registering **2** : entry in a register

reg•is•try \'rejəstrē\ *n, pl* -tries **1** : enrollment **2** : place of registration **3** : official record book

re•gress \ri'gres\ *vb* : go or cause to go

back or to a lower level — **re·gres·sion** \-'greshən\ *n* — **re·gres·sive** *adj*

re·gret \ri'gret\ *vb* -tt- **1** : mourn the loss or death of **2** : be very sorry for ～ *n* **1** : sorrow or the expression of sorrow **2** *pl* : message declining an invitation — **re·gret·ful** \-fəl\ *adj* — **re·gret·ful·ly** *adv* — **re·gret·ta·ble** \-əbəl\ *adj* — **re·gret·ta·bly** \-blē\ *adv* — **re·gret·ter** *n*

reg·u·lar \'regyələr\ *adj* **1** : conforming to what is usual, normal, or average **2** : steady, uniform, or unvarying — **regular** *n* — **reg·u·lar·i·ty** \,regyə-'larətē\ *n* — **reg·u·lar·ize** \'regyələ-,rīz\ *vb* — **reg·u·lar·ly** *adv*

reg·u·late \'regyə,lāt\ *vb* -lat·ed; -lat·ing **1** : govern according to rule **2** : adjust to a standard — **reg·u·la·tive** \-,lātiv\ *adj* — **reg·u·la·tor** \-,lātər\ *n* — **reg·u·la·to·ry** \-lə,tōrē\ *adj*

reg·u·la·tion \,regyə'lāshən\ *n* **1** : act of regulating **2** : rule dealing with details of procedure

re·gur·gi·tate \rē'gərjə,tāt\ *vb* -tat·ed; -tat·ing : vomit — **re·gur·gi·ta·tion** \-,gərjə'tāshən\ *n*

re·ha·bil·i·tate \,rēhə'bilə,tāt\ *vb* -tat·ed; -tat·ing **1** : reinstate **2** : make good or usable again — **re·ha·bil·i·ta·tion** \-,bilə'tāshən\ *n*

re·hears·al \ri'hərsəl\ *n* : practice session or performance

re·hearse \-'hərs\ *vb* -hearsed; -hearsing **1** : repeat or recount **2** : engage in a rehearsal of — **re·hears·er** *n*

reign \'rān\ *n* : sovereign's authority or rule ～ *vb* : rule as a sovereign

re·im·burse \,rēəm'bərs\ *vb* -bursed; -burs·ing : repay — **re·im·burs·able** *adj* — **re·im·burse·ment** *n*

rein \'rān\ *n* **1** : strap fastened to a bit to control an animal **2** : restraining influence ～ *vb* : direct by reins

re·in·car·na·tion \,rē,in,kär'nāshən\ *n* : rebirth of the soul — **re·in·car·nate** \,rēin'kär,nāt\ *vb*

rein·deer \'rān,dir\ *n* : caribou

re·in·force \,rēən'fōrs\ *vb* : strengthen or support — **re·in·force·ment** *n* — **re·in·forc·er** *n*

re·in·state \,rēən'stāt\ *vb* : restore to a former position — **re·in·state·ment** *n*

re·it·er·ate \rē'itə,rāt\ *vb* : say again — **re·it·er·a·tion** \-,itə'rāshən\ *n*

re·ject \ri'jekt\ *vb* **1** : refuse to grant or consider **2** : refuse to admit, believe, or receive **3** : throw out as useless or unsatisfactory ～ \'rē,-\ *n* : rejected person or thing — **re·jec·tion** \-'jekshən\ *n*

re·joice \ri'jóis\ *vb* -joiced; -joic·ing : feel joy — **re·joic·er** *n*

re·join *vb* **1** \rē'jóin\ : join again **2** \ri'-\ : say in answer

re·join·der \ri'joindər\ *n* : answer

re·ju·ve·nate \ri'jüvə,nāt\ *vb* -nat·ed; -nat·ing : make young again — **re·ju·ve·na·tion** \-,jüvə'nāshən\ *n*

re·lapse \ri'laps, 'rē,laps\ *n* : recurrence of illness after a period of improvement ～ \ri'-\ *vb* : suffer a relapse

re·late \ri'lāt\ *vb* -lat·ed; -lat·ing **1** : give a report of **2** : show a connection between **3** : have a relationship — **re·lat·able** *adj* — **re·lat·er, re·la·tor** *n*

re·la·tion \-'lāshən\ *n* **1** : account **2** : connection **3** : relationship **4** : reference **5** *pl* : dealings

re·la·tion·ship \-,ship\ *n* : state of being related or interrelated

rel·a·tive \'relətiv\ *n* : person connected with another by blood or marriage ～ *adj* : considered in comparison with something else — **rel·a·tive·ly** *adv* — **rel·a·tive·ness** *n*

re·lax \ri'laks\ *vb* **1** : make or become less tense or rigid **2** : make less severe **3** : seek rest or recreation — **re·lax·er** *n*

re·lax·a·tion \,rē,lak'sāshən\ *n* **1** : lessening of tension **2** : recreation

re·lay \'rē,lā\ *n* : fresh supply (as of horses or people) arranged to relieve others ～ \'rē,-, ri'-\ *vb* -layed; -lay·ing : pass along in stages

re·lease \ri'lēs\ *vb* -leased; -leas·ing **1** : free from confinement or oppression **2** : relinquish **3** : permit publication, performance, exhibition, or sale ~ n 1 : relief from trouble 2 : discharge from an obligation 3 : act of releasing or what is released

rel•e•gate \'relə͵gāt\ vb -gat•ed; -gat•ing 1 : remove to some less prominent position 2 : assign to a particular class or sphere — rel•e•ga•tion \͵relə-'gāshən\ n

re•lent \ri'lent\ vb : become less severe

re•lent•less \-ləs\ adj : mercilessly severe or persistent — re•lent•less•ly adv — re•lent•less•ness n

rel•e•vance \'reləvəns\ n : relation to the matter at hand — rel•e•vant \-vənt\ adj — rel•e•vant•ly adv

re•li•able \ri'līəbəl\ adj : fit to be trusted — re•li•abil•i•ty \-͵līə'bilətē\ n — re•li•able•ness n — re•li•ably \-'līəblē\ adv

re•li•ance \ri'līəns\ n : act or result of relying

re•li•ant \ri'līənt\ adj : dependent

rel•ic \'relik\ n 1 : object venerated because of its association with a saint or martyr 2 : remaining trace

re•lief \ri'lēf\ n 1 : lightening of something oppressive 2 : welfare

re•lieve \ri'lēv\ vb -lieved; -liev•ing 1 : free from a burden or distress 2 : release from a post or duty 3 : break the monotony of — re•liev•er n

re•li•gion \ri'lijən\ n 1 : service and worship of God 2 : set or system of religious beliefs — re•li•gion•ist n

re•li•gious \-'lijəs\ adj 1 : relating or devoted to an ultimate reality or deity 2 : relating to religious beliefs or observances 3 : faithful, fervent, or zealous — re•li•gious•ly adv

re•lin•quish \-'liŋkwish, -'lin-\ vb 1 : renounce 2 : let go of — re•lin•quish•ment n

rel•ish \'relish\ n 1 : keen enjoyment 2 : highly seasoned sauce (as of pickles) ~ vb : enjoy — rel•ish•able adj

re•live \͵rē'liv\ vb : live over again (as in the imagination)

re•lo•cate \͵rē'lō͵kāt, ͵rēlō'kāt\ vb : move to a new location — re•lo•ca•tion \͵rēlō'kāshən\ n

re•luc•tant \ri'ləktənt\ adj : feeling or showing doubt or unwillingness — re•luc•tance \ri'ləktəns\ n — re•luc•tant•ly adv

re•ly \ri'lī\ vb -lied; -ly•ing : place faith or confidence — often with on

re•main \ri'mān\ vb 1 : be left after others have been removed 2 : be something yet to be done 3 : stay behind 4 : continue unchanged

re•main•der \-'māndər\ n : that which is left over

re•mains \-'mānz\ n pl 1 : remaining part or trace 2 : dead body

re•mark \ri'märk\ vb : express as an observation ~ n : passing comment

re•mark•able \-'märkəbəl\ adj : extraordinary — re•mark•able•ness n — re•mark•ably \-blē\ adv

re•me•di•al \ri'mēdēəl\ adj : intended to remedy or improve

rem•e•dy \'remədē\ n, pl -dies 1 : medicine that cures 2 : something that corrects an evil or compensates for a loss ~ vb -died; -dy•ing : provide or serve as a remedy for

re•mem•ber \ri'membər\ vb 1 : think of again 2 : keep from forgetting 3 : convey greetings from

re•mem•brance \-brəns\ n 1 : act of remembering 2 : something that serves to bring to mind

re•mind \ri'mīnd\ vb : cause to remember — re•mind•er n

rem•i•nisce \͵remə'nis\ vb -nisced; -nisc•ing : indulge in reminiscence

rem•i•nis•cence \-'nisᵊns\ n 1 : recalling of a past experience 2 : account of a memorable experience

rem•i•nis•cent \-ᵊnt\ adj 1 : relating to reminiscence 2 : serving to remind — rem•i•nis•cent•ly adv

re•miss \ri'mis\ adj : negligent or careless in performance of duty — re•miss•ly adv — re•miss•ness n

re•mis•sion \ri'mishən\ n 1 : act of forgiving 2 : period of relief from or easing of symptoms of a disease

re•mit \ri'mit\ vb -tt- 1 : pardon 2 : send money in payment

re•mit•tance \ri'mitᵊns\ n : sum of money remitted

---

rem·nant \'remnənt\ *n* : small part or trace remaining

re·mod·el \rē'mäd°l\ *vb* : alter the structure of

re·mon·strance \ri'mänstrəns\ *n* : act or instance of remonstrating

re·mon·strate \ri'män,strāt\ *vb* -strat·ed; -strat·ing : speak in protest, reproof, or opposition — **re·mon·stra·tion** \ri,män'strāshən, ,remən-\ *n*

re·morse \ri'mȯrs\ *n* : distress arising from a sense of guilt — **re·morse·ful** *adj* — **re·morse·less** *adj*

re·mote \ri'mōt\ *adj* -mot·er; -est 1 : far off in place or time 2 : hard to reach or find 3 : acting, acted on, or controlled indirectly or from afar 4 : slight 5 : distant in manner — **re·mote·ly** *adv* — **re·mote·ness** *n*

re·move \ri'müv\ *vb* -moved; -mov·ing 1 : move by lifting or taking off or away 2 : get rid of — **re·mov·able** *adj* — **re·mov·al** \-vəl\ *n* — **re·mov·er** *n*

re·mu·ner·ate \ri'myünə,rāt\ *vb* -at·ed; -at·ing : pay — **re·mu·ner·a·tion** *n* — **re·mu·ner·a·tor** \-,rātər\ *n*

re·mu·ner·a·tive \ri'myünərətiv, -,rāt-\ *adj* : gainful

re·nais·sance \,renə'säns, -'zäns\ *n* : rebirth or revival

re·nal \'rēn°l\ *adj* : relating to the kidneys

rend \'rend\ *vb* rent \'rent\; rend·ing : tear apart forcibly

ren·der \'rendər\ *vb* 1 : extract by heating 2 : hand over or give up 3 : do (a service) for another 4 : cause to be or become

ren·dez·vous \'rändi,vü, -dā-\ *n, pl* ren·dez·vous \-,vüz\ 1 : place appointed for a meeting 2 : meeting at an appointed place ~ *vb* -voused; -vous·ing : meet at a rendezvous

ren·di·tion \ren'dishən\ *n* : version

ren·e·gade \'reni,gād\ *n* : deserter of one faith or cause for another

re·nege \ri'nig, -'neg, -'nēg, -'nāg\ *vb* -neged; -neg·ing : go back on a promise — **re·neg·er** *n*

re·new \ri'nü, -'nyü\ *vb* 1 : make or become new, fresh, or strong again 2 : begin again 3 : grant or obtain an extension of — **re·new·able** *adj* — **re·new·al** *n* — **re·new·er** *n*

re·nounce \ri'naúns\ *vb* -nounced; -nounc·ing : give up, refuse, or resign — **re·nounce·ment** *n*

ren·o·vate \'renə,vāt\ *vb* -vat·ed; -vat·ing : make like new again — **ren·o·va·tion** \,renə'vāshən\ *n* — **ren·o·va·tor** \'renə,vātər\ *n*

re·nown \ri'naún\ *n* : state of being widely known and honored — **renowned** \-'naúnd\ *adj*

¹rent \'rent\ *n* : money paid or due periodically for the use of another's property ~ *vb* : hold or give possession and use of for rent — **rent·al** *n or adj* — **rent·er** *n*

²rent *n* : a tear in cloth

re·nun·ci·a·tion \ri,nənsē'āshən\ *n* : act of renouncing

¹re·pair \ri'par\ *vb* : go

²repair *vb* : restore to good condition ~ *n* 1 : act or instance of repairing 2 : condition — **re·pair·er** *n* — **re·pair·man** \-,man\ *n*

rep·a·ra·tion \,repə'rāshən\ *n* : money paid for redress — usu. pl.

rep·ar·tee \,repər'tē\ *n* : clever replies

re·past \ri'past, 'rē,past\ *n* : meal

re·pa·tri·ate \rē'pātrē,āt\ *vb* -at·ed; -at·ing : send back to one's own country — **re·pa·tri·ate** \-trēət, -trē,āt\ *n* — **re·pa·tri·a·tion** \-,pātrē'āshən\ *n*

re·pay \rē'pā\ *vb* -paid; -pay·ing : pay back — **re·pay·able** *adj* — **re·pay·ment** *n*

re·peal \ri'pēl\ *vb* : annul by legislative action — **repeal** *n* — **re·peal·er** *n*

re·peat \ri'pēt\ *vb* : say or do again ~ *n* 1 : act of repeating 2 : something repeated — **re·peat·able** *adj* — **re·peat·ed·ly** *adv* — **re·peat·er** *n*

re·pel \ri'pel\ *vb* -pelled; -pel·ling 1 : drive away 2 : disgust — **re·pel·lent** \-'pelənt\ *adj or n*

re·pent \ri'pent\ *vb* 1 : turn from sin 2 : regret — **re·pen·tance** \ri'pent°ns\ *n* — **re·pen·tant** \-°nt\ *adj*

re·per·cus·sion \,rēpər'kəshən,

ˌrep-\ *n* : effect of something done or said

rep•er•toire \ˈrepərˌtwär\ *n* : pieces a company or performer can present

rep•er•to•ry \ˈrepərˌtōrē\ *n, pl* **-ries 1** : repertoire **2** : theater with a resident company doing several plays

rep•e•ti•tion \ˌrepəˈtishən\ *n* : act or instance of repeating

rep•e•ti•tious \-ˈtishəs\ *adj* : tediously repeating — **rep•e•ti•tious•ly** *adv* — **rep•e•ti•tious•ness** *n*

re•pet•i•tive \riˈpetətiv\ *adj* : repetitious — **re•pet•i•tive•ly** *adv* — **re•pet•i•tive•ness** *n*

re•pine \riˈpīn\ *vb* **re•pined; re•pin•ing** : feel or express discontent

re•place \riˈplās\ *vb* **1** : restore to a former position **2** : take the place of **3** : put something new in the place of — **re•place•able** *adj* — **re•place•ment** *n* — **re•plac•er** *n*

re•plen•ish \riˈplenish\ *vb* : stock or supply anew — **re•plen•ish•ment** *n*

re•plete \riˈplēt\ *adj* : full — **re•plete•ness** *n* — **re•ple•tion** \-ˈplēshən\ *n*

rep•li•ca \ˈreplikə\ *n* : exact copy

rep•li•cate \ˈrepləˌkāt\ *vb* **-cat•ed; -cat•ing** : duplicate or repeat — **rep•li•cate** \-likət\ *n* — **rep•li•ca•tion** \-ləˈkāshən\ *n*

re•ply \riˈplī\ *vb* **-plied; -ply•ing** : say or do in answer ~ *n, pl* **-plies** : answer

re•port \riˈpōrt\ *n* **1** : rumor **2** : statement of information (as events or causes) **3** : explosive noise ~ *vb* **1** : give an account of **2** : present an account of (an event) as news **3** : present oneself **4** : make known to authorities — **re•port•age** \riˈpōrtij, ˌreparˈtäzh, ˌrepˌȯrˈ-\ *n* — **re•port•ed•ly** *adv* — **re•port•er** *n* — **re•por•to•ri•al** \ˌreparˈtōrēəl\ *adj*

re•pose \riˈpōz\ *vb* **-posed; -pos•ing** : lay or lie at rest ~ *n* **1** : state of resting **2** : calm or peace — **re•pose•ful** *adj*

re•pos•i•to•ry \riˈpäzəˌtōrē\ *n, pl* **-ries** : place where something is stored

re•pos•sess \ˌrēpəˈzes\ *vb* : regain possession and legal ownership of — **re•pos•ses•sion** \-ˈzeshən\ *n*

rep•re•hend \ˌrepriˈhend\ *vb* : censure — **rep•re•hen•sion** \-ˈhenchən\ *n*

rep•re•hen•si•ble \-ˈhensəbəl\ *adj* : deserving condemnation — **rep•re•hen•si•bly** *adv*

rep•re•sent \ˌrepriˈzent\ *vb* **1** : serve as a sign or symbol of **2** : act or speak for **3** : describe as having a specified quality or character — **rep•re•sen•ta•tion** \ˌrepriˌzenˈtāshən\ *n*

rep•re•sen•ta•tive \ˌrepriˈzentətiv\ *adj* **1** : standing or acting for another **2** : carried on by elected representatives ~ *n* **1** : typical example **2** : one that represents another **3** : member of usu. the lower house of a legislature — **rep•re•sen•ta•tive•ly** *adv* — **rep•re•sen•ta•tive•ness** *n*

re•press \riˈpres\ *vb* : restrain or suppress — **re•pres•sion** \-ˈpreshən\ *n* — **re•pres•sive** \-ˈpresiv\ *adj*

re•prieve \riˈprēv\ *n* **1** : a delay in punishment **2** : temporary respite — **re•prieve** *vb*

rep•ri•mand \ˈrepräˌmand\ *n* : formal or severe criticism — **reprimand** *vb*

re•pri•sal \riˈprīzəl\ *n* : act in retaliation

re•prise \riˈprēz\ *n* : musical repetition

re•proach \riˈprōch\ *n* **1** : disgrace **2** : rebuke ~ *vb* : express disapproval to — **re•proach•ful** *adj* — **re•proach•ful•ly** *adv* — **re•proach•ful•ness** *n*

rep•ro•bate \ˈrepräˌbāt\ *n* : scoundrel — **reprobate** *adj*

rep•ro•ba•tion \ˌrepräˈbāshən\ *n* : strong disapproval

re•pro•duce \ˌrēpräˈdüs, -ˈdyüs\ *vb* **1** : produce again or anew **2** : produce offspring — **re•pro•duc•ible** \-ˈdüsəbəl, -ˈdyü-\ *adj* — **re•pro•duc•tion** \-ˈdəkshən\ *n* — **re•pro•duc•tive** \-ˈdəktiv\ *adj*

re•proof \riˈprüf\ *n* : blame or censure for a fault

re•prove \riˈprüv\ *vb* **-proved; -prov•ing** : express disapproval to or of

rep•tile \ˈreptᵊl, -ˌtīl\ *n* : air-breathing scaly vertebrate — **rep•til•ian** \repˈtilēən\ *adj or n*

---

reinsert	**reintegrate**	**reinvestigate**
reinsertion	**reintegration**	**reinvestigation**
reinspect	**reinter**	**reinvigorate**
reinstall	**reintroduce**	**rejudge**
reinstitute	**reinvent**	**rekindle**

re·pub·lic \ri'pəblik\ *n* : country with representative government

re·pub·li·can \-likən\ *adj* **1** : relating to or resembling a republic **2** : supporting a republic — **republican** *n* — **re·pub·li·can·ism** *n*

re·pu·di·ate \ri'pyüdē͟ăt\ *vb* **-at·ed; -at·ing** : refuse to have anything to do with — **re·pu·di·a·tion** \-ˌpyüdē'ā-shən\ *n*

re·pug·nant \ri'pəgnənt\ *adj* : contrary to one's tastes or principles — **re·pug·nance** \-nəns\ *n* — **re·pug·nant·ly** *adv*

re·pulse \ri'pəls\ *vb* **-pulsed; -puls·ing 1** : drive or beat back **2** : rebuff **3** : be repugnant to — **repulse** *n* — **re·pul·sion** \-'pəlshən\ *n*

re·pul·sive \-siv\ *adj* : arousing aversion or disgust — **re·pul·sive·ly** *adv* — **re·pul·sive·ness** *n*

rep·u·ta·ble \'repyətəbəl\ *adj* : having a good reputation — **rep·u·ta·bly** \-blē\ *adv*

rep·u·ta·tion \ˌrepyə'tāshən\ *n* : one's character or public esteem

re·pute \ri'pyüt\ *vb* **-put·ed; -put·ing** : think of as being ～ *n* : reputation — **re·put·ed** *adj* — **re·put·ed·ly** *adv*

re·quest \ri'kwest\ *n* : act or instance of asking for something or a thing asked for ～ *vb* **1** : make a request of **2** : ask for — **re·quest·er** *n*

re·qui·em \'rekwēəm, 'räk-\ *n* : Mass for a dead person or a musical setting for this

re·quire \ri'kwīr\ *vb* **-quired; -quir·ing 1** : insist on **2** : call for as essential — **re·quire·ment** *n*

req·ui·site \'rekwəzət\ *adj* : necessary — **requisite** *n*

req·ui·si·tion \ˌrekwə'zishən\ *n* : formal application or demand — **requisition** *vb*

re·quite \ri'kwīt\ *vb* **-quit·ed; -quit·ing** : make return for or to — **re·quit·al** \-'kwīt³l\ *n*

re·scind \ri'sind\ *vb* : repeal or cancel — **re·scis·sion** \-'sizhən\ *n*

res·cue \'reskyü\ *vb* **-cued; -cu·ing** : set free from danger or confinement — **rescue** *n* — **res·cu·er** *n*

re·search \ri'sərch, 'rēˌsərch\ *n* : careful or diligent search esp. for new knowledge — **research** *vb* — **re·search·er** *n*

re·sem·ble \ri'zembəl\ *vb* **-sem·bled; -sem·bling** : be like or similar to — **re·sem·blance** \-'zembləns\ *n*

re·sent \ri'zent\ *vb* : feel or show annoyance at — **re·sent·ful** *adj* — **re·sent·ful·ly** *adv* — **re·sent·ment** *n*

res·er·va·tion \ˌrezər'vāshən\ *n* **1** : act of reserving or something reserved **2** : limiting condition

re·serve \ri'zərv\ *vb* **-served; -serv·ing 1** : store for future use **2** : set aside for special use ～ *n* **1** : something reserved **2** : restraint in words or bearing **3** : military forces withheld from action or not part of the regular services — **re·served** *adj*

res·er·voir \'rezərˌvwär, -ˌvwȯr, -ˌvȯr, -ˌvȯi\ *n* : place where something (as water) is kept in store

re·side \ri'zīd\ *vb* **-sid·ed; -sid·ing 1** : make one's home **2** : be present

res·i·dence \'rezədəns\ *n* **1** : act or fact of residing in a place **2** : place where one lives — **res·i·dent** \-ənt\ *adj or n* — **res·i·den·tial** \ˌrezə'den-chəl\ *adj*

res·i·due \'rezəˌdü, -ˌdyü\ *n* : part remaining — **re·sid·u·al** \ri'zijəwəl\ *adj*

re·sign \ri'zīn\ *vb* **1** : give up deliberately **2** : give (oneself) over without resistance — **res·ig·na·tion** \ˌrezig-'nāshən\ *n* — **re·sign·ed·ly** \-'zīnədlē\ *adv*

re·sil·ience \ri'zilyəns\ *n* : ability to recover or adjust easily

re·sil·ien·cy \-yənsē\ *n* : resilience

re·sil·ient \-yənt\ *adj* : elastic

res·in \'rez³n\ *n* : substance from the gum or sap of trees — **res·in·ous** *adj*

re·sist \ri'zist\ *vb* **1** : withstand the force or effect of **2** : fight against — **re·sist·ible** \-'zistəbəl\ *adj* — **re·sist·less** *adj*

re·sis·tance \ri'zistəns\ *n* **1** : act of resisting **2** : ability of an organism to

reknit relight rematch
relabel reline remelt
relandscape reload remobilize
relaunch remarriage remoisten
relearn remarry remold

resist disease **3** : opposition to electric current

re·sis·tant \-tənt\ *adj* : giving resistance

res·o·lute \'rezə,lüt\ *adj* : having a fixed purpose — **res·o·lute·ly** *adv* — **res·o·lute·ness** *n*

res·o·lu·tion \,rezə'lüshən\ *n* **1** : process of resolving **2** : firmness of purpose **3** : statement of the opinion, will, or intent of a body

re·solve \ri'zälv\ *vb* **-solved; -solving 1** : find an answer to **2** : make a formal resolution ~ *n* **1** : something resolved **2** : steadfast purpose — **re·solv·able** *adj*

res·o·nant \'rez°nənt\ *adj* **1** : continuing to sound **2** : relating to intensification or prolongation of sound (as by a vibrating body) — **res·o·nance** \-əns\ *n* — **res·o·nant·ly** *adv*

re·sort \ri'zȯrt\ *n* **1** : source of help **2** : place to go for vacation ~ *vb* **1** : go often or habitually **2** : have recourse

re·sound \ri'zaùnd\ *vb* : become filled with sound

re·sound·ing \-iŋ\ *adj* : impressive — **re·sound·ing·ly** *adv*

re·source \'rē,sȯrs, ri'sȯrs\ *n* **1** : new or reserve source **2** *pl* : available funds **3** : ability to handle situations — **re·source·ful** *adj* — **re·source·ful·ness** *n*

re·spect \ri'spekt\ *n* **1** : relation to something **2** : high or special regard **3** : detail ~ *vb* : consider deserving of high regard — **re·spect·er** *n* — **re·spect·ful** *adj* — **re·spect·ful·ly** *adv* — **re·spect·ful·ness** *n*

re·spect·able \ri'spektəbəl\ *adj* **1** : worthy of respect **2** : fair in size, quantity, or quality — **re·spect·abil·i·ty** \-,spektə'bilətē\ *n* — **re·spect·ably** \-'spektəblē\ *adv*

re·spec·tive \-tiv\ *adj* : individual and specific

re·spec·tive·ly \-lē\ *adv* **1** : as relating to each **2** : each in the order given

res·pi·ra·tion \,respə'rāshən\ *n* : act or process of breathing — **re·spi·ra·to·ry** \'respərə,tōrē, ri'spīrə-\ *adj* — **re·spire** \ri'spīr\ *vb*

res·pi·ra·tor \'respə,rātər\ *n* : device for artificial respiration

re·spite \'respət\ *n* : temporary delay or rest

re·splen·dent \ri'splendənt\ *adj* : shining brilliantly — **re·splen·dence** \-dəns\ *n* — **re·splen·dent·ly** *adv*

re·spond \ri'spänd\ *vb* **1** : answer **2** : react — **re·spon·dent** \-'spändənt\ *n or adj* — **re·spond·er** *n*

re·sponse \ri'späns\ *n* **1** : act of responding **2** : answer

re·spon·si·ble \ri'spänsəbəl\ *adj* **1** : answerable for acts or decisions **2** : able to fulfill obligations **3** : having important duties — **re·spon·si·bil·i·ty** \ri-,spänsə'bilətē\ *n* — **re·spon·si·ble·ness** *n* — **re·spon·si·bly** \-blē\ *adv*

re·spon·sive \-siv\ *adj* : quick to respond — **re·spon·sive·ly** *adv* — **re·spon·sive·ness** *n*

¹**rest** \'rest\ *n* **1** : sleep **2** : freedom from work or activity **3** : state of inactivity **4** : something used as a support ~ *vb* **1** : get rest **2** : cease action or motion **3** : give rest to **4** : sit or lie fixed or supported **5** : depend — **rest·ful** *adj* — **rest·ful·ly** *adv*

²**rest** *n* : remainder

res·tau·rant \'restərənt, -tə,ränt\ *n* : public eating place

res·ti·tu·tion \,restə'tüshən, -'tyü-\ *n* : act or fact of restoring something or repaying someone

res·tive \'restiv\ *adj* : uneasy or fidgety — **res·tive·ly** *adv* — **res·tive·ness** *n*

rest·less \'restləs\ *adj* **1** : lacking or giving no rest **2** : always moving **3** : uneasy — **rest·less·ly** *adv* — **rest·less·ness** *n*

re·store \ri'stōr\ *vb* **-stored; -stor·ing 1** : give back **2** : put back into use or into a former state — **re·stor·able** *adj* — **res·to·ra·tion** \,restə'rāshən\ *n* — **re·stor·ative** \ri'stōrətiv\ *n or adj* — **re·stor·er** *n*

re·strain \ri'strān\ *vb* : limit or keep under control — **re·strain·able** *adj* — **re·strained** \-'strānd\ *adj* — **re·strain·ed·ly** \-'strānədlē\ *adv* — **re·strain·er** *n*

---

remotivate	**reoccurrence**	**reorient**
rename	**reoperate**	**repack**
renegotiate	**reorchestrate**	**repave**
reoccupy	**reorganization**	**rephotograph**
reoccur	**reorganize**	**replan**

restraining order *n* : legal order directing one person to stay away from another

re•straint \-'strānt\ *n* **1** : act of restraining **2** : restraining force **3** : control over feelings

re•strict \ri'strikt\ *vb* **1** : confine within bounds **2** : limit use of — **re•stric•tion** \-'strikshən\ *n* — **re•stric•tive** *adj* — **re•stric•tive•ly** *adv*

re•sult \ri'zəlt\ *vb* : come about because of something else ~ *n* **1** : thing that results **2** : something obtained by calculation or investigation — **re•sul•tant** \-'zəlt°nt\ *adj or n*

re•sume \ri'züm\ *vb* **-sumed; -sum•ing** : return to or take up again after interruption — **re•sump•tion** \-'zəmpshən\ *n*

ré•su•mé,   re•su•me,   re•su•mé \'rezə,mā, ,rezə'-\ *n* : summary of one's career and qualifications

re•sur•gence \ri'sərjəns\ *n* : a rising again — **re•sur•gent** \-jənt\ *adj*

res•ur•rect \,rezə'rekt\ *vb* **1** : raise from the dead **2** : bring to attention or use again — **res•ur•rec•tion** \-'rekshən\ *n*

re•sus•ci•tate \ri'səsə,tāt\ *vb* **-tat•ed; -tat•ing** : bring back from apparent death — **re•sus•ci•ta•tion** \ri,səsə-'tāshən, ,rē-\ *n* — **re•sus•ci•ta•tor** \-,tātər\ *n*

re•tail \'rē,tāl\ *vb* : sell in small quantities directly to the consumer ~ *n* : business of selling to consumers — **retail** *adj or adv* — **re•tail•er** *n*

re•tain \ri'tān\ *vb* **1** : keep or hold onto **2** : engage the services of

re•tain•er *n* **1** : household servant **2** : retaining fee

re•tal•i•ate \ri'talē,āt\ *vb* **-at•ed; -at•ing** : return (as an injury) in kind — **re•tal•i•a•tion** \-,talē'āshən\ *n* — **re•tal•ia•to•ry** \-'talyə,tōrē\ *adj*

re•tard \ri'tärd\ *vb* : hold back — **re•tar•da•tion** \,rē,tär'dāshən, ri-\ *n*

re•tard•ed \ri'tärdəd\ *adj* : slow or limited in intellectual development

retch \'rech\ *vb* : try to vomit

re•ten•tion \ri'tenchən\ *n* **1** : state of being retained **2** : ability to retain — **re•ten•tive** \-'tentiv\ *adj*

ret•i•cent \'retəsənt\ *adj* : tending not to talk — **ret•i•cence** \-səns\ *n* — **ret•i•cent•ly** *adv*

ret•i•na \'ret°nə\ *n, pl* **-nas** *or* **-nae** \-°n,ē\ : sensory membrane lining the eye — **ret•i•nal** \'ret°nəl\ *adj*

ret•i•nue \'ret°n,ü, -,yü\ *n* : attendants or followers of a distinguished person

re•tire \ri'tīr\ *vb* **-tired; -tir•ing** **1** : withdraw for privacy **2** : end a career **3** : go to bed — **re•tir•ee** \ri,tī'rē\ *n* — **re•tire•ment** *n*

re•tir•ing \ri'tīrin\ *adj* : shy

re•tort \ri'tort\ *vb* : say in reply ~ *n* : quick, witty, or cutting answer

re•trace \,rē'trās\ *vb* : go over again or in reverse

re•tract \ri'trakt\ *vb* **1** : draw back or in **2** : withdraw a charge or promise — **re•tract•able** *adj* — **re•trac•tion** \-'trakshən\ *n*

re•treat \ri'trēt\ *n* **1** : act of withdrawing **2** : place of privacy or safety or meditation and study ~ *vb* : make a retreat

re•trench \ri'trench\ *vb* : cut down (as expenses) — **re•trench•ment** *n*

ret•ri•bu•tion \,retrə'byushən\ *n* : retaliation — **re•trib•u•tive** \ri'tribyətiv\ *adj* — **re•trib•u•to•ry** \-yə,tōrē\ *adj*

re•trieve \ri'trēv\ *vb* **-trieved; -triev•ing** **1** : search for and bring in game **2** : recover — **re•triev•able** *adj* — **re•triev•al** \-'trēvəl\ *n*

re•triev•er \-'trēvər\ *n* : dog for retrieving game

ret•ro•ac•tive \,retrō'aktiv\ *adj* : made effective as of a prior date — **ret•ro•ac•tive•ly** *adv*

ret•ro•grade \'retrə,grād\ *adj* **1** : moving backward **2** : becoming worse

ret•ro•gress \,retrə'gres\ *vb* : move backward — **ret•ro•gres•sion** \-'greshən\ *n*

ret•ro•spect \'retrə,spekt\ *n* : review of past events — **ret•ro•spec•tion** \,retrə'spekshən\ *n* — **ret•ro•spec•tive** \-'spektiv\ *adj* — **ret•ro•spec•tive•ly** *adv*

---

replaster	repressurize	reread
replay	reprice	rereading
replot	reprint	rerecord
repolish	reprocess	reregister
repopulate	reprogram	reroof

re•turn \ri'tərn\ vb **1** : go or come back **2** : pass, give, or send back to an earlier possessor **3** : answer **4** : bring in as a profit **5** : give or do in return ∼ n **1** : act of returning or something returned **2** pl : report of balloting results **3** : statement of taxable income **4** : profit — **return** adj — **re•turn•able** adj or n — **re•turn•er** n

re•union \rē'yünyən\ n **1** : act of re-uniting **2** : a meeting of persons after a separation

re•vamp \ˌrē'vamp\ vb : renovate or revise

re•veal \ri'vēl\ vb **1** : make known **2** : show plainly

rev•eil•le \'revəlē\ n : military signal sounded about sunrise

rev•el \'revəl\ vb **-eled** or **-elled; -el•ing** or **-el•ling** **1** : take part in a revel **2** : take great pleasure ∼ n : wild party or celebration — **rev•el•er, rev•el•ler** \-ər\ n — **rev•el•ry** \-rē\ n

rev•e•la•tion \ˌrevə'lāshən\ n **1** : act of revealing **2** : something enlightening or astonishing

re•venge \ri'venj\ vb : avenge ∼ n **1** : desire for retaliation **2** : act of retaliation — **re•venge•ful** adj — **re•veng•er** n

rev•e•nue \'revəˌnü, -ˌnyü\ n : money collected by a government

re•ver•ber•ate \ri'vərbəˌrāt\ vb **-at•ed; -at•ing** : resound in a series of echoes — **re•ver•ber•a•tion** \-ˌvərbə'rāshən\ n

re•vere \ri'vir\ vb **-vered; -ver•ing** : show honor and devotion to — **rev•er•ence** \'revərəns\ n — **rev•er•ent** \-rənt\ adj — **rev•er•ent•ly** adv

rev•er•end \'revərənd\ adj : worthy of reverence ∼ n : clergy member

rev•er•ie \'revərē\ n, pl **-er•ies** : day-dream

re•verse \ri'vərs\ adj **1** : opposite to a previous or normal condition **2** : acting in an opposite way ∼ vb **-versed; -vers•ing** **1** : turn upside down or completely around **2** : change to the contrary or in the opposite direction ∼ n **1** : something contrary **2**

: change for the worse **3** : back of something — **re•ver•sal** \-səl\ n — **re•verse•ly** adv — **re•vers•ible** \-'vərsəbəl\ adj

re•vert \ri'vərt\ vb : return to an original type or condition — **re•ver•sion** \-'vərzhᵊn\ n

re•view \ri'vyü\ n **1** : formal inspection **2** : general survey **3** : critical evaluation **4** : second or repeated study or examination ∼ vb **1** : examine or study again **2** : reexamine judicially **3** : look back over **4** : examine critically **5** : inspect — **re•view•er** n

re•vile \ri'vīl\ vb **-viled; -vil•ing** : abuse verbally — **re•vile•ment** n — **re•vil•er** n

re•vise \-'vīz\ vb **-vised; -vis•ing** **1** : look over something written to correct or improve **2** : make a new version of — **re•vis•able** adj — **revise** n — **re•vis•er, re•vi•sor** \-'vīzər\ n — **re•vi•sion** \-'vizhən\ n

re•viv•al \-'vīvəl\ n **1** : act of reviving or state of being revived **2** : evangelistic meeting

re•vive \-'vīv\ vb **-vived; -viv•ing** : bring back to life or consciousness or into use — **re•viv•er** n

re•vo•ca•tion \ˌrevə'kāshən\ n : act or instance of revoking

re•voke \ri'vōk\ vb **-voked; -vok•ing** : annul by recalling — **re•vok•er** n

re•volt \-'vōlt\ vb **1** : throw off allegiance **2** : cause or experience disgust or shock ∼ n : rebellion or revolution — **re•volt•er** n

re•volt•ing \-iŋ\ adj : extremely offensive — **re•volt•ing•ly** adv

rev•o•lu•tion \ˌrevə'lüshən\ n **1** : rotation **2** : progress in an orbit **3** : sudden, radical, or complete change (as overthrow of a government) — **rev•o•lu•tion•ary** \-shəˌnerē\ adj or n

rev•o•lu•tion•ize \-shəˌnīz\ vb **-ized; -iz•ing** : change radically — **rev•o•lu•tion•iz•er** n

re•volve \ri'välv\ vb **-volved; -voiv•ing** **1** : ponder **2** : move in an orbit **3** : rotate — **re•volv•able** adj

re•volv•er \ri'välvər\ n : pistol with a revolving cylinder

reroute	resegregate	resew
resalable	resell	reshoot
resale	resentence	reshow
reschedule	reset	resocialization
reseal	resettle	resod

re·vue \ri'vyü\ *n* : theatrical production of brief numbers

re·vul·sion \ri'vəlshən\ *n* : complete dislike or repugnance

re·ward \ri'word\ *vb* : give a reward to or for ~ *n* : something offered for service or achievement

re·write \,rē'rīt\ *vb* -wrote; -writ·ten; -writ·ing : revise — **rewrite** *n*

rhap·so·dy \'rapsədē\ *n, pl* -dies 1 : expression of extravagant praise 2 : flowing free-form musical composition — **rhap·sod·ic** \rap'sädik\ *adj* — **rhap·sod·i·cal·ly** \-iklē\ *adv* — **rhap·so·dize** \'rapsə,dīz\ *vb*

rhet·o·ric \'retərik\ *n* : art of speaking or writing effectively — **rhe·tor·i·cal** \ri'tórikəl\ *adj* — **rhet·o·ri·cian** \,retə'rishən\ *n*

rheu·ma·tism \'rümə,tizəm, 'rüm-\ *n* : disorder marked by inflammation or pain in muscles or joints — **rheu·mat·ic** \rü'matik\ *adj*

rhine·stone \'rīn,stōn\ *n* : a colorless imitation gem

rhi·no \'rīnō\ *n, pl* -no *or* -nos : rhinoceros

rhi·noc·er·os \rī'näsərəs\ *n, pl* -noc·er·os·es *or* -noc·er·os *or* -noc·eri \-'näsə,rī\ : large thick-skinned mammal with 1 or 2 horns on the snout

rho·do·den·dron \,rōdə'dendrən\ *n* : flowering evergreen shrub

rhom·bus \'rämbəs\ *n, pl* -bus·es *or* -bi \-,bī\ : parallelogram with equal sides

rhu·barb \'rü,bärb\ *n* : garden plant with edible stalks

rhyme \'rīm\ *n* 1 : correspondence in terminal sounds 2 : verse that rhymes

~ *vb* **rhymed; rhym·ing** : make or have rhymes

rhythm \'rithəm\ *n* : regular succession of sounds or motions — **rhyth·mic** \'rithmik\, **rhyth·mi·cal** \-mikəl\ *adj* — **rhyth·mi·cal·ly** *adv*

rhythm and blues *n* : popular music based on blues and black folk music

rib \'rib\ *n* 1 : curved bone joined to the spine 2 : riblike thing ~ *vb* -**bb**- 1 : furnish or mark with ribs 2 : tease — **rib·ber** *n*

rib·ald \'ribəld\ *adj* : coarse or vulgar — **rib·ald·ry** \-əldrē\ *n*

rib·bon \'ribən\ *n* 1 : narrow strip of fabric used esp. for decoration 2 : strip of inked cloth (as in a typewriter)

ri·bo·fla·vin \,rībə'flāvən, 'rībə,-\ *n* : growth-promoting vitamin

rice \'rīs\ *n, pl* **rice** : starchy edible seeds of an annual cereal grass

rich \'rich\ *adj* 1 : having a lot of money or possessions 2 : valuable 3 : containing much sugar, fat, or seasoning 4 : abundant 5 : deep and pleasing in color or tone 6 : fertile — **rich·ly** *adv* — **rich·ness** *n*

rich·es \'richəz\ *n pl* : wealth

rick·ets \'rikəts\ *n* : childhood bone disease

rick·ety \'rikətē\ *adj* : shaky

rick·sha, rick·shaw \'rik,shó\ *n* : small covered 2-wheeled carriage pulled by one person

ric·o·chet \'rikə,shā, *Brit also* -,shet\ *vb* -**cheted** \-,shād\ *or* -**chet·ted** \-,shetəd\; -**chet·ing** \-,shāiŋ\ *or* -**chet·ting** \-,shetiŋ\ : bounce off at an angle — **ricochet** *n*

rid \'rid\ *vb* **rid; rid·ding** : make free of

something unwanted — **rid•dance** \'rid⁰ns\ n

rid•den \'rid⁰n\ adj : overburdened with — used in combination

¹**rid•dle** \'rid⁰l\ n : puzzling question ~ vb **-dled; -dling** : speak in riddles

²**riddle** vb **-dled; -dling** : fill full of holes

ride \'rīd\ vb **rode** \'rōd\; **rid•den** \'rid⁰n\; **rid•ing** \'rīdiŋ\ **1** : be carried along **2** : sit on and cause to move **3** : travel over a surface **4** : tease or nag ~ n **1** : trip on an animal or in a vehicle **2** : mechanical device ridden for amusement

rid•er n **1** : one that rides **2** : attached clause or document — **rid•er•less** adj

ridge \'rij\ n **1** : range of hills **2** : raised line or strip **3** : line of intersection of 2 sloping surfaces — **ridgy** adj

rid•i•cule \'ridə,kyül\ vb : laugh at or make fun of — **ridicule** n

ri•dic•u•lous \rə'dikyələs\ adj : arousing ridicule — **ri•dic•u•lous•ly** adv — **ri•dic•u•lous•ness** n

rife \'rīf\ adj : abounding — **rife** adv

riff•raff \'rif,raf\ n : mob

¹**ri•fle** \'rīfəl\ vb **-fled; -fling** : ransack esp. with intent to steal — **ri•fler** \-flər\ n

²**rifle** n : long shoulder weapon with spiral grooves in the bore — **ri•fle•man** \-mən\ n — **ri•fling** n

rift \'rift\ n : separation — **rift** vb

¹**rig** \'rig\ vb **-gg- 1** : fit out with rigging **2** : set up esp. as a makeshift ~ n **1** : distinctive shape, number, and arrangement of sails and masts of a sailing ship **2** : equipment **3** : carriage with its horse

²**rig** vb **-gg-** : manipulate esp. by deceptive or dishonest means

rig•ging \'rigiŋ, -ən\ n : lines that hold and move the masts, sails, and spars of a sailing ship

right \'rīt\ adj **1** : meeting a standard of conduct **2** : correct **3** : genuine **4** : normal **5** : opposite of left ~ n **1** : something that is correct, just, proper, or honorable **2** : something to which one has a just claim **3** : something that is on the right side ~ adv **1** : according to what is right **2** : immediately **3** : completely **4** : on or to the right ~ vb **1** : restore to a proper state **2** : bring or become upright again — **right•er** n — **right•ness** n — **right•ward** \-wərd\ adj

right angle n : angle whose sides are perpendicular to each other — **right–**

an•gled \'rīt'aŋgəld\, **right–an•gle** \-gəl\ adj

righ•teous \'rīchəs\ adj : acting or being in accordance with what is just or moral — **righ•teous•ly** adv — **righ•teous•ness** n

right•ful \'rītfəl\ adj : lawful — **right•ful•ly** \-ē\ adv — **right•ful•ness** n

right•ly \'rītlē\ adv **1** : justly **2** : properly **3** : correctly

rig•id \'rijəd\ adj : lacking flexibility — **ri•gid•i•ty** \rə'jidətē\ n — **rig•id•ly** adv

rig•ma•role \'rigmə,rōl, 'rigə-\ n **1** : meaningless talk **2** : complicated often unnecessary procedure

rig•or \'rigər\ n : severity — **rig•or•ous** adj — **rig•or•ous•ly** adv

rig•or mor•tis \,rigər'mórtəs\ n : temporary stiffness of muscles occurring after death

rile \'rīl\ vb **riled; ril•ing** : anger

rill \'ril\ n : small brook

rim \'rim\ n : edge esp. of something curved ~ vb **-mm-** : border

¹**rime** \'rīm\ n : frost — **rimy** \'rīmē\ adj

²**rime** var of RHYME

rind \'rīnd\ n : usu. hard or tough outer layer

¹**ring** \'riŋ\ n **1** : circular band used as an ornament or for holding or fastening **2** : something circular **3** : place for contest or display **4** : group with a selfish or dishonest aim ~ vb : surround — **ringed** \'riŋd\ adj — **ring•like** adj

²**ring** vb **rang** \'raŋ\; **rung** \'rəŋ\; **ring•ing 1** : sound resonantly when struck **2** : cause to make a metallic sound by striking **3** : resound **4** : call esp. by a bell ~ n **1** : resonant sound or tone **2** : act or instance of ringing

ring•er \'riŋər\ n **1** : one that sounds by ringing **2** : illegal substitute **3** : one that closely resembles another

ring•lead•er \'riŋ,lēdər\ n : leader esp. of troublemakers

ring•let n : long curl

ring•worm n : contagious skin disease caused by fungi

rink \'riŋk\ n : enclosed place for skating

rinse \'rins\ vb **rinsed; rins•ing 1** : cleanse usu. with water only **2** : treat (hair) with a rinse ~ n : liquid used for rinsing — **rins•er** n

ri•ot \'rīət\ n **1** : violent public disorder **2** : random or disorderly profusion — **riot** vb — **ri•ot•er** n — **ri•ot•ous** adj

rip \'rip\ *vb* -**pp**- : cut or tear open ∼ *n* : rent made by ripping — **rip•per** *n*

ripe \'rīp\ *adj* **rip•er; rip•est** : fully grown, developed, or prepared — **ripe•ly** *adv* — **rip•en** \'rīpən\ *vb* — **ripe•ness** *n*

rip—off *n* : theft — **rip off** *vb*

rip•ple \'ripəl\ *vb* -**pled; -pling** 1 : become lightly ruffled on the surface 2 : sound like rippling water — **ripple** *n*

rise \'rīz\ *vb* **rose** \'rōz\; **ris•en** \'riz³n\; **ris•ing** \'rīziŋ\ 1 : get up from sitting, kneeling, or lying 2 : take arms 3 : appear above the horizon 4 : ascend 5 : gain a higher position or rank 6 : increase ∼ *n* 1 : act of rising 2 : origin 3 : elevation 4 : increase 5 : upward slope 6 : area of high ground — **ris•er** \'rīzər\ *n*

risk \'risk\ *n* : exposure to loss or injury — **risk** *vb* — **risk•i•ness** *n* — **risky** *adj*

ris•qué \ris'kā\ *adj* : nearly indecent

rite \'rīt\ *n* 1 : set form for conducting a ceremony 2 : liturgy of a church 3 : ceremonial action

rit•u•al \'richəwəl\ *n* : rite — **ritual** *adj* — **rit•u•al•ism** \-ˌizəm\ *n* — **rit•u•al•is•tic** \ˌrichəwəl'istik\ *adj* — **rit•u•al•is•ti•cal•ly** \-tiklē\ *adv* — **rit•u•al•ly** \'richəwəlē\ *adv*

ri•val \'rīvəl\ *n* 1 : competitor 2 : peer ∼ *vb* -**valed** *or* -**valled; -val•ing** *or* -**val•ling** 1 : be in competition with 2 : equal — **rival** *adj* — **ri•val•ry** \-rē\ *n*

riv•er \'rivər\ *n* : large natural stream of water — **riv•er•bank** *n* — **riv•er•bed** *n* — **riv•er•boat** *n* — **riv•er•side** *n*

riv•et \'rivət\ *n* : headed metal bolt ∼ *vb* : fasten with a rivet — **riv•et•er** *n*

riv•u•let \'rivyələt\ *n* : small stream

roach \'rōch\ *n* : cockroach

road \'rōd\ *n* : open way for vehicles, persons, and animals — **road•bed** *n* — **road•side** *n or adj* — **road•way** *n*

road•block *n* : obstruction on a road

road•run•ner *n* : large fast-running bird

roam \'rōm\ *vb* : wander

roan \'rōn\ *adj* : of a dark color sprinkled with white ∼ *n* : animal with a roan coat

roar \'rōr\ *vb* : utter a full loud prolonged sound — **roar** *n* — **roar•er** *n*

roast \'rōst\ *vb* 1 : cook by dry heat 2 : criticize severely ∼ *n* : piece of meat suitable for roasting — **roast** *adj* — **roast•er** *n*

rob \'räb\ *vb* -**bb**- 1 : steal from 2 : commit robbery — **rob•ber** *n*

rob•bery \'räbərē\ *n, pl* -**ber•ies** : theft of something from a person by use of violence or threat

robe \'rōb\ *n* 1 : long flowing outer garment 2 : covering for the lower body ∼ *vb* **robed; rob•ing** : clothe with or as if with a robe

rob•in \'räbən\ *n* : No. American thrush with a reddish breast

ro•bot \'rō,bät, -bət\ *n* 1 : machine that looks and acts like a human being 2 : efficient but insensitive person — **ro•bot•ic** \rō'bätik\ *adj*

ro•bust \rō'bəst, 'rō,bəst\ *adj* : strong and vigorously healthy — **ro•bust•ly** *adv* — **ro•bust•ness** *n*

¹**rock** \'räk\ *vb* : sway or cause to sway back and forth ∼ *n* 1 : rocking movement 2 : popular music marked by repetition and a strong beat

²**rock** *n* : mass of hard mineral material — **rock** *adj* — **rocky** *adj*

rock•er *n* 1 : curved piece on which a chair rocks 2 : chair that rocks

rock•et \'räkət\ *n* 1 : self-propelled firework or missile 2 : jet engine that carries its own oxygen ∼ *vb* : rise abruptly and rapidly — **rock•et•ry** \-ətrē\ *n*

rod \'räd\ *n* 1 : straight slender stick 2 : unit of length equal to 5 yards

rode *past of* RIDE

ro•dent \'rōd³nt\ *n* : usu. small gnawing mammal

ro•deo \'rōdē,ō, rō'dāō\ *n, pl* -**de•os** : contest of cowboy skills

roe \'rō\ *n* : fish eggs

rogue \'rōg\ *n* : dishonest or mischievous person — **rogu•ery** \'rōgərē\ *n* — **rogu•ish** \'rōgish\ *adj* — **rogu•ish•ly** *adv* — **rogu•ish•ness** *n*

roil \'ròil\ *vb* 1 : make cloudy or muddy by stirring up 2 : make angry

role \'rōl\ *n* 1 : part to play 2 : function

roll \'rōl\ *n* 1 : official record or list of names 2 : something rolled up or rounded 3 : bread baked in a small rounded mass 4 : sound of rapid drum strokes 5 : heavy reverberating sound 6 : rolling movement ∼ *vb* 1 : move by turning over 2 : move on wheels 3 : flow in a continuous stream 4 : swing from side to side 5 : shape or be shaped in rounded form 6 : press with a roller

roll•er *n* 1 : revolving cylinder 2 : rod on which something is rolled up 3 : long heavy ocean wave

roller skate *n* : a skate with wheels instead of a runner — **roller–skate** *vb*

rol·lick·ing \'rälikiŋ\ *adj* : full of good spirits

Ro·man Catholic \'rōmən-\ *n* : member of a Christian church led by a pope — **Roman Catholic** *adj* — **Roman Catholicism** *n*

ro·mance \rō'mans, 'rō͟,mans\ *n* **1** : medieval tale of knightly adventure **2** : love story **3** : love affair ~ *vb* **-manced; -manc·ing 1** : have romantic fancies **2** : have a love affair with — **ro·manc·er** *n*

ro·man·tic \rō'mantik\ *adj* **1** : visionary or imaginative **2** : appealing to one's emotions — **ro·man·ti·cal·ly** \-iklē\ *adv*

romp \'rämp\ *vb* : play actively and noisily — **romp** *n*

roof \'rüf, 'ru̇f\ *n, pl* **roofs** \'rüfs, 'ru̇fs; 'rüvz, 'ru̇vz\ : upper covering part of a building ~ *vb* : cover with a roof — **roofed** \'rüft, 'ru̇ft\ *adj* — **roof·ing** *n* — **roof·less** *adj* — **roof·top** *n*

¹rook \'ru̇k\ *n* : crowlike bird

²rook *vb* : cheat

rook·ie \'ru̇kē\ *n* : novice

room \'rüm, 'ru̇m\ *n* **1** : sufficient space **2** : partitioned part of a building ~ *vb* : occupy lodgings — **room·er** *n* — **room·ful** *n* — **roomy** *adj*

room·mate *n* : one sharing the same lodgings

roost \'rüst\ *n* : support on which birds perch ~ *vb* : settle on a roost

roost·er \'rüstər, 'ru̇s-\ *n* : adult male domestic chicken

¹root \'rüt, 'ru̇t\ *n* **1** : leafless underground part of a seed plant **2** : rootlike thing or part **3** : source **4** : essential core ~ *vb* : form, fix, or become fixed by roots — **root·less** *adj* — **root·let** \-lət\ *n* — **root·like** *adj*

²root *vb* : turn up with the snout

³root \'rüt, 'ru̇t\ *vb* : applaud or encourage noisily — **root·er** *n*

rope \'rōp\ *n* : large strong cord of strands of fiber ~ *vb* **roped; rop·ing 1** : tie with a rope **2** : lasso

ro·sa·ry \'rōzərē\ *n, pl* **-ries 1** : string of beads used in praying **2** : Roman Catholic devotion

¹rose *past of* RISE

²rose \'rōz\ *n* **1** : prickly shrub with bright flowers **2** : purplish red — **rose** *adj* — **rose·bud** *n* — **rose·bush** *n*

rose·mary \'rōz͟,merē\ *n, pl* **-mar·ies** : fragrant shrubby mint

ro·sette \rō'zet\ *n* : rose-shaped ornament

Rosh Ha·sha·nah \͟,räshhä'shänə, ͟,rōsh-\ *n* : Jewish New Year observed as a religious holiday in September or October

ros·in \'räz°n\ *n* : brittle resin

ros·ter \'rästər\ *n* : list of names

ros·trum \'rästrəm\ *n, pl* **-trums** *or* **-tra** \-trə\ : speaker's platform

rosy \'rōzē\ *adj* **ros·i·er; -est 1** : of the color rose **2** : hopeful — **ros·i·ly** *adv* — **ros·i·ness** *n*

rot \'rät\ *vb* **-tt-** : undergo decomposition ~ *n* **1** : decay **2** : disease in which tissue breaks down

ro·ta·ry \'rōtərē\ *adj* **1** : turning on an axis **2** : having a rotating part

ro·tate \'rō͟,tāt\ *vb* **-tat·ed; -tat·ing 1** : turn about an axis or a center **2** : alternate in a series — **ro·ta·tion** \rō'tāshən\ *n* — **ro·ta·tor** \'rō͟,tātər\ *n*

rote \'rōt\ *n* : repetition from memory

ro·tor \'rōtər\ *n* **1** : part that rotates **2** : system of rotating horizontal blades for supporting a helicopter

rot·ten \'rät°n\ *adj* **1** : having rotted **2** : corrupt **3** : extremely unpleasant or inferior — **rot·ten·ness** *n*

ro·tund \rō'tənd\ *adj* : rounded — **ro·tun·di·ty** \-'təndətē\ *n*

ro·tun·da \rō'təndə\ *n* : building or room with a dome

roué \ru̇'ā\ *n* : man given to debauched living

rouge \'rüzh, 'rüj\ *n* : cosmetic for the cheeks — **rouge** *vb*

rough \'rəf\ *adj* **1** : not smooth **2** : not calm **3** : harsh, violent, or rugged **4** : crudely or hastily done ~ *n* : rough state or something in that state ~ *vb* **1** : roughen **2** : manhandle **3** : make roughly — **rough·ly** *adv* — **rough·ness** *n*

rough·age \'rəfij\ *n* : coarse bulky food

rough·en \'rəfən\ *vb* : make or become rough

rough·neck \'rəf͟,nek\ *n* : rowdy

rou·lette \rü'let\ *n* : gambling game using a whirling numbered wheel

¹round \'rau̇nd\ *adj* **1** : having every part the same distance from the center **2** : cylindrical **3** : complete **4** : approximate **5** : blunt **6** : moving in or forming a circle ~ *n* **1** : round or curved thing **2** : series of recurring actions or events **3** : period of time or a unit of action **4** : fired shot **5** : cut of beef ~ *vb* **1** : make or become round **2** : go around **3** : finish **4** : express as an approximation — **round•ish** *adj* — **round•ly** *adv* — **round•ness** *n*

²**round** *prep or adv* : around

round•about *adj* : indirect

round•up \'raund,əp\ *n* **1** : gathering together of range cattle **2** : summary — **round up** *vb*

rouse \'rauz\ *vb* **roused; rous•ing 1** : wake from sleep **2** : stir up

rout \'raut\ *n* **1** : state of wild confusion **2** : disastrous defeat ~ *vb* : defeat decisively

route \'rüt, 'raut\ *n* : line of travel ~ *vb* **rout•ed; rout•ing** : send by a selected route

rou•tine \rü'tēn\ *n* **1** : regular course of procedure **2** : an often repeated speech, formula, or part — **routine** *adj* — **rou•tine•ly** *adv*

rove \'rōv\ *vb* **roved; rov•ing** : wander or roam — **rov•er** *n*

¹**row** \'rō\ *vb* **1** : propel a boat with oars **2** : carry in a rowboat ~ *n* : act of rowing — **row•boat** *n* — **row•er** \'rōər\ *n*

²**row** *n* : number of objects in a line

³**row** \'rau\ *n* : noisy quarrel — **row** *vb*

row•dy \'raudē\ *adj* **-di•er; -est** : coarse or boisterous in behavior — **row•di•ness** *n* — **rowdy** *n*

roy•al \'rōiəl\ *adj* : relating to or befitting a king ~ *n* : person of royal blood — **roy•al•ly** *adv*

roy•al•ty \'rōiəltē\ *n, pl* **-ties 1** : state of being royal **2** : royal persons **3** : payment for use of property

rub \'rəb\ *vb* **-bb- 1** : use pressure and friction on a body **2** : scour, polish, erase, or smear by pressure and friction **3** : chafe with friction ~ *n* : difficulty

rub•ber \'rəbər\ *n* **1** : one that rubs **2** : waterproof elastic substance or something made of it — **rubber** *adj* — **rub•ber•ize** \-,īz\ *vb* — **rub•bery** *adj*

rub•bish \'rəbish\ *n* : waste or trash

rub•ble \'rəbəl\ *n* : broken fragments esp. of a destroyed building

ru•ble \'rübəl\ *n* : monetary unit of Russia

ru•by \'rübē\ *n, pl* **-bies** : precious red stone or its color — **ruby** *adj*

rud•der \'rədər\ *n* : steering device at the rear of a ship or aircraft

rud•dy \'rədē\ *adj* **-di•er; -est** : reddish — **rud•di•ness** *n*

rude \'rüd\ *adj* **rud•er; rud•est 1** : roughly made **2** : impolite — **rude•ly** *adv* — **rude•ness** *n*

ru•di•ment \'rüdəmənt\ *n* **1** : something not fully developed **2** : elementary principle — **ru•di•men•ta•ry** \,rüdə'mentərē\ *adj*

rue \'rü\ *vb* **rued; ru•ing** : feel regret for ~ *n* : regret — **rue•ful** \-fəl\ *adj* — **rue•ful•ly** *adv* — **rue•ful•ness** *n*

ruf•fi•an \'rəfēən\ *n* : brutal person

ruf•fle \'rəfəl\ *vb* **-fled; -fling 1** : draw into or provide with pleats **2** : roughen the surface of **3** : irritate ~ *n* : strip of fabric pleated on one edge — **ruf•fly** \'rəfəlē, -flē\ *adj*

rug \'rəg\ *n* : piece of heavy fabric used as a floor covering

rug•ged \'rəgəd\ *adj* **1** : having a rough uneven surface **2** : severe **3** : strong — **rug•ged•ly** *adv* — **rug•ged•ness** *n*

ru•in \'rüən\ *n* **1** : complete collapse or destruction **2** : remains of something destroyed — usu. in pl. **3** : cause of destruction ~ *vb* **1** : destroy **2** : damage beyond repair **3** : bankrupt

ru•in•ous \'rüənəs\ *adj* : causing ruin — **ru•in•ous•ly** *adv*

rule \'rül\ *n* **1** : guide or principle for governing action **2** : usual way of doing something **3** : government **4** : straight strip (as of wood or metal) marked off in units for measuring ~ *vb* **ruled; rul•ing 1** : govern **2** : give as a decision — **rul•er** *n*

rum \'rəm\ *n* : liquor made from molasses or sugarcane

rum•ble \'rəmbəl\ *vb* **-bled; -bling** : make a low heavy rolling sound — **rumble** *n*

ru•mi•nant \'rümənənt\ *n* : hoofed mammal (as a cow or deer) that chews the cud — **ruminant** *adj*

ru•mi•nate \'rümə,nāt\ *vb* **-nat•ed; -nat•ing** : contemplate — **ru•mi•na•tion** \,rümə'nāshən\ *n*

rum•mage \'rəmij\ *vb* **-maged; -mag•ing** : search thoroughly

rum•my \'rəmē\ *n* : card game

ru•mor \'rümər\ *n* **1** : common talk **2** : widespread statement not authenticated — **rumor** *vb*

rump \'rəmp\ *n* : rear part of an animal

rum•ple \'rəmpəl\ *vb* **-pled; -pling** : tousle or wrinkle — **rumple** *n*

rum·pus \'rəmpəs\ *n* : disturbance

run \'rən\ *vb* **ran** \'ran\; **run; run·ning** **1** : go rapidly or hurriedly **2** : enter a race or election **3** : operate **4** : continue in force **5** : flow rapidly **6** : take a certain direction **7** : manage **8** : incur ∼ *n* **1** : act of running **2** : brook **3** : continuous series **4** : usual kind **5** : freedom of movement **6** : lengthwise ravel

run·around *n* : evasive or delaying action esp. in response to a request

run·away \'rənə,wā\ *n* : fugitive ∼ *adj* **1** : fugitive **2** : out of control

run–down *adj* : being in poor condition

¹rung *past part of* RING

²rung \'rəŋ\ *n* : horizontal piece of a chair or ladder

run·ner \'rənər\ *n* **1** : one that runs **2** : thin piece or part on which something slides **3** : slender creeping branch of a plant

run·ner–up *n, pl* **run·ners–up** : competitor who finishes second

run·ning \'rəniŋ\ *adj* **1** : flowing **2** : continuous

runt \'rənt\ *n* : small person or animal — **runty** *adj*

run·way \'rən,wā\ *n* : strip on which aircraft land and take off

ru·pee \rü'pē, 'rü,-\ *n* : monetary unit (as of India)

rup·ture \'rəpchər\ *n* **1** : breaking or tearing apart **2** : hernia ∼ *vb* **-tured; -tur·ing** : cause or undergo rupture

ru·ral \'rúrəl\ *adj* : relating to the country or agriculture

ruse \'rüs, 'rüz\ *n* : trick

¹rush \'rəsh\ *n* : grasslike marsh plant

²rush *vb* **1** : move forward or act with too great haste **2** : perform in a short time ∼ *n* : violent forward motion ∼ *adj* : requiring speed — **rush·er** *n*

rus·set \'rəsət\ *n* **1** : reddish brown color **2** : a baking potato — **russet** *adj*

rust \'rəst\ *n* **1** : reddish coating on exposed iron **2** : reddish brown color — **rust** *vb* — **rusty** *adj*

rus·tic \'rəstik\ *adj* : relating to or suitable for the country or country dwellers ∼ *n* : rustic person — **rus·ti·cal·ly** *adv*

rus·tle \'rəsəl\ *vb* **-tled; -tling** **1** : make or cause a rustle **2** : forage food **3** : steal cattle from the range ∼ *n* : series of small sounds — **rus·tler** \-ələr\ *n*

rut \'rət\ *n* **1** : track worn by wheels or feet **2** : set routine — **rut·ted** *adj*

ruth·less \'rüthləs\ *adj* : having no pity — **ruth·less·ly** *adv* — **ruth·less·ness** *n*

RV \,är-'vē\ *n* recreational vehicle

-ry \rē\ *n suffix* : -ery

rye \'rī\ *n* **1** : cereal grass grown for grain **2** : whiskey from rye

S

s \'es\ *n, pl* **s's** *or* **ss** \'esəz\ : 19th letter of the alphabet

¹-s \s *after sounds* f, k, k̲, p, t, th; əz *after sounds* ch, j, s, sh, z, zh; z *after other sounds*\ — used to form the plural of most nouns

²-s *vb suffix* — used to form the 3d person singular present of most verbs

Sab·bath \'sabəth\ *n* **1** : Saturday observed as a day of worship by Jews and some Christians **2** : Sunday observed as a day of worship by Christians

sa·ber, sa·bre \'sābər\ *n* : curved cavalry sword

sa·ble \'sābəl\ *n* **1** : black **2** : dark brown mammal or its fur

sab·o·tage \'sabə,täzh\ *n* : deliberate destruction or hampering ∼ *vb* **-taged; -tag·ing** : wreck through sabotage

sab·o·teur \,sabə'tər\ *n* : person who sabotages

sac \'sak\ *n* : anatomical pouch

sac·cha·rin \'sakərən\ *n* : low-calorie artificial sweetener

sac·cha·rine \-ərən\ *adj* : nauseatingly sweet

sa·chet \sa'shā\ *n* : small bag with perfumed powder (**sachet powder**)

¹sack \'sak\ *n* : bag ∼ *vb* : fire

²sack *vb* : plunder a captured place

sack·cloth *n* : rough garment worn as a sign of penitence

sac•ra•ment \'sakrəmənt\ *n* : formal religious act or rite — **sac•ra•men•tal** \ˌsakrə'ment°l\ *adj*

sa•cred \'sākrəd\ *adj* 1 : set apart for or worthy of worship 2 : worthy of reverence 3 : relating to religion — **sa•cred•ly** *adv* — **sa•cred•ness** *n*

sac•ri•fice \'sakrəˌfīs\ *n* 1 : the offering of something precious to a deity or the thing offered 2 : loss or deprivation ~ *vb* **-ficed; -fic•ing** : offer or give up as a sacrifice — **sac•ri•fi•cial** \ˌsakrə'fishəl\ *adj*

sac•ri•lege \'sakrəlij\ *n* : violation of something sacred — **sac•ri•le•gious** \ˌsakrə'lijəs, -'lējəs\ *adj*

sac•ro•sanct \'sakrō,saŋkt\ *adj* : sacred

sad \'sad\ *adj* **-dd-** 1 : affected with grief or sorrow 2 : causing sorrow — **sad•den** \'sad°n\ *vb* — **sad•ly** *adv* — **sad•ness** *n*

sad•dle \'sad°l\ *n* : seat for riding on horseback ~ *vb* **-dled; -dling** : put a saddle on

sa•dism \'sā,dizəm, 'sad,iz-\ *n* : delight in cruelty — **sa•dist** \'sādist, 'sad-\ *n* — **sa•dis•tic** \sə'distik\ *adj* — **sa•dis•ti•cal•ly** *adv*

sa•fa•ri \sə'färē, -'far-\ *n* : hunting expedition in Africa

safe \'sāf\ *adj* **saf•er; saf•est** 1 : free from harm 2 : providing safety ~ *n* : container to keep valuables safe — **safe•keep•ing** *n* — **safe•ly** *adv*

safe•guard *n* : measure or device for preventing accidents — **safeguard** *vb*

safe•ty \'sāftē\ *n, pl* **-ties** 1 : freedom from danger 2 : protective device

saf•flow•er \'saf,laủər\ *n* : herb with seeds rich in edible oil

saf•fron \'safrən\ *n* : orange powder from a crocus flower used in cooking

sag \'sag\ *vb* **-gg-** : droop, sink, or settle — **sag** *n*

sa•ga \'sägə\ *n* : story of heroic deeds

sa•ga•cious \sə'gāshəs\ *adj* : shrewd — **sa•gac•i•ty** \-'gasətē\ *n*

¹**sage** \'sāj\ *adj* : wise or prudent ~ *n* : wise man — **sage•ly** *adv*

²**sage** *n* : mint used in flavoring

sage•brush *n* : low shrub of the western U.S.

said *past of* SAY

sail \'sāl\ *n* 1 : fabric used to catch the wind and move a boat or ship 2 : trip on a sailboat ~ *vb* 1 : travel on a ship or sailboat 2 : move with ease or grace — **sail•boat** *n* — **sail•or** \'sālər\ *n*

sail•fish *n* : large fish with a very large dorsal fin

saint \'sānt, *before a name* ˌsānt *or* sənt\ *n* : holy or godly person — **saint•ed** \-əd\ *adj* — **saint•hood** \-ˌhủd\ *n* — **saint•li•ness** *n* — **saint•ly** *adj*

¹**sake** \'sāk\ *n* 1 : purpose or reason 2 : one's good or benefit

²**sa•ke, sa•ki** \'säkē\ *n* : Japanese rice wine

sa•la•cious \sə'lāshəs\ *adj* : sexually suggestive — **sa•la•cious•ly** *adv*

sal•ad \'saləd\ *n* : dish usu. of raw lettuce, vegetables, or fruit

sal•a•man•der \'saləˌmandər\ *n* : lizardlike amphibian

sa•la•mi \sə'lämē\ *n* : highly seasoned dried sausage

sal•a•ry \'salərē\ *n, pl* **-ries** : regular payment for services

sale \'sāl\ *n* 1 : transfer of ownership of property for money 2 : selling at bargain prices 3 **sales** *pl* : activities involved in selling — **sal•able, sale•able** \'sāləbəl\ *adj* — **sales•man** \-mən\ *n* — **sales•per•son** *n* — **sales•wom•an** *n*

sa•lient \'sālyənt\ *adj* : standing out conspicuously

sa•line \'sā,lēn, -,līn\ *adj* : containing salt — **sa•lin•i•ty** \sā'linətē, sə-\ *n*

sa•li•va \sə'līvə\ *n* : liquid secreted into the mouth — **sal•i•vary** \'salə,verē\ *adj* — **sal•i•vate** \-,vāt\ *vb* — **sal•i•va•tion** \ˌsalə'vāshən\ *n*

sal•low \'salō\ *adj* : of a yellowish sickly color

sal•ly \'salē\ *n, pl* **-lies** 1 : quick attack on besiegers 2 : witty remark — **sally** *vb*

salm•on \'samən\ *n, pl* **salmon** 1 : food fish with pink or red flesh 2 : deep yellowish pink color

sa•lon \sə'län, 'sal,än, sa'lōⁿ\ *n* : elegant room or shop

sa•loon \sə'lün\ *n* 1 : public cabin on a passenger ship 2 : barroom

sal•sa \'sôlsə, 'säl-\ *n* : spicy sauce of tomatoes, onions, and hot peppers

salt \'sôlt\ *n* 1 : white crystalline substance that consists of sodium and chlorine 2 : compound formed usu. from acid and metal — **salt** *vb or adj* — **salt•i•ness** *n* — **salty** *adj*

salt•wa•ter *adj* : relating to or living in salt water

sa•lu•bri•ous \sə'lübrēəs\ *adj* : good for health

sal·u·tary \'salyə,terē\ *adj* : health=
giving or beneficial

sal·u·ta·tion \,salyə'tāshən\ *n* : greeting

sa·lute \sə'lüt\ *vb* **-lut·ed; -lut·ing**
: honor by ceremony or formal movement — **salute** *n*

sal·vage \'salvij\ *n* : something saved
from destruction ∼ *vb* **-vaged; -vag-
ing** : rescue or save

sal·va·tion \sal'vāshən\ *n* : saving of a
person from sin or danger

salve \'sav, 'såv\ *n* : medicinal ointment ∼ *vb* **salved; salv·ing** : soothe

sal·ver \'salvər\ *n* : small tray

sal·vo \'salvō\ *n, pl* **-vos** *or* **-voes** : simultaneous discharge of guns

same \'sām\ *adj* : being the one referred to ∼ *pron* : the same one or
ones ∼ *adv* : in the same manner —
same·ness *n*

sam·ple \'sampəl\ *n* : piece or part that
shows the quality of a whole ∼ *vb*
-pled; -pling : judge by a sample

sam·pler \'samplər\ *n* : piece of needlework testing skill in embroidering

san·a·to·ri·um \,sanə'tōrēəm\ *n, pl*
-riums *or* **-ria** \-ēə\ : hospital for the
chronically ill

sanc·ti·fy \'saŋktə,fī\ *vb* **-fied; -fy·ing**
: make holy — **sanc·ti·fi·ca·tion**
\,saŋktəfə'kāshən\ *n*

sanc·ti·mo·nious \,saŋktə'mōnēəs\
adj : hypocritically pious — **sanc·ti-
mo·nious·ly** *adv*

sanc·tion \'saŋkshən\ *n* **1** : authoritative approval **2** : coercive measure —
usu. pl ∼ *vb* : approve

sanc·ti·ty \'saŋktətē\ *n, pl* **-ties** : quality or state of being holy or sacred

sanc·tu·ary \'saŋkchə,werē\ *n, pl* **-ar-
ies 1** : consecrated place **2** : place of
refuge

sand \'sand\ *n* : loose granular particles of rock ∼ *vb* : smooth with an
abrasive — **sand·bank** *n* — **sand·er**
n — **sand·storm** *n* — **sandy** *adj*

san·dal \'sand°l\ *n* : shoe consisting of
a sole strapped to the foot

sand·pa·per *n* : abrasive paper —
sandpaper *vb*

sand·pip·er \-,pīpər\ *n* : long-billed
shorebird

sand·stone *n* : rock made of naturally
cemented sand

sand·wich \'sand,wich\ *n* : 2 or more
slices of bread with a filling between
them ∼ *vb* : squeeze or crowd in

sane \'sān\ *adj* **san·er; san·est 1**

: mentally healthy **2** : sensible —
sane·ly *adv*

sang *past of* SING

san·gui·nary \'saŋgwə,nerē\ *adj*
: bloody

san·guine \'saŋgwən\ *adj* **1** : reddish
2 : cheerful

san·i·tar·i·um \,sanə'terēəm\ *n, pl*
-i·ums *or* **-ia** \-ēə\ : sanatorium

san·i·tary \'sanəterē\ *adj* **1** : relating
to health **2** : free from filth or infec-
tive matter

san·i·ta·tion \,sanə'tāshən\ *n* : protection of health by maintenance of san-
itary conditions

san·i·ty \'sanətē\ *n* : soundness of mind

sank *past of* SINK

¹sap \'sap\ *n* **1** : fluid that circulates
through a plant **2** : gullible person

²sap *vb* **-pp- 1** : undermine **2** : weaken
or exhaust gradually

sa·pi·ent \'sāpēənt, 'sapē-\ *adj* : wise
— **sa·pi·ence** \-əns\ *n*

sap·ling \'sapliŋ\ *n* : young tree

sap·phire \'saf,īr\ *n* : hard transparent
blue gem

sap·py \'sapē\ *adj* **-pi·er; -est 1** : full
of sap **2** : overly sentimental

sap·suck·er \'sap,səkər\ *n* : small No.
American woodpecker

sar·casm \'sär,kazəm\ *n* **1** : cutting
remark **2** : ironical criticism or reproach — **sar·cas·tic** \sär'kastik\
adj — **sar·cas·ti·cal·ly** *adv*

sar·coph·a·gus \sär'käfəgəs\ *n, pl* **-gi**
\-,gī, -,jī\ : large stone coffin

sar·dine \sär'dēn\ *n* : small fish preserved for use as food

sar·don·ic \sär'dänik\ *adj* : disdainfully humorous — **sar·don·i·cal·ly** *adv*

sa·rong \sə'röŋ, -'räŋ\ *n* : loose garment worn esp. by Pacific islanders

sar·sa·pa·ril·la \,saspə'rilə, ,särs-\ *n*
: dried roots of a tropical American
plant used esp. for flavoring or a carbonated drink flavored with this

sar·to·ri·al \sär'tōrēəl\ *adj* : relating to
a tailor or men's clothes

¹sash \'sash\ *n* : broad band worn
around the waist or over the shoulder

²sash *n, pl* **sash 1** : frame for a pane of
glass in a door or window **2** : movable part of a window

sas·sa·fras \'sasə,fras\ *n* : No. American tree or its dried root bark

sassy \'sasē\ *adj* **sass·i·er; -est** : saucy

sat *past of* SIT

Sa·tan \'sāt³n\ *n* : devil — **sa·tan·ic** \sə-'tanik, sā-\ *adj* — **sa·tan·i·cal·ly** *adv*

satch·el \'sachəl\ *n* : small bag

sate \'sāt\ *vb* **sat·ed; sat·ing** : satisfy fully

sat·el·lite \'sat³l,īt\ *n* 1 : toady 2 : body or object that revolves around a larger celestial body

sa·ti·ate \'sāshē,āt\ *vb* -at·ed; -at·ing : sate — **sa·ti·ety** \sə'tīətē\ *n*

sat·in \'sat³n\ *n* : glossy fabric — **sat·iny** *adj*

sat·ire \'sa,tīr\ *n* : literary ridicule done with humor — **sa·tir·ic** \sə'tirik\, **sa·tir·i·cal** \-ikəl\ *adj* — **sa·tir·i·cal·ly** *adv* — **sat·i·rist** \'satərist\ *n* — **sat·i·rize** \-ə,rīz\ *vb*

sat·is·fac·tion \,satəs'fakshən\ *n* : state of being satisfied — **sat·is·fac·to·ri·ly** \-'faktərəlē\ *adv* — **sat·is·fac·to·ry** \-'faktərē\ *adj*

sat·is·fy \'satəs,fī\ *vb* -fied; -fy·ing 1 : make happy 2 : pay what is due to or on — **sat·is·fy·ing·ly** *adv*

sat·u·rate \'sachə,rāt\ *vb* -rat·ed; -rat·ing : soak or charge thoroughly — **sat·u·ra·tion** \,sachə'rāshən\ *n*

Sat·ur·day \'satərdā, -dē\ *n* : 7th day of the week

sat·ur·nine \'satər,nīn\ *adj* : sullen

sa·tyr \'sātər, 'sat-\ *n* : pleasure-loving forest god of ancient Greece

sauce \'sós\ *n* : fluid dressing or topping for food — **sauce·pan** *n*

sau·cer \'sósər\ *n* : small shallow dish under a cup

saucy \'sasē, 'sósē\ *adj* **sauc·i·er; -est** : insolent — **sauc·i·ly** *adv* — **sauc·i·ness** *n*

sau·er·kraut \'saúər,kraút\ *n* : finely cut and fermented cabbage

sau·na \'saúnə\ *n* : steam or dry heat bath or a room or cabinet used for such a bath

saun·ter \'sóntər, 'sänt-\ *vb* : stroll

sau·sage \'sósij\ *n* : minced and highly seasoned meat

sau·té \sȯ'tā, sō-\ *vb* -téed *or* -téd; -té·ing : fry in a little fat — **sauté** *n*

sav·age \'savij\ *adj* 1 : wild 2 : cruel ～ *n* : person belonging to a primitive society — **sav·age·ly** *adv* — **sav·age·ness** *n* — **sav·age·ry** *n*

¹save \'sāv\ *vb* **saved; sav·ing** 1 : rescue from danger 2 : guard from destruction 3 : redeem from sin 4 : put aside as a reserve — **sav·er** *n*

²save *prep* : except

sav·ior, sav·iour \'sāvyər\ *n* 1 : one who saves 2 *cap* : Jesus Christ

sa·vor \'sāvər\ *n* : special flavor ～ *vb* : taste with pleasure — **sa·vory** *adj*

¹saw *past of* SEE

²saw \'sȯ\ *n* : cutting tool with teeth ～ *vb* **sawed; sawed** *or* **sawn; saw·ing** : cut with a saw — **saw·dust** \-,dəst\ *n* — **saw·mill** *n* — **saw·yer** \-yər\ *n*

saw·horse *n* : support for wood being sawed

sax·o·phone \'saksə,fōn\ *n* : wind instrument with a reed mouthpiece and usu. a bent metal body

say \'sā\ *vb* **said** \'sed\; **say·ing** \'sāiŋ\; **says** \'sez\ 1 : express in words 2 : state positively ～ *n, pl* **says** \'sāz\ 1 : expression of opinion 2 : power of decision

say·ing \'sāiŋ\ *n* : commonly repeated statement

scab \'skab\ *n* 1 : protective crust over a sore or wound 2 : worker taking a striker's job ～ *vb* **-bb-** 1 : become covered with a scab 2 : work as a scab — **scab·by** *adj*

scab·bard \'skabərd\ *n* : sheath for the blade of a weapon

scaf·fold \'skafəld, -,ōld\ *n* 1 : raised platform for workmen 2 : platform on which a criminal is executed

scald \'skȯld\ *vb* 1 : burn with hot liquid or steam 2 : heat to the boiling point

¹scale \'skāl\ *n* : weighing device ～ *vb* **scaled; scal·ing** : weigh

²scale *n* 1 : thin plate esp. on the body of a fish or reptile 2 : thin coating or layer ～ *vb* **scaled; scal·ing** : strip of scales — **scaled** \'skāld\ *adj* — **scaleless** *adj* — **scaly** *adj*

³scale *n* 1 : graduated series 2 : size of a sample (as a model) in proportion to the size of the actual thing 3 : standard of estimation or judgment 4 : series of musical tones ～ *vb* **scaled; scal·ing** 1 : climb by a ladder 2 : arrange in a graded series

scal·lion \'skalyən\ *n* : bulbless onion

scal·lop \'skäləp, 'skal-\ *n* 1 : marine mollusk 2 : rounded projection on a border

scalp \'skalp\ *n* : skin and flesh of the head ～ *vb* 1 : remove the scalp from 2 : resell at a greatly increased price — **scalp·er** *n*

scal·pel \'skalpəl\ *n* : surgical knife

scamp \'skamp\ *n* : rascal

scam·per \'skampər\ *vb* : run nimbly
  — **scamper** *n*

scan \'skan\ *vb* **-nn-** **1** : read (verses) so
as to show meter **2** : examine closely
or hastily **3** : examine with a sensing
device — **scan** *n* — **scan·ner** *n*

scan·dal \'skand³l\ *n* **1** : disgraceful
situation **2** : malicious gossip —
scan·dal·ize *vb* — **scan·dal·ous** *adj*

scant \'skant\ *adj* : barely sufficient
  ~ *vb* : stint — **scant·i·ly** *adv* —
scanty *adj*

scape·goat \'skāp͵gōt\ *n* : one that
bears the blame for others

scap·u·la \'skapyələ\ *n, pl* **-lae** \-͵lē\
or **-las** : shoulder blade

scar \'skär\ *n* : mark where a wound
has healed — **scar** *vb*

scar·ab \'skarəb\ *n* : large dark beetle
or an ornament representing one

scarce \'skers\ *adj* **scarc·er; scarc-
est** : lacking in quantity or number —
scar·ci·ty \'skersətē\ *n*

scarce·ly \'skerslē\ *adv* **1** : barely **2**
: almost not

scare \'sker\ *vb* **scared; scar·ing**
: frighten ~ *n* : fright — **scary** *adj*

scare·crow \'sker͵krō\ *n* : figure for
scaring birds from crops

scarf \'skärf\ *n, pl* **scarves** \'skärvz\
or **scarfs** : cloth worn about the
shoulders or the neck

scar·let \'skärlət\ *n* : bright red color
  — **scarlet** *adj*

scarlet fever *n* : acute contagious disease marked by fever, sore throat, and
red rash

scath·ing \'skāthiŋ\ *adj* : bitterly severe

scat·ter \'skatər\ *vb* **1** : spread about
irregularly **2** : disperse

scav·en·ger \'skavənjər\ *n* **1** : person
that collects refuse or waste **2** : animal that feeds on decayed matter —
scav·enge \'skavənj\ *vb*

sce·nar·io \sə'narē͵ō, -'när-\ *n, pl* **-i·os**
1 : plot of a play or movie **2** : possible sequence of events

scene \'sēn\ *n* **1** : single situation in a
play or movie **2** : stage setting **3**
: view **4** : display of emotion — **sce-
nic** \'sēnik\ *adj*

scen·ery \'sēnərē\ *n, pl* **-er·ies** **1**
: painted setting for a stage **2** : pictur-
esque view

scent \'sent\ *vb* **1** : smell **2** : fill with
odor ~ *n* **1** : odor **2** : sense of smell
3 : perfume — **scent·ed** \'sentəd\ *adj*

scep·ter \'septər\ *n* : staff signifying
authority

scep·tic \'skeptik\ *var of* SKEPTIC

sched·ule \'skejül, *esp Brit* 'shedyül\
n : list showing sequence of events ~
vb **-uled; -ul·ing** : make a schedule of

scheme \'skēm\ *n* **1** : crafty plot **2**
: systematic design ~ *vb* **schemed;
schem·ing** : form a plot — **sche·mat-
ic** \ski'matik\ *adj* — **schem·er** *n*

schism \'sizəm, 'skiz-\ *n* : split —
schis·mat·ic \siz'matik, skiz-\ *n
or adj*

schizo·phre·nia \͵skitsə'frēnēə\ *n*
: severe mental illness — **schiz·oid**
\'skit͵sóid\ *adj or n* — **schizo-
phren·ic** \͵skitsə'frenik\ *adj or n*

schol·ar \'skälər\ *n* : student or learned
person — **schol·ar·ly** *adj*

schol·ar·ship \-͵ship\ *n* **1** : qualities or
learning of a scholar **2** : money given
to a student to pay for education

scho·las·tic \skə'lastik\ *adj* : relating
to schools, scholars, or scholarship

¹**school** \'skül\ *n* **1** : institution for
learning **2** : pupils in a school **3**
: group with shared beliefs ~ *vb*
: teach — **school·boy** *n* — **school·girl**
n — **school·house** *n* — **school-
mate** *n* — **school·room** *n* — **school-
teach·er** *n*

²**school** *n* : large number of fish swimming together

schoo·ner \'skünər\ *n* : sailing ship

sci·ence \'sīəns\ *n* : branch of systematic study esp. of the physical world
  — **sci·en·tif·ic** \͵sīən'tifik\ *adj* —
sci·en·tif·i·cal·ly *adv* — **sci·en·tist**
\'sīəntist\ *n*

scin·til·late \'sint³l͵āt\ *vb* **-lat·ed; -lat-
ing** : flash — **scin·til·la·tion** \͵sint³l-
'āshən\ *n*

scin·til·lat·ing *adj* : brilliantly lively or
witty

sci·on \'sīən\ *n* : descendant

scis·sors \'sizərz\ *n pl* : small shears

scoff \'skäf\ *vb* : mock — **scoff·er** *n*

scold \'skōld\ *n* : person who scolds
  ~ *vb* : criticize severely

scoop \'sküp\ *n* : shovellike utensil ~
vb **1** : take out with a scoop **2** : dig out

scoot \'süt\ *vb* : move swiftly

scoot·er \'skütər\ *n* : child's foot-
propelled vehicle

¹**scope** \'skōp\ *n* **1** : extent **2** : room for
development

²**scope** *n* : viewing device (as a micro-
scope)

scorch \'skórch\ *vb* : burn the surface of

score \'skōr\ *n, pl* **scores 1** *or pl* **score** : twenty **2** : cut **3** : record of points made (as in a game) **4** : debt **5** : music of a composition ∼ *vb* **scored; scor•ing 1** : record **2** : mark with lines **3** : gain in a game **4** : assign a grade to **5** : compose a score for — **score•less** *adj* — **scor•er** *n*

scorn \'skórn\ *n* : emotion involving both anger and disgust ∼ *vb* : hold in contempt — **scorn•er** *n* — **scorn•ful** \-fəl\ *adj* — **scorn•ful•ly** *adv*

scor•pi•on \'skórpēən\ *n* : poisonous long-tailed animal

scoun•drel \'skaúndrəl\ *n* : villain

¹**scour** \'skaúər\ *vb* : examine thoroughly

²**scour** *vb* : rub in order to clean

scourge \'skərj\ *n* **1** : whip **2** : punishment ∼ *vb* **scourged; scourg•ing 1** : lash **2** : punish severely

scout \'skaút\ *vb* : inspect or observe to get information ∼ *n* : person sent out to get information

scow \'skaú\ *n* : large flat-bottomed boat with square ends

scowl \'skaúl\ *vb* : make a frowning expression of displeasure — **scowl** *n*

scrag•gly \'skraglē\ *adj* : irregular or unkempt

scram \'skram\ *vb* **-mm-** : go away at once

scram•ble \'skrambəl\ *vb* **-bled; -bling 1** : clamber clumsily around **2** : struggle for possession of something **3** : mix together **4** : cook (eggs) by stirring during frying — **scramble** *n*

¹**scrap** \'skrap\ *n* **1** : fragment **2** : discarded material ∼ *vb* **-pp-** : get rid of as useless

²**scrap** *vb* **-pp-** : fight — **scrap** *n* — **scrap•per** *n*

scrap•book *n* : blank book in which mementos are kept

scrape \'skrāp\ *vb* **scraped; scrap•ing 1** : remove by drawing a knife over **2** : clean or smooth by rubbing **3** : draw across a surface with a grating sound **4** : damage by contact with a rough surface **5** : gather or proceed with difficulty ∼ *n* **1** : act of scraping **2** : predicament — **scrap•er** *n*

scratch \'skrach\ *vb* **1** : scrape or dig with or as if with claws or nails **2** : cause to move gratingly **3** : delete by or as if by drawing a line through

∼ *n* : mark or sound made in scratching — **scratchy** *adj*

scrawl \'skról\ *vb* : write hastily and carelessly — **scrawl** *n*

scraw•ny \'skrónē\ *adj* **-ni•er; -est** : very thin

scream \'skrēm\ *vb* : cry out loudly and shrilly ∼ *n* : loud shrill cry

screech \'skrēch\ *vb or n* : shriek

screen \'skrēn\ *n* **1** : device or partition used to protect or decorate **2** : surface on which pictures appear (as in movies) ∼ *vb* : shield or separate with or as if with a screen

screw \'skrü\ *n* **1** : grooved fastening device **2** : propeller ∼ *vb* **1** : fasten by means of a screw **2** : move spirally

screw•driv•er \'skrü,drīvər\ *n* : tool for turning screws

scrib•ble \'skribəl\ *vb* **-bled; -bling** : write hastily or carelessly — **scrib•ble** *n* — **scrib•bler** \-ələr\ *n*

scribe \'skrīb\ *n* : one who writes or copies writing

scrimp \'skrimp\ *vb* : economize greatly

scrip \'skrip\ *n* **1** : paper money for less than a dollar **2** : certificate entitling one to something (as stock)

script \'skript\ *n* : text (as of a play)

scrip•ture \'skripchər\ *n* : sacred writings of a religion — **scrip•tur•al** \'skripchərəl\ *adj*

scroll \'skrōl\ *n* **1** : roll of paper for writing a document **2** : spiral or coiled design

scro•tum \'skrōtəm\ *n, pl* **-ta** \-ə\ *or* **-tums** : pouch containing the testes

scrounge \'skraúnj\ *vb* **scrounged; scroung•ing** : collect by or as if by foraging

¹**scrub** \'skrəb\ *n* : stunted tree or shrub or a growth of these — **scrub** *adj* — **scrub•by** *adj*

²**scrub** *vb* **-bb-** : clean or wash by rubbing — **scrub** *n*

scruff \'skrəf\ *n* : loose skin of the back of the neck

scrump•tious \'skrəmpshəs\ *adj* : delicious

scru•ple \'skrüpəl\ *n* : reluctance due to ethical considerations — **scruple** *vb* — **scru•pu•lous** \-pyələs\ *adj* — **scru•pu•lous•ly** *adv*

scru•ti•ny \'skrüt³nē\ *n, pl* **-nies** : careful inspection — **scru•ti•nize** \-³n,īz\ *vb*

scud \'skəd\ *vb* **-dd-** : move speedily

scuff \'skəf\ *vb* : scratch, scrape, or wear away — **scuff** *n*

scuf·fle \'skəfəl\ *vb* -fled; -fling **1** : struggle at close quarters **2** : shuffle one's feet — **scuffle** *n*

scull \'skəl\ *n* **1** : oar **2** : racing shell propelled with sculls ∼ *vb* : propel a boat by an oar over the stern

scul·lery \'skələrē\ *n, pl* -ler·ies : room for cleaning dishes and cookware

sculpt \'skəlpt\ *vb* : sculpture

sculp·ture \'skəlpchər\ *n* : work of art carved or molded ∼ *vb* -tured; -turing : form as sculpture — **sculp·tor** \-tər\ *n* — **sculp·tur·al** \-chərəl\ *adj*

scum \'skəm\ *n* : slimy film on a liquid

scur·ri·lous \'skərələs\ *adj* : vulgar or abusive

scur·ry \'skərē\ *vb* -ried; -ry·ing : scamper

scur·vy \'skərvē\ *n* : vitamin-deficiency disease

¹**scut·tle** \'skətᵊl\ *n* : pail for coal

²**scuttle** *vb* -tled; -tling : sink (a ship) by cutting holes in its bottom

³**scuttle** *vb* -tled; -tling : scamper

scythe \'sīth\ *n* : tool for mowing by hand — **scythe** *vb*

sea \'sē\ *n* **1** : large body of salt water **2** : ocean **3** : rough water — **sea** *adj* — **sea·coast** *n* — **sea·food** *n* — **sea·port** *n* — **sea·shore** *n* — **sea·wa·ter** *n*

sea·bird *n* : bird frequenting the open ocean

sea·board *n* : country's seacoast

sea·far·er \-ˌfarər\ *n* : seaman — **sea·far·ing** \-ˌfariŋ\ *adj or n*

sea horse *n* : small fish with a horselike head

¹**seal** \'sēl\ *n* : large sea mammal of cold regions — **seal·skin** *n*

²**seal** *n* **1** : device for stamping a design **2** : something that closes ∼ *vb* **1** : affix a seal to **2** : close up securely **3** : determine finally — **seal·ant** \-ənt\ *n* — **seal·er** *n*

sea lion *n* : large Pacific seal with external ears

seam \'sēm\ *n* **1** : line of junction of 2 edges **2** : layer of a mineral ∼ *vb* : join by sewing — **seam·less** *adj*

sea·man \'sēmən\ *n* **1** : one who helps to handle a ship **2** : naval enlisted man ranking next below a petty officer third class — **sea·man·ship** *n*

seaman apprentice *n* : naval enlisted man ranking next below a seaman

seaman recruit *n* : naval enlisted man of the lowest rank

seam·stress \'sēmstrəs\ *n* : woman who sews

seamy \'sēmē\ *adj* **seam·i·er; -est** : unpleasant or sordid

sé·ance \'sāˌäns\ *n* : meeting for communicating with spirits

sea·plane *n* : airplane that can take off from and land on the water

sear \'sir\ *vb* : scorch — **sear** *n*

search \'sərch\ *vb* **1** : look through **2** : seek — **search** *n* — **search·er** *n* — **search·light** *n*

search engine *n* : computer software used to search for specified information on the World Wide Web

sea·sick *adj* : nauseated by the motion of a ship — **sea·sick·ness** *n*

¹**sea·son** \'sēzᵊn\ *n* **1** : division of the year **2** : customary time for something — **sea·son·al** \'sēzᵊnəl\ *adj* — **sea·son·al·ly** *adv*

²**season** *vb* **1** : add spice to (food) **2** : make strong or fit for use — **sea·son·ing** \-ᵊniŋ\ *n*

sea·son·able \'sēznəbəl\ *adj* : occurring at a suitable time — **sea·son·ably** \-blē\ *adv*

seat \'sēt\ *n* **1** : place to sit **2** : chair, bench, or stool for sitting on **3** : place that serves as a capital or center ∼ *vb* **1** : place in or on a seat **2** : provide seats for

sea·weed *n* : marine alga

sea·wor·thy *adj* : strong enough to hold up to a sea voyage

se·cede \si'sēd\ *vb* -ced·ed; -ced·ing : withdraw from a body (as a nation)

se·clude \si'klüd\ *vb* -clud·ed; -cluding : shut off alone — **se·clu·sion** \si'klüzhən\ *n*

¹**sec·ond** \'sekənd\ *adj* : next after the 1st ∼ *n* **1** : one that is second **2** : one who assists (as in a duel) — **second, se·cond·ly** *adv*

²**second** *n* **1** : 60th part of a minute **2** : moment

sec·ond·ary \'sekənˌderē\ *adj* **1** : second in rank or importance **2** : coming after the primary or elementary

sec·ond·hand *adj* **1** : not original **2** : used before

second lieutenant *n* : lowest ranking commissioned officer of the army, air force, or marines

se·cret \'sēkrət\ *adj* **1** : hidden **2**

: kept from general knowledge — **se·cre·cy** \-krəsē\ *n* — **secret** *n* — **se·cre·tive** \'sēkrətiv, si'krēt-\ *adj* — **se·cret·ly** *adv*

sec·re·tar·i·at \ˌsekrə'terēət\ *n* : administrative department

sec·re·tary \'sekrəˌterē\ *n, pl* **-tar·ies** 1 : one hired to handle correspondence and other tasks for a superior 2 : official in charge of correspondence or records 3 : head of a government department — **sec·re·tari·al** \ˌsekrə-'terēəl\ *adj*

¹**se·crete** \si'krēt\ *vb* **-cret·ed; -cret·ing** : produce as a secretion

²**se·crete** \si'krēt, 'sēkrət\ *vb* **-cret·ed; -cret·ing** : hide

se·cre·tion \si'krēshən\ *n* 1 : process of secreting 2 : product of glandular activity

sect \'sekt\ *n* : religious group

sec·tar·i·an \sek'terēən\ *adj* 1 : relating to a sect 2 : limited in character or scope ∼ *n* : member of a sect

sec·tion \'sekshən\ *n* : distinct part — **sec·tion·al** \-shənəl\ *adj*

sec·tor \'sektər\ *n* 1 : part of a circle between 2 radii 2 : distinctive part

sec·u·lar \'sekyələr\ *adj* 1 : not sacred 2 : not monastic

se·cure \si'kyúr\ *adj* **-cur·er; -est** : free from danger or loss ∼ *vb* 1 : fasten safely 2 : get — **se·cure·ly** *adv*

se·cu·ri·ty \si'kyúrətē\ *n, pl* **-ties** 1 : safety 2 : something given to guarantee payment 3 *pl* : bond or stock certificates

se·dan \si'dan\ *n* 1 : chair carried by 2 men 2 : enclosed automobile

¹**se·date** \si'dāt\ *adj* : quiet and dignified — **se·date·ly** *adv*

²**sedate** *vb* **-dat·ed; -dat·ing** : dose with sedatives — **se·da·tion** \si'dāshən\ *n*

sed·a·tive \'sedətiv\ *adj* : serving to relieve tension ∼ *n* : sedative drug

sed·en·tary \'sed³nˌterē\ *adj* : characterized by much sitting

sedge \'sej\ *n* : grasslike marsh plant

sed·i·ment \'sedəmənt\ *n* : material that settles to the bottom of a liquid or is deposited by water or a glacier — **sed·i·men·ta·ry** \ˌsedə'mentərē\ *adj* — **sed·i·men·ta·tion** \-mən'tā-shən, -ˌmen-\ *n*

se·di·tion \si'dishən\ *n* : revolution against a government — **se·di·tious** \-əs\ *adj*

se·duce \si'düs, -'dyüs\ *vb* **-duced; -duc·ing** 1 : lead astray 2 : entice to sexual intercourse — **se·duc·er** *n* — **se·duc·tion** \-'dəkshən\ *n* — **se·duc·tive** \-tiv\ *adj*

sed·u·lous \'sejələs\ *adj* : diligent

¹**see** \'sē\ *vb* **saw** \'sò\; **seen** \'sēn\; **see·ing** 1 : perceive by the eye 2 : have experience of 3 : understand 4 : make sure 5 : meet with or escort

²**see** *n* : jurisdiction of a bishop

seed \'sēd\ *n, pl* **seed** *or* **seeds** 1 : part by which a plant is propagated 2 : source ∼ *vb* 1 : sow 2 : remove seeds from — **seed·less** *adj*

seed·ling \-liŋ\ *n* : young plant grown from seed

seedy \-ē\ *adj* **seed·i·er; -est** 1 : full of seeds 2 : shabby

seek \'sēk\ *vb* **sought** \'sòt\; **seek·ing** 1 : search for 2 : try to reach or obtain — **seek·er** *n*

seem \'sēm\ *vb* : give the impression of being — **seem·ing·ly** *adv*

seem·ly \-lē\ *adj* **seem·li·er; -est** : proper or fit

seep \'sēp\ *vb* : leak through fine pores or cracks — **seep·age** \'sēpij\ *n*

seer \'sēər\ *n* : one who foresees or predicts events

seer·suck·er \'sirˌsəkər\ *n* : light puckered fabric

see·saw \'sēˌsò\ *n* : board balanced in the middle — **seesaw** *vb*

seethe \'sēth\ *vb* **seethed; seeth·ing** : become violently agitated

seg·ment \'segmənt\ *n* : division of a thing — **seg·ment·ed** \-ˌmentəd\ *adj*

seg·re·gate \'segriˌgāt\ *vb* **-gat·ed; -gat·ing** 1 : cut off from others 2 : separate by races — **seg·re·ga·tion** \ˌsegri'gāshən\ *n*

seine \'sān\ *n* : large weighted fishing net ∼ *vb* : fish with a seine

seis·mic \'sīzmik, 'sīs-\ *adj* : relating to an earthquake

seis·mo·graph \-məˌgraf\ *n* : apparatus for detecting earthquakes

seize \'sēz\ *vb* **seized; seiz·ing** : take by force — **sei·zure** \'sēzhər\ *n*

sel·dom \'seldəm\ *adv* : not often

se·lect \sə'lekt\ *adj* 1 : favored 2 : discriminating ∼ *vb* : take by preference — **se·lec·tive** \-'lektiv\ *adj*

se·lec·tion \sə'lekshən\ *n* : act of selecting or thing selected

se·lect·man \si'lektˌman, -mən\ *n* : New England town official

self \\'self\ *n, pl* **selves** \\'selvz\ : essential person distinct from others

self- *comb form* **1** : oneself or itself **2** : of oneself or itself **3** : by oneself or automatic **4** : to, for, or toward oneself

self–cen•tered *adj* : concerned only with one's own self

self–con•scious *adj* : uncomfortably aware of oneself as an object of observation — **self–con•scious•ly** *adv* — **self–con•scious•ness** *n*

self•ish \\'selfish\ *adj* : excessively or exclusively concerned with one's own well-being — **self•ish•ly** *adv* — **self•ish•ness** *n*

self•less \\'selfləs\ *adj* : unselfish — **self•less•ness** *n*

self–made *adj* : having succeeded by one's own efforts

self–righ•teous *adj* : strongly convinced of one's own righteousness

self•same \\'self‚sām\ *adj* : precisely the same

sell \\'sel\ *vb* **sold** \\'sōld\; **sell•ing 1** : transfer (property) esp. for money **2**

: deal in as a business **3** : be sold — **sell•er** *n*

selves *pl of* SELF

se•man•tic \si'mantik\ *adj* : relating to meaning in language — **se•man•tics** \-iks\ *n sing or pl*

sem•a•phore \\'semə‚fōr\ *n* **1** : visual signaling apparatus **2** : signaling by flags

sem•blance \\'sembləns\ *n* : appearance

se•men \\'sēmən\ *n* : male reproductive fluid

se•mes•ter \sə'mestər\ *n* : half a school year

semi- \‚semi, 'sem-, -‚ī\ *prefix* **1** : half **2** : partial

semi•co•lon \\'semi‚kōlən\ *n* : punctuation mark **;**

semi•con•duc•tor *n* : substance between a conductor and a nonconductor in ability to conduct electricity — **semi•con•duct•ing** *adj*

semi•fi•nal *adj* : being next to the final — **semifinal** *n*

semi•for•mal *adj* : being or suitable for an occasion of moderate formality

---

List of self-explanatory words with the prefix *self-*

self–addressed	self–destructive	self–operating
self–administered	self–determination	self–pity
self–analysis	self–determined	self–portrait
self–appointed	self–discipline	self–possessed
self–assertive	self–doubt	self–possession
self–assurance	self–educated	self–preservation
self–assured	self–employed	self–proclaimed
self–awareness	self–employment	self–propelled
self–cleaning	self–esteem	self–propelling
self–closing	self–evident	self–protection
self–complacent	self–explanatory	self–reliance
self–conceit	self–expression	self–reliant
self–confessed	self–fulfilling	self–respect
self–confidence	self–fulfillment	self–respecting
self–confident	self–governing	self–restraint
self–contained	self–government	self–sacrifice
self–contempt	self–help	self–satisfaction
self–contradiction	self–image	self–satisfied
self–contradictory	self–importance	self–service
self–control	self–important	self–serving
self–created	self–imposed	self–starting
self–criticism	self–improvement	self–styled
self–defeating	self–indulgence	self–sufficiency
self–defense	self–indulgent	self–sufficient
self–denial	self–inflicted	self–supporting
self–denying	self–interest	self–taught
self–destruction	self–love	self–winding

sem·i·nal \'semən^əl\ *adj* **1** : relating to seed or semen **2** : causing or influencing later development

sem·i·nar \'semə₁när\ *n* : conference or conferencelike study

sem·i·nary \'semə₁nerē\ *n, pl* **-nar·ies** : school and esp. a theological school — **sem·i·nar·i·an** \₁semə'nerēən\ *n*

sen·ate \'senət\ *n* : upper branch of a legislature — **sen·a·tor** \-ər\ *n* — **sen·a·to·rial** \₁senə'tōrēəl\ *adj*

send \'send\ *vb* **sent** \'sent\: **send·ing 1** : cause to go **2** : propel — **send·er** *n*

se·nile \'sēn₁īl, 'sen-\ *adj* : mentally deficient through old age — **se·nil·i·ty** \si'nilətē\ *n*

se·nior \'sēnyər\ *adj* : older or higher ranking — **senior** *n* — **se·nior·i·ty** \₁sēn'yȯrətē\ *n*

senior chief petty officer *n* : petty officer in the navy or coast guard ranking next below a master chief petty officer

senior master sergeant *n* : noncommissioned officer in the air force ranking next below a chief master sergeant

sen·sa·tion \sen'sāshən\ *n* **1** : bodily feeling **2** : condition of excitement or the cause of it — **sen·sa·tion·al** \-shənəl\ *adj*

sense \'sens\ *n* **1** : meaning **2** : faculty of perceiving something physical **3** : sound mental capacity ∼ *vb* **sensed; sens·ing 1** : perceive by the senses **2** : detect automatically — **sense·less** *adj* — **sense·less·ly** *adv*

sen·si·bil·i·ty \₁sensə'bilətē\ *n, pl* **-ties** : delicacy of feeling

sen·si·ble \'sensəbəl\ *adj* **1** : capable of sensing or being sensed **2** : aware or conscious **3** : reasonable — **sen·si·bly** \-blē\ *adv*

sen·si·tive \'sensətiv\ *adj* **1** : subject to excitation by or responsive to stimuli **2** : having power of feeling **3** : easily affected — **sen·si·tive·ness** *n* — **sen·si·tiv·i·ty** \₁sensə'tivətē\ *n*

sen·si·tize \'sensə₁tīz\ *vb* **-tized; -tiz·ing** : make or become sensitive

sen·sor \'sen₁sȯr, -sər\ *n* : device that responds to a physical stimulus

sen·so·ry \'sensərē\ *adj* : relating to sensation or the senses

sen·su·al \'senchəwəl, -shəwəl\ *adj* **1** : pleasing the senses **2** : devoted to the pleasures of the senses — **sen·su·al·ist** *n* — **sen·su·al·i·ty** \₁senchə-'walətē\ *n* — **sen·su·al·ly** *adv*

sen·su·ous \'senchəwəs\ *adj* : having strong appeal to the senses

sent *past of* SEND

sen·tence \'sent^əns, -^ənz\ *n* **1** : judgment of a court **2** : grammatically self-contained speech unit ∼ *vb* **-tenced; -tenc·ing** : impose a sentence on

sen·ten·tious \sen'tenchəs\ *adj* : using pompous language

sen·tient \'senchēənt\ *adj* : capable of feeling

sen·ti·ment \'sentəmənt\ *n* **1** : belief **2** : feeling

sen·ti·men·tal \₁sentə'ment^əl\ *adj* : influenced by tender feelings — **sen·ti·men·tal·ism** *n* — **sen·ti·men·tal·ist** *n* — **sen·ti·men·tal·i·ty** \-₁men-'talətē, -mən-\ *n* — **sen·ti·men·tal·ize** \-'ment^əl₁īz\ *vb* — **sen·ti·men·tal·ly** *adv*

sen·ti·nel \'sent^ənəl\ *n* : sentry

sen·try \'sentrē\ *n, pl* **-tries** : one who stands guard

se·pal \'sēpəl, 'sep-\ *n* : modified leaf in a flower calyx

sep·a·rate \'sepə₁rāt\ *vb* **-rat·ed; -rat·ing 1** : set or keep apart **2** : become divided or detached ∼ \'seprət, 'sepə-\ *adj* **1** : not connected or shared **2** : distinct from each other — **sep·a·ra·ble** \'sepərəbəl\ *adj* — **sep·a·rate·ly** *adv* — **sep·a·ra·tion** \₁sepə'rāshən\ *n* — **sep·a·ra·tor** \'sepə₁rātər\ *n*

se·pia \'sēpēə\ *n* : brownish gray

Sep·tem·ber \sep'tembər\ *n* : 9th month of the year having 30 days

sep·ul·chre, sep·ul·cher \'sepəlkər\ *n* : burial vault — **se·pul·chral** \sə'pəlkrəl\ *adj*

se·quel \'sēkwəl\ *n* **1** : consequence or result **2** : continuation of a story

se·quence \'sēkwəns\ *n* : continuous or connected series — **se·quen·tial** \si-'kwenchəl\ *adj* — **se·quen·tial·ly** *adv*

se·ques·ter \si'kwestər\ *vb* : segregate

se·quin \'sēkwən\ *n* : spangle

se·quoia \si'kwȯiə\ *n* : huge California coniferous tree

sera *pl of* SERUM

ser·aph \'serəf\ *n, pl* **-a·phim** \-ə₁fim\ *or* **-aphs** : angel — **se·raph·ic** \sə'rafik\ *adj*

sere \'sir\ *adj* : dried up or withered

ser·e·nade \₁serə'nād\ *n* : music sung or played esp. to a woman being courted — **serenade** *vb*

ser·en·dip·i·ty \,serən'dipətē\ n : good luck in finding things not sought for — **ser·en·dip·i·tous** \-əs\ adj

se·rene \sə'rēn\ adj : tranquil — **se·rene·ly** adv — **se·ren·i·ty** \sə-'renətē\ n

serf \'sərf\ n : peasant obligated to work the land — **serf·dom** \-dəm\ n

serge \'sərj\ n : twilled woolen cloth

ser·geant \'särjənt\ n : noncommissioned officer (as in the army) ranking next below a staff sergeant

sergeant first class n : noncommissioned officer in the army ranking next below a master sergeant

sergeant major n, pl **sergeants major** or **sergeant majors** 1 : noncommissioned officer serving as an enlisted adviser in a headquarters 2 : noncommissioned officer in the marine corps ranking above a first sergeant

se·ri·al \'sirēəl\ adj : being or relating to a series or sequence ~ n : story appearing in parts — **se·ri·al·ly** adv

se·ries \'sirēz\ n, pl **series** : number of things in order

se·ri·ous \'sirēəs\ adj 1 : subdued in appearance or manner 2 : sincere 3 : of great importance — **se·ri·ous·ly** adv — **se·ri·ous·ness** n

ser·mon \'sərmən\ n : lecture on religion or behavior

ser·pent \'sərpənt\ n : snake — **ser·pen·tine** \-pən,tēn, -,tīn\ adj

ser·rated \'ser,ātəd\ adj : saw-toothed

se·rum \'sirəm\ n, pl **-rums** or **-ra** \-ə\ : watery part of blood

ser·vant \'sərvənt\ n : person employed for domestic work

serve \'sərv\ vb **served; serv·ing** 1 : work through or perform a term of service 2 : be of use 3 : prove adequate 4 : hand out (food or drink) 5 : be of service to — **serv·er** n

ser·vice \'sərvəs\ n 1 : act or means of serving 2 : meeting for worship 3 : branch of public employment or the persons in it 4 : set of dishes or silverware 5 : benefit ~ vb **-viced; -vic·ing** : repair — **ser·vice·able** adj — **ser·vice·man** \-,man, -mən\ n — **ser·vice·wom·an** n

ser·vile \'sərvəl, -,vīl\ adj : behaving like a slave — **ser·vil·i·ty** \,sər-'vilətē\ n

serv·ing \'sərviŋ\ n : helping

ser·vi·tude \'sərvə,tüd, -,tyüd\ n : slavery

ses·a·me \'sesəmē\ n : annual herb or its seeds that are used in flavoring

ses·sion \'seshən\ n : meeting

set \'set\ vb **set; set·ting** 1 : cause to sit 2 : place 3 : settle, arrange, or adjust 4 : cause to be or do 5 : become fixed or solid 6 : sink below the horizon ~ adj : settled ~ n 1 : group classed together 2 : setting for the scene of a play or film 3 : electronic apparatus 4 : collection of mathematical elements — **set forth** : begin a trip — **set off** vb : set forth — **set out** vb : begin a trip or undertaking — **set up** vb 1 : assemble or erect 2 : cause

set·back n : reverse

set·tee \se'tē\ n : bench or sofa

set·ter \'setər\ n : large long-coated hunting dog

set·ting \'setiŋ\ n : the time, place, and circumstances in which something occurs

set·tle \'setᵊl\ vb **-tled; -tling** 1 : come to rest 2 : sink gradually 3 : establish in residence 4 : adjust or arrange 5 : calm 6 : dispose of (as by paying) 7 : decide or agree on — **set·tle·ment** \-mənt\ n — **set·tler** \'setᵊlər\ n

sev·en \'sevən\ n : one more than 6 — **seven** adj or pron — **sev·enth** \-ənth\ adj or adv or n

sev·en·teen \,sevən'tēn\ n : one more than 16 — **seventeen** adj or pron — **sev·en·teenth** \-'tēnth\ adj or n

sev·en·ty \'sevəntē\ n, pl **-ties** : 7 times 10 — **sev·en·ti·eth** \-tēəth\ adj or n — **seventy** adj or pron

sev·er \'sevər\ vb **-ered; -er·ing** : cut off or apart — **sev·er·ance** \'sevrəns, -vərəns\ n

sev·er·al \'sevrəl, 'sevə-\ adj 1 : distinct 2 : consisting of an indefinite but not large number — **sev·er·al·ly** adv

se·vere \sə'vir\ adj **-ver·er; -est** 1 : strict 2 : restrained or unadorned 3 : painful or distressing 4 : hard to endure — **se·vere·ly** adv — **se·ver·i·ty** \-'verətē\ n

sew \'sō\ vb **sewed; sewn** \'sōn\ or **sewed; sew·ing** : join or fasten by stitches — **sew·ing** n

sew·age \'süij\ n : liquid household waste

¹**sew·er** \'sōər\ n : one that sews

²**sew·er** \'süər\ n : pipe or channel to carry off waste matter

sex \'seks\ n 1 : either of 2 divisions

into which organisms are grouped according to their reproductive roles or the qualities which differentiate them **2** : copulation — **sexed** \'sekst\ *adj* — **sex•less** *adj* — **sex•u•al** \'sekshəwəl\ *adj* — **sex•u•al•i•ty** \ˌsekshə'walətē\ *n* — **sex•u•al•ly** *adv* — **sexy** *adj*

sex•ism \'sekˌsizəm\ *n* : discrimination based on sex and esp. against women — **sex•ist** \'seksist\ *adj or n*

sex•tant \'sekstənt\ *n* : instrument for navigation

sex•tet \sek'stet\ *n* **1** : music for 6 performers **2** : group of 6

sex•ton \'sekstən\ *n* : church caretaker

shab•by \'shabē\ *adj* **-bi•er; -est 1** : worn and faded **2** : dressed in worn clothes **3** : not generous or fair — **shab•bi•ly** *adv* — **shab•bi•ness** *n*

shack \'shak\ *n* : hut

shack•le \'shakəl\ *n* : metal device to bind legs or arms ⁓ *vb* **-led; -ling** : bind or fasten with shackles

shad \'shad\ *n* : Atlantic food fish

shade \'shād\ *n* **1** : space sheltered from the light esp. of the sun **2** : gradation of color **3** : small difference **4** : something that shades ⁓ *vb* **shaded; shad•ing 1** : shelter from light and heat **2** : add shades of color to **3** : show slight differences esp. in color or meaning

shad•ow \'shadō\ *n* **1** : shade cast upon a surface by something blocking light **2** : trace **3** : gloomy influence ⁓ *vb* **1** : cast a shadow **2** : follow closely — **shad•owy** *adj*

shady \'shādē\ *adj* **shad•i•er; -est 1** : giving shade **2** : of dubious honesty

shaft \'shaft\ *n* **1** : long slender cylindrical part **2** : deep vertical opening (as of a mine)

shag \'shag\ *n* : shaggy tangled mat

shag•gy \'shagē\ *adj* **-gi•er; -est 1** : covered with long hair or wool **2** : not neat and combed

shake \'shāk\ *vb* **shook** \'shuk\; **shak•en** \'shākən\; **shak•ing 1** : move or cause to move quickly back and forth **2** : distress **3** : clasp (hands) as friendly gesture — **shake** *n* — **shak•er** \-ər\ *n*

shake–up *n* : reorganization

shaky \'shākē\ *adj* **shak•i•er; -est** : not sound, stable, or reliable — **shak•i•ly** *adv* — **shak•i•ness** *n*

shale \'shāl\ *n* : stratified rock

shall \'shal\ *vb, past* **should** \'shud\; *pres sing & pl* **shall** — used as an auxiliary to express a command, futurity, or determination

shal•low \'shalō\ *adj* **1** : not deep **2** : not intellectually profound

shal•lows \-ōz\ *n pl* : area of shallow water

sham \'sham\ *adj or n or vb* : fake

sham•ble \'shambəl\ *vb* **-bled; -bling** : shuffle along — **sham•ble** *n*

sham•bles \'shambəlz\ *n* : state of disorder

shame \'shām\ *n* **1** : distress over guilt or disgrace **2** : cause of shame or regret ⁓ *vb* **shamed; sham•ing 1** : make ashamed **2** : disgrace — **shame•ful** \-fəl\ *adj* — **shame•fully** \-ē\ *adv* — **shame•less** *adj* — **shame•less•ly** *adv*

shame•faced \'shām'fāst\ *adj* : ashamed

sham•poo \sham'pü\ *vb* : wash one's hair ⁓ *n, pl* **-poos** : act of or preparation used in shampooing

sham•rock \'shamˌräk\ *n* : plant of legend with 3-lobed leaves

shank \'shaŋk\ *n* : part of the leg between the knee and ankle

shan•ty \'shantē\ *n, pl* **-ties** : hut

shape \'shāp\ *vb* **shaped; shap•ing** : form esp. in a particular structure or appearance ⁓ *n* **1** : distinctive appearance or arrangement of parts **2** : condition — **shape•less** \-ləs\ *adj* — **shape•li•ness** *n* — **shape•ly** *adj*

shard \'shärd\ *n* : broken piece

share \'sher\ *n* **1** : portion belonging to one **2** : interest in a company's stock ⁓ *vb* **shared; shar•ing** : divide or use with others — **share•hold•er** *n* — **shar•er** *n*

share•crop•per \-ˌkräpər\ *n* : farmer who works another's land in return for a share of the crop — **share•crop** *vb*

shark \'shärk\ *n* : voracious sea fish

sharp \'shärp\ *adj* **1** : having a good point or cutting edge **2** : alert, clever, or sarcastic **3** : vigorous or fierce **4** : having prominent angles or a sudden change in direction **5** : distinct **6** : higher than the true pitch ⁓ *adv* : exactly ⁓ *n* : sharp note — **sharp•ly** *adv* — **sharp•ness** *n*

sharp•en \'shärpən\ *vb* : make sharp — **sharp•en•er** \-ənər\ *n*

sharp•shoot•er *n* : expert marksman — **sharp•shoot•ing** *n*

shat·ter \'shatər\ *vb* : smash or burst into fragments — **shat·ter·proof** \-ˌprüf\ *adj*

shave \'shāv\ *vb* **shaved; shaved** *or* **shav·en** \'shāvən\; **shav·ing 1** : cut off with a razor **2** : make bare by cutting the hair from **3** : slice very thin ~ *n* : act or instance of shaving — **shav·er** *n*

shawl \'shȯl\ *n* : loose covering for the head or shoulders

she \'shē\ *pron* : that female one

sheaf \'shēf\ *n, pl* **sheaves** \'shēvz\ : bundle esp. of grain stalks

shear \'shir\ *vb* **sheared; sheared** *or* **shorn** \'shȯrn\; **shear·ing 1** : trim wool from **2** : cut off with scissorlike action

shears \'shirz\ *n pl* : cutting tool with 2 blades fastened so that the edges slide by each other

sheath \'shēth\ *n, pl* **sheaths** \'shēthz, 'shēths\ : covering (as for a blade)

sheathe \'shēth\ *vb* **sheathed; sheath·ing** : put into a sheath

shed \'shed\ *vb* **shed; shed·ding 1** : give off (as tears or hair) **2** : cause to flow or diffuse ~ *n* : small storage building

sheen \'shēn\ *n* : subdued luster

sheep \'shēp\ *n, pl* **sheep** : domesticated mammal covered with wool — **sheep·skin** *n*

sheep·ish \'shēpish\ *adj* : embarrassed by awareness of a fault

sheer \'shir\ *adj* **1** : pure **2** : very steep **3** : very thin or transparent

sheet \'shēt\ *n* : broad flat piece (as of cloth or paper)

sheikh, sheik \'shēk, 'shāk\ *n* : Arab chief — **sheikh·dom, sheik·dom** \-dəm\ *n*

shelf \'shelf\ *n, pl* **shelves** \'shelvz\ **1** : flat narrow structure used for storage or display **2** : sandbank or rock ledge

shell \'shel\ *n* **1** : hard or tough outer covering **2** : case holding explosive powder and projectile for a weapon ~ *vb* **1** : light racing boat with oars ~ *vb* **1** : remove the shell of **2** : bombard — **shelled** \'sheld\ *adj* — **shell·er** *n*

shel·lac \shə'lak\ *n* : varnish ~ *vb* **-lacked; -lack·ing 1** : coat with shellac **2** : defeat — **shel·lack·ing** *n*

shell·fish *n* : water animal with a shell

shel·ter \'sheltər\ *n* : something that gives protection ~ *vb* : give refuge to

shelve \'shelv\ *vb* **shelved; shelv·ing 1** : place or store on shelves **2** : dismiss or put aside

she·nan·i·gans \shə'nanigənz\ *n pl* : mischievous or deceitful conduct

shep·herd \'shepərd\ *n* : one that tends sheep ~ *vb* : act as a shepherd or guardian

shep·herd·ess \'shepərdəs\ *n* : woman who tends sheep

sher·bet \'shərbət\, **sher·bert** \-bərt\ *n* : fruit-flavored frozen dessert

sher·iff \'sherəf\ *n* : county law officer

sher·ry \'sherē\ *n, pl* **-ries** : type of wine

shield \'shēld\ *n* **1** : broad piece of armor carried on the arm **2** : something that protects — **shield** *vb*

shier *comparative of* SHY

shiest *superlative of* SHY

shift \'shift\ *vb* **1** : change place, position, or direction **2** : get by ~ *n* **1** : loose-fitting dress **2** : an act or instance of shifting **3** : scheduled work period

shift·less \-ləs\ *adj* : lazy

shifty \'shiftē\ *adj* **shift·i·er; -est** : tricky or untrustworthy

shil·le·lagh \shə'lālē\ *n* : club or stick

shil·ling \'shiliŋ\ *n* : former British coin

shil·ly–shally \'shilē,shalē\ *vb* **-shallied; -shally·ing 1** : hesitate **2** : dawdle

shim·mer \'shimər\ *vb or n* : glimmer

shin \'shin\ *n* : front part of the leg below the knee ~ *vb* **-nn-** : climb by sliding the body close along

shine \'shīn\ *vb* **shone** \-shōn\ *or* **shined; shin·ing 1** : give off or cause to give off light **2** : be outstanding **3** : polish ~ *n* : brilliance

shin·gle \'shiŋgəl\ *n* **1** : small thin piece used in covering roofs or exterior walls — **shingle** *vb*

shin·gles \'shiŋgəlz\ *n pl* : acute inflammation of spinal nerves

shin·ny \'shinē\ *vb* **-nied; -ny·ing** : shin

shiny \'shīnē\ *adj* **shin·i·er; -est** : bright or polished

ship \'ship\ *n* **1** : large oceangoing vessel **2** : aircraft or spacecraft ~ *vb* **-pp-** : put on a ship **2** : transport by carrier — **ship·board** *n* — **ship·build·er** *n* — **ship·per** *n* — **ship·wreck** *n or vb* — **ship·yard** *n*

-ship \ˌship\ *n suffix* **1** : state, condition, or quality **2** : rank or profession

3 : skill **4** : something showing a state or quality

ship•ment \-mənt\ *n* : an act of shipping or the goods shipped

ship•ping \'shipiŋ\ *n* **1** : ships **2** : transportation of goods

ship•shape *adj* : tidy

shire \'shīr, *in place-name compounds* ‚shir, shər\ *n* : British county

shirk \'shərk\ *vb* : evade — **shirk•er** *n*

shirr \'shər\ *vb* **1** : gather (cloth) by drawing up parallel lines of stitches **2** : bake (eggs) in a dish

shirt \'shərt\ *n* : garment for covering the torso — **shirt•less** *adj*

shiv•er \'shivər\ *vb* : tremble — **shiver** *n* — **shiv•ery** *adj*

shoal \'shōl\ *n* : shallow place (as in a river)

¹shock \'shäk\ *n* : pile of sheaves set up in a field

²shock *n* **1** : forceful impact **2** : violent mental or emotional disturbance **3** : effect of a charge of electricity **4** : depression of the vital bodily processes ～ *vb* **1** : strike with surprise, horror, or disgust **2** : subject to an electrical shock — **shock•proof** *adj*

³shock *n* : bushy mass (as of hair)

shod•dy \'shädē\ *adj* **-di•er; -est** : poorly made or done — **shod•di•ly** \'shäd³lē\ *adv* — **shod•di•ness** *n*

shoe \'shü\ *n* **1** : covering for the human foot **2** : horseshoe ～ *vb* **shod** \'shäd\; **shoe•ing** : put horseshoes on — **shoe•lace** *n* — **shoe•ma•ker** *n*

shone *past of* SHINE

shook *past of* SHAKE

shoot \'shüt\ *vb* **shot** \'shät\; **shooting** **1** : propel (as an arrow or bullet) **2** : wound or kill with a missile **3** : discharge (a weapon) **4** : drive (as a ball) at a goal **5** : photograph **6** : move swiftly ～ *n* : new plant growth — **shoot•er** *n*

shop \'shäp\ *n* : place where things are made or sold ～ *vb* **-pp-** : visit stores — **shop•keep•er** *n* — **shop•per** *n*

shop•lift *vb* : steal goods from a store — **shop•lift•er** \-‚liftər\ *n*

¹shore \'shōr\ *n* : land along the edge of water — **shore•line** *n*

²shore *vb* **shored; shor•ing** : prop up ～ *n* : something that props

shore•bird *n* : bird of the seashore

shorn *past part of* SHEAR

short \'shȯrt\ *adj* **1** : not long or tall or extending far **2** : brief in time **3**

: curt **4** : not having or being enough ～ *adv* : curtly ～ *n* **1** *pl* : short drawers or trousers **2** : short circuit — **short•en** \-³n\ *vb* — **short•ly** *adv* — **short•ness** *n*

short•age \'shȯrtij\ *n* : deficiency

short•cake *n* : dessert of biscuit with sweetened fruit

short•change *vb* : cheat esp. by giving too little change

short circuit *n* : abnormal electric connection — **short–circuit** *vb*

short•com•ing *n* : fault or failing

short•cut \-‚kət\ *n* **1** : more direct route than that usu. taken **2** : quicker way of doing something

short•hand *n* : method of speed writing

short–lived \'shȯrt'līvd, -‚livd\ *adj* : of short life or duration

short•sight•ed *adj* : lacking foresight

shot \'shät\ *n* **1** : act of shooting **2** : attempt (as at making a goal) **3** : small pellets forming a charge **4** : range or reach **5** : photograph **6** : injection of medicine **7** : small serving of liquor — **shot•gun** *n*

should \'shȯd\ *past of* SHALL — used as an auxiliary to express condition, obligation, or probability

shoul•der \'shōldər\ *n* **1** : part of the body where the arm joins the trunk **2** : part that projects or lies to the side ～ *vb* : push with or bear on the shoulder

shoulder blade *n* : flat triangular bone at the back of the shoulder

shout \'shaut\ *vb* : give voice loudly — **shout** *n*

shove \'shəv\ *vb* **shoved; shov•ing** : push along or away — **shove** *n*

shov•el \'shəvəl\ *n* : broad tool for digging or lifting ～ *vb* **-eled** *or* **-elled; -el•ing** *or* **-el•ling** : take up or dig with a shovel

show \'shō\ *vb* **showed** \'shōd\; **shown** \'shōn\ *or* **showed; showing** **1** : present to view **2** : reveal or demonstrate **3** : teach **4** : prove **5** : conduct or escort **6** : appear or be noticeable ～ *n* **1** : demonstrative display **2** : spectacle **3** : theatrical, radio, or television program — **showcase** *n* — **show off** *vb* **1** : display proudly **2** : act so as to attract attention — **show up** *vb* : arrive

show•down *n* : decisive confrontation

show•er \'shaùər\ *n* **1** : brief fall of rain **2** : bath in which water sprinkles down on the person or a facility for such a bath **3** : party at which someone gets gifts ∼ *vb* **1** : rain or fall in a shower **2** : bathe in a shower — **show•ery** *adj*

showy \'shōē\ *adj* **show•i•er; -est** : very noticeable or overly elaborate — **show•i•ly** *adv* — **show•i•ness** *n*

shrap•nel \'shrapn°l\ *n, pl* **shrapnel** : metal fragments of a bomb

shred \'shred\ *n* : narrow strip cut or torn off ∼ *vb* **-dd-** : cut or tear into shreds

shrew \'shrü\ *n* **1** : scolding woman **2** : mouselike mammal — **shrew•ish** \-ish\ *adj*

shrewd \'shrüd\ *adj* : clever — **shrewd•ly** *adv* — **shrewd•ness** *n*

shriek \'shrēk\ *n* : shrill cry — **shriek** *vb*

shrill \'shril\ *adj* : piercing and high-pitched — **shril•ly** *adv*

shrimp \'shrimp\ *n* : small sea crustacean

shrine \'shrīn\ *n* **1** : tomb of a saint **2** : hallowed place

shrink \'shriŋk\ *vb* **shrank** \'shraŋk\; **shrunk** \'shrəŋk\ *or* **shrunk•en** \'shrəŋkən\; **shrink•ing** **1** : draw back or away **2** : become smaller — **shrink•able** *adj*

shrink•age \'shriŋkij\ *n* : amount lost by shrinking

shriv•el \'shrivəl\ *vb* **-eled** *or* **-elled; -el•ing** *or* **-el•ling** : shrink or wither into wrinkles

shroud \'shraùd\ *n* **1** : cloth put over a corpse **2** : cover or screen ∼ *vb* : veil or screen from view

shrub \'shrəb\ *n* : low woody plant — **shrub•by** *adj*

shrub•bery \'shrəbərē\ *n, pl* **-ber•ies** : growth of shrubs

shrug \'shrəg\ *vb* **-gg-** : hunch the shoulders up in doubt, indifference, or uncertainty — **shrug** *n*

shuck \'shək\ *vb* : strip of a shell or husk — **shuck** *n*

shud•der \'shədər\ *vb* : tremble — **shudder** *n*

shuf•fle \'shəfəl\ *vb* **-fled; -fling** **1** : mix together **2** : walk with a sliding movement — **shuffle** *n*

shuf•fle•board \'shəfəl,bōrd\ *n* : game of sliding disks into a scoring area

shun \'shən\ *vb* **-nn-** : keep away from

shunt \'shənt\ *vb* : turn off to one side

shut \'shət\ *vb* **shut; shut•ting** **1** : bar passage into or through (as by moving

a lid or door) **2** : suspend activity — **shut out** *vb* : exclude — **shut up** *vb* : stop or cause to stop talking

shut–in *n* : invalid

shut•ter \'shətər\ *n* **1** : movable cover for a window **2** : camera part that exposes film

shut•tle \'shət°l\ *n* **1** : part of a weaving machine that carries thread back and forth **2** : vehicle traveling back and forth over a short route ∼ *vb* **-tled; -tling** : move back and forth frequently

shut•tle•cock \'shət°l,käk\ *n* : light conical object used in badminton

shy \'shī\ *adj* **shi•er** *or* **shy•er** \'shīər\; **shi•est** *or* **shy•est** \'shīəst\ **1** : sensitive and hesitant in dealing with others **2** : wary **3** : lacking ∼ *vb* **shied; shy•ing** : draw back (as in fright) — **shy•ly** *adv* — **shy•ness** *n*

sib•i•lant \'sibələnt\ *adj* : having the sound of the *s* or the *sh* in *sash* — **sibilant** *n*

sib•ling \'sibliŋ\ *n* : brother or sister

sick \'sik\ *adj* **1** : not in good health **2** : nauseated **3** : relating to or meant for the sick — **sick•bed** *n* — **sick•en** \-ən\ *vb* — **sick•ly** *adj* — **sick•ness** *n*

sick•le \'sikəl\ *n* : curved short-handled blade

side \'sīd\ *n* **1** : part to left or right of an object or the torso **2** : edge or surface away from the center or at an angle to top and bottom or ends **3** : contrasting or opposing position or group — **sid•ed** *adj*

side•board *n* : piece of dining-room furniture for table service

side•burns \-,bərnz\ *n pl* : whiskers in front of the ears

side•long \'sīd,lòŋ\ *adv or adj* : to or along the side

side•show *n* : minor show at a circus

side•step *vb* **1** : step aside **2** : avoid

side•swipe \-,swīp\ *vb* : strike with a glancing blow — **sideswipe** *n*

side•track *vb* : lead aside or astray

side•walk *n* : paved walk at the side of a road

side•ways \-,wāz\ *adv or adj* **1** : to or from the side **2** : with one side to the front

sid•ing \'sīdiŋ\ *n* **1** : short railroad track **2** : material for covering the outside of a building

si•dle \'sīd°l\ *vb* **-dled; -dling** : move sideways or unobtrusively

siege \'sēj\ *n* : persistent attack (as on a fortified place)

si·es·ta \sē'estə\ *n* : midday nap

sieve \'siv\ *n* : utensil with holes to separate particles

sift \'sift\ *vb* 1 : pass through a sieve 2 : examine carefully — **sift·er** *n*

sigh \'sī\ *n* : audible release of the breath (as to express weariness) — **sigh** *vb*

sight \'sīt\ *n* 1 : something seen or worth seeing 2 : process, power, or range of seeing 3 : device used in aiming 4 : view or glimpse ~ *vb* : get sight of — **sight·ed** *adj* — **sight·less** *adj* — **sight–see·ing** *adj* — **sight·seer** \-ˌsēər\ *n*

sign \'sīn\ *n* 1 : symbol 2 : gesture expressing a command or thought 3 : public notice to advertise or warn 4 : trace ~ *vb* 1 : mark with or make a sign 2 : write one's name on — **sign·er** *n*

sig·nal \'signºl\ *n* 1 : sign of command or warning 2 : electronic transmission ~ *vb* **-naled** *or* **-nalled; -nal·ing** *or* **-nal·ling** : communicate or notify by signals ~ *adj* : distinguished

sig·na·to·ry \'signəˌtōrē\ *n, pl* **-ries** : person or government that signs jointly with others

sig·na·ture \'signəˌchùr\ *n* : one's name written by oneself

sig·net \'signət\ *n* : small seal

sig·nif·i·cance \sig'nifikəns\ *n* 1 : meaning 2 : importance — **sig·nif·i·cant** \-kənt\ *adj* — **sig·nif·i·cant·ly** *adv*

sig·ni·fy \'signəˌfī\ *vb* **-fied; -fy·ing** 1 : show by a sign 2 : mean — **sig·ni·fi·ca·tion** \ˌsignəfə'kāshən\ *n*

si·lence \'sīləns\ *n* : state of being without sound ~ *vb* **-lenced; -lenc·ing** : keep from making noise or sound — **si·lenc·er** *n*

si·lent \'sīlənt\ *adj* : having or producing no sound — **si·lent·ly** *adv*

sil·hou·ette \ˌsilə'wet\ *n* : outline filled in usu. with black ~ *vb* **-ett·ed; -ett·ing** : represent by a silhouette

sil·i·ca \'silikə\ *n* : mineral found as quartz and opal

sil·i·con \'silikən, -ˌkän\ *n* : nonmetallic chemical element

silk \'silk\ *n* 1 : fine strong lustrous protein fiber from moth larvae (**silkworms** \-ˌwərmz\) 2 : thread or cloth made from silk — **silk·en** \'silkən\ *adj* — **silky** *adj*

sill \'sil\ *n* : bottom part of a window frame or a doorway

sil·ly \'silē\ *adj* **sil·li·er; -est** : foolish or stupid — **sil·li·ness** *n*

si·lo \'sīlō\ *n, pl* **-los** : tall building for storing animal feed

silt \'silt\ *n* : fine earth carried by rivers ~ *vb* : obstruct or cover with silt

sil·ver \'silvər\ *n* 1 : white ductile metallic chemical element 2 : silverware ~ *adj* : having the color of silver — **sil·very** *adj*

sil·ver·ware \-ˌwar\ *n* : eating and serving utensils esp. of silver

sim·i·lar \'simələr\ *adj* : resembling each other in some ways — **sim·i·lar·i·ty** \ˌsimə'larətē\ *n* — **sim·i·lar·ly** \'simələrlē\ *adv*

sim·i·le \'siməˌlē\ *n* : comparison of unlike things using *like* or *as*

sim·mer \'simər\ *vb* : stew gently

sim·per \'simpər\ *vb* : give a silly smile — **simper** *n*

sim·ple \'simpəl\ *adj* **-pler; -plest** 1 : free from dishonesty, vanity, or pretense 2 : of humble origin or modest position 3 : not complex 4 : lacking education, experience, or intelligence — **sim·ple·ness** *n* — **sim·ply** \-plē\ *adv*

sim·ple·ton \'simpəltən\ *n* : fool

sim·plic·i·ty \sim'plisətē\ *n* : state or fact of being simple

sim·pli·fy \'simpləˌfī\ *vb* **-fied; -fy·ing** : make easier — **sim·pli·fi·ca·tion** \ˌsimpləfə'kāshən\ *n*

sim·u·late \'simyəˌlāt\ *vb* **-lat·ed; -lat·ing** : create the effect or appearance of — **sim·u·la·tion** \ˌsimyə'lāshən\ *n* — **sim·u·la·tor** \'simyəˌlātər\ *n*

si·mul·ta·ne·ous \ˌsīməl'tānēəs\ *adj* : occurring or operating at the same time — **si·mul·ta·ne·ous·ly** *adv* — **simul·ta·ne·ous·ness** *n*

sin \'sin\ *n* : offense against God ~ *vb* **-nn-** : commit a sin — **sin·ful** \-fəl\ *adj* — **sin·less** *adj* — **sin·ner** *n*

since \'sins\ *adv* 1 : from a past time until now 2 : backward in time ~ *prep* 1 : in the period after 2 : continuously from ~ *conj* 1 : from the time when 2 : because

sin·cere \sin'sir\ *adj* **-cer·er; -cer·est** : genuine or honest — **sin·cere·ly** *adv* — **sin·cer·i·ty** \-'serətē\ *n*

si·ne·cure \'sīniˌkyùr, 'sini-\ *n* : well-paid job that requires little work

sin•ew \'sinyü\ *n* **1** : tendon **2** : physical strength — **sin•ewy** *adj*

sing \'siŋ\ *vb* **sang** \'saŋ\ *or* **sung** \'səŋ\; **sung; sing•ing** : produce musical tones with the voice — **sing•er** *n*

singe \'sinj\ *vb* **singed; singe•ing** : scorch lightly

sin•gle \'siŋgəl\ *adj* **1** : one only **2** : unmarried ∼ *n* : separate one — **single•ness** *n* — **sin•gly** \-glē\ *adv* — **single out** *vb* : select or set aside

sin•gu•lar \'siŋgyələr\ *adj* **1** : relating to a word form denoting one **2** : outstanding or superior **3** : queer — **singular** *n* — **sin•gu•lar•i•ty** \,siŋgyə-'larətē\ *n* — **sin•gu•lar•ly** \'siŋgyə-lərlē\ *adv*

sin•is•ter \'sinəstər\ *adj* : threatening evil

sink \'siŋk\ *vb* **sank** \'saŋk\ *or* **sunk** \'səŋk\; **sunk; sink•ing 1** : submerge or descend **2** : grow worse **3** : make by digging or boring **4** : invest ∼ *n* : basin with a drain

sink•er \'siŋkər\ *n* : weight to sink a fishing line

sin•u•ous \'sinyəwəs\ *adj* : winding in and out — **sin•u•os•i•ty** \,sinyə-'wäsətē\ *n* — **sin•u•ous•ly** *adv*

si•nus \'sīnəs\ *n* : skull cavity usu. connecting with the nostrils

sip \'sip\ *vb* **-pp-** : drink in small quantities — **sip** *n*

si•phon \'sīfən\ *n* : tube that draws liquid by suction — **siphon** *vb*

sir \'sər\ *n* **1** — used before the first name of a knight or baronet **2** — used as a respectful form of address

sire \'sīr\ *n* : father ∼ *vb* **sired; sir•ing** : beget

si•ren \'sīrən\ *n* **1** : seductive woman **2** : wailing warning whistle

sir•loin \'sər,lòin\ *n* : cut of beef

sirup *var of* SYRUP

si•sal \'sīsəl, -zəl\ *n* : strong rope fiber

sis•sy \'sisē\ *n, pl* **-sies** : timid or effeminate boy

sis•ter \'sistər\ *n* : female sharing one or both parents with another person — **sis•ter•hood** \-,hùd\ *n* — **sis•ter•ly** *adj*

sis•ter–in–law *n, pl* **sis•ters–in–law** : sister of one's spouse or wife of one's brother

sit \'sit\ *vb* **sat** \'sat\; **sit•ting 1** : rest on the buttocks or haunches **2** : roost **3** : hold a session **4** : pose for a portrait **5** : have a location **6** : rest or fix in place — **sit•ter** *n*

site \'sīt\ *n* **1** : place **2** : Web site

sit•u•at•ed \'sichə,wātəd\ *adj* : located

sit•u•a•tion \,sichə'wāshən\ *n* **1** : location **2** : condition **3** : job

six \'siks\ *n* : one more than 5 — **six** *adj or pron* — **sixth** \'siksth\ *adj or adv or n*

six•teen \siks'tēn\ *n* : one more than 15 — **sixteen** *adj or pron* — **six•teenth** \-'tēnth\ *adj or n*

six•ty \'sikstē\ *n, pl* **-ties** : 6 times 10 — **six•ti•eth** \-əth\ *adj or n* — **sixty** *adj or pron*

siz•able, size•able \'sīzəbəl\ *adj* : quite large — **siz•ably** \-blē\ *adv*

size \'sīz\ *n* : measurement of the amount of space something takes up ∼ *vb* : grade according to size

siz•zle \'sizəl\ *vb* **-zled; -zling** : fry with a hissing sound — **sizzle** *n*

skate \'skāt\ *n* **1** : metal runner on a shoe for gliding over ice **2** : roller skate — **skate** *vb* — **skat•er** *n*

skein \'skān\ *n* : loosely twisted quantity of yarn or thread

skel•e•ton \'skelət°n\ *n* : bony framework — **skel•e•tal** \-ət°l\ *adj*

skep•tic \'skeptik\ *n* : one who is critical or doubting — **skep•ti•cal** \-tikəl\ *adj* — **skep•ti•cism** \-tə,sizəm\ *n*

sketch \'skech\ *n* **1** : rough drawing **2** : short story or essay — **sketch** *vb* — **sketchy** *adj*

skew•er \'skyüər\ *n* : long pin for holding roasting meat — **skewer** *vb*

ski \'skē\ *n, pl* **skis** : long strip for gliding over snow or water — **ski** *vb* — **ski•er** *n*

skid \'skid\ *n* **1** : plank for supporting something or on which it slides **2** : act of skidding ∼ *vb* **-dd-** : slide sideways

skiff \'skif\ *n* : small boat

skill \'skil\ *n* : developed or learned ability — **skilled** \'skild\ *adj* — **skill•ful** \-fəl\ *adj* — **skill•ful•ly** *adv*

skil•let \'skilət\ *n* : pan for frying

skim \'skim\ *vb* **-mm- 1** : take off from the top of a liquid **2** : read or move over swiftly ∼ *adj* : having the cream removed — **skim•mer** *n*

skimp \'skimp\ *vb* : give too little of something — **skimpy** *adj*

skin \'skin\ *n* **1** : outer layer of an animal body **2** : rind ∼ *vb* **-nn-** : take

the skin from — **skin·less** *adj* —
skinned *adj* — **skin·tight** *adj*
skin diving *n* : sport of swimming under water with a face mask and flippers
skin·flint \'skin,flint\ *n* : stingy person
skin·ny \'skinē\ *adj* **-ni·er; -est** : very
thin
skip \'skip\ *vb* **-pp-** **1** : move with leaps
2 : read past or ignore — **skip** *n*
skip·per \'skipər\ *n* : ship's master —
skipper *vb*
skir·mish \'skərmish\ *n* : minor combat — **skirmish** *vb*
skirt \'skərt\ *n* : garment or part of a
garment that hangs below the waist
~ *vb* : pass around the edge of
skit \'skit\ *n* : brief usu. humorous play
skit·tish \'skitish\ *adj* : easily frightened
skulk \'skəlk\ *vb* : move furtively
skull \'skəl\ *n* : bony case that protects
the brain
skunk \'skəŋk\ *n* : mammal that can
forcibly eject an ill-smelling fluid
sky \'skī\ *n, pl* **skies** **1** : upper air **2**
: heaven — **sky·line** *n* — **sky·ward**
\-wərd\ *adv or adj*
sky·lark \'skī,lärk\ *n* : European lark
noted for its song
sky·light *n* : window in a roof or ceiling
sky·rock·et *n* : shooting firework **~** *vb*
: rise suddenly
sky·scrap·er \-,skrāpər\ *n* : very tall
building
slab \'slab\ *n* : thick slice
slack \'slak\ *adj* **1** : careless **2** : not
taut **3** : not busy **~** *n* **1** : part hanging loose **2** *pl* : casual trousers —
slack·en *vb* — **slack·ly** *adv* — **slack·
ness** *n*
slag \'slag\ *n* : waste from melting of ores
slain *past part of* SLAY
slake \'slāk\ *vb* **slaked; slak·ing**
: quench
slam \'slam\ *n* : heavy jarring impact
~ *vb* **-mm-** : shut, strike, or throw violently and loudly
slan·der \'slandər\ *n* : malicious gossip
~ *vb* : hurt (someone) with slander
— **slan·der·er** *n* — **slan·der·ous** *adj*
slang \'slaŋ\ *n* : informal nonstandard
vocabulary — **slangy** *adj*
slant \'slant\ *vb* **1** : slope **2** : present
with a special viewpoint **~** *n* : sloping direction, line, or plane
slap \'slap\ *vb* **-pp-** : strike sharply
with the open hand — **slap** *n*

slash \'slash\ *vb* **1** : cut with sweeping
strokes **2** : reduce sharply **~** *n* : gash
slat \'slat\ *n* : thin narrow flat strip
slate \'slāt\ *n* **1** : dense fine-grained
layered rock **2** : roofing tile or writing
tablet of slate **3** : list of candidates
~ *vb* **slat·ed; slat·ing** : designate
slat·tern \'slatərn\ *n* : untidy woman
— **slat·tern·ly** *adj*
slaugh·ter \'slotər\ *n* **1** : butchering of
livestock for market **2** : great and
cruel destruction of lives **~** *vb*
: commit slaughter upon — **slaughterhouse** *n*
slave \'slāv\ *n* : one owned and forced
into service by another **~** *vb* **slaved;
slav·ing** : work as or like a slave —
slave *adj* — **slav·ery** \'slāvərē\ *n*
sla·ver \'slavər, 'slāv-\ *vb or n* : slobber
slav·ish \'slāvish\ *adj* : of or like a
slave — **slav·ish·ly** *adv*
slay \'slā\ *vb* **slew** \'slü\; **slain** \'slān\;
slay·ing : kill — **slay·er** *n*
slea·zy \'slēzē, 'slā-\ *adj* **-zi·er; -est**
: shabby or shoddy
sled \'sled\ *n* : vehicle on runners —
sled *vb*
¹sledge \'slej\ *n* : sledgehammer
²sledge *n* : heavy sled
sledge·ham·mer *n* : heavy long-handled
hammer — **sledgehammer** *adj or vb*
sleek \'slēk\ *adj* : smooth or glossy —
sleek *vb*
sleep \'slēp\ *n* : natural suspension of
consciousness **~** *vb* **slept** \'slept\;
sleep·ing : rest in a state of sleep —
sleep·er *n* — **sleep·less** *adj* —
sleep·walk·er *n*
sleepy \'slēpē\ *adj* **sleep·i·er; -est** **1**
: ready for sleep **2** : quietly inactive
— **sleep·i·ly** \'slēpəlē\ *adv* — **sleep-
i·ness** \-pēnəs\ *n*
sleet \'slēt\ *n* : frozen rain — **sleet** *vb*
— **sleety** *adj*
sleeve \'slēv\ *n* : part of a garment for
the arm — **sleeve·less** *adj*
sleigh \'slā\ *n* : horse-drawn sled with
seats **~** *vb* : drive or ride in a sleigh
sleight of hand \'slīt-\ : skillful manual
manipulation or a trick requiring it
slen·der \'slendər\ *adj* **1** : thin esp. in
physique **2** : scanty
sleuth \'slüth\ *n* : detective
slew \'slü\ *past of* SLAY
slice \'slīs\ *n* : thin flat piece **~** *vb*
sliced; slic·ing : cut a slice from
slick \'slik\ *adj* **1** : very smooth **2**
: clever — **slick** *vb*

slick•er \'slikər\ *n* : raincoat

slide \'slīd\ *vb* **slid** \'slid\; **slid•ing** \'slīdiŋ\ : move smoothly along a surface ~ *n* **1** : act of sliding **2** : surface on which something slides **3** : transparent picture for projection

slier *comparative of* SLY

sliest *superlative of* SLY

slight \'slīt\ *adj* **1** : slender **2** : frail **3** : small in degree ~ *vb* **1** : ignore or treat as unimportant — **slight** *n* — **slight•ly** *adv*

slim \'slim\ *adj* **-mm- 1** : slender **2** : scanty ~ *vb* **-mm-** : make or become slender

slime \'slīm\ *n* : dirty slippery film (as on water) — **slimy** *adj*

sling \'sliŋ\ *vb* **slung** \'sləŋ\; **sling•ing** : hurl with or as if with a sling ~ *n* **1** : strap for swinging and hurling stones **2** : looped strap or bandage to lift or support

sling•shot *n* : forked stick with elastic bands for shooting pebbles

slink \'sliŋk\ *vb* **slunk** \'sləŋk\; **slink•ing** : move stealthily or sinuously — **slinky** *adj*

¹**slip** \'slip\ *vb* **-pp- 1** : escape quietly or secretly **2** : slide along smoothly **3** : make a mistake **4** : to pass without being noticed or done **5** : fall off from a standard ~ *n* **1** : ship's berth **2** : sudden mishap **3** : mistake **4** : woman's undergarment

²**slip** *n* **1** : plant shoot **2** : small strip (as of paper)

slip•per \'slipər\ *n* : shoe that slips on easily

slip•pery \'slipərē\ *adj* **-peri•er; -est 1** : slick enough to slide on **2** : tricky — **slip•peri•ness** *n*

slip•shod \'slip,shäd\ *adj* : careless

slit \'slit\ *vb* **slit; slit•ting** : make a slit in ~ *n* : long narrow cut

slith•er \'slithər\ *vb* : glide along like a snake — **slith•ery** *adj*

sliv•er \'slivər\ *n* : splinter

slob \'släb\ *n* : untidy person

slob•ber \'släbər\ *vb* : dribble saliva — **slobber** *n*

slo•gan \'slōgən\ *n* : word or phrase expressing the aim of a cause

sloop \'slüp\ *n* : one-masted sailboat

slop \'släp\ *n* : food waste for animal feed ~ *vb* **-pp-** : spill

slope \'slōp\ *vb* **sloped; slop•ing** : deviate from the vertical or horizontal ~ *n* : upward or downward slant

slop•py \'släpē\ *adj* **-pi•er; -est 1** : muddy **2** : untidy

slot \'slät\ *n* : narrow opening

sloth \'slȯth, 'slōth\ *n, pl* **sloths** *with* ths *or* thz\ **1** : laziness **2** : slow-moving mammal — **sloth•ful** *adj*

slouch \'slaúch\ *n* **1** : drooping posture **2** : lazy or incompetent person ~ *vb* : walk or stand with a slouch

¹**slough** \'slü, 'slaú\ *n* : swamp

²**slough, sluff** \'sləf\ *vb* : cast off (old skin)

slov•en•ly \'sləvənlē\ *adj* : untidy

slow \slō\ *adj* **1** : sluggish or stupid **2** : moving, working, or happening at less than the usual speed ~ *vb* **1** : make slow **2** : go slower — **slow** *adv* — **slow•ly** *adv* — **slow•ness** *n*

sludge \'sləj\ *n* : slushy mass (as of treated sewage)

slug \'sləg\ *n* **1** : mollusk related to the snails **2** : bullet **3** : metal disk ~ *vb* **-gg-** : strike forcibly — **slug•ger** *n*

slug•gish \'sləgish\ *adj* : slow in movement or flow — **slug•gish•ly** *adv* — **slug•gish•ness** *n*

sluice \'slüs\ *n* : channel for water ~ *vb* **sluiced; sluic•ing** : wash in running water

slum \'sləm\ *n* : thickly populated area marked by poverty

slum•ber \'sləmbər\ *vb or n* : sleep

slump \'sləmp\ *vb* **1** : sink suddenly **2** : slouch — **slump** *n*

slung *past of* SLING

slunk *past of* SLINK

¹**slur** \'slər\ *vb* **-rr-** : run (words or notes) together — **slur** *n*

²**slur** *n* : malicious or insulting remark

slurp \'slərp\ *vb* : eat or drink noisily — **slurp** *n*

slush \'sləsh\ *n* : partly melted snow — **slushy** *adj*

slut \'slət\ *n* **1** : untidy woman **2** : lewd woman — **slut•tish** *adj*

sly \'slī\ *adj* **sli•er** \'slīər\; **sli•est** \'slīəst\ : given to or showing secrecy and deception — **sly•ly** *adv* — **sly•ness** *n*

¹**smack** \'smak\ *n* : characteristic flavor ~ *vb* : have a taste or hint

²**smack** *vb* **1** : move (the lips) so as to make a sharp noise **2** : kiss or slap with a loud noise ~ *n* **1** : sharp noise made by the lips **2** : noisy slap

³**smack** *adv* : squarely and sharply

⁴**smack** *n* : fishing boat

small \'smȯl\ *adj* **1** : little in size or

amount **2** : few in number **3** : trivial
— **small•ish** *adj* — **small•ness** *n*
small•pox \'smȯl͵paks\ *n* : contagious
virus disease
smart \'smärt\ *vb* **1** : cause or feel
stinging pain **2** : endure distress ~
adj **1** : intelligent or resourceful **2**
: stylish — **smart** *n* — **smart•ly** *adv*
— **smart•ness** *n*
smash \'smash\ *vb* : break or be broken into pieces ~ *n* **1** : smashing
blow **2** : act or sound of smashing
smat•ter•ing \'smatəriŋ\ *n* **1** : superficial knowledge **2** : small scattered
number or amount
smear \'smir\ *n* : greasy stain ~ *vb* **1**
: spread (something sticky) **2** : smudge
3 : slander
smell \'smel\ *vb* **smelled** \'smeld\ *or*
smelt \'smelt\: **smell•ing 1** : perceive the odor of **2** : have or give off
an odor ~ *n* **1** : sense by which one
perceives odor **2** : odor — **smelly** *adj*
¹**smelt** \'smelt\ *n, pl* **smelts** *or* **smelt**
: small food fish
²**smelt** *vb* : melt or fuse (ore) in order to
separate the metal — **smelt•er** *n*
smile \'smīl\ *n* : facial expression with
the mouth turned up usu. to show
pleasure — **smile** *vb*
smirk \'smərk\ *vb* : wear a conceited
smile — **smirk** *n*
smite \'smīt\ *vb* **smote** \'smōt\: **smit-
ten** \'smit³n\ *or* **smote; smit•ing**
\'smītiŋ\ **1** : strike heavily or kill **2**
: affect strongly
smith \'smith\ *n* : worker in metals and
esp. a blacksmith
smithy \'smithē\ *n, pl* **smith•ies** : a
smith's workshop
smock \'smäk\ *n* : loose dress or protective coat
smog \'smäg, 'smȯg\ *n* : fog and smoke
— **smog•gy** *adj*
smoke \'smōk\ *n* : sooty gas from
burning ~ *vb* **smoked; smok•ing 1**
: give off smoke **2** : inhale the fumes
of burning tobacco **3** : cure (as meat)
with smoke — **smoke•less** *adj* —
smok•er *n* — **smoky** *adj*
smoke•stack *n* : chimney through
which smoke is discharged
smol•der, smoul•der \'smōldər\ *vb* **1**
: burn and smoke without flame **2**
: be suppressed but active — **smolder** *n*
smooth \'smüth\ *adj* **1** : having a surface without irregularities **2** : not jar-

ring or jolting ~ *vb* : make smooth
— **smooth•ly** *adv* — **smooth•ness** *n*
smor•gas•bord \'smȯrgəs͵bȯrd\ *n*
: buffet consisting of many foods
smoth•er \'sməthər\ *vb* **1** : kill by de-
priving of air **2** : cover thickly
smudge \'sməj\ *vb* **smudged;
smudg•ing** : soil or blur by rubbing
~ *n* **1** : thick smoke **2** : dirty spot
smug \'sməg\ *adj* **-gg-** : content in
one's own virtue or accomplishment
— **smug•ly** *adv* — **smug•ness** *n*
smug•gle \'sməgəl\ *vb* **-gled; -gling**
: import or export secretly or illegally
— **smug•gler** \'sməglər\ *n*
smut \'smət\ *n* **1** : something that soils
2 : indecent language or matter **3**
: disease of plants caused by fungi —
smut•ty *adj*
snack \'snak\ *n* : light meal
snag \'snag\ *n* : unexpected difficulty
~ *vb* **-gg-** : become caught on something that sticks out
snail \'snāl\ *n* : small mollusk with a
spiral shell
snake \'snāk\ *n* : long-bodied limbless
reptile — **snake•bite** *n*
snap \'snap\ *vb* **-pp- 1** : bite at something **2** : utter angry words **3** : break
suddenly with a sharp sound ~ *n* **1**
: act or sound of snapping **2** : fastening that closes with a click **3** : something easy to do — **snap•per** *n* —
snap•pish *adj* — **snap•py** *adj*
snap•drag•on *n* : garden plant with
spikes of showy flowers
snap•shot \'snap͵shät\ *n* : casual photograph
snare \'snar\ *n* : trap for catching game
~ *vb* : capture or hold with or as if
with a snare
¹**snarl** \'snärl\ *n* : tangle ~ *vb* : cause to
become knotted
²**snarl** *vb or n* : growl
snatch \'snach\ *vb* **1** : try to grab
something suddenly **2** : seize or take
away suddenly ~ *n* **1** : act of snatch-
ing **2** : something brief or fragmentary
sneak \'snēk\ *vb* : move or take in a
furtive manner ~ *n* : one who acts
in a furtive manner — **sneak•i•ly**
\'snēkəlē\ *adv* — **sneak•ing•ly** *adv*
— **sneaky** *adj*
sneak•er \'snēkər\ *n* : sports shoe
sneer \'snir\ *vb* : smile scornfully —
sneer *n*
sneeze \'snēz\ *vb* **sneezed; sneez•ing**

: force the breath out with sudden and involuntary violence — **sneeze** n

snick•er \'snikər\ n : partly suppressed laugh — **snicker** vb

snide \'snīd\ adj : subtly ridiculing

sniff \'snif\ vb **1** : draw air audibly up the nose **2** : detect by smelling — **sniff** n

snip \'snip\ n : fragment snipped off ～ vb **-pp-** : cut off by bits

¹**snipe** \'snīp\ n, pl **snipes** or **snipe** : game bird of marshy areas

²**snipe** vb **sniped; snip•ing** : shoot at an enemy from a concealed position — **snip•er** n

snips \'snips\ n pl : scissorslike tool

sniv•el \'snivəl\ vb **-eled** or **-elled; -el•ing** or **-el•ling** **1** : have a running nose **2** : whine

snob \'snäb\ n : one who acts superior to others — **snob•bery** \-ərē\ n — **snob•bish** adj — **snob•bish•ly** adv — **snob•bish•ness** n

snoop \'snüp\ vb : pry in a furtive way ～ n : prying person

snooze \'snüz\ vb **snoozed; snooz•ing** : take a nap — **snooze** n

snore \'snōr\ vb **snored; snor•ing** : breathe with a hoarse noise while sleeping — **snore** n

snort \'snȯrt\ vb : force air noisily through the nose — **snort** n

snout \'snaut\ n : long projecting muzzle (as of a swine)

snow \'snō\ n : crystals formed from water vapor ～ vb : fall as snow — **snow•ball** n — **snow•bank** n — **snow•drift** n — **snow•fall** n — **snow•plow** n — **snow•storm** n — **snowy** adj

snow•shoe n : frame of wood strung with thongs for walking on snow

snub \'snəb\ vb **-bb-** : ignore or avoid through disdain — **snub** n

¹**snuff** \'snəf\ vb : put out (a candle) — **snuff•er** n

²**snuff** vb : draw forcibly into the nose ～ n : pulverized tobacco

snug \'snəg\ adj **-gg-** **1** : warm, secure, and comfortable **2** : fitting closely — **snug•ly** adv — **snug•ness** n

snug•gle \'snəgəl\ vb **-gled; -gling** : curl up comfortably

so \'sō\ adv **1** : in the manner or to the extent indicated **2** : in the same way **3** : therefore **4** : finally **5** : thus ～ conj : for that reason

soak \'sōk\ vb **1** : lie in a liquid **2** : absorb ～ n : act of soaking

soap \'sōp\ n : cleaning substance — **soap** vb — **soapy** adj

soar \'sōr\ vb : fly upward on or as if on wings

sob \'säb\ vb **-bb-** : weep with convulsive heavings of the chest — **sob** n

so•ber \'sōbər\ adj **1** : not drunk **2** : serious or solemn — **so•ber•ly** adv

so•bri•ety \sə'brīətē, sō-\ n : quality or state of being sober

soc•cer \'säkər\ n : game played by kicking a ball

so•cia•ble \'sōshəbəl\ adj : friendly — **so•cia•bil•i•ty** \,sōshə'bilətē\ n — **so•cia•bly** \'sōshəblē\ adv

so•cial \'sōshəl\ adj **1** : relating to pleasant companionship **2** : naturally living or growing in groups **3** : relating to human society ～ n : social gathering — **so•cial•ly** adv

so•cial•ism \'sōshə,lizəm\ n : social system based on government control of the production and distribution of goods — **so•cial•ist** \'sōshəlist\ n or adj — **so•cial•is•tic** \,sōshə'listik\ adj

so•cial•ize \'sōshə,līz\ vb **-ized; -iz•ing** **1** : regulate by socialism **2** : adapt to social needs **3** : participate in a social gathering — **so•cial•i•za•tion** \,sōshələ'zāshən\ n

social work n : services concerned with aiding the poor and socially maladjusted — **social worker** n

so•ci•ety \sə'sīətē\ n, pl **-et•ies** **1** : companionship **2** : community life **3** : rich or fashionable class **4** : voluntary group

so•ci•ol•o•gy \,sōsē'äləjē\ n : study of social relationships — **so•ci•o•log•i•cal** \-ə'läjikəl\ adj — **so•ci•ol•o•gist** \-'äləjist\ n

¹**sock** \'säk\ n, pl **socks** or **sox** : short stocking

²**sock** vb or n : punch

sock•et \'säkət\ n : hollow part that holds something

sod \'säd\ n : turf ～ vb **-dd-** : cover with sod

so•da \'sōdə\ n **1** : carbonated water or a soft drink **2** : ice cream drink made with soda

sod•den \'säd²n\ adj **1** : lacking spirit **2** : soaked or soggy

so•di•um \'sōdēəm\ n : soft waxy silver white metallic chemical element

so•fa \'sōfə\ n : wide padded chair

soft \'sȯft\ adj **1** : not hard, rough, or harsh **2** : nonalcoholic — **soft•en**

\\'sófən\ *vb* — **soft•en•er** \-ənər\ *n*
— **soft•ly** *adv* — **soft•ness** *n*
soft•ball *n* : game like baseball
soft•ware \\'sóft¸wär\ *n* : computer programs
sog•gy \\'sägē\ *adj* **-gi•er; -est** : heavy with moisture — **sog•gi•ness** \-ēnəs\ *n*
¹**soil** \\'sóil\ *vb* : make or become dirty ~ *n* : embedded dirt
²**soil** *n* : loose surface material of the earth
so•journ \\'sō¸jərn, sō'jərn\ *n* : temporary stay ~ *vb* : reside temporarily
so•lace \\'säləs\ *n or vb* : comfort
so•lar \\'sōlər\ *adj* : relating to the sun or the energy in sunlight
sold *past of* SELL
sol•der \\'sädər, 'sód-\ *n* : metallic alloy melted to join metallic surfaces ~ *vb* : cement with solder
sol•dier \\'sōljər\ *n* : person in military service ~ *vb* : serve as a soldier — **sol•dier•ly** *adj or adv*
¹**sole** \\'sōl\ *n* : bottom of the foot or a shoe — **soled** *adj*
²**sole** *n* : flatfish caught for food
³**sole** *adj* : single or only — **sole•ly** *adv*
sol•emn \\'säləm\ *adj* **1** : dignified and ceremonial **2** : highly serious — **so•lem•ni•ty** \sə'lemnətē\ *n* — **sol•emn•ly** *adv*
so•lic•it \sə'lisət\ *vb* : ask for — **so•lic•i•ta•tion** \-¸lisə'tāshən\ *n*
so•lic•i•tor \sə'lisətər\ *n* **1** : one that solicits **2** : lawyer
so•lic•i•tous \sə'lisətəs\ *adj* : showing or expressing concern — **so•lic•i•tous•ly** *adv* — **so•lic•i•tude** \sə'lisə¸tüd, -¸tyüd\ *n*
sol•id \\'säləd\ *adj* **1** : not hollow **2** : having 3 dimensions **3** : hard **4** : of good quality **5** : of one character ~ *n* **1** : 3-dimensional figure **2** : substance in solid form — **solid** *adv* — **so•lid•i•ty** \sə'lidətē\ *n* — **sol•id•ly** *adv* — **sol•id•ness** *n*
sol•i•dar•i•ty \¸sälə'darətē\ *n* : unity of purpose
so•lid•i•fy \sə'lidə¸fī\ *vb* **-fied; -fy•ing** : make or become solid — **so•lid•i•fi•ca•tion** \-¸lidəfə'kāshən\ *n*
so•lil•o•quy \sə'liləkwē\ *n, pl* **-quies** : dramatic monologue — **so•lil•o•quize** \-¸kwīz\ *vb*
sol•i•taire \\'sälə¸tar\ *n* **1** : solitary gem **2** : card game for one person

sol•i•tary \-¸terē\ *adj* **1** : alone **2** : secluded **3** : single
sol•i•tude \-¸tüd, -¸tyüd\ *n* : state of being alone
so•lo \\'sōlō\ *n, pl* **-los** : performance by only one person ~ *adv* : alone — **solo** *adj or vb* — **so•lo•ist** *n*
sol•stice \\'sälstəs\ *n* : time of the year when the sun is farthest north or south of the equator
sol•u•ble \\'sälyəbəl\ *adj* **1** : capable of being dissolved **2** : capable of being solved — **sol•u•bil•i•ty** \¸sälyə'bilətē\ *n*
so•lu•tion \sə'lüshən\ *n* **1** : answer to a problem **2** : homogeneous liquid mixture
solve \\'sälv\ *vb* **solved; solv•ing** : find a solution for — **solv•able** *adj*
sol•vent \\'sälvənt\ *adj* **1** : able to pay all debts **2** : dissolving or able to dissolve ~ *n* : substance that dissolves or disperses another substance — **sol•ven•cy** \-vənsē\ *n*
som•ber, som•bre \\'sämbər\ *adj* **1** : dark **2** : grave — **som•ber•ly** *adv*
som•bre•ro \səm'brerō\ *n, pl* **-ros** : broad-brimmed hat
some \\'səm\ *adj* **1** : one unspecified **2** : unspecified or indefinite number of **3** : at least a few or a little ~ *pron* : a certain number or amount
-some \səm\ *adj suffix* : characterized by a thing, quality, state, or action
some•body \\'səmbədē, -¸bäd-\ *pron* : some person
some•day \\'səm¸dā\ *adv* : at some future time
some•how \-¸hau\ *adv* : by some means
some•one \-¸wən\ *pron* : some person
som•er•sault \\'səmər¸sólt\ *n* : body flip — **somersault** *vb*
some•thing \\'səmthiŋ\ *pron* : some undetermined or unspecified thing
some•time \\'səm¸tīm\ *adv* : at a future, unknown, or unnamed time
some•times \-¸tīmz\ *adv* : occasionally
some•what \-¸hwət, -¸hwät\ *adv* : in some degree
some•where \-¸hwer\ *adv* : in, at, or to an unknown or unnamed place
som•no•lent \\'sämnələnt\ *adj* : sleepy — **som•no•lence** \-ləns\ *n*
son \\'sən\ *n* : male offspring
so•nar \\'sō¸när\ *n* : device that detects and locates underwater objects using sound waves

so·na·ta \sə'nätə\ *n* : instrumental composition

song \'soŋ\ *n* : music and words to be sung

song·bird *n* : bird with musical tones

son·ic \'sänik\ *adj* : relating to sound waves or the speed of sound

son–in–law *n, pl* **sons–in–law** : husband of one's daughter

son·net \'sänət\ *n* : poem of 14 lines

so·no·rous \sə'nōrəs, 'sänərəs\ *adj* 1 : loud, deep, or rich in sound 2 : impressive — **so·nor·i·ty** \sə'nórətē\ *n*

soon \'sün\ *adv* 1 : before long 2 : promptly 3 : early

soot \'sut, 'sət, 'süt\ *n* : fine black substance formed by combustion — **sooty** *adj*

soothe \'süth\ *vb* **soothed; sooth·ing** : calm or comfort — **sooth·er** *n*

sooth·say·er \'süth,sāər\ *n* : prophet — **sooth·say·ing** \-iŋ\ *n*

sop \'säp\ *n* : conciliatory bribe, gift, or concession ~ *vb* **-pp-** 1 : dip in a liquid 2 : soak 3 : mop up

so·phis·ti·cat·ed \sə'fistə,kātəd\ *adj* 1 : complex 2 : wise, cultured, or shrewd in human affairs — **so·phis·ti·ca·tion** \-,fistə'kāshən\ *n*

soph·ist·ry \'säfəstrē\ *n* : subtly fallacious reasoning or argument — **sophist** \'säfist\ *n*

soph·o·more \'säf°m,ōr, 'säf,mōr\ *n* : 2d-year student

so·po·rif·ic \,säpə'rifik, ,sōp-\ *adj* : causing sleep or drowsiness

so·pra·no \sə'pranō\ *n, pl* **-nos** : highest singing voice

sor·cery \'sórsərē\ *n* : witchcraft — **sor·cer·er** \-rər\ *n* — **sor·cer·ess** \-rəs\ *n*

sor·did \'sórdəd\ *adj* : filthy or vile — **sor·did·ly** *adv* — **sor·did·ness** *n*

sore \'sōr\ *adj* **sor·er; sor·est** 1 : causing pain or distress 2 : severe or intense 3 : angry ~ *n* : sore usu. infected spot on the body — **sore·ly** *adv* — **sore·ness** *n*

sor·ghum \'sórgəm\ *n* : forage grass

so·ror·i·ty \sə'rórətē\ *n, pl* **-ties** : women's student social group

¹sor·rel \'sórəl\ *n* : brownish orange to light brown color or an animal of this color

²sorrel *n* : herb with sour juice

sor·row \'särō\ *n* : deep distress, sadness, or regret or a cause of this — **sor·row·ful** \-fəl\ *adj* — **sor·row·ful·ly** *adv*

sor·ry \'särē\ *adj* **-ri·er; -est** 1 : feeling sorrow, regret, or penitence 2 : dismal

sort \'sórt\ *n* 1 : kind 2 : nature ~ *vb* : classify — **out of sorts** : grouchy

sor·tie \'sórtē, sór'tē\ *n* : military attack esp. against besiegers

SOS \,es,ō'es\ *n* : call for help

so–so \'sō'sō\ *adj or adv* : barely acceptable

sot \'sät\ *n* : drunkard — **sot·tish** *adj*

souf·flé \sü'flā\ *n* : baked dish made light with beaten egg whites

sought *past of* SEEK

soul \'sōl\ *n* 1 : immaterial essence of an individual life 2 : essential part 3 : person

soul·ful \'sōlfəl\ *adj* : full of or expressing deep feeling — **soul·ful·ly** *adv*

¹sound \'saund\ *adj* 1 : free from fault, error, or illness 2 : firm or hard 3 : showing good judgment — **sound·ly** *adv* — **sound·ness** *n*

²sound *n* 1 : sensation of hearing 2 : energy of vibration sensed in hearing 3 : something heard ~ *vb* 1 : make or cause to make a sound 2 : seem — **sound·less** *adj* — **sound·less·ly** *adv* — **sound·proof** *adj or vb*

³sound *n* : wide strait ~ *vb* 1 : measure the depth of (water) 2 : investigate

soup \'süp\ *n* : broth usu. containing pieces of solid food — **soupy** *adj*

sour \'sauər\ *adj* 1 : having an acid or tart taste 2 : disagreeable ~ *vb* : become or make sour — **sour·ish** *adj* — **sour·ly** *adv* — **sour·ness** *n*

source \'sōrs\ *n* 1 : point of origin 2 : one that provides something needed

souse \'saus\ *vb* **soused; sous·ing** 1 : pickle 2 : immerse 3 : intoxicate ~ *n* 1 : something pickled 2 : drunkard

south \'sauth\ *adv* : to or toward the south ~ *adj* : situated toward, at, or coming from the south ~ *n* 1 : direction to the right of sunrise 2 *cap* : regions to the south — **south·er·ly** \'səthərlē\ *adv or adj* — **south·ern** \'səthərn\ *adj* — **South·ern·er** *n* — **south·ern·most** \-,mōst\ *adj* — **southward** \'sauthwərd\ *adv or adj* — **south·wards** \-wərdz\ *adv*

south·east \sauth'ēst, *naut* sau'ēst\ *n* 1 : direction between south and east 2 *cap* : regions to the southeast — **southeast** *adj or adv* — **south·east-**

er•ly *adv or adj* — **south•east•ern** \-ərn\ *adj*

south pole *n* : the southernmost point of the earth

south•west \saüth'west, *naut* saò-'west\ *n* **1** : direction between south and west **2** *cap* : regions to the southwest — **southwest** *adj or adv* — **south•west•er•ly** *adv or adj* — **south•west•ern** \-ərn\ *adj*

sou•ve•nir \'süvə,nir\ *n* : something that is a reminder of a place or event

sov•er•eign \'sävərən\ *n* **1** : supreme ruler **2** : gold coin of the United Kingdom ∼ *adj* **1** : supreme **2** : independent — **sov•er•eign•ty** \-tē\ *n*

¹sow \'saü\ *n* : female swine

²sow \'sō\ *vb* **sowed**; **sown** \'sōn\ *or* **sowed**; **sow•ing** **1** : plant or strew with seed **2** : scatter abroad — **sow•er** \'sōər\ *n*

sox *pl of* SOCK

soy•bean \'sòi,bēn\ *n* : legume with edible seeds

spa \'spä\ *n* : resort at a mineral spring

space \'spās\ *n* **1** : period of time **2** : area in, around, or between **3** : region beyond earth's atmosphere **4** : accommodations ∼ *vb* **spaced**; **spac•ing** : place at intervals — **space•craft** *n* — **space•flight** *n* — **space•man** *n* — **space•ship** *n*

spa•cious \'spāshəs\ *adj* : large or roomy — **spa•cious•ly** *adv* — **spa•cious•ness** *n*

¹spade \'spād\ *n or vb* : shovel — **spade•ful** *n*

²spade *n* : playing card marked with a black figure like an inverted heart

spa•ghet•ti \spə'getē\ *n* : pasta strings

spam \'spam\ *n* : unsolicited commercial e-mail

span \'span\ *n* **1** : amount of time **2** : distance between supports ∼ *vb* **-nn-** : extend across

span•gle \'spaŋgəl\ *n* : small disk of shining metal or plastic — **spangle** *vb*

span•iel \'spanyəl\ *n* : small or medium-sized dog with drooping ears and long wavy hair

spank \'spaŋk\ *vb* : hit on the buttocks with an open hand

¹spar \'spär\ *n* : pole or boom

²spar *vb* **-rr-** : practice boxing

spare \'spar\ *adj* **1** : held in reserve **2** : thin or scanty ∼ *vb* **spared**; **spar•ing** **1** : reserve or avoid using **2** : avoid punishing or killing — **spare** *n*

spar•ing \'spariŋ\ *adj* : thrifty — **spar•ing•ly** *adv*

spark \'spärk\ *n* **1** : tiny hot and glowing particle **2** : smallest beginning or germ **3** : visible electrical discharge ∼ *vb* **1** : emit or produce sparks **2** : stir to activity

spar•kle \'spärkəl\ *vb* **-kled**; **-kling** **1** : flash **2** : effervesce ∼ *n* : gleam — **spark•ler** \-klər\ *n*

spar•row \'sparō\ *n* : small singing bird

sparse \'spärs\ *adj* **spars•er**; **spars•est** : thinly scattered — **sparse•ly** *adv*

spasm \'spazəm\ *n* **1** : involuntary muscular contraction **2** : sudden, violent, and temporary effort or feeling — **spas•mod•ic** \spaz'mädik\ *adj* — **spas•mod•i•cal•ly** *adv*

spas•tic \'spastik\ *adj* : relating to, marked by, or affected with muscular spasm — **spastic** *n*

¹spat \'spat\ *past of* SPIT

²spat *n* : petty dispute

spa•tial \'späshəl\ *adj* : relating to space — **spa•tial•ly** *adv*

spat•ter \'spatər\ *vb* : splash with drops of liquid — **spatter** *n*

spat•u•la \'spachələ\ *n* : flexible knifelike utensil

spawn \'spón\ *vb* **1** : produce eggs or offspring **2** : bring forth ∼ *n* : egg cluster — **spawn•er** *n*

spay \'spā\ *vb* : remove the ovaries of (a female)

speak \'spēk\ *vb* **spoke** \'spōk\; **spoken** \'spōkən\; **speak•ing** **1** : utter words **2** : express orally **3** : address an audience **4** : use (a language) in talking — **speak•er** *n*

spear \'spir\ *n* : long pointed weapon ∼ *vb* : strike or pierce with a spear

spear•head *n* : leading force, element, or influence — **spearhead** *vb*

spear•mint *n* : aromatic garden mint

spe•cial \'speshəl\ *adj* **1** : unusual or unique **2** : particularly favored **3** : set aside for a particular use — **special** *n* — **spe•cial•ly** *adv*

spe•cial•ist \'speshəlist\ *n* **1** : person who specializes in a particular branch of learning or activity **2** : any of four enlisted ranks in the army corresponding to the grades of corporal through sergeant first class

spe•cial•ize \'speshə,līz\ *vb* **-ized**; **-izing** : concentrate one's efforts — **spe•cial•i•za•tion** \,speshələ'zāshən\ *n*

spe·cial·ty \\'speshəltē\ *n, pl* **-ties** : area or field in which one specializes

spe·cie \\'spēshē, -sē\ *n* : money in coin

spe·cies \\'spēshēz, -sēz\ *n, pl* **species** : biological grouping of closely related organisms

spe·cif·ic \spi'sifik\ *adj* : definite or exact — **spe·cif·i·cal·ly** *adv*

spec·i·fi·ca·tion \ˌspesəfə'kāshən\ *n* **1** : act or process of specifying **2** : detailed description of work to be done — usu. pl.

spec·i·fy \\'spesəˌfī\ *vb* **-fied; -fy·ing** : mention precisely or by name

spec·i·men \-əmən\ *n* : typical example

spe·cious \\'spēshəs\ *adj* : apparently but not really genuine or correct

speck \\'spek\ *n* : tiny particle or blemish — **speck** *vb*

speck·led \\'spekəld\ *adj* : marked with spots

spec·ta·cle \\'spektikəl\ *n* **1** : impressive public display **2** *pl* : eyeglasses

spec·tac·u·lar \spek'takyələr\ *adj* : sensational or showy

spec·ta·tor \\'spek,tātər\ *n* : person who looks on

spec·ter, spec·tre \\'spektər\ *n* **1** : ghost **2** : haunting vision

spec·tral \\'spektrəl\ *adj* : relating to or resembling a specter or spectrum

spec·trum \\'spektrəm\ *n, pl* **-tra** \-trə\ *or* **-trums** : series of colors formed when white light is dispersed into its components

spec·u·late \\'spekyəˌlāt\ *vb* **-lat·ed; -lat·ing** **1** : think about things yet unknown **2** : risk money in a business deal in hope of high profit — **spec·u·la·tion** \ˌspekyə'lāshən\ *n* — **spec·u·la·tive** \\'spekyəˌlātiv\ *adj* — **spec·u·la·tor** \-ˌlātər\ *n*

speech \\'spēch\ *n* **1** : power, act, or manner of speaking **2** : talk given to an audience — **speech·less** *adj*

speed \\'spēd\ *n* **1** : quality of being fast **2** : rate of motion or performance ∼ *vb* **sped** \\'sped\ *or* **speed·ed; speed·ing** : go at a great or excessive rate of speed — **speed·boat** *n* — **speed·er** *n* — **speed·i·ly** \\'spēd°lē\ *adv* — **speed·up** \-ˌəp\ *n* — **speedy** *adj*

speed·om·e·ter \spi'dämətər\ *n* : instrument for indicating speed

¹spell \\'spel\ *n* : influence of or like magic

²spell *vb* **1** : name, write, or print the letters of **2** : mean — **spell·er** *n*

³spell *vb* : substitute for or relieve (someone) ∼ *n* **1** : turn at work **2** : period of time

spell·bound *adj* : held by a spell

spend \\'spend\ *vb* **spent** \\'spent\; **spend·ing** **1** : pay out **2** : cause or allow to pass — **spend·er** *n*

spend·thrift \\'spend,thrift\ *n* : wasteful person

sperm \\'spərm\ *n, pl* **sperm** *or* **sperms** : semen or a germ cell in it

spew \\'spyü\ *vb* : gush out in a stream

sphere \\'sfir\ *n* **1** : figure with every point on its surface at an equal distance from the center **2** : round body **3** : range of action or influence — **spher·i·cal** \\'sfirikəl, 'sfer-\ *adj*

spher·oid \\'sfir-\ *n* : spherelike figure

spice \\'spīs\ *n* **1** : aromatic plant product for seasoning food **2** : interesting quality — **spice** *vb* — **spicy** *adj*

spi·der \\'spīdər\ *n* : small insectlike animal with 8 legs — **spi·dery** *adj*

spig·ot \\'spigət, 'spikət\ *n* : faucet

spike \\'spīk\ *n* : very large nail — *vb* **spiked; spik·ing** : fasten or pierce with a spike — **spiked** \\'spīkt\ *adj*

spill \\'spil\ *vb* **1** : fall, flow, or run out unintentionally **2** : divulge ∼ *n* **1** : act of spilling **2** : something spilled — **spill·able** *adj*

spill·way *n* : passage for surplus water

spin \\'spin\ *vb* **spun** \\'spən\; **spin·ning** **1** : draw out fiber and twist into thread **2** : form thread from a sticky body fluid **3** : revolve or cause to revolve extremely fast ∼ *n* : rapid rotating motion — **spin·ner** *n*

spin·ach \\'spinich\ *n* : garden herb with edible leaves

spi·nal \\'spīn°l\ *adj* : relating to the backbone — **spi·nal·ly** *adv*

spinal cord *n* : thick strand of nervous tissue that extends from the brain along the back within the backbone

spin·dle \\'spind°l\ *n* **1** : stick used for spinning thread **2** : shaft around which something turns

spin·dly \\'spindlē\ *adj* : tall and slender

spine \\'spīn\ *n* **1** : backbone **2** : stiff sharp projection on a plant or animal — **spine·less** *adj* — **spiny** *adj*

spin·et \\'spinət\ *n* : small piano

spin·ster \\'spinstər\ *n* : woman who has never married

spi·ral \\'spīrəl\ *adj* : circling or wind-

ing around a single point or line —
spiral *n or vb* — **spi•ral•ly** *adv*
spire \'spīr\ *n* : steeple — **spiry** *adj*
spir•it \'spirət\ *n* **1** : life-giving force
2 *cap* : presence of God **3** : ghost **4**
: mood **5** : vivacity or enthusiasm **6**
pl : alcoholic liquor ∼ *vb* : carry off
secretly — **spir•it•ed** *adj* — **spir•it•
less** *adj*
spir•i•tu•al \'spirichəwəl\ *adj* **1** : relating to the spirit or sacred matters **2**
: deeply religious ∼ *n* : religious folk
song — **spir•i•tu•al•i•ty** \ˌspirichə-
'walətē\ *n* — **spir•i•tu•al•ly** *adv*
spir•i•tu•al•ism \'spirichəwəˌlizəm\ *n*
: belief that spirits communicate with
the living — **spir•i•tu•al•ist** \-list\ *n*
or adj
¹**spit** \'spit\ *n* **1** : rod for holding and
turning meat over a fire **2** : point of
land that runs into the water
²**spit** *vb* **spit** *or* **spat** \'spat\; **spit•ting**
: eject saliva from the mouth ∼ *n* **1**
: saliva **2** : perfect likeness
spite \'spīt\ *n* : petty ill will ∼ *vb* **spit-
ed; spit•ing** : annoy or offend —
spite•ful \-fəl\ *adj* — **spite•ful•ly** *adv*
— **in spite of** : in defiance or contempt of
spit•tle \'spit⁰l\ *n* : saliva
spit•toon \spiˈtün\ *n* : receptacle for spit
splash \'splash\ *vb* : scatter a liquid on
— **splash** *n*
splat•ter \'splatər\ *vb* : spatter —
splatter *n*
splay \'splā\ *vb* : spread out or apart —
splay *n or adj*
spleen \'splēn\ *n* **1** : organ for maintenance of the blood **2** : spite or anger
splen•did \'splendəd\ *adj* **1** : impressive in beauty or brilliance **2** : outstanding — **splen•did•ly** *adv*
splen•dor \'splendər\ *n* **1** : brilliance
2 : magnificence
splice \'splīs\ *vb* **spliced; splic•ing**
: join (2 things) end to end — **splice** *n*
splint \'splint\ *n* **1** : thin strip of wood
2 : something that keeps an injured
body part in place
splin•ter \'splintər\ *n* : thin needlelike
piece ∼ *vb* : break into splinters
split \'split\ *vb* **split; split•ting** : divide
lengthwise or along a grain — **split** *n*
splotch \'spläch\ *n* : blotch
splurge \'splərj\ *vb* **splurged; splurg-
ing** : indulge oneself — **splurge** *n*
splut•ter \'splətər\ *n* : sputter — **splut-
ter** *vb*

spoil \'spóil\ *n* : plunder ∼ *vb* **spoiled**
\'spóild, 'spóilt\ *or* **spoilt** \'spóilt\;
spoil•ing 1 : pillage **2** : ruin **3** : rot
— **spoil•age** \'spóilij\ *n* — **spoil•er** *n*
¹**spoke** \'spōk\ *past of* SPEAK
²**spoke** *n* : rod from the hub to the rim of
a wheel
spo•ken *past part of* SPEAK
spokes•man \'spōksmən\ *n* : person
who speaks for others
spokes•wom•an \-ˌwümən\ *n* : woman
who speaks for others
sponge \'spənj\ *n* **1** : porous water=
absorbing mass that forms the skeleton
of some marine animals **2** : sponge-
like material used for wiping ∼ *vb*
sponged; spong•ing 1 : wipe with a
sponge **2** : live at another's expense
— **spongy** \'spənjē\ *adj*
spon•sor \'spänsər\ *n* : one who assumes responsibility for another or
who provides financial support —
sponsor *vb* — **spon•sor•ship** *n*
spon•ta•ne•ous \spänˈtānēəs\ *adj*
: done, produced, or occurring naturally or without planning — **spon•ta-
ne•i•ty** \ˌspäntənˈēətē\ *n* — **spon-
ta•ne•ous•ly** \spänˈtānēəslē\ *adv*
spoof \'süf\ *vb* : make good-natured
fun of — **spoof** *n*
spook \'spük\ *n* : ghost ∼ *vb* : frighten
— **spooky** *adj*
spool \'spül\ *n* : cylinder on which
something is wound
spoon \'spün\ *n* : utensil consisting of
a small shallow bowl with a handle —
spoon *vb* — **spoon•ful** \-ˌfül\ *n*
spoor \'spür, 'spōr\ *n* : track or trail
esp. of a wild animal
spo•rad•ic \spəˈradik\ *adj* : occasional
— **spo•rad•i•cal•ly** *adv*
spore \'spōr\ *n* : primitive usu. one=
celled reproductive body
sport \'spōrt\ *vb* **1** : frolic **2** : show off
∼ *n* **1** : physical activity engaged in
for pleasure **2** : jest **3** : person who
shows good sportsmanship — **sport-
ive** \-iv\ *adj* — **sporty** *adj*
sports•cast \'spōrtsˌkast\ *n* : broadcast of a sports event — **sports•cast-
er** \-ˌkastər\ *n*
sports•man \-mən\ *n* : one who enjoys
hunting and fishing
sports•man•ship \-mənˌship\ *n* : ability to be gracious in winning or losing
spot \'spät\ *n* **1** : blemish **2** : distinctive small part **3** : location ∼ *vb* **-tt-
1** : mark with spots **2** : see or recog-

nize ~ *adj* : made at random or in limited numbers — **spot·less** *adj* — **spot·less·ly** *adv*

spot·light *n* **1** : intense beam of light **2** : center of public interest — **spotlight** *vb*

spot·ty \'spätē\ *adj* **-ti·er; -est** : uneven in quality

spouse \'spaús\ *n* : one's husband or wife

spout \'spaút\ *vb* **1** : shoot forth in a stream **2** : say pompously ~ *n* **1** : opening through which liquid spouts **2** : jet of liquid

sprain \'sprān\ *n* : twisting injury to a joint ~ *vb* : injure with a sprain

sprat \'sprat\ *n* : small or young herring

sprawl \'spról\ *vb* : lie or sit with limbs spread out — **sprawl** *n*

¹spray \'sprā\ *n* : branch or arrangement of flowers

²spray *n* **1** : mist **2** : device that discharges liquid as a mist — **spray** *vb* — **spray·er** *n*

spread \'spred\ *vb* **spread; spreading 1** : open up or unfold **2** : scatter or smear over a surface **3** : cause to be known or to exist over a wide area ~ *n* **1** : extent to which something is spread **2** : cloth cover **3** : something intended to be spread — **spread·er** *n*

spread·sheet \'spred,shēt\ *n* : accounting program for a computer

spree \'sprē\ *n* : burst of indulging in something

sprig \'sprig\ *n* : small shoot or twig

spright·ly \'sprītlē\ *adj* **-li·er; -est** : lively — **spright·li·ness** *n*

spring \spriŋ\ *vb* **sprang** \'spraŋ\ *or* **sprung** \'sprəŋ\; **sprung; springing 1** : move or grow quickly or by elastic force **2** : come from by descent **3** : make known suddenly ~ *n* **1** : source **2** : flow of water from underground **3** : season between winter and summer **4** : elastic body or device (as a coil of wire) **5** : leap **6** : elastic power — **springy** *adj*

sprin·kle \'spriŋkəl\ *vb* **-kled; -kling** : scatter in small drops or particles ~ *n* : light rainfall — **sprin·kler** *n*

sprint \'sprint\ *n* : short run at top speed — **sprint** *vb* — **sprint·er** *n*

sprite \'sprīt\ *n* : elf or elfish person

sprock·et \'spräkət\ *n* : toothed wheel whose teeth engage the links of a chain

sprout \'spraút\ *vb* : send out new growth ~ *n* : plant shoot

¹spruce \'sprüs\ *n* : conical evergreen tree

²spruce *adj* **spruc·er; spruc·est** : neat and stylish in appearance ~ *vb* **spruced; spruc·ing** : make or become neat

spry \'sprī\ *adj* **spri·er** *or* **spry·er** \'sprīər\; **spri·est** *or* **spry·est** \'sprīəst\ : agile and active

spume \'spyüm\ *n* : froth

spun *past of* SPIN

spunk \'spəŋk\ *n* : courage — **spunky** *adj*

spur \'spər\ *n* **1** : pointed device used to urge on a horse **2** : something that urges to action **3** : projecting part ~ *vb* **-rr-** : urge on — **spurred** *adj*

spu·ri·ous \'spyúrēəs\ *adj* : not genuine

spurn \'spərn\ *vb* : reject

¹spurt \'spərt\ *n* : burst of effort, speed, or activity ~ *vb* : make a spurt

²spurt *vb* : gush out ~ *n* : sudden gush

sput·ter \'spətər\ *vb* **1** : talk hastily and indistinctly in excitement **2** : make popping sounds — **sputter** *n*

spy \'spī\ *vb* **spied; spy·ing** : watch or try to gather information secretly — **spy** *n*

squab \'skwäb\ *n, pl* **squabs** *or* **squab** : young pigeon

squab·ble \'skwäbəl\ *n or vb* : dispute

squad \'skwäd\ *n* : small group

squad·ron \'skwädrən\ *n* : small military unit

squal·id \'skwäləd\ *adj* : filthy or wretched

squall \'skwól\ *n* : sudden violent brief storm — **squally** *adj*

squa·lor \'skwälər\ *n* : quality or state of being squalid

squan·der \'skwändər\ *vb* : waste

square \'skwar\ *n* **1** : instrument for measuring right angles **2** : flat figure that has 4 equal sides and 4 right angles **3** : open area in a city **4** : product of number multiplied by itself ~ *adj* **squar·er; squar·est 1** : being a square in form **2** : having sides meet at right angles **3** : multiplied by itself **4** : being a square unit of area **5** : honest ~ *vb* **squared; squar·ing 1** : form into a square **2** : multiply (a number) by itself **3** : conform **4** : settle — **square·ly** *adv*

¹squash \'skwäsh, 'skwósh\ *vb* **1** : press flat **2** : suppress

²squash *n, pl* **squash·es** *or* **squash** : garden vegetable

squat \'skwät\ *vb* **-tt-** **1** : stoop or sit on one's heels **2** : settle on land one does not own ～ *n* : act or posture of squatting ～ *adj* **squat•ter; squattest** : short and thick — **squat•ter** *n*

squawk \'skwȯk\ *n* : harsh loud cry — **squawk** *vb*

squeak \'skwēk\ *vb* : make a thin high≈ pitched sound — **squeak** *n* — **squeaky** *adj*

squeal \'skwēl\ *vb* **1** : make a shrill sound or cry **2** : protest — **squeal** *n*

squea•mish \'skwēmish\ *adj* : easily nauseated or disgusted

squeeze \'skwēz\ *vb* **squeezed; squeez•ing** **1** : apply pressure to **2** : extract by pressure — **squeeze** *n* — **squeez•er** *n*

squelch \'skwelch\ *vb* : suppress (as with a retort) — **squelch** *n*

squid \'skwid\ *n, pl* **squid** *or* **squids** : 10-armed long-bodied sea mollusk

squint \'skwint\ *vb* : look with the eyes partly closed — **squint** *n or adj*

squire \'skwīr\ *n* **1** : knight's aide **2** : country landholder **3** : lady's devoted escort ～ *vb* **squired; squir•ing** : escort

squirm \'skwərm\ *vb* : wriggle

squir•rel \'skwərəl\ *n* : rodent with a long bushy tail

squirt \'skwərt\ *vb* : eject liquid in a spurt — **squirt** *n*

stab \'stab\ *n* **1** : wound made by a pointed weapon **2** : quick thrust **3** : attempt ～ *vb* **-bb-** : pierce or wound with or as if with a pointed weapon

¹**sta•ble** \'stābəl\ *n* : building for domestic animals ～ *vb* **-bled; -bling** : keep in a stable

²**stable** *adj* **sta•bler; sta•blest** **1** : firmly established **2** : mentally and emotionally healthy **3** : steady — **sta•bili•ty** \stə'bilətē\ *n* — **sta•bil•iza•tion** \ˌstābələ'zāshən\ *n* — **sta•bi•lize** \'stābəˌlīz\ *vb* — **sta•bi•liz•er** *n*

stac•ca•to \stə'kätō\ *adj* : disconnected

stack \'stak\ *n* : large pile ～ *vb* : pile up

sta•di•um \'stādēəm\ *n* : outdoor sports arena

staff \'staf\ *n, pl* **staffs** \'stafs, stavz\ *or* **staves** \'stavz, 'stāvz\ **1** : rod or supporting cane **2** : people assisting a leader **3** : 5 horizontal lines on which music is written ～ *vb* : supply with workers — **staff•er** *n*

staff sergeant *n* : noncommissioned officer ranking next above a sergeant in the army, air force, or marine corps

stag \'stag\ *n, pl* **stags** *or* **stag** : male deer ～ *adj* : only for men ～ *adv* : without a date

stage \'stāj\ *n* **1** : raised platform for a speaker or performers **2** : theater **3** : step in a process ～ *vb* **staged; stag•ing** : produce (a play)

stage•coach *n* : passenger coach

stag•ger \'stagər\ *vb* **1** : reel or cause to reel from side to side **2** : overlap or alternate — **stagger** *n* — **stagger•ing•ly** *adv*

stag•nant \'stagnənt\ *adj* : not moving or active — **stag•nate** \-ˌnāt\ *vb* — **stag•na•tion** \stag'nāshən\ *n*

¹**staid** \'stād\ *adj* : sedate

²**staid** *past of* STAY

stain \'stān\ *vb* **1** : discolor **2** : dye (as wood) **3** : disgrace ～ *n* **1** : discolored area **2** : mark of guilt **3** : coloring preparation — **stain•less** *adj*

stair \'star\ *n* **1** : step in a series for going from one level to another **2** *pl* : flight of steps — **stair•way** *n*

stair•case *n* : series of steps with their framework

stake \'stāk\ *n* **1** : usu. small post driven into the ground **2** : bet **3** : prize in a contest ～ *vb* **staked; stak•ing** **1** : mark or secure with a stake **2** : bet

sta•lac•tite \stə'lakˌtīt\ *n* : icicle≈ shaped deposit hanging in a cavern

sta•lag•mite \stə'lagˌmīt\ *n* : icicle≈ shaped deposit on a cavern floor

stale \'stāl\ *adj* **stal•er; stal•est** **1** : having lost good taste and quality from age **2** : no longer new, strong, or effective — **stale•ness** *n*

stale•mate \'stālˌmāt\ *n* : deadlock — **stalemate** *vb*

¹**stalk** \'stȯk\ *vb* **1** : walk stiffly or proudly **2** : pursue stealthily

²**stalk** *n* : plant stem — **stalked** \'stȯkt\ *adj*

¹**stall** \'stȯl\ *n* **1** : compartment in a stable **2** : booth where articles are sold

²**stall** *vb* : bring or come to a standstill unintentionally

³**stall** *vb* : delay, evade, or keep a situation going to gain advantage or time

stal•lion \'stalyən\ *n* : male horse

stal•wart \'stȯlwərt\ *adj* : strong or brave

sta•men \'stāmən\ *n* : flower organ that produces pollen

stam•i•na \'stamənə\ *n* : endurance

stam•mer \\'stamər\\ *vb* : hesitate in speaking — **stammer** *n*

stamp \\'stamp\\ *vb* **1** : pound with the sole of the foot or a heavy implement **2** : impress or imprint **3** : cut out with a die **4** : attach a postage stamp to ∼ *n* **1** : device for stamping **2** : act of stamping **3** : government seal showing a tax or fee has been paid

stam•pede \\stam'pēd\\ *n* : headlong rush of frightened animals ∼ *vb* **-ped•ed; -ped•ing** : flee in panic

stance \\'stans\\ *n* : way of standing

¹**stanch** \\'stȯnch, 'stänch\\ *vb* : stop the flow of (as blood)

²**stanch** *var of* STAUNCH

stan•chion \\'stanchən\\ *n* : upright support

stand \\'stand\\ *vb* **stood** \\'stu̇d\\; **stand•ing 1** : be at rest in or assume an upright position **2** : remain unchanged **3** : be steadfast **4** : maintain a relative position or rank **5** : set upright **6** : undergo or endure ∼ *n* **1** : act or place of standing, staying, or resisting **2** : sales booth **3** : structure for holding something upright **4** : group of plants growing together **5** *pl* : tiered seats **6** : opinion or viewpoint

stan•dard \\'standərd\\ *n* **1** : symbolic figure or flag **2** : model, rule, or guide **3** : upright support — **standard** *adj* — **stan•dard•i•za•tion** \\ˌstandərdə-'zāshən\\ *n* — **stan•dard•ize** \\'stan-dərdˌīz\\ *vb*

standard time *n* : time established over a region or country

stand•ing \\'standiŋ\\ *n* **1** : relative position or rank **2** : duration

stand•still *n* : state of rest

stank *past of* STINK

stan•za \\'stanzə\\ *n* : division of a poem

¹**sta•ple** \\'stāpəl\\ *n* : U-shaped wire fastener — **staple** *vb* — **sta•pler** \\-plər\\ *n*

²**staple** *n* : chief commodity or item — **staple** *adj*

star \\'stär\\ *n* **1** : celestial body visible as a point of light **2** : 5- or 6-pointed figure representing a star **3** : leading performer ∼ *vb* **-rr- 1** : mark with a star **2** : play the leading role — **star•dom** \\'stärdəm\\ *n* — **star•less** *adj* — **star•light** *n* — **star•ry** *adj*

star•board \\'stärbərd\\ *n* : right side of a ship or airplane looking forward — **starboard** *adj*

starch \\'stärch\\ *n* : nourishing carbohydrate from plants also used in adhe-

sives and laundering ∼ *vb* : stiffen with starch — **starchy** *adj*

stare \\'star\\ *vb* **stared; star•ing** : look intently with wide-open eyes — **stare** *n* — **star•er** *n*

stark \\'stärk\\ *adj* **1** : absolute **2** : severe or bleak ∼ *adv* : completely — **stark•ly** *adv*

star•ling \\'stärliŋ\\ *n* : bird related to the crows

start \\'stärt\\ *vb* **1** : twitch or jerk (as from surprise) **2** : perform or show performance of the first part of an action or process ∼ *n* **1** : sudden involuntary motion **2** : beginning — **start•er** *n*

star•tle \\'stärtᵊl\\ *vb* **-tled; -tling** : frighten or surprise suddenly

starve \\'stärv\\ *vb* **starved; starv•ing 1** : suffer or die from hunger **2** : kill with hunger — **star•va•tion** \\stär'vā-shən\\ *n*

stash \\'stash\\ *vb* : store in a secret place for future use — **stash** *n*

state \\'stāt\\ *n* **1** : condition of being **2** : condition of mind **3** : nation or a political unit within it ∼ *vb* **stat•ed; stat•ing 1** : express in words **2** : establish — **state•hood** \\-ˌhu̇d\\ *n*

state•ly \\'stātlē\\ *adj* **-li•er; -est** : having impressive dignity — **state•li•ness** *n*

state•ment \\'stātmənt\\ *n* **1** : something stated **2** : financial summary

state•room *n* : private room on a ship

states•man \\'stātsmən\\ *n* : one skilled in government or diplomacy — **states•man•like** *adj* — **states•man•ship** *n*

stat•ic \\'statik\\ *adj* **1** : relating to bodies at rest or forces in equilibrium **2** : not moving **3** : relating to stationary charges of electricity ∼ *n* : noise on radio or television from electrical disturbances

sta•tion \\'stāshən\\ *n* **1** : place of duty **2** : regular stop on a bus or train route **3** : social standing **4** : place where radio or television programs originate ∼ *vb* : assign to a station

sta•tion•ary \\'stāshəˌnerē\\ *adj* **1** : not moving or not movable **2** : not changing

sta•tio•nery \\'stāshəˌnerē\\ *n* : letter paper with envelopes

sta•tis•tic \\stə'tistik\\ *n* : single item of statistics

sta•tis•tics \\-tiks\\ *n pl* : numerical facts collected for study — **sta•tis•ti•cal**

\-tikəl\ *adj* — **sta·tis·ti·cal·ly** *adv* — **stat·is·ti·cian** \ˌstatə'stishən\ *n*

stat·u·ary \'stachəˌwerē\ *n, pl* **-ar·ies** : collection of statues

stat·ue \'stachü\ *n* : solid 3-dimensional likeness — **stat·u·ette** \ˌstachə'wet\ *n*

stat·u·esque \ˌstachə'wesk\ *adj* : tall and shapely

stat·ure \'stachər\ *n* **1** : height **2** : status gained by achievement

sta·tus \'stātəs, 'stat-\ *n* : relative situation or condition

sta·tus quo \-'kwō\ *n* : existing state of affairs

stat·ute \'stachüt\ *n* : law — **stat·u·to·ry** \'stachəˌtōrē\ *adj*

staunch \'stónch\ *adj* : steadfast — **staunch·ly** *adv*

stave \'stāv\ *n* : narrow strip of wood ~ *vb* **staved** *or* **stove** \'stōv\; **stav·ing 1** : break a hole in **2** : drive away

staves *pl of* STAFF

[1]stay \'stā\ *n* : support ~ *vb* **stayed; stay·ing** : prop up

[2]stay *vb* **stayed** \'stād\ *or* **staid** \'stād\; **stay·ing 1** : pause **2** : remain **3** : reside **4** : stop or postpone **5** : satisfy for a time ~ *n* : a staying

stead \'sted\ *n* : one's place, job, or function — **in good stead** : to advantage

stead·fast \-ˌfast\ *adj* : faithful or determined — **stead·fast·ly** *adv*

steady \'stedē\ *adj* **stead·i·er; -est 1** : firm in position or sure in movement **2** : calm or reliable **3** : constant **4** : regular ~ *vb* **stead·ied; steady·ing** : make or become steady — **steadi·ly** \'sted³lē\ *adv* — **steadi·ness** *n* — **steady** *adv*

steak \'stāk\ *n* : thick slice of meat

steal \'stēl\ *vb* **stole** \'stōl\; **sto·len** \'stōlən\; **steal·ing 1** : take and carry away wrongfully and with intent to keep **2** : move secretly or slowly

stealth \'stelth\ *n* : secret or unobtrusive procedure — **stealth·i·ly** \-thəlē\ *adv* — **stealthy** *adj*

steam \'stēm\ *n* : vapor of boiling water ~ *vb* : give off steam — **steam·boat** *n* — **steam·ship** *n* — **steamy** *adj*

steed \'stēd\ *n* : horse

steel \'stēl\ *n* : tough carbon-containing iron ~ *vb* : fill with courage — **steel** *adj* — **steely** *adj*

[1]steep \'stēp\ *adj* : having a very sharp slope or great elevation — **steep·ly** *adv* — **steep·ness** *n*

[2]steep *vb* : soak in a liquid

stee·ple \'stēpəl\ *n* : usu. tapering church tower

stee·ple·chase *n* : race over hurdles

[1]steer \'stir\ *n* : castrated ox

[2]steer *vb* **1** : direct the course of (as a ship or car) **2** : guide

steer·age \'stirij\ *n* : section in a ship for people paying the lowest fares

stein \'stīn\ *n* : mug

stel·lar \'stelər\ *adj* : relating to stars or resembling a star

[1]stem \'stem\ *n* : main upright part of a plant ~ *vb* **-mm- 1** : derive **2** : make progress against — **stem·less** *adj* — **stemmed** *adj*

[2]stem *vb* **-mm-** : stop the flow of

stem cell *n* : undifferentiated cell that may give rise to many different types of cells

stench \'stench\ *n* : stink

sten·cil \'stensəl\ *n* : printing sheet cut with letters to let ink pass through — **stencil** *vb*

ste·nog·ra·phy \stə'nägrəfē\ *n* : art or process of writing in shorthand — **ste·nog·ra·pher** \-fər\ *n* — **steno·graph·ic** \ˌstenə'grafik\ *adj*

sten·to·ri·an \sten'tōrēən\ *adj* : extremely loud and powerful

step \'step\ *n* **1** : single action of a leg in walking or running **2** : rest for the foot in going up or down **3** : degree, rank, or stage **4** : way of walking ~ *vb* **-pp- 1** : move by steps **2** : press with the foot

step- \'step-\ *comb form* : related by a remarriage and not by blood

step·lad·der *n* : light portable set of steps in a hinged frame

steppe \'step\ *n* : dry grassy treeless land esp. of Asia

-ster \stər\ *n suffix* **1** : one that does, makes, or uses **2** : one that is associated with or takes part in **3** : one that is

ste·reo \'sterēˌō, 'stir-\ *n, pl* **-reos** : stereophonic sound system — **stereo** *adj*

ste·reo·phon·ic \ˌsterēə'fänik, ˌstir-\ *adj* : relating to a 3-dimensional effect of reproduced sound

ste·reo·type \'sterēəˌtīp, 'stir-\ *n* : gross often mistaken generalization — **stereotype** *vb* — **ste·reo·typ·i·cal** \ˌsterēə'tipikəl\ *adj* — **ste·reo·typi·cal·ly** *adv*

ste·reo·typed \'sterēəˌtīpt, 'stir-\ *adj* : lacking originality or individuality

ster·ile \'sterəl\ *adj* **1** : unable to bear fruit, crops, or offspring **2** : free from disease germs — **ster·il·i·ty** \stə-'rilətē\ *n* — **ster·il·i·za·tion** \,sterələ-'zāshən\ *n* — **ster·il·ize** \-ə,līz\ *vb* — **ster·il·iz·er** *n*

ster·ling \'stərliŋ\ *adj* **1** : being or made of an alloy of 925 parts of silver with 75 parts of copper **2** : excellent

¹**stern** \'stərn\ *adj* : severe — **stern·ly** *adv* — **stern·ness** *n*

²**stern** *n* : back end of a boat

ster·num \'stərnəm\ *n, pl* **-nums** *or* **-na** \-nə\ : long flat chest bone joining the 2 sets of ribs

stetho·scope \'stethə,skōp\ *n* : instrument used for listening to sounds in the chest

ste·ve·dore \'stēvə,dōr\ *n* : worker who loads and unloads ships

stew \'stü, 'styü\ *n* **1** : dish of boiled meat and vegetables **2** : state of worry or agitation — **stew** *vb*

stew·ard \'stüərd, 'styü-\ *n* **1** : manager of an estate or an organization **2** : person on a ship or airliner who looks after passenger comfort — **stew·ard·ship** *n*

stew·ard·ess \-əs\ *n* : woman who is a steward (as on an airplane)

¹**stick** \'stik\ *n* **1** : cut or broken branch **2** : long thin piece of wood or something resembling it

²**stick** *vb* **stuck** \'stək\; **stick·ing 1** : stab **2** : thrust or project **3** : hold fast to something **4** : attach **5** : become jammed or fixed

stick·er \'stikər\ *n* : adhesive label

stick·ler \'stiklər\ *n* : one who insists on exactness or completeness

sticky \'stikē\ *adj* **stick·i·er; -est 1** : adhesive or gluey **2** : muggy **3** : difficult

stiff \'stif\ *adj* **1** : not bending easily **2** : tense **3** : formal **4** : strong **5** : severe — **stiff·en** \'stifən\ *vb* — **stiff·en·er** \-ənər\ *n* — **stiff·ly** *adv* — **stiff·ness** *n*

sti·fle \'stīfəl\ *vb* **-fled; -fling 1** : smother or suffocate **2** : suppress

stig·ma \'stigmə\ *n, pl* **-ma·ta** \stig-'mätə, 'stigmətə\ *or* **-mas** : mark of disgrace — **stig·ma·tize** \'stigmə-,tīz\ *n*

stile \'stīl\ *n* : steps for crossing a fence

sti·let·to \stə'letō\ *n, pl* **-tos** *or* **-toes** : slender dagger

¹**still** \'stil\ *adj* **1** : motionless **2** : silent — **~** *vb* : make or become still **~** *adv* **1** : without motion **2** : up to and during this time **3** : in spite of that **~** *n* : silence — **still·ness** *n*

²**still** *n* : apparatus used in distillation

still·born *adj* : born dead — **still·birth** *n*

stilt \'stilt\ *n* : one of a pair of poles for walking

stilt·ed \'stiltəd\ *adj* : not easy and natural

stim·u·lant \'stimyələnt\ *n* : substance that temporarily increases the activity of an organism — **stimulant** *adj*

stim·u·late \-,lāt\ *vb* **-lat·ed; -lat·ing** : make active — **stim·u·la·tion** \,stimyə'lāshən\ *n*

stim·u·lus \'stimyələs\ *n, pl* **-li** \-,lī\ : something that stimulates

sting \'stiŋ\ *vb* **stung** \'stəŋ\; **sting·ing 1** : prick painfully **2** : cause to suffer acutely **~** *n* : act of stinging or a resulting wound — **sting·er** *n*

stin·gy \'stinjē\ *adj* **stin·gi·er; -est** : not generous — **stin·gi·ness** *n*

stink \'stiŋk\ *vb* **stank** \'staŋk\ *or* **stunk** \'stəŋk\; **stunk; stink·ing** : have a strong offensive odor — **stink** *n* — **stink·er** *n*

stint \'stint\ *vb* : be sparing or stingy **~** *n* **1** : restraint **2** : quantity or period of work

sti·pend \'stī,pend, -pənd\ *n* : money paid periodically

stip·ple \'stipəl\ *vb* **-pled; -pling** : engrave, paint, or draw with dots instead of lines — **stipple** *n*

stip·u·late \'stipyə,lāt\ *vb* **-lat·ed; -lat·ing** : demand as a condition — **stip·u·la·tion** \,stipyə'lāshən\ *n*

stir \'stər\ *vb* **-rr- 1** : move slightly **2** : prod or push into activity **3** : mix by continued circular movement **~** *n* : act or result of stirring

stir·rup \'stərəp\ *n* : saddle loop for the foot

stitch \'stich\ *n* **1** : loop formed by a needle in sewing **2** : sudden sharp pain **~** *vb* **1** : fasten or decorate with stitches **2** : sew

stock \'stäk\ *n* **1** : block or part of wood **2** : original from which others derive **3** : farm animals **4** : supply of goods **5** : money invested in a large business **6** *pl* : instrument of punishment like a pillory with holes for the feet or feet and hands **~** *vb* : provide with stock

stock•ade \stä'kād\ *n* : defensive or confining enclosure

stock•ing \'stäkiŋ\ *n* : close-fitting covering for the foot and leg

stock•pile *n* : reserve supply — **stock•pile** *vb*

stocky \'stäkē\ *adj* **stock•i•er; -est** : short and relatively thick

stock•yard *n* : yard for livestock to be slaughtered or shipped

stodgy \'stäjē\ *adj* **stodg•i•er; -est 1** : dull **2** : old-fashioned

sto•ic \'stōik\, **sto•i•cal** \-ikəl\ *adj* : showing indifference to pain — **stoic** *n* — **sto•i•cal•ly** *adv* — **sto•i•cism** \'stōə,sizəm\ *n*

stoke \'stōk\ *vb* **stoked; stok•ing** : stir up a fire or supply fuel to a furnace — **stok•er** *n*

¹**stole** \'stōl\ *past of* STEAL

²**stole** *n* : long wide scarf

stolen *past part of* STEAL

stol•id \'stäləd\ *adj* : having or showing little or no emotion — **stol•id•ly** \'stälədlē\ *adv*

stom•ach \'stəmək, -ik\ *n* **1** : saclike digestive organ **2** : abdomen **3** : appetite or desire ~ *vb* : put up with — **stom•ach•ache** *n*

stomp \'stämp, 'stómp\ *vb* : stamp

stone \'stōn\ *n* **1** : hardened earth or mineral matter **2** : small piece of rock **3** : seed that is hard or has a hard covering ~ *vb* **stoned; ston•ing** : pelt or kill with stones — **stony** *adj*

stood *past of* STAND

stool \'stül\ *n* **1** : seat usu. without back or arms **2** : footstool **3** : discharge of feces

¹**stoop** \'stüp\ *vb* **1** : bend over **2** : lower oneself ~ *n* **1** : act of bending over **2** : bent position of shoulders

²**stoop** *n* : small porch at a house door

stop \'stäp\ *vb* **-pp- 1** : block an opening **2** : end or cause to end **3** : pause for rest or a visit in a journey ~ *n* **1** : plug **2** : act or place of stopping **3** : delay in a journey — **stop•light** *n* — **stop•page** \-ij\ *n* — **stop•per** *n*

stop•gap *n* : temporary measure or thing

stor•age \'stōrij\ *n* : safekeeping of goods (as in a warehouse)

store \'stōr\ *vb* **stored; stor•ing** : put aside for future use ~ *n* **1** : something stored **2** : retail business establishment — **store•house** *n* — **store•keep•er** *n* — **store•room** *n*

stork \'stórk\ *n* : large wading bird

storm \'stórm\ *n* **1** : heavy fall of rain or snow **2** : violent outbreak ~ *vb* **1** : rain or snow heavily **2** : rage **3** : make an attack against — **stormy** *adj*

¹**sto•ry** \'stōrē\ *n, pl* **-ries 1** : narrative **2** : report — **sto•ry•tell•er** *n*

²**story** *n, pl* **-ries** : floor of a building

stout \'staút\ *adj* **1** : firm or strong **2** : thick or bulky — **stout•ly** *adv* — **stout•ness** *n*

¹**stove** \'stōv\ *n* : apparatus for providing heat (as for cooking or heating)

²**stove** *past of* STAVE

stow \'stō\ *vb* **1** : pack in a compact mass **2** : put or hide away

strad•dle \'stradᵊl\ *vb* **-dled; -dling** : stand over or sit on with legs on opposite sides — **straddle** *n*

strafe \'strāf\ *vb* **strafed; straf•ing** : fire upon with machine guns from a low=flying airplane

strag•gle \'stragəl\ *vb* **-gled; -gling** : wander or become separated from others — **strag•gler** \-ələr\ *n*

straight \'strāt\ *adj* **1** : having no bends, turns, or twists **2** : just, proper, or honest **3** : neat and orderly ~ *adv* : in a straight manner — **straight•en** \'strātᵊn\ *vb*

straight•for•ward \strāt'fórwərd\ *adj* : frank or honest

straight•way *adv* : immediately

¹**strain** \'strān\ *n* **1** : lineage **2** : trace

²**strain** *vb* **1** : exert to the utmost **2** : filter or remove by filtering **3** : injure by improper use ~ *n* **1** : excessive tension or exertion **2** : bodily injury from excessive effort — **strain•er** *n*

strait \'strāt\ *n* **1** : narrow channel connecting 2 bodies of water **2** *pl* : distress

strait•en \'strātᵊn\ *vb* **1** : hem in **2** : make distressing or difficult

¹**strand** \'strand\ *vb* **1** : drive or cast upon the shore **2** : leave helpless

²**strand** *n* **1** : twisted fiber of a rope **2** : length of something ropelike

strange \'strānj\ *adj* **strang•er; strang•est 1** : unusual or queer **2** : new — **strange•ly** *adv* — **strange•ness** *n*

strang•er \'strānjər\ *n* : person with whom one is not acquainted

stran•gle \'straŋgəl\ *vb* **-gled; -gling** : choke to death — **stran•gler** \-glər\ *n*

stran•gu•la•tion \,straŋgyə'lāshən\ *n* : act or process of strangling

strap \\'strap\ *n* : narrow strip of flexible material used esp. for fastening ~ *vb* **1** : secure with a strap **2** : beat with a strap — **strap•less** *n*

strap•ping \\'strapiŋ\ *adj* : robust

strat•a•gem \\'stratəjəm, -ˌjem\ *n* : deceptive scheme or maneuver

strat•e•gy \\'stratəjē\ *n, pl* **-gies** : carefully worked out plan of action — **strate•gic** \strə'tējik\ *adj* — **strat•e•gist** \\'stratəjist\ *n*

strat•i•fy \\'stratəˌfī\ *vb* **-fied; -fy•ing** : form or arrange in layers — **strat•i•fi•ca•tion** \ˌstratəfə'kāshən\ *n*

strato•sphere \\'stratəˌsfir\ *n* : earth's atmosphere from about 7 to 31 miles above the surface

stra•tum \\'strātəm, 'strat-\ *n, pl* **-ta** \\'strātə, 'strat-\ : layer

straw \\'strȯ\ *n* **1** : grass stems after grain is removed **2** : tube for drinking ~ *adj* : made of straw

straw•ber•ry \\'strȯˌberē\ *n* : juicy red pulpy fruit

stray \\'strā\ *vb* : wander or deviate ~ *n* : person or animal that strays ~ *adj* : separated from or not related to anything close by

streak \\'strēk\ *n* **1** : mark of a different color **2** : narrow band of light **3** : trace **4** : run (as of luck) or series ~ *vb* **1** : form streaks in or on **2** : move fast

stream \\'strēm\ *n* **1** : flow of water on land **2** : steady flow (as of water or air) ~ *vb* **1** : flow in a stream **2** : pour out streams

stream•er \\'strēmər\ *n* : long ribbon or ribbonlike flag

stream•lined \-ˌlīnd, -'līnd\ *adj* **1** : made with contours to reduce air or water resistance **2** : simplified **3** : modernized — **streamline** *vb*

street \\'strēt\ *n* : thoroughfare esp. in a city or town

street•car *n* : passenger vehicle running on rails in the streets

strength \\'streŋth\ *n* **1** : quality of being strong **2** : toughness **3** : intensity

strength•en \\'streŋthən\ *vb* : make, grow, or become stronger — **strength•en•er** \\'streŋthənər\ *n*

stren•u•ous \\'strenyəwəs\ *adj* **1** : vigorous **2** : requiring or showing energy — **stren•u•ous•ly** *adv*

stress \\'stres\ *n* **1** : pressure or strain that tends to distort a body **2** : relative prominence given to one thing among others **3** : state of physical or mental tension or something inducing it ~ *vb* : put stress on — **stress•ful** \\'stresfəl\ *adj*

stretch \\'strech\ *vb* **1** : spread or reach out **2** : draw out in length or breadth **3** : make taut **4** : exaggerate **5** : become extended without breaking ~ *n* : act of extending beyond normal limits

stretch•er \\'strechər\ *n* : device for carrying a sick or injured person

strew \\'strü\ *vb* **strewed; strewed** *or* **strewn** \\'strün\; **strew•ing** **1** : scatter **2** : cover by scattering something over

strick•en \\'strikən\ *adj* : afflicted with disease

strict \\'strikt\ *adj* **1** : allowing no escape or evasion **2** : precise — **strict•ly** *adv* — **strict•ness** *n*

stric•ture \\'strikchər\ *n* : hostile criticism

stride \\'strīd\ *vb* **strode** \\'strōd\; **strid•den** \\'strid°n\; **strid•ing** : walk or run with long steps ~ *n* **1** : long step **2** : manner of striding

stri•dent \\'strīd°nt\ *adj* : loud and harsh

strife \\'strīf\ *n* : conflict

strike \\'strīk\ *vb* **struck** \\'strək\; **struck; strik•ing** \\'strīkiŋ\ **1** : hit sharply **2** : delete **3** : produce by impressing **4** : cause to sound **5** : afflict **6** : occur to or impress **7** : cause (a match) to ignite by rubbing **8** : refrain from working **9** : find **10** : take on (as a pose) ~ *n* **1** : act or instance of striking **2** : work stoppage **3** : military attack — **strik•er** *n* —

strike out *vb* : start out vigorously —

strike up *vb* : start

strik•ing \\'strīkiŋ\ *adj* : very noticeable — **strik•ing•ly** *adv*

string \\'striŋ\ *n* **1** : line usu. of twisted threads **2** : series **3** *pl* : stringed instruments ~ *vb* **strung** \\'strəŋ\; **string•ing** **1** : thread on or with a string **2** : hang or fasten by a string

stringed \\'striŋd\ *adj* : having strings

strin•gent \\'strinjənt\ *adj* : severe

stringy \\'striŋē\ *adj* **string•i•er; -est** : tough or fibrous

¹strip \\'strip\ *vb* **-pp-** **1** : take the covering or clothing from **2** : undress — **strip•per** *n*

²strip *n* : long narrow flat piece

stripe \\'strīp\ *n* : distinctive line or long narrow section ~ *vb* **striped**

\'strīpt\; **strip•ing** : make stripes on
— **striped** \'strīpt, 'strīpəd\ *adj*
strive \'strīv\ *vb* **strove** \'strōv\; **stri•ven** \'strivən\ *or* **strived; striv•ing**
\'strīviŋ\ **1** : struggle **2** : try hard
strode *past of* STRIDE
stroke \'strōk\ *vb* **stroked; strok•ing**
: rub gently ～ *n* **1** : act of swinging
or striking **2** : sudden action
stroll \'strōl\ *vb* : walk leisurely —
stroll *n* — **stroll•er** *n*
strong \'stròŋ\ *adj* **1** : capable of exerting great force or of withstanding
stress or violence **2** : healthy **3**
: zealous — **strong•ly** *adv*
strong•hold *n* : fortified place
struck *past of* STRIKE
struc•ture \'strəkchər\ *n* **1** : building
2 : arrangement of elements ～ *vb*
-tured; -tur•ing : make into a structure — **struc•tur•al** \-chərəl\ *adj*
strug•gle \'strəgəl\ *vb* **-gled; -gling 1**
: make strenuous efforts to overcome an adversary **2** : proceed with
great effort ～ *n* **1** : strenuous effort
2 : intense competition for superiority
strum \'strəm\ *vb* **-mm-** : play (a musical
instrument) by brushing the strings
with the fingers
strum•pet \'strəmpət\ *n* : prostitute
strung *past of* STRING
strut \'strət\ *vb* **-tt-** : walk in a proud or
showy manner ～ *n* **1** : proud walk **2**
: supporting bar or rod
strych•nine \'strik,nīn, -nən, -,nēn\ *n*
: bitter poisonous substance
stub \'stəb\ *n* : short end or section ～
vb **-bb-** : strike against something
stub•ble \'stəbəl\ *n* : short growth left
after cutting — **stub•bly** *adj*
stub•born \'stəbərn\ *adj* **1** : determined not to yield **2** : hard to control
— **stub•born•ly** *adv* — **stub•born•ness** *n*
stub•by \'stəbē\ *adj* : short, blunt, and
thick
stuc•co \'stəkō\ *n, pl* **-cos** *or* **-coes**
: plaster for coating outside walls —
stuc•coed \'stəkōd\ *adj*
stuck *past of* STICK
stuck–up \'stək'əp\ *adj* : conceited
¹**stud** \'stəd\ *n* : male horse kept for
breeding
²**stud** *n* **1** : upright beam for holding
wall material **2** : projecting nail, pin,
or rod ～ *vb* **-dd-** : supply or dot with
studs

stu•dent \'stüd³nt, 'styü-\ *n* : one who
studies
stud•ied \'stədēd\ *adj* : premeditated
stu•dio \'stüdē,ō, 'styü-\ *n, pl* **-dios 1**
: artist's workroom **2** : place where
movies are made or television or radio shows are broadcast
stu•di•ous \'stüdēəs, 'styü-\ *adj* : devoted to study — **stu•di•ous•ly** *adv*
study \'stədē\ *n, pl* **stud•ies 1** : act or
process of learning about something
2 : branch of learning **3** : careful examination **4** : room for reading or
studying ～ *vb* **stud•ied; study•ing**
: apply the attention and mind to a
subject
stuff \'stəf\ *n* **1** : personal property **2**
: raw or fundamental material **3** : unspecified material or things ～ *vb*
: fill by packing things in — **stuff•ing** *n*
stuffy \'stəfē\ *adj* **stuff•i•er; -est 1**
: lacking fresh air **2** : unimaginative
or pompous
stul•ti•fy \'stəltə,fī\ *vb* **-fied; -fy•ing 1**
: cause to appear foolish **2** : impair or
make ineffective **3** : have a dulling
effect on
stum•ble \'stəmbəl\ *vb* **-bled; -bling
1** : lose one's balance or fall in walking
or running **2** : speak or act clumsily
3 : happen by chance — **stumble** *n*
stump \'stəmp\ *n* : part left when
something is cut off ～ *vb* : confuse
— **stumpy** *adj*
stun \'stən\ *vb* **-nn- 1** : make senseless
or dizzy by or as if by a blow **2** : bewilder
stung *past of* STING
stunk *past of* STINK
stun•ning \'stəniŋ\ *adj* **1** : astonishing
or incredible **2** : strikingly beautiful
— **stun•ning•ly** *adv*
¹**stunt** \'stənt\ *vb* : hinder the normal
growth or progress of
²**stunt** *n* : spectacular feat
stu•pe•fy \'stüpə,fī, 'styü-\ *vb* **-fied;
-fy•ing 1** : make insensible by or as if
by drugs **2** : amaze
stu•pen•dous \stù'pendəs, styù-\ *adj*
: very big or impressive — **stu•pendous•ly** *adv*
stu•pid \'stüpəd, 'styü-\ *adj* : not sensible or intelligent — **stu•pid•i•ty** \stù-'pidətē, styü-\ *n* — **stu•pid•ly** *adv*
stu•por \'stüpər, 'styü-\ *n* : state of
being conscious but not aware or sensible
stur•dy \'stərdē\ *adj* **-di•er; -est**

: strong — **stur•di•ly** \\'stərd°lē\\ *adv*
— **stur•di•ness** *n*

stur•geon \\'stərjən\\ *n* : fish whose roe is caviar

stut•ter \\'stətər\\ *vb or n* : stammer

¹sty \\'stī\\ *n, pl* **sties** : pig pen

²sty, stye \\'stī\\ *n, pl* **sties** *or* **styes** : inflamed swelling on the edge of an eyelid

style \\'stīl\\ *n* **1** : distinctive way of speaking, writing, or acting **2** : elegant or fashionable way of living ~ *vb* **styled; styl•ing 1** : name **2** : give a particular design or style to — **styl•ish** \\'stīlish\\ *adj* — **styl•ish•ly** *adv* — **styl•ish•ness** *n* — **styl•ist** \\-ist\\ *n* — **styl•ize** \\'stīəl,īz\\ *vb*

sty•lus \\'stīləs\\ *n, pl* **-li** \\'stīl,ī\\ **1** : pointed writing tool **2** : phonograph needle

sty•mie \\'stīmē\\ *vb* **-mied; -mie•ing** : block or frustrate

suave \\'swäv\\ *adj* : well-mannered and gracious — **suave•ly** *adv*

¹sub \\'səb\\ *n or vb* : substitute

²sub *n* : submarine

sub- \\,səb, 'səb\\ *prefix* **1** : under or beneath **2** : subordinate or secondary **3** : subordinate portion of **4** : with repetition of a process so as to form, stress, or deal with subordinate parts or relations **5** : somewhat **6** : nearly

sub•con•scious \\,səb'känchəs\\ *adj* : existing without conscious awareness ~ *n* : part of the mind concerned with subconscious activities — **sub•con•scious•ly** *adv*

sub•di•vide \\,səbdə'vīd, 'səbdə,vīd\\ *vb* **1** : divide into several parts **2** : divide (land) into building lots — **sub•di•vi•sion** \\-'vizhən, -,vizh-\\ *n*

sub•due \\səb'dü, -'dyü\\ *vb* **-dued;**

-du•ing 1 : bring under control **2** : reduce the intensity of

sub•ject \\'səbjikt\\ *n* **1** : person under the authority of another **2** : something being discussed or studied **3** : word or word group about which something is said in a sentence ~ *adj* **1** : being under one's authority **2** : prone **3** : dependent on some condition or act ~ \\səb'jekt\\ *vb* **1** : bring under control **2** : cause to undergo — **sub•jec•tion** \\-'jekshən\\ *n*

sub•jec•tive \\,səb'jektiv\\ *adj* : deriving from an individual viewpoint or bias — **sub•jec•tive•ly** *adv* — **sub•jec•tiv•i•ty** \\-,jek'tivətē\\ *n*

sub•ju•gate \\'səbji,gāt\\ *vb* **-gat•ed; -gat•ing** : bring under one's control — **sub•ju•ga•tion** \\,səbji'gāshən\\ *n*

sub•junc•tive \\səb'jənktiv\\ *adj* : relating to a verb form which expresses possibility or contingency — **sub•junctive** *n*

sub•let \\'səb,let\\ *vb* **-let; -let•ting** : rent (a property) from a lessee

sub•lime \\sə'blīm\\ *adj* : splendid — **sub•lime•ly** *adv*

sub•ma•rine \\'səbmə,rēn, ,səbmə'-\\ *adj* : existing, acting, or growing under the sea ~ *n* : underwater boat

sub•merge \\səb'mərj\\ *vb* **-merged; -merg•ing** : put or plunge under the surface of water — **sub•mer•gence** \\-'mərjəns\\ *n* — **sub•mers•ible** \\səb-'mərsəbəl\\ *adj or n* — **sub•mer•sion** \\-'mərzhən\\ *n*

sub•mit \\səb'mit\\ *vb* **-tt- 1** : yield **2** : give or offer — **sub•mis•sion** \\-'mishən\\ *n* — **sub•mis•sive** \\-'misiv\\ *adj*

sub•nor•mal \\,səb'nórməl\\ *adj* : falling below what is normal

sub•or•di•nate \\sə'bórd°nət\\ *adj* : lower

List of self-explanatory words with the prefix *sub-*

subacute
subagency
subagent
subarctic
subarea
subatmospheric
subaverage
subbase
subbasement
subbranch
subcabinet

subcategory
subclass
subclassification
subclassify
subcommission
subcommittee
subcommunity
subcomponent
subcontract
subcontractor
subculture

subdean
subdepartment
subdistrict
subentry
subfamily
subfreezing
subgroup
subhead
subheading
subhuman
subindex

in rank ~ *n* : one that is subordinate ~ \sə'bȯrdᵊn,āt\ *vb* **-nat•ed; -nat•ing** : place in a lower rank or class — **sub•or•di•na•tion** \-,bȯrdᵊn'āshən\ *n*

sub•poe•na \sə'pēnə\ *n* : summons to appear in court ~ *vb* **-naed; -na•ing** : summon with a subpoena

sub•scribe \səb'skrīb\ *vb* **-scribed; -scrib•ing 1** : give consent or approval **2** : agree to support or to receive and pay for — **sub•scrib•er** *n*

sub•scrip•tion \səb'skripshən\ *n* : order for regular receipt of a publication

sub•se•quent \'səbsikwənt, -sə,kwent\ *adj* : following after — **sub•se•quent•ly** \-,kwentlē, -kwənt-\ *adv*

sub•ser•vi•ence \səb'sərvēəns\ *n* : obsequious submission — **sub•ser•vi•ent** \-ənt\ *adj*

sub•side \səb'sīd\ *vb* **-sid•ed; -sid•ing** : die down in intensity

sub•sid•iary \səb'sidē,erē\ *adj* **1** : furnishing support **2** : of secondary importance ~ *n* : company controlled by another company

sub•si•dize \'səbsə,dīz\ *vb* **-dized; -diz•ing** : aid with a subsidy

sub•si•dy \'səbsədē\ *n, pl* **-dies** : gift of supporting funds

sub•sist \səb'sist\ *vb* : acquire the necessities of life — **sub•sis•tence** \-'sistəns\ *n*

sub•stance \'səbstəns\ *n* **1** : essence or essential part **2** : physical material **3** : wealth

sub•stan•dard \,səb'standərd\ *adj* : falling short of a standard or norm

sub•stan•tial \səb'stanchəl\ *adj* **1** : plentiful **2** : considerable — **sub•stan•tial•ly** *adv*

sub•stan•ti•ate \səb'stanchē,āt\ *vb* **-at•ed; -at•ing** : verify — **sub•stan•ti•a•tion** \-,stanchē'āshən\ *n*

sub•sti•tute \'səbstə,tüt, -,tyüt\ *n* : replacement ~ *vb* **-tut•ed; -tut•ing** : put or serve in place of another — **substitute** *adj* — **sub•sti•tu•tion** \,səbstə'tüshən, -'tyü-\ *n*

sub•ter•fuge \'səbtər,fyüj\ *n* : deceptive trick

sub•ter•ra•nean \,səbtə'rānēən\ *adj* : lying or being underground

sub•ti•tle \'səb,tītᵊl\ *n* : movie caption

sub•tle \'sətᵊl\ *adj* **-tler** \-ər\; **-tlest** \-ist\ **1** : hardly noticeable **2** : clever — **sub•tle•ty** \-tē\ *n* — **sub•tly** \-ᵊlē\ *adv*

sub•tract \səb'trakt\ *vb* : take away (as one number from another) — **sub•trac•tion** \-'trakshən\ *n*

sub•urb \'səb,ərb\ *n* : residential area adjacent to a city — **sub•ur•ban** \sə'bərbən\ *adj or n* — **sub•ur•ban•ite** \-bə,nīt\ *n*

sub•vert \səb'vərt\ *vb* : overthrow or ruin — **sub•ver•sion** \-'vərzhən\ *n* — **sub•ver•sive** \-'vərsiv\ *adj*

sub•way \'səb,wā\ *n* : underground electric railway

suc•ceed \sək'sēd\ *vb* **1** : follow (someone) in a job, role, or title **2** : attain a desired object or end

suc•cess \-'ses\ *n* **1** : favorable outcome **2** : gaining of wealth and fame **3** : one that succeeds — **suc•cess•ful** \-fəl\ *adj* — **suc•cess•ful•ly** *adv*

suc•ces•sion \sək'seshən\ *n* **1** : order, act, or right of succeeding **2** : series

suc•ces•sive \-'sesiv\ *adj* : following in order — **suc•ces•sive•ly** *adv*

suc•ces•sor \-'sesər\ *n* : one that succeeds another

suc•cinct \sək'siŋkt, sə'siŋkt\ *adj* : brief — **suc•cinct•ly** *adv* — **suc•cinct•ness** *n*

suc•cor \'səkər\ *n or vb* : help

suc·co·tash \'səkə,tash\ *n* : beans and corn cooked together

suc·cu·lent \'səkyələnt\ *adj* : juicy — **suc·cu·lence** \-ləns\ *n* — **succu·lent** *n*

suc·cumb \sə'kəm\ *vb* **1** : yield **2** : die

such \'səch\ *adj* **1** : of this or that kind **2** : having a specified quality — **such** *pron or adv*

suck \'sək\ *vb* **1** : draw in liquid with the mouth **2** : draw liquid from by or as if by mouth — **suck** *n*

suck·er \'səkər\ *n* **1** : one that sucks or clings **2** : easily deceived person

suck·le \'səkəl\ *vb* **-led; -ling** : give or draw milk from the breast or udder

suck·ling \'səkliŋ\ *n* : young unweaned mammal

su·crose \'sü,krōs, -,krōz\ *n* : cane or beet sugar

suc·tion \'səkshən\ *n* **1** : act of sucking **2** : act or process of drawing in by partially exhausting the air

sud·den \'səd⁴n\ *adj* **1** : happening unexpectedly **2** : steep **3** : hasty — **sud·den·ly** *adv* — **sud·den·ness** *n*

suds \'sədz\ *n pl* : soapy water esp. when frothy — **sudsy** \'sədzē\ *adj*

sue \'sü\ *vb* **sued; su·ing** **1** : petition **2** : bring legal action against

suede, suède \'swād\ *n* : leather with a napped surface

su·et \'süət\ *n* : hard beef fat

suf·fer \'səfər\ *vb* **1** : experience pain, loss, or hardship **2** : permit — **suf·fer·er** *n*

suf·fer·ing \-əriŋ\ *n* : pain or hardship

suf·fice \sə'fīs\ *vb* **-ficed; -fic·ing** : be sufficient

suf·fi·cient \sə'fishənt\ *adj* : adequate — **suf·fi·cien·cy** \-ənsē\ *n* — **suf·ficient·ly** *adv*

suf·fix \'səf,iks\ *n* : letters added at the end of a word — **suffix** \'səfiks, sə'fiks\ *vb* — **suf·fix·a·tion** \,səf,ik-'sāshən\ *n*

suf·fo·cate \'səfə,kāt\ *vb* **-cat·ed; -cat·ing** : suffer or die or cause to die from lack of air — **suf·fo·cat·ing·ly** *adv* — **suf·fo·ca·tion** \,səfə'kā-shən\ *n*

suf·frage \'səfrij\ *n* : right to vote

suf·fuse \sə'fyüz\ *vb* **-fused; -fus·ing** : spread over or through

sug·ar \'shùgər\ *n* : sweet substance — *vb* : mix, cover, or sprinkle with sugar — **sug·ar·cane** *n* — **sug·ary** *adj*

sug·gest \sə'jest, səg-\ *vb* **1** : put into someone's mind **2** : remind one by association of ideas — **sug·gest·ible** \-'jestəbəl\ *adj* — **sug·ges·tion** \'jeschən\ *n*

sug·ges·tive \-'jestiv\ *adj* : suggesting something improper — **sug·ges·tive·ly** *adv* — **sug·ges·tive·ness** *n*

sui·cide \'süə,sīd\ *n* **1** : act of killing oneself purposely **2** : one who commits suicide — **sui·cid·al** \,süə-'sīd⁴l\ *adj*

suit \'süt\ *n* **1** : action in court to recover a right or claim **2** : number of things used or worn together **3** : one of the 4 sets of playing cards ~ *vb* **1** : be appropriate or becoming to **2** : meet the needs of — **suit·abil·i·ty** \,sütə-'bilətē\ *n* — **suit·able** \'sütəbəl\ *adj* — **suit·ably** *adv*

suit·case *n* : case for a traveler's clothing

suite \'swēt, *for 2 also* 'süt\ *n* **1** : group of rooms **2** : set of matched furniture

suit·or \'sütər\ *n* : one who seeks to marry a woman

sul·fur \'səlfər\ *n* : nonmetallic yellow chemical element — **sul·fu·ric** \,səl-'fyùrik\ *adj* — **sul·fu·rous** \-'fyùrəs, 'səlfərəs, 'səlfyə-\ *adj*

sulk \'səlk\ *vb* : be moodily silent or irritable — **sulk** *n*

sulky \'səlkē\ *adj* : inclined to sulk ~ *n* : light 2-wheeled horse-drawn cart — **sulk·i·ly** \'səlkəlē\ *adv* — **sulk·i·ness** \-kēnəs\ *n*

sul·len \'sələn\ *adj* **1** : gloomily silent **2** : dismal — **sul·len·ly** *adv* — **sul·len·ness** *n*

sul·ly \'səlē\ *vb* **-lied; -ly·ing** : cast doubt or disgrace on

sul·tan \'səlt³n\ *n* : sovereign of a Muslim state — **sul·tan·ate** \-,āt\ *n*

sul·try \'səltrē\ *adj* **-tri·er; -est** **1** : very hot and moist **2** : sexually arousing

sum \'səm\ *n* **1** : amount **2** : gist **3** : result of addition ~ *vb* **-mm-** : find the sum of

su·mac \'shü,mak, 'sü-\ *n* : shrub with spikes of berries

sum·ma·ry \'səmərē\ *adj* **1** : concise **2** : done without delay or formality ~ *n, pl* **-ries** : concise statement — **sum·mar·i·ly** \sə'merəlē, 'səmərəlē\ *adv* — **sum·ma·rize** \'səmə,rīz\ *vb*

sum·ma·tion \sə'māshən\ *n* : a summing up esp. in court

sum·mer \'səmər\ *n* : season in which

the sun shines most directly — **sum-mery** *adj*

sum·mit \'səmət\ *n* **1** : highest point **2** : high-level conference

sum·mon \'səmən\ *vb* **1** : send for or call together **2** : order to appear in court — **sum·mon·er** *n*

sum·mons \'səmənz\ *n, pl* **summons·es** : an order to answer charges in court

sump·tu·ous \'səmpchəwəs\ *adj* : lavish

sun \'sən\ *n* **1** : shining celestial body around which the planets revolve **2** : light of the sun ∼ *vb* **-nn-** : expose to the sun — **sun·beam** *n* — **sun·block** *n* — **sun·burn** *n or vb* — **sun·glass-es** *n pl* — **sun·light** *n* — **sun·ny** *adj* — **sun·rise** *n* — **sun·set** *n* — **sun·shine** *n* — **sun·tan** *n*

sun·dae \'səndē\ *n* : ice cream with topping

Sun·day \'səndā, -dē\ *n* : 1st day of the week

sun·di·al \-ˌdīəl\ *n* : device for showing time by the sun's shadow

sun·dries \'səndrēz\ *n pl* : various small articles

sun·dry \-drē\ *adj* : several

sun·fish *n* : perchlike freshwater fish

sun·flow·er *n* : tall plant grown for its oil-rich seeds

sung *past of* SING

sunk *past of* SINK

sunk·en \'səŋkən\ *adj* **1** : submerged **2** : fallen in

sun·spot *n* : dark spot on the sun

sun·stroke *n* : heatstroke from the sun

sup \'səp\ *vb* **-pp-** : eat the evening meal

super \'süpər\ *adj* : very fine

super- \ˌsüpər, 'sü-\ *prefix* **1** : higher in quantity, quality, or degree than **2** : in addition **3** : exceeding a norm **4** : in excessive degree or intensity **5** : surpassing others of its kind **6** : situated above, on, or at the top of **7** : more inclusive than **8** : superior in status or position

su·perb \su̇'pərb\ *adj* : outstanding — **su·perb·ly** *adv*

su·per·cil·ious \ˌsüpər'silēəs\ *adj* : haughtily contemptuous

su·per·fi·cial \ˌsüpər'fishəl\ *adj* : relating to what is only apparent — **su·per·fi·ci·al·i·ty** \-ˌfishē'alətē\ *n* — **su·per·fi·cial·ly** *adv*

su·per·flu·ous \su̇'pərfləwəs\ *adj* : more than necessary — **su·per·flu·i·ty** \ˌsüpər'flüətē\ *n*

su·per·im·pose \ˌsüpərim'pōz\ *vb* : lay over or above something

su·per·in·tend \ˌsüpərin'tend\ *vb* : have charge and oversight of — **su·per·in·ten·dence** \-'tendəns\ *n* — **su·per·in·ten·den·cy** \-dənsē\ *n* — **su·per·in·ten·dent** \-dənt\ *n*

su·pe·ri·or \su̇'pirēər\ *adj* **1** : higher, better, or more important **2** : haughty — **superior** *n* — **su·pe·ri·or·i·ty** \-ˌpirē'ȯrətē\ *n*

su·per·la·tive \su̇'pərlətiv\ *adj* **1** : relating to or being an adjective or adverb form that denotes an extreme level **2** : surpassing others — **superlative** *n* — **su·per·la·tive·ly** *adv*

su·per·mar·ket \'süpərˌmärkət\ *n* : self-service grocery store

---

List of self-explanatory words with the prefix *super-*

superabundance	supergovernment	superport
superabundant	supergroup	superpowerful
superambitious	superhero	superrich
superathlete	superheroine	supersalesman
superbomb	superhuman	superscout
superclean	superintellectual	supersecrecy
supercolossal	superintelligence	supersecret
superconvenient	superintelligent	supersensitive
supercop	superman	supersize
superdense	supermodern	supersized
supereffective	superpatriot	superslick
superefficiency	superpatriotic	supersmooth
superefficient	superpatriotism	supersoft
superfast	superplane	superspecial
supergood	superpolite	superspecialist

su·per·nat·u·ral \ˌsüpər'nachərəl\ *adj* : beyond the observable physical world — **su·per·nat·u·ral·ly** *adv*

su·per·pow·er \'süpərˌpaủər\ *n* : politically and militarily dominant nation

su·per·sede \ˌsüpər'sēd\ *vb* **-sed·ed; sed·ing** : take the place of

su·per·son·ic \-'sänik\ *adj* : faster than the speed of sound

su·per·sti·tion \ˌsüpər'stishən\ *n* : beliefs based on ignorance, fear of the unknown, or trust in magic — **su·per·sti·tious** \-əs\ *adj*

su·per·struc·ture \'süpərˌstrəkchər\ *n* : something built on a base or as a vertical extension

su·per·vise \'süpərˌvīz\ *vb* **-vised; -vis·ing** : have charge of — **su·per·vi·sion** \ˌsüpər'vizhən\ *n* — **su·per·vi·sor** \'süpərˌvīzər\ *n* — **su·per·vi·so·ry** \ˌsüpər'vīzərē\ *adj*

su·pine \sủ'pīn\ *adj* **1** : lying on the back **2** : indifferent or abject

sup·per \'səpər\ *n* : evening meal

sup·plant \sə'plant\ *vb* : take the place of

sup·ple \'səpəl\ *adj* **-pler; -plest** : able to bend easily

sup·ple·ment \'səpləmənt\ *n* : something that adds to or makes up for a lack — **supplement** *vb* — **sup·ple·men·tal** \ˌsəplə'mentᵊl\ *adj* — **sup·ple·men·ta·ry** \-'mentərē\ *adj*

sup·pli·ant \'səplēənt\ *n* : one who supplicates

sup·pli·cate \'səpləˌkāt\ *vb* **-cat·ed; -cat·ing** **1** : pray to God **2** : ask earnestly and humbly — **sup·pli·cant** \-likənt\ *n* — **sup·pli·ca·tion** \ˌsəplə'kāshən\ *n*

sup·ply \sə'plī\ *vb* **-plied; -ply·ing** : furnish ~ *n, pl* **-plies** **1** : amount needed or available **2** *pl* : provisions — **sup·pli·er** \-'plīər\ *n*

sup·port \sə'pōrt\ *vb* **1** : take sides with **2** : provide with food, clothing, and shelter **3** : hold up or serve as a foundation for — **support** *n* — **sup·port·able** *adj* — **sup·port·er** *n*

sup·pose \sə'pōz\ *vb* **-posed; -pos**ing **1** : assume to be true **2** : expect **3** : think probable — **sup·po·si·tion** \ˌsəpə'zishən\ *n*

sup·pos·i·to·ry \sə'päzəˌtōrē\ *n, pl* **-ries** : medicated material for insertion (as into the rectum)

sup·press \sə'pres\ *vb* **1** : put an end to by authority **2** : keep from being known **3** : hold back — **sup·pres·sant** \sə'presᵊnt\ *n* — **sup·pres·sion** \-'preshən\ *n*

su·prem·a·cy \sủ'preməsē\ *n, pl* **-cies** : supreme power or authority

su·preme \sủ'prēm\ *adj* **1** : highest in rank or authority **2** : greatest possible — **su·preme·ly** *adv*

Supreme Being *n* : God

sur·charge \'sərˌchärj\ *n* **1** : excessive load or burden **2** : extra fee or cost

sure \'shủr\ *adj* **sur·er; sur·est** **1** : confident **2** : reliable **3** : not to be disputed **4** : bound to happen ~ *adv* : surely — **sure·ness** *n*

sure·ly \'shủrlē\ *adv* **1** : in a sure manner **2** : without doubt **3** : indeed

sure·ty \'shủrətē\ *n, pl* **-ties** **1** : guarantee **2** : one who gives a guarantee for another person

surf \'sərf\ *n* : waves that break on the shore ~ *vb* : ride the surf — **surf·board** *n* — **surf·er** *n* — **surf·ing** *n*

sur·face \'sərfəs\ *n* **1** : the outside of an object **2** : outward aspect ~ *vb* **-faced; -fac·ing** : rise to the surface

sur·feit \'sərfət\ *n* **1** : excess **2** : excessive indulgence (as in food or drink) **3** : disgust caused by excess ~ *vb* : feed, supply, or indulge to the point of surfeit

surge \'sərj\ *vb* **surged; surg·ing** : rise and fall in or as if in waves ~ *n* : sudden increase

sur·geon \'sərjən\ *n* : physician who specializes in surgery

sur·gery \'sərjərē\ *n, pl* **-ger·ies** : medical treatment involving cutting open the body

sur·gi·cal \'sərjikəl\ *adj* : relating to surgeons or surgery — **sur·gi·cal·ly** *adv*

superspy	superstrong	superthin
superstar	supersystem	supertight
superstate	supertanker	superweapon
superstrength	superthick	superwoman

sur·ly \'sərlē\ *adj* **-li·er; -est** : having a rude nature — **sur·li·ness** *n*

sur·mise \sər'mīz\ *vb* **-mised; -mis·ing** : guess — **surmise** *n*

sur·mount \-'maůnt\ *vb* **1** : prevail over **2** : get to or be the top of

sur·name \'sər,nām\ *n* : family name

sur·pass \sər'pas\ *vb* : go beyond or exceed — **sur·pass·ing·ly** *adv*

sur·plice \'sərpləs\ *n* : loose white outer ecclesiastical vestment

sur·plus \'sər,pləs\ *n* : quantity left over

sur·prise \sə'prīz, sər-\ *vb* **-prised; -pris·ing** **1** : come upon or affect unexpectedly **2** : amaze — **surprise** *n* — **sur·pris·ing** *adj* — **sur·pris·ing·ly** *adv*

sur·ren·der \sə'rendər\ *vb* : give up oneself or a possession to another ~ *n* : act of surrendering

sur·rep·ti·tious \,sərəp'tishəs\ *adj* : done, made, or acquired by stealth — **sur·rep·ti·tious·ly** *adv*

sur·rey \'sərē\ *n, pl* **-reys** : horse-drawn carriage

sur·ro·gate \'sərəgāt, -gət\ *n* : substitute

sur·round \sə'raůnd\ *vb* : enclose on all sides

sur·round·ings \sə'raůndiŋz\ *n pl* : objects, conditions, or area around something

sur·veil·lance \sər'vāləns, -'vālyəns, -'vāəns\ *n* : careful watch

sur·vey \sər'vā\ *vb* **-veyed; -vey·ing** **1** : look over and examine closely **2** : make a survey of (as a tract of land) ~ \'sər,-\ *n, pl* **-veys** **1** : inspection **2** : process of measuring (as land) — **sur·vey·or** \-ər\ *n*

sur·vive \sər'vīv\ *vb* **-vived; -viv·ing** **1** : remain alive or in existence **2** : outlive or outlast — **sur·viv·al** *n* — **sur·vi·vor** \-'vīvər\ *n*

sus·cep·ti·ble \sə'septəbəl\ *adj* : likely to allow or be affected by something — **sus·cep·ti·bil·i·ty** \-,septə'bilətē\ *n*

sus·pect \'səs,pekt, sə'spekt\ *adj* **1** : regarded with suspicion **2** : questionable ~ \'səs,pekt\ *n* : one who is suspected (as of a crime) ~ \sə'spekt\ *vb* **1** : have doubts of **2** : believe guilty without proof **3** : guess

sus·pend \sə'spend\ *vb* **1** : temporarily stop or keep from a function or job **2** : withhold (judgment) temporarily **3** : hang

sus·pend·er \sə'spendər\ *n* : one of 2 supporting straps holding up trousers and passing over the shoulders

sus·pense \sə'spens\ *n* : excitement and uncertainty as to outcome — **suspense·ful** *adj*

sus·pen·sion \sə'spenchən\ *n* : act of suspending or the state or period of being suspended

sus·pi·cion \sə'spishən\ *n* **1** : act of suspecting something **2** : trace

sus·pi·cious \-əs\ *adj* **1** : arousing suspicion **2** : inclined to suspect — **sus·pi·cious·ly** *adv*

sus·tain \sə'stān\ *vb* **1** : provide with nourishment **2** : keep going **3** : hold up **4** : suffer **5** : support or prove

sus·te·nance \'səstənəns\ *n* **1** : nourishment **2** : something that sustains or supports

svelte \'sfelt\ *adj* : slender and graceful

swab \'swäb\ *n* **1** : mop **2** : wad of absorbent material for applying medicine ~ *vb* **-bb-** : use a swab on

swad·dle \'swäd°l\ *vb* **-dled; -dling** \'swäd°liŋ\ : bind (an infant) in bands of cloth

swag·ger \'swagər\ *vb* **-gered; -ger·ing** **1** : walk with a conceited swing **2** : boast — **swagger** *n*

¹**swal·low** \'swälō\ *n* : small migratory bird

²**swallow** *vb* **1** : take into the stomach through the throat **2** : envelop or take in **3** : accept too easily — **swallow** *n*

swam *past of* SWIM

swamp \'swämp\ *n* : wet spongy land ~ *vb* : deluge (as with water) — **swampy** *adj*

swan \'swän\ *n* : white long-necked swimming bird

swap \'swäp\ *vb* **-pp-** : trade — **swap** *n*

swarm \'swȯrm\ *n* **1** : mass of honeybees leaving a hive to start a new colony **2** : large crowd ~ *vb* : gather in a swarm

swar·thy \'swȯrthē, -thē\ *adj* **-thi·er; -est** : dark in complexion

swash·buck·ler \'swäsh,bəklər\ *n* : swaggering or daring soldier or adventurer — **swash·buck·ling** \-,bəkliŋ\ *adj*

swat \'swät\ *vb* **-tt-** : hit sharply — **swat** *n* — **swat·ter** *n*

swatch \'swäch\ *n* : sample piece (as of fabric)

swath \'swäth, 'swȯth\, **swathe**

\'swäth, 'swȯth, 'swāth\ *n* : row or path cut (as through grass)

swathe \'swäth, 'swȯth, 'swāth\ *vb* **swathed; swath•ing** : wrap with or as if with a bandage

sway \'swā\ *vb* **1** : swing gently from side to side **2** : influence ~ *n* **1** : gentle swinging from side to side **2** : controlling power or influence

swear \'swar\ *vb* **swore** \'swōr\; **sworn** \'swōrn\; **swear•ing 1** : make or cause to make a solemn statement under oath **2** : use profane language — **swear•er** *n* — **swear•ing** *n*

sweat \'swet\ *vb* **sweat** *or* **sweat•ed; sweat•ing 1** : excrete salty moisture from skin glands **2** : form drops of moisture on the surface **3** : work or cause to work hard — **sweat** *n* — **sweaty** *adj*

sweat•er \'swetər\ *n* : knitted jacket or pullover

sweat•shirt \'swet,shərt\ *n* : loose collarless heavy cotton jersey pullover

sweep \'swēp\ *vb* **swept** \'swept\; **sweep•ing 1** : remove or clean by a brush or a single forceful wipe (as of the hand) **2** : move over with speed and force (as of the hand) **3** : move or extend in a wide curve ~ *n* **1** : a clearing off or away **2** : single forceful wipe or swinging movement **3** : scope — **sweep•er** *n* — **sweep•ing** *adj*

sweep•stakes \'swēp,stāks\ *n, pl* **sweep•stakes** : contest in which the entire prize may go to the winner

sweet \'swēt\ *adj* **1** : being or causing the pleasing taste typical of sugar **2** : not stale or spoiled **3** : not salted **4** : pleasant **5** : much loved ~ *n* : something sweet — **sweet•en** \'swēt³n\ *vb* — **sweet•ly** *adv* — **sweet•ness** *n* — **sweet•en•er** \-³nər\ *n*

sweet•heart *n* : person one loves

sweet potato *n* : sweet yellow edible root of a tropical vine

swell \'swel\ *vb* **swelled; swelled** *or* **swol•len** \'swōlən\; **swell•ing 1** : enlarge **2** : bulge **3** : fill or be filled with emotion ~ *n* **1** : long rolling ocean wave **2** : condition of bulging — **swell•ing** *n*

swel•ter \'sweltər\ *vb* : be uncomfortable from excessive heat

swept *past of* SWEEP

swerve \'swərv\ *vb* **swerved; swerv•ing** : move abruptly aside from a course — **swerve** *n*

¹**swift** \'swift\ *adj* **1** : moving with great speed **2** : occurring suddenly — **swift•ly** *adv* — **swift•ness** *n*

²**swift** *n* : small insect-eating bird

swig \'swig\ *vb* **-gg-** : drink in gulps — **swig** *n*

swill \'swil\ *vb* : swallow greedily ~ *n* **1** : animal food of refuse and liquid **2** : garbage

swim \'swim\ *vb* **swam** \'swam\; **swum** \'swəm\; **swim•ming 1** : propel oneself in water **2** : float in or be surrounded with a liquid **3** : be dizzy ~ *n* : act or period of swimming — **swim•mer** *n*

swin•dle \'swind³l\ *vb* **-dled; -dling** \-iŋ\ : cheat (someone) of money or property — **swindle** *n* — **swin•dler** \-ər\ *n*

swine \'swīn\ *n, pl* **swine** : short-legged hoofed mammal with a snout — **swinish** \'swīnish\ *adj*

swing \'swiŋ\ *vb* **swung** \'swəŋ\; **swing•ing 1** : move or cause to move rapidly in an arc **2** : sway or cause to sway back and forth **3** : hang so as to sway or sag **4** : turn on a hinge or pivot **5** : manage or handle successfully ~ *n* **1** : act or instance of swinging **2** : swinging movement (as in trying to hit something) **3** : suspended seat for swinging — **swing** *adj* — **swing•er** *n*

swipe \'swīp\ *n* : strong sweeping blow ~ *vb* **swiped; swip•ing 1** : strike or wipe with a sweeping motion **2** : steal esp. with a quick movement

swirl \'swərl\ *vb* : move or cause to move in a circle — **swirl** *n*

swish \'swish\ *n* : hissing, sweeping, or brushing sound — **swish** *vb*

switch \'swich\ *n* **1** : slender flexible whip or twig **2** : blow with a switch **3** : shift, change, or reversal **4** : device that opens or closes an electrical circuit ~ *vb* **1** : punish or urge on with a switch **2** : change or reverse roles, positions, or subjects **3** : operate a switch of

switch•board *n* : panel of switches to make and break telephone connections

swiv•el \'swivəl\ *vb* **-eled** *or* **-elled; -eling** *or* **-el•ling** : swing or turn on a pivot — **swivel** *n*

swollen *past part of* SWELL

swoon \'swün\ *n* : faint — **swoon** *vb*

swoop \'swüp\ *vb* : make a swift diving attack — **swoop** *n*

sword \'sȯrd\ *n* : thrusting or cutting weapon with a long blade

sword·fish *n* : large ocean fish with a long swordlike projection

swore *past of* SWEAR

sworn *past part of* SWEAR

swum *past part of* SWIM

swung *past of* SWING

syc·a·more \'sikə,mōr\ *n* : shade tree

sy·co·phant \'sikəfənt\ *n* : servile flatterer — **syc·o·phan·tic** \,sikə-'fantik\ *adj*

syl·la·ble \'siləbəl\ *n* : unit of a spoken word — **syl·lab·ic** \sə'labik\ *adj*

syl·la·bus \'siləbəs\ *n, pl* **-bi** \-,bī\ *or* **-bus·es** : summary of main topics (as of a course of study)

syl·van \'silvən\ *adj* **1** : living or located in a wooded area **2** : abounding in woods

sym·bol \'simbəl\ *n* : something that represents or suggests another thing — **sym·bol·ic** \sim'bälik\ *adj* — **sym·bol·i·cal·ly** *adv*

sym·bol·ism \'simbə,lizəm\ *n* : representation of meanings with symbols

sym·bol·ize \'simbə,līz\ *vb* **-ized; -iz·ing** : serve as a symbol of — **sym·bol·i·za·tion** \,simbələ'zāshən\ *n*

sym·me·try \'simətrē\ *n, pl* **-tries** : regularity and balance in the arrangement of parts — **sym·met·ri·cal** \sə'metrikəl\ *adj* — **sym·met·ri·cal·ly** *adv*

sym·pa·thize \'simpə,thīz\ *vb* **-thized; -thiz·ing** : feel or show sympathy — **sym·pa·thiz·er** *n*

sym·pa·thy \'simpəthē\ *n, pl* **-thies** **1** : ability to understand or share the feelings of another **2** : expression of sorrow for another's misfortune — **sym·pa·thet·ic** \,simpə'thetik\ *adj* — **sym·pa·thet·i·cal·ly** *adv*

sym·pho·ny \'simfənē\ *n, pl* **-nies** : composition for an orchestra or the orchestra itself — **sym·phon·ic** \sim'fänik\ *adj*

sym·po·sium \sim'pōzēəm\ *n, pl* **-sia** \-zēə\ *or* **-siums** : conference at which a topic is discussed

symp·tom \'simptəm\ *n* : unusual feeling or reaction that is a sign of disease — **symp·tom·at·ic** \,simptə-'matik\ *adj*

syn·a·gogue, syn·a·gog \'sinə,gäg, -,gȯg\ *n* : Jewish house of worship

syn·chro·nize \'siŋkrə,nīz, 'sin-\ *vb* **-nized; -niz·ing** **1** : occur or cause to occur at the same instant **2** : cause to agree in time — **syn·chro·ni·za·tion** \,siŋkrənə'zāshən, ,sin-\ *n*

syn·co·pa·tion \,siŋkə'pāshən, ,sin-\ *n* : shifting of the regular musical accent to the weak beat — **syn·co·pate** \'siŋkə,pāt, 'sin-\ *vb*

syn·di·cate \'sindikət\ *n* : business association ~ \-də,kāt\ *vb* **-cat·ed; -cat·ing** **1** : form a syndicate **2** : publish through a syndicate — **syn·di·ca·tion** \,sində'kāshən\ *n*

syn·drome \'sin,drōm\ *n* : particular group of symptoms

syn·onym \'sinə,nim\ *n* : word with the same meaning as another — **syn·on·y·mous** \sə'nänəməs\ *adj* — **syn·on·y·my** \-mē\ *n*

syn·op·sis \sə'näpsəs\ *n, pl* **-op·ses** \-,sēz\ : condensed statement or outline

syn·tax \'sin,taks\ *n* : way in which words are put together — **syn·tac·tic** \sin'taktik\, **syn·tac·ti·cal** \-tikəl\ *adj*

syn·the·sis \'sinthəsəs\ *n, pl* **-the·ses** \-,sēz\ : combination of parts or elements into a whole — **syn·the·size** \-,sīz\ *vb*

syn·thet·ic \sin'thetik\ *adj* : artificially made — **synthetic** *n* — **syn·thet·i·cal·ly** *adv*

syph·i·lis \'sifələs\ *n* : venereal disease

sy·ringe \sə'rinj, 'sirinj\ *n* : plunger device for injecting or withdrawing liquids

syr·up \'sərəp, 'sirəp\ *n* : thick sticky sweet liquid — **syr·upy** *adj*

sys·tem \'sistəm\ *n* **1** : arrangement of units that function together **2** : regular order — **sys·tem·at·ic** \,sistə'matik\ *adj* — **sys·tem·at·i·cal·ly** *adv* — **sys·tem·a·tize** \'sistəmə,tīz\ *vb*

sys·tem·ic \sis'temik\ *adj* : relating to the whole body

T

t \'tē\ *n, pl* **t's** *or* **ts** \'tēz\ : 20th letter of the alphabet

tab \'tab\ *n* **1** : short projecting flap **2** *pl* : careful watch

tab·by \'tabē\ *n, pl* **-bies** : domestic cat

tab·er·na·cle \'tabər,nakəl\ *n* : house of worship

ta·ble \'tābəl\ *n* **1** : piece of furniture having a smooth slab fixed on legs **2** : supply of food **3** : arrangement of data in columns **4** : short list — **ta·ble·cloth** *n* — **ta·ble·top** *n* — **ta·ble·ware** *n* — **tab·u·lar** \'tabyələr\ *adj*

tab·leau \'tab,lō\ *n, pl* **-leaux** \-,lōz\ **1** : graphic description **2** : depiction of a scene by people in costume

ta·ble·spoon *n* **1** : large serving spoon **2** : measuring spoon holding 1/2 fluid ounce — **ta·ble·spoon·ful** \-,fùl\ *n*

tab·let \'tablət\ *n* **1** : flat slab suited for an inscription **2** : collection of sheets of paper glued together at one edge **3** : disk-shaped pill

tab·loid \'tab,lòid\ *n* : newspaper of small page size

ta·boo \tə'bü, ta-\ *adj* : banned esp. as immoral or dangerous — **taboo** *n or vb*

tab·u·late \'tabyə,lāt\ *vb* **-lat·ed; -lat·ing** : put in the form of a table — **tab·u·la·tion** \,tabyə'lāshən\ *n* — **tab·u·la·tor** \'tabyə,lātər\ *n*

tac·it \'tasət\ *adj* : implied but not expressed — **tac·it·ly** *adv* — **tac·it·ness** *n*

tac·i·turn \'tasə,tərn\ *adj* : not inclined to talk

tack \'tak\ *n* **1** : small sharp nail **2** : course of action ~ *vb* **1** : fasten with tacks **2** : add on

tack·le \'takəl, *naut often* 'tāk-\ *n* **1** : equipment **2** : arrangement of ropes and pulleys **3** : act of tackling ~ *vb* **-led; -ling** **1** : seize or throw down **2** : start dealing with

¹tacky \'takē\ *adj* **tack·i·er; -est** : sticky to the touch

²tacky *adj* **tack·i·er; -est** : cheap or gaudy

tact \'takt\ *n* : sense of the proper thing to say or do — **tact·ful** \-fəl\ *adj* —

tact·ful·ly *adv* — **tact·less** *adj* — **tact·less·ly** *adv*

tac·tic \'taktik\ *n* : action as part of a plan

tac·tics \'taktiks\ *n sing or pl* **1** : science of maneuvering forces in combat **2** : skill of using available means to reach an end — **tac·ti·cal** \-tikəl\ *adj* — **tac·ti·cian** \tak'tishən\ *n*

tac·tile \'takt²l, -,tīl\ *adj* : relating to or perceptible through the sense of touch

tad·pole \'tad,pōl\ *n* : larval frog or toad with tail and gills

taf·fe·ta \'tafətə\ *n* : crisp lustrous fabric (as of silk)

taf·fy \'tafē\ *n, pl* **-fies** : candy stretched until porous

¹tag \'tag\ *n* : piece of hanging or attached material ~ *vb* **-gg-** **1** : provide or mark with a tag **2** : follow closely

²tag *n* : children's game of trying to catch one another ~ *vb* : touch a person in tag

tail \'tāl\ *n* **1** : rear end or a growth extending from the rear end of an animal **2** : back or last part **3** : the reverse of a coin ~ *vb* : follow — **tailed** \'tāld\ *adj* — **tail·less** *adj*

tail·gate \-,gāt\ *n* : hinged gate on the back of a vehicle that can be lowered for loading ~ *vb* **-gat·ed; -gat·ing** : drive too close behind another vehicle

tail·light *n* : red warning light at the back of a vehicle

tai·lor \'tālər\ *n* : one who makes or alters garments ~ *vb* **1** : fashion or alter (clothes) **2** : make or adapt for a special purpose

tail·spin *n* : spiral dive by an airplane

taint \'tānt\ *vb* : affect or become affected with something bad and esp. decay ~ *n* : trace of decay or corruption

take \'tāk\ *vb* **took** \'tùk\; **tak·en** \'tākən\; **tak·ing** **1** : get into one's possession **2** : become affected by **3** : receive into one's body (as by eating) **4** : pick out or remove **5** : use for transportation **6** : need or make use of **7** : lead, carry, or cause to go to another place **8** : undertake and do, make, or perform ⁓ *n* : amount taken — **take•over** *n* — **tak•er** *n* — **take advantage of** : profit by — **take exception** : object — **take off** *vb* **1** : remove **2** : go away **3** : mimic **4** : begin flight — **take over** *vb* : assume control or possession of or responsibility for — **take place** : happen

take•off *n* : act or instance of taking off

talc \'talk\ *n* : soft mineral used in making toilet powder (**tal•cum powder** \'talkəm-\)

tale \'tāl\ *n* **1** : story or anecdote **2** : falsehood

tal•ent \'talənt\ *n* : natural mental or creative ability — **tal•ent•ed** *adj*

tal•is•man \'taləsmən, -əz-\ *n, pl* **-mans** : object thought to act as a charm

talk \'tȯk\ *vb* **1** : express one's thoughts in speech **2** : discuss **3** : influence to a position or course of action by talking ⁓ *n* **1** : act of talking **2** : formal discussion **3** : rumor **4** : informal lecture — **talk•a•tive** \-ətiv\ *adj* — **talk•er** *n*

tall \'tȯl\ *adj* : extending to a great or specified height — **tall•ness** *n*

tal•low \'talō\ *n* : hard white animal fat used esp. in candles

tal•ly \'talē\ *n, pl* **-lies** : recorded amount ⁓ *vb* **-lied; -ly•ing 1** : add or count up **2** : match

tal•on \'talən\ *n* : bird's claw

tam \'tam\ *n* : tam-o'-shanter

tam•bou•rine \,tambə'rēn\ *n* : small drum with loose disks at the sides

tame \'tām\ *adj* **tam•er; tam•est 1** : changed from being wild to being controllable by man **2** : docile **3** : dull ⁓ *vb* **tamed; tam•ing** : make or become tame — **tam•able, tame•able** *adj* — **tame•ly** *adv* — **tam•er** *n*

tam–o'–shan•ter \'tamə,shantər\ *n* : Scottish woolen cap with a wide flat circular crown

tamp \'tamp\ *vb* : drive down or in by a series of light blows

tam•per \'tampər\ *vb* : interfere so as to change for the worse

tan \'tan\ *vb* **-nn- 1** : change (hide) into leather esp. by soaking in a liquid containing tannin **2** : make or become brown (as by exposure to the sun) ⁓ *n* **1** : brown skin color induced by the

sun **2** : light yellowish brown — **tan•ner** *n* — **tan•nery** \'tanərē\ *n*

tan•dem \'tandəm\ *adv* : one behind another

tang \'taŋ\ *n* : sharp distinctive flavor — **tangy** *adj*

tan•gent \'tanjənt\ *adj* : touching a curve or surface at only one point ⁓ *n* **1** : tangent line, curve, or surface **2** : abrupt change of course — **tan•gen•tial** \tan'jenchəl\ *adj*

tan•ger•ine \'tanjə,rēn, ,tanjə'-\ *n* : deep orange citrus fruit

tan•gi•ble \'tanjəbəl\ *adj* **1** : able to be touched **2** : substantially real — **tan•gi•bly** *adv*

tan•gle \'taŋgəl\ *vb* **-gled; -gling** : unite in intricate confusion ⁓ *n* : tangled twisted mass

tan•go \'taŋgō\ *n, pl* **-gos** : dance of Latin-American origin — **tango** *vb*

tank \'taŋk\ *n* **1** : large artificial receptacle for liquids **2** : armored military vehicle — **tank•ful** *n*

tan•kard \'taŋkərd\ *n* : tall one-handled drinking vessel

tank•er \'taŋkər\ *n* : vehicle or vessel with tanks for transporting a liquid

tan•nin \'tanən\ *n* : substance of plant origin used in tanning and dyeing

tan•ta•lize \'tant°l,īz\ *vb* **-lized; -liz•ing** : tease or torment by keeping something desirable just out of reach — **tan•ta•liz•er** *n* — **tan•ta•liz•ing•ly** *adv*

tan•ta•mount \'tantə,maůnt\ *adj* : equivalent in value or meaning

tan•trum \'tantrəm\ *n* : fit of bad temper

¹**tap** \'tap\ *n* **1** : faucet **2** : act of tapping ⁓ *vb* **-pp- 1** : pierce so as to draw off fluid **2** : connect into — **tap•per** *n*

²**tap** *vb* **-pp-** : rap lightly ⁓ *n* : light stroke or its sound

tape \'tāp\ *n* **1** : narrow flexible strip (as of cloth, plastic, or metal) **2** : tape measure ⁓ *vb* **taped; tap•ing 1** : fasten with tape **2** : record on tape

tape measure *n* : strip of tape marked in units for use in measuring

ta•per \'tāpər\ *n* **1** : slender wax candle **2** : gradual lessening of width in a long object ⁓ *vb* **1** : make or become smaller toward one end **2** : diminish gradually

tap•es•try \'tapəstrē\ *n, pl* **-tries** : heavy handwoven ruglike wall hanging

tape•worm *n* : long flat intestinal worm

tap•i•o•ca \,tapē'ōkə\ *n* : a granular starch used esp. in puddings

tar \'tär\ *n* : thick dark sticky liquid distilled (as from coal) ∼ *vb* **-rr-** : treat or smear with tar

ta·ran·tu·la \tə'ranchələ, -'rant°lə\ *n* : large hairy usu. harmless spider

tar·dy \'tärdē\ *adj* **-di·er; -est** : late — **tar·di·ly** \'tärd°lē\ *adv* — **tar·di·ness** *n*

tar·get \'tärgət\ *n* **1** : mark to shoot at **2** : goal to be achieved ∼ *vb* **1** : make a target of **2** : establish as a goal

tar·iff \'tarəf\ *n* **1** : duty or rate of duty imposed on imported goods **2** : schedule of tariffs, rates, or charges

tar·nish \'tärnish\ *vb* : make or become dull or discolored — **tarnish** *n*

tar·pau·lin \tär'pólən, 'tärpə-\ *n* : waterproof protective covering

¹**tar·ry** \'tarē\ *vb* **-ried; -ry·ing** : be slow in leaving

²**tar·ry** \'tärē\ *adj* : resembling or covered with tar

¹**tart** \'tärt\ *adj* **1** : pleasantly sharp to the taste **2** : caustic — **tart·ly** *adv* — **tart·ness** *n*

²**tart** *n* : small pie

tar·tan \'tärt°n\ *n* : woolen fabric with a plaid design

tar·tar \'tärtər\ *n* : hard crust on the teeth

task \'task\ *n* : assigned work

task·mas·ter *n* : one that burdens another with labor

tas·sel \'tasəl, 'täs-\ *n* : hanging ornament made of a bunch of cords fastened at one end

taste \'tāst\ *vb* **tast·ed; tast·ing 1** : test or determine the flavor of **2** : eat or drink in small quantities **3** : have a specific flavor ∼ *n* **1** : small amount tasted **2** : bit **3** : special sense that identifies sweet, sour, bitter, or salty qualities **4** : individual preference **5** : critical appreciation of quality — **taste·ful** \-fəl\ *adj* — **taste·ful·ly** *adv* — **taste·less** *adj* — **taste·less·ly** *adv* — **tast·er** *n*

tasty \'tāstē\ *adj* **tast·i·er; -est** : pleasing to the sense of taste — **tast·i·ness** *n*

tat·ter \'tatər\ *n* **1** : part torn and left hanging **2** *pl* : tattered clothing ∼ *vb* : make or become ragged

tat·tle \'tat°l\ *vb* **-tled; -tling** : inform on someone — **tat·tler** *n*

tat·tle·tale *n* : one that tattles

tat·too \ta'tü\ *vb* : mark the skin with indelible designs or figures — **tattoo** *n*

taught *past of* TEACH

taunt \'tónt\ *n* : sarcastic challenge or insult — **taunt** *vb* — **taunt·er** *n*

taut \'tót\ *adj* : tightly drawn — **taut·ly** *adv* — **taut·ness** *n*

tav·ern \'tavərn\ *n* : establishment where liquors are sold to be drunk on the premises

taw·dry \'tódrē\ *adj* **-dri·er; -est** : cheap and gaudy — **taw·dri·ly** \'tódrəlē\ *adv*

taw·ny \'tónē\ *adj* **-ni·er; -est** : brownish orange

tax \'taks\ *vb* **1** : impose a tax on **2** : charge **3** : put under stress ∼ *n* **1** : charge by authority for public purposes **2** : strain — **tax·able** *adj* — **tax·a·tion** \tak'sāshən\ *n* — **tax·pay·er** *n* — **tax·pay·ing** *adj*

taxi \'taksē\ *n, pl* **tax·is** \-sēz\ : automobile transporting passengers for a fare ∼ *vb* **tax·ied; taxi·ing** *or* **taxy·ing; tax·is** *or* **tax·ies 1** : transport or go by taxi **2** : move along the ground before takeoff or after landing

taxi·cab \'taksē‚kab\ *n* : taxi

taxi·der·my \'taksə‚dərmē\ *n* : skill or job of stuffing and mounting animal skins — **taxi·der·mist** \-mist\ *n*

tea \'tē\ *n* : cured leaves of an oriental shrub or a drink made from these — **tea·cup** *n* — **tea·pot** *n*

teach \'tēch\ *vb* **taught** \'tót\; **teaching 1** : tell or show the fundamentals or skills of something **2** : cause to know the consequences **3** : impart knowledge of — **teach·able** *adj* — **teach·er** *n* — **teach·ing** *n*

teak \'tēk\ *n* : East Indian timber tree or its wood

tea·ket·tle \'tē‚ket°l\ *n* : covered kettle with a handle and spout for boiling water

teal \'tēl\ *n, pl* **teal** *or* **teals** : small short-necked wild duck

team \'tēm\ *n* **1** : draft animals harnessed together **2** : number of people organized for a game or work ∼ *vb* : form or work together as a team — **team** *adj* — **team·mate** *n* — **team·work** *n*

team·ster \'tēmstər\ *n* **1** : one that drives a team of animals **2** : one that drives a truck

¹**tear** \'tir\ *n* : drop of salty liquid that moistens the eye — **tear·ful** \-fəl\ *adj* — **tear·ful·ly** *adv*

²**tear** \'tar\ *vb* **tore** \'tōr\; **torn** \'tōrn\; **tear·ing 1** : separate or pull apart by

force **2** : move or act with violence or haste **~** *n* : act or result of tearing

tease \'tēz\ *vb* **teased; teas•ing** : annoy by goading, coaxing, or tantalizing **~** *n* **1** : act of teasing or state of being teased **2** : one that teases

tea•spoon \'tē,spün\ *n* **1** : small spoon for stirring or sipping **2** : measuring spoon holding 1/6 fluid ounce — **tea•spoon•ful** \-,fúl\ *n*

teat \'tēt\ *n* : protuberance through which milk is drawn from an udder or breast

tech•ni•cal \'teknikəl\ *adj* **1** : having or relating to special mechanical or scientific knowledge **2** : by strict interpretation of rules — **tech•ni•cal•ly** *adv*

tech•ni•cal•i•ty \,teknə'kalətē\ *n, pl* **-ties** : detail meaningful only to a specialist

technical sergeant *n* : noncommissioned officer in the air force ranking next below a master sergeant

tech•ni•cian \tek'nishən\ *n* : person with the technique of a specialized skill

tech•nique \tek'nēk\ *n* : manner of accomplishing something

tech•nol•o•gy \tek'näləjē\ *n, pl* **-gies** : applied science — **tech•no•log•i•cal** \,teknə'läjikəl\ *adj*

te•dious \'tēdēəs\ *adj* : wearisome from length or dullness — **te•dious•ly** *adv* — **te•dious•ness** *n*

te•di•um \'tēdēəm\ *n* : tedious state or quality

tee \'tē\ *n* : mound or peg on which a golf ball is placed before beginning play — **tee** *vb*

teem \'tēm\ *vb* : become filled to overflowing

teen•age \'tēn,āj\, **teen•aged** \-,ājd\ *adj* : relating to people in their teens — **teen•ag•er** \-,ājər\ *n*

teens \'tēnz\ *n pl* : years 13 to 19 in a person's life

tee•pee *var of* TEPEE

tee•ter \'tētər\ *vb* **1** : move unsteadily **2** : seesaw — **teeter** *n*

teeth *pl of* TOOTH

teethe \'tēth̲\ *vb* **teethed; teeth•ing** : grow teeth

tele•cast \'teli,kast\ *vb* **-cast; -cast•ing** : broadcast by television — **tele•cast** *n* — **tele•cast•er** *n*

tele•com•mu•ni•ca•tion \'teləkəmyünə'kāshən\ *n* : communication at a distance (as by radio or telephone)

tele•gram \'telə,gram\ *n* : message sent by telegraph

tele•graph \-,graf\ *n* : system for communication by electrical transmission of coded signals **~** *vb* : send by telegraph — **te•leg•ra•pher** \tə'legrəfər\ *n* — **tele•graph•ic** \,telə'grafik\ *adj*

te•lep•a•thy \tə'lepəthē\ *n* : apparent communication without known sensory means — **tele•path•ic** \,telə'pathik\ *adj* — **tele•path•i•cal•ly** *adv*

tele•phone \'telə,fōn\ *n* : instrument or system for electrical transmission of spoken words **~** *vb* **-phoned; -phon•ing** : communicate with by telephone — **tele•phon•er** *n*

tele•scope \-,skōp\ *n* : tube-shaped optical instrument for viewing distant objects **~** *vb* **-scoped; -scop•ing** : slide or cause to slide inside another similar section — **tele•scop•ic** \,telə'skäpik\ *adj*

tele•vise \'telə,vīz\ *vb* **-vised; -vis•ing** : broadcast by television

tele•vi•sion \-,vizhən\ *n* : transmission and reproduction of images by radio waves

tell \'tel\ *vb* **told** \'tōld\; **tell•ing 1** : count **2** : relate in detail **3** : reveal **4** : give information or an order to **5** : find out by observing

tell•er \'telər\ *n* **1** : one that relates or counts **2** : bank employee handling money

te•mer•i•ty \tə'merətē\ *n, pl* **-ties** : boldness

temp \'temp\ *n* **1** : temperature **2** : temporary worker

tem•per \'tempər\ *vb* **1** : dilute or soften **2** : toughen **~** *n* **1** : characteristic attitude or feeling **2** : toughness **3** : disposition or control over one's emotions

tem•per•a•ment \'tempərəmənt\ *n* : characteristic frame of mind — **tem•per•a•men•tal** \,tempro'ment³l\ *adj*

tem•per•ance \'temprəns\ *n* : moderation in or abstinence from indulgence and esp. the use of intoxicating drink

tem•per•ate \'tempərət\ *adj* : moderate

tem•per•a•ture \'tempər,chùr, -prə-,chùr, -chər\ *n* **1** : degree of hotness or coldness **2** : fever

tem•pest \'tempəst\ *n* : violent storm — **tem•pes•tu•ous** \tem'peschəwəs\ *adj*

¹tem•ple \'tempəl\ *n* : place of worship

²temple *n* : flattened space on each side of the forehead

tem•po \'tempō\ *n, pl* **-pi** \-ˌpē\ *or* **-pos** : rate of speed

tem•po•ral \'tempərəl\ *adj* : relating to time or to secular concerns

tem•po•rary \'tempəˌrerē\ *adj* : lasting for a short time only — **tem•po•rar•i•ly** \ˌtempə'rerəlē\ *adv*

tempt \'tempt\ *vb* **1** : coax or persuade to do wrong **2** : attract or provoke — **tempt•er** *n* — **tempt•ing•ly** *adv* — **tempt•ress** \'temptrəs\ *n*

temp•ta•tion \temp'tāshən\ *n* **1** : act of tempting **2** : something that tempts

ten \'ten\ *n* **1** : one more than 9 **2** : 10th in a set or series **3** : thing having 10 units — **ten** *adj or pron* — **tenth** \'tenth\ *adj or adv or n*

ten•a•ble \'tenəbəl\ *adj* : capable of being held or defended — **ten•a•bil•i•ty** \ˌtenə'bilətē\ *n*

te•na•cious \tə'nāshəs\ *adj* **1** : holding fast **2** : retentive — **te•na•cious•ly** *adv* — **te•nac•i•ty** \tə'nasətē\ *n*

ten•ant \'tenənt\ *n* : one who occupies a rented dwelling — **ten•an•cy** \-ənsē\ *n*

¹tend \'tend\ *vb* : take care of or supervise something

²tend *vb* **1** : move in a particular direction **2** : show a tendency

ten•den•cy \'tendənsē\ *n, pl* **-cies** : likelihood to move, think, or act in a particular way

¹ten•der \'tendər\ *adj* **1** : soft or delicate **2** : expressing or responsive to love or sympathy **3** : sensitive (as to touch) — **ten•der•ly** *adv* — **ten•der•ness** *n*

²tend•er \'tendər\ *n* **1** : one that tends **2** : boat providing transport to a larger ship **3** : vehicle attached to a steam locomotive for carrying fuel and water

³ten•der *n* **1** : offer of a bid for a contract **2** : something that may be offered in payment — **tender** *vb*

ten•der•ize \'tendəˌrīz\ *vb* **-ized; -iz•ing** : make (meat) tender — **ten•der•iz•er** \'tendəˌrīzər\ *n*

ten•der•loin \'tenderˌlóin\ *n* : tender beef or pork strip from near the backbone

ten•don \'tendən\ *n* : cord of tissue attaching muscle to bone — **ten•di•nous** \-dənəs\ *adj*

ten•dril \'tendrəl\ *n* : slender coiling growth of some climbing plants

ten•e•ment \'tenəmənt\ *n* **1** : house divided into apartments **2** : shabby dwelling

te•net \'tenət\ *n* : principle of belief

ten•nis \'tenəs\ *n* : racket-and-ball game played across a net

ten•or \'tenər\ *n* **1** : general drift or meaning **2** : highest natural adult male voice

ten•pin \'tenˌpin\ *n* : bottle-shaped pin bowled at in a game (**tenpins**)

¹tense \'tens\ *n* : distinct verb form that indicates time

²tense *adj* **tens•er; tens•est 1** : stretched tight **2** : marked by nervous tension — **tense** *vb* — **tense•ly** *adv* — **tense•ness** *n* — **ten•si•ty** \'tensətē\ *n*

ten•sile \'tensəl, -ˌsīl\ *adj* : relating to tension

ten•sion \'tenchən\ *n* **1** : tense condition **2** : state of mental unrest or of potential hostility or opposition

tent \'tent\ *n* : collapsible shelter

ten•ta•cle \'tentikəl\ *n* : long flexible projection of an insect or mollusk — **ten•ta•cled** \-kəld\ *adj* — **ten•tac•u•lar** \ten'takyələr\ *adj*

ten•ta•tive \'tentətiv\ *adj* : subject to change or discussion — **ten•ta•tive•ly** *adv*

ten•u•ous \'tenyəwəs\ *adj* **1** : not dense or thick **2** : flimsy or weak — **ten•u•ous•ly** *adv* — **ten•u•ous•ness** *n*

ten•ure \'tenyər\ *n* : act, right, manner, or period of holding something — **ten•ured** \-yərd\ *adj*

te•pee \'tēˌpē\ *n* : conical tent

tep•id \'tepəd\ *adj* : moderately warm

term \'tərm\ *n* **1** : period of time **2** : mathematical expression **3** : special word or phrase **4** *pl* : conditions **5** *pl* : relations ∼ *vb* : name

ter•min•al \'tərmən⁹l\ *n* **1** : end **2** : device for making an electrical connection **3** : station at end of a transportation line — **terminal** *adj*

ter•mi•nate \'tərməˌnāt\ *vb* **-nat•ed; -nat•ing** : bring or come to an end — **ter•mi•na•ble** \-nəbəl\ *adj* — **ter•mi•na•tion** \ˌtərmə'nāshən\ *n*

ter•mi•nol•o•gy \ˌtərmə'näləjē\ *n* : terms used in a particular subject

ter•mi•nus \'tərmənəs\ *n, pl* **-ni** \-ˌnī\ *or* **-nus•es 1** : end **2** : end of a transportation line

ter•mite \'tərˌmīt\ *n* : wood-eating insect

tern \'tərn\ *n* : small sea bird

ter·race \'terəs\ *n* **1** : balcony or patio **2** : bank with a flat top ∼ *vb* **-raced; -rac·ing** : landscape in a series of banks

ter·ra-cot·ta \ˌterə'kätə\ *n* : reddish brown earthenware

ter·rain \tə'rān\ *n* : features of the land

ter·ra·pin \'terəpən\ *n* : No. American turtle

ter·rar·i·um \tə'rareəm\ *n, pl* **-ia** \-ēə\ *or* **-i·ums** : container for keeping plants or animals

ter·res·tri·al \tə'restrēəl\ *adj* **1** : relating to the earth or its inhabitants **2** : living or growing on land

ter·ri·ble \'terəbəl\ *adj* **1** : exciting terror **2** : distressing **3** : intense **4** : of very poor quality — **ter·ri·bly** \-blē\ *adv*

ter·ri·er \'terēər\ *n* : small dog

ter·rif·ic \tə'rifik\ *adj* **1** : exciting terror **2** : extraordinary

ter·ri·fy \'terəˌfī\ *vb* **-fied; -fy·ing** : fill with terror — **ter·ri·fy·ing·ly** *adv*

ter·ri·to·ry \'terəˌtōrē\ *n, pl* **-ries** : particular geographical region — **ter·ri·to·ri·al** \ˌterə'tōrēəl\ *adj*

ter·ror \'terər\ *n* : intense fear and panic or a cause of it

ter·ror·ism \-ˌizəm\ *n* : systematic covert warfare to produce terror for political coercion — **ter·ror·ist** \-ist\ *adj or n*

ter·ror·ize \-ˌīz\ *vb* **-ized; -iz·ing** **1** : fill with terror **2** : coerce by threat or violence

ter·ry \'terē\ *n, pl* **-ries** : absorbent fabric with a loose pile

terse \'tərs\ *adj* **ters·er; ters·est** : concise — **terse·ly** *adv* — **terse·ness** *n*

ter·tia·ry \'tərshēˌerē\ *adj* : of 3d rank, importance, or value

test \'test\ *n* : examination or evaluation ∼ *vb* : examine by a test — **test·er** *n*

tes·ta·ment \'testəmənt\ *n* **1** *cap* : division of the Bible **2** : will — **tes·ta·men·ta·ry** \ˌtestə'mentərē\ *adj*

tes·ti·cle \'testikəl\ *n* : testis

tes·ti·fy \'testəˌfī\ *vb* **-fied; -fy·ing** **1** : give testimony **2** : serve as evidence

tes·ti·mo·ni·al \ˌtestə'mōnēəl\ *n* **1** : favorable recommendation **2** : tribute — **testimonial** *adj*

tes·ti·mo·ny \'testəˌmōnē\ *n, pl* **-nies** : statement given as evidence in court

tes·tis \'testəs\ *n, pl* **-tes** \-ˌtēz\ : male reproductive gland

tes·ty \'testē\ *adj* **-ti·er; -est** : easily annoyed

tet·a·nus \'tetᵊnəs\ *n* : bacterial disease producing violent spasms

tête à tête \ˌtātə'tāt\ *adv* : privately ∼ *n* : private conversation ∼ *adj* : private

teth·er \'tethər\ *n* : leash ∼ *vb* : restrain with a leash

text \'tekst\ *n* **1** : author's words **2** : main body of printed or written matter on a page **3** : textbook **4** : scriptural passage used as the theme of a sermon **5** : topic — **tex·tu·al** \'tekschəwəl\ *adj*

text·book \-ˌbuk\ *n* : book on a school subject

tex·tile \'tekˌstīl, 'tekstᵊl\ *n* : fabric

tex·ture \'tekschər\ *n* **1** : feel and appearance of something **2** : structure

than \'than\ *conj or prep* — used in comparisons

thank \'thank\ *vb* : express gratitude to

thank·ful \-fəl\ *adj* : giving thanks — **thank·ful·ly** *adv* — **thank·ful·ness** *n*

thank·less *adj* : not appreciated

thanks \'thanks\ *n pl* : expression of gratitude

Thanks·giv·ing \thanks'givin\ *n* : 4th Thursday in November observed as a legal holiday for giving thanks for divine goodness

that \'that\ *pron, pl* **those** \thōz\ **1** : something indicated or understood **2** : the one farther away ∼ *adj, pl* **those** : being the one mentioned or understood or farther away ∼ *conj or pron* — used to introduce a clause ∼ *adv* : to such an extent

thatch \'thach\ *vb* : cover with thatch ∼ *n* : covering of matted straw

thaw \'thȯ\ *vb* : melt or cause to melt — **thaw** *n*

the \thə, *before vowel sounds usu* thē\ *definite article* : that particular one ∼ *adv* — used before a comparative or superlative

the·ater, the·atre \'thēətər\ *n* **1** : building or room for viewing a play or movie **2** : dramatic arts

the·at·ri·cal \thē'atrikəl\ *adj* **1** : relating to the theater **2** : involving exaggerated emotion

thee \'thē\ *pron, archaic objective case of* THOU

theft \'theft\ *n* : act of stealing

their \'ther\ *adj* : relating to them

theirs \'thearz\ *pron* : their one or ones

the·ism \'thē,izəm\ *n* : belief in the existence of a god or gods — **the·ist** \-ist\ *n or adj* — **the·is·tic** \thē-'istik\ *adj*

them \'them\ *pron, objective case of* THEY

theme \'thēm\ *n* **1** : subject matter **2** : essay **3** : melody developed in a piece of music — **the·mat·ic** \thi-'matik\ *adj*

them·selves \thəm'selvz, them-\ *pron pl* : they, them — used reflexively or for emphasis

then \'then\ *adv* **1** : at that time **2** : soon after that **3** : in addition **4** : in that case **5** : consequently ∼ *n* : that time ∼ *adj* : existing at that time

thence \'thens, 'thens\ *adv* : from that place or fact

the·oc·ra·cy \thē'äkrəsē\ *n, pl* **-cies** : government by officials regarded as divinely inspired — **the·o·crat·ic** \,thēə'kratik\ *adj*

the·ol·o·gy \thē'äləjē\ *n, pl* **-gies** : study of religion — **the·o·lo·gian** \,thēə'lōjən\ *n* — **the·o·log·i·cal** \-'läjikəl\ *adj*

the·o·rem \'thēərəm, 'thirəm\ *n* : provable statement of truth

the·o·ret·i·cal \,thēə'retikəl\ *adj* : relating to or being theory — **the·o·ret·i·cal·ly** *adv*

the·o·rize \'thēə,rīz\ *vb* **-rized; -riz·ing** : put forth theories — **the·o·rist** *n*

the·o·ry \'thēərē, 'thirē\ *n, pl* **-ries** **1** : general principles of a subject **2** : plausible or scientifically acceptable explanation **3** : judgment, guess, or opinion

ther·a·peu·tic \,therə'pyütik\ *adj* : offering or relating to remedy — **ther·a·peu·ti·cal·ly** *adv*

ther·a·py \'therəpē\ *n, pl* **-pies** : treatment for mental or physical disorder — **ther·a·pist** \-pist\ *n*

there \'ther\ *adv* **1** : in, at, or to that place **2** : in that respect ∼ *pron* — used to introduce a sentence or clause ∼ *n* : that place or point

there·abouts, there·about \,therə-'baúts, 'therə,-, -'baút\ *adv* : near that place, time, number, or quantity

there·af·ter \thar'aftər\ *adv* : after that

there·by \thar'bī, 'thar,bī\ *adv* **1** : by that **2** : connected with or with reference to that

there·fore \'thar,fōr\ *adv* : for that reason

there·in \thar'in\ *adv* **1** : in or into that place, time, or thing **2** : in that respect

there·of \-'əv, -'äv\ *adv* **1** : of that or it **2** : from that

there·upon \'thərə,pón, -,pän; ,thərə-'pón, -'pän\ *adv* **1** : on that matter **2** : therefore **3** : immediately after that

there·with \thar'with, -'with\ *adv* : with that

ther·mal \'thərməl\ *adj* : relating to, caused by, or conserving heat — **ther·mal·ly** *adv*

ther·mo·dy·nam·ics \,thərmədī-'namiks\ *n* : physics of heat

ther·mom·e·ter \thər'mämətər\ *n* : instrument for measuring temperature — **ther·mo·met·ric** \,thərmə-'metrik\ *adj*

ther·mos \'thərməs\ *n* : double-walled bottle used to keep liquids hot or cold

ther·mo·stat \'thərmə,stat\ *n* : automatic temperature control — **ther·mo·stat·ic** \,thərmə'statik\ *adj* — **ther·mo·stat·i·cal·ly** *adv*

the·sau·rus \thi'sórəs\ *n, pl* **-sau·ri** \-'sór,ī\ *or* **-sau·rus·es** \-'sórəsəz\ : book of words and esp. synonyms

these *pl of* THIS

the·sis \'thēsəs\ *n, pl* **the·ses** \'thē-,sēz\ **1** : proposition to be argued for **2** : essay embodying results of original research

thes·pi·an \'thespēən\ *adj* : dramatic ∼ *n* : actor

they \'thā\ *pron* **1** : those ones **2** : people in general

thi·a·mine \'thīəmən, -,mēn\ *n* : essential vitamin

thick \'thik\ *adj* **1** : having relatively great mass from front to back or top to bottom **2** : viscous ∼ *n* : most crowded or thickest part — **thick·ly** *adv* — **thick·ness** *n*

thick·en \'thikən\ *vb* : make or become thick — **thick·en·er** \-ənər\ *n*

thick·et \'thikət\ *n* : dense growth of bushes or small trees

thick–skinned \-'skind\ *adj* : insensitive to criticism

thief \'thēf\ *n, pl* **thieves** \'thēvz\ : one that steals

thieve \'thēv\ *vb* **thieved; thiev·ing** : steal — **thiev·ery** *n*

thigh \'thī\ *n* : upper part of the leg

thigh·bone \'thī,bōn\ *n* : femur

thim·ble \'thimbəl\ *n* : protective cap

for the finger in sewing — **thim•ble•ful** *n*

thin \'thin\ *adj* **-nn-** **1** : having relatively little mass from front to back or top to bottom **2** : not closely set or placed **3** : relatively free flowing **4** : lacking substance, fullness, or strength ~ *vb* **-nn-** : make or become thin — **thin•ly** *adv* — **thin•ness** *n*

thing \'thiŋ\ *n* **1** : matter of concern **2** : event or act **3** : object **4** *pl* : possessions

think \'thiŋk\ *vb* **thought** \'thȯt\; **think•ing** **1** : form or have in the mind **2** : have as an opinion **3** : ponder **4** : devise by thinking **5** : imagine — **think•er** *n*

thin–skinned *adj* : extremely sensitive to criticism

third \'thərd\ *adj* : being number 3 in a countable series ~ *n* **1** : one that is third **2** : one of 3 equal parts — **third**, **third•ly** *adv*

third dimension *n* : thickness or depth — **third–dimensional** *adj*

third world *n* : less developed nations of the world

thirst \'thərst\ *n* **1** : dryness in mouth and throat **2** : intense desire ~ *vb* : feel thirst — **thirsty** *adj*

thir•teen \,thər'tēn\ *n* : one more than 12 — **thirteen** *adj or pron* — **thirteenth** \-'tēnth\ *adj or n*

thir•ty \'thərtē\ *n, pl* **thirties** : 3 times 10 — **thir•ti•eth** \-ēəth\ *adj or n* — **thirty** *adj or pron*

this \'this\ *pron, pl* **these** \'thēz\ : something close or under immediate discussion ~ *adj, pl* **these** : being the one near, present, just mentioned, or more immediately under observation ~ *adv* : to such an extent or degree

this•tle \'thisəl\ *n* : tall prickly herb

thith•er \'thithər\ *adv* : to that place

thong \'thȯŋ\ *n* : strip of leather or hide

tho•rax \'thȯr,aks\ *n, pl* **-rax•es** or **-races** \'thȯrə,sēz\ **1** : part of the body between neck and abdomen **2** : middle of 3 divisions of an insect body — **tho•rac•ic** \thə'rasik\ *adj*

thorn \'thȯrn\ *n* : sharp spike on a plant or a plant bearing these — **thorny** *adj*

thor•ough \'thərō\ *adj* : omitting or overlooking nothing — **thor•ough•ly** *adv* — **thor•ough•ness** *n*

thor•ough•bred \'thərə,bred\ *n* **1** *cap* : light speedy racing horse **2** : one of excellent quality — **thoroughbred** *adj*

thor•ough•fare \'thərə,far\ *n* : public road

those *pl of* THAT

thou \'thau̇\ *pron, archaic* : you

though \'thō\ *adv* : however ~ *conj* **1** : despite the fact that **2** : granting that

thought \'thȯt\ *past of* THINK *n* **1** : process of thinking **2** : serious consideration **3** : idea

thought•ful \-fəl\ *adj* **1** : absorbed in or showing thought **2** : considerate of others — **thought•ful•ly** *adv* — **thought•ful•ness** *n*

thought•less \-ləs\ *adj* **1** : careless or reckless **2** : lacking concern for others — **thought•less•ly** *adv*

thou•sand \'thau̇zⁿnd\ *n, pl* **-sands** or **-sand** : 10 times 100 — **thousand** *adj* — **thou•sandth** \-ⁿnth\ *adj or n*

thrash \'thrash\ *vb* **1** : thresh **2** : beat **3** : move about violently — **thrash•er** *n*

thread \'thred\ *n* **1** : fine line of fibers **2** : train of thought **3** : ridge around a screw ~ *vb* **1** : pass thread through **2** : put together on a thread **3** : make one's way through or between

thread•bare *adj* **1** : worn so that the thread shows **2** : trite

threat \'thret\ *n* **1** : expression of intention to harm **2** : thing that threatens

threat•en \'thretⁿn\ *vb* **1** : utter threats **2** : show signs of being near or impending — **threat•en•ing•ly** *adv*

three \'thrē\ *n* **1** : one more than 2 **2** : 3d in a set or series — **three** *adj or pron*

three•fold \'thrē,fōld\ *adj* : triple — **three•fold** \-'fōld\ *adv*

three•score *adj* : being 3 times 20

thresh \'thresh, 'thrash\ *vb* : beat to separate grain — **thresh•er** *n*

thresh•old \'thresh,ōld\ *n* **1** : sill of a door **2** : beginning stage

threw *past of* THROW

thrice \'thrīs\ *adv* : 3 times

thrift \'thrift\ *n* : careful management or saving of money — **thrift•i•ly** \'thriftəlē\ *adv* — **thrifty** *adj*

thrill \'thril\ *vb* **1** : have or cause to have a sudden sharp feeling of excitement **2** : tremble — **thrill** *n* — **thrill•er** *n* — **thrill•ing•ly** *adv*

thrive \'thrīv\ *vb* **throve** \'thrōv\ *or*

thrived; thriv•en \'thrivən\ **1** : grow vigorously **2** : prosper

throat \'thrōt\ *n* **1** : front part of the neck **2** : passage to the stomach — **throat•ed** *adj* — **throaty** *adj*

throb \'thräb\ *vb* **-bb-** : pulsate — **throb** *n*

throe \'thrō\ *n* **1** : pang or spasm **2** *pl* : hard or painful struggle

throne \'thrōn\ *n* : chair representing power or sovereignty

throng \'thrȯŋ\ *n or vb* : crowd

throt•tle \'thrät°l\ *vb* **-tled; -tling** : choke ~ *n* : valve regulating volume of fuel and air delivered to engine cylinders

through \'thrü\ *prep* **1** : into at one side and out at the other side of **2** : by way of **3** : among, between, or all around **4** : because of **5** : throughout the time of ~ \'thrü\ *adv* **1** : from one end or side to the other **2** : from beginning to end **3** : to the core **4** : into the open ~ *adj* **1** : going directly from origin to destination **2** : finished

through•out \thrü'aut\ *adv* **1** : everywhere **2** : from beginning to end ~ *prep* **1** : in or to every part of **2** : during the whole of

throve *past of* THRIVE

throw \'thrō\ *vb* **threw** \'thrü\; **thrown** \'thrōn\; **throw•ing 1** : propel through the air **2** : cause to fall or fall off **3** : put suddenly in a certain position or condition **4** : move quickly as if throwing **5** : put on or off hastily — **throw** *n* — **throw•er** \'thrōər\ *n* — **throw up** *vb* : vomit

thrush \'thrəsh\ *n* : songbird

thrust \'thrəst\ *vb* **thrust; thrust•ing 1** : shove forward **2** : stab or pierce — **thrust** *n*

thud \'thəd\ *n* : dull sound of something falling — **thud** *vb*

thug \'thəg\ *n* : ruffian or gangster

thumb \'thəm\ *n* **1** : short thick division of the hand opposing the fingers **2** : glove part for the thumb ~ *vb* : leaf through with the thumb — **thumb•nail** *n*

thump \'thəmp\ *vb* : strike with something thick or heavy causing a dull sound — **thump** *n*

thun•der \'thəndər\ *n* : sound following lightning — **thunder** *vb* — **thun•der•clap** *n* — **thun•der•ous** \'thəndərəs\ *adj* — **thun•der•ous•ly** *adv*

thun•der•bolt \-ˌbōlt\ *n* : discharge of lightning with thunder

thun•der•show•er \'thəndərˌshauər\ *n* : shower with thunder and lightning

thun•der•storm *n* : storm with thunder and lightning

Thurs•day \'thərzdā, -dē\ *n* : 5th day of the week

thus \'thəs\ *adv* **1** : in this or that way **2** : to this degree or extent **3** : because of this or that

thwart \'thwȯrt\ *vb* : block or defeat

thy \'thī\ *adj, archaic* : your

thyme \'tīm, 'thīm\ *n* : cooking herb

thy•roid \'thīˌrȯid\ *adj* : relating to a large endocrine gland (**thyroid gland**)

thy•self \thī'self\ *pron, archaic* : yourself

ti•ara \tē'arə, -'är-\ *n* : decorative formal headband

tib•ia \'tibēə\ *n, pl* **-i•ae** \-ē,ē\ : bone between the knee and ankle

tic \'tik\ *n* : twitching of facial muscles

¹tick \'tik\ *n* : small 8-legged bloodsucking animal

²tick *n* **1** : light rhythmic tap or beat **2** : check mark ~ *vb* **1** : make ticks **2** : mark with a tick **3** : operate

tick•er \'tikər\ *n* **1** : something (as a watch) that ticks **2** : telegraph instrument that prints on paper tape

tick•et \'tikət\ *n* **1** : tag showing price, payment of a fee or fare, or a traffic offense **2** : list of candidates ~ *vb* : put a ticket on

tick•ing \'tikiŋ\ *n* : fabric covering of a mattress

tick•le \'tikəl\ *vb* **-led; -ling 1** : please or amuse **2** : touch lightly causing uneasiness, laughter, or spasmodic movements — **tickle** *n*

tick•lish \'tiklish\ *adj* **1** : sensitive to tickling **2** : requiring delicate handling — **tick•lish•ness** *n*

tid•al wave \'tīd°l-\ *n* : high sea wave following an earthquake

tid•bit \'tidˌbit\ *n* : choice morsel

tide \'tīd\ *n* : alternate rising and falling of the sea ~ *vb* **tid•ed; tid•ing** : be enough to allow (one) to get by for a time — **tid•al** \'tīd°l\ *adj* — **tide•water** *n*

tid•ings \'tīdiŋz\ *n pl* : news or message

ti•dy \'tīdē\ *adj* **-di•er; -est 1** : well ordered and cared for **2** : large or substantial — **ti•di•ness** *n* — **tidy** *vb*

tie \\'tī\ *n* **1** : line or ribbon for fastening, uniting, or closing **2** : cross support to which railroad rails are fastened **3** : uniting force **4** : equality in score or tally or a deadlocked contest **5** : necktie ~ *vb* **tied; ty•ing** *or* **tie•ing 1** : fasten or close by wrapping and knotting a tie **2** : form a knot in **3** : gain the same score or tally as an opponent

tier \\'tir\ *n* : one of a steplike series of rows

tiff \\'tif\ *n* : petty quarrel — **tiff** *vb*

ti•ger \\'tīgər\ *n* : very large black-striped cat — **ti•ger•ish** \-gərish\ *adj* — **ti•gress** \-grəs\ *n*

tight \\'tīt\ *adj* **1** : fitting close together esp. so as not to allow air or water in **2** : held very firmly **3** : taut **4** : fitting too snugly **5** : difficult **6** : stingy **7** : evenly contested **8** : low in supply — **tight** *adv* — **tight•en** \-ᵊn\ *vb* — **tight•ly** *adv* — **tight•ness** *n*

tights \\'tīts\ *n pl* : skintight garments

tight•wad \\'tīt,wäd\ *n* : stingy person

tile \\'tīl\ *n* : thin piece of stone or fired clay used on roofs, floors, or walls ~ *vb* : cover with tiles

¹till \\'til\ *prep or conj* : until

²till *vb* : cultivate (soil) — **till•able** *adj*

³till *n* : money drawer

¹till•er \\'tilər\ *n* : one that cultivates soil

²til•ler \\'tilər\ *n* : lever for turning a boat's rudder

tilt \\'tilt\ *vb* : cause to incline ~ *n* : slant

tim•ber \\'timbər\ *n* **1** : cut wood for building **2** : large squared piece of wood **3** : wooded land or trees for timber ~ *vb* : cover, frame, or support with timbers — **tim•bered** *adj* — **tim•ber•land** \-,land\ *n*

tim•bre \\'tambər, 'tim-\ *n* : sound quality

time \\'tīm\ *n* **1** : period during which something exists or continues or can be accomplished **2** : point at which something happens **3** : customary hour **4** : age **5** : tempo **6** : moment, hour, day, or year as indicated by a clock or calendar **7** : one's experience during a particular period ~ *vb* **timed; tim•ing 1** : arrange or set the time of **2** : determine or record the time, duration, or rate of — **time•keep•er** *n* — **time•less** *adj* — **time•less•ness** *n* — **time•li•ness** *n* — **time•ly** *adv* — **tim•er** *n*

time•piece *n* : device to show time

times \\'tīmz\ *prep* : multiplied by

time•ta•ble \\'tīm,tābəl\ *n* : table of departure and arrival times

tim•id \\'timəd\ *adj* : lacking in courage or self-confidence — **ti•mid•i•ty** \tə'midətē\ *n* — **tim•id•ly** *adv*

tim•o•rous \\'timərəs\ *adj* : fearful — **tim•o•rous•ly** *adv* — **tim•o•rous•ness** *n*

tim•pa•ni \\'timpənē\ *n pl* : set of kettledrums — **tim•pa•nist** \-nist\ *n*

tin \\'tin\ *n* **1** : soft white metallic chemical element **2** : metal food can

tinc•ture \\'tiŋkchər\ *n* : alcoholic solution of a medicine

tin•der \\'tindər\ *n* : substance used to kindle a fire

tine \\'tīn\ *n* : one of the points of a fork

tin•foil \\'tin,fȯil\ *n* : thin metal sheeting

tinge \\'tinj\ *vb* **tinged; tinge•ing** *or* **ting•ing** \\'tinjiŋ\ **1** : color slightly **2** : affect with a slight odor ~ *n* : slight coloring or flavor

tin•gle \\'tiŋgəl\ *vb* **-gled; -gling** : feel a ringing, stinging, or thrilling sensation — **tingle** *n*

tin•ker \\'tiŋkər\ *vb* : experiment in repairing something — **tin•ker•er** *n*

tin•kle \\'tiŋkəl\ *vb* **-kled; -kling** : make or cause to make a high ringing sound — **tinkle** *n*

tin•sel \\'tinsəl\ *n* : decorative thread or strip of glittering metal or paper

tint \\'tint\ *n* **1** : slight or pale coloration **2** : color shade ~ *vb* : give a tint to

ti•ny \\'tīnē\ *adj* **-ni•er; -est** : very small

¹tip \\'tip\ *vb* **-pp- 1** : overturn **2** : lean ~ *n* : act or state of tipping

²tip *n* : pointed end of something ~ *vb* **-pp- 1** : furnish with a tip **2** : cover the tip of

³tip *n* : small sum given for a service performed ~ *vb* : give a tip to

⁴tip *n* : piece of confidential information ~ *vb* **-pp-** : give confidential information to

tip—off \\'tip,ȯf\ *n* : indication

tip•ple \\'tipəl\ *vb* **-pled; -pling** : drink intoxicating liquor esp. habitually or excessively — **tip•pler** *n*

tip•sy \\'tipsē\ *adj* **-si•er; -est** : unsteady or foolish from alcohol

tip•toe \\'tip,tō\ *n* : the toes of the feet ~ *adv or adj* : supported on tiptoe ~ *vb* **-toed; -toe•ing** : walk quietly or on tiptoe

tip–top *n* : highest point ∼ *adj* : excellent

ti·rade \tī'rād, 'tī͵-\ *n* : prolonged speech of abuse

¹tire \'tīr\ *vb* **tired; tir·ing** **1** : make or become weary **2** : wear out the patience of — **tire·less** *adj* — **tire·less·ly** *adv* — **tire·some** \-səm\ *adj* — **tire·some·ly** *adv*

²tire *n* : rubber cushion encircling a car wheel

tired \'tīrd\ *adj* : weary

tis·sue \'tishü\ *n* **1** : soft absorbent paper **2** : layer of cells forming a basic structural element of an animal or plant body

ti·tan·ic \tī'tanik, tə-\ *adj* : gigantic

ti·ta·ni·um \tī'tānēəm, tə-\ *n* : gray light strong metallic chemical element

tithe \'tīth\ *n* : tenth part paid or given esp. for the support of a church — **tithe** *vb* — **tith·er** *n*

tit·il·late \'tit²l͵āt\ *vb* **-lat·ed; -lat·ing** : excite pleasurably — **tit·il·la·tion** \͵tit²l'āshən\ *n*

ti·tle \'tīt²l\ *n* **1** : legal ownership **2** : distinguishing name **3** : designation of honor, rank, or office **4** : championship — **ti·tled** *adj*

tit·ter \'titər\ *n* : nervous or affected laugh — **titter** *vb*

tit·u·lar \'tichələr\ *adj* **1** : existing in title only **2** : relating to or bearing a title

tiz·zy \'tizē\ *n, pl* **tizzies** : state of agitation or worry

TNT \͵tē͵en'tē\ *n* : high explosive

to \'tü\ *prep* **1** : in the direction of **2** : at, on, or near **3** : resulting in **4** : before or until **5** — used to show a relationship or object of a verb **6** — used with an infinitive ∼ *adv* **1** : forward **2** : to a state of consciousness

toad \'tōd\ *n* : tailless leaping amphibian

toad·stool \-͵stül\ *n* : mushroom esp. when inedible or poisonous

toady \'tōdē\ *n, pl* **toad·ies** : one who flatters to gain favors — **toady** *vb*

toast \'tōst\ *vb* **1** : make (as a slice of bread) crisp and brown **2** : drink in honor of someone or something **3** : warm ∼ *n* **1** : toasted sliced bread **2** : act of drinking in honor of someone — **toast·er** *n*

to·bac·co \tə'bakō\ *n, pl* **-cos** : broadleaved herb or its leaves prepared for smoking or chewing

to·bog·gan \tə'bägən\ *n* : long flatbottomed light sled ∼ *vb* : coast on a toboggan

to·day \tə'dā\ *adv* **1** : on or for this day **2** : at the present time ∼ *n* : present day or time

tod·dle \'täd²l\ *vb* **-dled; -dling** : walk with tottering steps like a young child — **toddle** *n* — **tod·dler** \'täd²lər\ *n*

to·do \tə'dü\ *n, pl* **to·dos** \-'düz\ : disturbance or fuss

toe \'tō\ *n* : one of the 5 end divisions of the foot — **toe·nail** *n*

tof·fee, tof·fy \'tófē, 'tä-\ *n, pl* **toffees** *or* **toffies** : candy made of boiled sugar and butter

to·ga \'tōgə\ *n* : loose outer garment of ancient Rome

to·geth·er \tə'gethər\ *adv* **1** : in or into one place or group **2** : in or into contact or association **3** : at one time **4** : as a group — **to·geth·er·ness** *n*

togs \'tägz, 'tógz\ *n pl* : clothing

toil \'tóil\ *vb* : work hard and long — **toil** *n* — **toil·er** *n* — **toil·some** *adj*

toi·let \'tóilət\ *n* **1** : dressing and grooming oneself **2** : bathroom **3** : water basin to urinate and defecate in

to·ken \'tōkən\ *n* **1** : outward sign or expression of something **2** : small part representing the whole **3** : piece resembling a coin

told *past of* TELL

tol·er·a·ble \'tälərəbəl\ *adj* **1** : capable of being endured **2** : moderately good — **tol·er·a·bly** \-blē\ *adv*

tol·er·ance \'tälərəns\ *n* **1** : lack of opposition for beliefs or practices differing from one's own **2** : capacity for enduring **3** : allowable deviation — **tol·er·ant** *adj* — **tol·er·ant·ly** *adv*

tol·er·ate \'tälə͵rāt\ *vb* **-at·ed; -at·ing** **1** : allow to be or to be done without opposition **2** : endure or resist the action of — **tol·er·a·tion** \͵tälə'rāshən\ *n*

¹toll \'tōl\ *n* **1** : fee paid for a privilege or service **2** : cost of achievement in loss or suffering — **toll·booth** *n* — **toll·gate** *n*

²toll *vb* **1** : cause the sounding of (a bell) **2** : sound with slow measured strokes ∼ *n* : sound of a tolling bell

tom·a·hawk \'tämə͵hók\ *n* : light ax used as a weapon by American Indians

to·ma·to \tə'mātō, -'mät-\ *n, pl* **-toes** : tropical American herb or its fruit

tomb \'tüm\ *n* : house, vault, or grave for burial

tom·boy \'täm,bȯi\ *n* : girl who behaves in a manner usu. considered boyish

tomb·stone *n* : stone marking a grave

tom·cat \'täm,kat\ *n* : male cat

tome \'tōm\ *n* : large or weighty book

to·mor·row \tə'märō\ *adv* : on or for the day after today — **tomorrow** *n*

tom–tom \'täm,täm\ *n* : small-headed drum beaten with the hands

ton \'tən\ *n* : unit of weight equal to 2000 pounds

tone \'tōn\ *n* **1** : vocal or musical sound **2** : sound of definite pitch **3** : manner of speaking that expresses an emotion or attitude **4** : color quality **5** : healthy condition **6** : general character or quality — *vb* : soften or muffle — often used with *down* — **ton·al** \-ᵊl\ *adj* — **to·nal·i·ty** \tō'nalətē\ *n*

tongs \'täŋz, 'tȯŋz\ *n pl* : grasping device of 2 joined or hinged pieces

tongue \'təŋ\ *n* **1** : fleshy movable organ of the mouth **2** : language **3** : something long and flat and fastened at one end — **tongued** \'təŋd\ *adj* — **tongue·less** *adj*

ton·ic \'tänik\ *n* : something (as a drug) that invigorates or restores health — **tonic** *adj*

to·night \tə'nīt\ *adv* : on this night — *n* : present or coming night

ton·sil \'tänsəl\ *n* : either of a pair of oval masses in the throat — **ton·sil·lec·to·my** \,tänsə'lektəmē\ *n* — **ton·sil·li·tis** \-'lītəs\ *n*

too \'tü\ *adv* **1** : in addition **2** : excessively

took *past of* TAKE

tool \'tül\ *n* : device worked by hand — *vb* : shape or finish with a tool

tool·bar \'tül,bär\ *n* : strip of icons on a computer display providing quick access to pictured functions

toot \'tüt\ *vb* : sound or cause to sound esp. in short blasts — **toot** *n*

tooth \'tüth\ *n, pl* **teeth** \'tēth\ **1** : one of the hard structures in the jaws for chewing **2** : one of the projections on the edge of a gear wheel — **tooth·ache** *n* — **tooth·brush** *n* — **toothed** \'tütht\ *adj* — **tooth·less** *adj* — **tooth·paste** *n* — **tooth·pick** *n*

tooth·some \'tüthsəm\ *adj* **1** : delicious **2** : attractive

¹**top** \'täp\ *n* **1** : highest part or level of something **2** : lid or covering — *vb* -**pp**- **1** : cover with a top **2** : surpass **3** : go over the top of — *adj* : being at the top — **topped** *adj*

²**top** *n* : spinning toy

to·paz \'tō,paz\ *n* : hard gem

top·coat *n* : lightweight overcoat

top·ic \'täpik\ *n* : subject for discussion or study

top·i·cal \-ikəl\ *adj* **1** : relating to or arranged by topics **2** : relating to current or local events — **top·i·cal·ly** *adv*

top·most \'täp,mōst\ *adj* : highest of all

top–notch \-'näch\ *adj* : of the highest quality

to·pog·ra·phy \tə'pägrəfē\ *n* **1** : art of mapping the physical features of a place **2** : outline of the form of a place — **to·pog·ra·pher** \-fər\ *n* — **top·o·graph·ic** \,täpə'grafik\, **top·o·graph·i·cal** \-ikəl\ *adj*

top·ple \'täpəl\ *vb* -**pled; -pling** : fall or cause to fall

top·sy–tur·vy \,täpsē'tərvē\ *adv or adj* **1** : upside down **2** : in utter confusion

torch \'tȯrch\ *n* : flaming light — **torch·bear·er** *n* — **torch·light** *n*

tore *past of* TEAR

tor·ment \'tȯr,ment\ *n* : extreme pain or anguish or a source of this — *vb* **1** : cause severe anguish to **2** : harass — **tor·men·tor** \-ər\ *n*

torn *past part of* TEAR

tor·na·do \tȯr'nādō\ *n, pl* -**does** *or* -**dos** : violent destructive whirling wind

tor·pe·do \tȯr'pēdō\ *n, pl* -**does** : self-propelled explosive submarine missile — *vb* : hit with a torpedo

tor·pid \'tȯrpəd\ *adj* **1** : having lost motion or the power of exertion **2** : lacking vigor — **tor·pid·i·ty** \tȯr'pidətē\ *n*

tor·por \'tȯrpər\ *n* : extreme sluggishness or lethargy

torque \'tȯrk\ *n* : turning force

tor·rent \'tȯrənt\ *n* **1** : rushing stream **2** : tumultuous outburst — **tor·ren·tial** \tȯ'renchəl, tə-\ *adj*

tor·rid \'tȯrəd\ *adj* **1** : parched with heat **2** : impassioned

tor·sion \'tȯrshən\ *n* : a twisting or being twisted — **tor·sion·al** \'tȯr-shənəl\ *adj* — **tor·sion·al·ly** *adv*

tor·so \'tȯrsō\ *n, pl* -**sos** *or* -**si** \-,sē\ : trunk of the human body

tor·ti·lla \tȯr'tēyə\ *n* : round flat cornmeal or wheat flour bread

tor·toise \'tórtəs\ *n* : land turtle

tor·tu·ous \'tórchəwəs\ *adj* **1** : winding **2** : tricky

tor·ture \'tórchər\ *n* **1** : use of pain to punish or force **2** : agony ~ *vb* **-tured; -tur·ing** : inflict torture on — **tor·tur·er** *n*

toss \'tós, 'täs\ *vb* **1** : move to and fro or up and down violently **2** : throw with a quick light motion **3** : move restlessly — **toss** *n*

toss–up *n* **1** : a deciding by flipping a coin **2** : even chance

tot \'tät\ *n* : small child

to·tal \'tōt³l\ *n* : entire amount ~ *vb* **-taled** *or* **-talled; -tal·ing** *or* **-tal·ling** **1** : add up **2** : amount to — **total** *adj* — **to·tal·ly** *adv*

to·tal·i·tar·i·an \tō̩talə'terēən\ *adj* : relating to a political system in which the government has complete control over the people — **totalitarian** *n* — **to·tal·i·tar·i·an·ism** \-ēə̩nizəm\ *n*

to·tal·i·ty \tō'talətē\ *n, pl* **-ties** : whole amount or entirety

tote \'tōt\ *vb* **tot·ed; tot·ing** : carry

to·tem \'tōtəm\ *n* : often carved figure used as a family or tribe emblem

tot·ter \'tätər\ *vb* **1** : sway as if about to fall **2** : stagger

touch \'təch\ *vb* **1** : make contact with so as to feel **2** : be or cause to be in contact **3** : take into the hands or mouth **4** : treat or mention a subject **5** : relate or concern **6** : move to sympathetic feeling ~ *n* **1** : light stroke **2** : act or fact of touching or being touched **3** : sense of feeling **4** : trace **5** : state of being in contact — **touch up** *vb* : improve with minor changes

touch·down \'təch̩daún\ *n* : scoring of 6 points in football

touch·stone *n* : test or criterion of genuineness or quality

touchy \'təchē\ *adj* **touch·i·er; -est** **1** : easily offended **2** : requiring tact

tough \'təf\ *adj* **1** : strong but elastic **2** : not easily chewed **3** : severe or disciplined **4** : stubborn ~ *n* : rowdy — **tough·ly** *adv* — **tough·ness** *n*

tough·en \'təfən\ *vb* : make or become tough

tou·pee \tü'pā\ *n* : small wig for a bald spot

tour \'túr\ *n* **1** : period of time spent at work or on an assignment **2** : journey with a return to the starting point ~

vb : travel over to see the sights — **tour·ist** \'túrist\ *n*

tour·na·ment \'túrnəmənt, 'tər-\ *n* **1** : medieval jousting competition **2** : championship series of games

tour·ney \-nē\ *n, pl* **-neys** : tournament

tour·ni·quet \'túrnikət, 'tər-\ *n* : tight bandage for stopping blood flow

tou·sle \'taúzəl\ *vb* **-sled; -sling** : dishevel (as someone's hair)

tout \'taút, 'tüt\ *vb* : praise or publicize loudly

tow \'tō\ *vb* : pull along behind — **tow** *n*

to·ward, to·wards \'tōrd, tə'wórd, 'tōrdz, tə'wórdz\ *prep* **1** : in the direction of **2** : with respect to **3** : in part payment on

tow·el \'taúəl\ *n* : absorbent cloth or paper for wiping or drying

tow·er \'taúər\ *n* : tall structure ~ *vb* : rise to a great height — **tow·ered** \'taúərd\ *adj* — **tow·er·ing** *adj*

tow·head \'tō̩hed\ *n* : person having whitish blond hair — **tow·head·ed** \-̩hedəd\ *adj*

town \'taún\ *n* **1** : small residential area **2** : city — **towns·peo·ple** \'taúnz̩pēpəl\ *n pl*

town·ship \'taún̩ship\ *n* **1** : unit of local government **2** : 36 square miles of U.S. public land

tox·ic \'täksik\ *adj* : poisonous — **tox·ic·i·ty** \täk'sisətē\ *n*

tox·in \'täksən\ *n* : poison produced by an organism

toy \'tói\ *n* : something for a child to play with ~ *vb* : amuse oneself or play with something ~ *adj* **1** : designed as a toy **2** : very small

¹trace \'trās\ *vb* **traced; trac·ing** **1** : mark over the lines of (a drawing) **2** : follow the trail or the development of ~ *n* **1** : track **2** : tiny amount or residue — **trace·able** *adj* — **trac·er** *n*

²trace *n* : line of a harness

tra·chea \'trākēə\ *n, pl* **-che·ae** \-kē̩ē\ : windpipe — **tra·che·al** \-kēəl\ *adj*

track \'trak\ *n* **1** : trail left by wheels or footprints **2** : racing course **3** : train rails **4** : awareness of a progression **5** : looped belts propelling a vehicle ~ *vb* **1** : follow the trail of **2** : make tracks on — **track·er** *n*

track–and–field *adj* : relating to athletic contests of running, jumping, and throwing events

¹tract \'trakt\ *n* **1** : stretch of land **2** : system of body organs

²**tract** *n* : pamphlet of propaganda

trac·ta·ble \'traktəbəl\ *adj* : easily controlled

trac·tion \'trakshən\ *n* : gripping power to permit movement — **trac·tion·al** \-shənəl\ *adj* — **trac·tive** \'traktiv\ *adj*

trac·tor \'traktər\ *n* **1** : farm vehicle used esp. for pulling **2** : truck for hauling a trailer

trade \'trād\ *n* **1** : one's regular business **2** : occupation requiring skill **3** : the buying and selling of goods **4** : act of trading ~ *vb* **trad·ed; trad·ing 1** : give in exchange for something **2** : buy and sell goods **3** : be a regular customer — **trades·peo·ple** \'trādz͵pēpəl\ *n pl*

trade-in \'trād͵in\ *n* : an item traded to a merchant at the time of a purchase

trade·mark \'trād͵märk\ *n* : word or mark identifying a manufacturer — **trademark** *vb*

trades·man \'trādzmən\ *n* : shopkeeper

tra·di·tion \trə'dishən\ *n* : belief or custom passed from generation to generation — **tra·di·tion·al** \-'dishənəl\ *adj* — **tra·di·tion·al·ly** *adv*

tra·duce \trə'düs, -'dyüs\ *vb* **-duced; -duc·ing** : lower the reputation of — **tra·duc·er** *n*

traf·fic \'trafik\ *n* **1** : business dealings **2** : movement along a route ~ *vb* : do business — **traf·fick·er** *n* — **traffic light** *n*

trag·e·dy \'trajədē\ *n, pl* **-dies 1** : serious drama describing a conflict and having a sad end **2** : disastrous event

trag·ic \'trajik\ *adj* : being a tragedy — **trag·i·cal·ly** *adv*

trail \'trāl\ *vb* **1** : hang down and drag along the ground **2** : draw along behind **3** : follow the track of **4** : dwindle ~ *n* **1** : something that trails **2** : path or evidence left by something

trail·er \'trālər\ *n* **1** : vehicle intended to be hauled **2** : dwelling designed to be towed to a site

train \'trān\ *n* **1** : trailing part of a gown **2** : retinue or procession **3** : connected series **4** : group of linked railroad cars ~ *vb* **1** : cause to grow as desired **2** : make or become prepared or skilled **3** : point — **train·ee** *n* — **train·er** *n* — **train·load** *n*

traipse \'trāps\ *vb* **traipsed; traips·ing** : walk

trait \'trāt\ *n* : distinguishing quality

trai·tor \'trātər\ *n* : one who betrays a trust or commits treason — **trai·tor·ous** *adj*

tra·jec·to·ry \trə'jektərē\ *n, pl* **-ries** : path of something moving through air or space

tram·mel \'traməl\ *vb* **-meled** *or* **-melled; -mel·ing** *or* **-mel·ling** : impede — **trammel** *n*

tramp \'tramp\ *vb* **1** : walk or hike **2** : tread on ~ *n* : beggar or vagrant

tram·ple \'trampəl\ *vb* **-pled; -pling** : walk or step on so as to bruise or crush — **trample** *n* — **tram·pler** \-plər\ *n*

tram·po·line \͵trampə'lēn, 'trampə͵-\ *n* : resilient sheet or web supported by springs and used for bouncing — **tram·po·lin·ist** \-ist\ *n*

trance \'trans\ *n* **1** : sleeplike condition **2** : state of mystical absorption

tran·quil \'traŋkwəl, 'tran-\ *adj* : quiet and undisturbed — **tran·quil·ize** \-kwə͵līz\ *vb* — **tran·quil·iz·er** *n* — **tran·quil·li·ty, tran·quil·i·ty** \tran-'kwilətē, traŋ-\ *n* — **tran·quil·ly** *adv*

trans·act \trans'akt, tranz-\ *vb* : conduct (business)

trans·ac·tion \-'akshən\ *n* **1** : business deal **2** *pl* : records of proceedings

tran·scend \trans'end\ *vb* : rise above or surpass — **tran·scen·dent** \-'endənt\ *adj* — **tran·scen·den·tal** \͵trans͵en'dent³l, -ən-\ *adj*

tran·scribe \trans'krīb\ *vb* **-scribed; -scrib·ing** : make a copy, arrangement, or recording of — **tran·scrip·tion** \trans'kripshən\ *n*

tran·script \'trans͵kript\ *n* : official copy

tran·sept \'trans͵ept\ *n* : part of a church that crosses the nave at right angles

trans·fer \trans'fər, 'trans͵fər\ *vb* **-rr- 1** : move from one person, place, or situation to another **2** : convey ownership of **3** : print or copy by contact **4** : change to another vehicle or transportation line ~ \'trans͵fər\ *n* **1** : act or process of transferring **2** : one that transfers or is transferred **3** : ticket permitting one to transfer — **trans·fer·able** \trans'fərəbəl\ *adj* — **trans·fer·al** \-əl\ *n* — **trans·fer·ence** \-əns\ *n*

trans·fig·ure \trans'figyər\ *vb* **-ured; -ur·ing 1** : change the form or appearance of **2** : glorify — **trans·fig·u·ra·tion** \ˌtransˌfigyə'rāshən\ n

trans·fix \trans'fiks\ vb **1** : pierce through **2** : hold motionless

trans·form \-'fórm\ vb **1** : change in structure, appearance, or character **2** : change (an electric current) in potential or type — **trans·for·ma·tion** \ˌtransfər'māshən\ n — **trans·form·er** \trans'fórmər\ n

trans·fuse \trans'fyüz\ vb **-fused; -fus·ing 1** : diffuse into or through **2** : transfer (as blood) into a vein — **trans·fu·sion** \-'fyüzhən\ n

trans·gress \trans'gres, tranz-\ vb : sin — **trans·gres·sion** \-'greshən\ n — **trans·gres·sor** \-'gresər\ n

tran·sient \'tranchənt\ adj : not lasting or staying long — **transient** n — **tran·sient·ly** adv

tran·sis·tor \tranz'istər, trans-\ n : small electronic device used in electronic equipment — **tran·sis·tor·ize** \-təˌrīz\ vb

tran·sit \'transət, 'tranz-\ n **1** : movement over, across, or through **2** : local and esp. public transportation **3** : surveyor's instrument

tran·si·tion \trans'ishən, tranz-\ n : passage from one state, stage, or subject to another — **tran·si·tion·al** \-'ishənəl\ adj

tran·si·to·ry \'transəˌtōrē, 'tranz-\ adj : of brief duration

trans·late \trans'lāt, tranz-\ vb **-lated; -lat·ing** : change into another language — **trans·lat·able** adj — **trans·la·tion** \-'lāshən\ n — **trans·la·tor** \-'lātər\ n

trans·lu·cent \trans'lüs°nt, tranz-\ adj : not transparent but clear enough to allow light to pass through — **trans·lu·cence** \-°ns\ n — **trans·lu·cen·cy** \-°nsē\ n — **trans·lu·cent·ly** adv

trans·mis·sion \-'mishən\ n **1** : act or process of transmitting **2** : system of gears between a car engine and drive wheels

trans·mit \-'mit\ vb **-tt- 1** : transfer from one person or place to another **2** : pass on by inheritance **3** : broadcast — **trans·mis·si·ble** \-'misəbəl\ adj — **trans·mit·ta·ble** \-'mitəbəl\ adj — **trans·mit·tal** \-'mit°l\ n — **trans·mit·ter** n

tran·som \'transəm\ n : often hinged window above a door

trans·par·ent \trans'parənt\ adj **1**

: clear enough to see through **2** : obvious — **trans·par·en·cy** \-ənsē\ n — **trans·par·ent·ly** adv

tran·spire \trans'pīr\ vb **-spired; -spir·ing** : take place — **tran·spi·ra·tion** \ˌtranspə'rāshən\ n

trans·plant \trans'plant\ vb **1** : dig up and move to another place **2** : transfer from one body part or person to another — **transplant** \'transˌ-\ n — **trans·plan·ta·tion** \ˌtransˌplan'tāshən\ n

trans·port \trans'pórt\ vb **1** : carry or deliver to another place **2** : carry away by emotion ～ \'transˌ-\ n **1** : act of transporting **2** : rapture **3** : ship or plane for carrying troops or supplies — **trans·por·ta·tion** \ˌtranspər'tāshən\ n — **trans·port·er** n

trans·pose \trans'pōz\ vb **-posed; -pos·ing** : change the position, sequence, or key — **trans·po·si·tion** \ˌtranspə'zishən\ n

trans·ship \tran'ship, trans-\ vb : transfer from one mode of transportation to another — **trans·ship·ment** n

trans·verse \trans'vərs, tranz-\ adj : lying across — **trans·verse** \'transˌvərs, 'tranz-\ n — **trans·verse·ly** adv

trap \'trap\ n **1** : device for catching animals **2** : something by which one is caught unawares **3** : device to allow one thing to pass through while keeping other things out ～ vb **-pp-** : catch in a trap — **trap·per** n

trap·door n : door in a floor or roof

tra·peze \tra'pēz\ n : suspended bar used by acrobats

trap·e·zoid \'trapəˌzóid\ n : plane 4-sided figure with 2 parallel sides — **trap·e·zoi·dal** \ˌtrapə'zóid°l\ adj

trap·pings \'trapiŋz\ n pl **1** : ornamental covering **2** : outward decoration or dress

trash \'trash\ n : something that is no good — **trashy** adj

trau·ma \'traúmə, 'tró-\ n : bodily or mental injury — **trau·mat·ic** \trə'matik, tró-, traú-\ adj

tra·vail \trə'vāl, 'travˌāl\ n : painful work or exertion ～ vb : labor hard

trav·el \'travəl\ vb **-eled** or **-elled; -el·ing** or **-el·ling 1** : take a trip or tour **2** : move or be carried from point to point ～ n : journey — often pl. — **trav·el·er, trav·el·ler** n

tra•verse \trə'vərs, tra'vərs, 'travərs\ vb -versed; -vers•ing : go or extend across — **tra•verse** \'travərs\ n

trav•es•ty \'travəstē\ n, pl -ties : imitation that makes crude fun of something — **travesty** vb

trawl \'tról\ vb : fish or catch with a trawl ~ n : large cone-shaped net — **trawl•er** n

tray \'trā\ n : shallow flat-bottomed receptacle for holding or carrying something

treach•er•ous \'trechərəs\ adj : disloyal or dangerous — **treach•er•ous•ly** adv

treach•ery \'trechərē\ n, pl -er•ies : betrayal of a trust

tread \'tred\ vb trod \'träd\; trod•den \'träd⁰n\ or trod; tread•ing 1 : step on or over 2 : walk 3 : press or crush with the feet ~ n 1 : way of walking 2 : sound made in walking 3 : part on which a thing runs

trea•dle \'tred⁰l\ n : foot pedal operating a machine — **treadle** vb

tread•mill n 1 : mill worked by walking persons or animals 2 : wearisome routine

trea•son \'trēz⁰n\ n : attempt to overthrow the government — **trea•son•able** \'trēz⁰nəbəl\ adj — **trea•son•ous** \-⁰nəs\ adj

trea•sure \'trezhər, 'trāzh-\ n 1 : wealth stored up 2 : something of great value ~ vb -sured; -sur•ing : keep as precious

trea•sur•er \'trezhərər, 'trāzh-\ n : officer who handles funds

trea•sury \'trezhərē, 'trāzh-\ n, pl -sur•ies : place or office for keeping and distributing funds

treat \'trēt\ vb 1 : have as a topic 2 : pay for the food or entertainment of 3 : act toward or regard in a certain way 4 : give medical care to ~ n 1 : food or entertainment paid for by another 2 : something special and enjoyable — **treat•ment** \-mənt\ n

trea•tise \'trētəs\ n : systematic written exposition or argument

trea•ty \'trētē\ n, pl -ties : agreement between governments

tre•ble \'trebəl\ n 1 : highest part in music 2 : upper half of the musical range ~ adj : triple in number or amount ~ vb -bled; -bling : make triple — **tre•bly** adv

tree \'trē\ n : tall woody plant ~ vb

treed; tree•ing : force up a tree — **tree•less** adj

trek \'trek\ n : difficult trip ~ vb -kk- : make a trek

trel•lis \'treləs\ n : structure of crossed strips

trem•ble \'trembəl\ vb -bled; -bling 1 : shake from fear or cold 2 : move or sound as if shaken

tre•men•dous \tri'mendəs\ adj : amazingly large, powerful, or excellent — **tre•men•dous•ly** adv

trem•or \'tremər\ n : a trembling

trem•u•lous \'tremyələs\ adj : trembling or quaking

trench \'trench\ n : long narrow cut in land

tren•chant \'trenchənt\ adj : sharply perceptive

trend \'trend\ n : prevailing tendency, direction, or style ~ vb : move in a particular direction — **trendy** \'trendē\ adj

trep•i•da•tion \ˌtrepə'dāshən\ n : nervous apprehension

tres•pass \'trespəs, -ˌpas\ n 1 : sin 2 : unauthorized entry onto someone's property ~ vb 1 : sin 2 : enter illegally — **tres•pass•er** n

tress \'tres\ n : long lock of hair

tres•tle \'tresəl\ n 1 : support with a horizontal piece and spreading legs 2 : framework bridge

tri•ad \'trīˌad, -əd\ n : union of 3

tri•age \trē'äzh, 'trēˌäzh\ n : system of dealing with cases (as patients) according to priority guidelines intended to maximize success

tri•al \'trīəl\ n 1 : hearing and judgment of a matter in court 2 : source of great annoyance 3 : test use or experimental effort — **trial** adj

tri•an•gle \'trīˌaŋgəl\ n : plane figure with 3 sides and 3 angles — **tri•an•gu•lar** \trī'aŋgyələr\ adj

tribe \'trīb\ n : social group of numerous families — **trib•al** \'trībəl\ adj — **tribes•man** \'trībzmən\ n — **tribes•peo•ple** \-ˌpēpəl\ n pl

trib•u•la•tion \ˌtribyə'lāshən\ n : suffering from oppression

tri•bu•nal \trī'byün⁰l, tri-\ n 1 : court 2 : something that decides

trib•u•tary \'tribyəˌterē\ n, pl -tar•ies : stream that flows into a river or lake

trib•ute \'tribˌyüt\ n 1 : payment to acknowledge submission 2 : tax 3 : gift or act showing respect

trick \'trik\ *n* **1** : scheme to deceive **2** : prank **3** : deceptive or ingenious feat **4** : mannerism **5** : knack **6** : tour of duty ∼ *vb* : deceive by cunning — **trick•ery** \-ərē\ *n* — **trick•ster** \-stər\ *n*

trick•le \'trikəl\ *vb* **-led; -ling** : run in drops or a thin stream — **trickle** *n*

tricky \'trikē\ *adj* **trick•i•er; -est 1** : inclined to trickery **2** : requiring skill or caution

tri•cy•cle \'trī,sikəl\ *n* : 3-wheeled bicycle

tri•dent \'trīd°nt\ *n* : 3-pronged spear

tri•en•ni•al \'trī'enēəl\ *adj* : lasting, occurring, or done every 3 years — **tri•ennial** *n*

tri•fle \'trīfəl\ *n* : something of little value or importance ∼ *vb* **-fled; -fling 1** : speak or act in a playful or flirting way **2** : toy — **tri•fler** *n*

tri•fling \'trīfliŋ\ *adj* : trivial

trig•ger \'trigər\ *n* : finger-piece of a firearm lock that fires the gun ∼ *vb* : set into motion — **trigger** *adj* — **trig•gered** \-ərd\ *adj*

trig•o•nom•e•try \,trigə'nämətrē\ *n* : mathematics dealing with triangular measurement — **trig•o•no•met•ric** \-nə'metrik\ *adj*

trill \'tril\ *n* **1** : rapid alternation between 2 adjacent tones **2** : rapid vibration in speaking ∼ *vb* : utter in or with a trill

tril•lion \'trilyən\ *n* : 1000 billions — **trillion** *adj* — **tril•lionth** \-yənth\ *adj or n*

tril•o•gy \'triləjē\ *n, pl* **-gies** : 3-part literary or musical composition

trim \'trim\ *vb* **-mm- 1** : decorate **2** : make neat or reduce by cutting ∼ *adj* **-mm-** : neat and compact ∼ *n* **1** : state or condition **2** : ornaments — **trim•ly** *adv* — **trim•mer** *n*

trim•ming \'trimiŋ\ *n* : something that ornaments or completes

Trin•i•ty \'trinətē\ *n* : divine unity of Father, Son, and Holy Spirit

trin•ket \'triŋkət\ *n* : small ornament

trio \'trēō\ *n, pl* **tri•os 1** : music for 3 performers **2** : group of 3

trip \'trip\ *vb* **-pp- 1** : step lightly **2** : stumble or cause to stumble **3** : make or cause to make a mistake **4** : release (as a spring or switch) ∼ *n* **1** : journey **2** : stumble **3** : drug-induced experience

tri•par•tite \trī'pär,tīt\ *adj* : having 3 parts or parties

tripe \'trīp\ *n* **1** : animal's stomach used as food **2** : trash

tri•ple \'tripəl\ *vb* **-pled; -pling** : make 3 times as great ∼ *n* : group of 3 ∼ *adj* **1** : having 3 units **2** : being 3 times as great or as many

trip•let \'triplət\ *n* **1** : group of 3 **2** : one of 3 offspring born together

trip•li•cate \'triplikət\ *adj* : made in 3 identical copies ∼ *n* : one of 3 copies

tri•pod \'trī,päd\ *n* : a stand with 3 legs — **tripod, tri•po•dal** \'tripəd°l, 'trī,päd-\ *adj*

tri•sect \'trī,sekt, trī'-\ *vb* : divide into 3 usu. equal parts — **tri•sec•tion** \'trī,sekshən\ *n*

trite \'trīt\ *adj* **trit•er; trit•est** : commonplace

tri•umph \'trīəmf\ *n, pl* **-umphs** : victory or great success ∼ *vb* : obtain or celebrate victory — **tri•um•phal** \trī'əmfəl\ *adj* — **tri•um•phant** \-fənt\ *adj* — **tri•um•phant•ly** *adv*

tri•um•vi•rate \trī'əmvərət\ *n* : ruling body of 3 persons

triv•et \'trivət\ *n* **1** : 3-legged stand **2** : stand to hold a hot dish

triv•ia \'trivēə\ *n sing or pl* : unimportant details

triv•i•al \'trivēəl\ *adj* : of little importance — **triv•i•al•i•ty** \,trivē'alətē\ *n*

trod *past of* TREAD

trodden *past part of* TREAD

troll \'trōl\ *n* : dwarf or giant of folklore inhabiting caves or hills

trol•ley \'trälē\ *n, pl* **-leys** : streetcar run by overhead electric wires

trol•lop \'träləp\ *n* : untidy or immoral woman

trom•bone \träm'bōn, 'träm,-\ *n* : musical instrument with a long sliding tube — **trom•bon•ist** \-'bōnist, -,bō-\ *n*

troop \'trüp\ *n* **1** : cavalry unit **2** *pl* : soldiers **3** : collection of people or things ∼ *vb* : move or gather in crowds

troop•er \'trüpər\ *n* **1** : cavalry soldier **2** : police officer on horseback or state police officer

tro•phy \'trōfē\ *n, pl* **-phies** : prize gained by a victory

trop•ic \'träpik\ *n* **1** : either of the 2 parallels of latitude one 23½ degrees north of the equator (**tropic of Cancer** \-'kansər\) and one 23½ degrees south of the equator (**tropic of Cap•ri•corn** \-'kaprə,kórn\) **2** *pl* : region lying between the tropics — **tropic, trop•i•cal** \-ikəl\ *adj*

trot \'trät\ *n* : moderately fast gait esp. of a horse with diagonally paired legs moving together ~ *vb* **-tt-** : go at a trot — **trot•ter** *n*

troth \'träth, 'tróth, 'trōth\ *n* **1** : pledged faithfulness **2** : betrothal

trou•ba•dour \'trübə,dōr\ *n* : medieval lyric poet

trou•ble \'trəbəl\ *vb* **-bled; -bling 1** : disturb **2** : afflict **3** : make an effort ~ *n* **1** : cause of mental or physical distress **2** : effort — **trou•ble•mak•er** *n* — **trou•ble•some** *adj* — **trou•ble•some•ly** *adv*

trough \'tróf\ *n, pl* **troughs** \'trófs, 'tróvz\ **1** : narrow container for animal feed or water **2** : long channel or depression (as between waves)

trounce \'traúns\ *vb* **trounced; trounc•ing** : thrash, punish, or defeat severely

troupe \'trüp\ *n* : group of stage performers — **troup•er** *n*

trou•sers \'traúzərz\ *n pl* : long pants — **trouser** *adj*

trous•seau \'trüsō, trü'sō\ *n, pl* **-seaux** \-sōz, -'sōz\ *or* **-seaus** : bride's collection of clothing and personal items

trout \'traút\ *n, pl* **trout** : freshwater food and game fish

trow•el \'traúəl\ *n* **1** : tool for spreading or smoothing **2** : garden scoop — **trowel** *vb*

troy \'trói\ *n* : system of weights based on a pound of 12 ounces

tru•ant \'trüənt\ *n* : student absent from school without permission — **tru•an•cy** \-ənsē\ *n* — **truant** *adj*

truce \'trüs\ *n* : agreement to halt fighting

truck \'trək\ *n* **1** : wheeled frame for moving heavy objects **2** : automotive vehicle for transporting heavy loads ~ *vb* : transport on a truck — **truck•er** *n* — **truck•load** *n*

truck•le \'trəkəl\ *vb* **-led; -ling** : yield slavishly to another

tru•cu•lent \'trəkyələnt\ *adj* : aggressively self-assertive — **truc•u•lence** \-ləns\ *n* — **tru•cu•lent•ly** *adv*

trudge \'trəj\ *vb* **trudged; trudg•ing** : walk or march steadily and with difficulty

true \'trü\ *adj* **tru•er; tru•est 1** : loyal

2 : in agreement with fact or reality **3** : genuine ~ *adv* **1** : truthfully **2** : accurately ~ *vb* **trued; true•ing** : make balanced or even — **tru•ly** *adv*

true–blue *adj* : loyal

truf•fle \'trəfəl\ *n* **1** : edible fruit of an underground fungus **2** : ball-shaped chocolate candy

tru•ism \'trü,izəm\ *n* : obvious truth

trump \'trəmp\ *n* : card of a designated suit any of whose cards will win over other cards ~ *vb* : take with a trump

trumped–up \'trəmpt'əp\ *adj* : made-up

trum•pet \'trəmpət\ *n* : tubular brass wind instrument with a flaring end ~ *vb* **1** : blow a trumpet **2** : proclaim loudly — **trum•pet•er** *n*

trun•cate \'trəŋ,kāt, 'trən-\ *vb* **-cat•ed; -cat•ing** : cut short — **trun•ca•tion** \,trəŋ'kāshən\ *n*

trun•dle \'trəndəl\ *vb* **-dled; -dling** : roll along

trunk \'trəŋk\ *n* **1** : main part (as of a body or tree) **2** : long muscular nose of an elephant **3** : storage chest **4** : storage space in a car **5** *pl* : shorts

truss \'trəs\ *vb* : bind tightly ~ *n* **1** : set of structural parts forming a framework **2** : appliance worn to hold a hernia in place

trust \'trəst\ *n* **1** : reliance on another **2** : assured hope **3** : credit **4** : property held or managed in behalf of another **5** : combination of firms that reduces competition **6** : something entrusted to another's care **7** : custody ~ *vb* **1** : depend **2** : hope **3** : entrust **4** : have faith in — **trust•ful** \-fəl\ *adj* — **trust•ful•ly** *adv* — **trust•ful•ness** *n* — **trust•worth•i•ness** *n* — **trust•wor•thy** *adj*

trust•ee \,trəs'tē\ *n* : person holding property in trust — **trust•ee•ship** *n*

trusty \'trəstē\ *adj* **trust•i•er; -est** : dependable

truth \'trüth\ *n, pl* **truths** \'trüthz, 'trüths\ **1** : real state of things **2** : true or accepted statement **3** : agreement with fact or reality — **truth•ful** \-fəl\ *adj* — **truth•ful•ly** *adv* — **truth•ful•ness** *n*

try \'trī\ *vb* **tried; try•ing 1** : conduct the trial of **2** : put to a test **3** : strain **4** : make an effort at ~ *n, pl* **tries** : act of trying

try–out *n* : competitive test of performance esp. for athletes or actors — **try out** *vb*

tryst \'trist, 'trīst\ *n* : secret rendezvous of lovers

tsar \'zär, 'tsär, 'sär\ *var of* CZAR

T–shirt \'tē,shərt\ *n* : collarless pullover shirt with short sleeves

tub \'təb\ *n* **1** : wide bucketlike vessel **2** : bathtub

tu•ba \'tübə, 'tyü-\ *n* : large low= pitched brass wind instument

tube \'tüb, 'tyüb\ *n* **1** : hollow cylinder **2** : round container from which a substance can be squeezed **3** : airtight circular tube of rubber inside a tire **4** : electronic device consisting of a sealed usu. glass container with electrodes inside — **tubed** \'tübd, 'tyübd\ *adj* — **tube•less** *adj*

tu•ber \'tübər, 'tyü-\ *n* : fleshy underground growth (as of a potato) — **tu•ber•ous** \-rəs\ *adj*

tu•ber•cu•lo•sis \tü,bərkyə'lōsəs, tyü-\ *n, pl* **-lo•ses** \-,sēz\ : bacterial disease esp. of the lungs — **tu•ber•cu•lar** \-'bərkyələr\ *adj* — **tu•ber•cu•lous** \-ləs\ *adj*

tub•ing \'tübiŋ, 'tyü-\ *n* : series or arrangement of tubes

tu•bu•lar \'tübyələr, 'tyü-\ *adj* : of or like a tube

tuck \'tək\ *vb* **1** : pull up into a fold **2** : put into a snug often concealing place **3** : make snug in bed — with *in* ~ *n* : fold in a cloth

tuck•er \'təkər\ *vb* : fatigue

Tues•day \'tüzdā, 'tyüz-, -dē\ *n* : 3d day of the week

tuft \'təft\ *n* : clump (as of hair or feathers) — **tuft•ed** \'təftəd\ *adj*

tug \'təg\ *vb* **-gg-** **1** : pull hard **2** : move by pulling ~ *n* **1** : act of tugging **2** : tugboat

tug•boat *n* : boat for towing or pushing ships through a harbor

tug–of–war \,təgə'wȯr\ *n, pl* **tugs–of–war** : pulling contest between 2 teams

tu•ition \tü'ishən, 'tyü-\ *n* : cost of instruction

tu•lip \'tüləp, 'tyü-\ *n* : herb with cup= shaped flowers

tum•ble \'təmbəl\ *vb* **-bled; -bling** **1** : perform gymnastic feats of rolling and turning **2** : fall or cause to fall suddenly **3** : toss ~ *n* : act of tumbling

tum•bler \'təmblər\ *n* **1** : acrobat **2** : drinking glass **3** : obstruction in a lock that can be moved (as by a key)

tu•mid \'tüməd, 'tyü-\ *adj* : turgid

tum•my \'təmē\ *n, pl* **-mies** : belly

tu•mor \'tümər, 'tyü-\ *n* : abnormal and useless growth of tissue — **tu•mor•ous** *adj*

tu•mult \'tü,məlt, 'tyü-\ *n* **1** : uproar **2** : violent agitation of mind or feelings — **tu•mul•tu•ous** \tü'məlchəwəs, tyü-\ *adj*

tun \'tən\ *n* : large cask

tu•na \'tünə, 'tyü-\ *n, pl* **-na** *or* **-nas** : large sea food fish

tun•dra \'təndrə\ *n* : treeless arctic plain

tune \'tün, 'tyün\ *n* **1** : melody **2** : correct musical pitch **3** : harmonious relationship ~ *vb* **tuned; tuning** **1** : bring or come into harmony **2** : adjust in musical pitch **3** : adjust a receiver so as to receive a broadcast **4** : put in first-class working order — **tun•able** *adj* — **tune•ful** \-fəl\ *adj* — **tun•er** *n*

tung•sten \'təŋstən\ *n* : metallic element used for electrical purposes and in hardening alloys (as steel)

tu•nic \'tünik, 'tyü-\ *n* **1** : ancient knee-length garment **2** : hip-length blouse or jacket

tun•nel \'tən²l\ *n* : underground passageway ~ *vb* **-neled** *or* **-nelled; -nel•ing** *or* **-nel•ling** : make a tunnel through or under something

tur•ban \'tərbən\ *n* : wound headdress worn esp. by Muslims

tur•bid \'tərbəd\ *adj* **1** : dark with stirred-up sediment **2** : confused — **tur•bid•i•ty** \,tər'bidətē\ *n*

tur•bine \'tərbən, -,bīn\ *n* : engine turned by the force of gas or water on fan blades

tur•bo•jet \'tərbō,jet\ *n* : airplane powered by a jet engine having a turbine= driven air compressor or the engine itself

tur•bo•prop \'tərbō,präp\ *n* : airplane powered by a propeller turned by a jet engine-driven turbine

tur•bu•lent \'tərbyələnt\ *adj* **1** : causing violence or disturbance **2** : marked by agitation or tumult — **tur•bu•lence** \-ləns\ *n* — **tur•bu•lent•ly** *adv*

tu•reen \tə'rēn, tyü-\ *n* : deep bowl for serving soup

turf \'tərf\ *n* : upper layer of soil bound by grass and roots

tur•gid \'tərjəd\ *adj* **1** : swollen **2** : too highly embellished in style — **tur•gid•i•ty** \,tər'jidətē\ *n*

tur·key \'tərkē\ *n, pl* **-keys** : large American bird raised for food

tur·moil \'tər,móil\ *n* : extremely agitated condition

turn \'tərn\ *vb* **1** : move or cause to move around an axis **2** : twist (a mechanical part) to operate **3** : wrench **4** : cause to face or move in a different direction **5** : reverse the sides or surfaces of **6** : upset **7** : go around **8** : become or cause to become **9** : seek aid from a source ~ *n* **1** : act or instance of turning **2** : change **3** : place at which something turns **4** : place, time, or opportunity to do something in order — **turn·er** *n* — **turn down** *vb* : decline to accept — **turn in** *vb* **1** : deliver or report to authorities **2** : go to bed — **turn off** *vb* : stop the functioning of — **turn out** *vb* **1** : expel **2** : produce **3** : come together **4** : prove to be in the end — **turn over** *vb* : transfer — **turn up** *vb* **1** : discover or appear **2** : happen unexpectedly

turn·coat *n* : traitor

tur·nip \'tərnəp\ *n* : edible root of an herb

turn·out \'tərn,aút\ *n* **1** : gathering of people for a special purpose **2** : size of a gathering

turn·over *n* **1** : upset or reversal **2** : filled pastry **3** : volume of business **4** : movement (as of goods or people) into, through, and out of a place

turn·pike \'tərn,pīk\ *n* : expressway on which tolls are charged

turn·stile \-,stīl\ *n* : post with arms pivoted on the top that allows people to pass one by one

turn·ta·ble *n* : platform that turns a phonograph record

tur·pen·tine \'tərpən,tīn\ *n* : oil distilled from pine-tree resin and used as a solvent

tur·pi·tude \'tərpə,tüd, -,tyüd\ *n* : inherent baseness

tur·quoise \'tər,kóiz, -,kwóiz\ *n* : blue or greenish gray gemstone

tur·ret \'tərət\ *n* **1** : little tower on a building **2** : revolving tool holder or gun housing

tur·tle \'tərt°l\ *n* : reptile with the trunk enclosed in a bony shell

tur·tle·dove *n* : wild pigeon

tur·tle·neck *n* : high close-fitting collar that can be turned over or a sweater or shirt with this collar

tusk \'təsk\ *n* : long protruding tooth (as of an elephant) — **tusked** \'təskt\ *adj*

tus·sle \'təsəl\ *n or vb* : struggle

tu·te·lage \'tüt°lij, 'tyüt-\ *n* **1** : act of protecting **2** : instruction esp. of an individual

tu·tor \'tütər, 'tyü-\ *n* : private teacher ~ *vb* : teach usu. individually

tux·e·do \,tək'sēdō\ *n, pl* **-dos** *or* **-does** : semiformal evening clothes for a man

TV \,tē'vē, 'tē,vē\ *n* : television

twain \'twān\ *n* : two

twang \'twaŋ\ *n* **1** : harsh sound like that of a plucked bowstring **2** : nasal speech or resonance ~ *vb* : sound or speak with a twang

tweak \'twēk\ *vb* : pinch and pull playfully — **tweak** *n*

tweed \'twēd\ *n* **1** : rough woolen fabric **2** *pl* : tweed clothing — **tweedy** *adj*

tweet \'twēt\ *n* : chirping note — **tweet** *vb*

twee·zers \'twēzərz\ *n pl* : small pincerlike tool

twelve \'twelv\ *n* **1** : one more than 11 **2** : 12th in a set or series **3** : something having 12 units — **twelfth** \'twelfth\ *adj or n* — **twelve** *adj or pron*

twen·ty \'twentē\ *n, pl* **-ties** : 2 times 10 — **twen·ti·eth** \-ēəth\ *adj or n* — **twenty** *adj or pron*

twen·ty–twen·ty, 20–20 *adj* : being vision of normal sharpness

twice \'twīs\ *adv* **1** : on 2 occasions **2** : 2 times

twig \'twig\ *n* : small branch — **twig·gy** *adj*

twi·light \'twī,līt\ *n* : light from the sky at dusk or dawn — **twilight** *adj*

twill \'twil\ *n* : fabric with a weave that gives an appearance of diagonal lines in the fabric

twilled \'twild\ *adj* : made with a twill weave

twin \'twin\ *n* : either of 2 offspring born together ~ *adj* **1** : born with one another or as a pair at one birth **2** : made up of 2 similar parts

twine \'twīn\ *n* : strong twisted thread ~ *vb* **twined; twin·ing 1** : twist together **2** : coil about a support — **twin·er** *n* — **twiny** *adj*

twinge \'twinj\ *vb* **twinged; twing·ing** *or* **twinge·ing** : affect with or feel a sudden sharp pain ~ *n* : sudden sharp stab (as of pain)

twin·kle \'twiŋkəl\ *vb* **-kled; -kling**

: shine with a flickering light ∼ *n* **1** : wink **2** : intermittent shining — **twin•kler** \-klər\ *n*

twirl \'twərl\ *vb* : whirl round ∼ *n* **1** : act of twirling **2** : coil — **twirl•er** *n*

twist \'twist\ *vb* **1** : unite by winding (threads) together **2** : wrench **3** : move in or have a spiral shape **4** : follow a winding course ∼ *n* **1** : act or result of twisting **2** : unexpected development

twist•er \'twistər\ *n* : tornado

¹**twit** \'twit\ *n* : fool

²**twit** *vb* **-tt-** : taunt

twitch \'twich\ *vb* : move or pull with a sudden motion ∼ *n* : act of twitching

twit•ter \'twitər\ *vb* : make chirping noises ∼ *n* : small intermittent noise

two \'tü\ *n, pl* **twos 1** : one more than one **2** : the 2d in a set or series **3** : something having 2 units — **two** *adj or pron*

two•fold \'tü,fōld\ *adj* : double — **two-fold** \-'fōld\ *adv*

two•some \'tüsəm\ *n* : couple

-ty *n suffix* : quality, condition, or degree

ty•coon \tī'kün\ *n* : powerful and successful businessman

tying *pres part of* TIE

tyke \'tīk\ *n* : small child

tym•pa•num \'timpənəm\ *n, pl* **-na** \-nə\ : eardrum or the cavity which it closes externally — **tym•pan•ic** \tim'panik\ *adj*

type \'tīp\ *n* **1** : class, kind, or group set apart by common characteristics **2** : special design of printed letters ∼ *vb* **typed; typ•ing 1** : write with a typewriter **2** : identify or classify as a particular type

type•writ•er *n* : keyboard machine that produces printed material by striking a ribbon with raised letters — **type-write** *vb*

ty•phoid \'tī,fòid, tī'-\ *adj* : relating to or being a communicable bacterial disease **(typhoid fever)**

ty•phoon \tī'fün\ *n* : hurricane of the western Pacific ocean

ty•phus \'tīfəs\ *n* : severe disease with fever, delirium, and rash

typ•i•cal \'tipikəl\ *adj* : having the essential characteristics of a group — **typ•i•cal•i•ty** \,tipə'kalətē\ *n* — **typ-i•cal•ly** *adv* — **typ•i•cal•ness** *n*

typ•i•fy \'tipə,fī\ *vb* **-fied; -fy•ing** : be typical of

typ•ist \'tīpist\ *n* : one who operates a typewriter

ty•pog•ra•phy \tī'pägrəfē\ *n* **1** : art of printing with type **2** : style, arrangement, or appearance of printed matter — **ty•po•graph•ic** \,tīpə'grafik\, **ty-po•graph•i•cal** \-ikəl\ *adj* — **ty•po-graph•i•cal•ly** *adv*

ty•ran•ni•cal \tə'ranikəl, tī-\ *adj* : relating to a tyrant — **ty•ran•ni•cal•ly** *adv*

tyr•an•nize \'tirə,nīz\ *vb* **-nized; -niz-ing** : rule or deal with in the manner of a tyrant — **tyr•an•niz•er** *n*

tyr•an•ny \'tirənē\ *n, pl* **-nies** : unjust use of absolute governmental power

ty•rant \'tīrənt\ *n* : harsh ruler having absolute power

ty•ro \'tīrō\ *n, pl* **-ros** : beginner

tzar \'zär, 'tsär, 'sär\ *var of* CZAR

U

u \'yü\ *n, pl* **u's** *or* **us** \'yüz\ : 21st letter of the alphabet

ubiq•ui•tous \yü'bikwətəs\ *adj* : omnipresent — **ubiq•ui•tous•ly** *adv* — **ubiq•ui•ty** \-wətē\ *n*

ud•der \'ədər\ *n* : animal sac containing milk glands and nipples

ug•ly \'əglē\ *adj* **ug•li•er; -est 1** : offensive to look at **2** : mean or quarrelsome — **ug•li•ness** *n*

uku•le•le \,yükə'lālē\ *n* : small 4-string guitar

ul•cer \'əlsər\ *n* : eroded sore — **ul•cer-ous** *adj*

ul•cer•ate \'əlsə,rāt\ *vb* **-at•ed; -at•ing** : become affected with an ulcer — **ul-cer•a•tion** \,əlsə'rāshən\ *n* — **ul-cer•a•tive** \'əlsə,rātiv\ *adj*

ul•na \'əlnə\ *n* : bone of the forearm opposite the thumb

ul•te•ri•or \,əl'tirēər\ *adj* : not revealed

ul•ti•mate \'əltəmət\ *adj* : final, maximum, or extreme — **ultimate** *n* — **ul-ti•mate•ly** *adv*

ul·ti·ma·tum \,əltə'mātəm, -'mät-\ *n,* *pl* **-tums** *or* **-ta** \-ə\ **:** final proposition or demand carrying or implying a threat

ul·tra·vi·o·let \,əltrə'vīələt\ *adj* **:** having a wavelength shorter than visible light

um·bi·li·cus \,əmbə'līkəs, ,əm'bili-\ *n, pl* **-li·ci** \-bə'lī,kī, -,sī; -'bilə,kī, -,kē\ *or* **-li·cus·es** **:** small depression on the abdominal wall marking the site of the cord (**umbilical cord**) that joins the unborn fetus to its mother — **um·bil·i·cal** \,əm'bilikəl\ *adj*

um·brage \'əmbrij\ *n* **:** resentment

um·brel·la \,əm'brelə\ *n* **:** collapsible fabric device to protect from sun or rain

um·pire \'əm,pīr\ *n* **1** **:** arbitrator **2** **:** sport official — **umpire** *vb*

ump·teen \'əmp'tēn\ *adj* **:** very numerous — **ump·teenth** \-'tēnth\ *adj*

un- \,ən, 'ən\ *prefix* **1** **:** not **2** **:** opposite of

un·ac·cus·tomed *adj* **1** **:** not customary **2** **:** not accustomed

un·af·fect·ed *adj* **1** **:** not influenced or changed by something **2** **:** natural and sincere — **un·af·fect·ed·ly** *adv*

unan·i·mous \yů'nanəməs\ *adj* **1** **:** showing no disagreement **2** **:** formed with the agreement of all — **una·nim·i·ty** \,yünə'nimətē\ *n* — **unan·i·mous·ly** *adv*

un·armed *adj* **:** not armed or armored

un·as·sum·ing *adj* **:** not bold or arrogant

un·at·tached *adj* **1** **:** not attached **2** **:** not married or engaged

un·aware *adv* **:** unawares ~ *adj* **:** not aware

un·awares \,ənə'warz\ *adv* **1** **:** without warning **2** **:** unintentionally

un·bal·anced *adj* **1** **:** not balanced **2** **:** mentally unstable

un·beat·en *adj* **:** not beaten

un·be·com·ing *adj* **:** not proper or suitable — **un·be·com·ing·ly** *adv*

un·be·liev·able *adj* **1** **:** improbable **2** **:** superlative — **un·be·liev·ably** *adv*

un·bend *vb* **-bent; -bend·ing** **:** make or become more relaxed and friendly

un·bend·ing *adj* **:** formal and inflexible

un·bind *vb* **-bound; -bind·ing** **1** **:** remove bindings from **2** **:** release

un·bolt *vb* **:** open or unfasten by withdrawing a bolt

un·born *adj* **:** not yet born

un·bo·som *vb* **:** disclose thoughts or feelings

un·bowed \,ən'baůd\ *adj* **:** not defeated or subdued

un·bri·dled \,ən'brīd°ld\ *adj* **:** unrestrained

un·bro·ken *adj* **1** **:** not damaged **2** **:** not interrupted

un·buck·le *vb* **:** unfasten the buckle of

un·bur·den *vb* **:** relieve (oneself) of anxieties

un·but·ton *vb* **:** unfasten the buttons of

un·called–for *adj* **:** too harsh or rude for the occasion

un·can·ny \ən'kanē\ *adj* **1** **:** weird **2** **:** suggesting superhuman powers — **un·can·ni·ly** \-'kan°lē\ *adv*

un·ceas·ing *adj* **:** never ceasing — **un·ceas·ing·ly** *adv*

un·cer·e·mo·ni·ous *adj* **:** acting without ordinary courtesy — **un·cer·e·mo·ni·ous·ly** *adv*

un·cer·tain *adj* **1** **:** not determined, sure, or definitely known **2** **:** subject to chance or change — **un·cer·tain·ly** *adv* — **un·cer·tain·ty** *n*

List of self-explanatory words with the prefix *un-*

unable	unannounced	unbearable
unabridged	unanswered	unbiased
unacceptable	unanticipated	unbranded
unaccompanied	unappetizing	unbreakable
unaccounted	unappreciated	uncensored
unacquainted	unapproved	unchallenged
unaddressed	unarguable	unchangeable
unadorned	unarguably	unchanged
unadulterated	unassisted	unchanging
unafraid	unattended	uncharacteristic
unaided	unattractive	uncharged
unalike	unauthorized	unchaste
unambiguous	unavailable	uncivilized
unambitious	unavoidable	unclaimed

un·chris·tian *adj* : not consistent with Christian teachings

un·cle \'əŋkəl\ *n* **1** : brother of one's father or mother **2** : husband of one's aunt

un·clean *adj* : not clean or pure — **un·clean·ness** *n*

un·clog *vb* : remove an obstruction from

un·coil *vb* : release or become released from a coiled state

un·com·mit·ted *adj* : not pledged to a particular allegiance or course of action

un·com·mon *adj* **1** : rare **2** : superior — **un·com·mon·ly** *adv*

un·com·pro·mis·ing *adj* : not making or accepting a compromise

un·con·cerned *adj* **1** : disinterested **2** : not anxious or upset — **un·con·cerned·ly** *adv*

un·con·di·tion·al *adj* : not limited in any way — **un·con·di·tion·al·ly** *adv*

un·con·scio·na·ble *adj* : shockingly unjust or unscrupulous — **un·con·scio·na·bly** *adv*

un·con·scious *adj* **1** : not awake or aware of one's surroundings **2** : not consciously done ~ *n* : part of one's mental life that one is not aware of — **un·con·scious·ly** *adv* — **un·con·scious·ness** *n*

un·con·sti·tu·tion·al *adj* : not according to or consistent with a constitution

un·con·trol·la·ble *adj* : incapable of being controlled — **un·con·trol·la·bly** *adv*

un·count·ed *adj* : countless

un·couth \ˌən'küth\ *adj* : rude and vulgar

un·cov·er *vb* **1** : reveal **2** : expose by removing a covering

unc·tion \'əŋkshən\ *n* **1** : rite of anointing **2** : exaggerated or insincere earnestness

unc·tu·ous \'əŋkchəwəs\ *adj* **1** : oily **2** : insincerely smooth in speech or manner — **unc·tu·ous·ly** *adv*

un·cut *adj* **1** : not cut down, into, off, or apart **2** : not shaped by cutting **3** : not abridged

un·daunt·ed *adj* : not discouraged — **un·daunt·ed·ly** *adv*

un·de·ni·able *adj* : plainly true — **un·de·ni·ably** *adv*

un·der \'əndər\ *adv* : below or beneath something ~ *prep* **1** : lower than and sheltered by **2** : below the surface of **3** : covered or concealed by **4** : subject to the authority of **5** : less than ~ *adj* **1** : lying below or beneath **2** : subordinate **3** : less than usual, proper, or desired

un·der·age \ˌəndər'āj\ *adj* : of less than legal age

un·der·brush \'əndərˌbrəsh\ *n* : shrubs and small trees growing beneath large trees

un·der·clothes \'əndərˌklōz, -ˌklōthz\ *n pl* : underwear

un·der·cloth·ing \-ˌklōthiŋ\ *n* : underwear

un·der·cov·er \ˌəndər'kəvər\ *adj* : employed or engaged in secret investigation

un·der·cur·rent \'əndərˌkərənt\ *n* : hidden tendency or opinion

un·der·cut \ˌəndər'kət\ *vb* **-cut; -cutting** : offer to sell or to work at a lower rate than

un·der·de·vel·oped \ˌəndərdi'veləpt\ *adj* : not normally or adequately developed esp. economically

---

unclear	unconventionally	undeserving
uncleared	unconverted	undesirable
unclothed	uncooked	undetected
uncluttered	uncooperative	undetermined
uncombed	uncoordinated	undeveloped
uncomfortable	uncovered	undeviating
uncomfortably	uncultivated	undifferentiated
uncomplimentary	undamaged	undignified
unconfirmed	undated	undisturbed
unconsummated	undecided	undivided
uncontested	undeclared	undomesticated
uncontrolled	undefeated	undrinkable
uncontroversial	undemocratic	unearned
unconventional	undependable	uneducated

un•der•dog \'əndər,dȯg\ n : contestant given least chance of winning

un•der•done \,əndər'dən\ adj : not thoroughly done or cooked

un•der•es•ti•mate \,əndər'estə,māt\ vb : estimate too low

un•der•ex•pose \,əndərik'spōz\ vb : give less than normal exposure to — **un•der•ex•po•sure** n

un•der•feed \,əndər'fēd\ vb -fed; -feed•ing : feed inadequately

un•der•foot \,əndər'fu̇t\ adv 1 : under the feet 2 : in the way of another

un•der•gar•ment \'əndər,gärmənt\ n : garment to be worn under another

un•der•go \,əndər'gō\ vb -went \-'went\; -gone; -go•ing 1 : endure 2 : go through (as an experience)

un•der•grad•u•ate \,əndər'grajəwət\ n : university or college student

un•der•ground \,əndər'gra͝und\ adv 1 : beneath the surface of the earth 2 : in secret ~ \'əndər,-\ adj 1 : being or growing under the surface of the ground 2 : secret ~ \'əndər,-\ n : secret political movement or group

un•der•growth \'əndər'grōth\ n : low growth on the floor of a forest

un•der•hand \'əndər,hand\ adv or adj 1 : with secrecy and deception 2 : with the hand kept below the waist

un•der•hand•ed \,əndər'handəd\ adj or adv : underhand — **un•der•hand•ed•ly** adv — **un•der•hand•ed•ness** n

un•der•line \'əndər,līn\ vb 1 : draw a line under 2 : stress — **underline** n

un•der•ling \'əndərliŋ\ n : inferior

un•der•ly•ing \,əndər,lïiŋ\ adj : basic

un•der•mine \,əndər'mīn\ vb 1 : excavate beneath 2 : weaken or wear away secretly or gradually

un•der•neath \,əndər'nēth\ prep : directly under ~ adv 1 : below a surface or object 2 : on the lower side

un•der•nour•ished \,əndər'nərisht\ adj : insufficiently nourished — **un•der•nour•ish•ment** n

un•der•pants \'əndər,pants\ n pl : short undergarment for the lower trunk

un•der•pass \-,pas\ n : passageway crossing underneath another

un•der•pin•ning \'əndər,piniŋ\ n : support

un•der•priv•i•leged adj : poor

un•der•rate \,əndər'rāt\ vb : rate or value too low

un•der•score \'əndər,skōr\ vb 1 : underline 2 : emphasize — **underscore** n

un•der•sea \,əndər'sē\ adj : being, carried on, or used beneath the surface of the sea ~ \,əndər'sē\, **un•der•seas** \-'sēz\ adv : beneath the surface of the sea

un•der sec•re•tary n : deputy secretary

un•der•sell \,əndər'sel\ vb -sold; -sell•ing : sell articles cheaper than

un•der•shirt \'əndər,shərt\ n : shirt worn as underwear

un•der•shorts \'əndər,shȯrts\ n pl : short underpants

un•der•side \'əndər,sīd, ,əndər'sīd\ n : side or surface lying underneath

un•der•sized \,əndər'sīzd\ adj : unusually small

un•der•stand \,əndər'stand\ vb -stood \-'stu̇d\; -stand•ing 1 : be aware of the meaning of 2 : deduce 3 : have a sympathetic attitude — **un•der•stand•able** \-'standəbəl\ adj — **un•der•stand•ably** \-blē\ adv

un•der•stand•ing \,əndər'standiŋ\ n 1 : intelligence 2 : ability to compre-

unemotional
unending
unendurable
unenforceable
unenlightened
unethical
unexcitable
unexciting
unexplainable
unexplored
unfair
unfairly
unfairness
unfavorable

unfavorably
unfeigned
unfilled
unfinished
unflattering
unforeseeable
unforeseen
unforgivable
unforgiving
unfulfilled
unfurnished
ungenerous
ungentlemanly
ungraceful

ungrammatical
unharmed
unhealthful
unheated
unhurt
unidentified
unimaginable
unimaginative
unimportant
unimpressed
uninformed
uninhabited
uninjured
uninsured

hend and judge **3** : mutual agreement ~ *adj* : sympathetic

un·der·state \ˌəndər'stāt\ *vb* **1** : represent as less than is the case **2** : state with restraint — **un·der·state·ment** *n*

un·der·stood \ˌəndər'stùd\ *adj* **1** : agreed upon **2** : implicit

un·der·study \'əndər,stədē, ˌəndər'-\ *vb* : study another actor's part in order to substitute — **understudy** \'əndər,-\ *n*

un·der·take \ˌəndər'tāk\ *vb* **-took; -tak·en; -tak·ing 1** : attempt (a task) or assume (a responsibility) **2** : guarantee

un·der·tak·er \'əndər,tākər\ *n* : one in the funeral business

un·der·tak·ing \'əndər,tākiŋ, ˌəndər'-\ *n* **1** : something (as work) that is undertaken **2** : promise

under–the–counter *adj* : illicit

un·der·tone \'əndər,tōn\ *n* : low or subdued tone or utterance

un·der·tow \-ˌtō\ *n* : current beneath the waves that flows seaward

un·der·val·ue \ˌəndər'valyü\ *vb* : value too low

un·der·wa·ter \-'wótər, -'wät-\ *adj* : being or used below the surface of the water — **underwater** *adv*

under way *adv* : in motion or in progress

un·der·wear \'əndər,war\ *n* : clothing worn next to the skin and under ordinary clothes

un·der·world \'əndər,wərld\ *n* **1** : place of departed souls **2** : world of organized crime

un·der·write \'əndər,rīt, ˌəndər,-\ *vb* **-wrote; -writ·ten; -writ·ing 1** : provide insurance for **2** : guarantee financial support of — **un·der·writ·er** *n*

un·dies \'əndēz\ *n pl* : underwear

un·do *vb* **-did; -done; -do·ing 1** : unfasten **2** : reverse **3** : ruin — **un·do·ing** *n*

un·doubt·ed *adj* : certain — **un·doubt·ed·ly** *adv*

un·dress *vb* : remove one's clothes ~ *n* : state of being naked

un·due *adj* : excessive — **un·du·ly** *adv*

un·du·late \'ənjə,lāt\ *vb* **-lat·ed; -lat·ing** : rise and fall regularly — **un·du·la·tion** \ˌənjə'lāshən\ *n*

un·dy·ing *adj* : immortal or perpetual

un·earth *vb* : dig up or discover

un·earth·ly *adj* : supernatural

un·easy *adj* **1** : awkward or embarrassed **2** : disturbed or worried — **un·eas·i·ly** *adv* — **un·eas·i·ness** *n*

un·em·ployed *adj* : not having a job — **un·em·ploy·ment** *n*

un·equal *adj* : not equal or uniform — **un·equal·ly** *adv*

un·equaled, un·equalled *adj* : having no equal

un·equiv·o·cal *adj* : leaving no doubt — **un·equiv·o·cal·ly** *adv*

un·err·ing *adj* : infallible — **un·err·ing·ly** *adv*

un·even *adj* **1** : not smooth **2** : not regular or consistent — **un·even·ly** *adv* — **un·even·ness** *n*

un·event·ful *adj* : lacking interesting or noteworthy incidents — **un·event·ful·ly** *adv*

un·ex·pect·ed \ˌənik'spektəd\ *adj* : not expected — **un·ex·pect·ed·ly** *adv*

un·fail·ing *adj* : steadfast — **un·fail·ing·ly** *adv*

un·faith·ful *adj* : not loyal — **un·faith·ful·ly** *adv* — **un·faith·ful·ness** *n*

un·fa·mil·iar *adj* **1** : not well known **2** : not acquainted — **un·fa·mil·iar·i·ty** *n*

unintelligent	unknowing	unmolested
unintelligible	unknowingly	unmotivated
unintelligibly	unknown	unmoving
unintended	unleavened	unnamed
unintentional	unlicensed	unnecessarily
unintentionally	unlikable	unnecessary
uninterested	unlimited	unneeded
uninteresting	unlovable	unnoticeable
uninterrupted	unmanageable	unnoticed
uninvited	unmarked	unobjectionable
unjust	unmarried	unobservable
unjustifiable	unmerciful	unobservant
unjustified	unmercifully	unobtainable
unjustly	unmerited	unobtrusive

un•fas•ten *vb* : release a catch or lock

un•feel•ing *adj* : lacking feeling or compassion — **un•feel•ing•ly** *adv*

un•fit *adj* : not suitable — **un•fit•ness** *n*

un•flap•pa•ble \,ən'flapəbəl\ *adj* : not easily upset or panicked — **un•flap•pa•bly** *adv*

un•fold *vb* **1** : open the folds of **2** : reveal **3** : develop

un•for•get•ta•ble *adj* : memorable — **un•for•get•ta•bly** *adv*

un•for•tu•nate *adj* **1** : not lucky or successful **2** : deplorable — **unfortunate** *n* — **un•for•tu•nate•ly** *adv*

un•found•ed *adj* : lacking a sound basis

un•freeze *vb* **-froze; -fro•zen; -freez•ing** : thaw

un•friend•ly *adj* : not friendly or kind — **un•friend•li•ness** *n*

un•furl *vb* : unfold or unroll

un•gain•ly *adj* : clumsy — **un•gain•li•ness** *n*

un•god•ly *adj* : wicked — **un•god•li•ness** *n*

un•grate•ful *adj* : not thankful for favors — **un•grate•ful•ly** *adv* — **un•grate•ful•ness** *n*

un•guent \'əŋgwənt, 'ən-\ *n* : ointment

un•hand *vb* : let go

un•hap•py *adj* **1** : unfortunate **2** : sad — **un•hap•pi•ly** *adv* — **un•hap•pi•ness** *n*

un•healthy *adj* **1** : not wholesome **2** : not well

un•heard-of \,ən'hərdəv, -,äv\ *adj* : unprecedented

un•hinge \,ən'hinj\ *vb* **1** : take from the hinges **2** : make unstable esp. mentally

un•hitch *vb* : unfasten

un•ho•ly *adj* : sinister or shocking — **un•ho•li•ness** *n*

un•hook *vb* : release from a hook

uni•cel•lu•lar \,yüni'selyələr\ *adj* : having or consisting of a single cell

uni•corn \'yünə,körn\ *n* : legendary animal with one horn in the middle of the forehead

uni•cy•cle \'yüni,sīkəl\ *n* : pedal-powered vehicle with only a single wheel

uni•di•rec•tion•al \,yünidə'rekshənəl, -dī-\ *adj* : working in only a single direction

uni•form \'yünə,förm\ *adj* : not changing or showing any variation ∼ *n* : distinctive dress worn by members of a particular group — **uni•for•mi•ty** \,yünə'förmətē\ *n* — **uni•form•ly** *adv*

uni•fy \'yünə,fī\ *vb* **-fied; -fy•ing** : make into a coherent whole — **uni•fi•ca•tion** \,yünəfə'kāshən\ *n*

uni•lat•er•al \,yünə'latərəl\ *adj* : having, affecting, or done by one side only — **uni•lat•er•al•ly** *adv*

un•im•peach•able *adj* : blameless

un•in•hib•it•ed *adj* : free of restraint — **un•in•hib•it•ed•ly** *adv*

union \'yünyən\ *n* **1** : act or instance of joining 2 or more things into one or the state of being so joined **2** : confederation of nations or states **3** : organization of workers (**labor union, trade union**)

union•ize \'yünyə,nīz\ *vb* **-ized; -iz•ing** : form into a labor union — **union•i•za•tion** \,yünyənə'zāshən\ *n*

unique \yu'nēk\ *adj* **1** : being the only one of its kind **2** : very unusual — **unique•ly** *adv* — **unique•ness** *n*

uni•son \'yünəsən, -nəzən\ *n* **1** : sameness in pitch **2** : exact agreement

unit \'yünət\ *n* **1** : smallest whole

---

unobtrusively	unpleasantness	unproven
unofficial	unpopular	unprovoked
unopened	unpopularity	unpunished
unopposed	unposed	unqualified
unorganized	unpredictability	unquenchable
unoriginal	unpredictable	unquestioning
unorthodox	unpredictably	unreachable
unorthodoxy	unprejudiced	unreadable
unpaid	unprepared	unready
unpardonable	unpretentious	unrealistic
unpatriotic	unproductive	unreasonable
unpaved	unprofitable	unreasonably
unpleasant	unprotected	unrefined
unpleasantly	unproved	unrelated

number **2** : definite amount or quantity used as a standard of measurement **3** : single part of a whole — **unit** adj

unite \yù'nīt\ vb **unit·ed; unit·ing** : put or join together

uni·ty \'yūnətē\ n, pl **-ties 1** : quality or state of being united or a unit **2** : harmony

uni·ver·sal \ˌyünə'vərsəl\ adj **1** : relating to or affecting everyone or everything **2** : present or occurring everywhere — **uni·ver·sal·ly** adv

uni·verse \'yünəˌvərs\ n : the complete system of all things that exist

uni·ver·si·ty \ˌyünə'vərsətē\ n, pl **-ties** : institution of higher learning

un·kempt \ˌən'kempt\ adj : not neat or combed

un·kind adj : not kind or sympathetic — **un·kind·li·ness** n — **un·kind·ly** adv — **un·kind·ness** n

un·law·ful adj : illegal — **un·law·ful·ly** adv

un·leash vb : free from control or restraint

un·less \ən'les\ conj : except on condition that

un·like \ən'līk, 'ənˌlīk\ adj **1** : not similar **2** : not equal ∼ prep : different from — **un·like·ly** \ən'līklē\ adv — **un·like·ness** \-nəs\ n — **un·like·li·hood** \-lēˌhu̇d\ n

un·load vb **1** : take (cargo) from a vehicle, vessel, or plane **2** : take a load from **3** : discard

un·lock vb **1** : unfasten through release of a lock **2** : release or reveal

un·lucky adj **1** : experiencing bad luck **2** : likely to bring misfortune — **un·luck·i·ly** adv

un·mis·tak·able adj : not capable of being mistaken or misunderstood — **un·mis·tak·ably** adv

un·moved adj **1** : not emotionally affected **2** : remaining in the same place or position

un·nat·u·ral adj **1** : not natural or spontaneous **2** : abnormal — **un·nat·u·ral·ly** adv — **un·nat·u·ral·ness** n

un·nerve vb : deprive of courage, strength, or steadiness

un·oc·cu·pied adj **1** : not busy **2** : not occupied

un·pack vb **1** : remove (things packed) from a container **2** : remove the contents of (a package)

un·par·al·leled adj : having no equal

un·plug vb **1** : unclog **2** : disconnect from an electric circuit by removing a plug

un·prec·e·dent·ed adj : unlike or superior to anything known before

un·prin·ci·pled adj : unscrupulous

un·ques·tion·able adj : acknowledged as beyond doubt — **un·ques·tion·ably** adv

un·rav·el vb **1** : separate the threads of **2** : solve

un·re·al adj : not real or genuine — **un·re·al·i·ty** n

un·rea·son·ing adj : not using or being guided by reason

un·re·lent·ing adj : not yielding or easing — **un·re·lent·ing·ly** adv

un·rest n : turmoil

un·ri·valed, un·ri·valled adj : having no rival

un·roll vb **1** : unwind a roll of **2** : become unrolled

un·ruf·fled adj : not agitated or upset

un·ruly \ˌən'rülē\ adj : not readily con-

---

unreliable	unsatisfactory	unsolved
unremembered	unsatisfied	unsophisticated
unrepentant	unscented	unsound
unrepresented	unscheduled	unsoundly
unrequited	unseasoned	unsoundness
unresolved	unseen	unspecified
unresponsive	unselfish	unspoiled
unrestrained	unselfishly	unsteadily
unrestricted	unselfishness	unsteadiness
unrewarding	unshaped	unsteady
unripe	unshaven	unstructured
unsafe	unskillful	unsubstantiated
unsalted	unskillfully	unsuccessful
unsanitary	unsolicited	unsuitable

trolled or disciplined — **un•rul•i•ness** *n*

un•scathed \ˌən'skā<u>th</u>d\ *adj* : unharmed

un•sci•en•tif•ic *adj* : not in accord with the principles and methods of science

un•screw *vb* : loosen or remove by withdrawing screws or by turning

un•scru•pu•lous *adj* : being or acting in total disregard of conscience, ethical principles, or rights of others — **un•scru•pu•lous•ly** *adv* — **un•scru•pu•lous•ness** *n*

un•seal *vb* : break or remove the seal of

un•sea•son•able *adj* : not appropriate or usual for the season — **un•sea•son•ably** *adv*

un•seem•ly \ˌən'sēmlē\ *adj* : not polite or in good taste — **un•seem•li•ness** *n*

un•set•tle *vb* : disturb — **un•set•tled** *adj*

un•sight•ly \ˌən'sītlē\ *adj* : not attractive

un•skilled *adj* : not having or requiring a particular skill

un•snap *vb* : loosen by undoing a snap

un•speak•able \ˌən'spēkəbəl\ *adj* : extremely bad — **un•speak•ably** \-blē\ *adv*

un•sta•ble *adj* **1** : not mentally or physically balanced **2** : tending to change

un•stop *vb* **1** : unclog **2** : remove a stopper from

un•stop•pa•ble \ˌən'stäpəbəl\ *adj* : not capable of being stopped

un•strung \ˌən'strəŋ\ *adj* : nervously tired or anxious

un•sung \ˌən'səŋ\ *adj* : not celebrated in song or verse

un•tan•gle *vb* **1** : free from a state of being tangled **2** : find a solution to

un•think•able \ˌən'thiŋkəbəl\ *adj* : not to be thought of or considered possible

un•think•ing *adj* : careless — **un•think•ing•ly** *adv*

un•tie *vb* **-tied; -ty•ing** *or* **-tie•ing** : open by releasing ties

un•til \ˌən'til\ *prep* : up to the time of ~ *conj* : to the time that

un•time•ly *adj* **1** : premature **2** : coming at an unfortunate time

un•to \ˌən'tü, 'ənˌ-\ *prep* : to

un•told *adj* **1** : not told **2** : too numerous to count

un•tow•ard \ˌən'tōrd\ *adj* **1** : difficult to manage **2** : inconvenient

un•truth *n* **1** : lack of truthfulness **2** : lie

un•used *adj* **1** \ˌən'yüst, -'yüzd\ : not accustomed **2** \-'yüzd\ : not used

un•well *adj* : sick

un•wieldy \ˌən'wēldē\ *adj* : too big or awkward to manage easily

un•wind *vb* **-wound; -wind•ing** **1** : undo something that is wound **2** : become unwound **3** : relax

un•wit•ting *adj* **1** : not knowing **2** : not intended — **un•wit•ting•ly** *adv*

un•wont•ed *adj* **1** : unusual **2** : not accustomed by experience

un•wrap *vb* : remove the wrappings from

un•writ•ten *adj* : made or passed on only in speech or through tradition

un•zip *vb* : zip open

up \'əp\ *adv* **1** : in or to a higher position or level **2** : from beneath a surface or level **3** : in or into an upright position **4** : out of bed **5** : to or with greater intensity **6** : into existence, evidence, or knowledge **7** : away **8** — used to indicate a degree of success, completion, or finality **9** : in or

unsuitably	untreated	unwelcome
unsuited	untrue	unwholesome
unsupervised	untrustworthy	unwilling
unsupported	untruthful	unwillingly
unsure	unusable	unwillingness
unsurprising	unusual	unwise
unsuspecting	unvarying	unwisely
unsweetened	unverified	unworkable
unsympathetic	unwanted	unworthily
untamed	unwarranted	unworthiness
untanned	unwary	unworthy
untidy	unwavering	unyielding
untouched	unweaned	
untrained	unwed	

into parts ∼ *adj* **1** : in the state of having risen **2** : raised to or at a higher level **3** : moving, inclining, or directed upward **4** : in a state of greater intensity **5** : at an end ∼ *vb* **upped** *or in 1* **up**; **upped**; **up•ping**; **ups** *or in 1* **up 1** : act abruptly **2** : move or cause to move upward ∼ *prep* **1** : to, toward, or at a higher point of **2** : along or toward the beginning of

up•braid \\ˌəp'brād\\ *vb* : criticize or scold

up•bring•ing \\'əpˌbriŋiŋ\\ *n* : process of bringing up and training

up•com•ing \\ˌəp'kəmiŋ\\ *adj* : approaching

up•date \\ˌəp'dāt\\ *vb* : bring up to date — **update** \\'əpˌdāt\\ *n*

up•end \\ˌəp'end\\ *vb* **1** : stand or rise on end **2** : overturn

up•grade \\'əpˌgrād\\ *n* **1** : upward slope **2** : increase ∼ \\'əpˌ-, ˌəp'-\\ *vb* : raise to a higher position

up•heav•al \\ˌəp'hēvəl\\ *n* **1** : a heaving up (as of part of the earth's crust) **2** : violent change

up•hill \\ˌəp'hil\\ *adv* : upward on a hill or incline ∼ \\'əpˌ-\\ *adj* **1** : going up **2** : difficult

up•hold \\ˌəp'hōld\\ *vb* -**held**; -**hold•ing** : support or defend — **up•hold•er** *n*

up•hol•ster \\ˌəp'hōlstər\\ *vb* : cover (furniture) with padding and fabric (**up•hol•stery** \\-stərē\\) — **up•hol•ster•er** *n*

up•keep \\'əpˌkēp\\ *n* : act or cost of keeping up or maintaining

up•land \\'əplənd, -ˌland\\ *n* : high land — **upland** *adj*

up•lift \\ˌəp'lift\\ *vb* **1** : lift up **2** : improve the condition or spirits of — **up•lift** \\'əpˌ-\\ *n*

up•on \\ə'pȯn, -'pän\\ *prep* : on

up•per \\'əpər\\ *adj* : higher in position, rank, or order ∼ *n* : top part of a shoe

upper•hand *n* : advantage

up•per•most \\'əpərˌmōst\\ *adv* : in or into the highest or most prominent position — **uppermost** *adj*

up•pi•ty \\'əpətē\\ *adj* : acting with a manner of undue importance

up•right \\'əpˌrīt\\ *adj* **1** : vertical **2** : erect in posture **3** : morally correct ∼ *n* : something that stands upright — **upright** *adv* — **up•right•ly** *adv* — **up•right•ness** *n*

up•ris•ing \\'əpˌrīziŋ\\ *n* : revolt

up•roar \\'əpˌrōr\\ *n* : state of commotion or violent disturbance

up•roar•i•ous \\ˌəp'rōrēəs\\ *adj* **1** : marked by uproar **2** : extremely funny — **up•roar•i•ous•ly** *adv*

up•root \\ˌəp'rüt, -'rùt\\ *vb* : remove by or as if by pulling up by the roots

up•set \\ˌəp'set\\ *vb* -**set**; -**set•ting 1** : force or be forced out of the usual position **2** : disturb emotionally or physically ∼ \\'əpˌ-\\ *n* **1** : act of throwing into disorder **2** : minor physical disorder ∼ *adj* : emotionally disturbed or agitated

up•shot \\'əpˌshät\\ *n* : final result

up•side down \\ˌəpˌsīd'daùn\\ *adv* **1** : turned so that the upper and lower parts are reversed **2** : in or into confusion or disorder — **upside–down** *adj*

up•stairs \\'əpˌstarz, ˌəp'-\\ *adv* : up the stairs or to the next floor ∼ *adj* : situated on the floor above ∼ *n sing or pl* : part of a building above the ground floor

up•stand•ing \\ˌəp'standiŋ, 'əpˌ-\\ *adj* : honest

up•start \\'əpˌstärt\\ *n* : one who claims more personal importance than is warranted — **up•start** *adj*

up•swing \\'əpˌswiŋ\\ *n* : marked increase (as in activity)

up•tight \\ˌəp'tīt\\ *adj* **1** : tense **2** : angry **3** : rigidly conventional

up–to–date *adj* : current — **up–to–date•ness** *n*

up•town \\'əpˌtaùn\\ *n* : upper part of a town or city — **uptown** *adj or adv*

up•turn \\'əpˌtərn\\ *n* : improvement or increase

up•ward \\'əpwərd\\, **up•wards** \\-wərdz\\ *adv* **1** : in a direction from lower to higher **2** : toward a higher or greater state or number ∼ *adj* : directed toward or situated in a higher place — **up•ward•ly** *adv*

up•wind \\ˌəp'wind\\ *adv or adj* : in the direction from which the wind is blowing

ura•ni•um \\yù'rānēəm\\ *n* : metallic radioactive chemical element

ur•ban \\'ərbən\\ *adj* : characteristic of a city

ur•bane \\ˌər'bān\\ *adj* : polished in manner — **ur•ban•i•ty** \\ˌər'banətē\\ *n*

ur•ban•ite \\'ərbəˌnīt\\ *n* : city dweller

ur•chin \\'ərchən\\ *n* : mischievous youngster

-ure *n suffix* : act or process

ure·thra \yù'rēthrə\ *n, pl* **-thras** *or* **-thrae** \-₁thrē\ : canal that carries off urine from the bladder — **ure·thral** \-thrəl\ *adj*

urge \'ərj\ *vb* **urged; urging 1** : earnestly plead for or insist on (an action) **2** : try to persuade **3** : impel to a course of activity ~ *n* : force or impulse that moves one to action

ur·gent \'ərjənt\ *adj* **1** : calling for immediate attention **2** : urging insistently — **ur·gen·cy** \-jənsē\ *n* — **ur·gent·ly** *adv*

uri·nal \'yùrən³l\ *n* : receptacle to urinate in

uri·nate \'yùrə₁nāt\ *vb* **-nat·ed; -nat·ing** : discharge urine — **uri·na·tion** \₁yùrə'nāshən\ *n*

urine \'yùrən\ *n* : liquid waste material from the kidneys — **uri·nary** \-ə₁nerē\ *adj*

URL \₁yü₁är'el\ *n* : address on the Internet

urn \'ərn\ *n* **1** : vaselike or cuplike vessel on a pedestal **2** : large coffee pot

us \'əs\ *pron, objective case of* WE

us·able \'yüzəbəl\ *adj* : suitable or fit for use — **us·abil·i·ty** \₁yüzə'bilətē\ *n*

us·age \'yüsij, -zij\ *n* **1** : customary practice **2** : way of doing or of using something

use \'yüs\ *n* **1** : act or practice of putting something into action **2** : state of being used **3** : way of using **4** : privilege, ability, or power to use something **5** : utility or function **6** : occasion or need to use ~ \'yüz\ *vb* **used** \'yüzd; *"used to" usu* 'yüstə\; **us·ing** \'yüzⁱŋ\ **1** : put into action or service **2** : consume **3** : behave toward **4** : to make use of **5** — used in the past tense with *to* to indicate a former practice — **use·ful** \'yüsfəl\ *adj* — **use·ful·ly** *adv* — **use·ful·ness** *n*

— **use·less** \'yüsləs\ *adj* — **use·less·ly** *adv* — **use·less·ness** *n* — **us·er** *n*

used \'yüzd\ *adj* : not new

ush·er \'əshər\ *n* : one who escorts people to their seats ~ *vb* : conduct to a place

ush·er·ette \₁əshə'ret\ *n* : woman or girl who is an usher

usu·al \'yüzhəwəl\ *adj* : being what is expected according to custom or habit — **usu·al·ly** \'yüzhəwəlē\ *adv*

usurp \yù'sərp, -'zərp\ *vb* : seize and hold by force or without right — **usur·pa·tion** \₁yüsər'pāshən, -zər-\ *n* — **usurp·er** *n*

usu·ry \'yüzhərē\ *n, pl* **-ries 1** : lending of money at excessive interest or the rate or amount of such interest — **usu·rer** \-zhərər\ *n* — **usu·ri·ous** \yù'zhùrēəs\ *adj*

uten·sil \yù'tensəl\ *n* **1** : eating or cooking tool **2** : useful tool

uter·us \'yütərəs\ *n, pl* **uteri** \-₁rī\ : organ for containing and nourishing an unborn offspring — **uter·ine** \-₁rīn, -rən\ *adj*

util·i·tar·i·an \yù₁tilə'terēən\ *adj* : being or meant to be useful rather than beautiful

util·i·ty \yù'tilətē\ *n, pl* **-ties 1** : usefulness **2** : regulated business providing a public service (as electricity)

uti·lize \'yüt³l₁īz\ *vb* **-lized; -liz·ing** : make use of — **uti·li·za·tion** \₁yüt³lə-'zāshən\ *n*

ut·most \'ət₁mōst\ *adj* **1** : most distant **2** : of the greatest or highest degree or amount — **utmost** *n*

uto·pia \yù'tōpēə\ *n* : place of ideal perfection — **uto·pi·an** \-pēən\ *adj or n*

ut·ter \'ətər\ *adj* : absolute ~ *vb* : express with the voice — **ut·ter·er** \-ərər\ *n* — **ut·ter·ly** *adv*

ut·ter·ance \'ətərəns\ *n* : what one says

V

v \'vē\ *n, pl* **v's** *or* **vs** \'vēz\ : 22d letter of the alphabet

va·can·cy \'vākənsē\ *n, pl* **-cies 1** : state of being vacant **2** : unused or unoccupied place or office

va·cant \-kənt\ *adj* **1** : not occupied, filled, or in use **2** : devoid of thought or expression — **va·cant·ly** *adv*

va·cate \-₁kāt\ *vb* **-cat·ed; -cat·ing 1** : annul **2** : leave unfilled or unoccupied

va•ca•tion \vā'kāshən, və-\ *n* : period of rest from routine — **vacation** *vb* — **va•ca•tion•er** *n*

vac•ci•nate \'vaksə,nāt\ *vb* -nat•ed; -nat•ing : administer a vaccine usu. by injection

vac•ci•na•tion \,vaksə'nāshən\ *n* : act of or the scar left by vaccinating

vac•cine \vak'sēn, 'vak,-\ *n* : substance to induce immunity to a disease

vac•il•late \'vasə,lāt\ *vb* -lat•ed; -lat•ing : waver between courses or opinions — **vac•il•la•tion** \,vasə'lāshən\ *n*

vac•u•ous \'vakyəwəs\ *adj* 1 : empty 2 : dull or inane — **va•cu•ity** \va-'kyüətē, və-\ *n* — **vac•u•ous•ly** *adv* — **vac•u•ous•ness** *n*

vac•u•um \'vak,yüm, -yəm\ *n, pl* **vac-u•ums** *or* **vac•ua** \-yəwə\ : empty space with no air ∼ *vb* : clean with a vacuum cleaner

vacuum cleaner *n* : appliance that cleans by suction

vag•a•bond \'vagə,bänd\ *n* : wanderer with no home — **vagabond** *adj*

va•ga•ry \'vāgərē, və'gerē\ *n, pl* **-ries** : whim

va•gi•na \və'jīnə\ *n, pl* **-nae** \-,nē\ *or* **-nas** : canal that leads out from the uterus — **vag•i•nal** \'vajən°l\ *adj*

va•grant \'vāgrənt\ *n* : person with no home and no job — **va•gran•cy** \-grənsē\ *n* — **vagrant** *adj*

vague \'vāg\ *adj* **vagu•er; vagu•est** : not clear, definite, or distinct — **vague•ly** *adv* — **vague•ness** *n*

vain \'vān\ *adj* 1 : of no value 2 : unsuccessful 3 : conceited — **vain•ly** *adv*

va•lance \'valəns, 'vāl-\ *n* : border drapery

vale \'vāl\ *n* : valley

vale•dic•to•ri•an \,valə,dik'tōrēən\ *n* : student giving the farewell address at commencement

vale•dic•to•ry \-'diktərē\ *adj* : bidding farewell — **valedictory** *n*

va•lence \'vāləns\ *n* : degree of combining power of a chemical element

val•en•tine \'valən,tīn\ *n* : sweetheart or a card sent to a sweetheart or friend on St. Valentine's Day

va•let \'valət, 'val,ā, va'lā\ *n* : male personal servant

val•iant \'valyənt\ *adj* : brave or heroic — **val•iant•ly** *adv*

val•id \'valəd\ *adj* 1 : proper and legally binding 2 : founded on truth or fact — **va•lid•i•ty** \və'lidətē, va-\ *n* — **val•id•ly** *adv*

val•i•date \'valə,dāt\ *vb* -dat•ed; -dat•ing : establish as valid — **val•i•da•tion** \,valə'dāshən\ *n*

va•lise \və'lēs\ *n* : suitcase

val•ley \'valē\ *n, pl* **-leys** : long depression between ranges of hills

val•or \'valər\ *n* : bravery or heroism — **val•or•ous** \'valərəs\ *adj*

valu•able \'valyəwəbəl\ *adj* 1 : worth a lot of money 2 : being of great importance or use — **valuable** *n*

val•u•a•tion \,valyə'wāshən\ *n* 1 : act or process of valuing 2 : market value of a thing

val•ue \'valyü\ *n* 1 : fair return or equivalent for something exchanged 2 : how much something is worth 3 : distinctive quality (as of a color or sound) 4 : guiding principle or ideal — usu. pl. ∼ *vb* **val•ued; valu•ing** 1 : estimate the worth of 2 : appreciate the importance of — **val•ue•less** *adj* — **val•u•er** *n*

valve \'valv\ *n* : structure or device to control flow of a liquid or gas — **valved** \'valvd\ *adj* — **valve•less** *adj*

vam•pire \'vam,pīr\ *n* 1 : legendary night-wandering dead body that sucks human blood 2 : bat that feeds on the blood of animals

¹van \'van\ *n* : vanguard

²van *n* : enclosed truck

va•na•di•um \və'nādēəm\ *n* : soft ductile metallic chemical element

van•dal \'vand°l\ *n* : person who willfully defaces or destroys property — **van•dal•ism** \-,izəm\ *n* — **van•dal•ize** \-,īz\ *vb*

vane \'vān\ *n* : bladelike device designed to be moved by force of the air or water

van•guard \'van,gärd\ *n* 1 : troops moving at the front of an army 2 : forefront of an action or movement

va•nil•la \və'nilə\ *n* : a flavoring made from the pods of a tropical orchid or this orchid

van•ish \'vanish\ *vb* : disappear suddenly

van•i•ty \'vanətē\ *n, pl* **-ties** 1 : futility or something that is futile 2 : undue pride in oneself 3 : makeup case or table

van•quish \'vaŋkwish, 'van-\ *vb* 1

: overcome in battle or in a contest **2**
: gain mastery over

van•tage \'vantij\ *n* : position of advantage or perspective

va•pid \'vapəd, 'vāpəd\ *adj* : lacking
spirit, liveliness, or zest — **va•pid•i•ty**
\va'pidətē\ *n* — **vap•id•ly** \'vapədlē\
adv — **vap•id•ness** *n*

va•por \'vāpər\ *n* **1** : fine separated
particles floating in and clouding the
air **2** : gaseous form of an ordinarily
liquid substance — **va•por•ous**
\-pərəs\ *adj*

va•por•ize \'vāpə‚rīz\ *vb* **-ized; -iz•ing**
: convert into vapor — **va•por•i•za-
tion** \‚vāpərə'zāshən\ *n* — **va•por-
iz•er** *n*

var•i•able \'verēəbəl\ *adj* : apt to vary
— **var•i•abil•i•ty** \‚verēə'bilətē\ *n* —
var•i•able *n* — **var•i•ably** *adv*

var•i•ance \'verēəns\ *n* **1** : instance or
degree of variation **2** : disagreement
or dispute **3** : legal permission to
build contrary to a zoning law

var•i•ant \-ənt\ *n* : something that differs from others of its kind — **variant**
adj

vari•a•tion \‚verē'āshən\ *n* : instance
or extent of varying

var•i•cose \'varə‚kōs\ *adj* : abnormally swollen and dilated

var•ied \'verēd\ *adj* : showing variety
— **var•ied•ly** *adv*

var•ie•gat•ed \'verēə‚gātēd\ *adj* : having patches, stripes, or marks of different colors — **var•ie•gate** \-‚gāt\ *vb*
— **var•ie•ga•tion** \‚verēə'gāshən\ *n*

va•ri•ety \və'rīətē\ *n, pl* **-et•ies 1**
: state of being different **2** : collection of different things **3** : something
that differs from others of its kind

var•i•ous \'verēəs\ *adj* : being many
and unlike — **var•i•ous•ly** *adv*

var•nish \'värnish\ *n* : liquid that dries
to a hard glossy protective coating ~
vb : cover with varnish

var•si•ty \'värsətē\ *n, pl* **-ties** : principal team representing a school

vary \'verē\ *vb* **var•ied; vary•ing 1**
: alter **2** : make or be of different kinds

vas•cu•lar \'vaskyələr\ *adj* : relating to
a channel for the conveyance of a
body fluid (as blood or sap)

vase \'vās, 'vāz\ *n* : tall usu. ornamental container to hold flowers

vas•sal \'vasəl\ *n* **1** : one acknowledging another as feudal lord **2** : one in

a dependent position — **vas•sal•age**
\-əlij\ *n*

vast \'vast\ *adj* : very great in size,
extent, or amount — **vast•ly** *adv* —
vast•ness *n*

vat \'vat\ *n* : large tub- or barrel-shaped
container

vaude•ville \'vódvəl, 'väd-, 'vōd-,
-‚vil, -əvəl, -ə‚vil\ *n* : stage entertainment of unrelated acts

¹vault \'vólt\ *n* **1** : masonry arch **2**
: usu. underground storage or burial
room ~ *vb* : form or cover with a
vault — **vault•ed** *adj* — **vaulty** *adj*

²vault *vb* : spring over esp. with the help
of the hands or a pole ~ *n* : act of
vaulting — **vault•er** *n*

vaunt \'vónt\ *vb* : boast — **vaunt** *n*

veal \'vēl\ *n* : flesh of a young calf

veer \'vir\ *vb* : change course esp. gradually — **veer** *n*

veg•e•ta•ble \'vejtəbəl, 'vejə-\ *adj* **1**
: relating to or obtained from plants
2 : like that of a plant ~ *n* **1** : plant
2 : plant grown for food

veg•e•tar•i•an \‚vejə'terēən\ *n* : person
who eats no meat — **vegetarian** *adj*
— **veg•e•tar•i•an•ism** \-ē‚nizəm\ *n*

veg•e•tate \'vejə‚tāt\ *vb* **-tat•ed; -tat-
ing** : lead a dull inert life

veg•e•ta•tion \‚vejə'tāshən\ *n* : plant
life — **veg•e•ta•tion•al** \-shənəl\ *adj*
— **veg•e•ta•tive** \'vejə‚tātiv\ *adj*

ve•he•ment \'vēəmənt\ *adj* : showing
strong esp. violent feeling — **ve-
he•mence** \-məns\ *n* — **ve•he•ment-
ly** *adv*

ve•hi•cle \'vē‚hikəl, 'vēəkəl\ *n* **1**
: medium through which something is
expressed, applied, or administered **2**
: structure for transporting something
esp. on wheels — **ve•hic•u•lar** \vē-
'hikyələr\ *adj*

veil \'vāl\ *n* **1** : sheer material to hide
something or to cover the face and
head **2** : something that hides ~ *vb*
: cover with a veil

vein \'vān\ *n* **1** : rock fissure filled with
deposited mineral matter **2** : vessel
that carries blood toward the heart **3**
: sap-carrying tube in a leaf **4** : distinctive element or style of expression — **veined** \'vānd\ *adj*

ve•loc•i•ty \və'läsətē\ *n, pl* **-ties** : speed

ve•lour, ve•lours \və'lùr\ *n, pl* **velours**
\-'lùrz\ : fabric with a velvetlike pile

vel•vet \'velvət\ *n* : fabric with a short
soft pile — **velvet** *adj* — **vel•vety** *adj*

ve·nal \\'vēn°l\ *adj* : capable of being corrupted esp. by money — **ve·nal·i·ty** \vi'nalətē\ *n* — **ve·nal·ly** *adv*

vend \\'vend\ *vb* : sell — **vend·ible** *adj* — **ven·dor** \\'vendər\ *n*

ven·det·ta \ven'detə\ *n* : feud marked by acts of revenge

ve·neer \və'nir\ *n* **1** : thin layer of fine wood glued over a cheaper wood **2** : superficial display ∼ *vb* : overlay with a veneer

ven·er·a·ble \\'venərəbəl\ *adj* : deserving of respect

ven·er·ate \\'venə,rāt\ *vb* **-at·ed; -at·ing** : respect esp. with reverence — **ven·er·a·tion** \venə'rāshən\ *n*

ve·ne·re·al disease \və'nirēəl-\ *n* : contagious disease spread through copulation

ven·geance \\'venjəns\ *n* : punishment in retaliation for an injury or offense

venge·ful \\'venjfəl\ *adj* : filled with a desire for revenge — **venge·ful·ly** *adv*

ve·nial \\'vēnēəl\ *adj* : capable of being forgiven

ven·i·son \\'venəsən, -əzən\ *n* : deer meat

ven·om \\'venəm\ *n* **1** : poison secreted by certain animals **2** : ill will — **ven·om·ous** \-əməs\ *adj*

vent \\'vent\ *vb* **1** : provide with or let out at a vent **2** : give expression to ∼ *n* : opening for passage or for relieving pressure

ven·ti·late \\'vent°l,āt\ *vb* **-lat·ed; -lat·ing** : allow fresh air to circulate through — **ven·ti·la·tion** \vent°l'āshən\ *n* — **ven·ti·la·tor** \\'vent°l,ātər\ *n*

ven·tri·cle \\'ventrikəl\ *n* : heart chamber that pumps blood into the arteries

ven·tril·o·quist \ven'trilə,kwist\ *n* : one who can make the voice appear to come from another source — **ven·tril·o·quism** \-,kwizəm\ *n* — **ven·tril·o·quy** \-kwē\ *n*

ven·ture \\'venchər\ *vb* **-tured; -tur·ing** **1** : risk or take a chance on **2** : put forward (an opinion) ∼ *n* : speculative business enterprise

ven·ture·some \-səm\ *adj* : brave or daring — **ven·ture·some·ly** *adv* — **ven·ture·some·ness** *n*

ven·ue \\'venyü\ *n* : scene of an action or event

ve·rac·i·ty \və'rasətē\ *n, pl* **-ties** : truthfulness or accuracy — **ve·ra·cious** \və'rāshəs\ *adj*

ve·ran·da, ve·ran·dah \və'randə\ *n* : large open porch

verb \\'vərb\ *n* : word that expresses action or existence

ver·bal \\'vərbəl\ *adj* **1** : having to do with or expressed in words **2** : oral **3** : relating to or formed from a verb — **ver·bal·i·za·tion** \,vərbələ'zāshən\ *n* — **ver·bal·ize** \\'vərbə,līz\ *vb* — **ver·bal·ly** \-ē\ *adv*

verbal auxiliary *n* : auxiliary verb

ver·ba·tim \vər'bātəm\ *adv or adj* : using the same words

ver·biage \\'vərbēij\ *n* : excess of words

ver·bose \vər'bōs\ *adj* : using more words than are needed — **ver·bos·i·ty** \-'bäsətē\ *n*

ver·dant \\'vərd°nt\ *adj* : green with growing plants — **ver·dant·ly** *adv*

ver·dict \\'vərdikt\ *n* : decision of a jury

ver·dure \\'vərjər\ *n* : green growing vegetation or its color

verge \\'vərj\ *vb* **verged; verg·ing** : be almost on the point of happening or doing something ∼ *n* **1** : edge **2** : threshold

ver·i·fy \\'verə,fī\ *vb* **-fied; -fy·ing** : establish the truth, accuracy, or reality of — **ver·i·fi·able** *adj* — **ver·i·fi·ca·tion** \,verəfə'kāshən\ *n*

ver·i·ly \\'verəlē\ *adv* : truly or confidently

veri·si·mil·i·tude \,verəsə'milə,tüd\ *n* : appearance of being true

ver·i·ta·ble \\'verətəbəl\ *adj* : actual or true — **ver·i·ta·bly** *adv*

ver·i·ty \\'verətē\ *n, pl* **-ties** : truth

ver·mi·cel·li \,vərmə'chelē, -'sel-\ *n* : thin spaghetti

ver·min \\'vərmən\ *n, pl* **vermin** : small animal pest

ver·mouth \vər'müth\ *n* : dry or sweet wine flavored with herbs

ver·nac·u·lar \vər'nakyələr\ *adj* : relating to a native language or dialect and esp. its normal spoken form ∼ *n* : vernacular language

ver·nal \\'vərn°l\ *adj* : relating to spring

ver·sa·tile \\'vərsət°l\ *adj* : having many abilities or uses — **ver·sa·til·i·ty** \,vərsə'tilətē\ *n*

¹verse \\'vərs\ *n* **1** : line or stanza of poetry **2** : poetry **3** : short division of a chapter in the Bible

²verse *vb* **versed; versing** : make familiar by experience, study, or practice

ver·sion \\'vərzhən\ *n* **1** : translation of the Bible **2** : account or description from a particular point of view

ver·sus \\'vərsəs\ *prep* : opposed to or against

ver•te•bra \'vərtəbrə\ *n, pl* **-brae** \-ˌbrā, -ˌbrē\ *or* **-bras** : segment of the backbone — **ver•te•bral** \vər'tēbrəl, 'vərtə-\ *adj*

ver•te•brate \'vərtəbrət, -ˌbrāt\ *n* : animal with a backbone — **verte•brate** *adj*

ver•tex \'vər‚teks\ *n, pl* **ver•ti•ces** \'vərtə‚sēz\ **1** : point of intersection of lines or surfaces **2** : highest point

ver•ti•cal \'vərtikəl\ *adj* : rising straight up from a level surface — **vertical** *n* — **ver•ti•cal•i•ty** \ˌvərtə-'kalətē\ *n* — **ver•ti•cal•ly** *adv*

ver•ti•go \'vərti‚gō\ *n, pl* **-goes** *or* **-gos** : dizziness

verve \'vərv\ *n* : liveliness or vividness

very \'verē\ *adj* **veri•er; -est 1** : exact **2** : exactly suitable **3** : mere or bare **4** : precisely the same ⁓ *adv* **1** : to a high degree **2** : in actual fact

ves•i•cle \'vesikəl\ *n* : membranous cavity — **ve•sic•u•lar** \və'sikyələr\ *adj*

ves•pers \'vespərz\ *n pl* : late afternoon or evening worship service

ves•sel \'vesəl\ *n* **1** : a container (as a barrel, bottle, bowl, or cup) for a liquid **2** : craft for navigation esp. on water **3** : tube in which a body fluid is circulated

¹vest \'vest\ *vb* **1** : give a particular authority, right, or property to **2** : clothe with or as if with a garment

²vest *n* : sleeveless garment usu. worn under a suit coat

ves•ti•bule \'vestə‚byül\ *n* : enclosed entrance — **ves•tib•u•lar** \ve'sti-byələr\ *adj*

ves•tige \'vestij\ *n* : visible trace or remains — **ves•ti•gial** \ve'stijēəl\ *adj* — **ves•ti•gial•ly** *adv*

vest•ment \'vestmənt\ *n* : clergy member's garment

ves•try \'vestrē\ *n, pl* **-tries** : church storage room for garments and articles

vet•er•an \'vetərən\ *n* **1** : former member of the armed forces **2** : person with long experience — **veteran** *adj*

Veterans Day *n* : 4th Monday in October or formerly November 11 observed as a legal holiday in commemoration of the end of war in 1918 and 1945

vet•er•i•nar•i•an \ˌvetərən'erēən\ *n* : doctor of animals — **vet•er•i•nary** \'vetərən‚erē\ *adj*

ve•to \'vētō\ *n, pl* **-toes 1** : power to forbid and esp. the power of a chief executive to prevent a bill from becoming law **2** : exercise of the veto ⁓ *vb* **1** : forbid **2** : reject a legislative bill

vex \'veks\ *vb* **vexed; vex•ing** : trouble, distress, or annoy — **vex•a•tion** \vek'sāshən\ *n* — **vex•a•tious** \-shəs\ *adj*

via \'vīə, 'vēə\ *prep* : by way of

vi•a•ble \'vīəbəl\ *adj* **1** : capable of surviving or growing **2** : practical or workable — **vi•a•bil•i•ty** \ˌvīə'bilətē\ *n* — **vi•a•bly** \'vīəblē\ *adv*

via•duct \'vīə‚dəkt\ *n* : elevated roadway or railway bridge

vi•al \'vīəl\ *n* : small bottle

vi•brant \'vībrənt\ *adj* **1** : vibrating **2** : pulsing with vigor or activity **3** : sounding from vibration — **vi•bran•cy** \-brənsē\ *n*

vi•brate \'vī‚brāt\ *vb* **-brat•ed; -brat•ing 1** : move or cause to move quickly back and forth or side to side **2** : respond sympathetically — **vi•bra•tion** \vī'brāshən\ *n* — **vi•bra•tor** \'vī-ˌbrātər\ *n* — **vi•bra•tory** \'vībrə-ˌtórē\ *adj*

vic•ar \'vikər\ *n* : parish clergy member — **vi•car•i•ate** \-ēət\ *n*

vi•car•i•ous \vī'karēəs\ *adj* : sharing in someone else's experience through imagination or sympathetic feelings — **vi•car•i•ous•ly** *adv* — **vi•car•i•ous•ness** *n*

vice \'vīs\ *n* **1** : immoral habit **2** : depravity

vice- \ˌvīs\ *prefix* : one that takes the place of

vice admiral *n* : commissioned officer in the navy or coast guard ranking above a rear admiral

vice•roy \'vīs‚rói\ *n* : provincial governor who represents the sovereign

vice ver•sa \ˌvīsī'vərsə, ˌvīs'vər-\ *adv* : with the order reversed

vi•cin•i•ty \və'sinətē\ *n, pl* **-ties** : surrounding area

vi•cious \'vishəs\ *adj* **1** : wicked **2**

List of self-explanatory words with the prefix *vice-*

vice–chancellor	vice presidency	vice presidential
vice–consul	vice president	vice–regent

: savage **3** : malicious — **vi•cious•ly** *adv* — **vi•cious•ness** *n*

vi•cis•si•tude \və'sisə,tüd, vī-, -,tyüd\ *n* : irregular, unexpected, or surprising change — usu. used in pl.

vic•tim \'viktəm\ *n* : person killed, hurt, or abused

vic•tim•ize \'viktə,mīz\ *vb* **-ized; -iz•ing** : make a victim of — **vic•tim•i•za•tion** \,viktəmə'zāshən\ *n* — **vic•tim•iz•er** \'viktə,mīzər\ *n*

vic•tor \'viktər\ *n* : winner

Vic•to•ri•an \vik'tōrēən\ *adj* : relating to the reign of Queen Victoria of England or the art, taste, or standards of her time ～ *n* : one of the Victorian period

vic•to•ri•ous \vik'tōrēəs\ *adj* : having won a victory — **vic•to•ri•ous•ly** *adv*

vic•to•ry \'viktərē\ *n, pl* **-ries** : success in defeating an enemy or opponent or in overcoming difficulties

vict•uals \'vit³lz\ *n pl* : food

vid•eo \'vidē,ō\ *adj* : relating to the television image

vid•eo•cas•sette \,vidē,ōkə'set\ *n* : cassette containing videotape

vid•eo•tape \'vidēō,tāp\ *vb* : make a recording of (a television production) on special tape — **videotape** *n*

vie \'vī\ *vb* **vied; vy•ing** : contend — **vi•er** \'vīər\ *n*

view \'vyü\ *n* **1** : process of seeing or examining **2** : opinion **3** : area of landscape that can be seen **4** : range of vision **5** : purpose or object ～ *vb* **1** : look at **2** : think about or consider — **view•er** *n*

view•point *n* : position from which something is considered

vigil \'vijəl\ *n* **1** : day of devotion before a religious feast **2** : act or time of keeping awake **3** : long period of keeping watch (as over a sick or dying person)

vig•i•lant \'vijələnt\ *adj* : alert esp. to avoid danger — **vig•i•lance** \-ləns\ *n* — **vig•i•lant•ly** *adv*

vig•i•lan•te \,vijə'lantē\ *n* : one of a group independent of the law working to suppress crime

vi•gnette \vin'yet\ *n* : short descriptive literary piece

vig•or \'vigər\ *n* **1** : energy or strength **2** : intensity or force — **vig•or•ous** \'vigərəs\ *adj* — **vig•or•ous•ly** *adv* — **vig•or•ous•ness** *n*

vile \'vīl\ *adj* **vil•er; vil•est** : thoroughly bad or contemptible — **vile•ly** *adv* — **vile•ness** *n*

vil•i•fy \'vilə,fī\ *vb* **-fied; -fy•ing** : speak evil of — **vil•i•fi•ca•tion** \,viləfə'kāshən\ *n* — **vil•i•fi•er** \'vilə,fīər\ *n*

vil•la \'vilə\ *n* : country estate

vil•lage \'vilij\ *n* : small country town — **vil•lag•er** *n*

vil•lain \'vilən\ *n* : bad person — **vil•lain•ess** \-ənəs\ *n* — **vil•lainy** *n*

vil•lain•ous \-ənəs\ *adj* : evil or corrupt — **vil•lain•ous•ly** *adv* — **vil•lain•ous•ness** *n*

vim \'vim\ *n* : energy

vin•di•cate \'vində,kāt\ *vb* **-cat•ed; -cat•ing 1** : avenge **2** : exonerate **3** : justify — **vin•di•ca•tion** \,vində'kāshən\ *n* — **vin•di•ca•tor** \'vində,kātər\ *n*

vin•dic•tive \vin'diktiv\ *adj* : seeking or meant for revenge — **vin•dic•tive•ly** *adv* — **vin•dic•tive•ness** *n*

vine \'vīn\ *n* : climbing or trailing plant

vin•e•gar \'vinigər\ *n* : acidic liquid obtained by fermentation — **vin•e•gary** \-gərē\ *adj*

vine•yard \'vinyərd\ *n* : plantation of grapevines

vin•tage \'vintij\ *n* **1** : season's yield of grapes or wine **2** : period of origin ～ *adj* : of enduring interest

vi•nyl \'vīn³l\ *n* : strong plastic

vi•o•la \vē'ōlə\ *n* : instrument of the violin family tuned lower than the violin — **vi•o•list** \-list\ *n*

vi•o•late \'vīə,lāt\ *vb* **-lat•ed; -lat•ing 1** : act with disrespect or disregard of **2** : rape **3** : desecrate — **vi•o•la•tion** \,vīə'lāshən\ *n* — **vi•o•la•tor** \'vīə,lātər\ *n*

vi•o•lence \'vīələns\ *n* : intense physical force that causes or is intended to cause injury or destruction — **vi•o•lent** \-lənt\ *adj* — **vi•o•lent•ly** *adv*

vi•o•let \'vīələt\ *n* **1** : small flowering plant **2** : reddish blue

vi•o•lin \,vīə'lin\ *n* : bowed stringed instrument — **vi•o•lin•ist** \-nist\ *n*

VIP \,vē,ī'pē\ *n, pl* **VIPs** \-'pēz\ : very important person

vi•per \'vīpər\ *n* **1** : venomous snake **2** : treacherous or malignant person

vi•ra•go \və'rägō, -'rā-; 'virə,gō\ *n, pl* **-goes** *or* **-gos** : shrew

vi•ral \'vīrəl\ *adj* : relating to or caused by a virus

vir•gin \'vərjən\ *n* **1** : unmarried woman **2** : a person who has never

had sexual intercourse ~ *adj* **1**
: chaste **2** : natural and unspoiled —
vir·gin·al \-əl\ *adj* — **vir·gin·al·ly**
adv — **vir·gin·i·ty** \vər'jinətē\ *n*
vir·gule \'vərgyül\ *n* : mark/used esp.
to denote "or" or "per"
vir·ile \'virəl\ *adj* : masculine — **vi·ril·
i·ty** \və'rilətē\ *n*
vir·tu·al \'vərchəwəl\ *adj* : being in
effect but not in fact or name — **vir·
tu·al·ly** *adv*
vir·tue \'vərchü\ *n* **1** : moral excellence **2** : effective or commendable
quality **3** : chastity
vir·tu·os·i·ty \ˌvərchə'wäsətē\ *n, pl*
-ties : great skill (as in music)
vir·tu·o·so \ˌvərchə'wōsō, -zō\ *n,
pl* **-sos** *or* **-si** \-ˌsē, -ˌzē\ : highly
skilled performer esp. of music —
virtuoso *adj*
vir·tu·ous \'vərchəwəs\ *adj* **1** : morally
good **2** : chaste — **vir·tu·ous·ly** *adv*
vir·u·lent \'virələnt, -yələnt\ *adj* **1**
: extremely severe or infectious **2**
: full of malice — **vir·u·lence** \-ləns\
n — **vir·u·lent·ly** *adv*
vi·rus \'vīrəs\ *n* **1** : tiny disease-
causing agent **2** : a computer program that performs a malicious action (as destroying data)
vi·sa \'vēzə, -sə\ *n* : authorization to
enter a foreign country
vis·age \'vizij\ *n* : face
vis·cera \'visərə\ *n pl* : internal bodily
organs esp. of the trunk
vis·cer·al \'visərəl\ *adj* **1** : bodily **2**
: instinctive **3** : deeply or crudely
emotional — **vis·cer·al·ly** *adv*
vis·cid \'visəd\ *adj* : viscous — **vis·cid·
i·ty** \vis'idətē\ *n*
vis·count \'vīˌkaunt\ *n* : British nobleman ranking below an earl and above
a baron
vis·count·ess \-əs\ *n* **1** : wife of a viscount **2** : woman with rank of a viscount
vis·cous \'viskəs\ *adj* : having a thick
or sticky consistency — **vis·cos·i·ty**
\vis'käsətē\ *n*
vise \'vīs\ *n* : device for clamping
something being worked on
vis·i·bil·i·ty \ˌvizə'bilətē\ *n, pl* **-ties**
: degree or range to which something
can be seen
vis·i·ble \'vizəbəl\ *adj* **1** : capable of
being seen **2** : manifest or apparent
— **vis·i·bly** *adv*
vi·sion \'vizhən\ *n* **1** : vivid picture

seen in a dream or trance or in the
imagination **2** : foresight **3** : power
of seeing ~ *vb* : imagine
vi·sion·ary \'vizhəˌnerē\ *adj* **1** : given
to dreaming or imagining **2** : illusory
3 : not practical ~ *n* : one with great
dreams or projects
vis·it \'vizət\ *vb* **1** : go or come to see
2 : stay with for a time as a guest **3**
: cause or be a reward, affliction, or
punishment ~ *n* : short stay as a
guest — **vis·it·able** *adj* — **vis·i·tor**
\-ər\ *n*
vis·i·ta·tion \ˌvizə'tāshən\ *n* **1** : official visit **2** : divine punishment or favor **3** : severe trial
vi·sor \'vīzər\ *n* **1** : front piece of a
helmet **2** : part (as on a cap or car
windshield) that shades the eyes
vis·ta \'vistə\ *n* : distant view
vi·su·al \'vizhəwəl\ *adj* **1** : relating to
sight **2** : visible — **vi·su·al·ly** *adv*
vi·su·al·ize \'vizhəwəˌlīz\ *vb* **-ized;
-iz·ing** : form a mental image of
— **vi·su·al·i·za·tion** \ˌvizhəwələ'zā-
shən\ *n* — **vi·su·al·iz·er** \'vizhəwə-
ˌlīzər\ *n*
vi·tal \'vīt°l\ *adj* **1** : relating to, necessary for, or characteristic of life **2**
: full of life and vigor **3** : fatal **4**
: very important — **vi·tal·ly** *adv*
vi·tal·i·ty \vī'talətē\ *n, pl* **-ties** **1** : life
force **2** : energy
vital signs *n pl* : body's pulse rate, respiration, temperature, and usu. blood
pressure
vi·ta·min \'vītəmən\ *n* : natural organic
substance essential to health
vi·ti·ate \'vishēˌāt\ *vb* **-at·ed; -at·ing** **1**
: spoil or impair **2** : invalidate — **vi·
ti·a·tion** \ˌvishē'āshən\ *n* — **vi·ti·a·
tor** \'vishēˌātər\ *n*
vit·re·ous \'vitrēəs\ *adj* : relating to or
resembling glass
vit·ri·ol \'vitrēəl\ *n* : something caustic,
corrosive, or biting — **vit·ri·ol·ic**
\ˌvitrē'älik\ *adj*
vi·tu·per·ate \vī'tüpəˌrāt, və, -'tyü-\ *vb*
-at·ed; -at·ing : abuse in words — **vi·
tu·per·a·tion** \-ˌtüpə'rāshən, -ˌtyü\
n — **vi·tu·per·a·tive** \-'tüpərətiv,
-'tyü-, -pəˌrāt-\ *adj* — **vi·tu·per·a·
tive·ly** *adv*
vi·va·cious \və'vāshəs, vī-\ *adj* : lively
— **vi·va·cious·ly** *adv* — **vi·va·cious·
ness** *n* — **vi·vac·i·ty** \-'vasətē\ *n*
viv·id \'vivəd\ *adj* **1** : lively **2** : bril-

liant **3** : intense or sharp — **viv•id•ly**
adv — **viv•id•ness** *n*

viv•i•fy \'vivə‚fī\ *vb* **-fied; -fy•ing** : give
life or vividness to

vivi•sec•tion \‚vivə'sekshən, 'vivə‚-\
n : experimental operation on a living
animal

vix•en \'viksən\ *n* **1** : scolding woman
2 : female fox

vo•cab•u•lary \vō'kabyə‚lerē\ *n, pl*
-lar•ies 1 : list or collection of words
2 : stock of words used by a person or
about a subject

vo•cal \'vōkəl\ *adj* **1** : relating to or
produced by or for the voice **2**
: speaking out freely and usu. emphatically

vocal cords *n pl* : membranous folds in
the larynx that are important in making vocal sounds

vo•cal•ist \'vōkəlist\ *n* : singer

vo•cal•ize \-‚līz\ *vb* **-ized; -iz•ing** : give
vocal expression to

vo•ca•tion \vō'kāshən\ *n* : regular
employment — **vo•ca•tion•al** \-shən-
əl\ *adj*

vo•cif•er•ous \vō'sifərəs\ *adj* : noisy
and insistent — **vo•cif•er•ous•ly** *adv*

vod•ka \'vädkə\ *n* : colorless distilled
grain liquor

vogue \'vōg\ *n* : brief but intense pop-
ularity — **vogu•ish** \'vōgish\ *adj*

voice \'vȯis\ *n* **1** : sound produced
through the mouth by humans and
many animals **2** : power of speaking
3 : right of choice or opinion ∼ *vb*
voiced; voic•ing : express in words
— **voiced** \'vȯist\ *adj*

void \'vȯid\ *adj* **1** : containing nothing
2 : lacking — with *of* **3** : not legally
binding ∼ *n* **1** : empty space **2**
: feeling of hollowness ∼ *vb* **1** : discharge (as body waste) **2** : make (as a
contract) void — **void•able** *adj* —
void•er *n*

vol•a•tile \'välətˀl\ *adj* **1** : readily vapor-
izing at a relatively low temperature
2 : likely to change suddenly — **vol•a-
til•i•ty** \‚välə'tilətē\ *n* — **vol•a•til•ize**
\'välətˀl‚īz\ *vb*

vol•ca•no \väl'kānō\ *n, pl* **-noes** *or*
-nos : opening in the earth's crust
from which molten rock and steam
come out — **vol•ca•nic** \-'kanik\ *adj*

vo•li•tion \vō'lishən\ *n* : free will —
vo•li•tion•al \-'lishənəl\ *adj*

vol•ley \'välē\ *n, pl* **-leys 1** : flight of

missiles (as arrows) **2** : simultaneous
shooting of many weapons

vol•ley•ball *n* : game of batting a large
ball over a net

volt \'vōlt\ *n* : unit for measuring the
force that moves an electric current

volt•age \'vōltij\ *n* : quantity of volts

vol•u•ble \'välyəbəl\ *adj* : fluent and
smooth in speech — **vol•u•bil•i•ty**
\‚välyə'bilətē\ *n* — **vol•u•bly** \'väl-
yəblē\ *adv*

vol•ume \'välyəm\ *n* **1** : book **2** : space
occupied as measured by cubic units
3 : amount **4** : loudness of a sound

vo•lu•mi•nous \və'lümənəs\ *adj* : large
or bulky

vol•un•tary \'välən‚terē\ *adj* **1** : done,
made, or given freely and without ex-
pecting compensation **2** : relating to
or controlled by the will — **vol•un-
tar•i•ly** *adv*

vol•un•teer \‚välən'tir\ *n* : person who
offers to help or work without expect-
ing payment or reward ∼ *vb* **1** : offer
or give voluntarily **2** : offer oneself
as a volunteer

vo•lup•tuous \və'ləpchəwəs\ *adj* **1**
: luxurious **2** : having a full and sexually attractive figure — **vo•lup•tu-
ous•ly** *adv* — **vo•lup•tuous•ness** *n*

vom•it \'vämət\ *vb* : throw up the contents of the stomach — **vomit** *n*

voo•doo \'vüdü\ *n, pl* **voodoos 1** : religion derived from African polythe-
ism and involving sorcery **2** : one
who practices voodoo **3** : charm or
fetish used in voodoo — **voodoo** *adj*
— **voo•doo•ism** \-‚izəm\ *n*

vo•ra•cious \vȯ'rāshəs, və-\ *adj*
: greedy or exceedingly hungry — **vo-
ra•cious•ly** *adv* — **vo•ra•cious•ness**
n — **vo•rac•i•ty** \-'rasətē\ *n*

vor•tex \'vȯr‚teks\ *n, pl* **vor•ti•ces**
\'vȯrtə‚sēz\ : whirling liquid

vo•ta•ry \'vōtərē\ *n, pl* **-ries 1** : devoted participant, adherent, admirer,
or worshiper

vote \'vōt\ *n* **1** : individual expression
of preference in choosing or reaching
a decision **2** : right to indicate one's
preference or the preference expressed ∼ *vb* **vot•ed; vot•ing 1**
: cast a vote **2** : choose or defeat by
vote — **vote•less** *adj* — **vot•er** *n*

vo•tive \'vōtiv\ *adj* : consisting of or
expressing a vow, wish, or desire

vouch \'vauch\ *vb* : give a guarantee or
personal assurance

vouch•er \'vauchər\ *n* : written record

or receipt that serves as proof of a transaction

vouch•safe \vaůch'sāf\ *vb* **-safed; -saf•ing** : grant as a special favor

vow \vaů\ *n* : solemn promise to do something or to live or act a certain way — **vow** *vb*

vow•el \'vaůəl\ *n* **1** : speech sound produced without obstruction or friction in the mouth **2** : letter representing such a sound

voy•age \'vȯiij\ *n* : long journey esp. by water or through space ~ *vb* **-aged; -ag•ing** : make a voyage — **voy•ag•er** *n*

vul•ca•nize \'vəlkə,nīz\ *vb* **-nized; -niz•ing** : treat (as rubber) to make more elastic or stronger

vul•gar \'vəlgər\ *adj* **1** : relating to the common people **2** : lacking refinement **3** : offensive in manner or language — **vul•gar•ism** \-,rizəm\ *n* — **vul•gar•ize** \-,rīz\ *vb* — **vul•gar•ly** *adv*

vul•gar•i•ty \,vəl'garətē\ *n, pl* **-ties 1** : state of being vulgar **2** : vulgar language or act

vul•ner•a•ble \'vəlnərəbəl\ *adj* : susceptible to attack or damage — **vul•ner•a•bil•i•ty** \,vəlnərə'bilətē\ *n* — **vul•ner•a•bly** *adv*

vul•ture \'vəlchər\ *n* : large flesh=eating bird

vul•va \'vəlvə\ *n, pl* **-vae** \-,vē, -,vī\ : external genital parts of the female

vying *pres part of* VIE

W

w \'dəbəl,yü\ *n, pl* **w's** *or* **ws** \-,yüz\ : 23d letter of the alphabet

wad \'wäd\ *n* **1** : little mass **2** : soft mass of fibrous material **3** : pliable plug to retain a powder charge **4** : considerable amount ~ *vb* **1** : form into a wad **2** : stuff with a wad

wad•dle \'wäd°l\ *vb* **-dled; -dling** : walk with short steps swaying from side to side — **waddle** *n*

wade \'wād\ *vb* **wad•ed; wad•ing 1** : step in or through (as water) **2** : move with difficulty — **wade** *n* — **wad•er** *n*

wa•fer \'wāfər\ *n* **1** : thin crisp cake or cracker **2** : waferlike thing

waf•fle \'wäfəl\ *n* : crisped cake of batter cooked in a hinged utensil (**waffle iron**) ~ *vb* : vacillate

waft \'wäft, 'waft\ *vb* : cause to move lightly by wind or waves — **waft** *n*

¹wag \'wag\ *vb* **-gg-** : sway or swing from side to side or to and fro — **wag** *n*

²wag *n* : wit — **wag•gish** *adj*

wage \'wāj\ *vb* **waged; wag•ing** : engage in ~ *n* **1** : payment for labor or services **2** : compensation

wa•ger \'wājər\ *n or vb* : bet

wag•gle \'wagəl\ *vb* **-gled; -gling** : wag — **waggle** *n*

wag•on \'wagən\ *n* **1** : 4-wheeled vehicle drawn by animals **2** : child's 4=wheeled cart

waif \'wāf\ *n* : homeless child

wail \'wāl\ *vb* **1** : mourn **2** : make a sound like a mournful cry — **wail** *n*

wain•scot \'wänskət, -,skōt, -,skät\ *n* : usu. paneled wooden lining of an interior wall — **wainscot** *vb*

waist \'wāst\ *n* **1** : narrowed part of the body between chest and hips **2** : waistlike part — **waist•line** *n*

wait \'wāt\ *vb* **1** : remain in readiness or expectation **2** : delay **3** : attend as a waiter ~ *n* **1** : concealment **2** : act or period of waiting

wait•er \'wātər\ *n* : person who serves others at tables

wait•per•son \'wāt,pərsən\ *n* : a waiter or waitress

wait•ress \'wātrəs\ *n* : woman who serves others at tables

waive \'wāv\ *vb* **waived; waiv•ing** : give up claim to

waiv•er \'wāvər\ *n* : act of waiving right, claim, or privilege

¹wake \'wāk\ *vb* **woke** \'wōk\; **wo•ken** \'wōkən\; **wak•ing 1** : keep watch **2** : bring or come back to consciousness after sleep ~ *n* **1** : state of being awake **2** : watch held over a dead body

²wake *n* : track left by a ship

wake•ful \'wākfəl\ *adj* : not sleeping or able to sleep — **wake•ful•ness** *n*

wak•en \'wākən\ *vb* : wake

wale \'wāl\ *n* : ridge on cloth

walk \'wok\ *vb* **1** : move or cause to move on foot **2** : pass over, through, or along by walking ∼ *n* **1** : a going on foot **2** : place or path for walking **3** : distance to be walked **4** : way of living **5** : way of walking **6** : slow 4= beat gait of a horse — **walk•er** *n*

wall \'wol\ *n* **1** : structure for defense or for enclosing something **2** : upright enclosing part of a building or room **3** : something like a wall ∼ *vb* : provide, separate, surround, or close with a wall — **walled** \'wold\ *adj*

wal•la•by \'wäləbē\ *n, pl* **-bies** : small or medium-sized kangaroo

wal•let \'wälət\ *n* : pocketbook with compartments

wall•flow•er *n* **1** : mustardlike plant with showy fragrant flowers **2** : one who remains on the sidelines of social activity

wal•lop \'wäləp\ *n* **1** : powerful blow **2** : ability to hit hard ∼ *vb* **1** : beat soundly **2** : hit hard

wal•low \'wälō\ *vb* **1** : roll about in deep mud **2** : indulge oneself excessively ∼ *n* : place for wallowing

wall•pa•per *n* : decorative paper for walls — **wallpaper** *vb*

wal•nut \'wol,nət\ *n* **1** : nut with a furrowed shell and adherent husk **2** : tree on which this nut grows or its brown wood

wal•rus \'wolrəs, 'wäl-\ *n, pl* **-rus** *or* **-rus•es** : large seallike mammal of northern seas having ivory tusks

waltz \'wolts\ *n* : gliding dance to music having 3 beats to the measure or the music — **waltz** *vb*

wam•pum \'wämpəm\ *n* : strung shell beads used by No. American Indians as money

wan \'wän\ *adj* **-nn-** : sickly or pale — **wan•ly** *adv* — **wan•ness** *n*

wand \'wänd\ *n* : slender staff

wan•der \'wändər\ *vb* **1** : move about aimlessly **2** : stray **3** : become delirious — **wan•der•er** *n*

wan•der•lust \'wändər,ləst\ *n* : strong urge to wander

wane \'wān\ *vb* **waned; wan•ing 1** : grow smaller or less **2** : lose power, prosperity, or influence — **wane** *n*

wan•gle \'waŋgəl\ *vb* **-gled; -gling** : obtain by sly or devious means

want \'wont\ *vb* **1** : lack **2** : need **3** : desire earnestly ∼ *n* **1** : deficiency **2** : dire need **3** : something wanted

want•ing \-iŋ\ *adj* **1** : not present or in evidence **2** : falling below standards **3** : lacking in ability ∼ *prep* **1** : less or minus **2** : without

wan•ton \'wont°n\ *adj* **1** : lewd **2** : having no regard for justice or for others' feelings, rights, or safety ∼ *n* : lewd or immoral person ∼ *vb* : be wanton — **wan•ton•ly** *adv* — **wan•ton•ness** *n*

wa•pi•ti \'wäpətē\ *n, pl* **-ti** *or* **-tis** : elk

war \'wor\ *n* **1** : armed fighting between nations **2** : state of hostility or conflict **3** : struggle between opposing forces or for a particular end ∼ *vb* **-rr-** : engage in warfare — **war•less** \-ləs\ *adj* — **war•time** *n*

war•ble \'worbəl\ *n* **1** : melodious succession of low pleasing sounds **2** : musical trill ∼ *vb* **-bled; -bling** : sing or utter in a trilling way

war•bler \'worblər\ *n* **1** : small thrushlike singing bird **2** : small bright= colored insect-eating bird

ward \'word\ *n* **1** : a guarding or being under guard or guardianship **2** : division of a prison or hospital **3** : electoral or administrative division of a city **4** : person under protection of a guardian or a law court ∼ *vb* : turn aside — **ward•ship** *n*

¹**-ward** \wərd\ *adj suffix* **1** : that moves, tends, faces, or is directed toward **2** : that occurs or is situated in the direction of

²**-ward, -wards** *adv suffix* **1** : in a (specified) direction **2** : toward a (specified) point, position, or area

war•den \'word°n\ *n* **1** : guardian **2** : official charged with supervisory duties or enforcement of laws **3** : official in charge of a prison

ward•er \'wordər\ *n* : watchman or warden

ward•robe \'word,rōb\ *n* **1** : clothes closet **2** : collection of wearing apparel

ware \'war\ *n* **1** : articles for sale — often pl. **2** : items of fired clay

ware•house \-,haus\ *n* : place for storage of merchandise — **warehouse** *vb* — **ware•house•man** \-mən\ *n* — **ware•hous•er** \-,hauzər, -sər\ *n*

war•fare \'wȯr‚far\ *n* **1** : military operations between enemies **2** : struggle

war•head \-‚hed\ *n* : part of a missile holding the explosive material

war•like *adj* : fond of, relating to, or used in war

warm \'wȯrm\ *adj* **1** : having or giving out moderate or adequate heat **2** : serving to retain heat **3** : showing strong feeling **4** : giving a pleasant impression of warmth, cheerfulness, or friendliness ⁓ *vb* **1** : make or become warm **2** : give warmth or energy to **3** : experience feelings of affection **4** : become increasingly ardent, interested, or competent — **warm•er** *n* — **warm•ly** *adv* — **warm up** *vb* : make ready by preliminary activity

war•mon•ger \'wȯr‚məngər, -‚män-\ *n* : one who attempts to stir up war

warmth \'wȯrmth\ *n* **1** : quality or state of being warm **2** : enthusiasm

warn \'wȯrn\ *vb* **1** : put on guard **2** : notify in advance — **warn•ing** \-iŋ\ *n or adj*

warp \'wȯrp\ *n* **1** : lengthwise threads in a woven fabric **2** : twist ⁓ *vb* **1** : twist out of shape **2** : lead astray **3** : distort

war•rant \'wȯrənt, 'wär-\ *n* **1** : authorization **2** : legal writ authorizing action ⁓ *vb* **1** : declare or maintain positively **2** : guarantee **3** : approve **4** : justify

warrant officer *n* **1** : officer in the armed forces ranking next below a commissioned officer **2** : commissioned officer in the navy or coast guard ranking below an ensign

war•ran•ty \'wȯrəntē, 'wär-\ *n, pl* **-ties** : guarantee of the integrity of a product

war•ren \'wȯrən, 'wär-\ *n* : area where rabbits are bred and kept

war•rior \'wȯryər, 'wȯrēər; 'wärē-, 'wäryər\ *n* : man engaged or experienced in warfare

war•ship \'wȯr‚ship\ *n* : naval vessel

wart \'wȯrt\ *n* **1** : small projection on the skin caused by a virus **2** : wartlike protuberance — **warty** *adj*

wary \'warē\ *adj* **war•i•er; -est** : careful in guarding against danger or deception

was *past 1st & 3d sing of* BE

wash \'wȯsh, 'wäsh\ *vb* **1** : cleanse with or as if with a liquid (as water) **2** : wet thoroughly with liquid **3** : flow along the border of **4** : flow in a stream **5** : move or remove by or as if by the action of water **6** : cover or daub lightly with a liquid **7** : undergo laundering ⁓ *n* **1** : act of washing or being washed **2** : articles to be washed **3** : surging action of water or disturbed air — **wash•able** \-əbəl\ *adj*

wash•board *n* : grooved board to scrub clothes on

wash•bowl *n* : large bowl for water for washing hands and face

wash•cloth *n* : cloth used for washing one's face and body

washed–up \'wȯsht'əp, 'wäsht-\ *adj* : no longer capable or usable

wash•er \'wȯshər, 'wäsh-\ *n* **1** : machine for washing **2** : ring used around a bolt or screw to ensure tightness or relieve friction

wash•ing \'wȯshiŋ, 'wäsh-\ *n* : articles to be washed

Washington's Birthday *n* : the 3d Monday in February or formerly February 22 observed as a legal holiday

wash•out *n* **1** : washing out or away of earth **2** : failure

wash•room *n* : bathroom

wasp \'wäsp, 'wȯsp\ *n* : slender-bodied winged insect related to the bees and having a formidable sting

wasp•ish \'wäspish, 'wȯs-\ *adj* : irritable

was•sail \'wäsəl, wä'säl\ *n* **1** : toast to someone's health **2** : liquor drunk on festive occasions **3** : riotous drinking — **wassail** *vb*

waste \'wāst\ *n* **1** : sparsely settled or barren region **2** : act or an instance of wasting **3** : refuse (as garbage or rubbish) **4** : material (as feces) produced but not used by a living body ⁓ *vb* **wast•ed; wast•ing 1** : ruin **2** : spend or use carelessly **3** : lose substance or energy ⁓ *adj* **1** : wild and uninhabited **2** : being of no further use — **wast•er** *n* — **waste•ful** \-fəl\ *adj* — **waste•ful•ly** *adv* — **waste•ful•ness** *n*

waste•bas•ket \-‚baskət\ *n* : receptacle for refuse

waste•land \-‚land, -lənd\ *n* : barren uncultivated land

wast•rel \'wāstrəl, 'wästrəl\ *n* : one who wastes

watch \'wäch, 'wȯch\ *vb* **1** : be or stay awake intentionally **2** : be on the lookout for danger **3** : observe **4** : keep oneself informed about ⁓ *n* **1** : act of keeping awake to guard **2** : close observation **3** : one that watches **4** : period of duty on a ship or those on duty during this period **5** : timepiece carried on the person — **watch•er** n

watch•dog n **1** : dog kept to guard property **2** : one that protects

watch•ful \-fəl\ adj : steadily attentive — **watch•ful•ly** adv — **watch•ful•ness** n

watch•man \-mən\ n : person assigned to watch

watch•word n **1** : secret word used as a signal **2** : slogan

wa•ter \'wȯtər, 'wät-\ n **1** : liquid that descends as rain and forms rivers, lakes, and seas **2** : liquid containing or resembling water ∼ vb **1** : supply with or get water **2** : dilute with or as if with water **3** : form or secrete watery matter

water buffalo n : common oxlike often domesticated Asian buffalo

wa•ter•col•or n **1** : paint whose liquid part is water **2** : picture made with watercolors

wa•ter•course n : stream of water

wa•ter•cress \-ˌkres\ n : perennial salad plant with white flowers

wa•ter•fall n : steep descent of the water of a stream

wa•ter•fowl n **1** : bird that frequents the water **2** **waterfowl** pl : swimming game birds

wa•ter•front n : land fronting a body of water

water lily n : aquatic plant with floating leaves and showy flowers

wa•ter•logged \-ˌlȯgd, -ˌlägd\ adj : filled or soaked with water

wa•ter•mark n **1** : mark showing how high water has risen **2** : a marking in paper visible under light ∼ vb : mark (paper) with a watermark

wa•ter•mel•on n : large fruit with sweet juicy usu. red pulp

water moccasin n : venomous snake of the southeastern U.S.

wa•ter•pow•er n : power of moving water used to run machinery

wa•ter•proof adj : not letting water through ∼ vb : make waterproof — **wa•ter•proof•ing** n

wa•ter•shed \-ˌshed\ n : dividing ridge between two drainage areas or one of these areas

water ski n : ski used on water when the

wearer is towed — **wa•ter–ski** vb — **wa•ter–ski•er** n

wa•ter•spout n **1** : pipe from which water is spouted **2** : tornado over a body of water

wa•ter•tight adj **1** : so tight as not to let water in **2** : allowing no possibility for doubt or uncertainty

wa•ter•way n : navigable body of water

wa•ter•works n pl : system by which water is supplied (as to a city)

wa•tery \'wȯtərē, 'wät-\ adj **1** : containing, full of, or giving out water **2** : being like water **3** : soft and soggy

watt \'wät\ n : unit of electric power — **watt•age** \'wätij\ n

wat•tle \'wät³l\ n **1** : framework of flexible branches used in building **2** : fleshy process hanging usu. about the head or neck (as of a bird) — **wat•tled** \-³ld\ adj

wave \'wāv\ vb **waved; wav•ing** **1** : flutter **2** : signal with the hands **3** : wave to and fro with the hand **4** : curve up and down like a wave ∼ n **1** : moving swell on the surface of water **2** : wave-like shape **3** : waving motion **4** : surge **5** : disturbance that transfers energy from point to point — **wave•let** \-lət\ n — **wave•like** adj — **wavy** adj

wave•length \'wāvˌleṇth\ n **1** : distance from crest to crest in the line of advance of a wave **2** : line of thought that reveals a common understanding

wa•ver \'wāvər\ vb **1** : fluctuate in opinion, allegiance, or direction **2** : flicker **3** : falter — **waver** n — **wa•ver•er** n — **wa•ver•ing•ly** adv

¹wax \'waks\ n **1** : yellowish plastic substance secreted by bees **2** : substance like beeswax ∼ vb : treat or rub with wax esp. for polishing

²wax vb **1** : grow larger **2** : become

wax•en \'waksən\ adj : made of or resembling wax

waxy \'waksē\ adj **wax•i•er; -est** : made of, full of, or resembling wax

way \'wā\ n **1** : thoroughfare for travel or passage **2** : route **3** : course of action **4** : method **5** : detail **6** : usual or characteristic state of affairs **7** : condition **8** : distance **9** : progress along a course — **by the way** : in a digression — **by way of** **1** : for the purpose of **2** : by the route through — **out of the way** : remote

way•bill n : paper that accompanies a

shipment and gives details of goods, route, and charges

way·far·er \'wā͟ˌfarər\ *n* : traveler esp. on foot — **way·far·ing** \-ˌfariŋ\ *adj*

way·lay \'wāˌlā\ *vb* **-laid** \-ˌlād\; **-lay·ing** : lie in wait for

way·side *n* : side of a road

way·ward \'wāwərd\ *adj* **1** : following one's own capricious inclinations **2** : unpredictable

we \'wē\ *pron* — used of a group that includes the speaker or writer

weak \'wēk\ *adj* **1** : lacking strength or vigor **2** : deficient in vigor of mind or character **3** : of less than usual strength **4** : not having or exerting authority — **weak·en** \'wēkən\ *vb* — **weak·ly** *adv*

weak·ling \-liŋ\ *n* : person who is physically, mentally, or morally weak

weak·ly \'wēklē\ *adj* : feeble

weak·ness \-nəs\ *n* **1** : quality or state of being weak **2** : fault **3** : object of special liking

wealth \'welth\ *n* **1** : abundant possessions or resources **2** : profusion

wealthy \'welthē\ *adj* **wealth·i·er**; **-est** : having wealth

wean \'wēn\ *vb* **1** : accustom (a young mammal) to take food by means other than nursing **2** : free from dependence

weap·on \'wepən\ *n* **1** : something (as a gun) that may be used to fight with **2** : means by which one contends against another — **weap·on·less** *adj*

wear \'war\ *vb* **wore** \'wōr\; **worn** \'wōrn\; **wear·ing** **1** : use as an article of clothing or adornment **2** : carry on the person **3** : show an appearance of **4** : decay by use or by scraping **5** : lessen the strength of **6** : endure use ~ *n* **1** : act of wearing **2** : clothing **3** : lasting quality **4** : result of use — **wear·able** \'warəbəl\ *adj* — **wear·er** *n* — **wear out** *vb* **1** : make or become useless by wear **2** : tire

wea·ri·some \'wirēsəm\ *adj* : causing weariness — **wea·ri·some·ly** *adv* — **wea·ri·some·ness** *n*

wea·ry \'wirē\ *adj* **-ri·er**; **-est** **1** : worn out in strength, freshness, or patience **2** : expressing or characteristic of weariness ~ *vb* **-ried**; **-ry·ing** : make or become weary — **wea·ri·ly** *adv* — **wea·ri·ness** *n*

wea·sel \'wēzəl\ *n* : small slender flesh-eating mammal

weath·er \'wethər\ *n* : state of the atmosphere ~ *vb* **1** : expose to or endure the action of weather **2** : endure

weath·er–beat·en *adj* : worn or damaged by exposure to the weather

weath·er·man \-ˌman\ *n* : one who forecasts and reports the weather

weath·er·proof *adj* : able to withstand exposure to weather — **weatherproof** *vb*

weather vane *n* : movable device that shows the way the wind blows

weave \'wēv\ *vb* **wove** \'wōv\ *or* **weaved**; **wo·ven** \'wōvən\ *or* **weaved**; **weav·ing** **1** : form by interlacing strands of material **2** : to make as if by weaving together parts **3** : follow a winding course ~ *n* : pattern or method of weaving — **weav·er** *n*

web \'web\ *n* **1** : cobweb **2** : animal or plant membrane **3** : network **4** *cap* : WORLD WIDE WEB ~ *vb* **-bb-** : cover or provide with a web — **webbed** \'webd\ *adj*

web·bing \'webiŋ\ *n* : strong closely woven tape

Web site *n* : group of World Wide Web pages available online

wed \'wed\ *vb* **-dd-** **1** : marry **2** : unite

wed·ding \'wediŋ\ *n* : marriage ceremony and celebration

wedge \'wej\ *n* : V-shaped object used for splitting, raising, forcing open, or tightening ~ *vb* **wedged**; **wedg·ing** **1** : tighten or split with a wedge **2** : force into a narrow space

wed·lock \'wedˌläk\ *n* : marriage

Wednes·day \'wenzdā, -dē\ *n* : 4th day of the week

wee \'wē\ *adj* : very small

weed \'wēd\ *n* : unwanted plant ~ *vb* **1** : remove weeds **2** : get rid of — **weed·er** *n* — **weedy** *adj*

weeds *n pl* : mourning clothes

week \'wēk\ *n* **1** : 7 successive days **2** : calendar period of 7 days beginning with Sunday and ending with Saturday **3** : the working or school days of the calendar week

week·day \'wēkˌdā\ *n* : any day except Sunday and often Saturday

week·end \-ˌend\ *n* : Saturday and Sunday ~ *vb* : spend the weekend

week·ly \'wēklē\ *adj* : occurring, appearing, or done every week ~ *n, pl* **-lies** : weekly publication — **weekly** *adv*

weep \'wēp\ *vb* **wept** \'wept\; **weep-**

ing : shed tears — **weep•er** *n* —
weepy *adj*

wee•vil \'wēvəl\ *n* : small injurious
beetle with a long head usu. curved
into a snout — **wee•vily, wee•vil•ly**
\'wēvəlē\ *adj*

weft \'weft\ *n* : crosswise threads or
yarn in weaving

weigh \'wā\ *vb* **1** : determine the heaviness of **2** : have a specified weight **3**
: consider carefully **4** : raise (an anchor) off the sea floor **5** : press down
or burden

weight \'wāt\ *n* **1** : amount that something weighs **2** : relative heaviness **3**
: heavy object **4** : burden or pressure
5 : importance ~ *vb* **1** : load with a
weight **2** : oppress — **weight•less**
\-ləs\ *adj* — **weight•less•ness** *n* —
weighty \'wātē\ *adj*

weird \'wird\ *adj* **1** : unearthly or mysterious **2** : strange — **weird•ly** *adv* —
weird•ness *n*

wel•come \'welkəm\ *vb* **-comed;**
-com•ing : accept or greet cordially
~ *adj* : received or permitted gladly
~ *n* : cordial greeting or reception

weld \'weld\ *vb* : unite by heating,
hammering, or pressing ~ *n* : union
by welding — **weld•er** *n*

wel•fare \'wel,far\ *n* **1** : prosperity **2**
: government aid for those in need

¹**well** \'wel\ *n* **1** : spring **2** : hole sunk in
the earth to obtain a natural deposit
(as of oil) **3** : source of supply **4**
: open space extending vertically
through floors ~ *vb* : flow forth

²**well** *adv* **bet•ter** \'betər\; **best** \'best\
1 : in a good or proper manner **2** : satisfactorily **3** : fully **4** : intimately **5**
: considerably ~ *adj* **1** : satisfactory **2** : prosperous **3** : desirable **4**
: healthy

well–adjusted \,welə'jəstəd\ *adj* : well-
balanced

well–ad•vised \,weləd'vīzd\ *adj* : prudent

well–balanced \'wel'balənst\ *adj* **1**
: evenly balanced **2** : emotionally or
psychologically sound

well–be•ing \'wel'bēiŋ\ *n* : state of being happy, healthy, or prosperous

well–bred \-'bred\ *adj* : having good
manners

well–done *adj* **1** : properly performed
2 : cooked thoroughly

well–heeled \-'hēld\ *adj* : financially
well-off

well–mean•ing *adj* : having good inten-
tions

well–nigh *adv* : nearly

well–off *adj* : being in good condition
esp. financially

well–read \-'red\ *adj* : well informed
through reading

well–round•ed \-'raündəd\ *adj* : broadly
developed

well•spring *n* : source

well–to–do \,weltə'dü\ *adj* : prosperous

welsh \'welsh, 'welch\ *vb* **1** : avoid
payment **2** : break one's word

Welsh rabbit *n* : melted often seasoned
cheese poured over toast or crackers

Welsh rare•bit \-'rarbət\ *n* : Welsh
rabbit

welt \'welt\ *n* **1** : narrow strip of leather
between a shoe upper and sole **2**
: ridge raised on the skin usu. by a
blow ~ *vb* : hit hard

wel•ter \'weltər\ *vb* **1** : toss about **2**
: wallow ~ *n* : confused jumble

wen \'wen\ *n* : abnormal growth or cyst

wench \'wench\ *n* : young woman

wend \'wend\ *vb* : direct one's course

went *past of* GO

wept *past of* WEEP

were *past 2d sing, past pl, or past subjunctive of* BE

were•wolf \'wer,wůlf, 'wir-, 'wər-\ *n,
pl* **-wolves** \-,wůlvz\ : person held to
be able to change into a wolf

west \'west\ *adv* : to or toward the west
~ *adj* : situated toward or at or coming from the west ~ *n* **1** : direction
of sunset **2** *cap* : regions to the west
— **west•er•ly** \'westərlē\ *adv or adj*
— **west•ward** \-wərd\ *adv or adj* —
west•wards \-wərdz\ *adv*

west•ern \'westərn\ *adj* **1** *cap* : of a
region designated West **2** : lying toward or coming from the west —
West•ern•er *n*

wet \'wet\ *adj* **-tt- 1** : consisting of or
covered or soaked with liquid **2** : not
dry ~ *n* : moisture ~ *vb* **-tt-** : make
or become moist — **wet•ly** *adv* —
wet•ness *n*

whack \'hwak\ *vb* : strike sharply ~ *n*
1 : sharp blow **2** : proper working order **3** : chance **4** : try

¹**whale** \'hwāl\ *n, pl* **whales** *or* **whale**
: large marine mammal ~ *vb* **whaled;**
whal•ing : hunt for whales — **whale-
boat** *n* — **whal•er** *n*

²**whale** *vb* **whaled; whal•ing** : strike or
hit vigorously

whale•bone *n* : horny substance attached to the upper jaw of some large whales (**whalebone whales**)

wharf \'hwȯrf\ *n, pl* **wharves** \'hwȯrvz\ : structure alongside which boats lie to load or unload

what \'hwät\ *pron* **1** — used to inquire the identity or nature of something **2** : that which **3** : whatever ~ *adv* : in what respect ~ *adj* **1** — used to inquire about the identity or nature of something **2** : how remarkable or surprising **3** : whatever

what•ev•er \hwät'evər\ *pron* **1** : anything or everything that **2** : no matter what ~ *adj* : of any kind at all

what•not \'hwät,nät\ *pron* : any of various other things that might be mentioned

what•so•ev•er \,hwätsō'evər\ *pron or adj* : whatever

wheal \'hwēl\ *n* : a welt on the skin

wheat \'hwēt\ *n* : cereal grain that yields flour — **wheat•en** *adj*

whee•dle \'hwēdᵊl\ *vb* **-dled; -dling** : coax or tempt by flattery

wheel \'hwēl\ *n* **1** : disk or circular frame capable of turning on a central axis **2** : device of which the main part is a wheel ~ *vb* **1** : convey or move on wheels or a wheeled vehicle **2** : rotate **3** : turn so as to change direction — **wheeled** *adj* — **wheel•er** *n* — **wheel•less** *adj*

wheel•bar•row \-,barō\ *n* : one-wheeled vehicle for carrying small loads

wheel•base *n* : distance in inches between the front and rear axles of an automotive vehicle

wheel•chair *n* : chair mounted on wheels esp. for the use of disabled persons

wheeze \'hwēz\ *vb* **wheezed; wheezing** : breathe with difficulty and with a whistling sound — **wheeze** *n* — **wheezy** *adj*

whelk \'hwelk\ *n* : large sea snail

whelp \'hwelp\ *n* : one of the young of various carnivorous mammals (as a dog) ~ *vb* : bring forth whelps

when \'hwen\ *adv* — used to inquire about or designate a particular time ~ *conj* **1** : at or during the time that **2** : every time that **3** : if **4** : although ~ *pron* : what time

whence \'hwens\ *adv or conj* : from what place, source, or cause

when•ev•er \hwen'evər\ *conj or adv* : at whatever time

where \'hwer\ *adv* **1** : at, in, or to what place **2** : at, in, or to what situation, position, direction, circumstances, or respect ~ *conj* **1** : at, in, or to what place, position, or circumstance **2** : at, in, or to which place ~ *n* : place

where•abouts \-ə,baùts\ *adv* : about where ~ *n sing or pl* : place where a person or thing is

where•as \hwer'az\ *conj* **1** : while on the contrary **2** : since

where•by *conj* : by, through, or in accordance with which

where•fore \'hwer,fōr\ *adv* **1** : why **2** : therefore ~ *n* : reason

where•in \hwer'in\ *adv* : in what respect

where•of \-'əv, -äv\ *conj* : of what, which, or whom

where•up•on \'hwerə,pȯn, -,pän\ *conj* **1** : on which **2** : and then

wher•ev•er \hwer'evər\ *adv* : where ~ *conj* : at, in, or to whatever place or circumstance

where•with•al \'hwerwith,ȯl, -with-\ *n* : resources and esp. money

whet \'hwet\ *vb* **-tt-** **1** : sharpen by rubbing (as with a stone) **2** : stimulate — **whet•stone** *n*

whether \'hwethər\ *conj* **1** : if it is or was true that **2** : if it is or was better **3** : whichever is the case

whey \'hwā\ *n* : watery part of sour milk

which \'hwich\ *adj* **1** : being what one or ones out of a group **2** : whichever ~ *pron* **1** : which one or ones **2** : whichever

which•ev•er \hwich'evər\ *pron or adj* : no matter what one

whiff \'hwif\ *n* **1** : slight gust **2** : inhalation of odor, gas, or smoke **3** : slight trace ~ *vb* : inhale an odor

while \'hwīl\ *n* **1** : period of time **2** : time and effort used ~ *conj* **1** : during the time that **2** : as long as **3** : although ~ *vb* **whiled; whil•ing** : cause to pass esp. pleasantly

whim \'hwim\ *n* : sudden wish, desire, or change of mind

whim•per \'hwimpər\ *vb* : cry softly — **whimper** *n*

whim•si•cal \'hwimzikəl\ *adj* **1** : full of whims **2** : erratic — **whim•si•cal•i•ty** \,hwimzə'kalətē\ *n* — **whim•si•cal•ly** *adv*

whim·sy, whim·sey \'hwimzē\ *n, pl* **-sies** *or* **-seys** 1 : whim 2 : fanciful creation

whine \'hwīn\ *vb* **whined; whin·ing** 1 : utter a usu. high-pitched plaintive cry 2 : complain — **whine** *n* — **whin·er** *n* — **whiny** *adj*

whin·ny \'hwinē\ *vb* **-nied; -ny·ing** : neigh — **whinny** *n*

whip \'hwip\ *vb* **-pp-** 1 : move quickly 2 : strike with something slender and flexible 3 : defeat 4 : incite 5 : beat into a froth ~ *n* 1 : flexible device used for whipping 2 : party leader responsible for discipline 3 : thrashing motion — **whip·per** *n*

whip·cord *n* 1 : thin tough cord 2 : cloth made of hard-twisted yarns

whip·lash *n* : injury from a sudden sharp movement of the neck and head

whip·per·snap·per \'hwipər,snapər\ *n* : small, insignificant, or presumptuous person

whip·pet \'hwipət\ *n* : small swift dog often used for racing

whip·poor·will \'hwipər,wil\ *n* : American nocturnal bird

whir \'hwər\ *vb* **-rr-** : move, fly, or revolve with a whir ~ *n* : continuous fluttering or vibratory sound

whirl \'hwərl\ *vb* 1 : move or drive in a circle 2 : spin 3 : move or turn quickly 4 : reel ~ *n* 1 : rapid circular movement 2 : state of commotion or confusion 3 : try

whirl·pool *n* : whirling mass of water having a depression in the center

whirl·wind *n* : whirling wind storm

whisk \'hwisk\ *n* 1 : quick light sweeping or brushing motion 2 : usu. wire kitchen implement for beating ~ *vb* 1 : move or convey briskly 2 : beat 3 : brush lightly

whisk broom *n* : small broom

whis·ker \'hwiskər\ *n* 1 *pl* : beard 2 : long bristle or hair near an animal's mouth — **whis·kered** \-kərd\ *adj*

whis·key, whis·ky \'hwiskē\ *n, pl* **-keys** *or* **-kies** : liquor distilled from a fermented mash of grain

whis·per \'hwispər\ *vb* 1 : speak softly 2 : tell by whispering ~ *n* 1 : soft low sound 2 : rumor

whist \'hwist\ *n* : card game

whis·tle \'hwisəl\ *n* 1 : device by which a shrill sound is produced 2 : shrill clear sound made by a whistle or through the lips ~ *vb* **-tled; -tling**

1 : make or utter a whistle 2 : signal or call by a whistle 3 : produce by whistling — **whis·tler** *n*

whis·tle—blow·er \'hwisəl,blōər\ *n* : informer

whis·tle—stop *n* : brief political appearance

whit \'hwit\ *n* : bit

white \'hwīt\ *adj* **whit·er; -est** 1 : free from color 2 : of the color of new snow or milk 3 : having light skin ~ *n* 1 : color of maximum lightness 2 : white part or thing 3 : person who is light-skinned — **white·ness** *n* — **whit·ish** *adj*

white blood cell *n* : blood cell that does not contain hemoglobin

white·cap \'hwīt,kap\ *n* : wave crest breaking into white foam

white—col·lar *adj* : relating to salaried employees with duties not requiring protective or work clothing

white elephant *n* : something costly but of little use or value

white·fish \'hwīt,fish\ *n* : freshwater food fish

whit·en \'hwīt³n\ *vb* : make or become white — **whit·en·er** \'hwīt³nər\ *n*

white slave *n* : woman or girl held unwillingly for purposes of prostitution — **white slavery** *n*

white·tail \'hwīt,tāl\ *n* : No. American deer

white·wash *vb* 1 : whiten with a composition (as of lime and water) 2 : gloss over or cover up faults or wrongdoing — **whitewash** *n*

whith·er \'hwithər\ *adv* 1 : to what place 2 : to what situation, position, degree, or end

¹**whit·ing** \'hwītiŋ\ *n* : usu. light or silvery food fish

²**whiting** *n* : pulverized chalk or limestone

whit·tle \'hwit³l\ *vb* **-tled; -tling** 1 : pare 2 : shape by paring 3 : reduce gradually

whiz, whizz \'hwiz\ *vb* **-zz-** : make a sound like a speeding object — **whiz, whizz** *n*

who \'hü\ *pron* 1 : what or which person or persons 2 : person or persons that 3 — used to introduce a relative clause

who·dun·it \hü'dənət\ *n* : detective or mystery story

who·ev·er \hü'evər\ *pron* : no matter who

whole \'hōl\ *adj* 1 : being in healthy or

sound condition **2** : having all its parts or elements **3** : constituting the total sum of ~ *n* **1** : complete amount or sum **2** : something whole or entire — **on the whole 1** : considering all circumstances **2** : in general — **whole·ness** *n*

whole·heart·ed \'hōl'härtəd\ *adj* : sincere

whole number *n* : integer

whole·sale *n* : sale of goods in quantity usu. for resale by a retail merchant ~ *adj* **1** : of or relating to wholesaling **2** : performed on a large scale ~ *vb* -saled; -sal·ing : sell at wholesale — **wholesale** *adv* — **whole·sal·er** *n*

whole·some \-səm\ *adj* **1** : promoting mental, spiritual, or bodily health **2** : healthy — **whole·some·ness** *n*

whole wheat *adj* : made of ground entire wheat kernels

whol·ly \'hōlē\ *adv* **1** : totally **2** : solely

whom \'hüm\ *pron, objective case of* WHO

whom·ev·er \hüm'evər\ *pron, objective case of* WHOEVER

whoop \'hwüp, 'hwûp, 'hüp, 'hûp\ *vb* : shout loudly ~ *n* : shout

whooping cough *n* : infectious disease marked by convulsive coughing fits

whop·per \'hwäpər\ *n* **1** : something unusually large or extreme of its kind **2** : monstrous lie

whop·ping \'hwäpiŋ\ *adj* : extremely large

whore \'hōr\ *n* : prostitute

whorl \'hwȯrl, 'hwərl\ *n* : spiral — **whorled** *adj*

whose \'hüz\ *adj* : of or relating to whom or which ~ *pron* : whose one or ones

who·so·ev·er \,hüsō'evər\ *pron* : whoever

why \'hwī\ *adv* : for what reason, cause, or purpose ~ *conj* **1** : reason for which **2** : for which ~ *n, pl* **whys** : reason ~ *interj* — used esp. to express surprise

wick \'wik\ *n* : cord that draws up oil, tallow, or wax to be burned

wick·ed \'wikəd\ *adj* **1** : morally bad **2** : harmful or troublesome **3** : very unpleasant **4** : very impressive — **wick·ed·ly** *adv* — **wick·ed·ness** *n*

wick·er \'wikər\ *n* **1** : small pliant branch **2** : wickerwork — **wicker** *adj*

wick·er·work *n* : work made of wickers

wick·et \'wikət\ *n* **1** : small gate, door,

or window **2** : frame in cricket or arch in croquet

wide \'wīd\ *adj* **wid·er; wid·est 1** : covering a vast area **2** : measured at right angles to the length **3** : having a great measure across **4** : opened fully **5** : far from the thing in question ~ *adv* **wid·er; wid·est 1** : over a great distance **2** : so as to leave considerable space between **3** : fully — **wide·ly** *adv* — **wid·en** \'wīdⁿn\ *vb*

wide-awake *adj* : alert

wide-eyed *adj* **1** : having the eyes wide open **2** : amazed **3** : naive

wide·spread *adj* : widely extended

wid·ow \'widō\ *n* : woman who has lost her husband by death and has not married again ~ *vb* : cause to become a widow — **wid·ow·hood** *n*

wid·ow·er \'widəwər\ *n* : man who has lost his wife by death and has not married again

width \'width\ *n* **1** : distance from side to side **2** : largeness of extent **3** : measured and cut piece of material

wield \'wēld\ *vb* **1** : use or handle esp. effectively **2** : exert — **wield·er** *n*

wie·ner \'wēnər\ *n* : frankfurter

wife \'wīf\ *n, pl* **wives** \'wīvz\ : married woman — **wife·hood** *n* — **wife·less** *adj* — **wife·ly** *adj*

wig \'wig\ *n* : manufactured covering of hair for the head

wig·gle \'wigəl\ *vb* -gled; -gling **1** : move with quick jerky or shaking movements **2** : wriggle — **wiggle** *n* — **wig·gler** *n*

wig·gly \-əlē\ *adj* **1** : tending to wiggle **2** : wavy

wig·wag \'wig,wag\ *vb* : signal by a flag or light waved according to a code

wig·wam \'wig,wäm\ *n* : American Indian hut consisting of a framework of poles overlaid with bark, rush mats, or hides

wild \'wīld\ *adj* **1** : living or being in a state of nature and not domesticated or cultivated **2** : unrestrained **3** : turbulent **4** : crazy **5** : uncivilized **6** : erratic ~ *n* **1** : wilderness **2** : undomesticated state ~ *adv* : without control — **wild·ly** *adv* — **wild·ness** *n*

wild·cat \-,kat\ *n* : any of various undomesticated cats (as a lynx) ~ *adj* **1** : not sound or safe **2** : unauthorized

wil·der·ness \'wildərnəs\ *n* : uncultivated and uninhabited region

wild•fire \\'wīld,fīr\\ *n* : sweeping and destructive fire

wild•fowl *n* : game waterfowl

wild•life \\'wīld,līf\\ *n* : undomesticated animals

wile \\'wīl\\ *n* : trick to snare or deceive ~ *vb* **wiled; wil•ing** : lure

will \\'wil\\ *vb, past* **would** \\'wùd\\; *pres sing & pl* **will** **1** : wish **2** — used as an auxiliary verb to express (1) desire or willingness (2) customary action (3) simple future time (4) capability (5) determination (6) probability (7) inevitability or (8) a command **3** : dispose of by a will ~ *n* **1** : often determined wish **2** : act, process, or experience of willing **3** : power of controlling one's actions or emotions **4** : legal document disposing of property after death

will•ful, wil•ful \\'wilfəl\\ *adj* **1** : governed by will without regard to reason **2** : intentional — **will•ful•ly** *adv*

will•ing \\'wiliŋ\\ *adj* **1** : inclined or favorably disposed in mind **2** : prompt to act **3** : done, borne, or accepted voluntarily or without reluctance — **will•ing•ly** *adv* — **will•ing•ness** *n*

will-o'-the-wisp \\,wiləthə'wisp\\ *n* **1** : light that appears at night over marshy grounds **2** : misleading or elusive goal or hope

wil•low \\'wilō\\ *n* : quick-growing shrub or tree with flexible shoots

wil•lowy \\'wiləwē\\ *adj* : gracefully tall and slender

will•pow•er \\'wil,paùər\\ *n* : energetic determination

wil•ly–nil•ly \\,wilē'nilē\\ *adv or adj* : without regard for one's choice

wilt \\'wilt\\ *vb* **1** : lose or cause to lose freshness and become limp esp. from lack of water **2** : grow weak

wily \\'wīlē\\ *adj* **wil•i•er; -est** : full of craftiness — **wil•i•ness** *n*

win \\'win\\ *vb* **won** \\'wən\\; **win•ning 1** : get possession of esp. by effort **2** : gain victory in battle or a contest **3** : make friendly or favorable ~ *n* : victory

wince \\'wins\\ *vb* **winced; winc•ing** : shrink back involuntarily — **wince** *n*

winch \\'winch\\ *n* : machine for hoisting or pulling with a drum around which rope is wound — **winch** *vb*

¹wind \\'wind\\ *n* **1** : movement of the air **2** : breath **3** : gas in the stomach or intestines **4** : air carrying a scent **5** : intimation ~ *vb* **1** : get a scent of **2** : cause to be out of breath

²wind \\'wīnd\\ *vb* **wound** \\'waùnd\\; **wind•ing 1** : have or follow a curving course **2** : move or lie to encircle **3** : encircle or cover with something pliable **4** : tighten the spring of ~ *n* : turn or coil — **wind•er** *n*

wind•break \\-,brāk\\ *n* : trees and shrubs to break the force of the wind

wind•break•er \\-,brākər\\ *n* : light wind-resistant jacket

wind•fall \\'wind,fól\\ *n* **1** : thing blown down by wind **2** : unexpected benefit

wind instrument *n* : musical instrument (as a flute or horn) sounded by wind and esp. by the breath

wind•lass \\'windləs\\ *n* : winch esp. for hoisting anchor

wind•mill \\'wind,mil\\ *n* : machine worked by the wind turning vanes

win•dow \\'windō\\ *n* **1** : opening in the wall of a building to let in light and air **2** : pane in a window **3** : span of time for something **4** : area of a computer display — **win•dow•less** *adj*

win•dow–shop *vb* : look at the displays in store windows — **win•dow–shop•per** *n*

wind•pipe \\'wind,pīp\\ *n* : passage for the breath from the larynx to the lungs

wind•shield \\'-,shēld\\ *n* : transparent screen in front of the occupants of a vehicle

wind–up \\'wīnd,əp\\ *n* : end — **wind up** *vb*

wind•ward \\'windwərd\\ *adj* : being in or facing the direction from which the wind is blowing ~ *n* : direction from which the wind is blowing

windy \\'windē\\ *adj* **wind•i•er; -est 1** : having wind **2** : indulging in useless talk

wine \\'wīn\\ *n* **1** : fermented grape juice **2** : usu. fermented juice of a plant product (as fruit) used as a beverage ~ *vb* : treat to or drink wine

wing \\'wiŋ\\ *n* **1** : movable paired appendage for flying **2** : winglike thing **3** *pl* : area at the side of the stage out of sight **4** : faction ~ *vb* **1** : fly **2** : propel through the air — **winged** *adj* — **wing•less** *adj* — **on the wing** : in flight — **under one's wing** : in one's charge or care

wink \\'wiŋk\\ *vb* **1** : close and open the eyes quickly **2** : avoid seeing or noticing something **3** : twinkle **4** : close and open one eye quickly as a signal or hint ⁓ *n* **1** : brief sleep **2** : act of winking **3** : instant — **wink·er** *n*

win·ner \'winər\ *n* : one that wins

win·ning \-iŋ\ *n* **1** : victory **2** : money won at gambling ⁓ *adj* **1** : victorious **2** : charming

win·now \'winō\ *vb* **1** : remove (as chaff) by a current of air **2** : sort or separate something

win·some \'winsəm\ *adj* **1** : causing joy **2** : cheerful or gay — **win·some·ly** *adv* — **win·some·ness** *n*

win·ter \'wintər\ *n* : season between autumn and spring ⁓ *adj* : sown in autumn for harvest the next spring or summer — **win·ter·time** *n*

win·ter·green \'wintər,grēn\ *n* : low heathlike evergreen plant with red berries

win·try \'wintrē\ *adj* **win·tri·er; -est 1** : characteristic of winter **2** : cold in feeling

wipe \'wīp\ *vb* **wiped; wip·ing 1** : clean or dry by rubbing **2** : remove by rubbing **3** : erase completely **4** : destroy **5** : pass over a surface ⁓ *n* : act or instance of wiping — **wip·er** *n*

wire \'wīr\ *n* **1** : thread of metal **2** : work made of wire **3** : telegram or cablegram ⁓ *vb* **1** : provide with wire **2** : bind or mount with wire **3** : telegraph — **wire·less** *adj*

wire·less \-ləs\ *n, chiefly Brit* : radio

wire·tap *vb* : connect into a telephone or telegraph wire to get information — **wiretap** *n* — **wire·tap·per** *n*

wir·ing \'wīriŋ\ *n* : system of wires

wiry \'wīrē\ *adj* **wir·i·er** \'wīrēər\; **-est 1** : resembling wire **2** : slender yet strong and sinewy — **wir·i·ness** *n*

wis·dom \'wizdəm\ *n* **1** : accumulated learning **2** : good sense

wisdom tooth *n* : last tooth on each half of each human jaw

¹wise \'wīz\ *n* : manner

²wise *adj* **wis·er; wis·est 1** : having or showing wisdom, good sense, or good judgment **2** : aware of what is going on — **wise·ly** *adv*

wise·crack *n* : clever, smart, or flippant remark ⁓ *vb* : make a wisecrack

wish \'wish\ *vb* **1** : have a desire **2** : express a wish concerning **3** : request ⁓ *n* **1** : a wishing or desire **2** : expressed will or desire

wish·bone *n* : forked bone in front of the breastbone in most birds

wish·ful \-fəl\ *adj* **1** : expressive of a wish **2** : according with wishes rather than fact

wishy–washy \'wishē,wȯshē, -,wäsh-\ *adj* : weak or insipid

wisp \'wisp\ *n* **1** : small bunch of hay or straw **2** : thin strand, strip, fragment, or streak **3** : something frail, slight, or fleeting — **wispy** *adj*

wis·te·ria \wis'tirēə\ *n* : pealike woody vine with long clusters of flowers

wist·ful \'wistfəl\ *adj* : full of longing — **wist·ful·ly** *adv* — **wist·ful·ness** *n*

wit \'wit\ *n* **1** : reasoning power **2** : mental soundness — usu. pl. **3** : quickness and cleverness in handling words and ideas **4** : talent for clever remarks or one noted for witty remarks — **wit·less** *adj* — **wit·less·ly** *adv* — **wit·less·ness** *n* — **wit·ted** *adj*

witch \'wich\ *n* **1** : person believed to have magic power **2** : ugly old woman ⁓ *vb* : bewitch

witch·craft \'wich,kraft\ *n* : power or practices of a witch

witch·ery \'wichərē\ *n, pl* **-er·ies 1** : witchcraft **2** : charm

witch ha·zel \'wich,hāzəl\ *n* **1** : shrub having small yellow flowers in fall **2** : alcoholic lotion made from witch hazel bark

witch–hunt *n* **1** : searching out and persecution of supposed witches **2** : harassment esp. of political opponents

with \'with, 'with\ *prep* **1** : against, to, or toward **2** : in support of **3** : because of **4** : in the company of **5** : having **6** : despite **7** : containing **8** : by means of

with·draw \with'drȯ, with-\ *vb* **-drew** \-'drü\; **-drawn** \-'drȯn\; **-draw·ing** \-'drȯiŋ\ **1** : take back or away **2** : call back or retract **3** : go away **4** : terminate one's participation in or use of — **with·draw·al** \-'drȯəl\ *n*

with·drawn \with'drȯn\ *adj* : socially detached and unresponsive

with·er \'withər\ *vb* **1** : shrivel **2** : lose or cause to lose energy, force, or freshness

with·ers \'withərz\ *n pl* : ridge between the shoulder bones of a horse

with·hold \with'hōld, with-\ *vb* **-held** \-'held\; **-hold·ing 1** : hold back **2** : refrain from giving

with·in \with'in, with-\ *adv* **1** : in or into the interior **2** : inside oneself ⁓

prep **1** : in or to the inner part of **2** : in the limits or compass of

with·out \with'aut, with-\ *prep* **1** : outside **2** : lacking **3** : unaccompanied or unmarked by — **without** *adv*

with·stand \with'stand, with-\ *vb* **-stood** \-'stud\; **-stand·ing** : oppose successfully

wit·ness \'witnəs\ *n* **1** : testimony **2** : one who testifies **3** : one present at a transaction to testify that it has taken place **4** : one who has personal knowledge or experience **5** : something serving as proof ~ *vb* **1** : bear witness **2** : act as legal witness of **3** : furnish proof of **4** : be a witness of **5** : be the scene of

wit·ti·cism \'witə,sizəm\ *n* : witty saying or phrase

wit·ting \'witiŋ\ *adj* : intentional — **wit·ting·ly** *adv*

wit·ty \'witē\ *adj* **-ti·er; -est** : marked by or full of wit — **wit·ti·ly** \'wit³lē\ *adv* — **wit·ti·ness** *n*

wives *pl of* WIFE

wiz·ard \'wizərd\ *n* **1** : magician **2** : very clever person — **wiz·ard·ry** \-ərdrē\ *n*

wiz·ened \'wiz³nd\ *adj* : dried up

wob·ble \'wäbəl\ *vb* **-bled; -bling** **1** : move or cause to move with an irregular rocking motion **2** : tremble **3** : waver — **wobble** *n* — **wob·bly** \'wäbəlē\ *adj*

woe \'wō\ *n* **1** : deep suffering **2** : misfortune

woe·be·gone \'wōbi,gòn\ *adj* : exhibiting woe, sorrow, or misery

woe·ful \'wōfəl\ *adj* **1** : full of woe **2** : bringing woe — **woe·ful·ly** *adv*

woke *past of* WAKE

woken *past part of* WAKE

wolf \'wulf\ *n, pl* **wolves** \'wulvz\ : large doglike predatory mammal ~ *vb* : eat greedily — **wolf·ish** *adj*

wol·fram \'wulfrəm\ *n* : tungsten

wol·ver·ine \,wulvə'rēn\ *n, pl* **-ines** : flesh-eating mammal related to the weasels

wom·an \'wumən\ *n, pl* **wom·en** \'wimən\ **1** : adult female person **2** : womankind **3** : feminine nature — **wom·an·hood** \-,hud\ *n* — **wom·an·ish** *adj*

wom·an·kind \-,kīnd\ *n* : females of the human race

wom·an·ly \-lē\ *adj* : having qualities

characteristic of a woman — **wom·an·li·ness** \-lēnəs\ *n*

womb \'wüm\ *n* : uterus

won *past of* WIN

won·der \'wəndər\ *n* **1** : cause of astonishment or surprise **2** : feeling (as of astonishment) aroused by something extraordinary ~ *vb* **1** : feel surprise **2** : feel curiosity or doubt

won·der·ful \'wəndərfəl\ *adj* **1** : exciting wonder **2** : unusually good — **won·der·ful·ly** *adv* — **won·der·ful·ness** *n*

won·der·land \-,land, -lənd\ *n* **1** : fairylike imaginary realm **2** : place that excites admiration or wonder

won·der·ment \-mənt\ *n* : wonder

won·drous \'wəndrəs\ *adj* : wonderful — **won·drous·ly** *adv* — **won·drous·ness** *n*

wont \'wònt, 'wōnt\ *adj* : accustomed ~ *n* : habit — **wont·ed** *adj*

woo \'wü\ *vb* : try to gain the love or favor of — **woo·er** *n*

wood \'wud\ *n* **1** : dense growth of trees usu. smaller than a forest — often pl. **2** : hard fibrous substance of trees and shrubs beneath the bark **3** : wood prepared for some use (as burning) ~ *adj* **1** : wooden **2** : suitable for working with wood **3** *or* **woods** \'wudz\ : living or growing in woods — **wood·chop·per** *n* — **wood·pile** *n* — **wood·shed** *n*

wood·bine \'wud,bīn\ *n* : climbing vine

wood·chuck \-,chək\ *n* : thick-bodied grizzled animal of No. America

wood·craft *n* **1** : skill and practice in matters relating to the woods **2** : skill in making articles from wood

wood·cut \-,kət\ *n* **1** : relief printing surface engraved on wood **2** : print from a woodcut

wood·ed \'wudəd\ *adj* : covered with woods

wood·en \'wud³n\ *adj* **1** : made of wood **2** : lacking resilience **3** : lacking ease, liveliness or interest — **wood·en·ly** *adv* — **wood·en·ness** *n*

wood·land \-lənd, -,land\ *n* : land covered with trees

wood·peck·er \'wud,pekər\ *n* : brightly marked bird with a hard bill for drilling into trees

woods·man \'wudzmən\ *n* : person who works in the woods

wood·wind \'wud,wind\ *n* : one of a

group of wind instruments (as a flute or oboe)

wood•work *n* : work (as interior house fittings) made of wood

woody \'wùdē\ *adj* **wood•i•er; -est** **1** : abounding with woods **2** : of, containing, or like wood fibers — **wood•i•ness** *n*

woof \'wùf\ *n* : weft

wool \'wùl\ *n* **1** : soft hair of some mammals and esp. the sheep **2** : something (as a textile) made of wool — **wooled** \'wùld\ *adj*

wool•en, wool•len \'wùlən\ *adj* **1** : made of wool **2** : relating to the manufacture of woolen products ~ *n* **1** : woolen fabric **2** : woolen garments — usu. pl.

wool•gath•er•ing *n* : idle daydreaming

wool•ly \'wùlē\ *adj* **-li•er; -est** **1** : of, relating to, or bearing wool **2** : consisting of or resembling wool **3** : confused or turbulent

woo•zy \'wüzē\ *adj* **-zi•er; -est** **1** : confused **2** : somewhat dizzy, nauseated, or weak — **woo•zi•ness** *n*

word \'wərd\ *n* **1** : brief remark **2** : speech sound or series of speech sounds that communicates a meaning **3** : written representation of a word **4** : order **5** : news **6** : promise **7** *pl* : dispute ~ *vb* : express in words — **word•less** *adj*

word•ing \'wərdiŋ\ *n* : verbal expression

word processing *n* : production of structured and printed documents through a computer program (**word processor**) — **word process** *vb*

wordy \'wərdē\ *adj* **word•i•er; -est** : using many words — **word•i•ness** *n*

wore *past of* WEAR

work \'wərk\ *n* **1** : labor **2** : employment **3** : task **4** : something (as an artistic production) produced by mental effort or physical labor **5** *pl* : place where industrial labor is done **6** *pl* : moving parts of a mechanism **7** : workmanship ~ *adj* **1** : suitable for wear while working **2** : used for work ~ *vb* **worked** \'wərkt\ *or* **wrought** \'ròt\; **work•ing** **1** : bring to pass **2** : create by expending labor upon **3** : bring or get into a form or condition **4** : set or keep in operation **5** : solve **6** : cause to labor **7** : arrange **8** : excite **9** : labor **10** : perform work regularly for wages **11** : function according to plan or design **12** : produce a desired

effect — **work•bench** *n* — **work•man** \-mən\ *n* — **work•room** *n* — **in the works** : in preparation

work•able \'wərkəbəl\ *adj* **1** : capable of being worked **2** : feasible — **work•able•ness** *n*

work•a•day \'wərkə,dā\ *adj* **1** : relating to or suited for working days **2** : ordinary

work•a•hol•ic \,wərkə'hòlik, -'häl-\ *n* : compulsive worker

work•day \'wərk,dā\ *n* **1** : day on which work is done **2** : period of time during which one is working

work•er \'wərkər\ *n* : person who works esp. for wages

work•horse *n* **1** : horse used for hard work **2** : person who does most of the work of a group task

work•house *n* : place of confinement for persons who have committed minor offenses

work•ing \'wərkiŋ\ *adj* **1** : adequate to allow work to be done **2** : adopted or assumed to help further work or activity ~ *n* : operation — usu. used in pl.

work•ing•man \'wərkiŋ,man\ *n* : worker

work•man•like \-,līk\ *adj* : worthy of a good workman

work•man•ship \-,ship\ *n* **1** : art or skill of a workman **2** : quality of a piece of work

work•out \'wərk,aùt\ *n* : exercise to improve one's fitness

work out *vb* **1** : bring about by effort **2** : solve **3** : develop **4** : to be successful **5** : perform exercises

work•shop *n* **1** : small establishment for manufacturing or handicrafts **2** : seminar emphasizing exchange of ideas and practical methods

world \'wərld\ *n* **1** : universe **2** : earth with its inhabitants and all things upon it **3** : people in general **4** : great number or quantity **5** : class of persons or their sphere of interest

world•ly \'wərldlē\ *adj* **1** : devoted to this world and its pursuits rather than to religion **2** : sophisticated — **world•li•ness** *n*

world•ly-wise *adj* : possessing understanding of human affairs

world•wide *adj* : extended throughout the entire world — **worldwide** *adv*

World Wide Web *n* : part of the Internet accessible through a browser

worm \'wərm\ *n* **1** : earthworm or a

similar animal **2** *pl* : disorder caused by parasitic worms ~ *vb* **1** : move or cause to move in a slow and indirect way **2** : to free from worms — **wormy** *adj*

worm·wood \'wərm,wüd\ *n* **1** : aromatic woody herb (as sagebrush) **2** : something bitter or grievous

worn *past part of* WEAR

worn–out \'wōrn'aút\ *adj* : exhausted or used up by or as if by wear

wor·ri·some \'wərēsəm\ *adj* **1** : causing worry **2** : inclined to worry

wor·ry \'wərē\ *vb* **-ried; -ry·ing 1** : shake and mangle with the teeth **2** : disturb **3** : feel or express anxiety ~ *n, pl* **-ries 1** : anxiety **2** : cause of anxiety — **wor·ri·er** *n*

worse \'wərs\ *adj, comparative of* BAD *or of* ILL **1** : bad or evil in a greater degree **2** : more unwell ~ *n* **1** : one that is worse **2** : greater degree of badness ~ *adv comparative of* BAD *or of* ILL : in a worse manner

wors·en \'wərsᵊn\ *vb* : make or become worse

wor·ship \'wərshəp\ *n* **1** : reverence toward a divine being or supernatural power **2** : expression of reverence **3** : extravagant respect or devotion ~ *vb* **-shiped** *or* **-shipped; -ship·ing** *or* **-ship·ping 1** : honor or reverence **2** : perform or take part in worship — **wor·ship·er, wor·ship·per** *n*

worst \'wərst\ *adj, superlative of* BAD *or of* ILL **1** : most bad, evil, ill, or corrupt **2** : most unfavorable, unpleasant, or painful ~ *n* : one that is worst ~ *adv superlative of* ILL *or of* BAD *or* BADLY : to the extreme degree of badness ~ *vb* : defeat

wor·sted \'wústəd, 'wərstəd\ *n* : smooth compact wool yarn or fabric made from such yarn

worth \'wərth\ *prep* **1** : equal in value to **2** : deserving of ~ *n* **1** : monetary value **2** : value of something measured by its qualities **3** : moral or personal merit

worth·less \-ləs\ *adj* **1** : lacking worth **2** : useless — **worth·less·ness** *n*

worth·while \-'hwīl\ *adj* : being worth the time or effort spent

wor·thy \'wərthē\ *adj* **-thi·er; -est 1** : having worth or value **2** : having sufficient worth ~ *n, pl* **-thies** : worthy person — **wor·thi·ly** *adv* — **wor·thi·ness** *n*

would \'wüd\ *past of* WILL — used to express **(1)** preference **(2)** intent **(3)** habitual action **(4)** contingency **(5)** probability or **(6)** a request

would–be \'wüd'bē\ *adj* : desiring or pretending to be

¹**wound** \'wünd\ *n* **1** : injury in which the skin is broken **2** : mental hurt ~ *vb* : inflict a wound to or in

²**wound** \'waúnd\ *past of* WIND

wove *past of* WEAVE

woven *past part of* WEAVE

wrack \'rak\ *n* : ruin

wraith \'rāth\ *n, pl* **wraiths** \'rāths, 'rāthz\ **1** : ghost **2** : insubstantial appearance

wran·gle \'raŋgəl\ *vb or n* : quarrel — **wran·gler** *n*

wrap \'rap\ *vb* **-pp- 1** : cover esp. by winding or folding **2** : envelop and secure for transportation or storage **3** : enclose, surround, or conceal wholly **4** : coil, fold, draw, or twine about something ~ *n* **1** : wrapper or wrapping **2** : outer garment (as a shawl)

wrap·per \'rapər\ *n* **1** : that in which something is wrapped **2** : one that wraps

wrap·ping *n* : something used to wrap an object

wrath \'rath\ *n* : violent anger — **wrath·ful** \-fəl\ *adj*

wreak \'rēk\ *vb* **1** : inflict **2** : bring about

wreath \'rēth\ *n, pl* **wreaths** \'rēthz, 'rēths\ : something (as boughs) intertwined into a circular shape

wreathe \'rēth\ *vb* **wreathed; wreath·ing 1** : shape into or take on the shape of a wreath **2** : decorate or cover with a wreath

wreck \'rek\ *n* **1** : broken remains (as of a ship or vehicle) after heavy damage **2** : something disabled or in a state of ruin **3** : an individual who has become weak or infirm **4** : action of breaking up or destroying something ~ *vb* : ruin or damage by breaking up

wreck·age \'rekij\ *n* **1** : act of wrecking **2** : remains of a wreck

wreck·er \-ər\ *n* **1** : automotive vehicle for removing disabled cars **2** : one that wrecks or tears down and removes buildings

wren \'ren\ *n* : small mostly brown singing bird

wrench \'rench\ *vb* **1** : pull with violent twisting or force **2** : injure or disable by a violent twisting or straining ~ *n* **1** : forcible twisting **2** : tool for exerting a twisting force

wrest \'rest\ *vb* **1** : pull or move by a forcible twisting movement **2** : gain with difficulty ~ *n* : forcible twist

wres•tle \'resəl, 'ras-\ *vb* **-tled; -tling 1** : scuffle with and attempt to throw and pin an opponent **2** : compete against in wrestling **3** : struggle (as with a problem) ~ *n* : action or an instance of wrestling — **wres•tler** \'reslər, 'ras-\ *n*

wres•tling \'resliŋ\ *n* : sport in which 2 opponents try to throw and pin each other

wretch \'rech\ *n* **1** : miserable unhappy person **2** : vile person

wretch•ed \'rechəd\ *adj* **1** : deeply afflicted, dejected, or distressed **2** : grievous **3** : inferior — **wretch•ed•ly** *adv* — **wretch•ed•ness** *n*

wrig•gle \'rigəl\ *vb* **-gled; -gling 1** : twist and turn restlessly **2** : move along by twisting and turning — **wrig•gle** *n* — **wrig•gler** \'rigələr\ *n*

wring \'riŋ\ *vb* **wrung** \'rəŋ\; **wring-ing 1** : squeeze or twist out moisture **2** : get by or as if by twisting or pressing **3** : twist together in anguish **4** : pain — **wring•er** *n*

wrin•kle \'riŋkəl\ *n* : crease or small fold on a surface (as in the skin or in cloth) ~ *vb* **-kled; -kling** : develop or cause to develop wrinkles — **wrin-kly** \-kəlē\ *adj*

wrist \'rist\ *n* : joint or region between the hand and the arm

writ \'rit\ *n* **1** : something written **2** : legal order in writing

write \'rīt\ *vb* **wrote** \'rōt\; **writ•ten** \'rit°n\; **writ•ing** \'rītiŋ\ **1** : form letters or words on a surface **2** : form the letters or the words of (as on paper) **3** : make up and set down for others to read **4** : write a letter to — **write off** *vb* : cancel

writ•er \'rītər\ *n* : one that writes esp. as a business or occupation

writhe \'rīth\ *vb* **writhed; writh•ing** : twist and turn this way and that

writ•ing \'rītiŋ\ *n* **1** : act of one that writes **2** : handwriting **3** : something written or printed

wrong \'rȯŋ\ *n* **1** : unfair or unjust act **2** : something that is contrary to justice **3** : state of being or doing wrong ~ *adj* **wrong•er** \'rȯŋər\; **wrong-est** \'rȯŋəst\ **1** : sinful **2** : not right according to a standard **3** : unsuitable **4** : incorrect ~ *adv* **1** : in a wrong direction or manner **2** : incorrectly ~ *vb* **wronged; wrong•ing 1** : do wrong to **2** : treat unjustly — **wrong•ly** *adv*

wrong•do•er \-'düər\ *n* : one who does wrong — **wrong•do•ing** \-'düiŋ\ *n*

wrong•ful \-fəl\ *adj* **1** : wrong **2** : illegal — **wrong•ful•ly** *adv* — **wrong•ful-ness** *n*

wrong•head•ed \'rȯŋ'hedəd\ *adj* : stubborn in clinging to wrong opinion or principles — **wrong•head•ed-ly** *adv* — **wrong•head•ed•ness** *n*

wrote *past of* WRITE

wrought \'rȯt\ *adj* **1** : formed **2** : hammered into shape **3** : deeply stirred

wrung *past of* WRING

wry \'rī\ *adj* **wri•er** \'rīər\; **wri•est** \'rīəst\ **1** : turned abnormally to one side **2** : twisted **3** : cleverly and often ironically humorous — **wry•ly** *adv* — **wry•ness** *n*

X

x \'eks\ *n, pl* **x's** *or* **xs** \'eksəz\ **1** : 24th letter of the alphabet **2** : unknown quantity ~ *vb* **x–ed; x–ing** *or* **x'ing** : cancel with a series of *x*'s — usu. with *out*

xe•non \'zē,nän,'zen,än\ *n* : heavy gaseous chemical element

xe•no•pho•bia \,zenə'fōbēə, ,zēn-\ *n* : fear and hatred of foreign people and things — **xe•no•phobe** \'zenə-,fōb, 'zēn-\ *n*

Xmas \'krisməs\ *n* : Christmas

x–ra•di•a•tion *n* **1** : exposure to X rays **2** : radiation consisting of X rays

x–ray \'eks,rā\ *vb* : examine, treat, or photograph with X rays

X ray *n* **1** : radiation of short wavelength that is able to penetrate solids **2** : photograph taken with X rays — **X–ray** *adj*

xy•lo•phone \'zīlə‚fōn\ *n* : musical instrument with wooden bars that are struck — **xy•lo•phon•ist** \-‚fōnist\ *n*

Y

y \'wī\ *n, pl* **y's** *or* **ys** \'wīz\ : 25th letter of the alphabet

¹-y \ē\ *adj suffix* **1** : composed or full of **2** : like **3** : performing or apt to perform an action

²-y \ē\ *n suffix, pl* **-ies** **1** : state, condition, or quality **2** : activity, place of business, or goods dealt with **3** : whole group

yacht \'yät\ *n* : luxurious pleasure boat ~ *vb* : race or cruise in a yacht

ya•hoo \'yāhü, 'yä-\ *n, pl* **-hoos** : uncouth or stupid person

yak \'yak\ *n* : big hairy Asian ox

yam \'yam\ *n* **1** : edible root of a tropical vine **2** : deep orange sweet potato

yam•mer \'yamər\ *vb* **1** : whimper **2** : chatter — **yammer** *n*

yank \'yaŋk\ *n* : strong sudden pull — **yank** *vb*

Yank \'yaŋk\ *n* : Yankee

Yan•kee \'yaŋkē\ *n* : native or inhabitant of New England, the northern U.S., or the U.S.

yap \'yap\ *vb* **-pp-** **1** : yelp **2** : chatter — **yap** *n*

¹yard \'yärd\ *n* **1** : 3 feet **2** : long spar for supporting and spreading a sail — **yard•age** \-ij\ *n*

²yard *n* **1** : enclosed roofless area **2** : grounds of a building **3** : work area

yard•arm \'yärd‚ärm\ *n* : end of the yard of a square-rigged ship

yard•stick *n* **1** : measuring stick 3 feet long **2** : standard for judging

yar•mul•ke \'yäməkə, 'yär-, -məl-\ *n* : a small brimless cap worn by Jewish males in a synagogue

yarn \'yärn\ *n* **1** : spun fiber for weaving or knitting **2** : tale

yaw \'yȯ\ *vb* : deviate erratically from a course — **yaw** *n*

yawl \'yȯl\ *n* : sailboat with 2 masts

yawn \'yȯn\ *vb* : open the mouth wide ~ *n* : deep breath through a wide-open mouth — **yawn•er** *n*

ye \'yē\ *pron* : you

yea \'yā\ *adv* **1** : yes **2** : truly ~ *n* : affirmative vote

year \'yir\ *n* **1** : period of about 365 days **2** *pl* : age

year•book *n* : annual report of the year's events

year•ling \'yirliŋ, 'yərlən\ *n* : one that is or is rated as a year old

year•ly \'yirlē\ *adj* : annual — **yearly** *adv*

yearn \'yərn\ *vb* **1** : feel desire esp. for what one cannot have **2** : feel tenderness or compassion

yearn•ing \-iŋ\ *n* : tender or urgent desire

yeast \'yēst\ *n* : froth or sediment in sugary liquids containing a tiny fungus and used in making alcoholic liquors and as a leaven in baking — **yeasty** *adj*

yell \'yel\ *vb* : utter a loud cry — **yell** *n*

yel•low \'yelō\ *adj* **1** : of the color yellow **2** : sensational **3** : cowardly ~ *vb* : make or turn yellow ~ *n* **1** : color of lemons **2** : yolk of an egg — **yel•low•ish** \'yeləwish\ *adj*

yellow fever *n* : virus disease marked by prostration, jaundice, fever, and often hemorrhage

yellow jacket *n* : wasp with yellow stripes

yelp \'yelp\ *vb* : utter a sharp quick shrill cry — **yelp** *n*

yen \'yen\ *n* : strong desire

yeo•man \'yōmən\ *n* **1** : attendant or officer in a royal or noble household **2** : small farmer **3** : naval petty officer with clerical duties — **yeo•man•ry** \-rē\ *n*

-yer — see **-ER**

yes \'yes\ *adv* — used to express consent or agreement ~ *n* : affirmative answer

ye•shi•va, ye•shi•vah \yə'shēvə\ *n, pl* **yeshivas** *or* **ye•shi•voth** \-‚shē'vōt, -'vōth\ : Jewish school

yes–man \'yes‚man\ *n* : person who agrees with every opinion or suggestion of a boss

yes•ter•day \'yestərdē\ *adv* **1** : on the

day preceding today **2** : only a short time ago ~ *n* **1** : day last past **2** : time not long past

yet \'yet\ *adv* **1** : in addition **2** : up to now **3** : so soon as now **4** : nevertheless ~ *conj* : but

yew \'yü\ *n* : evergreen tree or shrubs with dark stiff poisonous needles

yield \'yēld\ *vb* **1** : surrender **2** : grant **3** : bear as a crop **4** : produce **5** : cease opposition or resistance ~ *n* : quantity produced or returned

yo·del \'yōd°l\ *vb* **-deled** *or* **-delled; -del·ing** *or* **-del·ling** : sing by abruptly alternating between chest voice and falsetto — **yodel** *n* — **yo·del·er** \'yōd°lər\ *n*

yo·ga \'yōgə\ *n* : system of exercises for attaining bodily or mental control and well-being

yo·gi \'yōgē\ *n* : person who practices yoga

yo·gurt \'yōgərt\ *n* : fermented slightly acid soft food made from milk

yoke \'yōk\ *n* **1** : neck frame for coupling draft animals or for carrying loads **2** : clamp **3** : slavery **4** : tie or link **5** : piece of a garment esp. at the shoulder ~ *vb* **yoked; yok·ing 1** : couple with a yoke **2** : join

yo·kel \'yōkəl\ *n* : naive and gullible country person

yolk \'yōk\ *n* : yellow part of an egg — **yolked** \'yōkt\ *adj*

Yom Kip·pur \ˌyōmki'pùr, ˌyäm-, -'kipər\ *n* : Jewish holiday observed in September or October with fasting and prayer as a day of atonement

yon \'yän\ *adj or adv* : yonder

yon·der \'yändər\ *adv* : at or to that place ~ *adj* : distant

yore \'yōr\ *n* : time long past

you \'yü\ *pron* **1** : person or persons addressed **2** : person in general

young \'yəŋ\ *adj* **youn·ger** \'yəŋgər\; **youn·gest** \'yəŋgəst\ **1** : being in the first or an early stage of life, growth, or development **2** : recently come into being **3** : youthful ~ *n, pl* **young** : persons or animals that are young — **young·ish** \-ish\ *adj*

young·ster \-stər\ *n* **1** : young person **2** : child

your \yər, 'yùr, 'yōr\ *adj* : relating to you or yourself

yours \'yùrz, 'yōrz\ *pron* : the ones belonging to you

your·self \yər'self\ *pron, pl* **your·selves** \-'selvz\ : you — used reflexively or for emphasis

youth \'yüth\ *n, pl* **youths** \'yüthz, 'yüths\ **1** : period between childhood and maturity **2** : young man **3** : young persons **4** : state or quality of being young, fresh, or vigorous

youth·ful \'yüthfəl\ *adj* **1** : relating to or appropriate to youth **2** : young **3** : vigorous and fresh — **youth·ful·ly** *adv* — **youth·ful·ness** *n*

yowl \'yaùl\ *vb* : utter a loud long mournful cry — **yowl** *n*

yo–yo \'yō,yō\ *n, pl* **-yos** : toy that falls from or rises to the hand as it unwinds and rewinds on a string

yuc·ca \'yəkə\ *n* : any of several plants related to the lilies that grow in dry regions

yule \'yül\ *n* : Christmas — **yule·tide** \-ˌtīd\ *n*

yum·my \'yəmē\ *adj* **-mi·er; -est** : highly attractive or pleasing

---

Z

z \'zē\ *n, pl* **z's** *or* **zs** : 26th letter of the alphabet

za·ny \'zānē\ *n, pl* **-nies 1** : clown **2** : silly person ~ *adj* **-ni·er; -est** : crazy or foolish — **za·ni·ly** *adv* — **za·ni·ness** *n*

zeal \'zēl\ *n* : enthusiasm

zeal·ot \'zelət\ *n* : fanatical partisan

zeal·ous \'zeləs\ *adj* : filled with zeal — **zeal·ous·ly** *adv* — **zeal·ous·ness** *n*

ze·bra \'zēbrə\ *n* : horselike African mammal marked with light and dark stripes

zeit·geist \'tsīt,gīst, 'zīt-\ *n* : general spirit of an era

ze·nith \'zēnəth\ *n* : highest point

zeph•yr \'zefər\ *n* : gentle breeze

zep•pe•lin \'zepələn\ *n* : rigid airship like a blimp

ze•ro \'zērō\ *n, pl* **-ros 1** : number represented by the symbol 0 or the symbol itself **2** : starting point **3** : lowest point ~ *adj* : having no size or quantity

zest \'zest\ *n* **1** : quality of enhancing enjoyment **2** : keen enjoyment — **zest•ful** \-fəl\ *adj* — **zest•ful•ly** *adv* — **zest•ful•ness** *n*

zig•zag \'zig,zag\ *n* : one of a series of short sharp turns or angles ~ *adj* : having zigzags ~ *adv* : in or by a zigzag path ~ *vb* **-gg-** : proceed along a zigzag path

zil•lion \'zilyən\ *n* : large indeterminate number

zinc \'ziŋk\ *n* : bluish white crystaline metallic chemical element

zing \'ziŋ\ *n* **1** : shrill humming noise **2** : energy — **zing** *vb*

zin•nia \'zinēə, 'zēnyə\ *n* : American herb widely grown for its showy flowers

¹zip \'zip\ *vb* **-pp-** : move or act with speed ~ *n* : energy

²zip *vb* **-pp-** : close or open with a zipper

zip code *n* : number that identifies a U.S. postal delivery area

zip•per \'zipər\ *n* : fastener consisting of 2 rows of interlocking teeth

zip•py \'zipē\ *adj* **-pi•er; -est** : brisk

zir•con \'zər,kän\ *n* : zirconium-containing mineral sometimes used in jewelry

zir•co•ni•um \,zər'kōnēəm\ *n* : corrosion-resistant gray metallic element

zith•er \'zithər, 'zith-\ *n* : stringed musical instrument played by plucking

zi•ti \'zētē\ *n, pl* **ziti** : short tubular pasta

zo•di•ac \'zōdē,ak\ *n* : imaginary belt in the heavens encompassing the paths of the planets and divided into 12 signs used in astrology — **zo•di•a•cal** \zō'dīəkəl\ *adj*

zom•bie \'zämbē\ *n* : person thought to have died and been brought back to life without free will

zon•al \'zōn³l\ *adj* : of, relating to, or having the form of a zone — **zon•al•ly** *adv*

zone \'zōn\ *n* **1** : division of the earth's surface based on latitude and climate **2** : distinctive area ~ *vb* **zoned; zoning 1** : mark off into zones **2** : reserve for special purposes — **zo•na•tion** \zō'nāshən\ *n*

zoo \'zü\ *n, pl* **zoos** : collection of living animals usu. for public display — **zoo•keep•er** *n*

zo•ol•o•gy \zō'äləjē\ *n* : science of animals — **zo•o•log•i•cal** \,zōə'läjikəl\ *adj* — **zo•ol•o•gist** \zō'äləjist\ *n*

zoom \'züm\ *vb* **1** : move with a loud hum or buzz **2** : move or increase with great speed — **zoom** *n*

zuc•chi•ni \zu'kēnē\ *n, pl* **-ni** *or* **-nis** : summer squash with smooth cylindrical dark green fruits

zwie•back \'swēbak, 'swī-, 'zwē-, 'zwī-\ *n* : biscuit of baked, sliced, and toasted bread

zy•gote \'zī,gōt\ *n* : cell formed by the union of 2 sexual cells — **zy•got•ic** \zī'gätik\ *adj*

ABBREVIATIONS

Most of these abbreviations have been given in one form. Variation in use of periods, in type, and in capitalization is frequent and widespread (as *mph, MPH, m.p.h., Mph*).

abbr abbreviation
AC alternating current
acad academic, academy
AD in the year of our Lord
adj adjective
adv adverb, advertisement
advt advertisement
AF air force, audio frequency
agric agricultural, agriculture
AK Alaska
aka also known as
AL, Ala Alabama
alg algebra
Alta Alberta
a.m., AM before noon
Am, Amer America, American
amp ampere
amt amount
anc ancient
anon anonymous
ans answer
ant antonym
APO army post office
approx approximate, approximately
Apr April
apt apartment, aptitude
AR Arkansas
arith arithmetic
Ariz Arizona
Ark Arkansas
art article, artificial
assn association
assoc associate, associated, association
asst assistant
ATM automated teller machine
att attached, attention, attorney
attn attention
atty attorney
Aug August
auth authentic, author, authorized
aux, auxil auxiliary
av avoirdupois
AV audiovisual
ave avenue
avg average

AZ Arizona
BA bachelor of arts
bal balance
bar barometer, barrel
bbl barrel, barrels
BC before Christ, British Columbia
BCE before Christian Era, before Common Era
bet between
biog biographer, biographical, biography
biol biologic, biological, biologist, biology
bldg building
blvd boulevard
BO backorder, best offer, body odor, box office, branch office
Brit Britain, British
bro brother, brothers
bros brothers
BS bachelor of science
Btu British thermal unit
bu bureau, bushel
c carat, cent, centimeter, century, chapter, circa, cup
C Celsius, centigrade
ca circa
CA, Cal, Calif California
cal calendar, caliber, calorie
Can, Canad Canada, Canadian
cap capacity, capital, capitalize, capitalized
Capt captain
CB citizens band
CDT central daylight time
cen central
cert certificate, certification, certified, certify
cf compare
chap chapter
chem chemistry
cir circle, circuit, circular, circumference
civ civil, civilian
cm centimeter
co company, county

CO Colorado
c/o care of
COD cash on delivery, collect on delivery
col colonial, colony, color, colored, column, counsel
Col colonel, Colorado
Colo Colorado
comp comparative, compensation, compiled, compiler, composition, compound, comprehensive, comptroller
cong congress, congressional
conj conjunction
Conn Connecticut
cont continued
contr contract, contraction
corp corporal, corporation
corr corrected, correction
cp compare, coupon
CPR cardiopulmonary resuscitation
cr credit, creditor
CSA Confederate States of America
CST central standard time
ct carat, cent, count, court
CT central time, certified teacher, Connecticut
cu cubic
cur currency, current
CZ Canal Zone
d penny
DA district attorney
dag dekagram
dal dekaliter
dam dekameter
dbl double
DC direct current, District of Columbia
DDS doctor of dental science, doctor of dental surgery
DE Delaware
dec deceased, decrease
Dec December
deg degree
Del Delaware
Dem Democrat, Democratic
dept department
det detached, detachment, detail, determine
dg decigram
dia, diam diameter
diag diagonal, diagram
dict dictionary
dif, diff difference
dim dimension, diminished
dir director
disc discount
dist distance, district

div divided, dividend, division, divorced
dl deciliter
dm decimeter
DMD doctor of dental medicine
DOB date of birth
doz dozen
DP data processing
dr dram, drive, drum
Dr doctor
DST daylight saving time
DUI driving under the influence
DWI driving while intoxicated
dz dozen
e east, eastern, excellent
ea each
ecol ecological, ecology
econ economics, economist, economy
EDT eastern daylight time
e.g. for example
EKG electrocardiogram, electrocardiograph
elec electric, electrical, electricity
elem elementary
eng engine, engineer, engineering
Eng England, English
esp especially
EST eastern standard time
ET eastern time
et al and others
etc et cetera
ex example, express, extra
exec executive
f false, female, feminine
F, Fah, Fahr Fahrenheit
Feb February
fed federal, federation
fem female, feminine
FL, Fla Florida
fl oz fluid ounce
FPO fleet post office
fr father, friar, from
Fri Friday
ft feet, foot, fort
fut future
FYI for your information
g gram
Ga, GA Georgia
gal gallery, gallon
gen general
geog geographic, geographical, geography
geol geologic, geological, geology
geom geometric, geometrical, geometry
gm gram
GMT Greenwich mean time

GOP	Grand Old Party (Republican)	**long**	longitude
gov	government, governor	**m**	male, masculine, meter, mile
govt	government	**M**	medium
GP	general practice, general practitioner	**MA**	Massachusetts
		Man	Manitoba
gr	grade, grain, gram	**Mar**	March
gram	grammar, grammatical	**masc**	masculine
gt	great	**Mass**	Massachusetts
GU	Guam	**math**	mathematical, mathematician
hd	head	**max**	maximum
hf	half	**Md**	Maryland
hgt	height	**MD**	doctor of medicine, Maryland
hgwy	highway	**MDT**	mountain daylight time
HI	Hawaii	**Me, ME**	Maine
hist	historian, historical, history	**med**	medium
hon	honor, honorable, honorary	**mg**	milligram
hr	here, hour	**mgr**	manager
HS	high school	**MI, Mich**	Michigan
ht	height	**mid**	middle
HT	Hawaii time	**min**	minimum, minor, minute
hwy	highway	**Minn**	Minnesota
i	intransitive, island, isle	**misc**	miscellaneous
Ia, IA	Iowa	**Miss**	Mississippi
ICU	intensive care unit	**ml**	milliliter
ID	Idaho, identification	**mm**	millimeter
i.e.	that is	**MN**	Minnesota
IL, Ill	Illinois	**mo**	month
imp	imperative, imperfect	**Mo, MO**	Missouri
in	inch	**Mon**	Monday
IN	Indiana	**Mont**	Montana
inc	incomplete, incorporated	**mpg**	miles per gallon
ind	independent	**mph**	miles per hour
Ind	Indian, Indiana	**MRI**	magnetic resonance imaging
inf	infinitive	**MS**	Mississippi
int	interest	**MST**	mountain standard time
interj	interjection	**mt**	mount, mountain
intl, intnl	international	**MT**	Montana, mountain time
ital	italic, italicized	**n**	neuter, north, northern, noun
Jan	January	**NA**	North America, not applicable
JD	juvenile delinquent	**nat**	national, native, natural
jour	journal, journeyman	**natl**	national
JP	justice of the peace	**naut**	nautical
jr, jun	junior	**NB**	New Brunswick
JV	junior varsity	**NC**	North Carolina
Kan, Kans	Kansas	**ND, N Dak**	North Dakota
kg	kilogram	**NE, Neb, Nebr**	Nebraska
km	kilometer	**neg**	negative
KS	Kansas	**neut**	neuter
kW	kilowatt	**Nev**	Nevada
Ky, KY	Kentucky	**Nfld**	Newfoundland
l	late, left, liter, long	**NH**	New Hampshire
L	large	**NJ**	New Jersey
La	Louisiana	**NM, N Mex**	New Mexico
LA	Los Angeles, Louisiana	**no**	north, number
lat	latitude	**Nov**	November
lb	pound	**NR**	not rated
lg	large, long	**NS**	Nova Scotia
lib	liberal, librarian, library	**NV**	Nevada

NWT Northwest Territories
NY New York
NYC New York City
O Ohio
obj object, objective
occas occasionally
Oct October
off office, officer, official
OH Ohio
OJ orange juice
OK, Okla Oklahoma
ON, Ont Ontario
opp opposite
OR, Ore, Oreg Oregon
orig original, originally
oz ounce, ounces
p page
Pa Pennsylvania
PA Pennsylvania, public address
PAC political action committee
par paragraph, parallel
part participle, particular
pass passenger, passive
pat patent
PC percent, politically correct, post-card
pd paid
PD police department
PDT Pacific daylight time
PE physical education
PEI Prince Edward Island
Penn, Penna Pennsylvania
pg page
PIN personal identification number
pk park, peak, peck
pkg package
pl place, plural
p.m., PM afternoon
PMS premenstrual syndrome
PO post office
Port Portugal, Portuguese
pos position, positive
poss possessive
pp pages
PQ Province of Quebec
pr pair, price, printed
PR public relations, Puerto Rico
prep preposition
pres present, president
prob probable, probably, problem
prof professor
pron pronoun
prov province
PS postscript, public school
PST Pacific standard time
psych psychology
pt part, payment, pint, point
PT Pacific time, physical therapy

pvt private
qr quarter
qt quantity, quart
Que Quebec
quot quotation
r right, river
rd road, rod, round
RDA recommended daily allowance, recommended dietary allowance
recd received
reg region, register, registered, regular
rel relating, relative, religion
rep report, reporter, representative, republic
Rep Republican
res residence
rev reverse, review, revised, revision, revolution
Rev reverend
RFD rural free delivery
RI Rhode Island
rm room
RPM revolutions per minute
RR railroad, rural route
RSVP please reply
rt right
rte route
s small, south, southern
SA South America
SASE self-addressed stamped envelope
Sask Saskatchewan
Sat Saturday
SC South Carolina
sci science, scientific
SD, S Dak South Dakota
secy secretary
sen senate, senator, senior
Sept, Sep September
sing singular
sm small
so south, southern
soph sophomore
sp spelling
spec special, specifically
specif specific, specifically
SPF sun protection factor
sq square
sr senior
Sr sister
SSN Social Security number
SSR Soviet Socialist Republic
st street
St saint
std standard
subj subject
Sun Sunday

supt superintendent
SWAT Special Weapons and Tactics
syn synonym
t teaspoon, temperature, ton, transitive, troy, true
T tablespoon
tbs, tbsp tablespoon
TD touchdown
tech technical, technician, technology
Tenn Tennessee
terr territory
Tex Texas
Th, Thu, Thur, Thurs Thursday
TN Tennessee
trans translated, translation, translator
tsp teaspoon
Tu, Tue, Tues Tuesday
TX Texas
UK United Kingdom
UN United Nations
univ universal, university
US United States
USA United States of America
USSR Union of Soviet Socialist Republics

usu usual, usually
UT Utah
UV ultraviolet
v verb, versus
Va, VA Virginia
var variant, variety
vb verb
VG very good
VI Virgin Islands
vol volume, volunteer
VP vice president
vs versus
Vt, VT Vermont
w west, western
WA, Wash Washington
Wed Wednesday
WI, Wis, Wisc Wisconsin
wk week, work
wt weight
WV, W Va West Virginia
WY, Wyo Wyoming
XL extra large, extra long
yd yard
yr year, younger, your
YT Yukon Territory

BIOGRAPHICAL NAMES

This section gives basic information on many notable figures from contemporary culture, history, legend, mythology, and biblical tradition. Figures from the Bible, myth, and legend are clearly identified as such.

In cases where individuals have alternate names, they are generally entered under the name by which they are best known. Names are generally alphabetized by the main element of the surname, without regard for connectives such as *da, de, van,* or *von* (as **Gama** . . . Vasco da). Names appearing in the entry in italics are original names, maiden names, or nicknames.

The first dates given in the entry are birth/death dates; other dates refer to terms in office, reigns, achievements, or honors. Abbreviations used here are listed in the front section Abbreviations in This Work.

Aar·on \\'er-ən\\ brother of Moses and 1st high priest of the Hebrews in the Bible

Aaron Hank 1934–　　*Henry Louis Aaron* Amer. baseball player

Abel \\'ā-bəl\\ son of Adam and Eve and brother of Cain in the Bible

Abra·ham \\'ā-brə-ˌham\\ patriarch and founder of the Hebrew people in the Bible; also revered by Muslims

Achil·les \\ə-'ki-lēz\\ hero of the Trojan War in Greek mythology

Ad·am \\'a-dəm\\ the 1st man in biblical tradition

Ad·ams \\'a-dəmz\\ Abigail 1744–1818 née *Smith* Amer. writer; wife of John Adams

Adams Ansel Easton 1902–1984 Amer. photographer

Adams John 1735–1826 2d pres. of the U.S. (1797–1801)

Adams John Quin·cy \\'kwin-zē, -sē\\ 1767–1848 6th pres. of the U.S. (1825–29); son of John and Abigail Adams

Adams Samuel 1722–1803 patriot in the Amer. Revolution

Ad·dams \\'a-dəmz\\ Jane 1860–1935 Amer. social worker; Nobel Prize winner (1931)

Ado·nis \\ə-'dä-nəs, -'dō-\\ youth in Greek mythology loved by Aphrodite

Ae·ne·as \\i-'nē-əs\\ Trojan hero in Greek and Roman mythology

Ae·o·lus \\'ē-ə-ləs\\ god of the winds in Greek mythology

Aes·chy·lus \\'es-kə-ləs, 'ēs-\\ 525–456 B.C. Greek dramatist

Aes·cu·la·pi·us \\ˌes-k(y)ə-'lā-pē-əs\\ god of medicine in Roman mythology — compare ASCLEPIUS

Ae·sop \\'ē-ˌsäp, -səp\\ legendary Greek writer of fables

Ag·a·mem·non \\ˌa-gə-'mem-ˌnän, -nən\\ leader of the Greeks during the Trojan War in Greek mythology

Ag·nes \\'ag-nəs\\ Saint *died* 304 A.D. Christian martyr

Ahab \\'ā-ˌhab\\ king of Israel in the 9th cent. B.C. and husband of Jezebel

Ajax \\'ā-ˌjaks\\ hero in Greek mythology who kills himself because the armor of Achilles is awarded to Odysseus during the Trojan War

Alad·din \\ə-'la-dᵊn\\ youth in the *Arabian Nights' Entertainments* who acquires a magic lamp

Al·bright \\'ȯl-ˌbrīt\\ Madeleine 1937–　née *Korbel* Amer. (Czech-born) diplomat; U.S. secretary of state (1997–2001)

Al·cott \\'ȯl-kət, 'al-, -ˌkät\\ Louisa May 1832–1888 Amer. author

Al·ex·an·der \\ˌa-lig-'zan-dər, ˌe-\\ name of eight popes: esp. **VI** 1431–1503 (pope 1492–1503)

Alexander the Great 356–323 B.C. *Alexander III* king of Macedonia (336–323)

Al·fred \\'al-frəd, -fərd\\ 849–899 *Alfred the Great* king of the West Saxons (871–899)

Ali \\ä-'lē\\ Muhammed 1942–　orig. *Cassius Clay* Amer. boxer

Ali Ba·ba \\ˌa-lē-'bä-bə, ˌä-lē-\\ woodcutter in the *Arabian Nights' Entertainments* who enters the cave of the Forty Thieves by using the password *Sesame*

Al·len \\'a-lən\\ Ethan 1738–1789 Amer. Revolutionary soldier

Amerigo Vespucci — see VESPUCCI

Am·herst \\'a-(ˌ)mərst\\ Jeffery 1717–1797 Baron *Amherst* Brit. general in America

Amund·sen \\'ä-mən-sən\\ Roald 1872–1928 Norwegian explorer

An·a·ni·as \\ˌa-nə-'nī-əs\\ early Christian in the Bible struck dead for lying

An·der·sen \\'an-dər-sən\\ Hans Christian 1805–1875 Danish writer of fairy tales

An·der·son \\'an-dər-sən\\ Marian 1897–1993 Amer. contralto

An·ge·lou \\'an-jə-(ˌ)lō, *commonly* -ˌlü\\ Maya 1928–　orig. *Marguerite Johnson* Amer. author

Anne \\'an\\ 1665–1714 queen of Great Britain (1702–14)

An·tho·ny \\'an(t)-thə-nē\\ Susan Brownell 1820–1906 Amer. suffragist

An·tig·o·ne \\an-'ti-gə-(ˌ)nē\\ daughter of Oedipus and Jocasta in Greek mythology

An·to·ny \\'an-tə-nē\\ Mark *ca* 82–30 B.C.

Marc Anthony; Marcus *An·to·ni·us* \an-'tō-nē-əs\ Roman general and triumvir (43–30)

Aph·ro·di·te \ˌa-frə-'dī-tē\ goddess of love and beauty in Greek mythology — compare VENUS

Apol·lo \ə-'pä-(ˌ)lō\ god of sunlight, prophecy, music, and poetry in Greek and Roman mythology

Ap·ple·seed \'ap-əl-ˌsēd\ Johnny 1774–1845 orig. *John Chapman* Amer. pioneer

Aqui·nas \ə-'kwī-nəs\ Saint Thomas 1224/25–1274 Ital. theologian

Ar·chi·me·des \ˌär-kə-'mē-dēz\ *ca* 287–212 B.C. Greek mathematician and inventor

Ares \'a-(ˌ)rēz, 'er-(ˌ)ēz\ god of war in Greek mythology — compare MARS

Ar·is·toph·a·nes \ˌa-rə-'stä-fə-ˌnēz\ *ca* 450–*ca* 388 B.C. Greek playwright

Ar·is·tot·le \'a-rə-ˌstä-tᵊl\ 384–322 B.C. Greek philosopher

Arm·strong \'ärm-ˌströŋ\ Lance 1971– Amer. cyclist

Armstrong Louis 1901–1971 *Satch·mo* \'sach-ˌmō\ Amer. jazz musician

Armstrong Neil Alden 1930– Amer. astronaut; 1st man on the moon (1969)

Ar·nold \'är-nᵊld\ Benedict 1741–1801 Amer. Revolutionary general and traitor

Ar·te·mis \'är-tə-məs\ goddess of the moon, wild animals, and hunting in Greek mythology — compare DIANA

Ar·thur \'är-thər\ legendary king of the Britons whose story is based on traditions of a 6th-century military leader — **Ar·thu·ri·an** \är-'thür-ē-ən, -'thyür-\ *adj*

Arthur Chester Alan 1829–1886 21st pres. of the U.S. (1881–85)

As·cle·pi·us \ə-'sklē-pē-əs\ god of medicine in Greek mythology — compare AESCULAPIUS

As·tor \'as-tər\ John Jacob 1763–1848 Amer. (Ger.-born) fur trader and capitalist

Athe·na \ə-'thē-nə\ *or* Athe·ne \-nē\ goddess of wisdom in Greek mythology — compare MINERVA

At·las \'at-ləs\ Titan in Greek mythology forced to bear the heavens on his shoulders

At·ti·la \'a-tə-lə, ə-'ti-lə\ 406?–453 A.D. king of the Huns

At·tucks \'a-təks\ Crispus 1723?–1770 Amer. patriot

Au·du·bon \'ȯ-də-bən, -ˌbän\ John James 1785–1851 Amer. (Haitian-born) artist and naturalist

Au·gus·tine \'ȯ-gə-ˌstēn; ȯ-'gəs-tən, ə-\ Saint 354–430 A.D. church father; bishop of Hippo (396–430)

Au·gus·tus \ȯ-'gəs-təs, ə-\ *or* Caesar Augustus *or* Oc·ta·vi·an \äk-'tā-vē-ən\ 63 B.C.–14 A.D., 1st Roman emperor (27 B.C.–14 A.D.)

Au·ro·ra \ə-'rȯr-ə, ȯ-\ goddess of the dawn in Roman mythology — compare EOS

Aus·ten \'ȯs-tən, 'äs-\ Jane 1775–1817 Eng. author

Bac·chus \'ba-kəs, 'bä-\ — see DIONYSUS

Bach \'bäk, 'bäk\ Johann Sebastian 1685–1750 Ger. composer

Ba·con \'bā-kən\ Francis 1561–1626 Eng. philosopher and author

Ba·den–Pow·ell \'bā-dᵊn-'pō-əl\ Robert Stephenson Smyth 1857–1941 Baron *Baden-Powell* Brit. general and founder of Boy Scout movement

Baf·fin \'ba-fən\ William *ca* 1584–1622 Eng. navigator

Bal·boa \bal-'bō-ə\ Vasco Núñez de 1475–1519 Span. explorer

Bal·zac \'bȯl-ˌzak, 'bal-\ Honoré de 1799–1850 French author

Ba·rab·bas \bə-'ra-bəs\ prisoner in the Bible released in preference to Jesus at the demand of the multitude

Bar·num \'bär-nəm\ P. T. 1810–1891 *Phineas Taylor Barnum* Amer. showman

Bar·rie \'ba-rē\ Sir James Matthew 1860–1937 Scot. author

Bar·thol·di \bär-'täl-dē, -'tȯl-, -'thäl-, -'thȯl-\ Frédéric-Auguste 1834–1904 French sculptor of the Statue of Liberty

Bar·ton \'bär-tᵊn\ Clara 1821–1912 founder of American Red Cross

Beau·re·gard \'bȯr-ə-ˌgärd\ Pierre Gustave Toutant 1818–1893 Amer. Confederate general

Beck·et \'be-kət\ Saint Thomas *ca* 1118–1170 *Thomas à Becket* archbishop of Canterbury (1162–70)

Beck·ett \'be-kət\ Samuel 1906–1989 Irish playwright in France; Nobel Prize winner (1969)

Bee·tho·ven \'bā-ˌtō-vən\ Ludwig van 1770–1827 Ger. composer

Bell \'bel\ Alexander Graham 1847–1922 Amer. (Scot.-born) inventor of the telephone

Bel·low \'be-(ˌ)lō\ Saul 1915–2005 Amer. (Canad.–born) author

Ben·e·dict \'be-nə-ˌdikt\ name of 16 popes: esp. **XIV** 1675–1758 (pope 1740–58); **XV** 1854–1922 (pope 1914–22); **XVI** 1927– (pope 2005–)

Be·nét \bə-'nā\ Stephen Vincent 1898–1943 Amer. author

Ben·ja·min \'ben-jə-mən\ youngest son of Jacob and ancestor of one of the 12 tribes of Israel in the Bible

Ben·ton \'ben-tᵊn\ Thomas Hart 1889–1975 Amer. painter

Be·o·wulf \'bā-ə-ˌwulf\ legendary warrior and hero of the Old Eng. poem *Beowulf*

Be·ring \'ber-iŋ, 'bir-\ Vitus 1681–1741 Danish navigator and explorer for Russia

Ber·lin \(ˌ)bər-'lin\ Irving 1888–1989 Amer. (Russ.-born) composer

Ber·ni·ni \ber-'nē-nē\ Gian Lorenzo

1598–1680 Ital. sculptor, architect, and painter

Bes·se·mer \'be-sə-mər\ Sir Henry 1813–1898 Eng. engineer and inventor

Bi·den \'bī-dᵊn\ Joseph Robinette, Jr. 1942– vice pres. of the U.S. (2009–)

Bi·zet \bē-'zā\ Georges 1838–1875 French composer

Black Hawk \'blak-ˌhȯk\ 1767–1838 Amer. Indian chief

Black·well \'blak-ˌwel, -wəl\ Elizabeth 1821–1910 Amer. (Eng.-born) physician

Blair \'bler\ Tony 1953– *Anthony Charles Lynton Blair* Brit. prime minister (1997–2007)

Blake \'blāk\ William 1757–1827 Eng. poet and artist

Bloom·er \'blü-mər\ Amelia 1818–1894 née *Jenks* Amer. social reformer

Boc·cac·cio \bō-'kä-ch(ē-ˌ)ō\ Giovanni 1313–1375 Ital. author

Bohr \'bȯr\ Niels 1885–1962 Danish physicist; Nobel Prize winner (1922)

Bo·leyn \bu̇-'lin, -'lēn\ Anne 1507?–1536 2d wife of Henry VIII and mother of Elizabeth I of England

Bo·lí·var \bə-'lē-ˌvär; 'bä-lə-ˌvär, -vər\ Simón \sē-ˌmōn, ˌsī-mən\ 1783–1830 South Amer. liberator

Bon·i·face \'bä-nə-fəs, -ˌfās\ name of 9 popes: esp. **VIII** *ca* 1235 (or 1240)–1303 (pope 1294–1303)

Boone \'bün\ Daniel 1734–1820 Amer. pioneer

Booth \'büth\ John Wilkes 1838–1865 Amer. actor; assassin of Abraham Lincoln

Bo·re·as \'bȯr-ē-əs\ god of the north wind in Greek mythology

Bot·ti·cel·li \ˌbä-tə-'che-lē\ Sandro 1445–1510 Ital. painter

Bow·ie \'bü-ē, 'bō-\ Jim 1796–1836 *James Bowie* Amer. hero of the Texas revolution

Boyle \'bȯi(-ə)l\ Robert 1627–1691 Eng. physicist and chemist

Brad·bury \'brad-ˌber-ē, -b(ə-)rē\ Ray Douglas 1920– Amer. author

Brad·dock \'bra-dək\ Edward 1695–1755 Brit. general in America

Brad·ford \'brad-fərd\ William 1590–1657 Pilgrim leader

Brad·street \'brad-ˌstrēt\ Anne *ca* 1612–1672 Amer. poet

Bra·dy \'brā-dē\ Mathew B. 1823?–1896 Amer. photographer

Brahe \'brä; 'brä-hē, -hə\ Tycho 1546–1601 Danish astronomer

Brah·ma \'brä-mə\ creator god of the Hindu sacred triad — compare SHIVA; VISHNU

Brahms \'brämz\ Johannes 1833–1897 Ger. composer

Braille \'brāl, 'brī\ Louis 1809–1852 French blind teacher of the blind

Brant \'brant\ Joseph 1742–1807 *Thayendanegea* Mohawk Indian chief

Braun \'brau̇n\ Wernher von 1912–1977 Amer. (Ger.-born) rocket engineer

Brezh·nev \'brezh-ˌnef\ Leonid Ilich 1906–1982 Soviet leader of the Communist Party (1964–82); pres. of the U.S.S.R. (1960–64; 1977–82)

Bron·të \'brän-tē, -ˌtä\ family of Eng. writers: Charlotte 1816–1855 and her sisters Emily 1818–1848 and Anne 1820–1849

Brooks \'bru̇ks\ Gwendolyn Elizabeth 1917–2000 Amer. poet

Brown \'brau̇n\ John 1800–1859 Amer. abolitionist

Brown James Gordon 1951– Brit. prime minister

Brow·ning \'brau̇-niŋ\ Elizabeth Barrett 1806–1861 Eng. poet

Browning Robert 1812–1889 Eng. poet; husband of the preceding

Bru·tus \'brü-təs\ Marcus Junius 85–42 B.C. Roman politician; one of Julius Caesar's assassins

Bry·an \'brī-ən\ William Jennings 1860–1925 Amer. lawyer and politician

Bu·chan·an \byü-'ka-nən, bə-\ James 1791–1868 15th pres. of the U.S. (1857–61)

Buck \'bək\ Pearl S. 1892–1973 née *Sydenstricker* Amer. author; Nobel Prize winner (1938)

Bud·dha \'bü-də, 'bu̇-\ *ca* 563–*ca* 483 B.C. orig. *Siddhartha Gautama* Indian founder of Buddhism

Buffalo Bill — see W. F. CODY

Bun·yan \'bən-yən\ John 1628–1688 Eng. preacher and author

Bunyan Paul — see PAUL BUNYAN

Bur·bank \'bər-ˌbaŋk\ Luther 1849–1926 Amer. horticulturist

Bur·goyne \(ˌ)bər-'gȯin, 'bər-ˌ\ John 1722–1792 Brit. general in America

Burns \'bərnz\ Robert 1759–1796 Scot. poet

Burn·side \'bərn-ˌsīd\ Ambrose Everett 1824–1881 Amer. general

Burr \'bər\ Aaron 1756–1836 vice pres. of the U.S. (1801–5)

Bush \'bu̇sh\ George (Herbert Walker) 1924– 41st pres. of the U.S. (1989–93)

Bush George W. 1946– *George Walker Bush* 43rd pres. of the U.S. (2001–09); son of the preceding

By·ron \'bī-rən\ Lord 1788–1824 *George Gordon Byron*, 6th Baron *Byron* Eng. poet

Cab·ot \'ka-bət\ John *ca* 1450–*ca* 1499 orig. *Giovanni Ca·bo·to* \kä-'bō-tō\ Ital. navigator; explorer for England

Cabot Sebastian 1476?–1557 Eng. navigator; son of J. Cabot

Ca·bri·ni \kə-'brē-nē\ Saint Frances Xavier 1850–1917 *Mother Cabrini* 1st Amer. (Ital.-born) saint (1946)

Cae·sar \'sē-zər\ (Gaius) Julius 100?–44 B.C. Roman general, political leader, and writer

Cain \'kān\ son of Adam and Eve and brother of Abel in the Bible

Calamity Jane \kə-'la-mə-tē-\ 1852?–1903 *Martha Jane Burk* \'bərk\ née *Cannary* \'ka-nə-rē\ Amer. frontier figure

Cal·houn \kal-'hün\ John Caldwell 1782–1850 vice pres. of the U.S. (1825–32)

Ca·lig·u·la \kə-'li-gyə-lə\ 12–41 A.D. Roman emperor (37–41)

Cal·li·ope \kə-'lī-ə-(ˌ)pē\ muse of heroic poetry in Greek mythology

Cal·vert \'kal-vərt\ George 1580?–1632 Baron *Baltimore* Eng. colonist in America

Cal·vin \'kal-vən\ John 1509–1564 *Jean Calvin* or *Cau·vin* \kō-'vaⁿ\ French theologian and reformer

Ca·mus \kä-'mœ\ Albert 1913–1960 French author; Nobel Prize winner (1957)

Ca·nute \kə-'nüt, -'nyüt\ died 1035 *Canute the Great* Danish king of England (1016–35); of Denmark (1018–35); of Norway (1028–35)

Car·ne·gie \kär-'ne-gē, 'kär-nə-gē\ Andrew 1835–1919 Amer. (Scot.-born) industrialist and philanthropist

Car·roll \'ka-rəl\ Lewis 1832–1898 pseud. of *Charles Lutwidge Dodgson* Eng. author and mathematician

Car·son \'kär-sⁿn\ Kit 1809–1868 *Christopher Carson* Amer. frontiersman and guide

Carson Rachel Louise 1907–1964 Amer. scientist and writer

Car·ter \'kär-tər\ Jimmy 1924– orig. *James Earl Carter, Jr.* 39th pres. of the U.S. (1977–81); Nobel Prize winner (2002)

Car·tier \kär-'tyā, 'kär-tē-ˌā\ Jacques 1491–1557 French explorer

Ca·ru·so \kə-'rü-(ˌ)sō, -(ˌ)zō\ En·ri·co \en-'rē-kō\ 1873–1921 Ital. tenor

Car·ver \'kär-vər\ George Washington 1861?–1943 Amer. agricultural chemist and agronomist

Ca·sa·no·va \ˌka-zə-'nō-və, ˌka-sə-\ Giovanni Giacomo 1725–1798 Ital. adventurer

Cas·san·dra \kə-'san-drə, -'sän-\ daughter of Priam in Greek mythology who is endowed with the gift of prophecy but fated never to be believed

Cas·satt \kə-'sat\ Mary 1845–1926 Amer. painter

Cas·tro \'käs-(ˌ)trō\ **(Ruz)** \'rüs\ Fidel 1926– Cuban leader (1959–2008)

Cath·er \'ka-thər\ Willa 1873–1947 Amer. author

Cath·er·ine \'ka-th(ə-)rən\ name of 1st, 5th, and 6th wives of Henry VIII of England: Catherine of Aragon 1485–1536; Catherine Howard 1520?–1542; Catherine Parr 1512–1548

Catherine I 1684–1727 wife of Peter the Great; empress of Russia (1725–27)

Catherine II 1729–1796 *Catherine the Great* empress of Russia (1762–96)

Catherine de Mé·di·cis \-də-ˌmä-dē-'sēs, -'me-də-(ˌ)chē\ 1519–1589 Ital. *Ca·te·ri·na de' Me·di·ci* \ˌkä-tä-'rē-nä-dā-'me-dē-(ˌ)chē\ queen consort of Henry II of France (1547–59) and regent of France (1560–74)

Cav·en·dish \'ka-vən-(ˌ)dish\ Henry 1731–1810 Eng. scientist

Ce·ci·lia \sə-'sēl-yə, -'sil-\ Saint *fl.* 3d cent. A.D. Christian martyr; patron saint of music

Ce·res \'sir-(ˌ)ēz\ goddess of agriculture in Roman mythology — compare DEMETER

Cer·van·tes \sər-'van-ˌtēz, -'vän-ˌtās\ Miguel de 1547–1616 Span. author

Cé·zanne \sā-'zan\ Paul 1839–1906 French painter

Cha·gall \shə-'gäl, -'gal\ Marc 1887–1985 Russ. painter in France

Cham·plain \ˌsham-'plān, shäⁿ-'plaⁿ\ Samuel de 1567–1635 French explorer in America

Chap·lin \'cha-plən\ Charlie 1889–1977 Sir *Charles Spencer Chaplin* Brit. actor and producer

Chapman \'chap-mən\ John — see Johnny APPLESEED

Char·le·magne \'shär-lə-ˌmän\ 742–814 A.D. *Charles the Great* or *Charles I* Frankish king (768–814); emperor of the West (800–814)

Charles \'chär(-ə)lz\ name of 10 kings of France: esp. **II** 823–877 A.D. *Charles the Bald* (r. 840–77); Holy Roman emperor (875–77); **IV** 1294–1328 *Charles the Fair* (r. 1322–28); **V** 1337–1380 *Charles the Wise* (r. 1364–80); **VI** 1368–1422 *Charles the Mad* or *the Beloved* (r. 1380–1422); **VII** 1403–1461 *Charles the Well-Served* or *the Victorious* (r. 1422–61); **IX** 1550–1574 (r. 1560–74); **X** 1757–1836 (r. 1824–30)

Charles name of 2 kings of Great Britain: **I** 1600–1649 (r. 1625–49); **II** 1630–1685 (r. 1660–85); son of Charles I

Charles V 1500–1558 Holy Roman emperor (1519–56); king of Spain as *Charles I* (1516–56)

Charles Edward Stuart — see Charles Edward STUART

Charles Mar·tel \-mär-'tel\ *ca* 688–741 A.D. Frankish ruler (719–41); grandfather of Charlemagne

Cha·ryb·dis \kə-'rib-dəs\ whirlpool off the coast of Sicily personified in Greek mythology as a female monster

Chau·cer \'chò-sər\ Geoffrey *ca* 1342–1400 Eng. poet

Che·khov \'che-ˌkòf, -ˌkóv\ Anton Pavlovich 1860–1904 Russ. author

Che·ney \'chē-nē, *commonly* 'chā-\ Richard Bruce 1941– vice pres. of the U.S. (2001–2009)

Cheops — see KHUFU

Ches·ter·ton \'ches-tər-tən\ G. K. 1874–1936 *Gilbert Keith Chesterton* Eng. author

Cho·pin \'shō-ˌpan, -ˌpaⁿ\ Frédéric François 1810–1849 Polish composer

Chou En–lai *or* **Zhou Enlai** \'jō-'en-'lī\ 1898–1976 Chinese Communist politician; premier (1949–76)

Chré·tien \krā-'tyaⁿ\ Jean 1934– Canad. prime minister (1993–2003)

Christ Jesus — see JESUS

Chris·tie \'kris-tē\ Dame Agatha 1890–1976 née *Miller* Eng. author

Chur·chill \'chər-ˌchil, 'chərch-ˌhil\ Sir Winston Leonard Spencer 1874–1965 Brit. prime minister (1940–45; 1951–55) Nobel Prize winner (1953)

Clark \'klärk\ George Rogers 1752–1818 Amer. soldier and frontiersman

Clark William 1770–1838 Amer. explorer (with Meriwether Lewis)

Clay \'klā\ Henry 1777–1852 Amer. politician and orator

Clem·ens \'kle-mənz\ Samuel Langhorne — see Mark TWAIN

Cle·o·pa·tra \ˌklē-ə-'pa-trə, -'pä-\ 69–30 B.C. queen of Egypt (51–30)

Cleve·land \'klēv-lənd\ (Stephen) Grover 1837–1908 22nd and 24th pres. of the U.S. (1885–89; 1893–97)

Clin·ton \'klin-tᵊn\ Hillary Rodham née *Rodham* 1947– Amer. politician; U.S. secretary of state (2009–); wife of W.J. Clinton

Clinton William Jefferson 1946– *Bill Clinton* 42nd pres. of the U.S. (1993–2001)

Cly·tem·nes·tra \ˌklī-təm-'nes-trə\ wife of Agamemnon in Greek mythology

Cobb \'käb\ Ty 1886–1961 *Tyrus Raymond Cobb* Amer. baseball player

Co·chise \kō-'chēs\ 1812?–1874 Apache Indian chief

Co·dy \'kō-dē\ William Frederick 1846–1917 *Buffalo Bill* Amer. hunter, guide, and showman

Co·han \'kō-ˌhan\ George Michael 1878–1942 Amer. composer

Cole·ridge \'kōl-rij, 'kō-lə-rij\ Samuel Taylor 1772–1834 Eng. poet

Co·lette \kò-'let\ 1873–1954 orig. *Sidonie Gabrielle Colette* French author

Co·lum·bus \kə-'ləm-bəs\ Christopher 1451–1506 Ital. navigator and explorer for Spain

Con·fu·cius \kən-'fyü-shəs\ 551–479 B.C. Chinese philosopher

Con·rad \'kän-ˌrad\ Joseph 1857–1924 Brit. (Polish-born) author

Con·sta·ble \'kən(t)-stə-bəl, 'kän(t)-\ John 1776–1837 Eng. painter

Con·stan·tine I \'kän(t)-stən-ˌtēn, -ˌtīn\ *after* 280–337 A.D. *Constantine the Great* Roman emperor (306–37)

Cook \'kúk\ Captain James 1728–1779 Eng. navigator

Coo·lidge \'kü-lij\ (John) Calvin 1872–1933 30th pres. of the U.S. (1923–29)

Coo·per \'kü-pər, 'kú-\ James Fenimore 1789–1851 Amer. author

Co·per·ni·cus \kō-'pər-ni-kəs\ Nicolaus 1473–1543 Polish astronomer

Cop·land \'kō-plənd\ Aaron 1900–1990 Amer. composer

Cop·ley \'kä-plē\ John Singleton 1738–1815 Amer. painter

Corn·wal·lis \kòrn-'wä-ləs\ Charles 1738–1805 1st Marquess *Cornwallis* Brit. general in America

Co·ro·na·do \ˌkòr-ə-'nä-(ˌ)dō, ˌkär-\ Francisco Vásquez de *ca* 1510–1554 Span. explorer of southwestern U.S.

Cor·tés \kòr-'tez, 'kòr-ˌ\ Hernán *or* Hernando 1485–1547 Span. conqueror of Mexico

Cous·teau \kü-'stō\ Jacques-Yves 1910–1997 French marine explorer

Crane \'krān\ Stephen 1871–1900 Amer. author

Crazy Horse \'krā-zē-ˌhòrs\ 1842?–1877 *Ta-sunko-witko* Sioux Indian chief

Crock·ett \'krä-kət\ *Davy* 1786–1836 *David Crockett* Amer. frontiersman

Crom·well \'kräm-ˌwel, 'krəm-, -wəl\ Oliver 1599–1658 Eng. general; lord protector of England (1653–58)

Cro·nus \'krō-nəs, 'krä-\ Titan in Greek mythology overthrown by his son Zeus

Cum·mings \'kə-miŋz\ Edward Estlin 1894–1962 known as *e. e. cummings* Amer. poet

Cu·pid \'kyü-pəd\ god of love in Roman mythology — compare EROS

Cu·rie \kyù-'rē, 'kyùr-(ˌ)ē\ Marie 1867–1934 née *Sklo·dow·ska* \sklə-'dóf-skə\ French (Polish-born) chemist; Nobel Prize winner (1903, 1911)

Curie Pierre 1859–1906 French chemist; husband of M. Curie; Nobel Prize winner (1903)

Cus·ter \'kəs-tər\ George Armstrong 1839–1876 Amer. general

Cy·ra·no de Ber·ge·rac \'sir-ə-ˌnō-də-'ber-zhə-ˌrak\ Savinien 1619–1655 French playwright

Cy·rus II \'sī-rəs\ *ca* 585–*ca* 529 B.C. *Cyrus the Great* king of Persia (*ca* 550–529)

Dae·da·lus \'de-də-ləs, 'dē-\ builder in Greek mythology of the Cretan labyrinth and inventor of wings by which he and his son Icarus escape imprisonment

Da·lí \'dä-lē, *by himself* dä-'lē\ Salvador 1904–1989 Span. painter

Dal·ton \'dòl-tᵊn\ John 1766–1844 Eng. chemist and physicist

Da·na \'dä-nə\ Richard Henry 1815–1882 Amer. author

Dan·iel \'dan-yəl\ prophet in the Bible who is held captive in Babylon and delivered from a den of lions

Dan·te \'dän-(ˌ)tā, 'dan-, -(ˌ)tē\ 1265–1321 *Dante Ali·ghie·ri* \ˌa-lə-'gyer-ē\ Ital. poet

Dare \'der\ Virginia 1587–? 1st child born in America of Eng. parents

Da·ri·us I \də-'rī-əs\ 550–486 B.C. *Darius the Great* king of Persia (522–486)

Dar·row \'da-(ˌ)rō\ Clarence Seward 1857–1938 Amer. lawyer

Dar·win \'där-wən\ Charles Robert 1809–1882 Eng. naturalist

Da·vid \'dā-vəd\ a youth in the Bible who slays Goliath and succeeds Saul as king of Israel

Da·vis \'dā-vəs\ Jefferson 1808–1889 pres. of the Confederate States of America (1861–65)

Dawes \'dȯz\ William 1745–1799 Amer. patriot

Debs \'debz\ Eugene Victor 1855–1926 Amer. socialist and labor organizer

De·bus·sy \ˌde-byü-'sē, ˌdā-\ Claude 1862–1918 French composer

De·ca·tur \di-'kā-tər\ Stephen 1779–1820 Amer. naval officer

De·foe \di-'fō\ Daniel 1660–1731 Eng. author

De·gas \də-'gä\ Edgar 1834–1917 French painter

de Gaulle \di-'gōl, -'gȯl\ Charles 1890–1970 French general; pres. of Fifth Republic (1958–69)

De·li·lah \di-'lī-lə\ mistress and betrayer of Samson in the Bible

De·me·ter \di-'mē-tər\ goddess of agriculture in Greek mythology — compare CERES

de Mille \də-'mil\ Agnes 1905–1993 Amer. dancer and choreographer

De·mos·the·nes \di-'mäs-thə-ˌnēz\ 384–322 B.C. Athenian orator and statesman

Demp·sey \'dem(p)-sē\ Jack 1895–1983 orig. *William Harrison Dempsey* Amer. boxer

Des·cartes \dā-'kärt\ René 1596–1650 French mathematician and philosopher

de So·to \thā-'sō-(ˌ)tō, di-\ Hernando *ca* 1496–1542 Span. explorer

Dew·ey \'dü-ē, 'dyü-\ George 1837–1917 Amer. admiral

Dewey John 1859–1952 Amer. philosopher and educator

Dewey Melvil 1851–1931 Amer. librarian

Di·ana \dī-'a-nə\ ancient Ital. goddess of the forest and of childbirth who was identified with Artemis by the Romans

Dick·ens \'di-kənz\ Charles 1812–1870 pseud. *Boz* \'bäz, 'bōz\ Eng. author

Dick·in·son \'di-kən-sən\ Emily Elizabeth 1830–1886 Amer. poet

Di·do \'dī-(ˌ)dō\ legendary queen of Carthage who falls in love with Aeneas and kills herself when he leaves her

Di·Mag·gio \də-'mä-zhē-(ˌ)ō, -'ma-jē-(ˌ)ō\ Joe 1914–1999 *Joseph Paul DiMaggio* Amer. baseball player

Di·o·ny·sus \ˌdī-ə-'nī-səs, -'nē-\ god of wine and ecstasy in classical mythology

Dis·ney \'diz-nē\ Walt 1901–1966 *Walter Elias Disney* Amer. film producer and cartoonist

Dis·rae·li \diz-'rā-lē\ Benjamin 1804–1881 Earl of *Beaconsfield* Brit. prime minister (1868; 1874–80)

Dix \'diks\ Dorothea Lynde 1802–1887 Amer. social reformer

Dodg·son \'däd-sən, 'däj-\ Charles Lutwidge — see Lewis CARROLL

Donne \'dən\ John 1572–1631 Eng. poet and clergyman

Don Qui·xote \ˌdän-kē-'(h)ō-tē, ˌdän-\ hero of Cervantes' *Don Quixote*

Dos·to·yev·sky \ˌdäs-tə-'yef-skē, -'yev-\ Fyodor Mikhaylovich 1821–1881 Russ. novelist

Doug·las \'də-gləs\ Stephen Arnold 1813–1861 Amer. politician

Doug·lass \'də-gləs\ Frederick 1817–1895 Amer. abolitionist

Doyle \'dȯi(-ə)l\ Sir Arthur Conan 1859–1930 Brit. physician and author

Drake \'drāk\ Sir Francis *ca* 1540–1596 Eng. navigator, explorer, and admiral

Drei·ser \'drī-sər, -zər\ Theodore 1871–1945 Amer. author

DuBois \dü-'bȯis, dyü-\ William Edward Burghardt 1868–1963 Amer. educator and writer

Du·mas \dü-'mä, dyü-\ Alexandre 1802–1870 *Dumas père* \'per\ French author

Dumas Alexandre 1824–1895 *Dumas fils* \'fēs\ French author

Dun·can \'dən-kən\ Isadora 1877–1927 Amer. dancer

Dü·rer \'dȯr-ər, 'dyȯr-, 'dʉr-\ Albrecht 1471–1528 Ger. painter and engraver

Ea·kins \'ā-kənz\ Thomas 1844–1916 Amer. artist

Ear·hart \'er-ˌhärt, 'ir-\ Amelia 1897–1937 Amer. aviator

Earp \'ərp\ Wyatt 1848–1929 Amer. frontiersman and lawman

Ed·dy \'e-dē\ Mary Baker 1821–1910 Amer. founder of Christian Science

Ed·i·son \'e-də-sən\ Thomas Alva 1847–1931 Amer. inventor

Ed·ward \'ed-wərd\ name of 8 post-Norman kings of England: **I** 1239–1307 *Edward Longshanks* (r. 1272–1307); **II** 1284–1327 (r. 1307–27); **III** 1312–1377 (r. 1327–77); **IV** 1442–1483 (r. 1461–70; 1471–83); **V** 1470–1483 (r. 1483); **VI** 1537–1553 (r. 1547–53); son of Henry VIII and Jane Seymour; **VII** 1841–1910 (r. 1901–10); son of Queen Victoria; **VIII** 1894–1972 (r. 1936; abdicated) *Duke of Windsor*; son of George V

Ein·stein \'īn-ˌstīn\ Albert 1879–1955 Amer. (Ger.-born) physicist; Nobel Prize winner (1921)

Ei·sen·how·er \'ī-zᵊn-ˌhaȯ(-ə)r\ Dwight David 1890–1969 Amer. general; 34th pres. of the U.S. (1953–61)

Elec·tra \i-'lek-trə\ sister of Orestes in Greek mythology who aids him in avenging their father's murder

Eli·jah \i-ˈlī-jə\ Hebrew prophet of the 9th cent. B.C.

El·i·on \ˈe-lē-ən\ Gertrude Belle 1918–1999 Amer. pharmacologist; Nobel Prize winner (1988)

El·iot \ˈe-lē-ət, ˈel-yət\ George 1819–1880 pseud. of *Mary Ann Evans* Eng. author

Eliot T. S. 1888–1965 *Thomas Stearns Eliot* Brit. (Amer.-born) poet; Nobel Prize winner (1948)

Eliz·a·beth I \i-ˈli-zə-bəth\ 1533–1603 queen of England (1558–1603); daughter of Henry VIII and Anne Boleyn

Elizabeth II 1926– queen of the United Kingdom (1952–); daughter of George VI

El·ling·ton \ˈe-liŋ-tən\ Duke 1899–1974 *Edward Kennedy Ellington* Amer. bandleader and composer

Em·er·son \ˈe-mər-sən\ Ralph Waldo 1803–1882 Amer. essayist and poet

En·dym·i·on \en-ˈdi-mē-ən\ beautiful youth in Greek mythology loved by the goddess of the moon

Eos \ˈē-ˌäs\ goddess of the dawn in Greek mythology — compare AURORA

Ep·i·cu·rus \ˌe-pi-ˈkyùr-əs\ 341–270 B.C. Greek philosopher

Er·ik the Red \ˈer-ik\ *fl.* 10th cent. orig. *Erik Thorvaldson* Norwegian explorer; father of Leif Eriksson

Eriksson Leif — see LEIF ERIKSSON

Eros \ˈer-ˌäs, ˈir-\ god of love in Greek mythology — compare CUPID

Esau \ˈē-(ˌ)sô\ son of Isaac and Rebekah and elder twin brother of Jacob in the Bible

Es·ther \ˈes-tər\ Hebrew woman in the Bible who as the queen of Persia delivers her people from destruction

Eu·clid \ˈyü-kləd\ *fl. ca* 300 B.C. Greek mathematician

Eu·rip·i·des \yù-ˈri-pə-ˌdēz\ *ca* 484–406 B.C. Greek playwright

Eu·ro·pa \yù-ˈrō-pə\ princess in Greek mythology who was carried off by Zeus disguised as a white bull

Eu·ryd·i·ce \yù-ˈri-də-(ˌ)sē\ wife of Orpheus in Greek mythology

Eve \ˈēv\ the 1st woman in biblical tradition; wife of Adam

Eze·kiel \i-ˈzē-kyəl, -kē-əl\ Hebrew prophet of the 6th cent. B.C.

Fahr·en·heit \ˈfa-rən-ˌhīt, ˈfär-ən-\ Daniel Gabriel 1686–1736 Ger. physicist

Far·a·day \ˈfa-rə-ˌdā, -dē\ Michael 1791–1867 Eng. chemist and physicist

Far·ra·gut \ˈfa-rə-gət\ David Glasgow 1801–1870 Amer. admiral

Faulk·ner \ˈfôk-nər\ William 1897–1962 Amer. author; Nobel Prize winner (1949)

Faust \ˈfaùst\ *or* **Fau·stus** \ˈfaù-stəs, ˈfô-\ magician in Ger. legend who sells his soul to the devil for knowledge and power

Fawkes \ˈfóks\ Guy 1570–1606 Eng. conspirator

Fer·di·nand \ˈfər-də-ˌnand\ **V** of Castile *or* **II** of Aragon 1452–1516 *Ferdinand the Catholic* king of Castile (1474–1504), of Aragon (1479–1516), of Naples (1504–16); husband of Isabella I

Fer·mi \ˈfer-(ˌ)mē\ Enrico 1901–1954 Amer. (Ital.-born) physicist; Nobel Prize winner (1938)

Field·ing \ˈfēl-diŋ\ Henry 1707–1754 Eng. author

Fill·more \ˈfil-ˌmòr\ Millard 1800–1874 13th pres. of the U.S. (1850–53)

Fitz·ger·ald \fits-ˈjer-əld\ Ella 1917–1996 Amer. singer

Fitzgerald F. Scott 1896–1940 *Francis Scott Key Fitzgerald* Amer. author

Flem·ing \ˈfle-miŋ\ Sir Alexander 1881–1955 Brit. bacteriologist; Nobel Prize winner (1945)

Flo·ra \ˈflòr-ə\ goddess of flowers in Roman mythology

Flying Dutchman legendary Dutch mariner condemned to sail the seas until Judgment Day

Ford \ˈfòrd\ Gerald Rudolph 1913–2007 38th pres. of the U.S. (1974–77)

Ford Henry 1863–1947 Amer. automobile manufacturer

Fos·sey \ˈfò-sē, ˈfä-\ Dian 1932–1985 Amer. zoologist

Fos·ter \ˈfòs-tər, ˈfäs-\ Stephen Collins 1826–1864 Amer. songwriter

Fran·cis of As·si·si \ˈfran(t)-səs-əv-ə-ˈsi-sē, -sē-\ Saint 1181/1182–1226 Ital. friar; founder of Franciscan order

Fran·co \ˈfräŋ-(ˌ)kō, ˈfraŋ-\ Francisco 1892–1975 Span. general, dictator, and head of Span. state (1936–75)

Frank \ˈfraŋk, ˈfräŋk\ Anne 1929–1945 Ger.-born diarist during the Holocaust

Frank·lin \ˈfraŋ-klən\ Benjamin 1706–1790 Amer. patriot, author, and inventor

Fred·er·ick I \ˈfre-d(ə-)rik\ *ca* 1123–1190 *Frederick Barbarossa* Holy Roman emperor (1152–90)

Frederick II 1712–1786 *Frederick the Great* king of Prussia (1740–86)

Fré·mont \ˈfrē-ˌmänt\ John Charles 1813–1890 Amer. general and explorer

French \ˈfrench\ Daniel Chester 1850–1931 Amer. sculptor

Freud \ˈfròid\ Sigmund 1856–1939 Austrian neurologist; founder of psychoanalysis

Frig·ga \ˈfri-gə\ wife of Odin and goddess of married love and the hearth in Norse mythology

Frost \ˈfròst\ Robert Lee 1874–1963 Amer. poet

Ful·ler \ˈfù-lər\ (Richard) Buckminster 1895–1983 Amer. engineer and architect

Fuller (Sarah) Margaret 1810–1850 Amer. author and reformer

Ful·ton \ˈfùl-tᵊn\ Robert 1765–1815 Amer. inventor

Ga·bri·el \ˈgā-brē-əl\ archangel named in

Hebrew tradition — compare MICHAEL; RAPHAEL; URIEL

Ga·ga·rin \gə-'gär-ən\ Yury Alekseyevich 1934–1968 Russ. astronaut; 1st man in space (1961)

Gage \'gāj\ Thomas 1721–1787 Brit. general in America

Gal·a·had \'ga-lə-,had\ knight of the Round Table in medieval legend who finds the Holy Grail

Gal·a·tea \,ga-lə-'tē-ə\ female figure sculpted by Pygmalion in Greek mythology and given life by Aphrodite in answer to the sculptor's prayer

Ga·len \'gā-lən\ 129–ca 216 A.D. Greek physician and writer

Ga·li·leo \,ga-lə-'lē-(,)ō, -'lā-\ 1564–1642 Galileo Galilei Ital. astronomer and physicist

Gall \'gȯl\ 1840?–1894 Sioux Indian leader

Ga·ma \'ga-mə, 'gä-\ Vasco da ca 1460–1524 Portuguese navigator and explorer

Gan·dhi \'gän-dē, 'gan-\ Indira 1917–1984 Indian prime minister (1966–77; 1980–84); daughter of Jawaharlal Nehru

Gandhi Mohandas Karamchand 1869–1948 Ma·hat·ma \mə-'hät-mə, -'hat-\ Gandi Indian leader

Gar·field \'gär-,fēld\ James Abram 1831–1881 20th pres. of the U.S. (1881)

Gar·i·bal·di \,ga-rə-'bȯl-dē\ Giuseppe 1807–1882 Ital. patriot

Gar·ri·son \'ga-rə-sən\ William Lloyd 1805–1879 Amer. abolitionist

Gates \'gāts\ Bill 1955– William Henry Gates III Amer. computer software manufacturer

Gau·guin \gō-'gaⁿ\ Paul 1848–1903 French painter

Gau·ta·ma Buddha \'gau̇-tə-mə, -'gō-\ — see BUDDHA

Geh·rig \'ger-ig\ Lou 1903–1941 Henry Louis Gehrig Amer. baseball player

Gei·sel \'gī-zəl\ Theodor Seuss 1904–1991 pseud. Dr. Seuss Amer. author and illustrator

Gen·ghis Khan \,jeŋ-gəs-'kän, ,geŋ-\ ca 1162–1227 Mongol conqueror

George \'jȯrj\ name of 6 kings of Great Britain: I 1660–1727 (r. 1714–27); II 1683–1760 (r. 1727–60); III 1738–1820 (r. 1760–1820); IV 1762–1830 (r. 1820–30); V 1865–1936 (r. 1910–36); VI 1895–1952 (r. 1936–52); father of Elizabeth II

Ge·ron·i·mo \jə-'rä-nə-,mō\ 1829–1909 Apache Indian leader

Gersh·win \'gər-shwən\ George 1898–1937 Amer. composer

Gid·e·on \'gi-dē-ən\ Hebrew hero in the Bible

Gil·bert \'gil-bərt\ Sir William Schwenck 1836–1911 Eng. librettist and poet; collaborator with Sir Arthur Sullivan

Gins·burg \'ginz-,bərg\ Ruth Bader 1933–   Amer. jurist

Glad·stone \'glad-,stōn, chiefly Brit -stən\ William Ewart 1809–1898 Brit. prime minister (1868–74; 1880–85; 1886; 1892–94)

Glenn \'glen\ John Herschel 1921– Amer. astronaut and politician; 1st Amer. to orbit the earth (1962)

Go·di·va \gə-'dī-və\ an Eng. gentlewoman who in legend rode naked through Coventry to save its citizens from a tax

Goe·thals \'gō-thəlz\ George Washington 1858–1928 Amer. engineer who directed the building of the Panama Canal

Goe·the \'gə(r)-tə, 'gœ-tə\ Johann Wolfgang von 1749–1832 Ger. author

Gogh, van \van-'gō, -'gäk\ Vincent Willem 1853–1890 Dutch painter

Gol·ding \'gōl-diŋ\ William Gerald 1911–1993 Eng. author; Nobel Prize winner (1983)

Go·li·ath \gə-'lī-əth\ Philistine giant who is killed by David in the Bible

Gom·pers \'gäm-pərz\ Samuel 1850–1924 Amer. (Brit.-born) labor leader

Goo·dall \'gu̇-(,)dȯl, -(,)däl\ Jane 1934– Brit. zoologist

Good·year \'gu̇d-,yir\ Charles 1800–1860 Amer. inventor

Gor·ba·chev \,gȯr-bə-'chȯf, -'chef\ Mikhail Sergeyevich 1931–   Soviet leader of Communist party (1985–91); pres. of U.S.S.R. (1990–91); Nobel Prize winner (1990)

Gore \'gȯr\ Albert, Jr. 1948–   vice pres. of the U.S. (1993–2001); Nobel Prize winner (2007)

Gor·gas \'gȯr-gəs\ William Crawford 1854–1920 Amer. army surgeon

Gra·ham \'grā-əm, 'gra(-ə)m\ Martha 1893–1991 Amer. dancer and choreographer

Grant \'grant\ Ulysses S. 1822–1885 orig. Hiram Ulysses Grant Amer. general; 18th pres. of the U.S. (1869–77)

Gre·co, El \el-'gre-(,)kō\ 1541–1614 Doménikos Theotokópoulos Span. (Cretan-born) painter

Gree·ley \'grē-lē\ Horace 1811–1872 Amer. journalist and politician

Greene \'grēn\ (Henry) Graham 1904–1991 Brit. author

Greene Nathanael 1742–1786 Amer. Revolutionary general

Greg·o·ry \'gre-g(ə-)rē\ name of 16 popes: esp. I Saint ca 540–604 A.D. Gregory the Great (pope 590–604); VII Saint ca 1020–1085 (pope 1073–85); XIII 1502–1585 (pope 1572–85)

Grey \'grā\ Lady Jane 1537–1554 queen of England for 9 days (1553)

Grey Zane 1872–1939 Amer. author

Grieg \'grēg\ Edward Hagerup 1843–1907 Norwegian composer

Grimm \'grim\ Jacob 1785–1863 and his brother Wilhelm 1786–1859 Ger. philologists and folklorists

Guin·e·vere \'gwi-nə-,vir\ legendary wife of King Arthur and lover of Lancelot

Gu·ten·berg \'gü-t⁰n-ˌbərg\ Johannes *ca* 1400–1468 Ger. inventor of printing method from movable type

Ha·des \'hā-(ˌ)dēz\ — see PLUTO

Ha·dri·an \'hā-drē-ən\ 76–138 A.D. Roman emperor (117–138)

Hai·le Se·las·sie \'hī-lē-sə-'la-sē, -'lä-\ 1892–1975 emperor of Ethiopia (1930–36; 1941–74)

Hale \'hāl\ Edward Everett 1822–1909 Amer. minister and author

Hale Nathan 1755–1776 Amer. Revolutionary hero

Hal·ley \'ha-lē\ Edmond *or* Edmund 1656–1742 Eng. astronomer and mathematician

Hal·sey \'hȯl-sē, -zē\ William Frederick 1882–1959 Amer. admiral

Ham·il·ton \'ha-məl-tən\ Alexander 1755–1804 Amer. political leader

Ham·mu·ra·bi \ˌha-mə-'rä-bē\ *died ca* 1750 B.C. king of Babylon (*ca* 1792–50)

Han·cock \'han-ˌkäk\ John 1737–1793 Amer. Revolutionary patriot

Han·del \'han-d⁰l\ George Frideric 1685–1759 Brit. (Ger.-born) composer

Han·dy \'han-dē\ W. C. 1873–1958 *William Christopher Handy* Amer. blues musician and composer

Han·ni·bal \'ha-nə-bəl\ 247–183? B.C. Carthaginian general

Har·ding \'här-diŋ\ Warren Gamaliel 1865–1923 29th pres. of the U.S. (1921–23)

Har·dy \'här-dē\ Thomas 1840–1928 Eng. author

Har·per \'här-pər\ Stephen 1959– Canad. prime minister (2006–   )

Har·ri·son \'ha-rə-sən\ Benjamin 1833–1901 23rd pres. of the U.S. (1889–93); grandson of W. H. Harrison

Harrison William Henry 1773–1841 Amer. general; 9th pres. of the U.S. (1841)

Harte \'härt\ Bret 1836–1902 orig. *Francis Brett Harte* Amer. author

Har·vey \'här-vē\ William 1578–1657 Eng. physician and anatomist

Haw·thorne \'hȯ-ˌthȯrn\ Nathaniel 1804–1864 Amer. author

Haydn \'hī-d⁰n\ Franz Joseph 1732–1809 Austrian composer

Hayes \'hāz\ Rutherford Birchard 1822–1893 19th pres. of the U.S. (1877–81)

Hearst \'hərst\ William Randolph 1863–1951 Amer. newspaper publisher

Hec·tor \'hek-tər\ son of Priam and Hecuba; Trojan hero slain by Achilles in Greek mythology

Hec·u·ba \'he-kyə-bə\ wife of Priam in Greek mythology

Hel·en of Troy \ˌhe-lən-əv-'trȯi\ wife of Menelaus whose abduction by Paris in Greek mythology causes the Trojan War

He·li·os \'hē-lē-əs, -(ˌ)ȯs\ god of the sun in Greek mythology — compare SOL

Hem·ing·way \'he-miŋ-ˌwā\ Ernest Miller 1899–1961 Amer. author; Nobel Prize winner (1954)

Hen·ry \'hen-rē\ name of 8 kings of England: I 1068–1135 (r. 1100–35); II 1133–1189 (r. 1154–89); III 1207–1272 (r. 1216–72); IV 1366–1413 (r. 1399–1413); V 1387–1422 (r. 1413–22); VI 1421–1471 (r. 1422–61; 1470–71); VII 1457–1509 (r. 1485–1509); VIII 1491–1547 (r. 1509–47)

Henry name of 4 kings of France: I *ca* 1008–1060 (r. 1031–60); II 1519–1559 (r. 1547–59); III 1551–1589 (r. 1574–89); IV 1553–1610 *Henry of Navarre* (r. 1589–1610)

Henry O. 1862–1910 pseud. of *William Sydney Porter* Amer. author

Henry Patrick 1736–1799 Amer. patriot and orator

Hen·son \'hen(t)-sən\ Matthew Alexander 1866–1955 Amer. arctic explorer

He·phaes·tus \hi-'fes-təs, -'fēs-\ god of fire and of metalworking in Greek mythology — compare VULCAN

He·ra \'hir-ə, 'he-rə, 'her-ə\ sister and wife of Zeus and goddess of women and marriage in Greek mythology — compare JUNO

Her·cu·les \'hər-kyə-ˌlēz\ *or* **Her·a·cles** \'her-ə-ˌklēz-, 'he-rə-\ hero in Greek mythology noted for his strength

Her·maph·ro·di·tus \(ˌ)hər-ˌma-frə-'dī-təs\ son of Hermes and Aphrodite who in Greek mythology is joined with a nymph into one body

Her·mes \'hər-(ˌ)mēz\ god of commerce, eloquence, invention, travel, and theft who serves as herald and messenger of the other gods in Greek mythology — compare MERCURY

Her·od \'her-əd\ 73–4 B.C. *Herod the Great* Roman king of Judea (37–4)

Herod An·ti·pas \'an-tə-pəs, -ˌpas\ 21 B.C.–39 A.D., Roman governor of Galilee (4 B.C.–39 A.D.); son of Herod the Great

Hes·se \'he-sə\ Hermann 1877–1962 Ger. author; Nobel Prize winner (1946)

Hey·er·dahl \'hā-ər-ˌdäl\ Thor 1914–2002 Norwegian explorer and author

Hi·a·wa·tha \ˌhī-ə-'wȯ-thə, ˌhē-ə-, -'wä-\ legendary Iroquois Indian chief

Hick·ok \'hi-ˌkäk\ Wild Bill 1837–1876 orig. *James Butler Hickok* Amer. frontiersman and U.S. marshal

Hil·ton \'hil-t⁰n\ James 1900–1954 Eng. novelist

Hip·poc·ra·tes \hi-'pä-krə-ˌtēz\ *ca* 460–*ca* 377 B.C. Greek physician

Hi·ro·hi·to \ˌhir-ō-'hē-(ˌ)tō\ 1901–1989 emperor of Japan (1926–89)

Hit·ler \'hit-lər\ Adolf 1889–1945 Ger. (Austrian-born) chancellor and dictator (1933–45)

Hodg·kin \'häj-kin\ Dorothy Mary 1910–1994 née *Crowfoot* Brit. physicist; Nobel Prize winner (1964)

Holmes \'hōmz, 'hōlmz\ Oliver Wendell 1809–1894 Amer. physician and author

Holmes Oliver Wendell, Jr. 1841–1935 Amer. jurist; son of the preceding

Ho·mer \'hō-mər\ *fl.* 9th *or* 8th cent. B.C. Greek epic poet

Homer Winslow 1836–1910 Amer. painter

Hooke \'huk\ Robert 1635–1703 Eng. scientist

Hook·er \'hu-kər\ Thomas 1586?–1647 Eng. colonist; a founder of Connecticut

Hoo·ver \'hü-vər\ Herbert Clark 1874–1964 31st pres. of the U.S. (1929–33)

Hoover John Edgar 1895–1972 Amer. director of the Federal Bureau of Investigation (1924–72)

Hop·per \'hä-pər\ Grace 1906–1992 née *Murray* Amer. admiral, mathematician, and computer scientist

Hou·di·ni \hü-'dē-nē\ Harry 1874–1926 orig. *Erik Weisz* Amer. magician

Hous·ton \'hyü-stən, 'yü-\ Sam 1793–1863 *Samuel Houston* Amer. politician; pres. of the Republic of Texas (1836–38; 1841–44)

Howe \'hau\ Elias 1819–1867 Amer. inventor

Howe Julia 1819–1910 née *Ward* Amer. suffragist and reformer

Hud·son \'həd-sən\ Henry *ca* 1565–1611 Eng. explorer

Hughes \'hyüz\ (James) Langston 1902–1967 Amer. author

Hugo \'hyü-(ˌ)gō, 'yü-\ Victor 1802–1885 French author

Hus·sein I \hü-'sān\ 1935–1999 king of Jordan (1952–99)

Hussein Saddam 1937–2006 pres. of Iraq (1979–2003)

Hutch·in·son \'hə-chə(n)-sən\ Anne 1591–1643 née *Marbury* Eng. colonist and religious leader in America

Hutchinson Thomas 1711–1780 Amer. colonial administrator

Hux·ley \'həks-lē\ Aldous Leonard 1894–1963 Eng. author

Hy·men \'hī-mən\ god of marriage in Greek mythology

Ib·sen \'ib-sən, 'ip-\ Henrik 1828–1906 Norwegian playwright

Ic·a·rus \'i-kə-rəs\ son of Daedalus who in Greek mythology falls into the sea when the wax of his artificial wings melts as he flies too near the sun

Ig·na·tius \ig-'nā-sh(ē-)əs\ Saint 1491–1556 *Ignatius of Loyola* Span. priest; founder of Society of Jesus (Jesuits)

In·no·cent \'i-nə-sənt\ name of 13 popes: esp. **III** 1160/61–1216 (pope 1198–1216); **IV** *died* 1254 (pope 1243–54)

Ir·ving \'ər-viŋ\ Washington 1783–1859 Amer. author

Isaac \'ī-zik, -zək\ son of Abraham and father of Jacob in the Bible

Is·a·bel·la I \ˌi-zə-'be-lə\ 1451–1504 queen

of Castile (1474–1504) and of Aragon (1479–1504); wife of Ferdinand V

Isa·iah \ī-'zā-ə, *chiefly Brit* -'zī-\ Hebrew prophet of the 8th cent. B.C.

Ish·ma·el \'ish-(ˌ)mā-əl, -mē-\ outcast son of Abraham and Hagar in the Bible

Ives \'īvz\ Charles Edward 1874–1954 Amer. composer

Jack·son \'jak-sən\ Andrew 1767–1845 Amer. general; 7th pres. of the U.S. (1829–37)

Jackson Thomas Jonathan 1824–1863 *Stonewall Jackson* Amer. Confederate general

Ja·cob \'jā-kəb\ son of Isaac and Rebekah and younger twin brother of Esau in the Bible

James \'jāmz\ one of the 12 apostles in the Bible

James *the Less* one of the 12 apostles in the Bible

James name of 2 kings of Great Britain: **I** 1566–1625 (r. 1603–25); king of Scotland as *James VI* (r. 1567–1625); **II** 1633–1701 (r. 1685–88)

James Henry 1843–1916 Brit. (Amer.-born) author

Ja·nus \'jā-nəs\ god of gates and doors and of all beginnings in Roman mythology and that is pictured with two opposite faces

Ja·son \'jā-sᵊn\ hero in Greek mythology noted for his successful quest of the Golden Fleece

Jay \'jā\ John 1745–1829 Amer. jurist and statesman; 1st chief justice of the U.S. Supreme Court (1789–95)

Jef·fer·son \'je-fər-sən\ Thomas 1743–1826 3d pres. of the U.S. (1801–09)

Jer·e·mi·ah \ˌjer-ə-'mī-ə\ Hebrew prophet of the 7th–6th cent. B.C.

Je·sus \'jē-zəs, -zəz\ *or* **Jesus Christ** *ca* 6 B.C.–*ca* 30 A.D. source of the Christian religion and Savior in the Christian faith

Jez·e·bel \'je-zə-ˌbel\ queen of Israel and wife of Ahab who is noted for her wickedness in the Bible

Joan of Arc \ˌjōn-əv-'ärk\ Saint *ca* 1412–1431 *the Maid of Orléans* French national heroine

Job \'jōb\ man in the Bible who has many sufferings but keeps his faith

Jo·cas·ta \jō-'kas-tə\ queen of Thebes in Greek mythology who unknowingly marries her son Oedipus

John \'jän\ one of the 12 apostles believed to be the author of the 4th Gospel, three Epistles, and the Book of Revelation

John name of 21 popes: esp. **XXIII** 1881–1963 (pope 1958–63)

John 1167–1216 *John Lackland* king of England (1199–1216)

John Paul \'pól\ name of 2 popes: esp. **II** 1920–2005 (pope 1978–2005)

John·son \'jän(t)-sən\ Andrew 1808–1875 17th pres. of the U.S. (1865–69)

Johnson Lyndon Baines 1908–1973 36th pres. of the U.S. (1963–69)

Johnson Samuel 1709–1784 *Dr. Johnson* Eng. lexicographer and author

John the Baptist Saint, 1st cent. A.D. prophet and baptizer of Jesus in the Bible

Jol·liet *or* **Jo·liet** \zhȯl-ˈyā\ Louis 1645–1700 French-Canad. explorer

Jo·nah \ˈjō-nə\ Hebrew prophet who in the Bible spends three days in the belly of a great fish

Jones \ˈjōnz\ John Paul 1747–1792 Amer. (Scot.-born) naval officer

Jop·lin \ˈjä-plən\ Scott 1868–1917 Amer. pianist and composer

Jor·dan \ˈjȯr-dᵊn\ Michael 1963– Amer. basketball player

Jo·seph \ˈjō-zəf\ son of Jacob in the Bible who rises to high office in Egypt after being sold into slavery by his brothers

Joseph Chief *ca* 1840–1904 Nez Percé Indian chief

Joseph Saint, husband of Mary, the mother of Jesus, in the Bible

Josh·ua \ˈjä-sh(ə-)wə\ Hebrew leader in the Bible who succeeds Moses during the settlement of the Israelites in Canaan

Joyce \ˈjȯis\ James Augustine 1882–1941 Irish author

Juan Car·los \ˈ(h)wän-ˈkär-ˌlōs\ 1938– king of Spain (1975–)

Ju·dah \ˈjü-də\ son of Jacob and ancestor of one of the 12 tribes of Israel in the Bible

Ju·das \ˈjü-dəs\ *or* **Judas Is·car·i·ot** \-is-ˈka-rē-ət\ one of the 12 apostles and the betrayer of Jesus in the Bible

Jung \ˈyu̇ŋ\ Carl Gustav 1875–1961 Swiss psychologist

Ju·no \ˈjü-(ˌ)nō\ queen of heaven, wife of Jupiter, and goddess of light, birth, women, and marriage in Roman mythology — compare HERA

Ju·pi·ter \ˈjü-pə-tər\ chief god and god of light, of the sky and weather, and of the state in Roman mythology — compare ZEUS

Kalb \ˈkälp, ˈkalb\ Johann 1721–1780 Baron *de Kalb* \di-ˈkalb\ Ger. general in Amer. Revolutionary army

Ka·me·ha·me·ha \kə-ˌmā-ə-ˈmā-(ˌ)hä\ 1758?–1819 orig. *Paiea* Hawaiian king (1795–1819)

Keats \ˈkēts\ John 1795–1821 Eng. poet

Kel·ler \ˈke-lər\ Helen Adams 1880–1968 Amer. deaf and blind lecturer and author

Kel·vin \ˈkel-vən\ 1st Baron 1824–1907 *William Thomson* Brit. mathematician and physicist

Ken·ne·dy \ˈke-nə-dē\ John Fitzgerald 1917–1963 35th pres. of the U.S. (1961–63)

Kennedy Robert Francis 1925–1968 attorney general of the U.S. (1961–64); brother of the preceding

Ke·o·kuk \ˈkē-ə-ˌkək\ 1780?–1848 Amer. Indian chief

Key \ˈkē\ Francis Scott 1779–1843 Amer. lawyer; author of "The Star-Spangled Banner"

Khayyám Omar — see OMAR KHAYYÁM

Khru·shchev \krùsh-ˈchȯf, -ˈchȯv\ Nikita Sergeyevich 1894–1971 premier of U.S.S.R. (1958–64)

Khu·fu \ˈkü-(ˌ)fü\ *or Greek* **Che·ops** \ˈkē-ˌäps\ *fl.* 25th cent. B.C. king of Egypt and pyramid builder

Kidd \ˈkid\ William *ca* 1645–1701 *Captain Kidd* Scot. pirate

Kier·ke·gaard \ˈkir-kə-ˌgär(d), -ˌgȯr\ Søren 1813–1855 Danish philosopher

King \ˈkiŋ\ Billie Jean 1943– Amer. tennis player

King Martin Luther, Jr. 1929–1968 Amer. minister and civil rights leader; Nobel Prize winner (1964)

Kip·ling \ˈkip-liŋ\ Rudyard 1865–1936 Eng. author; Nobel Prize winner (1907)

Kis·sin·ger \ˈki-sᵊn-jər\ Henry Alfred 1923– Amer. (Ger.-born) government official; U.S. secretary of state (1973–77); Nobel Prize winner (1973)

Knox \ˈnäks\ John *ca* 1514–1572 Scot. religious reformer

Koch \ˈkȯk, ˈkȯḵ, ˈkōk, ˈkōḵ\ Robert 1843–1910 Ger. bacteriologist; Nobel Prize winner (1905)

Koś·ciusz·ko \ˌkȯsh-ˈchùsh-(ˌ)kō, ˌkä-sē-ˈəs-ˌkō\ Tadeusz 1746–1817 Polish patriot and general in Amer. Revolutionary army

Krish·na \ˈkrish-nə, ˈkrēsh-\ god worshipped in later Hinduism

Ku·blai Khan \ˈkü-ˌblə-ˈkän, -ˌblī-\ 1215–1294 Mongol leader; grandson of Genghis Khan

La·fa·yette \ˌlä-fē-ˈet, ˌla-\ Marquis de 1757–1834 French general in Amer. Revolutionary army

La·ius \ˈlā-əs, ˈlī-əs\ king of Thebes who in Greek mythology is killed by his son Oedipus

Lan·ce·lot \ˈlan(t)-sə-ˌlät, ˈlän(t)-, -s(ə-)lət\ legendary knight of the Round Table and lover of Queen Guinevere

Lange \ˈlaŋ\ Dorothea 1895–1965 Amer. photographer

Lao—tzu \ˈlau̇d-ˈzə\ *fl.* 6th cent. B.C. Chinese philosopher

La Salle \lə-ˈsal\ Sieur de 1643–1687 *René-Robert Cavelier* French explorer

La·voi·sier \ləv-ˈwä-zē-ˌā\ Antoine-Laurent 1743–1794 French chemist

Law·rence \ˈlȯr-ən(t)s, ˈlär-\ D. H. 1885–1930 *David Herbert Lawrence* Eng. author

Lawrence Thomas Edward 1888–1935 *Lawrence of Arabia* Brit. soldier and author

Laz·a·rus \ˈlaz-rəs, ˈla-zə-\ brother of Mary and Martha who in the Bible is raised by Jesus from the dead

Lazarus beggar in the biblical parable of the rich man and the beggar

Le·da \\'lē-də\ Spartan princess in Greek mythology who is courted by Zeus in the form of a swan

Lee \\'lē\ Ann 1736–1784 Eng. mystic; founder of Shaker society in the U.S.

Lee Henry 1756–1818 *Light-Horse Harry* Amer. general

Lee Robert Edward 1807–1870 Amer. Confederate general; son of the preceding

Leeu·wen·hoek \\'lā-vən-ˌhùk\ Antonie van 1632–1723 Dutch naturalist

Leif Er·iks·son *or* **Er·ics·son** \ˌlāv-'er-ik-sən, ˌlēf-\ *fl.* 1000 Norwegian explorer; son of Erik the Red

Le·nin \\'le-nən\ 1870–1924 orig. *Vladimir Ilyich Ul·ya·nov* \ül-'yän-əf, -ˌòf, -ˌòv\ Russ. Communist leader

Leo \\'lē-(ˌ)ō\ name of 13 popes: esp. **I** Saint *died* 461 A.D. *Leo the Great* (pope 440–61); **III** Saint *died* 816 (pope 795–816); **XIII** 1810–1903 (pope 1878–1903)

Le·o·nar·do da Vin·ci \ˌlē-ə-'när-(ˌ)dō-də-'vin-chē, ˌlā-, -'vēn-\ 1452–1519 Ital. painter, sculptor, architect, and engineer

Lew·is \\'lü-əs\ C. S. 1898–1963 *Clive Staples Lewis* Brit. author

Lewis John Llewellyn 1880–1969 Amer. labor leader

Lewis Meriwether 1774–1809 Amer. explorer (with William Clark)

Lewis Sinclair 1885–1951 Amer. author; Nobel Prize winner (1930)

Lin·coln \\'liŋ-kən\ Abraham 1809–1865 16th pres. of the U.S. (1861–65)

Lind·bergh \\'lin(d)-ˌbərg\ Charles Augustus 1902–1974 Amer. aviator

Lin·nae·us \lə-'nē-əs, -'nā-\ Carolus 1707–1778 *Carl von Linné* Swedish botanist

Lis·ter \\'lis-tər\ Joseph 1827–1912 Eng. surgeon and medical scientist

Liszt \\'list\ Franz 1811–1886 Hungarian pianist and composer

Liv·ing·stone \\'li-viŋ-stən\ David 1813–1873 Scot. missionary in Africa

Lon·don \\'lən-dən\ Jack 1876–1916 *John Griffith London* Amer. author

Long·fel·low \\'lòŋ-ˌfe-(ˌ)lō\ Henry Wadsworth 1807–1882 Amer. poet

Lou·is \\'lü-ē, lü-'ē\ name of 18 kings of France: esp. **IX** Saint 1214–1270 (r. 1226–70); **XI** 1423–1483 (r. 1461–83); **XII** 1462–1515 (r. 1498–1515); **XIII** 1601–1643 (r. 1610–43); **XIV** 1638–1715 (r. 1643–1715); **XV** 1710–1774 (r. 1715–74); **XVI** 1754–1793 (r. 1774–92; guillotined); **XVII** 1785–1795 (r. in name 1793–95); **XVIII** 1755–1824 (r. 1814–15; 1815–24)

Lou·is \\'lü-əs\ Joe 1914–1981 orig. *Joseph Louis Barrow* Amer. boxer

Low \\'lō\ Juliette 1860–1927 née *Gordon* Amer. founder of the Girl Scouts

Low·ell \\'lō-əl\ Amy 1874–1925 Amer. poet

Lowell James Russell 1819–1891 Amer. author

Luke \\'lük\ physician and companion of the apostle Paul believed to be the author of the 3d Gospel and the Book of Acts

Lu·ther \\'lü-thər\ Martin 1483–1546 Ger. Reformation leader

Ly·on \\'lī-ən\ Mary 1797–1849 Amer. educator

Mac·Ar·thur \mə-'kär-thər\ Douglas 1880–1964 Amer. general

Ma·cy \\'mā-sē\ Anne Sullivan 1866–1936 née *Sullivan* Amer. educator; teacher of Helen Keller

Mad·i·son \\'ma-də-sən\ James 1751–1836 4th pres. of the U.S. (1809–17)

Ma·gel·lan \mə-'je-lən, *chiefly Brit* -'ge-\ Ferdinand *ca* 1480–1521 Portuguese navigator and explorer

Mal·colm X \\'mal-kəm-'eks\ *Malcolm Little* 1925–1965 Amer. civil rights leader

Man·dela \man-'de-lə\ Nelson Rolihlahla 1918– pres. of South Africa (1994–99); Nobel Prize winner (1993)

Ma·net \ma-'nā, mä-\ Édouard 1832–1883 French painter

Mann \\'man\ Horace 1796–1859 Amer. educator

Mao Tse–tung *or* **Mao Zedong** \\'maù-(ˈ)(d)zə-'dùŋ, -(ˈ)tsə-\ 1893–1976 leader of People's Republic of China (1949–76)

Mar·co·ni \mär-'kō-nē\ Guglielmo 1874–1937 Ital. physicist and inventor; Nobel Prize winner (1909)

Marco Polo — see POLO

Ma·rie An·toi·nette \ˌan-twə-'net, -tə-\ 1755–1793 wife of Louis XVI of France

Mar·i·on \\'mer-ē-ən\ Francis 1732?–1795 *the Swamp Fox* Amer. commander in Revolution

Mark \\'märk\ evangelist believed to be the author of the 2d Gospel

Mark Antony — see ANTONY

Mar·quette \mär-'ket\ Jacques 1637–1675 *Père Marquette* French-born Jesuit missionary and explorer in America

Mars \\'märz\ god of war in Roman mythology — compare ARES

Mar·shall \\'mär-shəl\ George Catlett 1880–1959 Amer. general and diplomat; Nobel Prize winner (1953)

Marshall John 1755–1835 Amer. jurist; chief justice of the U.S. Supreme Court (1801–35)

Mar·tha \\'mär-thə\ sister of Lazarus and Mary and friend of Jesus in the Bible

Mar·tin \\'mär-tᵊn, mär-'taⁿ\ Saint 316–397 *Martin of Tours* \-'tùr\ patron saint of France

Martin \\'mär-tᵊn\ Paul (Edgar Phillipe) 1938– Canad. prime minister (2003–06)

Marx \\'märks\ Karl 1818–1883 Ger. political philosopher and socialist

Mary \'mer-ē, 'ma-rē, 'mā-rē\ *Saint Mary; Virgin Mary* mother of Jesus

Mary sister of Lazarus and Martha in the Bible

Mary I 1516–1558 *Mary Tudor; Bloody Mary* queen of England (1553–58)

Mary II 1662–1694 joint Brit. sovereign with William III (1689–94)

Mary Mag·da·lene \'mag-də-lən, -,lēn\ woman in the Bible who sees the risen Christ

Mary, Queen of Scots 1542–1587 *Mary Stuart* queen of Scotland (1542–67)

Mas·sa·soit \,ma-sə-'sòit\ *died* 1661 Amer. Indian chief

Math·er \'ma-thər, -thər\ Cotton 1663–1728 Amer. religious leader and author

Mather Increase 1639–1723 Amer. minister and author; father of Cotton Mather

Ma·tisse \ma-'tēs, mə-\ Henri 1869–1954 French painter

Mat·thew \'ma-(,)thyü\ apostle believed to be the author of the 1st Gospel

Mau·pas·sant \,mō-pə-'sä\ Guy de 1850–1893 French author

Mays \'māz\ Willie Howard 1931– Amer. baseball player

Mc·Au·liffe \mə-'kòl-əf\ Christa 1948–1986 Amer. teacher; 1st private citizen in space (1986)

Mc·Car·thy \mə-'kär-thē\ Joseph Raymond 1908–1957 Amer. politician

Mc·Clel·lan \mə-'kle-lən\ George Brinton 1826–1885 Amer. general

Mc·Clin·tock \mə-'klin-tək\ Barbara 1902–1992 Amer. botanist; Nobel Prize winner (1983)

Mc·Cor·mick \mə-'kòr-mik\ Cyrus Hall 1809–1884 Amer. inventor

Mc·Kin·ley \mə-'kin-lē\ William 1843–1901 25th pres. of the U.S. (1897–1901)

Mead \'mēd\ Margaret 1901–1978 Amer. anthropologist

Meade \'mēd\ George Gordon 1815–1872 Amer. Civil War general

Mea·ny \'mē-nē\ George 1894–1980 Amer. labor leader

Me·dea \mə-'dē-ə\ woman with magic powers in Greek mythology who helps Jason to win the Golden Fleece and who kills her children when he leaves her

Medici Catherine de' — see CATHERINE DE MÉDICIS

Me·di·ci \'me-də-chē\ Lorenzo de' 1449–1492 *Lorenzo the Magnificent* Florentine statesman, ruler, and patron of the arts

Me·du·sa \mi-'dü-sə, -'dyü-, -zə\ Gorgon in Greek mythology slain by Perseus

Me·ir \mā-'ir\ Golda 1898–1978 prime minister of Israel (1969–74)

Mel·ville \'mel-,vil\ Herman 1819–1891 Amer. author

Men·del \'men-dəl\ Gregor Johann 1822–1884 Austrian botanist

Men·dels·sohn (–Bar·thol·dy) \'men-dəl-sən(-bär-'tòl-dē, -'thòl-)\ Felix 1809–1847 Ger. composer

Men·e·la·us \,me-nə-'lā-əs\ king of Sparta, brother of Agamemnon, and husband of Helen of Troy in Greek mythology

Meph·is·toph·e·les \,me-fə-'stä-fə-,lēz\ chief devil in the Faust legend

Mer·ca·tor \(,)mər-'kā-tər\ Gerardus 1512–1594 orig. *Gerhard Kremer* Flemish cartographer

Mer·cu·ry \'mər-kyə-rē, -k(ə-)rē\ god of commerce, eloquence, travel, and theft who serves as messenger of the other gods in Roman mythology — compare HERMES

Mer·lin \'mər-lən\ prophet and magician in the legend of King Arthur

Met·a·com \'me-tə-,käm\ *or* **King Philip** *ca* 1638–1676 *Met·a·com·et* \,me-tə-'käm-ət\ Amer. Indian chief; son of Massasoit

Mi·chael \'mī-kəl\ archangel named in Hebrew tradition — compare GABRIEL; RAPHAEL; URIEL

Mi·chel·an·ge·lo \,mī-kə-'lan-jə-,lō, ,mi-, ,mē-kə-'län-\ 1475–1564 Ital. sculptor, painter, architect, and poet

Mi·das \'mī-dəs\ legendary king having the power to turn everything he touched into gold

Mil·lay \mi-'lā\ Edna St. Vincent 1892–1950 Amer. poet

Mil·ler \'mi-lər\ Arthur 1915–2005 Amer. playwright

Milne \'mil(n)\ A. A. 1882–1956 *Alan Alexander Milne* Eng. author

Mil·ton \'mil-t°n\ John 1608–1674 Eng. poet

Mi·ner·va \mə-'nər-və\ goddess of wisdom in Roman mythology — compare ATHENA

Mi·no·taur \'mi-nə-,tòr, 'mī-\ monster in Greek mythology shaped half like a man and half like a bull

Min·u·it \'min-yə-wət\ Peter *ca* 1580–1638 Dutch colonial administrator in America

Mitch·ell \'mi-chəl\ Maria 1818–1889 Amer. astronomer

Mo·lière \mōl-'yer, 'mōl-,\ 1622–1673 orig. *Jean-Baptiste Poquelin* French actor and playwright

Mo·net \mō-'nā\ Claude 1840–1926 French painter

Mon·roe \mən-'rō\ James 1758–1831 5th pres. of the U.S. (1817–25)

Mont·calm \mänt-'kälm-, -'käm-\ Marquis de 1712–1759 *Louis-Joseph de Montcalm-Grozon* French field marshal in Canada

Mon·tes·so·ri \,män-tə-'sòr-ē\ Maria 1870–1952 Ital. educator

Mon·te·zu·ma II \,män-tə-'zü-mə\ 1466–1520 last Aztec emperor of Mexico (1502–20)

Moore \'mòr, 'mùr\ Marianne 1887–1972 Amer. poet

More \'mòr\ Sir Thomas 1478–1535 *Saint*

Thomas More Eng. public official and author

Mor·gan \'mȯr-gən\ J. P. 1837–1913 *John Pierpont Morgan* Amer. financier

Mor·ri·son \'mȯr-ə-sən, 'mär-\ Toni 1931–   orig. *Chloe Anthony Wofford* Amer. author; Nobel Prize winner (1993)

Morse \'mȯrs\ Samuel Finley Breese 1791–1872 Amer. artist and inventor

Mo·ses \'mō-zəz\ Hebrew prophet and lawgiver in the Bible

Moses Grandma 1860–1961 *Anna Mary Moses* née *Robertson* Amer. painter

Mott \'mät\ Lucretia 1793–1880 Amer. reformer

Mo·zart \'mōt-ˌsärt\ Wolfgang Amadeus 1756–1791 Austrian composer

Mu·ham·mad \mō-'ha-məd, -'hä-\ *ca* 570–632 A.D. Arab prophet and founder of Islam

Mus·so·li·ni \ˌmü-sə-'lē-nē, ˌmü-\ Be·ni·to \bə-'nēt-ō\ 1883–1945 *Il Du·ce* \ēl-'dü-chā\ Ital. fascist premier (1922–43)

Na·bo·kov \nə-'bȯ-kəf\ Vladimir 1899–1977 Amer. (Russ.-born) author

Na·po·leon I \nə-'pōl-yən, -'pō-lē-ən\ *or* Napoleon Bo·na·parte \'bō-nə-ˌpärt\ 1769–1821 French general and emperor of the French (1804–15)

Nar·cis·sus \när-'si-səs\ beautiful youth in Greek mythology who pines away for love of his own reflection and is then turned into the narcissus flower

Nash \'nash\ Ogden 1902–1971 Amer. poet

Na·tion \'nā-shən\ Car·ry \'kar-ē\ Amelia 1846–1911 née *Moore* Amer. temperance agitator

Nav·ra·ti·lo·va \ˌnav-rə-tə-'lō-və\ Martina 1956–   Amer. (Czech-born) tennis player

Neb·u·cha·drez·zar II \ˌne-byə-kə-'dre-zər, -bə-\ *or* Neb·u·chad·nez·zar \-kəd-'ne-\ *ca* 630–*ca* 561 B.C. Chaldean king of Babylon (605–562)

Neh·ru \'ner-(ˌ)ü, 'nā-(ˌ)rü\ Ja·wa·har·lal \jə-'wä-hər-ˌläl\ 1889–1964 1st prime minister of Republic of India (1947–64)

Nel·son \'nel-sən\ Horatio 1758–1805 Viscount *Nelson* Brit. admiral

Nem·e·sis \'ne-mə-səs\ goddess of reward and punishment in Greek mythology

Nep·tune \'nep-ˌtün, -ˌtyün\ god of the sea in Roman mythology — compare PO-SEIDON

Ne·ro \'nē-(ˌ)rō, 'nir-(ˌ)ō\ 37–68 A.D. Roman emperor (54–68)

Nev·el·son \'ne-vəl-sən\ Louise 1900?–1988 Amer. sculptor

New·ton \'nütᵊn, 'nyü-\ Sir Isaac 1642–1727 Eng. mathematician and physicist

Nich·o·las \'ni-k(ə-)ləs\ Saint *fl.* 4th cent. A.D. Christian bishop

Nicholas I 1796–1855 czar of Russia (1825–55)

Nicholas II 1868–1918 last czar of Russia (1894–1917)

Nietz·sche \'nē-chə, -chē\ Friedrich Wilhelm 1844–1900 Ger. philosopher

Night·in·gale \'nī-tᵊn-ˌgāl, -tiŋ-\ Florence 1820–1910 *Lady of the Lamp* Eng. nurse and philanthropist

Ni·ke \'nī-kē\ goddess of victory in Greek mythology

Ni·o·be \'nī-ə-bē\ bereaved mother in Greek mythology who while weeping for her slain children is turned into a stone from which her tears continue to flow

Nix·on \'nik-sən\ Richard Milhous 1913–1994 37th pres. of the U.S. (1969–74)

No·ah \'nō-ə\ biblical builder of the ark in which he, his family, and living creatures of every kind survive the biblical Flood

No·bel \nō-'bel\ Alfred Bernhard 1833–1896 Swedish manufacturer, inventor, and philanthropist

Oak·ley \'ōk-lē\ Annie 1860–1926 orig. *Phoebe Anne Oakley Moses* Amer. sharpshooter

Oba·ma \ō-'bä-mə\ Ba·rack \bə-'räk\ Hussein, Jr. 1961–   44th pres. of the U.S. (2009–   )

Oce·a·nus \ō-'sē-ə-nəs\ Titan who rules over a great river encircling the earth in Greek mythology

O'·Con·nor \ō-'kä-nər\ (Mary) Flannery 1925–1964 Amer. author

O'Connor Sandra Day 1930–   Amer. jurist

Odin \'ō-dᵊn\ *or* Wo·den \'wō-dᵊn\ chief god, god of war, and patron of heroes in Norse mythology

Odys·seus \ō-'di-sē-əs, -'dis-yəs, -'di-shəs, -'di-ˌshüs\ *or* Ulys·ses \yù-'li-(ˌ)sēz\ king of Ithaca and hero in Greek mythology

Oe·di·pus \'e-də-pəs, 'ē-\ son of Laius and Jocasta who in Greek mythology kills his father and marries his mother not knowing their identity

Ogle·thorpe \'ō-gəl-ˌthȯrp\ James Edward 1696–1785 Eng. general and founder of Georgia

O'·Keeffe \ō-'kēf\ Georgia 1887–1986 Amer. painter

Olaf V \'ō-ləf, -läf, -laf; 'ü-läf\ 1903–1991 king of Norway (1957–91)

Omar Khay·yám \ˌō-ˌmär-ˌkī-'yäm, ˌō-mər-, -'yam\ 1048–1131 Persian poet and astronomer

O'·Neill \ō-'nēl\ Eugene Gladstone 1888–1953 Amer. playwright; Nobel Prize winner (1936)

Or·pheus \'ȯr-ˌfyüs, -fē-əs\ poet and musician in Greek mythology

Or·well \'ȯr-ˌwel, -wəl\ George 1903–1950 pseud. of *Eric Arthur Blair* Eng. author

Osce·o·la \ˌä-sē-'ō-lə, ˌō-\ *ca* 1804–1838 Seminole Indian chief

Otis \'ō-təs\ James 1725–1783 Amer. Revolutionary patriot

Ov·id \\'ä-vəd\\ 43 B.C.–17A.D.? Roman poet

Ow·en \\'ō-ən\\ Robert 1771–1858 Welsh social reformer

Ow·ens \\'ō-ənz\\ Jesse 1913–1980 orig. *James Cleveland Owens* Amer. track-and-field athlete

Paine \\'pān\\ Thomas 1737–1809 Amer. (Eng.-born) political philosopher and author

Pan \\'pan\\ god of pastures, flocks, and shepherds in Greek mythology who is usu. represented as having the legs, ears, and horns of a goat

Pan·do·ra \\pan-'dȯr-ə\\ woman in Greek mythology who out of curiosity opens a box and lets loose all of the evils that trouble humans

Pank·hurst \\'paŋk-ˌhərst\\ Emmeline 1858–1928 née *Goulden* Eng. suffragist

Par·is \\'pa-rəs\\ son of Priam whose abduction of Helen of Troy in Greek mythology leads to the Trojan War

Park·man \\'pärk-mən\\ Francis 1823–1893 Amer. historian

Parks \\'pärks\\ Rosa 1913–2005 née *McCauley* Amer. civil rights activist

Pas·cal \\pa-'skal, päs-'käl\\ Blaise 1623–1662 French mathematician and philosopher

Pas·ter·nak \\'pas-tər-ˌnak\\ Boris Leonidovich 1890–1960 Russ. author; Nobel Prize winner (1958)

Pas·teur \\pas-'tər\\ Louis 1822–1895 French chemist and microbiologist

Pat·rick \\'pa-trik\\ Saint *fl.* 5th cent. A.D. apostle and patron saint of Ireland

Pat·ton \\'pa-tᵊn\\ George Smith 1885–1945 Amer. general

Paul \\'pȯl\\ Saint *died ca* 67 A.D. Christian missionary and author of several New Testament epistles

Paul name of 6 popes: esp. **III** 1468–1549 (pope 1534–49); **V** 1552–1621 (pope 1605–21); **VI** 1897–1978 (pope 1963–78)

Paul Bun·yan \\'bən-yən\\ giant lumberjack in Amer. folklore

Pau·ling \\'pȯ-liŋ\\ Linus Carl 1901–1994 Amer. chemist; Nobel Prize winner (1954, 1962)

Pav·lov \\'päv-ˌlȯf, 'pav-, -ˌlȯv\\ Ivan Petrovich 1849–1936 Russ. physiologist; Nobel Prize winner (1904)

Pa·vlo·va \\'pav-lə-və, pav-'lō-\\ Anna 1881–1931 Russ. ballerina

Pea·ry \\'pir-ē\\ Robert Edwin 1856–1920 Amer. arctic explorer

Pe·cos Bill \\ˌpā-kəs-'bil\\ cowboy in Amer. folklore known for his extraordinary feats

Peg·a·sus \\'pe-gə-səs\\ winged horse in Greek mythology

Penn \\'pen\\ William 1644–1718 Eng. Quaker leader and founder of Pennsylvania

Per·i·cles \\'per-ə-ˌklēz\\ *ca* 495–429 B.C. Athenian political leader

Per·ry \\'per-ē\\ Matthew Calbraith 1794–1858 Amer. commodore

Perry Oliver Hazard 1785–1819 Amer. naval officer; brother of the preceding

Per·seph·o·ne \\pər-'se-fə-nē\\ daughter of Zeus and Demeter who in Greek mythology is abducted by Pluto to rule with him over the underworld

Per·shing \\'pər-shiŋ, -zhiŋ\\ John Joseph 1860–1948 Amer. general

Pe·ter \\'pē-tər\\ Saint *died ca* 64 A.D. orig. *Si·mon* \\'sī-mən-\\ one of the 12 apostles in the Bible

Peter I 1672–1725 *Peter the Great* czar of Russia (1682–1725)

Phil·ip \\'fi-ləp\\ Saint, one of the 12 apostles in the Bible

Philip King — see METACOM

Philip name of 6 kings of France: esp. **II** *or* **Philip Augustus** 1165–1223 (r. 1179–1223); **IV** 1268–1314 *Philip the Fair* (r. 1285–1314); **VI** 1293–1350 (r. 1328–50)

Philip name of 5 kings of Spain: esp. **II** 1527–1598 (r. 1556–98); **V** 1683–1746 (r. 1700–46)

Philip II 382–336 B.C. king of Macedon (359–336); father of Alexander the Great

Pi·cas·so \\pi-'kä-(ˌ)sō, -'ka-\\ Pablo 1881–1973 Span. painter and sculptor in France

Pic·card \\pi-'kär, -'kärd\\ Auguste 1884–1962 and his son Jacques 1922–2008 Swiss scientists and developers of the bathyscaphe

Pick·ett \\'pi-kət\\ George Edward 1825–1875 Amer. Confederate general

Pierce \\'pirs\\ Franklin 1804–1869 14th pres. of the U.S. (1853–57)

Pi·late \\'pī-lət\\ Pon·tius \\'pän-chəs, 'pən-chəs\\ *died after* 36 A.D. Roman governor of Judea (26–36)

Pinkerton \\'piŋ-kər-tᵊn\\ Allan 1819–1884 Amer. (Scot.-born) detective

Pis·sar·ro \\pə-'sär-(ˌ)ō\\ Camille 1830–1903 French (West Indian-born) painter

Pitt \\'pit\\ William 1759–1806 *the Younger Pitt* Eng. prime minister (1783–1801; 1804–6)

Pi·us \\'pī-əs\\ name of 12 popes: esp. **VII** 1742–1823 (pope 1800–23); **IX** 1792–1878 (pope 1846–78); **X** Saint 1835–1914 (pope 1903–14); **XI** 1857–1939 (pope 1922–39); **XII** 1876–1958 (pope 1939–58)

Pi·zar·ro \\pə-'zär-(ˌ)ō\\ Francisco *ca* 1475–1541 Span. conqueror of Peru

Pla·to \\'plā-(ˌ)tō\\ *ca* 428–348 (*or* 347) B.C. Greek philosopher

Plu·to \\'plü-(ˌ)tō\\ god of the underworld in Greek mythology

Po·ca·hon·tas \\ˌpō-kə-'hän-təs\\ *ca* 1595–1617 Amer. Indian friend of the colonists at Jamestown; daughter of Powhatan

Poe \\'pō\\ Edgar Allan 1809–1849 Amer. author

Polk \\'pōk\\ James Knox 1795–1849 11th pres. of the U.S. (1845–49)

Po·lo \'pō-(ˌ)lō\ Marco *ca* 1254–1324 Venetian merchant and traveler

Poly·phe·mus \ˌpä-lə-'fē-məs\ a one-eyed creature in Greek mythology that is blinded by Odysseus

Ponce de Le·ón \ˌpän(t)-sə-ˌdā-lē-'ōn, ˌpänts-də-, -'lē-ən\ Juan 1460–1521 Span. explorer

Pon·ti·ac \'pän-tē-ˌak\ *ca* 1720–1769 Ottawa Indian chief

Por·ter \'pòr-tər\ Cole Albert 1891–1964 Amer. composer

Porter Katherine Anne 1890–1980 Amer. author

Porter William Sydney — see O. HENRY

Po·sei·don \pə-'sī-dᵊn\ god of the sea in Greek mythology — compare NEPTUNE

Pot·ter \'pä-tər\ (Helen) Beatrix 1866–1943 Brit. author and illustrator

Pound \'paund\ Ezra Loomis 1885–1972 Amer. poet

Pound·mak·er \'paund-ˌmā-kər\ 1826–1886 Cree Indian chief

Pow·ell \'pau̇(-ə)l\ Colin Luther 1937– Amer. general; U.S. secretary of state (2001–05)

Pow·ha·tan \ˌpau̇-ə-'tan, pau̇-'ha-tᵊn\ 1550?–1618 Amer. Indian chief of a confederacy of Algonquian-speaking tribes; father of Pocahontas

Pres·ley \'pres-lē, 'prez-\ Elvis Aaron 1935–1977 Amer. popular singer

Pri·am \'prī-əm, -ˌam\ king of Troy during the Trojan War in Greek mythology

Price \'prīs\ (Mary) Leontyne 1927– Amer. soprano

Pro·me·theus \prə-'mē-thē-əs, -ˌthyüs\ Titan in Greek mythology who is punished by Zeus for stealing fire from heaven and giving it to humans

Pro·teus \'prō-tyüs, -tē-əs\ sea god in Greek mythology who is capable of assuming different forms

Ptol·e·my \'tä-lə-mē\ *fl.* 2d cent. A.D. Greco-Egyptian astronomer, geographer, and mathematician in Alexandria

Puc·ci·ni \pü-'chē-nē\ Giacomo 1858–1924 Ital. composer

Pu·las·ki \pə-'las-kē, pyü-\ Kazimierz 1747–1779 Polish soldier in Amer. Revolutionary army

Pu·lit·zer \'pu̇-lət-sər (*family's pron*), 'pyü-\ Joseph 1847–1911 Amer. (Hungarian-born) journalist

Pu·tin \'pü-tin\ Vladimir Vladimirovich 1952– pres. of Russia (2000–08)

Pyg·ma·lion \pig-'māl-yən, -'mā-lē-ən\ sculptor in Greek mythology who creates Galatea

Py·thag·o·ras \pə-'tha-gə-rəs, pī-\ *ca* 580–*ca* 500 B.C. Greek philosopher and mathematician

Ra \'rä\ god of the sun and chief deity of ancient Egypt

Ra·leigh *or* **Ra·legh** \'rò-lē, 'rä- *also* 'ra-\ Sir Walter 1554?–1618 Eng. navigator and writer

Ram·ses \'ram-ˌsēz\ *or* **Ram·e·ses** \'ra-mə-ˌsēz\ name of 12 kings of Egypt: esp. **II** (r. 1279–1213 B.C.,); **III** (r. 1187–1156 B.C.)

Ran·dolph \'ran-ˌdälf\ Asa Philip 1889–1979 Amer. labor and civil rights leader

Ra·pha·el \'ra-fē-əl, 'rä-, -ˌel\ archangel named in Hebrew tradition — compare GABRIEL; MICHAEL; URIEL

Ra·pha·el \'ra-fē-əl, 'rä-, 'rä-\ 1483–1520 orig. *Raffaello Sanzio or Santi* Ital. painter

Ras·pu·tin \ra-'spyü-tᵊn, -'spü-, -'spu̇-\ Grigory Yefimovich 1872–1916 Russ. mystic

Rea·gan \'rā-gən\ Ronald Wilson 1911–2004 40th pres. of the U.S. (1981–89)

Re·bek·ah \ri-'be-kə\ wife of Isaac and mother of Jacob in the Bible

Red Cloud \'red-ˌklau̇d\ 1822–1909 Sioux Indian chief

Red Jack·et \'red-ja-kət\ 1758?–1830 *Sago-ye-wa·tha* \sä-ˌgoi-(y)ə-'wä-thə\ Seneca Indian chief

Reed \'rēd\ Walter 1851–1902 Amer. army surgeon

Rem·brandt \'rem-ˌbrant *also* -ˌbränt\ 1606–1669 *Rembrandt (Harmenszoon) van Rijn* Dutch painter

Rem·ing·ton \'re-miŋ-tən\ Frederic 1861–1909 Amer. painter and sculptor

Re·mus \'rē-məs\ son of Mars who in Roman mythology is killed by his twin brother Romulus

Re·noir \'ren-ˌwär, rən-'\ (Pierre-) Auguste 1841–1919 French painter

Re·vere \ri-'vir\ Paul 1735–1818 Amer. patriot and silversmith

Rich·ard \'ri-chərd\ name of 3 kings of England: **I** 1157–1199 *Richard the Lion-Hearted* (r. 1189–99); **II** 1367–1400 (r. 1377–99); **III** 1452–1485 (r. 1483–85)

Ride \'rīd\ Sally Kristen 1951– Amer. astronaut; 1st Amer. woman in space (1983)

Rob·in Good·fel·low \'rä-bən-'gu̇d-ˌfe-(ˌ)lō\ mischievous elf in Eng. folklore

Robin Hood \ˌhu̇d\ legendary Eng. outlaw who gave to the poor what he stole from the rich

Rob·in·son \'rä-bən-sən\ Edwin Arlington 1869–1935 Amer. poet

Robinson Jackie 1919–1972 *Jack Roosevelt Robinson* Amer. baseball player

Rob·in·son Cru·soe \'rä-bə(n)-sən-'krü-(ˌ)sō\ shipwrecked sailor in Daniel Defoe's *Robinson Crusoe* who lives for many years on a desert island

Ro·cham·beau \ˌrō-ˌsham-'bō\ Comte de 1725–1807 French general in Amer. Revolution

Rocke·fel·ler \'rä-ki-ˌfe-lər\ John Davison 1839–1937 and his son John Davison, Jr. 1874–1960 Amer. oil magnates and philanthropists

Ro·ma·nov \rō-'mä-nəf, 'rō-mə-ˌnäf\ Michael 1596–1645 1st czar (1613–45) of Russ. Romanov dynasty (1613–1917)

Rom·u·lus \'räm-yə-ləs\ son of Mars in Roman mythology who is the twin brother of Remus and the founder of Rome

Rönt·gen or **Roent·gen** \'rent-gən, 'rənt-, -jən\ Wilhelm Conrad 1845–1923 Ger. physicist; Nobel Prize winner (1901)

Roo·se·velt \'rō-zə-vəlt, -ˌvelt\ (Anna) Eleanor 1884–1962 Amer. lecturer and writer; wife of F. D. Roosevelt

Roosevelt Franklin Delano 1882–1945 32nd pres. of the U.S. (1933–45)

Roosevelt Theodore 1858–1919 26th pres. of the U.S. (1901–09); Nobel Prize winner (1906)

Ross \'ròs\ Betsy 1752–1836 née *Griscom* reputed maker of 1st Amer. flag

Ros·si·ni \rò-'sē-nē, rə-\ Gioacchino Antonio 1792–1868 Ital. composer

Row·ling \'rō-liŋ\ J. K. 1965– *Joanne Kathleen Rowling* Brit. author

Ru·bens \'rü-bənz\ Peter Paul 1577–1640 Flemish painter

Ru·dolph \'rü-ˌdòlf, -ˌdälf\ Wilma Glodean 1940–1994 Amer. athlete

Rus·sell \'rə-səl\ Bertrand Arthur William 1872–1970 3d Earl *Russell* Eng. mathematician and philosopher; Nobel Prize winner (1950)

Ruth \'rüth\ woman in the Bible who was one of the ancestors of King David

Ruth Babe 1895–1948 *George Herman Ruth* Amer. baseball player

Ruth·er·ford \'rə-thə(r)-fərd, -thə(r)-\ Ernest 1871–1937 Baron *Rutherford* Brit. physicist; Nobel Prize winner (1908)

Sa·bin \'sā-bin\ Albert Bruce 1906–1993 Amer. (Polish-born) physician and microbiologist

Sac·a·ga·wea \ˌsa-kə-jə-'wē-ə\ 1786?–1812 Shoshone Indian guide to Lewis and Clark

Sa·dat \sə-'dat, -'dät\ Anwar el- 1918–1981 pres. of Egypt (1970–81); Nobel Prize winner (1978)

Sa·gan \'sā-gən\ Carl Edward 1934–1996 Amer. astronomer and science writer

Saint Nicholas — see Saint NICHOLAS; SANTA CLAUS

Sal·in·ger \'sa-lən-jər\ J. D. 1919– *Jerome David Salinger* Amer. author

Salk \'sò(l)k\ Jonas Edward 1914–1995 Amer. physician and medical researcher

Sa·lo·me \sə-'lō-mē, 'sa-lə-ˌ)mä\ niece of Herod Antipas who in the Bible is given the head of John the Baptist as a reward for her dancing

Sa·mo·set \'sa-mə-ˌset, sə-'mä-sət\ *died ca* 1653 Amer. Indian leader

Sam·son \'sam(p)-sən\ powerful Hebrew hero in the Bible who fights against the Philistines but is betrayed by Delilah

Sam·u·el \'sam-yə-wəl, -yəl\ Hebrew judge in the Bible who appoints Saul and then David king

Sand·burg \'san(d)-ˌbərg\ Carl 1878–1967 Amer. author

Sang·er \'saŋ-ər\ Margaret 1883–1966 née *Higgins* Amer. birth-control activist

San·ta Claus \'san-tə-ˌklòz\ plump white-bearded and red-suited old man in modern folklore who delivers presents to good children at Christmastime

Sap·pho \'sa-(ˌ)fō\ *fl. ca* 610–*ca* 580 B.C. Greek poet

Sa·rah \'ser-ə, 'sä-rə\ wife of Abraham and mother of Isaac in the Bible

Sar·gent \'sär-jənt\ John Singer 1856–1925 Amer. painter

Sar·tre \'särtrᵊ\ Jean-Paul 1905–1980 French philosopher and author

Sat·urn \'sa-tərn\ god of agriculture in Roman mythology

Saul \'sòl, 'säl\ 1st king of Israel in the Bible

Saul or **Saul of Tarsus** the apostle Paul in the Bible

Sche·her·a·zade \shə-ˌher-ə-'zäd\ fictional wife of a sultan and narrator of the tales in the *Arabian Nights' Entertainments*

Schin·dler \'shind-lər\ Oskar 1908–1974 Ger. humanitarian during the Holocaust

Schu·bert \'shü-bərt, -ˌbert\ Franz Peter 1797–1828 Austrian composer

Schu·mann \'shü-ˌmän, -mən\ Clara 1819–1896 née *Wieck* \'vēk\ Ger. pianist; wife of R. Schumann

Schumann Robert Alexander 1810–1856 Ger. composer

Schweit·zer \'shwīt-sər, 'shvīt-, 'swīt-\ Albert 1875–1965 French theologian, philosopher, physician, and music scholar; Nobel Prize winner (1952)

Scott \'skät\ Dred \'dred\ 1795?–1858 Amer. slave

Scott Robert Falcon 1868–1912 Brit. polar explorer

Scott Sir Walter 1771–1832 Scot. author

Scott Winfield 1786–1866 Amer. general

Scyl·la \'si-lə\ nymph in Greek mythology who is changed into a monster and inhabits a cave opposite the whirlpool Charybdis off the coast of Sicily

Se·at·tle \sē-'a-tᵊl\ 1786?–1866 Amer. Indian chief

Se·le·ne \sə-'lē-nē\ goddess of the moon in classical mythology

Se·quoy·ah or **Se·quoia** \si-'kwòi-ə\ *ca* 1760–1843 *George Guess* Cherokee Indian scholar

Ser·ra \'ser-ə\ Junípero 1713–1784 Span. missionary in Mexico and California

Se·ton \'se-tᵊn\ Saint Elizabeth Ann 1774–1821 *Mother Seton* née *Bayley* Amer. religious leader

Seu·rat \sə-'rä\ Georges 1859–1891 French painter

Sew·ard \'sü-ərd, 'sùrd\ William Henry

1801–1872 Amer. politician; U.S. secretary of state (1861–69)

Shack·le·ton \'sha-kəl-tən\ Sir Ernest Henry 1874–1922 Brit. polar explorer

Shake·speare \'shāk-ˌspir\ William 1564–1616 Eng. playwright and poet

Shaw \'shȯ\ George Bernard 1856–1950 Brit. playwright; Nobel Prize winner (1925)

Shaw Robert Gould 1837–1863 Amer. soldier

Shel·ley \'she-lē\ Mary Wollstonecraft 1797–1851 née *Godwin* Eng. author; wife of P. B. Shelley

Shelley Percy Bysshe \'bish\ 1792–1822 Eng. poet

Shep·ard \'she-pərd\ Alan Bartlett, Jr. 1923–1998 Amer. astronaut; 1st Amer. in space (1961)

Sher·i·dan \'sher-ə-dən\ Philip Henry 1831–1888 Amer. general

Sher·lock Holmes \'shər-ˌläk-'hōmz, -'hōlmz\ detective in stories by Sir Arthur Conan Doyle

Sher·man \'shər-mən\ John 1823–1900 Amer. statesman; brother of W. T. Sherman

Sherman William Tecumseh 1820–1891 Amer. general

Shi·va \'shi-və, 'shē-\ *or* **Si·va** \'si-və, 'shi-, 'sē-, 'shē-\ god of destruction and regeneration in the Hindu sacred triad — compare BRAHMA; VISHNU

Sieg·fried \'sig-ˌfrēd, 'sēg-\ hero in Germanic legend who kills a dragon guarding a gold hoard

Si·mon \sī-'mən\ *or* **Simon the Zealot** one of the 12 apostles in the Bible

Si·na·tra \sə-'nä-trə\ Frank 1915–1998 *Francis Albert Sinatra* Amer. singer and actor

Sind·bad the Sailor \'sin-ˌbad\ citizen of Baghdad whose adventures are narrated in the *Arabian Nights' Entertainments*

Sis·y·phus \'si-sə-fəs\ king of Corinth who in Greek mythology is condemned to roll a heavy stone up a hill in Hades only to have it roll down again as it nears the top

Sit·ting Bull \ˌsi-tiŋ-'bu̇l\ *ca* 1831–1890 Sioux Indian chief

Siva — see SHIVA

Smith \'smith\ Bessie 1894?–1937 Amer. blues singer

Smith John *ca* 1580–1631 Eng. colonist in America

Smith Joseph 1805–1844 Amer. founder of the Mormon Church

Soc·ra·tes \'sä-krə-ˌtēz\ *ca* 470–399 B.C. Greek philosopher

Sol \'säl\ god of the sun in Roman mythology — see HELIOS

Sol·o·mon \'sä-lə-mən\ 10th-century B.C. king of Israel noted for his wisdom

Soph·o·cles \'sä-fə-ˌklēz\ *ca* 496–406 B.C. Greek playwright

Sou·sa \'sü-zə, 'sü-sə\ John Philip 1854–1932 Amer. bandmaster and composer

Spar·ta·cus \'spär-tə-kəs\ *died* 71 B.C. Roman slave and gladiator

Sphinx \'sfiŋ(k)s\ monster in Greek mythology having a lion's body, wings, and the head and bust of a woman

Spiel·berg \'spēl-ˌbərg\ Steven 1947– Amer. filmmaker

Squan·to \'skwän-tō\ *died* 1622 Amer. Indian friend of the Pilgrims

Sta·lin \'stä-lən, 'sta-, -ˌlēn\ Joseph 1879–1953 Soviet Communist party leader (1922–53), premier (1941–53), and dictator

Stan·dish \'stan-dish\ Myles *or* Miles 1584?–1656 Amer. colonist

Stan·ley \'stan-lē\ Sir Henry Morton 1841–1904 Brit. explorer in Africa

Stan·ton \'stan-tᵊn\ Elizabeth Cady 1815–1902 Amer. suffragist

Stein \'stīn\ Gertrude 1874–1946 Amer. author

Stein·beck \'stīn-ˌbek\ John Ernst 1902–1968 Amer. author; Nobel Prize winner (1962)

Steu·ben \'stü-bən, 'styü-, 'shtȯi-\ Friedrich Wilhelm von 1730–1794 Prussian-born general in Amer. Revolution

Ste·ven·son \'stē-vən-sən\ Adlai Ewing 1900–1965 Amer. politician

Stevenson Robert Louis 1850–1894 Scot. author

Sto·ker \'stō-kər\ Bram 1847–1912 *Abraham Stoker* Irish author

Stowe \'stō\ Harriet Beecher 1811–1896 Amer. author

Stra·di·va·ri \ˌstra-də-'vär-ē, -'ver-\ Antonio 1644?–1737 Ital. violin maker

Strauss \'shtrau̇s, 'strau̇s\ Johann 1804–1849 and his sons Johann, Jr. 1825–1899 and Josef 1827–1870 Austrian composers

Strauss Richard 1864–1949 Ger. composer

Stra·vin·sky \strə-'vin(t)-skē\ Igor 1882–1971 Amer. (Russ.-born) composer

Stu·art \'stü-ərt, 'styü-; 'st(y)u̇rt\ Charles Edward 1720–1788 *the Young Pretender; Bonnie Prince Charlie* claimant to the Brit. throne

Stuart Gilbert Charles 1755–1828 Amer. painter

Stuart Jeb 1833–1864 *James Ewell Brown Stuart* Amer. Confederate general

Stuy·ve·sant \'stī-və-sənt\ Peter *ca* 1610–1672 Dutch colonial administrator in America

Sul·li·van \'sə-lə-vən\ Sir Arthur Seymour 1842–1900 Eng. composer; collaborator with Sir William Gilbert

Sullivan Louis Henri 1856–1924 Amer. architect

Sum·ner \'səm-nər\ Charles 1811–1874 Amer. politician

Sun Yat-sen \'su̇n-'yät-'sen\ 1866–1925 Chinese statesman

Sut·ter \'sə-tər, 'sü-\ John Augustus 1803–1880 Amer. (Ger.-born) pioneer in California

Swift \'swift\ Jonathan 1667–1745 Eng. (Irish-born) author

Synge \'siŋ\ John Millington 1871–1909 Irish playwright

Taft \'taft\ William Howard 1857–1930 27th pres. of the U.S. (1909–13); chief justice of the U.S. Supreme Court (1921–30)

Ta·gore \tə-'gòr\ Ra·bin·dra·nath \rə-'bin-drə-,nät\ 1861–1941 Indian poet; Nobel Prize winner (1913)

Tall·chief \'tòl-,chēf\ Maria 1925– Amer. dancer

Tan \'tan\ Amy 1952–   Amer. author

Ta·ney \'tò-nē\ Roger Brooke 1777–1864 Amer. jurist; chief justice of the U.S. Supreme Court (1836–64)

Tan·ta·lus \'tan-tə-ləs\ king in Greek mythology who is condemned to stand up to his chin in a pool of water in Hades and beneath fruit-laden boughs only to have the water or fruit go out of reach at each attempt to drink or eat

Tay·lor \'tā-lər\ Zachary 1784–1850 Amer. general; 12th pres. of the U.S. (1849–50)

Tchai·kov·sky \chī-'kòf-skē, chə-, -'kòv-\ Pyotr Ilich 1840–1893 Russ. composer

Te·cum·seh \tə-'kəm(p)-sə, -sē\ 1768–1813 Shawnee Indian chief

Tek·a·kwitha \,te-kə-'kwi-thə\ Kateri 1656–1680 *Lily of the Mohawks* beatified Mohawk Indian religious

Ten·ny·son \'te-nə-sən\ Alfred 1809–1892 Baron *Tennyson* known as *Alfred, Lord Tennyson* Eng. poet

Te·re·sa \tə-'rā-zə, -'rē-sə\ Mother 1910–1997 beatified Albanian religious in India; Nobel Prize winner (1979)

Teresa of Ávi·la \'ä-vi-lə\ Saint 1515–1582 Span. nun and mystic

Tes·la \'tes-lə\ Nikola 1856–1943 Amer. (Croatian-born) electrical engineer and inventor

Thatch·er \'tha-chər\ Margaret Hilda 1925–   Baroness *Thatcher of Kesteven* née *Roberts* Brit. prime minister (1979–90)

The·seus \'thē-,süs, -sē-əs\ hero in Greek mythology who kills the Minotaur and conquers the Amazons

Thom·as \'tä-məs\ apostle in the Bible who demanded proof of Jesus' resurrection

Thomas à Becket — see Saint Thomas BECKET

Thomas Aquinas Saint — see AQUINAS

Thor \'thòr\ god of thunder, weather, and crops in Norse mythology

Tho·reau \thə-'rō, thó-\ Henry David 1817–1862 Amer. author

Thorpe \'thòrp\ Jim 1888–1953 *James Francis Thorpe* Amer. athlete

Thur·ber \'thər-bər\ James Grover 1894–1961 Amer. author

Ti·be·ri·us \tī-'bir-ē-əs\ 42 B.C.–37 A.D. Roman emperor (14–37)

Tocque·ville \'tòk-,vil, 'tòk-, 'täk-, -,vēl, -vəl\ Alexis de 1805–1859 French politician and author

Tol·kien \'tòl-,kēn\ J. R. R. 1892–1973 *John Ronald Reuel Tolkien* Brit. author

Tol·stoy \tòl-'stòi, tōl-', täl-', 'tòl-,, 'tōl-,, 'täl-,\ Leo 1828–1910 Count *Lev Nikolayevich Tolstoy* Russ. author

Tou·louse–Lau·trec \tü-,lüz-lō-'trek\ Henri de 1864–1901 French painter

Tri·ton \'trī-t²n\ sea god in Greek mythology who is half man and half fish

Trots·ky \'trät-skē\ Leon 1879–1940 orig. *Lev Davidovich Bronstein* Russ. Communist leader

Tru·deau \'trü-(,)dō, trü-'\ Pierre Elliott 1919–2000 Canad. prime minister (1968–79, 1980–84)

Tru·man \'trü-mən\ Harry S. 1884–1972 33rd pres. of the U.S. (1945–53)

Truth \'trüth\ Sojourner 1797?–1883 Amer. abolitionist

Tub·man \'təb-mən\ Harriet *ca* 1820–1913 Amer. abolitionist

Tut·ankh·a·men \,tü-,taŋ-'kä-mən, -,täŋ-\ originally *Tut·ankh·a·ten* \-'kä-t²n\ *ca* 1370–1352 B.C., king of Egypt (1361–1352 B.C.)

Twain \'kle-mənz\ Mark 1835–1910 pseud. of *Samuel Langhorne Clem·ens* \'klem-ənz\ Amer. author

Tweed \'twēd\ William Marcy 1823–1878 *Boss Tweed* Amer. politician

Ty·ler \'tī-lər\ John 1790–1862 10th pres. of the U.S. (1841–45)

Ulysses — see ODYSSEUS

Ura·nus \'yùr-ə-nəs, yù-'rä-\ the sky personified as a god and father of the Titans in Greek mythology

Ur·ban \'ər-bən\ name of eight popes: esp. **II** *ca* 1035–1099 (pope 1088–99)

Uri·el \'yùr-ē-əl\ archangel named in Hebrew tradition — compare GABRIEL; MICHAEL; RAPHAEL

Val·en·tine \'va-lən-,tīn\ Saint, 3d cent. Christian martyr

Van Bu·ren \van-'byùr-ən, vən-\ Martin 1782–1862 8th pres. of the U.S. (1837–41)

Van Dyck *or* **Van·dyke** \van-'dīk, vən-\ Sir Anthony 1599–1641 Flemish painter

van Gogh Vincent — see GOGH, VAN

Ve·láz·quez \və-'las-kəs, -'läs-, -kwiz, -(,)kās\ Diego 1599–1660 Span. painter

Ve·nus \'vē-nəs\ goddess of love and beauty in Roman mythology — compare APHRODITE

Ver·di \'ver-dē\ Giuseppe 1813–1901 Ital. composer

Ver·meer \vər-'mer, -'mir\ Jan *or* Johannes 1632–1675 Dutch painter

Verne \'vərn, 'vern\ Jules \'jülz\ 1828–1905 French author

Ves·puc·ci \ve-'spü-chē, -'spyü-\ Ame·ri·go \ə-'mer-i-ˌgō\ 1454–1512 Latin *Amer·i·cus Ves·pu·cius* \ə-'mer-ə-kəs-ˌves-'pyü-sh(ē-)əs\ Ital. navigator for Spain and namesake of America

Vic·to·ria \vik-'tȯr-ē-ə\ 1819–1901 *Alexandrina Victoria* queen of the United Kingdom (1837–1901)

Vinci, da Leonardo — see LEONARDO DA VINCI

Vir·gil *also* **Ver·gil** \'vər-jəl\ 70–19 B.C. Roman poet

Vish·nu \'vish-(ˌ)nü\ god of preservation in the Hindu sacred triad — compare BRAHMA; SHIVA

Vol·ta \vȯl-'tar, väl-, vȯl-, -'ter\ Alessandro 1745–1827 Ital. physicist

Vol·taire \vȯl-'tar, väl-, vȯl-, -'ter\ 1694–1778 orig. *François-Marie Arouet* French author

Vul·can \'vəl-kən\ god of fire and metalworking in Roman mythology — compare HEPHAESTUS

Wag·ner \'väg-nər\ Ri·chard \'ri-ˌkärt, -ˌkärt\ 1813–1883 Ger. composer

Walk·er \'wȯ-kər\ Alice Malsenior 1944– Amer. writer

Wal·len·berg \'wä-lən-ˌbərg\ Raoul 1912–1947? Swedish diplomat and hero of the Holocaust

War·ren \'wȯr-ən, 'wär-\ Earl 1891–1974 Amer. jurist; chief justice of the U.S. Supreme Court (1953–69)

Wash·ing·ton \'wȯ-shiŋ-tən, 'wä-\ Booker Tal·ia·ferro \'tä-lə-vər\ 1856–1915 Amer. educator

Washington George 1732–1799 Amer. general; 1st pres. of the U.S. (1789–97)

Watt \'wät\ James 1736–1819 Scot. inventor

Wayne \'wān\ Anthony 1745–1796 *Mad Anthony* Amer. general

Web·ster \'web-stər\ Daniel 1782–1852 Amer. politician

Webster Noah 1758–1843 Amer. lexicographer

Wel·ling·ton \'we-liŋ-tən\ Duke of 1769–1852 *Arthur Wellesley*; *the Iron Duke* Brit. general and statesman

Wells \'welz\ H. G. 1866–1946 *Herbert George Wells* Eng. author and historian

Wel·ty \'wel-tē\ Eudora 1909–2001 Amer. author

Wes·ley \'wes-lē, 'wez-\ John 1703–1791 Eng. founder of Methodism

Wes·ting·house \'wes-tiŋ-ˌhaus\ George 1846–1914 Amer. inventor and industrialist

Whar·ton \'hwȯr-tᵊn, 'wȯr-\ Edith 1862–1937 née *Jones* Amer. author

Whis·tler \'hwis-lər, 'wis-\ James (Abbott) McNeill 1834–1903 Amer. artist

Whit·man \'hwit-mən, 'wit-\ Walt 1819–1892 Amer. poet

Whit·ney \'hwit-nē, 'wit-\ Eli 1765–1825 Amer. inventor

Whit·ti·er \'hwi-tē-ər, 'wit-\ John Greenleaf 1807–1892 Amer. poet

Wie·sel \vē-'zel, wē-\ Elie 1928– Amer. (Romanian-born) author; Nobel Prize winner (1986)

Wilde \'wī(-ə)ld\ Oscar 1854–1900 Irish author

Wil·der \'wī(-ə)l-dər\ Thornton Niven 1897–1975 Amer. author

Wil·liam \'wil-yəm\ name of 4 kings of England: I *ca* 1028–1087 *William the Conqueror* (r. 1066–87); II *ca* 1056–1100 *William Rufus* \'rü-fəs\ (r. 1087–1100); III 1650–1702 (r. 1689–1702); IV 1765–1837 (r. 1830–37)

Wil·liam Tell \ˌwil-yəm-'tel\ legendary Swiss patriot commanded to shoot an apple off his son's head

Wil·liams \'wil-yəmz\ Roger 1603?–1683 Eng. colonist

Williams Ted 1918–2002 *Theodore Samuel Williams* Amer. baseball player

Williams Tennessee 1911–1983 orig. *Thomas Lanier Williams* Amer. playwright

Williams Venus 1980–   and her sister Serena 1981–   Amer. tennis players

Wil·son \'wil-sən\ (Thomas) Woodrow 1856–1924 28th pres. of the U.S. (1913–21); Nobel Prize winner (1919)

Win·throp \'win(t)-thrəp\ John 1588–1649 1st governor of Massachusetts Bay Colony

Woden — see ODIN

Woll·stone·craft \'wul-stən-ˌkraft\ Mary 1759–1797 Eng. feminist and writer

Woods \'wudz\ Tiger 1975–   *Eldrick Woods* Amer. golfer

Woolf \'wulf\ Virginia 1882–1941 Eng. author

Words·worth \'wərdz-(ˌ)wərth\ William 1770–1850 Eng. poet

Wo·vo·ka \wō-'vō-kə\ 1858?–1932 *Jack Wilson* Paiute Indian mystic

Wren \'ren\ Sir Christopher 1632–1723 Eng. architect

Wright \'rīt\ Frank Lloyd 1867–1959 Amer. architect

Wright Orville 1871–1948 and his brother Wilbur 1867–1912 Amer. pioneers in aviation

Wright Richard 1908–1960 Amer. author

Wy·eth \'wī-əth\ Andrew Newell 1917–2009 Amer. painter

Yeats \'yāts\ William Butler 1865–1939 Irish author

Yel·tsin \'yelt-sən, 'yel-sin\ Boris Nikolayevich 1931–2007 pres. of Russia (1990–99)

York \'yȯrk\ Alvin Cullum 1887–1964 Amer. hero in World War I

Young \'yəŋ\ Brig·ham \'brig-əm\ 1801–1877 Amer. Mormon leader

Za·har·i·as \zə-'ha-rē-əs\ Babe Didrikson 1914–1956 *Mildred Ella Zaharias* née *Didrikson* Amer. athlete

Zech·a·ri·ah \ˌze-kə-'rī-ə\ Hebrew prophet of the 6th cent. B.C.

Zeng·er \'zeŋ-gər, -ər\ John Peter 1697–1746 Amer. (Ger.-born) journalist and printer

Zeph·y·rus \'ze-fə-rəs\ god of the west wind in Greek mythology

Zeus \'züs\ chief god and ruler of the sky and weather in Greek mythology — compare JUPITER

GEOGRAPHICAL NAMES

This section gives basic information about the world's countries, regions, cities, and major physical features. The latest population figures are given for nations, cities, and some regions. For many of these entries, derived nouns and adjectives are also listed (as **Iceland . . . Icelander . . .** *n*). Other derived words not shown here have been separately entered in the main A-Z section, because of the presence of additional senses (as **Chinese**).

Abbreviations used here are listed in the front section Abbreviations in This Work. The capital letters N, E, S, and W, used singly or in combination and without a period, indicate direction. For example, "N India" means "northern India." Where direction is a part of the name, the word is spelled out.

The symbol ✳ denotes a capital. Sizes are given in conventional U.S. units, with metric equivalents following.

Ab·er·deen \,a-bər-'dēn\ city NE Scotland; *pop* 211,080 — **Ab·er·do·ni·an** \,a-bər-'dō-nē-ən\ *adj or n*

Ab·i·djan \,ä-bē-'jän, ,a-bi-\ city, seat of government of Ivory Coast; *pop* 1,934,342

Abilene \'a-bə-,lēn\ city NW *cen* Texas; *pop* 115,930

Abu Dha·bi \,ä-bü-'dä-bē, -'thä-\ city, ✳ of United Arab Emirates; *pop* 347,000

Abu·ja \ä-'bü-jä\ city *cen* Nigeria; its ✳; *pop* 423,391

Ab·ys·sin·ia \,a-bə-'si-nē-ə, -nyə\ — see ETHIOPIA — **Ab·ys·sin·i·an** \-nē-ən, -nyən\ *adj or n*

Aca·dia \ə-'kā-dē-ə\ *or French* **Aca·die** \ä-kä-'dē\ NOVA SCOTIA — an early name — **Aca·di·an** \-ē-ən\ *adj or n*

Aca·pul·co \,ä-kä-'pül-(,)kō, ,a-\ city & port S Mexico on the Pacific; *pop* 687,292

Ac·cra \'ä-krə, 'a-; ə-'krä\ city & port, ✳ of Ghana; *pop* 867,459

Acon·ca·gua \,ä-kōn-'kä-gwä\ mountain 22,834 ft. (6960 m.) W Argentina; highest in the Andes & in Western Hemisphere

Ad·dis Aba·ba \'ä-dis-'ä-bä-,bä, ,a-dəs-'a-bə-bə\ city, ✳ of Ethiopia; *pop* 2,646,000

Ad·e·laide \'a-də-,lād\ city S Australia, ✳ of South Australia; *pop* 917,000

Aden \'ä-dᵊn, 'ä-\ city & port S Yemen; *pop* 240,370

Aden, Gulf of arm of Indian Ocean between Yemen (Arabia) & Somalia (Africa)

Ad·i·ron·dack \,a-də-'rän-,dak\ mountains NE New York; highest Mount Marcy 5344 ft. (1629 m.)

Admiralty \'ad-m(ə-)rəl-tē\ **1** island SE Alaska **2** islands W Pacific N of New Guinea; part of Papua New Guinea

Adri·at·ic Sea \,ā-drē-'a-tik, ,a-\ arm of Mediterranean between Italy & Balkan Peninsula

Ae·ge·an Sea \i-'jē-ən\ arm of Mediterranean between Asia Minor & Greece

Af·ghan·i·stan \af-'ga-nə-,stan, -'gä-nə-,stän\ country W Asia E of Iran; ✳, Kabul; *pop* (est.) 28,717,000

Af·ri·ca \'a-fri-kə\ continent S of the Mediterranean

Aga·na — see HAGÁTÑA

Agra \'ä-grə, 'ə-\ city N India SSE of Delhi; *pop* 1,259,979

Aguas·ca·lien·tes \,ä-gwäs-,käl-'yen-,täs\ city *cen* Mexico NE of Guadalajara; metropolitan area *pop* 637,303

Agul·has, Cape \ə-'gə-ləs\ cape Republic of South Africa; most southerly point of Africa, at 34° 52′ S latitude

Ahag·gar \ə-'hä-gər, ,ä-hə-'gär\ mountains S Algeria in W *cen* Sahara

Ah·mad·abad \'ä-mə-də-,bäd, -,bad\ city W India N of Bombay; *pop* 3,515,361

Ak·ron \'a-krən\ city NE Ohio; *pop* 217,074

Al·a·bama \,a-lə-'ba-mə\ state SE U.S.; ✳, Montgomery; *pop* 4,447,100 — **Al·a·bam·i·an** \-'ba-mē-ən\ *or* **Al·a·bam·an** \-'ba-mən\ *adj or n*

Alas·ka \ə-'las-kə\ **1** peninsula SW Alaska SW of Cook Inlet **2** state of U.S. in NW North America; ✳, Juneau; *pop* 626,932 **3** mountain range S Alaska extending from Alaska Peninsula to Yukon boundary — **Alas·kan** \-kən\ *adj or n*

Alaska, Gulf of inlet of Pacific off S Alaska between Alaska Peninsula on W & Alexander Archipelago on E

Al·ba·nia \al-'bā-nē-ə, -nyə\ country S Europe in Balkan Peninsula on Adriatic; ✳, Tirane; *pop* 3,069,275

Al·ba·ny \'ȯl-bə-nē\ city, ✳ of New York; *pop* 95,658

Albemarle Sound \'al-bə-,märl\ inlet of the Atlantic in NE North Carolina

Albert, Lake \'al-bərt\ lake E Africa between Uganda & Democratic Republic of the Congo in course of the Nile

Al·ber·ta \al-'bər-tə\ province W Canada;

✳, Edmonton; *pop* 2,974,807 — **Al·ber·tan** \-'bər-t°n\ *adj or n*

Al·bu·quer·que \'al-bə-ˌkər-kē\ city *cen* New Mexico; *pop* 448,607

Al·ca·traz \'al-kə-ˌtraz\ island California in San Francisco Bay

Al·da·bra \äl-'dä-brə\ island NW Indian Ocean N of Madagascar; belongs to Seychelles

Al·der·ney \'ȯl-dər-nē\ — see CHANNEL

Alep·po \ə-'le-(ˌ)pō\ city N Syria; *pop* 1,445,000

Aleu·tian \ə-'lü-shən\ islands SW Alaska extending 1700 mi. (2735 km.) W from Alaska Peninsula

Al·ex·an·der \ˌal-ig-'zan-dər, ˌel-\ archipelago SE Alaska

Al·ex·an·dria \ˌa-lig-'zan-drē-ə, ˌe-\ 1 city N Virginia S of District of Columbia; *pop* 128,283 2 city N Egypt on the Mediterranean; *pop* 3,170,000 — **Al·ex·an·dri·an** \-drē-ən\ *adj or n*

Al·ge·ria \al-'jir-ē-ə\ country NW Africa on Mediterranean; ✳, Algiers; *pop* 22,971,000 — **Al·ge·ri·an** \-ē-ən\ *adj or n*

Al·giers \al-'jirz\ city, ✳ of Algeria; *pop* 1,365,400 — **Al·ge·rine** \ˌal-jə-'rēn\ *adj or n*

Al·lah·a·bad \'ä-lä-hä-ˌbäd, 'a-lə-hə-ˌbad\ city N India on the Ganges; *pop* 990,298

Al·le·ghe·ny \ˌa-lə-'gā-nē\ 1 river 325 mi. (523 km.) long W Pennsylvania & SW New York 2 mountains of Appalachian system E U.S. in Pennsylvania, Maryland, Virginia, & West Virginia

Al·len·town \'a-lən-ˌtaùn\ city E Pennsylvania; *pop* 106,632

Al·maty \əl-'mä-tē\ *or* **Al·ma–Ata** \əl-'mä-ə-'tä; ˌal-mə-'ä-tə, -ə-'tä\ city, former ✳ of Kazakhstan; *pop* 1,156,200

Alps \'alps\ mountain system *cen* Europe — see MONT BLANC

Al·tai *or* **Al·tay** \ˌal-'tī\ mountain system *cen* Asia between Mongolia & W China & between Kazakhstan & Russia

Ama·ga·sa·ki \ˌä-mä-gä-'sä-kē\ city Japan in W *cen* Honshu; *pop* 466,187

Am·a·ril·lo \ˌa-mə-'ri-(ˌ)lō, -lə\ city NW Texas; *pop* 173,627

Am·a·zon \'a-mə-ˌzän, -zən\ river 3900 mi. (6436 km.) long N South America flowing from Peruvian Andes into Atlantic in N Brazil

Amer·i·ca \ə-'mer-ə-kə, -'me-rə-\ 1 either continent (**North America** *or* **South America**) of Western Hemisphere 2 *or* **the Amer·i·cas** \-kəz\ lands of Western Hemisphere including North, Central, & South America & West Indies 3 UNITED STATES OF AMERICA — **American** *adj or n*

American Falls — see NIAGARA FALLS

American Samoa *or* **Eastern Samoa** islands SW *cen* Pacific; U. S. territory; ✳, Pago Pago (on Tutuila Island); *pop* 57,291

Am·man \ä-'män, a-, -'man\ city, ✳ of Jordan; *pop* 627,505

Am·ster·dam \'am(p)-stər-ˌdam, 'äm(p)-stər-ˌdäm\ city, official ✳ of the Netherlands; *pop* 735,526

Amur \ä-'mur\ river 1780 mi. (2784 km.) long E Asia flowing into the Pacific & forming part of boundary between China & Russia

An·a·heim \'a-nə-ˌhīm\ city SW California E of Long Beach; *pop* 328,014

An·a·to·lia \ˌa-nə-'tō-lē-ə, -'tōl-yə\ — see ASIA MINOR — **An·a·to·li·an** \-'tō-lē-ən, -'tōl-yən\ *adj or n*

An·chor·age \'aŋ-k(ə-)rij\ city S *cen* Alaska; *pop* 260,283

An·da·man \'an-də-mən, -ˌman\ 1 islands India in Bay of Bengal S of Myanmar & N of Nicobar Islands 2 sea, arm of Bay of Bengal S of Myanmar — **An·da·man·ese** \ˌan-də-mə-'nēz, -'nēs\ *adj or n*

An·des \'an-(ˌ)dēz\ mountain system W South America extending from Panama to Tierra del Fuego — see ACONCAGUA — **An·de·an** \'an-(ˌ)dē-ən, an-'\ *adj* — **An·dine** \'an-ˌdēn, -ˌdīn\ *adj*

An·dor·ra \an-'dȯr-ə, -'där-ə\ country SW Europe in E Pyrenees between France & Spain; ✳, Andorra la Vella; *pop* 57,110 — **An·dor·ran** \-ən\ *adj or n*

Andorra la Vel·la \lä-'vel-yä\ town, ✳ of Andorra; *pop* 21,513

An·dros \'an-drəs\ island, largest of Bahamas

An·gel Falls \'än-jəl\ waterfall 3212 ft. (979 m.) SE Venezuela; world's highest waterfall

Ang·kor \'aŋ-ˌkȯr\ ruins of ancient city NW Cambodia

An·gle·sey \'aŋ-gəl-sē\ island NW Wales

An·go·la \aŋ-'gō-lə, an-\ country SW Africa S of mouth of Congo River; ✳, Luanda; *pop* 10,609,000 — **An·go·lan** \-lən\ *adj or n*

An·i·ak·chak Crater \ˌa-nē-'ak-ˌchak\ volcanic crater SW Alaska on Alaska Peninsula; 6 mi. (10 km.) in diameter

An·ka·ra \'aŋ-kə-rə, 'äŋ-\ city, ✳ of Turkey in N *cen* Anatolia; *pop* 2,559,471

An·nap·o·lis \ə-'na-pə-lis\ city, ✳ of Maryland; *pop* 35,838

Ann Ar·bor \(ˌ)an-'är-bər\ city SE Michigan; *pop* 114,024

An·shan \'än-'shän\ city NE China; *pop* 1,203,986

An·ta·nan·a·ri·vo \ˌän-tä-ˌnä-nä-'rē-(ˌ)vō\ city, ✳ of Madagascar; *pop* 958,929

Ant·arc·ti·ca \ˌand-'ärk-ti-kə, -'är-ti-\ body of land around the South Pole; plateau covered by great ice cap

An·ti·gua \an-'tē-gə, -gwə\ island West Indies in the Leewards; with Barbuda forms independent **Antigua and Barbuda**; ✳, Saint John's; *pop* 83,000

An·til·les \an-'ti-lēz\ the West Indies except for the Bahamas — see GREATER ANTILLES; LESSER ANTILLES — **An·til·le·an** \-lē-ən\ *adj*

An·trim \'an-trəm\ district E Northern Ireland; *pop* 44,322

Ant·werp \'ant-₁wərp, 'an-₁twərp\ city N Belgium; *pop* 448,709

Aomen — see MACAO

Aorangi — see COOK, MOUNT

Ap·en·nines \'a-pə-₁nīnz\ mountain chain Italy extending length of the peninsula; highest peak Monte Corno (NE of Rome) 9560 ft. (2897 m.) — **Ap·en·nine** \'a-pə-₁nīnz\ *adj*

Apia \ä-'pē-ä\ town, ✳ of Samoa; *pop* 38,000

Apo, Mount \'ä-(₁)pō\ volcano Philippines in SE Mindanao 9692 ft. (2954 m.); highest peak in the Philippines

Ap·pa·la·chia \₁a-pə-'lā-chə, -'la-chə, -'lā-shə\ region E U.S. including Appalachian Mountains from S *cen* New York to *cen* Alabama

Ap·pa·la·chian Mountains \₁a-pə-'lāch(ē-)ən, -sh(ē-)ən\ mountain system E North America extending from S Quebec to *cen* Alabama — see MITCHELL, MOUNT

Aqa·ba, Gulf of \'ä-kä-bə\ arm of Red Sea E of Sinai Peninsula

Aquid·neck \ə-'kwid-₁nek\ *or* **Rhode** island SE Rhode Island in Narragansett Bay

Ara·bia \ə-'rā-bē-ə\ peninsula of SW Asia including Saudi Arabia, Yemen, Oman, & Persian Gulf States

Ara·bi·an \ə-'rā-bē-ən\ **1** desert E Egypt between the Nile & Red Sea **2** sea NW section of Indian Ocean between Arabia & India

Ara·fu·ra \₁a-rä-'fü-rä\ sea between N Australia & W New Guinea

Ar·al Sea \'a-rəl\ *formerly* **Lake Aral** lake W Asia between Kazakhstan & Uzbekistan

Ar·a·rat \'a-rə-₁rat\ mountain 16,946 ft. (5165 m.) E Turkey near border of Iran

Arc·tic \'ärk-tik, 'är-tik\ **1** ocean N of Arctic Circle **2** Arctic regions **3** archipelago N Canada in Nunavut & Northwest Territories

Ar·da·bil *or* **Ar·de·bil** \₁är-də-'bēl\ city NW Iran; *pop* 281,973

Ards \'ärdz\ district E Northern Ireland; *pop* 64,026

Are·ci·bo \₁ä-rä-'sē-(₁)bō\ city & port N Puerto Rico; *pop* 100,131

Ar·gen·ti·na \₁är-jən-'tē-nə\ country S South America between the Andes & the Atlantic; ✳, Buenos Aires; *pop* 33,070,000 — **Ar·gen·tine** \'är-jən-₁tīn, -₁tēn\ *adj or n* — **Ar·gen·tin·ean** *or* **Ar·gen·tin·i·an** \₁är-jən-'ti-nē-ən\ *adj or n*

Ar·gos \'är-₁gós, -gəs\ ancient Greek city-state S Greece

Ar·i·zo·na \₁a-rə-'zō-nə\ state SW U.S.; ✳, Phoenix; *pop* 5,130,632 — **Ar·i·zo·nan** \-nən\ *or* **Ar·i·zo·nian** \-nē-ən, -nyən\ *adj or n*

Ar·kan·sas \'är-kən-₁só\ **1** river 1450 mi. (2334 km.) long SW *cen* U.S. flowing SE into the Mississippi **2** state S *cen* U.S.; ✳, Little Rock; *pop* 2,673,400 — **Ar·kan·san** \är-'kan-zən\ *adj or n*

Ar·ling·ton \'är-liŋ-tən\ city N Texas; *pop* 332,969

Ar·magh \är-'mä, 'är-₁\ **1** district S Northern Ireland; *pop* 51,331 **2** town *cen* Armagh district; *pop* 14,265

Ar·me·nia \är-'mē-nē-ə, -nyə\ **1** region W Asia in mountainous area SE of Black Sea & SW of Caspian Sea divided between Iran, Turkey, & Armenia (country) **2** country E Europe; ✳, Yerevan; *pop* 3,426,000

Arn·hem Land \'är-nəm\ region N Australia on N coast of Northern Territory

Ar·no \'är-(₁)nō\ river 150 mi. (241 km.) long *cen* Italy flowing through Florence

Aru·ba \ə-'rü-bə\ island Netherlands Antilles off coast of NW Venezuela; *pop* 69,000

Ar·vada \är-'va-də\ city N *cen* Colorado NW of Denver; *pop* 102,153

Ash·ga·bat \'äsh-gə-₁bät\ *or* **Ashkh·a·bad** \'ash-kə-₁bad, -₁bäd\ city, ✳ of Turkmenistan; *pop* 412,200

Asia \'ā-zhə, -shə\ continent of Eastern Hemisphere N of the Equator — see EURASIA

Asia Mi·nor \-'mī-nər\ *or* **An·a·to·lia** \₁a-nə-'tō-lē-ə, -'tōl-yə\ peninsula in modern Turkey between Black Sea on N & the Mediterranean on S

As·ma·ra \az-'mä-rə, -'ma-rə\ city, ✳ of Eritrea; *pop* 342,706

As·syr·ia \ə-'sir-ē-ə\ ancient empire W Asia extending along the middle Tigris & over foothills to the E — **As·syr·i·an** \-ən\ *adj or n*

As·ta·na \ä-stä-'nä\ city, ✳ of Kazakhstan; *pop* 319,318

Asun·ción \ä-sün-'syōn\ city, ✳ of Paraguay; *pop* 502,426

As·wân \a-'swän, ä-\ city S Egypt on the Nile near site of **Aswân High Dam**; *pop* 191,461

Ata·ca·ma \₁ä-tä-'kä-mä\ desert N Chile

Atchaf·a·laya \(ə-)₁cha-fə-'lī-ə\ river 225 mi. (362 km.) long S Louisiana flowing S into Gulf of Mexico

Ath·a·bas·ca *or* **Ath·a·bas·ka** \₁a-thə-'bas-kə, ₁ä-\ river 765 mi. (1231 km.) long NE Alberta flowing into **Lake Athabasca** on Alberta–Saskatchewan border

Ath·ens \'a-thənz\ **1** city NE Georgia; *pop* 101,489 **2** city, ✳ of Greece; *pop* 748,110 — **Athe·nian** \ə-'thē-nē-ən, -nyən\ *adj or n*

At·lan·ta \ət-'lan-tə, at-\ city, ✳ of Georgia; *pop* 416,474

At·lan·tic \ət-'lan-tik, at-\ ocean separating North America & South America from Europe & Africa; often divided into **North Atlantic** and **South Atlantic** — **Atlantic** *adj*

At·las \'at-ləs\ mountains NW Africa extending from SW Morocco to N Tunisia

At·ti·ca \'a-ti-kə\ ancient state E Greece; chief city Athens — **At·tic** \'at-ik\ *adj*

Auck·land \'ò-klənd\ city N New Zealand on NW North Island; urban area *pop* 1,074,510

Au·gus·ta \ò-'gəs-tə, ə-\ **1** city E Georgia; *pop* 199,775 **2** city, ✳ of Maine; *pop* 18,560

Au·ro·ra \ə-'ròr-ə, ò-\ **1** city NE *cen* Colorado; *pop* 276,393 **2** city NE Illinois; *pop* 142,990

Auschwitz — see OSWIECIM

Aus·tin \'òs-tən, 'äs-\ city, ✳ of Texas; *pop* 656,562

Aus·tral·asia \ˌòs-trə-'lā-zhə, ˌäs-, -'lā-shə\ Australia, Tasmania, New Zealand, & Melanesia — **Aus·tral·asian** \-zhən, -shən\ *adj or n*

Aus·tra·lia \ò-'strāl-yə, ä-, ə-\ **1** continent of Eastern Hemisphere SE of Asia **2** country including continent of Australia & island of Tasmania; ✳, Canberra; *pop* 17,562,000 — **Aus·tra·lian** \-yən\ *adj or n*

Australian Alps mountain range SE Australia in E Victoria & SE New South Wales; part of Great Dividing Range

Australian Capital Territory district SE Australia including two areas, one containing Canberra (✳ of Australia) & the other on Jervis Bay (inlet of the South Pacific); surrounded by New South Wales

Aus·tria \'òs-trē-ə, 'äs-\ country *cen* Europe; ✳, Vienna; *pop* 7,812,100 — **Aus·tri·an** \-ən\ *adj or n*

Aus·tria–Hun·ga·ry \-'həŋ-gə-rē\ country 1867–1918 *cen* Europe including Bohemia, Moravia, Transylvania, Galicia, and what are now Austria, Hungary, Slovenia, Crotia, & part of NE Italy — **Aus·tro–Hun·gar·i·an** \'òs-(ˌ)trō-ˌhəŋ-'ger-ē-ən, 'äs-\ *adj or n*

Aus·tro·ne·sia \ˌòs-trə-'nē-zhə, ˌäs-, -'nē-shə\ **1** islands of the South Pacific **2** area extending from Madagascar through Malay Peninsula & Malay Archipelago to Hawaii & Easter Island — **Aus·tro·ne·sian** \-zhən, -shən\ *adj or n*

Avon \'ā-vən, 'a-\ river 96 mi. (154 km.) long *cen* England flowing WSW into the Severn

Ayers Rock \'erz\ outcrop *cen* Australia in SW Northern Territory

Ayles·bury \'ālz-b(ə-)rē\ town SE *cen* England; *pop* 41,288

Ayr \'er\ *or* Ayr·shire \-ˌshir, -shər\ former county SW Scotland

Azer·bai·jan \ˌa-zər-ˌbī-'jän, ˌä-\ country SE Europe bordering on Caspian Sea; ✳, Baku; *pop* 7,029,000 — **Azer·bai·ja·ni** \ˌa-zər-ˌbī-'jä-nē, ˌä-\ *adj or n*

Azores \'ā-ˌzórz, ə-\ islands Portugal in North Atlantic lying 800 mi. (1287 km.) W of Portuguese coast; *pop* 241,763 — **Azor·e·an** *or* **Azor·i·an** \ā-'zór-ē-ən, ə-\ *adj or n*

Bab·y·lon \'ba-bə-lən, -ˌlän\ ancient city, ✳ of Babylonia; site 55 mi. (89 km.) S of Baghdad near the Euphrates — **Bab·y·lo·nian** \ˌba-bə-'lō-nyən, -nē-ən\ *adj or n*

Bab·y·lo·nia \ˌba-bə-'lō-nyə, -nē-ə\ ancient country W Asia in valley of lower Euphrates and Tigris rivers

Bac·tria \'bak-trē-ə\ ancient country W Asia in present NE Afghanistan — **Bac·tri·an** \'bak-trē-ən\ *adj or n*

Bad·lands barren region SW South Dakota & NW Nebraska

Baf·fin \'ba-fən\ **1** bay of the Atlantic between W Greenland & E Baffin Island **2** island NE Canada in Arctic Archipelago N of Hudson Strait

Bagh·dad \'bag-ˌdad, ˌbäg-'däd\ city, ✳ of Iraq on the Tigris; *pop* (est.) 5,949,000

Ba·guio \'bä-gē-'ò\ city, former summer ✳ of the Philippines in NW *cen* Luzon; *pop* 183,000

Ba·ha·mas \bə-'hä-məz\ islands in N Atlantic SE of Florida; ✳, Nassau; *pop* 303,611 — **Ba·ha·mi·an** \bə-'hā-mē-ən, -'hä-\ *or* **Ba·ha·man** \-'hä-mən, -'häm-ən\ *adj or n*

Bahia — see SALVADOR

Bah·rain \bä-'rān\ islands in Persian Gulf off coast of Arabia; country; ✳, Manama; *pop* 485,600 — **Bah·raini** \-'rä-nē\ *adj or n*

Bai·kal, Lake *or* Lake Bay·kal \bī-'käl, -'kal\ lake Russia, in mountains N of Mongolia

Ba·ja California \'bä-(ˌ)hä\ peninsula NW Mexico W of Gulf of California

Bakersfield \'bä-kərz-ˌfēld\ city S California; *pop* 247,057

Ba·ku \bä-'kü\ city, ✳ of Azerbaijan on W coast of Caspian Sea; *pop* 1,150,000

Bal·a·ton \'ba-lə-ˌtän, 'bò-lò-ˌtōn\ lake W Hungary

Bal·boa Heights \(ˌ)bal-'bō-ə\ town Panama; formerly the center of administration for Canal Zone

Bal·e·ar·ic Islands \ˌba-lē-'a-rik\ islands E Spain in the W Mediterranean

Ba·li \'bä-lē, 'ba-\ island Indonesia off E end of Java; *pop* 2,777,811 — **Ba·li·nese** \ˌbäl-i-nēz, ˌbal-, -'nēs\ *adj or n*

Bal·kan \'bòl-kən\ **1** mountains N Bulgaria extending from Serbia border to Black Sea; highest 7793 ft. (2375 m.) **2** peninsula SE Europe between Adriatic &

Ionian seas on the W & Aegean & Black seas on the E

Bal·kans \'bȯl-kənz\ *or* **Balkan States** countries occupying the Balkan Peninsula: Slovenia, Croatia, Bosnia and Herzegovina, Macedonia, Kosovo, Serbia, Montenegro, Romania, Bulgaria, Albania, Greece, Turkey (in Europe)

Bal·ly·me·na \ˌba-lē-'mē-nə\ district NE *cen* Northern Ireland; *pop* 56,032

Bal·ly·mon·ey \ˌba-lē-'mə-nē\ district N *cen* Northern Ireland; *pop* 23,984

Bal·tic Sea \'bȯl-tik\ arm of the Atlantic N Europe E of Scandinavian Peninsula

Bal·ti·more \'bȯl-tə-ˌmȯr, -mər\ city N *cen* Maryland; *pop* 651,154

Ba·ma·ko \'bä-mä-ˌkō\ city, ✳ of Mali on the Niger; *pop* 745,787

Ban·bridge \ban-'brij\ district SE *cen* Northern Ireland; *pop* 33,102

Ban·dar Se·ri Be·ga·wan \ˌbən-dər-ˌser-ē-bə-'gä-wän\ town, ✳ of Brunei; *pop* 27,285

Ban·dung \'bän-ˌdu̇ŋ\ city Indonesia in W Java SE of Jakarta; *pop* 2,057,442

Ban·ga·lore \'baŋ-gə-ˌlȯr\ city S India W of Madras; *pop* 4,292,223

Bang·kok \'baŋ-ˌkäk, baŋ-'\ city, ✳ of Thailand; *pop* 6,320,200

Ban·gla·desh \ˌbäŋ-glə-'desh, ˌbaŋ-, ˌbəŋ-, -'däsh\ country S Asia E of India; ✳, Dhaka; *pop* 115,075,000 — see EAST PAKISTAN — **Ban·gla·deshi** \-'de-shē, -'dä-\ *adj or n*

Ban·gor \'baŋ-ˌgȯr, 'ban-ˌgȯr\ town E Northern Ireland; *pop* 46,585

Ban·gui \bäŋ-'gē\ city, ✳ of Central African Republic; *pop* 300,723

Ban·jul \'bän-jül\ *formerly* **Bath·urst** \'bath-(ˌ)ərst\ city & port, ✳ of Gambia; *pop* 44,188

Bao·tou *or* **Pao–t'ou** \'bau̇-'tō\ city N China; *pop* 983,508

Bar·ba·dos \bär-'bā-(ˌ)dōs, -dəs, -(ˌ)dōz\ island West Indies in Lesser Antilles E of Windward Islands; country, ✳, Bridgetown; *pop* 250,010 — **Bar·ba·di·an** \-'bā-dē-ən\ *adj or n*

Bar·bu·da \bär-'bü-də\ island West Indies; part of independent Antigua and Barbuda

Bar·ce·lo·na \ˌbär-sə-'lō-nə\ city NE Spain on the Mediterranean; chief city of Catalonia; *pop* 1,503,884

Bar·king and Dag·en·ham \'bär-kiŋ-ən(d)-'da-gə-nəm\ borough of E Greater London, England; *pop* 139,960

Bar·na·ul \ˌbär-nə-'ül\ city S Russia; *pop* 606,000

Bar·net \'bär-nət\ borough of N Greater London, England; *pop* 283,000

Bar·ran·qui·lla \ˌbär-än-'kē-yä\ city N Colombia; *pop* 1,018,800

Barren Grounds treeless plains N Canada W of Hudson Bay

Bar·row, Point \'ba-(ˌ)rō\ most northerly point of Alaska & of U.S. at about 71°25′ N latitude

Ba·si·lan \bä-'sē-ˌlän\ island S Philippines SW of Mindanao

Bas·il·don \'ba-zəl-dən\ town SE England; *pop* 157,500

Bass \'bas\ strait separating Tasmania & continent of Australia

Basse·terre \bas-'ter, bäs-\ seaport Saint Kitts, ✳ of Saint Kitts-Nevis; *pop* 14,725

Basutoland — see LESOTHO

Bathurst — see BANJUL

Bat·on Rouge \ˌba-tᵊn-'rüzh\ city, ✳ of Louisiana; *pop* 227,818

Ba·var·ia \bə-'ver-ē-ə\ *or German* **Bay·ern** \'bī-ərn\ state SE Germany bordering on Czech Republic & Austria; *pop* 11,448,800 — **Ba·var·i·an** \bə-'ver-ē-ən, -'var-\ *adj or n*

Ba·ya·mon \ˌbī-ä-'mōn\ city NE *cen* Puerto Rico; *pop* 224,004

Beau·fort \'bō-fərt\ sea consisting of part of Arctic Ocean NE of Alaska & NW of Canada

Beau·mont \'bō-ˌmänt, bō-'\ city SE Texas; *pop* 113,866

Bech·u·a·na·land \ˌbech-'wä-nə-ˌland, -be-chə-\ **1** region S Africa N of Orange River **2** — see BOTSWANA — **Bech·u·a·na** \ˌbech-'wä-nə, -be-chə-\ *adj or n*

Bed·ford·shire \'bed-fərd-ˌshir, -shər\ *or* **Bedford** county SE England

Bedloe's — see LIBERTY

Bei·jing \'bā-'jiŋ\ *or* **Pe·king** \'pē-'kiŋ, 'pā-\ city, ✳ of China; *pop* 10,819,407

Bei·rut \bā-'rüt\ city, ✳ of Lebanon; urban area *pop* 1,100,000

Be·la·rus \ˌbē-lə-'rüs, ˌbye-lə-\ country *cen* Europe; ✳, Minsk; *pop* 9,899,000 — **Be·la·ru·si·an** \-'rü-sē-ən, -'rə-shən\ *or* **Be·la·rus·sian** \-'rə-shən\ *adj or n*

Belau — see PALAU

Be·lém \be-'lem\ city N Brazil; *pop* 1,280,614

Bel·fast \'bel-ˌfast, bel-'\ city, ✳ of Northern Ireland; *pop* 295,100

Bel·gium \'bel-jəm\ *or French* **Bel·gique** \bel-'zhēk\ *or Flemish* **Bel·gië** \'bel-kē-ə\ country W Europe; ✳, Brussels; *pop* 10,309,725 — **Bel·gian** \'bel-jən\ *adj or n*

Bel·grade \'bel-ˌgrād, -ˌgräd, -ˌgrad, bel-'\ *or* **Beo·grad** \bä-'ȯ-ˌgräd\ city, ✳ of Serbia on the Danube; *pop* 1,553,854

Be·lize \bə-'lēz\ *formerly* **British Honduras** country Central America on the Caribbean; ✳, Belmopan; *pop* 241,000 — **Be·liz·ean** *adj or n*

Belize City seaport E Belize; *pop* 45,158

Belle·vue \'bel-ˌvyü\ city W Washington E of Seattle; *pop* 109,569

Bel·mo·pan \ˌbel-mō-'pän\ city, ✳ of Belize; *pop* 6500

Be·lo Ho·ri·zon·te \'bā-lō-ˌȯr-ē-'zōn-tē\

city E Brazil N of Rio de Janeiro; *pop* 2,238,526

Be·lo·rus·sia \ˌbe-lō-ˈrə-shə, ˌbye-lō-\ *or* **Bye·lo·rus·sia** \ˌbē-ˌe-lō-, ˌbye-lō-\ former republic of U.S.S.R.; became independent Belarus in 1991 — **Belo·rus·sian** \ˌbe-lō-ˈrə-shən, ˌbye-\ *adj or n*

Ben·gal \ben-ˈgȯl, beŋ-, -ˈgäl\ region S Asia including delta of Ganges & Brahmaputra rivers; divided between Bangladesh & India — **Ben·gal·ese** \ˌbeŋ-gə-ˈlēz, ˌben-, -ˈlēs\ *adj or n*

Bengal, Bay of arm of Indian Ocean between India & Myanmar

Be·nin \bə-ˈnēn, -ˈnin; ˈbe-nin\ *formerly* **Da·ho·mey** \də-ˈhō-mē\ country W Africa on Gulf of Guinea; ✳, Porto-Novo; *pop* 5,074,000 — **Ben·i·nese** \ˌbə-ˌni-ˈnēz, -ˌnē-, -ˈnēs; ˌbe-ni-ˈnēz, -ˈnēs\ *adj or n*

Ben Nev·is \ben-ˈne-vəs\ mountain 4406 ft. (1343 m.) W Scotland in the Grampians; highest in Great Britain

Beograd — see BELGRADE

Ber·gen \ˈbər-gən, ˈber-\ city & port SW Norway; *pop* 209,375

Be·ring \ˈbir-iŋ, ˈber-\ **1** sea, arm of the North Pacific between Alaska & NE Siberia **2** strait at narrowest point 53 mi. (85 km.) wide between North America (Alaska) and Asia (Russia)

Berke·ley \ˈbər-klē\ city W California on San Francisco Bay N of Oakland; *pop* 102,743

Berk·shire \ˈbərk-ˌshir, -shər\ hills W Massachusetts; highest point Mount Greylock 3491 ft. (1064 m.)

Ber·lin \(ˌ)bər-ˈlin, *G* ber-ˈlēn\ city, ✳ of Germany; divided 1945–90 into **East Berlin** (✳ of East Germany) & **West Berlin** (city of West Germany lying within East Germany); *pop* 3,392,900 — **Ber·lin·er** \(ˌ)bər-ˈli-nər\ *n*

Ber·mu·da \(ˌ)bər-ˈmyü-də\ islands W Atlantic ESE of Cape Hatteras; a British colony; ✳, Hamilton; *pop* 62,059 — **Bermu·dan** \-dᵊn\ *or* **Ber·mu·di·an** \-dē-ən\ *adj or n*

Bern \ˈbərn, ˈbern\ city, ✳ of Switzerland; *pop* 122,469 — **Ber·nese** \(ˌ)bər-ˈnēz, -ˈnēs\ *adj or n*

Bes·sa·ra·bia \ˌbe-sə-ˈrā-bē-ə\ region SE Europe now chiefly in Moldova — **Bessa·ra·bi·an** \-bē-ən\ *adj or n*

Beth·le·hem \ˈbeth-li-ˌhem, -lē-həm, -lē-əm\ town of ancient Palestine in Judaea; the present-day town is SW of Jerusalem in the West Bank; *pop* 34,180

Bev·er·ly Hills \ˈbe-vər-lē\ city SW California within Los Angeles; *pop* 33,784

Bex·ley \ˈbek-slē\ borough of E Greater London, England; *pop* 211,200

Bho·pal \bō-ˈpäl\ city N *cen* India; *pop* 1,433,875

Bhu·tan \bü-ˈtän, -ˈtan\ country S Asia in the Himalayas on NE border of India; ✳,

Thimphu; *pop* 1,546,000 — **Bhu·ta·nese** \ˌbü-tə-ˈnēz, -ˈnēs\ *adj or n*

Bi·ki·ni \bi-ˈkē-nē\ atoll W Pacific in Marshall Islands

Bil·lings \ˈbi-liŋz\ city S *cen* Montana; largest in state; *pop* 89,847

Bi·lox·i \bə-ˈlək-sē, -ˈläk-\ city & port SE Mississippi on Gulf of Mexico; *pop* 50,644

Bi·o·ko \bē-ˈō-(ˌ)kō\ *formerly* **Fer·nan·do Póo** \fer-ˈnän-(ˌ)dō-ˈpō\ island portion of Equatorial Guinea in Gulf of Guinea

Bir·ken·head \ˈbər-kən-ˌhed, ˌbər-kən-ˈ\ borough NW England on the Mersey opposite Liverpool; *pop* 123,907

Bir·ming·ham \ˈbər-miŋ-ˌham\ **1** city N *cen* Alabama; *pop* 242,820 **2** city W *cen* England; *pop* 934,900

Bis·cay, Bay of \ˈbis-ˌkā, -kē\ inlet of the Atlantic between W coast of France & N coast of Spain

Bish·kek \bish-ˈkek\ *formerly 1926–91* **Frun·ze** \ˈfrün-zi\ city, ✳ of Kyrgyzstan; *pop* 641,400

Bis·marck \ˈbiz-ˌmärk\ **1** city, ✳ of North Dakota; *pop* 55,532 **2** archipelago W Pacific N of E end of New Guinea

Bis·sau \bi-ˈsau̇\ city, ✳ of Guinea-Bissau; *pop* 125,000

Bi·thyn·ia \bə-ˈthi-nē-ə\ ancient country NW Asia Minor bordering on Sea of Marmara and Black Sea — **Bi·thyn·i·an** \-nē-ən\ *adj or n*

Bit·ter·root \ˈbi-tə(r)-ˌrüt, -ˌru̇t\ range of the Rockies along Idaho–Montana boundary

Black·burn \ˈblak-(ˌ)bərn\ town NW England; *pop* 132,800

Black Forest forested mountain region Germany along E bank of the upper Rhine

Black Hills mountains W South Dakota & NE Wyoming

Black·pool \ˈblak-ˌpül\ town NW England on Irish Sea; *pop* 144,500

Black Sea sea between Europe & Asia connected with Aegean Sea through the Bosporus, Sea of Marmara, & Dardanelles

Blanc, Mont — see MONT BLANC

Blan·tyre \ˈblan-ˌtī(-ə)r\ city S Malawi; *pop* 554,578

Bloem·fon·tein \ˈblüm-fən-ˌtān, -ˌfän-\ city Republic of South Africa, judicial ✳ of the country; *pop* 149,836

Blue Ridge E range of the Appalachians E U.S. extending from S Pennsylvania to N Georgia

Bodh Gaya \ˈbȯd-ˈgī-ä\ village NE India; one of the holiest sites of Buddhism

Boe·o·tia \bē-ˈō-sh(ē-)ə\ ancient state E *cen* Greece NW of Attica; chief ancient city, Thebes — **Boe·o·tian** \bē-ˈō-shən\ *adj or n*

Bo·go·tá \ˌbō-gō-ˈtä, -ˈtȯ, ˈbō-gə-ˌ\ city, ✳ of Colombia; *pop* 4,921,300

Bo Hai *or* **Po Hai** \'bō-'hī\ *or* **Gulf of Chih·li** \'chē-'lē, 'jir-\ arm of Yellow Sea NE China

Bo·he·mia \bō-'hē-mē-ə\ region W Czech Republic; chief city, Prague

Bo·hol \bō-'hól\ island S *cen* Philippines

Boi·se \'bói-sē, -zē\ city, ✻ of Idaho; *pop* 185,787

Bo·liv·ia \bə-'li-vē-ə\ country W *cen* South America; administrative ✻, La Paz; constitutional ✻, Sucre; *pop* 8,274,325 — **Bo·liv·i·an** \-vē-ən\ *adj or n*

Bo·lo·gna \bō-'lō-nyä\ city N Italy; *pop* 379,964

Bol·ton \'bōl-tᵊn\ town NW England; *pop* 253,300

Bom·bay \bäm-'bā\ *or* **Mum·bai** \'məm-‚bī\ city & port W India; *pop* 11,914,398

Bonn \'bän, 'bón\ city Germany on the Rhine SSE of Cologne, formerly (1949–99) ✻ of West Germany; *pop* 296,244

Boo·thia \'bü-thē-ə\ peninsula N Canada W of Baffin Island; its N tip is most northerly point in mainland North America

Bor·ders \'bór-dərz\ former administrative region SE Scotland

Bor·neo \'bór-nē-‚ō\ island Malay Archipelago SW of the Philippines; divided between Brunei, Indonesia, and Malaysia

Bos·nia \'bäz-nē-ə, 'bóz\ region S Europe; with Herzegovina forms independent **Bosnia and Her·ze·go·vi·na** \‚hert-sə-gō-'vē-nə, ‚hert-, -'gō-və-nə\; ✻, Sarajevo; *pop* 4,422,000 — **Bos·ni·an** \-nē-ən\ *adj or n*

Bos·po·rus \'bäs-p(ə-)rəs\ strait 18 mi. (29 km.) long between Turkey in Europe & Turkey in Asia connecting Sea of Marmara & Black Sea

Bos·ton \'bós-tən\ city, ✻ of Massachusetts; *pop* 589,141 — **Bos·to·nian** \bó-'stō-nē-ən, -nyən\ *adj or n*

Bot·a·ny Bay \'bä-tə-nē\ inlet of South Pacific SE Australia in New South Wales S of Sydney

Both·nia, Gulf of \'bäth-nē-ə\ arm of Baltic Sea between Sweden & Finland

Bo·tswa·na \bät-'swä-nə\ *formerly* **Bech·u·a·na·land** \‚bech-'wä-nə-land\ country S Africa; ✻, Gaborone; *pop* 1,611,021

Boul·der \'bōl-dər\ city N *cen* Colorado; *pop* 94,673

Boulder Dam — see HOOVER DAM

Bourne·mouth \'bórn-məth, 'búrn-\ town S England on English Channel; *pop* 154,400

Brad·ford \'brad-fərd\ city N England; *pop* 280,691

Brah·ma·pu·tra \‚brä-mə-'pü-trə\ river about 1800 mi. (2900 km.) long S Asia flowing from the Himalayas in Tibet to Ganges Delta

Bra·sí·lia \brə-'zil-yə\ city, ✻ of Brazil; *pop* 2,051,146

Bra·ti·sla·va \‚bra-tə-'slä-və, ‚brä\ city on the Danube; ✻ of Slovakia; *pop* 428,672

Bra·zil \brə-'zil\ country E & *cen* South America; ✻, Brasília; *pop* 169,799,170 — **Bra·zil·ian** \brə-'zil-yən\ *adj or n*

Braz·za·ville \'bra-zə-‚vil, 'brä-zə-‚vēl\ city, ✻ of Republic of the Congo on W bank of lower Congo River; *pop* 937,579

Bre·men \'bre-mən, 'brā-\ city & port NW Germany; *pop* 552,746

Bren·ner \'bre-nər\ pass 4495 ft. (1370 m.) high in the Alps between Austria & Italy

Brent \'brent\ borough of W Greater London, England; *pop* 226,100

Bret·on, Cape \‚kāp-'bre-tᵊn, kə-'bre-, -'bri-\ cape Canada; most easterly point of Cape Breton Island & of Nova Scotia

Bridge·port \'brij-‚pórt\ city SW Connecticut on Long Island Sound; *pop* 139,529

Bridge·town \'brij-‚taún\ city, ✻ of Barbados; *pop* 5996

Brigh·ton \'brī-tᵊn\ town S England on English Channel; *pop* 133,400

Bris·bane \'briz-bən, -‚bān\ city & port E Australia; ✻ of Queensland; *pop* 751,115

Bris·tol \'bris-tᵊl\ **1** city & port SW England; *pop* 370,300 **2** channel between S Wales & SW England

Brit·ain \'bri-tᵊn\ **1** the island of Great Britain **2** UNITED KINGDOM

British Columbia province W Canada on Pacific coast; ✻, Victoria; *pop* 3,907,738

British Commonwealth — see COMMONWEALTH, THE

British Empire former empire consisting of Great Britain & the British dominions & dependencies

British Guiana — see GUYANA

British Honduras — see BELIZE

British India the part of India formerly under direct British administration

British Indian Ocean Territory British colony in Indian Ocean consisting of Chagos Archipelago

British Isles island group W Europe consisting of Great Britain, Ireland, & nearby islands

British Virgin Islands E islands of Virgin Islands; a British possession; *pop* 14,786

British West Indies islands of the West Indies including Jamaica, Trinidad and Tobago, & the Bahama & Cayman islands, Windward Islands, Leeward Islands, & British Virgin Islands

Brit·ta·ny \'bri-tə-nē\ region NW France SW of Normandy

Brom·ley \'bräm-lē\ borough of SE Greater London, England; *pop* 281,700

Bronx \'bräŋks\ *or* **The Bronx** borough of New York City NE of Manhattan; *pop* 1,332,650

Brook·lyn \'brúk-lən\ borough of New York City at SW end of Long Island; *pop* 2,465,326

Brooks Range \'brúks\ mountains N Alaska

Browns·ville \'braúnz-ˌvil, -vəl\ city S Texas on the Rio Grande; *pop* 139,722

Bru·nei \brü-'nī, 'brü-ˌnī\ country NE Borneo; ✳, Bandar Seri Begawan; *pop* 332,844 — **Bru·nei·an** \brü-'nī-ən\ *adj or n*

Brus·sels \'brə-səlz\ city, ✳ of Belgium; *pop* 136,730

Bu·cha·rest \'bü-kə-ˌrest, 'byü\ city, ✳ of Romania; *pop* 1,921,751

Buck·ing·ham·shire \'bə-kiŋ-əm-ˌshir\ *or* **Buckingham** county SE *cen* England

Bu·da·pest \'bü-də-ˌpest\ city, ✳ of Hungary; *pop* 2,008,546

Bue·nos Ai·res \ˌbwā-nəs-'a-rēz, *Sp* ˌbwā-nōs-'ī-rās\ city, ✳ of Argentina; *pop* 2,960,976

Buf·fa·lo \'bə-fə-ˌlō\ city W New York on Lake Erie; *pop* 292,648

Bu·jum·bu·ra \ˌbü-jəm-'búr-ə\ city, ✳ of Burundi; *pop* 236,334

Bu·ko·vi·na \ˌbü-kō-'vē-nə\ region E *cen* Europe in foothills of E Carpathians

Bul·gar·ia \ˌbəl-'ger-ē-ə, búl-\ country SE Europe on Black Sea; ✳, Sofia; *pop* 8,466,000 — **Bul·gar·i·an** \ˌbəl-'ger-ē-ən, búl-\ *adj or n*

Bull Run \'búl-'rən\ stream NE Virginia

Bun·ker Hill \'bəŋ-kər\ height in Boston, Massachusetts

Bur·bank \'bər-ˌbaŋk\ city SW California; *pop* 100,316

Bur·gun·dy \'bər-gən-dē\ region E France — **Bur·gun·di·an** \(ˌ)bər-'gən-dē-ən\ *adj or n*

Bur·ki·na Fa·so \búr-'kē-nə-'fä-sō, bər-\ *formerly* **Upper Vol·ta** \'vōl-tə, 'vól-\ country W Africa N of Ivory Coast, Ghana, & Togo; ✳, Ouagadougou; *pop* 9,780,000

Bur·ling·ton \'bər-liŋ-tən\ city NW Vermont; largest in state; *pop* 38,889

Bur·ma \'bər-mə\ — see MYANMAR — **Bur·mese** \ˌbər-'mēz, -'mēs\ *adj or n*

Bu·run·di \bù-'rün-dē, -'rùn-\ country E *cen* Africa; ✳, Bujumbura; *pop* 5,665,000 — **Bu·run·di·an** \-dē-ən\ *adj or n*

Busan — see PUSAN

Bute \'byüt\ island SW Scotland in Firth of Clyde

Butte \'byüt\ city SW Montana; county *pop* 34,606

Byelorussia — see BELORUSSIA

By·zan·tine Empire \'bi-zˀn-ˌtēn, 'bī-, -ˌtīn; bə-'zan-ˌtēn, -tīn, bī-\ empire of SE & S Europe and W Asia from 4th to 15th century

By·zan·ti·um \bə-'zan-sh(ē-)əm, -'zant-ē-əm\ ancient city on site of modern Istanbul

Caer·nar·von \kär-'när-vən, kə(r)-\ town & seaport NW Wales; *pop* 9506

Ca·guas \'kä-ˌgwäs\ town E *cen* Puerto Rico; *pop* 140,502

Cai·ro \'kī-(ˌ)rō\ city, ✳ of Egypt; *pop* 6,633,000 — **Cai·rene** \kī-'rēn\ *adj or n*

Ca·la·bria \kə-'lä-brē-ə, -'lä-\ district of ancient Italy consisting of area forming heel of Italian Peninsula — **Ca·la·bri·an** \kə-'lä-brē-ən, -'lä-\ *adj or n*

Cal·cut·ta \kal-'kə-tə\ *or* **Kol·ka·ta** \kōl-'kä-tä\ city E India on Hugli River; *pop* 4,580,544 — **Cal·cut·tan** \-'kə-tˀn\ *adj or n*

Cal·e·do·nia \ˌka-lə-'dō-nyə, -nē-ə\ — see SCOTLAND — **Cal·e·do·nian** \-nyən, -nē-ən\ *adj or n*

Cal·ga·ry \'kal-gə-rē\ city SW Alberta, Canada; *pop* 988,193

Ca·li \'kä-lē\ city W Colombia; *pop* 1,624,400

Cal·i·for·nia \ˌka-lə-'fòr-nyə\ state SW U.S.; ✳, Sacramento; *pop* 33,871,648 — **Cal·i·for·nian** \-nyən\ *adj or n*

California, Gulf of arm of the Pacific NW Mexico

Cal·va·ry \'kal-v(ə-)rē\ place outside ancient Jerusalem where Jesus was crucified

Cambay, Gulf of — see KHAMBHAT (Gulf of)

Cam·bo·dia \kam-'bō-dē-ə\ *or* **Kam·pu·chea** \ˌkam-pù-'chē-ə\ country SE Asia in S Indochina; ✳, Phnom Penh; *pop* 11,437,656 — **Cam·bo·di·an** \kam-'bō-dē-ən\ *adj or n*

Cam·bria \'kam-brē-ə\ WALES — an old name

Cam·bridge \'kām-brij\ 1 city E Massachusetts W of Boston; *pop* 101,355 2 city E England; *pop* 92,772

Cam·bridge·shire \'kām-brij-ˌshir, -shər\ *or* **Cambridge** county E England

Cam·den \'kam-dən\ borough of N Greater London, England; *pop* 170,500

Cam·er·oon *or French* **Cam·er·oun** \ˌka-mə-'rün\ country W Africa; ✳, Yaoundé; *pop* 13,103,000 — **Cam·er·oo·nian** \-'rü-nē-ən, -rü-nyən\ *adj or n*

Ca·mi·guin \ˌkä-mē-'gēn\ island Philippines, off N coast of Mindanao

Ca·naan \'kä-nən\ ancient region SW Asia; approximately the area later called Palestine — **Ca·naan·ite** \'kā-nə-ˌnīt\ *adj or n*

Can·a·da \'ka-nə-də\ country N North America; ✳, Ottawa; *pop* 31,612,897 — **Ca·na·di·an** \kə-'nä-dē-ən\ *adj or n*

Canadian Falls — see NIAGARA FALLS

Canadian Shield *or* **Lau·ren·tian Plateau** \lò-'ren(t)-shən\ plateau region E Canada & NE U.S. extending from Mackenzie River basin E to Davis Strait & S to S Quebec, S *cen* Ontario, NE Minnesota, N Wisconsin, NW Michigan, and NE New York including the Adirondacks

Canal Zone *or* **Panama Canal Zone**

strip of territory Panama leased to U.S. (until 1979) for Panama Canal

Ca·nary \kə-'ner-ē\ islands Spain in the Atlantic off NW coast of Africa; *pop* 1,493,784

Ca·nav·er·al, Cape \kə-'nav-rəl, -'na-və-\ *or 1963–73* **Cape Ken·ne·dy** \-'ken-ə-dē\ cape E Florida in the Atlantic on **Canaveral Peninsula** E of Indian River

Can·ber·ra \'kan-b(ə-)rə, -,ber-ə\ city, ✻ of Australia in Australian Capital Territory; *pop* 348,600

Cannes \'kan, 'kän\ port SE France; *pop* 69,363

Can·ter·bury \'kan-tə(r)-,ber-ē, -b(ə-)rē\ city SE England; *pop* 34,404

Canton — see GUANGZHOU

Cape Bret·on Island \kāp-'bre-tᵊn, kə-'bre-, -'bri-\ island NE Nova Scotia

Cape Coral city SW Florida; *pop* 102,286

Cape Horn — see HORN, CAPE

Cape of Good Hope — see GOOD HOPE, CAPE OF

Cape Province *or* **Cape of Good Hope** *or before 1910* **Cape Colony** former province S Republic of South Africa

Cape Town \'kāp-,taún\ city, legislative ✻ of Republic of South Africa and formerly ✻ of Cape Province; *pop* 776,617

Cape Verde \'vərd\ islands in the North Atlantic off W Africa; country; ✻, Praia; *pop* 350,000 — **Cape Verd·ean** \'vər-dē-ən\ *adj or n*

Cape York Peninsula \'yórk\ peninsula NE Australia in N Queensland

Ca·pri \ka-'prē, kə-; 'kä-(,)prē, 'ka-\ island Italy S of Bay of Naples; *pop* 7270

Ca·ra·cas \kä-'rä-käs\ city, ✻ of Venezuela; *pop* 1,824,892

Car·diff \'kär-dif\ city, ✻ of Wales; *pop* 272,600

Ca·rib·be·an Sea \,ka-rə-'bē-ən, kə-'ri-bē-\ arm of the Atlantic; on N & E are the West Indies, on S is South America, & on W is Central America — **Caribbean** *adj*

Car·lisle \kär-'lī(-ə)l, kər-, 'kär-,\ city NW England; *pop* 99,800

Carls·bad Caverns \'kärl(-ə)lz-,bad\ series of caves SE New Mexico

Car·mar·then \kär-'mär-thən, kə(r)-\ port S Wales; *pop* 54,800

Car·o·li·na \,ka-rə-'lī-nə\ English colony on E coast of North America founded 1663 & divided 1729 into North Carolina & South Carolina (the **Carolinas**) — **Car·o·lin·i·an** \,ka-rə-'li-nē-ən, -nyən\ *adj or n*

Ca·ro·li·na \,kä-rō-'lē-nä\ city NE Puerto Rico; *pop* 186,076

Car·o·line \'ka-rə-,līn, -lən\ islands W Pacific E of S Philippines; comprising Palau & the Federated States of Micronesia

Car·pa·thi·an \kär-'pā-thē-ən\ mountains E *cen* Europe along boundary between Slovakia & Poland & in N & *cen* Romania; highest Gerlachovksky 8711 ft. (2655 m.)

Car·pen·tar·ia, Gulf of \,kär-pən-'ter-ē-ə\ inlet of Arafura Sea N of Australia

Car·rick·fer·gus \,ka-rik-'fər-gəs\ district E Northern Ireland; *pop* 32,439

Car·roll·ton \'ka-rəl-tən\ city N Texas; *pop* 109,576

Car·son City \'kär-sᵊn\ city, ✻ of Nevada; *pop* 52,457

Car·thage \'kär-thij\ ancient city N Africa NE of modern Tunis; ✻ of an empire that once included much of NW Africa, E Spain, & Sicily — **Car·tha·gin·ian** \,kär-thə-'ji-nyən, -nē-ən\ *adj or n*

Ca·sa·blan·ca \,ka-sə-'blaŋ-kə, ,kä-sə-'bläŋ-, -zə-\ city W Morocco on the Atlantic; *pop* 3,102,000

Cas·cade Range \(,)kas-'kād\ mountains NW U.S. in Washington, Oregon, & N California — see RAINIER, MOUNT

Cas·per \'kas-pər\ city *cen* Wyoming; *pop* 49,644

Cas·pi·an Sea \'kas-pē-ən\ salt lake between Europe and Asia about 90 ft. (27 m.) below sea level

Cas·tile \ka-'stēl\ *or Spanish* **Cas·ti·lla** \kä-'stēl-yä, -'stē-yä\ region & ancient kingdom *cen* & N Spain

Cast·le·reagh \'ka-səl-(,)rā\ district E Northern Ireland; *pop* 60,649

Cas·tries \'kas-,trēz, -,trēs\ seaport, ✻ of Saint Lucia; *pop* 1814

Cat·a·lo·nia \,ka-tə-'lō-nyə, -nē-ə\ region NE Spain bordering on France & the Mediterranean; chief city, Barcelona; *pop* 6,059,494 — **Cat·a·lo·nian** \-'lō-nyən, -nē-ən\ *adj or n*

Ca·thay \ka-'thā\ an old name for China

Cats·kill \'kat-,skil\ mountains in Appalachian system SE New York W of the Hudson

Cau·ca·sus \'kó-kə-səs\ mountain system SE Europe between Black & Caspian seas in Russia, Georgia, Azerbaijan, & Armenia

Cay·enne \kī-'en, kā-\ city, ✻ of French Guiana; *pop* 37,097

Cay·man \(,)kā-'man, *attributively* 'kā-mən\ islands West Indies NW of Jamaica; a British colony; *pop* 23,881

Ce·bu \sā-'bü\ island E *cen* Philippines

Ce·dar Rapids \'sē-dər\ city E Iowa; *pop* 120,758

Cel·tic Sea \'kel-tik, 'sel-\ inlet of the Atlantic in British Isles SE of Ireland, SW of Wales, & W of SW England

Central African Republic country N *cen* Africa; ✻, Bangui; *pop* 2,998,000

Central America narrow portion of North America from S border of Mexico to South America — **Central American** *adj or n*

Central Valley valley of Sacramento &

San Joaquin rivers in California between Sierra Nevada & Coast Ranges

Cey·lon \si-ˈlän, sā-\ **1** island in Indian Ocean off S India **2** — see SRI LANKA — **Cey·lon·ese** \ˌsā-lə-ˈnēz, ˌsē-, ˌse-, -ˈnēs\ adj or n

Chad \ˈchad\ country N cen Africa; ✻, N'Djamena; pop 5,200,000 — **Chad·ian** \ˈcha-dē-ən\ adj or n

Chad, Lake shallow lake N cen Africa at junction of boundaries of Chad, Niger, & Nigeria

Cha·gos Archipelago \ˈchä-gəs\ island group cen Indian Ocean; forms British Indian Ocean Territory — see DIEGO GARCIA

Chal·dea \kal-ˈdē-ə\ ancient region SW Asia on Euphrates River & Persian Gulf — **Chal·de·an** \-ˈdē-ən\ adj or n — **Chal·dee** \ˈkal-ˌdē\ n

Cham·pagne \sham-ˈpān\ region NE France

Cham·plain, Lake \sham-ˈplān\ lake between New York & Vermont extending N into Quebec

Chan·di·garh \ˈchən-dē-gər\ city N India N of Delhi; pop 510,565

Chan·dler \ˈchan(d)-lər\ city SW cen Arizona; pop 176,581

Chang \ˈchäŋ\ or **Yang·tze** \ˈyaŋ-ˈsē, ˈyaŋ(k)t-ˈsē; ˈyäŋ-ˈtsə\ river 3434 mi. (5525 km.) long cen China flowing into East China Sea

Chang·chun \ˈchäŋ-ˈchùn\ city NE China; pop 1,679,270

Chang·sha \ˈchäŋ-ˈshä\ city SE cen China; pop 1,113,312

Channel islands in English Channel including Jersey, Guernsey, & Alderney & belonging to United Kingdom; pop 135,694

Charles \ˈchär(-ə)lz\ river 47 mi. (76 km.) long E Massachusetts flowing into Boston harbor

Charles, Cape cape E Virginia N of entrance to Chesapeake Bay

Charles·ton \ˈchär(-ə)l-stən\ **1** seaport SE South Carolina; pop 96,650 **2** city, ✻ of West Virginia; pop 53,421

Char·lotte \ˈshär-lət\ city S North Carolina; pop 540,828

Charlotte Ama·lie \ə-ˈmäl-yə, ˈa-mə-lē\ city, ✻ of Virgin Islands of the U.S.; on island of Saint Thomas; pop 12,331

Char·lottes·ville \ˈshär-ləts-ˌvil, -vəl\ city cen Virginia; pop 45,049

Char·lotte·town \ˈshär-lət-ˌtaùn\ city, ✻ of Prince Edward Island, Canada; pop 32,245

Chat·ta·noo·ga \ˌcha-tə-ˈnü-gə\ city SE Tennessee; pop 155,554

Chech·nya \chech-ˈnyä, ˈchech-nyə\ republic of SE Russia in Europe; ✻, Grozny

Chelms·ford \ˈchemz-fərd\ town SE England; pop 150,000

Che·lya·binsk \chel-ˈyä-bən(t)sk\ city W Russia; pop 1,143,000

Cheng·chou — see ZHENGZHOU

Cheng·du or **Ch'eng-tu** \ˈchəŋ-ˈdü\ city SW cen China; pop 1,713,255

Chennai — see MADRAS

Cher·no·byl \chər-ˈnō-bəl, (ˌ)cher-\ site N Ukraine of town abandoned after 1986 nuclear accident

Ches·a·peake \ˈche-sə-ˌpēk, ˈches-ˌpēk\ city SE Virginia; pop 199,184

Chesapeake Bay inlet of the Atlantic in Virginia & Maryland

Chesh·ire \ˈche-shər, -ˌshir\ or **Ches·ter** \ˈches-tər\ county W England bordering on Wales

Chester \ˈches-tər\ city NW England; pop 58,436

Chev·i·ot \ˈchē-vē-ət, ˈche-\ hills along English–Scottish border

Chey·enne \shī-ˈan, -ˈen\ city, ✻ of Wyoming; pop 53,011

Chi·ba \ˈchē-bä\ city E Japan in Honshu on Tokyo Bay E of Tokyo; pop 887,164

Chi·ca·go \shə-ˈkä-(ˌ)gō, -ˈkȯ-, -gə\ city & port NE Illinois on Lake Michigan; pop 2,896,016 — **Chi·ca·go·an** \-ˈkä-gō-ən, -ˈkȯ-\ n

Chi·chén It·zá \chē-ˌchen-ēt-ˈsä, -ˈēt-sə\ ruined Mayan city SE Mexico in Yucatán Peninsula

Chich·es·ter \ˈchi-chəs-tər\ city S England; pop 24,189

Ch'i-ch'i-ha-erh — see QIQIHAR

Chihli, Gulf of — see BO HAI

Chi·le \ˈchi-lē, ˈchē-(ˌ)lā\ country SW South America; ✻, Santiago; pop 15,116,435 — **Chil·ean** \ˈchi-lē-ən, chə-ˈlā-ən\ adj or n

Chim·bo·ra·zo \ˌchēm-bō-ˈrä-(ˌ)zō\ mountain 20,561 ft. (6267 m.) W cen Ecuador

Chi·na \ˈchī-nə\ **1** country E Asia; ✻, Beijing; pop 1,179,467,000 — see TAIWAN **2** sea section of the W Pacific; divided at Taiwan strait into East China & South China seas

Chin–chou or **Chinchow** — see JINZHOU

Chi·și·nău \ˌkē-shē-ˈnaù\ or **Ki·shi·nev** \ˈki-shi-ˈnyȯf; ˈki-shə-ˌnef, -ˌnev\ city cen Moldova; its ✻; pop 665,000

Chit·ta·gong \ˈchi-tə-ˌgäŋ, -ˌgȯŋ\ city SE Bangladesh on Bay of Bengal; pop 1,566,070

Chong·qing or **Ch'ung–ch'ing** \ˈchùŋ-ˈchiŋ\ or **Chung·king** \ˈchùŋ-ˈkiŋ\ city SW cen China; pop 2,266,772

Christ·church \ˈkrīs(t)-ˌchərch\ city New Zealand on E coast of South Island; urban area pop 334,107

Christ·mas \ˈkris-məs\ island E Indian Ocean SW of Java; governed by Australia; pop 1000

Chu·la Vis·ta \ˌchü-lə-ˈvis-tə\ city SW California S of San Diego; pop 173,556

Chuuk \\'chùk\\ *or* **Truk** \\'trək, 'trúk\\ islands *cen* Carolines, part of Federated States of Micronesia

Cin·cin·na·ti \\ˌsin(t)-sə-'na-tē, -'na-tə\\ city SW Ohio; *pop* 331,285

Ci·u·dad Juá·rez \\syü-'thäth-'hwär-es, 'wär-; ˌsē-ù-'dad-\\ city Mexico on Texas border; urban area *pop* 1,011,786

Ciudad Trujillo — see SANTO DOMINGO

Clarks·ville \\'klärks-ˌvil, -vəl\\ city N Tennessee NW of Nashville; *pop* 103,455

Clear·wa·ter \\'klir-ˌwó-tər, -ˌwä-\\ city W Florida NW of St. Petersburg; *pop* 108,787

Cleve·land \\'klēv-lənd\\ city & port NE Ohio on Lake Erie; *pop* 478,403

Clyde \\'klīd\\ river 106 mi. (171 km.) long SW Scotland flowing into **Firth of Clyde** (estuary)

Coast Mountains mountain range W British Columbia, Canada; the N continuation of Cascade Range

Coast Ranges chain of mountain ranges W North America extending along Pacific coast W of Sierra Nevada & Cascade Range & through Vancouver Island into S Alaska to Kenai Peninsula & Kodiak Island

Cod, Cape \\-'käd\\ peninsula SE Massachusetts

Coim·ba·tore \\ˌkóim-bə-'tór\\ city S India; *pop* 816,321

Cole·raine \\kōl-'rān, 'kōl-ˌ\\ **1** district N Northern Ireland; *pop* 51,062 **2** port in Coleraine district

Co·logne \\kə-'lōn\\ city W Germany on the Rhine; *pop* 956,690

Co·lom·bia \\kə-'ləm-bē-ə\\ country NW South America; *, Bogotá; *pop* 26,525,670 — **Co·lom·bi·an** \\-bē-ən\\ *adj or n*

Co·lom·bo \\kə-'ləm-(ˌ)bō\\ city, * of Sri Lanka; *pop* 615,000

Col·o·ra·do \\ˌkä-lə-'ra-(ˌ)dō\\ **1** river 1450 mi. (2334 km.) long SW U.S. & NW Mexico flowing from N Colorado into Gulf of California **2** desert SE California **3** plateau region SW U.S. W of Rocky Mountains **4** state W U.S.; *, Denver; *pop* 4,301,261 — **Col·o·rad·an** \\-'ra-d°n, -'rä-\\ *or* **Co·lo·ra·do·an** \\-'ra-dō-ən, -'rä-\\ *adj or n*

Colorado Springs city *cen* Colorado E of Pikes Peak; *pop* 360,890

Co·lum·bia \\kə-'ləm-bē-ə\\ **1** river 1214 mi. (1953 km.) long SW Canada & NW U.S. flowing S & W from SE British Columbia into the Pacific **2** plateau in Columbia River basin in E Washington, E Oregon, & SW Idaho **3** city, * of South Carolina; *pop* 116,278

Co·lum·bus \\kə-'ləm-bəs\\ **1** city W Georgia; *pop* 186,291 **2** city, * of Ohio; *pop* 711,470

Com·mon·wealth, the \\'käm-ən-ˌwel(t)th\\ *or* **Commonwealth of Na-**tions *formerly* **British Commonwealth** the United Kingdom & most of the countries formerly dependent on it

Com·o·ros \\'kä-mə-ˌrōz\\ islands off SE Africa NW of Madagascar; country (except for Mayotte Island); *, Moroni; *pop* 519,527

Con·a·kry \\'kä-nə-krē\\ city, * of Guinea; *pop* 581,000

Con·cord \\'kän-ˌkórd, 'käŋ-\\ **1** city W California; *pop* 121,780 **2** town E Massachusetts NW of Boston; *pop* 16,993 **3** city, * of New Hampshire; *pop* 40,687

Con·go \\'käŋ-(ˌ)gō\\ **1** *or* **Zaire** \\zä-'ir\\ river over 2700 mi. (4344 km.) long W Africa flowing into the Atlantic **2** *officially* **Democratic Republic of the Congo** *formerly 1971–97* **Zaire** country *cen* Africa consisting of most of Congo River basin E of lower Congo River; *, Kinshasa; *pop* 43,775,000 **3** *or officially* **Republic of the Congo** country W *cen* Africa W of lower Congo River; *, Brazzaville; *pop* 2,775,000 — **Con·go·lese** \\ˌkäŋ-gə-'lēz, -'lēs\\ *adj or n*

Con·nacht \\'kä-ˌnót\\ province W Ireland; *pop* 422,909

Con·nect·i·cut \\kə-'ne-ti-kət\\ **1** river 407 mi. (655 km.) long NE U.S. flowing S from N New Hampshire into Long Island Sound **2** state NE U.S.; *, Hartford; *pop* 3,405,565

Constantinople — see ISTANBUL

Continental Divide line of highest points of land separating the waters flowing W from those flowing N or E and extending SSE from NW Canada across W U.S. through Mexico & Central America to South America where it joins the Andes Mountains

Cook \\'kúk\\ **1** inlet of the Pacific S Alaska W of Kenai Peninsula **2** islands South Pacific SW of Society Islands belonging to New Zealand; *pop* 17,614 **3** strait New Zealand between North Island & South Island

Cook, Mount *formerly* **Ao·rangi** \\aú-'räŋ-ē\\ mountain 12,349 ft. (3764 m.) New Zealand in W *cen* South Island in Southern Alps; highest in New Zealand

Cooks·town \\'kúks-ˌtaún\\ district *cen* Northern Ireland; *pop* 30,808

Co·pen·ha·gen \\ˌkō-pən-'hä-gən, -'hä-\\ city, * of Denmark; *pop* 501,285

Cor·al Sea \\'kór-əl, 'kär-\\ arm of the W Pacific NE of Australia

Coral Springs city SE Florida; *pop* 117,549

Cór·do·ba \\'kór-də-bə, 'kór-thō-ˌvä\\ city N *cen* Argentina; *pop* 1,179,067

Cor·inth \\'kór-ən(t)th, 'kär-\\ **1** region of ancient Greece **2** ancient city; site SW of present city of Corinth — **Co·rin·thi·an** \\kə-'rin(t)-thē-ən\\ *adj or n*

Corinth, Gulf of inlet of Ionian Sea *cen* Greece N of the Peloponnese

Cork \'kòrk\ city S Ireland; *pop* 123,062

Corn·wall \'kòrn-ˌwòl, -wəl\ *or since 1974* **Cornwall and Isles of Scilly** \'si-lē\ county SW England

Co·ro·na \kə-'rō-nə\ city SW California E of Los Angeles; *pop* 124,966

Cor·pus Chris·ti \ˌkòr-pəs-'kris-tē\ city & port S Texas; *pop* 277,454

Cor·reg·i·dor \kə-'re-gə-ˌdòr\ island Philippines at entrance to Manila Bay

Cor·si·ca \'kòr-si-kə\ island France in the Mediterranean N of Sardinia; *pop* 260,149 — **Cor·si·can** \'kòr-si-kən\ *adj or n*

Cos·ta Me·sa \'mā-sə\ city SW California; *pop* 108,724

Costa Ri·ca \'rē-kə\ country Central America between Nicaragua & Panama; *, San José; *pop* 4,075,863 — **Cos·ta Ri·can** \-kən\ *adj or n*

Côte d'Ivoire — see IVORY COAST

Cots·wold \'kät-ˌswōld, -swəld\ hills SW *cen* England

Cov·en·try \'kə-vən-trē\ city *cen* England; *pop* 292,500

Craig·av·on \krā-'ga-vən\ district *cen* Northern Ireland; *pop* 74,494

Cra·ter \'krā-tər\ lake 1932 ft. (589 m.) deep SW Oregon in Cascade Range

Crete \'krēt\ island Greece in E Mediterranean; *pop* 536,980 — **Cre·tan** \'krē-tⁿn\ *adj or n*

Cri·mea \krī-'mē-ə, krə-\ peninsula SE Europe in S Ukraine, extending into Black Sea — **Cri·me·an** \krī-'mē-ən, krə-\ *adj*

Cro·atia \krō-'ā-sh(ē-)ə\ country SE Europe; *, Zagreb; *pop* 4,437,460 — **Croat** \'krō-ˌat\ *n*

Croy·don \'kròi-dⁿn\ borough of S Greater London, England; *pop* 299,600

Cu·ba \'kyü-bə, 'kü-vä\ island in the West Indies; country; *, Havana; *pop* 10,892,000 — **Cu·ban** \'kyü-bən\ *adj or n*

Cum·ber·land \'kəm-bər-lənd\ river 687 mi. (1106 km.) long S Kentucky & N Tennessee

Cumberland Gap pass through Cumberland Plateau NE Tennessee

Cumberland Plateau mountain region E U.S.; part of S Appalachian Mountains extending from S West Virginia to NE Alabama

Cum·bria \'kəm-brē-ə\ county NW England; *pop* 486,900

Cum·bri·an \'kəm-brē-ən\ mountains NW England chiefly in Cumbria county

Cu·par \'kü-pər\ town E Scotland; *pop* 6642

Cu·ri·ti·ba \ˌkùr-ə-'tē-bə\ city S Brazil SW of São Paulo; *pop* 1,587,315

Cush \'kəsh, 'kùsh\ ancient country NE Africa in upper Nile valley S of Egypt —

Cush·ite \'kə-ˌshīt, 'kù-\ *n* — **Cush·it·ic** \ˌkə-'shi-tik, kù-\ *adj*

Cuz·co \'küs-(ˌ)kō\ city S *cen* Peru; *pop* 316,804

Cymru — see WALES

Cy·prus \'sī-prəs\ island E Mediterranean S of Turkey; country; *, Nicosia; *pop* 793,100 — **Cyp·ri·ot** \'si-prē-ət, -ˌät\ *or* **Cyp·ri·ote** \-ˌōt, -ət\ *adj or n*

Cy·re·na·ica \ˌsir-ə-'nā-ə-kə, ˌsī-rə-\ ancient region N Africa on coast W of Egypt — **Cy·re·na·i·can** \-'nä-ə-kən\ *adj or n*

Czecho·slo·va·kia \ˌche-kə-slō-'vä-kē-ə, -slə-, -'va-\ former country *cen* Europe divided into the independent states of the Czech Republic & Slovakia — **Czecho·slo·vak** \'slō-ˌväk, -ˌvak\ *adj or n* — **Czecho·slo·va·ki·an** \-slō-'vä-kē-ən, -slə-, -'va-\ *adj or n*

Czech Republic country *cen* Europe; *, Prague; *pop* 10,332,000

Daegu — see TAEGU

Daejeon — see TAEJON

Dahomey — see BENIN

Dairen — see DALIAN

Da·kar \'da-ˌkär, dä-'kär\ city, * of Senegal; *pop* 1,729,823

Da·ko·ta **1** *or* **James** river 710 mi. (1143 km.) long North Dakota & South Dakota flowing S into the Missouri **2** territory 1861–89 NW U.S. divided 1889 into states of North Dakota & South Dakota (the **Dakotas** \-təz\ )

Da·lian \dä-'lyen\ *or* **Ta·lien** \'dä-'lyen\ *or* **Lü·da** *or* **Lü·ta** \'lü-'dä\ *or* **Dai·ren** \'dī-'ren\ city NE China; *pop* 1,723,302

Dal·las \'da-ləs, -lis\ city NE Texas; *pop* 1,188,580

Dal·ma·tia \dal-'mā-sh(ē-)ə\ region W Balkan Peninsula on the Adriatic — **Dal·ma·tian** \-shən\ *adj or n*

Da·ly City \'dā-lē\ city W California S of San Francisco; *pop* 103,621

Da·mas·cus \də-'mas-kəs\ city, * of Syria; *pop* 1,451,000

Dan·ube \'dan-(ˌ)yüb\ river 1771 mi. (2850 km.) long S Europe flowing from SW Germany into Black Sea — **Da·nu·bi·an** \da-'nü-bē-ən, da-, -'nyü-\ *adj*

Dar·da·nelles \ˌdär-də-'nelz\ *or* **Hel·les·pont** \'he-lə-ˌspänt\ strait NW Turkey connecting Sea of Marmara & the Aegean

Dar es Sa·laam \ˌdär-ˌe(s)-sə-'läm\ city, historic * of Tanzania; *pop* 1,360,850

Dar·ling \'där-liŋ\ river about 1700 mi. (2735 km.) long SE Australia in Queensland & New South Wales flowing SW into the Murray

Dar·win \'där-wən\ city Australia, * of Northern Territory; *pop* 70,071

Da·vao \'dä-ˌvaù, dä-'vaù\ city S Philippines in E Mindanao on Davao Gulf; *pop* 850,000

Dav·en·port \'da-vən-ˌpòrt\ city E Iowa; *pop* 98,359

Da·vis \'dā-vəs\ strait between SW Greenland & E Baffin Island connecting Baffin Bay & the Atlantic

Day·ton \'dā-ᵊn\ city SW Ohio; *pop* 166,169

Dead Sea salt lake between Israel & Jordan; 1312 ft. (400 m.) below sea level

Death Valley dry valley E California & S Nevada containing lowest point in U.S. (282 ft. *or* 86 m. below sea level)

Dec·can \'de-kən, -ˌkan\ plateau region S India

Del·a·ware \'de-lə-ˌwer, -wər\ 1 river 296 mi. (476 km.) long E U.S. flowing S from S New York into Delaware Bay 2 state E U.S.; ✳, Dover; *pop* 783,600 — **Del·a·war·ean** *or* **Del·a·war·ian** \ˌde-lə-'wer-ē-ən\ *adj or n*

Delaware Bay inlet of the Atlantic between SW New Jersey & E Delaware

Del·hi \'de-lē\ city N India; *pop* 9,817,439 — see NEW DELHI

De·los \'dē-ˌläs\ island Greece — **De·lian** \'dē-lē-ən, 'dēl-yən\ *adj or n*

Del·phi \'del-ˌfī\ ancient town *cen* Greece on S slope of Mt. Parnassus

Democratic Republic of the Congo — see CONGO 2

Denali — see MCKINLEY, MOUNT

Den·mark \'den-ˌmärk\ country N Europe occupying most of Jutland & neighboring islands; ✳, Copenhagen; *pop* 5,383,507

Den·ver \'den-vər\ city, ✳ of Colorado; *pop* 554,636

Der·by \'där-bē\ city N *cen* England; *pop* 214,000

Der·by·shire \'där-bē-ˌshir, -shər\ *or* **Derby** county N *cen* England

Der·ry \'der-ē\ *or* **Lon·don·der·ry** \ˌlən-dən-'der-ē\ city & port NW Northern Ireland; *pop* 62,697

Des Moines \di-'mòin\ city, ✳ of Iowa; *pop* 198,682

De·troit \di-'tròit\ 1 river 31 mi. (50 km.) long between SE Michigan & Ontario connecting Lake Saint Clair & Lake Erie 2 city SE Michigan; *pop* 951,270

Dev·on \'de-vən\ *or* **De·von·shire** \'de-vən-ˌshir, -shər\ county SW England

Dha·ka \'dä-kə\ city, ✳ of Bangladesh; *pop* 3,637,892

Die·go Gar·cia \dē-ˌā-gō-ˌgär-'sē-ə\ island in Indian Ocean; chief island of Chagos Archipelago

Dili *or* **Dilli** \'di-lē\ city & port N Timor, ✳ of East Timor

Di·nar·ic Alps \də-'na-rik\ range of the E Alps in W Slovenia, W Croatia, Bosnia and Herzegovina, & Montenegro

District of Co·lum·bia \kə-'ləm-bē-ə\ federal district E U.S. coextensive with city of Washington; *pop* 572,059

Djakarta — see JAKARTA

Dji·bou·ti \jə-'bü-tē\ 1 country E Africa on Gulf of Aden; *pop* 510,000 2 city, its ✳; *pop* 300,000

Dni·pro·pe·trovs'k *or* **Dne·pro·pe·trovsk** \də-ˌnye-prə-pə-'tròfsk\ city E *cen* Ukraine; *pop* 1,189,000

Dodge City \'däj\ city S Kansas on Arkansas River; *pop* 25,176

Do·do·ma \dō-'dō-ˌ)mä\ city, legislative ✳ of Tanzania; *pop* 203,833

Do·ha \'dō-ˌ)hä\ city & port, ✳ of Qatar on Persian Gulf; *pop* 217,294

Dom·i·ni·ca \ˌdä-mə-'nē-kə\ island West Indies in the Leeward Islands; country; ✳, Roseau; *pop* 71,242

Do·min·i·can Republic \də-'mi-ni-kən\ country West Indies in E Hispaniola; ✳, Santo Domingo; *pop* 8,533,744 — **Dominican** *adj or n*

Don \'dän\ river 1224 mi. (1969 km.) long SW Russia

Do·nets'k \də-'nyetsk\ city E Ukraine; *pop* 1,121,000

Dor·ches·ter \'dòr-chəs-tər, -ˌches-\ town S England; *pop* 14,049

Dor·set \'dòr-sət\ *or* **Dor·set·shire** \-ˌshir, -shər\ county S England on English Channel

Dort·mund \'dòrt-ˌmủnt, -mənd\ city W Germany in the Ruhr; *pop* 601,007

Dou·a·la \dü-'ä-lä\ seaport W Cameroon; *pop* 810,000

Dou·ro \'dòr-ˌ)ü\ *or* Spanish **Due·ro** \'dwe(ə)r-ō\ river 556 mi. (895 km.) long N Spain & N Portugal flowing into the Atlantic

Do·ver \'dō-vər\ city, ✳ of Delaware; *pop* 32,135

Dover, Strait of channel between SE England & N France; the most easterly section of English Channel

Down \'daủn\ district SE Northern Ireland; *pop* 57,511

Dow·ney \'daủ-nē\ city SW California SE of Los Angeles; *pop* 107,323

Down·pat·rick \daủn-'pa-trik\ town E Northern Ireland; *pop* 8245

Dra·kens·berg \'drä-kənz-ˌbərg\ mountain range E Republic of South Africa & Lesotho; highest peak Thabana Ntlenyana 11,425 ft. (3482 m.)

Dres·den \'drez-dən\ city E Germany; *pop* 485,132

Dub·lin \'də-blən\ city, ✳ of Ireland; *pop* 495,781

Dud·ley \'dəd-lē\ town W *cen* England; *pop* 300,000

Duis·burg \'dü-əs-ˌbərg, 'düz-ˌ, 'dyüz-ˌ\ city W Germany at junction of Rhine & Ruhr rivers; *pop* 537,441

Du·luth \də-'lüth\ city & port NE Minnesota at W end of Lake Superior; *pop* 86,918

Dum·fries \ˌdəm-'frēs, -'frēz\ burgh S Scotland; *pop* 32,084

Dumfries and Gal·lo·way \'ga-lə-ˌwā\ administrative subdivision of S Scotland

Dun·dee \ˌdən-'dē\ city E Scotland; *pop* 172,860

Dun·gan·non \ˌdən-'ga-nən\ district W Northern Ireland; *pop* 45,322

Dur·ban \'dər-bən\ city and seaport E Republic of South Africa; *pop* 736,852

Dur·ham \'dər-əm, 'də-rəm, 'dúr-əm\ city N *cen* North Carolina; *pop* 187,035

Du·shan·be \dü-'sham-bə, dyü-, -'shäm-, 'dyü-ˌ; ˌdyü-shäm-'bä\ city, ✻ of Tajikistan; *pop* 595,000

Düs·sel·dorf \'dü-səl-ˌdȯrf, 'dyü-, 'dᵫ-\ city W Germany on the Rhine; *pop* 577,561

Ea·ling \'ē-liŋ\ borough of W Greater London, England; *pop* 263,300

East An·glia \'aŋ-glē-ə\ region E England; *pop* 1,366,300

East China Sea — see CHINA

Eas·ter \'ē-stər\ island Chile SE Pacific about 2000 mi. (3200 km.) W of Chilean coast

Eastern Cape province SE Republic of South Africa; *pop* 6,504,000

Eastern Ghats \'gäts, 'gȯts, 'gəts\ chain of low mountains SE India along coast

Eastern Hemisphere the half of the earth E of the Atlantic Ocean including Europe, Asia, Australia, and Africa

Eastern Roman Empire the Byzantine Empire from 395 to 474

Eastern Samoa — see AMERICAN SAMOA

East Germany — see GERMANY

East Indies the Malay Archipelago — **East Indian** *adj or n*

East London city S Republic of South Africa; *pop* 119,727

East Pakistan the former E division of Pakistan consisting of E portion of Bengal; now Bangladesh

East River strait SE New York connecting upper New York Bay & Long Island Sound and separating Manhattan & Long Island

East Sea — see JAPAN, SEA OF

East Sus·sex \'sə-siks\ county SE England; *pop* 670,600

East Timor country SE Asia on E Timor; ✻, Dili; *pop* 747,750

Ebro \'ā-(ˌ)brō\ river 565 mi. (909 km.) long NE Spain flowing into the Mediterranean

Ec·ua·dor \'e-kwə-ˌdȯr, ˌe-kwä-'thȯr\ country W South America; ✻, Quito; *pop* 12,156,608 — **Ec·ua·dor·an** \ˌe-kwə-'dȯr-ən\ *or* **Ec·ua·dor·ean** *or* **Ec·ua·dor·ian** \-ē-ən\ *adj or n*

Ed·in·burgh \'e-d³n-ˌbərg\ city, ✻ of Scotland; *pop* 434,520

Ed·mon·ton \'ed-mən-tən\ city, ✻ of Alberta, Canada; *pop* 666,104

Edom \'ē-dəm\ ancient country SW Asia S of Judaea & Dead Sea — **Edom·ite** \'ēd-ə-ˌmīt\ *n*

Egypt \'ē-jipt\ country NE Africa & Sinai Peninsula of SW Asia bordering on Mediterranean & Red seas; ✻, Cairo; *pop* 67,313,000

Eire — see IRELAND

Elam \'ē-ləm\ ancient country SW Asia at head of Persian Gulf E of Babylonia — **Elam·ite** \'ē-lə-ˌmīt\ *n*

Elbe \'el-bə, 'elb\ river 720 mi. (1159 km.) long N Czech Republic & NE Germany flowing NW into North Sea

El·bert, Mount \'el-bərt\ mountain 14,433 ft. (4399 m.) W *cen* Colorado; highest in Colorado & the Rocky Mountains

El·brus, Mount \el-'brüz, -'brüs\ mountain 18,510 ft. (5642 m.) Russia; highest in the Caucasus & in Europe

El·burz \el-'búrz\ mountains N Iran

Eliz·a·beth \i-'li-zə-bəth\ city NE New Jersey; *pop* 120,568

Elles·mere \'elz-ˌmir\ island N Canada in Nunavut

Ellice — see TUVALU

El·lis Island \'e-ləs\ island SE New York S of Manhattan; served as immigration station 1892–1954

El Mon·te \el-'män-tē\ city SW California E of Los Angeles; *pop* 115,965

El Paso \el-'pa-(ˌ)sō\ city W Texas on Rio Grande; *pop* 563,662

El Sal·va·dor \el-'sal-və-ˌdȯr, -ˌsal-və-'; ˌel-ˌsäl-vä-'thȯr\ country Central America bordering on the Pacific; ✻, San Salvador; *pop* 5,517,000

Ely, Isle of \'ē-lē\ area of high ground amid marshes in East Anglia, England

En·field \'en-ˌfēld\ borough of N Greater London, England; *pop* 248,900

En·gland \'iŋ-glənd, 'iŋ-lənd\ country S Great Britain; a division of United Kingdom; ✻, London; *pop* 49,138,831

English Channel arm of the Atlantic between S England & N France

En·nis·kil·len \ˌe-nə-'ski-lən\ town SW Northern Ireland in Fermanagh district

Ephra·im \'ē-frē-əm\ **1** hilly region N Jordan E of Jordan River **2** — see ISRAEL — **Ephra·im·ite** \'ē-frē-ə-ˌmīt\ *n*

Equatorial Guinea *formerly* **Spanish Guinea** country W Africa including Mbini & Bioko; ✻, Malabo; *pop* 376,000

Erie \'ir-ē\ **1** city & port NW Pennsylvania; *pop* 103,717 **2** canal New York between Hudson River at Albany & Lake Erie at Buffalo; now superseded by New York State Barge Canal

Erie, Lake lake E *cen* North America in U.S. & Canada; one of the Great Lakes

Er·in \'er-ən\ poetic name of Ireland

Er·i·trea \ˌer-ə-'trē-ə, -'trä-\ country NE Africa; ✻, Asmara; *pop* 3,317,611 — **Er·i·tre·an** \-ən\ *adj or n*

Es·con·di·do \ˌes-kən-ˈdē-(ˌ)dō\ city SW California N of San Diego; *pop* 133,559

Es·fa·han \ˌes-fə-ˈhän, -ˈhan\ *or* **Is·fa·han** \ˌis-\ city W *cen* Iran; *pop* 986,753

Española — see HISPANIOLA

Es·sen \ˈe-sᵊn\ city W Germany in the Ruhr; *pop* 626,989

Es·sex \ˈe-siks\ county SE England on North Sea

Es·to·nia \e-ˈstō-nē-ə, -nyə\ country E Europe on Baltic Sea; ✳, Tallinn; *pop* 1,361,242 — **Es·to·nian** \e-ˈstō-nē-ən, -nyən\ *adj or n*

Ethi·o·pia \ˌē-thē-ˈō-pē-ə\ *formerly* **Ab·ys·sin·ia** \ˌa-bə-ˈsi-nē-ə, -nyə\ country E Africa; ✳, Addis Ababa; *pop* 67,220,000 — **Ethi·o·pi·an** \-pē-ən\ *adj or n*

Et·na, Mount \ˈet-nə\ volcano 10,902 ft. (3323 m.) Italy in NE Sicily

Eto·bi·coke \e-ˈtō-bi-ˌkō\ former city Canada in SE Ontario; now part of Toronto

Etru·ria \i-ˈtrùr-ē-ə\ ancient country *cen* peninsula of Italy

Eu·gene \yü-ˈjēn\ city W Oregon; *pop* 137,893

Eu·phra·tes \yù-ˈfrā-(ˌ)tēz\ river 1700 mi. (2736 km.) long SW Asia flowing from E Turkey & uniting with the Tigris to form the Shatt al Arab

Eur·asia \yù-ˈrā-zhə, -shə\ landmass consisting of Europe & Asia — **Eur·asian** \-zhən, -shən\ *adj or n*

Eu·rope \ˈyùr-əp\ continent of the Eastern Hemisphere between Asia & the Atlantic; *pop* 498,000,000

European Union economic, scientific, & political organization consisting of Belgium, France, Italy, Luxembourg, Netherlands, Germany, Denmark, Greece, Ireland, United Kingdom, Spain, Portugal, Austria, Finland, Sweden, Cyprus, Czech Republic, Estonia, Hungary, Latvia, Lithuania, Malta, Poland, Slovakia, Slovenia, Bulgaria, & Romania

Ev·ans·ville \ˈe-vənz-ˌvil\ city SW Indiana; *pop* 121,582

Ev·er·est, Mount \ˈev-rəst, ˈe-və-\ mountain 29,035 ft. (8850 m.) S Asia in the Himalayas on border between Nepal & Tibet; highest in the world

Ev·er·glades \ˈe-vər-ˌglādz\ swamp region S Florida now partly drained

Ex·e·ter \ˈek-sə-tər\ city SW England; *pop* 101,100

Faer·oe *or* **Far·oe** \ˈfer-(ˌ)ō\ islands NE Atlantic NW of the Shetlands belonging to Denmark; *pop* 47,653 — **Faero·ese** \ˌfar-ə-ˈwēz, ˌfer-, -ˈwēs\ *adj or n*

Fair·banks \ˈfer-ˌbaŋks\ city E *cen* Alaska; *pop* 30,224

Fai·sa·la·bad \ˌfī-ˌsä-lə-ˈbäd, -ˌsä-lə-ˈbad\ *formerly* **Ly·all·pur** \lē-ˌäl-ˈpùr\ city NE Pakistan W of Lahore; *pop* 2,008,861

Falk·land Islands \ˈfȯ-klənd, ˈfȯl-\ *or*

Spanish **Is·las Mal·vi·nas** \ˌēs-läs-mäl-ˈvē-näs\ island group SW Atlantic E of S end of Argentina; a British colony; ✳, Stanley; *pop* 2100

Far East the countries of E Asia & the Malay Archipelago — usually thought to consist of the Asian countries bordering on the Pacific but sometimes including also India, Sri Lanka, Bangladesh, Tibet, & Myanmar — **Far Eastern** *adj*

Far·go \ˈfär-(ˌ)gō\ city E North Dakota; largest in state; *pop* 90,599

Faroe — see FAEROE

Fay·ette·ville \ˈfā-ət-ˌvil, -vəl\ city SE *cen* North Carolina; *pop* 121,015

Fear, Cape \ˈfir\ cape SE North Carolina

Fer·man·agh \fər-ˈma-nə\ district SW Northern Ireland; *pop* 54,062

Fernando Póo — see BIOKO

Fez \ˈfez\ city N *cen* Morocco; *pop* 774,574

Fife \ˈfīf\ administrative subdivision of E Scotland

Fi·ji \ˈfē-(ˌ)jē\ islands SW Pacific; country; ✳, Suva; *pop* 775,077 — **Fi·ji·an** \ˈfē-(ˌ)jē-ən, fi-\ *adj or n*

Fin·land \ˈfin-lənd\ country NE Europe; ✳, Helsinki; *pop* 5,058,000 — **Fin·land·er** *n*

Flan·ders \ˈflan-dərz\ **1** region W Belgium & N France on North Sea **2** semiautonomous region W Belgium; *pop* 5,972,781

Flat·tery, Cape \ˈfla-tə-rē\ cape NW Washington at entrance to Strait of Juan de Fuca

Flint \ˈflint\ city SE Michigan; *pop* 124,943

Flor·ence \ˈflȯr-ən(t)s, ˈflär-\ *or Italian* **Fi·ren·ze** \fē-ˈrent-sā\ city *cen* Italy; *pop* 374,501 — **Flor·en·tine** \ˈflȯr-ən-ˌtēn, ˈflär-, -ˌtīn\ *adj or n*

Flor·i·da \ˈflȯr-ə-də, ˈflär-\ state SE U.S.; ✳, Tallahassee; *pop* 15,982,378 — **Flo·rid·i·an** \flə-ˈri-dē-ən\ *or* **Flor·i·dan** \ˈflȯr-ə-dən, ˈflär-\ *adj or n*

Florida, Straits of channel between Florida Keys on NW & Cuba & Bahamas on S & E connecting Gulf of Mexico & the Atlantic

Florida Keys chain of islands off S tip of Florida

Foochow — see FUZHOU

For·a·ker, Mount \ˈfȯr-i-kər, ˈfär-\ mountain 17,400 ft. (5304 m.) S *cen* Alaska in Alaska Range

For·mo·sa \fȯr-ˈmō-sə, fər-, -zə\ — see TAIWAN — **For·mo·san** \fȯr-ˈmō-sᵊn, fər-, -zᵊn\ *adj or n*

For·ta·le·za \ˌfȯr-tə-ˈlä-zə\ city & port NE Brazil on the Atlantic; *pop* 2,141,402

Fort Col·lins \ˈkä-lənz\ city N Colorado; *pop* 118,652

Fort–de–France \ˌfȯr-də-ˈfräⁿs\ city West Indies, ✳ of Martinique on W coast; *pop* 93,598

Forth \\'fȯrth\ river 116 mi. (187 km.) long
S *cen* Scotland flowing E into North Sea
through **Firth of Forth**

Fort Knox \\'näks\ military reservation N
cen Kentucky SSW of Louisville; location of U.S. Gold Bullion Depository

Fort Lau·der·dale \\'lȯ-dər-,dȧl\ city SE
Florida; *pop* 152,397

Fort Wayne \\'wān\ city NE Indiana; *pop*
205,727

Fort Worth \\'wərth\ city NE Texas; *pop*
534,694

Fox \\'fäks\ islands SW Alaska in the E
Aleutians

Foxe Basin \\'fäks\ inlet of the Atlantic N
Canada in E Nunavut W of Baffin Island

France \\'fran(t)s, 'fräⁿs\ country W Europe between the English Channel & the
Mediterranean; ✱, Paris; *pop* 58,520,688

Frank·fort \\'fraŋk-fərt\ city, ✱ of Kentucky; *pop* 27,741

Frank·furt \\'fraŋk-fərt, 'fräŋk-,fu̇rt\ *or in
full* **Frankfurt am Main** \\(,)ȧm-'mīn\ city
W Germany on Main River; *pop* 654,679

Frank·lin \\'fraŋ-klən\ former district N
Canada in Northwest Territories includ-
ing Arctic Archipelago & Boothia &
Melville peninsulas

Fra·ser \\'frā-zər, -zhər\ river 850 mi.
(1368 km.) long Canada in S *cen* British
Columbia flowing into the Pacific

Fred·er·ic·ton \\'fre-drik-tən, 'fre-də-rik-\
city, ✱ of New Brunswick, Canada; *pop*
47,560

Free State *formerly* **Or·ange Free State**
\\'ȯr-inj, 'är-, -ənj\ province E *cen* Republic of South Africa; *pop* 2,767,000

Free·town \\'frē-,tau̇n\ city, ✱ of Sierra
Leone; *pop* 178,600

Fre·mont \\'frē-,mänt\ city W California;
pop 203,413

French Guiana country N South America
on the Atlantic; an overseas division of
France; ✱, Cayenne; *pop* 128,000

French Indochina — see INDOCHINA

Fres·no \\'frez-(,)nō\ city S *cen* California
SE of San Francisco; *pop* 427,652

Frunze — see BISHKEK

Fu·ji, Mount \\'fü-jē\ *or* **Fu·ji·ya·ma** \,fü-
jē-'yä-mä\ mountain 12,388 ft. (3776 m.)
Japan in S *cen* Honshu; highest in Japan

Fu·ku·o·ka \,fü-kü-'ō-kä\ city Japan in N
Kyushu; *pop* 1,341,470

Ful·ler·ton \\'fu̇-lər-tən\ city SW California; *pop* 126,003

Fu·na·fu·ti \,fü-nä-'fü-tē\ city, ✱ of Tuvalu; *pop* 1328

Fun·dy, Bay of \\'fən-dē\ inlet of the Atlantic SE Canada between New
Brunswick & Nova Scotia

Fu·shun \\'fü-'shu̇n\ city NE China E of
Shenyang; *pop* 1,202,388

Fu·zhou \\'fü-'jō\ *or* **Foo·chow** \\'fü-'jō,
-'chau̇\ city & port SE China; *pop* 874,809

Ga·bon \gä-'bōⁿ\ country W Africa on the

Equator; ✱, Libreville; *pop* 1,014,976 —
Gab·o·nese \,ga-bə-'nēz, -'nēs\ *adj or n*

Ga·bo·rone \,gä-bō-'rō-(,)nā, ,kä-\ city, ✱
of Botswana; *pop* 133,468

Gads·den Purchase \\'gadz-dən\ area of
land S of Gila River in present Arizona &
New Mexico purchased 1853 by the U.S.
from Mexico

Ga·la·pa·gos Islands \gə-'lä-pə-gəs, -'la-,
-,gōs\ island group Ecuador in the Pacific
600 mi. (965 km.) W of South America;
pop 9785

Ga·la·tia \gə-'lā-sh(ē-)ə\ ancient country
cen Asia Minor in region around modern
Ankara, Turkey — **Ga·la·tian** \-shən\
adj or n

Ga·li·cia \gə-'li-sh(ē-)ə\ **1** region E *cen*
Europe now divided between Poland &
Ukraine **2** region NW Spain on the At-
lantic — **Ga·li·cian** \-'li-shən\ *adj or n*

Gal·i·lee \\'ga-lə-,lē\ hilly region N Israel
— **Gal·i·le·an** \,ga-lə-'lē-ən\ *adj or n*

Galilee, Sea of *or modern* **Lake Ti·be·ri·
as** \tī-'bir-ē-əs\ lake N Israel on Syrian
border; crossed by Jordan River

Gal·lo·way \\'ga-lə-,wā\ former administrative district of SW Scotland — see
DUMFRIES AND GALLOWAY

Gam·bia \\'gam-bē-ə, 'gäm-\ country W
Africa; ✱, Banjul; *pop* 687,817 — **Gam·
bi·an** \-bē-ən\ *adj or n*

Gan·ges \\'gan-jēz\ river 1550 mi. (2494
km.) long N India flowing from the Himalayas SE & E to unite with the
Brahmaputra and empty into Bay of Bengal through a vast delta — **Gan·get·ic**
\gan-'je-tik\ *adj*

Garden Grove city SW California; *pop*
165,196

Gar·land \\'gär-lənd\ city NE Texas NNE
of Dallas; *pop* 215,768

Ga·ronne \gə-'rän, gä-'rȯn\ river 355 mi.
(571 km.) long SE France flowing NW

Gary \\'ger-ē\ city NW Indiana on Lake
Michigan; *pop* 102,746

Gas·co·ny \\'gas-kə-nē\ region SW France
— **Gas·con** \\'gas-kən\ *adj or n*

Gas·pé \ga-'spā, 'ga-,\ peninsula SE Quebec E of mouth of the Saint Lawrence —
Gas·pe·sian \ga-'spē-zhən\ *adj or n*

Gaul \\'gȯl\ *or Latin* **Gal·lia** \\'ga-lē-ə\ ancient country W Europe chiefly consist-
ing of region occupied by modern France
& Belgium

Gau·teng \\'gau̇-,teŋ\ province *cen* NE Republic of South Africa; *pop* 6,864,000

Ga·za Strip \\'gä-zə, 'ga-\ district NE Sinai
Peninsula on the Mediterranean

Ge·ne·va \jə-'nē-və\ city SW Switzerland
on Lake Geneva; *pop* 175,998 — **Ge·ne·
van** \-vən\ *adj or n* — **Gen·e·vese** \,je-
nə-'vēz, -'vēs\ *adj or n*

Geneva, Lake lake on border between
SW Switzerland & E France

Gen·oa \\'je-nō-ə\ *or Italian* **Ge·no·va**

\'je-nō-(ˌ)vä\ city & port NW Italy; *pop* 632,366 — **Gen·o·ese** \ˌje-nō-'ēz, -'ēs\ *or* **Gen·o·vese** \-nə-'vēz, -'vēs\ *adj or n*

George·town \'jörj-ˌtaùn\ **1** a W section of Washington, District of Columbia **2** city & port, * of Guyana; *pop* 162,000

Geor·gia \'jör-jə\ **1** state SE U.S.; *, Atlanta; *pop* 8,186,453 **2** *or* **Republic of Georgia** country SE Europe on Black Sea S of Caucasus Mountains; *, Tbilisi; *pop* 5,493,000 — **Geor·gian** \'jör-jən\ *adj or n*

Georgia, Strait of channel Canada & U.S. between Vancouver Island & main part of British Columbia NW of Puget Sound

Georgian Bay inlet of Lake Huron in S Ontario

Ger·man·town \'jər-mən-ˌtaùn\ a NW section of Philadelphia, Pennsylvania

Ger·ma·ny \'jər-mə-nē\ country *cen* Europe bordering on North & Baltic seas; *, Berlin; divided 1946–90 into two independent states: the **Federal Republic of Germany** (West Germany; *, Bonn) & the **German Democratic Republic** (East Germany; *, East Berlin); *pop* 82,440,000

Get·tys·burg \'ge-tēz-ˌbərg\ town S Pennsylvania; *pop* 7490

Gha·na \'gä-nə, 'ga-\ *formerly* **Gold Coast** country W Africa on Gulf of Guinea; *, Accra; *pop* 15,636,000 — **Gha·na·ian** \gä-'nā-ən, ga-, -'nī-ən\ *or* **Gha·ni·an** \'gä-nē-ən, 'ga-, -nyən\ *adj or n*

Ghats \'göts\ two mountain chains S India consisting of **Eastern Ghats** & **Western Ghats**

Ghent \'gent\ city NW *cen* Belgium; *pop* 226,220

Gi·bral·tar \jə-'bról-tər\ British colony on S coast of Spain including Rock of Gibraltar; *pop* 29,760

Gibraltar, Rock of cape on S coast of Spain in Gibraltar at E end of Strait of Gibraltar; highest point 1396 ft. (426 m.)

Gibraltar, Strait of passage between Spain & Africa connecting the Atlantic & the Mediterranean

Gi·la \'hē-lə\ river 630 mi. (1014 km.) long SW New Mexico and S Arizona flowing W into the Colorado

Gil·bert \'gil-bərt\ town SW *cen* Arizona; *pop* 109,697

Gilbert and El·lice Islands \'e-lis\ island group W Pacific; divided into Kiribati and Tuvalu

Gil·e·ad \'gi-lē-əd\ mountain region of NE ancient Palestine E of Jordan River; now in NW Jordan — **Gil·e·ad·ite** \-lē-ə-ˌdīt\ *n*

Gi·za \'gē-zə\ city N Egypt on the Nile SW of Cairo; *pop* 2,096,000

Gla·cier Bay \'glā-shər\ inlet SE Alaska at S end of Saint Elias Range

Glas·gow \'glas-(ˌ)kō, 'glas-(ˌ)gō, 'glaz-(ˌ)gō\ city S *cen* Scotland on the Clyde; *pop* 681,470 — **Glas·we·gian** \gla-'swē-jən, glaz-\ *adj or n*

Glen·dale \'glen-ˌdāl\ **1** city *cen* Arizona NW of Phoenix; *pop* 218,812 **2** city S California NE of Los Angeles; *pop* 194,973

Glouces·ter \'gläs-tər, 'glòs\ town SW *cen* England; *pop* 91,800

Glouces·ter·shire \'gläs-tər-ˌshir, -shər, 'glòs-\ *or* **Gloucester** county SW *cen* England

Goa \'gō-ə\ district W India on Malabar coast

Goat Island island W New York in Niagara River — see NIAGARA FALLS

Go·bi \'gō-(ˌ)bē\ desert E *cen* Asia in Mongolia & N China

Godt·hab — see NUUK

Godwin Austen — see K2

Go·lan Heights \'gō-ˌlän, -lən\ hilly region NE of Sea of Galilee

Gol·con·da \gäl-'kän-də\ ruined city *cen* India W of Hyderabad

Gold Coast 1 — see GHANA **2** coast region W Africa on N shore of Gulf of Guinea E of Ivory Coast

Golden Gate strait W California connecting San Francisco Bay with Pacific Ocean

Good Hope, Cape of \ˌgùd-'hōp\ cape S Republic of South Africa on SW coast of Western Cape province

Gorki — see NIZHNIY NOVGOROD

Gö·te·borg \ˌyœ-tə-'bòr-ē\ city & port SW Sweden; *pop* 474,921

Gram·pi·an \'gram-pē-ən\ hills N *cen* Scotland

Grand Banks shallow area in the W North Atlantic SE of Newfoundland

Grand Canyon gorge of Colorado River NW Arizona

Grand Canyon of the Snake HELLS CANYON

Grande, Rio — see RIO GRANDE

Grand Prairie city NE *cen* Texas W of Dallas; *pop* 127,427

Grand Rapids city SW Michigan; *pop* 197,800

Graz \'gräts\ city S Austria; *pop* 226,244

Great Australian Bight wide bay on S coast of Australia

Great Barrier Reef coral reef Australia off NE coast of Queensland

Great Basin region W U.S. between Sierra Nevada & Wasatch Range including most of Nevada & parts of California, Idaho, Utah, Wyoming, & Oregon; has no drainage to ocean

Great Bear lake Canada in Northwest Territories draining through Great Bear River into Mackenzie River

Great Brit·ain \'bri-t²n\ **1** island W Europe NW of France consisting of England,

Scotland, & Wales; *pop* 53,917,000 **2** UNITED KINGDOM

Great Dividing Range mountain system E Australia extending S from Cape York Peninsula into Tasmania — see KOSCIUSKO, MOUNT

Greater Antilles group of islands of the West Indies including Cuba, Hispaniola, Jamaica, & Puerto Rico — see LESSER ANTILLES

Greater London metropolitan county SE England consisting of City of London & 32 surrounding boroughs

Greater Manchester metropolitan county NW England including city of Manchester

Greater Sudbury — see SUDBURY, GREATER

Great Lakes chain of five lakes (Superior, Michigan, Huron, Erie, & Ontario) *cen* North America in U.S. & Canada

Great Plains elevated plains region W *cen* U.S. & W Canada E of the Rockies; extending from W Texas to NE British Columbia & NW Alberta

Great Rift Valley basin SW Asia & E Africa extending with several breaks from valley of the Jordan S to *cen* Mozambique

Great Salt Lake lake N Utah having salty waters & no outlet

Great Slave Lake lake NW Canada in S Northwest Territories drained by Mackenzie River

Great Smoky mountains between W North Carolina & E Tennessee

Greece \'grēs\ country S Europe at S end of Balkan Peninsula; ✳, Athens; *pop* 10,964,020

Green \'grēn\ **1** mountains E North America in the Appalachians extending from S Quebec S through Vermont into W Massachusetts **2** river 730 mi. (1175 km.) long W U.S. flowing from W Wyoming S into the Colorado in SE Utah

Green Bay 1 inlet of NW Lake Michigan 120 mi. (193 km.) long in NW Michigan & NE Wisconsin **2** city NE Wisconsin on Green Bay; *pop* 102,313

Green·land \'grēn-lənd, -,land\ island in the North Atlantic off NE North America belonging to Denmark; ✳, Nuuk; *pop* 55,171

Greens·boro \'grēnz-,bər-ō\ city N *cen* North Carolina; *pop* 223,891

Green·wich \'gre-nich, 'grēn-,wich, 'grin-,wich\ borough of SE Greater London, England; *pop* 200,800

Green·wich Village \'gre-nich\ section of New York City in W Manhattan

Gre·na·da \grə-'nā-də\ island West Indies in S Windward Islands; independent country; ✳, Saint George's; *pop* 102,632

Gren·a·dines, the \,gre-nə-'dēnz, 'gre-nə-,\ islands West Indies in *cen* Windward Islands; N islands part of Saint Vincent and the Grenadines; S islands dependency of Grenada

Groz·ny \'gróz-nē, 'gräz-\ city S Russia in Europe; ✳ of Chechnya; *pop* 388,000

Gua·da·la·ja·ra \,gwä-də-lə-'här-ə, ,gwä-thä-lä-'hä-rä\ city W *cen* Mexico; *pop* 2,987,194

Gua·dal·ca·nal \,gwä-d°l-kə-'nal, ,gwä-də-kə-\ island W Pacific in the SE Solomons; *pop* 23,922

Gua·dal·qui·vir \,gwä-d°l-ki-'vir, -'kwi-vər\ river 408 mi. (656 km.) long S Spain flowing into the Atlantic

Gua·de·loupe \'gwä-də-,lüp\ two islands separated by a narrow channel in West Indies in *cen* Leeward Islands; an overseas division of France; *pop* 418,000

Gua·lla·ti·ri \,gwä-yə-'tir-ē, ,gwī-ə-\ volcano 19,882 ft. (6060 m.) high N Chile

Guam \'gwäm\ island W Pacific in S Marianas belonging to U.S.; ✳, Hagåtña; *pop* 154,805 — **Gua·ma·ni·an** \gwä-'mä-nē-ən\ *adj or n*

Gua·na·ba·ra Bay \,gwä-nä-'bär-ə\ inlet of the Atlantic SE Brazil on which city of Rio de Janeiro is located

Guang·dong \'gwän-'dùn\ *or* **Kwang·tung** \'gwän-'dùn, 'kwän-, -'tùn\ province SE China bordering on South China Sea & Gulf of Tonkin; ✳, Guangzhou; *pop* 62,829,236

Guang·zhou \'gwän-'jō\ *or* **Can·ton** \'kan-,tän, kan-'\ city & port SE China; *pop* 2,914,281

Guan·tá·na·mo Bay \gwän-'tä-nä-,mō\ inlet of the Caribbean in SE Cuba; site of U.S. naval station

Gua·te·ma·la \,gwä-tə-'mä-lə, -tä-'mä-lä\ **1** country Central America; *pop* 9,713,000 **2** *or* **Guatemala City** city, its ✳; *pop* 1,132,730 — **Gua·te·ma·lan** \-'mä-lən\ *adj or n*

Gua·ya·quil \,gwī-ə-'kēl, -'kil\ city & port W Ecuador; *pop* 1,508,444

Guay·na·bo \gwī-'nä-(,)bō, -(,)vō\ city NE *cen* Puerto Rico; *pop* 100,053

Guern·sey \'gərn-zē\ — see CHANNEL

Gui·a·na \gē-'a-nə, -'ä-nə; gī-'a-nə\ region N South America on the Atlantic; includes Guyana, French Guiana, Suriname, & nearby parts of Brazil & Venezuela — **Gui·a·nan** \-nən\ *adj or n*

Guin·ea \'gi-nē\ **1** region W Africa on the Atlantic extending along coast from Gambia to Angola **2** country W Africa N of Sierra Leone & Liberia; ✳, Conakry; *pop* 7,300,000 — **Guin·ean** \'gi-nē-ən\ *adj or n*

Guinea, Gulf of arm of the Atlantic W *cen* Africa

Guin·ea–Bis·sau \,gi-nē-bi-'saù\ country W Africa; ✳, Bissau; *pop* 1.036,000

Gui·yang \'gwä-'yän\ *or* **Kuei·yang** \'gwä-'yän\ city S China; *pop* 1,018,619

Gulf States states of U.S. bordering on Gulf of Mexico: Florida, Alabama, Mississippi, Louisiana, and Texas

Gulf Stream warm current of the Atlantic Ocean flowing from Gulf of Mexico NE along coast of U.S. to Nantucket Island and from there eastward

Guy·ana \gī-'an-ə\ *formerly* **British Guiana** country N South America on the Atlantic; *, Georgetown; *pop* 755,000 — **Guy·a·nese** \ˌgī-ə-'nēz, -'nēs\ *adj or n*

Gwangju — see KWANGJU

Gwent \'gwent\ former county SE Wales

Gwyn·edd \'gwi-neth\ former county NW Wales

Hack·ney \'hak-nē\ borough of N Greater London, England; *pop* 164,200

Ha·gåt·ña \hə-'gät-nyə\ *formerly* **Aga·na** \ä-'gä-nyä\ town, * of Guam; *pop* 1139

Hague, The \thə-'hāg\ city, seat of government of Netherlands; *pop* 457,726

Hai·kou \'hī-'kō\ city & port SE China; *pop* 280,153

Hai·phong \'hī-'fȯŋ, -'fäŋ\ city & port N Vietnam; *pop* 1,726,900

Hai·ti \'hā-tē\ country West Indies in W Hispaniola; *, Port-au-Prince; *pop* 6,902,000 — **Hai·tian** \'hā-shən\ *adj or n*

Ha·le·a·ka·la Crater \ˌhä-lā-ˌä-kä-'lä\ crater over 2500 ft. (762 m.) deep Hawaii in E Maui

Hal·i·fax \'ha-lə-ˌfaks\ municipality & port, * of Nova Scotia, Canada; *pop* 372,679

Ham·burg \'ham-ˌbərg; 'häm-ˌbu̇rg, -ˌbu̇rk\ city N Germany on the Elbe; *pop* 1,668,800 — **Ham·burg·er** \-ˌbər-gər, -ˌbu̇r-\ *n*

Ham·hung *or* **Ham·heung** \'häm-ˌhu̇ŋ\ city E *cen* North Korea; *pop* 701,000

Ham·il·ton \'ha-məl-tən\ **1** town, * of Bermuda; *pop* 969 **2** city & port, S Ontario, Canada on Lake Ontario; *pop* 504,559

Ham·mer·smith and Ful·ham \'ha-mər-ˌsmith-ənd-'fu̇-ləm\ borough of SW Greater London, England; *pop* 136,500

Hamp·shire \'hamp-ˌshir, -shər\ county S England on English Channel

Hamp·ton \'hamp-tən\ city SE Virginia; *pop* 146,437

Hampton Roads channel SE Virginia through which James River flows into Chesapeake Bay

Hang·zhou \'häŋ-'jō\ *or* **Hang·chow** \'haŋ-'chau̇, 'häŋ-'jō\ *or* **Hang–chou** \'jō\ city E China; *pop* 1,099,660

Han·ni·bal \'ha-nə-bəl\ city NE Missouri on the Mississippi River; *pop* 17,757

Han·no·ver *or* **Han·o·ver** \'ha-ˌnō-vər, -nə-vər, *G* hä-'nō-fər\ city N *cen* Germany; *pop* 517,746

Ha·noi \ha-'nȯi, hə-, hä-\ city, * of Vietnam; *pop* 2,931,400

Ha·ra·re \hə-'rä-(ˌ)rā\ *formerly* **Salis-**

bury \'sȯlz-ˌber-ē, -b(ə-)rē\ city, * of Zimbabwe; *pop* 1,184,169

Har·bin \'här-bən, här-'bin\ *or* **Ha–erh–pin** \'hä-'ər-'bin\ city NE China; *pop* 2,443,398

Har·in·gey \'ha-riŋ-ˌgā\ borough of N Greater London, England; *pop* 187,300

Har·lem \'här-ləm\ section of New York City in N Manhattan

Har·ris·burg \'ha-rəs-ˌbərg\ city, * of Pennsylvania; *pop* 48,950

Har·row \'ha-(ˌ)rō\ borough of NW Greater London, England; *pop* 194,300

Hart·ford \'härt-fərd\ city, * of Connecticut; *pop* 121,578

Hat·ter·as, Cape \'ha-tə-rəs\ cape North Carolina on **Hatteras Island**

Ha·vana \hə-'va-nə\ city, * of Cuba; *pop* 2,096,054

Hav·ant \'ha-vənt\ town S England; *pop* 117,400

Ha·ver·ing \'hāv-riŋ, 'hä-və-riŋ\ borough of NE Greater London, England; *pop* 224,400

Ha·waii \hə-'wä-yē, -'wä-ˌē\ **1** *or* **Hawai·ian Islands** *formerly* **Sand·wich Islands** \ˌsan-(d)wich-\ group of islands *cen* Pacific belonging to U.S. **2** island, largest of the group **3** state of U.S., *, Honolulu; *pop* 1,211,537

Hay·ward \'hä-wərd\ city W California SE of Oakland; *pop* 140,030

Heb·ri·des \'he-brə-ˌdēz\ islands W Scotland in the North Atlantic consisting of **Outer Hebrides** (to W) and **Inner Hebrides** (to E); *pop* 30,660 — **Heb·ri·de·an** \ˌhe-brə-'dē-ən\ *adj or n*

Hel·e·na \'he-lə-nə\ city, * of Montana; *pop* 25,780

Hellespont — see DARDANELLES

Hells Canyon \'helz\ canyon of Snake River on Idaho–Oregon boundary

Hel·sin·ki \'hel-ˌsiŋ-kē, hel-'\ city, * of Finland; *pop* 559,718

Hen·der·son \'hen-dər-sən\ city S Nevada; *pop* 175,381

Hen·ry, Cape \'hen-rē\ cape E Virginia S of entrance to Chesapeake Bay

Her·e·ford and Wor·ces·ter \'her-ə-fərd-ən-'wu̇s-tər\ former county W England

Hert·ford·shire \'här-fərd-ˌshir, 'härt-, -shər\ *or* **Hertford** county SE England

Her·ze·go·vi·na \ˌhert-sə-gō-'vē-nə, ˌhärt-, -'gō-və-nə\ *or Serb* **Her·ce·go·vi·na** \'kert-sə-gō-vē-nə\ region S Europe; with Bosnia to the N forms Bosnia and Herzegovina — **Her·ze·go·vi·nian** \ˌhert-sə-gō-'vē-nē-ən, ˌhärt-, -nyən\ *n*

Hi·a·le·ah \ˌhī-ə-'lē-ə\ city SE Florida; *pop* 226,419

Hi·ber·nia \hī-'bər-nē-ə\ — see IRELAND — **Hi·ber·ni·an** \-ən\ *adj or n*

Hi·ga·shi·ōsa·ka \hē-ˌgä-shē-'ō-sä-kä\ city Japan in S Honshu E of Osaka; *pop* 515,094

High·land \\'hī-lənd\ administrative subdivision of NW Scotland

High·lands \\'hī-lənd\ the mountainous N part of Scotland lying N & W of the Lowlands

High Plains the Great Plains esp. from Nebraska southward

Hil·ling·don \\'hi-liŋ-dən\ borough of W Greater London, England; *pop* 225,800

Hi·ma·la·yas, the \\,hi-mə-'lā-əz\ *or the* **Himalaya** mountain system S Asia on border between India & Tibet and in Kashmir, Nepal, & Bhutan — see EVEREST, MOUNT — **Hi·ma·la·yan** \\,him-ə-'lā-ən, hə-'mäl-(ə-)yən\ *adj*

Hin·du Kush \\'hin-(,)dü-'kush, -'kəsh\ mountain range *cen* Asia SW of the Pamirs on border of Kashmir and in Afghanistan

Hin·du·stan \\,hin-(,)dü-'stan, -də-, -'stän\ 1 a name for N India 2 the subcontinent of India 3 the country of India

Hi·ro·shi·ma \\,hir-ə-'shē-mə, hə-'rō-shə-mə\ city Japan in SW Honshu on Inland Sea; *pop* 1,126,239

His·pan·io·la \\,his-pə-'nyō-lə\ *or Spanish* **Es·pa·ño·la** \\,es-,pä-'nyō-lä\ island West Indies in Greater Antilles; divided between Haiti on W & Dominican Republic on E

Ho·bart \\'hō-bərt\ city Australia, ✱ of Tasmania; *pop* 47,106

Ho Chi Minh City \\'hō-,chē-'min\ *formerly* **Sai·gon** \\sī-'gän, 'sī-,\ city S Vietnam; *pop* 5,479,000

Hoh·hot \\'hō-'hōt\ *or* **Hu·he·hot** \\'hü-(,)hä-'hōt\ city N China, ✱ of Inner Mongolia; *pop* 652,534

Hok·kai·do \\hó-'kī-(,)dō\ island N Japan N of Honshu; *pop* 5,683,062

Hol·land \\'hä-lənd\ 1 county of Holy Roman Empire bordering on North Sea & consisting of area now forming part of W Netherlands 2 — see NETHERLANDS — **Hol·land·er** \-lən-dər\ *n*

Hol·ly·wood \\'hä-lē-,wúd\ 1 section of Los Angeles, California, NW of downtown district 2 city SE Florida; *pop* 139,357

Holy Roman Empire empire consisting mainly of German & Italian territories & existing from 9th or 10th century to 1806

Hon·du·ras \\hän-'dúr-əs, -'dyúr-; ón-'dü-räs\ country Central America; ✱, Tegucigalpa; *pop* 4,604,800 — **Hon·du·ran** \-ən\ *adj or n*

Hong Kong \\'häŋ-,käŋ, -'käŋ\ *or Chinese* **Xiang·gang** \\'shyäŋ-,gäŋ\ special administrative region China on SE coast including Hong Kong Island & Jiulong Peninsula; chief city Victoria; *pop* 6,843,000

Ho·ni·a·ra \\,hō-nē-'är-ə\ town, ✱ of Solomon Islands; *pop* 35,288

Ho·no·lu·lu \\,hä-nə-'lü-(,)lü, ,hō-nə-\ city, ✱ of Hawaii on Oahu; *pop* 371,657

Hon·shu \\'hän-(,)shü, 'hòn-\ island Japan; largest of the four chief islands; *pop* 102,324,961

Hood, Mount \\'húd\ mountain 11,235 ft. (3424 m.) NW Oregon in Cascade Range

Hoo·ver Dam \\'hü-vər\ *or* **Boul·der Dam** \\'bōl-dər\ dam 726 ft. (221 m.) high in Colorado River between Arizona & Nevada — see MEAD, LAKE

Hormuz, Strait of \\'(h)òr-,məz, (h)òr-'müz\ strait connecting Persian Gulf & Gulf of Oman

Horn, Cape \\'hòrn\ cape S Chile on an island in Tierra del Fuego; the most southerly point of South America at 56° S latitude

Horn of Africa the easternmost projection of Africa; variously used to refer to Somalia, SE or all of Ethiopia, & sometimes Djibouti

Horseshoe Falls — see NIAGARA FALLS

Houns·low \\'haúnz-(,)lō\ borough of SW Greater London, England; *pop* 193,400

Hous·ton \\'hyüs-tən, 'yüs\ city SE Texas; *pop* 1,953,631

How·rah \\'haú-rə\ city E India on Hugli River opposite Calcutta; *pop* 1,008,704

Hsi·an — see XI'AN

Huang *or* **Hwang** \\'hwän\ *or* **Yellow** river about 3000 mi. (4828 km.) long N China flowing into Bo Hai

Hud·ders·field \\'hə-dərz-,fēld\ town N England NE of Manchester; *pop* 123,888

Hud·son \\'həd-sən\ 1 river 306 mi. (492 km.) long E New York flowing S 2 bay, inlet of the Atlantic in N Canada 3 strait NE Canada connecting Hudson Bay & the Atlantic

Hu·gli *or* **Hoo·ghly** \\'hü-glē\ river 120 mi. (193 km.) long E India flowing S into Bay of Bengal

Huhehot — see HOHHOT

Hull \\'həl\ *or* **Kings·ton upon Hull** \\'kiŋ-stən\ city & port N England; *pop* 242,200

Hun·ga·ry \\'həŋ-gə-rē\ country *cen* Europe; ✱, Budapest; *pop* 10,142,000

Hunt·ing·ton Beach \\'hən-tiŋ-tən\ city SW California; *pop* 189,594

Hunts·ville \\'hənts-,vil, -vəl\ city N Alabama; *pop* 158,216

Hu·ron, Lake \\'hyúr-,än, 'yúr-\ lake E *cen* North America in U.S. & Canada; one of the Great Lakes

Hy·der·abad \\'hī-d(ə-)rə-,bad, -,bäd\ 1 city S *cen* India; *pop* 3,449,878 2 city SE Pakistan on the Indus; *pop* 1,166,894

Iba·dan \\i-'bä-dᵊn, -'ba-\ city SW Nigeria; *pop* 1,263,000

Ibe·ri·an \\ī-'bir-ē-ə\ peninsula SW Europe occupied by Spain & Portugal

Ice·land \\'īs-lənd, 'īs-,land\ island SE of Greenland between Arctic & Atlantic oceans; country; ✱, Reykjavik; *pop* 282,849 — **Ice·land·er** \\'īs-,lan-dər, 'īs-lən-\ *n*

Ida·ho \'ī-də-,hō\ state NW U.S.; *, Boise; *pop* 1,293,953 — **Ida·ho·an** \,ī-də-'hō-ən\ *adj or n*

Igua·çú *or* **Igua·zú** \,ē-gwə-'sü\ river 745 mi. (1199 km.) long S Brazil flowing W

IJs·sel *or* **Ijs·sel** \'ī-səl, 'ā-\ river 70 mi. (113 km.) long E Netherlands flowing out of Rhine N into IJsselmeer

IJs·sel·meer \'ī-səl-,mer, 'ā-\ *or* **Lake IJs·sel** freshwater lake N Netherlands separated from North Sea by a dike; part of former Zuider Zee (inlet of North Sea)

Ilium — see TROY

Il·li·nois \,i-lə-'noi\ state N *cen* U.S.; *, Springfield; *pop* 12,419,293 — **Il·li·nois·an** \,i-lə-'noi-ən\ *adj or n*

Il·lyr·ia \i-'lir-ē-ə\ ancient country S Europe and Balkan Peninsula on the Adriatic — **Il·lyr·i·an** \-ē-ən\ *adj or n*

Im·pe·ri·al Valley \im-'pir-ē-əl\ valley SE corner of California & partly in NE Baja California, Mexico

In·chon *or* **In·cheon** \'in-,chən\ city South Korea on Yellow Sea; *pop* 2,466,338

In·de·pen·dence \,in-də-'pen-dən(t)s\ city W Missouri E of Kansas City; *pop* 113,288

In·dia \'in-dē-ə\ **1** subcontinent S Asia S of the Himalayas between Bay of Bengal & Arabian Sea **2** country consisting of major portion of the subcontinent; *, New Delhi; *pop* 896,567,000 **3** *or* **Indian Empire** before 1947 those parts of the subcontinent of India under British rule or protection

In·di·an \'in-dē-ən\ ocean E of Africa, S of Asia, W of Australia, & N of Antarctica

In·di·ana \,in-dē-'a-nə\ state E *cen* U.S.; *, Indianapolis; *pop* 6,080,485 — **In·di·an·an** \-'a-nən\ *or* **In·di·an·i·an** \-'a-nē-ən\ *adj or n*

In·di·a·nap·o·lis \,in-dē-ə-'na-pə-lis\ city, * of Indiana; *pop* 791,926

Indian River lagoon 165 mi. (266 km.) long E Florida between main part of the state & coastal islands

Indian Territory former territory S U.S. in present state of Oklahoma

In·dies \'in-(,)dēz\ **1** EAST INDIES **2** WEST INDIES

In·do·chi·na \,in-(,)dō-'chī-nə\ **1** peninsula SE Asia including Myanmar, Malay Peninsula, Thailand, Cambodia, Laos, & Vietnam **2** *or* **French Indochina** former country SE Asia consisting of area now forming Cambodia, Laos, & Vietnam — **In·do–Chi·nese** \-chī-'nēz, -'nēs\ *adj or n*

In·do·ne·sia \,in-də-'nē-zhə, -shə\ country SE Asia in Malay Archipelago consisting of Sumatra, Java, S & E Borneo, Sulawesi, W New Guinea, & many smaller islands; *, Jakarta; *pop* 187,468,250 — **In·do·ne·sian** \-zhən, -shən\ *adj or n*

In·dore \in-'dor\ city W *cen* India; *pop* 1,597,441

In·dus \'in-dəs\ river 1800 mi. (2897 km.) long S Asia flowing from Tibet NW & SSW through Pakistan into Arabian Sea

In·gle·wood \'in-gəl-,wud\ city SW California; *pop* 112,580

In·land Sea \'in-,land, -lənd\ inlet of the Pacific in SW Japan between Honshu on N and Shikoku and Kyushu on S

Inner Hebrides — see HEBRIDES

Inner Mon·go·lia \män-'gōl-yə, män-, -'gō-lē-ə\ *or* **Nei Mong·gol** \'nä-'män-,gōl, -'män-\ region N China; *pop* 21,456,798

Inside Passage protected shipping route between Puget Sound, Washington, & the lower part of Alaska

In·ver·ness \,in-vər-'nes\ town NW Scotland; *pop* 63,090

Io·ni·an \ī-'ō-nē-ən\ sea, arm of the Mediterranean between SE Italy & W Greece

Io·wa \'ī-ə-wə\ state N *cen* U.S.; *, Des Moines; *pop* 2,926,324 — **Io·wan** \-wən\ *adj or n*

Ips·wich \'ip-(,)swich\ town SE England; *pop* 115,500

Iqa·lu·it \ē-'ka-lü-ət\ city Canada, * of Nunavut on Baffin Island; *pop* 6184

Iran \i-'rän, -'ran\ *formerly* **Per·sia** \'pər-zhə\ country SW Asia; *, Tehran; *pop* 59,570,000 — **Irani** \i-'rä-nē, -'ra-\ *adj or n* — **Ira·nian** \i-'rā-nē-ən, -'ran-ē-, -'rän-ē-\ *adj or n*

Iraq \i-'räk, -'rak\ country SW Asia in Mesopotamia; *, Baghdad; *pop* (est.) 24,683,000 — **Iraqi** \i-'räk-ē, -'rak-\ *adj or n*

Ire·land \'ī(-ə)r-lənd\ **1** *or Latin* **Hi·ber·nia** \hī-'bər-nē-ə\ island W Europe in the North Atlantic; one of the British Isles **2** *or* **Eire** \'er-ə\ country occupying major portion of the Ireland (island); *, Dublin; *pop* 3,917,203

Irish Sea arm of the North Atlantic between Great Britain & Ireland

Ir·kutsk \ir-'kütsk, ,ər-\ city S Russia near Lake Baikal; *pop* 639,000

Ir·ra·wad·dy \,ir-ə-'wä-dē\ river 1300 mi. (2092 km.) long Myanmar flowing S into Bay of Bengal

Ir·tysh \ir-'tish, ,ər-\ river over 2600 mi. (4180 km.) long *cen* Asia flowing NW & N from Altay Mountains in China, through Kazakhstan, & into W *cen* Russia

Ir·vine \'ər-,vīn\ city SW California; *pop* 143,072

Ir·ving \'ər-vin\ city NE Texas NW of Dallas; *pop* 191,615

Isfahan — see ESFAHAN

Is·lam·a·bad \is-'lä-mə-,bäd, iz-, -'la-mə-,bad\ city, * of Pakistan; *pop* 529,180

Islas Malvinas — see FALKLAND ISLANDS

Isle of Man — see MAN, ISLE OF

Isle of Wight \'wīt\ island England in English Channel

Isle Roy·ale \'ī(-ə)l-'ròi(-ə)l\ island Michigan in Lake Superior

Isles of Scilly 1 — see CORNWALL AND ISLES OF SCILLY 2 — see SCILLY

Is·ling·ton \'iz-liŋ-tən\ borough of N Greater London, England; *pop* 155,200

Ispahan — see ESFAHAN

Is·ra·el \'iz-rē(-ə)l, -(ₐ)rā(-ə)l\ 1 kingdom in ancient Palestine consisting of lands occupied by the Hebrew people 2 *or* **Ephra·im** \'ē-frē-əm\ the N part of the Hebrew kingdom after about 933 B.C. 3 country SW Asia; *, Jerusalem; *pop* 4,037,620 — **Is·rae·li** \iz-'rā-lē\ *adj or n*

Is·tan·bul \ˌis-tən-'bül, -ˌtan-, -ˌtän-, -'bùl, 'is-tən-ˌ, *or with* m *for* n\ *formerly* **Con·stan·ti·no·ple** \ˌkän-ˌstan-tə-'nō-pəl\ city NW Turkey on the Bosporus & Sea of Marmara; *pop* 6,620,241

Is·tria \'is-trē-ə\ peninsula in Croatia & Slovenia extending into the N Adriatic — **Is·tri·an** \-trē-ən\ *adj or n*

It·a·ly \'i-tə-lē\ country S Europe including a boot-shaped peninsula & the islands of Sicily & Sardinia; *, Rome; *pop* 57,844,017

Itas·ca, Lake \ī-'tas-kə\ lake NW *cen* Minnesota; source of the Mississippi

Ivory Coast *or* **Côte d'Ivoire** \ˌkōt-dē-'vwär\ country W Africa on Gulf of Guinea; official *, Yamoussoukro; seat of government, Abidjan; *pop* 13,459,000 — **Ivor·i·an** \(ₐ)ī-'vòr-ē-ən\ *adj or n* — **Ivory Coast·er** \'kō-stər\ *n*

Iwo Ji·ma \ˌē-(ₐ)wō-'jē-mə\ *or* **Iwo To** \-'tō\ island Japan in W Pacific SSE of Tokyo

Izhevsk \'ē-ˌzhefsk\ *or 1985–87* **Usti·nov** \'üs-ti-ˌnòf, -ˌnòv\ city W Russia; *pop* 651,000

Iz·mir \iz-'mir\ *formerly* **Smyr·na** \'smər-nə\ city W Turkey; *pop* 1,757,414

Jack·son \'jak-sən\ city, * of Mississippi; *pop* 184,256

Jack·son·ville \'jak-sən-ˌvil\ city NE Florida; *pop* 735,617

Jai·pur \'jī-ˌpùr\ city NW India; *pop* 2,324,319

Ja·kar·ta *formerly* **Dja·kar·ta** \jə-'kär-tə\ city, * of Indonesia in NW Java; *pop* 6,503,449

Ja·mai·ca \jə-'mā-kə\ island West Indies in Greater Antilles; country; *, Kingston; *pop* 2,599,334 — **Ja·mai·can** \-kən\ *adj or n*

James \'jāmz\ 1 — see DAKOTA 2 river 340 mi. (547 km.) long Virginia flowing E into Chesapeake Bay

James Bay the S extension of Hudson Bay between NE Ontario & W Quebec

James·town \'jāmz-ˌtaùn\ ruined village E Virginia on James River; first permanent English settlement in America (1607)

Jam·shed·pur \'jäm-ˌshed-ˌpùr\ city E India; *pop* 570,349

Ja·pan \jə-'pan, ja-\ country E Asia consisting of Honshu, Hokkaido, Kyushu, Shikoku, & other islands in the W Pacific; *, Tokyo; *pop* 126,925,843

Japan, Sea of *also* **East Sea** arm of the Pacific W of Japan

Ja·va \'jä-və, 'ja-\ island Indonesia SW of Borneo; chief city, Jakarta; *pop* 107,581,306 — **Ja·va·nese** \ˌja-və-'nēz, jä-, -'nēs\ *n*

Jef·fer·son City \'je-fər-sən\ city, * of Missouri; *pop* 39,636

Jer·sey \'jər-zē\ — see CHANNEL

Jersey City city NE New Jersey on Hudson River; *pop* 240,055

Je·ru·sa·lem \jə-'rü-s(ə-)ləm, -'rü-z(ə-)ləm\ city NW of Dead Sea, * of Israel; *pop* 544,200

Jid·da *or* **Jid·dah** \'ji-də\ *or* **Jed·da** *or* **Jed·dah** \'je-də\ city W Saudi Arabia on Red Sea; *pop* 561,104

Ji·lin \'jē-'lin\ *or* **Ki·rin** \'kē-'rin\ city NE China; *pop* 1,036,858

Ji·nan *or* **Tsi·nan** \'jē-'nän\ city E China; *pop* 1,500,000

Jin·zhou *or* **Chin–chou** *or* **Chin·chow** \'jin-'jō\ city NE China; *pop* 400,000

Jiu·long \'jü-'lòŋ\ *or* **Kow·loon** \'kaù-'lün\ 1 peninsula SE China in Hong Kong opposite Hong Kong Island 2 city on Jiulong Peninsula; *pop* 1,975,265

Jo·han·nes·burg \jō-'hä-nəs-ˌbərg, -'ha-\ city NE Republic of South Africa; *pop* 654,232

Jo·li·et \ˌjō-lē-'et\ city NE Illinois; *pop* 106,221

Jor·dan \'jòr-dᵊn\ 1 river 200 mi. (322 km.) long Israel & Jordan flowing S from Syria into Dead Sea 2 country SW Asia in NW Arabia; *, Amman; *pop* 5,182,000 — **Jor·da·ni·an** \jòr-'dā-nē-ən\ *adj or n*

Juan de Fu·ca, Strait of \ˌwän-də-'fyü-kə, ˌhwän-\ strait 100 mi. (161 km.) long between Vancouver Island, British Columbia, & Olympic Peninsula, Washington

Ju·daea *or* **Ju·dea** \jù-'dē-ə, -'dā-\ region of ancient Palestine forming its S division under Persian, Greek, & Roman rule — **Ju·dae·an** *or* **Ju·dean** \-ən\ *adj or n*

Ju·neau \'jü-(ₐ)nō, jú-'\ city, * of Alaska; *pop* 30,711

Ju·ra \'jùr-ə\ mountain range extending along boundary between France & Switzerland N of Lake of Geneva

Jut·land \'jət-lənd\ 1 peninsula N Europe extending into North Sea and consisting of main part of Denmark & N portion of Germany 2 the main part of Denmark

Ka·bul \'kä-bəl, -ˌbül; kə-'bül\ city, * of Afghanistan; *pop* (est.) 2,272,000

Ka Lae \kä-'lä-ā\ *or* **South Cape** *or*

South Point most southerly point of Hawaii & of U.S.

Ka·la·ha·ri \ˌka-lə-ˈhär-ē, ˌkä-\ desert region S Africa N of Orange River in S Botswana & NW Republic of South Africa

Kalgan — see ZHANGJIAKOU

Ka·li·man·tan \ˌka-lə-ˈman-ˌtan, ˌkä-lē-ˈmän-ˌtän\ **1** BORNEO — its Indonesian name **2** the S & E portion of Borneo belonging to Indonesia

Ka·li·nin·grad \kə-ˈlē-nən-ˌgrad, -nyən-, -ˌgrät\ *formerly* **Kö·nigs·berg** \ˈkā-nigz-ˌbərg\ city & port W Russia; *pop* 424,000

Kam·chat·ka \kam-ˈchat-kə, -ˈchät-\ peninsula 750 mi. (1207 km.) long E Russia

Kam·pa·la \käm-ˈpä-lä, kam-\ city, ✳ of Uganda; *pop* 773,463

Kampuchea — see CAMBODIA

Kan·da·har \ˈkən-də-ˌhär\ city SE Afghanistan; *pop* (est.) 359,700

Ka·no \ˈkä-(ˌ)nō\ city N *cen* Nigeria; *pop* 594,800

Kan·pur \ˈkän-ˌpur\ city N India on the Ganges; *pop* 2,532,138

Kan·sas \ˈkan-zəs\ state W *cen* U.S.; ✳, Topeka; *pop* 2,688,418 — **Kan·san** \ˈkan-zən\ *adj or n*

Kansas City **1** city NE Kansas bordering on Kansas City, Missouri; *pop* 146,866 **2** city W Missouri; *pop* 441,545

Kao–hsiung \ˈkaù-ˈshyüŋ, ˈgaù-\ city & port SW Taiwan; *pop* 1,405,860

Ka·ra·chi \kə-ˈrä-chē\ city S Pakistan on Arabian Sea; *pop* 9,339,023

Ka·ra·gan·da \ˌkär-ə-ˈgän-də\ *or* **Qa·ra·ghan·dy** \-dē\ city *cen* Kazakhstan *pop* 608,600

Kar·a·ko·ram Pass \ˌkär-ə-ˈkór-əm\ mountain pass NE Kashmir in **Karakoram Range** (system connecting the Himalayas with the Pamirs)

Ka·re·lia \kə-ˈrē-lē-ə, -ˈrēl-yə\ region NE Europe in Finland & Russia; *pop* 800,000 — **Ka·re·lian** \kə-ˈrē-lē-ən, -ˈrēl-yən\ *adj or n*

Ka·roo *or* **Kar·roo** \kə-ˈrü\ plateau region W Republic of South Africa W of Drakensberg Mountains

Kash·mir \ˈkash-ˌmir, ˈkazh-, kash-ˈ, kazh-ˈ\ disputed territory N subcontinent of India; claimed by India & Pakistan — **Kash·miri** \kash-ˈmi(ə)r-ē, kazh-\ *adj or n*

Ka·thi·a·war \ˌkä-tē-ə-ˈwär\ peninsula W India N of Gulf of Cambay

Kath·man·du *or* **Kat·man·du** \ˌkat-ˌman-ˈdü, ˌkät-ˌmän-\ city, ✳ of Nepal; metropolitan area *pop* 671,846

Kat·mai, Mount \ˈkat-ˌmī\ volcano 6715 ft. (2047 m.) S Alaska on Alaska Peninsula

Kat·te·gat \ˈka-ti-ˌgat\ arm of North Sea between Sweden & E coast of Jutland Peninsula of Denmark

Kau·ai \kä-ˈwä-ē\ island Hawaii NW of Oahu

Kau·nas \ˈkaù-nəs, -ˌnäs\ city *cen* Lithuania; *pop* 378,943

Ka·wa·sa·ki \ˌkä-wä-ˈsä-kē\ city Japan in E Honshu S of Tokyo; *pop* 1,249,905

Ka·zakh·stan *or* **Ka·zak·stan** \ˌka-(ˌ)zak-ˈstan\ country NW *cen* Asia; ✳, Astana; *pop* 17,186,000 — **Ka·zakh** *also* **Ka·zak** \kə-ˈzak, -ˈzäk\ *n*

Ka·zan \kə-ˈzan\ city W Russia; *pop* 1,098,000

Kee·wa·tin \kē-ˈwä-tᵊn, -ˈwä-\ former district N Canada in E Northwest Territories NW of Hudson Bay; area now part of Nunavut

Ke·me·ro·vo \ˈkye-mə-rə-və\ city S *cen* Russia; *pop* 521,000

Ke·nai \ˈkē-ˌnī\ peninsula S Alaska E of Cook Inlet

Kennedy, Cape — see CANAVERAL, CAPE

Ken·sing·ton and Chel·sea \ˈken-ziŋ-tən-ənd-ˈchel-sē, ˈken(t)-siŋ-\ borough of W Greater London, England; *pop* 127,600

Kent \ˈkent\ county SE England — **Kentish** \ˈken-tish\ *adj*

Ken·tucky \kən-ˈtə-kē\ state E *cen* U.S.; ✳, Frankfort; *pop* 4,041,769 — **Kentuck·i·an** \-kē-ən\ *adj or n*

Ken·ya \ˈke-nyə, ˈkē-\ **1** mountain 17,058 ft. (5199 m.) *cen* Kenya **2** country E Africa S of Ethiopia; ✳, Nairobi; *pop* 28,662,239 — **Ken·yan** \-nyən\ *adj or n*

Key West \ˈwest\ city SW Florida on Key West (island); *pop* 25,478

Kha·ba·rovsk \kə-ˈbär-əfsk, kə-\ city SE Russia; *pop* 615,000

Kham·bhat, Gulf of \ˈkəm-bət\ *or* **Gulf of Cam·bay** \kam-ˈbä\ inlet of Arabian Sea in India N of Bombay

Khar·kiv \ˈkär-kəf, ˈkär-\ *or* **Khar·kov** \ˈkär-ˌkóf, ˈkär-, -ˌkòv, -kəf\ city NE Ukraine; *pop* 1,623,000

Khar·toum \kär-ˈtüm\ city, ✳ of Sudan; *pop* 1,950,000

Khy·ber \ˈkī-bər\ pass 33 mi. (53 km.) long on border between Afghanistan & Pakistan

Ki·bo \ˈkē-(ˌ)bō\ mountain peak 19,340 ft. (5895 m.) NE Tanzania; highest peak of Kilimanjaro & highest point in Africa

Kiel \ˈkēl\ — see NORD-OSTSEE

Ki·ev \ˈkē-ˌef, -ˌev, -if\ *or Ukrainian* **Kyiv** \ˈkyē-ü\ city, ✳ of Ukraine; *pop* 2,587,000

Ki·ga·li \kē-ˈgä-lē\ city, ✳ of Rwanda; *pop* 232,733

Ki·lau·ea \ˌkē-ˌlä-ˈwä-ä\ volcanic crater Hawaii on Hawaii Island on E slope of Mauna Loa

Kil·i·man·ja·ro \ˌki-lə-mən-ˈjär-(ˌ)ō, -ˈja-(ˌ)rō\ mountain NE Tanzania; highest in Africa — see KIBO

Kil·lar·ney, Lakes of \ki-'lär-nē\ three lakes SW Ireland

Kings·ton \'kiŋ-stən\ city & port, ✻ of Jamaica; *pop* 103,771

Kingston upon Hull — see HULL

Kingston upon Thames borough of SW Greater London, England; *pop* 130,600

Kings·town \'kiŋz-ˌtaún\ seaport, ✻ of Saint Vincent and the Grenadines; *pop* 15,670

Kin·sha·sa \kin-'shä-sə\ city, ✻ of Democratic Republic of the Congo; *pop* 3,804,000

Ki·ri·bati \'kir-ə-ˌbas\ island group W Pacific; country; ✻, Tarawa; *pop* 78,600

Kirin — see JILIN

Kirk·wall \'kər-ˌkwól\ town and port N Scotland, ✻ of Orkney Islands; *pop* 5947

Kishinev — see CHIŞINĂU

Ki·ta·kyu·shu \kē-ˌtä-'kyü-(ˌ)shü\ city Japan in N Kyushu; *pop* 1,011,471

Kitch·e·ner \'kich-nər, 'ki-chə-\ city SE Ontario, Canada; *pop* 204,668

Kit·ty Hawk \'kit-ē-ˌhók\ town E North Carolina; *pop* 2991

Klon·dike \'klän-ˌdīk\ region NW Canada in *cen* Yukon Territory in valley of Klondike River

Knox·ville \'näks-ˌvil, -vəl\ city E Tennessee; *pop* 173,890

Ko·be \'kō-bē, -ˌbā\ city Japan in S Honshu; *pop* 1,493,398

Ko·di·ak \'kō-dē-ˌak\ island S Alaska E of Alaska Peninsula

Ko·la \'kō-lə\ peninsula NW Russia bordering on Finland

Ko·rea \kə-'rē-ə\ peninsula E Asia between Yellow Sea & Sea of Japan (East Sea); divided 1948 into independent countries of North Korea & South Korea — **Ko·re·an** \kə-'rē-ən\ *adj or n*

Ko·ror \'kór-ˌór\ town, former ✻ of Palau; *pop* 13,303

Kos·ci·us·ko, Mount \ˌkä-zē-'əs-(ˌ)kō, ˌkä-sē-\ mountain 7310 ft. (2228 m.) SE Australia in SE New South Wales; highest in Great Dividing Range & in Australia

Ko·so·vo \'kó-sə-ˌvō, 'kä-\ country S Europe in the Balkans; *pop* 2,092,000

Kowloon — see JIULONG

Krak·a·tau \ˌkra-kə-'taú\ *or* **Krak·a·toa** \-'tō-ə\ island & volcano Indonesia between Sumatra & Java

Kra·kow \'krä-ˌkaú, 'kra-, 'krä-, -(ˌ)kō, *Pol* 'krä-ˌküf\ city S Poland; *pop* 748,356

Kras·no·dar \ˌkräs-nə-'där\ city SW Russia; *pop* 635,000

Kras·no·yarsk \ˌkräs-nə-'yärsk\ city S *cen* Russia; *pop* 925,000

Kry·vyy Rih \kri-'vē-'rik\ *or* **Kri·voy Rog** \ˌkri-ˌvói-'róg, -'rók\ city SE *cen* Ukraine; *pop* 724,000

K2 \ˌkā-'tü\ *or* **God·win Aus·ten** \ˌgädwən-'ós-tən, ˌgó-, -'äs-\ mountain 28,250 ft. (8611 m.) N Kashmir in Karakoram Range; second highest in the world

Kua·la Lum·pur \ˌkwä-lə-'lùm-ˌpúr, -'ləm-, -ˌlùm-'\ city, ✻ of Malaysia; *pop* 1,145,075

Kuei·yang — see GUIYANG

Kun·lun \'kün-'lün\ mountain system W China extending E from the Pamirs; highest peak Ulugh Muztagh 25,340 ft. (7724 m.)

Kun·ming \'kùn-'miŋ\ city S China; *pop* 1,127,411

Kur·di·stan \ˌkúr-də-'stan, ˌkər-, -'stän; 'kər-də-ˌ\ region SW Asia chiefly in E Turkey, NW Iran, & N Iraq — **Kurd** \'kúrd, 'kərd\ *n* — **Kurd·ish** \'kúr-dish, 'kər-\ *adj*

Ku·ril *or* **Ku·rile** \'kyúr-ˌēl, 'kúr-; kyü-'rēl, kú-\ islands Russia in W Pacific between Kamchatka Peninsula & Hokkaido Island

Ku·wait \kú-'wät\ **1** country SW Asia in Arabia at head of Persian Gulf; *pop* 1,355,827 **2** city, its ✻; *pop* 181,774 — **Ku·waiti** \-'wä-tē\ *adj or n*

Kuybyshev — see SAMARA

Kuz·netsk Basin \kúz-'netsk\ *or* **Kuzbas** *or* **Kuz·bass** \'kúz-ˌbas\ basin S *cen* Russia

Kwa·ja·lein \'kwä-jə-lən, -ˌlän\ island W Pacific in Marshall Islands

Kwang·ju *or* **Gwang·ju** \'gwän-(ˌ)jü\ city SW South Korea; *pop* 1,350,948

Kwa·Zu·lu–Na·tal \kwä-'zü-(ˌ)lü-nə-'täl\ province E Republic of South Africa; *pop* 8,553,000

Kyo·to \kē-'ōt-ō\ city Japan in W *cen* Honshu; *pop* 1,467,785

Kyr·gyz·stan \ˌkir-gi-'stan, -'stän\ country W *cen* Asia; ✻, Bishkek; *pop* 4,526,000

Kyu·shu \'kyü-(ˌ)shü\ island Japan S of W end of Honshu; *pop* 13,445,561

Lab·ra·dor \'la-brə-ˌdór\ **1** peninsula E Canada between Hudson Bay & the Atlantic divided between the provinces of Quebec & Newfoundland and Labrador **2** the part of the peninsula belonging to the province of Newfoundland and Labrador — **Lab·ra·dor·ean** *or* **Lab·ra·dor·ian** \ˌla-brə-'dór-ē-ən\ *adj or n*

Lac·ca·dive \'la-kə-ˌdēv, -ˌdīv, -div\ islands India in Arabian Sea N of Maldive Islands

La·co·nia \lə-'kō-nē-ə, -nyə\ ancient country S Greece in SE Peloponnese; ✻, Sparta — **La·co·nian** \-nē-ən, -nyən\ *adj or n*

La·fay·ette \ˌla-fē-'et, ˌlä-\ city S Louisiana; *pop* 110,257

La·gos \'lä-ˌgäs, -ˌgós\ city, former ✻ (1960–91) of Nigeria; *pop* 1,340,000

La·hore \lə-'hór\ city E Pakistan; *pop* 5,143,495

Lake District region NW England containing many lakes & mountains

Lake·hurst \\'lāk-(ˌ)hərst\\ borough E New Jersey; *pop* 2522

Lake·wood \\'lāk-ˌwùd\\ city *cen* Colorado; *pop* 144,126

Lam·beth \\'lam-bəth, -ˌbeth\\ borough of S Greater London, England; *pop* 220,100

La·nai \\lə-'nī, lä-\\ island Hawaii W of Maui

Lan·ca·shire \\'laŋ-kə-ˌshir, -shər\\ *or* **Lan·cas·ter** \\'laŋ-kəs-tər\\ county NW England — **Lan·cas·tri·an** \\laŋ-'kas-trē-ən, lan-\\ *adj or n*

Lan·cas·ter \\'laŋ-kəs-tər, 'lan-ˌkas-tər\\ city NW England; *pop* 125,600

Land's End \\'landz-'end\\ cape SW England; most westerly point of England

Lan·sing \\'lan-siŋ\\ city, * of Michigan; *pop* 119,128

Lan·zhou *or* **Lan·chou** \\'län-'jō\\ city W China; *pop* 1,194,640

Laos \\'laùs, 'lä-(ˌ)ōs, 'lā-ˌäs\\ country SE Asia in Indochina NE of Thailand; *, Vientiane; *pop* 4,533,000 — **Lao·tian** \\lā-'ō-shən, 'laù-shən\\ *adj or n*

La Paz \\lä-'päz, -'päs\\ city, administrative * of Bolivia; *pop* 711,036

Lap·land \\'lap-ˌland, -lənd\\ region N Europe above the Arctic Circle in N Norway, N Sweden, N Finland, & Kola Peninsula of Russia — **Lap·land·er** \\-ˌlan-dər, -lən-\\ *n*

La·re·do \\lə-'rā-(ˌ)dō\\ city S Texas on the Rio Grande; *pop* 176,576

Larne \\'lärn\\ district NE Northern Ireland; *pop* 29,181

Las·sen Peak \\'la-sⁿn\\ volcano 10,457 ft. (3187 m.) N California at S end of Cascade Range

Las Ve·gas \\läs-'vā-gəs\\ city SE Nevada; *pop* 478,434

Latin America 1 Spanish America and Brazil 2 all of the Americas S of the U.S. — **Latin–American** *adj* — **Latin American** *n*

Latin Quarter section of Paris, France S of the Seine

Lat·via \\'lat-vē-ə\\ country E Europe on Baltic Sea; *, Riga; *pop* 2,345,768

Lau·ren·tian Mountains \\lȯ-'ren(t)-shən\\ hills E Canada in S Quebec N of the Saint Lawrence on S edge of Canadian Shield

Laurentian Plateau — *see* CANADIAN SHIELD

La·val \\lə-'val\\ city S Quebec NW of Montreal; *pop* 343,005

Law·rence \\'lȯr-ən(t)s, 'lär-\\ city NE corner of Massachusetts; *pop* 72,043

League of Nations political organization established at the end of World War I; replaced by United Nations 1946

Leb·a·non \\'le-bə-nən\\ 1 mountains Lebanon (country) running parallel to coast 2 country SW Asia on the Mediterranean; *, Beirut; *pop* 2,909,000 — **Leb·a·nese** \\ˌle-bə-'nēz, -'nēs\\ *adj or n*

Leeds \\'lēdz\\ city N England; *pop* 674,400

Lee·ward Islands \\'lē-wərd, 'lü-ərd\\ 1 islands Hawaii extending WNW from main islands of the group 2 islands South Pacific in W Society Islands 3 islands West Indies in N Lesser Antilles extending from Virgin Islands (on N) to Dominica (on S)

Le Ha·vre \\lə-'hävrᵊ, -'häv\\ city N France on English Channel; *pop* 190,924

Leh·man Caves \\'lē-mən\\ limestone caverns E Nevada

Leices·ter \\'les-tər\\ city *cen* England ENE of Birmingham; *pop* 270,600

Leices·ter·shire \\'les-tər-ˌshir, -shər\\ *or* **Leicester** county *cen* England

Lein·ster \\'len(t)-stər\\ province E Ireland; *pop* 2,105,579

Leip·zig \\'līp-sig, -sik\\ city E Germany; *pop* 503,191

Le·na \\'lē-nə, 'lā-\\ river about 2700 mi. (4345 km.) long E Russia, flowing NE & N from mountains W of Lake Baikal into Arctic Ocean

Leningrad — *see* SAINT PETERSBURG

Le·ón \\lā-'ōn\\ city *cen* Mexico; metropolitan area *pop* 1,174,180

Ler·wick \\'lər-(ˌ)wik, 'ler-\\ town and port N Scotland in the Shetlands; *pop* 7223

Le·so·tho \\lə-'sō-(ˌ)tō, -'sü-(ˌ)tü\\ *formerly* **Ba·su·to·land** \\bə-'sü-tō-ˌland\\ country S Africa surrounded by Republic of South Africa; *, Maseru; *pop* 1,903,000

Lesser Antilles islands in the West Indies including Virgin Islands, Leeward Islands, & Windward Islands, Barbados, Trinidad, Tobago, & islands in the S Caribbean N of Venezuela — *see* GREATER ANTILLES

Le·vant \\lə-'vant\\ the countries bordering on the E Mediterranean — **Lev·an·tine** \\'lev-ən-ˌtīn, -ˌtēn, lə-'van-\\ *adj or n*

Lew·es \\'lü-əs\\ town S England

Lew·i·sham \\'lü-ə-shəm\\ borough of SE Greater London, England; *pop* 215,300

Lew·is with Har·ris \\'lü-əs-with-'ha-rəs, -with-\\ island NW Scotland in Outer Hebrides

Lex·ing·ton \\'lek-siŋ-tən\\ 1 city NE *cen* Kentucky; county *pop* 260,512 2 town NE Massachusetts; *pop* 30,355

Ley·te \\'lā-tē\\ island Philippines S of Samar

Lha·sa \\'lä-sə, 'la-\\ city SW China, * of Tibet; *pop* 106,885

Li·be·ria \\lī-'bir-ē-ə\\ country W Africa on the North Atlantic; *, Monrovia; *pop* 2,101,628 — **Li·be·ri·an** \\-ē-ən\\ *adj or n*

Lib·er·ty \\'li-bər-tē\\ *formerly* **Bed·loe's** \\'bed-ˌlōz\\ island SE New York; site of the Statue of Liberty

Li·bre·ville \\'lē-brə-ˌvil, -ˌvēl\\ city, * of Gabon; *pop* 419,596

Lib·ya \\'li-bē-ə\\ country N Africa on the

Mediterranean W of Egypt; **✳**, Tripoli; *pop* 4,573,000 — **Lib·y·an** \'li-bē-ən\ *adj or n*

Libyan desert N Africa W of the Nile in Libya, Egypt, & Sudan

Liech·ten·stein \'lik-tən-ˌstīn, 'lik-tən-ˌshtīn\ country W Europe between Austria & Switzerland; **✳**, Vaduz; *pop* 33,525 — **Liech·ten·stein·er** \-ˌstī-nər, -ˌshtī-\ *n*

Lif·fey \'li-fē\ river 50 mi. (80 km.) long E Ireland

Li·gu·ria \lə-'gyùr-ē-ə\ region NW on Ligurian Sea — **Li·gu·ri·an** \-ē-ən\ *adj or n*

Ligurian Sea arm of the Mediterranean N of Corsica

Li·lon·gwe \li-'lòn̄-(ˌ)gwä\ city, **✳** of Malawi; *pop* 498,185

Li·ma \'lē-mə\ city, **✳** of Peru; *pop* 5,825,900

Lim·a·vady \ˌli-mə-'va-dē\ district NW Northern Ireland; *pop* 29,201

Lim·po·po \lim-'pō-(ˌ)pō\ river 1000 mi. (1609 km.) long Africa flowing from Republic of South Africa into Indian Ocean in Mozambique

Lin·coln \'liŋ-kən\ **1** city, **✳** of Nebraska; *pop* 225,581 **2** city E England; *pop* 81,900

Lin·coln·shire \'liŋ-kən-ˌshir, -shər\ *or* **Lincoln** county E England

Line \'līn\ islands Kiribati S of Hawaii; *pop* 4782

Lis·bon \'liz-bən\ *or Portuguese* **Lis·boa** \lēzh-'vō-ə\ city, **✳** of Portugal; *pop* 564,657

Lis·burn \'liz-(ˌ)bərn\ district E Northern Ireland; *pop* 99,162

Lith·u·a·nia \ˌli-thə-'wā-nē-ə, ˌli-thyə-, -nyə\ country E Europe; **✳**, Vilnius; *pop* 3,483,972

Lit·tle Rock \'li-t³l-ˌräk\ city, **✳** of Arkansas; *pop* 183,133

Liv·er·pool \'li-vər-ˌpül\ city NW England; *pop* 448,300

Li·vo·nia \lə-'vō-nē-ə, -nyə\ city SE Michigan; *pop* 100,545

Lju·blja·na \lē-ˌü-blē-'ä-nə\ city, **✳** of Slovenia; *pop* 323,291

Lla·no Es·ta·ca·do \'la-(ˌ)nō-ˌes-tə-'kä-(ˌ)dō, 'lä-, 'yä-\ *or* **Staked Plain** \'stäk(t)-\ plateau region SE New Mexico & NW Texas

Lo·bam·ba \lō-'bäm-bə\ town, legislative **✳** of Swaziland; *pop* (est.) 10,000

Lodz \'lüj, 'lädz\ city *cen* Poland WSW of Warsaw; *pop* 851,690

Lo·fo·ten \'lō-ˌfō-t³n\ islands NW Norway

Lo·gan, Mount \'lō-gən\ mountain 19,524 ft. (5951 m.) NW Canada in Saint Elias Range; highest in Canada & second highest in North America

Loire \lə-'wär, 'lwär\ river 634 mi. (1020 km.) long *cen* France flowing NW & W into Bay of Biscay

Lo·mé \lō-'mā\ city, **✳** of Togo; *pop* 229,400

Lo·mond, Loch \'lō-mənd\ lake S *cen* Scotland

Lon·don \'lən-dən\ **1** city SE Ontario, Canada; *pop* 336,539 **2** city, **✳** of England & of United Kingdom on the Thames; consists of **City of London** & **Greater London** metropolitan county; *pop* 6,377,900 — **Lon·don·er** \-də-nər\ *n*

Londonderry — see DERRY

Long Beach city SW California S of Los Angeles; *pop* 461,522

Long Island island 118 mi. (190 km.) long SE New York S of Connecticut

Long Island Sound inlet of the Atlantic between Connecticut & Long Island, New York

Lon·gueuil \lòn̄-'gāl\ city Canada in S Quebec E of Montreal; *pop* 128,016

Lor·raine \lə-'rān, lò-\ region NE France

Los An·ge·les \lòs-'an-jə-ləs\ city SW California; *pop* 3,694,820

Lou·ise, Lake \lú-'ēz\ lake SW Alberta, Canada

Lou·i·si·ana \lù-ˌē-zē-'a-nə, ˌlü-ə-zē-, ˌlü-zē-\ state S U.S.; **✳**, Baton Rouge; *pop* 4,468,976 — **Lou·i·si·an·ian** \-'a-nē-ən, -'a-nyən\ *or* **Lou·i·si·an·an** \-'a-nən\ *adj or n*

Louisiana Purchase area W *cen* U.S. between Rocky Mountains & the Mississippi purchased 1803 from France

Lou·is·ville \'lü-i-ˌvil, -vəl\ city N Kentucky on the Ohio River; *pop* 256,231

Low Countries region W Europe consisting of modern Belgium, Luxembourg, & the Netherlands

Lowell \'lō-əl\ city NE Massachusetts NW of Boston; *pop* 105,167

Lower 48 the continental states of the U.S. excluding Alaska

Low·lands \'lō-ləndz, -ˌlandz\ the *cen* & E part of Scotland

Lu·an·da \lù-'än-də\ city, **✳** of Angola; *pop* 1,544,400

Lub·bock \'lə-bək\ city NW Texas; *pop* 199,564

Lu·bum·ba·shi \ˌlü-büm-'bä-shē\ city SE Democratic Republic of the Congo; *pop* (est.) 1,138,000

Luck·now \'lək-ˌnaủ\ city N India ESE of Delhi; *pop* 2,207,340

Lüda *or* **Lü–ta** — see DALIAN

Lu·ray Caverns \'lü-ˌrā, lü-'\ series of caves N Virginia

Lu·sa·ka \lü-'sä-kä\ city, **✳** of Zambia; *pop* 982,362

Lü·shun \'lü-'shùn, 'lⴱ-\ *or* **Port Ar·thur** \-'är-thər\ seaport NE China; part of greater Dalian

Lu·ton \'lü-t³n\ town SE *cen* England; *pop* 167,300

Lux·em·bourg *or* **Lux·em·burg** \'lək-səm-ˌbərg, 'lük-səm-ˌbủrk\ **1** country W

Europe bordered by Belgium, France, & Germany; *pop* 392,000 **2** city, its **＊**; *pop* 75,377 — **Lux·em·bourg·er** \-ˌbər-gər, -ˌbür-\ *n* — **Lux·em·bourg·ian** \ˌlək-səm-ˈbər-gē-ən, ˌlük-səm-ˈbür-\ *adj*

Lu·zon \lü-ˈzän\ island N Philippines; *pop* 23,900,796

L'viv \lə-ˈvē-ū, -ˈvēf\ *or* **L'vov** \lə-ˈvóf, -ˈvòv\ *or Polish* **Lwów** \lə-ˈvüf, -ˈvüv\ city W Ukraine; *pop* 802,000

Lyallpur — see FAISALABAD

Lyd·ia \ˈli-dē-ə\ ancient country W Asia Minor on the Aegean — **Lyd·i·an** \-ē-ən\ *adj or n*

Lyon \ˈlyōⁿ\ *or* **Lyons** \lē-ˈōⁿ, ˈlī-ənz\ city SE *cen* France; *pop* 445,274

Ma·cao *or Portuguese* **Ma·cau** \mə-ˈkaú\ *or Chinese* **Ao·men** \ˈaú-ˈmən\ **1** special administrative region on coast of SE China W of Hong Kong; *pop* 488,000 **2** city, its **＊**; *pop* 161,252 — **Mac·a·nese** \ˌmä-kə-ˈnēz, -ˈnēs\ *n*

Mac·e·do·nia \ˌma-sə-ˈdō-nē-ə, -nyə\ **1** region S Europe in Balkan Peninsula in NE Greece, the former Yugoslav section & now independent country of Macedonia, & SW Bulgaria including territory of ancient kingdom of Macedonia (**Mac·e·don** \ˈmas-ə-dən, -ə-ˌdän\ ) **2** country S *cen* Balkan Peninsula; **＊**, Skopje; a former republic of Yugoslavia; *pop* 2,038,059 — **Mac·e·do·nian** \ˌmas-ə-ˈdō-nyən, -nē-ən\ *adj or n*

Mac·gil·li·cud·dy's Reeks \mə-ˈgi-lə-ˌkə-dēz-ˈrēks\ mountains SW Ireland; highest Carrantuohill 3414 ft. (1041 m.)

Ma·chu Pic·chu \ˌmä-(ˌ)chü-ˈpē-(ˌ)chü, -ˈpēk-\ site SE Peru of ancient Inca city

Mac·ken·zie \mə-ˈken-zē\ river 1120 mi. (1802 km.) long NW Canada flowing from Great Slave Lake NW into Beaufort Sea

Mack·i·nac, Straits of \ˈma-kə-ˌnó, -ˌnak\ channel N Michigan connecting Lake Huron & Lake Michigan

Ma·con \ˈmā-kən\ city *cen* Georgia; *pop* 97,255

Mad·a·gas·car \ˌma-də-ˈgas-kər, -kär\ *formerly* **Mal·a·gasy Re·public** \ˌma-lə-ˈga-sē\ island country W Indian Ocean off SE Africa; **＊**, Antananarivo; *pop* 16,694,272 — **Mad·a·gas·can** \ˌma-də-ˈgas-kən\ *adj or n*

Ma·dei·ra \mə-ˈdir-ə, -ˈder-ə\ **1** river 2013 mi. (3239 km.) long W Brazil flowing NE into the Amazon **2** islands Portugal in the North Atlantic N of the Canary Islands; *pop* 245,011 **3** island; chief of the Madeira group — **Ma·dei·ran** \-ˈdir-ən, -ˈder-\ *adj or n*

Ma·di·nat ash Sha'b \mə-ˌdē-ˌnə-tash-ˈshab\ city S Yemen

Mad·i·son \ˈma-də-sən\ city, **＊** of Wisconsin; *pop* 208,054

Ma·dras \mə-ˈdras, -ˈdräs\ *or* **Chen·nai** \ˈche-ˌnī\ city SE India; *pop* 4,216,268

Ma·drid \mə-ˈdrid\ city, **＊** of Spain; *pop* 2,938,723

Ma·du·rai \ˌmä-də-ˈrī\ city S India; *pop* 922,913

Mag·da·len Islands \ˈmag-də-lən\ *or F* **Îles de la Ma·de·leine** \ˌēl-də-lä-mäd-ˈlen, -mä-də-ˈlen\ islands Canada in Gulf of Saint Lawrence between Newfoundland & Prince Edward Island

Ma·gel·lan, Strait of \mə-ˈje-lən, *chiefly Brit* -ˈge-\ strait at S end of South America between mainland & Tierra del Fuego

Magh·er·a·felt \ˈmär-ə-ˌfelt, ˈma-kə-rə-ˌfelt\ district *cen* Northern Ireland; *pop* 35,874

Maid·stone \ˈmäd-stən, -ˌstōn\ town SE England; *pop* 133,200

Main \ˈmīn, ˈmän\ river 325 mi. (523 km.) long S *cen* Germany flowing W into the Rhine

Maine \ˈmän\ state NE U.S.; **＊**, Augusta; *pop* 1,274,923 — **Main·er** \ˈmä-nər\ *n*

Ma·jor·ca \mä-ˈjòr-kə, mə-, -ˈyòr-\ *or Spanish* **Ma·llor·ca** \mä-ˈyòr-kä\ island Spain in W Mediterranean — **Ma·jor·can** \-ˈjòr-kən, -ˈyòr\ *adj or n*

Ma·ju·ro \mə-ˈjúr-(ˌ)ō\ atoll, **＊** of Marshall Islands; *pop* (est.) 20,000

Mal·a·bar Coast \ˈma-lə-ˌbär\ region SW India on Arabian Sea

Ma·la·bo \mä-ˈlä-(ˌ)bō\ city, **＊** of Equatorial Guinea; *pop* 37,237

Ma·lac·ca, Strait of \mə-ˈla-kə, -ˈlä-\ channel between S Malay Peninsula & island of Sumatra

Ma·la·wi \mə-ˈlä-wē\ *formerly* **Ny·asa·land** \nī-ˈa-sə-ˌland, nē-\ country SE Africa on Lake Nyasa; **＊**, Lilongwe; *pop* 10,475,257 — **Ma·la·wi·an** \-ən\ *adj or n*

Ma·lay \mə-ˈlā, ˈmä-(ˌ)lā\ **1** archipelago SE Asia including Sumatra, Java, Borneo, Sulawesi, Moluccas, & Timor; usu. thought to include the Philippines & sometimes New Guinea **2** peninsula SE Asia divided between Thailand & Malaysia (country)

Ma·laya \mə-ˈlā-ə, mä-\ **1** the Malay Peninsula **2** former country SE Asia on Malay Peninsula; now part of Malaysia

Ma·lay·sia \mə-ˈlā-zh(ē-)ə, -sh(ē-)ə\ **1** the Malay Archipelago **2** the Malay Peninsula & Malay Archipelago **3** country SE Asia; **＊**, Kuala Lumpur; *pop* 19,077,000 — **Ma·lay·sian** \mə-ˈlā-zhən, -shən\ *adj or n*

Mal·dives \ˈmól-ˌdēvz, -ˌdīvz\ islands in Indian Ocean SW of Sri Lanka; country; **＊**, Male Atoll; *pop* 270,101 — **Mal·div·i·an** \mól-ˈdi-vē-ən, mal-\ *adj or n*

Ma·le \ˈmä-lē\ atoll, **＊** of Maldives; *pop* (est.) 63,000

Ma·li \ˈmä-lē, ˈma-\ country W Africa; **＊**, Bamako; *pop* 8,646,000 — **Ma·li·an** \-lē-ən\ *adj or n*

Mal·ta \ˈmól-tə\ islands in the Mediterranean S of Sicily; country since 1964; ✱, Valletta; *pop* 397,296 — **Mal·tese** \mȯl-'tēz, -'tēs\ *adj or n*

Malvinas, Islas — see FALKLAND IS-LANDS

Mam·moth Cave \'ma-məth\ limestone caverns SW *cen* Kentucky

Man, Isle of \'man\ island British Isles in Irish Sea; has own legislature & laws; *pop* 60,496

Ma·na·gua \mä-'nä-gwä\ city, ✱ of Nicaragua; *pop* 552,900

Ma·na·ma \mə-'na-mə\ city, ✱ of Bahrain; *pop* 136,999

Man·ches·ter \'man-ˌches-tər, -chəs-tər\ 1 city S *cen* New Hampshire; *pop* 107,006 2 city NW England; *pop* 406,900

Man·chu·ria \man-'chu̇r-ē-ə\ region NE China S of the Amur — **Man·chu·ri·an** \-ē-ən\ *adj or n*

Man·hat·tan \man-'ha-tᵊn, mən-\ 1 island SE New York in New York City 2 borough of New York City consisting chiefly of Manhattan Island; *pop* 1,537,195

Ma·nila \mə-'ni-lə\ city, ✱ of Philippines in W Luzon; *pop* 1,587,000

Man·i·to·ba \ˌma-nə-'tō-bə\ province *cen* Canada; ✱, Winnipeg; *pop* 1,150,034 — **Man·i·to·ban** \-bən\ *adj or n*

Man·i·tou·lin \ˌma-nə-'tü-lən\ island 80 mi. (129 km.) long S Ontario in Lake Huron

Ma·pu·to \mä-'pü-(ˌ)tō, -(ˌ)tü\ city, ✱ of Mozambique; *pop* 966,800

Mar·a·cai·bo \ˌma-rə-'kī-(ˌ)bō, ˌmär-ä-\ city NW Venezuela; *pop* 1,207,513

Maracaibo, Lake extension of a gulf of the Caribbean NW Venezuela

Mar·a·thon \'ma-rə-ˌthän\ plain E Greece NE of Athens

Mar·i·ana \ˌmer-ē-'a-nə\ islands W Pacific N of Caroline Islands; comprise Commonwealth of Northern Mariana Islands & Guam

Mariana Trench ocean trench W Pacific extending from SE of Guam to NW of Mariana Islands; deepest in world

Ma·rin·du·que \ˌma-rən-'dü-(ˌ)kä, ˌmär-ēn-\ island *cen* Philippines; *pop* 173,715

Maritime Provinces the Canadian provinces of New Brunswick, Nova Scotia, & Prince Edward Island & sometimes thought to include Newfoundland and Labrador

Ma·ri·u·pol \ˌma-rē-'ü-ˌpȯl, -pəl\ *or* *1949–89* **Zhda·nov** \zhə-'dä-nəf\ city E Ukraine; *pop* 417,000

Mar·ma·ra, Sea of \'mär-mə-rə\ sea NW Turkey connected with Black Sea by the Bosporus & with Aegean Sea by the Dardanelles

Marne \'märn\ river 325 mi. (523 km.) long NE France flowing W into the Seine

Mar·que·sas \mär-'kā-zəz, -zəs, -səz, -səs\ islands South Pacific; belonging to France; *pop* 7358 — **Mar·que·san** \-zən, -sən\ *adj or n*

Mar·ra·kech \ˌma-rə-'kesh, 'ma-rə-ˌ, mə-'rä-kish\ city *cen* Morocco; *pop* 439,728

Mar·seille \mär-'sā\ *or* **Mar·seilles** \mär-'sā, -'sālz\ city SE France; *pop* 797,491

Mar·shall Islands \'mär-shəl\ islands W Pacific E of the Carolines; republic, in association with U.S.; ✱, Majuro; *pop* 70,822

Mar·tha's Vineyard \'mär-thəz\ island SE Massachusetts off SW coast of Cape Cod WNW of Nantucket

Mar·ti·nique \ˌmär-tə-'nēk\ island West Indies in the Windward Islands; an overseas division of France; ✱, Fort-de-France; *pop* 377,000

Mary·land \'mer-ə-lənd\ state E U.S.; ✱, Annapolis; *pop* 5,296,486 — **Mary·land·er** \-lən-dər, -ˌlan-\ *n*

Mas·ba·te \mäz-'bä-tē, mäs-\ island *cen* Philippines

Mas·e·ru \'ma-sə-ˌrü, -zə-\ city, ✱ of Lesotho; *pop* 71,500

Mash·had \mə-'shad\ city NE Iran; *pop* 1,463,508

Ma·son–Dix·on Line \'mā-sᵊn-'dik-sən\ boundary between Maryland & Pennsylvania; often considered the boundary between N & S states

Mas·qat \'məs-ˌkät\ *or* **Mus·cat** \-ˌkät, -ˌkat, -kət\ town E Arabia, ✱ of Oman; *pop* 100,000

Mas·sa·chu·setts \ˌma-sə-'chü-səts, -zəts\ state NE U.S.; ✱, Boston; *pop* 6,349,097

Mat·a·be·le·land \ˌma-tə-'bē-lē-ˌland, ˌmä-tä-'bä-lä-\ region SW Zimbabwe

Mat·lock \'mat-ˌläk\ town N England; *pop* 20,610

Mat·ter·horn \'ma-tər-ˌhȯrn, 'mä-\ mountain 14,691 ft. (4478 m.) on border between Switzerland & Italy

Maui \'mau̇-ē\ island Hawaii NW of Hawaii Island

Mau·na Kea \ˌmau̇-nä-'kā-ä, ˌmȯ-\ extinct volcano 13,796 ft. (4205 m.) Hawaii in N *cen* Hawaii Island

Mau·na Loa \-'lō-ə\ volcano 13,680 ft. (4170 m.) Hawaii in S *cen* Hawaii Island

Mau·re·ta·nia *or* **Mau·ri·ta·nia** \ˌmȯr-ə-'tā-nē-ə, ˌmär-, -nyə\ ancient country NW Africa in modern Morocco & W Algeria — **Mau·re·ta·ni·an** *or* **Mau·ri·ta·ni·an** \-nē-ən, -nyən\ *adj or n*

Mauritania country NW Africa on the Atlantic N of Senegal River; ✱, Nouakchott; *pop* 2,171,000 — **Mauritanian** *adj or n*

Mau·ri·tius \mȯ-'ri-sh(ē-)əs\ island in Indian Ocean E of Madagascar; country; ✱, Port Louis; *pop* 1,210,196 — **Mau·ri·tian** \-'ri-shən\ *adj or n*

May, Cape \'mā\ cape S New Jersey at entrance to Delaware Bay

Ma·yon, Mount \mä-ˈyȯn\ volcano 8077 ft. (2462 m.) Philippines in SE Luzon

Ma·yotte \mä-ˈyät, -ˈyȯt\ island Comoros group; French dependency; *pop* 90,000 — see COMOROS

Ma·za·ma, Mount \mə-ˈzäm-ə\ prehistoric mountain SW Oregon the collapse of whose top formed Crater Lake

Mba·bane \ˌəm-bä-ˈbä-nä\ city, ✱ of Swaziland; *pop* 57,992

Mbi·ni \em-ˈbē-nē\ *formerly* **Río Mu·ni** \ˌrē-ō-ˈmü-nē\ mainland portion of Equatorial Guinea

Mc·Al·len \mə-ˈka-lən\ city S Texas; *pop* 106,414

Mc·Kin·ley, Mount \mə-ˈkin-lē\ *or* **De·na·li** \də-ˈnä-lē\ mountain 20,320 ft. (6194 m.) S *cen* Alaska in Alaska Range; highest in U.S. & North America

Mead, Lake \ˈmēd\ reservoir NW Arizona & SE Nevada formed by Hoover Dam in Colorado River

Mec·ca \ˈme-kə\ city W Saudi Arabia contains Islam's Great Mosque; *pop* 366,801

Me·dan \mā-ˈdän\ city Indonesia, in N Sumatra; *pop* 1,730,752

Me·de·llín \ˌme-də-ˈlēn, ˌmä-thä-ˈyēn\ city NW Colombia; *pop* 1,581,400

Me·di·na \mə-ˈdī-nə\ city W Saudi Arabia; *pop* 608,295

Med·i·ter·ra·nean \ˌme-də-tə-ˈrā-nē-ən, -nyən\ sea 2300 mi. (3700 km.) long between Europe & Africa connecting with the Atlantic through Strait of Gibraltar

Me·kong \ˈmā-ˈkȯŋ, -ˈkäŋ; ˈmā-ˌ\ river 2600 mi. (4184 km.) long SE Asia flowing from E Tibet S & SE into South China Sea in S Vietnam

Mel·a·ne·sia \ˌme-lə-ˈnē-zhə, -shə\ islands of the Pacific NE of Australia & S of Micronesia including Bismarck, the Solomons, Vanuatu, New Caledonia, & the Fijis

Mel·bourne \ˈmel-bərn\ city SE Australia, ✱ of Victoria; metropolitan area *pop* 2,761,995

Mel·e·ke·ok \ˈme-lə-ˌkä-ˌȯk\ town, ✱ of Palau

Melos — see MÍLOS

Mel·ville \ˈmel-ˌvil\ **1** island N Canada, split between Northwest Territories & Nunavut **2** peninsula Canada in Nunavut

Mem·phis \ˈmem(p)-fəs\ **1** city SW Tennessee; *pop* 650,100 **2** ancient city N Egypt S of modern Cairo

Mem·phre·ma·gog, Lake \ˌmem(p)-fri-ˈmä-ˌgäg\ lake on border between Canada (Quebec) & United States (Vermont)

Men·do·ci·no, Cape \ˌmen-də-ˈsē-(ˌ)nō\ cape NW California

Mer·cia \ˈmər-sh(ē-)ə\ ancient Anglo-Saxon kingdom *cen* England — **Mer·cian** \ˈmər-shən\ *adj or n*

Mer·sey \ˈmər-zē\ river 70 mi. (113 km.) long NW England flowing NW & W into Irish Sea

Mer·sey·side \ˈmər-zē-ˌsīd\ metropolitan county NW England; includes Liverpool

Mer·ton \ˈmər-tᵊn\ borough of SW Greater London, England; *pop* 161,800

Me·sa \ˈmā-sə\ city S *cen* Arizona; *pop* 396,375

Me·sa·bi Range \mə-ˈsä-bē\ region NE Minnesota that contains iron ore

Mes·o·po·ta·mia \ˌme-s(ə-)pə-ˈtä-mē-ə, -myə\ **1** region SW Asia between Euphrates & Tigris rivers **2** the entire Tigris–Euphrates valley — **Mes·o·po·ta·mian** \-mē-ən, -myən\ *adj or n*

Mes·quite \mə-ˈskēt, me-\ city NE Texas E of Dallas; *pop* 124,523

Meuse \ˈmyüz, ˈmə(r)z, ˈmœz\ river 580 mi. (933 km.) long W Europe flowing from NE France into North Sea in the Netherlands

Mex·i·co \ˈmek-si-ˌkō\ **1** country S North America; *pop* 89,995,000 **2** *or* **Mexico City** city, its ✱; metropolitan area *pop* 16,674,160 — **Mex·i·can** \ˈmek-si-kən\ *adj or n*

Mexico, Gulf of inlet of the Atlantic SE North America

Mi·ami \mī-ˈa-mē\ city & port SE Florida; *pop* 362,470

Miami Beach city SE Florida; *pop* 87,933

Mich·i·gan \ˈmi-shi-gən\ state N *cen* U.S.; ✱, Lansing; *pop* 9,938,444 — **Mich·i·gan·der** \ˌmi-shi-ˈgan-dər\ *n* — **Mich·i·gan·i·an** \ˌmi-shə-ˈgä-nē-ən, -ˈga-\ *n* — **Mich·i·gan·ite** \ˈmi-shi-gə-ˌnīt\ *n*

Michigan, Lake lake N *cen* U.S.; one of the Great Lakes

Mi·cro·ne·sia \ˌmī-krə-ˈnē-zhə, -shə\ islands of the W Pacific E of the Philippines & N of Melanesia including Caroline, Kiribati, Mariana, & Marshall groups — **Mi·cro·ne·sian** \-zhən, -shən\ *adj or n*

Micronesia, Federated States of islands W Pacific in the Carolines; country in association with U.S.; ✱, Palikir; *pop* 134,597

Middle East the countries of SW Asia & N Africa — usually thought to include the countries extending from Libya on the W to Afghanistan on the E — **Middle Eastern** *adj*

Mid·dles·brough \ˈmi-dᵊlz-brə\ town N England; *pop* 141,100

Middle West — see MIDWEST

Mid Gla·mor·gan \ˈmid-glə-ˈmȯr-gən\ former county SE Wales

Mid·i·an \ˈmi-dē-ən\ ancient region NW Arabia E of Gulf of Aqaba — **Mid·i·an·ite** \-ē-ə-ˌnīt\ *n*

Mid·lands \ˈmid-ləndz\ the *cen* counties of England

Mid·way \ˈmid-ˌwā\ islands *cen* Pacific 1300 mi. (2092 km.) WNW of Honolulu belonging to U.S.

Mid·west \,mid-'west\ *or* Middle West region N *cen* U.S. including area around Great Lakes & in upper Mississippi valley from Ohio on the E to North Dakota, South Dakota, Nebraska, & Kansas on the W — Mid·west·ern \,mid-'wes-tərn\ *or* Middle Western *adj* — Mid·west·ern·er \,mid-'wes-tə(r)-nər\ *or* Middle Westerner *n*

Mi·lan \mə-'lan, -'län\ *or Italian* Mi·la·no \mē-'lä-(,)nō\ city NW Italy; *pop* 1,449,403 — Mil·a·nese \,mi-lə-'nēz, -'nēs\ *adj or n*

Mí·los *or* Me·los \'mē-,lós\ island Greece

Mil·wau·kee \mil-'wó-kē\ city SE Wisconsin on Lake Michigan; *pop* 596,974

Mi·nas Basin \'mī-nəs\ bay *cen* Nova Scotia; NE extension of Bay of Fundy

Min·da·nao \,min-də-'nä-,ō, -'naú\ island S Philippines; *pop* 13,966,000

Min·do·ro \min-'dór-(,)ō\ island *cen* Philippines; *pop* 473,940

Min·ne·ap·o·lis \,mi-nē-'a-pə-lis\ city SE Minnesota; *pop* 382,618

Min·ne·so·ta \,mi-nə-'sō-tə\ state N *cen* U.S.; ✳, Saint Paul; *pop* 4,919,479 — Min·ne·so·tan \-'sō-tᵊn\ *adj or n*

Mi·nor·ca \mə-'nór-kə\ island Spain in W Mediterranean — Mi·nor·can \mə-'nór-kən\ *adj or n*

Minsk \'min(t)sk\ city, ✳ of Belarus; *pop* 1,589,000

Mis·sis·sau·ga \,mi-sə-'sò-gə\ city Canada in S Ontario; *pop* 612,925

Mis·sis·sip·pi \,mi-sə-'si-pē\ 1 river 2340 mi. (3765 km.) long *cen* U.S. flowing into Gulf of Mexico — see ITASCA, LAKE 2 state S U.S.; ✳, Jackson; *pop* 2,844,658

Mis·sou·ri \mə-'zúr-ē\ 1 river 2466 mi. (3968 km.) long W U.S. flowing from SW Montana to the Mississippi in E Missouri (state) 2 state *cen* U.S.; ✳, Jefferson City; *pop* 5,595,211 — Mis·sou·ri·an \-'zúr-ē-ən\ *adj or n*

Mitch·ell, Mount \'mi-chəl\ mountain 6684 ft. (2037 m.) W North Carolina in the Appalachians; highest in U.S. E of the Mississippi

Mo·bile \mō-'bēl, 'mō-,bēl\ city SW Alabama on Mobile Bay (inlet of Gulf of Mexico); *pop* 198,915

Mo·des·to \mə-'des-(,)tō\ city *cen* California; *pop* 188,856

Mog·a·di·shu \,mä-gə-'di-(,)shü, ,mō-, -'dē-\ *or* Mog·a·di·scio \-(,)shō\ city, ✳ of Somalia; *pop* 349,245

Mo·hawk \'mō-,hók\ river E *cen* New York flowing into the Hudson

Mo·hen·jo Da·ro \mō-'hen-(,)jō-'där-(,)ō\ prehistoric city in valley of the Indus NE of modern Karachi, Pakistan

Mo·ja·ve *or* Mo·ha·ve \mə-'hä-vē, mō-\ desert S California SE of S end of Sierra Nevada

Mol·da·via \mäl-'dā-vē-ə, -vyə\ region E Europe in NE Romania & Moldova — Mol·da·vian \-vē-ən, -vyən\ *adj or n*

Mol·do·va \mäl-'dō-və, mòl-\ country E Europe in E Moldavia region; ✳, Chişinău; *pop* 4,362,000 — Mol·do·van \-vən\ *adj or n*

Mol·o·kai \,mä-lə-'kī, ,mō-lō-'kä-ē\ island Hawaii ESE of Oahu

Mo·luc·cas \mə-'lə-kəz\ islands Indonesia E of Sulawesi; *pop* 1,857,790 — Mo·luc·ca \mə-'lə-kə\ *adj* — Mo·luc·can \-kən\ *adj or n*

Mom·ba·sa city & port S Kenya; *pop* 665,018

Mo·na·co \'mä-nə-,kō\ country W Europe on Mediterranean coast of France; ✳, Monaco; *pop* 30,500 — Mo·na·can \'mä-nə-kən, mə-'nä-kən\ *adj or n* — Mon·e·gasque \,mä-ni-'gask\ *n*

Mon·go·lia \män-'gōl-yə, mäŋ-, -'gō-lē-ə\ 1 region E Asia E of Altay Mountains; includes Gobi Desert 2 country E Asia consisting of major portion of Mongolia region; ✳, Ulaanbaatar; *pop* 2,182,000

Mo·non·ga·he·la \mə-,nän-gə-'hē-lə, -,näŋ-gə-, -'hā-lə\ river N West Virginia & SW Pennsylvania

Mon·ro·via \(,)mən-'rō-vē-ə\ city, ✳ of Liberia; *pop* 243,243

Mon·tana \män-'ta-nə\ state NW U.S.; ✳, Helena; *pop* 902,195 — Mon·tan·an \-nən\ *adj or n*

Mont Blanc \,mōⁿ-'bläⁿ\ mountain 15,771 ft. (4807 m.) SE France on Italian border; highest in the Alps

Mon·te·go Bay \män-'tē-(,)gō\ city & port NW Jamaica on Montego Bay (inlet of the Caribbean); *pop* 83,446

Mon·te·ne·gro \,män-tə-'nē-(,)grō, -'nā-, -'ne-\ country S Europe on the Adriatic Sea; ✳, Podgorica; *pop* 616,327

Mon·ter·rey \,män-tə-'rā\ city NE Mexico; metropolitan area *pop* 3,022,268

Mon·te·vi·deo \,män-tə-və-'dā-(,)ō, -'vi-dē-,ō; ,män-tā-vē-'thä-ō\ city, ✳ of Uruguay; *pop* 1,260,753

Mont·gom·ery \(,)mən(t)-'gə-mə-rē, män(t)-, -'gä-; -'gəm-rē, -'gäm-\ city, ✳ of Alabama; *pop* 201,568

Mont·pe·lier \mänt-'pēl-yər, -'pil-\ city, ✳ of Vermont; *pop* 8035

Mon·tre·al \,män-trē-'ól, ,mən-\ city S Quebec, Canada on Montreal Island in the Saint Lawrence; *pop* 1,039,534

Mont·ser·rat \,män(t)-sə-'rat\ island British West Indies in the Leeward Islands; *pop* 12,100

Mo·ra·via \mə-'rä-vē-ə\ region E Czech Republic — Mo·ra·vi·an \mə-'rä-vē-ən\ *adj or n*

Mo·rea \mə-'rē-ə\ PELOPONNESE — an old name — Mo·re·an \-'rē-ən\ *adj or n*

Mo·re·no Valley \mə-'rē-(,)nō\ city S California; *pop* 142,381

Mo·roc·co \mə-'rä-(,)kō\ country NW

Africa; ✱, Rabat; *pop* 29,631,000 — **Mo-roc-can** \-kən\ *adj or n*

Mo-ro-ni \mō-'rō-nē\ city, ✱ of Comoros; *pop* 23,432

Mos-cow \'mäs-(ˌ)kō, -ˌkaù\ *or Russian* **Mos-kva** \mäsk-'vä\ city, ✱ of Russia; *pop* 8,769,000

Mo-selle \mō-'zel\ river about 340 mi. (545 km.) long E France & W Germany

Moyle \'mòi(-ə)l\ district N Northern Ireland; *pop* 14,617

Mo-zam-bique \ˌmō-zəm-'bēk\ **1** channel SE Africa between Mozambique (country) & Madagascar **2** country SE Africa; ✱, Maputo; *pop* 16,099,246 — **Mo-zam-bi-can** \ˌmō-zəm-'bē-kən\ *adj or n*

Mpu-ma-lan-ga \əm-ˌpü-mä-'län-gä\ province NE Republic of South Africa; *pop* 2,911,000

Mukden — see SHENYANG

Mul-tan \mùl-'tän\ city NE Pakistan SW of Lahore; *pop* 1,197,384

Mumbai — see BOMBAY

Mu-nich \'myü-nik\ *or German* **Mün-chen** \'mùen-kən\ city S Germany in Bavaria; *pop* 1,229,052

Mun-ster \'mən(t)-stər\ province S Ireland; *pop* 1,100,614

Mur-cia \'mər-sh(ē-)ə\ region & ancient kingdom SE Spain

Mur-ray \'mər-ē, 'mə-rē\ river 1609 mi. (2589 km.) long SE Australia flowing W from E Victoria into Indian Ocean in South Australia

Mur-rum-bidg-ee \ˌmər-əm-'bi-jē, ˌmə-rəm-\ river almost 1000 mi. (1609 km.) long SE Australia in New South Wales flowing W into the Murray

Muscat — see MASQAT

Myan-mar \'myän-ˌmär\ *or* **Bur-ma** \'bər-mə\ country SE Asia; ✱, Naypyidaw; *pop* 45,573,000

My-ce-nae \mī-'sē-(ˌ)nē\ ancient city S Greece in NE Peloponnese

Myr-tle Beach \'mər-tᵊl\ city E South Carolina on the Atlantic; *pop* 22,759

My-sore \mī-'sór\ city S India; *pop* 742,261

Nab-a-taea *or* **Nab-a-tea** \ˌna-bə-'tē-ə\ ancient Arab kingdom SE of Palestine — **Nab-a-tae-an** *or* **Nab-a-te-an** \-'tē-ən\ *adj or n*

Na-goya \nə-'gòi-ə, 'nä-gò-(ˌ)yä\ city Japan in S cen Honshu; *pop* 2,171,557

Nag-pur \'näg-ˌpùr\ city E cen India; *pop* 2,051,320

Nai-ro-bi \nī-'rō-bē\ city, ✱ of Kenya; *pop* 2,083,509

Na-mib-ia \nə-'mi-bē-ə\ *formerly* **South-West Africa** country SW Africa on the Atlantic; ✱, Windhoek; *pop* 1,511,600 — **Na-mib-ian** \-bē-ən, -byən\ *adj or n*

Nan-chang \'nän-'chäŋ\ city SE China; *pop* 1,086,124

Nan-jing \'nän-'jiŋ\ *or* **Nan-king** \'nan-'kiŋ, 'nän-\ city E China; *pop* 2,090,204

Nan-tuck-et \nan-'tə-kət\ island SE Massachusetts S of Cape Cod; *pop* 6012

Na-per-ville \'nä-pər-ˌvil\ city NE Illinois W of Chicago; *pop* 128,358

Na-ples \'nä-pəlz\ *or Italian* **Na-po-li** \'nä-pō-lē\ *ancient* **Ne-ap-o-lis** \nē-'a-pə-ləs\ city S Italy on Bay of Naples; *pop* 1,000,470 — **Ne-a-pol-i-tan** \ˌnē-ə-'päl-ə-tən\ *adj or n*

Nar-ra-gan-sett Bay \ˌna-rə-'gan(t)-sət\ inlet of the Atlantic SE Rhode Island

Nash-ville \'nash-ˌvil, -vəl\ city, ✱ of Tennessee; *pop* 569,891

Nas-sau \'na-ˌsò\ city, ✱ of Bahamas on New Providence Island; *pop* 172,196

Na-tal \nə-'tal, -'täl\ former province E Republic of South Africa

Na-u-ru \nä-'ü-(ˌ)rü\ island W South Pacific; country; ✱, Yaren; *pop* 10,000 — **Na-u-ru-an** \-'ü-rə-wən\ *adj or n*

Nay-pyi-daw \'nə-ˌpyē-ˌdò\ site of ✱ of Myanmar

Naz-a-reth \'na-zə-rəth\ town of ancient Palestine in cen Galilee; now a city of N Israel; *pop* 49,800

N'Dja-me-na \ən-jä-'mä-nä, -'mē-\ city, ✱ of Chad; *pop* 687,800

Neagh, Lough \ˌläk-'nä\ lake Northern Ireland; largest in British Isles

Near East the countries of NE Africa & SW Asia — **Near Eastern** *adj*

Ne-bras-ka \nə-'bras-kə\ state cen U.S.; ✱, Lincoln; *pop* 1,711,263 — **Ne-bras-kan** \-kən\ *adj or n*

Neg-ev \'ne-ˌgev\ desert region S Israel

Ne-gro \'nā-(ˌ)grō, 'ne-\ river 1400 mi. (2253 km.) long in E Colombia & N Brazil flowing into the Amazon

Ne-gros \'nā-(ˌ)grōs, 'ne-\ island cen Philippines

Nei Monggol — see INNER MONGOLIA

Ne-pal \nə-'pól, nä-\ country Asia on NE border of India in the Himalayas; ✱, Kathmandu; *pop* 23,151,423 — **Nep-a-lese** \ˌne-pə-'lēz, -'lēs\ *adj or n* — **Ne-pali** \nə-'pól-ē, -'päl-, -'pal-\ *adj or n*

Ness, Loch \'nes\ lake NW Scotland

Neth-er-lands \'ne-thər-ləndz\ **1** *or Dutch* **Ne-der-land** \'nād-ər-ˌlänt\ *also* **Holland** country NW Europe on North Sea; ✱, Amsterdam; seat of the government, The Hague; *pop* 15,009,000 **2** LOW COUNTRIES — an historical usage — **Neth-er-land** \'ne-thər-lənd\ *adj* — **Neth-er-land-er** \-ˌlan-dər, -lən-\ *n* — **Neth-er-land-ish** \-ˌlan-dish, -lən-\ *adj*

Netherlands Antilles islands of the West Indies belonging to the Netherlands; ✱, Willemstad; *pop* 190,566

Ne-va \'nē-və, 'nä-, nye-'vä\ river 40 mi. (64 km.) long W Russia; flows through Saint Petersburg

Ne-vada \nə-'va-də\ state W U.S.; ✱, Carson City; *pop* 1,998,257 — **Ne·vad·an** \-'va-d³n, -'vä-\ *or* **Ne·vad·i·an** \-'va-dē-ən, -'vä-\ *adj or n*

Ne·vis \'nē-vəs\ island West Indies in the Leeward Islands — see SAINT KITTS

New Amsterdam town founded 1625 on island of Manhattan by the Dutch; renamed New York 1664 by the British

New·ark \'nü-ərk, 'nyü-\ city NE New Jersey; *pop* 273,546

New Britain island W Pacific in Bismarck group; *pop* 263,500

New Bruns·wick \-'brənz-(,)wik\ province SE Canada; ✳, Fredericton; *pop* 757,077

New Caledonia island SW Pacific SW of Vanuatu; an overseas department of France; ✳, Nouméa; *pop* 183,100

New·cas·tle \'nü-,ka-səl, 'nyü-\ city SE Australia in E New South Wales; metropolitan area *pop* 262,331

Newcastle *or* **Newcastle upon Tyne** \'tīn\ city N England; *pop* 263,000

New Delhi city, ✳ of India S of Delhi; *pop* 294,783

New England section of NE U.S. consisting of states of Maine, New Hampshire, Vermont, Massachusetts, Rhode Island, & Connecticut — **New En·gland·er** \'iŋ-glən-dər\ *n*

New·found·land \'nü-fən(d)-lənd, 'nyü-, -,land; ,nü-fən(d)-'land, ,nyü-\ island Canada in the Atlantic — **New·found·land·er** \-lən-dər, -,lan-\ *n*

Newfoundland and Labrador province E Canada consisting of Newfoundland Island and Labrador; ✳, Saint John's; *pop* 533,761

New France the possessions of France in North America before 1763

New Guinea 1 island W Pacific N of E Australia; divided between West Papua, Indonesia & independent Papua New Guinea **2** the NE portion of the island of New Guinea together with some nearby islands; now part of Papua New Guinea — **New Guinean** *adj or n*

New·ham \'nü-əm, 'nyü-\ borough of E Greater London, England; *pop* 200,200

New Hamp·shire \'hamp-shər, -,shir\ state NE U.S.; ✳, Concord; *pop* 1,235,786 — **New Hamp·shire·man** \-mən\ *n* — **New Hamp·shir·ite** \-,īt\ *n*

New Ha·ven \'hā-vən\ city S Connecticut; *pop* 123,626

New Hebrides — see VANUATU

New Jersey state E U.S.; ✳, Trenton; *pop* 8,414,350 — **New Jer·sey·an** \-ən\ *n* — **New Jer·sey·ite** \-,īt\ *n*

New Mex·i·co \'mek-si-,kō\ state SW U.S.; ✳, Santa Fe; *pop* 1,819,046 — **New Mex·i·can** \-si-kən\ *adj or n*

New Neth·er·land \'ne-thər-lənd\ former Dutch colony (1613–64) North America along Hudson & lower Delaware rivers

New Or·leans \'òr-lē-ənz, 'òr-lənz, 'òrl-yənz, (,)òr-'lēnz\ city SE Louisiana; *pop* 484,674

New·port \'nü-,pòrt, 'nyü-, -,pòrt\ **1** town S England in Isle of Wight; *pop* 23,570 **2** city SE Wales; *pop* 129,900

Newport News \'nü-,pòrt-'nüz, 'nyü-,pòrt-'nyüz, -pərt-\ city SE Virginia; *pop* 180,150

New Providence island NW *cen* Bahamas; chief town, Nassau; *pop* 210,832

New·ry \'nü-rē, 'nyü-\ urban district S Northern Ireland

New South Wales state SE Australia; ✳, Sydney; *pop* 5,732,032

New Spain former Spanish possessions in North America, Central America, West Indies, & the Philippines

New Sweden former Swedish colony (1638–55) North America on W bank of Delaware River

New·town·ab·bey \,nü-t³n-'a-bē, ,nyü-\ district E Northern Ireland; *pop* 73,832

Newtown Saint Bos·wells \'nü-,taùn-sənt-'bäz-wəlz, 'nyü-, -sänt-\ village S Scotland

New World the Western Hemisphere including North America and South America

New York 1 state NE U.S.; ✳, Albany; *pop* 18,976,457 **2** *or* **New York City** city SE New York (state); *pop* 8,008,278 — **New York·er** \'yòr-kər\ *n*

New York State Barge Canal — see ERIE

New Zea·land \'zē-lənd\ country SW Pacific ESE of Australia; ✳, Wellington; *pop* 3,737,277 — **New Zea·land·er** \-lən-dər\ *n*

Ni·ag·a·ra Falls \(,)nī-'a-g(ə-)rə\ falls New York & Ontario in **Niagara River** (flowing N from Lake Erie into Lake Ontario); divided by Goat Island into Horseshoe Falls, or Canadian Falls (158 ft. or 48 m. high) & American Falls (167 ft. or 51 m. high)

Nia·mey \nē-'ä-(,)mā, nyä-'mā\ city, ✳ of Niger; *pop* 392,165

Ni·caea \nī-'sē-ə\ *or* **Nice** \'nīs\ ancient city W Bithynia; site at modern village in NW Turkey — **Ni·cae·an** \nī-'sē-ən\ *adj or n* — **Ni·cene** \'nī-,sēn, nī-'sēn\ *adj*

Ni·ca·ra·gua \,ni-kə-'rä-gwə, ,nē-kä-'rä-gwä\ **1** lake about 100 mi. (160 km.) long S Nicaragua **2** country Central America; ✳, Managua; *pop* 4,265,000 — **Ni·ca·ra·guan** \-'rä-gwən-'rä-gwən\ *adj or n*

Nice \'nēs\ city & port SE France on the Mediterranean; *pop* 345,892

Nic·o·bar \'ni-kə-,bär\ islands India in Bay of Bengal S of the Andamans; *pop* 14,563

Nic·o·sia \,ni-kə-'sē-ə\ city, ✳ of Cyprus; *pop* 206,200

Ni·ger \'nī-jər, nē-'zher\ **1** river 2600 mi. (4184 km.) long W Africa flowing into Gulf of Guinea **2** country W Africa N of Nigeria; *, Niamey; *pop* 8,516,000 — **Ni·ger·ien** \ˌnī-ˌjir-ē-'en, nē-'zher-ē-ən\ *adj or n* — **Ni·ger·ois** \ˌnē-zhər-'wä, -zher-\ *n*

Ni·ge·ria \nī-'jir-ē-ə\ country W Africa on Gulf of Guinea; *, Abuja; *pop* 88,514,501 — **Ni·ge·ri·an** \-ē-ən\ *adj or n*

Nii·hau \'nē-ˌhaů\ island Hawaii WSW of Kauai

Nile \'nī(-ə)l\ river 4160 mi. (6693 km.) long E Africa flowing from Lake Victoria in Uganda N into the Mediterranean in Egypt

Nil·gi·ri \'nil-gə-rē\ hills S India

Nin·e·veh \'ni-nə-və\ ancient city, * of Assyria; ruins in Iraq on the Tigris

Nip·i·gon, Lake \'ni-pə-ˌgän\ lake Canada in W Ontario N of Lake Superior

Nizh·niy Nov·go·rod \'nizh-nē-'näv-gə-ˌräd, -'nóv-gə-rət\ *formerly 1932–89* **Gor·ki** \'gór-kē\ city W Russia; *pop* 1,433,000

Nord–Ost·see \'nórt-'óst-'zā\ *or* **Kiel** \'kēl\ canal 61 mi. (98 km.) long N Germany across base of Jutland Peninsula connecting Baltic Sea & North Sea

Nor·folk \'nór-fək\ city & port SE Virginia; *pop* 234,403

Nor·man·dy \'nór-mən-dē\ region NW France NE of Brittany

North 1 river estuary of the Hudson between NE New Jersey & SE New York **2** sea, arm of the Atlantic E of Great Britain **3** island N New Zealand; *pop* 2,829,798

North·al·ler·ton \nór-'tha-lər-tən\ town N England; *pop* 9556

North America continent of Western Hemisphere NW of South America & N of the Equator — **North American** *adj or n*

North·amp·ton \nór-'tham(p)-tən, nórth-'ham(p)-\ town *cen* England; *pop* 145,421

North·amp·ton·shire \-ˌshir, -shər\ *or* **Northampton** county *cen* England

North Cape cape New Zealand at N end of North Island

North Car·o·li·na \ˌker-(ə)-'lī-nə, ˌka-rə-\ state E U.S.; *, Raleigh; *pop* 8,049,313 — **North Car·o·lin·ian** \-'li-nē-ən, -'li-nyən\ *adj or n*

North Da·ko·ta \də-'kō-tə\ state N U.S.; *, Bismarck; *pop* 642,200 — **North Da·ko·tan** \-'kō-tᵊn\ *adj or n*

North Down district E Northern Ireland; *pop* 70,308

Northern Cape province W Republic of South Africa; *pop* 749,000

Northern Cook islands S *cen* Pacific N of Cook Islands

Northern Hemisphere the half of the earth that lies N of the Equator

Northern Ireland region N Ireland comprising 26 districts of Ulster; a division of United Kingdom; *, Belfast; *pop* 1,685,267

Northern Mar·i·ana Islands \ˌmer-ē-'a-nə\ islands W Pacific; commonwealth in association with U.S.; seat of the government on Saipan; *pop* 69,221

Northern Rhodesia — see ZAMBIA

Northern Territory territory N & *cen* Australia; *, Darwin; *pop* 169,300

North Korea *or* **Democratic People's Republic of Korea** country N half of Korean Peninsula in E Asia; *, Pyongyang; *pop* 22,646,000

North Las Vegas city SE Nevada; *pop* 115,448

North Slope region N Alaska between Brooks Range & Arctic Ocean

North·um·ber·land \nór-'thəm-bər-lənd\ county N England

North·um·bria \nór-'thəm-brē-ə\ ancient country Great Britain in what is now N England and S Scotland — **North·um·bri·an** \-brē-ən\ *adj or n*

North Vietnam — see VIETNAM

North West province N Republic of South Africa; *pop* 3,349,000

Northwest Passage sea passage between the Atlantic and the Pacific along the N coast of North America

Northwest Territories territory NW Canada consisting of the area of the mainland north of 60° between Yukon Territory & Nunavut; *, Yellowknife; *pop* 41,464

North York former city Canada in SE Ontario; now part of Toronto

North Yorkshire county N England

Norwalk \'nór-ˌwók\ city SW California SE of Los Angeles; *pop* 103,298

Nor·way \'nór-ˌwā\ country N Europe in Scandinavia; *, Oslo; *pop* 4,552,200

Nor·wich \'nór-(ˌ)wich\ city E England; *pop* 120,700

Not·ting·ham \'nä-tiŋ-əm\ city N *cen* England; *pop* 261,500

Not·ting·ham·shire \'nä-tiŋ-əm-ˌshir, -shər\ *or* **Nottingham** county N *cen* England

Nouak·chott \nú-'äk-ˌshät\ city, * of Mauritania; *pop* 393,325

Nou·méa \nü-'mā-ə\ city, * of New Caledonia; *pop* 65,110

No·va Sco·tia \ˌnō-və-'skō-shə\ province SE Canada; *, Halifax; *pop* 913,462 — **No·va Sco·tian** \-shən\ *adj or n*

No·vo·kuz·netsk \ˌnō-(ˌ)vō-kůz-'netsk, ˌnó-və-kůz-'nyetsk\ city S Russia in Asia; *pop* 600,000

No·vo·si·birsk \ˌnō-(ˌ)vō-sə-'birsk, ˌnó-və-\ city S Russia in Asia; *pop* 1,442,000

Nu·bia \'nü-bē-ə, 'nyü-\ region NE Africa in Nile valley in S Egypt & N Sudan — **Nu·bi·an** \'nü-bē-ən, 'nyü-\ *adj or n*

Nu·ku·a·lo·fa \,nü-kü-ä-'lō-fä\ seaport, ✳ of Tonga; *pop* 22,400

Nu·mid·ia \nü-'mi-dē-ə, nyü-\ ancient country N Africa E of Mauretania in modern Algeria — **Nu·mid·i·an** \-dē-ən\ *adj or n*

Nu·na·vut \'nü-nə-,vüt\ semiautonomous territory NE Canada; ✳, Iqaluit; *pop* 28,159

Nu·rem·berg \'nur-əm-,bərg, 'nyur-\ *or* German **Nürn·berg** \'nurn-,berk\ city S Germany; *pop* 497,496

Nuuk \'nük\ *or* **Godt·håb** \'gȯt-,hȯp\ town, ✳ of Greenland on SW coast; *pop* 12,181

Ny·asa, Lake \nī-'as-ə, nē-\ lake SE Africa in Malawi, Mozambique, & Tanzania

Nyasaland — see MALAWI

Oa·hu \ō-'ä-(,)hü\ island Hawaii; site of Honolulu

Oak·land \'ō-klənd\ city W California on San Francisco Bay E of San Francisco; *pop* 399,484

Ob' \'äb, 'ȯb\ river over 2250 mi. (3620 km.) long W Russia in Asia flowing NW & N into Arctic Ocean

Oce·a·nia \,ō-shē-'a-nē-ə, -'ä-\ lands of the *cen* & S Pacific: Micronesia, Melanesia, Polynesia including New Zealand, & sometimes Australia & Malay Archipelago

Ocean·side \'ō-shən-,sīd\ city SW California NNW of San Diego; *pop* 161,029

Oder \'ō-dər\ *or* **Odra** \'ō-drə\ river about 565 mi. (909 km.) long *cen* Europe flowing from Silesia NW into Baltic Sea; forms part of boundary between Poland & Germany

Odes·sa \ō-'de-sə\ city & port S Ukraine on Black Sea; *pop* 1,101,000

Ohio \ō-'hī-(,)ō, ə-, -ə\ **1** river about 981 mi. (1578 km.) long E U.S. flowing from W Pennsylvania into the Mississippi **2** state E *cen* U.S.; ✳, Columbus; *pop* 11,353,140 — **Ohio·an** \-'hī-ō-ən\ *adj or n*

Oka·ya·ma \,ō-kä-'yä-mä\ city Japan in W Honshu on Inland Sea; *pop* 626,642

Okee·cho·bee, Lake \,ō-kə-'chō-bē\ lake S *cen* Florida

Oke·fe·no·kee \,ō-kə-fə-'nō-kē, ,ō-kē-\ swamp SE Georgia & NE Florida

Okhotsk, Sea of \ō-'kätsk, ə-'kȯtsk\ inlet of the North Pacific E Russia in Asia

Oki·na·wa \,ō-kə-'nä-wə, -'naů-ə\ **1** islands Japan in *cen* Ryukyus **2** island, chief of group — **Oki·na·wan** \-'nä-wən, -'naů-ən\ *adj or n*

Okla·ho·ma \,ō-klə-'hō-mə\ state S *cen* U.S.; ✳, Oklahoma City; *pop* 3,450,654 — **Okla·ho·man** \-mən\ *adj or n*

Oklahoma City city, ✳ of Oklahoma; *pop* 506,132

Old·ham \'ōl-dəm\ city NW England; *pop* 211,400

Old Point Comfort cape SE Virginia N of entrance to Hampton Roads

Ol·du·vai Gorge \'ȯl-də-,vī\ canyon N Tanzania SE of Serengeti Plain; site of fossil beds

Old World the half of the earth to the E of the Atlantic Ocean including Europe, Asia, and Africa & esp. the continent of Europe

Olym·pia \ə-'lim-pē-ə, ō-\ **1** city, ✳ of Washington; *pop* 42,514 **2** plain S Greece in NW Peloponnese

Olym·pic \-pik\ mountains NW Washington on Olympic Peninsula; highest Mt. Olympus 7965 ft. (2428 m.)

Olym·pus \ə-'lim-pəs, ō-\ mountains NE Greece

Omagh \'ō-mə, -(,)mä\ **1** district W Northern Ireland; *pop* 45,343 **2** town in Omagh district; *pop* 17,280

Oma·ha \'ō-mə, -(,)mä\ **1** beach NW France in Normandy **2** city E Nebraska on Missouri River; *pop* 390,007

Oman \ō-'män, -'man\ country SW Asia in SE Arabia; ✳, Masqat; *pop* 2,477,687 — **Omani** \ō-'mä-nē, -'ma-\ *adj or n*

Oman, Gulf of arm of Arabian Sea between Oman & SE Iran

Omsk \'ȯm(p)sk, 'äm(p)sk\ city SW Russia in Asia; *pop* 1,169,000

On·tar·io \än-'ter-ē-,ō\ **1** city SW California; *pop* 158,007 **2** province E Canada; ✳, Toronto; *pop* 11,874,436 — **Ontar·i·an** \-ē-ən\ *adj or n*

Ontario, Lake lake E *cen* North America in U.S. & Canada; one of the Great Lakes

Oran \ȯ-'rän\ city & port NW Algeria; *pop* 628,558

Or·ange \'är-inj, 'är(-ə)nj, 'ȯr-inj, 'ȯr(-ə)nj\ **1** city SW California; *pop* 128,821 **2** river 1300 mi. (2092 km.) long S Africa flowing W from Drakensberg Mountains into the Atlantic

Orange Free State — see FREE STATE

Or·e·gon \'ȯr-i-gən, 'är-\ state NW U.S.; ✳, Salem; *pop* 3,421,399 — **Or·e·go·nian** \,ȯr-i-'gō-nē-ən, ,är-, -nyən\ *adj or n*

Oregon Trail pioneer route to the NW about 2000 mi. (3220 km.) long from Missouri to Washington

Ori·no·co \,ȯr-ē-'nō-(,)kō\ river 1336 mi. (2150 km.) long Venezuela flowing into the Atlantic

Ork·ney \'ȯrk-nē\ islands N Scotland; *pop* 19,570

Or·lan·do \ȯr-'lan-(,)dō\ city *cen* Florida; *pop* 185,951

Osa·ka \ō-'sä-kä, 'ō-sä-,kä\ city Japan in S Honshu; *pop* 2,598,774

Osh·a·wa \'ä-shə-wə, -,wä, -,wȯ\ city SE Ontario, Canada on Lake Ontario ENE of Toronto; *pop* 139,051

Os·lo \'äz-(,)lō, 'äs-\ city, ✳ of Norway; *pop* 507,831

Oś·wię·cim \,ȯsh-'fyen-chēm\ *or* German

Ausch·witz \\'aùsh-ˌvits\\ town S Poland W of Krakow; *pop* 45,282

Ot·ta·wa \\'ä-tə-wə, -ˌwä, -ˌwȯ\\ **1** river 696 mi. (1120 km.) E Canada in SE Ontario & S Quebec flowing E into the Saint Lawrence **2** city, * of Canada in SE Ontario on Ottawa River; *pop* 812,129

Ot·to·man Empire \\'ä-tə-mən\\ former Turkish sultanate in SE Europe, W Asia, & N Africa

Oua·ga·dou·gou \\ˌwä-gä-'dü-(ˌ)gü\\ city, * of Burkina Faso; *pop* 366,000

Outer Hebrides — see HEBRIDES

Over·land Park \\'ō-vər-lənd\\ city NE Kansas; *pop* 149,080

Ox·ford \\'äks-fərd\\ city *cen* England; *pop* 109,000

Ox·ford·shire \\'äks-fərd-ˌshir, -shər\\ *or* **Oxford** county *cen* England

Ox·nard \\'äks-ˌnärd\\ city SW California; *pop* 170,358

Ozark Plateau \\'ō-ˌzärk\\ *or* **Ozark Mountains** eroded plateau N Arkansas, S Missouri, & NE Oklahoma with E extension into S Illinois

Pa·cif·ic \\pə-'si-fik\\ ocean extending from Arctic Circle to the Equator (**North Pacific**) and from the Equator to the Antarctic regions (**South Pacific**) & from W North America & W South America to E Asia & Australia — **Pacific** *adj*

Pacific Islands, Trust Territory of the grouping of islands in W Pacific formerly under U.S. administration: the Carolines & the Marshalls

Pacific Rim the countries bordering on or located in the Pacific Ocean — used esp. of Asian countries on the Pacific

Pa·dang \\'pä-ˌdäŋ\\ city Indonesia in W Sumatra; *pop* 631,543

Pa·dre \\'pä-drē, -drā\\ island 113 mi. (182 km.) long S Texas in Gulf of Mexico

Pa·go Pa·go \\pä-(ˌ)gō-'pä-(ˌ)gō, ˌpäŋ-(ˌ)ō-'päŋ-(ˌ)ō\\ town, * of American Samoa on Tutuila Island; *pop* 4278

Painted Desert region N *cen* Arizona

Pak·i·stan \\'pa-ki-ˌstan, ˌpä-ki-'stän\\ country S Asia NW of India; *, Islamabad; *pop* 131,434,000 — see EAST PAKISTAN — **Pak·i·stani** \\ˌpa-ki-'sta-nē, ˌpä-ki-'stä-\\ *adj or n*

Pa·lau \\pə-'laù\\ *or* **Be·lau** \\bə-\\ island group W Pacific in the W Carolines in association with U.S.; country; *, Melekeok; *pop* 17,225 — **Pa·lau·an** \\pə-'laù-ən\\ *n*

Pa·la·wan \\pə-'lä-wən, -ˌwän\\ island W Philippines between South China & Sulu seas; *pop* 528,287

Pa·lem·bang \\'pä-ləm-ˌbäŋ\\ city Indonesia in SE Sumatra; *pop* 1,141,036

Pa·ler·mo \\pə-'lər-(ˌ)mō, pä-'ler-\\ city Italy, * of Sicily; *pop* 679,290

Pal·es·tine \\'pa-lə-ˌstīn\\ **1** ancient region SW Asia bordering on E coast of the Mediterranean and extending E of Jordan River **2** region bordering on the Mediterranean on W and Dead Sea on E; now approximately coextensive with Israel & the West Bank — **Pal·es·tin·ian** \\ˌpa-lə-'sti-nē-ən, -nyən\\ *adj or n*

Pa·li·kir \\ˌpä-lē-'kir\\ town, * of Federated States of Micronesia on Pohnpei Island; *pop* 6227

Pal·i·sades \\ˌpa-lə-'sādz\\ line of high cliffs 15 mi. (24 km.) long on W bank of the Hudson in SE New York & NE New Jersey

Palm·dale \\'päm-ˌdāl, 'pälm-\\ city SW California NE of Los Angeles; *pop* 116,670

Pa·mirs \\pə-'mirz\\ elevated mountainous region *cen* Asia in E Tajikistan & on borders of China, India, Pakistan, & Afghanistan; many peaks over 20,000 ft. (6096 m.)

Pam·li·co Sound \\'pam-li-ˌkō\\ inlet of the North Atlantic E North Carolina between main part of the state & offshore islands

Pam·pa \\'pam-pə\\ city NW Texas; *pop* 17,887

Pan·a·ma \\'pan-ə-ˌmä, -ˌmȯ, ˌpan-ə-'mä, -'mȯ\\ **1** country S Central America; *pop* 2,839,177 **2** *or* **Panama City** city, its * on the Pacific; *pop* 411,549 **3** canal 40 mi. (64 km.) long Panama connecting Atlantic & Pacific oceans — **Pan·a·ma·ni·an** \\ˌpan-ə-'mä-nē-ən\\ *adj or n*

Panama, Isthmus of *formerly* **Isthmus of Dar·i·en** \\ˌder-ē-'en\\ strip of land *cen* Panama connecting North America & South America

Panama Canal Zone — see CANAL ZONE

Pa·nay \\pə-'nī\\ island *cen* Philippines in the Visayas

Pan·gaea \\pan-'jē-ə\\ hypothetical land area believed to have once connected the landmasses of the Southern Hemisphere with those of the Northern Hemisphere

Pan·mun·jom *or* **Pan·mun·jeom** \\ˌpän-ˌmùn-'jäm\\ village on North Korea–South Korea border

Pao–t'ou — see BAOTOU

Pap·ua, Territory of \\'pa-pyü-wə, 'pä-pù-wə\\ former British territory consisting of SE New Guinea & offshore islands; now part of Papua New Guinea

Papua New Guinea country SW Pacific *, Port Moresby; *pop* 5,190,736

Par·a·guay \\'pa-rə-ˌgwī, -ˌgwä\\ **1** river 1584 mi. (2549 km.) long *cen* South America flowing from Brazil S into the Paraná in Paraguay **2** country *cen* South America; *, Asunción; *pop* 4,643,000 — **Par·a·guay·an** \\ˌpa-rə-'gwī-ən, -'gwä-\\ *adj or n*

Par·a·mar·i·bo \\ˌpa-rə-'ma-rə-ˌbō\\ city, * of Suriname; *pop* 200,000

Pa·ra·ná \\ˌpär-ə-'nä\\ river about 2500 mi.

(4022 km.) long *cen* South America flowing S from Brazil into Argentina

Pa·ri·cu·tin \pä-ˌrē-kü-'tēn\ volcano Mexico on site of a former village

Par·is \'pa-rəs\ city, ✳ of France; *pop* 2,125,851 — **Pa·ri·sian** \pə-'ri-zhən, -'rē-\ *adj or n*

Par·nas·sus \pär-'na-səs\ mountain *cen* Greece

Par·os \'pär-ˌös\ island Greece — **Par·i·an** \'par-ē-ən, 'per-\ *adj*

Par·ra·mat·ta \ˌpa-rə-'ma-tə\ city SE Australia in New South Wales; *pop* 132,798

Par·thia \'pär-thē-ə\ ancient country SW Asia in NE modern Iran — **Par·thi·an** \-thē-ən\ *adj or n*

Pas·a·de·na \ˌpa-sə-'dē-nə\ **1** city SW California E of Glendale; *pop* 133,936 **2** city SE Texas; *pop* 141,674

Pat·a·go·nia \ˌpa-tə-'gō-nyə, -nē-ə\ region South America S of about 40° S latitude in S Argentina & S tip of Chile; sometimes thought to include Tierra del Fuego — **Pat·a·go·nian** \-nyən, -nē-ən\ *adj or n*

Pat·er·son \'pa-tər-sən\ city NE New Jersey; *pop* 149,222

Pat·mos \'pat-məs\ island Greece SSW of Samos

Pat·na \'pət-nə\ city NE India on the Ganges; *pop* 1,376,950

Pearl Harbor inlet Hawaii on S coast of Oahu W of Honolulu

Peking — see BEIJING

Pe·li·on \'pē-lē-ən\ mountain 5089 ft. (1551 m.) NE Greece

Pel·o·pon·nese \'pe-lə-pə-ˌnēz, -ˌnēs\ *or* **Pel·o·pon·ni·sos** \ˌpe-lə-pə-'nē-səs\ peninsula forming S part of mainland of Greece

Pem·broke Pines \'pem-ˌbrōk\ city SE Florida; *pop* 137,427

Pen·nine Chain \'pe-ˌnīn\ mountains N England; highest Cross Fell 2930 ft. (893 m.)

Penn·syl·va·nia \ˌpen(t)-səl-'vā-nyə, -nē-ə\ state E U.S.; ✳, Harrisburg; *pop* 12,281,054

Pe·o·ria \pē-'ór-ē-ə\ **1** town SW *cen* Arizona; *pop* 108,364 **2** city N *cen* Illinois; *pop* 112,936

Per·ga·mum \'pər-gə-məm\ *or* **Per·ga·mus** \-məs\ ancient Greek kingdom including most of Asia Minor

Perm \'pərm, 'perm\ city E Russia in Europe; *pop* 1,099,000

Pernambuco — see RECIFE

Persia — see IRAN

Per·sian Gulf \'pər-zhən\ arm of Arabian Sea between Iran & Arabia

Perth \'pərth\ city, ✳ of Western Australia; *pop* 80,517

Pe·ru \pə-'rü, pā-\ country W South America; ✳, Lima; *pop* 22,916,000 — **Pe·ru·vi·an** \-'rü-vē-ən\ *adj or n*

Pe·tra \'pē-trə, 'pe-\ ancient city NW Arabia; site in SW Jordan

Petrograd — see SAINT PETERSBURG

Phil·a·del·phia \ˌfi-lə-'del-fyə, -fē-ə\ city SE Pennsylvania; *pop* 1,517,550 — **Phil·a·del·phian** \-fyən, -fē-ən\ *adj or n*

Phil·ip·pines \ˌfi-lə-'pēnz, 'fi-lə-ˌpēnz\ island group approximately 500 mi. (805 km.) off SE coast of Asia; country; ✳, Manila; *pop* 64,954,000 — **Phil·ip·pine** \ˌfi-lə-'pēn, 'fi-lə-ˌ\ *adj*

Phnom Penh \(pə-)'näm-'pen, (pə-)'nóm-\ city, ✳ of Cambodia; *pop* 800,000

Phoe·ni·cia \fi-'ni-sh(ē-)ə, -'nē-\ ancient country SW Asia on the Mediterranean in modern Syria & Lebanon

Phoe·nix \'fē-niks\ city, ✳ of Arizona; *pop* 1,321,045

Phry·gia \'fri-j(ē-)ə\ ancient country W *cen* Asia Minor

Pic·ar·dy \'pi-kər-dē\ *or F* **Pi·car·die** \pē-kär-'dē\ region & former province N France bordering on English Channel N of Normandy — **Pi·card** \'pi-ˌkärd, -kərd\ *adj or n*

Pied·mont \'pēd-ˌmänt\ plateau region E U.S. E of the Appalachians between SE New York & NE Alabama

Pierre \'pir\ city, ✳ of South Dakota; *pop* 13,876

Pie·ter·mar·itz·burg \ˌpē-tər-'ma-rəts-ˌbərg\ city E Republic of South Africa; *pop* 128,598

Pigs, Bay of \'pigz\ *or* **Ba·hía de Co·chi·nos** \bä-'ē-ä-thä-kō-'chē-nōs\ bay W Cuba on S coast

Pikes Peak \'pīks\ mountain 14,110 ft. (4301 m.) E *cen* Colorado in a range of the Rockies

Pin·dus \'pin-dəs\ mountains W Greece; highest point 8136 ft. (2480 m.)

Pi·sa \'pē-zə, *It* -sä\ city W *cen* Italy W of Florence; *pop* 91,977

Pit·cairn \'pit-ˌkern\ island South Pacific; a British colony; *pop* less than 100

Pitts·burgh \'pits-ˌbərg\ city SW Pennsylvania; *pop* 334,563

Plac·id, Lake \'pla-səd\ lake NE New York

Pla·no \'plā-(ˌ)nō\ city NE Texas N of Dallas; *pop* 222,030

Plov·div \'plóv-ˌdif, -ˌdiv\ city S Bulgaria; *pop* 379,083

Plym·outh \'pli-məth\ **1** town SE Massachusetts; *pop* 51,701 **2** city & port SW England; *pop* 238,800

Po \'pō\ river 405 mi. (652 km.) N Italy flowing into the Adriatic

Pod·go·ri·ca \'pòd-ˌgór-ēt-sä\ city, ✳ of Montenegro; *pop* 152,242

Po Hai — see BO HAI

Pohn·pei \'pón-ˌpā\ *or* **Po·na·pe** \'pō-nə-ˌpā\ island W Pacific in the E Carolines; part of Federated States of Micronesia

Po·land \'pō-lənd\ country *cen* Europe on

Baltic Sea; ✳, Warsaw; *pop* 38,038,400 —
Pole *n*

Pol·y·ne·sia \ˌpä-lə-'nē-zhə, -shə\ islands
of the *cen* & S Pacific including Hawaii,
the Line, Tonga, Cook, & Samoa islands,
& often New Zealand among others

Pom·er·a·nia \ˌpä-mə-'rā-nē-ə, -nyə\ region N Europe on Baltic Sea; formerly in
Germany, now mostly in Poland

Po·mo·na \pə-'mō-nə\ city SW California
E of Los Angeles; *pop* 149,473

Pom·peii \päm-'pā, -'pā-ē\ ancient city S
Italy SE of Naples destroyed 79 A.D. by
eruption of Vesuvius — **Pom·pe·ian**
\-'pā-ən\ *adj or n*

Pon·ce \'pòn(t)-(ˌ)sā\ city S Puerto Rico;
pop 186,475

Pon·do·land \'pän-(ˌ)dō-ˌland\ region S
Republic of South Africa

Pon·ta Del·ga·da \ˌpòn-tə-del-'gä-də\ city
& port Portugal, largest in the Azores;
pop 65,854

Pont·char·train, Lake \'pänt-shər-ˌtrān,
ˌpänt-shər-'\ lake SE Louisiana E of the
Mississippi & N of New Orleans

Pon·tus \'pän-təs\ ancient country NE
Asia Minor — **Pon·tic** \'pänt-ik\ *adj or n*

Poole \'pül\ town S England on English
Channel; *pop* 130,900

Po·po·ca·te·petl \ˌpō-pə-'ka-tə-ˌpe-t'l,
-ˌka-tə-'\ volcano 17,887 ft. (5452 m.) SE
cen Mexico

Port Arthur — see LÜSHUN

Port–au–Prince \ˌpòrt-ō-'prin(t)s, ˌpòr-
(t)ō-'praⁿs\ city, ✳ of Haiti; *pop* 752,600

Port Jack·son \'jak-sən\ inlet of South
Pacific SE Australia in New South Wales;
harbor of Sydney

Port·land \'pòrt-lənd\ **1** city SW Maine;
largest in state; *pop* 64,249 **2** city NW
Oregon; *pop* 529,121

Port Lou·is \'lü-əs, 'lü-ē\ city, ✳ of Mau-
ritius; *pop* 146,876

Port Mores·by \'mòrz-bē\ city, ✳ of
Papua New Guinea; *pop* 254,158

Por·to \'pòr-(ˌ)tü\ city & port NW Portugal; *pop* 310,600

Por·to Ale·gre \'pòr-(ˌ)tü-ä-'lä-grē\ city &
port S Brazil; *pop* 1,360,590

Port of Spain city NW Trinidad, ✳ of
Trinidad and Tobago; *pop* 49,031

Por·to–No·vo \ˌpòr-tō-'nō-(ˌ)vō\ city, ✳
of Benin; *pop* 192,000

Port Phil·lip Bay \'fi-ləp\ inlet of South
Pacific SE Australia in Victoria; harbor
of Melbourne

Port Said \sä-'ēd, 'sīd\ city & port NE
Egypt on the Mediterranean at N end of
the Suez Canal; *pop* 262,760

Ports·mouth \'pòrts-məth\ **1** city SE
Virginia; *pop* 100,565 **2** city S England;
pop 174,400

Por·tu·gal \'pòr-chi-gəl, ˌpùr-tü-'gäl\
country SW Europe; ✳, Lisbon; *pop*
10,356,117

Portuguese India former Portuguese
possession on W coast of India; became
part of India 1962

Port–Vi·la \pòrt-'vē-lə\ *or* **Vila** city, ✳ of
Vanuatu; *pop* 18,905

Po·to·mac \pə-'tō-mək, -mik\ river 287
mi. (462 km.) long flowing from West Virginia into Chesapeake Bay and forming
boundary between Maryland & Virginia

Pough·keep·sie \pə-'kip-sē, pō-\ city &
river port SE New York on the Hudson;
pop 29,871

Po·wys \'pō-əs\ administrative subdivision E *cen* Wales

Prague \'präg\ *or Czech* **Pra·ha** \'prä-
(ˌ)hä\ city, ✳ of Czech Republic; *pop*
1,162,179

Praia \'prī-ə\ town, ✳ of Cape Verde; *pop*
61,797

Prairie Provinces the Canadian provinces of Alberta, Manitoba, & Saskatchewan

Pres·ton \'pres-tən\ town NW England;
pop 126,200

Pre·to·ria \pri-'tòr-ē-ə\ city Republic of
South Africa, administrative ✳ of the
country; *pop* 303,684

Prib·i·lof \'pri-bə-ˌlòf\ islands Alaska in
Bering Sea

Prince Ed·ward Island \'ed-wərd\ island
SE Canada in Gulf of Saint Lawrence; a
province; ✳, Charlottetown; *pop* 138,514

Prince Ru·pert's Land \'rü-pərts\ historical region N & W Canada consisting of
drainage basin of Hudson Bay

Prince·ton \'prin(t)-stən\ borough W *cen*
New Jersey; *pop* 14,203

Prín·ci·pe \'prin(t)-si-pē\ island W Africa
in Gulf of Guinea — see SÃO TOMÉ AND
PRÍNCIPE

Pro·vence \prə-'vän(t)s, prō-'väⁿs\ region
SE France on the Mediterranean

Prov·i·dence \'prä-və-dən(t)s, -ˌden(t)s\
city, ✳ of Rhode Island; *pop* 173,618

Pro·vo \'prō-(ˌ)vō\ city N *cen* Utah; *pop*
105,166

Prud·hoe Bay \'prü-(ˌ)dō, 'prə-\ inlet of
Beaufort Sea N Alaska

Prus·sia \'prə-shə\ former kingdom, &
later, state Germany — **Prus·sian** \'prə-
shən\ *adj or n*

Pueb·lo \'pwe-ˌblō\ city SE *cen* Colorado
SSE of Colorado Springs; *pop* 102,121

Puer·to Ri·co \ˌpòr-tə-'rē-(ˌ)kō, ˌpwer-
tō-\ island West Indies E of Hispaniola; a
self-governing commonwealth associated
with U.S.; ✳, San Juan; *pop* 3,808,610 —
Puer·to Ri·can \'rē-kən\ *adj or n*

Pu·get Sound \'pyü-jət\ arm of the
North Pacific W Washington

Pu·ne \'pü-nə\ city W India; ESE of Bombay; *pop* 2,540,069

Pun·jab \pən-'jäb, -'jab, 'pən-ˌ\ region in
Pakistan & NW India in valley of the
Indus

Pu·san \'pü-ˌsän, 'bü-\ *or* **Bu·san** \'bü-\ city SE South Korea; *pop* 3,655,437

Pyong·yang *or* **Pyeong·yang** \'pyoŋ-ˈyaŋ, 'pyoŋ-, -ˈyäŋ\ city, ✳ of North Korea; *pop* 2,355,000

Pyr·e·nees \'pir-ə-ˌnēz\ mountains on French–Spanish border extending from Bay of Biscay to the Mediterranean

Qaraghandy — see KARAGANDA

Qa·tar \'kä-tər, 'gä-, 'gə-; kə-'tär\ country E Arabia on peninsula extending into Persian Gulf; ✳, Doha; *pop* 539,000 — **Qatari** \kə-'tär-ē, gə-\ *adj or n*

Qing·dao \'chiŋ-'dau̇\ *or* **Tsing·tao** \'chiŋ-'dau̇, '(t)siŋ-'dau̇\ city & port E China; *pop* 1,459,195

Qi·qi·har \'chē-'chē-'här\ *or* **Ch'i-ch'i-ha-erh** \'chē-'chē-'hä-'ər\ city NE China; *pop* 1,500,000

Que·bec \kwi-'bek, ki-\ *or French* **Qué·bec** \kā-'bek\ **1** province E Canada; *pop* 7,546,131 **2** city, its ✳, on the Saint Lawrence; *pop* 491,142

Queens \'kwēnz\ borough of New York City on Long Island E of Brooklyn; *pop* 2,229,379

Queens·land \'kwēnz-ˌland, -lənd\ state NE Australia; ✳, Brisbane; *pop* 3,116,200 — **Queens·land·er** \-ˌlan-dər, -ˌlən-\ *n*

Que·zon City \'kā-ˌsȯn\ city Philippines in Luzon; formerly ✳ of the country; *pop* 1,632,000

Qui·to \'kē-(ˌ)tō\ city, ✳ of Ecuador; *pop* 1,100,847

Ra·bat \rə-'bät\ city, ✳ of Morocco; *pop* 668,000

Rai·nier, Mount \rə-'nir, rā-\ mountain 14,410 ft. (4392 m.) W *cen* Washington; highest in Cascade Range

Raj·pu·ta·na \ˌräj-pə-'tä-nə\ *or* **Ra·ja·sthan** \'räj-ə-ˌstän\ region NW India S of Punjab

Ra·leigh \'rȯ-lē, 'rä-lē\ city, ✳ of North Carolina; *pop* 276,093

Ran·cho Cu·ca·mon·ga \'ran-(ˌ)chō-ˌkü-kə-'məŋ-gə, 'rän-, -'mäŋ-\ city SW California; *pop* 127,743

Rand — see WITWATERSRAND

Rand·wick \'ran-(ˌ)dwik\ municipality SE Australia in E New South Wales; *pop* 115,349

Rangoon — see YANGON

Ra·wal·pin·di \ˌrä-wəl-'pin-dē, rau̇l-', rȯl-'\ city NE Pakistan NNW of Lahore; *pop* 1,409,768

Read·ing \'re-diŋ\ town S England; *pop* 122,600

Re·ci·fe \ri-'sē-fē\ *formerly* **Per·nam·bu·co** \ˌpər-nəm-'bü-(ˌ)kō, -'byü-\ city NE Brazil; *pop* 1,422,905

Red \'red\ **1** river 1018 mi. (1638 km.) long flowing E on Oklahoma–Texas boundary and into the Atchafalaya & the Mississippi in Louisiana **2** sea between Arabia & NE Africa

Red·bridge \'red-(ˌ)brij\ borough of NE Greater London, England; *pop* 220,600

Re·gi·na \ri-'jī-nə\ city, ✳ of Saskatchewan, Canada; *pop* 179,246

Re·no \'rē-(ˌ)nō\ city NW Nevada; *pop* 180,480

Republic of the Congo — see CONGO 3

Ré·union \rē-'yü-nyən, ˌrä-ᴜᴇ-'nyōⁿ\ island W Indian Ocean; an overseas division of France; ✳, Saint-Denis; *pop* 634,000

Reyk·ja·vik \'rā-kyə-ˌvik, -ˌvēk\ city, ✳ of Iceland; *pop* 112,490

Rhine \'rīn\ river 820 mi. (1320 km.) long W Europe flowing from SE Switzerland to North Sea in the Netherlands — **Rhen·ish** \'re-nish, 'rē-\ *adj*

Rhine·land \'rīn-ˌland, -lənd\ *or German* **Rhein·land** \'rīn-ˌlänt\ the part of Germany W of the Rhine — **Rhine·land·er** \'rīn-ˌlan-dər, -lən-\ *n*

Rhode Is·land \rōd-'ī-lənd\ **1** *or officially* **Rhode Island and Providence Plantations** state NE U.S.; ✳, Providence; *pop* 1,048,319 **2** — see AQUIDNECK — **Rhode Is·land·er** \-lən-dər\ *n*

Rhodes \'rōdz\ island Greece in the SE Aegean

Rho·de·sia \rō-'dē-zh(ē-)ə\ — see ZIMBABWE — **Rho·de·sian** \-zh(ē-)ən\ *adj or n*

Rhone *or French* **Rhône** \'rōn\ river 505 mi. (813 km.) long Switzerland & SE France

Rich·mond \'rich-mənd\ **1** — see STATEN ISLAND **2** city, ✳ of Virginia; *pop* 197,790

Richmond upon Thames borough of SW Greater London, England; *pop* 154,600

Ri·ga \'rē-gə\ city, ✳ of Latvia; *pop* 747,157

Rio de Ja·nei·ro \'rē-(ˌ)ō-dā-zhə-'ner-(ˌ)ō, -dē-\ city SE Brazil on Guanabara Bay; *pop* 5,857,904

Rio Grande \ˌrē-(ˌ)ō-'grand, -'gran-dē\ *or Mexican* **Rio Bra·vo** \ˌrē-(ˌ)ō-'brä-(ˌ)vō\ river 1885 mi. (3034 km.) long SW U.S. forming part of U.S.–Mexico boundary and flowing into Gulf of Mexico

Río Muni — see MBINI

Riv·er·side \'ri-vər-ˌsīd\ city S California; *pop* 255,166

Riv·i·era \ˌri-vē-'er-ə\ coast region SE France & NW Italy

Ri·yadh \rē-'yäd\ city, ✳ of Saudi Arabia; *pop* 4,700,000

Ro·a·noke \'rō-(ə-)ˌnōk\ city W Virginia; *pop* 94,911

Roanoke Island island North Carolina S of entrance to Albemarle Sound

Rob·son, Mount \'räb-sən\ mountain 12,972 ft. (3954 m.) W Canada in E British Columbia; highest in the Canadian Rockies

Roch·es·ter \'rä-chəs-tər, -ˌches-tər\ city W New York; *pop* 219,773

Rock·ford \'räk-fərd\ city N Illinois; *pop* 150,115

Rocky Mountains *or* **Rock·ies** \'rä-kēz\ mountains W North America extending SE from N Alaska to *cen* New Mexico

Roman Empire the empire of ancient Rome

Ro·ma·nia \rů-'mā-nē-ə, rō-, -nyə\ *or* **Ru·ma·nia** \ru̇-\ country SE Europe on Black Sea; ✳, Bucharest; *pop* 21,698,181

Rom·blon \räm-'blōn\ island group *cen* Philippines

Rome \'rōm\ *or Italian* **Ro·ma** \'rō-mä\ city, ✳ of Italy; *pop* 2,655,970

Ro·sa·rio \rō-'zär-ē-ˌō, -'sär-\ city E *cen* Argentina on the Paraná; *pop* 591,428

Ro·seau \rō-'zō\ seaport, ✳ of Dominica; *pop* 14,847

Ros·tov—on—Don \rä-'stȯf-ˌän-'dän, -'stȯv, -ˌȯn-\ city S Russia in Europe; *pop* 1,027,000

Ros·well \'räz-ˌwel, -wəl\ city SE New Mexico; *pop* 45,293

Ro·ta \'rō-tə\ island W Pacific in the Marianas

Rot·ter·dam \'rä-tər-ˌdam, -ˌdäm\ city & port SW Netherlands; *pop* 598,660

Ru·an·da–Urun·di \rü-ˈän-dä-ü-'rün-dē\ former trust territory E *cen* Africa bordering on Lake Tanganyika; now divided into Burundi & Rwanda

Rudolf, Lake — see TURKANA, LAKE

Ruhr \'rur\ 1 river 146 mi. (235 km.) long W Germany flowing NW & W to the Rhine 2 industrial district W Germany E of the Rhine in valley of Ruhr River

Rumania — see ROMANIA

Rupert's Land PRINCE RUPERT'S LAND

Rush·more, Mount \'rəsh-ˌmȯr\ mountain 5600 ft. (1707 m.) W South Dakota in Black Hills

Rus·sia \'rə-shə\ 1 former empire largely having the same boundaries as U.S.S.R. 2 UNION OF SOVIET SOCIALIST REPUBLICS 3 country E Europe & N Asia; ✳, Moscow; *pop* 148,000,000

Ru·the·nia \rü-'thē-nyə, -nē-ə\ region W Ukraine W of the N Carpathians — **Ru·the·nian** \-'thē-nyən, -nē-ən\ *adj or n*

Ru·wen·zo·ri \ˌrü-ən-'zȯr-ē\ mountain group E *cen* Africa between Uganda & Democratic Republic of the Congo; highest Mount Margherita 16,763 ft. (5109 m.)

Rwan·da *formerly* **Ru·an·da** \rü-'än-dä\ country E *cen* Africa; ✳, Kigali; *pop* 7,584,000 — **Rwan·dan** \-dən\ *adj or n*

Ryu·kyu \rē-'yü-(ˌ)kyü, -(ˌ)kü\ islands Japan extending in an arc from S Japan, to N tip of Taiwan; *pop* 1,222,458 — **Ryu·kyu·an** \-ˌkyü-ən, -ˌkü-\ *adj or n*

Saar \'sär, 'zär\ 1 river about 150 mi. (241 km.) long Europe flowing from E France to W Germany 2 *or* **Saar·land** \'sär-ˌland, 'zär-\ region W Europe in valley of Saar River between France & Germany

Sac·ra·men·to \ˌsa-krə-'men-(ˌ)tō\ 1 river 382 mi. (615 km.) long N California flowing S into Suisun Bay 2 city, ✳ of California; *pop* 407,018

Sag·ue·nay \'sa-gə-ˌnā, ˌsa-gə-'\ 1 river 105 mi. (169 km.) long Canada in S Quebec flowing E into the Saint Lawrence 2 city Canada in S Quebec; *pop* 143,692

Sa·ha·ra \sə-'her-ə, -'här-\ desert region N Africa extending from Atlantic coast to Red Sea — **Sa·ha·ran** \-ən\ *adj*

Sa·hel \'sa-hil, sə-'hil\ the S fringe of the Sahara

Saigon — see HO CHI MINH CITY

Saint Al·bans \'ȯl-bənz\ city SE England; *pop* 122,400

Saint Cath·a·rines \'ka-th(ə-)rənz\ city Canada in SE Ontario; *pop* 131,989

Saint Christopher — see SAINT KITTS

Saint Clair, Lake \'kler\ lake SE Michigan & SE Ontario connected by **Saint Clair River** (40 mi. or 64 km. long) with Lake Huron & draining by Detroit River into Lake Erie

Saint Croix \sänt-'krȯi, sənt-\ 1 river 129 mi. (208 km.) long Canada & U.S. on border between New Brunswick & Maine 2 island West Indies; largest of Virgin Islands of the U.S.; *pop* 50,139

Saint Eli·as, Mount \i-'lī-əs\ mountain 18,008 ft. (5489 m.) on Alaska–Canada boundary in **Saint Elias Range**

Saint George's \'jȯr-jəz\ town, ✳ of Grenada; *pop* 29,400

Saint George's Channel channel British Isles between SW Wales & Ireland

Saint Gott·hard \sänt-'gä-tərd, sənt-, 'gät-hərd\ pass S *cen* Switzerland in Saint Gotthard Range of the Alps

Saint He·le·na \ˌsänt-ə-'lē-nə, ˌsänt-hə-'lē-\ island South Atlantic; a British colony; *pop* 5644

Saint Hel·ens, Mount \sänt-'he-lənz, sənt-\ volcano S Washington

Saint John \sänt-'jän, sənt-\ city & port Canada in New Brunswick; *pop* 68,043

Saint John's \sänt-'jänz, sənt-\ 1 city, ✳ of Antigua and Barbuda; *pop* 22,342 2 city, ✳ of Newfoundland and Labrador, Canada; *pop* 100,646

Saint Kitts \'kits\ *or* **Saint Chris·to·pher** \'kris-tə-fər\ island West Indies in the Leeward Islands; with Nevis forms independent **Saint Kitts–Nevis**; ✳, Basseterre (on Saint Kitts); *pop* 41,800

Saint Law·rence \sänt-'lȯr-ən(t)s, sənt-, -'lär-\ 1 river 760 mi. (1223 km.) long E Canada in Ontario & Quebec bordering on U.S. in New York and flowing from Lake Ontario NE into the **Gulf of Saint Lawrence** (inlet of the Atlantic) 2 seaway Canada & U.S. in and along the Saint

Lawrence between Lake Ontario & Montreal

Saint Lou·is \sänt-'lü-əs, sənt-\ city E Missouri on the Mississippi; *pop* 348,189

Saint Lu·cia \sänt-'lü-shə, sənt-\ island West Indies in the Windwards S of Martinique; country; ✻, Castries; *pop* 157,775

Saint Mo·ritz \sänt-mə-'rits, ‚saⁿ-mə-\ *or* G **Sankt Mo·ritz** \‚zäŋkt-mə-'rits\ town E Switzerland; *pop* 5900

Saint Paul \'pȯl\ city, ✻ of Minnesota; *pop* 287,151

Saint Pe·ters·burg \'pē-tərz-‚bərg\ **1** city W Florida; *pop* 248,232 **2** *formerly 1914–24* **Pet·ro·grad** \'pe-trə-‚grad, -‚grät\ *or* **1924–91 Le·nin·grad** \'le-nən-‚grad, -‚grät\ city W Russia in Europe; *pop* 4,952,000

Saint Thom·as \'tä-məs\ island West Indies, one of Virgin Islands of the U.S.; chief town, Charlotte Amalie

Saint Vin·cent \sänt-'vin(t)-sənt, sənt-\ island West Indies in the *cen* Windward Islands; with N Grenadines forms independent **Saint Vincent and the Grenadines**; ✻, Kingstown (on Saint Vincent); *pop* 109,000

Sai·pan \sī-'pan, -'pän, 'sī-‚\ island W Pacific in S *cen* Marianas; *pop* 38,896

Sa·kai \(‚)sä-'kī\ city Japan in S Honshu; *pop* 792,018

Sa·kha·lin \'sa-kə-‚lēn, -lən; ‚sä-kä-'lēn\ island SE Russia in W Pacific N of Hokkaido, Japan

Sal·a·mis \'sa-lə-məs\ ancient city Cyprus on E coast

Sa·lem \'sä-ləm\ city, ✻ of Oregon; *pop* 136,924

Sa·li·nas \sə-'lē-nəs\ city W California; *pop* 151,060

Salisbury — see HARARE

Salisbury Plain plateau S England; site of Stonehenge

Salop — see SHROPSHIRE

Salt Lake City city, ✻ of Utah; *pop* 181,743

Sal·ton Sea \'sȯl-tⁿn\ saline lake about 235 ft. (72 m.) below sea level SE California; formed by diversion of water from Colorado River

Sal·va·dor \'sal-və-‚dȯr, ‚sal-və-'\ *or* Bahia \bä-ē-ə\ city NE Brazil on the Atlantic; *pop* 2,443,107 — **Sal·va·dor·an** \‚sal-və-'dȯr-ən\ *or* **Sal·va·dor·ean** *or* **Sal·va·dor·ian** \-ē-ən\ *adj or n*

Sal·ween \'sal-‚wēn\ river about 1500 mi. (2415 km.) long SE Asia flowing from Tibet S into Bay of Bengal in Myanmar

Sa·mar \'sä-‚mär\ island *cen* Philippines

Sa·ma·ra \sə-'mär-ə\ *or* *1935–91* **Kuy·by·shev** \'kwē-bə-‚shef, 'kü-ē-bə-, -‚shev\ city W Russia, on the Volga; *pop* 1,239,000

Sa·mar·ia \sə-'mer-ē-ə\ district of ancient

Palestine W of the Jordan between Galilee & Judaea

Sam·ar·qand *or* **Sam·ar·kand** \'sa-mər-‚kand\ city E Uzbekistan; *pop* 370,500

Sam·ni·um \'sam-nē-əm\ ancient country S *cen* Italy — **Sam·nite** \'sam-‚nīt\ *adj or n*

Sa·moa \sə-'mō-ə\ **1** islands SW *cen* Pacific N of Tonga; divided at longitude 171° W into American Samoa (or Eastern Samoa) & independent Samoa **2** *formerly* **Western Samoa** islands Samoa W of 171° W; country; ✻ Apia; *pop* 156,349 — **Sa·mo·an** \sə-'mō-ən\ *adj or n*

Sa·mos \'sā-‚mäs, 'sä-‚mȯs\ island Greece in the Aegean off coast of Turkey

San·aa *or* **Sana** \sa-'nä, 'sa-‚nä\ city SW Arabia, ✻ of Yemen; *pop* 125,093

San An·dre·as Fault \‚san-an-'drā-əs\ zone of faults in California extending from N coast toward head of Gulf of California

San An·to·nio \‚san-ən-'tō-nē-‚ō\ city S Texas; *pop* 1,144,646

San Ber·nar·di·no \‚san-‚bər-nə(r)-'dē-(‚)nō\ city S California; *pop* 185,401

San Di·ego \‚san-dē-'ā-(‚)gō\ coastal city SW California; *pop* 1,223,400

San·i·bel Island \'sa-nə-bəl, -‚bel\ island SW Florida

Sand·wich \'san(d)-(‚)wich\ town SE England; *pop* 4227

Sandwich Islands — see HAWAII

San Fran·cis·co \‚san-frən-'sis-(‚)kō\ city W California on San Francisco Bay & Pacific Ocean; *pop* 776,733

San Joa·quin \‚san-wä-'kēn, -wȯ-\ river 350 mi. (563 km.) long *cen* California flowing NW into the Sacramento

San Jo·se \‚san-(h)ō-'zā\ city W California SE of San Francisco; *pop* 894,943

San Jo·sé \‚sän-hō-'sā, ‚san-(h)ō-'zā\ city, ✻ of Costa Rica; *pop* 330,529

San Juan \san-'wän, ‚sän-'hwän\ city, ✻ of Puerto Rico; *pop* 434,374

San Ma·ri·no \‚san-mə-'rē-(‚)nō\ **1** small country S Europe surrounded by Italy ENE of Florence near Adriatic Sea; *pop* 24,000 **2** town, its ✻; *pop* 2300 — **Sam·mar·i·nese** \‚sa(m)-‚ma-rə-'nēz, -'nēs\ *n* — **San Mar·i·nese** \‚san-‚ma-\ *adj or n*

San Pe·dro Su·la \‚sän-‚pā-(‚)thrō-'sü-lä\ city NW Honduras; *pop* 300,400

San Sal·va·dor \san-'sal-və-‚dȯr, ‚sän-'säl-vä-‚thȯr\ **1** island *cen* Bahamas **2** city, ✻ of El Salvador; *pop* 349,333

San·ta Ana \‚san-tə-'a-nə, ‚sän-tä-'ä-nä\ city SW California ESE of Long Beach; *pop* 337,977

San·ta Bar·ba·ra \'bär-b(ə-)rə\ *or* **Channel** islands California off SW coast in the North Pacific

Santa Clara \'kler-ə\ city W California NW of San Jose; *pop* 102,361

San·ta Cla·ri·ta \klə-ˈrē-tə\ city S California N of Los Angeles; *pop* 151,088

San·ta Fe \ˌsan-tə-ˈfā\ city, ✳ of New Mexico; *pop* 62,203

Santa Fe Trail pioneer route to the SW U.S. about 1200 mi. (1930 km.) long used esp. 1821–80 from vicinity of Kansas City, Missouri, to Santa Fe, New Mexico

Santa Rosa \ˌsan-tə-ˈrō-zə\ city W California N of San Francisco; *pop* 147,595

San·ti·a·go \ˌsan-tē-ˈä-(ˌ)gō, ˌsän-\ city, ✳ of Chile; *pop* 200,792

San·to Do·min·go \ˌsan-tə-də-ˈmiŋ-(ˌ)gō\ *formerly* **Tru·ji·llo** \trü-ˈhē-(ˌ)yō\ city, ✳ of Dominican Republic; metropolitan area *pop* 2,677,056

São Pau·lo \saůⁿ-ˈpaů-(ˌ)lü, -(ˌ)lō\ city SE Brazil; *pop* 10,434,252

São To·mé \ˌsaůⁿ-tə-ˈmä\ town, ✳ of São Tomé and Príncipe; *pop* 43,420

São Tomé and Príncipe country W Africa; ✳ São Tomé; *pop* 128,000

Sap·po·ro \ˈsä-pō-ˌrō; sä-ˈpór-(ˌ)ō\ city Japan on W Hokkaido; *pop* 1,822,368

Sa·ra·je·vo \ˌsar-ə-ˈyä-(ˌ)vō, ˌsär-ə-\ city SE *cen* Bosnia and Herzegovina, its ✳; *pop* (est.) 602,500

Sa·ra·tov \sə-ˈrä-təf\ city W Russia, on the Volga; *pop* 909,000

Sar·din·ia \sär-ˈdi-nē-ə, -ˈdi-nyə\ island Italy in the Mediterranean S of Corsica; *pop* 1,648,044 — **Sar·din·ian** \sär-ˈdi-nē-ən, -ˈdin-yən\ *adj or n*

Sar·gas·so Sea \sär-ˈga-(ˌ)sō\ area of nearly still water in the North Atlantic lying chiefly between 20° & 35° N latitude & 30° & 70° W longitude

Sas·katch·e·wan \sə-ˈska-chə-wən, sa-, -ˌwän\ province W Canada; ✳, Regina; *pop* 1,015,783

Sas·ka·toon \ˌsas-kə-ˈtün\ city *cen* Saskatchewan, Canada; *pop* 196,811

Sau·di Ara·bia \ˈsaů-dē, ˈsó-dē, sä-ˈü-dē\ country SW Asia occupying largest part of Arabian Peninsula; ✳, Riyadh; *pop* 20,800,000 — **Saudi** *adj or n* — **Saudi Arabian** *adj or n*

Sault Sainte Ma·rie Canals \ˈsü-(ˌ)sänt-mə-ˈrē\ *or* **Soo Canals** \ˈsü\ three ship canals, two in U.S. (Michigan) & one in Canada (Ontario), at rapids in river connecting Lake Superior & Lake Huron

Sa·vaii \sə-ˈvī-ˌē\ island, largest in independent Samoa

Sa·van·nah \sə-ˈva-nə\ city & port E Georgia; *pop* 131,510

Sa·voy \sə-ˈvói\ *or French* **Sa·voie** \sä-ˈvwä\ region SE France SW of Switzerland bordering on Italy — **Sa·voy·ard** \sə-ˈvói-ˌärd, ˌsa-ˌvói-ˈärd, ˌsa-ˌvwä-ˈyär(d)\ *adj or n*

Sca·fell Pike \ˌskó-ˈfel\ mountain 3210 ft. (978 m.) NW England; highest in Cumbrian Mountains & in England

Scan·di·na·via \ˌskan-də-ˈnä-vē-ə, -vyə\ **1** peninsula N Europe occupied by Norway & Sweden **2** Denmark, Norway, Sweden, & sometimes also Iceland & Finland — **Scan·di·na·vian** \ˌskan-də-ˈnä-vē-ən, -vyən\ *adj or n*

Scar·bor·ough \ˈskär-ˌbər-ō\ former city Canada in SE Ontario; now part of Toronto

Schel·de \ˈskel-də\ *or* **Scheldt** \ˈskelt\ river 270 mi. (434 km.) long W Europe flowing from N France through Belgium into North Sea in Netherlands

Schuyl·kill \ˈskü-kᵊl, ˈskül-ˌkil\ river 131 mi. (211 km.) long SE Pennsylvania flowing SE into the Delaware River at Philadelphia

Scil·ly, Isles of \ˈsi-lē\ island group SW England off Land's End; *pop* 2900

Sco·tia \ˈskō-shə\ SCOTLAND — the Medieval Latin name

Scot·land \ˈskät-lənd\ *or Latin* **Cal·e·do·nia** \ˌka-lə-ˈdō-nyə, -nē-ə\ country N Great Britain; a division of United Kingdom; ✳, Edinburgh; *pop* 5,062,011

Scotts·dale \ˈskäts-ˌdäl\ city SW *cen* Arizona E of Phoenix; *pop* 202,705

Scyth·ia \ˈsi-thē-ə, -thē\ ancient area of Europe & Asia N & NE of Black Sea & E of Aral Sea — **Scyth·i·an** \ˈsi-thē-ən, -thē-\ *adj or n*

Se·at·tle \sē-ˈa-tᵊl\ city & port W Washington; *pop* 563,374

Seine \ˈsān, ˈsen\ river 480 mi. (772 km.) long N France flowing NW into English Channel

Sel·kirk \ˈsel-ˌkərk\ range of the Rocky Mountains SE British Columbia, Canada; highest peak, 11,555 ft. (3522 m.)

Se·ma·rang \sə-ˈmär-ˌäŋ\ city Indonesia in *cen* Java; *pop* 1,250,971

Sen·dai \(ˌ)sen-ˈdī\ city Japan in NE Honshu; *pop* 1,008,130

Sen·e·ca Falls \ˈse-ni-kə\ village W *cen* New York; *pop* 6861

Sen·e·gal \ˌse-ni-ˈgól, -ˈgäl, ˈse-ni-ˌ\ **1** river 1015 mi. (1633 km.) long W Africa flowing W into the North Atlantic **2** country W Africa; ✳, Dakar; *pop* 7,899,000 — **Sen·e·ga·lese** \ˌse-ni-gə-ˈlēz, -ˈlēs\ *adj or n*

Seoul \ˈsōl\ city, ✳ of South Korea; *pop* 9,853,972

Ser·bia \ˈsər-bē-ə\ country S Europe in the Balkans; ✳, Belgrade; *pop* 9,823,000

Serbia and Montenegro *or 1992–2003* **Yugoslavia** former country S Europe on Balkan Peninsula

Ser·en·ge·ti Plain \ˌser-ən-ˈge-tē\ area N Tanzania

Seven Hills the seven hills upon and about which was built the city of Rome, Italy

Sev·ern \ˈse-vərn\ river 210 mi. (338 km.)

long Wales & England flowing from E *cen* Wales into Bristol Channel

Se·ville \sə-'vil\ *or Spanish* **Se·vi·lla** \sā-'vē-(ˌ)yä\ city SW Spain; *pop* 684,633

Sew·ard Peninsula \'sü-ərd\ peninsula 180 mi. (290 km.) long W Alaska projecting into Bering Sea

Sey·chelles \sā-'shel(z)\ islands W Indian Ocean NE of Madagascar; country; ✱, Victoria; *pop* 72,700 — **Sey·chel·lois** \ˌsā-shəl-'wä, -ˌshel-\ *n*

Shang·hai \shaŋ-'hī\ municipality & port E China; *pop* 7,469,509

Shan·non \'sha-nən\ river 230 mi. (370 km.) long W Ireland flowing S & W into the North Atlantic

Sharon, Plain of \'sher-ən\ region Israel on the coast

Shas·ta, Mount \'shas-tə\ mountain 14,162 ft. (4316 m.) N California in Cascade Range

Shatt al Ar·ab \ˌshat-al-'a-rəb\ river 120 mi. (193 km.) long SE Iraq formed by flowing together of Euphrates & Tigris rivers and flowing SE into Persian Gulf

Shef·field \'she-ˌfēld\ city N England; *pop* 499,700

Shen·an·do·ah \ˌshe-nən-'dō-ə, ˌsha-nə-'dō-ə\ valley Virginia between the Allegheny & Blue Ridge mountains

Shen·yang \'shən-'yäŋ\ *or traditionally* **Muk·den** \'mūk-dən, 'mək-; mūk-'den\ city NE China; chief city of Manchuria; *pop* 3,603,712

Sher·brooke \'shər-ˌbrūk\ city Quebec, Canada E of Montreal; *pop* 75,916

Sher·wood Forest \'shər-ˌwūd\ ancient royal forest *cen* England

Shet·land \'shet-lənd\ islands N Scotland NE of the Orkneys; *pop* 22,270

Shi·jia·zhuang *or* **Shih–chia–chuang** \'shir-'jyä-'jwäŋ, 'shē-\ city NE China; *pop* 1,068,439

Shi·ko·ku \shē-'kō-(ˌ)kü\ island S Japan E of Kyushu; *pop* 4,195,106

Shi·raz \shi-'räz, -'raz\ city SW *cen* Iran; *pop* 848,289

Shreve·port \'shrēv-ˌpòrt\ city NW Louisiana on Red River; *pop* 200,145

Shrews·bury \'sh(r)üz-ˌber-ē, -b(ə-)rē\ town W England; *pop* 31,640

Shrop·shire \'shräp-shər, -ˌshir\ *or 1974–80* **Sal·op** \'sal-əp\ county W England bordering on Wales

Shu·ma·gin \'shü-mə-gən\ islands SW Alaska S of Alaska Peninsula

Siam — see THAILAND

Siam, Gulf of — see THAILAND, GULF OF

Si·be·ria \sī-'bir-ē-ə\ region N Asia in Russia between the Urals & the North Pacific — **Si·be·ri·an** \-ən\ *adj or n*

Sic·i·ly \'si-s(ə-)lē\ *or Italian* **Si·ci·lia** \sē-'chēl-yä\ island S Italy SW of toe of peninsula of Italy; ✱, Palermo; *pop*

5,076,700 — **Si·cil·ian** \sə-'sil-yən\ *adj or n*

Si·er·ra Le·one \sē-ˌer-ə-lē-'ōn, ˌsir-ə-, -lē-'ō-nē\ country W Africa on the North Atlantic; ✱, Freetown; *pop* 4,491,000 — **Si·er·ra Le·on·ean** \-'ō-nē-ən\ *adj or n*

Si·er·ra Ma·dre \sē-ˌer-ə-'mä-drä, 'syer-ä-'mä-thrä\ mountain system Mexico including **Sierra Madre Oc·ci·den·tal** \ˌäk-sə-ˌden-'täl, ˌòk-sē-ˌthen-'täl\ range W of the *cen* plateau, **Sierra Madre Ori·en·tal** \ˌòr-ē-ˌen-'täl\ range E of the plateau, & **Sierra del Sur** \'sùr, 'sür\ range to the S

Sierra Ne·va·da \nə-'va-də, -'vä-\ **1** mountain range E California & W Nevada — see WHITNEY, MOUNT **2** mountain range S Spain

Sik·kim \'si-kəm, -ˌkim\ former country SE Asia on S slope of the Himalayas between Nepal & Bhutan; part of India (country); *pop* 406,457

Si·le·sia \sī-'lē-zh(ē-)ə, sə-, -sh(ē-)ə\ region E *cen* Europe in valley of the upper Oder; formerly chiefly in Germany now chiefly in E Czech Republic & SW Poland — **Si·le·sian** \-zh(ē-)ən, -sh(ē-)ən\ *adj or n*

Silk Road *or* **Silk Route** ancient trade route that extended from China to the Mediterranean

Sim·coe, Lake \'sim-(ˌ)kō\ lake Canada in SE Ontario

Si·mi Valley \sē-'mē\ city SW California W of Los Angeles; *pop* 111,351

Sim·plon Pass \'sim-ˌplän\ mountain pass 6590 ft. (2009 m.) between Switzerland & Italy

Si·nai \'sī-ˌnī\ **1** mountain on Sinai Peninsula where according to the Bible the Law was given to Moses **2** peninsula extension of continent of Asia NE Egypt between Red Sea & the Mediterranean

Sin·ga·pore \'siŋ-ə-ˌpòr\ **1** island off S end of Malay Peninsula; country; *pop* 4,163,700 **2** city, its ✱; *pop* 206,500 — **Sin·ga·por·ean** \ˌsiŋ-ə-'pòr-ē-ən\ *adj or n*

Sinkiang Uighur — see XINJIANG UYGUR

Sioux Falls \'sü\ city SE South Dakota; largest in state; *pop* 123,975

Skag·ge·rak \'ska-gə-ˌrak\ arm of North Sea between S Norway & N Denmark

Skop·je \'skò-pye, -pyə\ city, ✱ of independent Macedonia; *pop* 563,301

Sla·vo·nia \slə-'vō-nē-ə, -nyə\ region E Croatia — **Sla·vo·ni·an** \-nē-ən, -nyən\ *adj or n*

Slo·va·kia \slō-'vä-kē-ə, -'va-\ country *cen* Europe; ✱, Bratislava; *pop* 5,379,455

Slo·ve·nia \slō-'vē-nē-ə, -nyə\ country S Europe; ✱, Ljubljana; *pop* 1,975,164

Smyrna — see IZMIR

Snake \'snāk\ river NW U.S. flowing from NW Wyoming into the Columbia in SE Washington

Snow·don \'snō-dᵊn\ massif 3560 ft. (1085 m.) in **Snow·do·nia** \snō-'dō-nē-ə, -nyə\ (mountainous district) NW Wales; highest point in Wales

So·ci·e·ty \sə-'sī-ə-tē\ islands South Pacific; belonging to France; chief island, Tahiti; *pop* 162,573

So·fia \'sō-fē-ə, 'sò-, sō-'\ city, ✶ of Bulgaria; *pop* 1,141,142

So·ho \'sō-ˌhō\ district of *cen* London, England

So·li·hull \ˌsō-li-'həl\ city *cen* England; *pop* 194,100

Sol·o·mon \'sä-lə-mən\ **1** islands W Pacific E of New Guinea divided between Papua New Guinea & independent Solomon Islands **2** sea, arm of Coral Sea W of the Solomons

Solomon Islands country, SW Pacific E of New Guinea; ✶, Honiara (on Guadalcanal); *pop* 349,000

So·ma·lia \sō-'mä-lē-ə, sə-, -'mäl-yə\ country E Africa on Gulf of Aden & Indian Ocean; ✶, Mogadishu; *pop* 8,050,000 — **So·ma·li·an** \-'mä-lē-ən, -'mäl-yən\ *adj or n*

So·ma·li·land \sō-'mä-lē-ˌland, sə-\ region E Africa consisting of Somalia, Djibouti, & part of E Ethiopia — **So·ma·li** \sō-'mä-lē, sə-\ *n*

Som·er·set \'sə-mər-ˌset, -sət\ *or* **Som·er·set·shire** \-ˌshir, -shər\ county SW England

So·nor·an \sə-'nòr-ən\ *or* **So·no·ra** \sə-'nòr-ə\ desert SW U.S. & NW Mexico

Soo Canals — see SAULT SAINTE MARIE CANALS

South island S New Zealand; *pop* 906,756

South Africa, Republic of *formerly* **Union of South Africa** country S Africa; administrative ✶, Pretoria; legislative ✶, Cape Town; judicial ✶, Bloemfontein; *pop* 30,193,000 — **South African** *adj or n*

South America continent of Western Hemisphere SE of North America and chiefly S of the Equator — **South American** *adj or n*

South·amp·ton \saù-'tham(p)-tən, saùth-'ham(p)-\ city S England; *pop* 194,400

South Australia state S Australia; ✶, Adelaide; *pop* 1,462,900 — **South Australian** *adj or n*

South Bend \'bend\ city N Indiana; *pop* 107,789

South Cape *or* **South Point** — see KA LAE

South Car·o·li·na \ˌker(-ə)-'lī-nə, ˌka-rə-\ state SE U.S.; ✶, Columbia; *pop* 4,012,012 — **South Car·o·lin·i·an** \-'li-nē-ən, -'li-nyən\ *adj or n*

South China Sea — see CHINA

South Da·ko·ta \də-'kō-tə\ state NW *cen* U.S.; ✶, Pierre; *pop* 754,844 — **South Da·ko·tan** \-'kō-tᵊn\ *adj or n*

South·end—on—Sea \ˌsaù-ˌthend-ˌòn-'sē, -ˌän-\ seaside resort SE England E of London; *pop* 153,700

Southern Alps mountain range New Zealand in W South Island extending almost the length of the island

Southern Hemisphere the half of the earth that lies S of the Equator

South Georgia island S Atlantic E of Tierra del Fuego; administered by United Kingdom

South Korea *or* **Republic of South Korea** country S half of Korean Peninsula in E Asia; ✶, Seoul; *pop* 45,985,289

South Seas the areas of the Atlantic, Indian, & Pacific oceans in the Southern Hemisphere

South Shields \'shēldz\ seaport N England; *pop* 87,203

South Vietnam — see VIETNAM

South·wark \'sə-thərk, 'saùth-wərk\ borough of S Greater London, England; *pop* 196,500

South—West Africa — see NAMIBIA

South Yorkshire metropolitan county N England; *pop* 1,248,500

Soviet Central Asia portion of *cen* & SW Asia formerly belonging to U.S.S.R. and including the former soviet socialist republics of present-day Kyrgyzstan, Tajikistan, Uzbekistan & sometimes Kazakhstan

Soviet Union — see UNION OF SOVIET SOCIALIST REPUBLICS

So·we·to \sō-'wä-tō, -'we-, -tü\ residential area NE Republic of South Africa adjoining SW Johannesburg

Spain \'spān\ country SW Europe on Iberian Peninsula; ✶, Madrid; *pop* 39,141,000

Spanish America **1** the Spanish-speaking countries of America **2** the parts of America settled and formerly governed by the Spanish

Spanish Guinea — see EQUATORIAL GUINEA

Spanish Sahara — see WESTERN SAHARA

Spar·ta \'spär-tə\ ancient city S Greece in Peloponnese; ✶ of Laconia

Spo·kane \spō-'kan\ city E Washington; *pop* 195,629

Spring·field \'sprin-ˌfēld\ **1** city, ✶ of Illinois; *pop* 111,454 **2** city SW Massachusetts; *pop* 152,082 **3** city SW Missouri; *pop* 151,580

Sri Lan·ka \(ˌ)srē-'läŋ-kə, (ˌ)shrē-, -'laŋ-\ *formerly* **Cey·lon** \si-'län, sä-\ country having the same boundaries as island of Ceylon; ✶, Colombo; *pop* 17,829,500 — **Sri Lan·kan** \-'läŋ-kən, -'laŋ-\ *adj or n*

Sri·na·gar \srē-'nə-gər\ city N India; *pop* 894,940

Staf·ford \'sta-fərd\ town W *cen* England; *pop* 117,000

Staf·ford·shire \'sta-fərd-ˌshir, -shər\ *or* **Stafford** county W *cen* England

Staked Plain — see LLANO ESTACADO

Stam·ford \'stam-fərd\ city SW Connecticut; *pop* 117,083

Stan·ley \'stan-lē\ town, ✳ of Falkland Islands; *pop* 1559

Stat·en Island \'sta-tᵊn\ **1** island SE New York SW of mouth of the Hudson **2** *formerly* **Rich·mond** \'rich-mənd\ borough of New York City including Staten Island; *pop* 443,728

Ster·ling Heights \'stər-liŋ\ city SE Michigan; *pop* 124,471

Stir·ling \'stər-liŋ\ town *cen* Scotland; *pop* 38,638

Stock·holm \'stäk-ˌhō(l)m\ city, ✳ of Sweden; *pop* 758,148

Stock·port \'stäk-ˌpȯrt\ town NW England; *pop* 276,800

Stock·ton \'stäk-tən\ city *cen* California; *pop* 243,771

Stoke—on—Trent \'stōk-ˌän-'trent, -ˌȯn-\ city *cen* England; *pop* 244,800

Stone·henge \'stōn-ˌhenj, (ˌ)stōn-'\ prehistoric assemblage of megaliths S England in Wiltshire on Salisbury Plain

Stone Mountain mountain 1686 ft. (514 m.) NW Georgia E of Atlanta

Stor·no·way \'stȯr-nə-ˌwā\ seaport NW Scotland; chief town of Lewis with Harris Island; *pop* 8660

Stra·bane \strə-'ban\ district W Northern Ireland; *pop* 35,668

Strath·clyde \strath-'klīd\ former region SW Scotland; included Glasgow

Strom·bo·li \'sträm-bō-(ˌ)lē\ volcano 2500 ft. (758 m.) Italy on **Stromboli Island** in Tyrrhenian Sea

Stutt·gart \'shtu̇t-ˌgärt, 'stu̇t-, 'stət-\ city SW Germany; *pop* 591,946

Styx \'stiks\ chief river of the underworld in Greek mythology

Süchow — see XUZHOU

Su·cre \'sü-(ˌ)krā\ city, constitutional ✳ of Bolivia; *pop* 130,952

Su·dan \sü-'dan, -'dän\ **1** region N Africa S of the Sahara between the Atlantic & the upper Nile **2** country NE Africa S of Egypt; ✳, Khartoum; *pop* 25,000,000 — **Su·da·nese** \ˌsü-də-'nēz, -'nēs\ *adj or n*

Sud·bury, Greater \'səd-ˌber-ē, -b(ə-)rē\ city SE Ontario, Canada; *pop* 157,857

Su·ez, Gulf of \sü-'ez, 'sü-ˌez\ arm of Red Sea

Suez, Isthmus of isthmus NE Egypt between Mediterranean & Red seas connecting Africa & Asia

Suez Canal canal 100 mi. (161 km.) long NE Egypt across the Isthmus of Suez

Suf·folk \'sə-fək\ county E England on North Sea

Sui·sun Bay \sə-'sün\ inlet of San Francisco Bay, W *cen* California

Su·la·we·si \ˌsü-lä-'wā-sē\ island Indonesia E of Borneo; *pop* 12,520,711

Su·lu \'sü-(ˌ)lü\ **1** archipelago SW Philippines SW of Mindanao **2** sea W Philippines

Su·ma·tra \su̇-'mä-trə\ island W Indonesia S of Malay Peninsula — **Su·ma·tran** \-trən\ *adj or n*

Su·mer \'sü-mər\ the S division of ancient Babylonia — **Su·me·ri·an** \sü-'mer-ē-ən, -'mir-\ *adj or n*

Sun·belt \'sən-ˌbelt\ region S & SW U.S.

Sun·da \'sün-də, 'sən-\ strait between Java & Sumatra

Sun·der·land \'sən-dər-lənd\ seaport N England; *pop* 286,800

Sun·ny·vale \'sə-nē-ˌvāl\ city W California; *pop* 131,760

Sun Valley resort center *cen* Idaho

Su·pe·ri·or, Lake \su̇-'pir-ē-ər\ lake E *cen* North America in U.S. & Canada; largest of the Great Lakes

Su·ra·ba·ya \ˌsu̇r-ə-'bī-ə\ city Indonesia in NE Java; *pop* 2,483,871

Su·ri·na·me \ˌsu̇r-ə-'nä-mə\ country N South America between Guyana & French Guiana; ✳, Paramaribo; *pop* 403,000 — **Su·ri·nam·er** \'su̇r-ə-ˌnä-mər, ˌsu̇r-ə-'nä-\ *n* — **Su·ri·nam·ese** \ˌsu̇r-ə-nə-'mēz, -'mēs\ *adj or n*

Sur·rey \'sər-ē, 'sə-rē\ city Canada in SW British Columbia; *pop* 394,976

Sut·ton \'sə-tᵊn\ borough of S Greater London, England; *pop* 164,300

Su·va \'sü-və\ city & port, ✳ of Fiji on Viti Levu Island; *pop* 63,628

Su·wan·nee \sə-'wä-nē, 'swä-\ river 250 mi. (400 km.) SE U.S. flowing SW into Gulf of Mexico

Sverdlovsk — see YEKATERINBURG

Swan·sea \'swän-zē\ city & port SE Wales; *pop* 182,100

Swa·zi·land \'swä-zē-ˌland\ country SE Africa between Republic of South Africa & Mozambique; ✳, Mbabane; *pop* 929,718 — **Swa·zi** \'swä-zē\ *adj or n*

Swe·den \'swē-dᵊn\ country N Europe on Scandinavia (peninsula) bordering on Baltic Sea; ✳, Stockholm; *pop* 8,940,788

Swit·zer·land \'swit-sər-lənd\ country W Europe in the Alps; ✳, Bern; *pop* 6,996,000

Syd·ney \'sid-nē\ city SE Australia, ✳ of New South Wales; metropolitan area *pop* 3,097,956

Syr·a·cuse \'sir-ə-ˌkyüs, -ˌkyüz\ city *cen* New York; *pop* 147,306

Syr·ia \'sir-ē-ə\ **1** ancient region SW Asia bordering on the Mediterranean **2** country S of Turkey; ✳, Damascus; *pop* 13,398,000 — **Syr·i·an** \'sir-ē-ən\ *adj or n*

Syrian Desert desert region between Mediterranean coast & the Euphrates in N Saudi Arabia, SE Syria, W Iraq, & NE Jordan

Table Bay harbor of Cape Town, Republic of South Africa

Ta·briz \tə-'brēz\ city NW Iran; *pop* 971,482

Ta·co·ma \tə-'kō-mə\ city & port W Washington S of Seattle; *pop* 193,556

Tae·gu \'tā-gü, 'dā-\ *or* **Dae·gu** \'dā-\ city SE South Korea; *pop* 2,473,990

Tae·jon \'tā-'jən, 'dā-\ *or* **Dae·jeon** \'dā-\ city *cen* South Korea NW of Taegu; *pop* 1,365,961

Ta·gus \'tā-gəs\ *or Spanish* **Ta·jo** \'tä-(‚)hō\ *or Portuguese* **Te·jo** \'tā-(‚)zhü\ river 626 mi. (1007 km.) long Spain & Portugal flowing W into the North Atlantic

Ta·hi·ti \tə-'hē-tē\ island South Pacific in Society Islands; *pop* 131,309

Tai·chung \'tī-'chün\ city W Taiwan; *pop* 779,370

T'ai–nan \'tī-'nän\ city SW Taiwan; *pop* 702,237

Tai·pei \'tī-'pā, -'bā\ city, ✳ of (Nationalist) China in N Taiwan; *pop* 2,651,419

Tai·wan \'tī-'wän\ *formerly* **For·mo·sa** \fȯr-'mō-sə, fər-, -zə\ **1** island off SE coast of Asia; seat of government of (Nationalist) Republic of China; ✳, Taipei; *pop* 20,926,000 **2** strait between Taiwan & mainland of China connecting East China & South China seas — **Tai·wan·ese** \‚tī-wə-'nēz, -'nēs\ *adj or n*

Tai·yuan \'tī-'ywen, -'ywän\ city N China; *pop* 1,533,884

Ta·jik·i·stan \tä-ji-ki-'stan, tə-, -jē-, -'stän\ country W *cen* Asia bordering on China & Afghanistan; ✳, Dushanbe; *pop* 5,705,000

Ta·kli·ma·kan *or* **Ta·kla Ma·kan** \‚tä-klə-mə-'kän\ desert W China

Ta–lien — see DALIAN

Tal·la·has·see \‚ta-lə-'ha-sē\ city, ✳ of Florida; *pop* 150,624

Tal·linn \'ta-lən, 'tä-\ city, ✳ of Estonia; *pop* 398,434

Tam·pa \'tam-pə\ city W Florida on **Tampa Bay** (inlet of Gulf of Mexico); *pop* 303,447

Tan·gan·yi·ka \‚tan-gə-'nyē-kə, ‚taŋ-gə-, -'nē-\ former country E Africa S of Kenya; now part of Tanzania

Tanganyika, Lake lake E Africa between Tanzania & Democratic Republic of the Congo

Tang·shan \'däŋ-'shän, 'täŋ-\ city NE China; *pop* 1,044,194

Tan·za·nia \‚tan-zə-'nē-ə, ‚tän-\ country E Africa on Indian Ocean, including Zanzibar; designated ✳, Dodoma; seat of government, Dar es Salaam; *pop* 26,542,000 — **Tan·za·ni·an** \-'nē-ən\ *adj or n*

Ta·ra·wa \tə-'rä-wə, 'ta-rə-‚wä\ island *cen* Pacific, contains ✳ of Kiribati; *pop* 28,802

Tar·ry·town \'ta-rē-‚taün\ village SE New York; *pop* 11,090

Tar·sus \'tär-səs\ ancient city of S Asia Minor; now a city in S Turkey

Tash·kent \tash-'kent, täsh-\ city, ✳ of Uzbekistan; *pop* 2,073,000

Tas·ma·nia \taz-'mā-nē-ə, -nyə\ *or earlier* **Van Die·men's Land** \van-'dē-mənz-\ island SE Australia S of Victoria; a state; ✳, Hobart; *pop* 471,400 — **Tas·ma·nian** \taz-'mā-nē-ən, -nyən\ *adj or n*

Tas·man Sea \'taz-mən\ the part of the South Pacific between SE Australia & New Zealand

Ta·try \'tä-trē\ *or* **Ta·tra** \'tä-trə\ mountains N Slovakia & S Poland in *cen* Carpathian Mountains

Taun·ton \'tȯn-tᵊn, 'tän-\ town SW England; *pop* 35,326

Tbi·li·si \tə-'bē-lə-sē, tə-bə-'lē-sē\ *or* **Tif·lis** \'ti-fləs, tə-'flēs\ city, ✳ of Republic of Georgia; *pop* 1,260,000

Te·gu·ci·gal·pa \tə-‚gü-sə-'gal-pə, tä-‚gü-sē-'gäl-pä\ city, ✳ of Honduras; *pop* 608,100

Teh·ran \‚tā-(ə-)'ran, te-'ran, -'rän\ city, ✳ of Iran; at foot of S slope of Elburz Mountains; *pop* 6,042,584

Tel Aviv \‚tel-ə-'vēv\ city W Israel on the Mediterranean; *pop* 353,200

Tem·pe \tem-'pē\ city S *cen* Arizona; *pop* 158,625

Ten·nes·see \‚te-nə-'sē, 'te-nə-‚\ **1** river 652 mi. (1049 km.) long in Tennessee, N Alabama, & W Kentucky **2** state E *cen* U.S.; ✳, Nashville; *pop* 5,689,283 — **Ten·nes·se·an** *or* **Ten·nes·see·an** \‚te-nə-'sē-ən\ *adj or n*

Te·noch·ti·tlan \tä-‚nȯch-tēt-'län\ ancient name of Mexico City

Tex·as \'tek-səs, -siz\ state S U.S.; ✳, Austin; *pop* 20,851,820 — **Tex·an** \-sən\ *adj or n*

Texas Panhandle the NW projection of land in Texas

Thai·land \'tī-‚land, -lənd\ *formerly* **Si·am** \sī-'am\ country SE Asia on Gulf of Thailand; ✳, Bangkok; *pop* 60,617,200 — **Thai·land·er** \-‚lan-dər, -lən-\ *n*

Thailand, Gulf of *formerly* **Gulf of Siam** arm of South China Sea between Indochina & Malay Peninsula

Thames \'temz\ river over 200 mi. (322 km.) long S England flowing E from the Cotswolds into the North Sea

Thar \'tär\ desert E Pakistan & NW India (country) E of Indus River

Thebes \'thēbz\ **1** *or* **The·bae** \'thē-(‚)bē\ ancient city S Egypt on the Nile **2** ancient city E Greece NNW of Athens — **The·ban** \'thē-bən\ *adj or n*

Thes·sa·lo·ní·ki \‚the-sä-lō-'nē-kē\ city N Greece; *pop* 402,443

Thim·phu \tim-'pü\ city, ✳ of Bhutan; *pop* 45,000

Thousand Islands island group Canada

& U.S. in the Saint Lawrence River in Ontario & New York

Thousand Oaks city SW California W of Los Angeles; *pop* 117,005

Thrace \'thrās\ *or ancient* **Thra·cia** \'thrā-sh(ē-)ə\ region SE Europe in Balkan Peninsula N of the Aegean now divided between Greece & Turkey; in ancient times extended N to the Danube — **Thra·cian** \'thrā-shən\ *adj or n*

Thunder Bay city SW Ontario, Canada on Lake Superior; *pop* 109,016

Tian·jin \'tyän-'jin\ *or* **Tien·tsin** \'tyen-'tsin, 'tin-\ city NE China SE of Beijing; *pop* 7,764,141

Tian Shan *or* **Tien Shan** \'tyen-'shän, -'shan\ mountain system *cen* Asia extending NE from Pamirs

Ti·ber \'tī-bər\ *or Italian* **Te·ve·re** \'tā-vā-rä\ river 252 mi. (405 km.) long *cen* Italy flowing through Rome into Tyrrhenian Sea

Tiberias, Lake — see GALILEE, SEA OF

Ti·bes·ti \tə-'bes-tē\ mountains N *cen* Africa in *cen* Sahara in NW Chad; highest 11,204 ft. (3415 m.)

Ti·bet \tə-'bet\ *or* **Xi·zang** \'shēd-'zäŋ\ region SW China on high plateau at average altitude 16,000 ft. (4877 m.) N of the Himalayas; *, Lhasa; *pop* 2,196,010

Tier·ra del Fue·go \tē-'er-ə-(,)del-fü-'ā-(,)gō, 'tyer-ä-(,)thel-'fwä-gō\ 1 island group off S South America 2 chief island of the group; divided between Argentina & Chile

Tiflis — see TBILISI

Ti·gris \'tī-grəs\ river 1180 mi. (1899 km.) long Turkey & Iraq flowing SSE and uniting with the Euphrates to form the Shatt al Arab

Ti·jua·na \,tē-ə-'wä-nə, tē-'hwä-nä\ city NW Mexico on the U.S. border; *pop* 991,592

Tim·buk·tu \,tim-,bək-'tü, tim-'bək-(,)tü\ *or* **Tom·bouc·tou** \tōⁿ-bük-'tü\ town Mali near Niger River; *pop* 31,925

Ti·mor \'tē-,mȯr, tē-'\ island S Malay archipelago SE of Sulawesi; W half part of Indonesia, E half independent East Timor

Ti·ra·ne *or* **Ti·ra·na** \ti-'rä-nə, tē-\ city, * of Albania; *pop* 519,720

Ti·rol *or* **Ty·rol** \tə-'rōl\ *or Italian* **Ti·ro·lo** \tē-'rȯ-(,)lō\ region in E Alps in W Austria & NE Italy — **Ti·ro·le·an** \tə-'rō-lē-ən, tī-\ *or* **Tir·o·lese** \,tir-ə-'lēz, ,tī-rə-, -'lēs\ *adj or n*

Ti·ti·ca·ca, Lake \,ti-ti-'kä-kä, ,tē-tē-\ lake on Bolivia–Peru boundary at altitude of 12,500 ft. (3810 m.)

To·ba·go \tə-'bā-(,)gō\ island West Indies NE of Trinidad; part of independent Trinidad and Tobago; *pop* 54,084 — **To·ba·go·ni·an** \,tō-bə-'gō-nē-ən, -nyən\ *n*

To·go \'tō-(,)gō\ country W Africa on Gulf of Guinea; *, Lomé; *pop* 3,810,000 — **To·go·lese** \,tō-gə-'lēz, -'lēs\ *adj or n*

To·kyo \'tō-kē-,ō, -,kyō\ city, * of Japan in SE Honshu on Tokyo Bay; *pop* 12,064,101 — **To·kyo·ite** \'tō-kē-(,)ō-,īt\ *n*

To·le·do \tə-'lē-(,)dō, -'lē-də\ city NW Ohio; *pop* 313,619

Tol'·yat·ti \tȯl-'yä-tē\ city W Russia; NW of Samara; *pop* 666,000

Ton·ga \'täŋ-gə, 'täŋ-ə, 'tȯŋ-ä\ islands SW Pacific E of Fiji Islands; country; *, Nukualofa; *pop* 101,002 — **Ton·gan** \-(g)ən\ *adj or n*

Tonkin, Gulf of \'täŋ-kən\ arm of South China Sea E of N Vietnam

To·pe·ka \tə-'pē-kə\ city, * of Kansas; *pop* 122,377

Tor·bay \(,)tȯr-'bā\ urban area SW England; *pop* 122,500

To·ron·to \tə-'rän-(,)tō, -'rän-tə\ city, * of Ontario, Canada; *pop* 2,481,494

Tor·rance \'tȯr-ən(t)s, 'tär-\ city SW California; *pop* 137,946

Tor·res \'tȯr-əs\ strait between New Guinea & Cape York Peninsula, Australia

Tou·louse \tü-'lüz\ city SW France; *pop* 390,301

Tower Hamlets borough of E Greater London, England; *pop* 153,500

Trans·vaal \tran(t)s-'väl, tranz-\ former province NE Republic of South Africa

Tran·syl·va·nia \,tran(t)-səl-'vā-nyə, -nē-ə\ region W Romania — **Tran·syl·va·nian** \-nyən, -nē-ən\ *adj or n*

Transylvanian Alps a S extension of Carpathian Mountains in *cen* Romania

Tren·ton \'tren-tⁿn\ city, * of New Jersey; *pop* 85,403

Trin·i·dad \'tri-nə-,dad\ island West Indies off NE coast of Venezuela; with Tobago forms the independent country of **Trinidad and Tobago**; *, Port of Spain; *pop* 1,262,386 — **Trin·i·da·di·an** \,tri-nə-'dä-dē-ən, -'da-\ *adj or n*

Trip·o·li \'tri-pə-lē\ 1 city & port NW Lebanon; *pop* 127,611 2 city & port, * of Libya; *pop* 591,062

Tris·tan da Cu·nha \,tris-tən-də-'kü-nə, -nyə\ island South Atlantic, chief of the Tristan da Cunha Islands (part of British colony of Saint Helena); *pop* 296

Tri·van·drum \tri-'van-drəm\ city S India; *pop* 744,739

Tro·bri·and \'trō-brē-,änd, -,and\ islands SW Pacific in Solomon Sea belonging to Papua New Guinea

Trond·heim \'trän-,hām\ city & port *cen* Norway; *pop* 137,346

Trow·bridge \'trō-(,)brij\ town S England; *pop* 22,984

Troy \'trȯi\ *or* **Il·i·um** \'i-lē-əm\ *or* **Tro·ja** \'trō-jə, -yə\ ancient city NW Asia Minor SW of the Dardanelles

Truk — see CHUUK

Truk — see CHUUK

Tru·ro \'trür-(,)ō\ city SW England; *pop* 16,277

Tsinan — see JINAN

Tsingtao — see QINGDAO

Tuc·son \'tü-,sän\ city SE Arizona; *pop* 486,699

Tu·la \'tü-lä\ city W Russia S of Moscow; *pop* 541,000

Tul·sa \'təl-sə\ city NE Oklahoma; *pop* 393,049

Tu·nis \'tü-nəs, 'tyü-\ city ✻ of Tunisia; *pop* 620,149

Tu·ni·sia \tü-'nē-zh(ē-)ə, tyü-, -'ni-\ country N Africa on the Mediterranean E of Algeria; ✻, Tunis; *pop* 9,673,600 — **Tu·ni·sian** \-zh(ē-)ən\ *adj or n*

Tu·rin \'tür-ən, 'tyür-\ city NW Italy on the Po; *pop* 900,987

Tur·ka·na, Lake \tər-'ka-nə\ *or* **Lake Ru·dolf** \'rü-,dólf, -,dälf\ lake N Kenya in Great Rift Valley

Tur·key \'tər-kē\ country W Asia & SE Europe between Mediterranean & Black seas; ✻, Ankara; *pop* 50,664,458 — **Turk** \'tərk\ *n*

Turk·men·i·stan \(,)tərk-,me-nə-'stan, -'stän\ country *cen* Asia; ✻, Ashkhabad; *pop* 3,958,000 — **Turk·me·ni·an** \,tərk-'mē-nē-ən\ *adj*

Turks and Cai·cos \'tərks-ənd-'kā-kəs, -,kōs\ two groups of islands West Indies at SE end of the Bahamas; a British colony; *pop* 12,350

Tu·tu·ila \,tü-tü-'wē-lä\ island South Pacific, chief of American Samoa group

Tu·va·lu \tü-'vä-(,)lü, -'vär-(,)ü\ *formerly* **El·lice** \'e-lis\ islands W Pacific N of Fiji; country; ✻, Funafuti; *pop* 9700 — see GILBERT AND ELLICE ISLANDS

Tyne and Wear \'tīn-ənd-'wir\ metropolitan county N England

Tyre \'tī(-ə)r\ ancient city ✻ of Phoenicia; now a town of S Lebanon — **Tyr·i·an** \'tir-ē-ən\ *adj or n*

Tyrol — see TIROL — **Ty·ro·le·an** \tə-'rō-lē-ən, tī-\ *adj or n* — **Ty·ro·lese** \,tir-ə-'lēz, ,tī-rə-, -'lēs\ *adj or n*

Tyr·rhe·ni·an Sea \tə-'rē-nē-ən\ the part of the Mediterranean SW of Italy N of Sicily & E of Sardinia & Corsica

Ufa \ü-'fä\ city W Russia NE of Samara; *pop* 1,097,000

Ugan·da \ü-'gän-də, yü-, -'gan-\ country E Africa N of Lake Victoria; ✻, Kampala; *pop* 24,551,021 — **Ugan·dan** \-dən\ *adj or n*

Ukraine \yü-'krān, 'yü-,\ country E Europe on N coast of Black Sea; ✻, Kiev; *pop* 52,344,000 — **Ukrai·ni·an** \yü-'krā-nē-ən\ *adj or n*

Ulaan·baa·tar *or* **Ulan Ba·tor** \,ü-,län-'bä-,tòr\ city ✻ of Mongolia; *pop* 548,400

Ul·san \'ül-'sän\ city SE South Korea; *pop* 1,012,110

Ul·ster \'əl-stər\ **1** region N Ireland (island) consisting of Northern Ireland & N Ireland (country) **2** province N Ireland (country); *pop* 246,714 **3** NORTHERN IRELAND

Um·bria \'əm-brē-ə\ region *cen* Italy in the Apennines; *pop* 840,482

Un·ga·va \,ən-'ga-və\ **1** bay, inlet of Hudson Strait NE Canada **2** peninsula region NE Canada in N Quebec

Union of South Africa — see SOUTH AFRICA, REPUBLIC OF

Union of Soviet Socialist Republics *or* **U.S.S.R.** *or* **Soviet Union** country 1922–91 E Europe & N Asia; former union of 15 republics comprising present-day countries of Armenia, Azerbaijan, Belarus, Estonia, Georgia, Kazakhstan, Kyrgyzstan, Latvia, Lithuania, Moldova, Russia, Tajikistan, Turkmenistan, Ukraine, & Uzbekistan

United Arab Emir·ates \'e-mə-rət, -,rāts\ country E Arabia on Persian Gulf; composed of seven emirates; ✻, Abu Dhabi; *pop* 1,986,000

United Kingdom *or in full* **United Kingdom of Great Britain and Northern Ireland** country W Europe in British Isles consisting of England, Scotland, Wales, Northern Ireland, Channel Islands, & Isle of Man; ✻, London; *pop* 58,789,194

United Nations international territory; a small area in New York City in E *cen* Manhattan; seat of permanent headquarters of a political organization established in 1945

United States of America *or* **United States** country North America bordering on Atlantic, Pacific, & Arctic oceans & including Hawaii; ✻, Washington; *pop* 281,421,906

Upper Volta — see BURKINA FASO — **Upper Vol·tan** \'väl-t²n, 'vōl-, 'vòl-\ *adj or n*

Ural \'yùr-əl\ **1** mountains Russia & Kazakhstan extending about 1640 mi. (2640 km.); usually thought of as dividing line between Europe & Asia; highest about 6214 ft. (1894 m.) **2** river over 1500 mi. (2414 km.) long Russia & Kazakhstan flowing from S end of Ural Mountains into Caspian Sea

Uru·guay \'ùr-ə-,gwī, 'yùr-\ **1** river about 1000 mi. (1609 km.) long SE South America **2** country SE South America; ✻, Montevideo; *pop* 3,149,000 — **Uru·guay·an** \,ùr-ə-'gwī-ən, ,yùr-\ *adj or n*

Ürüm·qi \'ue-'rùm-'chē\ *or* **Urum·chi** \ü-'rùm-chē, ,ùr-əm-'\ city NW China; *pop* 1,046,898

Us·pa·lla·ta \,üs-pä-'yä-tä, -'zhä-\ mountain pass S South America in the Andes between Argentina & Chile

Ustinov — see IZHEVSK

Utah \'yü-,tó, -,tä\ state W U.S.; ✻, Salt

Lake City; *pop* 2,233,169 — **Utah·an** \-ˌtȯ(-ə)n, -ˌtä(-ə)n\ *adj or n* — **Utahn** \-ˌtȯ(-ə)n, -ˌtä(-ə)n\ *n*

Uz·bek·i·stan \(ˌ)üz-ˌbe-ki-ˈstan, ˌəz-, -ˈstän\ country W *cen* Asia between Aral Sea & Afghanistan; ✳, Tashkent; *pop* 21,179,000

Va·duz \vä-ˈdüts\ town, ✳ of Liechtenstein; *pop* 4949

Val·dez \val-ˈdēz\ city & port S Alaska; *pop* 4036

Va·len·cia \və-ˈlen(t)-sh(ē-)ə, -sē-ə\ **1** region & ancient kingdom E Spain **2** city, its ✳, on the Mediterranean; *pop* 738,441

Val·le·jo \və-ˈlā-(ˌ)ō\ city W California; *pop* 116,760

Valley Forge locality SE Pennsylvania

Val·let·ta \və-ˈle-tə\ city, ✳ of Malta; *pop* 9210

Van·cou·ver \van-ˈkü-vər\ **1** city SW Washington on Columbia River opposite Portland, Oregon; *pop* 143,560 **2** island W Canada in SW British Columbia **3** city & port SW British Columbia, Canada; *pop* 545,671

Van Diemen's Land — see TASMANIA

Van·u·atu \ˌvan-ˌwä-ˈtü, ˌvän-\ *formerly* **New Heb·ri·des** \ˈhe-brə-ˌdēz\ islands SW Pacific W of Fiji; country; ✳, Port-Vila; *pop* 142,419

Va·ra·na·si \və-ˈrä-nə-sē\ city N India; *pop* 1,100,748

Vat·i·can City \ˈva-ti-kən\ independent state within Rome, Italy; *pop* 911

Ven·e·zu·e·la \ˌve-nə-ˈzwā-lə, -zə-ˈwā-; ˌbā-nā-ˈswä-lä\ country N South America; ✳, Caracas; *pop* 20,609,000 — **Ven·e·zu·e·lan** \-lən\ *adj or n*

Ven·ice \ˈve-nəs\ *or Italian* **Ve·ne·zia** \ve-ˈnet-sē-ä\ city N Italy on islands in Lagoon of Venice; *pop* 275,368 — **Ve·ne·tian** \və-ˈnē-shən\ *adj or n*

Ven·tu·ra \ven-ˈtu̇r-ə, -ˈtyu̇r-\ city & port SW California; *pop* 100,916

Ve·ra·cruz \ˌver-ə-ˈkrüz, -ˈkrüs\ city E Mexico; metropolitan area *pop* 560,200

Ver·mont \vər-ˈmänt\ state NE U.S.; ✳, Montpelier; *pop* 608,827 — **Ver·mont·er** \-ˈmän-tər\ *n*

Ve·ro·na \ve-ˈrō-nä\ city N Italy W of Venice; *pop* 257,477

Ver·sailles \(ˌ)vər-ˈsī, ver-\ city N France, WSW suburb of Paris; *pop* 91,029

Ve·su·vi·us \və-ˈsü-vē-əs\ volcano about 4190 ft. (1277 m.) S Italy near Bay of Naples

Vicks·burg \ˈviks-ˌbərg\ city W Mississippi; *pop* 26,407

Vic·to·ria \vik-ˈtȯr-ē-ə\ **1** city, ✳ of British Columbia, Canada on Vancouver Island; *pop* 74,125 **2** island N Canada in Arctic Archipelago **3** state SE Australia; ✳, Melbourne; *pop* 4,244,221 **4** city & port, Hong Kong; *pop* 1,026,870 **5** sea-

port, ✳ of Seychelles; *pop* 28,000 — **Vic·to·ri·an** \vik-ˈtȯr-ē-ən\ *adj or n*

Victoria, Lake lake E Africa in Tanzania, Kenya, & Uganda

Victoria Falls waterfall 355 ft. (108 m.) S Africa in the Zambezi on border between Zambia & Zimbabwe

Vi·en·na \vē-ˈe-nə\ *or German* **Wien** \ˈvēn\ city, ✳ of Austria on the Danube; *pop* 1,550,123 — **Vi·en·nese** \ˌvē-ə-ˈnēz, -ˈnēs\ *adj or n*

Vien·tiane \(ˌ)vyen-ˈtyän\ city, ✳ of Laos; *pop* 132,253

Vie·ques \vē-ˈā-kās\ island Puerto Rico off E end of main island

Viet·nam \vē-ˈet-ˈnäm, vyet-, ˌvē-ət-, vēt-, -ˈnam\ country SE Asia in Indochina; ✳, Hanoi; divided 1954–75 into the independent states of **North Vietnam** (✳, Hanoi) & **South Vietnam** (✳, Saigon); *pop* 79,727,400 — **Viet·nam·ese** \vē-ˌet-nə-ˈmēz, ˌvyet-, ˌvē-ət-, ˌvēt-, -na-, -nä-, -ˈmēs\ *adj or n*

Vila — see PORT-VILA

Vi·la No·va de Ga·ia \ˈvē-lə-ˈnȯ-və-dē-ˈgī-ə\ city NW Portugal; *pop* 288,749

Vil·ni·us \ˈvil-nē-əs\ city, ✳ of Lithuania; *pop* 542,287

Vin·land \ˈvin-lənd\ a portion of the coast of North America visited & so called by Norse voyagers about 1000 A.D.; thought to be located along the North Atlantic in what is now E or NE Canada

Vir·gin·ia \vər-ˈji-nyə, -ˌji-nē-ə\ state E U.S.; ✳, Richmond; *pop* 7,078,515 — **Vir·gin·ian** \-nyən, -nē-ən\ *adj or n*

Virginia Beach city SE Virginia; *pop* 425,257

Virginia City locality W Nevada

Virgin Islands island group West Indies E of Puerto Rico — see BRITISH VIRGIN ISLANDS; VIRGIN ISLANDS OF THE UNITED STATES

Virgin Islands of the United States the W islands of the Virgin Islands; U.S. territory; ✳, Charlotte Amalie (on Saint Thomas); *pop* 108,612

Vi·sa·yan \və-ˈsī-ən\ islands *cen* Philippines

Vish·a·kha·pat·nam \vi-ˌshä-kə-ˈpət-nəm\ *or* **Vis·a·kha·pat·nam** \vi-ˌsä-\ city E India; *pop* 969,608

Vis·tu·la \ˈvis-chə-lə, ˈvish-chə-, ˈvis-tə-\ river over 660 mi. (1062 km.) long Poland flowing N from the Carpathians

Vi·ti Le·vu \ˌvē-tē-ˈle-(ˌ)vü\ island SW Pacific; largest of the Fiji group

Vlad·i·vos·tok \ˌvla-də-və-ˈstäk, -ˈväs-ˌtäk\ city & port SE Russia on Sea of Japan; *pop* 648,000

Vol·ga \ˈväl-gə, ˈvȯl-, ˈvōl-\ river about 2300 mi. (3700 km.) long W Russia; longest river in Europe

Vol·go·grad \ˈväl-gə-ˌgrad, ˈvȯl-, ˈvōl-,

-ˌgrät\ city S Russia in Europe, on the Volga; *pop* 1,006,000

Vol·ta \'väl-tə, 'vȯl-, 'vōl-\ river about 300 mi. (485 km.) long Ghana flowing from **Lake Volta** (reservoir) into Gulf of Guinea

Vo·ro·nezh \və-'rȯ-nish\ city S *cen* Russia in Europe; *pop* 902,000

Vosges \'vōzh\ mountains NE France on W side of Rhine valley

Wa·co \'wā-(ˌ)kō\ city *cen* Texas; *pop* 113,726

Wad·den·zee \ˌvä-dⁿn-'zā\ inlet of the North Sea N Netherlands

Wake \'wāk\ island North Pacific N of Marshall Islands; U.S. territory

Wake·field \'wāk-ˌfēld\ city N England; *pop* 60,540

Wa·la·chia *or* **Wal·la·chia** \wä-'lā-kē-ə\ region S Romania between Transylvanian Alps & the Danube

Wales \'wālz\ *or Welsh* **Cym·ru** \'kəm-ˌrē\ principality SW Great Britain; a division of United Kingdom; ✳, Cardiff; *pop* 2,903,085

Wal·lo·nia \wä-'lō-nē-ə\ semiautonomous region S Belgium; *pop* 3,358,560

Wal·sall \'wȯl-ˌsȯl, -səl\ town W *cen* England; *pop* 255,600

Wal·tham Forest \'wȯl-thəm\ borough of NE Greater London, England; *pop* 203,400

Wal·vis Bay \'wȯl-vəs\ town & port W Namibia on Walvis Bay (inlet of the Atlantic); formerly administered by Republic of South Africa

Wands·worth \'wän(d)z-(ˌ)wərth\ borough of SW Greater London, England; *pop* 237,500

War·ley \'wȯr-lē\ town W *cen* England; *pop* 152,455

War·ren \'wȯr-ən, 'wär-\ city SE Michigan; *pop* 138,247

War·saw \'wȯr-ˌsȯ\ *or Polish* **War·sza·wa** \vär-'shä-vä\ city, ✳ of Poland; *pop* 1,655,063

War·wick \'wär-ik\ town *cen* England; *pop* 21,936

War·wick·shire \'wär-ik-ˌshir, -shər\ *or* **Warwick** county *cen* England

Wa·satch \'wȯ-ˌsach\ range of the Rockies SE Idaho & N *cen* Utah; highest Mount Timpanogos 12,008 ft. (3660 m.), in Utah

Wash·ing·ton \'wȯ-shiŋ-tən, 'wä-\ **1** state NW U.S.; ✳, Olympia; *pop* 5,894,121 **2** city, ✳ of U.S.; having the same boundaries as District of Columbia; *pop* 572,059 — **Wash·ing·to·nian** \ˌwȯ-shiŋ-'tō-nē-ən, ˌwä-, -nyən\ *adj or n*

Washington, Mount mountain 6288 ft. (1916 m.) N New Hampshire; highest in White Mountains

Wa·ter·bury \'wȯ-tə(r)-ˌber-ē, 'wä-\ city W *cen* Connecticut; *pop* 107,271

Wa·ver·ley \'wā-vər-lē\ municipality SE Australia in E New South Wales; *pop* 59,095

Wei·mar Republic \'vī-ˌmär, 'wī-\ the German republic 1919–33

Wel·land \'we-lənd\ canal 27 mi. (44 km.) long SE Ontario connecting Lake Erie & Lake Ontario

Wel·ling·ton \'we-liŋ-tən\ city, ✳ of New Zealand; urban area *pop* 339,747

Wes·sex \'we-siks\ ancient kingdom S England

West Bank area Middle East W of Jordan River; occupied by Israel since 1967 with parts having been transferred to Palestinian administration since 1993

West Brom·wich \'brä-mich\ town W *cen* England; *pop* 154,930

West Co·vi·na \kō-'vē-nə\ city SW California; *pop* 105,080

Western Australia state W Australia; ✳, Perth; *pop* 1,676,400 — **Western Australian** *adj or n*

Western Cape province SW Republic of South Africa; *pop* 3,635,000

Western Ghats — see GHATS

Western Hemisphere the half of the earth lying W of the Atlantic Ocean & comprising North America, South America, & surrounding waters

Western Isles English name for the administrative area of W Scotland consisting of the Outer Hebrides

Western Sahara *formerly* **Spanish Sahara** territory NW Africa; occupied by Morocco

Western Samoa — see SAMOA

West Germany — see GERMANY

West Indies islands lying between SE North America & N South America & consisting of the Greater Antilles, Lesser Antilles, & Bahamas — **West Indian** *adj or n*

West Midlands metropolitan county W *cen* England; includes Birmingham

West·min·ster \'wes(t)-ˌmin(t)-stər\ city N *cen* Colorado NW of Denver; *pop* 100,940

West Pakistan the former W division of Pakistan now having the same boundaries as Pakistan

West·pha·lia \west-'fāl-yə, -'fā-lē-ə\ region W Germany E of the Rhine — **West·pha·lian** \west-'fāl-yən, -'fā-lē-ən\ *adj or n*

West Point site SE New York of United States Military Academy on W bank of Hudson River N of New York City

West Quod·dy Head \'kwä-dē\ cape; most easterly point of Maine & of the Lower 48

West Sus·sex \'sə-siks\ county SE England

West Valley City city N Utah S of Salt Lake City; *pop* 108,896

West Virginia state E U.S.; ✳, Charleston; *pop* 1,808,344 — **West Virginian** *adj or n*

West York·shire metropolitan county NW England; includes Wakefield

White sea NW Russia in Europe

White·horse \'hwit-ˌhȯrs, 'wīt-\ city, ✳ of Yukon Territory, Canada; *pop* 19,058

White Mountains mountains N New Hampshire in the Appalachians — see WASHINGTON, MOUNT

Whit·ney, Mount \'hwit-nē, 'wit-\ mountain 14,495 ft. (4418 m.) SE *cen* California in Sierra Nevada; highest in U.S. outside of Alaska

Wich·i·ta \'wi-chə-ˌtȯ\ city S Kansas; *pop* 344,284

Wichita Falls city N Texas; *pop* 104,197

Wien — see VIENNA

Wight, Isle of — see ISLE OF WIGHT

Wil·lem·stad \'vi-ləm-ˌstät\ city, ✳ of Netherlands Antilles; *pop* 43,547

Wil·liams·burg \'wil-yəmz-ˌbərg\ city SE Virginia; *pop* 11,998

Wil·ming·ton \'wil-miŋ-tən\ city N Delaware; largest in state; *pop* 72,664

Wilt·shire \'wilt-ˌshir, -shər\ county S England

Win·ches·ter \'win-ˌches-tər, -chəs-tər\ city S England; *pop* 30,642

Win·der·mere \'win-də(r)-ˌmir\ lake NW England in Lake District

Wind·hoek \'vint-ˌhu̇k\ city, ✳ of Namibia; *pop* 144,558

Wind·sor \'win-zər\ city S Ontario, Canada on Detroit River; *pop* 216,473

Wind·ward Islands \'wind-wərd\ islands West Indies in the S Lesser Antilles extending S from Martinique but not including Barbados, Tobago, or Trinidad

Win·ni·peg \'wi-nə-ˌpeg\ city, ✳ of Manitoba, Canada; *pop* 633,451

Winnipeg, Lake lake S *cen* Manitoba, Canada

Win·ni·pe·sau·kee, Lake \ˌwi-nə-pə-'sȯ-kē\ lake *cen* New Hampshire

Win·ston-Sa·lem \ˌwin(t)-stən-'sā-ləm\ city N *cen* North Carolina; *pop* 185,776

Wis·con·sin \wi-'skän(t)-sən\ state N *cen* U.S.; ✳, Madison; *pop* 5,363,675 — **Wis·con·sin·ite** \-sə-ˌnīt\ *n*

Wit·wa·ters·rand \'wit-ˌwȯ-tərz-ˌrand, -ˌwä-, -ˌränt\ *or* **Rand** ridge of gold-bearing rock NE Republic of South Africa

Wol·lon·gong \'wu̇-lən-ˌgäŋ, -ˌgȯŋ\ city SE Australia in E New South Wales S of Sydney; *pop* 211,417

Wol·ver·hamp·ton \ˌwu̇l-vər-'ham(p)-tən\ town W *cen* England NW of Birmingham; *pop* 236,582

Worces·ter \'wu̇s-tər\ city E *cen* Massachusetts; *pop* 172,648

Wran·gell, Mount \'raŋ-gəl\ volcano 14,163 ft. (4317 m.) S Alaska in **Wrangell Mountains**

Wro·claw \'vrȯt-ˌswäf, -ˌsläv\ city SW Poland in Silesia; *pop* 642,334

Wu·han \'wü-'hän\ city E *cen* China; *pop* 3,284,229

Wu·xi *or* **Wu–hsi** \'wü-'shē\ city E China; *pop* 826,833

Wy·o·ming \wī-'ō-miŋ\ state NW U.S.; ✳, Cheyenne; *pop* 493,782 — **Wy·o·ming·ite** \-miŋ-ˌīt\ *n*

Xi'·an *or* **Hsi–an** \'shē-'än\ city E *cen* China; *pop* 1,959,044

Xianggang — see HONG KONG

Xin·jiang Uy·gur *or* **Sin·kiang Ui·ghur** \'shin-'jyäŋ-'wē-gər\ region W China between the Kunlun & Altai mountains; *pop* 15,155,778

Xizang — see TIBET

Xu·zhou \'shü-'jō\ *or* **Sü·chow** \'shü-'jō, 'sü-\ city E China; *pop* 805,695

Yak·i·ma \'ya-kə-ˌmȯ\ city S *cen* Washington; *pop* 71,845

Ya·lu \'yä-(ˌ)lü\ river 500 mi. (804 km.) long SE Manchuria & North Korea

Ya·mous·sou·kro \ˌyä-mə-'sü-krō\ town, official ✳ of Ivory Coast; *pop* 110,000

Yan·gon \ˌyän-'gōn\ *formerly* **Ran·goon** \ran-'gün, raŋ-\ city, former ✳ of Myanmar; *pop* 1,717,649

Yangtze — see CHANG

Yaoun·dé \yau̇n-'dā\ city, ✳ of Cameroon; *pop* 649,000

Yap \'yap, 'yäp\ island W Pacific in the W Carolines

Ya·ren \'yä-ˌrən\ town, ✳ of Nauru; *pop* 1100

Ya·ro·slavl \ˌyär-ə-'slä-vəl\ city *cen* Russia in Europe, NE of Moscow; *pop* 637,000

Yaz·oo \ya-'zü, 'ya-(ˌ)zü\ river W *cen* Mississippi

Ye·ka·te·rin·burg \yi-'ka-tə-rən-ˌbərg, yi-ˌkä-ti-rēm-'bu̇rk\ *formerly* **Sverd·lovsk** \sverd-'lȯfsk\ city W Russia, in *cen* Ural Mountains; *pop* 1,371,000

Yellow 1 — see HUANG **2** sea, section of East China Sea between N China, North Korea, & South Korea

Yel·low·knife \'ye-lō-ˌnif\ town, ✳ of Northwest Territories, Canada; *pop* 16,541

Ye·men \'ye-mən\ country S Arabia bordering on Red Sea & Gulf of Aden; ✳, Sanaa; *pop* 12,961,000 — **Ye·me·ni** \'ye-mə-nē\ *adj or n* — **Ye·men·ite** \-mə-ˌnīt\ *adj or n*

Ye·ni·sey *or* **Ye·ni·sei** \ˌyi-ni-'sā\ river over 2500 mi. (4022 km.) long *cen* Russia, flowing N into Arctic Ocean

Ye·re·van \ˌyer-ə-'vän\ city, ✳ of Armenia; *pop* 1,199,000

Yo·ko·ha·ma \ˌyō-kō-'hä-mä\ city Japan in SE Honshu on Tokyo Bay S of Tokyo; *pop* 3,426,651

Yon·kers \'yäŋ-kərz\ city SE New York N of New York City; *pop* 196,086

York \'yȯrk\ city N England; *pop* 100,600

York, Cape cape NE Australia in Queensland at N tip of Cape York Peninsula

York·shire \-ˌshir, -shər\ former county N England

Yo·sem·i·te Falls \yō-ˈse-mə-tē\ waterfall E California in Yosemite Valley; includes two falls, the upper 1430 ft. (436 m.) & the lower 320 ft. (98 m.)

Youngs·town \ˈyəŋz-ˌtaún\ city NE Ohio; *pop* 82,026

Yu·ca·tán \ˌyü-kə-ˈtan, -kä-ˈtän\ peninsula SE Mexico & N Central America including Belize & N Guatemala

Yu·go·sla·via \ˌyü-gō-ˈslä-vē-ə, ˌyü-gə-\ **1** former country S Europe including Serbia, Montenegro, Slovenia, Croatia, Bosnia and Herzegovina, & Macedonia; ✻, Belgrade **2** — see SERBIA AND MONTENEGRO — **Yu·go·slav** \ˌyü-gō-ˈsläv, -ˈslav; ˈyü-gō-ˌ\ *or* **Yu·go·sla·vi·an** \ˌyü-gō-ˈslä-vē-ən, -gə-\ *adj or n*

Yu·kon \ˈyü-ˌkän\ **1** river 1979 mi. (3185 km.) long NW Canada & Alaska flowing into Bering Sea **2** *or* **Yukon Territory** territory NW Canada; ✻, Whitehorse; *pop* 29,885

Yu·ma \ˈyü-mə\ city SW corner of Arizona on the Colorado; *pop* 77,515

Za·greb \ˈzä-ˌgreb\ city, ✻ of Croatia; *pop* 779,145

Zaire \zä-ˈir\ **1** river in Africa — see CONGO 1 **2** country in Africa — see CONGO 2 — **Zair·ean** *or* **Zair·ian** \zä-ˈir-ē-ən\ *adj or n*

Zam·be·zi *or* **Zam·be·si** \zam-ˈbē-zē, zäm-ˈbä-zē\ river about 1700 mi. (2735 km.) long SE Africa flowing from NW Zambia into Mozambique Channel

Zam·bia \ˈzam-bē-ə\ *formerly* **Northern Rhodesia** country S Africa N of the Zambezi; ✻, Lusaka; *pop* 9,132,000 — **Zam·bi·an** \ˈzam-bē-ən\ *adj or n*

Zan·zi·bar \ˈzan-zə-ˌbär\ island Tanzania off NE Tanganyika coast; united 1964 with Tanganyika forming Tanzania

Za·po·rizh·zhya *or* **Za·po·ro·zh'ye** \ˌzä-pə-ˈrēzh-zhyə\ city SE Ukraine; *pop* 897,000

Zhang·jia·kou \ˈjäŋ-ˈjyä-ˈkō\ *or* **Kal·gan** \ˈkal-ˈgan\ city NE China NW of Beijing; *pop* 529,136

Zhdanov — see MARIUPOL

Zheng·zhou *or* **Cheng–chou** \ˈjəŋ-ˈjō\ city NE *cen* China; *pop* 1,159,679

Zim·ba·bwe \zim-ˈbä-bwē, -(ˌ)bwā\ *formerly* **Rhodesia** country S Africa S of Zambezi River; ✻, Harare; *pop* 7,550,000 — **Zim·ba·bwe·an** \-ən\ *adj or n*

Zui·der Zee \ˌzī-dər-ˈzā, -ˈzē\ — see IJSSELMEER

Zu·lu·land \ˈzü-(ˌ)lü-ˌland\ territory E Republic of South Africa on Indian Ocean

Zu·rich \ˈzúr-ik\ city N Switzerland; *pop* 340,873

ENGLISH WORD ROOTS

The capitalized word elements here are the ancient roots of the derived modern English words that appear in italics in the discussion and following in boldface.

AB/ABS comes to us from Latin, and means "from," "away," or "off." *Abuse* is the use of something in the wrong way. To *abduct* is to "lead away from" or kidnap. *Aberrant* behavior is behavior that "wanders away from" what is usually acceptable. But there are so many words that include these roots, it would be *absurd* to try to list them all here. **abscond, abstemious, abstraction, abstruse**

AM/IM comes from the Latin word *amor*, "love." *Amiable* means "friendly or good-natured," and *amigo* is Spanish for "friend." **amicable, enamored, inimical, paramour**

AMBI/AMPHI means "on both sides" or "around"; *ambi-* comes from Latin and *amphi-* from Greek. An *ambidextrous* person can use the right and the left hand equally well. An *amphibian*, such as a frog or salamander, is able to live both on land and in the water. **ambient, ambiguous, ambivalent, amphitheater**

ANIM comes from Latin *anima*, meaning "breath" or "soul," and it generally describes something that is alive or lively. An *animal* is a living, breathing thing. *Animism* is the belief that all things have a spirit and an awareness. **animated, animosity, inanimate, magnanimous**

ANN/ENN comes from Latin *annus* and means "year." An *annual* event occurs yearly. A wedding or birthday *anniversary* is an example, although the older you get the more frequent they seem to be. **annuity, millennium, perennial, superannuated**

ANT/ANTI is opposite to or opposes something else. An *antiseptic* or an *antibiotic* fights germs; an *anticlimax* is the opposite of a climax; an *antidote* is given against a poison; and an *antacid* fights acid in the stomach. Be careful not to confuse *anti-* with *ante-*, meaning "before": *antebellum* means "before a war," not "opposed to war." **antagonist, antigen, antipathy, antithesis**

ANTE is Latin for "before" or "in front of." *Antediluvian*, a word describing something very old or outdated, literally means "before the flood"—that is,

the flood described in the Bible. *Antebellum* literally means "before the war," usually the American Civil War. **antechamber, antedate, ante meridiem, anterior**

ANTHROP comes from the Greek word for "human being." An *anthropomorphic* god, such as Zeus or Athena, basically looks and acts like a human. **anthropoid, anthropology, misanthropic, philanthropy**

ART comes from the Latin word for "skill." Until a few centuries ago, almost no one made a strong distinction between skilled craftsmanship and what we would call "art." *Art* could also mean simply "cleverness." The result is that this root appears in some words where we might not expect it. **artful, artifact, artifice, artisan**

AUD, from the Latin verb *audire*, is the root that has to do with hearing. What is *audible* is hearable, and an *audience* is a group of people that listen, sometimes in an *auditorium*. **audition, auditor, auditory, inaudible**

BELL comes from a Latin word meaning "war." Bellona was the little-known Roman goddess of war; her husband, Mars, was the god of war. **antebellum, bellicose, belligerence, rebellion**

BI means "two" or "double." A *bicycle* has two wheels; *binoculars* consist of two little telescopes; *bigamy* is marriage to two people at once. A road through the middle of a neighborhood *bisects* it into two pieces. **biennial, binary, bipartisan, bipolar**

BIO comes from the Greek word for "life." It forms the base for many English words: a *biosphere* is a body of life forms in an environment; *biology* is the study of all living forms and life processes; and *biotechnology* uses the knowledge acquired through biology. **biodegradable, bionic, biopsy, symbiosis**

CAD/CID/CAS all come from the same Latin verb, *cadere*, meaning "to fall, fall down, drop," or from the related noun *casus*, "fall or chance." An *accident* happens to you out of the blue. By *coincidence*, things fall together in a pattern. *Casual* dress is what you put on almost by chance. **cadaver, casualty, decadent, recidivism**

CANT, from the Latin verbs *canere* and *cantare,* meaning "sing," produces several words that come directly from Latin, and others that come by way of French and add an *h* to the root: for example, *chant* and *chantey.* **cantata, cantor, descant, incantation**

CAP/CEP comes from *capere,* the Latin verb meaning "take, seize." *Capture,* which is what a *captor* does to a *captive,* has the same meaning. *Captivate* once meant literally "capture," but now means only to capture mentally through charm or appeal. In some other English words this root produces, its meaning is harder to find. **incipient, perceptible, reception, susceptible**

CAPIT, from the Latin word for "head," *caput,* turns up in some pretty important places. The *captain* of a ship is the head of the whole operation; the *capital* of a state or country is the seat of government, where the head of state is located. A *capital* letter stands head and shoulders above a lowercase letter, as well as at the head of a sentence. **capitalism, capitulate, decapitate, recapitulate**

CARN comes from *caro,* the Latin word for "flesh," and words including this root usually refer to flesh in some form. The word *carnivore,* for example, means "an eater of meat." **carnage, carnal, carnival, incarnation**

CATA comes from Greek *kata,* one of whose meanings was "down." A *catalogue* is a list of items put down on paper. A *catapult* is an ancient military weapon for hurling missiles down on one's enemies. **cataclysm, catalyst, cataract, catatonic**

CED/CESS, from the Latin verb *cedere,* meaning "to go" or "to proceed," produces many English words, from *procession,* meaning something that goes forward, to *recession,* which is a moving back or away. **accede, antecedent, concession, precedent**

CENT means "one hundred," from Latin *centum.* The dollar is made up of a hundred *cents;* other monetary systems use *centavos* or *centimes* as the smallest coin. A *centipede* has what appears to be a hundred pairs of legs, though the actual number varies greatly. But there really are a hundred years in a *century.* **centenary, centigrade, centimeter, centurion**

CENTR/CENTER comes from Greek *kentron* and Latin *centrum,* meaning "sharp point" or "exact middle of a circle." A *centrifuge* is a spinning machine that throws things outward from the *center*; the apparent force that pushes them outward is called *centrifugal* force. **concentrate, eccentric, egocentric, epicenter**

CHRON comes from the Greek word for "time." A *chronicle* records the events of a particular time. A *chronometer* is a device for measuring time, usually one that's more accurate (and more expensive) than an ordinary watch or clock. **anachronism, chronic, chronology, synchronous**

CIRCU/CIRCUM means "around" in Latin. So *circumnavigate* is "to navigate around," often describing a trip around the world, and *circumambulate* means "to walk around." A *circuit* can be a tour around an area or territory, or the complete path of an electric current. **circuitous, circumference, circumspect, circumvent**

CIS comes from the Latin verb meaning "to cut, cut down, or slay." An *incisor* is one of the big front biting teeth; beavers and woodchucks have especially large ones. A *decision* "cuts off" previous discussion and uncertainty. **concise, excise, incisive, precision**

CLAM/CLAIM comes from the Latin verb *clamare,* meaning, "to shout or cry out." An *exclamation* is a cry of shock, joy, or surprise. A *proclamation* is read loudly enough so that all can hear its important message. **acclamation, clamor, declaim, reclamation**

CLUD/CLUS, from Latin *claudere,* "to close," appears in *include,* which originally meant "to shut up or enclose" and now means "to contain." *Exclude,* its opposite, means "to expel or keep out"—that is, to close the door to something. **occlusion, preclude, recluse, seclusion**

COD/CODI comes from Latin *codex,* meaning "trunk of a tree" or "document written on wooden tablets." A *code* can be either a set of laws or a system of symbols used to write messages. To *encode* a message is to write it in code. A genetic code, transmitted by genes, is a set of instructions for everything from blood type to eye color. **codex, codicil, codify, decode**

COGN comes from the Latin verb *cognoscere,* "to get to know." We may *recognize* ("know again") the root in some words, but in *quaint* and *acquaint* French has altered it beyond *recognition.* **cognitive, cognizance, cognoscente, incognito**

CONTRA is the Latin equivalent of *anti-* and it too means essentially "against" or "contrary to" or "in contrast to." *Con-*

trary itself comes directly from this prefix and means simply "opposite" or "opposed." A *contrast* "stands against" something else to which it is compared. *Contrapuntal* music sets one melody against another and produces harmony, which no one is opposed to. **contraband, contradict, contraindication, contravene**

CORD, from the Latin word for "heart," turns up in many common English words. For example, the word *concord* (which includes the prefix *con-*, "with") means literally that one heart is *with* another heart, and thus that they are in agreement. So *discord* (with its prefix *dis-*, "apart") means "disagreement" or "conflict." **accord, concordance, cordial, discordant**

CORP comes from *corpus*, the Latin word for "body." A *corporation* is one kind of body, a *corpse* is another, and a *corps*, such as the Marine Corps, is yet another. **corporal, corporeal, corpulent, incorporate**

COSM, from the Greek word meaning both "ornament" and "order," gives us two different groups of words. *Cosmetics* are the stuff we use to ornament our faces. The "order" meaning combines with the Greek belief that the universe was an orderly place, so words in this group relate to the universe and the worlds within it. *Cosmonaut*, for instance, is the word for a space traveler from the former Soviet Union. **cosmogony, cosmology, cosmopolitan, cosmos**

CRAC/CRAT comes from a Greek word meaning "power." Attached to another root, it indicates which group holds the power. With *demos*, the Greek word for "people," it forms *democracy*, a form of government in which the people rule. In a *meritocracy*, people earn power by their own merit. A *theocracy*, from Greek *theos*, "god," is government based on divine guidance. **aristocrat, autocratic, bureaucrat, plutocracy**

CRE/CRET comes from the Latin verb *crescere*, which means both "to come into being" and "to grow." A *crescendo* in music occurs when the music is growing louder, a *decrescendo* when it is growing softer. **accretion, crescent, excrescence, increment**

CRED comes from *credere*, the Latin verb meaning "to believe." If something is *credible* it is believable, and if it is *incredible* it is almost unbelievable. We have a good *credit* rating when institutions believe in our ability to repay a loan, and we carry *credentials* so that others will believe we are who we say

we are. **credence, creditable, credulity, creed**

CRIT comes from a Greek verb that means "to judge" or "to decide." A film *critic* judges a movie and tells us what is good or bad about it. Her *critical* opinion may convince us not to go, or we may overlook any negative *criticism* and see it anyway. **criterion, critique, diacritic, hypercritical**

CRYPT comes from a Greek verb meaning "to hide." *Cryptography* is the practice of putting a message into code—that is, hiding its meaning in a secret language. A medical term beginning with *crypto-* means there is something hidden about the condition. **apocryphal, crypt, cryptic, cryptogram**

CUMB/CUB can be traced to the Latin verbs *cubare*, "to lie," and *-cumbere*, "to lie down." A *cubicle* was originally a small room for sleeping that was separated from a larger room, though now it can be any small area set off by partitions, as in an office. An *incubus* is an evil spirit that was once believed to seek out women in order to "lie on" them in their sleep. **incubate, incumbent, recumbent, succumb**

CUR, from the Latin verb *curare*, means basically "care for." Our verb *cure* comes from this root, as do *manicure* ("care of the hands") and *pedicure* ("care of the feet"). **curative, curator, procure, sinecure**

CURR/CURS comes from *currere*, the Latin verb meaning "to run." Although the sense of speed may be lacking from words based on this root, the sense of movement remains. *Current*, for instance, refers to running water in a stream or river. And an *excursion* is a trip from one place to another. **concurrent, cursory, discursive, precursor**

DE/DIV comes from two related Roman words, *deus*, "god," and *divus*, "divine." *Deism*, a philosophy that teaches natural religion, emphasizes morality, and denies that the creator god interferes with the laws of the universe, was the basic faith of many of America's Founding Fathers. **deity, divination, divine, divinity**

DEC comes from both Greek and Latin and means "ten." A *decade* lasts for ten years, and the *decimal* system is based on 10. **decalogue, decathlon, decibel, decimate**

DEMI/HEMI/SEMI all mean "half." *Hemi-* comes from Greek, *semi-* from Latin, and *demi-* from French. A *hemisphere* is half a sphere. A *demitasse* (the word comes directly from French) is a dainty after-dinner coffee cup, half the size of a regular cup. And a *semicircle* is half a circle. **demigod, demimonde, semiconductor, semisweet**

DEMO comes from the Greek word meaning "people." A *demagogue* leads the people, usually into trouble, by lying and appealing to their prejudices. **demographic, demotic, endemic, pandemic**

DI/DU, the Greek and Latin prefixes meaning "two," show up in both technical and nontechnical terms. A *duel* is a battle between two people. A *duet* is music for a *duo*, or a pair of musicians. If you have *dual* citizenship, you belong to two countries at once. Most birds are *dimorphic*, with feathers of one color for males and another color for females. **dichotomy, diploma, duplex, duplicity**

DIC, from *dicere*, the Latin word meaning "to speak," says a lot. A *contradiction* (with the prefix *contra-*, "against") speaks against or denies something. A *dictionary* is a treasury of words. And *diction* is another word for speech. **edict, interdiction, jurisdiction, malediction**

DIS comes from Latin, where it means "apart." In English, its meanings have increased to include "do the opposite of" (as in *disestablish*), "deprive of" (as in *disfranchise*), "exclude or expel from" (*disbar*), "the opposite or absence of" (*disaffection*), and "not" (*disagreeable*). The original meaning can still be seen in a word like *dissipate*, which means "to break up and scatter." **diffraction, disseminate, dissension, dissipate**

DOC/DOCT comes from the Latin *docere*, which means "to teach." A *doctor* is a highly educated person capable of instructing others in the *doctrines*, or basic principles, of his or her field—which is not necessarily medicine. **docile, doctrinaire, doctrine, indoctrinate**

DOM comes from Latin *domus*, "house," or *dominus*, "master," or the verb *domare*, "to tame or subdue." A *domain* is the area where a person has authority or is *dominant*. Unfortunately, dominant people can also be *domineering*, seeing themselves as the masters of those they live and work with. **domicile, domination, dominion, predominant**

DUC, from the Latin verb *ducere*, "to lead," shows up constantly in English. *Duke* means basically "leader." The Italian dictator Mussolini was known simply as "Il Duce." But such words as *produce* and *reduce* also contain the root, even though their meanings show it less clearly. **conducive, deduction, induce, seduction**

DYNA/DYNAM come from a Greek verb that means "to be able" or "to have power." *Dynamite* has enough power to blow up the hardest granite bedrock. An instrument that measures force is called a *dynamometer*. **dynamic, dynamo, dynasty, hydrodynamic**

EP/EPI comes from Greek and means variously "upon," "besides," "attached to," "over," "outer," or "after." An *epicenter* is the portion of the earth's surface directly over the focus of an earthquake. The *epidermis* is the outer layer of the skin, overlying the inner layer or "dermis." **ephemeral, epitaph, epithet, epoch**

ERR, from the Latin verb *errare*, means "to wander" or "to stray." This root is easily seen in the word *error*, which means a wandering or straying from what is correct or true. We also use the word *erratum* to mean "a mistake" in a book or other printed material; its plural is *errata*, and the *errata* page is the book page that lists mistakes found too late to correct before publication. **aberrant, errant, erratic, erroneous**

EU comes from the Greek word for "well"; in English words it can also mean "good" or "true." A person delivering a *eulogy* is full of good words, or praise, for the honoree. *Euthanasia* is regarded as a way of providing a hopelessly sick or injured person a "good" or easy death. **eugenic, euphemism, euphoria, evangelism**

EV comes from Latin *aevum*, "age" or "lifetime." This root occurs in only a few English words, but it is related to Greek *aion*, "age," from which we get the English word *eon*, meaning a very long period of time. **coeval, longevity, medieval, primeval**

EXTRA places words outside or beyond their usual or routine territory. *Extraterrestrial* affairs take place beyond the earth. Something *extravagant*, such as an *extravaganza*, goes beyond the limits of reason or necessity. And of course *extra* itself is a word, a shortening of *extraordinary*, "beyond the ordinary." **extracurricular, extramarital, extraneous, extrapolate**

FAC/FEC/FIC comes from the Latin verb *facere*, meaning "to make or do." Thus, a *benefactor* is someone who does good. To *manufacture* is to make, usually in a *factory*. **confection, facile, olfactory, proficient**

FER, from the Latin verb *ferre*, means "to carry." If you *refer* to an incident in your past, you "carry back" to that time. And *transfer* means "to carry across." **confer, deferential, fertile, proliferate**

FID comes from *fides*, the Latin word for "faith." *Fidelity* is another word for "faithfulness." *Confidence* is having faith in someone or something. And an *infidel* is someone who lacks a particular kind of religious faith. **affidavit, diffident, fiduciary, perfidy**

FIG comes from the Latin verb *fingere*, which means "to shape or mold," and the related noun *figura*, meaning "a form or shape." A *transfiguration* changes the shape or appearance or nature of something. A *disfiguring* injury changes the shape of part of the body. **configuration, effigy, figment, figurative**

FIN comes from the Latin word for "end" or "boundary." *Final* describes last things, and a *finale* or a *finish* is an ending. But its meaning is harder to trace in some of the other English words derived from it. **affinity, definitive, finite, infinitesimal**

FLECT/FLEX comes from *flectere*, the Latin verb meaning "to bend." Things that are *flexible* can be bent. When light is *reflected*, it is bent and bounces back to us. **circumflex, deflect, genuflect, inflection**

FLU comes from the Latin verb *fluere*, "to flow." A *flume* is a narrow gorge with a stream flowing through it. A *fluent* speaker is one from whom words *flow* easily. Originally, *influence* referred to an invisible *fluid* that was believed to flow from the stars and to affect the actions of humans. **affluence, effluent, fluctuation, mellifluous**

FORM is a Latin root meaning "shape" or "form." Marching in *formation* is marching in ordered patterns. A *formula* is a standard form for expressing information, such as a recipe or a rule written in mathematical symbols. **conform, formality, format, formative**

FRAG/FRACT comes from the Latin verb *frangere*, "to break or shatter." A *fraction* is one of the pieces into which a whole can be broken; recipes typically call for *fractional* parts of a stick of butter or a cup of flour. The dinnerware on which food is served is often *fragile* or easily broken. **fractious, fragmentary, infraction, refraction**

FUG comes from the Latin verb *fugere*, meaning "to flee or escape." A *refugee* flees from some threat or danger to a *refuge*, which is a place that provides shelter and safety. **centrifugal, fugitive, fugue, subterfuge**

FUND/FUS, from the Latin verb *fundere*, "to pour out" or "to melt," pours forth English words. A *fuse* depends on melting metal to break an overloaded circuit. A *refund* pours money back into your pocket. *Confusion* results when so many things are poured together that they can't be sorted out. **diffuse, effusive, profusion, suffuse**

FUNG/FUNCT comes from the Latin verb *fungi*, "to perform, carry out, or undergo." A car that is *functional* is able to perform its *function* of providing transportation. A functional illiterate is a person who lacks the skills necessary to carry out the ordinary tasks of reading and writing required by day-to-day life. **defunct, functionary, malfunction, perfunctory**

GEN *generates* many English words. Their basic meaning is "come into being" or "be born." The root occurs in *gene*, the most fundamental of biological architects, and in *genealogy*, the study of family roots. **carcinogenic, congenial, generic, indigenous**

GRAD comes from Latin *gradus*, "step" or "degree." A *grade* is a step up or down on a scale of some kind. A *gradual* change takes place in small steps. The *gradient* of a steep slope might be 45 *degrees*. **degrade, gradation, graduate, retrograde**

GRAT comes from *gratus*, the Latin word meaning "pleasing, welcome, or agreeable," or from *gratia*, meaning "grace, agreeableness, or pleasantness." A meal that is served *graciously* will be received with *gratitude* by *grateful* diners, unless they want to risk being called *ingrates*. **congratulate, gratuitous, gratuity, ingratiate**

GRAV comes from the Latin word meaning "heavy, weighty, serious." Thus, a *grave* matter is serious and important. **aggravate, gravid, gravitate, gravity**

GREG comes from Latin *grex*, "herd" or "flock." Bees, wolves, people—any creatures that like to live together in flocks or herds—are *gregarious* animals. People who greatly enjoy companionship, who are happiest when part of a rowdy herd, are highly gregarious. **aggregate, congregation, egregious, segregate**

HABIT/HIBIT comes from Latin *habere*, "to have" or "to hold." A *habit*, bad or good, has a hold on you. To *prohibit* is to "hold back" or prevent. **exhibitionist, habitual, inhibit, prohibition**

HER/HES, from the Latin verb *haerere*, means "to stick." This has produced words with two kinds of meaning. A word such as *adhesive* means basically "sticking," whereas a word such as *hesitate* means more or less "stuck in one place." **adherent, cohesion, incoherent, inherent**

HOM/HOMO comes from *homos*, the Greek word for "same." In an English word it can mean "one and the same" or "similar" or "alike." A *homograph* is one of two or more words spelled alike but different in meaning or derivation or pronunciation. A *homosexual* is a person who exhibits sexual desire toward others of the same sex. **homogeneous, homologous, homonym, homophone**

HOSP/HOST comes from a Latin word meaning "host." *Hospitality* is what a good *host* or *hostess* offers to a guest. A *hospital* was once a house for religious pilgrims and other travelers or a home for the aged. **hospice, hostage, hostel, inhospitable**

HYDR flows from the Greek word for "water." In the Northwest, rushing rivers provide an abundance of *hydrodynamic* power to convert to electricity. "Water" can also be found in the lovely flower called *hydrangea*: its seed capsules resemble ancient Greek water vessels. **dehydrate, hydraulic, hydroelectric, hydroponics**

HYPER is a Greek prefix that means "above or beyond it all." To be *hypercritical* or *hypersensitive* is to be critical or sensitive above and beyond what is normal. **hyperactive, hyperbole, hypertension, hyperventilate**

HYPO/HYP as a prefix can mean variously "under," "beneath," "down," or "below normal." Many *hypo-* words are medical. A *hypodermic* needle injects medication under the skin. *Hypoglycemia*, low blood sugar, is an unhealthy condition. **hypochondriac, hypocrisy, hypothetical, hypothyroidism**

JAC/JEC comes from *jacere*, the Latin verb meaning "throw" or "hurl." To *reject* something is to throw (or push) it back. To *eject* something is to throw (or drive) it out. To *object* is to throw something in the way of something else. **adjacent, conjecture, dejected, trajectory**

JUR comes from the Latin verb *jurare*, "to swear or take an oath," and the noun *jur-*, "right or law." A *jury*, made up of *jurors*, makes judgments based on the law. A personal *injury* caused by another person is "not right." **abjure, jurisprudence, objurgate, perjury**

LAT comes from a Latin verb that means "to carry or bear." From this root come *relation* and *relative*, a person you are *related* to, whether you like it or not. You might be *elated*, or "carried away by joy," to get free tickets to a rock concert, but your elderly relative might not share your *elation*. **collate, correlate, prelate, relativity**

LEV comes from the Latin adjective *levis*, meaning "light," and the verb *levare*, meaning "to raise or lighten." *Levitation* is the magician's trick in which a body seems to rise into the air by itself. And a *lever* is a bar used to lift something by means of *leverage*. **alleviate, elevate, leavening, levity**

LOCU/LOQU comes from the Latin verb *loqui*, "to talk." An *eloquent* preacher speaks fluently, forcefully, and expressively. A dummy's words come out of a *ventriloquist's* mouth. **circumlocution, colloquial, elocution, loquacious**

LOG, from the Greek word *logos*, meaning "word, speech, reason," is found particularly in English words that end in *-logy* and *-logue*. The ending *-logy* often means "the study of": *biology* is the study of life, and *anthropology* is the study of humans. The ending *-logue* usually indicates a type of discussion: *dialogue* is conversation between two people or groups, and an *epilogue* is an author's last words on a subject. **eulogy, genealogy, monologue, neologism**

LUC comes from the Latin noun *lux*, "light," and the verb *lucere*, "to shine or glitter." *Lucid* prose is clear in meaning, as if light were shining through it. *Lucifer*, a name for the devil, means "Light-bearer," the name he had before he fell from heaven. **elucidate, lucent, lucubration, translucent**

LUD/LUS comes from Latin *ludere*, "to play," and *ludum*, "play" or "game." An *interlude* thus is something "between games" (*inter-* meaning "between"). A *delusion* or an *illusion* plays tricks on a person. **allude, collusion, ludicrous, prelude**

MAL as a combining form means "bad." *Malpractice* is bad medical practice. A *malady* is a bad condition—a disease or illness—of the body or mind. *Malodorous* things smell bad. And a *malefactor* is someone guilty of bad deeds. **malevolent, malicious, malign, malnourished**

MAND/MEND comes from *mandare*, Latin for "entrust" or "order." A *command* and a *commandment* are both orders. A *commando* unit carries out orders for special military actions. A *recommendation* may entrust, praise, or advise. **commendation, mandate, mandatory, remand**

MAR, from the Latin word *mare,* meaning "sea," brings its salty tang to English in words like *marine,* "having to do with the sea," and *submarine,* "under the sea." **aquamarine, marina, mariner, maritime**

MATR/METR comes from the Greek and Latin words for "mother." A *matron* is a mature woman with children; *matrimony* is marriage itself, traditionally a first step toward motherhood; and a *matrix* is something in which something else is embedded or takes form, the way a baby takes form inside the mother. **maternity, matriarch, matriculate, metropolitan**

MENS comes from the Latin noun *mensura,* "measure," and the verb *metiri,* "to measure." **commensurate, dimension, immensity, mensurable**

METR comes to us from Greek by way of Latin; in both languages it refers to "measure." A *thermometer* measures heat; a *perimeter* is the measure around something; and things that are *isometric* are equal in measure. **metric, odometer, symmetrical, tachometer**

MIT/MIS, from the Latin verb *mittere,* "to send," appears in such English words as *missionary, missile,* and *emit.* A missionary is sent out to convert others to a new faith; a missile is sent to explode on some far spot; and to emit is to send something out. **emissary, manumission, missive, remittance**

MONI comes from the Latin verb *monere,* "to warn" or "to remind." Warning and reminding often are rather similar, since some reminders warn against the consequences of forgetting. **admonish, monitor, monitory, premonition**

MONO is Greek for "one" or "only." So a *monorail* is a railroad that has only one rail, a *monotonous* voice seems to have only one tone, and a *monopoly* puts all ownership in the hands of a single company, eliminating any competition. **monogamous, monograph, monolithic, monotheism**

MOR/MORT comes from the Latin noun *mors* (stem *mort-*), meaning "death," and verb *mori,* meaning "to die." A *mortuary* is a place where dead bodies are kept until burial. A *postmortem* examination is one conducted on a recently dead body. And a *memento mori* (a Latin phrase meaning literally "Remember that you must die") is a reminder of death; the death's head

carved onto an old gravestone is an example. **immortality, moribund, mortician, mortify**

MORPH comes from the Greek word for "shape." *Morph* is itself an English word with a brand-new meaning; by morphing, filmmakers can now alter photographic images or shapes digitally, making them move or transform themselves in astonishing ways. **amorphous, anthropomorphic, metamorphosis, morphology**

MUT comes from the Latin *mutare,* "to change." Plenty of science-fiction movies have been made on the subject of weird *mutations,* changes in normal people or animals that end up causing no end of death and destruction. More often than not, it is some mysterious or alien force that causes the unfortunate victim to *mutate.* **commutation, immutable, permutation, transmute**

NASC/NAT/NAI comes from the Latin verb *nasci,* meaning "to be born." Words that have come directly from Latin carry the root *nasc-* or *nat-,* but those that took a detour through French bear a telltale *nai-* —words like *renaissance,* "rebirth," or *naive,* "unsophisticated." **cognate, innate, nascent, native**

NEC/NIC/NOX, from the Latin nouns *nex* (stem *nec-*) and *noxa,* have to do with violent death. These roots are related to Greek *nekros,* "corpse," found in such words as *necrology,* "a list of the recently dead," and *necromancy,* "the art of conjuring up spirits of the dead." **internecine, necrosis, noxious, pernicious**

NEG and its variants *nec-* and *ne-* are the prefixes of denial or refusal in Latin. The Latin verb *negare,* "to say no," is the source of our English verb *negate.* A *negative* is something that denies, contradicts, refuses, or reverses. **abnegation, negligible, renegade, renege**

NOM comes from the Latin word for "name." A *nominee* is "named"—or *nominated*—to run for or serve in office. A *binomial* ("two names") is the scientific name for a species; the domestic cat, for example, has the binomial *Felis catus.* A *polynomial,* with "many names," is an algebraic equation involving several terms. **ignominious, misnomer, nomenclature, nominal**

PAN comes from Greek with its spelling and meaning intact. It simply means "all" in Greek; as an English prefix it can also mean "completely," "whole," or "general." A *panoramic* view is a complete view in every direction. *Panchromatic* film is sensitive to the reflected light of all colors in the spectrum. *Pantheism* is the worship of all gods. A *pantheon* is a temple dedicated to all the gods of a particular religion. **panacea, pandemonium, panegyric, panoply**

PARA can mean "beside": *parallel* lines run beside each other. It can mean "beyond or outside": *paranoid*, in which *para-* combines with the Greek word *nous*, "mind," means a little outside of one's mind. Finally, *para-* can mean "associated with, especially as an assistant": *paramedics* and *paralegals* assist doctors and lawyers, and a *paramilitary* force assists regular military forces. **paradigm, paradox, paragon, parameter**

PART, from the Latin word *pars*, meaning "part," comes into English most obviously in our word *part* but also in words like *apartment*, *compartment*, and *particle*, all of which are parts of a larger whole. **impart, impartial, participle, partisan**

PATER/PATR, from both the Greek and the Latin word for "father," is the source of many English words. A *patriarchy* is a society or institution in which ultimate authority rests with the father or with the men of the family. A *patron* is one who assumes a fatherly role toward an institution or project, typically giving moral and financial support. **expatriate, paternal, patrician, patrimony**

PED comes from the Greek word for "child". It is like the PED that means "foot". The two usually aren't hard to tell apart—but don't mistake a *pediatrician* for a *podiatrist*. **encyclopedic, orthpedics, pedagogy, pediatrics**

PED comes from the Latin word *pes*, closely related to the Greek roots *pod* and *pous*, meaning "foot." From *ped-* we get *pedicure*, "care of the feet, toes, and toenails." From *pod-* we get *podiatrist*, "a foot doctor." **expedient, expedite, impediment, pedestrian**

PEL/PULS comes from the Latin verb *pellere*, meaning "to move or drive." A *propeller* moves an airplane forward. When soldiers *repel* an enemy charge, they drive it back. And to *dispel* something is to drive it away. **compel, expel, impel, repulsion**

PEN/PUN comes from the Latin words *poena*, "penalty," and *poenire* or *punire*, "to punish." From them come such English words as *penalty* and *repentance*; when a penalty is given to someone, it is expected that he or she will be moved to repentance. **impunity, penal, penance, punitive**

PEND/PENS, meaning "to hang, weigh, or cause to hang down," comes from the Latin verb *pendere*. We find it in English in words like *pensive*, meaning "thoughtful," and *appendix*, that useless and sometimes troublesome piece that hangs from the intestine. **appendage, expend, propensity, suspend**

PER, a Latin prefix that generally means "through," "throughout," or "thoroughly," has been a thoroughly useful root throughout its history and through all its many meanings. The "through" and "throughout" meanings are seen in *perforate*, "to bore through," *perennial*, "throughout the years," and *permanent*, "remaining throughout." And the "thoroughly" sense shows up in *persuade*, for "thoroughly advise," and *perverted*, "thoroughly turned around." **percolate, peremptory, permeate, persevere**

PERI usually means "going around something." With a *periscope*, you can see around corners. *Peristalsis* is the bodily function that moves food around the intestines; without it, digestion would grind to a halt. The moon's *perigee* is the point in its orbit where it is closest to the earth. The point in the earth's orbit around the sun that brings it closest to the sun is its *perihelion*. **perimeter, periodontal, peripatetic, peripheral**

PHAN/PHEN, from the Greek verbs that mean "to appear or seem" or "to present to the mind," has to do with the way things seem or appear rather than the way they really are. From these roots come words such as *fanciful* and *fantasy*, in which the imagination plays an important part. **diaphanous, phantasm, phantasmagoria, phenomenon**

PHIL comes from the Greek word meaning "love." In *philosophy*, it is joined with *sophia*, "wisdom," so philosophy means literally "love of wisdom." When joined with *biblio-*, "book," the result is *bibliophile*, or "lover of books." *Philadelphia*, containing the Greek word *adelphos*, "brother," is the city of "brotherly love." **philanthropy, philatelist, philology, philter**

PHON is a Greek root meaning "sound," "voice," or "speech." It is similar to the Latin *voc* in meaning but typically means only "sound" when used in such words as *telephone* ("far sound"), *microphone* ("small sound"), or *xylophone* ("wood sound"). **cacophony, phonetic, polyphonic, symphony**

PHOS/PHOT comes from the Greek word for "light." *Phos* can be seen in the word *phosphorus*, which refers generally to anything that glows in the dark and also to a particular glowing chemical element. *Phot*, the more familiar root, appears in words like *photography*, which is the use of light to create an image on film or paper. **phosphorescent, photogenic, photon, photosynthesis**

PLE comes from a Latin word meaning "to fill." It can be seen in the word *complete*, meaning "possessing all necessary parts." A *supplement* is an addition that makes something fuller. **complement, deplete, implement, replete**

PLIC comes from the Latin verb *plicare*, "to fold." A *complicated* subject has many folds or wrinkles. A person who is *implicated* in a crime is "wrapped up" in it somehow. The person's involvement may become *explicit*—"unwrapped" or revealed—when the details of the crime unfold. **complicity, explicate, implicit, replicate**

POLIS/POLIT comes from the Greek word for "city." "City-states" operated much like separate nations in ancient Greece, so all their *politics* was local, like all their public *policy*. **acropolis, cosmopolitan, megalopolis, politic**

POLY comes from *polys*, the Greek word for "many." *Polysyllabic* words are words of many syllables. *Polygamy* is marriage in which one has many spouses, or at least more than the legal limit of one. A *polygraph* is an instrument for recording variations in many different bodily pulsations simultaneously to reveal whether someone is lying. **polyglot, polyhedron, polymer, polyphony**

PON/POS, from the Latin verb *ponere*, means "put" or "place." You *expose* film by "placing it out" in the light. You *oppose* an *opponent* by "putting yourself against" him or her. You *postpone* a trip by "placing it after" its original date. **component, disposition, repository, superimpose**

POPUL comes from the Latin word meaning "people," and in fact forms the basis of the word *people* itself. *Popular* means not only "liked by many people" but also "relating to the general public." The *population* is the people of an area. **populace, populist, populous, vox populi**

POST comes from a Latin word meaning "after" or "behind." A *postscript* is a note that comes after an otherwise completed letter, usually as an afterthought. *Postpartum* refers to the period following childbirth and all of its related events and complications. To *postdate* a check is to give it a date after the day when it was written. **posterior, posterity, posthumous, postmortem**

PRE, one of the most common of all English *prefixes*, comes from *prae*, the Latin word meaning "before" or "in front of." A television program *precedes* another by coming on the air earlier. You make a *prediction* by saying something will happen before it occurs. A person who *presumes* to know makes an assumption before he or she has all the facts. Someone with a *prejudice* against a class of people has formed an opinion of individuals before having met them. **precept, precocious, predispose, prerequisite**

PRIM comes from *primus*, the Latin word for "first." Something that is *primary* is first in time, development, rank, or importance. A *primer* is a book of first instructions on a subject. A *primate* is a bishop or archbishop of the first rank. Something *primitive* is in its first stage of development. **primal, primeval, primogeniture, primordial**

PRO comes from Latin, where it means "before," "forward," or "for." As a prefix, it can also mean "earlier than," "front," or "in front of." A lifetime of anger or bitterness can *proceed*, or "come forth," from an unhappy childhood. An ambitious army officer expects to be *promoted*, or "moved forward," rapidly. Those who *provide* for the future by laying away money are "looking ahead." **procrastinate, prodigious, progress, propitious**

PROB/PROV comes from Latin words meaning "good, honest" and "show to be good, prove." *Probate* court is where the genuineness of the wills of deceased people must be *proved*. **approbation, disprove, probity, reprobate**

PROPER/PROPR come from the Latin word *proprius*, meaning "own." A *proprietor* is an owner. *Property* is what he or she owns. **appropriate, expropriate, proprietary, propriety**

PROT/PROTO comes from Greek and has the basic meaning "first in time" or "first formed." *Protozoans* are one-celled animals, such as amoebas and paramecia, that are among the most basic members of the biological kingdom. A *proton* is an elementary particle that, along with neutrons, can be found in all atomic nuclei. **protagonist, protocol, protoplasm, prototype**

PUNG/PUNCT comes from the Latin verb *pungere*, meaning "to prick or stab," and the noun *punctum*, meaning "point." A period is a form of *punctua-*

tion that is literally a point. A *punctured* tire, pricked by a sharp point, can make it hard to be *punctual*—that is, to arrive "on the dot" or at a precise point in time. **compunction, expunge, punctilious, pungent**

PURG comes from the Latin verb *purgare*, "to clean or cleanse." An *unexpurgated* version of Ovid's *Metamorphoses* has not been cleansed of its vulgar or "dirty" sections. *Purging* literature of passages that might harm youthful readers has kept many an editor occupied; even in ancient times, some of Ovid's poetry was carefully *purged*. **expurgate, purgation, purgative, purgatory**

PUT, from the Latin verb *putare*, meaning "to think, consider, or reckon," has come into English in a variety of forms. A *reputation*, for example, is what others think of you; a *deputy* is someone "considered as" the person who appointed him or her. **disputatious, impute, putative, reputed**

QUADR/QUART means "four" and comes from Latin *quadr-*, "four," "fourth," and *quartus*, "fourth." In English, a *quart* is one-fourth of a gallon, just as a *quarter* is one-fourth of a dollar. A *quadrangle* has four sides but is not necessarily square; a *quadrant* is one of four equal parts. **quadrennial, quadrille, quadruple, quartet**

QUINT comes from the Latin word meaning "fifth." A *quintessence* is literally the "fifth essence," the fifth and highest element of ancient and medieval philosophy, which was supposed to be in the celestial bodies. **quintessential, quintet, quintuplet**

QUIS is derived from the Latin verb *quaerere*, meaning "to seek or obtain." You can see it in our word *acquisitive*, which means "having a strong wish to possess things." The roots *quir* and *ques* are also derived from this word and give us words such as *inquiry*, "a search or request for information," and *question*, "something asked." **acquisitive, inquisition, perquisite, requisition**

RECT comes from the Latin word *rectus*, which means "straight" or "right." A *rectangle* is a four-sided figure whose parallel, straight sides meet at right angles. *Rectus*, short for Latin *rectus musculus*, may refer to any of several straight muscles, such as those of the abdomen. To *correct* something is to make it right. **rectify, rectilinear, rectitude, rector**

RETRO means "back," "behind," or "backward" in Latin. A *retrospective* is a "looking back" at events from the past.

retroactive, retrofit, retrograde, retrogress

ROG comes from *rogare*, the Latin verb meaning "to ask." The ancient Romans also used this word to mean "to propose," thinking perhaps that when we propose an idea, we are actually asking someone to consider it. So *interrogate* means "to question systematically," and a *surrogate* (for example, a surrogate mother) is a substitute, someone who is proposed to stand in for another. **abrogate, arrogate, derogatory, prerogative**

SACR/SANCT, meaning "holy," comes from the Latin words *sacer*, "holy," and *sancire*, "to make holy." A *sacrament* such as the bread and wine of Christian communion is a way of receiving holy grace. The person who receives it is *sanctified* or "made holy" by it; this holiness or *sanctity* is believed to result from God's grace. **sacrilege, sacrosanct, sanction, sanctuary**

SCAND/SCEND comes from the Latin verb *scandere*, "to climb." *Ascend*, "go up," and *descend*, "go down," are the most familiar of the English words it has produced. **ascendancy, condescend, descendant, transcend**

SCI comes from the Latin verb *scire*, "to know" or "to understand." This root appears in the word *science*, which refers to factual knowledge, and in *conscience*, which refers to moral knowledge. And to be *conscious* is to be in a state where you are able to know or understand. **conscientious, omniscience, prescient, unconscionable**

SCRIB/SCRIP comes from the Latin verb *scribere*, "to write." *Scribble* is a word meaning to write or draw carelessly. A written work that hasn't been published is a *manuscript*. To *describe* is to picture something in words. **circumscribe, conscription, inscription, proscribe**

SECU/SEQU comes from the Latin verb *sequi*, meaning "to follow." A *sequel* follows the original novel, film, or television show. The *second* follows the first. But a *non sequitur* is a conclusion that does "not follow" from what was said before. **consequential, execute, obsequious, sequential**

SERV means "to be subject to." A *servant* is the person who *serves* you with meals and provides other necessary *services*. A tennis or volleyball *serve* puts the ball in play much as a servant puts food on the table. **serviceable, servile, servitude, subservient**

SIGN comes from the Latin noun *signum*, "sign or mark." An architect's *design* marks out the pattern for a building; if the owner *designates* that design as the one he wants, he so indicates by putting a *signature,* his own special mark, on an agreement. **assignation, resign, signatory, signet**

SOLV/SOLU comes from the Latin verb *solvere,* "to loosen, free, release." The number of English words that have been spawned by this root is seemingly without end. For example, to *solve* a problem—that is, to find its *solution*—is to free up a situation, and a *solvent dissolves* and releases oil or paint. **absolve, dissolution, resolve, soluble**

SON is the Latin root meaning "sound," as in our word *sonata,* meaning a kind of music usually played by one or two instruments, and *sonorous,* usually meaning "full, loud, or rich in sound." **assonance, dissonant, resonance, sonic**

SOPH is a Greek root from the word meaning "wise" or "wisdom." In our language, the root often appears in words where the "wise" is of the "wiseguy" variety. But in words such as *philosophy* we see a more respectful attitude toward wisdom. **sophisticated, sophistry, sophomoric, theosophy**

SPHER comes from the Greek word for "ball," and it appears in words for things that have something round about them. A ball is itself a *sphere.* The *stratosphere* and the *ionosphere* are parts of the *atmosphere* that encircles the earth. **biosphere, hemisphere, spherical, troposphere**

SPIC/SPEC comes from the Latin verb *specere* or *spicere,* meaning "to look at or behold." Closely related is the root *specta-,* which produces such words as *spectator, spectacles,* and *spectacular.* **auspicious, conspicuous, introspection, perspicacious**

STRU/STRUCT comes from the Latin verb *struere,* meaning "to put together," "to put in order," and "to build or devise." A *structure* is something *constructed,* "built" or "put together"; *instructions* tell how the pieces should be arranged. Something that *obstructs* is "built up in the way." **construe, destructive, infrastructure, instrumental**

SUB means "under," as in *subway, submarine,* and *substandard.* A *subject* is a person who is under the authority of another. The word *subscribe* once meant "to write one's name underneath," and *subscription* was the act of signing at the end of a document or agreement. **subconscious, subjugate, subliminal, subversion**

TANG/TACT comes from the Latin verb *tangere,* "to touch." A person who shows *tact* has a delicate touch when it comes to dealing with other people. To make *contact* is to touch or "get in touch." **intact, tactile, tangential, tangible**

TELE has as its basic meanings "distant" or "at a distance." A *telescope* looks at faraway objects, a *telephoto* lens on a camera magnifies distant objects for a photograph, and a *television,* for better or worse, allows us to watch things taking place far away. **telecommunication, telegenic, telemetry, telepathic**

TEMPER comes from the Latin verb *temperare,* "to moderate or keep within limits" or "to mix." It comes into English in words like *temperature.* *Tempered* (as in tempered steel) means "hardened by reheating and cooling in oil or water." *Tempered* enthusiasm, similarly, is enthusiasm that has cooled a bit. **intemperate, temper, tempera, temperance**

TEMPOR comes from Latin *tempus,* meaning "time." The Latin phrase *tempus fugit* means "time flies," an observation that somehow seems more true during summer vacation than in the dead of winter. A *temporary* repair is meant to last only a short time. The *tempo,* or speed, of a country-and-western ballad is usually different from that of a heavy metal song. **contemporary, extemporaneous, temporal, temporize**

TEN/TIN, from the Latin verb *tenere* and the related word *tenax,* basically means "hold" or "hold on to." A *tenant* is the "holder" of an apartment, house, or land, but not necessarily the owner. A *lieutenant* governor may "hold the position" or "serve in lieu" of the governor when necessary. **abstinence, sustenance, tenable, tenacious**

TEND/TENT, from Latin *tendere,* meaning "to stretch, extend, or spread," can be seen most simply in the English word *tent,* meaning "a piece of material stretched or extended over a frame." It can also be seen in the word *extend,* which means "to stretch forth or stretch out," and in *tendon,* the word for a tough band of tissue that stretches from a muscle to a bone. **contentious, distend, portend, tendentious**

TERM/TERMIN comes from the Latin verb *terminare,* "to limit, bound, or set limits to," or the related noun *terminus,* a "limit or boundary." In English, those boundaries or limits tend to be final: to *terminate* a sentence or a meeting or a ballgame means to end it, and a *term* goes on for a given amount of time and then ends. **coterminous, indeterminate, interminable, terminal**

TERR comes from Latin *terra,* "earth." *Terra firma* is a Latin phrase that means "firm ground" as opposed to the swaying seas; a *terrace* is a leveled area along a sloping hill; the French call potatoes *pommes de terre,* literally "apples of the earth"; *territory* is a specific piece of land. **parterre, subterranean, terrarium, terrestrial**

THE comes from the Greek word meaning "god." *Theology* is the study of gods or religion. *Monotheism* is the worship of a single god; someone who is *polytheistic,* however, worships many gods. **apotheosis, atheistic, pantheistic, theocracy**

THERM/THERMO comes from the Greek word meaning "heat." A *thermometer* measures the amount of warmth in a body, the air, or an oven; a *thermostat* makes sure the temperature stays at the same level. In a *thermodynamic* process, heat affects the behavior of atoms, particles, or molecules. **thermal, thermocline, thermocouple, thermonuclear**

TOP comes from *topos,* the Greek word for "place." A *topic* is the subject of a paper or discussion. Its root originally meant "commonplace"—that is, a common subject. **isotope, topical, topography, utopia**

TORS/TORT comes from two forms of the Latin verb *torquere,* meaning "to twist" or "to wind" or "to wrench." A sideshow *contortionist* twists his or her body into bizarre shapes. This may appear to be a form of *torture,* which itself often involves a merciless wrenching and twisting of the body. **extort, torsion, tort, tortuous**

TRACT comes from *trahere,* the Latin verb meaning "drag or draw." Something *attractive* draws us toward it. A *tractor* drags other vehicles behind it, with the help of the *traction* of its wheels. **detract, intractable, protracted, retraction**

TRANS comes from Latin to indicate movement "through, across, or beyond" something. *Translation* carries the meaning from one language to another. A television signal is sent or *transmitted* through the air (or a cable) to your set. When making your way through a city on public *transportation,* you may have to *transfer* from one bus or subway across to another. **transcendent, transfiguration, transfuse, transient**

TRI means "three," whether derived from Greek or Latin. A *tricycle* has three wheels. A *triangle* has three sides and three angles. And a *triumvirate* is a board or government of three people. **triceratops, trident, trilogy, trinity**

TURB comes from the Latin verb *turbare,* "to throw into disorder," and the noun *turba,* "crowd" or "confusion." A *disturbance,* for example, confuses and upsets normal order or routine. **perturb, turbid, turbine, turbulent**

TUT/TUI, from the Latin verb *tueri,* originally meant "to look at," but the English meaning of the root gradually came to be "to guide, guard, or teach." A *tutor* guides a student through a subject, saving the most careful tutoring for the most difficult areas. **intuition, tuition, tutelage, tutorial**

UMBR, from Latin *umbra,* "shadow," is a shady customer. The familiar *umbrella,* with its ending meaning "little," casts a "little shadow" to keep off the sun or the rain. **adumbrate, penumbra, umber, umbrage**

UND comes into English from the Latin words *unda,* "wave," and *undare,* "to rise in waves," "to surge or flood." *Undulations* are waves or wavelike things or motions. To *undulate* is to rise and fall in a wavelike way. **abundant, inundate, redundancy, undulant**

UNI comes from the Latin word for "one." A *uniform* is a single design worn by everyone. A *united* group has one single opinion or forms a single *unit.* A *unicorn* is a mythical animal with one horn; a *unicycle* has only one wheel. **unicameral, unilateral, unison, unitarian**

UT/US comes from the Latin verb *uti,* "to use, make use of, employ," and the related adjective *utilis,* "useful, fit." It is *used* in such words as *abuse,* "improper use," and *reuse,* "to use again." **usufruct, usury, utilitarian, utility**

VEN/VENT comes from *venire,* the Latin verb meaning "come." To *intervene* in a case or an argument is to "come between" the two opponents. An *avenue* is a street, or originally an access road by which to "come toward" something. Groups "come together" at a *convention.* **advent, provenance, venturesome, venue**

VER comes from the Latin word for "truth." A *verdict* in a trial is "the truth spoken." But a just verdict may depend on the *veracity,* or "truthfulness," of the witnesses. **aver, verify, verisimilitude, verity**

VERB comes from Latin *verbum,* meaning "word." A *verb*—or action word—

appears in some form in every complete sentence. To express something *verbally*—or to *verbalize* something—is to say it or write it. **proverb, verbatim, verbiage, verbose**

VERT/VERS, from the Latin verb *vertere*, means "to turn" or "to turn around." An *advertisement* turns your attention to a product or service. *Vertigo* is the dizziness that results from turning too rapidly or that makes you feel as if everything else is turning. **avert, divert, perverse, versatile**

VEST comes from the Latin verb *vestire*, "to clothe" or "to dress," and the related noun *vestis*, "clothing" or "garment." *Vest* is the shortest English word we have from this root, and is the name of a rather small piece of clothing. **divest, investiture, transvestite, travesty**

VID/VIS comes from the Latin verb *videre*, and appears in words having to do with seeing and sight. A *videotape* is a collection of *visual* images—that is, images *visible* to our eyes. To *envision* something, for instance, is to see it with your imagination. **revise, visage, visionary, visitation**

VINC/VICT comes from the Latin verb *vincere*, which means "to conquer" or "to overcome." The *victor* defeats an enemy, whether on a battlefield or a football field. To *convince* someone that you're right is a *victory* of another kind. **conviction, evince, invincible, victorious**

VIR is Latin for "man." A *virtue* is a good quality—originally, the kind of quality an ideal man possessed. And *virtuous* behavior is morally excellent. All in all, the Romans seemed to believe that being a man was a good thing. **triumvirate, virago, virility, virtuosity**

VIV comes from *vivere*, the Latin verb meaning "to live or be alive." A *survivor* has lived through something terrible. A *revival* brings something back to life, whether an old film, interest in a long-dead novelist, or the religious faith of a group. **convivial, revivify, vivacious, vivisection**

VOC/VOK, from the Latin noun *vox* and the verb *vocare*, has to do with speaking and calling and the use of the voice. So a *vocation* is a calling to a type of work; an *evocative* sight or smell calls forth memories and feelings; and a *vocal* ensemble is a singing group. **equivocate, irrevocable, provoke, vociferous**

VOLU/VOLV comes from the Latin verb *volvere*, meaning "to roll, wind, turn around, or twist around." From this source come words like *volume*, which was originally the name of a scroll or roll of papyrus, and *revolve*, which simply means "turn in circles." **convoluted, devolution, evolution, voluble**

VOR, from the Latin verb *vorare*, means "to eat." The ending *-ivorous* shows up in words that refer to eaters of certain kinds of food. Some *-ivorous* words such as *insectivorous* are easy to understand at a glance. **carnivorous, herbivorous, omnivorous, voracious**

BASIC ENGLISH GRAMMAR

The essence of the English language is the sentence. A sentence is a grammatically self-contained group of words that expresses a statement, a question, a command, a wish, or an exclamation. It is composed of a *subject*, about which something is said, and a *predicate*, which expresses what is said about the subject. The subject can be a single noun, a noun phrase, such as "*the strong wind,*" or a noun clause, such as "*what he decides* is important to all of us." The predicate can be a single verb, a verb phrase, such as "*will be going,*" a verb and all its modifiers, such as "*will be going as soon as the bus arrives,*" or a verb and its complements, such as "*gave his client the bad news.*"

In English, word order is important. The subject usually comes first, but not necessarily:

> *An amusement park* is across the river.
> Across the river is *an amusement park.*
> Is *an amusement park* across the river?

The grammar of English is concerned with the structure of these elements that make up a sentence. Every word in a sentence can be classified as a particular part of speech (*noun, verb, adjective,* etc.), according to its function in the sentence. The major parts of speech are briefly discussed in the following guide to basic English grammar.

THE ADJECTIVE

The adjective gives information about a noun or pronoun, such as what kind

> the *black* cat   a *joyful* occasion

or which one

> a *first* draft   *that* suggestion

or how many

> *ten* players   *few* new ideas

The adjective usually precedes the noun it modifies, but some adjectives can also follow certain verbs:

> the house is *white* (→ *white* house)
> the speeches seemed *long* (→ *long* speeches)
> the chair felt *comfortable* (→ *comfortable* chair)
> the tree grew *tall* (→ *tall* tree)

A few adjectives will follow their nouns, but usually only in set phrases:

> court-martial   secretary-general

POSITIVE, COMPARATIVE, AND SUPERLATIVE DEGREES OF ADJECTIVES

The positive degree is the basic form of the adjective. It gives basic information about the noun without reference to anything else (a *white* house). The comparative degree relates a noun to another—as having more or less of some quality (this house is *whiter* than that); the superlative degree relates the noun to all others of its class (this is the *whitest* house in the neighborhood).

When the adjective consists of a single syllable, the suffix *-er* is added to form the comparative degree, and the suffix *-est* is added to form the superlative degree. When the adjective consists of two syllables, the suffixes are often used to form the comparative (as *gentler*) and superlative (as *gentlest*), but the adverbs *more/less* can also be used to form the comparative (as *more skillful* and *less skillful*), and likewise, the adverbs *most/least* can be used to form the superlative (as *most skillful* and *least skillful*). For adjectives of more than two syllables, the adverbs are usually used to form the comparative and superlative forms (as *more fortunate, most fortunate*).

There are a few adjectives that have unique comparative and superlative forms:

Positive	Comparative	Superlative
good	better	best
bad	worse	worst
some	more	most
little (amount)	less	least
but		
little (size)	littler	littlest

There are a few adjectives that have no comparative or superlative forms:

an *utter* failure   the *principal* objections

DEMONSTRATIVE ADJECTIVES

The demonstrative adjectives *this* and *that* are used to point out the one person or thing referred to (as "not *this* coat but *that* one"). The plural forms are *these* and *those*, respectively.

These books are mine and **those** books are yours.

DESCRIPTIVE ADJECTIVES

A descriptive adjective describes or indicates a quality, type, or condition:

a *fascinating* conversation   a *positive* attitude   a *fast* computer

INDEFINITE ADJECTIVES

An indefinite adjective is used to designate unspecified person(s) or thing(s):

some children   *other* projects   *any* book

INTERROGATIVE ADJECTIVES

An interrogative adjective is used to form a question:

Whose office is this?   *Which* book do you want?

THE NOUN USED AS ADJECTIVE

A noun sometimes serves to modify another noun and thus functions as an adjective:

the *Vietnam* War   *word* processing

POSSESSIVE ADJECTIVES

The possessive form of a personal pronoun is called a *possessive adjective*. Following is a list of possessive adjectives and a few examples of how they are used:

Singular	Plural
my	our
your	your
his/her/its	their

Where's *my* magazine?   *Your* cab is here.   They can read *his* story.
It was *her* idea.   The box and *its* contents were inspected.
She's *our* mother.   *Your* photos are ready.   We paid for *their* tickets.

PREDICATE ADJECTIVES

A predicate adjective modifies the subject of a linking verb, such as *be*, *become*, *feel*, *taste*, *smell*, or *seem*:

He is *lucky*.   She became *angry*.   They are *happy* with the outcome.
The milk smells *bad*.   The student seems *lonely*.

PROPER ADJECTIVES

A proper adjective is derived from a proper noun and is capitalized:

Victorian furniture   a *Chinese* custom   a *Shakespearean* scholar

THE ADVERB

Adverbs, whether single words or phrases, usually give information about the verbs, such as *when*

We arrived *yesterday*   He woke up *late*

or *where*

I found them *at the restaurant*   He spent time *in [the] hospital*

or *how*

They arose *quickly*   She worked *hard*

Most single-word adverbs end in *-ly* and are formed by adding the suffix *-ly* to an adjective:

mad → madly   *wonderful → wonderfully*

When the adjective ends in *-y*, the adverb is formed by changing *-y* to *-i* and adding the suffix *-ly*:

happy → happily   *dainty → daintily*

When the adjective ends in *-ic*, the adverb is formed by adding the suffix *-ally*:

basic → basically   *numeric → numerically*

When an adjective ends in *-ly*, the adverb retains the same spelling:

a *daily* routine (adjective)
she calls her mother *daily* (adverb)
an *early* meeting (adjective)
the show started *early* (adverb)

Also, there are adverbs that do not end in *-ly*, for example:

again   *now*   *soon*
too   *there*   *how*

POSITIVE, COMPARATIVE, AND SUPERLATIVE DEGREES OF ADVERBS

Adverbs, like adjectives, can have three degrees of comparison: the *positive* form exists without reference to anything else; the *comparative* degree relates to another—as being more or less of the adverb quality; and *superlative* relates to all members of a class. As a general rule, a single-syllable adverb ends in *-er* when it is comparative (as *faster*) and in *-est* when it is superlative (as *fastest*). For adverbs of three or more syllables, the comparative and superlative degrees are formed by using the adverbs *more/less* and *most/least*. The comparative and superlative degrees of an adverb of two syllables are formed by following either one of these methods:

Positive	Comparative	Superlative
early	earlier	earliest
easy	easier	easiest
nearly	more nearly	most nearly
quickly	more quickly	most quickly
satisfactorily	less satisfactorily	least satisfactorily

Some adverbs, such as *only*, *quite*, and *very*, have no comparative or superlative forms.

INTENSIVE ADVERBS

Intensive adverbs, such as *just* and *only*, are usually used only to emphasize other words. The emphasis varies according to the placement of the adverb within the sentence:

He *just* nodded to me as he passed.   He nodded to me *just* as he passed.
I *only* wanted to speak with you.   I wanted to speak *only* with you.

INTERROGATIVE ADVERBS

Interrogative adverbs, such as *when*, *where*, and *why*, are used chiefly to introduce questions:

When will he return?   *Where* is the remote control?   *Why* did you hide it?

THE ARTICLE

Articles, sometimes called "determiners," are elements of a noun phrase that indicate whether the noun is "definite," that is, a specific individual, or "indefinite," that is, very general in nature.

THE DEFINITE ARTICLE

There is only one form of the definite article: *the.*

The boys were expelled.   It was *the* best movie I have seen.

THE INDEFINITE ARTICLE

The indefinite article *a* is used with every noun or abbreviation beginning with either a consonant or the sound of a consonant:

a door	*a* union	*a* one-way street
a B.A. degree	*a* hat	*a* U.S. Senator

The indefinite article *an* is used with every noun or abbreviation that begins with a vowel sound, whether or not the first letter of the noun or abbreviation is a vowel or consonant:

an icicle   *an* MP   *an* honor   *an* FAQ

When the first syllable of a noun beginning with *h* is not stressed or has only a slight stress, the article *a* is frequently used:

a historian   *a* heroic attempt   *a* hilarious performance

However, the article *an* is sometimes used in these cases:

an historian   **an** heroic attempt   **an** hilarious performance

Both forms are acceptable.

THE CONJUNCTION

There are three main types of conjunctions: *coordinating conjunctions*, *correlative conjunctions*, and *subordinating conjunctions*.

COORDINATING CONJUNCTIONS

Coordinating conjunctions, such as *and*, *but*, *for*, *or*, *nor*, *so*, and *yet*, are used to connect grammatical elements of the same type. These elements may be words, phrases, clauses, or complete sentences. Coordinating conjunctions are used to connect similar elements, to make exclusions or contrasts, to indicate an alternative, to indicate a cause, or to specify a result:

connecting similar elements:	She ordered pencils, pens, **and** erasers.
exclusion or contrast:	He is a brilliant **but** arrogant man.
	They offered a promising plan, **but** it had not yet been tested.
alternative:	She can wait here **or** go on ahead.
cause:	The report is useless, **for** its information is no longer current.
result:	His diction is excellent, **so** every word is clear.

CORRELATIVE CONJUNCTIONS

Correlative conjunctions are used in groups of two to connect choices or elements of the same grammatical type:

Both Rita **and** Jane attended the conference.
Either you go **or** you stay.
He had **neither** looks **nor** wit.

SUBORDINATING CONJUNCTIONS

Subordinating conjunctions are used to connect a subordinate clause to an independent clause. These conjunctions express cause, condition or concession, manner, intention or result, time, place, or circumstance, as well as a possibility.

cause:	**Because** she learns quickly, she is doing well in her new job.
condition or concession:	Don't call **unless** you are coming.
manner:	We'll do it **however** you tell us.
intention or result:	They burned all the bridges **so** that the enemy could not use them.
time:	She kept the meeting to a minimum **when** she could.
place:	**Wherever** he goes, he is welcomed with open arms.

THE NOUN

BASIC USES

The noun may be a single word or a phrase (noun phrase). The noun phrase may consist of an article and/or adjectives and/or prepositional phrases. The noun can function as subject of a sentence, object of a verb, object of a preposition, predicate nominative, complement of an object, in apposition, and in direct discourse:

subject:	*The office* was quiet.
	The house with the green shutters was for sale.
direct object of a verb:	He locked *the office*.
indirect object of a verb:	He gave *his client* the papers.
object of a preposition:	The business was in *bankruptcy*.
	The file is in *the office*.
predicate nominative:	Ms. Adams is *the managing partner*.
complement of an object:	They made Ms. Adams *managing partner*.
in apposition:	Ms. Adams, *the managing partner*, wrote that memo.
in direct discourse:	*Ms. Adams*, may I present Mr. Wilson.

Nouns are often classified as proper nouns (*Eiffel Tower*, *White House*), common nouns (*tower*, *house*), abstract nouns (*honor*, *love*), concrete nouns (*desk*, *flower*), or collective nouns (*team*, *government*). American English typically uses a singular verb with a collective noun (the team *is*), while British English typically uses a plural verb (the government *are*).

Most nouns are neuter, showing no distinction as to whether having a masculine or feminine reference. However, a few nouns ending in -*ess* (as *empress*, *hostess*) are feminine in gender, and some others have a specific gender. For example: *husband*, *wife*, *father*, *mother*, *brother*, *sister*. The names of certain animals also have a specific gender, for example, *bull/cow*, *stag/doe*. When it is necessary to specify the gender of a neuter noun, the noun is usually modified with words like *male*, *female*, *man*, *woman* (a *male* parrot, *women* painters).

THE NOUN AS ADJECTIVE

The noun has the function of an adjective when it precedes another noun:

olive oil	*business* management	*emergency* room	*dog* house

THE FORMATION OF THE PLURAL

The plural of most nouns is formed by adding the suffix -*s* to the singular noun:

book → books   *cat → cats*

When the singular noun ends in -*s*, -*x*, -*z*, -*ch*, or -*sh*, the suffix -*es* is added to the singular:

cross → crosses   *fox → foxes*
witch → witches   *wish → wishes*

For a singular noun ending in -*z*, the last letter is doubled before adding the suffix -*es*:

buzz → buzzes   *quiz → quizzes*

For a singular noun ending in -*y* preceded by a consonant, the -*y* changes to -*i* and the suffix -*es* is added:

fairy → fairies   *pony → ponies*   *guppy → guppies*

For a singular noun ending in -*y* preceded by a vowel, the -*y* usually does not change when the suffix -*s* is added:

boy → boys   *attorney → attorneys*

Some words that end in -*uy* sometimes change the -*y* to -*i*:

guy → guys   *soliloquy → soliloquies*

There are a few nouns that do not always change in the plural:

fish → fish (or *fishes* when referring to more than one species)
caribou → caribou (sometimes *caribous*)
moose → moose

There are also some nouns that have a unique plural:

foot → feet   *mouse → mice*   *knife → knives*

THE POSSESSIVE CASE

The possessive case of most singular nouns is formed by adding an apostrophe followed by an -s:

Jackie's passport   This hat is **Billy's**

For plural nouns ending in -s, only the apostrophe is added:

the **neighbors'** dog   both **boys'** behavior

Proper nouns that end in -s often present a special case:

Mr. Douglas's car   **Socrates'** teachings

THE PREPOSITION

The preposition is used with an object (a noun, pronoun, or the equivalent of a noun) to form a phrase that functions generally as an adjective or an adverb.

The man **in the car** is his father. (adjective)
The river winds **through the valley**. (adverb)

There are two types of prepositions: the simple preposition, which consists of a single word (for example, *against, from, near, of, on, out, in*) and the compound preposition, which consists of more than one element (for example, *according to, on account of, because of, in spite of*).

THE CONJUNCTION VS. THE PREPOSITION

The words *after, before, but, for,* and *since* can be used as prepositions or conjunctions. Their part of speech is determined by their function in the sentence. Conjunctions are usually used to connect two elements of the same grammatical type, while prepositions are followed by an object to form a phrase.

conjunction:	The playful **but** thoughtful youngsters did well in school. (**but** connects two adjectives)
preposition:	I was left with nothing **but** hope. (**but** followed by an object)
conjunction:	The device conserves fuel, **for** it is battery-powered. (**for** connects two clauses)
preposition:	The device conserves fuel **for** better mileage. (**for** followed by an object)

PLACE IN THE SENTENCE

A preposition comes in front of a noun or a pronoun (*under* the desk, *beside* them), after an adjective (antagonistic *to*, insufficient *for*, symbolic *of*), or after a verb as a particle (take *over*, put *on*, come *across*).
The preposition may end a sentence, especially if it is a verb particle.

What does this all **add up to**?
After Amy left, Sandra **took over**.

THE PRONOUN

Pronouns are often said to stand in place of the noun or noun phrase in a sentence. Usually, the pronoun stands for something previously specified or generally understood.

Pronouns have the following characteristics: *case* (nominative, possessive, or objective); *number* (singular or plural); *person* (first, second, or third); and *gender* (masculine, feminine, or neuter). Pronouns can be classed in seven main categories, each having a specific function.

DEMONSTRATIVE PRONOUNS

The words *this*, *that*, *these*, and *those* are demonstrative pronouns when they function as nouns. (They are classed as demonstrative adjectives when they modify a noun.) The demonstrative pronoun distinguishes a person or thing from another person or thing:

> ***This*** is the one I want.   I was happy about ***that***.
> ***These*** are the best designs.   I picked ***those*** as the prettiest flowers.

The demonstrative pronoun also serves to distinguish a person or thing nearby from one that is farther away (*this* is my desk; *that* is yours).

INDEFINITE PRONOUNS

Indefinite pronouns are used to designate a person or thing of which the identity is unknown or is not immediately evident. The indefinite pronouns include the following:

all	either	none	another	everybody	no one
any	everyone	one	anybody	everything	other(s)
anyone	few	several	anything	many	some
both	much	somebody	each	neither	someone
each one	nobody	something			

The indefinite pronoun and the verb that follows it should agree in number. The following pronouns are used with a singular verb: *another*, *anything*, *each one*, *everything*, *much*, *nobody*, *no one*, *other*, *someone*, *something*:

> ***Much*** is being done.   ***No one*** wants to go.

The indefinite pronouns *both*, *few*, *many*, and *several* are used with plural verbs:

> ***Many*** are called; ***few*** are chosen.

Certain pronouns, such as *all*, *any*, *none*, and *some*, sometimes present difficulties, since they can be used with a singular or a plural verb. As a general rule, a pronoun that is used with a noun that cannot be counted requires a singular verb, while a pronoun that is used with a noun that can be counted requires a plural verb.

> **with an uncountable noun:**   All of the property is affected.
> None of the soup was spilled.
> Some of the money was spent.
> **with a countable noun:**   All of my shoes are black.
> None of the clerks were available.
> Some of your friends were here.

INTERROGATIVE PRONOUNS

The interrogative pronouns *what*, *which*, *who*, *whom*, and *whose*, as well as those bound with the word *-ever* (*whatever*, *whichever*, etc.) are used to introduce a direct or an indirect question:

> ***Who*** is she?   He asked me ***who*** she was.
> ***Whoever*** can that be?   We wondered ***whoever*** that could be.

PERSONAL PRONOUNS

The personal pronoun reflects the person, number, and gender of the entity it represents. Each category is made up of distinct personal pronouns:

Person	Nominative	Possessive	Objective
First (sing.)	I	my, mine	me
(pl.)	we	our, ours	us
Second (sing.)	you	your, yours	you
(pl.)	you	your, yours	you
Third (sing.)	he	his	him
	she	her, hers	her
	it	its	it
(pl.)	they	their, theirs	them

RECIPROCAL PRONOUNS

The reciprocal pronouns *each other* and *one another* indicate a mutual action or relationship:

> Jim and Andy saw *each other* at the party.
> They do not quarrel with *one another*.

The reciprocal pronoun is also used as a possessive:

> The two companies depend on *each other's* success.
> The members enjoyed *one another's* company.

REFLEXIVE PRONOUNS

Reflexive pronouns are formed from the personal pronouns *him*, *her*, *it*, *my*, *our*, *them*, and *your*, to which the combining form *-self* or *-selves* is added. The reflexive pronoun is usually used to express a reflexive action or to emphasize the subject of a sentence, clause, or phrase:

> She dressed *herself*.
> He asked *himself* if it was worth it.
> I *myself* am not involved.
> They wanted to do it *themselves*.

RELATIVE PRONOUNS

The relative pronouns are *who*, *whom*, *whose*, *which*, and *that*, as well as the compounds formed by adding the ending *-ever*. These pronouns are used to introduce subordinate clauses that function as a noun or an adjective.

> a man *who* sought success
> a woman *whom* we can trust
> an author *whose* first novel was a success
> a move *which* was unforeseen
> a boy *that* behaves well
> give it to *whomever* you wish
> *whoever* thought of it
> pick *whichever* you want

In certain cases the relative pronoun may be omitted:

> The man [*whom*] I was talking to is the senator.

THE VERB

Verbs have essentially three classes: ordinary verbs of action, such as *go*, auxiliary verbs, like *can* and *shall*, and fundamental verbs like *be*, *have*, and *do*, which can function as both ordinary verbs and as auxiliaries.

The verb has the following characteristics: *inflection* (for example, helps, helping, helped), *person* (first, second, third), *number* (singular, plural), *tense* (present, past, future), *aspect* (categories of time other than the simple tenses of present, past, future), *voice* (active, passive), and *mood* (indicative, subjunctive, and imperative).

INFLECTION

Regular verbs have three inflections that are formed by adding the suffixes *-s* or *-es*, *-ed*, and *-ing* (for example, *asks, asked, asking*) Most of the irregular verbs have four inflections (for example, *sees, saw, seen, seeing*). The verb *be* has seven inflections: *is, am, are, was, were, being, been*).

Verbs ending in silent *-e* in general keep the *-e* when a consonantal suffix (such as *-s*) is added to the word, but the *-e* is dropped when the suffix begins with a vowel (such as *-ed, -ing*):

> *arrange; arranges; arranged; arranging*
> *hope; hopes; hoped; hoping*

However, certain verbs keep the *-e* in order to avoid confusion with another verb:

> *dye* (color); *dyes; dyed; dyeing*
>   *but*
> *die* (cease to live); *dies; died; dying*
> *singe* (burn); *singes; singed; singeing*
>   *but*
> *sing* (produce music); *sings; sang; singing*

If a single-syllable verb ends in a single consonant preceded by a single vowel, the final consonant is often doubled before the addition of *-ed* or *-ing*:

> *brag; brags; bragged; bragging*
> *grip; grips; gripped; gripping*

When a multi-syllable verb ends in the same way, and the last syllable is stressed, the final consonant is also doubled:

> *commit; commits; committed; committing*
> *occur; occurs; occurred; occurring*

It frequently happens that a verb ending in *-y* preceded by a consonant changes *-y* to *-i*, except when the suffix is *-ing*:

> *carry; carries; carried; carrying*
> *study; studies; studied; studying*

When a verb ends in *-c*, a *-k* is added to inflections if the suffix begins with *-e* or *-i*:

> *mimic; mimics; mimicked; mimicking*
> *traffic; traffics; trafficked; trafficking*

TENSE AND ASPECT

The present and past tenses are generally formed as a single word:

> I *do*, I *did*
> we *write*, we *wrote*

The future tense is conjugated with the auxiliary verbs *shall* or *will* and the present or progressive forms:

> I *shall do* it.
> We *will come* tomorrow.
> I *shall be leaving* tomorrow.

Aspect concerns the tense of the verb other than the present, the past, or the future. Aspect has four forms: the *progressive*, the *present perfect*, the *past perfect*, and the *future perfect*.

The *progressive* is used to express an ongoing action that takes place in the present, past, or future:

> He *is reading* the paper at the moment.
> I *was studying* for the test when you called.
> I *will be going* to India next year.

The *present perfect* tense is used to express an action done in the past but which may be continuing in the present, or to express an action that occurred at an indefinite moment in the past. It is conjugated with the auxiliary verbs *has* or *have* and the past participle:

> She *has written* many books.
> They *have regretted* their mistake.

The *past perfect* expresses a completed action that occurred before another action in the past. It is conjugated with the auxiliary verb *had* and the past participle:

> She *had written* several books previously.
> We *had left* the house before they arrived.

The *future perfect* tense indicates that a future action will take place before another action or occurrence still to come. It is conjugated with the auxiliary verbs *will* or *shall* and *have* and the past participle:

> We *will have finished* the project by then.
> They *will have gone* before we will arrive.

VOICE

The *active* voice indicates that the subject of the sentence is the doer of the action of the verb; the *passive* voice, consisting of a form of the verb *be* and a past participle, indicates that the subject of the sentence is the object of the action:

> **Active voice:**   His colleagues *respect* him.
> **Passive voice:**   He *was respected* by his colleagues.

MOOD

There are three moods: the *indicative*, the *subjunctive*, and the *imperative*. The *indicative* is used to indicate a fact or to ask a question:

> He *is* here.
> *Is* he here?

The *subjunctive* is used to express a condition contrary to fact, especially in clauses introduced by *if*, and after the verb *wish*:

> If she *were* there, she could answer that.
> I wish he *were* here.

The *subjunctive* is also used in clauses beginning with the word *that* following verbs that request, demand, or recommend:

> They asked that the books *be* returned.
> She insisted that the door *remain* open.
> The law required that he *report* his earnings.

The imperative is used to express a command or a demand:

> *Come* here!
> *Pay* attention!

TRANSITIVE AND INTRANSITIVE VERBS

A transitive verb takes a direct object:

> She *sold* her car.

An intransitive verb has no direct object:

> He *talked* all day.